THE POWER OF
FINE LITERATURE
THE MASTERY OF
LANGUAGE ARTS

PRENTICE HALL
LITERATURE

Begin each selection with the Guide for Reading.

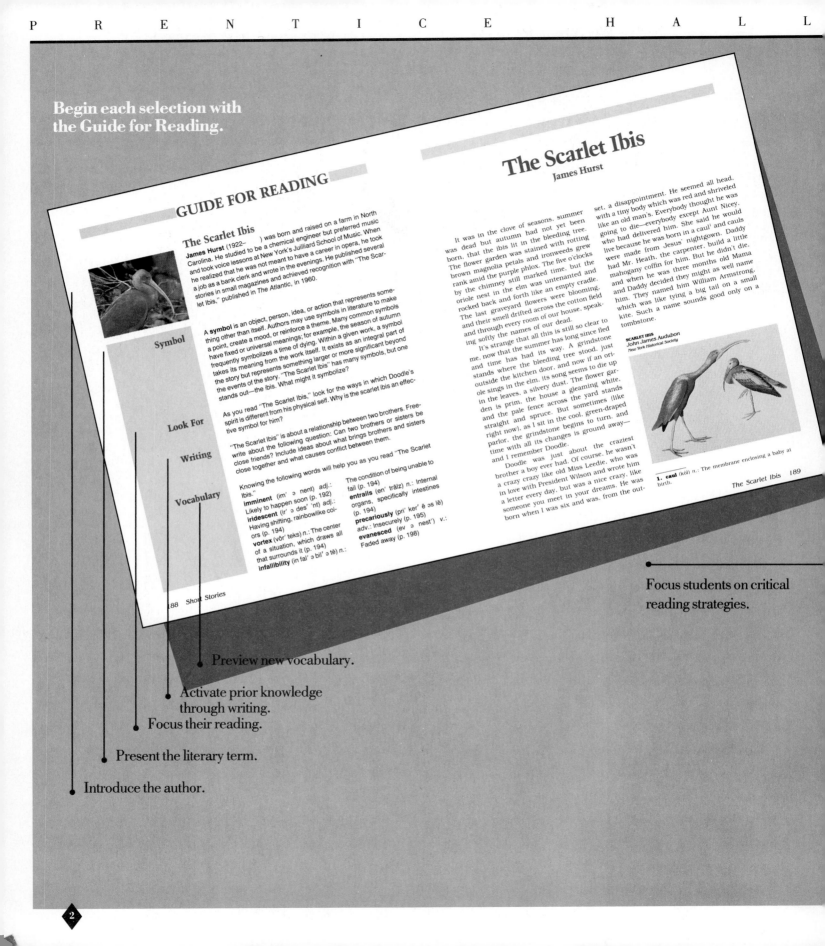

GUIDE FOR READING

The Scarlet Ibis

James Hurst (1922–   ) was born and raised on a farm in North Carolina. He studied to be a chemical engineer but preferred music and took voice lessons at New York's Juilliard School of Music. When he realized that he was not meant to have a career in opera, he took a job as a bank clerk and wrote in the evenings. He published several stories in small magazines and achieved recognition with "The Scarlet Ibis," published in *The Atlantic*, in 1960.

Symbol

A **symbol** is an object, person, idea, or action that represents something other than itself. Authors may use symbols in literature to make a point, create a mood, or reinforce a theme. Many common symbols have fixed or universal meanings; for example, the season of autumn frequently symbolizes a time of dying. Within a given work, a symbol takes its meaning from the work itself. It exists as an integral part of the story but represents something larger or more significant beyond the events of the story. "The Scarlet Ibis" has many symbols, but one stands out—the ibis. What might it symbolize?

Look For

As you read "The Scarlet Ibis," look for the ways in which Doodle's spirit is different from his physical self. Why is the scarlet ibis an effective symbol for him?

Writing

"The Scarlet Ibis" is about a relationship between two brothers. Free-write about the following question: Can two brothers or sisters be close friends? Include ideas about what brings brothers and sisters close together and what causes conflict between them.

Vocabulary

Knowing the following words will help you as you read "The Scarlet Ibis."

imminent (im′ ə nent) *adj.*: Likely to happen soon (p. 192)

iridescent (ir′ ə des′ ′nt) *adj.*: Having shifting, rainbowlike colors (p. 194)

vortex (vôr′ teks) *n.*: The center of a situation, which draws all that surrounds it (p. 194)

infallibility (in fal′ ə bil′ ə tē) *n.*:

The condition of being unable to fail (p. 194)

entrails (en′ trālz) *n.*: Internal organs, specifically intestines (p. 194)

precariously (pri′ ker′ ē əs lē) *adv.*: Insecurely (p. 195)

evanesced (ev ə nest′) *v.*: Faded away (p. 198)

188 Short Stories

The Scarlet Ibis
James Hurst

It was in the clove of seasons, summer was dead but autumn had not yet been born, that the ibis lit in the bleeding tree. The flower garden was stained with rotting brown magnolia petals and ironweeds grew rank amid the purple phlox. The five o'clocks by the chimney still marked time, but the oriole nest in the elm was untenanted and rocked back and forth like an empty cradle. The last graveyard flowers were blooming, and their smell drifted across the cotton field and through every room of our house, speaking softly the names of our dead.

It's strange that all this is still so clear to me, now that the summer has long since fled and time has had its way. A grindstone stands where the bleeding tree stood, just outside the kitchen door, and now if an oriole sings in the elm, its song seems to die up in the leaves, a silvery dust. The flower garden is prim, the house a gleaming white, and the pale fence across the yard stands straight and spruce. But sometimes (like right now), as I sit in the cool, green-draped parlor, the grindstone begins to turn, and time with all its changes is ground away—and I remember Doodle.

Doodle was just about the craziest brother a boy ever had. Of course, he wasn't a crazy crazy like old Miss Leedie, who was in love with President Wilson and wrote him a letter every day, but was a nice crazy, like someone you meet in your dreams. He was born when I was six and was, from the out-

set, a disappointment. He seemed all head, with a tiny body which was red and shriveled like an old man's. Everybody thought he was going to die—everybody except Aunt Nicey, who had delivered him. She said he would live because he was born in a caul[1] and cauls were made from Jesus' nightgown. Daddy had Mr. Heath, the carpenter, build a little mahogany coffin for him. But he didn't die, and when he was three months old Mama and Daddy decided they might as well name him. They named him William Armstrong, which was like tying a big tail on a small kite. Such a name sounds good only on a tombstone.

SCARLET IBIS
John James Audubon
New York Historical Society

1. **caul** (kôl) *n.*: The membrane enclosing a baby at birth.

The Scarlet Ibis   189

Preview new vocabulary.

Activate prior knowledge through writing.

Focus their reading.

Present the literary term.

Introduce the author.

Focus students on critical reading strategies.

The Power of Fine Literature, The Mastery of Critical Reading.

Integrate the power of fine literature with critical reading to stimulate an active response.

Begin each unit with Reading Actively.

Nonfiction

Some people seem to gain more from their reading of nonfiction than others. Why? Most likely, they gain more because they read with an active mind. To read nonfiction successfully, you must interact with the information the author presents. Ask questions about this information and make predictions about where the information is leading. Pause to answer your predictions and to check your predictions. At appropriate points, stop to summarize the information you have received so far.

Use the following strategies to help you read actively.

Question

Ask questions about the information the author presents. What does the author reveal about the topic? Determine whether the author's conclusions seem based on the information given. In addition, question the author's purpose for writing.

Predict

Think about what you already know about the topic. Make predictions about the conclusions you think the author will reach based on this information. As you read, you will find out whether your predictions are accurate.

Clarify

As you read, try to find the answers to your questions and check the accuracy of your predictions. In this way, you will monitor, or guide, your own reading and so gain the fullest understanding of the information presented.

Summarize

Every now and then, pause to summarize, or review, the information the author has presented so far. What important points has the author made? How has the author supported this information?

Pull It Together

Determine the main idea of the entire selection. What did you find out about the topic? How do you feel about the topic?

On the facing page is a model showing how an active reader might read an essay.

310 Nonfiction

from In Search of Our Mothers' Gardens

Alice Walker

Questions: What is the meaning of the title? What is the author's purpose for writing this essay?

My mother made all the clothes we wore, even my brothers' overalls. She made all the towels and sheets we used. She spent the summers canning vegetables and fruits. She spent the winter evenings making quilts enough to cover all our beds.

During the "working" day, she labored beside—not behind—my father in the fields. Her day began before sunup, and did not end until late at night. There was never a moment for her to sit down, undisturbed, to unravel her own private thoughts; never a time free from interruption—by work or the noisy inquiries of her many children. And yet, it is to my mother—and all our mothers who were not famous—that I went in search of the secret of what has fed that muzzled[1] and often mutilated,[2] but vibrant,[3] creative spirit that the black woman has inherited, and that pops out in wild and unlikely places to this day.

Clarification: The author's purpose is to uncover the secret of the black woman's creative spirit.

from *In Search of Our Mother's Gardens* 311

Direct students to a model showing examples of active reading.

3

Up to 100 Grammar in Action lessons in each ATE . . . the teachable moment for skills mastery.

Enrich your skills teaching with Grammar in Action lessons.

5 Discussion What sides of the narrator's character are revealed in this paragraph?

6 Reading Strategy Ask students to summarize Doodle's progress and to predict what further progress he might make.

7 Discussion Is Doodle a good name for William Armstrong? Why?

8 Discussion What character traits does the narrator's behavior reveal?

9 Discussion What kind of unspoken pact develops between the brothers?

tains billowed out in the afternoon sea breeze, rustling like palmetto fronds.[2]

It was bad enough having an invalid brother, but having one who possibly was not all there was unbearable, so I began to make plans to kill him by smothering him with a pillow. However, one afternoon as I watched him, my head poked between the irons posts of the foot of the bed, he looked straight at me and grinned. I skipped through the rooms, down the echoing halls, shouting, "Mama, he smiled. He's all there! He's all there!" and he was.

When he was two, if you laid him on his stomach, he began to try to move himself, straining terribly. The doctor said that with his weak heart this strain would probably kill him, but it didn't. Trembling, he'd push himself up, turning first red, then a soft purple, and finally collapse back onto the bed like an old worn-out doll. I can still see Mama watching him, her hand pressed tight across her mouth, her eyes wide and unblinking. But he learned to crawl (it was his third winter), and we brought him out of the front bedroom, putting him on the rug before the fireplace. For the first time he became one of us.

As long as he lay all the time in bed, we called him William Armstrong, even though it was formal and sounded as if we were referring to one of our ancestors, but with his creeping around on the deerskin rug and beginning to talk, something had to be done about his name. It was I who renamed him. When he crawled, he crawled backwards, as if he were in reverse and couldn't change gears. If you called him, he'd turn around as if he were going in the other direction, then he'd back right up to you to be picked up. Crawling backward made him look like a

2. palmetto fronds: Palm leaves.

190   Short Stories

doodle-bug, so I began to call him Doodle, and in time even Mama and Daddy thought it was a better name than William Armstrong. Only Aunt Nicey disagreed. She said caul babies should be treated with special respect since they might turn out to be saints. Renaming my brother was perhaps the kindest thing I ever did for him, because nobody expects much from someone called Doodle.

Although Doodle learned to crawl, he showed no signs of walking, but he wasn't idle. He talked so much that we all quit listening to what he said. It was about this time that Daddy built him a go-cart and I had to pull him around. At first I just paraded him up and down the piazza, but then he started crying to be taken out into the yard and it ended up by my having to lug him wherever I went. If I so much as picked up my cap, he'd start crying to go with me and Mama would call from wherever she was, "Take Doodle with you."

He was a burden in many ways. The doctor had said that he mustn't get too excited, too hot, too cold, or too tired and that he must always be treated gently. A long list of don'ts went with him, all of which I ignored once we got out of the house. To discourage his coming with me, I'd run with him across the ends of the cotton rows and careen him around corners on two wheels. Sometimes I accidentally turned him over, but he never told Mama. His skin was very sensitive, and he had to wear a big straw hat whenever he went out. When the going got rough and he had to cling to the sides of the go-cart, the hat slipped all the way down over his ears. He was a sight. Finally, I could see I was licked. Doodle was my brother and he was going to cling to me forever, no matter what I did, so I dragged him across the burning cotton field to share with him the only beauty I knew, Old Woman Swamp. I pulled the go-cart through the saw-tooth fern, down into the green dimness where the pal-

Grammar in Action

When a writer uses **concrete details,** readers can see, hear, smell, taste, and feel what the writer is describing. For instance, if a writer merely says "dog," the reader will only have a vague or general idea of the type of animal the writer has in mind. If a writer specifies "German shepherd," however, readers will have a much more specific picture.

Notice how James Hurst uses concrete, specific details to enliven the following description:

190

. . . I dragged him across the *burning cotton field* to share with him the only beauty I knew, Old Woman Swamp. I pulled the go-cart through the *saw-tooth fern,* down into the *green dimness* where the *palmetto fronds* whispered by the stream, lifted him out and set him down in the *soft rubber grass* beside a *tall pine.* His eyes were round with wonder as he gazed about him, and his little hands began to stroke the *rubber grass.* Then he began to cry.

Without the concrete details, this passage would be much less effective:

The Power of Fine Literature,
The Mastery of Grammar and Usage Skills.

Use fine literature as a springboard to teach grammar and usage skills.

BOYS IN A PUNT
N. C. Wyeth
Courtesy of Dr. and Mrs. William A. Morton, Jr.

Humanities Note

Fine art, *Boys in a Punt*, by N.C. Wyeth. Newel Convers Wyeth (1882–1945), who was born in Needham, Massachusetts, lived during the time that is now known as the Golden Age of American Illustration—the time from the mid-1870's to approximately the 1920's. The age was so named because of the number of creative and well-known illustrators whose work was published during that period, including Winslow Homer, Howard Pyle, and N.C. Wyeth.

By the time he was a teenager, Wyeth knew he wanted to be an artist and enrolled in the Howard Pyle School of Illustration in Philadelphia, where he was taught by Howard Pyle.

While in school, Wyeth frequently took trips to Pyle's home at Chadds Ford, Pennsylvania, to roam the hills and woods of the Brandywine Valley. He later permanently moved to this area to raise his own family. Much of Wyeth's finest work, including *Boys in a Punt* was inspired by the rural life around him.

You might use the following questions for discussion.

1. The tone of a painting is the painter's attitude toward the subject. It may be established through the colors the artist chose or the composition. What is the tone of this painting? How does the tone of the painting complement the tone of the story?
2. Do you think Wyeth's illustration is appropriate for this story? Explain.

I pulled him across the field into a pretty swamp. It was dark and wet. I set him on the ground. He was startled and cried.

he many concrete details that Hurst includes enable readers to xperience the swamp along with the two boys.

Student Activity 1. Identify the vague, general terms in the horter passage above. Then locate the concrete details in Hurst's passage that bring the description to life.

Student Activity 2. Rewrite the vague shorter passage so that it s more concrete. However, make your description of Old Woman wamp different from Hurst's.

191

Reinforce learning with blackline masters in the Teaching Portfolio.

Guide learning with on-the-spot practice.

A writing program within a literature program.

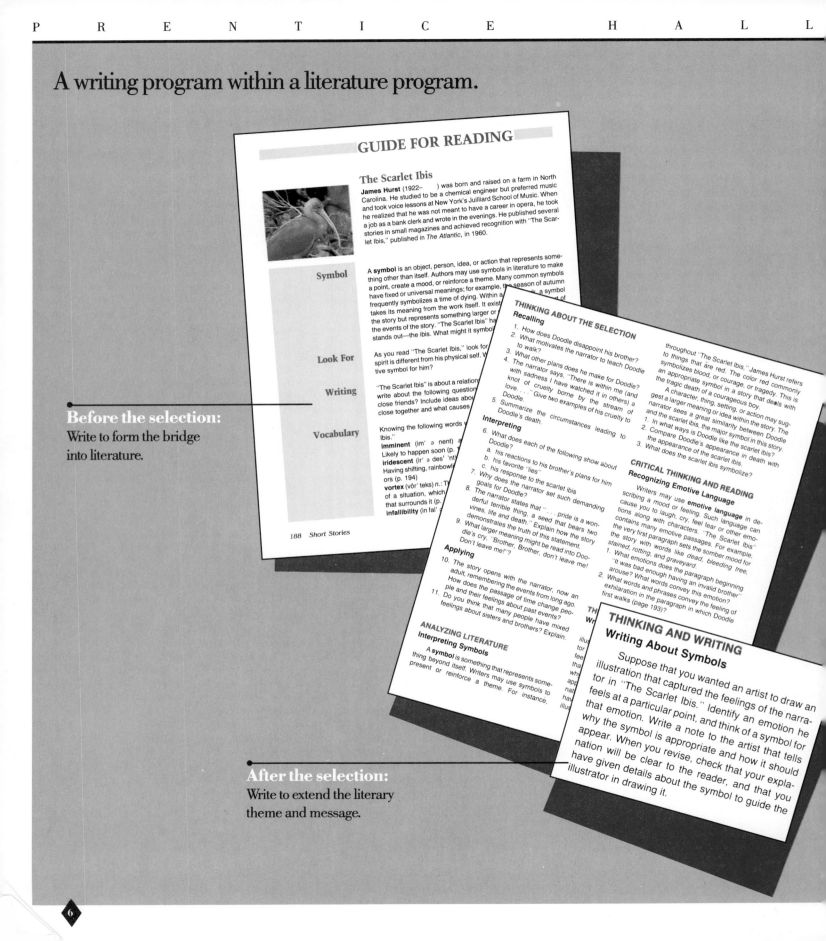

GUIDE FOR READING

The Scarlet Ibis

James Hurst (1922–) was born and raised on a farm in North Carolina. He studied to be a chemical engineer but preferred music and took voice lessons at New York's Juilliard School of Music. When he realized that he was not meant to have a career in opera, he took a job as a bank clerk and wrote in the evenings. He published several stories in small magazines and achieved recognition with "The Scarlet Ibis," published in *The Atlantic*, in 1960.

Symbol

A **symbol** is an object, person, idea, or action that represents something other than itself. Authors may use symbols in literature to make a point, create a mood, or reinforce a theme. Many common symbols have fixed or universal meanings; for example, the season of autumn frequently symbolizes a time of dying. Within a ___ a symbol takes its meaning from the work itself. It exist ___ the story but represents something larger or ___ the events of the story. "The Scarlet Ibis" ha ___ stands out—the ibis. What might it symbol ___

Look For

As you read "The Scarlet Ibis," look for ___ spirit is different from his physical self. W ___ tive symbol for him?

Writing

"The Scarlet Ibis" is about a relation ___ write about the following question ___ close friends? Include ideas abo ___ close together and what causes ___

Vocabulary

Knowing the following words ___ Ibis."

imminent (im′ ə nent) ___ Likely to happen soon (p. ___
iridescent (ir′ ə des′ ʹnt ___ Having shifting, rainbowli ___ ors (p. 194)
vortex (vôr′ teks) *n.*: T ___ of a situation, which ___ that surrounds it (p. ___
infallibility (in fal′ ___

188   *Short Stories*

THINKING ABOUT THE SELECTION

Recalling

1. How does Doodle disappoint his brother?
2. What motivates the narrator to teach Doodle to walk?
3. What other plans does he make for Doodle?
4. The narrator says, "There is within me (and with sadness I have watched it in others) a knot of cruelty borne by the stream of love. . . ." Give two examples of his cruelty to Doodle.
5. Summarize the circumstances leading to Doodle's death.

Interpreting

6. What does each of the following show about Doodle?
   a. his reactions to his brother's plans for him
   b. his favorite "lies"
   c. his response to the scarlet ibis
7. Why does the narrator set such demanding goals for Doodle?
8. The narrator states that ". . . pride is a wonderful terrible thing, a seed that bears two vines, life and death." Explain how the story demonstrates the truth of this statement.
9. What larger meaning might be read into Doodle's cry, "Brother, Brother, don't leave me! Don't leave me!"?

Applying

10. The story opens with the narrator, now an adult, remembering the events from long ago. How does the passage of time change people and their feelings about past events?
11. Do you think that many people have mixed feelings about sisters and brothers? Explain.

ANALYZING LITERATURE

Interpreting Symbols

A **symbol** is something that represents something beyond itself. Writers may use symbols to present or reinforce a theme. For instance, ___

throughout "The Scarlet Ibis," James Hurst refers to things that are red. The color red commonly symbolizes blood, or courage, or tragedy. This is an appropriate symbol in a story that deals with the tragic death of a courageous boy.

A character, thing, setting, or action may suggest a larger meaning or idea within the story. The narrator sees a great similarity between Doodle and the scarlet ibis, the major symbol in this story.

1. In what ways is Doodle like the scarlet ibis?
2. Compare Doodle's appearance in death with the appearance of the scarlet ibis.
3. What does the scarlet ibis symbolize?

CRITICAL THINKING AND READING

Recognizing Emotive Language

Writers may use **emotive language** in describing a mood or feeling. Such language can cause you to laugh, cry, feel fear or other emotions along with characters. "The Scarlet Ibis" contains many emotive passages. For example, the very first paragraph sets the somber mood for the story with words like *dead, bleeding tree, stained, rotting,* and *graveyard.*

1. What emotions does the paragraph beginning "It was bad enough having an invalid brother" arouse? What words convey this emotion?
2. What words and phrases convey the feeling of exhilaration in the paragraph in which Doodle first walks (page 193)?

THINKING AND WRITING

Writing About Symbols

Suppose that you wanted an artist to draw an illustration that captured the feelings of the narrator in "The Scarlet Ibis." Identify an emotion he feels at a particular point, and think of a symbol for that emotion. Write a note to the artist that tells why the symbol is appropriate and how it should appear. When you revise, check that your explanation will be clear to the reader, and that you have given details about the symbol to guide the illustrator in drawing it.

Before the selection:
Write to form the bridge
into literature.

After the selection:
Write to extend the literary
theme and message.

The Power of Fine Literature, The Mastery of Writing.

Choose from 5 writing activities for each selection.

Extend the power and breadth of your writing program with these additional activities:

- Fine Art Writing activities
- Selection Test essay questions
- Unit Test essay questions
- You the Writer Writing assignment
- You the Critic Writing assignment
- Writing Across the Curriculum activities
- Student writing models

Plus — Writing About Literature Handbook

A writing course right in the student book

Three additional writing activities in the Teaching Portfolio meet the needs of all ability levels:

- Less Challenging
- More Challenging
- The Student as Critic

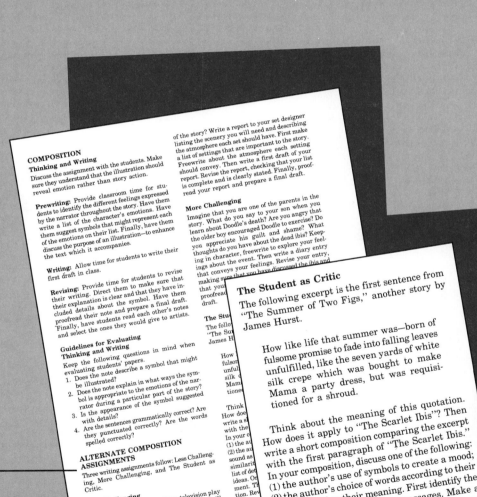

COMPOSITION
Thinking and Writing
Discuss the assignment with the students. Make sure they understand that the illustration should reveal emotion rather than story action.

Prewriting: Provide classroom time for students to identify the different feelings expressed by the narrator throughout the story. Have them write a list of the character's emotions. Have them suggest symbols that might represent each of the emotions on their list. Finally, have them discuss the purpose of an illustration—to enhance the text which it accompanies.

Writing: Allow time for students to write their first draft in class.

Revising: Provide time for students to revise their writing. Direct them to make sure that their explanation is clear and that they have included details about the symbol. Have them proofread their note and prepare a final draft. Finally, have students read each other's notes and select the ones they would give to artists.

Guidelines for Evaluating Thinking and Writing
Keep the following questions in mind when evaluating students' papers.
1. Does the note describe a symbol that might be illustrated?
2. Does the note explain in what ways the symbol is appropriate to the emotions of the narrator during a particular part of the story?
3. Is the appearance of the symbol suggested with details?
4. Are the sentences grammatically correct? Are they punctuated correctly? Are the words spelled correctly?

ALTERNATE COMPOSITION ASSIGNMENTS
Three writing assignments follow: Less Challenging, More Challenging, and The Student as Critic.

Less Challenging
Imagine that you are directing a television play of "The Scarlet Ibis." What stage settings will you need to convey the atmosphere and action

of the story? Write a report to your set designer listing the scenery you will need and describing the atmosphere each set should have. First make a list of settings that are important to the story. Freewrite about the atmosphere each setting should convey. Then write a first draft of your report. Revise the report, checking that your list is complete and is clearly stated. Finally, proofread your report and prepare a final draft.

More Challenging
Imagine that you are one of the parents in the story. What do you say to your son when you learn about Doodle's death? Are you angry that the older boy encouraged Doodle to exercise? Do you appreciate his guilt and shame? What thoughts do you have about the dead ibis? Keeping in character, freewrite to explore your feelings about the event. Then write a diary entry that conveys your feelings. Revise your entry, making sure that you have discussed the ibis and that your . . . proofread . . . draft.

The Student as Critic
The following excerpt is the first sentence from "The Summer of Two Figs," another story by James Hurst.

> How like life that summer was—born of fulsome promise to fade into falling leaves unfulfilled, like the seven yards of white silk crepe which was bought to make Mama a party dress, but was requisitioned for a shroud.

Think about the meaning of this quotation. How does it apply to "The Scarlet Ibis"? Then write a short composition comparing the excerpt with the first paragraph of "The Scarlet Ibis." In your composition, discuss one of the following: (1) the author's use of symbols to create a mood; (2) the author's choice of words according to their sound as well as their meaning. First identify the similarities between the two passages. Make a list of details from each passage that support your ideas. Organize your ideas around a thesis statement. Then write a first draft of your composi-

192   Short Stories

Teacher Backup
Selection background, check test, suggested readings, composition activities and evaluation guidelines, and answers to worksheets and tests.

Vocabulary Check
Reinforce or test the words taught before the selection.

Selection Test
Measure understanding of the literature through short answer questions and essay questions.

Usage and Mechanic Worksheet
Integrate grammar and editing skills with literature.

Grammar in Action Worksheet
Deepen the understanding of grammar and usage skills.

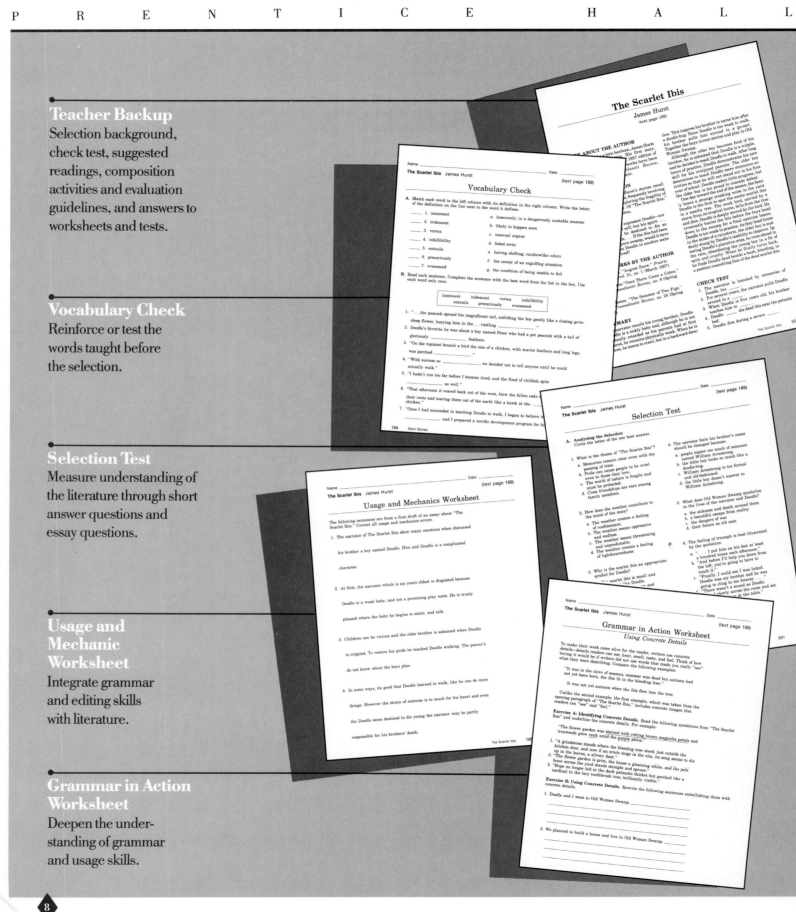

The Teaching Portfolio – Redefining the Concept of Support for all the Language Arts.

Everything you need to teach a selection is in one place.

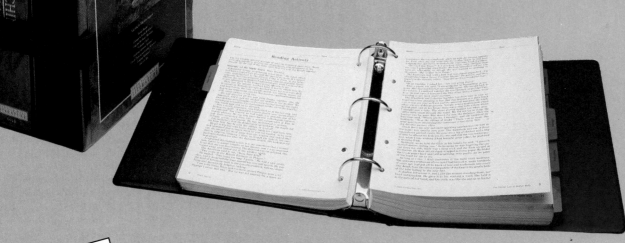

Analyzing Literature Worksheet
Extends understanding of the literary element.

Critical Thinking and Reading Worksheet
Promotes reading and reasoning.

Language Worksheet
Beyond vocabulary to word origins, synonyms, dialects — and more.

Fine Art Transparencies

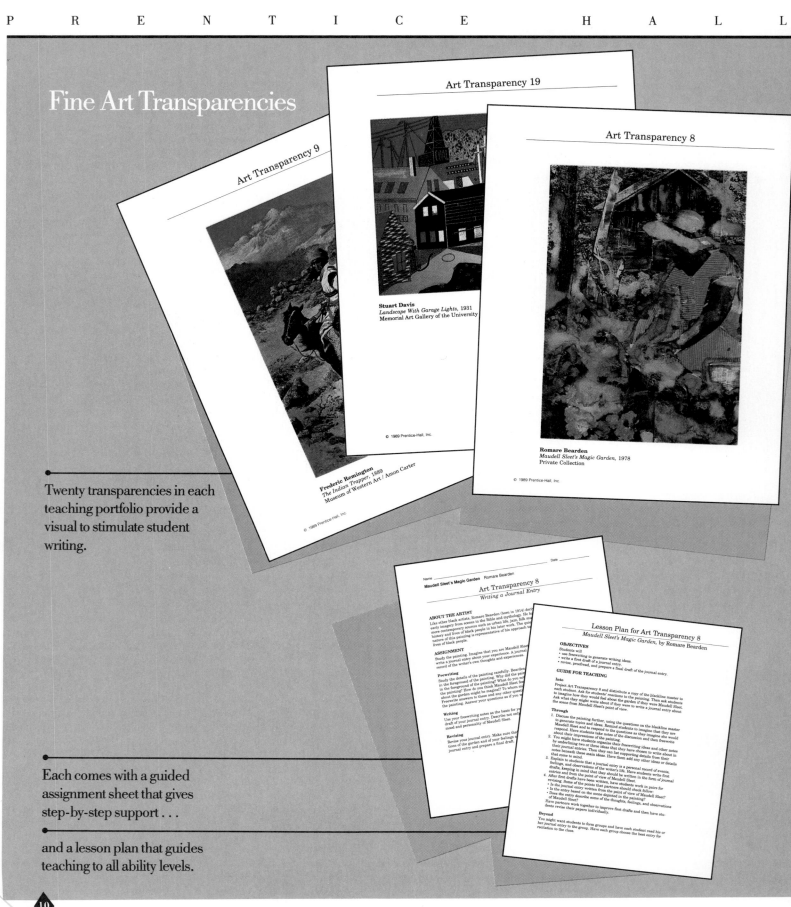

Stuart Davis
Landscape With Garage Lights, 1931
Memorial Art Gallery of the University

© 1989 Prentice-Hall, Inc.

Romare Bearden
Maudell Sleet's Magic Garden, 1978
Private Collection

© 1989 Prentice-Hall, Inc.

Frederic Remington
The Indian Trapper, 1889
Museum of Western Art / Amon Carter

© 1989 Prentice-Hall, Inc.

Twenty transparencies in each teaching portfolio provide a visual to stimulate student writing.

Each comes with a guided assignment sheet that gives step-by-step support . . .

and a lesson plan that guides teaching to all ability levels.

Capture the Power of Integrating Fine Literature and the Humanities.

A fine arts program and classic cinema connected with literature.

The Library of Video Classics

- Four feature length films per grade level, including the novel and the play.

- Viewing guides link the film with the literature to stimulate new ideas.

Each Viewing Guide provides:

- Previewing and After Viewing Questions — enhance critical thinking skills.

- Speaking and Listening activities — promote oral language skills through the impact of film.

- Writing activities — creative topics enhance students responsiveness.

- Ability level notes — ideas to challenge each student.

Direct students to new discoveries with the dynamic combination of literature and cinema.

Study Guides

What if your favorite novel or play is not in Prentice Hall Literature? We still provide you with teaching support. Complete teaching guides for 40 novels and plays give you fresh insights to make the classic even more interesting and relevant. Each guide contains:

- Author Background
- Synopses of Plot, Setting, Theme and More
- Chapter-by-Chapter Teaching Plans
- Writing Assignments
- Guidelines for Dealing With Provocative Themes
- Blackline Master Handouts and Test

Tailor the Literature Program to Your Own Classes.

Library of Great Works

Now, the time-honored longer works of American, British, and world cultures available with Prentice Hall Literature

- Classic, unabridged editions
- Hardbound versions insure lasting value
- A Novel Study Guide for expert teaching support to bring the work to life

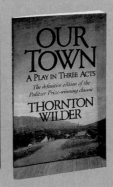
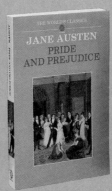

Great Works

Adventures of Huckleberry Finn	Nineteen Eighty Four
Brothers Karamazov	Our Town
Candide	Pride and Prejudice
Death of a Salesman	Red Badge of Courage
Don Quixote	Scarlet Letter
Great Gatsby	Siddartha
Hamlet	Tartuffe
Importance of Being Earnest	Things Fall Apart
Lord of the Flies	Wuthering Heights

Computer Test Bank

Customize your literature testing program with instant tests on each selection

For each selection choose from:
- Selection test
- Essay questions with evaluation guidelines
- Answer key

For each unit, choose from:
- Short answer test
- Essay tests

Powerful word processor for your made to order options.
- Write an unlimited number of new questions
- Delete questions

User friendly format for quick answers.
- Menus
- 800 customer service number

Annotated Teacher's Edition

PRENTICE HALL
LITERATURE

BRONZE

SECOND EDITION

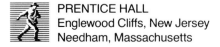
PRENTICE HALL
Englewood Cliffs, New Jersey
Needham, Massachusetts

ISBN 0-13-712944-0

10 9 8 7 6 5 4 3 2 1

Cover: *Sally,* Joseph DeCamp, Worcester Art Museum, Worcester, Massachusetts.

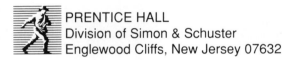

PRENTICE HALL
Division of Simon & Schuster
Englewood Cliffs, New Jersey 07632

ACKNOWLEDGMENT
Grateful acknowledgment is made to the following for permission
    to reprint copyrighted material:

Viking Penguin Inc.: Lines from "November By the Sea" in *The Complete Poems of D.H. Lawrence* Collected and Edited by Vivian de Sola Pinto and F. Warren Roberts. Copyright © 1964, 1971 by Angelo Ravagli and C.M. Weekley, Executors of The Estate of Frieda Lawrence Ravagli. Reprinted by permission of Viking Penguin Inc.

CONTENTS

The Prentice Hall Literature Program
OVERVIEW

THE STUDENT BOOK

The Prentice Hall Literature Program is a complete literature program, offering high-quality, appealing, traditional and contemporary literary selections, with study aids that will guide students into, through, and beyond the literature.

Organization

The selections are organized by genre to encourage comprehensive study of the types of literature. The following list show the units and the sections within each unit into which the selections are organized.

The Short Story: Plot, Character, Setting, Theme

Drama: One-act Plays, a Full-length Play

Nonfiction: Biographies and Personal Accounts, Essays for Enjoyment, Essays in the Content Areas

Poetry: Narrative Poetry, Figurative Language and Imagery, Lyric Poetry, The Changing Seasons, People in Their Variety

Fables, Myths, and Legends: Fables; Greek and Roman Myths; Myths, Legends, and Folk Tales From Around the World

The Novel: A complete novel

The number and variety of selections offers choice and flexibility in meeting curriculum requirements as well as student needs and interests.

Unique Features

Because the Prentice Hall Literature Program puts emphasis on the reading and appreciation of literature, it offers several unique features to help students become active readers.

Reading Actively Each unit begins with a feature called Reading Actively, which includes a set of strategies for effectively reading the literature in the unit. The strategies involve the reader in the text before reading and while reading. Such involvement and reaction are necessary if students are to learn. The active reading strategies include the following:

For prose: questioning, predicting, summarizing, clarifying

For drama: visualizing, questioning, predicting, clarifying, and summarizing

For poetry: questioning, clarifying, listening, paraphrasing, summarizing

In the short story, nonfiction, and poetry units, this feature is followed by a Model for Reading Actively, which is annotated to demonstrate and explain to students how a good reader might use the active reading strategies to understand a selection. Students are encouraged to use these strategies as they read other selections in the unit. This feature provides a method of scaffolding—giving students help and support while they acquire the skills to become successful readers of literature. To give students further practice with this process, there is an additional selection in the Teaching Portfolio, which students can annotate themselves.

Guide for Reading All other selections begin with a Guide for Reading. This page, which precedes the selection, contains useful prereading information. The Guide for Reading prepares students for successful reading in five ways:

- A biography of the author provides insight into how the author came to write the selection.
- A literary focus section introduces the literary concept that is taught with the selection.
- The Look For provides a specific goal—thematic, stylistic or meaning-oriented—to guide the students' reading of the selection.
- A motivational writing activity puts students in an appropriate frame of mind.
- A vocabulary list presents, in glossary format, words from the selection that might present difficulty in reading.

This Guide for Reading provides the necessary background to encourage comprehension, motivates students to read, and gives them technical support to read successfully.

Putting It Together The short story, nonfiction, and poetry units also end with a feature called Putting It Together. This feature serves as a summary for reading and analyzing the particular types of literature and comprehending the literary elements and devices that are in them. For example, the Putting It Together for short stories reviews plot, character, theme, and setting and analyzes the application of these elements in a particular story. There is an additional selection in the Teaching Portfolio, which students can annotate themselves.

Each selection is self-contained and complete so that you can use the selections in any order that you like.

After Reading

Features at the end of the selection are designed to foster comprehension and encourage constructive response, either personal or literary. These features encourage the growth of skills needed by students to become independent readers. These features comprise five areas:

Thinking About The Selection: These study questions are built upon three levels of comprehension: the literal, the interpretive, and the applied. The questions are grouped by the levels of increasing complexity: recalling (literal), interpreting (inference, analysis), and applying (generalization, extension, judgment). The different levels may be used as appropriate for different ability levels, or may be used to take all students through different levels of thinking.

Analyzing Literature: This section develops and reinforces the literary concept or skill introduced on the Guide for Reading page and applies it to the selection. It helps students to understand literary concepts and appreciate writers' techniques, thereby enabling them to respond appropriately to literature.

Critical Thinking and Reading: This section introduces students to those critical thinking and critical reading skills that are necessary for understanding literature. It gives them an opportunity to apply these skills to the literary selections.

Understanding Language: Knowledge and appreciation of language are developed in this section, which contains activities on language prompted by the selection. The activities may be geared toward helping students appreciate writers' use of language, master skills needed to increase their vocabulary, or prepare for SATs.

Thinking and Writing: This is a composition assignment arising from the selection. This assignment, which may be creative or analytical, is process-oriented, suggesting steps for prewriting, drafting, and revising.

End of Unit

Focus on Reading At the end of each unit is a two-page lesson focusing on one reading skill appropriate to the type of literature students have read. For example, at the end of the short story unit, students take an in-depth look at relationships and see how patterns of relationships affect the stories they have read. At the end of the poetry unit, students review and practice making inferences about poetry. Each lesson is structured so that it provides an explanation of the skill, examples, and activities.

You the Writer, You the Critic At the end of each unit, there are six additional writing activities. Three of them, under You the Writer, are creative; three of them, under You the Critic, are analytical. Each activity is developed through the steps of the writing process.

End of Book

Three handbooks are provided at the end of *Prentice Hall Literature:* Handbook of Writing About Literature, Handbook of Critical Thinking and Reading Terms, and Handbook of Literary Terms and Techniques.

Handbook of Writing About Literature The Handbook of Writing About Literature is divided into five sections. The first section introduces the process of writing. The second requires students to analyze and interpret literature and teaches them how to write about the specific elements of literary works. The third requires students to interpret and synthesize while teaching how to write about the work as a whole. The fourth provides instruction in evaluating literary works. The fifth guides the students in the creation of their own literary works.

This Handbook may be used for direct instruction or as support for the individual writing assignments in *Prentice Hall Literature.*

Handbook of Critical Thinking and Reading Terms The Handbook of Critical Thinking and Reading Terms provides an alphabetical arrangement of the terms taught in the Critical Thinking and Reading activities at the end of selections. Some entries expand upon the original definition and provide one or more examples. Other entries provide additional terms and definitions. This Handbook can be used to preteach terminology or to review information. It can also be used as an easy reference guide for students as they work on individual Critical Thinking and Reading assignments.

Handbook of Literary Terms and Techniques The Handbook of Literary Terms and Techniques provides an alphabetical guide to the literary terms introduced on the Guide for Reading page and taught in the Analyzing Literature activities at the end of selections. Each entry provides a full definition of the term or technique with one or more examples. The handbook can be used for preteaching, for review, or as a support for students as they work on individual Analyzing Literature activities.

TEACHING SUPPORT

THE ANNOTATED TEACHER'S EDITION

The Annotated Teacher's Edition of *Prentice Hall Literature* is designed to be used both for planning and for actual in-class teaching. It offers planning aids and specific teaching suggestions for all selections. This planning and teaching material appears in the side columns next to the reduced students pages of each selection. These annotations, which correspond to the student material on that page, help you give your students positive and relevant experiences with literature by asking the right question at the right time and by pointing out what is significant.

Preparing the Lesson: Focus

The annotations on the opening pages of the selection help you plan your presentation of the material. Each selection begins with notes that suggest ways to introduce or enhance the prereading instruction or activities presented in the students' Guide for Reading. These notes help you present the material or adapt it for **less advanced** or **more advanced** students. In addition, an occasional **spelling tip** gives a hint for remembering the spelling of a troublesome word. Objectives for each selection are keyed to the end-of-selection material. This page also includes a complete list of support material for this selection in the Teaching Portfolio and other program components. In the column next to the first page of the selection, you will find a **motivation/prior knowledge** suggestion and a **purpose-setting question** to prepare the students to read the selection. Frequently, **thematic ideas** are given. These suggest other selections in this book that treat themes similar to those under discussion. You may want to use these selections together to integrate and reinforce universal concepts and themes. **ESL strategies** suggest ways to make selections accessible to ESL students. All of these annotations help you effectively prepare your lesson.

Teaching the Lesson: Presentation

You may use the notes throughout the pages of the selection to direct your discussion in class. As you and your students read the selection, you will find additional notes, that enable you to customize the lesson for your class. They let you increase your students' involvement in the work and enrich their reading of it, while enabling them to deal with the particular genres. The following kinds of notes may direct your class discussions:

Master Teacher Notes These classroom tips from master teachers give an approach, a strategy, or a very special bit of information that enlivens the selection or increases appreciation.

Humanities Notes For each piece of fine art in the student book, there is a humanities note giving information on the work of art and the artist. These notes generally point out features of the piece of art that relate it to the work of literature with which it is presented. Additionally, the humanities note concludes with questions that you may use if you wish to discuss the art as part of your discussion of the work.

Enrichment Enrichment notes provide additional information on points of interest that arise in selection. You may use this information to enrich your students' knowledge of the background of a selection and appreciation of it.

Reading Strategies Strategies to promote student comprehension of the literary text reinforce the emphasis on enabling students to read literature.

Clarification Words, phrases, or ideas that might be obstacles to students understanding are clarified to ensure comprehension.

Discussion Throughout the selection, you will find additional questions and points for discussion. These help you proceed through the selection with students, eliciting their understanding and appreciation of significant passages.

Literary Focus To promote understanding of the writer's techniques, literary focus annotations direct attention to those aspects of the selection that reflect the literary concept presented with it.

Critical Thinking and Reading These notes reinforce the critical thinking and reading skills developed throughout the program.

Reader's Response These notes ask a question designed to prompt the students' personal response to the selection.

Grammar in Action Grammar in Action notes integrate language arts skills. These notes demonstrate the writer's use of particular grammatical or style points. They present a direct link between grammar and writing.

Occasional **commentary** and **primary source** notes add background or insight to the selection.

There are probably more notes than you need for presenting any given selection. We emphasize the importance of selecting those annotations that are best suited to your classes and to your course of instruction.

Closure and Extension

Answers are provided for all questions in each feature following the selection. Where questions are open-ended, we present a suggested response or we suggest points that students should note in their answers.

The annotations after the selection also include the following:

Challenge These questions take students beyond those given with the instruction.

Publishing Student Writing For many selections, additional notes suggest ways to publishing the writing students have done in the Thinking and Writing feature.

Writing Across the Curriculum Where appropriate, you will see suggestions for additional assignments or suggestions for relating the Thinking and Writing assignment to students' work in another discipline.

In addition, you will find teaching suggestions for the special features in the student book—Reading Actively, Putting It Together, Focus on Reading, and You the Writer, You the Critic.

THE TEACHING PORTFOLIO

The Teaching Portfolio provides support for teaching and testing all of the selections and skills in *Prentice Hall Literature*.

Fine Art Transparencies

Twenty fine-art transparencies with blackline masters are provided in the Teaching Portfolio. These can be used to introduce selections and motivate students to read, or they may be used as additional writing assignments in response to art. The fine art is keyed into the selections through Master Teacher Notes in the Annotated Teacher's Edition. In the portfolio, each transparency is accompanied by a writing assignment for students and a lesson plan for teaching that assignment.

Beginning of Unit

Each unit begins with a list of objectives and a skills chart listing literary elements and skills covered in the unit. The skills chart also identifies all the blackline masters in the Teaching Portfolio that correlate to each selection.

The Selections

Full teaching support is provided for each selection. This support material is organized by selection for your convenience. The support for each selection consists of the following: Teaching Backup, Grammar in Action Worksheet, Usage and Mechanics Worksheet, Vocabulary Check, Analyzing Literature Worksheet*, Critical Thinking and Reading Worksheet*, Language Worksheet* (there are always two of the starred three), and a Selection Test.

Teacher Backup Teacher Backup material is provided for each selection. This material consists of more information about the author, a critical quotation about the author, a summary of the selection, and a list of other works by the author. In addition, there is a Check Test that you can use to check if students have read the selection. Help in teaching and evaluating the writing assignment in the student text is provided as well as three alternative composition assignments for the students. One of these is less challenging than the assignment in the student text, one is more challenging, and one requires the student to write in response to literary criticism. Finally, answers to all worksheets and tests are provided.

Grammar in Action Worksheets These worksheets provide additional instruction and practice on the topic presented with a selection in the Annotated Teacher's Edition.

Usage and Mechanics The Usage and Mechanics Worksheet provides sentences dealing with the selection that contain errors in usage and mechanics. They provide additional practice with the skill presented in the Grammar in Action worksheet. Such common problems as run-on sentences, sentences fragments, and subject-verb agreement are incorporated into these sentences are well as errors in spelling and punctuation. We suggest you have your students correct these sentences orally so that they can discuss each problem.

Vocabulary Check The Vocabulary Check tests mastery of the vocabulary words listed on the Guide for Reading page before each selection. This blackline master can be used as a test or as an in-class or at-home assignment.

Worksheets The Analyzing Literature Worksheet, Critical Thinking and Reading Worksheet, and Language Worksheet support and expand upon the skills taught at the end of the selection in the student book.

Selection Test A Selection Test is provided for each selection. This test requires students to demonstrate comprehension and interpretation of the selection and to apply the skills taught at the end of the selection. The test includes an essay question and a reader's response question.

Annotated Models For each selection that is annotated as a model in the student book (at the beginning of the short story, nonfiction, and poetry units), a selection is provided in the Teaching Portfolio for students to annotate themselves.

End of Unit

Each unit ends with two unit tests: a short-answer test and an essay test, with guidelines for evaluating student responses to the essay test questions. In addition, a list of suggested projects, a bibliography, and list of audio-visual aids are included.

End of Portfolio

At the end of the Teaching Portfolio are models of strong and weak student writing and a guide to evaluating student writing.

STUDY GUIDES

Study Guides for major novels and plays are available with *Prentice Hall Literature*. These guides will help you teach many of the works of your choice as part of your total literature program. Each guide contains an overview of the novel or play, chapter-by-chapter lessons, assignments leading to essays and imaginative writing, guidelines for dealing with provocative themes, a bibliography, and blackline masters of skills and a test for the work.

COMPUTER TEST BANK

The computer test bank provides the selection test and unit tests from the Teaching Portfolio on a computer disk. The program allows you to modify the selection tests by deleting items from the short-answer selection tests supplied, choosing a different essay question, and writing your own test questions. You can save your test for future use.

LIBRARY OF VIDEO CLASSICS

The Library of Video Classics provides videotapes of films made of major works in this level. Each tape is accompanied by a Viewing Guide, which gives background on the film or director, a planning overview for the film, and pre-viewing and after-viewing questions and activities.

Composition Strand in Prentice Hall Literature

The following chart shows all composition activities and their location in the program. The activities are organized to take students into, through, and beyond the literature.

Feature	In the Student Materials	In the Teacher Materials	Benefit
Into the Literature			
"Writing" activity *before* each selection	"Guide for Reading" page before each selection in student text	"Guide for Reading" teaching note in margin of Annotated Teacher's Edition	Writing before reading is an ideal technique for getting students into literature.
Through the Literature			
"Thinking and Writing" composition activity after *each* selection	End of each selection in student text	In Teaching Portfolio: Teaching notes for activity labeled with writing process steps. Evaluation checklist for grading writing. In ATE: Suggestions for publishing student writing	The writing activity that follows each selection provides an immediate opportunity to respond to the literary experience. The activity is in writing process format.
Three additional composition activities for *each* selection: Less Challenging, More Challenging, The Student as Critic		Additional activities are in the Teaching Portfolio. These can be used as assignments, or as essay questions for tests.	Three additional activities for *each* selection let you meet the needs for lower ability levels, or provide enrichment.
"Handbook of Writing About Literature," made up of two-page writing lessons	Handbook section of at least 50 pages at the end of each student text	Notes and support for using the handbook in the Teaching Portfolio	Guided lessons lead students step-by-step through case studies and activities.
"Unit Test" essay questions that address several selections in a unit		Tests in Teaching Portfolio comes with evaluation checklists	Sharpen critical thinking and writing with thoughtful topics that compare and contrast thematic ideas, literary elements, and unit content.
Beyond the Literature			
"You the Writer" creative writing activity with each unit	End of each unit in student text	Guidelines for evaluating student writing are in Annotated Teacher's Edition	Students try their hand at expressive writing aided by imaginative prompts and step-by-step encouragement.
"You the Critic" literary criticism activity with each unit	End of each unit in student text	Teaching notes and guidelines for evaluating student writing in Annotated Teacher's Edition	Challenge analytical skills as your students respond to literary criticism.
"Writing Across the Curriculum" suggestions		Suggestions in Annotated Teacher's Edition	Broaden writing opportunities to other subjects. Notes suggest assignments and interactions with other departments.
"Fine Art Writing Activity" (from full color art transparency)	Handout sheet	Twenty fine art color transparencies with accompanying blackline masters in Teaching Portfolio	Use the dynamic combination of literature and writing for a humanities-based writing activity.
"Student Writing Models"		In the Teaching Portfolio: Examples of strong and weak student compositions	Use the powerful motivator of peer learning to prompt better writing responses.

Skills Chart for Selections in Each Unit

The following chart shows the literary elements and integrated language arts skills covered with each selection. An asterisk (*) indicates that a worksheet appears in the Teaching Portfolio.

SHORT STORIES

Selection	Analyzing Literature	Critical Thinking and Reading	Understanding Language/ Speaking and Listening	Thinking and Writing	Grammar in Action
Reading Actively					
"The Third Wish," Joan Aiken, p. 3	Understanding the title	Finding fantastic and realistic details Making inferences*	Finding word origins Using a glossary*	Writing a fantasy	Locating Vivid Adjectives*
Plot					
"Rikki-tikki-tavi," Rudyard Kipling, p. 13	Understanding plot*	Putting events in chronological order*	Using context clues	Writing a story with a strong plot	Recognizing Appositives* Identifying Synonyms*
"The Ransom of Red Chief," O. Henry, p. 25	Understanding conflict*	Recognizing stereotypes*	Appreciating diction	Writing about conflict	Exaggeration* Subordinate Clauses*
"A Boy and a Man," James Ramsay Ullman, p. 37	Understanding suspense*	Identifying details that create suspense	Using context clues*	Writing about suspense	Using Dashes*
"A Secret for Two," Quentin Reynolds, p. 45	Recognizing a hidden problem	Finding clues to a hidden problem*	Finding origins of English words*	Writing a short story	Recognizing Verb Tense*
"Zoo," Edward Hoch, p. 51	Understanding plot and point of view	Considering other points of view*	Appreciating vivid verbs*	Writing from another point of view	Identifying Proper Nouns and Proper Adjectives*
Character					
"Last Cover," Paul Annixter, p. 57	Understanding character traits*	Comparing and contrasting characters*	Using vivid words	Writing a character sketch	Making Subjects and Verbs Agree* Finding Compound Sentences*
"The Sneaker Crisis," Shirley Jackson, p. 67	Understanding humorous character traits*	Recognizing humorous situations	Recognizing slang*	Writing about a humorous incident	Recognizing Adverbs*
"The Luckiest Time of All," Lucille Clifton p. 75	Identifying major and minor characters	Making inferences about characters*	Appreciating action verbs*	Writing about luck	
"Amigo Brothers," Piri Thomas, p. 79	Considering two major characters	Comparing and contrasting characters*	Using words in comparisons*	Writing a comparison and contrast	Using Commas*

SHORT STORIES (continued)

Selection	Analyzing Literature	Critical Thinking and Reading	Understanding Language/ Speaking and Listening	Thinking and Writing	Grammar in Action
"Stolen Day," Sherwood Anderson, p. 89	Understanding motivation*	Making inferences about motivation	Using the root *flam* Understanding Latin roots*	Writing a diary entry	Varying Sentence Length*
"Two Kinds," Amy Tan, p. 95	Understanding characterization*	Making inferences about character	Understanding the information found in a dictionary*	Writing about characters	Beginning Sentences with Coordinating Conjunctions* Compound Predicates*
Setting					
"All Summer in a Day," Ray Bradbury, p. 107	Understanding setting*	Understanding the effect of setting	Using vivid adjectives*	Writing about setting	Concrete Words*
"The Trout," Sean O'Faolain, p. 113	Understanding atmosphere	Identifying details of atmosphere*	Using the adverb suffix-*ly*￼*	Extending a story	Pronoun and Antecedent Agreement*
"Caleb's Brother," James Baldwin, p. 119	Understanding atmosphere and meaning	Identifying details of atmosphere*	Choosing meaning to fit the context*	Writing about atmosphere	Repeating Words, Phases, and Sentence Patterns*
"The Third Level," Jack Finney, p. 127	Recognizing time in a setting*	Understanding the effects of time	Finding the meaning that fits the context*	Writing a time-travel story	Semicolons*
"Rip Van Winkle," Washington Irving, p. 133	Recognizing the passage of time*	Comparing and contrasting settings*	Looking up words in a dictionary	Describing a place then and now	Adjective Phrases* Adjectives* Adjective Clauses*
Theme					
"Utzel and His Daughter, Poverty," Isaac Bashevis Singer, p. 149	Identifying the stated theme	Paraphrasing the stated theme Paraphrasing*	Reading dialogue in a story Using precise words*	Writing about a motto	Paragraphing Dialogue*
"The Old Demon," Pearl Buck, p. 155	Recognizing an implied theme	Summarizing a story*	Using context clues*	Responding to an implied theme	Punctuating Direct Quotations* Participial Phrases*
"Humaweepi, the Warrior Priest," Leslie Marmon Silko, p. 167	Understanding theme	Recognizing the writer's purpose*	Abstract words and concrete words*	Responding to theme	Concrete Words*
"Home," Gwendolyn Brooks, p. 175	Understanding universal themes	Reading between the lines*	Finding synonyms*	Writing about theme	

SHORT STORIES (continued)

Selection	Analyzing Literature	Critical Thinking and Reading	Understanding Language/ Speaking and Listening	Thinking and Writing	Grammar in Action
"Hallucination," Isaac Asimov, p. 179	Recognizing theme in science fiction Recognizing theme*	Looking at reasoning*		Writing science fiction	Agreement Between Subjects and Verbs* Commas and Coordinating Conjunctions* Sentence Fragments in Dialogue*
"The Hummingbird That Lived Through Winter," William Saroyan, p. 197	Understanding symbols in literature*	Recognizing symbols in everyday life	Antonyms*	Creating a symbol	
"The Gentlemen of the Jungle," Jomo Kenyatta, p. 201	Interpreting symbols	Recognizing bias*	Understanding connotations*	Using a symbol	
Putting it Together					
"A Day's Wait," Ernest Hemingway, p. 205	Reviewing the short story	Making inferences about conflict*	Recognizing the Greek root *demos**	Planning a television program	Prepositional phrases*

DRAMA

Selection	Analyzing Literature	Critical Thinking and Reading	Understanding Language/ Speaking and Listening	Thinking and Writing	Grammar in Action
Grandpa and the Statue, Arthur Miller, p. 219	Reading dialogue*	Making inferences about characters*	Recognizing dialect	Writing dialogue	Inverted Word Order*
The Dying Detective, from a story by Sir Arthur Conan Doyle, Michael and Mollie Hardwick, p. 233	Understanding staging*	Relating staging to dramatic purpose*	Presenting a scene from the play	Writing about staging	Three Cases of Personal Pronouns*
The Monsters Are Due on Maple Street, Rod Serling, p. 247	Recognizing conflict in drama*	Identifying invalid conclusions*	Recognizing colloquial English	Extending the play	Agreement Between Subject and Verbs* Apostrophes in Contractions*

DRAMA (continued)

Selection	Analyzing Literature	Critical Thinking and Reading	Understanding Language/ Speaking and Listening	Thinking and Writing	Grammar in Action
A Christmas Carol: Scrooge and Marley, from A Christmas Carol by Charles Dickens, Israel Horovitz Act I p. 263, Act II, p. 284	Understanding plot and exposition* Connecting character and theme	Recognizing foreshadowing* Supporting an opinion of a character*	Understanding Latin roots Synonyms and antonyms*	Retelling A Christmas Carol Writing a review of a play	Predicate Nouns* The Four Functions of Sentences* Ellipses* Agreement Between Pronouns and Antecedents*

NONFICTION

Selection	Analyzing Literature	Critical Thinking and Reading	Understanding Language/ Speaking and Listening	Thinking and Writing	Grammar in Action
Reading Actively					
From In Search of Our Mothers' Gardens, Alice Walker, p. 311	Understanding essays about people	Understanding the main idea*	Appreciating vivid adjectives*	Writing about a remembered person	Using Transitions*
Biographies and Personal Accounts					
"Eugenie Clark and the Sleeping Sharks," Margery Facklam, p. 319	Understanding biography*	Learning about the scientific method*	Analyzing the word part -logy	Writing a biography	Identifying Infinitive Phrases*
"No Gumption," Russell Baker, p. 329	Understanding autobiography*	Comparing and contrasting characters*		Writing autobiographical sketch	Using Semicolons*
From Barrio Boy, Ernesto Galarza, p. 337	Thinking about the narrator*	Understanding stereotypes*	Learning words from Spanish	Writing about a school experience	Recognizing Personal Pronouns*
"A Time of Beginnings," Jade Snow Wong, p. 343	Understanding third-person narrative	Distinguishing details*	Jargon*	Writing a third-person sketch	Recognizing Antonyms*
Essays for Enjoyment					
"Cat on the Go," James Herriot, p. 351	Understanding the narrative essay	Considering another perspective*	Recognizing British English*	Creating a television program	Using Contractions* Combining Sentences*

NONFICTION (continued)

Selection	Analyzing Literature	Critical Thinking and Reading	Understanding Language/ Speaking and Listening	Thinking and Writing	Grammar in Action
"The Night the Bed Fell," James Thurber, p. 363	Understanding the humorous essay	Identifying exaggeration*	Formal language*	Creating a humorous essay	Using Pronouns*
"Rattlesnake Hunt," Marjorie Kinnan Rawlings, p. 369	Understanding description in essays*	Separating fact from opinion*		Writing a description	Recognizing Compound-Complex Sentences*
"How to Enjoy Poetry," James Dickey, p. 375	Understanding the expository essay	Experimenting with a suggestion*	Recognizing the Latin root *vita* Latin and Greek roots for the word *life**	Writing an expository essay	Identifying Indefinite Pronouns*
"Letter Writing," Andrew A. Rooney, p. 381	Understanding the persuasive essay*	Understanding contrasts*	Debating a premise	Writing a persuasive essay	Writing Friendly Letters*
Essay in the Content Areas					
"Endlessness," Isaac Asimov, p. 387	Outlining*	Explaining mathematic inductively Inductive reasoning*	Understanding mathematical terms	Writing about mathematics	Using Transitions*
"Winslow Homer: America's Greatest Painter," H.N. Levitt p. 395	Setting a purpose for reading*	Evaluating the writer	Learning about art terms*	Writing about a painting	Recognizing Three Degrees of Comparision*
"The Mystery and Wonder of Words," Maxwell Nurnberg, p. 401	Varying rates of reading	Distinguishing fact from speculation*	Punctuating interjections*	Speculating about words	Making Verbs Agree with Their Subjects*
From *A Circle of Seasons*, Edwin Way Teale, p. 407	Journal writing	Observing and inferring*	Building words from Latin roots*	Writing a journal entry	
From *These Were the Sioux*, Mari Sandoz, p. 411	Taking notes*	Understanding cause and effect*	Signaling cause and effect	Writing an article about Sioux visitor	Understanding Adverb Clauses*
Putting It Together					
"Morning—'The Bird Perched for Flight,'" Anne Morrow Lindbergh, p. 419	Understanding an essay	Separating fact and opinion*	Homophones*	Describing an event	Recognizing Vivid Verbs*

POETRY

Selection	Analyzing Literature	Critical Thinking and Reading	Understanding Language/ Speaking and Listening	Thinking and Writing	Grammar in Action
Reading Actively					
"The Village Black-smith," Henry Wadsworth Longfellow, p. 431	Understanding theme in poetry	Understanding the poet's purpose*	Interpreting similes*	Writing about work	Recognizing Specific Nouns*
Narrative Poetry					
"The Highwayman," Alfred Noyes, p. 437	Understanding narrative poetry	Following the sequence of events*	Reading with expression*	Summarizing a narrative poem	Using Exclamation Marks*
"The Cremation of Sam McGee," Robert Service, p. 445	Understanding rhythm*	Evaluating the effects of rhythm	Practicing choral reading*	Patterning the rhythm of a poem	
"Sarah Cynthia Sylvia Stout Would Not Take the Garbage Out," Shel Silverstein, p. 451	Understanding rhyme*	Evaluating the effects of rhyme	Appreciating specific words*	Writing a rhymed poem	
"Annabel Lee," Edgar Allan Poe, p. 455	Understanding repetition in poetry*	Evaluating the effects of repetition	Appreciating old fashioned words*	Writing about a narrative poem	
"Oranges," Gary Soto, p. 459	Understanding the speaker	Making inferences about a speaker*	Sensory words*	Adding to a narrative poem	
Figurative Language and Imagery					
"Upon Mistress Susanna Southwell, Her Feet," Robert Herrick, p. 464	Understanding simile				
"The Pheasant," Robert P. Tristram Coffin, p. 466	Understanding metaphor	Evaluating the effect of a metaphor	Appreciating vivid verbs*		
"Fog," Carl Sandburg, p. 468	Understanding extended metaphor Understanding figurative language*			Writing an extended metaphor	
"The Bat," Theodore Roethke, p. 472	Understanding images*			Writing a poem about an animal	

Selection	Analyzing Literature	Critical Thinking and Reading	Understanding Language/ Speaking and Listening	Thinking and Writing	Grammar in Action
"The Pasture," Robert Frost, p. 475			Synonyms and antonyms*		
"Seal," William Jay Smith, p. 475	Understanding concrete poetry	Writing about animals*	Recognizing words that are both nouns and verbs*	Writing a concrete poem	
Three Haiku, translated from Japanese by Harry Behn, p. 478	Understanding haiku	Interpreting images*			
Three Haiku, by Bashō, translated by Daniel C. Buchanan, p. 479			The suffix -less*	Writing a haiku	
Lyric poetry					
"Washed in Silver," James Stephens, p. 484	Understanding lyric poetry				
"Feelings About Words," Mary O'Neill, p. 486		Understanding connotation*			
"The Flower-Fed Buffaloes," Vachel Lindsay, p. 488			Appreciating vivid verbs*	Writing about a lyric poem	
"The Courage That My Mother Had," Edna St. Vincent Millay, p. 492	Understanding figuarative language*	Paraphrasing a poem			
"My Mother Pieced Quilts," Teresa Palomo Acosta, p. 494			Appreciating concrete language*	Writing a lyric poem	
The Changing Seasons					
"in Just–" E.E. Cummings, p. 500	Understanding sensory language*				
"Winter," Nikki Giovanni, p. 502			Understanding compound words*	Writing a poem	Recognizing Examples, Details, and Facts*
"Stopping by Woods on a Snowy Evening," Robert Frost, p. 504			Reading a lyric poem	Writing about a poem	

POETRY (continued)

Selection	Analyzing Literature	Critical Thinking and Reading	Understanding Language/ Speaking and Listening	Thinking and Writing	Grammar in Action
"Season at the Shore," Phyllis McGinley, p. 508	Understanding alliteration*			Writing a poem with alliteration	Using prepositional phrases*
"When the Frost Is on the Punkin," James Whitcomb Riley, p. 512	Understanding onomatopoeia*		Understanding dialect	Writing a travel article	Recognizing Dialect*
People in Their Variety					
"Mother to Son," Langston Hughes, p. 518	Understanding tone				
"A Song of Greatness," Chippewa Traditional/Mary Austin, p. 520		Comparing and contrasting tone*			
"I'm Nobody," Emily Dickinson, p. 521		Paraphrasing a poem			
"Life," Naomi Long Madgett, p. 522			Appreciating vivid adjectives		
"Martin Luther King," Raymond Richard Patterson, p. 523				Writing to express tone	
"Father William," Lewis Carroll, p. 525	Understanding humor in poetry*		Punctuating dialogue*	Writing a humorous poem	
Two Limericks, Oliver Herford, p. 529	Understanding limericks	Using context to choose the meaning of words*	Appreciating words from place names*	Writing a limerick	
Putting it Together					
"Miracles" Walt Whitman, p. 531	Understanding free verse	Categorizing*	Building new words*	Writing a poem about miracles	

FABLES, MYTHS, AND LEGENDS

Selection	Analyzing Literature	Critical Thinking and Reading	Understanding Language/ Speaking and Listening	Thinking and Writing	Grammar in Action
Fables					
"The Town Mouse and the Country Mouse" and "The Fox and the Crow," Aesop, pp. 545 and 547	Understanding fables*		Word analogies*	Writing a fable	
"The Fox and the Crow," James Thurber, p. 549	Understanding satire*	Recognizing satire in foolish boasts*	Finding homo-phones	Comparing and contrasting fables	
"The Boy and the Wolf," Louis Untermeyer, p. 553	Understanding a common expres-sion*	Predicting probable future actions*	Reading a fable aloud Completing word analogies	Writing a fable in verse	
Greek and Roman Myths					
"Demeter and Persephone," Anne Terry White, p. 557	Appreciating myth*	Contrasting science and myth*	Analyzing words with the Latin root *mors*	Writing a myth	Recognizing Appositives*
"Prometheus the Fire-Bringer," Jere-my Ingalls, p. 563	Understanding con-flict in myth*	Evaluating the rea-sons for a conflict*	Interpreting the adjective *Promethean*	Predicting the out-come of a conflict	Identifying Participi-al Phrases*
"Phaëthon, Son of Apollo," Olivia E. Coolidge, p. 571	Understanding hubris*	Recognizing clues to the outcome of a myth*	Understanding word histories	Creating a modern myth	Finding Compound Adjectives*
"Baucis and Phile-mon," Edith Hamil-ton, p. 577	Understanding lessons in myth*	Learning about a culture from its myths*	Analyzing words with the Greek root *phil*	Writing a dialogue for a myth	
"Icarus and Daedalus," Josephine Preston Peabody, p. 581	Understanding characters in myth	Comparing and contrasting charac-ters*	Creating a dramatic dialogue Choosing the meaning that fits the context*	Writing about char-acters in a myth	
"Narcissus," Jay Macpherson, p. 585	Understanding metamorphosis*	Evaluating general-izations*	Understanding word origins	Writing sketches about metamorpho-sis	
Myths, Legends, and Folktales from Around the World					
"The Legend of the Hummingbird," Pura Belpré, p. 589	Understanding uni-versal theme*	Recognizing clues to outcomes*	Completing verbal analogies	Writing a legend	

FABLES, MYTHS, AND LEGENDS (continued)

Selection	Analyzing Literature	Critical Thinking and Reading	Understanding Language/ Speaking and Listening	Thinking and Writing	Grammar in Action
"Ojeeg, the Hunter, and the Ice Man," Dorothy de Wit, p. 593	Understanding conflict in a legend*	Evaluating a personification*	Presenting a readers' theater	Creating a personification	Understanding Verb Tense*
"Popocatepetl and Ixtlaccihuatl," Juliet Piggott, p. 599	Understanding motivation in a legend*	Identifying imaginative details	Using synonyms as context clues Using synonyms*	Writing about a legend	Recognizing Specific Nouns and Specific Adjectives*
"The Pointing Finger," Carol Kendall and Yao-wen Li, p. 607	Understanding a folk tale*	Evaluating generalizations	Matching meaning with context*	Summarizing a folk tale	
"All Stories Are Anansi's," Harold Courlander, p. 611	Understanding the trickster in folklore*	Making inferences about characters in folklore*		Writing a folk tale with animal characters	
"The Little Lizard's Sorrow," Mai Vo-Dinh, p. 615	Understanding symbols in folktales Understanding symbols*	Making generalizations*	Recognizing the root word mit	Writing a folk tale with a symbol	

THE NOVEL: *WHERE THE RED FERN GROWS,* Wilson Rawls

Selection	Analyzing Literature	Critical Thinking and Reading	Understanding Language/ Speaking and Listening	Thinking and Writing	Grammar in Action
Chapters 1–7, p. 629	Understanding character*	Making inferences about characters	Discovering word origins*	Writing about character	Recognizing Compound Nouns* Using Action Verbs* Varying Sentence Openers* Understanding Subordinate Conjunctions*
Chapters 8–11, p. 667	Understanding plot development	Solving problems*	Using similes*	Writing a news article	Finding Present Participles* Understanding Infinitives* Identifying Transitions* Using Specific Words*

THE NOVEL: *WHERE THE RED FERN GROWS,* Wilson Rawls (continued)

Selection	Analyzing Literature	Critical Thinking and Reading	Understanding Language/ Speaking and Listening	Thinking and Writing	Grammar in Action
Chapters 12–15, p. 629	Appreciating setting in a novel*	Inferring the effect of setting	Using synonyms*	Writing about setting	Finding Adverbs* Recognizing Linking Verbs* Using Prepositional Phrases* Understanding *Lay* and *Lie**
Chapters 16–20, p. 733	Understanding theme	Evaluating a novel*	Understanding derived words*	Writing a book review	Identifying Transitive Verbs* Identifying Intransitive Verbs* Varying Sentence Length* Making Comparisons*

PRENTICE HALL
LITERATURE

COPPER

BRONZE

SILVER

GOLD

PLATINUM

THE AMERICAN EXPERIENCE

THE ENGLISH TRADITION

WORLD MASTERPIECES

PRENTICE HALL
LITERATURE

BRONZE

SECOND EDITION

 PRENTICE HALL
Englewood Cliffs, New Jersey
Needham, Massachusetts

Humanities Note

Fine art, *Sally,* by Joseph de-Camp. Decamp (1852-1923) was a portrait painter who began his career as an impressionist in the American style. After studying in Cincinnati and Munich, he opened a studio in Boston.

Along with such painters as Childe Hassam and J. Alden Weir, DeCamp formed an alliance, which the members called "The Ten American Painters." "The Ten" exhibited together, forming a kind of academy of American impressionism. Though each of the painters in the group had a different personal outlook and delicate stylistic differences, they were all skillful, traditional, and genteel in their depictions of proper American society. Pretty scenes, well-dressed ladies in drawing rooms, and vases of flowers were their primary subjects.

DeCamp was part of the proper world of Boston art. His painting was solid, sober, and skillfully crafted. His portrait studio became successful, and he spent his days off painting impressionist landscapes.

Sally was one of the many portraits he made of the Bostonians of his time. Little of the exuberance of impressionist brushwork or color is visible in this traditional work. At this point in his career, he was using a straightforward, academic approach to portraiture. Like so many American artists at the turn of the century, he led a conservative life, picturing society as he found it.

Art credits begin on page 881.

COVER AND TITLE PAGE: *Sally* (detail), Joseph DeCamp, Worcester Art Museum, Worcester, Massachusetts

PRENTICE HALL
A Division of Simon & Schuster
Englewood Cliffs, New Jersey 07632

STAFF CREDITS FOR PRENTICE HALL LITERATURE

Editorial: Eileen Thompson, Ellen Bowler, Philip Fried, Daniel Jackson, Doug McCollum, Jane Standen, Richard Hickox, Carol Schneider, Kelly Ackley

Design: Sue Walrath, Nancy Sharkey, Leslie Osher

Photo Research: Libby Forsyth

Production: Penny Hull, Suse Cioffi, Joan McCulley, Marlys Lehmann, Lisa Meyerhoff, Cleasta Wilburn

Editorial Systems: Andrew Grey Bommarito, Ralph O'Brien

Marketing: Carol Newman, Mollie Ledwith, Tom Maksym

Manufacturing: Laura Sanderson, Denise Herckenrath

Permissions: Doris Robinson

ACKNOWLEDGMENTS

Grateful acknowledgment is made to the following for permission to reprint copyrighted material:

Teresa Palomo Acosta
"My Mother Pieced Quilts" by Teresa Palomo Acosta. Reprinted by permission of the author.

T. D. Allen
"Grandfather" by Shirley Crawford. Copyright 1970. Used by permission of T. D. Allen.

Isaac Asimov
"Hallucination" by Isaac Asimov, published in *Boy's Life*. Copyright © 1985 by the Boy Scouts of America. Reprinted by permission of the author.

(contiued on page 878)

iv

CONTENTS

v

DRAMA

NONFICTION

POETRY

FABLES, MYTHS, AND LEGENDS

THE NOVEL

PRENTICE HALL
LITERATURE
BRONZE

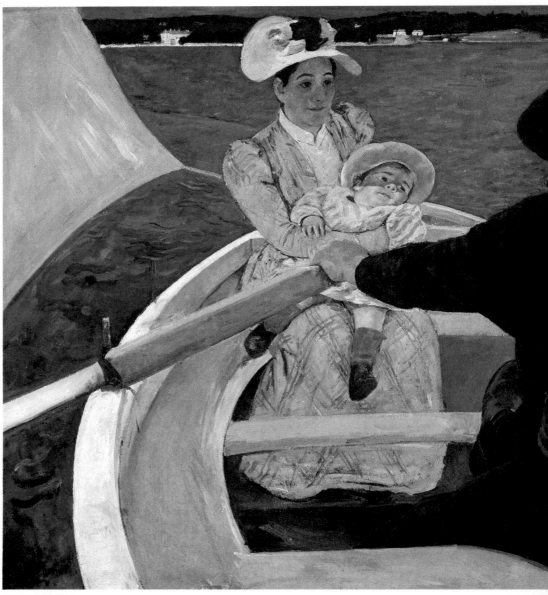

THE BOATING PARTY
Mary Cassatt
The National Gallery of Art, Washington

SHORT STORIES

One of the best loved forms of literature is the short story. It is a brief work of fiction containing made-up characters and events. Because short stories are brief, they do not take long to read. Usually you can start and finish one in a single sitting. Short stories are fun to read, presenting us with an endless variety of characters, places, and situations. In addition, they often reveal truths about life and so deepen our understanding of the human condition.

The basic meaning of the word *fiction* is "anything made up." Because short stories are made up from a writer's imagination, they are not just reports of events that actually happened. However, they are "made up" in another sense, too. They are put together from several basic elements: plot, characters, setting, and theme. The plot is the sequence of events in the story. The characters are, of course, the people, or sometimes the animals, that take part in the events. The setting is the time and place of the story. The theme is the central idea or insight into life that is revealed through the events of the story.

You will be learning more about these elements as you read the stories in this unit. As your understanding of these elements grows, so will the pleasure you gain from reading good fiction.

Humanities Note
Fine art, *The Boating Party,* Mary Cassatt. Mary Cassatt (1844–1926) was an American Impressionist painter. Born to a wealthy Philadelphia family, Cassatt met with opposition when she wanted to go abroad to study art. Undeterred, she established herself in Paris and her work soon attracted the attention of Edgar Degas, the famous French Impressionist. At his invitation, she joined the circle of Impressionists. She became an important figure in the Impressionist movement and her work with them won acclaim in Europe. She is well known today for her paintings of women and children.

The Boating Party was painted at Antibes, France, in the years 1893–94. This study of a mother with a tired child shows a calm and easy pose. The point of view is over the shoulder of the rower. The color scheme is predominantly yellow and blue. The large areas of color, such as the sea and the clothing of the man, are minimally detailed. This flatness of treatment shows the influence of the Japanese print on Mary Cassatt's painting. The pleasant familial scene could hold the story of an afternoon.

1

Reading Actively The process outlined on this page is based on research into the ways that good readers get meaning from fiction. These strategies enable readers to become thoughtful, active readers. The process also teaches them to monitor their own comprehension, learning how to find meaning in any text.

To introduce the process, have students discuss the difference between *active* and *passive*. Explain that to be effective readers, students must first become active readers. You might ask students to discuss the way they normally read a story. What strategies have they found that work for them? What difficulties have they encountered? Finally introduce the strategies listed here and explain that these strategies will help students become more effective readers. The model on the following pages is annotated with questions, predictions, clarifications, and summaries that an active reader might make. It also shows the way an active reader might pull together these details after reading. Ask students to pay attention to these annotations as they read. Also ask them to create their own questions, predictions, clarifications, and summaries, and finally to react to the story.

Consider having the students read this story aloud. This would allow you to have the students share their questions, predictions, clarifications, and summaries. It would also provide the students with the opportunity to comment on the annotations with the story.

For further practice with the process, use the selection in the Teaching Portfolio, "The Dinner Party" by Mona Gardner, page 8, which students can annotate themselves. Encourage students to continue to use these strategies when reading other stories.

READING ACTIVELY

The Short Story

To read a short story successfully, you must become actively involved. You do this by thinking about the story as you read. In other words, you bring ideas to mind by stopping to ask questions and to predict what will happen. You occasionally pause to answer your questions and check your predictions and to summarize what has happened so far.

Use the following strategies to help you read actively. These strategies will help you "figure out" what is important in a story and what makes the story effective.

Question

Before you begin, think about what you expect to happen in the story. What does the title suggest to you? As you read, you might ask yourself questions about what is happening. What causes the events to occur as they do? What are the characters like? Is the setting, or place of the story, important? Why does the author include certain information? Then look for the answers to your questions as you read on.

Predict

Bring your own experience to the story. Consider what you already know about similar situations or people in your own life. Use your knowledge of how stories work. Then try to predict what will happen based on what you already know. As you read on, you will find out if your predictions are correct.

Clarify

When something in the story is not clear or does not seem to make sense, stop and try to clarify the confusion. Look for the answers to your questions, and check your predictions. By continually clarifying in these ways, you will be able to get meaning from a story.

Summarize

Occasionally pause to review what has happened so far. Identify what seems important, and try to determine how that piece of information works with everything else in terms of how the story is developing.

Pull It Together

Try to determine the central idea or point of the story. What did the story say to you? How do you feel about the story?

Using these strategies will help you to be a more effective reader. You will better be able to recall details from the story, interpret what you have read to find meaning, and apply this meaning to your world.

On the following pages is a model of how an active reader might read a story.

Objectives

1 To learn how to read a short story actively
2 To understand the use of a title in a short story
3 To identify fantastic and realistic details
4 To recognize how word origins relate to meaning
5 To write a fantasy

Support Material

Teaching Portfolio
Teacher Backup, p. 5
Reading Actively, "The Dinner Party" by Mona Gardner, p. 8
Grammar in Action Worksheet, *Locating Vivid Adjectives,* p. 10
Usage and Mechanics Worksheet, p. 12
Critical Thinking and Reading Worksheet, *Making Inferences,* p. 13

Language Worksheet, *Using a Glossary,* p. 14
Selection Test, p. 15

The Third Wish

Joan Aiken

Once there was a man who was driving in his car at dusk on a spring evening through part of the forest of Savernake. His name was Mr. Peters. The primroses were just beginning but the trees were still bare, and it was cold; the birds had stopped singing an hour ago.

As Mr. Peters entered a straight, empty stretch of road he seemed to hear a faint crying, and a struggling and thrashing, as if somebody was in trouble far away in the trees. He left his car and climbed the mossy bank beside the road. Beyond the bank was an open slope of beech trees leading down to thorn bushes through which he saw the gleam of water. He stood a moment waiting to try and discover where the noise was coming from, and presently heard a rustling and some strange cries in a voice which was almost human—and yet there was something too hoarse about it at one time and too clear and sweet at another. Mr. Peters ran down the hill and as he neared the bushes he saw something white among them which was trying to extricate itself; coming closer he found that it was a swan that had become entangled in the thorns growing on the bank of the canal.

The bird struggled all the more frantically as he approached, looking at him with hate in its yellow eyes, and when he took hold of it to free it, it hissed at him, pecked him, and thrashed dangerously with its wings which were powerful enough to break his arm. Nevertheless he managed to release it from the thorns, and carrying it tightly with one arm, holding the snaky head well away with the other hand (for he did not wish his eyes pecked out), he took it to the verge of the canal and dropped it in.

The swan instantly assumed great dignity and sailed out to the middle of the water, where it put itself to rights with much dabbling and preening, smoothing its feathers with little showers of drops. Mr. Peters waited, to make sure that it was all right and had suffered no damage in its struggles. Presently the swan, when it was satisfied with its appearance, floated in to the bank once more, and in a moment, instead of

The Third Wish 3

Questions: Will this story be about three wishes? Why does the title mention only the third wish?

Question: Who is in trouble?

Prediction: Mr. Peters will help this person.

Clarification: The thing in trouble is not a person but a swan.

Clarification: Mr. Peters does help this creature.

Reading Strategy Remind students that the questions, predictions, clarifications, and summaries shown with "The Third Wish" are samples. Not all students would ask the same questions or need the same material clarified. Also remind students that predictions are risks; not all predictions are accurate, but it's all right to make predictions that turn out to be incorrect.

Clarification: So this story *is* about three wishes.

Summary: Mr. Peters saves the King of the Forest from a difficulty and is granted three wishes.

Question: How will Mr. Peters use his three wishes?

Prediction: Mr. Peters seems a practical person. Perhaps he will not regret his wishes.

Question: What happens to the leaf after he makes his wish?

the great white bird, there was a little man all in green with a golden crown and long beard, standing by the water. He had fierce glittering eyes and looked by no means friendly.

"Well, Sir," he said threateningly, "I see you are presumptuous enough to know some of the laws of magic. You think that because you have rescued—by pure good fortune—the King of the Forest from a difficulty, you should have some fabulous reward."

"I expect three wishes, no more and no less," answered Mr. Peters, looking at him steadily and with composure.

"Three wishes, he wants, the clever man! Well, I have yet to hear of the human being who made any good use of his three wishes—they mostly end up worse off than they started. Take your three wishes then"—he flung three dead leaves in the air—"don't blame me if you spend the last wish in undoing the work of the other two."

Mr. Peters caught the leaves and put two of them carefully in his briefcase. When he looked up, the swan was sailing about in the middle of the water again, flicking the drops angrily down its long neck.

Mr. Peters stood for some minutes reflecting on how he should use his reward. He knew very well that the gift of three magic wishes was one which brought trouble more often than not, and he had no intention of being like the forester who first wished by mistake for a sausage, and then in a rage wished it on the end of his wife's nose, and then had to use his last wish in getting it off again. Mr. Peters had most of the things which he wanted and was very content with his life. The only thing that troubled him was that he was a little lonely, and had no companion for his old age. He decided to use his first wish and to keep the other two in case of an emergency. Taking a thorn he pricked his tongue with it, to remind himself not to utter rash wishes aloud. Then holding the third leaf and gazing round him at the dusky undergrowth, the primroses, great beeches and the blue-green water of the canal, he said:

"I wish I had a wife as beautiful as the forest."

A tremendous quacking and splashing broke out on the surface of the water. He thought that it was the swan laughing at him. Taking no notice he made his way through the darkening woods to his car, wrapped himself up in the rug and went to sleep.

4   Short Stories

Grammar in Action

Writers use **vivid adjectives** to present a clear and precise picture. Vivid, specific words help the reader imagine what the author is describing distinctly and correctly. Notice how Joan Aiken uses vivid adjectives to convey a clear and precise picture in the following sentences:

Presently the swan, . . . floated in to the bank once more, and in a moment, instead of the *great white* bird, there was a *little* man all in green with a *golden* crown and *long* beard, standing by the water. He had *fierce glittering* eyes and looked by no means *friendly*.

It is easy for the reader to imagine a swan described as *great* and *white*. The author also presents a clear, precise picture of the King of the Forest, using the adjectives *little, golden, long, fierce,* and *glittering*. Compare Aiken's sentences, with vivid adjectives, with the following sentence.

BOUQUET WITH FLYING LOVERS, c. 1934—47
Marc Chagall
The Tate Gallery

The Third Wish 5

Humanities Note

Fine art, *Bouquet With Flying Lovers,* 1947, by Marc Chagall. Marc Chagall (1887–1985) was born in Russia but lived and worked in France. His work is chiefly fantasy, showing his roots in his Russian past and in Russian folklore.

Bouquet With Flying Lovers is one of many of Chagall's paintings of bouquets and lovers. This one has a soft, dreamy atmosphere appropriate for the sentimental emotions evoked by the subject.

1. Have students identify the figures and objects in the painting.
2. What aspects of this painting make it an appropriate illustration for this story?

Presently the swan, . . . floated in to the bank once more, and in a moment, instead of the bird, there was a man all in green with a crown and beard, standing by the water. He had mean eyes and looked by no means friendly.

Student Activity 1. Find three other sentences from the story in which the author uses vivid adjectives to describe people or things. Identify the adjectives and explain how they enhance the noun or pronoun they modify.

Student Activity 2. Write five original sentences that use vivid adjectives in describing nouns and pronouns.

Questions: Who is she? Where does she come from?

Question: Why is she so interested in swans?

Question: Where does she go?

Question: Who is this swan? Why is Leita weeping?

Clarification: Leita is really a swan, and this swan is her sister. So this is how the King of the Forest grants his wishes.

When he awoke it was morning and the birds were beginning to call. Coming along the track towards him was the most beautiful creature he had ever seen, with eyes as blue-green as the canal, hair as dusky as the bushes, and skin as white as the feathers of swans.

"Are you the wife that I wished for?" asked Mr. Peters.

"Yes, I am," she replied. "My name is Leita."

She stepped into the car beside him and they drove off to the church on the outskirts of the forest, where they were married. Then he took her to his house in a remote and lovely valley and showed her all his treasures—the bees in their white hives, the Jersey cows, the hyacinths, the silver candlesticks, the blue cups and the luster bowl for putting primroses in. She admired everything, but what pleased her most was the river which ran by the foot of his garden.

"Do swans come up there?" she asked.

"Yes, I have often seen swans there on the river," he told her, and she smiled.

Leita made him a good wife. But as time went by Mr. Peters began to feel that she was not happy. She seemed restless, wandered much in the garden, and sometimes when he came back from the fields he would find the house empty and she would only return after half an hour or so with no explanation of where she had been. On these occasions she was always especially tender and would put out his slippers to warm and cook his favorite dish—Welsh rarebit[1] with wild strawberries—for supper.

One evening he was returning home along the river path when he saw Leita in front of him, down by the water. A swan had sailed up to the verge and she had her arms round its neck and the swan's head rested against her cheek. She was weeping, and as he came nearer he saw that tears were rolling, too, from the swan's eyes.

"Leita, what is it?" he asked, very troubled.

"This is my sister," she answered. "I can't bear being separated from her."

Now he understood that Leita was really a swan from the forest, and this made him very sad because when a human being marries a bird it always leads to sorrow.

---

1. Welsh rarebit: A dish of melted cheese served on crackers or toast.

"I could use my second wish to give your sister human shape, so that she could be a companion to you," he suggested.

"No, no," she cried, "I couldn't ask that of her."

"Is it so very hard to be a human being?" asked Mr. Peters sadly.

"Very, very hard," she answered.

"Don't you love me at all, Leita?"

"Yes, I do, I do love you," she said, and there were tears in her eyes again. "But I missed the old life in the forest, the cool grass and the mist rising off the river at sunrise and the feel of the water sliding over my feathers as my sister and I drifted along the stream."

"Then shall I use my second wish to turn you back into a swan again?" he asked, and his tongue pricked to remind him of the old King's words, and his heart swelled with grief inside him.

"Who will take care of you?"

"I'd do it myself as I did before I married you," he said, trying to sound cheerful.

She shook her head. "No, I could not be as unkind to you as that. I am partly a swan, but I am also partly a human being now. I will stay with you."

Poor Mr. Peters was very distressed on his wife's account and did his best to make her life happier, taking her for drives in the car, finding beautiful music for her to listen to on the radio, buying clothes for her and even suggesting a trip round the world. But she said no to that; she would prefer to stay in their own house near the river.

He noticed that she spent more and more time baking wonderful cakes—jam puffs, petits fours, eclairs and meringues. One day he saw her take a basketful down to the river and he guessed that she was giving them to her sister.

He built a seat for her by the river, and the two sisters spent hours together there, communicating in some wordless manner. For a time he thought that all would be well, but then he saw how thin and pale she was growing.

One night when he had been late doing the account he came up to bed and found her weeping in her sleep and calling:

"Rhea! Rhea! I can't understand what you say! Oh, wait for me, take me with you!"

Summary: Mr. Peters uses his first wish to ask for a wife. She turns out to be a swan. Mr. Peters offers to use his second wish to turn Leita's sister into a human or to turn Leita back into a swan. Leita will have none of this and instead decides to bear her loneliness and stay with Mr. Peters.

Prediction: There seems to be no good solution to this problem. Perhaps the King of the Forest's words will prove to be true and Mr. Peters will wind up worse off than when he started.

Clarification: Rhea must be Leita's sister.

The Third Wish 7

Enrichment Sorcerers change human beings into swans in ballet and opera. In Tchaikovsky's ballet *Swan Lake,* a girl is transformed into a swan and must remain one until a man marries her and remains faithful in his love. In Wagner's opera *Lohengrin* the evil Ortrud puts Godfrey into the form of a swan to deny him his dukedom. Lohengrin, a knight of the Holy Grail, breaks her spell and restores Godfrey to human form.

Humanities Note

Fine art, *Landscape—Base and Fountain,* Tiffany Studios. The American artist, craftsman, and inventor Lewis Comfort Tiffany (1848–1933) is best remembered as the creator of the "Tiffany-glass lampshade." First a painter, then an interior designer, Tiffany finally concentrated his greatest efforts on the design and manufacture of art glass. He invented Favrile glass, a composite of various colored glass worked together while still molten, which produced varied and exotic effects of bold metallic tones and iridescence. This glass, for which he remains famous, was fashioned into lamps, vases, stained glass, mosaic tiles, and jewelry.

The *Glass Mosaic Wall Mural: Landscape—Base and Fountain* was made as a showy display piece for Tiffany's design studio in New York City. It is composed of glass manufactured by Tiffany and is a prime example of the elaborate designs produced by his studios. It shows a scene of absolute peace.

1. Ask students about the mood or feeling the piece suggests.
2. What scene in the story does it suggest?

Master Teacher Note Three wishes have a religious association. Pythagoras called three the perfect number, expressive of "beginning, middle, and end"; he makes it a symbol of deity. Ask the class how the progression of three wishes in this story matches the Pythagorean description of the number three.

GLASS MOSAIC WALL MURAL: LANDSCAPE—BASE AND FOUNTAIN, c. 1905–1915 (detail)
Tiffany Studios
The Metropolitan Museum of Art

Clarification: So this is how Mr. Peters uses his second wish. He turns Leita back into a swan. This explains what happens to the leaf when he uses his wish. He blows it away.

Then he knew that it was hopeless and she would never be happy as a human. He stooped down and kissed her goodbye, then took another leaf from his notecase, blew it out of the window, and used up his second wish.

Next moment instead of Leita there was a sleeping swan lying across the bed with its head under its wing. He carried it out of the house and down to the brink of the river, and then he said, "Leita! Leita!" to waken her, and gently put her into the water. She gazed round her in astonishment for a moment, and then came up to him and rested her head lightly against his hand; next instant she was flying away over the trees towards the heart of the forest.

He heard a harsh laugh behind him, and turning round saw the old King looking at him with a malicious expression.

Questions: Will Mr. Peters use his third wish? I still don't know why this story is called "The *Third* Wish."

"Well, my friend! You don't seem to have managed so wonderfully with your first two wishes, do you? What will you do with the last? Turn yourself into a swan? Or turn Leita back into a girl?"

"I shall do neither," said Mr. Peters calmly. "Human beings and swans are better in their own shapes."

But for all that he looked sadly over towards the forest

8   *Short Stories*

where Leita had flown, and walked slowly back to his house.

Next day he saw two swans swimming at the bottom of the garden, and one of them wore the gold chain he had given Leita after their marriage; she came up and rubbed her head against his hand.

Mr. Peters and his two swans came to be well known in that part of the country; people used to say that he talked to swans and they understood him as well as his neighbors. Many people were a little frightened of him. There was a story that once when thieves tried to break into his house they were set upon by two huge white birds which carried them off bodily and dropped them in the river.

As Mr. Peters grew old everyone wondered at his contentment. Even when he was bent with rheumatism[2] he would not think of moving to a drier spot, but went slowly about his work, with the two swans always somewhere close at hand.

Sometimes people who knew his story would say to him: "Mr. Peters, why don't you wish for another wife?"

"Not likely," he would answer serenely. "Two wishes were enough for me, I reckon. I've learned that even if your wishes are granted they don't always better you. I'll stay faithful to Leita."

One autumn night, passers-by along the road heard the mournful sound of two swans singing. All night the song went on, sweet and harsh, sharp and clear. In the morning Mr. Peters was found peacefully dead in his bed with a smile of great happiness on his face. In his hands, which lay clasped on his breast, were a withered leaf and a white feather.

Clarification: Mr. Peters dies without using his third wish. I know this because he still has the third leaf. This leaf seems to symbolize his victory over the King of the Forest.

Putting It Together: Mr. Peters did gain his first wish, which was really for a companion for his old age. Thus, he had no need to use his third wish to undo the first two.

---

2. **rheumatism** (rōō′ mə tĭz′ m) n. · Pain and stiffness of the joints and muscles.

Joan Aiken (1924–   ), the daughter of the American poet Conrad Aiken, always planned to be a writer. She has written several novels, as well as stories and plays for young people. She lives part of the year in England, which is the setting of "The Third Wish." Many of her stories deal with fantastic or mysterious events. In fact, her approach to writing can best be summed up by the title of the book from which "The Third Wish" was taken—*Not What You Expected.*

The Third Wish 9

More About the Author Joan Aiken writes with equal ease for children and adults. One of her books, *A Touch of Chill: Tales for Sleepless Nights,* an adult collection of short stories, was also reviewed in the children's book section of *The New York Times Book Review.* Ask what qualities a writer would need to have to appeal to both children and adults. What other authors come to mind?

Reader's Response Do you think that Mr. Peters used his wishes wisely? Why or why not?

Closure and Extension

(Questions begin on p. 10)

ANSWERS TO THINKING ABOUT THE SELECTION
Recalling

1. He rescues a swan entangled in thorns growing on the bank of the canal. When the freed swan turns out to be the King of the Forest who is willing to reward his liberator, Mr. Peters asks for and receives three wishes.
2. His first wish is for a wife as beautiful as the forest.
3. After making his first wish, Mr. Peters goes to sleep in his car. When he awakes in the morning, the most beautiful creature he has ever seen comes toward him, acknowledges that she is the wife he wished for, and goes with him to the church to be married.
4. His second wish is for his wife to be turned back into a swan.
5. He spends his life contentedly in the company of the two swans, Leita and her sister, Rhea. He is able to communicate with them, and they protect him from harm.

Interpreting

6. The action shows that he is loving, considerate, and unselfish.
7. After Leita was turned back into a swan, the two swans are always close at hand to keep him company. The three have a strong attachment and affection for each other.
8. Mr. Peters has had a good, contented life and has spent his final years in the company of the loving swans. He used his wishes wisely and therefore has no regrets.

(Answers begin on p. 9.)

9. The withered leaf proves that Mr. Peters never made his third wish but kept the leaf with him. The white feather is symbolic of his love and faithfulness to Leita and of his caring relationship with both swans.

Applying

10. Answers will differ. Suggested Response: Mr. Peters was aware that the King of the Forest said he would not take the blame if Mr. Peters spent the last wish undoing the work of the other two. Seeing how unhappy Leita was made him aware that swans could not be happy as humans, and conversely, he could deduce that he could not be happy as a swan. Therefore, the safe and wise thing for Mr. Peters to do was not to use the third wish.

ANSWERS TO ANALYZING LITERATURE

1. While the first two wishes were very important in that they propelled the plot forward, the last was the most important because it suggested the theme of the story. The title "The Three Wishes" would not suggest the theme.
2. Answers will differ, but students should see that this is an effective title because it excites the reader's curiosity about his third wish and also hints at the theme of the story. If a different title is chosen, it should be judged on the basis of what it suggests about the story and how intriguing it is.
3. Answers will differ, but students should suggest that when someone is given three wishes in a story, the reader expects all three wishes to be used, especially when the title is "The Third Wish." The expectation is that this third wish would be something really special, and thus one is surprised that it is never made.

Challenge What other stories or tales do you know concerning three wishes? How are they similar to and different from "The Third Wish"?

THINKING ABOUT THE SELECTION
Recalling

1. How does Mr. Peters gain his three wishes?
2. What is his first wish?
3. How is his first wish granted?
4. What is Mr. Peters' second wish?
5. Briefly describe his life after his second wish.

Interpreting

6. What does Mr. Peters' turning his wife back into a swan show about him?
7. Mr. Peters wished for a wife so that he would not be lonely in his old age. In what way is this wish fulfilled, despite the intentions of the King of the Forest?
8. Why does Mr. Peters die with a look of happiness on his face?
9. Explain why Mr. Peters is found with "a withered leaf and a white feather."

Applying

10. If you were Mr. Peters, would you have used your third wish? Why or why not?

ANALYZING LITERATURE
Understanding the Title

The **title** of a story gives you a hint about the work. An author might choose a title to call attention to a character or to suggest something about the plot. Often the title gives you a clue to a story's central idea, or the theme that the writer wishes to present. This is the case in "The Third Wish."

1. Why does the author call this story "The Third Wish" instead of, for example, "The Three Wishes"?
2. Would you have chosen another title for this story? If so, what would it be? Explain your answer.
3. The Third Wish" is taken from a collection of short stories called *Not What You Expected*. How is the ending of this story "not what you expected"?

CRITICAL THINKING AND READING
Finding Fantastic and Realistic Details

Fantastic details are strange and unusual. They are based on imagination rather than real life. In "The Third Wish," for example, the King of the Forest is a fantastic character. **Realistic details,** however, show life as we know it. Mr. Peters in this story is presented in a true-to-life fashion. A story based on fantasy often uses both realistic and fantastic details.

Find three realistic details in this selection and three fantastic details.

UNDERSTANDING LANGUAGE
Finding Word Origins

The word *fantasy* comes from the Greek word *phantasia,* which means "the appearance of a thing." In English, *fantasy* has come to mean the appearance of something imagined or dreamed as opposed to something real.

Many other words come from this same Greek word. Look up each word below in a dictionary and write its meaning. Note how each of these words relates to the idea of something dreamed or imagined. Then use each word in a sentence.
1. fantasize
2. fantasia
3. phantom
4. phantasmagoria

THINKING AND WRITING
Writing a Fantasy

Write your own story about the gift of three wishes. First brainstorm to decide what those three wishes will be. Remembering that the gift of three magic wishes can be more trouble than not, consider the complications that can be caused by each wish. Choose your characters with care, and make the person who grants the wishes a fantastic creature like the King of the Forest. Then prepare the first draft of your story. Read over this draft and make any necessary changes. Finally, proofread your story and share it with your classmates.

ANSWERS TO CRITICAL THINKING AND READING

Answers will differ. Suggested Responses: Three realistic details are: Mr. Peters frees a swan entangled in thorns; Mr. Peters and his bride drive to a church; Mr. Peters sees two swans swimming in the river at the bottom of his garden. Three fantastic details are: The swan changes into the King of the Forest; Mr. Peters is granted three magical wishes; Mr. Peters' wife is a swan from the forest.

ANSWERS TO UNDERSTANDING LANGUAGE

1. *Fantasize* means "to create or imagine in a fantasy."
2. A fantasia is a musical or literary composition of no fixed form, with a structure determined by the composer's or writer's fancy. The word relates to something dreamed or imagined.
3. A phantom is something that appears to the sight but has no physical existence, or it may mean something that exists only in the mind. Because this thing does not really exist, it must be imagined.
4. *Phantasmagoria* means "a rapidly changing series of things seen or imagined, as in a dream."

THINKING AND WRITING
Publishing Student Writing Students will enjoy reading each other's stories. You might prepare a class booklet of students' stories about three wishes.

Plot

THE CALLERS
Walter Ufer
Smithsonian Institution

Humanities Note

Fine art, *The Callers*, 1926, by Walter Ufer. Walter Ufer (1876–1936), an American painter of Native Americans, belonged to the Taos School. Ufer studied art at the Royal Academy in Dresden, Germany; the Royal Applied Art Schools in Dresden; the Art Institute of Chicago; and the J. Francis Smith Art School in Chicago. In subsequent years he taught, worked as a commercial artist, and traveled through Europe and North Africa. In 1914 he moved to Taos, the New Mexican artists' colony, and began to paint the desert landscape and the Pueblo Indians for which he would be remembered.

The Callers was painted in Taos, New Mexico. Ufer did not view or paint native Americans as an anthropological curiosity to preserve for posterity; he saw them as people in transition, caught between their past and the technology of the white person's world. His paintings caught their dilemma. In this painting he narrates an everyday incident from this world. A Native American servant opens the gate to two callers, Native Americans dressed in store-bought clothing. Painted in Ufer's broad style, it utilizes strong, bright colors. It is left to the viewer to decide the story that goes with this painting.

Focus

More About the Author Rudyard Kipling was such a prolific writer that his complete works encompass thirty-five volumes of stories, novels, essays, sketches, poetry, speeches, and an unfinished biography. Have the class discuss where a person might get so many ideas for writing.

Literary Focus Help students to realize that plot is more than a sequence of events. The events must all center on a conflict with a resolution at the end.

Look For Most students should readily be able to recognize conflict and sequence of events. For less advanced students, who might have difficulty with the concept of climax, suggest that they look for the turning point, the event after which the events move in a different direction and the conflict is resolved.

Writing/Prior Knowledge For less advanced students, simply summarizing might be sufficient. Students should be able to show how one event leads to the next and how the events build to a climax.

Vocabulary Most students will not find these words difficult. You might help them with the pronunciations before they read.

Spelling Tip Make sure students do not confuse the spelling of the word *mourning* with that of its homophone, *morning*.

Teaching to Ability Levels For more advanced students, you may want to indicate that within the context of the conflict–climax–resolution structure are other plot elements, one of which is the complication. The conflict leads to a series of complications as the dangers and setbacks besetting the main character become increasingly serious.

12

Rikki-tikki-tavi

Rudyard Kipling (1865–1936) was born in India, to British parents. While still a young man, he became famous for his stirring accounts of adventure and courage. In 1907 he received a major award, the Nobel Prize for Literature, for his novels, short stories, and poetry. "Rikki-tikki-tavi" comes from one of Kipling's most popular collections of short stories, *The Jungle Book*. Notice how Kipling makes "the great war" between the animal characters in this story seem just as important as a human conflict.

Plot

The **plot** is the sequence of events in a short story. In many stories the events follow a pattern you can recognize. First, the writer describes a **conflict,** which is a struggle between opposing sides or forces. As the story develops, this struggle becomes more and more intense. Then the story reaches a **climax,** the point at which the conflict is greatest. After the climax you learn the **resolution,** or outcome of the conflict, before the story ends. You will be able to see this sequence of events as you read "Rikki-tikki-tavi."

Look For

As you read this action-packed story about a mongoose in India, look for the pattern beneath the surface. Can you identify the three most important elements of the plot: the conflict, the climax, and the resolution?

Writing

Recall an exciting movie or television drama you have seen. Briefly summarize the plot in this movie or program. Then freewrite about why you enjoyed this show.

Vocabulary

Knowing the following words will help you as you read "Rikki-tikki-tavi."

draggled (drag′ld) *adj.:* Wet and dirty (p. 13)
flinched (flinch′t) *v.:* Moved back, as if away from a blow (p. 16)
mourning (morn′ iŋ) *v.:* Feeling sorrow for the death of a loved one (p. 20)

consolation (kän′ sə lā′ shən) *n.:* Something that makes you feel better (p. 20)
cunningly (kun′ iŋ lē) *adv.:* Cleverly (p. 20)

Objectives

1 To understand plot elements in a short story
2 To recognize a chronological sequence of events
3 To use context clues to learn new words
4 To write a story with a strong plot

Support Material

Teaching Portfolio
Teacher Backup, p. 17
Grammar in Action Worksheet, *Recognizing Appositives,* p. 21
Grammar in Action Worksheet, *Identifying Synonyms,* p. 23
Usage and Mechanics Worksheet, p. 25
Vocabulary Check, p. 26
Analyzing Literature Worksheet, *Understanding Plot,* p. 27

Critical Thinking and Reading Worksheet, *Understanding Chronological Order,* p. 28
Selection Test, p. 29

Rikki-tikki-tavi

Rudyard Kipling

1 This is the story of the great war that Rikki-tikki-tavi fought single-handed, through the bathrooms of the big bungalow in Segowlee cantonment.[1] Darzee, the tailorbird, helped him, and Chuchundra,[2] the muskrat, who never comes out into the middle of the floor, but always creeps round by the wall, gave him advice; but Rikki-tikki did the real fighting.

He was a mongoose, rather like a little cat in his fur and his tail, but quite like a weasel in his head and his habits. His eyes and the end of his restless nose were pink; he could scratch himself anywhere he pleased, with any leg, front or back, that he chose to use; he could fluff up his tail till it looked like a bottle brush, and his war cry as he scuttled through the long grass, was:

2 *"Rikk-tikk-tikki-tikki-tchk!"*

3 One day, a high summer flood washed him out of the burrow where he lived with his father and mother, and carried him, kicking and clucking, down a roadside ditch. He found a little wisp of grass floating there, and clung to it till he lost his senses. When he revived, he was lying in the hot sun on the middle of a garden path, very draggled indeed, and a small boy was saying: "Here's a dead mongoose. Let's have a funeral."

"No," said his mother; "let's take him in and dry him. Perhaps he isn't really dead."

---

1. Segowlee cantonment (sē gou′ lē kan tän′ mənt), *n.*: The living quarters for British troops in Segowlee, India.

2. Chuchundra (chōō chun′ drə)

They took him into the house, and a big man picked him up between his finger and thumb and said he was not dead but half choked; so they wrapped him in cotton wool, and warmed him, and he opened his eyes and sneezed.

"Now," said the big man (he was an Englishman who had just moved into the bungalow); "don't frighten him, and we'll see what he'll do."

It is the hardest thing in the world to frighten a mongoose, because he is eaten up from nose to tail with curiosity. The motto of all the mongoose family is, "Run and find out"; and Rikki-tikki was a true mongoose. He looked at the cotton wool, decided that it was not good to eat, ran all round the table, sat up and put his fur in order, scratched himself, and jumped on the small boy's shoulder.

"Don't be frightened, Teddy," said his father. "That's his way of making friends."

"Ouch! He's tickling under my chin," said Teddy.

Rikki-tikki looked down between the boy's collar and neck, snuffed at his ear, and climbed down to the floor, where he sat rubbing his nose.

"Good gracious," said Teddy's mother, "and that's a wild creature! I suppose he's so tame because we've been kind to him."

"All mongooses are like that," said her husband. "If Teddy doesn't pick him up by the tail, or try to put him in a cage, he'll run in and out of the house all day long. Let's give him something to eat."

Rikki-tikki-tavi   13

5 **Discussion** How does Rikki show that his family motto, "Run and find out," fits him?

6 **Literary Focus** This is the first mention of the snake, the "bad guy" in the story. It is an example of foreshadowing, another plot element. What does this mention foreshadow?

They gave him a little piece of raw meat. Rikki-tikki liked it immensely, and when it was finished he went out into the veranda and sat in the sunshine and fluffed up his fur to make it dry to the roots. Then he felt better.

"There are more things to find out about in this house," he said to himself, "than all my family could find out in all their lives. I shall certainly stay and find out."

He spent all that day roaming over the house. He nearly drowned himself in the bathtubs, put his nose into the ink on a writing table, and burned it on the end of the big man's cigar, for he climbed up in the big man's lap to see how writing was done. At nightfall he ran into Teddy's nursery to watch how kerosene lamps were lighted, and when Teddy went to bed Rikki-tikki climbed up too; but he was a restless companion, because he had to get up and attend to every noise all through the night, and find out what made it. Teddy's mother and father came in, the last thing, to look at their boy, and Rikki-tikki was awake on the pillow. "I don't like that," said Teddy's mother; "he may bite the child." "He'll do no such thing," said the father. "Teddy's safer with that little beast than if he had a bloodhound to watch him. If a snake came into the nursery now—"

But Teddy's mother wouldn't think of anything so awful.

Early in the morning Rikki-tikki came to early breakfast in the veranda riding on Teddy's shoulder, and they gave him banana and some boiled egg; and he sat on all their laps one after the other, because every well-brought-up mongoose always hopes to be a house mongoose some day and have rooms to run about in, and Rikki-tikki's mother (she used to live in the General's house at Segowlee) had carefully told Rikki what to do if ever he came across Englishmen.

Then Rikki-tikki went out into the garden to see what was to be seen. It was a large

14   Short Stories

garden, only half cultivated, with bushes as big as summer houses of Marshal Niel roses, lime and orange trees, clumps of bamboos, and thickets of high grass. Rikki-tikki licked his lips. "This is a splendid hunting ground," he said, and his tail grew bottle-brushy at the thought of it, and he scuttled up and down the garden, snuffing here and there till he heard very sorrowful voices in a thornbush.

It was Darzee, the tailorbird, and his wife. They had made a beautiful nest by pulling two big leaves together and stitching them up the edges with fibers, and had filled the hollow with cotton and downy fluff. The nest swayed to and fro, as they sat on the rim and cried.

"What is the matter?" asked Rikki-tikki.

"We are very miserable," said Darzee.

Grammar in Action

An **appositive** is a noun or pronoun that is placed after another noun or pronoun to rename, identify, or explain it. An appositive phrase consists of the appositive and its modifiers. Appositives or appositive phrases that are not essential to the meaning of the sentence are set off by commas. The commas show that the appositive can be left out of the sentence without changing the meaning of the sentence. Appositives add sophistication and coherence to writing. Notice the way Rudyard Kipling uses appositives to introduce an animal character in this story.

> Then inch by inch out of the grass rose up the head and spread hood of Nag, *the big black cobra,* . . . .

The appositive phrase identifies the noun it is placed after, Nag. The identification is done smoothly and coherently. Compare it to the following:

> Then inch by inch out of the grass rose up the head and spread hood of Nag. Nag was the big black cobra.

"One of our babies fell out of the nest yesterday and Nag[3] ate him."

"H'm!" said Rikki-tikki, "that is very sad—but I am a stranger here. Who is Nag?"

Darzee and his wife only cowered down in the nest without answering, for from the thick grass at the foot of the bush there came a low hiss—a horrid cold sound that made Rikki-tikki jump back two clear feet. Then inch by inch out of the grass rose up the head and spread hood of Nag, the big black cobra, and he was five feet long from tongue to tail. When he had lifted one third of himself clear of the ground, he stayed balancing to and fro exactly as a dandelion tuft balances in the wind, and he looked at Rikki-tikki with the wicked snake's eyes that never change their expression, whatever the snake may be thinking of.

"Who is Nag?" he said. "I am Nag. The great god Brahm[4] put his mark upon all our people when the first cobra spread his hood to keep the sun off Brahm as he slept. Look, and be afraid!"

He spread out his hood more than ever, and Rikki-tikki saw the spectacle mark on the back of it that looks exactly like the eye part of a hook-and-eye fastening. He was afraid for the minute; but it is impossible for a mongoose to stay frightened for any length of time, and though Rikki-tikki had never met a live cobra before, his mother had fed him on dead ones, and he knew that all a grown mongoose's business in life was to fight and eat snakes. Nag knew that too, and at the bottom of his cold heart he was afraid.

"Well," said Rikki-tikki, and his tail began to fluff up again, "marks or no marks, do you think it is right for you to eat fledglings out of a nest?"

Nag was thinking to himself, and watching the least little movement in the grass behind Rikki-tikki. He knew that mongooses in the garden meant death sooner or later for him and his family; but he wanted to get Rikki-tikki off his guard. So he dropped his head a little, and put it on one side.

"Let us talk," he said, "You eat eggs. Why should not I eat birds?"

"Behind you! Look behind you!" sang Darzee.

Rikki-tikki knew better than to waste time in staring. He jumped up in the air as high as he could go, and just under him whizzed by the head of Nagaina,[5] Nag's wicked wife. She had crept up behind him as he was talking, to make an end of him; and he heard her savage hiss as the stroke missed. He came down almost across her back, and if he had been an old mongoose he would have known that then was the time to break her back with one bite; but he was afraid of the terrible lashing return stroke of the cobra. He bit, indeed, but did not bite long enough, and he jumped clear of the whisking tail, leaving Nagaina torn and angry.

"Wicked, wicked Darzee!" said Nag, lashing up as high as he could reach toward the nest in the thornbush; but Darzee had built it out of reach of snakes; and it only swayed to and fro.

Rikki-tikki felt his eyes growing red and hot (when a mongoose's eyes grow red, he is angry), and he sat back on his tail and hind legs like a little kangaroo, and looked all around him, and chattered with rage. But Nag and Nagaina had disappeared into the grass. When a snake misses its stroke, it never says anything or gives any sign of what it means to do next. Rikki-tikki did not care to follow them, for he did not feel sure that he could manage two snakes at once. So he trotted off to the gravel path near the

---

3. **Nag** (Näg).

4. **Brahm** (bräm): An abbreviation of Brahma, the name of the chief god in the Hindu religion.

---

5. **Nagaina** (nə gī nə)

Rikki-tikki-tavi 15

---

7 **Discussion** What words in this paragraph convey the image of evil?

8 **Literary Focus** At this point the conflict is entered. What are the two sides that will be involved in the conflict? What words of Nag are a challenge?

9 **Enrichment** When a cobra is frightened, it flattens its neck by moving its ribs. The flattened neck gives the appearance of a hood. On the back of the Indian cobra's hood is a mark that looks like a pair of spectacles, so it is sometimes called "spectacled cobra."

10 **Discussion** What is each character thinking and feeling in this first confrontation?

11 **Discussion** Why might Nag want to get Rikki off guard?

12 **Discussion** In what ways does Rikki's inexperience show?

13 **Discussion** What characteristics does Rikki show when he gets angry?

Student Activity 1. Find three examples where Kipling uses appositives to identify or explain the animal characters in this story. Make sure one of the examples is an appositive phrase.

Student Activity 2. Combine each of the following sentences to include an appositive or appositive phrase. Then write a third sentence of your own that includes an appositive phrase.

1. Ever since I was a young child I have had two favorite foods. My favorite foods are ice cream and bananas.

2. Pierre is quickly learning the English language. Pierre is a native of a small town in southern France.

14 Reading Strategy Have students summarize the story to this point. Suggest that they predict what might happen with Nag and Nagaina.

15 **Discussion** What did Rikki learn in his encounter with Nagaina that he is able to apply in this battle with Karait?

14 house, and sat down to think. It was a serious matter for him.

If you read the old books of natural history, you will find they say that when the mongoose fights the snake and happens to get bitten, he runs off and eats some herb that cures him. That is not true. The victory is only a matter of quickness of eye and quickness of foot—snake's blow against mongoose's jump—and as no eye can follow the motion of a snake's head when it strikes, that makes things much more wonderful than any magic herb. Rikki-tikki knew he was a young mongoose, and it made him all the more pleased to think that he had managed to escape a blow from behind. It gave him confidence in himself, and when Teddy came running down the path, Rikki-tikki was ready to be petted.

But just as Teddy was stooping, something flinched a little in the dust, and a tiny voice said: "Be careful. I am death!" It was Karait,[6] the dusty brown snakeling that lies for choice on the dusty earth; and his bite is as dangerous as the cobra's. But he is so small that nobody thinks of him, and so he does the more harm to people.

Rikki-tikki's eyes grew red again, and he danced up to Karait with the peculiar rocking, swaying motion that he had inherited from his family. It looks very funny, but it is so perfectly balanced a gait that you can fly off from it at any angle you please; and in dealing with snakes this is an advantage. If Rikki-tikki had only known, he was doing a much more dangerous thing than fighting Nag, for Karait is so small, and can turn so quickly, that unless Rikki bit him close to the back of the head, he would get the return stroke in his eye or lip. But Rikki did not know: his eyes were all red, and he rocked back and forth, looking for a good place to hold. Karait struck out. Rikki jumped side-

---

6. **Karait** (kə rīt′)

16   Short Stories

ways and tried to run in, but the wicked little dusty gray head lashed within a fraction of his shoulder, and he had to jump over the body, and the head followed his heels close.

Teddy shouted to the house: "Oh, look here! Our mongoose is killing a snake"; and Rikki-tikki heard a scream from Teddy's mother. His father ran out with a stick, but by the time he came up, Karait had lunged out once too far, and Rikki-tikki had sprung, jumped on the snake's back, dropped his head far between his fore legs, bitten as high up the back as he could get hold, and rolled away. That bite paralyzed Karait, and Rikki-tikki was just going to eat him up from the tail, after the custom of his family at dinner, when he remembered that a full meal makes a slow mongoose, and if he wanted all his strength and quickness ready, he must keep himself thin.

He went away for a dust bath under the castor-oil bushes, while Teddy's father beat the dead Karait. "What is the use of that?" thought Rikki-tikki. "I have settled it all"; and then Teddy's mother picked him up from the dust and hugged him, crying that he had saved Teddy from death, and Teddy's father said that he was a providence,[7] and Teddy looked on with big scared eyes. Rikki-tikki was rather amused at all the fuss, which, of course, he did not understand. Teddy's mother might just as well have petted Teddy for playing in the dust. Rikki was thoroughly enjoying himself.

That night, at dinner, walking to and fro among the wineglasses on the table, he could have stuffed himself three times over with nice things; but he remembered Nag and Nagaina, and though it was very pleasant to be patted and petted by Teddy's mother, and to sit on Teddy's shoulder, his eyes would get red from time to time, and he

---

7. **a providence** (präv′ ə dəns): A godsend; a valuable gift.

15

Grammar in Action

Synonyms are words that have similar definition. However, it is rare for synonyms to have exactly the same definition. A writer carefully chooses a word for its exact meaning, and in some cases there are two or three words that could be used. Using the appropriate synonym adds vividness and precision to writing. Notice how Rudyard Kipling's use of synonyms makes the passage more lively.

. . . and a *tiny* voice said: "Be careful. I am death!" But he is so *small* that nobody thinks of him, ...

. . . the wicked *little* dusty gray head lashed within a fraction of his shoulder, ...

Because these words are so similar in meaning, any one of them could have been used in any one of the sentences. The effect of using all of them is to make the passage more interesting and vivid.

Synonyms are effective when they give a precise shade of meaning. To select the most appropriate word, you may want to

would go off into his long war cry of "Rikk-tikk-tikki-tikki-tchk!"

Teddy carried him off to bed, and insisted on Rikki-tikki sleeping under his chin. Rikki-tikki was too well bred to bite or scratch, but as soon as Teddy was asleep he went off for his nightly walk round the house, and in the dark he ran up against Chuchundra, the muskrat, creeping round by the wall. Chuchundra is a brokenhearted little beast. He whimpers and cheeps all the night, trying to make up his mind to run into the middle of the room, but he never gets there.

"Don't kill me," said Chuchundra, almost weeping. "Rikki-tikki don't kill me."

"Do you think a snake-killer kills muskrats?" said Rikki-tikki scornfully.

"Those who kill snakes get killed by snakes," said Chuchundra, more sorrowfully than ever. "And how am I to be sure that Nag won't mistake me for you some dark night?"

"There's not the least danger," said Rikki-tikki; "but Nag is in the garden, and I know you don't go there."

"My cousin Chua, the rat, told me—" said Chuchundra, and then he stopped.

"Told you what?"

"H'sh! Nag is everywhere, Rikki-tikki. You should have talked to Chua in the garden."

"I didn't—so you must tell me. Quick, Chuchundra, or I'll bite you!"

Chuchundra sat down and cried till the tears rolled off his whiskers. "I am a very poor man," he sobbed. "I never had spirit enough to run out into the middle of the room. H'sh! I mustn't tell you anything. Can't you *hear*, Rikki-tikki?"

Rikki-tikki listened. The house was as still as still, but he thought he could just catch the faintest *scratch-scratch* in the world—a noise as faint as that of a wasp walking on a windowpane—the dry scratch of a snake's scales on brickwork.

"That's Nag or Nagaina," he said to himself; "and he is crawling into the bathroom sluice. You're right, Chuchundra; I should have talked to Chua."

He stole off to Teddy's bathroom, but there was nothing there, and then to Teddy's mother's bathroom. At the bottom of the smooth plaster wall there was a brick pulled out to make a sluice for the bath water, and as Rikki-tikki stole in by the masonry curb where the bath is put, he heard Nag and Nagaina whispering together outside in the moonlight.

"When the house is emptied of people," said Nagaina to her husband, "*he* will have to go away, and then the garden will be our own again. Go in quietly, and remember that the big man who killed Karait is the first one to bite. Then come out and tell me, and we will hunt for Rikki-tikki together."

"But are you sure that there is anything to be gained by killing the people?" said Nag.

"Everything. When there were no people in the bungalow, did we have any mongoose in the garden? So long as the bungalow is empty, we are king and queen of the garden; and remember that as soon as our eggs in the melon bed hatch (as they may tomorrow), our children will need room and quiet."

"I had not thought of that," said Nag. "I will go, but there is no need that we should hunt for Rikki-tikki afterward. I will kill the big man and his wife, and the child if I can, and come away quietly. Then the bungalow will be empty, and Rikki-tikki will go."

Rikki-tikki tingled all over with rage and hatred at this, and then Nag's head came through the sluice, and his five feet of cold body followed it. Angry as he was, Rikki-tikki was very frightened as he saw the size of the big cobra. Nag coiled himself up, raised his head, and looked into the bathroom in the dark, and Rikki could see his eyes glitter.

"Now, if I kill him here, Nagaina will know;—and if I fight him on the open floor,

consult a thesaurus to find synonyms and then a dictionary to determine the meaning of each of the synonyms.

Student Activity 1. Explain the difference in meaning of the synonyms in each group below. You may need to use a dictionary to find their differences in meaning.

1. story   tale   yarn   report
2. bungalow   house   cottage   hut
3. help   assist   serve   aid
4. restless   nervous   impatient   fidgety

Student Activity 2. Choose one of the groups of synonyms and write a sentence for each word in the group. Make sure that each sentence uses the exact meaning of the word.

21 Literary Focus How does the incident with Nag increase the tension in the conflict? What is its part in the "great war" between Rikki and the snakes?

the odds are in his favor. What am I to do?" said Rikki-tikki-tavi.

Nag waved to and fro, and then Rikki-tikki heard him drinking from the biggest water jar that was used to fill the bath. "That is good," said the snake. "Now, when Karait was killed, the big man had a stick. He may have that stick still, but when he comes in to bathe in the morning he will not have a stick. I shall wait here till he comes. Nagaina—do you hear me?—I shall wait here in the cool till daytime."

There was no answer from outside, so Rikki-tikki knew Nagaina had gone away. Nag coiled himself down, coil by coil, round the bulge at the bottom of the waterjar, and Rikki-tikki stayed still as death. After an hour he began to move, muscle by muscle, toward the jar. Nag was asleep, and Rikki-tikki looked at his big back, wondering which would be the best place for a good hold. "If I don't break his back at the first jump," said Rikki, "he can still fight; and if he fights—O Rikki!" He looked at the thickness of the neck below the hood, but that was too much for him; and a bite near the tail would only make Nag savage.

"It must be the head," he said at last; "the head above the hood; and, when I am once there, I must not let go."

21 Then he jumped. The head was lying a little clear of the water jar, under the curve of it; and, as his teeth met, Rikki braced his back against the bulge of the red earthenware to hold down the head. This gave him just one second's purchase,[8] and he made the most of it. Then he was battered to and fro as a rat is shaken by a dog—to and fro on the floor, up and down, and round in great

circles; but his eyes were red, and he held on as the body cartwhipped over the floor, upsetting the tin dipper and the soap dish and the fleshbrush, and banged against the tin side of the bath. As he held he closed his jaws tighter and tighter, for he made sure he would be banged to death, and, for the honor of his family, he preferred to be found with his teeth locked. He was dizzy, aching, and felt shaken to pieces when something went off like a thunderclap just behind him; a hot wind knocked him senseless and red fire singed his fur. The big man had been wakened by the noise, and had fired both barrels of a shotgun into Nag just behind the hood.

Rikki-tikki held on with his eyes shut, for now he was quite sure he was dead; but the head did not move, and the big man

---

8. purchase (pur' chəs): In this case, a good hold on something.

22 Discussion What still needs to be done before the conflict can be resolved, before the "war" is won?

picked him up and said: "It's the mongoose again, Alice; the little chap has saved *our* lives now." Then Teddy's mother came in with a very white face, and saw what was left of Nag, and Rikki-tikki dragged himself to Teddy's bedroom and spent half the rest of the night shaking himself tenderly to find out whether he really was broken into forty pieces, as he fancied.

When morning came he was very stiff, but well pleased with his doings. "Now I have Nagaina to settle with, and she will be worse than five Nags, and there's no knowing when the eggs she spoke of will hatch. Goodness! I must go and see Darzee," he said.

Without waiting for breakfast, Rikki-tikki ran to the thornbush where Darzee was singing a song of triumph at the top of his voice. The news of Nag's death was all over

the garden, for the sweeper had thrown the body on the rubbish heap.

"Oh, you stupid tuft of feathers!" said Rikki-tikki, angrily. "Is this the time to sing?"

"Nag is dead—is dead—is dead!" sang Darzee. "The valiant Rikki-tikki caught him by the head and held fast. The big man brought the bang-stick and Nag fell in two pieces! He will never eat my babies again."

"All that's true enough; but where's Nagaina?" said Rikki-tikki, looking carefully round him.

"Nagaina came to the bathroom sluice and called for Nag," Darzee went on; "and Nag came out on the end of a stick—the sweeper picked him up on the end of a stick

Rikki-tikki-tavi 19

and threw him upon the rubbish heap. Let us sing about the great, the red-eyed Rikki-tikki!" and Darzee filled his throat and sang.

"If I could get up to your nest, I'd roll all your babies out!" said Rikki-tikki. "You don't know when to do the right thing at the right time. You're safe enough in your nest there, but it's war for me down here. Stop singing a minute, Darzee."

"For the great, the beautiful Rikki-tikki's sake, I will stop," said Darzee. "What is it, O Killer of the terrible Nag!"

"Where is Nagaina, for the third time?"

"On the rubbish heap by the stables, mourning for Nag. Great is Rikki-tikki with the white teeth."

"Bother my white teeth! Have you ever heard where she keeps her eggs?"

"In the melon bed, on the end nearest the wall, where the sun strikes nearly all day. She had them there weeks ago."

"And you never thought it worthwhile to tell me? The end nearest the wall, you said?"

"Rikki-tikki, you are not going to eat her eggs?"

"Not eat exactly; no. Darzee, if you have a grain of sense you will fly off to the stables and pretend that your wing is broken, and let Nagaina chase you away to this bush! I must get to the melon bed, and if I went there now she'd see me."

Darzee was a featherbrained little fellow who could never hold more than one idea at a time in his head; and just because he knew that Nagaina's children were born in eggs like his own, he didn't think at first that it was fair to kill them. But his wife was a sensible bird, and she knew that cobra's eggs meant young cobras later on; so she flew off from the nest, and left Darzee to keep the babies warm, and continue his song about the death of Nag. Darzee was very like a man in some ways.

She fluttered in front of Nagaina by the rubbish heap, and cried out, "Oh, my wing is broken! The boy in the house threw a stone at me and broke it." Then she fluttered more desperately than ever.

Nagaina lifted up her head and hissed, "You warned Rikki-tikki when I would have killed him. Indeed and truly, you've chosen a bad place to be lame in." And she moved toward Darzee's wife, slipping along over the dust.

"The boy broke it with a stone!" shrieked Darzee's wife.

"Well! It may be some consolation to you when you're dead to know that I shall settle accounts with the boy. My husband lies on the rubbish heap this morning, but before night the boy in the house will lie very still. What is the use of running away? I am sure to catch you. Little fool, look at me!"

Darzee's wife knew better than to do *that*, for a bird who looks at a snake's eyes gets so frightened that she cannot move. Darzee's wife fluttered on, piping sorrowfully, and never leaving the ground, and Nagaina quickened her pace.

Rikki-tikki heard them going up the path from the stables, and he raced for the end of the melon patch near the wall. There, in the warm litter about the melons, very cunningly hidden, he found twenty-five eggs, about the size of a bantam's[9] eggs, but with whitish skin instead of shell.

"I was not a day too soon," he said; for he could see the baby cobras curled up inside the skin, and he knew that the minute they were hatched they could each kill a man or a mongoose. He bit off the tops of the eggs as fast as he could, taking care to crush the young cobras, and turned over the litter from time to time to see whether he had missed any. At last there were only three eggs left, and Rikki-tikki began to chuckle to himself, when he heard Darzee's wife screaming:

---

9. bantam's : A small chicken's.

"Rikki-tikki, I led Nagaina toward the house, and she has gone into the veranda, and—oh, come quickly—she means killing!"

Rikki-tikki smashed two eggs, and tumbled backward down the melon bed with the third egg in his mouth, and scuttled to the veranda as hard as he could put foot to the ground. Teddy and his mother and father were there at early breakfast; but Rikki-tikki saw that they were not eating anything. They sat stone-still, and their faces were white. Nagaina was coiled up on the matting by Teddy's chair, within easy striking distance of Teddy's bare leg, and she was swaying to and fro singing a song of triumph.

"Son of the big man that killed Nag," she hissed, "stay still. I am not ready yet. Wait a little. Keep very still, all you three. If you move I strike, and if you do not move I strike. Oh, foolish people, who killed my Nag!"

Teddy's eyes were fixed on his father, and all his father could do was to whisper, "Sit still, Teddy. You mustn't move. Teddy, keep still."

24 Then Rikki-tikki came up and cried: "Turn round, Nagaina; turn and fight!"

"All in good time," said she, without moving her eyes. "I will settle my account with *you* presently. Look at your friends, Rikki-tikki. They are still and white; they are afraid. They dare not move, and if you come a step nearer I strike."

"Look at your eggs," said Rikki-tikki, "in the melon bed near the wall. Go and look, Nagaina."

The big snake turned half round, and saw the egg on the veranda. "Ah-h! Give it to me," she said.

Rikki-tikki put his paws one on each side of the egg, and his eyes were blood-red. "What price for a snake's egg? For a young cobra? For a young king cobra? For the last—the very last of the brood? The ants are eating all the others down by the melon bed."

Nagaina spun clear round, forgetting everything for the sake of the one egg; and Rikki-tikki saw Teddy's father shoot out a big hand, catch Teddy by the shoulder, and drag him across the little table with the teacups, safe and out of reach of Nagaina.

"Tricked! Tricked! Tricked! *Rikk-tck-tck!*" chuckled Rikki-tikki. "The boy is safe, and it was I—I—I that caught Nag by the hood last night in the bathroom." Then he began to jump up and down, all four feet together, his head close to the floor. "He threw me to and fro, but he could not shake me off. He was dead before the big man blew him in two. I did it. *Rikki-tikki-tck-tck!* Come then, Nagaina. Come and fight with me. You shall not be a widow long."

Nagaina saw that she had lost her chance of killing Teddy, and the egg lay between Rikki-tikki's paws. "Give me the egg, Rikki-tikki. Give me the last of my eggs, and I will go away and never come back," she said, lowering her hood.

"Yes, you will go away, and you will never come back; for you will go to the rubbish heap with Nag. Fight, widow! The big man has gone for his gun! Fight!"

Rikki-tikki was bounding all round Nagaina, keeping just out of reach of her stroke, his little eyes like hot coals. Nagaina gathered herself together, and flung out at him. Rikki-tikki jumped up and backward. Again and again and again she struck, and each time her head came with a whack on the matting of the veranda and she gathered herself together like a watchspring. Then Rikki-tikki danced in a circle to get behind her, and Nagaina spun round to keep her head to his head, so that the rustle of her tail on the matting sounded like dry leaves blown along by the wind.

He had forgotten the egg. It still lay on the veranda, and Nagaina came nearer and nearer to it, till at last, while Rikki-tikki was drawing breath, she caught it in her mouth,

Rikki-tikki-tavi 21

24 **Critical Thinking and Reading**
Rikki challenges Nagaina. Have students predict the outcome of the final confrontation.

25 **Literary Focus** The actual events in the climax are left to our imaginations. What details create a feeling of suspense?

26 **Literary Focus** What is the outcome of the final battle? How is the conflict, the "great war," resolved? Explain whether you think the resolution is satisfying.

27 **Discussion** The creatures of the garden praise Rikki for his "brave deeds." How does Rikki regard their praise?

28 **Discussion** In what ways does Rikki act like a true hero?

Master Teacher Note To dramatize the battles between Rikki and the cobras, you might play excerpts from the music written by Prokofiev for the film *Aleksandr Neksky*. The scene of the galloping charge of the German Knights across the frozen lake carries the same buildup in ominous intensity as the cobras' advance on Rikki. Also play selections from the soundtrack *Victory at Sea* and the stirring *1812 Overture*. Ask students which music best applies to the story.

Reader's Response Which part of the story did you find most exciting? Why?

Closure and Extension

ANSWERS TO THINKING ABOUT THE SELECTION
Recalling

1. Mongooses typically show curiosity, are friendly, and kill snakes.
2. Rikki meets the cobras when he is in the garden talking with Darzee, the tailorbird. Darzee has just finished telling Rikki that Nag ate one of his babies when Nag arrives.

turned to the veranda steps, and flew like an arrow down the path, with Rikki-tikki behind her. When the cobra runs for her life, she goes like a whiplash flicked across a horse's neck.

Rikki-tikki knew that he must catch her, or all the trouble would begin again. She headed straight for the long grass by the thornbush, and as he was running Rikki-tikki heard Darzee still singing his foolish little song of triumph. But Darzee's wife was wiser. She flew off her nest as Nagaina came along, and flapped her wings about Nagaina's head. If Darzee had helped they might have turned her; but Nagaina only lowered her hood and went on. Still, the instant's delay brought Rikki-tikki up to her, and as she plunged into the rat hole where she and Nag used to live, his little white teeth were clenched on her tail, and he went down with her—and very few mongooses, however wise and old they may be, care to follow a cobra into its hole. It was dark in the hole; and Rikki-tikki never knew when it might open out and give Nagaina room to turn and strike at him. He held on savagely, and struck out his feet to act as brakes on the dark slope of the hot, moist earth.

Then the grass by the mouth of the hole stopped waving, and Darzee said: "It is all over with Rikki-tikki! We must sing his death song. Valiant Rikki-tikki is dead! For Nagaina will surely kill him underground."

So he sang a very mournful song that he made up all on the spur of the minute, and just as he got to the most touching part the grass quivered again, and Rikki-tikki, covered with dirt, dragged himself out of the hole leg by leg, licking his whiskers. Darzee stopped with a little shout. Rikki-tikki shook some of the dust out of his fur and sneezed. "It is all over," he said. "The widow will never come out again." And the red ants that live between the grass stems heard him, and began to troop down one after another to see if he had spoken the truth.

Rikki-tikki curled himself up in the grass and slept where he was—slept and slept till it was late in the afternoon, for he had done a hard day's work.

"Now," he said, when he awoke, "I will go back to the house. Tell the Coppersmith, Darzee, and he will tell the garden that Nagaina is dead."

The Coppersmith is a bird who makes a noise exactly like the beating of a little hammer on a copper pot; and the reason he is always making it is because he is the town crier to every Indian garden, and tells all the news to everybody who cares to listen. As Rikki-tikki went up the path, he heard his "attention" notes like a tiny dinner gong; and then the steady "*Ding-dong-tock! Nag is dead—dong! Nagaina is dead! Ding-dong-tock!*" That set all the birds in the garden singing, and the frogs croaking; for Nag and Nagaina used to eat frogs as well as little birds.

When Rikki got to the house, Teddy and Teddy's mother and Teddy's father came out and almost cried over him; and that night he ate all that was given him till he could eat no more, and went to bed on Teddy's shoulder, where Teddy's mother saw him when she came to look late at night.

"He saved our lives and Teddy's life," she said to her husband. "Just think, he saved all our lives."

Rikki-tikki woke up with a jump, for all the mongooses are light sleepers.

"Oh, it's you," said he. "What are you bothering for? All the cobras are dead; and if they weren't, I'm here."

Rikki-tikki had a right to be proud of himself; but he did not grow too proud, and he kept that garden as a mongoose should keep it, with tooth and jump and spring and bite, till never a cobra dared show its head inside the walls.

3. While Nagaina is outside, Nag will hide in the bathroom water jar until the father comes into the bathroom at which time Nag will strike and kill him. Then he will kill the mother and child. The cobras do not plan to kill Rikki as they think he will leave once the people are gone.
4. Rikki kills Nag while he is coiled inside the water jar. Then Rikki protects Teddy from Nagaina by diverting her attention when she is poised to strike the boy. He does this by telling her that he has the only one of her eggs that is left. She leaves the boy to attack Rikki and get her egg.
5. Nagaina snatches up her egg and races to her rat-hole home. Rikki catches her tail in his teeth as she is descending and goes down the hole where he kills her.

Interpreting

6. The animals resemble humans by talking and acting like them and by having the same kinds of relationships and character traits that humans do. Rikki is curious, self-confident, lovable, angered by evil, and fearless in the face of trouble. Darzee is feather-brained, fearful, and ruled by emotions rather than reason, whereas his wife is sensible and brave. Chuchundra is so fearful that he never accomplishes much. Nag and Nagaina are wicked, conniving, power hungry, sly, and selfish. Karait is very sly, using camou-

THINKING ABOUT THE SELECTION

Recalling

1. What kinds of behavior are typical of mongooses?
2. When does Rikki first meet the cobras?
3. What is Nag and Nagaina's plan to get control of the bungalow?
4. How does Rikki protect Teddy's father and then Teddy from the cobras?
5. What happens to Nagaina at the end of the story?

Interpreting

6. How does each of these animals resemble humans?
7. Compare and contrast the personalities of Rikki and the two cobras.
8. How is "the great war" in this story a battle between good and evil?

Applying

9. Why would Rikki's approach to problems in life work better than Darzee's?

ANALYZING LITERATURE

Understanding Plot

Plot is the sequence of events in a story. These events usually involve a **conflict,** or struggle between opposing sides. This struggle becomes the most intense at the **climax,** the point just before the conflict is resolved. The rest of the story is devoted to the **resolution,** or solving of the conflict.

The conflict in "Rikki-tikki-tavi" occurs between Rikki and the two cobras.
1. How does the first meeting between Rikki and the cobras make you want to read further?
2. Which battle occurs at the climax?
3. How is the conflict resolved?

CRITICAL THINKING AND READING

Putting Events in Chronological Order

In "Rikki-tikki-tavi" the events take place in **chronological order.** This means that they follow one another as time goes forward.
1. List the main events of the story in the order they occur.
2. About how much time passes between the first event in the story and the last?

UNDERSTANDING LANGUAGE

Using Context Clues

The **context** of a word consists of the words that surround it. When you see an unfamiliar word as you read, you can sometimes figure out its meaning by looking at its context. In the third paragraph of the story, for example, Rikki is described as being *draggled*. Since Rikki has just been in a flood, you can deduce that *draggled* means "wet and dirty."

Use context clues to figure out the meaning of the following *italicized* words from the story. Then check your answer in the glossary.
1. ". . . he *scuttled* up and down the garden, snuffing here and there. . . ."
2. "At the bottom of the smooth plaster wall there was a brick pulled out to make a *sluice* for the bath water. . . ."

THINKING AND WRITING

Writing a Story with a Strong Plot

In a story with a strong plot like "Rikki-tikki-tavi," the conflict rises to a climax and is then resolved. Imagine that a movie director has asked you to write such a story to serve as the basis for her next film. Brainstorm to think of a good idea for a conflict. Then use this idea to write a story with a strong plot. As you revise it, check to see that it has a climax and a resolution.

Rikki-tikki-tavi 23

(Answers begin on p.22.)

b. Rikki meets the cobras and is almost killed by Nagaina.
c. Rikki protects Teddy by killing Karait.
d. Rikki kills Nag.
e. Rikki destroys all but one of the cobra eggs.
f. Rikki distracts Nagaina when she is about to strike Teddy.
g. Nagaina flees with the egg to her home.
h. Rikki catches and kills her in the hole.
i. Rikki is greeted as a hero by everyone.
2. The story takes place over a period of three days.

ANSWERS TO UNDERSTANDING LANGUAGE
1. *Scuttled* means "to run quickly."
2. A sluice is a trough or channel for conducting water.

THINKING AND WRITING
For help with this assignment, students can refer to Lesson 12, "Writing About a Short Story," in the Handbook of Writing About Literature.

Writing Across the Curriculum
Students might do research on the climate, conditions, and animals natural to India. Or they might do research on the British rule in India and suggest what it might have been like for the Indians and for the British. Perhaps you could inform the social studies department. Social studies teachers might like to have students report their findings in their social studies classes.

---

flage to hide himself. Coppersmith is the town crier.
7. Rikki is lovable, good, considerate, and caring for others, whereas the cobras are selfish, evil, inconsiderate, and sly. Both Rikki and the cobras are intelligent, crafty, and wise.
8. Answers will differ. Suggested Response: The great war is a battle between good (Rikki who is loving and wants to help others) and evil (the snakes who want to harm and destroy for their own ends).

Applying
9. Answers will differ. Suggested Response: Rikki is alert, responds quickly, and takes action when necessary, whereas Darzee isn't very smart and doesn't know the correct actions to take to solve problems.

ANSWERS TO ANALYZING LITERATURE
1. Students should see that Rikki and the cobras are worthy opponents

and that their battles will be exciting.
2. The battle between Rikki and Nagaina occurs at the climax.
3. Rikki kills the cobras and lives thereafter a happy life with the British family.

ANSWERS TO CRITICAL THINKING AND READING
1. The main events listed sequentially are as follows:
   a. Rikki arrives at the bungalow and is allowed to stay.

Challenge Kipling wrote this story while he lived in India. Which details in the story could have come from his life there? Which came from his imagination?

Focus

More About the Author O. Henry left school at the age of fifteen and worked in a series of places, including a bank, a drugstore, a ranch, and eventually, for a newspaper in New York. How might his many and varied experiences have helped O. Henry to develop characters and situations for short stories?

Literary Focus Elicit from students that it is curiosity about how conflicts will be resolved that motivates the reader to read to the end of the story. Also emphasize that there are several conflicts in this story.

Look For You might suggest that students be alert for how the plot twists, or changes, during the course of the story. How do these plot twists affect the conflict?

Writing/Prior Knowledge Students might consider whether their "brats" possess any positive qualities that they could include in their descriptions.

Spelling Tip Point out that the endings -ent and -ant are pronounced exactly alike. The best way to remember that the vocabulary words *fraudulent,* and *somnolent* end with -ent is to memorize them.

The Ransom of Red Chief

O. Henry (1862–1910) was born William Sidney Porter in Greensboro, North Carolina. Under the pen name of O. Henry, he wrote about ordinary people with warmth, humor, and a touch of romance. After spending time in prison for embezzlement (a crime for which he may not have been guilty), O. Henry moved to New York City, where he gathered material for his stories. His understanding of human nature and of people on both sides of the law is evident in "The Ransom of Red Chief."

Conflict

A **conflict** is a struggle between opposing sides or forces. When conflict in a story occurs between one person and another or between a person and a force of nature, we say the conflict is **external**. When it occurs between opposing ideas or feelings within a character, we say the conflict is **internal**. "The Ransom of Red Chief" contains both external and internal conflicts.

Look For

Conflict lends excitement to a story. As you read "The Ransom of Red Chief," look for what happens when the town brat gets kidnapped. How does the conflict resolve itself in an unexpected way?

Writing

"Red Chief" is a mischief-maker, a rascal, the kind of kid most people would be quick to label "brat." He makes life very difficult for others. What is your image of a "brat"? From books, television, movies, or real life, choose one character who is a real rascal and write a brief description. Recount an incident that typifies this person's behavior.

Vocabulary

Knowing the following words will help you as you read "The Ransom of Red Chief."

undeleterious (un del′ ə tir′ ē əs) *adj.*: Healthy, full of well-being (p. 25)

fraudulent (frô′ jə lənt) *adj.*: Acting with fraud; deceit (p. 25)

lackadaisical (lak′ ə dā′ zi kəl) *adj.*: Showing a lack of interest (p. 25)

elevation (el′ ə vā′ shən) *n.*: A high place (p. 25)

provisions (prō vizh′ ənz) *n.*:

Food and supplies (p. 25)

stealthy (stel′ thē) *adj.*: Secret; sly (p. 27)

sylvan (sil′ vən) *adj.*: Of or characteristic of woods and forests (p. 28)

somnolent (säm′ nə lent) *adj.*: Sleepy; drowsy (p. 28)

collaborated (kə lab′ ə rāt′ 'd) *v.*: Worked together (p. 29)

Objectives

1 To understand conflict in a short story
2 To recognize stereotypes in a short story
3 To appreciate the use of diction to create humor
4 To write a diary entry for a character in a short story

Support Material

Teaching Portfolio
Teacher Backup, p. 31
Grammar in Action Worksheets, *Understanding Exaggeration,* p. 35; *Recognizing Subordinate Clauses,* p. 37
Usage and Mechanics Worksheet, p. 39
Vocabulary Check, p. 40

Analyzing Literature Worksheet, *Understanding Conflict,* p. 41
Critical Thinking and Reading Worksheet, *Understanding Stereotypes,* p. 42
Selection Test, p. 43

The Ransom of Red Chief

O. Henry

1   It looked like a good thing: but wait till I tell you. We were down South, in Alabama—Bill Driscoll and myself—when this kidnapping idea struck us. It was, as Bill afterward expressed it, "during a moment of temporary mental apparition"[1]; but we didn't find that out till later.

2   There was a town down there, as flat as a flannel-cake, and called Summit, of course. It contained inhabitants of as undeleterious and self-satisfied a class of peasantry as ever clustered around a Maypole.

  Bill and me had a joint capital of about six hundred dollars, and we needed just two thousand dollars more to pull off a fraudu-

3 lent town-lot scheme in Western Illinois with. We talked it over on the front steps of

4 the hotel. Philoprogenitoveness,[2] says we, is strong in semi-rural communities; therefore, and for other reasons, a kidnapping project ought to do better there than in the radius of newspapers that send reporters out in plain clothes to stir up talk about such things. We knew that Summit couldn't get after us with anything stronger than constables and, maybe, some lackadaisical bloodhounds and

a diatribe[3] or two in the *Weekly Farmers' Budget*. So, it looked good.

  We selected for our victim the only child of a prominent citizen named Ebenezer Dor-set. The father was respectable and tight, a

5 mortgage fancier and a stern, upright collection-plate passer and forecloser. The kid was a boy of ten, with bas-relief[4] freckles, and

6 hair the color of the cover of the magazine you buy at the newsstand when you want to catch a train. Bill and me figured that Ebe-nezer would melt down for a ransom of two thousand dollars to a cent. But wait till I tell

7 you.

  About two miles from Summit was a little mountain, covered with a dense cedar brake.[5] On the rear elevation of this mountain was a cave. There we stored provisions.

  One evening after sundown, we drove in a buggy past old Dorset's house. The kid was

8 in the street, throwing rocks at a kitten on the opposite fence.

  "Hey, little boy!" says Bill, "would you like to have a bag of candy and a nice ride?"

  The boys catches Bill neatly in the eye with a piece of brick.

  "That will cost the old man an extra five hundred dollars," says Bill, climbing over the wheel.

---

1. apparition (ap′ ə rish′ ən).: Bill is confusing words here. Instead of *apparition*, which is a strange ghostly figure, he means *aberration* (ab′ ər ā′ shən), which is a departure from the normal, or a mental lapse.

2. philoprogenitoveness (fil′ ō prō jen′ ə tiv′ nəs) *n*.: Again the characters make an error with a word. The correct spelling of the word is philoprogenitiveness, not -toveness. The word means "the love of parents for their offspring."

---

3. diatribe (dī′ ə trīb′) *n*.: Attack; criticism.
4. bas-relief (bä′ ri lēf′) *adj*.: Standing out from the background; like a sculpture in which figures are carved on a flat surface so that they project.
5. brake (brāk) *n*.: A thicket, or area of thick underbrush and trees.

The Ransom of Red Chief   25

Art Transparency 6
The Lafayette, by John Sloan
Thematic Idea You might want to pair this selection with the play, "The Dying Detective," on page 233 to reinforce the theme that crime doesn't pay.

Presentation

Motivation/Prior Knowledge Ask students if they have ever taken care of a child whose behavior was difficult. How did they try to get the younger child behave? If they have not had such an experience, have them imagine what they might do.

Purpose-Setting Question How does the kidnap victim turn the tables on his kidnappers?

1 **Reading Strategy** Explain how the opening sentence hints at unexpected events.

2 **Clarification** A flannel-cake is a pancake, perhaps named because pancakes are soft and warm like flannel.

3 **Clarification** A town-lot scheme is a confidence game—a con game or swindle—in which a person called a con man makes false promises about the sale of property.

4 **Discussion** What might be the author's purpose in having the two kidnappers use fancy language while they misuse words and speak ungrammatically?

5 **Clarification** The narrator means *mortgage financier*, not *mortgage fancier*. A mortgage financier lends money to people who pledge their property as security. A forecloser takes legal action against a person who has not repaid the mortgage.

6 **Clarification** The author is probably referring to a magazine such as *Time*, which has always had a bright red cover.

7 **Discussion** Why does the narrator repeat, "wait till I tell you"?

8 **Critical Thinking and Reading** What do the boy's actions indicate about his personality? How do these actions fit the stereotype of "brat"?

That boy put up a fight like a welterweight cinnamon bear; but, at last, we got him down in the bottom of the buggy and drove away. We took him up to the cave, and I hitched the horse in the cedar brake. After dark I drove the buggy to the little village, three miles away, where we had hired it, and walked back to the mountain.

Bill was pasting court-plaster[6] over the scratches and bruises on his features. There was a fire burning behind the big rock at the entrance of the cave, and the boy was watching a pot of boiling coffee, with two buzzard tail-feathers stuck in his red hair. He points a stick at me when I come up, and says:

"Ha! cursed paleface, do you dare to enter the camp of Red Chief, the terror of the plains?"

"He's all right now," says Bill, rolling up his trousers and examining some bruises on his shins. "We're playing Indian. We're making Buffalo Bill's show[7] look like magic-lantern[8] views of Palestine in the town hall. I'm Old Hank, the Trapper, Red Chief's captive, and I'm to be scalped at daybreak. By Geronimo! that kid can kick hard."

Yes, sir, that boy seemed to be having the time of his life. The fun of camping out in a cave had made him forget that he was a captive himself. He immediately christened me Snake-eye, the Spy, and announced that, when his braves returned from the warpath, I was to be broiled at the stake at the rising of the sun.

Then we had supper; and he filled his mouth full of bacon and bread and gravy, and began to talk. He made a during-dinner speech something like this:

"I like this fine. I never camped out before; but I had a pet 'possum once, and I was nine last birthday. I hate to go to school. Rats ate up sixteen of Jimmy Talbot's aunt's speckled hen's eggs. Are there any real Indians in these woods? I want some more gravy. Does the trees moving make the wind blow? We had five puppies. What makes your nose so red, Hank? My father has lots of money. Are the stars hot? I whipped Ed Walker twice, Saturday. I don't like girls. You dassent catch toads unless with a string. Do oxen make any noise? Why are oranges round? Have you got beds to sleep on in this cave? Amos Murray has got six toes. A parrot can talk, but a money or a fish can't. How many does it take to make twelve?"

Every few minutes he would remember that he was a pesky redskin, and pick up his stick rifle and tiptoe to the mouth of the cave to rubber[9] for the scouts of the hated paleface. Now and then he would let out a war-whoop that made Old Hank the Trapper shiver. That boy had Bill terrorized from the start.

"Red Chief," says I to the kid, "would you like to go home?"

"Aw, what for?" says he. "I don't have any fun at home. I hate to go to school. I like to camp out. You won't take me back home again, Snake-eye, will you?"

"Not right away," says I. "We'll stay here in the cave awhile."

"All right!" says he. "That'll be fine. I never had such fun in all my life."

We went to bed about eleven o'clock. We spread down some wide blankets and quilts and put Red Chief between us. We weren't afraid he'd run away. He kept us awake for three hours, jumping up and reaching for his rifle and screeching: "Hist! pard," in

---

6. **court-plaster:** Sticky cloth used to cover minor wounds.
7. **Buffalo Bill's show:** William F. Cody (1846–1917), known as Buffalo Bill, was a frontier scout turned showman. His famous wild-West show featured extravagant displays of trick-shooting and horseback riding.
8. **magic-lantern:** Old-fashioned term for a projector showing still pictures from transparent slides.

9. **rubber** (rub′ ər) *n.:* Short for *rubberneck*, old slang term meaning "to stretch one's neck and gaze around with curiosity."

26   Short Stories

mine and Bill's ears, as the fancied crackle of a twig or the rustle of a leaf revealed to his young imagination the stealthy approach of the outlaw band. At last, I fell into a troubled sleep, and dreamed that I had been kidnapped and chained to a tree by a ferocious pirate with red hair.

Just at daybreak, I was awakened by a series of awful screams from Bill. They weren't yells, or howls, or shouts, or whoops, or yawps, such as you'd expect from a manly set of vocal organs—they were simply indecent, terrifying, humiliating screams, such as women emit when they see ghosts or caterpillars. It's an awful thing to hear a strong, desperate, fat man scream incontinently in a cave at daybreak.

I jumped up to see what the matter was. Red Chief was sitting on Bill's chest, with one hand twined in Bill's hair. In the other he had the sharp case-knife we used for slicing bacon; and he was industriously and re-

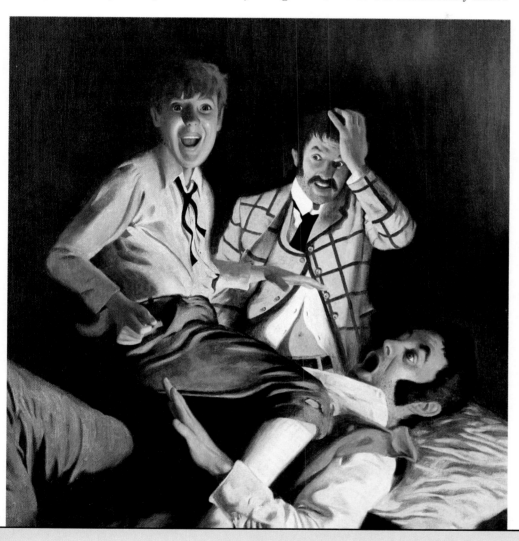

13 Discussion What does Sam's dream indicate about the unexpected turn of events?

Master Teacher Note This story is set near a southern town around the turn of the century. To give students an idea of the way buildings, automobiles, and people looked at the time, you might put Art Transparency 6, *The Lafayette* by John Sloan, on the overhead projector. Have students discuss the differences in how cities are perceived today compared to the scene portrayed in the painting. What elements found in short stories—setting, plot, character, and theme—can be found or imagined in this painting? For example, what is the setting? What role would characters like Bill and Sam have in such a scene? What scheme would they be embroiled in?

ESL Teaching Strategy You might want to explain that playing "cowboys and Indians" has been a popular game with young people in the United States because of our frontier heritage. Make sure they understand why the boy chooses the names "Red Chief," "Old Hank, the Trapper," and "Snake-eye, the Spy" for himself and the men. You could also explain that the pranks and the games he plays with Bill are based on his role-playing as Red Chief.

You might also introduce the terms *kidnap, ransom,* and *victim* to ESL students.

14 Critical Thinking and Reading In a story about a kidnapping, how would you expect to feel about the characters? Who would be the "bad guys?" ... the "good guys?" ... the victims?

15 Reading Strategy At this point, you might ask students to summarize the events in the story. Based on these events, they could make another prediction about the outcome of the story. Is their second prediction different from their first? Why or why not?

16 Discussion How do you think Sam feels when he realizes that no one is searching for the boy?

17 Discussion Bill asks Sam if he has a gun, presumably so he can protect himself from the boy. Based on what you know about Bill and Sam, why is this question humorous and not scary?

18 Discussion What do you think Bill is secretly hoping when he asks Sam if he thinks Red Chief will run away?

alistically trying to take Bill's scalp, according to the sentence that had been pronounced upon him the evening before.

14 I got the knife away from the kid and made him lie down again. But, from that moment, Bill's spirit was broken. He laid down on his side of the bed, but he never closed an eye again in sleep as long as that boy was with us. I dozed off for a while, but along toward sun-up I remembered that Red Chief had said I was to be burned at the stake at the rising of the sun. I wasn't nervous or afraid; but I sat up and lit my pipe and leaned against a rock.

"What you getting up so soon for, Sam?" asked Bill.

"Me?" says I. "Oh, I got a kind of pain in my shoulder. I thought sitting up would rest it."

15 "You're a liar!" says Bill. "You're afraid. You was to be burned at sunrise, and you was afraid he'd do it. And he would, too, if he could find a match. Ain't it awful, Sam? Do you think anybody will pay out money to get a little imp like that back home?"

"Sure," said I. "A rowdy kid like that is just the kind that parents dote on. Now, you and the Chief get up and cook breakfast, while I go up on the top of this mountain and reconnoiter."[10]

16 I went up on the peak of the little mountain and ran my eye over the contiguous[11] vicinity.[12] Over towards Summit I expected to see the sturdy yeomanry[13] of the village armed with scythes and pitchforks beating the countryside for the dastardly kidnappers. But what I saw was a peaceful landscape dotted with one man ploughing with a

---

10. **reconnoiter** (rek′ ə noit′ ər) v.: Examine an area to discover information.
11. **contiguous** (kən tig′ yōō əs) adj.: Near; next; touching.
12. **vicinity** (və sin′ ə tē) n.: Area; neighborhood.
13. **yeomanry** (yō′ mən rē) n.: Landowners.

dun mule. Nobody was dragging the creek; no couriers dashed hither and yon, bringing tidings of no news to the distracted parents. There was a sylvan attitude of somnolent sleepiness pervading that section of the external outward surface of Alabama that lay exposed to my view. "Perhaps," says I to myself, "it has not yet been discovered that the wolves have borne away the tender lambkin from the fold. Heaven help the wolves!" says I, and I went down the mountain to breakfast.

When I got to the cave I found Bill backed up against the side of it, breathing hard, and the boy threatening to smash him with a rock half as big as a cocoanut.

17 "He put a red-hot boiled potato down my back," explained Bill, "and then mashed it with his foot; and I boxed his ears. Have you got a gun about you, Sam?"

I took the rock away from the boy and kind of patched up the argument. "I'll fix you," says the kid to Bill. "No man ever yet struck the Red Chief but he got paid for it. You better beware!"

After breakfast the kid takes a piece of leather with strings wrapped around it out of his pocket and goes outside the cave unwinding it.

18 "What's he up now?" says Bill, anxiously. "You don't think he'll run away, do you, Sam?"

"No fear of it," says I. "He don't seem to be much of a home body. But we've got to fix up some plan about the ransom. There don't seem to be much excitement around Summit on account of his disappearance; but maybe they haven't realized yet that he's gone. His folks may think he's spending the night with Aunt Jane or one of the neighbors. Anyhow, he'll be missed today. Tonight we must get a message to his father demanding the two thousand dollars for his return."

Just then we heard a kind of war-whoop,

28 Short Stories

Grammar in Action

Exaggeration is speaking, writing, or thinking that overstates what is actually so. We all exaggerate in our everyday conversation. For example, you would be using exaggeration if you described someone with big feet by saying, "His shoes were the size of a canoe"; or a very hot place by saying, "It must be four hundred degrees in this room."

O. Henry often uses exaggeration to describe characters and events in order to make them humorous and striking for the reader. For example, he tells us that Red Chief has "hair the color of the cover of the magazine you buy at the newsstand when you want to catch a train." Of course, the boy's hair is not really the same color as a magazine. But using exaggeration creates a description that is both humorous and expressive. O. Henry's exaggerated description is much more vivid than "The boy had very bright red hair" or "The boy's hair was really red."

It is important to remember that there are improper as well as proper times for using exaggeration, just as there are proper and improper times to use humor in general. For example, you would not use exaggeration in writing factual newspaper articles or in writing realistic descriptions of a person or object.

19 such as David might have emitted when he knocked out the champion Goliath. It was a sling that Red Chief had pulled out of his pocket, and he was whirling it around his head.

I dodged, and heard a heavy thud and a kind of a sigh from Bill, like a horse gives out when you take his saddle off. A rock the size of an egg had caught Bill just behind his left ear. He loosened himself all over and fell in the fire across the frying pan of hot water for washing the dishes. I dragged him out and poured cold water on his head for half an hour.

20 By and by, Bill sits up and feels behind his ear and says: "Sam, do you know who my favorite Biblical character is?"

"Take it easy," says I. "You'll come to your senses presently."

21 "King Herod,"[14] says he. "You won't go away and leave me here alone, will you, Sam?"

I went out and caught that boy and shook him until his freckles rattled.

"If you don't behave," says I, "I'll take you straight home. Now, are you going to be good, or not?"

22 "I was only funning," says he, sullenly. "I didn't mean to hurt Old Hank. But what did he hit me for? I'll behave, Snake-eye, if you won't send me home, and if you'll let me play the Black Scout today."

23 "I don't know the game," says I. "That's for you and Mr. Bill to decide. He's your playmate for the day. I'm going away for a while, on business. Now, you come in and make friends with him and say you are sorry for hurting him, or home you go, at once."

I made him and Bill shake hands, and then I took Bill aside and told him I was going to Poplar Grove, a little village three

---

14. King Herod (73–74 B.C.): King of Judea who ordered the killing of all male children under two years of age.

---

miles from the cave, and find out what I could about how the kidnapping had been regarded in Summit. Also, I thought it best to send a peremptory[15] letter to old man Dorset that day, demanding the ransom and dictating how it should be paid.

"You know, Sam," says Bill, "I've stood by you without batting an eye in earthquakes, fire and flood—in poker games, dynamite outrages, police raids, train robberies, and cyclones. I never lost my nerve yet till we kidnapped that two-legged skyrocket of a kid. He's got me going. You won't leave me long with him, will you, Sam?"

"I'll be back some time this afternoon," says I. "You must keep the boy amused and quiet till I return. And now we'll write the letter to old Dorset."

Bill and I got paper and pencil and worked on the letter while Red Chief, with a blanket wrapped around him, strutted up and down, guarding the mouth of the cave. Bill begged me tearfully to make the ransom fifteen hundred dollars instead of two thousand. "I ain't attempting," says he, "to decry[16] the celebrated moral aspect of parental affection, but we're dealing with humans, **24** and it ain't human for anybody to give up two thousand dollars for that forty-pound chunk of freckled wildcat. I'm willing to take a chance at fifteen hundred dollars. You can charge the difference up to me."

So, to relieve Bill, I acceded, and we collaborated a letter that ran this way:

Ebenezer Dorset, Esq.:
We have your boy concealed in a place far from Summit. It is useless for you or the most skilful detectives to attempt to find him. Absolutely, the only terms on which you can

---

15. peremptory (pər emp' tə rē) *adj.*: Decisive, commanding.
16. decry (dē krī') *v.*: Speak out against strongly.

The Ransom of Red Chief 29

19 Clarification If some students are unfamiliar with this allusion to David and Goliath, explain that the story is from the Bible and is about a young boy, David, who slew a great and powerful warrior, Goliath, with a rock hurled from a sling.

20 Clarification King Herod was the reigning king of Palestine at the time of Jesus's birth. He ordered the slaughter of all newborn babies because he was warned that one of them would someday be the cause of his downfall.

21 Discussion Why does Bill tell Sam that his favorite Biblical character is King Herod? If some students are alarmed by the thought that Bill's favorite character ordered the killing of children, you might remind them that both Bill and Sam have shown themselves to be harmless. This statement was intended to be a humorous way of showing Bill's frustration.

22 Reading Strategy Have students summarize Red Chief's mischievous activities so far in the story. Then ask them to predict what might happen when Red Chief and Bill play the "Black Scout" game.

23 Discussion How do you think Sam feels when he tells Red Chief that Bill will be his playmate for the day? How do you think Bill feels?

24 Critical Thinking and Reading Why is Bill asking Sam to lower the ransom amount by five hundred dollars? How is his behavior different from what you might expect from a criminal?

Student Activity 1. Find two other vivid descriptions in the story in which O. Henry uses exaggeration. For each, tell in your own words what the author makes the reader see.

Student Activity 2. Rewrite the following sentences, using exaggeration to make them humorous and memorable.
1. Red Chief's behavior was wild and unruly.
2. Bill and Sam ran away quickly from the Dorsets' house after they returned Red Chief.
3. It seemed to Bill that Sam was gone for a long time when he left Bill alone with Red Chief.

Student Activity 3. Write three original sentences using exaggeration to describe imaginary people or animals.

25 Discussion Notice how the boy has affected Bill's behavior. Who seems to be the victim and who the villain in this scene? What clues are given about Bill's inner feelings?

26 Discussion Now Bill wishes they had asked for even less money in return for the boy. Why is this funny?

27 Clarification The word *whiskerando* is a slang term for an old man with whiskers or a beard.

have him restored to you are these: We demand fifteen hundred dollars in large bills for his return; the money to be left at midnight tonight at the same spot and in the same box as your reply—as hereinafter described. If you agree to these terms, send your answer in writing by a solitary messenger tonight at half-past eight o'clock. After crossing Owl Creek on the road to Poplar Grove, there are three large trees about a hundred yards apart, close to the fence of the wheat field on the right-hand side. At the bottom of the fence-post, opposite the third tree, will be found a small pasteboard box.

The messenger will place the answer in this box and return immediately to Summit.

If you attempt any treachery or fail to comply with our demand as stated, you will never see your boy again.

If you pay the money as demanded, he will be returned to you safe and well within three hours. These terms are final, and if you do not accede to them no further communication will be attempted.

Two Desperate Men

I addressed this letter to Dorset, and put it in my pocket. As I was about to start, the kid comes up to me and says:

"Aw, Snake-eye, you said I could play the Black Scout while you was gone."

"Play it, of course," says I. "Mr. Bill will play with you. What kind of a game is it?"

"I'm the Black Scout," says Red Chief, "and I have to ride to the stockade to warn the settlers that the Indians are coming. I'm tired of playing Indian myself. I want to be the Black Scout."

"All right," says I. "It sounds harmless to me. I guess Mr. Bill will help you foil the pesky savages."

"What am I to do?" asks Bill, looking at the kid suspiciously.

"You are the hoss," says Black Scout. "Get down on your hands and knees. How can I ride to the stockade without a hoss?"

"You'd better keep him interested," said I, "till we get the scheme going. Loosen up."

Bill gets down on his all fours, and a look comes in his eye like a rabbit's when you catch it in a trap.

"How far is it to the stockade, kid?" he asks, in a husky manner of voice.

"Ninety miles," says the Black Scout. "And you have to hump yourself to get there on time. Whoa, now!"

The Black Scout jumps on Bill's back and digs his heels in his side.

"For Heaven's sake," says Bill, "hurry back, Sam, as soon as you can. I wish we hadn't made the ransom more than a thousand. Say, you quit kicking me or I'll get up and warm you good."

I walked over to Poplar Grove and sat around the post-office and store, talking with the chaw-bacons[17] that came in to trade. One whiskerando says that he hears Summit is all upset on account of Elder Ebenezer Dorset's boy having been lost or stolen. That was all I wanted to know. I bought some smoking tobacco, referred casually to the price of black-eyed peas, posted my letter surreptitiously,[18] and came away. The postmaster said the mail-carrier would come by in an hour to take the mail to Summit.

When I got back to the cave Bill and the boy were not to be found. I explored the vicinity of the cave, and risked a yodel or two, but there was no response.

So I lighted my pipe and sat down on a

---

17. chaw-bacons: Old slang for yokels or hicks.
18. surreptitiously (sur′ əp tish′ əs lē) *adv.:* In a secret or sneaky way.

30 Short Stories

Grammar in Action

Writers use **subordinate clauses** to vary the length and structure of their sentences. A clause is a group of words with its own subject and verb. While an independent clause can stand by itself as a complete sentence, a subordinate clause, although it contains a subject and a verb, does not express a complete thought and cannot stand alone as a sentence. For example, "after we finished our breakfast" is a subordinate clause because more information is needed to complete the thought.

Subordinate clauses begin with words called subordinate conjunctions, words like *after, although, because, whenever, that, in order that, as if* and many others. A subordinate conjunction indicates that the clause is subordinate. When a subordinate clause appears at the beginning of a sentence, it is followed by a comma. If a subordinate clause follows an independent clause, no comma is usually needed.

Read the following sentences from "The Ransom of Red Chief." The subordinate clauses are in italics.

If you pay the money as demanded, he will be returned to you safe and well within three hours.

mossy bank to await developments.

In about half an hour I heard the bushes rustle, and Bill wabbled out into the little glade in front of the cave. Behind him was the kid, stepping softly like a scout, with a broad grin on his face. Bill stopped, took off his hat, and wiped his face with a red handkerchief. The kid stopped about eight feet behind him.

"Sam," says Bill, "I suppose you'll think

Master Teacher Note Tell students that the author of this story is noted for his unexpected endings. After teaching "The Ransom of Red Chief," you might want to read aloud to the class O. Henry's story, "The Gift of the Magi," to show that an ending can be unexpected without being humorous. Interrupt the story shortly before the end to ask if students can predict the ending.

As I was about to start, the kid comes up to me and says: . . .

I walked over to Poplar Grove and sat around the post-office and store, talking with the chaw-bacons *that came in to trade.*

Student Activity 1. Identify the subordinate clauses in each of the following sentences:
1. "I'll behave, Snake-eye, if you won't send me home. . . ."
2. When I got back to the cave, Bill and the boy were not to be found.
3. He laid down on his side of the bed, but he never closed an eye again in sleep as long as that boy was with us.

Student Activity 2. Find four other sentences with subordinate clauses in "The Ransom of Red Chief."

Student Activity 2. Write four original sentences using subordinate clauses. Place some of the clauses at the beginning of the sentences and some at the end.

28 Discussion What is funny about the language Bill uses in this speech?

29 Discussion What is Sam implying when he asks Bill if there is any heart disease in his family?

I'm a renegade,[19] but I couldn't help it. I'm a grown man with masculine proclivities[20] and habits of self-defense, but there is a time when all systems of egotism[21] and predominance[22] fail. The boy is gone. I sent him home. All is off. There was martyrs in old times," goes on Bill, "that suffered death rather than give up the particular graft they enjoyed. None of 'em ever was subjugated[23] to such supernatural tortures as I have been. I tried to be faithful to our articles of depredation;[24] but there came a limit."

"What's the trouble, Bill?" I asks him.

"I was rode," says Bill, "the ninety miles to the stockade, not barring an inch. Then, when the settlers was rescued, I was given oats. Sand ain't a palatable[25] substitute. And then, for an hour I had to try to explain to him why there was nothin' in holes, how a road can run both ways, and what makes the grass green. I tell you, Sam, a human can only stand so much. I takes him by the neck of his clothes and drags him down the mountain. On the way he kicks my legs black and blue from the knees down; and I've got to have two or three bites on my thumb and hand cauterized.[26]

"But he's gone"—continues Bill—"gone home. I showed him the road to Summit and kicked him about eight feet nearer there at one kick. I'm sorry we lose the ransom; but it was either that or Bill Driscoll to the madhouse."

Bill is puffing and blowing, but there is a look of ineffable[27] peace and growing content on his rose-pink features.

"Bill," says I, "there isn't any heart disease in your family, is there?"

"No," says Bill, "nothing chronic except malaria and accidents. Why?"

"Then you might turn around," says I, "and have a look behind you."

Bill turns and sees the boy, and loses his complexion and sits down plump on the ground and begins to pluck aimlessly at grass and little sticks. For an hour I was afraid of his mind. And then I told him that my scheme was to put the whole job through immediately and that we would get the ransom and be off with it by midnight if old Dorset fell in with our proposition. So Bill braced up enough to give the kid a weak sort of smile and a promise to play the Russian in a Japanese war[28] with him as soon as he felt a little better.

I had a scheme for collecting that ransom without danger of being caught by counterplots that ought to commend itself to professional kidnappers. The tree under which the answer was to be left—and the money later on—was close to the road fence with big, bare fields on all sides. If a gang of constables should be watching for anyone to come for the note, they could see him a long way off crossing the fields or in the road. But no, sirree! At half-past eight I was up in that tree as well hidden as a tree toad, waiting for the messenger to arrive.

Exactly on time, a half-grown boy rides up the road on a bicycle, locates the pasteboard box at the foot of the fence-post, slips

---

19. renegade (ren′ ə gād) *n.*: Traitor; turncoat.
20. proclivities (prō kliv′ ə tēz) *n.*: Tendencies; habits.
21. egotism (ē′ gō tiz′ əm) *n.*: Selfishness; self-conceit.
22. predominance (prē däm′ ə nəns) *n.*: Authority; superiority.
23. subjugated (sub′ jə gāt′ əd) *v.*: Put under the control of.
24. depredation (dep′ rə dā′ shən) *n.*: Robbing; here Bill is referring to the rules they set up for the kidnapping.
25. palatable (pal′ ə tə bəl) *adj.*: Pleasant; acceptable.
26. cauterized (kôt′ ər īz′ d) *v.*: Burned so as to stop the spread of infection.

27. ineffable (in ef′ ə bəl) *adj.*: Too overwhelming to be described.
28. the Russian in a Japanese war: Reference to the Russo-Japanese War of 1905.

32   Short Stories

Commentary

O. Henry's fiction entertains us, touches our emotions, delights us with its twists and surprises, and transforms ordinary people into unforgettable characters. What it does not do is preach, teach, or moralize. That is, it does not try to teach its readers a lesson about how the author believes they should think or act.

O. Henry himself wrote in "Strictly Business," from his book *The Gold That Glittered,* "A story with a moral appended is like the bill of a mosquito. It bores you and then injects a stinging drop to irritate your conscience." In fact, many of O. Henry's stories include criminals and others who are not part of society's mainstream. Although these characters often pay for their misdeeds, they are treated as realistic and sympathetic people.

In this story, for example, although Bill and Sam are portrayed as bungling and inept, we come to sympathize with them more than with the "victim," Red Chief. What event from O. Henry's life may have led him to his belief that moralizing was boring and irritating?

a folded piece of paper into it, and pedals away again back toward Summit.

I waited an hour and then concluded the thing was square. I slid down the tree, got the note, slipped along the fence till I struck the woods, and was back at the cave in another half an hour. I opened the note, got near the lantern, and read it to Bill. It was written with a pen in a crabbed hand,[29] and the sum and substance of it was this:

Two Desperate Men.
  Gentlemen: I received your letter today by post, in regard to the ransom you ask for the return of my son.

I think you are a little high in your demands, and I hereby make you a counter-proposition, which I am inclined to believe you will accept. You bring Johnny home and pay me two hundred and fifty dollars in cash, and I agree to take him off your hands. You had better come at night, for the neighbors believe he is lost, and I couldn't be responsible for what they would do to anybody they saw bringing him back. Very respectfully,

Ebenezer Dorset

"Great pirates of Penzance," says I; "of all the impudent——"

But I glanced at Bill, and hesitated. He

---

29. crabbed hand: Handwriting that is hard to read because it is cramped and irregular.

The Ransom of Red Chief 33

30 Literary Focus This letter indicates a twist in the plot. How does this twist affect the conflict?

31 Clarification "The Pirates of Penzance" is the title of an operetta by Gilbert and Sullivan. Here, Sam is using the title as an expression. In fact, the expression "great pirates of Penzance" is quite meaningless.

Reader's Response Ask students: Did you have more sympathy for the kidnappers or for the victim? Explain.

Speaking and Listening Have groups of three students work together to read aloud their favorite scene from the story. Groups should first choose a scene they wish to read, then assign the parts of Bill, Sam, or Red Chief to each member. They should then practice reading their scenes. Remind students to try to imitate the way they imagine their characters would speak. After they have practiced reading their scenes, have groups volunteer to present their reading to the class.

had the most appealing look in his eyes I ever saw on the face of a dumb or a talking brute.

"Sam," says he, "what's two hundred and fifty dollars, after all? We've got the money. One more night of this kid will send me to a bed in Bedlam.[30] Besides being a thorough gentleman, I think Mr. Dorset is a spendthrift for making us such a liberal offer. You ain't going to let the chance go, are you?"

32 "Tell you the truth, Bill," says I, "this little he ewe lamb has somewhat got on my nerves too. We'll take him home, pay the ransom, and make our getaway."

We took him home that night. We got him to go by telling him that his father had bought a silver-mounted rifle and a pair of moccasins for him, and we were to hunt bears the next day.

It was just twelve o'clock when we knocked at Ebenezer's front door. Just at

that moment when I should have been abstracting the fifteen hundred dollars from the box under the tree, according to the original proposition, Bill was counting out two hundred and fifty dollars into Dorset's hand.

When the kid found out we were going to leave him at home he started up a howl like a calliope[31] and fastened himself as tight as a leech to Bill's leg. His father peeled him away gradually, like a porous plaster.

"How long can you hold him?" asks Bill.

"I'm not as strong as I used to be," says old Dorset, "but I think I can promise you ten minutes."

"Enough," says Bill. "In ten minutes I shall cross the Central, Southern, and Middle Western States, and be legging it trippingly for the Canadian border."

And, as dark as it was, and as fat as Bill was, and as good a runner as I am, he was a good mile and a half out of Summit before I could catch up with him.

---

30. Bedlam: Short for St. Mary of Bethlehem, an old asylum for the insane in London.

31. calliope (kə lī′ ə pē′) n.: A keyboard instrument that has a series of steam whistles.

THINKING ABOUT THE SELECTION

Recalling

1. Why do Bill and Sam choose Ebenezer Dorset's son to kidnap?
2. Tell two things the boy does before he is kidnapped that should have warned Bill and Sam that he would be nothing but trouble.
3. What are the terms of the kidnapper's note?
4. What does Red Chief's father's note propose in response?

Interpreting

5. Outlaws are often described as "desperate criminals." Here the word *desperate* means

"extremely dangerous." No doubt, this is the meaning Bill and Sam intend when they sign their ransom note "two desperate men." What meaning does O. Henry also want you to read into this word?

6. Why does Bill and Sam's plan backfire?
7. What clues at the beginning of the story hint at the humorous, unexpected events to come?

Applying

8. Have you or someone you know ever started a task that was thought to be very simple and easy, only to have unforseen problems turn the simple project into a gigantic pain in the neck? Describe the experience.

34   Short Stories

Closure and Extension

ANSWERS TO THINKING ABOUT THE SELECTION
Recalling

1. They choose Dorset's son because Dorset is a wealthy man and because the boy is an only child.
2. Before he is kidnapped, the boy throws rocks at a kitten and hits Bill with a piece of brick.
3. The terms of the note are that Mr. Dorset must give the kidnappers fifteen hundred dollars in large bills for the boy's return.
4. Red Chief's father proposes that the kidnappers pay him two hundred fifty dollars to take back his son.

Interpreting

5. The kidnappers are desperate in the sense that they cannot handle Red Chief, and they are willing to do anything to get rid of him.
6. Bill and Sam's plan backfires because Red Chief turns out to be such a brat that his father doesn't really want him back.
7. Answers will differ. Some of the clues to the unexpected events

include the phrases, "wait till I tell you;" "during a moment of temporary mental apparition;" and "we didn't find that out till later."

Applying

8. Answers will differ. You might want students to emphasize the humor in their recollections. Students may relate stories of family vacation plans that went awry, or foiled attempts to earn extra spending money.

CRITICAL THINKING AND READING
Recognizing Stereotypes

In literature, **stereotypes** can be characters, expressions, or situations that conform to what is familiar and expected. In this story, O. Henry sets up a stereotypical situation, a kidnapping. He then turns it upside down to make what would normally be a tragic story quite funny.

1. What aspects of this situation fit the stereotype of a kidnapping story?
2. How are Bill and Sam not like typical kidnappers? Find evidence to support your answer.
3. How does Red Chief's behavior differ from that of a stereotypical kidnap victim?
4. How is Ebenezer Dorset's reply to the kidnap note different from what you would expect in a kidnap story?
5. Why is the story humorous?
6. What advice would you give to Bill and Sam before they set out to kidnap anyone else? (Keep your advice humorous.)

ANALYZING LITERATURE
Understanding Conflict

A **conflict** is a struggle between opposing forces. Sometimes a conflict can get so out of hand, taking so many unexpected twists and turns, that the outcome is quite humorous.

1. How do the kidnappers come into conflict with Ebenezer Dorset?
2. Describe the conflict between the kidnappers and Red Chief.
3. Red Chief's antics force Bill to face an internal conflict: Should he betray the compact with his friend to preserve his sanity? While Sam is in Poplar Grove sending the ransom note, what does Bill decide to do? What suprise awaits Bill as he tells Sam of his treachery?
4. How are the conflicts resolved?

UNDERSTANDING LANGUAGE
Appreciating Diction

Diction refers to the choice and use of words. The diction of Bill and Sam is inappropriately sophisticated or fancy. They choose long, difficult words to express simple ideas. For example, Sam says "Philoprogenitovenes, says we, is strong in semirural communities . . . ," meaning "Parents' love and concern for their children is strong in small towns." Even funnier is when Bill and Sam misuse fancy words because they are confused by two words that sound alike. Bill says "during a moment of temporary mental apparition," when he meant to say "abberation." O. Henry chose this diction carefully to add to the humor of the characters.

1. How does Sam and Bill's diction contrast with their profession?
2. How does their diction contrast with their actions and behavior?
3. Why do these contrasts add to the humor of the story?

THINKING AND WRITING
Writing Diary Entries

Imagine that you are the boy, Red Chief. Step into his shoes and become a mischievous, obnoxious brat. Thinking as Red Chief thinks, write two diary entries for the two days of your adventure with Sam and Bill. Explain how you feel about camping out in the woods and playing with "Snake-eye" and "Old Hank." What are you thinking about? How are you feeling? As you look over your first draft, ask yourself, "Is this Red Chief speaking?" Revise any sentences that are not from his point of view.

The Ransom of Red Chief 35

3. A typical kidnap victim would be frightened and want to go home. Red Chief is not afraid; in fact, he is having a great time and does not want to go home.
4. A typical reply to a kidnap note would reflect fear and worry, and would probably promise to pay the ransom, instead of proposing to have the kidnappers pay to be able to return the victim.
5. The story is humorous because the characters, the conflicts, and the outcome are all unexpected.
6. Answers will differ. Suggested Responses: Before choosing a victim, check at the local school to be sure the child is well-behaved; hire a professional entertainer to keep the victim amused.

ANSWERS TO UNDERSTANDING LANGUAGE

1. The reader does not expect small-time con men to use long, difficult words.
2. Their diction is pretentious, whereas their actions and behavior are bumbling and incompetent.
3. These contrasts add humor because they are unexpected and reflect the kidnappers' mistaken belief that they are professionals, while in fact they are amateurs.

THINKING AND WRITING

For help with this assignment, students can refer to Lesson 10, "Writing About Narration and Point of View," on page 800 in the Handbook of Writing About Literature.

Publishing Student Writing You might want to ask for student volunteers to read their diary entries aloud to the class. Encourage students read as if they're Red Chief, speaking in his tone of voice.

Challenge Write a diary entry, imagining that you are Bill. Tell about your experience playing the Black Scout game with Red Chief. Make your entry humorous by working in long, difficult words used incorrectly.

ANSWERS TO ANALYZING LITERATURE

1. The kidnappers come into conflict with Mr. Dorset by kidnapping his son.
2. The conflict between the kidnappers and Red Chief starts with Red Chief as the victim of the kidnappers. Because of his behavior and his captors' incompetence, however, the kidnappers become the victims of Red Chief.
3. Bill decides to send Red Chief home but is surprised to learn that the boy does not want to go home and has returned.
4. The conflicts are resolved when the kidnappers agree to pay two hundred fifty dollars to Dorset in return for taking Red Chief off their hands.

ANSWERS TO CRITICAL THINKING AND READING

1. The typical aspects of the situation are the roles the characters play: kidnappers, victim, and victim's parent.
2. Bill and Sam are different from typical kidnappers in three ways: They are bumbling and incompetent, they are incapable of harming their victim, and they agree to Dorset's counterproposal. Evidence might include the kidnapper's bumbling use of language, their refusal to harm Red Chief, their becoming intimidated by Red Chief.

Focus

Focus

More About the Author James Ullman's fame rests on his books about mountaineering. In 1964, he published *Americans on Everest,* which chronicled the first American attempt to ascend Everest. He had been a member of that team, serving as journalist and climber. Ask students to discuss the relationship between what a person loves to do and what the person writes about. Could Ullman have written as effectively about other sports? How much does a writer have to "feel" for his subjects?

Literary Focus By using suspense, a writer makes the reader curious, tense, and unsure of the outcome of the story. Point out to students that suspense is a part of everyday life. Students may be tense about the tryouts for a team or taking a test and uncertain about the outcome. Have students come up with other examples of suspense in everyday life.

Look For More advanced students may find it interesting to make a list of all the ways in which a writer creates suspense in a story. Using Ullman's story, have them make lists and compare them to see how many items the lists have in common.

Writing/Prior Knowledge Have students discuss how the unknown is often used to create suspense. Then have them complete the freewriting assignment.

Vocabulary Have less advanced students read the words aloud so that you can be sure they can pronounce them.

Spelling Tip Point out that three words in the vocabulary list have a double consonant: *crevasse, pummeled,* and *reconnoiter.*

A Boy and a Man

James Ramsey Ullman (1907–1971) was born in New York City, but his interest in mountain climbing made him "more familiar with Tibet than with Times Square." His work as a reporter, playwright, and play producer did not prevent him from traveling in pursuit of adventure. Though too ill to climb Mount Everest in Tibet himself, he assisted the American expedition that conquered this mountain in 1963. "A Boy and a Man" captures Ullman's love of climbing.

Suspense

Suspense is the quality of a story that makes you want to keep reading until you learn how the events turn out. The word *suspense* comes from a Latin word meaning "suspended" or "uncertain," and uncertainty is an important part of suspense. You keep reading because the story is like a fascinating puzzle that fits together only at the end. Danger is another key ingredient in creating suspense. In many tales of suspense, the outcome is a matter of life or death. However, the danger in a suspenseful story does not have to be a physical threat. It can involve, for example, the possibility of losing a friend or failing a test.

The writer of "A Boy and a Man" wastes no time in creating suspense. As soon as the story opens, you are faced with a situation that is both uncertain and dangerous.

Look For

As you read "A Boy and a Man," a story about a mountain rescue in the Alps, look for the ways that the writer uses uncertainty and danger to create suspense. Which parts of the story keep you sitting on the edge of your seat?

Writing

Describe an episode from a suspenseful movie or television program you have seen. Explain why this show kept you sitting at the edge of your seat.

Vocabulary

Knowing the following words will help you as you read "A Boy and a Man."

crevasse (kri vas') *n.:* Deep crack (p. 37)

glacier (glā' shər) *n.:* Large mass of ice and snow (p. 37)

despair (di sper') *n.:* Loss of hope (p. 37)

prone (prōn) *adj.:* Lying face downward (p. 38)

taut (tôt) *adj.:* Tightly stretched (p. 39)

pummeled (pum' ld) *v.:* Beat (p. 39)

reconnoiter (rē' kə noit' ər) *v.:* Look around (p. 41)

Objectives

1 To understand the use of suspense in a short story

2 To identify details that create suspense

3 To determine the meaning of a word from its context

4 To write a letter proposing a suspenseful short story to a magazine

Support Material

Teaching Portfolio
Teacher Backup, p. 45
Grammar in Action Worksheet, *Using Dashes,* p. 49
Usage and Mechanics Worksheet, p. 51
Vocabulary Check, p. 52
Analyzing Literature Worksheet, *Understanding Suspense,* p. 53
Language Worksheet, *Understanding Context Clues,* p. 54
Selection Test, p. 55

A Boy and a Man

from *Banner in the Sky*

James Ramsey Ullman

The crevasse was about six feet wide at the top and narrowed gradually as it went down. But how deep it was Rudi could not tell. After a few feet the blue walls of ice curved away at a sharp slant, and what was below the curve was hidden from sight.

"Hello!" Rudi called.

"Hello—" A voice answered from the depths.

"How far down are you?"

"I'm not sure. About twenty feet, I'd guess."

"On the bottom?"

"No. I can't even see the bottom. I was lucky and hit a ledge."

The voice spoke in German, but with a strange accent. Whoever was down there, Rudi knew, it was not one of the men of the valley.

"Are you hurt?" he called.

"Nothing broken—no," said the voice. "Just shaken up some. And cold."

"How long have you been there?"

"About three hours."

Rudi looked up and down the crevasse. He was thinking desperately of what he could do.

"Do you have a rope?" asked the voice.

"No."

"How many of you are there?"

"Only me."

There was a silence. When the voice spoke again, it was still quiet and under strict control. "Then you'll have to get help," it said.

Rudi didn't answer. To get down to Kurtal would take at least two hours, and for a party to climb back up would take three. By that time it would be night, and the man would have been in the crevasse for eight hours. He would be frozen to death.

"No," said Rudi, "it would take too long."

"What else is there to do?"

Rudi's eyes moved over the ice-walls: almost vertical, smooth as glass. "Have you an ax?" he asked.

"No. I lost it when I fell. It dropped to the bottom."

"Have you tried to climb?"

"Yes. But I can't get a hold."

There was another silence. Rudi's lips tightened, and when he spoke again his voice was strained. "I'll think of something," he cried. "I'll think of *something!*"

"Don't lose your head," the voice said. "The only way is to go down for help."

"But you'll—"

"Maybe. And maybe not. That's a chance we'll have to take."

The voice was as quiet as ever. And, hearing it, Rudi was suddenly ashamed. Here was he, safe on the glacier's surface, showing fear and despair, while the one below, facing almost certain death, remained calm and controlled. Whoever it was down there, it was a real man. A brave man.

Presentation

Motivation/Prior Knowledge
Have students imagine that they have climbed high up on a mountain in the Alps. Suddenly, they hear a cry for help breaking the stillness. Someone has fallen into a crevasse. Only they can rescue the person because there's no one else around for miles. Would they feel pure excitement or would their excitement be mixed with fear? What would they do to rescue the person?

Purpose-Setting Question
What role does suspense play in this story?

1 **Thematic Idea** Have students consider this title and contrast it with "Caleb's Brother," p. 119. If "Caleb's Brother" could not have been retitled "Caleb and Leo," why is "A Boy and a Man" an appropriate title for this story? Point out to students that, because of the way the boy reacts to the crisis, he and the man become equals.

2 **Discussion** How is the man in the crevasse able to stay so calm?

3 **Enrichment** Mountain climbing as a sport began in Europe about 1800. There are three basic forms of mountain climbing: rock climbing, snow and ice climbing, and mixed climbing. Snow and ice climbing, the basis for this story, includes climbing in winter, on glaciers, in ice gullies, or on slopes covered with snow and ice. Climbers must know how to use ice hammers and ice screws, which can be hammered into the ice and threaded with rope. Only the best climbers should ever climb alone.

4 **Discussion** What impresses Rudi about the man in the crevasse? Why is Rudi "suddenly ashamed"? How does this help him to think of a possible solution?

Master Teacher Note This story takes place in the Swiss Alps. Set the scene for the story by bringing in pictures of the Alps from travel guide books, such as Baedeker's *Switzerland*. The view from the Jungfraujoch towards the Wengernalp is particularly impressive.

5 **Discussion** What is Rudi's idea? Why couldn't he go for help?

6 **Critical Thinking and Reading** What kind of boy is Rudi? What do his actions tell you about his character?

Rudi drew in a long, slow breath. With his climbing-staff he felt down along the smooth surface of the ice walls.

"Are you still there?" said the voice.

"Yes," he said.

"You had better go."

"Wait—"

Lying flat on the glacier, he leaned over the rim of the crevasse and lowered the staff as far as it would go. Its end came almost to the curve in the walls.

"Can you see it?" he asked.

"See what?" said the man.

Obviously he couldn't. Standing up, Rudi removed his jacket and tied it by one sleeve to the curved end of the staff. Then, holding the other end, he again lay prone and lowered his staff and jacket.

"Can you see it now?" he asked.

"Yes," said the man.

"How far above you is it?"

"About ten feet."

Again the staff came up. Rudi took off his shirt and tied one of its sleeves to the dangling sleeve of the jacket. This time, as he lay down, the ice bit, cold and rough, into his bare chest; but he scarcely noticed it. With his arms extended, all the shirt and half the jacket were out of sight beneath the curve in the crevasse.

"How near are you now?" he called.

"Not far," said the voice.

"Can you reach it?"

"I'm trying."

There was the sound of scraping boot-nails; of labored breathing. But no pull on the shirtsleeve down below.

"I can't make it," said the voice. It was fainter than before.

"Wait," said Rudi.

For the third time he raised the staff. He took off his trousers. He tied a trouser-leg to the loose sleeve of the shirt. Then he pulled, one by one, at all the knots he had made: between staff and jacket, jacket and shirt, shirt and trousers. He pulled until the blood pounded in his head and the knots were as tight as his strength could make them. This done, he stepped back from the crevasse to the point where his toes had rested when he lay flat. With feet and hands he kicked and scraped the ice until he had made two holes. Then, lying down as before, he dug his toes deep into them. He was naked now, except for his shoes, stockings and underpants. The cold rose from the ice into his blood and bones. He lowered the staff and knotted clothes like a sort of crazy fishing line.

The trousers, the shirt and half of the jacket passed out of sight. He was leaning over as far as he could.

"Can you reach it now?" he called.

"Yes," the voice answered.

"All right. Come on."

38 *Short Stories*

Grammar in Action

Dashes are used to set off certain information, such as an explanation or an example, that is not essential to the sentence. Dashes are also used to indicate that someone's words are being interrupted or to show that there is a sudden break in the sentence.

Like a comma, a dash indicates that the reader should pause before continuing to read; however, the pause should be longer for a dash than for a comma. As a result, the dash puts emphasis on the element that is being set off or on the break in the sentence. Notice how James Ramsey Ullman effectively uses dashes to add emphasis in the following sentences.

"But you'll—"
"Maybe, maybe not. That's a chance we'll have to take."
"Why—you're just a boy!" he said in astonishment.
"And I—I have saved—I mean—" Rudi stopped in confusion.

The dash in the first example indicates that the speaker is being interrupted. In the second example, the dash is used for emphasis; it makes Captain Winter's discovery that Rudi is just a

"You won't be able to hold me. I'll pull you in."

"No you won't."

He braced himself. The pull came. His toes went taut in their ice-holds and his hands tightened on the staff until the knuckles showed white. Again he could hear a scraping sound below, and he knew that the man was clawing his boots against the ice-wall, trying both to lever himself up and to take as much weight as possible off the improvised lifeline. But the wall obviously offered little help. Almost all his weight was on the lifeline. Suddenly there was a jerk, as one of the knots in the clothing slipped, and the staff was almost wrenched from Rudi's hands. But the knot held. And his hands held. He tried to call down, "All right?" but he had no breath for words. From below, the only sound was the scraping of boots on ice.

How long it went on Rudi could never have said. Perhaps only for a minute or so. But it seemed like hours. And then at last—at last—it happened. A hand came into view around the curve of the crevasse wall: a hand gripping the twisted fabric of his jacket, and then a second hand rising slowly above it. A head appeared. A pair of shoulders. A face was raised for an instant and then lowered. Again one hand moved slowly up past the other.

But Rudi no longer saw it, for now his eyes were shut tight with the strain. His teeth were clamped, the cords of his neck bulged, the muscles of his arm felt as if he were being drawn one by one from the bones that held them. He began to lose his toe-holds. He was being dragged forward. Desperately, frantically, he dug in with his feet, pressed his whole body down, as if he could make it part of the glacier. Though all but naked on the ice, he was pouring with sweat. Somehow he stopped the slipping. Somehow he held on. But now suddenly the strain was even worse, for the man had reached the lower end of the staff. The slight "give" of the stretched clothing was gone, and in its place, was rigid deadweight on a length of wood. The climber was close now. But heavy. Indescribably heavy. Rudi's hands ached and burned, as if it were a rod of hot lead that they clung to. It was not a mere man he was holding, but a giant; or a block of granite. The pull was unendurable. The pain unendurable. He could hold on no longer. His hands were opening. It was all over.

And then it *was* over. The weight was gone. There was a scraping sound close beneath him; a hand on the rim of ice; a figure pulling itself up onto the lip of the crevasse. The man was beside Rudi, turning to him, staring at him.

"Why—you're just a boy!" he said in astonishment.

Rudi was too numb to move or speak. Taking the staff from him, the man pulled up the line of clothes, untied the knots and shook them out.

"Come on now. Quickly!" he said.

Pulling the boy to his feet, he helped him dress. Then he rubbed and pummeled him until at last Rudi felt the warmth of returning circulation.

"Better?" the man asked, smiling.

Rudi nodded. And finally he was able to speak again. "And you, sir," he said, "you are all right?"

The man nodded. He was warming himself now: flapping his arms and kicking his feet together. "A few minutes of sun and I'll be as good as new."

Nearby, a black boulder lay embedded in the glacial ice, and, going over to it, they sat down. The sunlight poured over them like a warm bath. Rudi slowly flexed his aching fingers and saw that the man was doing the same. And then the man had raised his eyes and was looking at him.

A Boy and a Man 39

7 **Literary Focus** How does Ullman build suspense in these paragraphs? List the suspenseful devices.

8 **Reading Strategy** Predict what will happen to Rudi and the man. Do you have confidence in Rudi's ability to hold on to the staff?

9 **Discussion** Are you surprised to learn that Rudi is young? Has he acted like a boy or like a man?

boy seem much more wondrous and important. In the last sentence dashes are used for both of the above reasons.

Dashes can be very effective, but they must be used properly and sparingly. Use a single dash after an introductory element or before a final sentence element. Use a pair of dashes to set off an element within the sentence. Only use dashes when the meaning of the sentence requires their use. Avoid the overuse of dashes!

Student Activity 1. Find two other sentences from "A Boy and a Man" in which Ullman uses dashes. Explain why Ullman uses dashes in these sentences.

Student Activity 2. In the following sentences, a period and comma have been used when dashes would have been more effective. Copy the sentences using dashes where they are appropriate.

1. "Hurry." The small, frightened boy was frantically clutching at the rope, clutching for his life.

2. "But."
   "Don't make any excuses!" she snapped.

10 Discussion Why is Rudi embarrassed when he learns the man's identity?

11 Discussion Is it surprising that Rudi comes from a mountaineering background? Could anyone have done what he did? What advantages does Rudi have in being the son of Josef Matt?

"It's a miracle how you did it," he said. "A boy of your size. All alone."

"It was nothing," Rudi murmured.

"Nothing?"

"I—I only—"

"Only saved my life," said the man.

For the first time, now, Rudi was really seeing him. He was a man of perhaps thirty, very tall and thin, and his face, too, was thin, with a big hawklike nose and a strong jutting chin. His weather-browned cheeks were clean-shaven, his hair black, his eyes deep-set and gray. And when he spoke, his voice was still almost as quiet as when it had been muffled by the ice-walls of the crevasse. He is—what?—Rudi thought. Not Swiss, he knew. Not French or German. English, perhaps? Yes, English. . . . And then suddenly a deep excitement filled him, for he knew who the man was.

"You are Captain Winter?" he murmured.

"That's right."

"And I—I have saved—I mean—"

Rudi stopped in confusion, and the Englishman grinned. "You've saved," he said, smiling, "one of the worst imbeciles that ever walked on a glacier. An imbecile who was so busy looking up at a mountain that he couldn't even see what was at his feet."

10 Rudi was wordless—almost stunned. He looked at the man, and then away in embarrassment, and he could scarcely believe what had happened. The name of Captain John Winter was known through the length and breadth of the Alps. He was the foremost mountaineer of his day, and during the past ten years had made more first ascents of great peaks than any other man alive. Rudi had heard that he had come to Kurtal a few days before. He had hoped that at least he would see him in the hotel or walking by in the street. But actually to meet him—and in this way! To pull him from a crevasse—save him. . . . It was incredible!

Captain Winter was watching him. "And you, son," he asked. "What is your name?"

Somehow the boy got his voice back. "Rudi," he said. "Rudi Matt."

"Matt?" Now it was the man's turn to be impressed. "Not of the family of the great Josef Matt?"

"He was my father," Rudi said. **11**

Captain Winter studied him with his gray eyes. Then he smiled again. "I should have known," he said. "A boy who could do what you've done—"

"Did you know my father, sir?"

"No, unfortunately I didn't. He was before my day. But ever since I was a boy I have heard of him. In twenty years no one has come to the Alps and not heard of the great guide, Josef Matt."

Rudi's heart swelled. He looked away. His eyes fixed on the vast mountain that rose before them, and then he saw that Captain Winter was watching it too.

Unconsciously the Englishman spoke his thoughts. "Your father was—" He caught himself and stopped.

"Yes," said Rudi softly, "he was killed on the Citadel."

There was a silence. Captain Winter reached into a pocket and brought out an unbroken bar of chocolate. "Lucky I fell on the other side," he grinned.

He broke the bar in two and handed half to Rudi.

"Oh, no, sir, thank you. I couldn't."

"When I meet a boy your age who can't eat chocolate," said Winter, "I'll be glad to stay in a crevasse for good."

Rudi took it, and they sat munching. The sun was warm on their thawing bodies. Far above, it struck the cliffs and snowfields of the Citadel, so brightly that they had to squint against the glare.

Then there was Winter's quiet voice again. "What do you think, Rudi?"

"Think, sir?"

"Can it be climbed?"

"Climbed? The Citadel?"

"Your father thought so. Alone among all the guides of Switzerland, he thought so." There was another pause. "And I think so too," said Captain Winter.

12

The boy was peering again at the shining heights. And suddenly his heart was pounding so hard that he was sure the Englishman must be able to hear it. "Is—is that why you have come here, sir?" he asked. "To try to climb the Citadel?"

"Well, now—" Winter smiled. "It's not so simple, you know. For one thing, there's not a guide in the valley who would go with me."

"I have an uncle, sir. He is—"

"Yes, I know your uncle. Franz Lerner. He is the best in Kurtal, and I've spoken to him. But he would not go. Anything but that, he said. Any other peak, any route, any venture. But not *that*, he said. Not the Citadel."

"He remembers my father—"

"Yes, he remembers your father. They all remember him. And while they love and respect his memory, they all think he was crazy." Winter chuckled softly. "Now they think *I'm* crazy," he added. "And maybe they're right too," he said.

"What will you do, sir?" asked Rudi. "Not try it alone?"

"No, that crazy I'm not." Winter slowly stroked his long jaw. "I'm not certain what I'll do," he went on. "Perhaps I'll go over to the next valley. To Broli. I've been told there is a guide there—a man called Saxo. Do you know him?"

"Yes—Emil Saxo. I have never met him, but I have heard of him. They say he is a very great guide."

"Well, I thought perhaps I'd go and talk with him. After a while. But first I must rec-

onnoiter some more. Make my plans. Pick the route. If there *is* a route."

"Yes, there is! Of course there is!"

Rudi had not thought the words. They simply burst out from him. And now again he was embarrassed as the man looked at him curiously.

13

"So?" said Captain Winter. "That is interesting, Rudi. Tell me why you think so."

"I have studied the Citadel many times, sir."

"Why?"

"Because—because—" He stopped. He couldn't say it.

"Because you want to climb it yourself?"

"I am not yet a grown man, sir. I know I cannot expect—"

"I wasn't a grown man either," said the Captain, "when I first saw the Citadel. I was younger than you—only twelve—and my parents had brought me here for a summer holiday. But I can still remember how I felt when I looked up at it, and the promise I made myself that some day I was going to climb it." He paused. His eyes moved slowly upward. "Youth is the time for dreams, boy," he murmured. "The trick is, when you get older, not to forget them."

14

Rudi listened, spellbound. He had never heard anyone speak like that. He had not known a grown man could think and feel like that.

Then Winter asked:

"This east face, Rudi—what do you think of it?"

"Think of it, sir?"

"Could it be climbed?"

Rudi shook his head. "No, it is no good. The long chimney[1] there—you see. It looks all right; it could be done. And to the left, the

---

1. chimney (chim′ nē) *n.*: In mountain climbing, this word means a deep, narrow crack in a cliff face.

12 Discussion Why is Rudi so excited to hear that John Winter intends to attempt to climb the Citadel?

13 Critical Thinking and Reading What suggests that Rudi may one day follow in his father's footsteps?

14 Critical Thinking and Reading What kind of man is John Winter? Do you think most people follow their childhood ambitions? Why or why not?

15 Critical Thinking and Reading
Both Rudi and John Winter have given a lot of thought to climbing the Citadel. Compare and contrast each one's reasons for wanting to do it.

16 Discussion How likely is it that Rudi will go into the hotel business considering the encounter that he has just had?

17 Discussion How does Rudi change back from a man into a boy when he comes down from the mountain?

18 Literary Focus When John Winter calls Rudi "dishwasher," he is being ironic. He is saying one thing but obviously meaning another. In Winter's estimation, Rudi is clearly a climber, not a dishwasher.

19 Critical Thinking and Reading
The mountain is portrayed almost as a wild animal here. Do you think Winter or Rudi will eventually "tame" the Citadel? Do you believe that Winter and Rudi will meet again?

Reader's Response What thoughts and feelings might you have had if you were Rudi and were trying to save Captain Winter?

ledges"—he pointed—"they could be done too. But higher up, no. They stop. The chimney stops, and there is only smooth rock."

"What about the northeast ridge?"

"That is not good either."

"It's not so steep."

"No, it is not so steep," said Rudi. "But the rocks are bad. They slope out, with few places for holds."

"And the north face?"

Rudi talked on. About the north face, the west ridge, the southwest ridge. He talked quietly and thoughtfully, but with deep inner excitement, for this was the first time in his life that he had been able to speak to anyone of these things which he had thought and studied for so long. . . . And then suddenly he stopped, for he realized what he was doing. He, Rudi Matt, a boy of sixteen who worked in the kitchen of the Beau Site Hotel, was presuming to give his opinions to one of the greatest climbers in the world.

But Captain Winter had been listening intently. Sometimes he nodded. "Go on," he said now, as Rudi paused.

"But I am only—"

"Go on."

And Rudi went on . . .

"That doesn't leave much," said the captain a little later.

"No, sir," said the boy.

"Only the southeast ridge."

"Yes, sir."

"That was the way your father tried, wasn't it?"

"Yes, sir."

"And you believe it's the *only* way?"

"Yes, sir."

Captain Winter rubbed his jaw for a moment before speaking again. Then—"That also is very interesting to me, Rudi," he said quietly, "because it is what I believe too."

Later, they threaded their way down the Blue Glacier. For a while they moved in silence. Then Captain Winter asked:

"What do you do, Rudi?"

"Do, sir?"

"Are you an apprentice guide? A porter?"

Rudi swallowed. "No sir."

"What then?"

He could hardly say it. "A—dishwasher."

"A dishwasher?"

"In the Beau Site Hotel. It is my mother, sir. Since my father died, you see, she is afraid—she does not want—" Rudi swallowed again. "I am to go into the hotel business," he murmured.

"Oh."

Again they moved on without speaking. It was now late afternoon, and behind them the stillness was broken by a great roaring, as sun-loosened rock and ice broke off from the heights of the Citadel.

When they reached the path Rudi spoke again, hesitantly. "Will you please do me a favor, sir," he asked.

"Of course," said Winter.

"Before we come to the town we will separate. And you will please not tell anyone that I have been up here today?"

The Englishman looked at him in astonishment. "Not tell anyone? You save my life, boy, and you want me to keep it a secret?"

"It was nothing, sir. Truly. And if you say that I have been in the mountains, my mother and uncle will hear, and I will be in trouble." Rudi's voice took on a note of urgency. "You will not do it, sir? You will promise—please?"

Winter put a hand on his shoulder. "Don't worry," he said. "I won't get you in trouble." Then he smiled and added: "Master Rudi Matt—dishwasher."

They walked down the path. The sun sank. Behind them, the mountain roared.

Closure and Extension

ANSWERS TO THINKING ABOUT THE SELECTION
Recalling

1. Rudi can't go to Kurtal because it would take too long, and the man would freeze to death waiting.
2. Rudi makes a lifeline by tying his clothes to his staff.
3. Rudi is stunned because he has just saved the life of one of the

THINKING ABOUT THE SELECTION

Recalling

1. Why doesn't Rudi go to Kurtal for help?
2. How does Rudi make a lifeline?
3. Why is Rudi "almost stunned" when he learns the identity of the man he has saved?
4. How did Rudi's father die?

Interpreting

5. Captain Winter says, "Youth is the time for dreams." What is Rudi's secret dream?
6. Why has Rudi been unable to fulfill his dream?
7. Why do you think this story is called "A Boy and a Man"?

Applying

8. Why do people sometimes keep secret their dreams and plans?

ANALYZING LITERATURE

Understanding Suspense

Writers create **suspense** by describing situations that are both uncertain and dangerous. Such dangers can be either physical or emotional. Many readers enjoy suspenseful stories because they want to discover what happens in the end and whether the characters avoid the dangers that face them. "A Boy and a Man" is a story that is filled with suspense.

1. How is Captain Winter's situation at the start of the story uncertain and dangerous?
2. How do Rudi's repeated attempts to rescue Captain Winter increase the suspense?
3. What future dangers are hinted at in the conversation between Rudi and the Captain?

CRITICAL THINKING AND READING

Identifying Details that Create Suspense

A writer creates suspense through details that increase the uncertainty and danger. Notice the details in the following description of Rudi's fourth attempt to make a lifeline for Captain Winter.

"He tied a trouser-leg to the loose sleeve of the shirt. Then he pulled, one by one, at all the knots he had made: between staff and jacket, jacket and shirt, shirt and trousers."

As you read, you wonder whether these knots will hold.

1. Find the paragraph that begins "He braced himself . . ." (page 39). Point out the details in this and the next few paragraphs that help create suspense.
2. Which specific words and phrases make you feel this suspense?

UNDERSTANDING LANGUAGE

Using Context Clues

The **context** of a word consists of the words that surround it. If you do not know a word's meaning, you can look for clues in the context. For example, from the description of a *crevasse* at the beginning of the story (p. 37), you could guess that the word *crevasse* means "a deep crack."

1. Find the reference to Rudi's "improvised lifeline" (p. 39). How does the description of the lifeline give you a clue to the meaning of the word *improvised*?
2. What does *improvised* mean?

THINKING AND WRITING

Writing About Suspense

Imagine that a magazine for teenagers is planning a special issue containing suspenseful stories. Think of stories you have read that would keep readers on the edge of their seats. Then choose the best one and write a letter to the editors of the magazine persuading them to use your story. (You may, of course, recommend "A Boy and a Man.") When revising your letter, make sure you have explained how your story contains the key ingredients of suspense: uncertainty and danger.

A Boy and a Man 43

(Answers begin on p. 42.)

wrenched from Rudi's hands." "And then at last—at last—it happened." " . . . His eyes were shut tight with the strain. His teeth were clamped, the cords of his neck bulged, the muscles of his arm felt as if he were being drawn one by one from the bones that held them." "He could hold on no longer. His hands were opening. It was all over."

2. The specific words and phrases that make you feel this suspense are: "toes taut," "knuckles white," "sudden jerk," "knots slipped," "staff wrenched; at last—at last," "shut tight with the strain," "teeth clamped," "cords bulged," "muscles drawn from bones," "lose his toehold," "dragged forward," "desperately, frantically," "strain worse," " 'give' of clothing gone," "rigid deadweight," "could hold on no longer, hands opening, all over."

ANSWERS TO UNDERSTANDING LANGUAGE

1. The fact that he tied his jacket to his staff, his shirt to the jacket, and his trousers to the shirt and then pulled the knots as tightly as he could makes you aware that *improvised* means something that was made on the spot out of necessity because standard equipment was not available.
2. *Improvised* means "made on the spur of the moment from whatever material is available."

Challenge Is it surprising that John Winter doesn't ask Rudi to join him in attempting to climb the Citadel? Why do you think he doesn't? Were you disappointed at the conclusion? Why or why not?

THINKING AND WRITING

For help with this assignment, students can refer to Lesson 8, "Writing About Plot," in the Handbook of Writing About Literature.

most famous mountain climbers in the world.

4. Rudi's father died trying to climb the Citadel.

Interpreting

5. Rudi's secret dream is to climb the Citadel.
6. Since his father died, Rudi's mother has been afraid of mountain climbing and wants her son to go into the hotel business.
7. The title suggests their isolation on the mountain together and implies that they are equals.

Applying

8. Answers will differ. Students might suggest that young people fear failing and having others know about it. They also might say that young people fear ridicule, hurting someone, or being dissuaded by others.

ANSWERS TO ANALYZING LITERATURE

1. Winter could fall deeper into the crevasse and be killed instantly or could freeze to death.
2. They increase the suspense because the reader grows less certain of Rudi's success, and if he fails, the man dies.
3. The dangers of climbing the Citadel are suggested.

ANSWERS TO CRITICAL THINKING AND READING

1. Some of the details that help create suspense are: "his toes went taut" "the knuckles showed white" "Suddenly there was a jerk, and one of the knots in the clothing slipped. The staff was almost

More About the Author Quentin Reynolds has been described as World's War II's most adventurous and most read war correspondent. He covered the war fronts in North Africa, Italy, Teheran, Palestine, and Europe. Ask students to discuss the relationship between writing about people in wartime and writing about people engaged in common, everyday activities. How are these types of writing alike? How are they different?

Literary Focus Most stories revolve around a character's problem and how it is or is not resolved. A problem can be external, such as a conflict between two characters, or internal, such as a character's inability to make an important decision. Consider other stories you have read, and decide whether the problem in each was external, internal, or a combination of the two.

Look For Less advanced students may find it difficult to identify the clues that point to a problem. Have students stop and explore the characters' meaningful comments and what they may imply as they read the story.

Writing/Prior Knowledge Have students discuss the special relationship between people and various animals as portrayed in the media and in literature. For example, Tarzan is a well-known character in books, films, and television programs based, in part, on his unique relationship with jungle animals. Then have students complete the freewriting assignment.

Vocabulary These words may also give students some difficulty: *mustache* (p. 46), *cobbled* (p. 46), *pension* (p. 46), *mirroring* (p. 48), and *hobbling* (p. 48). Be sure students know what these words mean as they read the story.

44

A Secret for Two

Quentin Reynolds (1902–1965), born in Brooklyn, New York, was active as a newspaper reporter, a sportswriter, and an author of short stories. One of his best-selling books, *The Wounded Don't Cry,* is about the courage of the English people during World War II. He covered the war for a popular magazine, writing fast-moving reports from combat areas. His reporting won high praise from England's prime minister, Winston Churchill. Reynolds also found bravery in ordinary life, as you will see in "A Secret for Two."

A Hidden Problem

The **problem,** or conflict, on which a story is based is not always clearly indicated. Sometimes a writer will disguise the problem until the story is nearly over. Only at that point do you understand that something important has been going on under the surface of the action. In fact, you may be quite surprised to learn what a writer has been keeping back.

In "A Secret for Two," the writer includes clues to the "secret," but does not reveal the problem until the end.

Look For

As you read "A Secret for Two," look for clues that point to the story's hidden problem. When is the hidden problem finally revealed?

Writing

The "secret" of this story is shared by a man and a horse who feel affection for each other. Write a description of a "friendship" you have had with a pet or one you have seen between another person and his or her pet.

Vocabulary

Knowing the following words will help you as you read "A Secret for Two."
henceforth (hens fôrth′) *adv.*: From this time on (p. 45)
sheen (shēn) *n.*: Brightness; shininess (p. 45)
stalk (stôk) *v.*: Walk slowly and stiffly (p. 45)

44　*Short Stories*

A Secret for Two

Quentin Reynolds

Montreal is a very large city, but, like all large cities, it has some very small streets. Streets, for instance, like Prince Edward Street, which is only four blocks long, ending in a cul-de-sac.[1] No one knew Prince Edward Street as well as did Pierre Dupin, for Pierre had delivered milk to the families on the street for thirty years now.

During the past fifteen years the horse which drew the milk wagon used by Pierre was a large white horse named Joseph. In Montreal, especially in that part of Montreal which is very French, the animals, like children, are often given the names of saints. When the big white horse first came to the Provincale Milk Company, he didn't have a name. They told Pierre that he could use the white horse henceforth. Pierre stroked the softness of the horse's neck; he stroked the sheen of its splendid belly, and he looked into the eyes of the horse.

"This is a kind horse, a gentle and a faithful horse," Pierre said, "and I can see a beautiful spirit shining out of the eyes of the horse. I will name him after good St. Joseph, who was also kind and gentle and faithful and a beautiful spirit."

Within a year Joseph knew the milk route as well as Pierre. Pierre used to boast that he didn't need reins—he never touched them. Each morning Pierre arrived at the stables of the Provincale Milk Company at five o'clock. The wagon would be loaded and Joseph hitched to it. Pierre would call "*Bon jour, vieille ami*,"[2] as he climbed into his seat and Joseph would turn his head and the other drivers would smile and say that the horse would smile at Pierre. Then Jacques, the foreman, would say, "All right, Pierre, go on," and Pierre would call softly to Joseph, "*Avance, mon ami*,"[3] and this splendid combination would stalk proudly down the street.

The wagon, without any direction from Pierre, would roll three blocks down St. Catherine Street, then turn right two blocks along Roslyn Avenue; then left, for that was Prince Edward Street. The horse would stop at the first house, allow Pierre perhaps thirty seconds to get down from his seat and put a bottle of milk at the front door and would then go on, skipping two houses and stopping at the third. So down the length of the street. Then Joseph, still without any direction from Pierre, would turn around and come back along the other side. Yes, Joseph was a smart horse.

Pierre would boast at the stable of Joseph's skill. "I never touch the reins. He knows just where to stop. Why, a blind man could handle my route with Joseph pulling the wagon."

---

1. cul-de-sac (kul′ də sak′) *n.*: A blind alley; a dead-end street.

2. Bon jour, vieille ami (bōn zhōōr′ vē ā′ äm ē′): French for "Hello, old friend."

3. Avance, mon ami (ä väns′ mōn äm ē′): French for "Go forward, my friend."

A Secret for Two 45

---

4 Critical Thinking and Reading
Why else besides unsteady legs might a person carry a walking stick?

5 Discussion How else might the cooks calling out their orders benefit Pierre? Since he could not read or write, what physical handicap could he keep secret under the right circumstances?

6 Critical Thinking and Reading
Can you guess what secret is shared by Pierre and Joseph? Does Jacques know what it is? Why does Jacques suspect that they share a secret?

So it went on for years—always the same. Pierre and Joseph both grew old together, but gradually, not suddenly. Pierre's huge walrus mustache was pure white now and Joseph didn't lift his knees so high or raise his head quite as much. Jacques, the foreman of the stables, never noticed that they were both getting old until Pierre appeared one day carrying a heavy walking stick.

"Hey, Pierre," Jacques laughed. "Maybe you got the gout,[4] hey?"

"*Mais oui*,[5] Jacques," Pierre said uncertainly. "One grows old. One's legs get tired."

"You should teach the horse to carry the milk to the front door for you," Jacques told him. "He does everything else."

He knew every one of the forty families he served on Prince Edward Street. The cooks knew that Pierre could neither read nor write, so instead of following the usual custom of leaving a note in an empty bottle if an additional quart of milk was needed they would sing out when they heard the rumble of his wagon wheels over the cobbled street, "Bring an extra quart this morning, Pierre."

"So you have company for dinner tonight," he would call back gaily.

Pierre had a remarkable memory. When he arrived at the stable he'd always remember to tell Jacques, "The Paquins took an extra quart this morning; the Lemoines bought a pint of cream."

Jacques would note these things in a little book he always carried. Most of the drivers had to make out the weekly bills and collect the money, but Jacques, liking Pierre, had always excused him from this task. All Pierre had to do was to arrive at five in the morning, walk to his wagon, which was always in the same spot at the curb, and deliver his milk. He returned some two hours

later, got stiffly from his seat, called a cheery "*Au 'voir*"[6] to Jacques and then limped slowly down the street.

One morning the president of the Provincale Milk Company came to inspect the early morning deliveries. Jacques pointed Pierre out to him and said, "Watch how he talks to that horse. See how the horse listens and how he turns his head toward Pierre? See the look in that horse's eyes? You know, I think those two share a secret. I have often noticed it. It is as though they both sometimes chuckle at us as they go off on their route. Pierre is a good man, Monsieur[7] President, but he gets old. Would it be too bold for me to suggest that he be retired and be given perhaps a small pension?" he added anxiously.

---

6. *au 'voir* (ō vwär'): French for "until we meet again"; "goodbye."
7. *monsieur* (mə syur') *n.*: French for "mister" or "sir."

---

4. gout (gowt) *n.*: a disease characterized by swelling and pain in the hands and feet.
5. mais oui (mä wē): French for "but yes."

Grammar in Action

Verb tense is important to writers. The tense of the verb indicates when the action takes place. The present tense tells of an action that is occurring at the present moment, whereas the past tense refers to an action that was completed in the past. The future tense describes an action that will take place in the future.

Writers use verb tense to indicate the time in which events are occurring. The proper use of verb tense adds clarity to writ-

ing. Notice how Quentin Reynolds changes the tenses of his verbs to convey time.

> "This *is* a kind horse, a gentle and a faithful horse," Pierre *said*, "and I *can see* a beautiful spirit shining out of the eyes of the horse. I *will name* him after good St. Joseph, who *was* also kind and gentle and faithful and a beautiful spirit."

The verbs *is* and *can see* indicate that Pierre is speaking about something occurring in the present. The verb *will name* indicates an action Pierre will do in the future. Since St. Joseph is now dead, Reynolds uses the past form, *was*, when describing what St. Joseph was like. The verb *said* is also past tense because the

entire story is being told in the past tense. Thus through the use of verb tense, the writer has made the time order of events clear.

Student Activity 1. Find another example from "A Secret for Two" in which Quentin Reynolds uses the present, past, and future tenses of verbs in the same passage. Explain how the use of verb tense in the passage effectively conveys when events are taking place.

Student Activity 2. Copy the following sentences, supplying the correct tense of the verb *move* for each blank. Note that you will have to use *will* with the future form of the verb. Use each tense only once.

1. Yesterday, we _____ the television set to my bedroom as my parents were entertaining friends in the living room.

2. _____ over, or I will fall off the bleachers.

3. We _____ to Arizona in three weeks.

7 Discussion Why does Pierre refuse to retire? What effect would Pierre's retirement have on Joseph?

8 Clarification Animals age faster than people, although scientists disagree about the ratio. In the story, Jacques believes that a horse ages three years to a man's one.

9 Reading Strategy Why might Jacques not understand? What do you predict will happen to Pierre now?

10 Critical Thinking and Reading What other reason might Pierre have had for keeping his cap low over his eyes? Is it common for a person who drives a truck to keep his eyes obscured? How did Pierre manage this?

11 Discussion Why didn't Pierre know that a huge truck was coming toward him? Were you surprised when Pierre died so soon after Joseph? Why or why not?

12 Discussion Were you surprised to learn that Pierre was blind? What made you suspect that something was wrong with his eyes?

13 Literary Focus Point out that Jacques counts Joseph as one of the men. He does not identify Joseph as Pierre's horse but as Pierre's friend. This is a measure of Jacques's respect for the relationship that Pierre and Joseph had.

Reader's Response What do you think was the most special aspect of the friendship between Pierre and Joseph? Why?

"But of course," the president laughed. "I know his record. He has been on this route now for thirty years and never once has there been a complaint. Tell him it is time he rested. His salary will go on just the same."

But Pierre refused to retire. He was panic-stricken at the thought of not driving Joseph every day. "We are two old men," he said to Jacques. "Let us wear out together. When Joseph is ready to retire—then I, too, will quit."

Jacques, who was a kind man, understood. There was something about Pierre and Joseph which made a man smile tenderly. It was as though each drew some hidden strength from the other. When Pierre was sitting in his seat, and when Joseph was hitched to the wagon, neither seemed old. But when they finished their work, then Pierre would limp down the street slowly, seeming very old indeed, and the horse's head would drop and he would walk very wearily to his stall.

Then one morning Jacques had dreadful news for Pierre when he arrived. It was a cold morning and still pitch-dark. The air was like iced wine that morning and the snow which had fallen during the night glistened like a million diamonds piled together.

Jacques said, "Pierre, your horse, Joseph, did not wake this morning. He was very old, Pierre, he was twenty-five, and that is like seventy-five for a man."

"Yes," Pierre said, slowly, "Yes. I am seventy-five. And I cannot see Joseph again."

"Of course you can," Jacques soothed. "He is over in his stall, looking very peaceful. Go over and see him."

Pierre took one step forward then turned. "No . . . no . . . you don't understand, Jacques."

Jacques clapped him on the shoulder. "We'll find another horse just as good as Joseph. Why, in a month you'll teach him to know your route as well as Joseph did. We'll . . ."

The look in Pierre's eyes stopped him. For years Pierre had worn a heavy cap, the peak of which came low over his eyes, keeping the bitter morning wind out of them. Now Jacques looked into Pierre's eyes and he saw something which startled him. He saw a dead, lifeless look in them. The eyes were mirroring the grief that was in Pierre's heart and his soul. It was as though his heart and soul had died.

"Take today off, Pierre," Jacques said, but already Pierre was hobbling off down the street, and had one been near one would have seen tears streaming down his cheeks and have heard half-smothered sobs. Pierre walked to the corner and stepped into the street. There was a warning yell from the driver of a huge truck that was coming fast and there was a scream of brakes, but Pierre apparently heard neither.

Five minutes later an ambulance driver said, "He's dead. Was killed instantly."

Jacques and several of the milk-wagon drivers had arrived and they looked down at the still figure.

"I couldn't help it." the driver of the truck protested, "he walked right into my truck. He never saw it, I guess. Why, he walked into it as though he was blind."

The ambulance doctor bent down. "Blind? Of course the man was blind. See those cataracts?[8] This man has been blind for five years." He turned to Jacques, "You say he worked for you? Didn't you know he was blind?"

"No . . . no . . ." Jacques said softly. "None of us knew. Only one knew—a friend of his named Joseph. . . . It was a secret, I think, just between those two."

---

8. cataracts (kat′ə rakts′) *n*.: An eye disease in which the lens becomes clouded over, causing partial or total blindness.

THINKING ABOUT THE SELECTION

Recalling

1. What does Pierre do on his job?
2. What is the "dreadful news" Jacques has for Pierre one morning?
3. How does Pierre die?
4. How do we learn Pierre's "secret"?

Interpreting

5. Why do Pierre and Joseph not seem old when they are together?
6. What makes Pierre keep his blindness a secret?

Applying

7. How is the friendship between Pierre and Joseph like a friendship between two people?

ANALYZING LITERATURE

Recognizing a Hidden Problem

In "A Secret for Two," the problem is hidden until the very end. Events continue, but you are not aware of an important fact that would explain the action. Going back over the story, however, you can find clues to the secret.

1. What is the hidden problem in "A Secret for Two"?
2. How might the story be different if the writer revealed the hidden problem sooner?
3. What is the meaning of the story's title?

CRITICAL THINKING AND READING

Finding Clues to a Hidden Problem

In "A Secret for Two," the writer gives you hints about the hidden problem. You can find these clues by looking for statements by the characters that seem exaggerated or unusual.

1. How does Pierre's boast about Joseph's skill give you a clue to the "secret"?
2. How does Jacques's unusual remark that Pierre and Joseph seem to "share a secret" hint at the hidden problem?

UNDERSTANDING LANGUAGE

Finding the Origins of English Words

Many English words have their origins, or beginnings, in other languages. Usually, a dictionary will tell you the language from which a word comes. For example, when you look up *cataract,* you will see the letters *Gr.* in brackets to indicate the origin of this word. The abbreviation *Gr.* stands for Greek. Other common abbreviations are *L.* for Latin, *Fr.* for French and *It.* for Italian.

Look up the following words from the story and identify the language or languages from which they come.

1. gout
2. ambulance
3. mustache
4. stable

THINKING AND WRITING

Writing a Short Story

You have just read a short story in which the main character faced a hidden problem. Now write a short story of your own in which a character has a secret difficulty. Get together with two or three classmates to think of ideas for this type of story. Remember that the problem does not have to be as serious as Pierre's. It can relate to an argument with a friend or a situation in school. Choose the idea you like best and develop it into a story. When you revise your story, make sure you have not revealed the hidden problem until the end.

A Secret for Two   49

Closure and Extension

ANSWERS TO THINKING ABOUT THE SELECTION

Recalling

1. He delivers dairy products to families on Prince Edward Street.
2. Jacques tells Pierre that Joseph is dead.
3. Pierre dies when he is hit by a truck while crossing a street.
4. The ambulance doctor examines Pierre's eyes and finds cataracts, which have made him blind.

Interpreting

5. Being together makes them happy. They draw strength from each other.
6. Pierre wants to keep working.

Applying

7. Answers will differ. Suggested Response: They share common experiences, do the same work, love each other, and are considerate of each other. They also share a secret.

ANSWERS TO ANALYZING LITERATURE

1. The hidden problem is that Pierre is blind.
2. The story would be much weaker because there would be no surprise ending. The reader would expect Pierre to act as he does because of his blindness.
3. The title refers to the secret between Pierre and Joseph that Pierre is blind and Joseph acts as his eyes.

ANSWERS TO CRITICAL THINKING AND READING

1. Pierre boasts that Joseph is so smart that even a blind man could handle the route with Joseph's help. This boast hints at Pierre's own future blindness.
2. The remark prepares the reader for an unusual revelation. It hints at a secret between the two that no one else knows about.

ANSWERS TO UNDERSTANDING LANGUAGE

1. gout—Old French
2. ambulance—Latin
3. mustache—Old French
4. stable—Latin

THINKING AND WRITING

For help with this assignment, students can refer to Lesson 17, "Writing a Short Story," in the Handbook of Writing About Literature.

Zoo

Edward D. Hoch (1930–   ), whose last name rhymes with "poke," was born in Rochester, New York. After graduating from the University of Rochester, he worked as a researcher for the Rochester Public Library and as a copy writer for an advertising company. Hoch has written many stories and novels in the mystery and science fiction fields. In 1967, he won an award from the Mystery Writers of America for his short story "The Oblong Room." As you will see in "Zoo," Hoch has a lively imagination and a good sense of humor.

Plot and Point of View

Point of view refers to the angle or position from which a writer tells a story. By choosing to look through the eyes of a particular character or group, a writer gives you a certain impression of the sequence of events. In "Zoo," the writer views the events from two different angles. He tells the first part of the story from the point of view of the Earth people. Then he lets you look through the eyes of the horse-spider people of Kaan. This change in point of view affects the way you understand the events of the story.

Look For

Be alert to the change in point of view as you read about the "strange creatures" that Professor Hugo brings in his great silver spaceship. How would the sequence of events seem different if the writer let you see it from only one angle?

Writing

Remember a time when you cheered for a team at a sports event. Write a description of this event. Then imagine that you were a fan supporting the other team and tell about the contest from the opposite point of view. By doing so, you will be thinking about the same event from two perspectives.

Vocabulary

Knowing the following words will help you as you read "Zoo."

interplanetary (in'tər plan'ə ter'ē) *adj.*: Between planets (p. 51)

wonderment (wun'dər mənt) *n.*: Astonishment (p. 51)

awe (ô) *n.*: A mixed feeling of fear and wonder (p. 51)

Zoo

Edward D. Hoch

The children were always good during the month of August, especially when it began to get near the twenty-third. It was on this day that the great silver spaceship carrying Professor Hugo's Interplanetary Zoo settled down for its annual six-hour visit to the Chicago area.

Before daybreak the crowds would form, long lines of children and adults both, each one clutching his or her dollar, and waiting with wonderment to see what race of strange creatures the Professor had brought this year.

In the past they had sometimes been treated to three-legged creatures from

Venus, or tall, thin men from Mars, or even snakelike horrors from somewhere more distant. This year, as the great round ship settled slowly to earth in the huge tri-city parking area just outside of Chicago, they watched with awe as the sides slowly slid up to reveal the familiar barred cages. In them were some wild breed of nightmare—small, horse-like animals that moved with quick, jerking motions and constantly chattered in a high-pitched tongue. The citizens of Earth clustered around as Professor Hugo's crew quickly collected the waiting dollars, and soon the good Professor himself made an appearance, wearing his many-colored rainbow cape and top hat. "Peoples of Earth," he called into his microphone.

The crowd's noise died down and he continued. "Peoples of Earth, this year you see a real treat for your single dollar— the little-known horse-spider people of Kaan—brought to you across a million miles of

Master Teacher Note Place Art Transparency 1, *Medicine Show* by Jack Levine, on the overhead projector. It is a painting of a man trying to attract an audience to a medicine show. Have students discuss what is taking place in the painting. What might the man have to show the people? Are the people interested? What is the effect of blurring and distorting the figures? How is this scene similar to the scene of Professor Hugo and his Interplanetary Zoo as described in the story? How are the scenes dissimilar?

4 Discussion How is Professor Hugo like the old-time carnival barkers displaying such phenomena as the bearded lady and the man with two heads? How is he different?

space at great expense. Gather around, see them, study them, listen to them, tell your friends about them. But hurry! My ship can remain here only six hours!"

And the crowds slowly filed by, at once horrified and fascinated by these strange creatures that looked like horses but ran up

52   *Short Stories*

Grammar in Action

Proper nouns name specific persons, places, or things. Proper adjectives are proper nouns used to describe other nouns. You should capitalize both proper nouns and proper adjectives. Edward D. Hoch indicates both proper nouns and proper adjectives by capitalizing them in the following sentence:

It was on this day that the great silver spaceship carrying *Professor Hugo's Interplanetary Zoo* settled down for its annual six-hour visit to the *Chicago* area.

Professor Hugo's Interplanetary Zoo is a proper noun naming a specific thing. *Chicago* is a proper adjective describing the common noun, *area*.

Student Activity 1. Find three other sentences where Hoch indicates proper nouns or proper adjectives by capitalization. For the proper nouns, indicate whether the noun is a specific person, place, or thing. For the proper adjectives, identify the noun being described.

Student Activity 2. Write three original sentences using proper nouns and proper adjectives, making sure to capitalize both.

52

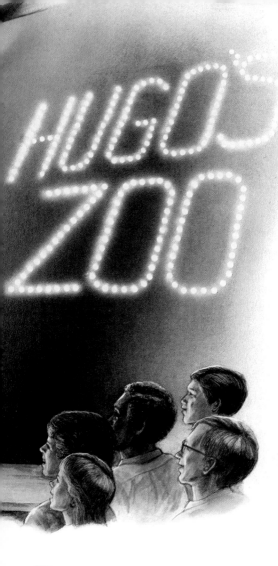

Then, as the six-hour limit ran out, Professor Hugo once more took the microphone in hand. "We must go now, but we will return next year on this date. And if you enjoyed our zoo this year, telephone your friends in other cities about it. We will land in New York tomorrow, and next week on to London, Paris, Rome, Hong Kong, and Tokyo. Then on to other worlds!"

He waved farewell to them, and as the ship rose from the ground, the Earth peoples agreed that this had been the very best Zoo yet. . . .

Some two months and three planets later, the silver ship of Professor Hugo settled at last onto the familiar jagged rocks of Kaan, and the odd horse-spider creatures filed quickly out of their cages. Professor Hugo was there to say a few parting words, and then they scurried away in a hundred different directions, seeking their homes among the rocks.

In one house, the she-creature was happy to see the return of her mate and offspring. She babbled a greeting in the strange tongue and hurried to embrace them. "It was a long time you were gone. Was it good?"

And the he-creature nodded. "The little one enjoyed it especially. We visited eight worlds and saw many things."

The little one ran up the wall of the cave. "On the place called Earth it was the best. The creatures there wear garments over their skins, and they walk on two legs."

"But isn't it dangerous?" asked the she-creature.

"No," her mate answered. "There are bars to protect us from them. We remain right in the ship. Next time you must come with us. It is well worth the nineteen commocs it costs."

And the little one nodded. "It was the very best Zoo ever. . . ."

the walls of their cages like spiders. "This is certainly worth a dollar," one man remarked, hurrying away. "I'm going home to get the wife."

All day long it went like that, until ten thousand people had filed by the barred cages set into the side of the spaceship.

Zoo 53

5 **Literary Focus** If the Earth man is impressed with the people of Kaan, how do you think the people of Kaan feel about the humans they are seeing?

6 **Discussion** What does the she-creature's reaction to her family's return remind you of?

7 **Discussion** Have you ever thought of yourself as a creature who wears garments and walks on two legs? Why doesn't this seem unusual to you? Are there any creatures in your life who might perceive you this way?

8 **Discussion** Does this dialogue sound familiar? Who else in the story had these reactions?

Answers

ANSWERS TO THINKING ABOUT THE SELECTION

Recalling

1. There is excitement because Professor Hugo's Interplanetary Zoo is coming.
2. Earthlings are fascinated by the people of Kaan because they seem strange, nightmarish, and bizarre.
3. The Kaanians describe humans as creatures who "wear garments over their skins, and . . . walk on two legs."

Interpreting

4. Both the Earthlings and the Kaanians were fascinated by the strangeness of one another, thought it was the best zoo they had ever seen, and thought it was worth the cost. The Earthlings were horrified at the way the Kaanians looked and behaved, while the Kaanians were glad that there were bars on their cages to protect them from the Earthlings. They each viewed the other as strange for different reasons.
5. Professor Hugo is obviously a shrewd businessman because he charges both the Earthlings and the Kaanians to look at each other.

Applying

6. Answers will differ. Suggested Response: By viewing situations from more than one perspective, you gain a broader understanding of the factors involved.

ANSWERS TO ANALYZING LITERATURE

1. The point of view changes with the paragraph that begins "Some two months and three planets later, ..."
2. The story would have lacked humor and the broad understanding that comes from seeing more than one point of view.
3. Changing the point of view makes the story effective because it spotlights the perceptions of the Earthlings and Kaanians by contrasting them.

ANSWERS TO CRITICAL THINKING AND READING

1. Answers will differ. Suggested Response: Cars are slow, small,

---

THINKING ABOUT THE SELECTION

Recalling

1. Why is there great excitement in Chicago?
2. What impression do Earthlings have of the people from Kaan?
3. How do the Kaanians describe humans?

Interpreting

4. Compare and contrast the ways in which Earthlings and Kaanians view each other.
5. What does the way Professor Hugo runs his zoo suggest about him?

Applying

6. Why is it easier to understand a situation if you see it from more than one angle?

ANALYZING LITERATURE

Understanding Plot and Point of View

Point of view is the position from which a writer tells a story. Often a writer will describe the sequence of events as they are seen by a particular person or group. In "Zoo," however, the writer treats point of view in an unusual way. He allows you to see the events from two different angles.

1. Identify the place in the story where the point of view changes.
2. How would the story have been different if it were told only from the Earthlings' point of view?
3. How does the change in point of view make the story effective?

CRITICAL THINKING AND READING

Considering Other Points of View

In "Zoo," the Earthlings think of the Kaanians as "small, horse-like animals" that are best viewed in a zoo. The Kaanians think of themselves as nor-

mal but regard the Earthlings as possibly dangerous "creatures." Neither group considers the other group's point of view. When studying people whose ideas or customs appear strange, you can keep an open mind by imagining what they think of *your* customs and ideas.

1. Imagine that you are a visitor to Earth from a planet where people travel by rockets. Describe your first impression of cars.
2. Describe your reaction to humans if on your planet people had eyes in the front *and* back of their heads.

UNDERSTANDING LANGUAGE

Appreciating Vivid Verbs

Writers use vivid, specific verbs so that you can picture what they are describing. A general word like *walk,* for example, can sometimes be effective. However, words that describe specific ways of walking—like *stumble, trudge, strut,* or even *tiptoe*—can make a description more lively.

Find the meaning of the vivid verbs printed in *italics* in the following descriptions from "Zoo."

1. ". . . the odd horse-spider creatures *filed* quickly out of their cages."
2. ". . . then they *scurried* away in a hundred different directions. . . ."

THINKING AND WRITING

Writing from Another Point of View

You have learned how the Earthlings and the Kaanians view the events of this story. However, Professor Hugo also must have a point of view. Imagine that the professor has kept a diary giving *his* impression of the story's events. List the type of entries the professor would make in his diary. Then use this list to write two diary pages indicating what the professor feels and thinks at each point of the story. When you revise these entries, make sure that the professor refers to himself as "I."

54   *Short Stories*

---

and brightly colored; they cannot leave the ground, lack sophisticated equipment, and have rubber wheels and bright lights front and back.
2. Answers will differ. Suggested Response: Humans are missing a pair of eyes, which limits their vision and makes them more vulnerable.

ANSWERS TO UNDERSTANDING LANGUAGE

1. *Filed* means "marched in a line."

2. *Scurried* means "ran or moved rapidly, especially with quick, short steps."

Challenge Discuss the universality of certain perceptions and reactions. Are all organisms fascinated by each other, fearful of each other, and so on? Think of other common emotions that were displayed by both the Earthlings and Kaanians in the story.

THINKING AND WRITING

Publishing Student Writing

Have students read their diary pages aloud. Based on what the students in the persona of the professor have written, have students illustrate some of the sights "Professor Hugo" describes in his diary. Then display both the diaries and illustrations in the classroom.

54

Character

FOUR GIRLS
August Macke
Three Lions

Humanities Note
Fine art, *Four Girls,* by August Macke. The German Expressionist artist August Macke (1887–1914) was educated at the Düsseldorf Academy and The Arts and Crafts School. His close association with the artists Franz Marc and Wassily Kandinsky involved him in the Blue-Rider (*Blaue-Reiter*) Movement, an exhibiting society for the less representational expressionist painters. Macke painted scenes from everyday life in bright, sunny colors. His death at age 27 on the front during World War I was a severe loss to Modern art.

A happy, uncomplicated man, Macke was able to transfer his inner harmony to his paintings. In the painting *Four Girls,* Macke takes a Cubistic approach to his subject without resorting to the somber colors favored by that school. The charming grouping of girls is typical of the simple scenes favored by Macke. The curving forms of the figures contrast pleasantly with the linear, stylized landscape.

Master Teacher Note Place Art Transparency 2, *In a Southern Garden* by Pierre Bonnard, on the overhead projector. It is a painting of four young people in a garden. Have students discuss the figures in the painting. You might point out that artists must use colors, expressions, and poses, instead of words to convey character. What might be the character of the girl in the center of the painting, as revealed by her relaxed pose, contented expression and beautiful face? How do the expressions of the other characters reveal what they are thinking or feeling? What is the effect of the artist's use of color on the mood of the painting?

GUIDE FOR READING

Last Cover

Paul Annixter (1894–   ) was born Howard Allison Sturtzel in Minneapolis, Minnesota. While working a timber claim in northern Minnesota, Annixter began writing. He published more than five hundred stories and worked with his wife writing novels for young people. He said, "Our stories deal with some phase of human and animal interrelation, which offers to our minds a different and deeper sort of heart interest." "Last Cover" deals with this special relationship between a boy and a fox.

Character Traits

Character traits are the qualities that make a person an individual. For example, one person may appear to be calm, another excitable. One person may be musical, another athletic. Writers give their characters qualities that make them seem like real people. It is these character traits that determine how each character behaves and interacts with others.

Look For

At one point in this story, the narrator, Stan, says of his brother Colin: "It was a rare moment in which I really 'met' my brother, when something of his essence flowed into me. . . ." As you read the story, try to discover Colin's essence, or nature, for yourself, by looking for the character traits that make him special.

Writing

What is talent? How is it different from the type of learning we gain from books? Freewrite, exploring your answer.

Vocabulary

Knowing the following words will help you as you read "Last Cover."
abetting (ə bet′iŋ) *v.*: Helping or encouraging (p. 59)
passive (pas′iv) *adj.*: Inactive (p. 59)
vixen (vik′s'n) *n.*: A female fox (p. 59)
confound (kən found′) *v.*: Confuse (p. 62)
sanction (saŋk′shən) *v.*: Support (p. 62)
crafty (kraf′tē) *adj.*: Sly, cunning (p. 63)
wily (wī′lē) *adj.*: Sly (p. 64)
sanctuary (saŋk′chōō wer′ē) *n.*: A place of protection (p. 64)

Last Cover

Paul Annixter

I'm not sure I can tell you what you want to know about my brother; but everything about the pet fox is important, so I'll tell all that from the beginning.

It goes back to a winter afternoon after I'd hunted the woods all day for a sign of our lost pet. I remember the way my mother looked up as I came into the kitchen. Without my speaking, she knew what had happened. For six hours I had walked, reading signs, looking for a delicate print in the damp soil or even a hair that might have told of a red fox passing that way—but I had found nothing.

"Did you go up in the foothills?" Mom asked.

I nodded. My face was stiff from held-back tears. My brother, Colin, who was going on twelve, got it all from one look at me and went into a heartbroken, almost silent, crying.

Three weeks before, Bandit, the pet fox Colin and I had raised from a tiny kit, had disappeared, and not even a rumor had been heard of him since.

"He'd have to go off soon anyway," Mom comforted. "A big, lolloping[1] fellow like him, he's got to live his life same as us. But he may come back. That fox set a lot of store by you boys in spite of his wild ways."

"He set a lot of store by our food, anyway," Father said. He sat in a chair by the kitchen window mending a piece of harness. "We'll be seeing a lot more of that fellow, never fear. That fox learned to pine for table scraps and young chickens. He was getting to be an egg thief, too, and he's not likely to forget that."

"That was only pranking when he was little," Colin said desperately.

From the first, the tame fox had made tension in the family. It was Father who said we'd better name him Bandit, after he'd made away with his first young chicken.

"Maybe you know," Father said shortly. "But when an animal turns to egg sucking he's usually incurable. He'd better not come pranking around my chicken run again."

It was late February, and I remember the bleak, dead cold that had set in, cold that was a rare thing for our Carolina hills. Flocks of sparrows and snowbirds had appeared to peck hungrily at all that the pigs and chickens didn't eat.

"This one's a killer," Father would say of a morning, looking out at the whitened barn roof. "This one will make the shoats[2] squeal."

A fire snapped all day in our cookstove and another in the stone fireplace in the living room, but still the farmhouse was never warm. The leafless woods were bleak and empty, and I spoke of that to Father when I came back from my search.

---

1. lolloping (läl′ əp iŋ) *adj.*: Moving in a clumsy or relaxed way, bobbing up and down or from side to side.

2. shoats (shōts) *n.*: Young hogs.

Presentation

Motivation/Prior Knowledge Have students imagine that they have a pet who has run away. The situation is complicated by the fact that the pet is destructive, and the neighbors are trying to stop it. Would they, the students, understand the community's need to control the animal? Would their love for the animal blind them to their neighbors' losses? Would they try to protect their pet, regardless of the consequences?

Enrichment This story concerns a sensitive boy coming to terms with the loss of his pet. One of the factors essential to understanding the character's feelings is that the pet, Bandit, is a wild animal. Another work that deals with this subject is the novel *The Yearling* by Marjorie Kinnan Rawlings.

As an enrichment assignment, suggest that students read this book to obtain a broader perspective on the emotional maturity of the main characters in both stories.

Thematic Idea A story in this book that deals with a similar subject is "Luke Baldwin's Vow," page 95. Both stories concern the special relationship between a boy and his pet.

Purpose-Setting Question What role does nature play in this story?

1 Discussion What do you learn about the characters of the parents? Contrast their different feelings regarding the fox.

Master Teacher Note Place Art Transparency 3, *Fox Hunt* by Winslow Homer, on the overhead projector. It is a painting of a fox running through snow, with birds hovering just overhead. Have students study the painting and discuss the animals. What are students' reactions to the scene? Who is the hunter and who is the hunted? Is something happening that is not visible in the painting? How has the painter used color and positioning to produce specific animal characters? A fox is also a main character in this story. What characteristics do foxes possess that tend to attract many peoples' attention and affection?

2 Critical Thinking and Reading

By looking at other characters' reactions to a specific character and by analyzing the character themselves, students can understand what the character is like. Have students discuss what they learn about Stan and Colin through their words and actions. How are the brothers alike and how are they different from each other?

Humanities Note

Fine art, *Brer Fox* by Bob Kuhn. Bob Kuhn (1920–) was born in Buffalo, New York, and studied art at the Pratt Institute.

Animals are a favorite subject of Kuhn. He has paintings in the Wildlife World Museum and was exhibited in the Animals in Art exhibit in the Royal Ontario Museum in Toronto. Kuhn has also won three Medals of Honor from the Society of Animal Artists.

His love for painting animals can be seen in the care he has taken in painting *Brer Fox*. You might tell students that "Brer" is a term found in folk tales that is used before someone's name. "Brer" is dialect for "brother."

The following questions might be used for discussion.
1. Considering Kuhn's love for painting animals, why did he use the term "Brer" to describe the fox?
2. How does the artist use color and form—shapes and structure—to portray the close tie between the fox and its surroundings?
3. What might Brer Fox's character be, based on the painting? Is he how you picture Bandit? How is "Brer Fox" similar to and how is he different from how you imagine Bandit to be?

Grammar in Action

The subject and verb must agree in number in a sentence. If the subject is singular, then the verb should be singular. Likewise, a plural subject requires a plural verb. Deciding which form of a

"It's always a sad time in the woods when the seven sleepers are under cover," he said.

"What sleepers are they?" I asked. Father was full of woods lore.

"Why, all the animals that have got sense enough to hole up and stay hid in weather like this. Let's see, how was it the old rhyme named them?

> Surly bear and sooty bat,
> Brown chuck and masked coon,
> Chippy-munk and sly skunk,
> And all the mouses
> 'Cept in men's houses.

"And man would have joined them and made it eight, Granther Yeary always said, if he'd had a little more sense."

"I was wondering if the red fox mightn't make it eight," Mom said.

Father shook his head. "Late winter's a high time for foxes. Time when they're out deviling, not sleeping."

My chest felt hollow. I wanted to cry like Colin over our lost fox, but at fourteen a boy doesn't cry. Colin had squatted down on the floor and got out his small hammer and nails to start another new frame for a new picture. Maybe then he'd make a drawing for the frame and be able to forget his misery. It had been that way with him since he was five.

I thought of the new dress Mom had brought home a few days before in a heavy cardboard box. That box cover would be fine for Colin to draw on. I spoke of it, and Mom's glance thanked me as she went to get it. She and I worried a lot about Colin. He was small for his age, delicate and blond, his hair much lighter and softer than mine, his eyes deep and wide and blue. He was often sick, and I knew the fear Mom had that he might be predestined.[3] I'm just ordinary, like Father. I'm the sort of stuff that can take it—tough and strong—but Colin was always sort of special.

---

3. predestined (prē des' tind) *adj.*: In this case, marked to die early.

BRER FOX
Bob Kuhn
Sportsman's Edge/King Gallery

verb to use becomes more difficult when you are working with an irregular verb such as *be* or *have*. For irregular verbs, you must be aware of all the forms of the verb to know which one to choose. Notice how Paul Annixter uses different forms of the irregular verbs *be* and *have* to agree with the subjects in the following sentences:

It *was* late February. . . .
The leafless woods *were* bleak and empty. . . .
"What sleepers *are* they?" I asked.
I'm the sort of stuff that can take it. . . .
"Not a single frame of Colin's *has* ever gone to waste."
"In a way it *is*. Ever since you started talking up Colin's art,
    "I've had an invalid for help around the place."

Mom lighted the lamp. Colin began cutting his white cardboard carefully, fitting it into his frame. Father's sharp glance turned on him now and again.

"There goes the boy making another frame before there's a picture for it," he said. "It's too much like cutting out a man's suit for a fellow that's, say, twelve years old. Who knows whether he'll grow into it?"

Mom was into him then, quick. "Not a single frame of Colin's has ever gone to waste. The boy has real talent, Sumter, and it's time you realized it."

"Of course he has," Father said. "All kids have 'em. But they get over 'em."

"It isn't the pox[4] we're talking of," Mom sniffed.

"In a way it is. Ever since you started talking up Colin's art, I've had an invalid for help around the place."

Father wasn't as hard as he made out, I knew, but he had to hold a balance against all Mom's frothing.[5] For him the thing was the land and all that pertained to it. I was following in Father's footsteps, true to form, but Colin threatened to break the family tradition with his leaning toward art, with Mom "aiding and abetting him," as Father liked to put it. For the past two years she had had dreams of my brother becoming a real artist and going away to the city to study.

It wasn't that Father had no understanding of such things. I could remember, through the years, Colin lying on his stomach in the front room making pencil sketches, and how a good drawing would catch Father's eye halfway across the room, and how he would sometimes gather up two or three of them to study, frowning and muttering, one hand in his beard, while a great pride rose in Colin, and in me too. Most of Colin's drawings were of the woods and wild things, and there Father was a master critic. He made out to scorn what seemed to him a passive "white-livered" interpretation of nature through brush and pencil instead of rod and rifle.

At supper that night Colin could scarcely eat. Ever since he'd been able to walk, my brother had had a growing love of wild things, but Bandit had been like his very own, a gift of the woods. One afternoon a year and a half before, Father and Laban Small had been running a vixen through the hills with their dogs. With the last of her strength the she-fox had made for her den, not far from our house. The dogs had overtaken her and killed her just before she reached it. When father and Laban came up, they'd found Colin crouched nearby holding her cub in his arms.

Father had been for killing the cub, which was still too young to shift for itself, but Colin's grief had brought Mom into it. We'd taken the young fox into the kitchen, all of us, except Father, gone a bit silly over the little thing. Colin had held it in his arms and fed it warm milk from a spoon.

"Watch out with all your soft ways," Father had warned, standing in the doorway. "You'll make too much of him. Remember, you can't make a dog out of a fox. Half of that little critter has to love, but the other half is a wild hunter. You boys will mean a whole lot to him while he's kit, but there'll come a day when you won't mean a thing to him and he'll leave you shorn."

For two weeks after that Colin had nursed the cub, weaning it from milk to bits of meat. For a year they were always together. The cub grew fast. It was soon following Colin and me about the barnyard. It turned out to be a patch fox, with a saddle of darker fur across its shoulders.

---

4. the pox (päks): Any of a variety of diseases—like smallpox or chicken pox—that cause a rash on the skin.
5. frothing (frôth′ iŋ) vb.: Here, speaking angrily.

3 Clarification The expression "aiding and abetting" is emotionally charged because it is usually used to describe someone helping a criminal.

4 Discussion What does the father mean when he says "you can't make a dog out of a fox"?

The verbs *was, am, has* and *is* are used with singular subjects whereas the verbs *were* and *are* are used with plural subjects. The verb *have* can be used with both singular and plural subjects. Because these verbs are irregular, you must be careful in deciding which form to use to agree with the subject.

Student Activity 1. Find four other sentences from "Last Cover" in which Annixter uses the forms of the verbs *be* and *have* agree with the subject. Make sure each sentence contains a different form of either or these verbs. Tell whether the subject is singular or plural in number.

Student Activity 2. On your paper write the verb from the choices in parentheses that agrees in number with the noun or pronoun. Then write a sentence using each subject/verb combination.

1. he	(has/have)		5. men	(was/were)
2. I	(am/be)		6. it	(is/are)
3. fox	(was/were)		7. they	(has/have)
4. we	(is/are)		8. I	(has/have)

I haven't the words to tell you what the fox meant to us. It was far more wonderful owning him than owning any dog. There was something rare and secret like the spirit of the woods about him, and back of his calm, straw-gold eyes was the sense of a brain the equal of a man's. The fox became Colin's whole life.

Each day, going and coming from school, Colin and I took long side trips through the woods, looking for Bandit. Wild things' memories were short, we knew; we'd have to find him soon or the old bond would be broken.

Ever since I was ten I'd been allowed to hunt with Father, so I was good at reading signs. But, in a way, Colin knew more about the woods and wild things than Father or me. What came to me from long observation, Colin seemed to know by instinct.

It was Colin who felt out, like an Indian, the stretch of woods where Bandit had his den, who found the first slim, small fox-print in the damp earth. And then, on an afternoon in March, we saw him. I remember the day well, the racing clouds, the wind rattling the tops of the pine trees and swaying the Spanish moss. Bandit had just come out of a clump of laurel; in the maze of leaves behind him we caught a glimpse of a slim red vixen, so we knew he had found a mate. She melted from sight like a shadow, but Bandit turned to watch us, his mouth open, his tongue lolling as he smiled his old foxy smile. On his thin chops, I saw a telltale chicken feather.

Colin moved silently forward, his movements so quiet and casual he seemed to be standing still. He called Bandit's name, and the fox held his ground, drawn to us with all his senses. For a few moments he let Colin actually put an arm about him. It was then I knew that he loved us still, for all of Father's warnings. He really loved us back, with a fierce, secret love no tame thing ever gave. But the urge of his life just then was toward his new mate. Suddenly, he whirled about and disappeared in the laurels.

Colin looked at me with glowing eyes. "We haven't really lost him, Stan. When he gets through with his spring sparking[6] he may come back. But we've got to show ourselves to him a lot, so he won't forget."

"It's a go," I said.

"Promise not to say a word to Father," Colin said, and I agreed. For I knew by the chicken feather that Bandit had been up to no good.

A week later the woods were budding and the thickets were rustling with all manner of wild things scurrying on the love scent. Colin managed to get a glimpse of Bandit every few days. He couldn't get close though, for the spring running was a lot more important to a fox than any human beings were.

Every now and then Colin got out his framed box cover and looked at it, but he never drew anything on it; he never even picked up his pencil. I remember wondering if what Father had said about framing a picture before you had one had spoiled something for him.

I was helping Father with the planting now, but Colin managed to be in the woods every day. By degrees he learned Bandit's range, where he drank and rested and where he was likely to be according to the time of day. One day he told me how he had petted Bandit again, and how they had walked together a long way in the woods. All this time we had kept his secret from Father.

As summer came on, Bandit began to live up to the prediction Father had made. Accustomed to human beings he moved without fear about the scattered farms of the

---

6. **sparking** (spär' kiŋ) *n.*: An old-fashioned term for courting.

THE COURTSHIP
Bonnie Marris
The Greenwich Workshop, Inc.

Last Cover 61

Fine art, *The Courtship* by Bonnie Marris. Bonnie Marris had to do a great deal of field observation in order to realistically depict these foxes in the wild. "During the fall," she says, "I began observing a young female fox practicing in earnest all her mother's hunting lessons. By December, she had two suitors, one of whom she vehemently chased away. The other she enticed with playful games, yips, nips, and high-pitched whines. Observing this fellow was not easy. Usually he was just a flash of red amid brown field grass or an orange flutter on a distant hill as he pounced on or dug for mice. But after the young female had chosen him, I saw them together on many of their winter morning romps." Foxes mate for life, although they generally live together only in winter.

You might use the following questions for discussion with the class.

1. How is the artist's experience observing foxes similar to the boys' experiences trying to locate Bandit?
2. How does the artist use the positions of the foxes and their expressions to indicate a "courtship"?
3. Which of the two foxes do you think is the female, and which the male? Support your answer.

9 **Enrichment** Fox hunting has been a sport of the leisure class in England since the middle 1700's. The sport of fox hunting, also called riding to hounds, involves tracking a wild fox by scent with a pack of specially trained hounds. There are strict rules to follow, and the fox is not always killed because it is the excitement of the chase itself that interests many hunters. How is the hunt for Bandit in the story different from the traditional fox hunt?

10 **Discussion** What does this tell you about what the boys' father is really thinking, despite his gruff manner?

region, raiding barns and hen runs that other foxes wouldn't have dared go near. And he taught his wild mate to do the same. Almost every night they got into some poultry house, and by late June Bandit was not only killing chickens and ducks but feeding on eggs and young chicks whenever he got the chance.

Stories of his doings came to us from many sources, for he was still easily recognized by the dark patch on his shoulders. Many a farmer took a shot at him as he fled and some of them set out on his trail with dogs, but they always returned home without even sighting him. Bandit was familiar with all the dogs in the region, and he knew a hundred tricks to confound them. He got a reputation that year beyond that of any fox our hills had known. His confidence grew, and he gave up wild hunting altogether and lived entirely off the poultry farmers. By September the hill farmers banded together to hunt him down.

It was father who brought home that news one night. All time-honored rules of the fox chase were to be broken in this hunt; if the dogs couldn't bring Bandit down, he was to be shot on sight. I was stricken and furious. I remember the misery of Colin's face in the lamplight. Father, who took pride in all the ritual of the hunt, had refused to be a party to such an affair, though in justice he could do nothing but sanction any sort of hunt, for Bandit, as old Sam Wetherwax put it, had been "purely getting in the Lord's hair."

The hunt began next morning, and it was the biggest turnout our hills had known. There were at least twenty mounted men in the party and as many dogs. Father and I were working in the lower field as they passed along the river road. Most of the hunters carried rifles, and they looked ugly. Twice during the morning I went up to

the house to find Colin, but he was nowhere around. As we worked, Father and I could follow the progress of the hunt by the distant hound music on the breeze. We could tell just where the hunters first caught sight of the fox and where Bandit was leading the dogs during the first hour. We knew as well as if we'd seen it how Bandit roused another fox along Turkey Branch and forced it to run for him, and how the dogs swept after it for twenty minutes before they sensed their mistake.

Noon came, and Colin had not come in to eat. After dinner Father didn't go back to the field. He moped about, listening to the hound talk. He didn't like what was on any more than I did, and now and again I caught his smile of satisfaction when we heard the broken, angry notes of the hunting horn, telling that the dogs had lost the trail or had run another fox.

I was restless, and I went up into the hills in midafternoon. I ranged the woods for miles, thinking all the time of Colin. Time lost all meaning for me, and the short day was nearing an end, when I heard the horn talking again, telling that the fox had put over another trick. All day he had deviled the dogs and mocked the hunters. This new trick and the coming night would work to save him. I was wildly glad, as I moved down toward Turkey Branch and stood listening for a time by the deep, shaded pool where for years we boys had gone swimming, sailed boats, and dreamed summer dreams.

Suddenly, out of the corner of my eye, I saw the sharp ears and thin, pointed mask of a fox—in the water almost beneath me. It was Bandit, craftily submerged there, all but his head, resting in the cool water of the pool and the shadow of the two big beeches that spread above it. He must have run forty miles or more since morning. And he must have hidden in this place before. His know-

Grammar in Action

A **compound sentence** is a sentence consisting of two or more independent clauses. Usually, the independent clauses are joined by a comma and one of the coordinating conjunctions: *and, but, for, nor, or, so, yet.* Less frequently, the independent clauses are joined by a semicolon. Writers use compound sentences to join closely related ideas of equal importance. The following sentences from "Last Cover" are compound:

> Stories of his doings came to us from many sources, for he was easily recognized by the dark patch on his shoulders.

> All time-honored rules of the fox chase were to be broken in this hunt; if the dogs couldn't bring Bandit down, he was to be shot on sight.

> The hunt began next morning, and it was the biggest turnout our hills had known.

In each sentence, two or more closely related ideas are joined together. Compare how they sound in comparison to the following short sentences:

> Stories of his doings came to us from many sources. He was easily recognized by the dark patch on his shoulders.

ing, crafty mask blended perfectly with the shadows and a mass of drift and branches that had collected by the bank of the pool. He was so still that a pair of thrushes flew up from the spot as I came up, not knowing he was there.

Bandit's bright, harried eyes were looking right at me. But I did not look at him direct. Some woods instinct, swifter than thought, kept me from it. So he and I met as in another world, indirectly, with feeling but without sign or greeting.

Suddenly I saw that Colin was standing almost beside me. Silently as a water snake, he had come out of the bushes and stood there. Our eyes met, and a quick and secret smile passed between us. It was a rare mo-ment in which I really "met" my brother, when something of his essence flowed into me and I knew all of him. I've never lost it since.

My eyes still turned from the fox, my heart pounding. I moved quietly away, and Colin moved with me. We whistled softly as we went, pretending to busy ourselves along the bank of the stream. There was magic in it, as if by will we wove a web of protection about the fox, a ring-pass-not that none might penetrate. It was so, too, we felt, in the brain of Bandit, and that doubled the charm. To us he was still our little pet that we had carried about in our arms on countless summer afternoons.

Two hundred yards upstream, we

SEPTEMBER GATHERING
George Harkins
Glenn C. Janss Collection

All time-honored rules of the fox chase were to be broken in this hunt. If the dogs couldn't bring Bandit down, he was to be shot on sight.

The hunt began next morning. It was the biggest turnout our hills had known.

Student Activity 1. Find four other examples of compound sentences in the story. For each example, explain how the ideas expressed in the independent clauses are related.

Student Activity 2. Write four pairs of simple but related sentences. Exchange papers with a partner, and combine your partner's pairs of sentences into compound sentences. Be sure to use a comma and the appropriate coordinating conjunction to join each pair of sentences.

11

11 Literary Focus Have students think of a special moment in their own lives when they felt that they were "meeting" a loved one for the first time through some shared secret or experience.

Humanities Note

Fine art, *September Gathering* by George Harkins. Harkins enjoys painting landscapes of places that are special to him in Vermont and New York. However, his paintings also try to convey important messages about the fragile balance of nature. "The further we get from our direct ties to the earth," he says, "the more trouble we get into."

You might use the following questions for a class discussion.
1. What in the painting suggests the fragile balance of nature?
2. What might the artist mean by the title *September Gathering*?
3. How do Colin and Stan demonstrate their close ties with nature?
4. Where might Bandit have successfully hidden in this scene?

12 Discussion Why is Colin able to draw again after he hears that Bandit has been killed? What are some other ways for people to express their grief?

13 Discussion How might his father's harsh criticism have motivated Colin to be a better artist? Could the father's criticism have been constructive if it forced Colin to look at nature more carefully?

14 Discussion How has Bandit's death brought Stan, Colin, and their father closer together? Why has Colin's father changed his mind about sending Colin to art school? How might Bandit be indirectly responsible for Colin's success as an artist?

15 Reading Strategy Ask students what they think is the central idea in this story. How do they feel about the main characters by the end of the story?

Reader's Response Do you think that the ending was happy or sad? Why?

stopped beside slim, fresh tracks in the mud where Bandit had entered the branch. The tracks angled upstream. But in the water the wily creature had turned down.

We climbed the far bank to wait, and Colin told me how Bandit's secret had been his secret ever since an afternoon three months before, when he'd watched the fox swim downstream to hide in the deep pool. Today he'd waited on the bank, feeling that Bandit, hard pressed by the dogs, might again seek the pool for sanctuary.

We looked back once as we turned homeward. He still had not moved. We didn't know until later that he was killed that same night by a chance hunter, as he crept out from his hiding place.

That evening Colin worked a long time on his framed box cover that had lain about the house untouched all summer. He kept at it all the next day too. I had never seen him work so hard. I seemed to sense in the air the feeling he was putting into it, how he was *believing* his picture into being. It was evening before he finished it. Without a word he handed it to Father. Mom and I went and looked over his shoulder.

It was a delicate and intricate pencil drawing of the deep branch pool, and there was Bandit's head and watching, fear-filled eyes hiding there amid the leaves and shadows, woven craftily into the maze of twigs and branches, as if by nature's art itself. Hardly a fox there at all, but the place where he was—or should have been. I recognized it instantly, but Mom gave a sort of incredulous sniff.

"I'll declare," she said, "It's mazy as a puzzle. It just looks like a lot of sticks and leaves to me."

Long minutes of study passed before Father's eye picked out the picture's secret, as few men's could have done. I laid that to Father's being a born hunter. That was a picture that might have been done especially for him. In fact, I guess it was.

Finally he turned to Colin with his deep, slow smile. "So that's how Bandit fooled them all," he said. He sat holding the picture with a sort of tenderness for a long time, while we glowed in the warmth of the shared secret. That was Colin's moment. Colin's art stopped being a pox[7] to Father right there. And later, when the time came for Colin to go to art school, it was Father who was his solid backer.

---

7. **pox** (päks) *n.*: In this case, a bother or trouble.

Closure and Extension

ANSWERS TO THINKING ABOUT THE SELECTION
Recalling

1. The fox stole chickens like a thief or bandit.
2. Colin's mother supports him while his father disapproves of art and wants Colin to be a farmer like himself.
3. They decide to shoot the fox on sight.
4. Bandit enters the water and changes direction so that the hunting dogs lose his scent.
5. Colin draws a finely detailed picture of Bandit submerged in the water. Even in the drawing the fox is difficult to spot.

Interpreting

6. Although the father pretended to disapprove of Colin's drawings, he often showed interest in them. However, he couldn't accept the idea of Colin being an artist because the father loved the land and wanted both his sons to follow in his footsteps.
7. The mother did not understand the picture Colin drew of Bandit. She was not able to "read" the drawing. The father had disapproved of Colin's drawings because he said they were a "passive, 'white-livered' interpretation of nature." Through the drawing of Bandit in hiding, however, the father realizes that Colin has a keen woodsman's eye and that

THINKING ABOUT THE SELECTION

Recalling

1. Why does the father name the fox Bandit?
2. How does Colin's art cause tension in the family?
3. What do the farmers do when Bandit continues to attack their animals?
4. How does Bandit elude the farmers?
5. How does Colin use his art to explain this trick to his father?

Interpreting

6. The father has mixed feelings about Colin and his art. What are they?
7. How are the mother's and the father's attitudes about Colin's art changed at the end of the story when Colin shows them his picture?
8. In the next to the last paragraph, Stan says, "That was a picture that might have been done especially for him. In fact, I guess it was." Explain what Stan means.
9. What are two possible meanings of the title "Last Cover"?

Applying

10. Much of the communication in this story is done nonverbally—that is, without words. Give two examples of nonverbal communication in daily life.

ANALYZING LITERATURE

Understanding Character Traits

Character traits are the qualities that make a person an individual. There are many aspects of Colin's personality that make him special. As the story unfolds, Colin reveals these special traits in what he says and what he does.

1. Which of Colin's character traits make his mother and Stan worry about him?
2. Which of Colin's traits does his father at first not appreciate?
3. Which character traits allow Colin to find Bandit when no one else can?

CRITICAL THINKING AND READING

Comparing and Contrasting Characters

You can understand more about characters if you compare and contrast them. When you **compare** characters, you look at ways in which they are alike. When you **contrast** them, you look at ways in which they are different.

1. Name two character traits that Colin and Stan share.
2. Stan describes himself as "tough and strong." How does Colin differ?
3. Stan says, "Colin knew more about the woods and wild things than Father or me." While Stan learns of the woods through observation, how does Colin seem to know?

UNDERSTANDING LANGUAGE

Using Vivid Words

Vivid words present a lively and sharp picture. Words are usually more vivid when they are specific. For example, *clutch* is a more specific and more vivid word than *hold*. Authors use vivid words and expressions to make you see and feel a scene or action more clearly.

Find the paragraph on page 58 that begins "It was late February . . ." Point out three vivid words in it that help create a strong picture.

THINKING AND WRITING

Writing a Character Sketch

Think of a person you know well. Write a character sketch describing this person to someone who does not know him or her at all. First list all the traits that make this person special. Then write your first draft. As you revise your sketch, be sure you have included enough details to make this person come alive for your reader. Replace any tired words with more vivid words. Finally, correct all spelling and punctuation mistakes and prepare a final draft.

Last Cover 65

(Answers begin on p. 64.)

ANSWERS TO CRITICAL THINKING AND READING

1. They share a love of nature and wild animals and are both sensitive.
2. Colin is delicate, fragile, and often sick. His mother feared that he might die young.
3. Colin seems to know about the woods and wild animals by instinct. He is so in tune with nature that understanding it is second nature to him.

ANSWERS TO UNDERSTANDING LANGUAGE

Answers will differ, but students may suggest *bleak, dead, rare, flocks, sparrows, snowbirds, peck,* or *hungrily.*

Challenge Explain what first-person narrator means. Stan is telling the story as first-person narrator. Have students analyze how this device heightens tension as the story progresses.

THINKING AND WRITING

For help with this assignment, students can refer to Lesson 9, "Writing About Character," in the Handbook of Writing About Literature.

Writing Across the Curriculum
You might work with the science department on this assignment. Have students research and write a report on the instincts of wild animals that make them defy taming despite outward appearances. Students could also explore why it is unwise to keep wild animals as pets. Life science teachers might provide guidance for students on conducting their research.

he is truly talented. Now the father is a "solid backer" of Colin's going to art school.

8. These words mean that Colin had put his heart into his drawing of Bandit to share the secret of the fox's hiding place with his father. The drawing made the father realize that Colin, like a good hunter, had discovered Bandit's hiding place and was capable of rendering a realistic picture of it. Colin won his father's respect with his drawing.

9. "Last Cover" can mean Bandit's last hiding place. It can also refer to the last box cover that Colin would have to use for his art. In the future, he would use proper art supplies.

Applying

10. Suggested Response: Students should note that our actions, facial expressions, and body language convey our thoughts and feelings.

ANSWERS TO ANALYZING LITERATURE

1. Colin is delicate and fragile.
2. Colin's sensitivity, loving and artistic nature, and persistence in pursuing his art are not qualities that his father appreciates.
3. Colin's fine instincts, patience, and sensitivity to animals allow him to find Bandit.

Focus

More About the Author Shirley Jackson wrote in two very different styles. She produced domestic comedies as well as chilling works of suspense and violence. Ask students to discuss how writers can be so strikingly multifaceted. Have students explore the relationship between comedy and horror.

Literary Focus Character traits can build a character who is primarily humorous or primarily serious. Point out that real people are often described as being funny or serious. A person who is always joking or who has a funny habit is perceived to be funny, while a person who, for example, frowns often is perceived to be serious. In literature, such character traits are exaggerated for comic effect.

Look For Most students will have no difficulty recognizing the humor in this story. You may want your **more advanced** students to list those character traits that are blown out of proportion in the story to achieve a humorous effect.

Writing/Prior Knowledge Before students write, you might have them discuss the causes and effects of losing things. What circumstances might contribute to losing items? What effect might a lost item have on their lives? Then have them complete the freewriting assignment.

Vocabulary Have your **less advanced** students read the words aloud so that you can be sure they can pronounce them.

The Sneaker Crisis

Shirley Jackson (1919–1965) wrote two kinds of stories. On the one hand she wrote stories, like her novel *We Have Always Lived in the Castle,* which are laced with horror and mystery. On the other hand, she wrote books like *Life Among the Savages* and *Raising Demons,* which build on events in the hectic family life she shared with her husband and four children. "The Sneaker Crisis," from *Raising Demons,* is a comical story about family life from the humorous side of Shirley Jackson.

Humorous Characters

Like real people, characters in stories may have a variety of traits, like honesty, strength, or dependability. In order to make a story amusing or funny, an author may choose to emphasize certain traits in a character, like forgetfulness or sloppiness, that lead to humorous situations. The characters display these traits in situations that become comical as small details are built up or overstated.

Look For

As you read "The Sneaker Crisis," notice the traits the author emphasizes in order to make the characters and situations seem humorous. Also notice how the author blows small details out of proportion so that a lost sneaker becomes a crisis.

Writing

The story you are about to read involves a search for a lost sneaker. Have you had the experience of searching for a lost item? What went through your mind as you searched? Freewrite about your experience, noting especially if there was anything funny in the situation.

Vocabulary

Knowing the following words will help you as you read "The Sneaker Crisis."

buffet (bə fā′) *n.*: A piece of furniture with drawers and cupboards for dishes, table linen, and so on (p. 67)
incredulously (in krej′oo ləs lē) *adv.*: In a disbelieving manner (p. 68)
resignedly (ri zīn′id lē) *adj.*: In a yielding and uncomplaining manner (p. 69)

ominously (äm′ə nəs lē) *adv.*: In a threatening manner (p. 69)
triumphant (trī um′fənt) *adj.*: Rejoicing for victory; exulting in success (p. 70)
rigorously (rig′ər əs lē) *adv.*: In a strict, thorough way (p. 71)

Objectives

1 To understand how character traits can make a character humorous
2 To recognize why situations are humorous
3 To understand the meaning of slang expressions
4 To write a story about a humorous incident

Support Material

Teaching Portfolio
Teacher Backup, p. 95
Grammar in Action Worksheet, *Recognizing Adverbs,* p. 99
Usage and Mechanics Worksheet, p. 101
Vocabulary Check, p. 102
Analyzing Literature Worksheet, *Understanding Humorous Characters,* p. 103

Language Worksheet, *Recognizing Slang,* p. 104
Selection Test, p. 105

The Sneaker Crisis

Shirley Jackson

Day after day after day I went around my house picking things up. I picked up books and shoes and toys and socks and shirts and gloves and boots and hats and handkerchiefs and puzzle pieces and pennies and pencils and stuffed rabbits and bones the dogs had left under the living room chairs. I also picked up tin soldiers and plastic cars and baseball gloves and sweaters and children's pocketbooks with nickels inside and little pieces of lint off the floor.

Every time I picked up something I put it down again somewhere else where it belonged better than it did in the place I found it. Nine times out of ten I did not notice what I was picking up or where I put it until sometime later when someone in the family needed it; then, when Sally said where were her crayons I could answer at once: kitchen windowsill, left. If Barry wanted his cowboy hat I could reply: playroom, far end of bookcase. If Jannie wanted her arithmetic homework, I could tell her it was under the ashtray on the dining room buffet.

I could locate the little nut that came off Laurie's bike wheel, and the directions for winding the living room clock. I could find the recipe for the turkey cutlets Sally admired and the top to my husband's fountain

pen; I could even find, ordinarily, the little celluloid strips which went inside the collar of his nylon shirt.

That was, of course, entirely automatic, like still remembering the home telephone number of my college roommate and being able to recite "Oh, what is so rare as a day in June." If I could not respond at once, identifying object and location in unhesitating answer to the question, the article was very apt to remain permanently lost. Like Jannie's pink Easter-egg hat, which disappeared—let me see—it was the day Laurie got into the fight with the Haynes boys, and the porch rocker got broken—
make it the end
of October.

1 Discussion What do you learn about the character of the narrator? How much does she really mind picking up after her family?

We had many small places in our big house where an Easter-egg hat could get itself hopelessly hidden, so when Jannie asked one night at dinner, the end of October, "Who took my Easter-egg hat?" and I found myself without an immediate answer, it was clear that the hat had taken itself off, and although we searched halfheartedly, Jannie had to wear a scarf around her head until the weather got cold enough to wear her long-tailed knitted cap.

1 Laurie's sneaker was of considerably more moment, since, of course, he could not play basketball with a scarf tied around his left foot. He came to the top of the back stairs of a Saturday morning and inquired gently who had stolen his sneaker. I opened my mouth to answer, found my mind blank, and closed my mouth again. Laurie came halfway down the stairs and bawled, "Mooooooom, where'd my *sneaker* get to?" and I still could not answer. "I neeeeeed my *sneaker*," Laurie howled, "I got to play baaaaaaasketball."

"I don't know," I called.

"But I need it," Laurie said. He crashed down the stairs and into the study, where I sat reading the morning paper and drinking a cup of coffee. "I got to play basketball, so I need my sneakers. I can't play on the basketball court without sneakers. So I need—"

"Have you looked? In your room? Under your bed?"

"Yeah, sure." He thought. "It's not there, though."

"Outdoors?"

"Now what would my sneaker be doing outdoors, I ask you? You think I get dressed and undressed out on the lawn, maybe, for the neighbors?"

"Well," I said helplessly, "you had it last Saturday."

"I *know* I had it last Saturday, you think I'm foolish or something?"

"Wait." I went and stood at the foot of the back stairs and called, "Jannie?"

There was a pause and then Jannie said, sniffling, "Yes?"

"Good heavens," I said, "are you reading *Little Women*[1] again?"

Jannie sniffled. "Just the part where Beth dies."

"Look," I said, "the sun is shining and the sky is blue and—"

"You seen my sneaker?" Laurie yelled from in back of me.

"No."

"You *sure*?"

Jannie came to the top of the stairs, wiping her eyes with her hand. "Hey," she said, "maybe some girl took it. For a keepsake."

"Wha?" said Laurie incredulously. "Took my *sneaker*? Who?"

"Like Mr. Brooke did Meg's glove, in *Little Women*, because he was in love with her and they got married."

"*Wha*?" For a minute Laurie stared at her, and then he turned deliberately and went back to the door of the study. "My sister," he announced formally to his father, "has snapped her twigs."

"That so?" said his father.

"I ask you." Laurie gestured. "Junk from books," he said.

"Well, he did," Jannie insisted, coming down the stairs. "He took it and hid it for ever so long and when Jo found out she—"

"Sally, Barry," I was calling from the back door. "Has either of you seen Laurie's sneaker?"

Sally and Barry were dancing on the lawn, turning and flickering among the last fallen leaves; when I called they circled and came toward the house, going "cheep-cheep." "We're little birds," Sally explained, coming closer. "Cheep-cheep."

"Have you seen Laurie's sneaker?"

1. *Little Women*: A novel by Louisa May Alcott about four sisters, Meg, Jo, Beth, and Amy, growing up in New England during the Civil War.

Grammar in Action

Adverbs are used to modify verbs, adjectives, or other adverbs. They enrich the meaning of the word they modify besides making the meaning of the sentence more precise and vivid. Without adverb modifiers, the sentence would be less specific. Notice how Shirley Jackson uses vivid adverbs to expand the meaning of the verbs they modify.

He threw his arms *dramatically* into the air and let them fall *resignedly*.

The adverbs *dramatically* and *resignedly* give insights into Laurie's personality and mood at the moment. His demonstrative behavior and anguish over his mother's actions are readily apparent. Compare Jackson's sentence to the following sentence to see the effect of using vivid adverbs.

He threw his arms into the air and let them fall.

Also, notice the importance of placement of the adverbs in the sentence. If *dramatically* had been placed before *his* and *resignedly* before *let*, the sentence would not have been as effective. When you write, try placing adverbs in different positions in your sentences to find the most effective placement.

"Cheep-cheep."

"Well?"

Barry thought. "I have unseen it," he remarked. "I did unsee Laurie's sneaker a day and a day and a day and a day and *many* mornings ago."

"Splendid," I said. "Sally?"

"No. But don't worry. I shall get it back for dear Laurie, dear Mommy."

"If you mean magic you better not let your father hear you, young lady. No," I said over my shoulder to Laurie, "they haven't."

"But I will find it, Laurie dear, never fear, Laurie dear, I will find your sneaker find for you."

"Yeah. So what'm I gonna do?" he asked me. "Play basketball in my socks or something?"

"Are you *sure* you looked under your bed?"

He looked at me in the manner his favorite television detective reserves for ladies who double-talk the cops. "Yeah," he said. "Yeah, lady. I'm sure."

"Daddy won't notice," Sally said busily to Barry. "All this will take is just a little bit of golden magic and Daddy will never notice and there will be dear Laurie's sneaker just right here."

"Can I do magic too?"

"You can be my dear helper and you can carry the shovel."

I went into the study and sat down and Laurie followed me. "And he kept it for weeks and weeks next to his heart," Jannie was explaining to her father, "and she was looking for it just like Laurie but Mr. Brooke had it all the time."

"How about that little dark-haired girl?" my husband asked Laurie. "The one who keeps calling you so much?"

"Nah," Laurie said. "She's tipped, anyhow. Besides, how could she get my sneaker?" He slapped his forehead. "A veritable madhouse," he said. "Lose a sneaker and they start criticizing your friends and trying to make out she stole it. Bah."

He flung himself violently into one of our good plastic leather chairs, which slid back across the floor and into the bookcase. "Bah," said Laurie. He threw his arms dramatically into the air and let them fall resignedly. "Never *find* anything around here, that's the *big* trouble," he explained. "Nothing's ever where you put it. If *she*—"

"If by *she* you mean *me*—" I began ominously.

"Always coming and picking things up and putting them away where a person can't find them. Always—"

"If you'd put things away neatly when you take them off instead of just throwing everything under your bed—" I stopped to think. "Have you looked under your bed?" I asked.

Laurie stood up and threw his arms wide. "Why was I ever born?" he demanded.

Jannie nodded. "In *Beverley Lee, Girl Detective*," she pointed out, "when the secret plans for the old armory get lost, Beverley Lee and her girlfriend Piggy, *they* look for clues."

"A broken shoelace?" my husband suggested.

"Well, when did you see them last?" I asked reasonably. "Seems to me if you could remember when you had them last, you might remember where you put them then."

"Yeah. Well," Laurie said, scowling, "I *know* I had them last Saturday. But then I took them off and I remember they were on my bookcase because I had to remember to make that map for geography and that was for Wednesday when we had gym—say!" He opened his eyes and his mouth wide. "Gym. I wore them Wednesday to school for gym. So I had them on Wednesday."

"And Wednesday," I put in, "was the day you were so late getting home from school because you were hanging around Joe's with

The Sneaker Crisis 69

2 Critical Thinking and Reading There are many ways to make characters humorous. In this story, Jackson provides her characters with specific traits which cause them to behave ridiculously over the lost sneaker. Have students notice how each character reacts to the "crisis" in his or her own absurd way.

3 Discussion How effective are the character tags? Is each character immediately recognizable through action and dialogue?

4 Reading Strategy Have students identify and describe each of the characters in the story. Have them include the children's approximate ages, based on clues in the story.

Student Activity 1. Find three other sentences in "The Sneaker Crisis" in which Jackson uses vivid adverbs. Explain why her use of each adverb increases the precision and vividness of the sentence.

Student Activity 2. Add vivid adverbs to the following sentences to enrich and expand the meaning of each sentence. Notice how the choice of adverb can affect the mood and feeling of the sentence.

1. She tore open the package and looked at her present.

2. Martin put down his glass and stared into space.

5 **Literary Focus** How does tracing the chain of events leading up to the loss of the sneaker heighten the humor of the story?

6 **Critical Thinking and Reading** What does this comment tell you about the father? What kind of person is he? Contrast the ways the parents handle this episode of the missing sneaker.

7 **Enrichment** The strains of raising a large family are hidden behind banter and humor here. Have students compare this story with a story from a favorite family television show, such as *The Cosby Show*, to see if they can identify parallels in humor masking hard truths.

that pack of juvenile delinquents and—"

"I told you six times already, those girls just happened to come by there by *accident*, how'd *I* know they'd be around Joe's? And anyway you got no right to go calling my friends—"

"And you never got your chores done and I kept dinner till six-thirty."

"That girl called, too," my husband put in.

"And I must of had my sneakers on all that time, because I never had time because *she* made me do my chores and then I had to rush through dinner because—because—"

"You were going to the dance," Jannie said, triumphant. "You got all dressed up, so *naturally* you put on shoes."

"Hey!" Laurie swung around and gestured wildly. "I got dressed—"

"You took a shower," I said. "I remember because—"

He shuddered. "I took a shower because *she* wouldn't let me have my good blue pants from the cleaners *unless* I took a shower.'

"No gentleman escorts a lady to a public function unless he has bathed and dressed himself in completely clean clothes," my husband said.

"So I undressed in the bathroom because I always do and then when I went out I had this towel around me and I was carrying my clothes and the sneaker and I—"

"I saw it," I said suddenly. "I did see it after all. I came upstairs to get two aspirin after you had finally gone to the dance and I remember the way the bathroom looked; the floor was sopping and dirty towels all over and the soap and—"

"The sneaker," Laurie said impatiently, "keep on the subject. The sneaker, the sneaker."

I meditated. "It was lying just inside the door and one wet towel was half on top of it.

And I . . . and I . . . " I thought. "What *did* I do?"

"Think, think, think." Laurie stood over me flapping his hands.

"Look," I said. "I go around this house and I go around this house and I *go* around this house and I pick up shoes and socks and shirts and hats and gloves and handkerchiefs and books and toys and I always put them down again, someplace where they belong. Now when I went upstairs and saw that mess of a bathroom I had to clean up, I would have taken the soap and put it in the soapdish. And I would have taken the bathmat and put it over the edge of the tub. And I would have taken the towels—"

"And put them in the hamper," Laurie said impatiently. "We know."

"You do? Because I have often wondered what happens all the times I say to you to put the towels—"

"Yeah, so next time I'll remember, sure. What about the *sneaker*?"

"Anyway they were wet so I couldn't put them in the hamper. I would have hung them over the shower rail to dry so *then* I could put them in the hamper. And then I would have picked up the sneaker—"

"Laurie's sneaker is weaker and creaker and cleaker and breaker and fleaker and greaker . . . " Sally wound through the study, eyes shut, chanting. Barry came behind her, doing an odd little two-step. Sally had a pail of sand and a shovel and she was making scattering motions.

"Now *wait* a minute here," my husband began.

"It's all right," Sally said, opening one eye. "I'm just pretending. This is only sand."

"We're just untending," Barry explained reassuringly. "Bleaker and sneaker and weaker and deaker."

They filed out. My husband studied the floor morosely. "That certainly looked like magic to *me* ," he said. "and I don't *like* it. Going to have footwear popping up all over, right through the floor, probably wreck the foundations."

"Reconstruct the scene of the crime," Jannie said suddenly. "Because Beverley Lee Girl Detective and her girlfriend Piggy, that's what they did. In *The Mystery of the Broken Candle*, when they had to find the missing will. They reconstructed the scene of the crime. They got everybody there and put everything the way it was—"

"Say!" Laurie looked at her admiringly. "You're charged, girl. Come on," he said, making for the stairs, and stopped in the doorway to look compellingly at me. "Come *on*," he said.

"And creaker and beaker and leaker and veaker."

"Gangway, birdbait," Laurie said. He stopped to pat his younger sister on the head. "You keep sprinkling that there magic, Perfessor. Size six-and-a-half, white."

"Kindly do not poke the Sally," said Sally, drawing away stiffly.

"Unpoke, unpoke," Barry said.

"Come *on*," Laurie said to me. He called ahead to Jannie, "You get the towels wet and throw them on the floor. I'll get the other sneaker and when she comes we'll have it all ready."

"You might as well take two more aspirin," my husband said.

"I might as well," I said.

Wearily, I headed up the stairs, sand grinding underfoot. The bathroom is at the head of the stairs, and by the time I was near the top I could see that everything was prepared. Rigorously, I put my mind back three days. It is eight-thirty in the evening, I told myself. I am coming upstairs to get myself two aspirin. Laurie has just gone to the dance, I have just told him goodbye, get home early, behave yourself, be careful, do you have a clean handkerchief? Jannie is reading. Sally and Barry are asleep. It is eight-thirty Wednesday evening, I am coming to get two aspirin.

I came to the top of the stairs, and sighed. The bathroom floor was sopping, the bathmat was soaked and crumpled, wet towels lay on the floor. In the corner, half under a wet towel, was one white sneaker. I asked myself through my teeth how old people had to get before they learned to pick up after themselves and after all our efforts to raise our children in a decent and clean house here they still behaved like pigs and the sooner Laurie grew up and got married and had a wife to pick up after him the better off I would be and maybe I would just take his allowance and hire a full-time nursemaid for him.

I picked up the bathmat and hung it over the edge of the tub. I put the soap in the soap dish and hung the towels over the shower rail. I picked up the sneaker and resisted the temptation to slam it into the wastebasket. Then, with the sneaker in my hand, I went to the other side of the hall to the linen closet to get clean towels and a dry bathmat and Laurie and Jannie burst out of the guest room shouting, "You see? You see?"

Jannie said excitedly, "Just like Beverley Lee and it turned out it *was* the caretaker all the time."

"Look, look," Laurie said, pointing. I had the door of the linen closet open and I reached up onto the towel shelf and took down Jannie's Easter-egg hat.

"What?" I said, surprised.

"That's my hat," Jannie said.

"Why would I want to put your hat in the linen closet?" I demanded. "Don't be silly."

"My nice pink Easter-egg hat," Jannie said, pleased.

"Craazy," Laurie remarked. "Opens the closet and there's the hat. Craazy." He pushed

8 **Reading Strategy** Have students predict the outcome of the story. Will the sneaker be found? Is reconstructing the "scene of the crime" necessary and effective? How and by whom will the sneaker be found? Who was responsible for losing it in the first place?

9 **Discussion** How surprising is the discovery of the Easter-egg hat? Why is this a funny discovery? Are people always as organized as they think they are?

past me and began to paw through the towels.

"Ridiculous," I said. "I *never* put hats in linen closets. Linen closets are where I keep towels and sheets and extra blankets, not hats."

"Not sneakers, either." Laurie stood back and dusted his hands.

"You pick up every one of those towels," I said, annoyed. "And then you and your sister can get right in there and clean up that bathroom. And the next time I find that pink hat lying around I am going to burn it. And you can tell Beverley Lee Girl Detective—"

"Any luck?" my husband called from the foot of the stairs.

10 "Certainly not." I started down. "Of all the idiotic notions and now it's too late in the year *any*way for a little hat like that."

"Sneaker, sneaker, sneaker!" It was Sally and Barry, in glory. Laurie raced past me down the stairs. "Got it? Sal," he yelled, "you *got* it?"

11 Proudly the little procession wound around to the front hall. Sally was still scattering sand but Barry was bearing the sneaker on high. "Gee," Laurie said. "Hey, kids, thanks. Where was it?"

"Under your bed," Sally said. "We did a lot of —" she glanced at her father "—blagic," she said. "And then we went up and looked. Very good, Barry." "Very good, Sally," Barry said. "Gosh." Laurie was pleased. He turned

and gave me an affectionate pat on the head. "Boy," he said, "are *you* ever a tippy old lady." Then, in a burst of gratitude, he added, "I'm going to go down right now on my bike and get you kids each a popsicle."

"Well, me, too, I should *think*," Jannie said indignantly. "After all, it was me thought of reconstructing the crime, and in *Elsie Dinsmore*[2] when Elsie—"

"What is this crime talk?" I said. "Anyone would think that instead of spending all my time picking up and putting away—"

"The sneaker," Laurie said to me, gesturing. "The other sneaker. I got to get down and get those popsicles, so let's have it."

_____

2. Elsie Dinsmore: A series of twenty-six novels by Martha F. Finley (1828–1909).

"What?" I said.

"The sneaker, dear. The one you just had upstairs, for heaven's sake."

Uncomfortably, I looked down at my empty hands. "Now let's see," I said. "I had it just a minute ago. . . ." 12

THINKING ABOUT THE SELECTION

Recalling

1. Who does most of the picking up in this family?
2. What advice does Jannie give to help find the missing sneaker?
3. How do the younger children help to find the sneaker?
4. Where is the missing sneaker finally found?
5. At the end of the story, what other object is missing?

Interpreting

6. Although the family members all react differently to the missing sneaker, in what way is their behavior alike?
7. What does the title indicate about this family's handling of their everyday problems?

Applying

8. What advice might you give this family to prevent another "crisis" like this one?

ANALYZING LITERATURE

Understanding Humorous Characters

A writer may create humor in a story by emphasizing character traits that lead to unexpected or humorous situations. For example, Shirley Jackson builds this episode of the family's searching for a lost sneaker on Laurie's sloppiness and on the mother's forgetfulness.

1. How does Laurie's sloppiness contribute to the humor in this story?
2. The mother's forgetting where she puts two items causes the events of this story to happen. What are the two items?
3. What traits of the younger children contribute to making this story humorous?

CRITICAL THINKING AND READING

Recognizing Humorous Situations

Humor depends largely on the unexpected. An author creates a humorous situation by presenting a series of events that lead you to expect a certain outcome. Instead, something amusingly different from what you expect happens.

1. Imagine that the family had looked in the linen closet and found nothing but linens there. Would this situation have been as humorous as their finding the Easter-egg hat there? Why?
2. Once the sneaker is found at the end of the story, you expect that the "sneaker crisis" is solved. What unexpected event occurs then?

UNDERSTANDING LANGUAGE

Recognizing Slang

The way a character speaks can make him or her seem humorous. The author of "The Sneaker Crisis" has Laurie speak using **slang** to imitate the casual language of many teenagers.

Find three slang expressions in the story and explain what they mean. Why is each humorous?

THINKING AND WRITING

Writing About a Humorous Incident

Think of a time when you looked for a lost object or helped someone else find a lost item. Write about the incident, making it seem humorous. Perhaps you might exaggerate the importance of the lost item or emphasize what you learned about the way the other person thinks and acts under the circumstances. As you revise, consider adding or emphasizing details to make your story funny.

The Sneaker Crisis 73

Focus

More About the Author Lucille Clifton, who is descended from slaves, has fought hard to overcome racial discrimination and to achieve a reputation as a writer. She says, "I try to tell the truth as I see it." Have students discuss Clifton's perspective on events based on her background. What truths would Clifton be likely to tell?

Literary Focus The identity of the major character is this story, Mrs. Elzie F. Pickens, is obvious from the start. She opens the short story by beginning a story of her own in which she is the major character. Point out that the major character is not always so easy to identify. If Mrs. Pickens' story were about someone other than herself, she might have been primarily a narrator, a minor character, rather than the major character.

Look For Your **less advanced** students might have difficulty understanding the time and place of the story and the pleasure people used to get out of simple shows. You may want to fill in some background on traveling "medicine" shows and remind students that, for many people, this type of show was exciting entertainment and a rare treat. (See Art Transparency, 1 *Medicine Show*, by Jack Levine.

Writing/Prior Knowledge Have students discuss what part luck plays in their daily lives. Then have them complete the freewriting assignment.

Vocabulary Some of the regional phrasing in the story may give students difficulty. Be sure students know the meaning of such phrases as "plaited our hair," "lit out," "bottoms of Virginia," and "grinnin fit to bust."

Teaching to Ability Levels Have more **advanced** students write a brief story with dialogue showing regionalisms from your own area.

Major and Minor Characters

Look For

Writing

Vocabulary

The Luckiest Time of All

Lucille Clifton (1936–   ) was born in Depew, New York. She has written about the strength of the courageous black women who raised their families with dignity during the harsh period of slavery and its aftermath. In addition to several books of poetry, she has written a book called *Generations,* which contains anecdotes that celebrate the lives of her father and mother. "The Luckiest Time of All" deals with a theme common in her work: the importance of a strong black woman in handing on a family's traditions to a new generation.

A **major character** is the one on whom a story focuses. It is the character who plays the most important role. Because a major character shows several character traits, you learn the most about this character as you read a story. In contrast, a **minor character** plays only a small part in a story. Therefore, you learn only a little about each minor character.

As you read "The Luckiest Time of All," you will meet several characters. Identify the major and minor characters by noticing which character plays the most important role and which characters play less important parts. Why does the author include both major and minor characters?

In the story you are about to read, the great-grandmother tells about her "luckiest time of all." Make a list of lucky incidents that have happened to you or to someone you know. Then briefly describe one of these incidents, telling what happened and what made it a lucky time.

In "The Luckiest Time of All" some words, particularly verbs, are spelled the way they are pronounced by the characters, such as *dancin* for *dancing* or *twirlin* for *twirling*. These spelling changes reflect spoken language. Since many people, particularly the characters in this story, drop the final *g* when they speak, these spellings reflect the way the words sound. You will be able to recognize these words from their context when you see them.

Objectives

1 To identify the major and minor characters
2 To make inferences about characters
3 To identify vivid action verbs
4 To write a composition about luck

Support Material

Teaching Portfolio
Teacher Backup, p. 107
Usage and Mechanics Worksheet, p. 110
Critical Thinking and Reading Worksheet, *Making Inferences About Characters,* p. 111
Language Worksheet, *Appreciating Action Verbs,* p. 112
Selection Test, p. 113

The Luckiest Time of All

from *The Lucky Stone*

Lucille Clifton

Mrs. Elzie F. Pickens was rocking slowly on the porch one afternoon when her Great-granddaughter, Tee, brought her a big bunch of dogwood blooms, and that was the beginning of a story.

"Ahhh, now that dogwood reminds me of the day I met your Great-granddaddy, Mr. Pickens, Sweet Tee.

"It was just this time, spring of the year, and me and my best friend Ovella Wilson, who is now gone, was goin to join the Silas Greene. Usta be a kinda show went all through the South, called it the Silas Greene show. Somethin like the circus. Me and Ovella wanted to join that thing and see the world. Nothin wrong at home or nothin, we just wanted to travel and see new things and have high times. Didn't say nothin to nobody but one another. Just up and decided to do it.

"Well, this day we plaited our hair and put a dress and some things in a crokasack[1] and started out to the show. Spring day like this.

"We got there after a good little walk and it was the world, Baby, such music and won-

ders as we never had seen! They had everything there, or seemed like it.

"Me and Ovella thought we'd walk around for a while and see the show before goin to the office to sign up and join.

"While we was viewin it all we come up

MOM AND DAD
William H. Johnson
National Museum of American Art

---

1. crokasack, usually spelled *croker sack* (krō' kər sak) *n.*: A bag made of burlap or similar material.

1 **Enrichment** Mr. and Mrs. Pickens were immediately attracted to one another. Can you name any other stories that involve love at first sight?

2 **Reading Strategy** Ask students what they expect to happen now. Why is Mrs. Pickens telling this story to her great-granddaughter? How does Mrs. Pickens feel about her husband?

3 **Discussion** Does Tee understand the point of her great-grandmother's story? Discuss the events from Mrs. Pickens's point of view and from Tee's.

4 **Discussion** How much of these events had to do with luck and how much with fate?

5 **Discussion** Why are Mrs. Pickens and Tee smiling at the conclusion of the story?

Reader's Response Does this story cause you to want to read the rest of *The Lucky Stone*? Explain.

on this dancin dog. Cutest one thing in the world next to you, Sweet Tee, dippin and movin and head bowin to that music. Had a little ruffly skirt on itself and up on two back legs twistin and movin to the music. Dancin dancin dancin till people started throwin pennies out of they pockets.

"Me and Ovella was caught up too and laughin so. She took a penny out of her pocket and threw it to the ground where that dog was dancin, and I took two pennies and threw 'em both.

"The music was faster and faster and that dog .was turnin and turnin. Ovella reached in her sack and threw out a little pin she had won from never being late at Sunday school. And me, laughin and all excited, reached in my bag and threw out my lucky stone!

"Well, I knew right off what I had done. Soon as it left my hand it seemed like I reached back out for it to take it back. But the stone was gone from my hand and Lord, it hit that dancin dog right on his nose!

"Well, he lit out after me, poor thing. He lit out after me and I flew! Round and round the Silas Greene we run, through every place me and Ovella had walked before, but now that dancin dog was a runnin dog and all the people was laughin at the new show, which was us!

"I felt myself slowin down after a while and I thought I would turn around a little bit to see how much gain that cute little dog was makin on me. When I did I got such a surprise! Right behind me was the dancin dog and right behind him was the finest fast runnin hero in the bottoms of Virginia.

"And that was Mr. Pickens when he was still a boy! He had a length of twine in his hand and he was twirlin it around in the air just like the cowboy at the Silas Greene and grinnin fit to bust.

"While I was watchin how the sun shined on him and made him look like an angel come to help a poor sinner girl, why, he twirled that twine one extra fancy twirl and looped it right around one hind leg of that dancin dog and brought him low.

"I stopped then and walked slow and shy to where he had picked up that poor dog to see if he was hurt, cradlin him and talkin to him soft and sweet. That showed me how kind and gentle he was, and when we walked back to the dancin dog's place in the show he let the dog loose and helped me to find my stone. I told him how shiny black it was and how it had the letter *A* scratched on one side. We searched and searched and at last he spied it!

"Ovella and me lost heart for shows then and we walked on home. And a good little way, the one who was gonna be your Great-granddaddy was walkin on behind. Seein us safe. Us walkin kind of slow. Him seein us safe. Yes." Mrs. Pickens' voice trailed off softly and Tee noticed she had a little smile on her face.

"Grandmama, that stone almost got you bit by a dog that time. It wasn't so lucky that time, was it?"

Tee's Great-grandmother shook her head and laughed out loud.

"That was the luckiest time of all, Tee Baby. It got me acquainted with Mr. Amos Pickens, and if that ain't luck, what could it be! Yes, it was luckier for me than for anybody, I think. Least mostly I think it."

Tee laughed with her Great-grandmother though she didn't exactly know why.

"I hope I have that kind of good stone luck one day," she said.

"Maybe you will someday," her Great-grandmother said.

And they rocked a little longer and smiled together.

Closure and Extension

ANSWERS TO THINKING ABOUT THE SELECTION
Recalling

1. Mrs. Elzie F. Pickens tells the story about the lucky stone and the Silas Greene show.
2. They are excited because of the dancing dog and want to show their appreciation for his performance.
3. She felt that the stone was re-
sponsible for her meeting Amos Pickens.

Interpreting

4. Mr. Pickens wanted to meet Elzie and find out where she lived.
5. Students' answers may include any of the following points: Mrs. Pickens speaks of Mr. Pickens only in flattering terms. She calls him the "finest fast runnin hero" in her first reference to him. She says how "kind and gentle" he was.

THINKING ABOUT THE SELECTION

Recalling

1. "The Luckiest Time of All" is a story within a story. Who tells the story about the lucky stone and the Silas Greene Show?
2. Why do the people at the Silas Greene Show start throwing pennies?
3. What is Great-grandmother's reason for believing that the stone was lucky for her?

Interpreting

4. What was Mr. Pickens's real intention in saving Great-grandmother from being bitten by the dog and in following her home?
5. What evidence does the story provide to show that Great-grandmother and Mr. Pickens had a happy life?

Applying

6. Which do you think brings success more, hard work or luck? Give reasons for your answer.

ANALYZING LITERATURE

Identifying Major and Minor Characters

The **major character** in a story is the one on whom the story focuses and thus the one you learn the most about. **Minor characters** play small roles in the development of a story.

1. Who is the major character in "The Luckiest Time of All"?
2. Point out three facts you learn about the major character.
3. Name one minor character.
4. What do you learn about this minor character?

CRITICAL THINKING AND READING

Making Inferences About Characters

An **inference** is a conclusion that you make based on the information given. An author does not always tell you everything there is to know about a character. Sometimes you must make inferences about the character's personality traits based on what the character says and does.

1. What inference can you make about Mr. Pickens based on the following facts?
   a. He cradles the dog and speaks softly to it.
   b. He sees the young women safely home.
2. Find two details in the story that support the inference that Great-grandmother is a happy, good-natured person.

UNDERSTANDING LANGUAGE

Appreciating Vivid Action Verbs

Writers use strong action verbs to create clear pictures. For example, when Lucille Clifton writes ". . . he *twirled* that twine one extra fancy twirl and *looped* it right around one hind leg of that dancin dog . . . ," you see Mr. Pickens's actions very clearly.

1. Find three other examples of vivid action verbs in "The Luckiest Time of All."
2. Tell which is the more vivid verb in each of the following pairs:
   a. talk, chatter   c. wash, scrub
   b. try, struggle   d. shine, glitter

THINKING AND WRITING

Writing About Luck

Think about a person you know who is successful. Make notes about how much of this person's success is due to luck and how much is due to hard work. Then prepare the first draft of a composition to present before your class telling whether you think luck or hard work is more important to success. Begin with a topic sentence that summarizes your opinion. Then give examples to support your opinion. When you revise, be sure you have given enough examples to convince your classmates of your opinion.

The Luckiest Time of All   77

And, most of all, Mrs. Pickens considered her meeting with Amos Pickens to be the luckiest event in her life.

Applying
6. Suggested Response: Most students should see that hard work is more likely to bring about success because a person is actively doing something to achieve it. Luck cannot be counted on; success must be earned.

ANSWERS TO ANALYZING LITERATURE

1. Mrs. Elzie F. Pickens is the major character.
2. When she was young, she wanted to join the Silas Greene show to "see the world." She liked a good time and got very excited about the dancing dog act. She believes in luck and carries a lucky stone. She and Mr. Pickens were interested in each other immediately. She had a happy marriage and is a contented person with pleasant memories.
3. Suggested Response: Although students' answers will vary, they may name Tee, Ovella Wilson, or Mr. Pickens.
4. Students learn that Tee is Mrs. Pickens' great-granddaughter, that Tee is fond of her great-grandmother because she brought her dogwood blossoms, and that Tee would like to find a good man like her great-grandfather someday. Students learn that Ovella Wilson

(Answers begin on p. 76.)

was Mrs. Pickens' best friend, that she is now dead, that she too wanted to join the Silas Greene show, and that she also loved the dancing dog act and then lost interest in joining the show. Students learn that Mr. Pickens was a fast runner, was kind and gentle to animals, was sensitive to Elzie losing her lucky stone and helpful in finding it, and was immediately attracted to the woman he would one day marry.

ANSWERS TO CRITICAL THINKING AND READING

1. (a) He is gentle and kind. (b) He is a gentleman and is interested in one of the girls. He wants to make sure the girls get home safely, and he wants to see where Elzie lives.
2. She has happy memories of going to the Silas Greene show with her best friend and meeting her future husband. She laughs "out loud" when she explains to Tee that the "luckiest time of all" was when she met Amos Pickens.

ANSWERS TO UNDERSTANDING LANGUAGE

1. Other examples of vivid verbs are *plaited, viewin, dippin, twistin, lit, flew, twirlin, grinnin, cradlin, scratched, searched, spied, trailed, noticed,* and *acquainted.*
2. a. chatter b. struggle c. scrub d. glitter.

Challenge Explain how Mrs. Pickens' personality, more than luck, might have been responsible for her happy life. How true is it that people often "make their own luck"?

THINKING AND WRITING
Writing Across the Curriculum
You might work with the social studies department to have students research the social background of the main character. Students can describe what life was like for a young black girl growing up in the south in the early 1900's.

Focus

More About the Author Piri Thomas's stories are set in the Puerto Rican communities of New York City. Sent to prison for five years in 1950 for attempted robbery, Thomas used his time there to embark on a writing career. When he was released, he began working on rehabilitation programs for drug addicts. Ask students if based on these facts, they believe Thomas was "into street negatives" or "dreamt positive."

Literary Focus Antonio and Felix are the two major characters in the story. Although they are very much alike in many ways, they are also distinct individuals. Point out the character traits that make each boy a major character and that distinguish one boy from the other.

Look For Your less advanced students may have difficulty distinguishing between Antonio and Felix. As they read the story, have them make a list of characteristics for each boy. The lists should help to individualize the characters.

Writing/Prior Knowledge Have students discuss the meaning of this saying: "Winning isn't everything; it's the only thing." Then have them complete the freewriting assignment.

Vocabulary Have your less advanced students read the words aloud so that you can be sure they can pronounce them. Have all students practice saying the Spanish words aloud, using the respellings at the bottoms of the pages. If there are any Spanish-speaking students in class, have them guide the other students in pronouncing the Spanish words.

Spelling Tip Have students look at the spelling of the words *dignitary, dignitaries*. Tell students that we form the plural of most words ending in *y* by changing the *y* to *i* and adding *es*.

Amigo Brothers

Piri Thomas (1928–   ) grew up in the Spanish Harlem section of New York City. While serving time in jail as a young man, he began to write about his life. Later he published an autobiography called *Down These Mean Streets,* which describes his experiences in some of the city's toughest neighborhoods. Like Thomas himself, the two major characters in "Amigo Brothers" have a dream that helps them overcome the problems they encounter in their environment.

More Than One Major Character

Many stories tell about the experiences of just one major character. Sometimes, however, a story contains two or more major characters. Each of them may have a variety of character traits, or ways of acting and looking at the world. The focus of this type of story is often on the relationship between the major characters.

"Amigo Brothers" has two major characters. During the story, the friendship between them is put to a difficult test.

Look For

In "Amigo Brothers" the two major characters are Antonio and Felix. As you read, notice what character traits they share. Also pay attention to how the two boys differ from each other. Why are they such good friends?

Writing

In "Amigo Brothers" two friends compete against each other. Think of a time when you have competed against a close friend in the classroom, at an athletic event, or in a social situation. If you prefer, make up a situation. Then freewrite about the event.

Vocabulary

Knowing the following words will help you as you read "Amigo Brothers."

barrage (bə räzh′) *n.*: A heavy attack (p. 80)

gnawing (nô′ iŋ) *adj.*: Tormenting; bothering (p. 82)

perpetual (pər pech′oo wəl) *adj.*: Never stopping (p. 82)

dignitaries (dig′nə ter′ ēz) *n.*: People holding high positions or offices (p. 83)

interwoven (in′tər wōv′ən) *v.*: Mixed together (p. 83)

nimble (nim′b'l) *adj.*: Moving quickly and lightly (p. 84)

dispelled (dis peld′) *v.*: Driven away (p. 85)

feinted (fānt′ əd) *v.*: Pretended to make an attack (p. 85)

Objectives

1 To understand the development of two major characters
2 To compare and contrast characters
3 To use words that show comparison and contrast
4 To write a paragraph using comparison and contrast

Support Material

Teaching Portfolio
Teacher Backup, p. 115
Grammar in Action Worksheet, *Using Commas,* p. 118
Usage and Mechanics Worksheet, p. 120
Vocabulary Check, p. 121
Critical Thinking and Reading Worksheet, *Comparing and Contrasting Characters,* p. 122

Language Worksheet, *Using Words for Comparison and Contrast,* p. 123
Selection Test, p. 124

Amigo[1] Brothers

Piri Thomas

Antonio Cruz and Felix Varga were both seventeen years old. They were so together in friendship that they felt themselves to be brothers. They had known each other since childhood, growing up on the lower east side of Manhattan in the same tenement building on Fifth Street between Avenue A and Avenue B.

Antonio was fair, lean, and lanky, while Felix was dark, short, and husky. Antonio's hair was always falling over his eyes, while Felix wore his black hair in a natural Afro style.

Each youngster had a dream of someday becoming lightweight champion of the world. Every chance they had the boys worked out, sometimes at the Boys Club on 10th Street and Avenue A and sometimes at the pro's gym on 14th Street. Early morning sunrises would find them running along the East River Drive, wrapped in sweat shirts, short towels around their necks, and handkerchiefs Apache style around their foreheads.

While some youngsters were into street negatives, Antonio and Felix slept, ate, rapped,[2] and dreamt positive. Between them, they had a collection of *Fight* magazines second to none, plus a scrapbook filled with torn tickets to every boxing match they had ever attended, and some clippings of their own. If asked a question about any given fighter, they would immediately zip out from their memory banks divisions, weights, records of fights, knock-outs, technical knock-outs,[3] and draws or losses.

Each had fought many bouts representing their community and had won two gold-plated medals plus a silver and bronze medallion. The difference was in their style. Antonio's lean form and long reach made him the better boxer, while Felix's short and muscular frame made him the better slugger.[4] Whenever they had met in the ring for sparring sessions, it had always been hot and heavy.

Now, after a series of elimination bouts,[5] they had been informed that they were to meet each other in the division finals that were scheduled for the seventh of August, two weeks away—the winner to represent the Boys Club in the Golden Gloves Championship Tournament.

The two boys continued to run together along the East River Drive. But even when joking with each other, they both sensed a wall rising between them.

One morning less than a week before their bout, they met as usual for their daily work-out. They fooled around with a few jabs at the air, slapped skin, and then took off, running lightly along the dirty East River's edge.

---

3. technical knock-outs: Occasions when a fight is stopped because one of the fighters is too hurt to continue, even though he is on his feet.
4. slugger (slug′ ər) *n.*: A boxer who relies more on the power of his punches than on his grace and form.
5. elimination bouts: A series of matches in which only the winners go on to fight in other matches.

1. amigo (ə mē′ gō) *adj.*: Spanish for "friend" (usually a noun).
2. rapped (rapt) *v.*: A slang term meaning "talked."

Enrichment This is a story both about friendship and about boxing. As in any other sport, the participants play to win, but boxing is a particularly dramatic sport because the fighters are literally fighting each other to win. This is perhaps why so many films about boxers have been made. Ask students if they have seen the *Rocky* films or other fight films, such as *The Champ* or *Raging Bull*. Have students discuss the main character in a fight film and the significance for the fighter of winning or losing a fight.

3 Discussion What do you expect Felix to say to Antonio? Why did they need to talk?

Antonio glanced at Felix who kept his eyes purposely straight ahead, pausing from time to time to do some fancy leg work while throwing one-twos followed by upper cuts to an imaginary jaw. Antonio then beat the air with a barrage of body blows and short devastating lefts with an overhand jaw-breaking right. After a mile or so, Felix puffed and said, "Let's stop a while, bro. I think we both got something to say to each other." Antonio nodded. It was not natural to be

3

80   *Short Stories*

Grammar in Action

One of the ways that **commas** are used is to set off words of direct address, introductory words, and other similar types of information that are not essential to the meaning of the sentence. The comma indicates that you should pause slightly before reading the next word. This helps your writing echo the way people speak.

The comma guides the reader to a better understanding of the meaning of the sentence. Notice how Piri Thomas' commas add clarity in the following sentences:

"Man, I don't know how to come out with it."
"Yeah, right."
"If it's fair, hermano, I'm for it."
"It's fair, Tony."

Without the commas in the last two sentences, their meanings would be very different. Commas can be very helpful, but it is important to follow the rules for using them and have a clear reason for including them. Keep in mind that a single comma is needed after an introductory element or before a final sentence element, as shown in the first, second, and fourth sentences above. Two commas are used to set off an element within the sentence, as shown in the third sentence.

acting as though nothing unusual was happening when two ace-boon buddies were going to be blasting each other within a few short days.

They rested their elbows on the railing separating them from the river. Antonio wiped his face with his short towel. The sunrise was now creating day.

Felix leaned heavily on the river's railing and stared across to the shores of Brooklyn. Finally, he broke the silence.

"Man, I don't know how to come out with it."

Antonio helped. "It's about our fight, right?"

"Yeah, right." Felix's eyes squinted at the rising orange sun.

"I've been thinking about it too, *panín*.[6] In fact, since we found out it was going to be me and you, I've been awake at night, pulling punches on you, trying not to hurt you."

"Same here. It ain't natural to think about the fight. I mean, we both are *cheverote*[7] fighters and we both want to win. But only one of us can win. There ain't no draws in the eliminations."

Felix tapped Antonio gently on the shoulder. "I don't mean to sound like I'm bragging, bro. But I wanna win, fair and square."

Antonio nodded quietly. "Yeah. We both know that in the ring the better man wins. Friend or no friend, brother or no . . . "

Felix finished it for him. "Brother. Tony, let's promise something right here. Okay?"

"If it's fair, *hermano*,[8] I'm for it." Antonio admired the courage of a tugboat pulling a barge five times its welterweight size.

"It's fair, Tony. When we get into the ring, it's gotta be like we never met. We gotta be like two heavy strangers that want the same thing and only one can have it. You understand, don'tcha?"

"*Sí*, I know." Tony smiled. "No pulling punches. We go all the way."

"Yeah, that's right. Listen, Tony. Don't you think it's a good idea if we don't see each other until the day of the fight? I'm going to stay with my Aunt Lucy in the Bronx. I can use Gleason's Gym for working out. My manager says he got some sparring partners with more or less your style."

Tony scratched his nose pensively. "Yeah, it would be better for our heads." He held out his hand, palm upward. "Deal?"

"Deal." Felix lightly slapped open skin.

"Ready for some more running?" Tony asked lamely.

"Naw, bro. Let's cut it here. You go on. I kinda like to get things together in my head."

"You ain't worried, are you?" Tony asked.

"No way, man." Felix laughed out loud. "I got too much smarts for that. I just think it's cooler if we split right here. After the fight, we can get it together again like nothing ever happened."

The amigo brothers were not ashamed to hug each other tightly.

"Guess you're right. Watch yourself, Felix. I hear there's some pretty heavy dudes up in the Bronx. *Suavecito*,[9] okay?"

"Okay. You watch yourself too, *sabe*?"[10]

Tony jogged away. Felix watched his friend disappear from view, throwing rights and lefts. Both fighters had a lot of psyching up[11] to do before the big fight.

The days in training passed much too slowly. Although they kept out of each other's way, they were aware of each other's progress via the ghetto grapevine.

The evening before the big fight, Tony made his way to the roof of his tenement. In

---

6. panín (pä nēn'): Spanish for "pal."
7. cheverote (che ve rô' tā): Spanish for "great."
8. hermano (er mä' nô): Spanish for "brother."

9. suavecito (swä vā sē' tô): Spanish for "take it easy."
10. sabe (sä' bā): Spanish for "understand?"
11. psyching (sīk iŋ) **up:** A slang term meaning "getting themselves mentally ready."

Amigo Brothers   81

4 Literary Focus Felix and Antonio are such good friends that they can be totally honest with each other about wanting to win. Notice how they address each other in their native language as pal and brother, showing their love and respect for one another.

5 Reading Strategy Have students predict what might happen to the boys' friendship as a result of this fight.

6 Enrichment For a deeper understanding of inner-city life and the importance of gangs in the ghetto, introduce students to the plot of *West Side Story*. Some students may have seen the movie version and may be able to explain how inner-city street gangs operate. You can also play some of the music from *West Side Story*, and let the lyrics speak for themselves.

Student Activity 1. Find three other sentences from "Amigo Brothers" in which Thomas uses commas to set off words of direct address and introductory words. Explain how the use of commas in these sentences helps your understanding of their meanings.

Student Activity 2. Copy the following sentences, inserting commas where the rules and reason indicate they would be helpful.

1. Could I please Mother go to the party.

2. That is lovely Mary.

3. Yes that is what I mean.

7 **Discussion** How did each of the boys rationalize fighting his best friend? What do you learn about the character of Felix and Antonio?

8 **Discussion** Why did the fight attract so much attention in the community?

the quiet early dark, he peered over the ledge. Six stories below the lights of the city blinked and the sounds of cars mingled with the curses and the laughter of children in the street. He tried not to think of Felix, feeling he had succeeded in psyching his mind. But only in the ring would he really know. To spare Felix hurt, he would have to knock him out, early and quick.

Up in the South Bronx, Felix decided to take in a movie in an effort to keep Antonio's face away from his fists. The flick was *The Champion* with Kirk Douglas, the third time Felix was seeing it.

The champion was getting hit hard. He was saved only by the sound of the bell.

Felix became the champ and Tony the challenger.

The movie audience was going out of its head. The challenger, confident that he had the championship in the bag, threw a left. The champ countered with a dynamite right.

Felix's right arm felt the shock. Antonio's face, superimposed on the screen, was hit by the awesome blow. Felix saw himself in the ring, blasting Antonio against the ropes. The challenger fell to the canvas.

When Felix finally left the theatre, he had figured out how to psyche himself for tomorrow's fight. It was Felix the Champion vs. Antonio the Challenger.

He walked up some dark streets, deserted except for small pockets of wary-looking kids wearing gang colors. Despite the fact that he was Puerto Rican like them, they eyed him as a stranger to their turf.[12] Felix did a fast shuffle, bobbing and weaving, while letting loose a torrent of blows that would demolish whatever got in its way. It seemed to impress the brothers, who went about their own business.

Finding no takers, Felix decided to split

___
12. turf (tʉrf): A slang term meaning "a gang's territory."

to his aunt's. Walking the streets had not relaxed him, neither had the fight flick. All it had done was to stir him up. He let himself quietly into his Aunt Lucy's apartment and went straight to bed, falling into a fitful sleep with sounds of the gong for Round One.

Antonio was passing some heavy time on his rooftop. How would the fight tomorrow affect his relationship with Felix? After all, fighting was like any other profession. Friendship had nothing to do with it. A gnawing doubt crept in. He cut negative thinking real quick by doing some speedy fancy dance steps, bobbing and weaving like mercury.[13] The night air was blurred with perpetual motions of left hooks and right crosses. Felix, his *amigo* brother, was not going to be Felix at all in the ring. Just an opponent with another face. Antonio went to sleep, hearing the opening bell for the first round. Like his friend in the South Bronx, he prayed for victory, via a quick clean knock-out in the first round.

Large posters plastered all over the walls of local shops announced the fight between Antonio Cruz and Felix Vargas as the main bout.

The fight had created great interest in the neighborhood. Antonio and Felix were well liked and respected. Each had his own loyal following. Antonio's fans counted on his boxing skills. On the other side, Felix's admirers trusted in his dynamite-packed fists.

Felix had returned to his apartment early in the morning of August 7th and stayed there, hoping to avoid seeing Antonio. He turned the radio on to *salsa* music[14] sounds

___
13. mercury (mʉr' kyoo rē): The element mercury, also known as quicksilver because it is so quick and fluid. This element was named after the Roman god Mercury, who because of his quick thinking and speed served as the messenger of the gods.
14. salsa (säl' sə) **music:** Latin American dance music.

and then tried to read while waiting for word from his manager.

The fight was scheduled to take place in Tompkins Square Park. It had been decided that the gymnasium of the Boys Club was not large enough to hold all the people who were sure to attend. In Tompkins Square Park, everyone who wanted could view the fight, whether from ringside or window fire escapes or tenement rooftops.

The morning of the fight Tompkins Square was a beehive of activity with numerous workers setting up the ring, the seats, and the guest speakers' stand. The scheduled bouts began shortly after noon and the park had begun filling up even earlier.

The local junior high school across from Tompkins Square Park served as the dressing room for all the fighters. Each was given a separate classroom with desk tops, covered with mats, serving as resting tables. Antonio thought he caught a glimpse of Felix waving to him from a room at the far end of the corridor. He waved back just in case it had been him.

The fighters changed from their street clothes into fighting gear. Antonio wore white trunks, black socks, and black shoes. Felix wore sky blue trunks, red socks, and white boxing shoes. Each had dressing gowns to match their fighting trunks with their names neatly stitched on the back.

9 The loudspeakers blared into the open windows of the school. There were speeches by dignitaries, community leaders, and great boxers of yesteryear. Some were well prepared, some improvised on the spot. They all carried the same message of great pleasure and honor at being part of such a historic event. This great day was in the tradition of champions emerging from the streets of the lower east side.

Interwoven with the speeches were the sounds of the other boxing events. After the sixth bout, Felix was much relieved when his trainer Charlie said, "Time change. Quick knock-out. This is it. We're on."

Waiting time was over. Felix was escorted from the classroom by a dozen fans in white T-shirts with the word FELIX across their fronts.

Antonio was escorted down a different stairwell and guided through a roped-off path.

10 As the two climbed into the ring, the crowd exploded with a roar. Antonio and Felix both bowed gracefully and then raised their arms in acknowledgment.

Antonio tried to be cool, but even as the roar was in its first birth, he turned slowly to meet Felix's eyes looking directly into his. Felix nodded his head and Antonio responded. And both as one, just as quickly, turned away to face his own corner.

Bong—bong—bong. The roar turned to stillness.

"Ladies and Gentlemen, *Señores y Señoras*."[15]

The announcer spoke slowly, pleased at his bilingual efforts.

11 "Now the moment we have all been waiting for—the main event between two fine young Puerto Rican fighters, products of our lower east side. In this corner, weighing 134 pounds, Felix Vargas. And in this corner, weighing 133 pounds, Antonio Cruz. The winner will represent the Boys Club in the tournament of champions, the Golden Gloves. There will be no draw. May the best man win."

The cheering of the crowd shook the window panes of the old buildings surrounding Tompkins Square Park. At the center of the ring, the referee was giving instructions to the youngsters.

"Keep your punches up. No low blows. No punching on the back of the head. Keep

---

15. señores y señoras (se nyô räs ē se nyô räs): Spanish for "Gentlemen and Ladies."

your heads up. Understand. Let's have a clean fight. Now shake hands and come out fighting."

Both youngsters touched gloves and nodded. They turned and danced quickly to their corners. Their head towels and dressing gowns were lifted neatly from their shoulders by their trainers' nimble fingers. Antonio crossed himself. Felix did the same.

BONG! BONG! ROUND ONE. Felix and 12

Antonio turned and faced each other squarely in a fighting pose. Felix wasted no time. He came in fast, head low, half hunched toward his right shoulder, and lashed out with a straight left. He missed a right cross as Antonio slipped the punch and countered with one-two-three lefts that snapped Felix's head back, sending a mild shock coursing through him. If Felix had any small doubt about their friendship affecting their fight, it was being neatly dispelled.

Antonio danced, a joy to behold. His left hand was like a piston pumping jabs one right after another with seeming ease. Felix bobbed and weaved and never stopped boring in. He knew that at long range he was at a disadvantage. Antonio had too much reach on him. Only by coming in close could Felix hope to achieve the dreamed-of knockout.

13 Antonio knew the dynamite that was stored in his *amigo* brother's fist. He ducked a short right and missed a left hook. Felix trapped him against the ropes just long enough to pour some punishing rights and lefts to Antonio's hard midsection. Antonio slipped away from Felix, crashing two lefts to his head, which set Felix's right ear to ringing.

Bong! Both *amigos* froze a punch well on its way, sending up a roar of approval for good sportsmanship.

Felix walked briskly back to his corner. His right ear had not stopped ringing. Antonio gracefully danced his way toward his stool none the worse, except for glowing glove burns, showing angry red against the whiteness of his midribs.

"Watch that right, Tony." His trainer talked into his ear. "Remember Felix always goes to the body. He'll want you to drop your hands for his overhand left or right. Got it?"

Antonio nodded, spraying water out between his teeth. He felt better as his sore midsection was being firmly rubbed.

Felix's corner was also busy.

"You gotta get in there, fella." Felix's trainer poured water over his curly Afro locks. "Get in there or he's gonna chop you up from way back."

Bong! Bong! Round two. Felix was off his stool and rushed Antonio like a bull, sending a hard right to his head. Beads of water exploded from Antonio's long hair.

Antonio, hurt, sent back a blurring barrage of lefts and rights that only meant pain to Felix, who returned with a short left to the head followed by a looping right to the body. Antonio countered with his own flurry, forcing Felix to give ground. But not for long.

Felix bobbed and weaved, bobbed and weaved, occasionally punching his two gloves together.

Antonio waited for the rush that was sure to come. Felix closed in and feinted with his left shoulder and threw his right instead. Lights suddenly exploded inside Felix's head as Antonio slipped the blow and hit him with a pistonlike left catching him flush on the point of his chin.

Bedlam broke loose as Felix's legs momentarily buckled. He fought off a series of rights and lefts and came back with a strong right that taught Antonio respect.

Antonio danced in carefully. He knew Felix had the habit of playing possum when hurt, to sucker an opponent within reach of the powerful bombs he carried in each fist.

A right to the head slowed Antonio's pretty dancing. He answered with his own left at Felix's right eye that began puffing up within three seconds.

Antonio, a bit too eager, moved in too close and Felix had him entangled into a rip-roaring, punching toe-to-toe slugfest that brought the whole Tompkins Square Park screaming to its feet.

Rights to the body. Lefts to the head. Neither fighter was giving an inch. Suddenly a short right caught Antonio squarely on the

Amigo Brothers 85

14

15

13 Discussion Does the fact that the boys know each other so well make the fight physically easier or more difficult for them?

14 Clarification A feint is a faked punch. To create openings for his punches, a boxer uses feints to throw an opponent off guard.

15 Discussion Describe the fighting tactics that each of the boys uses during the match.

16 Discussion Does it seem possible that two friends as close as Felix and Antonio could fight each other so brutally? What is motivating each boy to fight so hard?

17 Discussion Were you surprised when the boys embraced at the end of the fight? Why or why not?

18 Discussion Why didn't Felix and Antonio wait to hear the name of the winner announced? Whose name do you think was announced?

Reader's Response Were you happy with the story's ending? Explain.

chin. His long legs turned to jelly and his arms flailed out desperately. Felix, grunting like a bull, threw wild punches from every direction. Antonio, groggy, bobbed and weaved, evading most of the blows. Suddenly his head cleared. His left flashed out hard and straight catching Felix on the bridge of his nose.

Felix lashed back with a haymaker,[16] right off the ghetto streets. At the same instant, his eye caught another left hook from Antonio. Felix swung out trying to clear the pain. Only the frenzied screaming of those along ringside let him know that he had dropped Antonio. Fighting off the growing haze, Antonio struggled to his feet, got up, ducked, and threw a smashing right that dropped Felix flat on his back.

Felix got up as fast as he could in his own corner, groggy but still game. He didn't even hear the count. In a fog, he heard the roaring of the crowd, who seemed to have gone insane. His head cleared to hear the bell sound at the end of the round. He was very glad. His trainer sat him down on the stool.

In his corner, Antonio was doing what all fighters do when they are hurt. They sit and smile at everyone.

The referee signaled the ring doctor to check the fighters out. He did so and then gave his okay. The cold water sponges brought clarity to both *amigo* brothers. They were rubbed until their circulation ran free.

Bong! Round three—the final round. Up to now it had been tic-tac-toe, pretty much even. But everyone knew there could be no draw and that this round would decide the winner.

This time, to Felix's surprise, it was Antonio who came out fast, charging across the ring. Felix braced himself but couldn't ward off the barrage of punches. Antonio drove Felix hard against the ropes.

The crowd ate it up. Thus far the two had fought with *mucho corazón.*[17] Felix tapped his gloves and commenced his attack anew. Antonio, throwing boxer's caution to the winds, jumped in to meet him.

Both pounded away. Neither gave an inch and neither fell to the canvas. Felix's left eye was tightly closed. Claret red[18] blood poured from Antonio's nose. They fought toe-to-toe.

The sounds of their blows were loud in contrast to the silence of a crowd gone completely mute. The referee was stunned by their savagery.

Bong! Bong! Bong! The bell sounded over and over again. Felix and Antonio were past hearing. Their blows continued to pound on each other like hailstones.

Finally the referee and the two trainers pried Felix and Antonio apart. Cold water was poured over them to bring them back to their senses.

They looked around and then rushed toward each other. A cry of alarm surged through Tompkins Square Park. Was this a fight to the death instead of a boxing match?

The fear soon gave way to wave upon wave of cheering as the two *amigos* embraced.

No matter what the decision, they knew they would always be champions to each other.

BONG! BONG! BONG! "Ladies and Gentlemen. *Señores* and *Señoras.* The winner and representative to the Golden Gloves Tournament of Champions is . . ."

The announcer turned to point to the winner and found himself alone. Arm in arm the champions had already left the ring.

---

16. haymaker: A punch thrown with full force.

17. mucho corazón (m$\overline{oo}$′ chô kô rä sôn′): Spanish for "much courage."

18. claret (klar′ it) **red:** Purplish red.

Closure and Extension

ANSWERS TO THINKING ABOUT THE SELECTION
Recalling

1. Antonio is fair, lean, and lanky, while Felix is dark, husky, and short. Antonio's hair falls over his eyes, while Felix's hair is worn in a natural Afro.

2. They both dream of becoming lightweight champion of the world.

3. The boys must fight each other in the division finals to determine which of them will represent the Boys Club in the Golden Gloves Championship Tournament.

4. They make an agreement that they will fight each other as if they are strangers and fight to win.

5. The boys leave the ring arm in arm.

Interpreting

6. Boxing is one way that the boys

THINKING ABOUT THE SELECTION

Recalling

1. How do Antonio and Felix differ in appearance?
2. What dream do the boys share?
3. What event creates a wall between them?
4. What agreement do they make while jogging?
5. Describe the way the boys leave the ring at the end of the fight.

Interpreting

6. Why is boxing so important to Antonio and Felix?
7. Why do the boys decide not to see each other until the fight?
8. What do the boys discover they value as much as or more than winning?
9. *Amigo* means "friend." Why is "Amigo Brothers" an appropriate title for this story?

Applying

10. Why can it be hard for friends to compete?

ANALYZING LITERATURE

Considering Two Major Characters

Some stories deal with more than one major character. In "Amigo Brothers," both Antonio and Felix are fully developed and have a variety of character traits. The writer gives them equal attention. You learn about these two characters as you watch the dream they share become the barrier that divides them.

1. Explain how the boys' relationship is tested in this story.
2. Show how the boys' friendship is stronger or weaker as a result of this test.

CRITICAL THINKING AND READING

Comparing and Contrasting Characters

When you **compare** two characters you show how they are similar. When you **contrast** them, you show how they are different. Often, you can better understand stories with more than one major character by comparing and contrasting the characters. In "Amigo Brothers," for example, Antonio and Felix are different in height but similar in their love of boxing.

1. List three other ways in which the boys are similar.
2. Now list three ways in which they are different.
3. Which of these similarities and differences may have brought them together as friends?

UNDERSTANDING LANGUAGE

Using Words in Comparisons

Certain words are very helpful when you compare and contrast characters. Some words that express similarities are *like, identical to, the same as,* and *similar to.* For example, you could say: *Like* Felix, Antonio loves boxing. Words that express differences include *however, unlike, different from, while,* and *nevertheless.* For example, you could say: Felix and Antonio are both boxers; *nevertheless* (or *however*), Antonio is tall *while* Felix is short.

1. Express a similarity between Felix and Antonio using one of the words or phrases mentioned above.
2. Now express a difference between the two boys using one of the preceding words or phrases.

THINKING AND WRITING

Writing a Comparison and Contrast

Compare and contrast Antonio and Felix. As you brainstorm for ideas, recall your lists of the ways that the boys are similar and different. Also, remember to use some of the key words that show similarities and differences. When you have finished, revise your work to make sure it is clear.

Amigo Brothers 87

---

has survived a tremendous ordeal, both psychological and physical.

ANSWERS TO CRITICAL THINKING AND READING

1. The boys are both seventeen, both Puerto Rican, both had won boxing medals and dreamed of becoming lightweight champion of the world. Both boys grew up in the same tenement building on the Lower East Side. They dressed the same and worked out the same way. They both wanted a quick victory in the first round, and they both valued their friendship more than winning the boxing match.
2. They were physically different and had different boxing styles and abilities. They dressed in different colors for the fight. They dealt with their prefight anxiety differently, and each came up with a different strategy for fighting his friend.
3. Their backgrounds, their common dream, their love of boxing, and their positive attitudes brought them together as friends.

ANSWERS TO UNDERSTANDING LANGUAGE

1. Students' answers will differ. For example, students may say, "Felix's dream is *the same as* Antonio's: to become lightweight champion of the world."
2. Students' answers will differ. For example, students may say, "*Unlike* Felix, Antonio stayed home on the night before the fight."

Challenge What part does environment play in this story? How are Antonio and Felix a product of their environment? How are they different from the boys in the street gangs?

THINKING AND WRITING

For help with this assignment, students can refer to Lesson 16, "Writing a Comparative Evaluation," in the Handbook of Writing About Literature.

---

can excel in the ghetto and achieve recognition.

7. The boys decide not to see each other to lessen the pressure of the upcoming fight and to give themselves some breathing space. The tension of the fight was affecting their friendship in a negative way.
8. They value each other and their friendship.
9. It is an appropriate title because the boys are such good friends that they are like brothers, and

their relationship is more important to them, by the conclusion of the story, than winning the fight.

Applying

10. Students' answers will vary. However, answer should include the idea that competing with a friend puts a strain on the relationship. The trust and loyalty that underlie a friendship are overshadowed by the pressure to win.

ANSWERS TO ANALYZING LITERATURE

1. The boys' relationship is tested because each has a strong desire to win. But both Felix and Antonio know that one of them must lose, and they fear that one's bitterness over the lost match could destroy their friendship.
2. Students' answers will differ. Suggested Response: The friendship is stronger because it

Focus

More About the Author Sherwood Anderson was forced to drop out of high school in order to go to work to help support his family. However, at the age of 24, Anderson resumed his studies, impelled by a need for more education. Ask the class to write a portrait of Anderson based on this and on the fact that, in later life, he left a successful business to become a writer. Do you think it takes courage to pursue your dreams? How was Anderson a courageous man?

Literary Focus Motivation can be either a negative or a positive force. For example, a person, motivated by greed or jealousy, can be driven to commit a crime. But people motivated by generosity or a desire to help others can offer a great deal to society. Often, people are not even aware of what motivates them to act as they do.

Look For Your less advanced students may find motivation a difficult concept to grasp because it is so often unconscious. It may be helpful to preview the Analyzing Literature questions on page 93 so that these questions can guide their reading.

Writing/Prior Knowledge Have students analyze daily actions in terms of motivation. Students can examine a typical day in the life of a person they know, and write down what made that person act as he or she did. Then have them complete the freewriting assignment.

Vocabulary Have your less advanced students read the words aloud so that you can be sure they can pronounce them.

Spelling Tip Point out the silent *n* in the word *solemn*.

Stolen Day

Sherwood Anderson (1876–1941) was born in Camden, Ohio. Although Anderson had almost no formal education, he became a successful businessman, the manager of a paint factory. Then one day, surprisingly, he walked out of his job and went off to Chicago to become a writer. His most successful works were based on his boyhood, and many of his stories are about growing up. "Stolen Day" deals with a boy who has an experience that might help him to grow up.

Motivation

In stories as in life, people do things because they have reasons, or motives, for doing them. **Motivation** refers to the reasons behind actions. The word *motivation* contains the root *mot*, meaning "to move." Motivation moves a person forward, causing him or her to do something, to pursue some goal. Another word with the root *mot* is *emotion*. A powerful emotion, which causes a person to behave in certain ways, can be a strong motivation.

Look For

Motivation may be unconscious. For example, in "Stolen Day" the boy does not fully realize the reasons why he acts as he does. As you read "Stolen Day," look for the motivation behind the boy's behavior.

Writing

Has a beautiful spring day ever made you feel like stealing a day from a chore that had to be done? Freewrite, explaining the reasons you might give for taking a day off.

Vocabulary

Knowing the following words will help you as you read "Stolen Day."
inflammatory (in flam′ə tôr′ē) *adj.*: Characterized by pain and swelling (p. 89)
rheumatism (rōō′mə tiz′m) *n.*: A painful condition of the joints and muscles (p. 89)
solemn (säl′əm) *adj.*: Serious, somber (p. 90)
carp (kärp) *n.*: A fresh-water fish living in a pond or other quiet water (p. 92)

Objectives

1 To understand a character's motivations
2 To make inferences about a character's motivations
3 To use the root *flam* to figure out the meaning of words
4 To write a diary entry explaining motivations for actions

Support Material

Teaching Portfolio
Teacher Backup, p. 127
Grammar in Action Worksheet, *Varying Sentence Length,* p. 130
Usage and Mechanics Worksheet, p. 132
Vocabulary Check, p. 133
Analyzing Literature Worksheet, *Understanding Motivation,* p. 134

Language Worksheet, *Understanding Latin Roots,* p. 135
Selection Test, p. 136

Stolen Day
Sherwood Anderson

It must be that all children are actors. The whole thing started with a boy on our street named Walter, who had inflammatory rheumatism. That's what they called it. He didn't have to go to school.

Still he could walk about. He could go fishing in the creek or the waterworks pond. There was a place up at the pond where in the spring the water came tumbling over the dam and formed a deep pool. It was a good place. Sometimes you could get some good big ones there.

I went down that way on my way to school one spring morning. It was out of my way but I wanted to see if Walter was there.

He was, inflammatory rheumatism and all. There he was, sitting with a fish pole in his hand. He had been able to walk down there all right.

It was then that my own legs began to hurt. My back too. I went on to school but, at the recess time, I began to cry. I did it when the teacher, Sarah Suggett, had come out into the schoolhouse yard.

She came right over to me.

"I ache all over," I said. I did, too.

I kept on crying and it worked all right.

"You'd better go on home," she said.

So I went. I limped painfully away. I kept on limping until I got out of the schoolhouse street.

Then I felt better. I still had inflammatory rheumatism pretty bad but I could get along better.

I must have done some thinking on the way home.

"I'd better not say I have inflammatory rheumatism." I decided. "Maybe if you've got that you swell up."

A COUNTRY LAD, 1873
Winslow Homer
Cooper-Hewitt Museum

Stolen Day 89

2 Critical Thinking and Reading
Part of what makes this story humorous is that the narrator actually fools himself into thinking he's ill whenever it's convenient. Students should be aware of the speaker's motivation each time he has an "attack." Does the speaker know what he's doing? Discuss the meaning of the term "self-awareness."

3 Discussion What does this tell you about the real condition of the speaker?

4 Discussion What does the mother's reaction to her son's illness suggest about her and the seriousness of his condition?

5 Literary Focus How does knowing the speaker's thoughts heighten the humor of the story?

I thought I'd better go around to where Walter was and ask him about that, so I did—but he wasn't there.

"They must not be biting today," I thought.

I had a feeling that, if I said I had inflammatory rheumatism, Mother or my brothers and my sister Stella might laugh. They did laugh at me pretty often and I didn't like it at all.

"Just the same," I said to myself, "I have got it." I began to hurt and ache again.

I went home and sat on the front steps of our house. I sat there a long time. There wasn't anyone at home but Mother and the two little ones. Ray would have been four or five then and Earl might have been three.

It was Earl who saw me there. I had got tired sitting and was lying on the porch. Earl was always a quiet, solemn little fellow.

He must have said something to Mother for presently she came.

"What's the matter with you? Why aren't you in school?" she asked.

I came pretty near telling her right out that I had inflammatory rheumatism but I thought I'd better not. Mother and Father had been speaking of Walter's case at the table just the day before. "It affects the heart," Father had said. That frightened me when I thought of it. "I might die," I thought. "I might just suddenly die right here; my heart might stop beating."

On the day before I had been running a race with my brother Irve. We were up at the fairgrounds after school and there was a half-mile track.

"I'll bet you can't run a half-mile," he said. "I bet you I could beat you running clear around the track."

And so we did it and I beat him, but afterwards my heart did seem to beat pretty hard. I remembered that lying there on the porch. "It's a wonder, with my inflammatory

rheumatism and all, I didn't just drop down dead," I thought. The thought frightened me a lot. I ached worse than ever.

"I ache, Ma," I said. "I just ache."

She made me go in the house and upstairs and get into bed.

It wasn't so good. It was spring. I was up there for perhaps an hour, maybe two, and then I felt better.

I got up and went downstairs. "I feel better, Ma," I said.

Mother said she was glad. She was pretty busy that day and hadn't paid much attention to me. She had made me get into bed upstairs and then hadn't even come up to see how I was.

I didn't think much of that when I was up there but when I got downstairs where she was, and when, after I had said I felt better and she only said she was glad and went right on with her work, I began to ache again.

I thought, "I'll bet I die of it. I bet I do."

I went out to the front porch and sat down. I was pretty sore at Mother.

"If she really knew the truth, that I have the inflammatory rheumatism and I may just drop down dead any time, I'll bet she wouldn't care about that either," I thought.

I was getting more and more angry the more thinking I did.

"I know what I'm going to do," I thought; "I'm going to go fishing."

I thought that, feeling the way I did, I might be sitting on the high bank just above the deep pool where the water went over the dam, and suddenly my heart would stop beating.

And then, of course, I'd pitch forward, over the bank into the pool and, if I wasn't dead when I hit the water, I'd drown sure.

They would all come home to supper and they'd miss me.

"But where is he?"

90   *Short Stories*

Grammar in Action

Why do writers vary the length of their sentences? **Varying sentence length** between long and short sentences makes a passage smooth and flowing. The reader's interest is captured by the mixture of simple, compound, and complex sentences.

Too many of the same type of sentence can make a passage boring and difficult to read. Notice the way that Sherwood Anderson varies the length of his sentences in the following passage:

And so we did it and I beat him, but afterwards my heart did seem to beat pretty hard. I remembered that lying there on the porch. "It's a wonder, with my inflammatory rheumatism and all, I didn't just drop down dead," I thought. The thought frightened me a lot. I ached worse than ever.

Student Activity 1. Find another passage where Anderson varies the length of his sentences. Explain why the passage is effective.

Student Activity 2. Rewrite the following passages so that the sentence length is varied and each passage is, consequently, more lively and interesting.

Then Mother would remember that I'd come home from school aching.

She'd go upstairs and I wouldn't be there. One day during the year before, there was a child got drowned in a spring. It was one of the Wyatt children.

Right down at the end of the street there was a spring under a birch tree and there had been a barrel sunk in the ground.

Everyone had always been saying the spring ought to be kept covered, but it wasn't.

So the Wyatt child went down there, playing around alone, and fell in and got drowned.

Mother was the one who had found the drowned child. She had gone to get a pail of water and there the child was, drowned and dead.

This had been in the evening when we were all at home, and Mother had come run-

YOUNG FISHERMAN, 1889
Louis Michel Eilshemius
Hirshhorn Museum and Sculpture Garden

Stolen Day 91

6

6 Discussion How does the brief description of a real tragedy contrast with what the speaker is going through?

Humanities Note

Fine art, *Young Fisherman*, by Louis Michel Eilshemius. Louis Michel Eilshemius (1864–1941) was born in New Jersey and had extensive training in academic art at Cornell University, the Art Students' League in New York City, and at Academie Julien in Paris under the famous French artist Bouguereau. In addition to painting, Eilshemius published songs, poems, and essays on art.

Eilshemius is remembered as a "primitive" painter. But his early art was in the classical style. The painting *Young Fisherman*, painted in 1889, is from his classical period. This well-mannered and sensitively painted landscape reveals the painter's love of nature. Although there is a hint of the simplification of form that later dominated his work, this painting reflects the skill and polish of the academic tradition in which Eilshemius was trained.

1. Would this scene have caused the narrator of the story an "attack" of inflammatory rheumatism? Why?
2. Do you think the narrator would have had an "attack" if he lived in the city? How well does he relate to nature?

1. When Jane came home from school that Friday afternoon, she immediately saw that the back door, which lead into the dark, seldom-used basement and which was always locked, was wide open, and she faintly heard muffled footsteps making their careful way around the unlit room, and she felt scared stiff, but just then her mother appeared at the door and asked Jane to get her a lightbulb; whew, what a relief.

2. Over the grass a land turtle crawled. The turtle was brown and golden. He moved along clumsily. He dragged his rounded shell over the grass. The turtle was not really walking. He was just hoisting and tugging along his shell. He made a beaten path on the grass.

7 Critical Thinking and Reading
Point out this contradiction, and have students identify the incongruity between the phrases "grand time" and "having died." How is this typical of what makes the story funny?

8 Discussion What is wrong with the speaker's thinking? Why is it not valid or logical? Why is self-diagnosis generally not a good idea?

9 Clarification The word "freshet" means that there was a sudden overflowing of the pond probably due to the spring thaw. The rush of water caused the dam to break and water and fish to spill into the creek.

10 Reading Strategy Have students summarize the events that have occurred so far in the story and predict how the story will end.

11 Discussion Contrast how the mother acts now with her actions earlier in the story when her son came home from school.

12 Discussion What does the speaker mean now when he says the aching isn't in his legs or back? Compare his "suffering" throughout the story with how he feels at the end of the story.

Reader's Response At the end of the story, do you feel sorry for the narrator or do you think he got what he deserved? Explain.

ning up the street with the dead, dripping child in her arms. She was making for the Wyatt house as hard as she could run, and she was pale.

She had a terrible look on her face. I remembered then.

"So," I thought, "they'll miss me and there'll be a search made. Very likely there'll be someone who has seen me sitting by the pond fishing, and there'll be a big alarm and all the town will turn out and they'll drag the pond."

7 I was having a grand time, having died. Maybe, after they found me and had got me out of the deep pool, Mother would grab me up in her arms and run home with me as she had run with the Wyatt child.

I got up from the porch and went around the house. I got my fishing pole and lit out for the pool below the dam. Mother was busy—she always was—and didn't see me go. When I got there I thought I'd better not sit too near the edge of the high bank.

By this time I didn't ache hardly at all, but I thought.

8 "With inflammatory rheumatism you can't tell," I thought.

"It probably comes and goes," I thought.

"Walter has it and he goes fishing," I thought.

I had got my line into the pool and suddenly I got a bite. It was a regular whopper. I knew that. I'd never had a bite like that.

I knew what it was. It was one of Mr. Fenn's big carp.

Mr. Fenn was a man who had a big pond of his own. He sold ice in the summer and the pond was to make the ice. He had bought some big carp and put them into his pond and then, earlier in the spring **9** when there was a freshet, his dam had gone out.

So the carp had got into our creek and one or two big ones had been caught—but none of them by a boy like me.

The carp was pulling and I was pulling and I was afraid he'd break my line, so I just tumbled down the high bank holding onto the line and got right into the pool. We had **10** it out, there in the pool. We struggled. We wrestled. Then I got a hand under his gills and got him out.

He was a big one all right. He was nearly half as big as I was myself. I had him on the bank and I kept one hand under his gills and I ran.

I never ran so hard in my life. He was slippery, and now and then he wriggled out of my arms; once I stumbled and fell on him, but I got him home.

So there it was. I was a big hero that day. Mother got a washtub and filled it with water. She put the fish in it and all the neighbors came to look. I got into dry clothes and went down to supper—and then I made a break that spoiled my day.

There we were, all of us, at the table, and suddenly Father asked what had been the matter with me at school. He had met the teacher, Sarah Suggett, on the street and she had told him how I had become ill.

"What was the matter with you?" Father asked, and before I thought what I was saying I let it out.

"I had the inflammatory rheumatism," I said—and a shout went up. It made me sick to hear them, the way they all laughed.

It brought back all the aching again, and like a fool I began to cry.

"Well, I *have* got it—I *have*, I *have*," I cried, and I got up from the table and ran upstairs.

I stayed there until Mother came up. I **11** knew it would be a long time before I heard the last of the inflammatory rheumatism. I **12** was sick all right, but the aching I now had wasn't in my legs or in my back.

THINKING ABOUT THE SELECTION

Recalling

1. What happens to the boy in school?
2. How does the father find out that his son left school that day?
3. How do the members of the boy's family respond when he tells them he has inflammatory rheumatism?

Interpreting

4. Why does the boy stop limping once he gets away from the schoolhouse street?
5. What does the boy mean when he says, "I was having a grand time, having died."?
6. Why does he say this?
7. At the end of the story, the boy says, "I was sick all right, but the aching I now had wasn't in my legs or in my back." What do these words indicate?

Applying

8. To *justify* means "to provide good grounds or reasons for something." Why do people sometimes try to justify their behavior, even when they know that what they have done is wrong?

ANALYZING LITERATURE

Understanding Motivation

Motivation is the cause for characters' actions. It moves them to do what they do, to pursue their goals. Often, a powerful emotion can be a strong motivation. Understanding a character's motives gives you deeper insight into a story.

1. Why does the boy think he is ill?
2. Why does the boy at first not tell his family that he has inflammatory rheumatism?
3. Do you think the boy is fully conscious of his motives? Why or why not?

CRITICAL THINKING AND READING

Making Inferences About Motivation

Sometimes a character's motives are not directly stated. You must use the information avail-

able in the story to make an **inference,** or draw a reasonable conclusion, about them. For example, you can infer that the narrator would like to be able to go fishing on this spring day. The author does not tell you that directly, but you can infer it from the following information: The narrator goes by the pond on his way to school to see if Walter is there; and he feels that Walter can go fishing despite having inflammatory rheumatism.

What inference can you make about the narrator's motivation from the following sentences?

a. "Mother . . . hadn't paid much attention to me. She had made me get into bed upstairs and then hadn't even come up to see how I was."

b. "Maybe . . . Mother would grab me up in her arms and run home with me as she had run in with the Wyatt child."

UNDERSTANDING LANGUAGE

Using the Root *flam*

A **root** of a word is the part from which others grow. For example, the root in *inflammatory* is *flam,* meaning "flame." Knowing word roots can help you figure out the meaning of new words.

In a dictionary, find the definition of each of the following words. Show how it comes from the meaning of *flam*. Then use each word in a sentence.

1. inflame
2. flammable
3. flamboyant

THINKING AND WRITING

Writing a Diary Entry

Imagine that you are the narrator of this story. Write a diary entry in which you explain your behavior on this day. Include why you left school, why you got out of bed and went fishing, and what you imagined might happen if you fell in the pool. As you revise, check that what you have written explains your motivation.

Stolen Day   93

Focus

More About the Author Although Amy Tan always considered herself American, when she visited China for the first time she said, "As soon as my feet touched China, I became Chinese." Why do you think she had this reaction? Her mother predicted she would have this reaction. How could her mother know what her reaction would be?

Literary Focus Lead students to see that the characterization in television shows or movies is most often indirect. Because it is visual, it is preferable for the viewers to see and hear what the characters say and do, rather than be told directly.

Look For You might tell students that this story is told by a character in the story, the narrator. Discuss with students how this limits what we can know.

Writing/Prior Knowledge Before students freewrite, have them comment about the meaning of the sentence, "You can be anything you want to be in America." Discuss possible interpretations, such as "People have equal opportunities" or "People have no limitations."

Vocabulary Have students work with partners to write a short paragraph using all the vocabulary words.

Objectives

1 To understand characterization
2 To make inferences about character
3 To write about characters

Two Kinds

Amy Tan (1952–   ) was born in Oakland, California, two and a half years after her parents moved to the United States from China. Her parents expected her to become a doctor full-time and be a concert pianist in her spare time. Instead, Tan became a writer. "Two Kinds," an episode from the novel *Joy Luck Club,* expresses a similar conflict between the hopes and expectations of Chinese-immigrant parents and the desire of their Americanized child to make her own choices.

Direct and Indirect Characterization

Characterization is the art of making people in a story real. Authors can present characters in a **direct** or an **indirect** way. They present characters directly by simply telling you what they want you to know about a character. They develop characters indirectly by letting the characters reveal their personalities through what they think, say, or do. The narrator in "Two Kinds" is a woman recounting a part of her childhood. Sometimes the narrator makes direct statements about the characters, including herself, while at other times she lets you learn about the characters indirectly through what they say and do.

Look For

As you read "Two Kinds," imagine that you are meeting two new neighbors—a young girl and her mother. What are they like? Are they similar to you or to people you know? Look for what the narrator directly tells you about the characters. Also notice what she reveals about herself and her mother indirectly, through their behavior and their words.

Writing

"Two Kinds" begins with the following sentence: "My mother believed you could be anything you wanted to be in America." Freewrite, explaining whether you agree or disagree with the mother's belief.

Vocabulary

Knowing the following words will help you as you read "Two Kinds."
prodigy (präd′ ə jē) *n.*: A child of unusually high talent (p. 95)
reproach (ri prōch′) *n.*: Disgrace; blame (p. 96)
mesmerizing (mez′ mər īz′ iŋ) *adj.*: Hypnotizing (p. 97)
sauciness (sô′ sē nes) *n.*: Liveliness, spirit (p. 97)
reverie (rev′ ər ē) *n.*: Dreamy thinking or imagining (p. 99)
dawdled (dôd′ 'ld) *v.*: Wasted time by being slow (p. 100)
debut (dā byoo′) *n.*: First appearance in public (p. 100)
fiasco (fē as′ kō) *n.*: A complete failure (p. 101)

94   *Short Stories*

Support Material

Teaching Portfolio
Teacher Backup, p. 139
Grammar in Action Worksheets, *Recognizing Coordinating Conjunctions,* p. 143; *Understanding Compound Predicates,* p. 145
Usage and Mechanics Worksheet, p. 147
Vocabulary Check, p. 148

Analyzing Literature Worksheet, *Understanding Direct and Indirect Characterization,* p. 149
Language Worksheet, *Understanding Information Found in a Dictionary,* p. 150
Selection Test, p. 151

Two Kinds

from *The Joy Luck Club*

Amy Tan

My mother believed you could be anything you wanted to be in America. You could open a restaurant. You could work for the government and get good retirement. You could buy a house with almost no money down. You could become rich. You could become instantly famous.

"Of course you can be prodigy, too," my mother told me when I was nine. "You can be best anything. What does Auntie Lindo know? Her daughter, she is only best tricky."

America was where all my mother's hopes lay. She had come here in 1949 after losing everything in China: her mother and father, her family home, her first husband, and two daughters, twin baby girls. But she never looked back with regret. There were so many ways for things to get better.

We didn't immediately pick the right kind of prodigy. At first my mother thought I could be a Chinese Shirley Temple.[1] We'd watch Shirley's old movies on TV as though they were training films. My mother would poke my arm and say, *"Ni kan"*[2]—You watch. And I would see Shirley tapping her feet, or singing a sailor song, or pursing her lips into a very round O while saying, "Oh my goodness."

"Ni kan," said my mother as Shirley's eyes flooded with tears. "You already know how. Don't need talent for crying!"

Soon after my mother got this idea about Shirley Temple, she took me to a beauty training school in the Mission district[3] and put me in the hands of a student who could barely hold the scissors without shaking. Instead of getting big fat curls, I emerged with an uneven mass of crinkly black fuzz. My mother dragged me off to the bathroom and tried to wet down my hair.

"You look like Negro Chinese," she lamented, as if I had done this on purpose.

The instructor of the beauty training school had to lop off these soggy clumps to make my hair even again. "Peter Pan[4] is very popular these days," the instructor assured my mother. I now had hair the length of a boy's, with straight-across bangs that hung at a slant two inches above my eyebrows. I liked the haircut and it made me actually look forward to my future fame.

In fact, in the beginning, I was just as excited as my mother, maybe even more so. I

---

1. Shirley Temple: Shirley Temple was the most popular child movie star of the 1930's. She starred in her first picture at the age of three and achieved stardom in *Stand Up and Cheer* in 1934.
2. Ni (nē) **kan** (kän)

3. Mission district: A residential district in San Francisco, a city on the coast of California.
4. Peter Pan: The main character of J. M. Barrie's play of the same name, Peter Pan is a young boy who runs away to Never-Never Land to escape growing up. The success of the play led to the popularity of a short, boyish hairstyle for young girls.

Two Kinds 95

Presentation

Motivation/Prior Knowledge What are some of the things parents expect from their children? Why might parents have such expectations? Tell students that they are about to read a story about a mother's hopes for her daughter and her daughter's reaction to these hopes.

Purpose-Setting Question How do the daughter's expectations for herself differ from her mother's expectations for her.

Master Teacher Note Explain that the term, "generation gap," was first used in the 1960's when young people were questioning and breaking away from previously accepted ideas of older generations. What other "gaps" exist between groups of people? Tell students to look for evidence of a cultural gap as well as a generational gap in this story.

1 **Discussion** Are all these expectations realistic? What do her expectations indicate about the mother's character?

2 **Literary Focus** How does the use of dialect help to bring the character to life?

3 **Critical Thinking and Reading** What does this comment reveal about the mother's character?

4 **Reading Strategy** What does this statement suggest about what might happen?

5 **Clarification** Shirley Temple had long hair with big, fat curls.

Thematic Idea Conflict resulting from parental expectations is also a theme in the short story "Last Cover," on page 57, and in the nonfiction selection "No Gumption," on page 329. You might want to present these selections as a group.

ESL Teaching Strategy Students may not be aware that the mother's dialogue in this selection is in nonstandard English. Point this out, emphasizing that the author is not being derogatory, but using the mother's speech patterns as another way of making the character real to readers. With students, analyze the nonstandard elements in the mother's speech.

6 **Literary Focus** In which sentences in this paragraph does the author use direct characterization? Which sentences are examples of indirect characterization?

7 **Discussion** Why does the narrator fear she will be nothing?

8 **Critical Thinking and Reading** How does the fact that the mother cleans other people's houses help you to understand her expectations for a better life for her daughter?

9 **Critical Thinking and Reading** What do these tests reveal about the mother's character? About her hopes and expectations?

10 **Discussion** What began to die? Why does the mother's disappointment affect her daughter so strongly?

11 **Discussion** Why is the narrator's angry side her "prodigy side"? Why does she feel powerful?

pictured this prodigy part of me as many different images, trying each one on for size. I was a dainty ballerina girl standing by the curtains, waiting to hear the right music that would send me floating on my tiptoes. I was like the Christ child lifted out of the straw manger, crying with holy indignity. I was Cinderella[5] stepping from her pumpkin carriage with sparkly cartoon music filling the air.

In all of my imaginings, I was filled with a sense that I would soon become *perfect*. My mother and father would adore me. I would be beyond reproach. I would never feel the need to sulk for anything.

But sometimes the prodigy in me became impatient. "If you don't hurry up and get me out of here, I'm disappearing for good," it warned. "And then you'll always be nothing.

Every night after dinner, my mother and I would sit at the Formica[6] kitchen table. She would present new tests, taking her examples from stories of amazing children she had read in *Ripley's Believe It or Not*, or *Good Housekeeping, Reader's Digest*, and a dozen other magazines she kept in a pile in our bathroom. My mother got these magazines from people whose houses she cleaned. And since she cleaned many houses each week, we had a great assortment. She would look through them all, searching for stories about remarkable children.

The first night she brought out a story about a three-year-old boy who knew the capitals of all the states and even most of the European countries. A teacher was quoted as saying the little boy could also pronounce the names of the foreign cities correctly.

"What's the capital of Finland?" my mother asked me, looking at the magazine story.

All I knew was the capital of California, because Sacramento was the name of the street we lived on in Chinatown. "Nairobi!"[7] I guessed, saying the most foreign word I could think of. She checked to see if that was possibly one way to pronounce "Helsinki"[8] before showing me the answer.

The tests got harder—multiplying numbers in my head, finding the queen of hearts in a deck of cards, trying to stand on my head without using my hands, predicting the daily temperatures in Los Angeles, New York, and London.

One night I had to look at a page from the Bible for three minutes and then report everything I could remember. "Now Jehoshaphat had riches and honor in abundance and . . . that's all I remember, Ma," I said.

And after seeing my mother's disappointed face once again, something inside of me began to die. I hated the tests, the raised hopes and failed expectations. Before going to bed that night, I looked in the mirror above the bathroom sink and when I saw only my face staring back—and that it would always be this ordinary face—I began to cry. Such a sad, ugly girl! I made high-pitched noises like a crazed animal, trying to scratch out the face in the mirror.

And then I saw what seemed to be the prodigy side of me—because I had never seen that face before. I looked at my reflection, blinking so I could see more clearly. The girl staring back at me was angry,

---

5. Cinderella: The main character in a fairy tale about a young girl who has been mistreated by her stepmother. Her fairy godmother appears and magically changes her dress into a beautiful gown. A pumpkin is changed into a carriage, allowing her to go to the prince's ball.

6. Formica (fôr mī′ kə): Tradename for heat-resistant plastic used for table and counter tops.

7. Nairobi (nī rō′ bē): The capital of Kenya, a country in eastern Africa.

8. Helsinki (hel′ siŋ kē)

Grammar in Action

Writers use **coordinating conjunctions** to join ideas. The words *and, or, but, for, so, yet,* and *nor* are coordinating conjunctions. Usually, coordinating conjunctions are used to connect two independent clauses in a compound sentence. For example, in the compound sentence, "I would like to join you, but I am too busy," but is a coordinating conjunction. As a rule, it is considered incorrect to begin a sentence with a coordinating conjunction. Writers, however, sometimes break this rule to make a sentence stand out.

Notice how Amy Tan emphasizes the second sentence in the following pair by beginning it with the coordinating conjunction *and*:

"Too late change this," said my mother shrilly.
And I could sense her anger rising to its breaking point.

Had Tan followed the traditional grammar rule, she would have written the following:

"Too late change this," said my mother shrilly, and I could sense her anger rising to its breaking point.

As you can see, the emphasis is lost by combining the two thoughts into one sentence.

powerful. This girl and I were the same. I had new thoughts, willful thoughts, or rather thoughts filled with lots of won'ts. I won't let her change me, I promised myself. I won't be what I'm not.

So now on nights when my mother presented her tests, I performed listlessly, my head propped on one arm. I pretended to be bored. And I was. I got so bored I started counting the bellows of the foghorns out on the bay while my mother drilled me in other areas. The sound was comforting and reminded me of the cow jumping over the moon. And the next day, I played a game with myself, seeing if my mother would give up on me before eight bellows. After a while I usually counted only one, maybe two bellows at most. At last she was beginning to give up hope.

Two or three months had gone by without any mention of my being a prodigy again. And then one day my mother was watching *The Ed Sullivan Show*[9] on TV. The TV was old and the sound kept shorting out. Every time my mother got halfway up from the sofa to adjust the set, the sound would go back on and Ed would be talking. As soon as she sat down, Ed would go silent again. She got up, the TV broke into loud piano music. She sat down. Silence. Up and down, back and forth, quiet and loud. It was like a stiff embraceless dance between her and the TV set. Finally she stood by the set with her hand on the sound dial.

She seemed entranced by the music, a little frenzied piano piece with this mesmerizing quality, sort of quick passages and then teasing lilting ones before it returned to the quick playful parts.

"*Ni kan*," my mother said, calling me

over with hurried hand gestures, "Look here."

I could see why my mother was fascinated by the music. It was being pounded out by a little Chinese girl, about nine years old, with a Peter Pan haircut. The girl had the sauciness of a Shirley Temple. She was proudly modest like a proper Chinese child. And she also did this fancy sweep of a curtsy, so that the fluffy skirt of her white dress cascaded slowly to the floor like the petals of a large carnation.

In spite of these warning signs, I wasn't worried. Our family had no piano and we couldn't afford to buy one, let alone reams of sheet music and piano lessons. So I could be generous in my comments when my mother bad-mouthed the little girl on TV.

"Play note right, but doesn't sound good! No singing sound," complained my mother.

"What are you picking on her for?" I said carelessly. "She's pretty good. Maybe she's not the best, but she's trying hard." I knew almost immediately I would be sorry I said that.

"Just like you," she said. "Not the best. Because you not trying." She gave a little huff as she let go of the sound dial and sat down on the sofa.

The little Chinese girl sat down also to play an encore of "Anitra's Dance" by Grieg.[10] I remember the song, because later on I had to learn how to play it.

Three days after watching *The Ed Sullivan Show*, my mother told me what my schedule would be for piano lessons and piano practice. She had talked to Mr. Chong, who lived on the first floor of our apartment

---

9. The Ed Sullivan Show: A popular variety show hosted by Ed Sullivan that ran from 1955 to 1971.

10. Grieg (grēg): Edvard Grieg (1843–1907) was a Norwegian composer. He became known as "the Voice of Norway" because he used material from his native country—folk tales and native poetry—for composing his music.

Two Kinds 97

---

12 Clarification The setting is San Francisco, California, and the bay referred to is San Francisco Bay.

13 Clarification This is a reference to a line from the following nursery rhyme: "Hey, diddle, diddle,/ The cat and the fiddle,/The cow jumped over the moon;/The little dog laughed/To see such sport,/ And the dish ran away with the spoon." Perhaps the rhythm of the foghorns reminded the narrator of the rhythm of the poem.

14 Discussion What might have happened if the daughter had confronted her mother with her feelings about the tests instead of playing this game? What does this game indicate about the narrator's character?

15 Reading Stragedy You might want students to summarize the "warning signs" to which the narrator is referring. Then, they might predict what these signs warn of.

16 Reading Strategy How is this statement a clue of what is to come? What do you think will be the mother's next plan for the daughter?

It is important to remember that while writers sometimes bend grammar rules, they do it sparingly, and only to achieve a specific effect.

Student Activity 1. Find three other sentences in the selection that begin with a coordinating conjunction. Following traditional grammar rules, rewrite each sentence, combining it with another sentence if necessary.

Student Activity 2. Rewrite the following compound sentences. Break each sentence into two and begin the second sentence with the coordinating conjunction.

1. The narrator was sure no one would notice her mistakes, but the whispering in the audience proved her wrong.

2. She finally reached the end of the piece, and she was relieved.

3. She knew that she could survive the embarrassment, for the recital would soon be over.

Fine art, *Atelier*, by Byron Birdsall. Birdsall (1937–) is an American artist who works with watercolor and stone.

The title of this painting, *Atelier*, (at''l ya), is the French word for an artist's studio or workroom. Here, it is a room in which someone plays the piano. In the painting, we see both the piano and the music book only in part. We do not see the keyboard at all. The space is dominated by the lamp and the framed picture. Perhaps this is what the invisible pianist sees as she or he plays.

You might use the following questions for class discussion:
1. Which parts of the painting are dark? Which parts are light?
2. What is the mood of the painting? How do color and light contribute to the mood?
3. Who or what else might be in this room? Try to imagine what scenes might take place here.
4. Which characters in the story may have had this vision?

17 Discussion Do you agree that the mother is acting only for her daughter's sake? For whose sake might she also be acting?

18 Literary Focus Is this description direct or indirect characterization? Explain.

building. Mr. Chong was a retired piano teacher and my mother had traded house-cleaning services for weekly lessons and a piano for me to practice on every day, two hours a day, from four until six.

When my mother told me this, I felt as though I had been sent to hell. I whined and then kicked my foot a little when I couldn't stand it anymore.

"Why don't you like me the way I am? I'm *not* a genius! I can't play the piano. And even if I could, I wouldn't go on TV if you paid me a million dollars!" I cried.

ATELIER
Byron Birdsall
Artique, Ltd.

My mother slapped me. "Who ask you be genius?" she shouted. "Only ask you be your best. For you sake. You think I want you be genius? Hnnh! What for! Who ask you!"

"So ungrateful," I heard her mutter in Chinese. "If she had as much talent as she has temper, she would be famous now."

Mr. Chong, whom I secretly nicknamed Old Chong, was very strange, always tapping his fingers to the silent music of an invisible orchestra. He looked ancient in my eyes. He had lost most of the hair on top of his head and he wore thick glasses and had eyes that always looked tired and sleepy. But he must have been younger than I thought, since he lived with his mother and was not yet married.

I met Old Lady Chong once and that was enough. She had this peculiar smell like a baby that had done something in its pants. And her fingers felt like a dead person's, like an old peach I once found in the back of the refrigerator; the skin just slid off the meat when I picked it up.

I soon found out why Old Chong had retired from teaching piano. He was deaf. "Like Beethoven!"[11] he shouted to me. "We're both listening only in our head!" And he would start to conduct his frantic silent sonatas.[12]

Our lessons went like this. He would open the book and point to different things, explaining their purpose: "Key! Treble! Bass! No sharps or flats! So this is C major![13] Listen now and play after me!"

---
11. Beethoven (bā' tō vən): Ludvig van Beethoven (1770–1827) is considered to be one of the greatest composers ever. Like Old Chong, Beethoven became deaf. His illness began in 1801 and became worse until he was completely deaf by 1817. Despite this handicap, Beethoven continued to compose and created some of his best pieces during this time.
12. sonatas (sə nät' əz) *n.*: Musical compostions for one or two instruments.
13. Key! Treble! . . . C major!: Musical terms used for composing and reading sheet music.

Grammar in Action

Two or more verbs that have the same subject are called a compound predicate. The verbs in a compound predicate are joined by a conjunction--usually *or, but,* or *and*. Writers use compound predicates to combine related ideas from shorter sentences. In the following three short sentences, notice how the predicates are related and can be combined in the fourth sentence:

The narrator's mother *was born* in China.

The narrator's mother *grew up* in China.

The narrator's mother *moved to* the United States after the war.

The narrator's mother *was born* and *grew up* in China but *moved to* the United States after the war.

Notice that the conjunctions *and* and *but* join the predicates in the fourth sentence. What subject do the predicates share?

Amy Tan uses compound predicates in sentences such as the following:

I *whined* and then *kicked* my foot a little when I couldn't stand it anymore.

And then he would play the C scale a few times, a simple chord, and then, as if inspired by an old, unreachable itch, he gradually added more notes and running trills and a pounding bass until the music was really something quite grand.

I would play after him, the simple scale, the simple chord, and then I just played some nonsense that sounded like a cat running up and down on top of garbage cans. Old Chong smiled and applauded and then said, "Very good! But now you must learn to keep time!"

So that's how I discovered that Old Chong's eyes were too slow to keep up with the wrong notes I was playing. He went through the motions in half-time. To help me keep rhythm, he stood behind me, pushing down on my right shoulder for every beat. He balanced pennies on top of my wrists so I would keep them still as I slowly played scales and arpeggios.[14] He had me curve my hand around an apple and keep that shape when playing chords. He marched stiffly to show me how to make each finger dance up and down, staccato[15] like an obedient little soldier.

He taught me all these things, and that was how I also learned I could be lazy and get away with mistakes, lots of mistakes. If I hit the wrong notes because I hadn't practiced enough, I never corrected myself. I just kept playing in rhythm. And Old Chong kept conducting his own private reverie.

So maybe I never really gave myself a fair chance. I did pick up the basics pretty quickly, and I might have become a good pianist at that young age. But I was so determined not to try, not to be anybody different

that I learned to play only the most ear-splitting preludes, the most discordant hymns.

Over the next year, I practiced like this, dutifully in my own way. And then one day I heard my mother and her friend Lindo Jong both talking in a loud bragging tone of voice so others could hear. It was after church, and I was leaning against the brick wall wearing a dress with stiff white petticoats.[16] Auntie Lindo's daughter, Waverly, who was about my age, was standing farther down the wall about five feet away. We had grown up together and shared all the closeness of two sisters squabbling over crayons and dolls. In other words, for the most part, we hated each other. I thought she was snotty. Waverly Jong had gained a certain amount of fame as "Chinatown's Littlest Chinese Chess Champion."

"She bring home too many trophy," lamented Auntie Lindo that Sunday. "All day she play chess. All day I have no time do nothing but dust off her winnings." She threw a scolding look at Waverly, who pretended not to see her.

"You lucky you don't have this problem," said Auntie Lindo with a sigh to my mother.

And my mother squared her shoulders and bragged: "Our problem worser than yours. If we ask Jing-mei wash dish, she hear nothing but music. It's like you can't stop this natural talent."

And right then, I was determined to put a stop to her foolish pride.

A few weeks later, Old Chong and my mother conspired to have me play in a talent show which would be held in the church hall. By then, my parents had saved up enough to buy me a secondhand piano, a black Wurlitzer spinet[17] with a scarred

---

14. **arpeggios** (är pej′ ōz) *n.*: The notes in a chord played in quick succession instead of at the same time.
15. **staccato** (stə kät′ ō) *adj.*: Played with distinct breaks between notes.

16. **petticoats** (pet′ ē kōts′) *n.*: Lace or ruffles at the hemline of a skirt.
17. **spinet** (spin′ it) *n.*: A small, upright piano.

Two Kinds　99

---

19 Discussion Why was the narrator so determined not to be successful with her piano lessons?

20 Reading Strategy What is the humor in this passage?

21 Reading Strategy Now the reader understands what the mother was referring to when she called Auntie Lindo's daughter "best tricky" at the beginning of the selection. Why did the author wait until now to make this clear?

22 Critical Thinking and Reading What does the mother's lie reveal about her?

23 Reading Strategy On the basis of this sentence, what can you predict about what is to come?

We *had grown up* together and *shared* all the closeness of two sisters . . .

Old Chong *smiled* and *applauded* and then *said* . . .

Tan uses the compound predicates to connect two closely related thoughts in one sentence. In all three cases, she uses the conjunction *and* to join the predicates.

Student Activity 1. Find four other examples of compound verbs, from "Two Kinds." For each example, identify the predicates, the conjunction or conjunctions that join the predicates, and the subject that the predicates share.

Student Activity 2. Combine the following pairs of short sentences into a single sentence with a compound predicate.

1. a. The narrator did not want to change.
   b. The narrator resented her mother's efforts to make her a prodigy.
2. a. The narrator thought she would perform well at the recital.
   b. The narrator made many mistakes during her performance.

24 Enrichment/Master Teacher Note *Scenes from Childhood* is a series of short pieces in which Schumann musically depicts events and feelings of childhood. The titles of other pieces in the work are "A Curious Story," "Catch Me," "Frightening," "Dreaming," and "The Night of the Rockinghorse." You might play a recording of "Pleading Child" for the class. If you plan to play the other pieces, wait until the end of the selection.

25 Clarification The "repeat parts" are the sections of the piece that are to be repeated. If the repeats are taken twice, the section of the piece would be played three times, making the piece longer.

26 Discussion What might be some reasons for this being the narrator's favorite part of her performance?

27 Reading Strategy Have students predict how the narrator's performance will go. On what events or statements do they base their predictions?

bench. It was the showpiece of our living room.

For the talent show, I was to play a piece called "Pleading Child" from Schumann's[18] *Scenes from Childhood*. It was a simple, moody piece that sounded more difficult than it was. I was supposed to memorize the whole thing, playing the repeat parts twice to make the piece sound longer. But I dawdled over it, playing a few bars and then cheating, looking up to see what notes followed. I never really listened to what I was playing. I daydreamed about being somewhere else, about being someone else.

The part I liked to practice best was the fancy curtsy: right foot out, touch the rose on the carpet with a pointed foot, sweep to the side, left leg bends, look up and smile.

My parents invited all the couples from the Joy Luck Club[19] to witness my debut. Auntie Lindo and Uncle Tin were there. Waverly and her two older brothers had also come. The first two rows were filled with children both younger and older than I was. The littlest ones got to go first. They recited simple nursery rhymes, squawked out tunes on miniature violins, twirled Hula Hoops,[20] pranced in pink ballet tutus,[21] and when they bowed or curtsied, the audience would sigh in unison, "Awww," and then clap enthusiastically.

When my turn came, I was very confident. I remember my childish excitement. It was as if I knew, without a doubt, that the

---

18. Schumann (shōō' män): Robert Alexander Schumann (1810–1856) was a German composer and music critic and a leader of classical music's Romantic Movement.

19. The Joy Luck Club: Four chinese women who have been meeting for years to socialize, play games, and tell stories from the past.

20. Hula (hōō' lə) **Hoops:** Light hoops twirled around the body by rotating the hips.

21. tutus (tōō' tōōz') *n.*: Very short skirts worn by ballerinas.

prodigy side of me really did exist. I had no fear whatsoever, no nervousness. I remember thinking to myself, This is it! This is it! I looked out over the audience, at my mother's blank face, my father's yawn, Auntie Lindo's stiff-lipped smile, Waverly's sulky expression. I had on a white dress layered with sheets of lace, and a pink bow in my Peter Pan haircut. As I sat down I envisioned people jumping to their feet and Ed Sullivan rushing up to introduce me to everyone on TV.

And I started to play. It was so beautiful. I was so caught up in how lovely I looked that at first I didn't worry how I would sound. So it was a surprise to me when I hit the first wrong note and I realized something didn't sound quite right. And then I hit another and another followed that. A chill started at the top of my head and began to trickle down. Yet I couldn't stop playing, as though my hands were bewitched. I kept thinking my fingers would adjust themselves back, like a train switching to the right track. I played this strange jumble through two repeats, the sour notes staying with me all the way to the end.

When I stood up, I discovered my legs were shaking. Maybe I had just been nervous and the audience, like Old Chong, had seen me go through the right motions and had not heard anything wrong at all. I swept my right foot out, went down on my knee, looked up and smiled. The room was quiet, except for Old Chong, who was beaming and shouting, "Bravo! Bravo! Well done!" But then I saw my mother's face, her stricken face. The audience clapped weakly, and as I walked back to my chair, with my whole face quivering as I tried not to cry, I heard a little boy whisper loudly to his mother, "That was awful," and the mother whispered back, "Well, she certainly tried."

And now I realized how many people were in the audience, the whole world it

Commentary

Earlier in Amy Tan's novel, *The Joy Luck Club,* the reader learns that the narrator's mother lost her first two children fleeing from the Japanese Army in China. Japan began its attacks on China in 1931, and launched an all-out invasion in 1937. By 1939, the Japanese controlled most of eastern China. From that point until the end of World War II in 1945, Japan continued its attacks. The conclusion of the war brought no relief for the Chinese people, as the country became torn by civil war. All of this strife led to the deaths of countless Chinese people. It is no wonder then that the narrator's mother, along with many other Chinese people, looked to the United States for a better life for herself and her family. How might the mother's experiences in China affect her attitude about life in the United States? What problems for Amy Tan might result from growing up influenced by two cultures? What advantages?

seemed. I was aware of eyes burning into my back. I felt the shame of my mother and father as they sat stiffly throughout the rest of the show.

We could have escaped during intermission. Pride and some strange sense of honor must have anchored my parents to their chairs. And so we watched it all: the eighteen-year-old boy with a fake mustache who did a magic show and juggled flaming hoops while riding a unicycle. The breasted girl with white makeup who sang from *Madama Butterfly* and got honorable mention. And the eleven-year-old boy who won first prize playing a tricky violin song that sounded like a busy bee.

After the show, the Hsus, the Jongs, and the St. Clairs from the Joy Luck Club came up to my mother and father.

"Lots of talented kids," Auntie Lindo said vaguely, smiling broadly.

"That was somethin' else," said my father, and I wondered if he was referring to me in a humorous way, or whether he even remembered what I had done.

Waverly looked at me and shrugged her shoulders. "You aren't a genius like me," she said matter-of-factly. And if I hadn't felt so bad, I would have pulled her braids and punched her stomach.

But my mother's expression was what devastated me: a quiet, blank look that said she had lost everything. I felt the same way, and it seemed as if everybody were now coming up, like gawkers at the scene of an accident, to see what parts were actually missing. When we got on the bus to go home, my father was humming the busy-bee tune and my mother was silent. I kept thinking she wanted to wait until we got home before shouting at me. But when my father unlocked the door to our apartment, my mother walked in and then went to the back, into the bedroom. No accusations. No blame.

Amy Tan as a child playing the piano

And in a way, I felt disappointed. I had been waiting for her to start shouting, so I could shout back and cry and blame her for all my misery.

I assumed my talent-show fiasco meant I never had to play the piano again. But two days later, after school, my mother came out of the kitchen and saw me watching TV.

"Four clock," she reminded me as if it were any other day. I was stunned, as though she were asking me to go through the talent-show torture again. I wedged myself more tightly in front of the TV.

"Turn off TV," she called from the kitchen five minutes later.

I didn't budge. And then I decided. I didn't have to do what my mother said anymore. I wasn't her slave. This wasn't China. I had listened to her before and look what happened. She was the stupid one.

She came out from the kitchen and stood in the arched entryway of the living

Two Kinds 101

28 Critical Thinking and Reading Why is Auntie Lindo smiling? What does this action tell you about her?

29 Discussion This is the first and only time the father speaks. What does the fact that he speaks only once indicate about his importance in this story?

30 Discussion Why does the narrator, like her mother, feel that "she had lost everything," just because she performed badly in a piano recital? What has each lost?

31 Clarification One aspect of traditional Chinese culture is that children are expected to be completely obedient to the wishes of their elders, especially their parents. Why might this custom be more difficult for Chinese children growing up in the United States to accept than children growing up in China?

Primary Source

Although many of the ideas and feelings in *The Joy Luck Club*—the novel from which "Two Kinds" is a chapter—come from the author's experience, Amy Tan says that the stories are fictional. "It sounds like a paradox, but fiction is a much better vehicle for writing about an emotional truth." (*Newsweek*, April 17, 1989) Explain to students that a paradox is a statement that seems to be contradictory but, on reflection, is based on truth. You might ask students why fiction might be a better way for some people to write about true emotions than nonfiction.

32 Critical Thinking and Reading
What had been inside the narrator all along? What does she mean by her "true self"? What does this reveal about her?

33 Critical Thinking and Reading
Why do the narrator's words scare her? Why does it also make her feel good that her "awful side . . . had surfaced"? What is her "awful side"?

34 Discussion Why do the "magic words" seem to defeat the mother, rather than make her angry?

35 Literary Focus How does the author's use of figurative language in this passage affect your feelings about the mother?

36 Discussion Do you agree that falling short of her mother's expectations was the narrator's right? Support your answer.

37 Clarification Stanford is a very prestigious and highly competitive university in California.

38 Discussion How do you interpret these lines? Do you think the narrator was incapable of getting A's or graduating from college? Or might something else have stopped her? If so, what?

39 Discussion What is the effect of her mother's giving up hope?

40 Discussion What might have been the mother's reason for offering the piano to her daughter? What do you think the piano represented to the mother?

room. "Four clock," she said once again, louder.

"I'm not going to play anymore," I said nonchalantly. "Why should I? I'm not a genius."

She walked over and stood in front of the TV. I saw her chest was heaving up and down in an angry way.

32 "No!" I said, and I now felt stronger, as if my true self had finally emerged. So this was what had been inside me all along.

"No! I won't!" I screamed

She yanked me by the arm, pulled me off the floor, snapped off the TV. She was frighteningly strong, half pulling, half carrying me toward the piano as I kicked the throw rugs under my feet. She lifted me up and onto the hard bench. I was sobbing by now, looking at her bitterly. Her chest was heaving even more and her mouth was open, smiling crazily as if she were pleased I was crying.

"You want me to be someone that I'm not!" I sobbed. "I'll never be the kind of daughter you want me to be!"

"Only two kinds of daughters," she shouted in Chinese. "Those who are obedient and those who follow their own mind! Only one kind of daughter can live in this house. Obedient daughter!"

33 "Then I wish I wasn't your daughter. I wish you weren't my mother," I shouted. As I said these things I got scared. It felt like worms and toads and slimy things crawling out of my chest, but it also felt good, as if this awful side of me had surfaced, at last.

"Too late change this," said my mother shrilly.

And I could sense her anger rising to its breaking point. I wanted to see it spill over. And that's when I remembered the babies she had lost in China, the ones we never talked about. "Then I wish I'd never been **34** born!" I shouted. "I wish I were dead! Like them."

It was as if I had said the magic words. Alakazam!—and her face went blank, her mouth closed, her arms went slack, and she backed out of the room, stunned, as if she were blowing away like a small brown leaf, **35** thin, brittle, lifeless.

It was not the only disappointment my mother felt in me. In the years that followed, I failed her so many times, each time asserting my own will, my right to fall short of expectations. I didn't get straight A's. I didn't **36** become class president. I didn't get into Stanford. I dropped out of college. **37**

For unlike my mother, I did not believe I could be anything I wanted to be. I could **38** only be me.

And for all those years, we never talked about the disaster at the recital or my terrible accusations afterward at the piano bench. All that remained unchecked, like a betrayal that was now unspeakable. So I never found a way to ask her why she had hoped for something so large that failure was inevitable.

And even worse, I never asked her what **39** frightened me the most: Why had she given up hope?

For after our struggle at the piano, she never mentioned my playing again. The lessons stopped. The lid to the piano was closed, shutting out the dust, my misery, and her dreams.

So she surprised me. A few years ago, **40** she offered to give me the piano, for my thirtieth birthday. I had not played in all those years. I saw the offer as a sign of forgiveness, a tremendous burden removed.

"Are you sure?" I asked shyly. "I mean, won't you and Dad miss it?"

"No, this your piano," she said firmly. "Always your piano. You only one can play."

"Well, I probably can't play anymore," I said. "It's been years."

Collaborative Learning Working in groups, students could write the dialogue that might have taken place between mother and daughter if the narrator had "found a way to ask her (mother) why she had hoped for something so large that failure was inevitable." Have groups get together and brainstorm two lists of character traits, one for the narrator and one for the mother. As they write their dialogues, they should use their lists as a guide to what each character might say. After groups complete first drafts, suggest they read their dialogues aloud to get a good idea of whether their characters sound true to the story. As they revise, they could include notes on the appropriate tones of voice to use, and make sure characters use details and examples from the story to bring life to their discussion. After groups have proofread their dialogues, they can present them to the class.

"You pick up fast," said my mother, as if she knew this was certain. "You have natural talent. You could been genius if you want to."

"No I couldn't."

"You just not trying," said my mother. And she was neither angry nor sad. She said it as if to announce a fact that could never be disproved. "Take it," she said.

But I didn't at first. It was enough that she had offered it to me. And after that, every time I saw it in my parents' living room, standing in front of the bay windows, it made me feel proud, as if it were a shiny trophy I had won back.

Last week I sent a tuner over to my parents' apartment and had the piano reconditioned, for purely sentimental reasons. My mother had died a few months before and I had been getting things in order for my father, a little bit at a time. I put the jewelry in special silk pouches. The sweaters she had knitted in yellow, pink, bright orange—all the colors I hated—I put those in moth-proof boxes. I found some old Chinese silk dresses, the kind with little slits up the sides. I rubbed the old silk against my skin, then wrapped them in tissue and decided to take them home with me.

After I had the piano tuned, I opened the lid and touched the keys. It sounded even richer than I remembered. Really, it was a very good piano. Inside the bench were the same exercise notes with handwritten scales, the same secondhand music books with their covers held together with yellow tape.

I opened up the Schumann book to the dark little piece I had played at the recital. It was on the left-hand side of the page, "Pleading Child." It looked more difficult than I remembered. I played a few bars, surprised at how easily the notes came back to me.

And for the first time, or so it seemed, I noticed the piece on the right-hand side. It was called "Perfectly Contented." I tried to play this one as well. It had a lighter melody but the same flowing rhythm and turned out to be quite easy. "Pleading Child" was shorter but slower; "Perfectly Contented" was longer, but faster. And after I played them both a few times, I realized they were two halves of the same song.

THINKING ABOUT THE SELECTION

Recalling

1. Name the ways the mother tries to make her daughter a prodigy.
2. How does the narrator react to her mother's efforts to make her a prodigy?
3. How does the mother arrange to get her daughter access to a piano and lessons?
4. Describe the narrator's experience at the talent show.
5. What happens when the mother tries to get the narrator to continue practicing the piano after the talent show?

Interpreting

6. The narrator's mother does not regret her losses in China because, in America, "There were so many ways for things to get better." How are her hopes for her daughter a reflection of this attitude?
7. Why does the narrator react as she does to

Two Kinds 103

41 **Discussion** Why didn't the daughter take the piano at first?

42 **Critical Thinking and Reading** Why does the narrator tell us that the sweaters were in all the colors that she hated? What does this indicate about the narrator?

43 **Discussion** Why do you think the narrator took the Chinese silk dresses home with her?

44 **Clarification** When a piece of music, or any work of art, is described as "dark," it usually means that the work, in some way, evokes the unpleasant side of human nature. In this case "Pleading Child," has a moody, brooding quality, in contrast to "Perfectly Contented," which sounds lighter and sunnier. Based on this information, why is it appropriate that the piece she played at the recital was a "dark piece"? Why is it appropriate that she only now realizes that "Perfectly Contented" is part of the same set of songs?

Enrichment The author of this selection uses dialect as a way of making a character real to the reader. Recommend to students other works in which characters speak in dialect (the short story "The Luckiest Time of All" on page 75, the poem "When the Frost Is on the Punkin" on page 512).

Reader's Response With which character in this selection do you sympathize—the mother or the daughter? Is it possible to sympathize with both? Explain your response.

Closure and Extension

ANSWERS TO THINKING ABOUT THE SELECTION
Recalling

1. The mother wants her daughter to be a child actress, to be like the amazing children she reads about, to be a concert pianist.
2. First, the narrator tries to fulfill her mother's expectations; then she rebels.
3. The mother trades housecleaning services for access to a piano and lessons.
4. Although she did not practice, the narrator felt confident before she began playing. When she began to play and make mistakes, she hoped no one would notice. When she finished and realized how bad she sounded, she was humiliated.
5. The narrator refuses.

Interpreting

6. The mother hopes that her daughter will become important or even famous in America and believes there are many ways for her to achieve fame.
7. Answers may differ. Suggested Response: At first the narrator goes along with her mother's efforts because she, too, wants to become famous. However, the narrator soon comes to believe that her mother is trying to make her into someone other than herself, and she wants to be loved for who she is.

8. Answers will differ. Suggested Response: The narrator may fear that her mother has given up on her completely.

9. Suggested Response: The narrator may feel that by reclaiming the piano she is making peace with her mother.

10. Suggested Response: Perhaps both songs represent the narrator's feelings about her childhood. She had remembered "Pleading Child" before she made peace with her mother. This represented all their difficult times. She realizes that "Perfectly Contented" is part of the same song after she resolves these bad feelings. This might represent many of the good memories she has of childhood that she did not think of before.

Applying

11. Answers will differ. Suggested Response: The daughter could have been anything she wanted to be if she had realized that all she wanted was to be herself and then tried to make the most of herself. It is possible to agree with both the mother and the daughter if being anything you want to be is interpreted to mean having the opportunity to fulfill one's potential.

ANALYZING LITERATURE

1. Answers will differ. One possible example is the narrator's refusal to make a serious effort to play the piano well.

2. Anwers will differ. One example is Old Chong's conducting "frantic silent sonatas."

CRITICAL THINKING AND READING

1. Answers may differ. Suggested response: The mother was determined and willing to make sacrifices to get what she wanted for her daughter.

2. Answers may differ. One possible answer is that the mother was determined to maintain complete control over her daughter.

her mother's efforts to change her?

8. The narrator recalls that what frightened her most about her mother was that she had "given up hope" after their last fight. Why does this frighten the narrator most?

9. Why does the narrator reclaim the piano years later?

10. Reread the last paragraph. How can "Perfectly Contented" and "Pleading Child" be two halves of the same song?

Applying

11. The narrator in the story says, "For unlike my mother, I did not believe I could be anything I wanted to be. I could only be me." Do you agree or disagree with her? Explain your answer. Is it possible to agree with both the mother and the daughter? Explain.

ANALYZING LITERATURE
Understanding Characterization

In "Two Kinds" Amy Tan uses both **direct** and **indirect characterization** to give flesh and blood to her characters—to bring them to life. For example, the narrator states directly, "My mother believed you could be anything you wanted to be in America." The author reveals this indirectly through her mother's actions and statements, such as when her mother says, "Of course you can be prodigy, too . . . You can be best anything."

Read the following direct statements made the narrator. For each, find one example in the story that reveals the same trait indirectly.
1. "I had new thoughts, willful thoughts, or rather thoughts filled with lots of won'ts. I won't let her change me."

2. "Mr. Chong, whom I secretly nicknamed Old Chong, was very strange . . ."

CRITICAL THINKING AND READING
Making Inferences About Character

An **inference** is a reasonable conclusion that you draw from information given. When an author uses indirect characterization, you must make inferences based on a character's thoughts, words, and actions.

What can you infer about the narrator's mother from the following lines from "Two Kinds"?
1. ". . . my mother had traded housecleaning services for weekly lessons and a piano for me to practice on every day . . ."
2. " 'Only two kinds of daughters,' . . . 'Those who are obedient and those who follow their own mind! Only one kind of daughter can live in this house. Obedient daughter!' "

THINKING AND WRITING
Writing About Characters

Often, people view the same situation differently. In this story, the narrator and her mother view the narrator's abilities differently. Make two columns on a sheet of paper. In one column write the narrator's view of her abilities and hopes. In the other column, write the mother's view of her daughter's abilities and her hopes for her daughter. Write a description of these two views, and explain how the hopes and desires of the narrator and the mother determine how each views the narrator's abilities. When you revise, be sure you have clearly presented the reasons for the different views.

THINKING AND WRITING

For help with this assignment, students can refer to Lesson 9, "Writing About Character," on page 797 in the Handbook of Writing About Literature.

Challenge "Two Kinds" is a work of fiction, yet the girl in the selection resembles the author in many ways. Have students write a piece about a fictional event in which they are the main character.

Setting

EARLY SUMMER ON THE FARM
Karl Rodko
Three Lions

Humanities Note

Fine art, *Early Summer on the Farm,* Karl Rodko. *Early Summer on the Farm* by Karl Rodko is painted in the great landscape tradition. The rural setting with brook, farm, and boy fishing is reminiscent of the works of John Constable and Thomas Gainsborough. The truth of form and fresh, bright colors add to the balance and harmony of the composition. An able painter, Rodko handles the difficulties of rendering foliage and water with skill. His admiration for the out of doors is apparent in this lovely setting for the delights of a summer afternoon.

Focus

More About the Author Ray Bradbury does not drive a car and has never flown. Yet his fantastic imagination allows his readers to enter all kinds of strange worlds, some as far away as Venus. Ask students to account for the gap between an author's fiction and his life. Why do people assume that a science-fiction writer leads an adventurous life?

Literary Focus Setting can be crucial to plot since where the action takes place often affects the outcome. For example, a debate among students in a classroom does not have far-reaching implications, while a debate among justices in the Supreme Court could have results that would affect millions of people.

Look For Students who are **less advanced** may not be aware of all the details that go into describing a setting. It may be helpful to preview the Analyzing Literature questions on page 111 so that these questions can guide their reading.

Writing/Prior Knowledge Have students discuss the importance of the sun in their lives and how they feel on a rainy day. Then have them complete the freewriting assignment. For extra credit, you might ask them to use their freewriting as the basis for a formal composition.

Vocabulary Have **less advanced** students read these words aloud so that you can be sure they can pronounce them.

Teaching to Ability Levels You may want to have **more advanced** students try writing a poem about the sun or an ode to the sun along the lines of Margot's poem on the first page of the story.

All Summer in a Day

Ray Bradbury (1920–   ) was born in Waukegan, Illinois. As a boy, he was fascinated with magicians, circuses, and the stories of Edgar Allan Poe. These early interests influenced Bradbury's development as one of our best writers of fantasy and science fiction. His many honors and awards include membership in the National Institute of Arts and Letters. In "All Summer in a Day," you will enter Bradbury's world of gripping fantasy—a strange yet oddly believable world.

Setting

Setting is the time and place of a short story's action. In some stories, setting is little more than background, but in others it is of central importance. In "All Summer in a Day," for example, everything that happens depends on the setting: Venus, at a time when interplanetary travel is possible.

Look For

As you read the story, picture the strange world of Bradbury's Venus. Look for the details the author includes to make this place come alive for you. Imagine what it would be like to live and go to school there with the young people you are reading about. Would you like to live on Venus?

Writing

Imagine that you have traveled by rocket to Venus and, wearing a spacesuit, can explore the planet. What sights might you see? What might it feel like to be there? Freewrite about Venus as you imagine it.

Vocabulary

Knowing the following words will help you as you read "All Summer in a Day."

concussion (kən kush′ən) *n.*: Violent shaking (p. 107)

slackening (slak′'n iŋ) *v.*: Becoming less active (p. 107)

surged (sʉrjd) *v.*: Moved in a violent swelling motion (p. 109)

immense (i mens′) *adj.*: Vast (p. 109)

tumultuously (tōō mul′choo wəs lē) *adv.*: Noisy and violently (p. 110)

resilient (ri zil′yənt) *adj.*: Springing back into shape (p. 110)

savored (sā′vərd) *v.*: Enjoyed (p. 110)

Objectives

1 To understand the setting of a short story
2 To understand the effect of the setting on the plot
3 To write a letter describing a place

Support Material

Teaching Portfolio
Teacher Backup, p. 153
Grammar in Action Worksheet, *Concrete Words*, p. 156
Usage and Mechanics Worksheet, p. 158
Vocabulary Check, p. 159
Analyzing Literature Worksheet, *Understanding Setting*, p. 160

Language Worksheet, *Using Vivid Adjectives*, p. 161
Selection Test, p. 162
Library of Video Classics: *All Summer In a Day*

All Summer in a Day

Ray Bradbury

"Ready?"

"Ready."

"Now?"

"Soon."

"Do the scientists really know? Will it happen today, will it?"

"Look, look; see for yourself!"

The children pressed to each other like so many roses, so many weeds, intermixed, peering out for a look at the hidden sun.

It rained.

It had been raining for seven years; thousands upon thousands of days compounded and filled from one end to the other with rain, with the drum and gush of water, with the sweet crystal fall of showers and the concussion of storms so heavy they were tidal waves come over the islands. A thousand forests had been crushed under the rain and grown up a thousand times to be crushed again. And this was the way life was forever on the planet Venus and this was the schoolroom of the children of the rocket men and women who had come to a raining world to set up civilization and live out their lives.

"It's stopping, it's stopping!"

"Yes, yes!"

Margot stood apart from them, from these children who could never remember a time when there wasn't rain and rain and rain. They were all nine years old, and if there had been a day, seven years ago, when the sun came out for an hour and showed its face to the stunned world, they could not recall. Sometimes, at night, she heard them stir, in remembrance, and she knew they were dreaming and remembering gold or a yellow crayon or a coin large enough to buy the world with. She knew they thought they remembered a warmness, like a blushing in the face, in the body, in the arms and legs and trembling hands. But then they always awoke to the tatting drum, the endless shaking down of clear bead necklaces upon the roof, the walk, the gardens, the forests, and their dreams were gone.

All day yesterday they had read in class about the sun. About how like a lemon it was, and how hot. And they had written small stories or essays or poems about it:

> *I think the sun is a flower,*
> *That blooms for just one hour.*

That was Margot's poem, read in a quiet voice in the still classroom while the rain was falling outside.

"Aw, you didn't write that!" protested one of the boys.

"I did," said Margot. "I *did*."

"William!" said the teacher.

But that was yesterday. Now the rain was slackening, and the children were crushed in the great thick windows.

"Where's teacher?"

"She'll be back."

"She'd better hurry, we'll miss it!"

They turned on themselves, like a feverish wheel, all fumbling spokes.

Margot stood alone. She was a very frail girl who looked as if she had been lost in the rain for years and the rain had washed out

All Summer in a Day   107

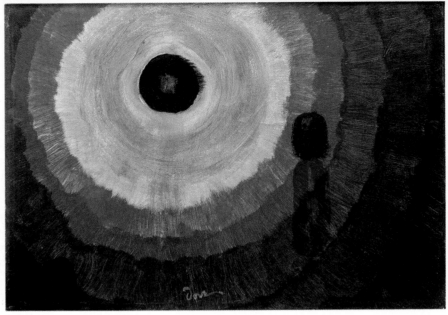

SUNRISE IV
Arthur Dove
Hirshhorn Museum and Scupture Garden

the blue from her eyes and the red from her mouth and the yellow from her hair. She was
3 an old photograph dusted from an album, whitened away, and if she spoke at all her voice would be a ghost. Now she stood, separate, staring at the rain and the loud wet world beyond the huge glass.

"What're *you* looking at?" said William. Margot said nothing.

"Speak when you're spoken to." He gave her a shove. But she did not move; rather she let herself be moved only by him and nothing else.

4 They edged away from her, they would not look at her. She felt them go away. And this was because she would play no games with them in the echoing tunnels of the underground city. If they tagged her and ran, she stood blinking after them and did not follow. When the class sang songs about happiness and life and games her lips barely moved. Only when they sang about the sun and the summer did her lips move as she watched the drenched windows.

And then, of course, the biggest crime of all was that she had come here only five years ago from Earth, and she remembered the sun and the way the sun was and the sky was when she was four in Ohio. And they, they had been on Venus all their lives, and they had been only two years old when last the sun came out and had long since forgotten the color and heat of it and the way it really was. But Margot remembered.

"It's like a penny," she said once, eyes closed.

"No, it's not!" the children cried.

"It's like a fire," she said, "in the stove."

"You're lying, you don't remember!" cried the children.

But she remembered and stood quietly

108   Short Stories

apart from all of them and watched the patterning windows. And once, a month ago, she had refused to shower in the school shower rooms, had clutched her hands to her ears and over her head, screaming the water mustn't touch her head. So after that, dimly, dimly, she sensed it, she was different and they knew her difference and kept away.

There was talk that her father and mother were taking her back to Earth next year; it seemed vital to her that they do so, though it would mean the loss of thousands of dollars to her family. And so, the children hated her for all these reasons of big and little consequence. They hated her pale snow face, her waiting silence, her thinness, and her possible future.

"Get away!" The boy gave her another push. "What're you waiting for?"

Then, for the first time, she turned and looked at him. And what she was waiting for was in her eyes.

"Well, don't wait around here!" cried the boy savagely. "You won't see nothing!"

Her lips moved.

"Nothing!" he cried. "It was all a joke, wasn't it?" He turned to the other children. "Nothing's happening today. *Is* it?"

They all blinked at him and then, understanding, laughed and shook their heads. "Nothing, nothing!"

"Oh, but," Margot whispered, her eyes helpless. "But this is the day, the scientists predict, they say, they *know*, the sun . . ."

"All a joke!" said the boy, and seized her roughly. "Hey, everyone, let's put her in a closet before teacher comes!"

"No," said Margot, falling back.

They surged about her, caught her up and bore her, protesting, and then pleading, and then crying, back into a tunnel, a room, a closet, where they slammed and locked the door. They stood looking at the door and saw it tremble from her beating and throwing herself against it. They heard her muffled cries. Then, smiling, they turned and went out and back down the tunnel, just as the teacher arrived.

"Ready, children?" She glanced at her watch.

"Yes!" said everyone.

"Are we all here?"

"Yes!"

The rain slackened still more.

They crowded to the huge door.

The rain stopped.

It was as if, in the midst of a film concerning an avalanche, a tornado, a hurricane, a volcanic eruption, something had, first, gone wrong with the sound apparatus, thus muffling and finally cutting off all noise, all of the blasts and repercussions and thunders, and then, second, ripped the film from the projector and inserted in its place a peaceful tropical slide which did not move or tremor. The world ground to a standstill. The silence was so immense and unbelievable that you felt your ears had been stuffed or you had lost your hearing altogether. The children put their hands to their ears. They stood apart. The door slid back and the smell of the silent, waiting world came in to them.

The sun came out.

It was the color of flaming bronze and it was very large. And the sky around it was a blazing blue tile color. And the jungle burned with sunlight as the children, released from their spell, rushed out, yelling, into the springtime.

"Now, don't go too far," called the teacher after them. "You've only two hours, you know. You wouldn't want to get caught out!"

But they were running and turning their faces up to the sky and feeling the sun on their cheeks like a warm iron; they were taking off their jackets and letting the sun burn their arms.

"Oh, it's better than the sun lamps, isn't it?"

"Much, much better!"

All Summer in a Day   109

5 Discussion What role does jealousy play in the students' hostility toward Margot?

6 Reading Strategy What do you predict will happen now?

7 Literary Focus Onomatopeia plays a major role in establishing the setting and atmosphere of the story. Venus is a noisy place because of the continuous rain. Now, as preparation for the appearance of the sun, the author quiets the setting down.

Master Teacher Note The Hudson River School was the name of the first group of American artists to develop a characteristic style of landscape painting. Some artists of this school were Thomas Cole, Asher B. Durand, Frederick E. Church, and Jasper F. Cropsey. Their style was popular from about 1825 to the late 1800's.

Bring in some examples of paintings from the Hudson River School in which the sun's rays illuminate and deeply enrich the entire painting. These paintings are a tribute to the beauty and importance of the sun.

Student Activity 1. Find three other sentences from "All Summer in a Day" in which Bradbury effectively uses concrete words that appeal to your senses of sight, hearing, and feeling.

Student Activity 2. Write five original sentences using concrete words to appeal to the five senses: sight, sound, touch, taste, and smell. Write one sentence for each sense.

8 Clarification The Venusian atmosphere consists mostly of carbon dioxide. The surface of Venus is covered with thick clouds made mostly of sulfuric acid. Venus has only very small traces of water vapor. The surface temperature is about 480°C. Obviously, there is no plant life on Venus.

9 Discussion Why can you relate to what the children are feeling as they play in the sun? Why is their play so frenzied?

10 Discussion How do the children feel now? Did they seem to change while the sun was shining? How will they act now?

11 Literary Focus The reappearance of the rain is introduced with a "boom of thunder." The equation in this story has been rain-noise, sun-silence. Have students scan the story for "sound" words and "silence" words.

12 Discussion How did the children feel about what they did to Margot? How serious a prank was locking her in a closet?

13 Reading Strategy Predict what Margot will say to the children who locked her in the closet. Summarize the impact this incident will have on Margot.

Reader's Response How do you feel about the children in Margot's class? Why?

---

8 They stopped running and stood in the great jungle that covered Venus, that grew and never stopped growing, tumultuously, even as you watched it. It was a nest of octopi, clustering up great arms of fleshlike weed, wavering, flowering in this brief spring. It was the color of rubber and ash, this jungle, from the many years without sun. It was the color of stones and white cheeses and ink, and it was the color of the moon.

9 The children lay out, laughing, on the jungle mattress, and heard it sigh and squeak under them, resilient and alive. They ran among the trees, they slipped and fell, they pushed each other, they played hide-and-seek and tag, but most of all they squinted at the sun until tears ran down their faces, they put their hands up to that yellowness and that amazing blueness and they breathed of the fresh, fresh air and listened and listened to the silence which suspended them in a blessed sea of no sound and no motion. They looked at everything and savored everything. Then, wildly, like animals escaped from their caves, they ran and ran in shouting circles. They ran for an hour and did not stop running.

And then—

In the midst of their running one of the girls wailed.

Everyone stopped.

The girl, standing in the open, held out her hand.

"Oh, look, look," she said, trembling.

They came slowly to look at her opened palm.

In the center of it, cupped and huge, was a single raindrop.

She began to cry, looking at it.

They glanced quietly at the sky.

"Oh. Oh."

10 A few cold drops fell on their noses and their cheeks and their mouths. The sun faded behind a stir of mist. A wind blew cool around them. They turned and started to walk back toward the underground house, their hands at their sides, their smiles vanishing away.

11 A boom of thunder startled them and like leaves before a new hurricane, they tumbled upon each other and ran. Lightning struck ten miles away, five miles away, a mile, a half mile. The sky darkened into midnight in a flash.

They stood in the doorway of the underground for a moment until it was raining hard. Then they closed the door and heard the gigantic sound of the rain falling in tons and avalanches, everywhere and forever.

"Will it be seven more years?"

"Yes. Seven."

Then one of them gave a little cry.

"Margot!"

"What?"

"She's still in the closet where we locked her."

"Margot."

12 They stood as if someone had driven them, like so many stakes, into the floor. They looked at each other and then looked away. They glanced out at the world that was raining now and raining and raining steadily. They could not meet each other's glances. Their faces were solemn and pale. They looked at their hands and feet, their faces down.

"Margot."

One of the girls said, "Well . . .?"

No one moved.

"Go on," whispered the girl.

They walked slowly down the hall in the sound of cold rain. They turned through the doorway to the room in the sound of the storm and thunder, lightning on their faces, blue and terrible. They walked over to the closet door slowly and stood by it.

Behind the closet door was only silence.

13 They unlocked the door, even more slowly, and let Margot out.

110   Short Stories

Closure and Extension

THINKING ABOUT THE SELECTION

Recalling

1. At the start of the story, why are all the children excited?
2. In what way is Margot's experience of the sun different from the experience of all the other children on Venus?
3. How does this difference affect the way Margot gets along with her classmates?
4. What do the children do to Margot just before the rain stops?
5. What do the children do during the two hours that they are outdoors?.
6. What happens to Margot at the very end?

Interpreting

7. What point is made about Margot when the story says that the rain had washed the blue from her eyes and the red from her mouth and the yellow from her hair?
8. How do the children feel when they remember what they have done to Margot?
9. Having read the story, what do you think the title, "All Summer in a Day," means?

Applying

10. What does this story suggest about the problems individuals face if their backgrounds or experiences make them different from other people?

ANALYZING LITERATURE

Understanding Setting

The **setting** of a story is the time and place of the action. In "All Summer in a Day," Bradbury gives you many details that help you see what Venus is like. For example, in describing the con-

stant rain he says that the children "always awoke to the tatting drum, the endless shaking down of clear bead necklaces upon the roof, the walk, the gardens, the forests . . . ."

1. Point out three other passages that give you a vivid impression of Venus.
2. What is the most significant feature of the setting?
3. Find at least two details that suggest that the time of the action is the future.

CRITICAL THINKING AND READING

Understanding the Effect of Setting

"All Summer in a Day" is a story in which the setting greatly affects the plot. Since the events occur only in a place where it rains almost constantly, this setting affects the way the characters behave.

1. What details of the setting make the story possible?
2. How is Margot affected by Venus?
3. How are the other children affected by it?

THINKING AND WRITING

Writing About Setting

Imagine that you have just arrived on Ray Bradbury's imagined Venus. After spending a day or so looking around, you decide to write a letter to a friend on Earth telling what Venus is like. First list on paper those sights and other details you will focus on. Then write a letter that will give your friend a clear picture of where you are. When you revise your writing, ask "Will my friend see what I am trying to convey? Is every sentence clear and specific?"

(Answers begin on p. 110.)

"Then they closed the door and heard the gigantic sound of rain falling in tons and avalanches, everywhere and forever." (page 110)

2. The most significant feature of the setting is the lack of sun.
3. Two details that suggest that the time of the action is the future are the facts that civilization had been established on Venus by the rocket men and women and that Margot's parents are able to take her back to Earth.

ANSWERS TO CRITICAL THINKING AND READING

1. The details are the constant noise, the rain, the darkness, the strange vegetation, and the children's underground world.
2. Margot has been adversely affected by Venus. She is sensitive, pale, unhappy, and withdrawn. She would not play with the other children and misses Earth and seeing the sun in the sky.
3. The other children on Venus are able to enjoy life, play games, sing songs, and form friendships with one another even though they, too, long for the appearance of the sun and revel in it once it appears. The conditions on Venus may also have made the children insensitive and cruel, as shown by their treatment of Margot.

Challenge How do you think Margot will feel about having missed the sun? Describe her feelings.

THINKING AND WRITING
For help with this assignment, students can refer to Lesson 7, "Writing About Setting," in the Handbook of Writing About Literature.

Writing Across the Curriculum
You might want to inform the science department of this Thinking and Writing assignment. Science teachers might contrast the real Venus with Bradbury's Venus.

Interpreting
7. The rain is draining the life out of Margot.
8. The children feel guilty and somber when they remember Margot.
9. Answers will differ. Suggested Response: The title means that the children were forced to live a whole summer's worth of fun and pleasure in just one day.

Applying
10. Answers will differ. Suggested

Response: People who are different often face a lack of understanding and a certain amount of hostility from other people.

ANSWERS TO ANALYZING LITERATURE
1. Three passages that give you a vivid impression of Venus follow.

"A thousand forests had been crushed under the rain and grown up a thousand times to be crushed again." (page 107)

"It was as if, in the midst of a film concerning an avalanche, a tornado, a hurricane, a volcanic eruption, something had, first, gone wrong with the sound apparatus, thus muffling and finally cutting off all noise, all of the blasts and repercussions and thunders, and then, second, ripped the film from the projector and inserted in its place a peaceful tropical slide which did not move or tremor." (page 109)

More About the Author Sean O'Faolain is one of the major twentieth-century Irish writers. However, his writing has not always been accepted because of his advocacy of an independent Ireland. Ever since the so-called Easter Rebellion of 1916, O'Faolain has been an outspoken supporter of Irish independence from British involvement. Have students discuss how political activism can affect a literary career.

Literary Focus Point out that atmosphere is present in everyday life. For example, there is a certain atmosphere at a pep rally and a completely different atmosphere in a room where a test is being taken.

Look For Less advanced students may find atmosphere a difficult concept to grasp. Explain that atmosphere can be created in many ways. Certain words, colors, smells, and sounds, as well as the setting of a story, can affect atmosphere.

Writing/Prior Knowledge Have students discuss the relationship between setting and literary effect. How important is setting to a story? Then have them complete the freewriting assignment.

Vocabulary These words may also give students some difficulty: *sinewy* (p. 113), *squabbled* (p. 113), *lightsome* (p. 115), and *scuttled* (p. 116). Be sure students know what these words mean as they read the story.

Spelling Tip Have students look at the words *haughty, haughtily*. Tell students that when a word ends in *y*, the *y* usually is changed to *i* when adding a suffix.

GUIDE FOR READING

The Trout

Sean O'Faolain (1900–   ) was born in Cork, Ireland. When he was fifteen, he saw a play about the lives of ordinary Irish people. This play inspired him to write. He has written stories about his country's struggle for independence from England and about life in the Irish countryside, with its pastures, bogs, mountains, and moody charm. In "The Trout" the spirit of rural Ireland is memorably captured.

Atmosphere

Atmosphere, or mood, is the feeling a place awakens in the reader. Such words as *gloomy, haunted, joyful, peaceful, restful, scary,* and *romantic* will give you some idea of the kinds of atmosphere frequently found in stories. The opening paragraphs of "The Trout," for example, present a place whose atmosphere might be described as pleasantly spooky.

Look For

As you read the story, look for the details that make the Laurel walk seem a pleasantly spooky place. Why does the author call it "The Dark Walk"?

Writing

What place have you visited that stands out clearly in your memory because of its beauty, peacefulness, scariness, or other quality of atmosphere? Freewrite about it. Try to describe it in a way that communicates its atmosphere.

Vocabulary

Knowing the following words will help you as you read "The Trout."
incredulous (in krej′oo ləs) *adj.*: unwilling or unable to believe (p. 113)
haughtily (hôt′ə lē) *adv.*: Showing pride in oneself and contempt for others (p. 113)
shrouded (shrou′ d'd) *v.*: Hidden from view (p. 113)

resolutely (rez′ə lo͞ot′lē) *adv.*: In a determined way (p. 115)
superciliously (so͞o′pər sil′ē əs lē) *adv.*: Pridefully, scornfully (p. 116)

Objectives
1 To understand the use of atmosphere
2 To identify the details that create atmosphere
3 To use the suffix *-ly* to create new words
4 To write a paragraph that creates atmosphere

Support Material
Teaching Portfolio
Teacher Backup, p. 165
Grammar in Action Worksheet, *Agreement Between Pronouns and Antecedents*, p. 169
Usage and Mechanics Worksheet, p. 171
Vocabulary Check, p. 172
Critical Thinking and Reading Worksheet, *Identifying Details That Create Atmosphere,* p. 173

Language Worksheet, *Using the Suffix -ly,* p. 174
Selection Test, p. 175
Art Transparency 4, *A Hilly Scene* by Samuel Palmer

The Trout

Sean O'Faolain

One of the first places Julia always ran to when they arrived in G— was The Dark Walk. It is a laurel walk, very old; almost gone wild, a lofty midnight tunnel of smooth, sinewy branches. Underfoot the tough brown leaves are never dry enough to crackle: there is always a suggestion of damp and cool trickle.

She raced right into it. For the first few yards she always had the memory of the sun behind her, then she felt the dusk closing swiftly down on her so that she screamed with pleasure and raced on to reach the light at the far end; and it was always just a little too long in coming so that she emerged gasping, clasping her hands, laughing, drinking in the sun. When she was filled with the heat and glare she would turn and consider the ordeal again.

This year she had the extra joy of showing it to her small brother, and of terrifying him as well as herself. And for him the fear lasted longer because his legs were so short and she had gone out at the far end while he was still screaming and racing.

When they had done this many times they came back to the house to tell everybody that they had done it. He boasted. She mocked. They squabbled.

"Cry baby!"

"You were afraid yourself, so there!"

"I won't take you any more."

"You're a big pig."

"I hate you."

Tears were threatening so somebody said, "Did you see the well?" She opened her eyes at that and held up her long lovely neck suspiciously and decided to be incredulous. She was twelve and at that age little girls are beginning to suspect most stories: they have already found out too many, from Santa Claus to the Stork. How could there be a well! In The Dark Walk? That she had visited year after year? Haughtily she said, "Nonsense."

But she went back, pretending to be going somewhere else, and she found a hole scooped in the rock at the side of the walk, choked with damp leaves, so shrouded by ferns that she only uncovered it after much searching. At the back of this little cavern there was about a quart of water. In the water she suddenly perceived a panting trout. She rushed for Stephen and dragged him to see, and they were both so excited that they were no longer afraid of the darkness as they hunched down and peered in at the fish panting in his tiny prison, his silver stomach going up and down like an engine.

Nobody knew how the trout got there.

Presentation

Motivation/Prior Knowledge Have students imagine that they have found an animal in distress. It is possible for them to rescue the creature, but it involves some risk. Would they rescue the animal? Would it depend on what kind of animal it was? Is a dog more "worth saving" than a fish? Should nature be left alone to "take its course"?

Purpose-Setting Question What significance does the trout have in this story?

Master Teacher Note You might help set the scene for this story with Art Transparency 4, *A Hilly Scene* by Samuel Palmer. Place the transparency on the overhead projector and have students discuss the dark and mysterious atmosphere of the painting. How does the artist create this effect? What kind of a story might be set in such a place?

1 **Discussion** What significance does Julia's age have?

Humanities Note

Fine Art: *Forest Interior,* Thomas Worthington Whittredge. Whittredge (1820–1910) was an American artist of the Hudson River School of painting. The artists in this group specialized in landscape painting. Whittredge found many subjects for his paintings along the banks of the Hudson River and at Lake George. *Forest Interior* was painted in 1882. It is an example of the sort of picturesque scene favored by Whittredge. As in many of his other works, Whittredge uses the landscape to study light. The trees are delineated with beauty and sensitivity but with a minimum of color. The filtered light glows with a special luminosity characteristic of the artists of the Hudson River School. Throughout his career, Whittredge sought to capture the beauty of the Hudson River valley in his paintings.

1. How does the scene in this painting remind you of Julia's Dark Walk? How is it different?
2. Would the beauty of such a landscape contribute to the poignancy of the trout's dilemma?

FOREST INTERIOR, 1882
Thomas Worthington Whittredge
© 1987 The Art Institute of Chicago

Grammar in Action

Writing would become tedious if the writer always had to use nouns to refer to someone or something. Substituting pronouns for nouns makes passages read more smoothly. The word for which the pronoun is substituted is called the **antecedent. Pronouns** have to agree with their **antecedents** in both number and person for a sentence to make sense. If they do not agree in both number and person, then misunderstandings can occur. This is especially true when the pronoun is in a different sentence or passage from its antecedent. Notice in the following passage, how Sean O'Faolain uses pronouns that agree with their antecedents:

> Nobody knew how the trout got there. Even old Martin in the kitchen-garden laughed and refused to believe that *it* was there, ... until she forced *him* to come down and see.

Trout is the antecedent for the pronoun *it,* and *Martin* is the antecedent for the pronoun *him.* Notice how these pronouns agree with their antecedents in both number (they are both singular) and person (*it* refers to the trout, and *him* refers to Martin, who is a

Even old Martin in the kitchen-garden laughed and refused to believe that it was there, or pretended not to believe, until she forced him to come down and see. Kneeling and pushing back his tattered old cap he peered in.

"Be cripes, you're right. How did that fella get there?"

She stared at him suspiciously.

"You knew?" she accused; but he said, "The divil a know"; and reached down to lift it out. Convinced she hauled him back. If she had found it then it was her trout.

Her mother suggested that a bird had carried the spawn. Her father thought that in the winter a small streamlet might have carried it down there as a baby, and it had been safe until the summer came and the water began to dry up. She said, "I see," and went back to look again and consider the matter in private. Her brother remained behind, wanting to hear the whole story of the trout, not really interested in the actual trout but much interested in the story which his mummy began to make up for him on the lines, of, "So one day Daddy Trout and Mammy Trout . . ." When he retailed[1] it to her she said, "Pooh."

It troubled her that the trout was always in the same position; he had no room to turn; all the time the silver belly went up and down; otherwise he was motionless. She wondered what he ate and in between visits to Joey Pony, and the boat and a bath to get cool, she thought of his hunger. She brought him down bits of dough; once she brought him a worm. He ignored the food. He just went on panting. Hunched over him she thought how, all the winter, while she was at school he had been in there. All the winter, in The Dark Walk, all day, all night,

floating around alone. She drew the leaf of her hat down around her ears and chin and stared. She was still thinking of it as she lay in bed.

It was late June, the longest days of the year. The sun had sat still for a week, burning up the world. Although it was after ten o'clock it was still bright and still hot. She lay on her back under a single sheet, with her long legs spread, trying to keep cool. She could see the D of the moon through the fir tree—they slept on the ground floor. Before they went to bed her mummy had told Stephen the story of the trout again, and she, in her bed, had resolutely presented her back to them and read her book. But she had kept one ear cocked.

"And so, in the end, this naughty fish who would not stay at home got bigger and bigger and bigger, and the water got smaller and smaller. . . ."

Passionately she had whirled and cried, "Mummy, don't make it a horrible old moral story!" Her mummy had brought in a Fairy Godmother, then, who sent lots of rain, and filled the well, and a stream poured out and the trout floated away down to the river below. Staring at the moon she knew that there are no such things as Fairy Godmothers and that the trout, down in The Dark Walk, was panting like an engine. She heard somebody unwind a fishing reel. Would the *beasts* fish him out!

She sat up. Stephen was a hot lump of sleep, lazy thing. The Dark Walk would be full of little scraps of moon. She leaped up and looked out the window, and somehow it was not so lightsome now that she saw the dim mountains far away and the black firs against the breathing land and heard a dog say, bark-bark. Quietly she lifted the ewer[2] of

---

1. **retailed** (rē tāld′) *v*.: In this case, it means "told."

2. **ewer** (yōō ər): A large water pitcher with a wide mouth.

2 **Critical Thinking and Reading** Contrast Julia's reaction to the trout with her brother's. What do you learn about each of them? How are they alike and how are they different from one another?

3 **Discussion** Why does Julia get angry at her mother's story about the trout?

The Trout 115

man). There are two other pronouns in these sentences: *there* and *she*. The antecedents for both of these pronouns can be found earlier.

Student Activity 1. Find another passage from "The Trout" in which the pronouns agree with their antecedents. Identify the pronouns and their antecedents, and explain why they agree.

Student Activity 2. Copy the following sentences and fill in the blanks with pronouns that agree in number and person with their antecedents.

1. Mary and Jim are the smartest students in _____ class.

2. My brother learned to cook so that _____ could get a job as a chef.

3. I hoped that Sally would bring some jeans with _____.

4 water, and climbed out the window and scuttled along the cool but cruel gravel down to the maw[3] of the tunnel. Her pajamas were very short so that when she splashed water it wet her ankles. She peered into the tunnel. Something alive rustled inside there.

5 She raced in, and up and down she raced, and flurried, and cried aloud, "Oh, Gosh, I can't find it," and then at last she did. Kneeling down in the damp she put her hand into the slimy hole. When the body lashed they were both mad with fright. But she gripped him and shoved him into the ewer and raced, with her teeth ground, out to the other end of the tunnel and down the steep paths to the river's edge.

All the time she could feel him lashing his tail against the side of the ewer. She was

---

3. **maw** (mô) *n.*: In this case, it means the opening or mouth of the tunnel. This word usually refers to the throat or jaws of an animal.

afraid he would jump right out. The gravel cut into her soles until she came to the cool ooze of the river's bank where the moon mice on the water crept into her feet. She poured out watching until he plopped. For a second he was visible in the water. She hoped he was not dizzy. Then all she saw was the glimmer of the moon in the silent-flowing river, the dark firs, the dim mountains, and the radiant pointed face laughing down at her out of the empty sky. 6

She scuttled up the hill, in the window, plonked down the ewer and flew through the air like a bird into bed. The dog said bark-bark. She heard the fishing reel whirring. She hugged herself and giggled. Like a river of joy her holiday spread before her.

In the morning Stephen rushed to her, shouting that "he" was gone, and asking "where" and "how." Lifting her nose in the air she said superciliously, "Fairy Godmother, I suppose?" and strolled away patting the palms of her hands. 7

THINKING ABOUT THE SELECTION
Recalling

1. Where does Julia find the trout?
2. What is Julia's mother's suggestion for how the trout got into the hole?
3. How does her father think the trout got there?
4. What troubles Julia about the position the trout is in?
5. Summarize the story about the trout that the mother makes up for Stephen.
6. What does Julia do to help the trout?

Interpreting

7. What do you learn about Julia's character from her going into a dark, scary place at night to help the trout?
8. What emotion do you think Julia is feeling in the last paragraph of the story?
9. What effect do you think the whole incident involving the trout has had on Julia?

Applying

10. Imagine Julia as an adult looking back on this incident. What importance to her life might she see in it?

ANALYZING LITERATURE
Understanding Atmosphere

Atmosphere may be thought of as the spirit, or personality, of a place. It is what makes The Dark Walk, for example, more than just a path shaded by trees.

1. Reread the paragraph that begins "It was late June, the longest days of the year" (page 115). How would you describe the atmosphere of Julia's room?
2. Describe the atmosphere of the river where Julia releases the trout.
3. Which three of the following adjectives could be used to describe the atmosphere created by the whole story: *joyful, mysterious, secretive, tense, comical, haunting, sad, peaceful, zany, tragic?*

CRITICAL THINKING AND READING
Identifying Details of Atmosphere

A skillful writer creates atmosphere by using specific details that allow you to "see" a place and feel its atmosphere. In the opening paragraph, for example, O'Faolain says of The Dark Walk, "It is a laurel walk, very old; almost gone wild, a lofty midnight tunnel of smooth, sinewy branches."

What specific details create atmosphere in the description of the river near the end of the story?

UNDERSTANDING LANGUAGE
Using the Adverb Suffix -ly

A **suffix** is one or more syllables added to the end of a word to form a new word. When the suffix -ly is added to an adjective, the adjective is changed into an adverb; for example, the adjective *slow* becomes the adverb *slowly.*

The following six adjectives are from "The Trout." Add the suffix -ly to make each one an adverb. Use the word in a sentence.
1. incredulous   3. mad
2. dim   4. radiant

THINKING AND WRITING
Extending a Story

Extend the story. Describe the river on the morning after Julia has freed the trout. First decide how the river looks. Then decide what atmosphere you wish to convey. Be sure to include specific details to give the reader both the look and the feel of the river as you imagine it. When you revise, concentrate on making your expression of atmosphere as vivid as you can.

The Trout   117

---

life when she changed from a child into a young adult, more aware of the world around her.

ANSWERS TO ANALYZING LITERATURE

1. The atmosphere of Julia's room is peaceful but oppressive because of the heat.
2. The atmosphere of the river is cool, peaceful, quiet, and beautiful.
3. The three adjectives that describe the atmosphere of the whole story are joyful, mysterious, and peaceful.

ANSWERS TO CRITICAL THINKING AND READING

Answers will differ. Suggested Responses: "moon mice on the water," "glimmer of the moon in the silent-flowing river," "the dark firs, the dim mountains, and the radiant pointed face laughing down at her out of the empty sky."

ANSWERS TO UNDERSTANDING LANGUAGE

1. incredulously   3. madly
2. dimly   4. radiantly
Sentences will differ

Challenge What do you think The Dark Walk symbolizes?

THINKING AND WRITING

Publishing Student Writing Have students read their descriptions of atmosphere aloud. Then have students vote for the most evocative descriptions and post them on the bulletin board. Students may want to bring in pictures from magazines that illustrate the written descriptions. These may be added to the bulletin board.

---

3. Her father suggests that in the winter a small streamlet might have carried it down there as a baby fish. Then when the water dried up in the summer, the fish was trapped in the cavern.
4. Julia is troubled that the trout is always in the same position, with no room to turn around.
5. The mother says that the trout was a naughty fish who wouldn't stay home. As he got bigger, the water in the cavern got smaller. Finally, a Fairy Godmother sent lots of rain which filled the well. A stream then poured out of the cavern, carrying the trout with it to the river.
6. Julia carries the trout to the river in a ewer of water. She then releases it into the river.

Interpreting

7. Julia is a strong person and has a well-developed conscience that impels her to do the right thing despite obstacles in her path.

8. Answers will differ. Suggested Response: She feels very proud, triumphant, and joyous.
9. Answers will differ. Suggested Response: Julia has become more self-confident and mature and has become more aware of nature and the value of life.

Applying

10. Answers will differ. Suggested Response: Julia might see this incident as a turning point in her

Caleb's Brother

James Baldwin (1924–1987) was born and raised in New York City. Though he had lived abroad, in Paris, for many years, much of his work was based on his youth in New York. *Go Tell It on the Mountain,* a novel that brought him early fame and recognition as a major black writer, tells of the adolescent experiences of a boy whose life is closely linked to the church in his Harlem neighborhood. In "Caleb's Brother," Baldwin again draws on his youthful experiences in the neighborhood where he grew up.

Atmosphere and Meaning

Atmosphere is the feeling a place awakens in the reader. In many short stories, the atmosphere may be an important part of the story's meaning. It gives you the feeling of what it is like to be in a particular place and helps you to understand the characters and situations you read about.

Look For

As you read "Caleb's Brother," look for the details that make the setting of the story cheerless and even threatening. Try to imagine how Leo's life and feelings are affected by his living in a world whose atmosphere is at times very dreary, and perhaps dangerous.

Writing

"Caleb's Brother" deals in part with a widespread situation, namely, that older boys and girls sometimes hurt the feelings of their younger brothers and sisters by ignoring them and their needs. List reasons why you think they behave this way.

Vocabulary

Knowing the following words will help you as you read "Caleb's Brother."

bravado (brə vä′dō) *n.*: Pretended courage (p. 119)

demeanor (di mēn′ ər) *n.*: Outward behavior, manner (p. 120)

indifferently (in dif′ər ənt lē) *adv.*: As if uninterested (p. 120)

distracted (dis trakt′ id) *adj.*: With the mind drawn away in another direction (p. 120)

decipher (di sī′fər) *v.*: To make out the meaning of (p. 120)

irrevocably (i rev′ ə kə blē) *adv.*: Unchangeably (p. 121)

susceptible (sə sep′tə b'l) *adj.*: Responsive (p. 121)

lethal (lē′thəl) *adj.*: Deadly (p. 121)

tempest (tem′pist) *n.*: A violent storm (p. 123)

Objectives

1 To understand how atmosphere affects characters in a short story
2 To identify the details that create atmosphere
3 To choose the meaning that fits the context
4 To write a comparison/contrast paper about atmosphere

Caleb's Brother

from *Tell Me How Long the Train's Been Gone*

James Baldwin

The hall was dark, smelling of cooking and of boiling diapers. We dropped down the stairs, Caleb going two at a time, pausing at each landing, briefly, to glance back up at me. I dropped down behind him as fast as I could. Sometimes Caleb was in a bad mood and then everything I did was wrong. But when Caleb was in a good mood, it didn't matter that everything I did was wrong. When I reached the street level, Caleb was already on the stoop, joking with some of his friends who were standing in the doorway— who seemed always to be in the doorway, no matter what hour one passed through. I didn't like Caleb's friends because I was afraid of them. I knew the only reason they didn't try to make life miserable for me the way they did for a lot of the other kids was because they were afraid of Caleb. I came through the door, passing between my brother and his friends, down to the sidewalk, feeling, as they looked briefly at me and then continued joking with Caleb, what they felt: that here was Caleb's round-eyed, frail and useless sissy of a little brother. They pitied Caleb for having to take me out. On the other hand, they also wanted to go to the show, but didn't have the money. Therefore, in silence, I could crow over them[1] even as they despised me. But this was always a terribly risky, touch-and-go business, for Caleb might always, at any moment, and with no warning, change his mind and drive me away, and, effectively, take their side against me. I always stood, those Saturday afternoons, in fear and trembling, holding on to the small shield of my bravado, while waiting for Caleb to come down the steps of the stoop, to come down the steps, away from his friends, to me. I prepared myself, always,

_____
1. **crow over them:** To take great pleasure in their bad luck.

JIM, 1930
William H. Johnson
National Museum of American Art

Humanities Note

Fine Art: *Jim,* William Henry Johnson. Johnson (1901–1970) was an American artist known for his paintings done in a primitive style. Even as a boy, Johnson knew that he wanted to be an artist, despite his family's poverty. When he was seventeen, he traveled to New York City and worked his way through the National Academy of Design. He later went to Paris to continue his studies. During the next ten years, he traveled throughout Europe, Scandinavia, and North Africa. His painting style evolved and changed from impressionistic to primitive.

Jim, painted in 1930, is done in the primitive style. The colors are basic and the forms are simple, combining to create a very powerful portrait of a black man. William Johnson was one of the first American painters to use black subjects extensively.

1. Does the man in the painting look like anyone in the story as you pictured him? Why or why not?
2. For Johnson, New York City represented the freedom to pursue his art. Contrast his view with Leo's in the story.

Presentation

Motivation/Prior Knowledge Have students imagine that their plans to accompany an older brother or sister to the movies have been canceled at the last minute. How would they react? Would they have the same problems that Leo has in the story? Can they relate to Leo's fears? Would it be difficult for them to pass the time safely and enjoyably?

Master Teacher Note This story takes place in New York City in the 1930's. The atmosphere of the tenements is dark and threatening, especially to a young boy. Set the mood for this story by bringing in some paintings by George Tooker or some of the inner-city photographs of Edward Steichen. Both Tooker's paintings and Steichen's city photos can lead to a discussion of what generates people's fears in the city.

Purpose-Setting Question How is the city setting responsible for the action in this story?

1 **Clarification** Before disposable diapers, people used cloth diapers, which had to be boiled in hot water to sanitize them before their next use.

2 **Discussion** What kind of boy is Caleb? What impression do you have of him from the friends he keeps?

3 **Discussion** How can you tell that the boys' parents are strict? Why would parents have to be strict in this neighborhood?

4 **Critical Thinking and Reading** Note the emphasis on eyes. Why does Leo always see people's eyes coming toward him? Point out to students that Leo's perceptions arise from his basic fear of his surroundings.

for the moment when he would turn to me, saying, "Okay, kid. You run along. I'll see you later."

This meant that I would have to go to the movies by myself and hang around in front of the box office, waiting for some grown-up to take me in. I could not go back upstairs, for this would be informing my mother and father that Caleb had gone off somewhere—after promising to take me to the movies. Neither could I simply hang around the block, playing with the kids on the block. For one thing, my demeanor, as I came out of the house, those Saturdays, very clearly indicated that I had better things to do than play with *them*; for another, they were not terribly anxious to play with *me*; and, finally, my remaining on the block would have had exactly the same effect as my going upstairs. Someone would surely inform my father and mother, or they might simply look out of the window, or one of them would come downstairs to buy something they had forgotten while shopping, or my father would pass down the block on his way somewhere. In short, to remain on the block after Caleb's dismissal was to put myself at the mercy of the block and to put Caleb at the mercy of our parents.

So I prepared myself, those Saturdays, to respond with a cool, "Okay. See you later," and prepared myself then to turn indifferently away, and walk. This was surely the most terrible moment. The moment I turned away I was committed, I was trapped, and I then had miles to walk, so it seemed to me, before I would be out of sight, before the block ended and I could turn onto the avenue. I wanted to run out of that block, but I never did. I never looked back. I forced myself to walk very slowly, looking neither right nor left, trying to look neither up nor down—striving to seem at once distracted and off-hand; concentrating on the cracks in the sidewalk, and stumbling over them, trying to

whistle, feeling every muscle in my body, from my pigeon toes[2] to my burning neck; feeling that all the block was watching me, and feeling—which was odd—that I deserved it. And then I reached the avenue, and turned, still not looking back, and was released from those eyes at least, but now faced other eyes, eyes coming toward me. These eyes were the eyes of children stronger than me, who would steal my movie money; these eyes were the eyes of cops, whom I feared; these eyes were the eyes of old folks who also thought I was a sissy and who might wonder what I was doing on this avenue by myself. And these eyes were the eyes of men and women standing on the corners, who certainly had no eyes for me, but who occupied the center of my bewildered attention because they seemed, at once, so abject and so free.

And then I got to the show. Sometimes, someone would take me in right away and sometimes I would have to wait. I looked at the posters which seemed magical indeed to me in those days. I was very struck, not altogether agreeably, by the colors. The faces of the movie stars were in red, in green, in blue, in purple, not at all like the colors of real faces and yet they looked more real than real. Or, rather, they looked like faces far from me, faces which I would never be able to decipher, faces which could be seen but never changed or touched, faces which existed only behind these doors. I don't know what I thought. Some great assault, certainly, was being made on my imagination, on my sense of reality. Caleb could draw, he was teaching me to draw, and I wondered if he could teach me to draw faces like these. I looked at the stills[3] from the show, seeing

---

2. **pigeon toes:** Toes or feet that turn inward.
3. **stills** (stilz) *n*.: Photographs made from single frames of a motion picture and used for advertising it.

Grammar in Action

One method you can use to vary your sentence structure when you revise an essay is to repeat elements within certain sentences or passages. Repeating words, phrases, and sentence patterns can strengthen the ideas presented, as well as make the passage more dramatic. In the following passage, James Baldwin uses repetition to emphasize all the eyes tormenting Leo:

These eyes were the *eyes* of children stronger than me, who would steal my movie money; *these eyes* were the *eyes* of cops, whom I feared; *these eyes* were the *eyes* of old folks who also thought I was a sissy and who might wonder what I was doing on this avenue by myself. And *these eyes* were the *eyes* of men and women standing on the corners, ...

By repeating the subject and the predicate nominative at the beginning of each sentence, Baldwin makes you feel Leo's fear and anguish over all the eyes that make him feel trapped. The repetition heightens the drama and makes the experience more vivid.

people in attitudes of danger, in attitudes of love, in atittudes of sorrow and loss. They were not like any people I had ever seen and this made them, irrevocably, better. With one part of my mind, of course, I knew that here was James Cagney—holding his gun like a prize; and here was Clark Gable, all dimples, teeth, and eyes; here was Joan Crawford, gleaming with astonishment, and here was proud, quivering Katharine Hepburn, who could never be astonished, and here was poor, downtrodden Sylvia Sidney, weeping in the clutches of yet another gangster. But only the faces and the attitudes were real, more real than the lives we led, more real than our days and nights, and the names were merely brand-names, like Campbell's Baked Beans or Kellogg's Corn Flakes. We went to see James Cagney because we had grown accustomed to that taste, we knew that we would like it.

But, then, I would have to turn my attention from the faces and the stills and watch the faces coming to the box office. And this was not easy, since I didn't, after all, want everyone in the neighborhood to know that I was loitering outside the moviehouse waiting for someone to take me in, exactly like an orphan. Eventually, I would see a face which looked susceptible and which I did not know. I would rush up beside him or her—but it was usually a man, for they were less likely to be disapproving—and whisper, "Take me in," and give him my dime. Sometimes the man simply took the dime and disappeared into the movies, sometimes he gave my dime back to me and took me in, anyway. Sometimes I ended up wandering around the streets—but I couldn't wander into a strange neighborhood because I would be beaten up if I did—until I figured the show was out. It was dangerous to get home too early and, of course, it was practically lethal to arrive too late. If all went well, I could cover for Caleb, saying that I had left him with some boys on the stoop. Then, if *he* came in too late and got a dressing down for it, it could not be considered my fault.

One time, it was raining and it was still too early for me to go home. I felt very, very low that day. It was one of the times that my tongue and my body refused to obey me—this happened often; when I was prey to my fantasies, or overwhelmed by my real condition; and I had not been able to work up the courage to ask anyone to take me into the show. I stood there, watching people go in, watching people come out. Every once in a while, when the doors opened, I caught a glimpse of the screen—huge, black and silver, moving all the time. The ticket-taker was watching me, or so I thought, with a hostile suspicion, as though he were thinking, You just *try* to get somebody to take you in. I dare you! Actually, it's very unlikely he was thinking at all, and certainly not of me. But I walked away from the show because I could no longer bear his eyes, or anybody's eyes.

I walked the long block east from the moviehouse. The street was empty, black, and glittering. The globes of the streetlamps, with the water slanting both behind them and before, told me how hard the rain was falling. The water soaked through my coat at the shoulders and water dripped down my neck from my cap. I began to be afraid. I could not stay out here in the rain because then my father and mother would know I had been wandering the streets. I would get a beating, and, though Caleb was too old to get a beating, he and my father would have a terrible fight and Caleb would blame it all on me and would not speak to me for days. I began to hate Caleb. I wondered where he was. If I had known where to find him, I would have gone to where he was and forced him, by screaming and crying even, to take me home or to take me wherever he was go-

Caleb's Brother   121

5 Discussion Why do the movie stars interest Leo so much? Are his feelings about the celebrities in the movie posters uncommon? Why do people go to the movies?

6 Discussion How does Leo feel about himself? Why does he lack self-confidence?

Student Activity 1. Find three sentences from "Caleb's Brother" in which Baldwin effectively uses a series of repeated words, phrases or sentence patterns to add emphasis. Explain how the use of repetition affects each passage.

Student Activity 2. Write three original sentences in which you use a series of repeated words, phrases or sentence patterns.

HARLEM NOCTURNE
Alice Neel
Robert Miller Gallery

ing. And I wouldn't have cared if he hit me, or even if he called me a sissy. Then it occurred to me that he might be in the same trouble as myself, since if I couldn't go home without *him*, he, even more surely, couldn't 7 go home without *me*. Perhaps he was also wandering around in the rain. If he was, then, I thought, it served him right: it would serve him right if he caught pneumonia and died; and I dwelt pleasantly on this possibility for the length of the block. But at the end of the block I realized that he was probably *not* wandering around in the rain—I was; and I, too, might catch pneumonia and die. I started in the direction of our house only because I did not know what else to do. Perhaps Caleb would be waiting for me on the stoop.

The avenue, too, was very long and silent. Somehow, it seemed old, like a picture in a book. It stretched straight before me, endless, and the streetlights did not so much illuminate it as prove how dark it was. The familiar buildings were now merely dark, silent shapes, great masses of wet rock; men stood against the walls or on the stoops, made faceless by the light in the hallway behind them. The rain was falling harder. Cars sloshed by, sending up sheets of water and bobbing like boats; from the bars I heard music faintly, and many voices. Straight ahead of me a woman walked, very fast, head down, carrying a shopping bag. I reached my corner and crossed the wide avenue. There was no one on my stoop.

Now, I was not even certain what time it was; and everything was so abnormally, wretchedly still that there was no way of guessing. But I knew it wasn't time yet for the show to be over. I walked into my hallway and wrung out my cap. I was sorry that I had not made someone take me into the show because now I did not know what to do. I *could* go upstairs and say that we had not liked the movie and had left early and that Caleb was with some boys on the stoop. But this would sound strange—I had never been known to dislike a movie; and if our father was home he might come downstairs to look for Caleb, who would not know what story I had told and who would, therefore, in any case, be greatly handicapped when he arrived. As far as Caleb knew, I was safely in the movies. That was our bargain, from which not even the rain released me. My nerve had failed me, but Caleb had no way of knowing that. I could not stay in my hallway because my father might not be at home and might come in. I could not go into the hallway of another building because if any of the kids who lived in the building found me they would have the right to beat me up. I could not go back out into the rain. I stood next to the big, cold radiator and I began to cry. But crying wasn't going to do me any good, either, especially as there was no one to hear me.

So I stepped out on my stoop again and looked carefully up and down the block. There was not a soul to be seen. The rain fell as hard as ever, with a whispering sound—like monstrous old gossips whispering together. The sky could not be seen. It was black. I stood there for a long time, wondering what to do. Then I thought of a condemned house, around the corner from us. We played there sometimes, though we were not supposed to, and it was very dangerous. The front door had been boarded up but the boards had been pried loose; and the basement windows had been broken and boys congregated in the basement and wandered through the rotting house. What possessed me to go there now I don't know, except that I could not think of another dry place in the whole world. I thought that I would just sit there, out of the rain, until I figured it was safe to come home. And I started running east, down our block. I turned two corners and I came to the house, with its black window sockets and garbage piled high around it and the rain moaning and whistling, clanging against the metal and drumming on the glass. The house stood by itself, for the house next to it had already been torn down. The house was completely dark. I had forgotten how afraid I was of the dark, but the rain was drenching me. I ran down the cellar steps and clambered into the house. I squatted there in a still, dry dread, in misery, not daring to look into the house but staring outward at the bright black area railing and the tempest beyond. I was holding my breath. I heard an endless scurrying in the darkness, a perpetual busy-ness, and I thought of rats, of their teeth and ferocity and fearful size and I began to cry again. If someone had come up then to murder me, I don't believe I could have moved or made any other sound.

I don't know how long I squatted there this way, or what was in my mind—I think there was nothing in my mind, I was as

Caleb's Brother 123

8 Critical Thinking and Reading Baldwin uses imagery to evoke the mood of the place. The weather contributes to the general feeling of foreboding in the story.

9 Discussion How would you handle this dilemma? What do you think Leo should do? Evaluate the consequences of each of his options.

10 Reading Strategy Summarize the story up to this point and predict what you think is going to happen to Leo.

11 Discussion Who do you think the person in the condemned house is? Do you think he meant to harm Leo? What do you think of Leo's decision to enter the condemned house?

12 Discussion What impression do you get of Caleb now? Contrast the Caleb who was on the stoop with his friends with the Caleb who is now comforting his brother.

13 Discussion Why doesn't Leo tell Caleb the truth?

14 Discussion How has this incident affected the relationship between the brothers? What lesson did Caleb learn about responsibility?

Reader's Response Do you believe that Leo won't let Caleb go to the movies alone again? Why or why not?

blank as a toothache. I listened to the rain and the rats. Then I was aware of another sound, I had been hearing it for awhile without realizing it. The sound came from the door which led to the backyard. I wanted to stand, but I crouched lower; wanted to run, but could not move. Sometimes the sound seemed to come closer and I knew that this meant my death; sometimes diminished or ceased altogether and then I knew that my assailant was looking for me. Oh, how I hated Caleb for bringing my life to an end so soon! How I wished I knew where to find him! I looked toward the backyard door and I seemed to see, silhouetted against the driving rain, a figure, half bent, moaning, leaning against the wall. I could not catch my breath to scream. Then I heard a laugh, a low, happy, wicked laugh, and the figure turned in my direction and seemed to start toward me. Then I screamed and stood straight up, bumping my head on the window frame and losing my cap, and scrambled up the cellar steps, into the rain. I ran head down, like a bull, away from that house and out of that block and it was my great good luck that no person and no vehicle were in my path. I ran up the steps of my stoop and bumped into Caleb.

"Where have you been? Hey! what's the matter with you?"

For I had jumped up on him, almost knocking him down, trembling and sobbing.

"You're *soaked*. Leo, what's the matter with you? Where's your cap?"

But I could not say anything. I held him around the neck with all my might, and I could not stop shaking.

"Come on, Leo," Caleb said, in a different tone, "tell me what's the matter. Don't carry on like this." He pried my arms loose and held me away from him so that he could look into my face. "Oh, little Leo. Little Leo. What's the matter, baby?" He looked as though he were about to cry himself and this made me cry harder than ever. He took out his handkerchief and wiped my face and made me blow my nose. My sobs began to lessen, but I could not stop trembling. He thought that I was trembling from cold and he rubbed his hands roughly up and down my back and rubbed my hands between his. "What's the matter?"

I did not know how to tell him.

"Somebody try to beat you up?"

I shook my head. "No."

"What movie did you see?"

"I didn't go. I couldn't find nobody to take me in."

"And you just been wandering around in the rain all night?"

I shook my head. "Yes."

He looked at me and sat down on the hallway steps. "Oh, Leo." Then, "You mad at me?"

I said, "No, I was scared."

He nodded. "I reckon you were, man," he said. "I reckon you were." He wiped my face again. "You ready to go upstairs? It's getting late."

"Okay."

"How'd you lose your cap?"

"I went in a hallway to wring it out—and—I put it on the radiator and I heard some people coming—and—I ran away and I forgot it."

"We'll say you forgot it in the movies."

"Okay."

We started up the stairs.

"Leo," he said, "I'm sorry about tonight. I'm really sorry. I won't let it happen again. You believe me?"

"Sure, I believe you."

"Give us a smile, then."

I smiled up at him. He squatted down.

"Give us a kiss."

I kissed him.

"Okay. Climb up. I'll give you a ride—hold on, now."

He carried me piggyback up the stairs.

Closure and Extension

ANSWERS TO THINKING ABOUT THE SELECTION
Recalling

1. Leo has to prepare himself in order not to show his fear of having to go to the movies alone. He prepares himself to "turn indifferently away, and walk" even though he is painfully self-conscious and afraid.

2. Leo can't go upstairs because then his parents would know that Caleb was with his friends instead of with his brother, as he was supposed to be. Leo can't stay on the block either because the kids there will beat him up or tell his parents that he was not with Caleb.

3. Leo fears the police, the children who might steal his movie money, the old people who, Leo thinks, perceive him as a sissy, and the men and women standing on the corners.

4. Leo is too shy to ask someone to take him into the movies. He can't go home without getting Caleb into trouble with their parents. He can't go into another building because the kids there will beat him up. Therefore, he goes to the condemned house to get out of the rain.

5. Leo runs out of the house when he realizes there's someone else there.

6. Caleb is apologetic, remorseful, and loving towards Leo.

THINKING ABOUT THE SELECTION
Recalling

1. Why does Leo feel that he must prepare himself for Caleb's saying, "Okay, kid. You run along. I'll see you later"?
2. When Caleb goes off with his friends, why can't Leo go upstairs or stay on his block?
3. What does Leo fear when he reaches the avenue?
4. On the rainy day, why does Leo walk away from the movie theater and go to the condemned house?
5. Why does he run out of the house?
6. How does Caleb behave toward Leo at the end of the story?

Interpreting

7. For what reason does Caleb sometimes send Leo off on his own?
8. How does Leo show his concern for Caleb even when Caleb ignores him?
9. In what way is the title "Caleb's Brother" more appropriate than some other possible title, such as "Leo and Caleb"?

Applying

10. Explain why you think that Caleb is, or is not, a typical older brother.

ANALYZING LITERATURE
Understanding Atmosphere and Meaning

The **atmosphere** of a place can have an effect on the characters in a story. The very first sentence of "Caleb's Brother"—"The hall was dark, smelling of cooking and of boiling diapers"—begins to establish the atmosphere that young Leo must live with every day.
1. What are three of the places described in the story whose atmosphere affects Leo?
2. Could "Caleb's Brother" be the same story if it were set in a time and place with a different atmosphere, for example, a suburban town on a clear, sunny day? Why or why not?

CRITICAL THINKING AND READING
Identifying Details of Atmosphere

Atmosphere is created by specific details that enable you to see, hear, and feel a place as if you were there. Choose three details that help create the atmosphere of this story. Explain why you chose each detail. To what sense does each detail appeal?

UNDERSTANDING LANGUAGE
Choosing Meaning to Fit Context

Many words have more than one meaning. When you read, you must choose the meaning that fits the context. For example, the word *committed* has a number of meanings, but in the context of the sentence "The moment I turned away I was committed . . ." it means "bound" or "engaged."

Choose the meaning of the *italicized* word that best fits the context of each sentence.
1. Bill would not *stoop* to rudeness.
   a. a platform with steps
   b. bend forward
   c. lower or degrade oneself
   d. pounce on
2. From the *landing* I could see the doorway.
   a. the act of coming to shore
   b. the place where a ship is loaded
   c. the act of coming to the ground
   d. a platform at the end of a flight of stairs

THINKING AND WRITING
Writing About Atmosphere

Imagine you are writing for your school magazine. Compare and contrast the atmosphere of the condemned house in "Caleb's Brother" with the atmosphere of a place in one of the other short stories you have recently read. If you cannot think of a place you have read about, select a place you know first hand. First think of an adjective or two to describe the atmosphere created by each of the two places. Then list those details you would use to develop and support each description. When you revise your writing, make sure you have pointed out the similarities and differences.

Caleb's Brother 125

(Answers begin on p. 124)

ANSWERS TO CRITICAL THINKING AND READING
Some details that contribute to the atmosphere follow.

"The avenue, too, was very long and silent." (Sense of hearing)

"It stretched straight before me, endless, ..." (Sense of sight)

". . . the streetlights did not so much illuminate it as prove how dark it was." (Sense of sight)

"The familiar buildings were now merely dark, silent shapes, great masses of wet rock; . . . ." (Senses of sight, sound, and touch)

"Cars sloshed by, sending up sheets of water and bobbing like boats; . . . ." (Senses of sight and sound)

". . . men stood against the walls or on the stoops, made faceless by the light in the hallway behind them." (Sense of sight)

". . . I came to the house, with its black window sockets and garbage piled high around it and the rain moaning and whistling, clanging against the metal and drumming on the glass." (Senses of smell and hearing)

"The house was completely dark." (Sense of sight)

"I heard an endless scurrying in the darkness, a perpetual busyness, and I thought of rats, of their teeth and ferocity and fearful size and I began to cry again." (Sense of hearing)

ANSWERS TO UNDERSTANDING LANGUAGE
1. c. lower or degrade oneself
2. d. a platform at the end of a flight of stairs

---

ashamed that he let Leo down and promises not to let it happen again.

Interpreting
7. Caleb wants to do things with friends his own age.
8. Leo will not go home early because Caleb would be in trouble with their parents if he did.
9. Answers will differ. Suggested Response: The story revolves around Caleb's relationship with his brother. Leo is the major character whose troubles spring from Caleb's treatment of him. This is not a relationship between equals, as the title "Leo and Caleb" would suggest.

Applying
10. Answers will differ. Suggested Response: Caleb is a typical older brother because he cares about Leo and yet is still more interested in doing what he likes with his peers.

ANSWERS TO ANALYZING LITERATURE
1. Suggested Responses: the tenement hallway and stoop, the block, the avenue, the movie theater, and the condemned house.
2. Answers will differ. Suggested Response: The atmosphere in "Caleb's Brother" is crucial to the plot and to the way the characters behave. The problems inherent in this type of environment precipitate the action.

Challenge What conclusions can you draw about the boys' relationships with their peers? Why doesn't Leo apper to have any friends his own age? What is Caleb's relationship with his friends like?

More About the Author Jack Finney has published mystery and detective stories, but he is considered a science-fiction writer. What makes him an unusual science-fiction writer is that he turns to the past rather than the future for his settings. He often depicts whole societies yearning to escape the harsh and complex present to return to an idealized past. Ask students to discuss a writer's need to conform to the guidelines established for a particular type of writing. How would writing about the past be a drawback for a science-fiction writer? Ask students to compare the settings of various science-fiction works with which they are familiar.

Literary Focus Time machines and time travel are concepts that have intrigued people for centuries. Point out to students that the time of a story can greatly affect the characters and the plot. Many television programs and movies have shown characters from the present or future somehow, often mistakenly, transported back to the past.

Look For More advanced students may be able to identify additional changes that have taken place in America since 1894. Have them discuss how they feel about these changes.

Writing/Prior Knowledge Have students discuss the meaning of this quotation: "All is change; all yields its place and goes." Then have them complete the freewriting assignment. For extra credit, you might ask them to use their freewriting as the basis for a formal composition.

Vocabulary These words may also give students some difficulty: *psychiatrist* (p. 127), *fulfillment* (p. 127), *mustache* (p. 129), and *nowadays* (p. 129). Be sure students know these words.

GUIDE FOR READING

The Third Level

Jack Finney (1911–   ), who was born in Milwaukee, Wisconsin, now lives in Northern California. He is best known for *Invasion of the Body Snatchers,* a novel about aliens who come to Earth and inhabit human bodies. Escape from the harsh present to a peaceful past is a common idea in Finney's writing. It appears in his novel *Time and Again* and runs through *I Love Galesburg in the Springtime,* a collection of short stories. It is also at the heart of the unusual story you are about to read.

Time

Setting consists of both the place and the time of a story. Think of all the changes that occur over time. A person who lived in a city in the 1980's would probably know a very different place from someone who had lived in the same city in the 1890's. In "The Third Level," the main character lives in the present but longs to go back to the past.

Look For

As you read "The Third Level," notice the contrast that is established between life in the present and life in the past. What details make the modern world seem unpleasant? What details make the past seem pleasant?

Writing

List some of the ways in which you think that life in America today is different from life in America one hundred years ago.

Vocabulary

Knowing the following words will help you as you read "The Third Level."

refuge (ref'yōoj) *n.*: A place of safety or shelter (p. 127)

arched (ärcht) *adj.*: curved (p. 127)

currency (kur'ən sē) *n.*: money (p. 129)

premium (prē'mē əm) *n.*: an additional charge (p. 129)

Objectives

1 To recognize time in a setting
2 To understand how time affects characters
3 To write a time-travel story

Support Material

Teaching Portfolio
Teacher Backup, p. 191
Grammar in Action Worksheet, *Semicolons,* p. 195
Usage and Mechanics Worksheet, p. 197
Vocabulary Check, p. 198
Analyzing Literature Worksheet, *Recognizing Time in a Setting,* p. 199

Language Worksheet, *Finding the Meaning That Fits the Context,* p. 200
Selection Test, p. 201

The Third Level

Jack Finney

The presidents of the New York Central and the New York, New Haven and Hartford railroads will swear on a stack of timetables that there are only two. But I say there are three, because I've *been* on the third level at Grand Central Station.[1] Yes, I've taken the obvious step: I talked to a psychiatrist friend of mine, among others. I told him about the third level at Grand Central Station, and he said it was a waking-dream wish fulfillment. He said I was unhappy. That made my wife kind of mad, but he explained that he meant the modern world is full of insecurity, fear, war, worry and all the rest of it, and that I just want to escape. Well, who doesn't? Everybody I know wants to escape, but they don't wander down into any third level at Grand Central Station.

But that's the reason, he said, and my friends all agreed. Everything points to it, they claimed. My stamp collecting, for example; that's a "temporary refuge from reality." Well, maybe, but my grandfather didn't need any refuge from reality; things were pretty nice and peaceful in his day, from all I hear, and he started my collection. It's a nice collection, too, blocks of four of practically every U.S. issue, first-day covers, and so on. President Roosevelt collected stamps, too, you know.

Anyway, here's what happened at Grand Central. One night last summer I worked late at the office. I was in a hurry to get uptown to my apartment so I decided to take the subway from Grand Central because it's faster than the bus.

Now, I don't know why this should have happened to me. I'm just an ordinary guy named Charley, thirty-one years old, and I was wearing a tan gabardine[2] suit and a straw hat with a fancy band; I passed a dozen men who looked just like me. And I wasn't trying to escape from anything; I just wanted to get home to Louisa, my wife.

I turned into Grand Central from Vanderbilt Avenue, and went down the steps to the first level, where you take trains like the Twentieth Century. Then I walked down another flight to the second level, where the suburban trains leave from, ducked into an arched doorway heading for the subway—and got lost. That's easy to do. I've been in and out of Grand Central hundreds of times, but I'm always bumping into new doorways and stairs and corridors. Once I got into a tunnel about a mile long and came out in the lobby of the Roosevelt Hotel. Another time I came up in an office building on Forty-sixth Street, three blocks away.

Sometimes I think Grand Central is

---

1. **Grand Central Station:** A large train station in New York City.

2. **gabardine** (gab' ər dēn'): A cloth of wool, cotton, rayon, or other material used for suits and dresses.

The Third Level 127

Motivation/Prior Knowledge Have students imagine that they could go back in time to the place and year of their choice. Where would they choose to go, and what year would they like it to be? Have students discuss the reasons for their choices.

Master Teacher Note This story can lead into a discussion of time dimensions, parallel worlds, and other topics familiar to science-fiction buffs. If students are not familiar with the classic H. G. Wells' book *The Time Machine,* bring in a copy and read some excerpts. Then ask students if they have seen any of the films based on this famous work. Or have students discuss such television programs as *Time Travelers* and *Star Trek,* which deal with travel to other times. Have students discuss the popular film *Star Trek IV: The Voyage Home,* in which the crew of the Enterprise returns from a distant century to Earth of the present.

Purpose-Setting Question How does time affect the major character in this story?

1 **Enrichment** Grand Central Terminal was completed in 1913. The building was designed by the architectural firm of Reed and Stem. It was given historic landmark status in 1978. The terminal separates train, auto, subway, and pedestrian traffic on different levels connected by sloping ramps.

2 **Discussion** Does Charley, the narrator of the story, seem unhappy? Is having a stamp collection any indication of his state of mind?

3 **Discussion** Do you think Charley has a happy home life? What else might lead you to believe that Charley is well adjusted?

4 Critical Thinking and Reading
Does this theory of Charley's imply that he is crazy? Why do you think he is or is not?

5 Discussion What is your immediate impression of the third level of Grand Central Station? How is it apparent that the time period has changed?

growing like a tree, pushing out new corridors and staircases like roots. There's probably a long tunnel that nobody knows about feeling its way under the city right now, on its way to Times Square, and maybe another to Central Park. And maybe—because for so many people through the years Grand Central *has* been an exit, a way of escape—maybe that's how the tunnel I got into . . . But I never told my psychiatrist friend about that idea.

The corridor I was in began angling left and slanting downward and I thought that was wrong, but I kept on walking. All I could hear was the empty sound of my own footsteps and I didn't pass a soul. Then I heard that sort of hollow roar ahead that means open space and people talking. The tunnel turned sharp left; I went down a short flight of stairs and came out on the third level at Grand Central Station. For just a moment I thought I was back on the second level, but I saw the room was smaller, there were fewer ticket windows and train gates, and the information booth in the center was wood and old-looking. And the man in the booth wore a green eyeshade and long black sleeve protectors. The lights were dim and sort of flickering. Then I saw why; they were open-flame gaslights.

Grammar in Action

Semicolons are often used to separate closely related independent clauses not joined by a coordinating conjunction. Using the semicolon signals a shorter pause than a period, but a stronger separation than a comma. Therefore, it pulls the related clauses together without completely breaking the flow of thought. Consequently, the semicolon can add unity and drama to writing. Notice how Jack Finney's use of the semicolon connects these independent clauses more effectively and clearly than a period or a comma.

My three hundred dollars bought less than two hundred old-style bills, but I didn't care; eggs were thirteen cents a dozen in 1894.

The semicolon points up the close relationship between the two clauses. Without breaking the flow of thought, it allows you to understand why Charley is not concerned about the uneven exchange of dollars and why 1894 is such a desirable time.

Semicolons should be used sparingly. Only use them when the clauses are closely related and when you want to draw the reader's attention to their relatedness.

There were brass spittoons[3] on the floor, and across the station a glint of light caught my eye; a man was pulling a gold watch from his vest pocket. He snapped open the cover, glanced at his watch, and frowned. He wore a derby hat,[4] a black four-button suit with tiny lapels, and he had a big, black, handlebar mustache. Then I looked around and saw that everyone in the station was dressed like eighteen-ninety-something; I never saw so many beards, sideburns and fancy mustaches in my life. A woman walked in through the train gate; she wore a dress with leg-of-mutton sleeves[5] and skirts to the top of her high-buttoned shoes. Back of her, out on the tracks, I caught a glimpse of a locomotive, a very small Currier & Ives[6] locomotive with a funnel-shaped stack. And then I knew.

To make sure, I walked over to a newsboy and glanced at the stack of papers at his feet. It was the *World*; and the *World* hasn't been published for years. The lead story said something about President Cleveland. I've found that front page since, in the Public Library files, and it was printed June 11, 1894.

I turned toward the ticket windows knowing that here—on the third level at Grand Central—I could buy tickets that would take Louisa and me anywhere in the United States we wanted to go. In the year 1894. And I wanted two tickets to Galesburg, Illinois.

Have you ever been there? It's a wonderful town still, with big old frame houses, huge lawns and tremendous trees whose branches meet overhead and roof the streets. And in 1894, summer evenings were twice as long, and people sat out on their lawns, the men smoking cigars and talking quietly, the women waving palm-leaf fans, with the fireflies all around, in a peaceful world. To be back there with the First World War still twenty years off, and World War II over forty years in the future . . . I wanted two tickets for that.

The clerk figured the fare—he glanced at my fancy hatband, but he figured the fare—and I had enough for two coach tickets, one way. But when I counted out the money and looked up, the clerk was staring at me. He nodded at the bills. "That ain't money, mister," he said, "and if you're trying to skin me[7] you won't get very far," and he glanced at the cash drawer beside him. Of course the money in his drawer was old-style bills, half again as big as the money we use nowadays, and different-looking. I turned away and got out fast. There's nothing nice about jail, even in 1894.

And that was that. I left the same way I came, I suppose. Next day, during lunch hour, I drew three hundred dollars out of the bank, nearly all we had, and bought old-style currency (that *really* worried my psychiatrist friend). You can buy old money at almost any coin dealer's, but you have to pay a premium. My three hundred dollars bought less than two hundred in old-style bills, but I didn't care; eggs were thirteen cents a dozen in 1894.

But I've never again found the corridor that leads to the third level at Grand Central Station, although I've tried often enough.

Louisa was pretty worried when I told her all this, and didn't want me to look for the third level any more, and after a while I

---

3. spittoons (spi tōōnz'): Jarlike containers into which people spit. Spitting in public was a more accepted habit in the past.
4. derby hat: A stiff felt hat with a round crown and curved brim.
5. leg-of-mutton sleeves: Sleeves that puff out toward the shoulder and resemble a leg of mutton (lamb or sheep).
6. Currier & Ives: These 19th-century American print makers became famous for their pictures of trains, yachts, horses, and scenes of nature.

7. skin me: An old-fashioned way of saying "cheat me."

The Third Level 129

---

6 Literary Focus What are some of the details that show you that Charley has stepped back into 1894? Think of other ways in which the world would be different for Charley if he were to remain in 1894. Point out to students that he would have to change in order to fit in. Ask them how.

7 Master Teacher Note Galesburg, Illinois, is Charley's Shangri-La, a mythical place in the Himalayas invented by James Hilton in 1933, where people lead peaceful lives and nothing ever changes. Point out to students that, like the Emerald City of Oz or Brigadoon, Galesburg represents for Charley a sheltered place that remains unspoiled by the horrors of the outside world. Bring in a recording of Lerner and Lowe's *Brigadoon* to set the mood of a world sheltered from the turmoil of the present.

8 Enrichment Paper money as we know it today dates from the 1860's. The bills were called legal tender notes or United States notes and were different in design from the paper money now in use.

9 Discussion Why couldn't Charley find the third level once he had left?

Student Activity 1. Find three examples where Finney uses semicolons to connect related, independent clauses. Explain how the semicolon unifies the two clauses.

Student Activity 2. Use semicolons to join each group of sentences below.

1. It was the most exciting event of the year.
   The circus had come to town with all its clowns, rides, animals and magic.

2. Although the presidents of the New York Central and the New York, New Haven and Hartford railroads will swear on a stack of timetables that there are only two, I know there are three. I have been on the third level at Grand Central Station.

10 **Discussion** How does Galesburg sound from Sam's letter? Is it a place in which you would like to live? Why or why not?

11 **Discussion** Why were you surprised to learn that Sam was Charley's psychiatrist?

12 **Critical Thinking and Reading** What impression do you form of Galesburg from the fact that Sam could not be a psychiatrist there? What does this indicate about the difference between New York City and Galesburg?

Reader's Response If you found your own Third Level and could travel in time—to the past or the future—where would you go? Why?

stopped; I went back to my stamps. But now we're *both* looking, every weekend, because now we have proof that the third level is still there. My friend Sam Weiner disappeared! Nobody knew where, but I sort of suspected because Sam's a city boy, and I used to tell him about Galesburg—I went to school there—and he always said he liked the sound of the place. And that's where he is, all right. In 1894.

Because one night, fussing with my stamp collection, I found—well, do you know what a first-day cover is? When a new stamp is issued, stamp collectors buy some and use them to mail envelopes to themselves on the very first day of sale; and the postmark proves the date. The envelope is called a first-day cover. They're never opened; you just put blank paper in the envelope.

That night, among my oldest first-day covers, I found one that shouldn't have been there. But there it was. It was there because someone had mailed it to my grandfather at his home in Galesburg; that's what the address on the envelope said. And it had been there since July 18, 1894—the postmark showed that—yet I didn't remember it at all. The stamp was a six-cent, dull brown, with a picture of President Garfield. Naturally, when the envelope came to Granddad in the mail, it went right into his collection and stayed there—till I took it out and opened it.

The paper inside wasn't blank. It read:

> 941 Willard Street
> Galesburg, Illinois
> July 18, 1894
>
> Charley:
> I got to wishing that you were right. Then I got to believing you were right. And, Charley, it's true; I found the third level! I've been here two weeks, and right now, down the street at the Daly's, someone is playing a piano, and they're all out on the front porch singing, "Seeing Nellie home." And I'm invited over for lemonade. Come on back, Charley and Louisa. Keep looking till you find the third level! It's worth it, believe me!

The note was signed *Sam.*

At the stamp and coin store I go to, I found out that Sam bought eight hundred dollars' worth of old-style currency. That ought to set him up in a nice little hay, feed and grain business; he always said that's what he really wished he could do, and he certainly can't go back to his old business. Not in Galesburg, Illinois, in 1894. His old business? Why, Sam was my psychiatrist.

10

11

12

Closure and Extension

ANSWERS TO THINKING ABOUT THE SELECTION
Recalling

1. According to Charley's psychiatrist, Charley thinks he has been on the third level as a result of waking-dream wish fulfillment. The psychiatrist believes Charley is trying to escape from the insecurity, fear, war, and worry of the modern world.
2. Grand Central Station is full of doorways, stairs, and corridors, which make it easy to get lost there.
3. The information booth was wood and old looking, and the man in the booth wore an eyeshade and long black sleeve protectors.
4. He can no longer find the third level.
5. He gets a letter from his friend Sam, dated July 18, 1894, who had found the third level himself and has traveled back to Galesburg, Illinois, in the year 1894.

THINKING ABOUT THE SELECTION

Recalling

1. According to Charley's psychiatrist, why does Charley think he has been on the third level of Grand Central Station?
2. What is it about Grand Central Station that makes it easy for Charley to get lost there?
3. What is the first clue that he is in the Grand Central Station of the past?
4. Why is he unable to travel to Galesburg even after he gets currency that the ticket clerk will accept?
5. What proof does Charley get that the third level exists?

Interpreting

6. Describe the contrast the story presents between life in the modern world and life in Galesburg at the turn of the century.
7. What is the connection between this contrast and Charley's wanting to go to Galesburg?
8. As a psychiatrist, Sam must listen to the problems and fears of people living in the modern world. How might his work have led to his going to Galesburg?
9. What effect do you think Sam's letter has on Charley?

Applying

10. Many stories, novels, and films deal with escaping from the present into a more pleasant time, usually in the past. Do you think the idea of a past that is better than the present is, or is not, realistic? Explain why.

ANALYZING LITERATURE

Recognizing Time in a Setting

Time refers to the *when* of the action. Sometimes a story will shift from the present to the past.

Then you have to determine from clues when the action is taking place.

1. What is the first detail that hints Charley has entered in the Grand Central Station of 1894?
2. Identify at least three other details that show the third level is in the past.

CRITICAL THINKING AND READING

Understanding the Effects of Time

The time in which a story is set affects the characters. There is a close connection between how people live and when they live. As time changes, a society changes. For example, in "The Third Level" Charley's and Sam's unhappiness is linked to life in general in the modern world.

1. What view of modern life is given in the first paragraph of the story?
2. According to Sam, how has modern life affected Charley's mind?
3. What does Sam's letter to Charley say that suggests life in Galesburg in 1894 is better than life in modern-day New York?

THINKING AND WRITING

Writing a Time-Travel Story

Write a brief story in which a character—maybe yourself—steps into the past, experiences life as it was then lived, and suddenly returns to the present (perhaps changed by the strange experience). First select the time period for your story. List details about this period that you might use in your story, for example, 1890's—gas lights, long dresses, street cars. Figure out a way to get your character into the past and a way to return him or her to the present. You might also think about how the experience of the past will change the character's life in the future. Go over your writing to see whether you have managed to convey a vivid glimpse of the past time that you are presenting. Then share your story with your classmates.

Interpreting

6. Life in the modern world is full of insecurity, fear, war, and worry, while life in Galesburg is peaceful, genteel, rural, and beautiful.
7. The connection is that Charley rejects the turmoil of the modern world for his vision of Galesburg, where people can lead more leisurely lives.
8. Listening to people's problems dealing with the modern world might have led Sam to seek the simpler life of Galesburg.
9. The letter will motivate Charley to look even harder for the third level.

Applying

10. Answers will differ. Suggested Responses: (1) Life is becoming more complex and, therefore, the past offers a more pleasant lifestyle. (2) Modern conveniences make the present more appealing than the past.

ANSWERS TO ANALYZING LITERATURE

1. The information booth was wood and old looking, the room was smaller, and there were fewer ticket windows. The man in the information booth is dressed in old-fashioned clothes.
2. Students should choose three of the following details: the lights were open-flame gaslights; there were brass spittoons on the floor; people were dressed in old-

(Answers begin on p. 130.)

fashioned clothes; men had sideburns and handlebar mustaches; the locomotive looked like a Currier and Ives print with a funnel-shaped stack; the date on the newspaper was July 11, 1894; the newspaper itself, the *World*, had not been published for years; and the currency was old style.

ANSWERS TO CRITICAL THINKING AND READING

1. The first paragraph presents modern life as insecure, anxious, frightening, and something to escape from.
2. Sam thinks modern life has made Charley fantasize to escape his unhappiness.
3. The letter refers to an invitation to come for lemonade and to someone playing a sweet old song, "Seeing Nellie Home," on the piano. These references make Galesburg seem like a warm-hearted, hospitable, tranquil place.

THINKING AND WRITING

For help with this assignment, students can refer to Lesson 17, "Writing a Short Story," in the Handbook of Writing About Literature.

Writing Across the Curriculum
You might want to inform the social studies and art departments that students are conducting research on Grand Central Station. History teachers might provide guidance for students on conducting their research on the architecture, preservation attempts, and so on. Specific reference books familiar to history teachers might provide just the level of detail students are looking for to set the time of their stories.

Challenge Imagine that you are related to someone who wants to live in another time period. Charley's wife in the story seems understanding and willing to go to Galesburg with him. Do you think most people would have this reaction?

Focus

More About the Author Washington Irving is one of the major nineteenth-century American Romantic writers. In his own time, however, Irving was considered by some critics to be a second-class writer because many of his stories are subtly humorous. Ask students to discuss the relationship between comic writing and literary merit. In what ways can humorous writing be as important as serious writing? What is the value of humorous literature?

Literary Focus The passage of time can be shown in many ways. In this story, it is shown through changes in the physical appearance of the setting and the characters. Point out that, over time, all things change. Have students think of examples of places and things that have changed with time.

Look For Less advanced students may find this story difficult to understand because of the old-fashioned terminology and elaborate sentence structure. Consider previewing Thinking About the Selection questions on page 146 so that the questions can guide their reading.

Writing/Prior Knowledge Show students a "before" and "after" picture of a location and have them note the differences. Then have them complete the freewriting assignment.

Vocabulary These words may also give students some difficulty: p. 134: *obsequious, malleable, insuperable, aversion;* p. 137: *approbation, august;* p. 138: *singularity, alacrity, amphitheater, perpendicular;* p. 141: *desolateness, assemblage, disputatious;* p. 143: *austerity;* p. 144: *corroborated;* p. 145: *patriarchs, torpor, despotism.* Be sure students know what these words mean as they read.

Rip Van Winkle

Washington Irving (1783–1859) was the first American author to achieve fame in both Europe and America. While living in England as a young man, he read old German folk tales in search of subjects he could use for stories of his own. One tale strongly appealed to him. He changed its setting from Europe to America, made other changes, and thus created "Rip Van Winkle." The magical quality of this story comes in part from its source—a strange old folk tale passed down from generation to generation of fascinated listeners.

Passage of Time

As a story moves forward in time, not only do characters and events change but the setting may change as well. How a place is described later in a story may be different from how it is described earlier. In "Rip Van Winkle," changes in the setting over time are especially important to the story as a whole.

Look For

As you read the story, try to picture the setting clearly. Look for the details that make the Catskill mountain region come vividly alive. How does the setting change as time passes?

Writing

Think of some place you know that has changed. It might be a piece of land, a house, a neighborhood, or another place. What did it look like before it changed? What did it look like after it changed? List details that would give a reader a clear picture of the "before" place. Then list the "after" details.

Vocabulary

Knowing the following words will help you as you read "Rip Van Winkle."

chivalrous (shiv′l rəs) *adj.*: Courteous (p. 134)

Martial (mär′shəl) *adj.*: Suitable for war (p. 134)

domestic (də mes′tik) *adj.*: Of the home and family (p. 134)

obliging (ə blī′jiŋ) *adj.*: Ready to do favors (p. 135)

keener (kēn′ ər) *adj.*: Sharper and quicker (p. 136)

wistfully (wist′fəl lē) *adj.*: Showing vague yearnings (p. 137)

majestic (mə jes′tik) *adj.*: Grand, lofty (p. 137)

incomprehensible (in′käm pri hen′sə b'l) *adj.*: not able to be understood (p. 138)

evidently (ev′ə dənt lē) *adj.*: Obviously (p. 139)

melancholy (mel′ən käl′ē) *adj.*: Sad, gloomy (p. 139)

Objectives

1 To recognize the passage of time in a short story
2 To compare and contrast a place over time
3 To look up words in a dictionary
4 To write a story in which you contrast a place over time

Support Material

Teaching Portfolio
Teacher Backup, p. 203
Grammar in Action Worksheet, *Adjective Phrases*, p. 207
Grammar in Action Worksheet, *Adjectives*, p. 209
Grammar in Action Worksheet, *Adjective Clauses*, p. 211
Usage and Mechanics Worksheet, p. 213
Vocabulary Check, p. 214

Analyzing Literature Worksheet, *Recognizing the Passage of Time*, p. 216
Critical Thinking and Reading Worksheet, *Comparing and Contrasting a Place Over Time*, p. 218
Selection Test, p. 219

Rip Van Winkle

Washington Irving

RIP IN THE MOUNTAINS
Albertus Del Orient Brower
Shelburne Museum, Shelburne, Vermont

Whoever has made a voyage up the Hudson must remember the Catskill mountains. They are a branch of the great Appalachian family,[1] and are seen away to the west of the river, swelling up to a noble height, and lording it over the surrounding country. Every change of season, every change of weather, indeed every hour of the day, produces some change in the magical hues and shapes of these mountains, and they are regarded by all the good wives, far and near, as perfect barometers. When the weather is fair and settled, they are clothed in blue and purple, and print their bold outlines on the clear evening sky; but sometimes, when the rest of the landscape is cloudless, they will gather a hood of gray vapors about their summits,

---

1. Appalachian (ap'ə lǎ' chən) **family:** A group of mountains extending from southern Quebec in Canada to northern Alabama.

Rip Van Winkle 133

Motivation/Prior Knowledge Have students imagine that they are hiking in the mountains and come upon a group of little men who are dressed in old-fashioned clothes and are bowling. What would they do? Would they be curious or frightened? If Rip Van Winkle had hurried away from his little men, how might the story be different? Is there a lesson to be learned from what happened to Rip?

Purpose-Setting Question How does the passage of twenty years affect Rip Van Winkle and his surroundings?

1 **Enrichment** The Catskill Mountains are a chain of low mountains along the western shore of the Hudson River in New York. The mountain chain is about fifty miles long and thirty miles wide, and the highest peak is more than four thousand feet high.

Humanities Note

Fine Art: *Rip in the Mountains,* Albertus Del Oriente Brower. *Rip in the Mountains* and the following two paintings, *Rip at the Inn* (p. 136), and *Rip Van Winkle Asleep* (p. 139), were also done by Albertus Del Oriente Brower. Note the similarity of style in all three paintings. Brower was obviously intrigued by the story of Rip Van Winkle and virtually illustrated it. Have students study each painting and discuss the following questions.

1. How can you tell that these three paintings were painted by the same artist? Identify common elements in the paintings.
2. What atmosphere and mood do the paintings evoke?
3. Is this the way you pictured Rip Van Winkle in your mind?
4. How is the tone of these three paintings different from that in John Quidor's painting of Rip on page 142?

which, in the last rays of the setting sun, will glow and light up like a crown of glory.

At the foot of these fairy mountains, the voyager may have seen the light smoke curling up from a village, whose shingle roofs gleam among the trees, just where the blue tints of the upland melt away into the fresh green of the nearer landscape. It is a little village, of great antiquity, having been founded by some of the Dutch colonists, in the early times of the province, just about the beginning of the government of the good Peter Stuyvesant,[2] (may he rest in peace!) and there were some of the houses of the original settlers standing within a few years,[3] built of small yellow bricks brought from Holland, having latticed windows and gable fronts,[4] surmounted with weathercocks.

In that same village, and in one of these very houses (which, to tell the precise truth, was sadly timeworn and weather-beaten), there lived many years since, while the country was yet a province of Great Britain, a simple good-natured fellow, of the name of Rip Van Winkle. He was a descendant of the Van Winkles who figured so gallantly in the chivalrous days of Peter Stuyvesant, and accompanied him to the siege of Fort Christina. He inherited, however, but little of the martial character of his ancestors. I have observed that he was a simple good-natured man; he was, moreover, a kind neighbor, and an obedient henpecked husband. Indeed, to the latter circumstance might be owing that meekness of spirit which gained him such universal popularity; for those men are most apt to be obsequious and conciliating abroad, who are under the discipline of shrews at home. Their tempers, doubtless, are rendered pliant and malleable in the fiery furnace of domestic tribulation which is worth all the sermons in the world for teaching the virtues of patience and long-suffering. A termagant[5] wife may, therefore, in some respects, be considered a tolerable blessing; and if so, Rip Van Winkle was thrice blessed.

Certain it is, that he was a great favorite among all the good wives of the village, who, as usual with the amiable sex, took his part in all family squabbles; and never failed, whenever they talked those matters over in their evening gossipings, to lay all the blame on Dame Van Winkle. The children of the village, too, would shout with joy whenever he approached. He assisted at their sports, made their playthings, taught them to fly kites and shoot marbles, and told them long stories of ghosts, witches, and Indians. Whenever he went dodging about the village, he was surrounded by a troop of them, hanging on his skirts, clambering on his back and playing a thousand tricks on him with impunity; and not a dog would bark at him throughout the neighborhood.

The great error in Rip's composition was an insuperable aversion to all kinds of profitable labor. It could not be from the want of perseverance; for he would sit on a wet rock, with a rod as long and heavy as a Tartar's lance,[6] and fish all day without a murmur, even though he should not be encouraged by a single nibble. He would carry a fowling piece[7] on his shoulder for hours together, trudging through woods and swamps, and up hill and down dale, to shoot

---

2. Peter Stuyvesant (stī′ və s'nt): The last governor of New Netherland, a Dutch colony, before it was taken over by the English in 1664 and renamed New York.
3. within a few years: Until recently. The story was written during the early part of the 19th century.
4. gable fronts: Triangular wall shapes where two roof slopes meet.

5. termagant (tər′ mə gənt) *adj.*: Scolding.
6. Tartar's (tär′ tərz) **lance:** The Tartars were a member of the Mongolian tribes that invaded Europe about 700 years ago; these warriors used lances, which are long and heavy spears.
7. fowling piece: A type of shotgun for hunting wild fowl or birds.

Grammar in Action

One way that writers add descriptive detail to their writing is to use prepositional phrases. A prepositional phrase is made up of a preposition and a noun or pronoun that is the object of the preposition. Prepositional phrases act as single parts of speech. When a prepositional phrase acts as an adjective in a sentence, it is called an **adjective phrase.** An adjective phrase modifies a noun or a pronoun by telling *what kind* or *which one*. Notice how

Washington Irving uses an adjective phrase to make this sentence more descriptive:

Rip Van Winkle, however, was one of those happy mortals, *of foolish, well-oiled dispositions* . . .

In the above sentence, the underlined phrase is made up of a preposition, *of,* its object, the noun *dispositions,* and two adjectives that modify the object of the preposition. The entire phrase acts as an adjective modifying *mortals.*

Student Activity 1. For each of the following sentences, identify the adjective phrase and the noun or pronoun that it modifies. Some sentences have more than one adjective phrase.

1. It is a little village, of great antiquity . . .

a few squirrels or wild pigeons. He would never refuse to assist a neighbor even in the roughest toil, and was a foremost man at all country frolics for husking Indian corn, or building stone fences; the women of the village, too, used to employ him to run their errands, and to do such little odd jobs as their less obliging husbands would not do for them. In a word, Rip was ready to attend to anybody's business but his own; but as to doing family duty, and keeping his farm in order, he found it impossible.

In fact, he declared it was of no use to work on his farm; it was the most pestilent[8] little piece of ground in the whole country; everything about it went wrong, and would go wrong, in spite of him. His fences were continually falling to pieces; his cow would either go astray, or get among the cabbages; weeds were sure to grow quicker in his fields than anywhere else; the rain always made a point of setting in just as he had some outdoor work to do; so that though his estate had dwindled away under his management, acre by acre, until there was little more left than a mere patch of Indian corn and potatoes, yet it was the worst conditioned farm in the neighborhood.

His children, too, were as ragged and wild as if they belonged to nobody. His son Rip, an urchin[9] begotten in his own likeness, promised to inherit the habits, with the old clothes of his father. He was generally seen trooping like a colt at his mother's heels, equipped in a pair of his father's castoff galligaskins,[10] which he had much ado to hold up with one hand, as a fine lady does her train in bad weather.

Rip Van Winkle, however, was one of those happy mortals, of foolish, well-oiled dispositions, who take the world easy, eat white bread or brown, whichever can be got with least thought or trouble, and would rather starve on a penny than work for a pound.[11] If left to himself, he would have whistled life away in perfect contentment; but his wife kept continually dinning in his ears about his idleness, his carelessness, and the ruin he was bringing on his family. Morning, noon, and night, her tongue was incessantly going, and everything he said or did was sure to produce a torrent of household eloquence. Rip had but one way of replying to all lectures of the kind, and that, by frequent use, had grown into a habit. He shrugged his shoulders, shook his head, cast up his eyes, but said nothing. This, however, always provoked a fresh volley from his wife; so that he was fain[12] to draw off his forces, and take to the outside of the house—the only side which, in truth, belongs to a henpecked husband.

Rip's sole domestic adherent was his dog Wolf, who was as much henpecked as his master; for Dame Van Winkle regarded them as companions in idleness, and even looked upon Wolf with an evil eye, as the cause of his master's going so often astray. True it is, in all points of spirit befitting an honorable dog, he was as courageous an animal as ever scoured the woods—but what courage can withstand the ever-enduring and all-besetting terrors of a woman's tongue? The moment Wolf entered the house his crest fell, his tail drooped to the ground or curled between his legs, he sneaked about with a gallows air, casting many a sidelong glance at Dame Van Winkle, and at the least flourish of a broomstick or ladle, he would fly to the door with yelping precipitation.[13]

---

8. pestilent (pes′ t'l ənt) *adj.*: In this case, it means "annoying."
9. urchin (ər′ ∂hin) *n.*: A mischievous boy.
10. galligaskins (gal′ i gas′ kinz) *n.*: Loosely fitting breeches worn in the 16th and 17th centuries.

11. pound (pound) *n.*: A British unit of money.
12. fain (fān) *adj.*: An old-fashioned word meaning "glad."
13. precipitation (pri sip′ ə tā′ sʰən) *n.*: Great speed.

4 **Critical Thinking and Reading**
Do you agree with the villagers or with Dame Van Winkle? Was Rip just simple and good-natured or was he lazy and negligent? How do you think Washington Irving feels about Rip?

5 **Critical Thinking and Reading**
How is the tone used to describe Wolf typical of the tone used in the story? How does Irving use language to create a humorous effect?

2. Certain it is, that he was a great favorite among all the good wives of the village . . .
3. The children of the village, too, would shout with joy whenever he approached.
4. Rip had but one way of replying to all lectures of the kind . . .
5. Times grew worse and worse with Rip Van Winkle as years of matrimony rolled on . . .

Student Activity 2. Find three other sentences from this story that use adjective phrases. Copy the sentences on a sheet of paper and exchange it with a partner. Identify the adjective phrases in your partner's sentences and work together to correct each other's work.

Student Activity 3. Write five original sentences describing the setting of "Rip Van Winkle." Use adjective phrases to enhance your description.

Times grew worse and worse with Rip Van Winkle as years of matrimony rolled on; a tart temper never mellows with age, and a sharp tongue is the only edged tool that grows keener with constant use. For a long while he used to console himself, when driven from home, by frequenting a kind of perpetual club of the sages, philosophers, and other idle personages of the village; which held its sessions on a bench before a small inn, designated by a portrait of His Majesty George the Third. Here they used to sit in the shade through a long, lazy summer's day, talking listlessly over village gossip, or telling endless sleepy stories about nothing. But it would have been worth any statesman's money to have heard the profound discussions that sometimes took place when by chance an old newspaper fell into their hands from some passing traveler. How solemnly they would listen to the contents, as drawled out by Derrick Van Bummel, the schoolmaster, a dapper, learned little man, who was not to be daunted by the most gigantic word in the dictionary; and how sagely they would deliberate upon public events some months after they had taken place.

The opinions of this group were completely controlled by Nicholas Vedder, a patriarch of the village, and landlord of the inn, at the door of which he took his seat from morning till night, just moving sufficiently to avoid the sun and keep in the shade of a large tree; so that the neighbors could tell the hour by his movements as accurately as by a sundial. It is true, he was rarely heard 6 to speak, but smoked his pipe incessantly. His adherents, however (for every great man has his adherents), perfectly understood

RIP AT THE INN
Albertus Del Orient Brower
Shelburne Museum, Shelburne, Vermont

him, and knew how to gather his opinions. When anything that was read or related displeased him, he was observed to smoke his pipe vehemently, and to send forth short, frequent, and angry puffs; but when pleased, he would inhale the smoke slowly and tranquilly, and emit it in light and placid clouds; and sometimes, taking the pipe from his mouth, and letting the fragrant vapor curl about his nose, would gravely nod his head in token of perfect approbation.

From even this stronghold the unlucky Rip was at length routed by his termagant wife, who would suddenly break in upon the tranquillity of the assemblage and call the members all to naught; nor was that august personage, Nicholas Vedder himself, sacred from the daring tongue of this terrible virago,[14] who charged him outright with encouraging her husband in habits of idleness.

Poor Rip was at last reduced almost to despair; and his only alternative, to escape from the labor of the farm and clamor of his wife, was to take gun in hand and stroll away into the woods. Here he would sometimes seat himself at the foot of a tree, and share the contents of his wallet[15] with Wolf, with whom he sympathized as a fellow-sufferer in persecution. "Poor Wolf," he would say, "thy mistress leads thee a dog's life of it; but never mind, my lad, whilst I live thou shalt never want a friend to stand by thee!" Wolf would wag his tail, look wistfully in his master's face, and if dogs can feel pity I verily believe he reciprocated the sentiment with all his heart.

In a long ramble of the kind on a fine autumnal day, Rip had unconsciously scrambled to one of the highest parts of the Catskill mountains. He was after his favorite sport of squirrel shooting, and the still solitudes had echoed and re-echoed with the reports of his gun. Panting and fatigued, he threw himself, late in the afternoon, on a green knoll, covered with mountain herbage, that crowned the brow of a precipice. From an opening between the trees he could overlook all the lower country for many a mile of rich woodland. He saw at a distance the lordly Hudson, far, far below him, moving on its silent but majestic course, with the reflection of a purple cloud, or the sail of a lagging bark,[16] here and there sleeping on its glassy bosom, and at last losing itself in the blue highlands.

On the other side he looked down into a deep mountain glen, wild, lonely, and shagged,[17] the bottom filled with fragments from the impending[18] cliffs, and scarcely lighted by the reflected rays of the setting sun. For some time Rip lay musing on this scene; evening was gradually advancing; the mountains began to throw their long blue shadows over the valleys; he saw that it would be dark long before he could reach the village, and he heaved a heavy sigh when he thought of encountering the terrors of Dame Van Winkle.

As he was about to descend, he heard a voice from a distance hallooing, "Rip Van Winkle! Rip Van Winkle!" He looked round, but could see nothing but a crow winging its solitary flight across the mountain. He thought his fancy[19] must have deceived him, and turned again to descend, when he heard the same cry ring through the still evening air: "Rip Van Winkle! Rip Van Winkle!"—at the same time Wolf bristled up his back, and giving a low growl, skulked to his master's

---

16. bark (bärk) n.: Any boat, especially a small sailing boat.
17. shagged (shagd) adj.: Shaggy or rough.
18. impending (im pend' iŋ) adj.: An old-fashioned word for "overhanging."
19. fancy (fan' sē) n.: An old-fashioned word for "imagination."

---

14. virago (vi rā' gō) n.: A quarrelsome woman.
15. wallet (wôl' it) n.: In this case, it means a bag for carrying provisions.

Rip Van Winkle 137

7 Discussion What is your impression of Dame Van Winkle? Does she have a right to scold Nicholas Vedder, "a patriarch of the village, and landlord of the inn"? Why or why not?

8 Thematic Idea Another story in this book, "Luke Baldwin's Vow" (page 95), deals with the theme of the relationship between a lonely boy and a dog and of how they find comfort in each other's company.

9 Enrichment Thunder Mountain in the Catskills is thought to be the setting for Rip's encounter.

138

10 **Discussion** What do you think of Rip's assumption that the stranger with the keg of liquor must be a neighbor? What should he, perhaps, have done?

11 **Master Teacher Note** For students to understand why the cloud-wreathed Catskills are the perfect setting for an elfin hideaway, bring in a reproduction of Samuel Colman's painting *Storm King on the Hudson.* The juxtaposition of light and cloud give the landscape a supernatural quality.

12 **Clarification** Ninepins is a form of bowling played with nine pins.

13 **Discussion** What leads you to believe that the men Rip encounters are not ordinary men from the village?

side, looking fearfully down into the glen. Rip now felt a vague apprehension stealing over him; he looked anxiously in the same direction, and perceived a strange figure slowly toiling up the rocks, and bending under the weight of something he carried on his back. He was surprised to see any human being in this lonely and unfrequented place, but supposing it to be some one of the neighborhood in need of his assistance, he hastened down to yield it.

On nearer approach he was still more surprised at the singularity of the stranger's appearance. He was a short, square-built old fellow, with thick bushy hair, and a grizzled[20] beard. His dress was of the antique Dutch fashion—a cloth jerkin[21] strapped round the waist—several pairs of breeches, the outer one of ample volume, decorated with rows of buttons down the sides and bunches at the knees. He bore on his shoulder a stout keg, that seemed full of liquor, and made signs for Rip to approach and assist him with the load. Though rather shy and distrustful of this new acquaintance, Rip complied with his usual alacrity; and mutually relieving one another, they clambered up a narrow gully, apparently the dry bed of a mountain torrent. As they ascended, Rip every now and then heard long rolling peals, like distant thunder, that seemed to issue out of a deep ravine, or rather cleft, between lofty rocks, toward which their rugged path conducted. He paused for an instant, but supposing it to be the muttering of one of these transient thundershowers which often take place in mountain heights, he proceeded. Passing through the ravine, they came to a hollow, like a small amphitheater, surrounded by perpendicular precipices,

over the brinks of which impending trees shot their branches, so that you only caught glimpses of the azure sky and the bright evening cloud. During the whole time, Rip and his companion had labored on in silence; for though the former marvelled greatly what could be the object of carrying a keg of liquor up this wild mountain, yet there was something strange and incomprehensible about the unknown that inspired awe and checked familiarity.

On entering the amphitheater, new objects of wonder presented themselves. On a level spot in the center was a company of odd-looking personages playing at ninepins. They were dressed in a quaint outlandish fashion; some wore short doublets,[22] others jerkins, with long knives in their belts, and most of them had enormous breeches, of similar style with that of the guide's. Their visages,[23] too, were peculiar; one had a large beard, broad face, and small piggish eyes; the face of another seemed to consist entirely of nose, and was surmounted by a white sugar-loaf hat,[24] set off with a little red cock's tail. They all had beards, of various shapes and colors. There was one who seemed to be the commander. He was a stout old gentleman, with a weather-beaten countenance,[25] he wore a laced doublet, broad belt and hanger,[26] high-crowned hat and feather, red stockings, and high-heeled shoes, with roses in them. The whole group reminded Rip of the figures in an old Flemish[27] painting, in the parlor of Dominie Van Shaick, the village parson, and which had been brought over from Holland at the time of the settlement.

---

20. grizzled (griz' ld) *adj.*: An old-fashioned word for "gray."
21. jerkin (jər' kin) *n.*: A short, closefitting jacket worn in the 16th and 17th centuries.

22. doublets (dub' lits) *n.*: Closefitting jackets.
23. visages (viz' ij iz) *n.*: An old-fashioned word for "faces."
24. sugar-loaf hat: A hat shaped like a cone.
25. countenance (koun' tə nəns) *n.*: An old-fashioned word for "face."
26. hanger (haŋ' ər) *n.*: A short sword that hangs from the belt.
27. Flemish (flem' ish) *adj.*: Referring to the former country of Flanders in northwest Europe.

138 Short Stories

Grammar in Action

An **adjective** is a word used to describe a noun or pronoun. By choosing vivid, specific adjectives, you can enrich your meaning and make your descriptions more precise and colorful. In the following passage, Washington Irving effectively uses adjectives to portray a vivid picture of the stranger:

He was a *short, square-built old* fellow, with *thick bushy* hair, and a *grizzled* beard.

By using a series of adjectives, Irving presents a short, smooth sentence that vividly describes the singular appearance of the stranger. Notice that most of the words in the sentence are adjectives and that the one prepositional phrase also functions as an adjective.

See how dull and colorless Irving's sentence becomes when the adjectives are omitted.

He was a fellow with hair and a beard.

Student Activity 1. Find three sentences where Irving uses adjectives to make the descriptions more vivid and precise.

RIP VAN WINKLE ASLEEP
Albertus Del Orient Brower
Shelburne Museum, Shelburne Vermont

14 What seemed particularly odd to Rip was, that though these folks were evidently amusing themselves, yet they maintained the gravest face, the most mysterious silence, and were, withal, the most melancholy party of pleasure he had ever witnessed. Nothing interrupted the stillness of the scene but the noise of the balls, which, whenever they were rolled, echoed along the mountains like rumbling peals of thunder.

As Rip and his companion approached them, they suddenly desisted from their play, and stared at him with such fixed, statuelike gaze, and such strange, lackluster[28]

---

28. lackluster (lak′ lus′ tər) *adj.*: Lacking brightness, dull.

countenances, that his heart turned within him, and his knees smote together. His companion, now emptied the contents of the keg into large flagons,[29] and made signs to him to wait upon the company. He obeyed with fear and trembling; they quaffed[30] the liquor in profound silence, and then returned to their game.

By degrees Rip's awe and apprehension subsided. He even ventured, when no eye was fixed upon him, to taste the beverage, which he found had much of the flavor of ex-

---

29. flagons (flag′ ənz) *n.*: A container for liquids, with a handle, narrow neck, spout, and sometimes a lid.
30. quaffed (kwäft) *v.*: Drank in a thirsty way.

Rip Van Winkle 139

15

---

14 **Clarification** This is just one of many mythical explanations for what causes thunder. Thunder is really caused by the violent expansion of the air after it has been heated by lightning. Some primitive people thought that thunder was the roar of angry gods.

15 **Discussion** What do you think of Rip's reaction to these strangers? Should he have drunk the strange liquor?

Student Activity 2. Add adjectives, especially adjectives in a series, to make the following sentences more colorful and interesting.

1. The girl watched the man pushing the cart.

2. The child had cheeks, eyes, and hair.

3. The woman in the hat rushed through the crowd.

16 **Literary Focus** What clues indicate that a great deal of time has passed?

17 **Reading Strategy** Summarize the events of the story up to this point, and predict what Rip is about to discover.

cellent Hollands.[31] He was naturally a thirsty soul, and was soon tempted to repeat the draft. One taste provoked another; and he reiterated his visits to the flagon so often that at length his senses were overpowered, his eyes swam in his head, his head gradually declined, and he fell into a deep sleep.

On waking, he found himself on the green knoll whence he had first seen the old man of the glen. He rubbed his eyes—it was a bright sunny morning. The birds were hopping and twittering among the bushes, and the eagle was wheeling aloft, and breasting the pure mountain breeze. "Surely," thought Rip, "I have not slept here all night." He recalled the occurrences before he fell asleep. The strange man with a keg of liquor—the mountain ravine—the wild retreat among the rocks—the woebegone party at ninepins—the flagon—"Oh! that flagon! that wicked flagon!" thought Rip—"what excuse shall I make to Dame Van Winkle?"

He looked round for his gun, but in place of the clean, well-oiled fowling piece, he found an old firelock lying by him, the barrel incrusted with rust, the lock falling of, and the stock worm-eaten. He now suspected that the grave roysters[32] of the mountain had put a trick upon him, and having dosed him with liquor, had robbed him of his gun. Wolf, too, had disappeared, but he might have strayed away after a squirrel or partridge. He whistled after him and shouted his name, but all in vain; the echoes repeated his whistle and shout, but no dog was to be seen.

He determined to revisit the scene of the last evening's gambol,[33] and if he met with any of the party, to demand his dog and gun. As he rose to walk, he found himself stiff in the joints, and wanting in his usual activity. "These mountain beds do not agree with me," thought Rip, "and if this frolic should lay me up with a fit of the rheumatism, I shall have a blessed time with Dame Van Winkle." With some difficulty he got down into the glen: he found the gully up which he and his companion had ascended the preceding evening; but to his astonishment a mountain stream was now foaming down it, leaping from rock to rock, and filling the glen with babbling murmurs. He, however, made shift to scramble up its sides, working his toilsome way through thickets of birch, sassafras, and witch hazel, and sometimes tripped up or entangled by the wild grapevines that twisted their coils or tendrils from tree to tree, and spread a kind of network in his path.

At length he reached to where the ravine had opened through the cliffs to the amphitheater; but no traces of such opening remained. The rocks presented a high impenetrable wall, over which the torrent came tumbling in a sheet of feathery foam, and fell into a broad deep basin, black from the shadows of the surrounding forest. Here, then, poor Rip was brought to a stand. He again called and whistled after his dog; he was only answered by the cawing of a flock of idle crows, sporting high in air about a dry tree that overhung a sunny precipice; and who, secure in their elevation, seemed to look down and scoff at the poor man's perplexities. What was to be done? The morning was passing away, and Rip felt famished for want of his breakfast. He grieved to give up his dog and gun; he dreaded to meet his wife; but it would not do to starve among the mountains. He shook his head, shouldered the rusty firelock, and with a heart full of trouble and anxiety, turned his steps homeward.

As he approached the village he met a number of people, but none whom he knew,

---

31. Hollands *n.*: Gin made in the Netherlands.
32. roysters (rois' tərs) *n.*: An old-fashioned word for people who are having a good time at a party.
33. gambol (gam' b'l) *v.*: Play, frolic.

which somewhat surprised him, for he had thought himself acquainted with everyone in the country round. Their dress, too, was of a different fashion from that to which he was accustomed. They all stared at him with equal marks of surprise, and whenever they cast their eyes upon him, invariably stroked their chins. The constant recurrence of this gesture induced Rip, involuntarily, to do the same, when, to his astonishment, he found his beard had grown a foot long!

He had now entered the outskirts of the village. A troop of strange children ran at his heels, hooting after him, and pointing at his gray beard. The dogs, too, not one of which he recognized for an old acquaintance, barked at him as he passed. The very village was altered; it was larger and more populous. There were rows of houses which he had never seen before, and those which had been his familiar haunts had disappeared. Strange names were over the doors—strange faces at the windows—every thing was strange. His mind now misgave him; he began to doubt whether both he and the world around him were not bewitched. Surely this was his native village, which he had left but the day before. There stood the Catskill mountains—there ran the silver Hudson at a distance—there was every hill and dale precisely as it had always been—Rip was sorely perplexed—"That flagon last night," thought he; "has addled[34] my poor head sadly!"

It was with some difficulty that he found the way to his own house, which he approached with silent awe, expecting every moment to hear the shrill voice of Dame Van Winkle. He found the house gone to decay—the roof fallen in, the windows shattered, and the doors off the hinges. A half-starved dog that looked like Wolf was skulking about it. Rip called him by name, but the cur snarled, showed his teeth, and passed on.

This was an unkind cut indeed—"My very dog," sighed poor Rip, "has forgotten me!"

He entered the house, which, to tell the truth, Dame Van Winkle had always kept in neat order. It was empty, forlorn, and apparently abandoned. This desolateness overcame all his fears—he called loudly for his wife and children—the lonely chambers rang for a moment with his voice, and then all again was silence.

He now hurried forth, and hastened to his old resort, the village inn—but it too was gone. A large rickety wooden building stood in its place, with great gaping windows, some of them broken and mended with old hats and petticoats, and over the door was painted, "The Union Hotel, by Jonathan Doolittle." Instead of the great tree that used to shelter the quiet little Dutch inn of yore, there now was reared a tall, naked pole, with something on the top that looked like a red nightcap,[35] and from it was fluttering a flag, on which was a singular assemblage of stars and stripes—all this was strange and incomprehensible. He recognized on the sign, however, the ruby face of King George, under which he had smoked so many a peaceful pipe; but even this was singularly metamorphosed.[36] The red coat was changed for one of blue and buff, a sword was held in the hand instead of a scepter, the head was decorated with a cocked hat, and underneath was painted in large characters, GENERAL WASHINGTON.

There was, as usual, a crowd of folk about the door, but none that Rip recollected. The very character of the people seemed changed. There was a busy, bustling, disputatious tone about it, instead of the accustomed drowsy tranquillity. He looked in vain for the sage Nicholas Vedder,

---

34. addled (ad'ld) v.: Muddled and confused.

35. red nightcap: A liberty cap, used by colonists to symbolize their freedom from Great Britain.
36. metamorphosed (met' ə môr' fōzd) v.: Changed.

Rip Van Winkle 141

18 Literary Focus As a story moves forward in time, not only do characters and events change but the setting changes as well. In this story, changes in the setting are especially important.

19 Discussion Was the dog Rip met really Wolf? Why did it look like Wolf?

20 Discussion Why had George Washington's picture replaced King George's picture on the sign over the inn?

Humanities Note

Fine Art: *Return of Rip Van Winkle,* John Quidor. Born in Tappan, New York, Quidor (1801–1881) is remembered as a painter of imaginative scenes inspired by literary themes. The painting *Return of Rip Van Winkle,* painted in 1829, was inspired by the writings of Washington Irving, who was a personal friend of Quidor's. It depicts a disheveled and confused Rip walking into town surrounded by an agitated group of townsfolk. The Dutch-style buildings in the background are appropriate to old New York. On the right flies an American flag, symbolic of the changes that have taken place during Rip's twenty-year sleep. John Quidor's romantic paintings were not popular in his own time but today are appreciated for their humor and vitality.

1. How is the subject of this painting like the Rip Van Winkle you visualized while reading the story? How is he different?
2. Explain how the town changed in twenty years based on evidence in the painting.

21 **Discussion** Why didn't any of these words make sense to Rip?

22 **Critical Thinking and Reading** Would a man dressed in clothes from another time attract any attention in your town? Why or why not?

with his broad face, double chin, and fair long pipe, uttering clouds of tobacco smoke instead of idle speeches; or Van Bummel, the school-master, doling forth the contents of an ancient newspaper. In places of these, a lean, bilious-looking[37] fellow, with his pockets full of handbills, was speaking vehemently about rights of citizens—elections—members of Congress—liberty—Bunker's Hill—heroes of seventy-six—and other words, which were a perfect Babylonish jargon[38] to the bewildered Van Winkle.

The appearance of Rip, with his long grizzled beard, his rusty fowling piece, his uncouth dress, and an army of women and children at his heels, soon attracted the attention of the tavern politicians. They crowded round him, eyeing him from head to foot with great curiosity. The orator bustled up to him, and, drawing him partly aside, inquired "on which side he voted?" Rip stared in vacant stupidity. Another short but busy little fellow pulled him by the arm, and, rising on tiptoe, inquired in his ear, "whether he was Federal or Democrat?"[39] Rip was equally at a loss to comprehend the question; when a knowing, self-important

---

37. bilious (bil′ yəs)**-looking** *adj.*: Looking cross or bad-tempered.
38. Babylonish (bab′ ə lō′ nish) **jargon:** A language he could not understand.

39. Federal or Democrat: Two political parties at that time.

RETURN OF RIP VAN WINKLE, 1829
John Quidor
National Gallery of Art, Washington

old gentleman in a sharp cocked hat made his way through the crowd, putting them to the right and left with his elbows as he passed, and planting himself before Van Winkle, with one arm akimbo,[40] the other resting on his cane, his keen eyes and sharp hat penetrating, as it were, into his very soul, demanded, in an austere tone, "what brought him to the election with a gun on his shoulder, and a mob at his heels, and whether he meant to breed a riot in the village?" "Alas! gentlemen," cried Rip, somewhat dismayed, "I am a poor, quiet man, a native of the place, and a loyal subject of the king, God bless him!"

Here a general shout burst from the bystanders—"A tory![41] a tory! a spy! a refugee! hustle him! away with him!" It was with great difficulty that the self-important man in the cocked hat restored order; and, having assumed a tenfold austerity of brow, demanded again of the unknown culprit, what he came there for, and whom he was seeking. The poor man humbly assured him that he meant no harm, but merely came there in search of some of his neighbors, who used to keep about the tavern.

"Well, who are they? Name them."

Rip bethought himself a moment, and inquired, "Where's Nicholas Vedder?"

There was a silence for a little while, when an old man replied, in a thin, piping voice, "Nicholas Vedder! why, he is dead and gone these eighteen years! There was a wooden tombstone in the churchyard that used to tell all about him, but that's rotten and gone too."

"Where's Brom Dutcher?"

"Oh, he went off to the army in the beginning of the war; some say he was killed at the storming of Stony Point[42]—others say he was drowned in a squall at the foot of Antony's Nose.[43] I don't know—he never came back again."

"Where's Van Bummel, the schoolmaster?"

"He went off to the wars, too, was a great militia general, and is now in Congress."

Rip's heart died away at hearing of these sad changes in his home and friends, and finding himself thus alone in the world. Every answer puzzled him too, by treating of such enormous lapses of time, and of matters which he could not understand; war—Congress—Stony Point—he had no courage to ask after any more friends, but cried out in despair, "Does nobody here know Rip Van Winkle?"

"Oh, Rip Van Winkle!" exclaimed two or three, "Oh, to be sure! that's Rip Van Winkle yonder, leaning against the tree."

Rip looked, and beheld a precise counterpart of himself, as he went up the mountain: apparently as lazy, and certainly as ragged. The poor fellow was now completely confounded. He doubted his own identity, and whether he was himself or another man. In the midst of his bewilderment, the man in the cocked hat demanded who he was, and what was his name.

"Goodness knows," exclaimed he, at his wit's end; "I'm not myself—I'm somebody else—that's me yonder—no—that's somebody else got into my shoes—I was myself last night, but I fell asleep on the mountain, and they've changed my gun, and everything's changed, and I'm changed, and I can't tell what's my name, or who I am!"

The bystanders began now to look at each other, nod, wink significantly, and tap

---

Rip Van Winkle 143

23 Discussion Why was this the worst thing Rip could have possibly said?

24 Enrichment Have students discuss the horror of a person outliving his or her own times and friends. Point out that in Jonathan Swift's *Gulliver's Travels,* one of the worst curses was to be born with the mark of eternal life on earth. People with this mark were doomed to live forever in an increasingly lonely and unfamiliar world. At this point, you might also touch on the similar plight of the elderly in society.

25 Discussion Who is this new Rip Van Winkle?

26 Critical Thinking and Reading Have students imagine how it would feel to go to sleep and wake up in another time. Ask students if any of them have seen the Woody Allen movie *Sleeper,* in which a man is put to sleep in a hospital in the present and wakes up in the future. Compare Allen's comic effects with Irving's.

27 Discussion Why might you say that Dame Van Winkle died as she had lived? Is Rip's reaction to the news of his wife's death surprising?

28 Discussion What was the reaction of Rip's neighbors when they heard his story? How did they know he was telling the truth?

29 Enrichment Henry Hudson was the first man to explore the Hudson River, which was named after him. He sailed from Amsterdam in 1609 in his ship the *Half Moon* and explored the North American coast.

30 Critical Thinking and Reading Can you think of any other regional legends that have been passed down for generations? An example is the Bigfoot legend of the Pacific Northwest.

their fingers against their foreheads. There was a whisper, also, about securing the gun, and keeping the old fellow from doing mischief, at the very suggestion of which the self-important man in the cocked hat retired with some precipitation. At this critical moment a fresh, comely[44] women pressed through the throng to get a peep at the gray-bearded man. She had a chubby child in her arms, which, frightened at his looks, began to cry. "Hush, Rip," cried she, "hush, you little fool; the old man won't hurt you." The name of the child, the air of the mother, the tone of her voice, all awakened a train of recollections in his mind. "What is your name, my good woman?" asked he.

"Judith Gardenier."

"And your father's name?"

"Ah! poor man, Rip Van Winkle was his name, but it's twenty years since he went away from home with his gun and never has been heard of since—his dog came home without him; but whether he shot himself, or was carried away by the Indians, nobody can tell. I was then but a little girl."

Rip had but one question more to ask; but he put it with a faltering voice:

"Where's your mother?"

27 "Oh, she too had died but a short time since; she broke a blood vessel in a fit of passion at a New England peddler."

There was a drop of comfort, at least, in this intelligence.[45] The honest man could contain himself no longer. He caught his daughter and her child in his arms. "I am your father!" cried he—"Young Rip Van Winkle once—old Rip Van Winkle now! Does nobody know poor Rip Van Winkle?"

All stood amazed, until an old woman, tottering out from among the crowd, put her

---

44. comely (kum′ lē) *adj.*: Attractive, pretty.
45. intelligence (in tel′ ə jəns) *n.*: In this case, it means "news."

hand to her brow, and peering under it in his face for a moment, exclaimed, "Sure enough! it is Rip Van Winkle—it is himself! Welcome home again, old neighbor. Why, where have you been these twenty long years?"

Rip's story was soon told, for the whole twenty long years had been to him but as one night. The neighbors stared when they heard it; some were seen to wink at each other, and put their tongues in their cheeks: and the self-important man in the cocked hat, who, when the alarm was over, had returned to the field, screwed down the corners of his mouth, and shook his head—upon which there was a general shaking of the head throughout the assemblage. **28**

It was determined, however, to take the opinion of old Peter Vanderdonk, who was seen slowly advancing up the road. He was a descendant of the historian of that name, who wrote one of the earliest accounts of the province. Peter was the most ancient inhabitant of the village, and well versed in all the wonderful events and traditions of the neighborhood. He recollected Rip at once, and corroborated his story in the most satisfactory manner. He assured the company that it was a fact, handed down from his ancestor the historian, that the Catskill mountains had always been haunted by strange beings. That it was affirmed that the great Henry Hudson, the first discoverer of the river and country,[46] kept a kind of vigil there **29** every twenty years, with his crew of the *Half-Moon*; being permitted in this way to revisit the scenes of his enterprise, and keep a guardian eye upon the river, and the great city called by his name. That his father had once seen them in their old Dutch dresses **30** playing at ninepins in a hollow of the mountain; and that he himself had heard, one

---

46. country: The area around the Catskills.

Grammar in Action

An **adjective clause** is a subordinate clause that modifies a noun or pronoun. An adjective clause describes, adds to, or limits the word it modifies and, therefore, makes the word more precise. Using subordinate clauses to add related information adds variety and smoothness to writing. Notice how Washington Irving effectively uses adjective clauses to identify Rip's son-in-law precisely and vividly:

She had a snug, well-furnished house, and a stout, cheery farmer for a husband, *whom Rip recollected for one of the urchins that used to climb upon his back.*

By using adjective clauses, Irving is able to add more depth to the reader's knowledge of the son-in-law.

It might be helpful to remember that, like adjectives, adjective clauses answer the questions *What kind?* or *Which one?* Also, most adjective clauses begin with the words *that, which, who, whom,* and *whose*. Sometimes adjective clauses begin with an adverb such as *since, where,* or *when*.

Student Activity 1. Combine each group of sentences to form a sentence with at least one adjective clause.

summer afternoon, the sound of their balls, like distant peals of thunder.

To make a long story short, the company broke up, and returned to the more important concerns of the election. Rip's daughter took him home to live with her; she had a snug, well-furnished house, and a stout, cheery farmer for a husband, whom Rip recollected for one of the urchins that used to climb upon his back. As to Rip's son and heir, who was the ditto of himself, seen leaning against the tree, he was employed to work on the farm; but evinced an hereditary disposition to attend to anything else but his business.

Rip now resumed his old walks and habits; he soon found many of his former cronies, though all rather the worse for the wear and tear of time; and preferred making friends among the rising generation, with whom he soon grew into great favor.

31 Having nothing to do at home, and being arrived at that happy age when a man can be idle with impunity, he took his place once more on the bench at the inn door, and was reverenced as one of the patriarchs of the village, and a chronicle of the old times "before the war." It was some time before he could get into the regular track of gossip, or could be made to comprehend the strange events that had taken place during his torpor. How that there had been a revolutionary war—that the country had thrown off the yoke of old England—and that, instead of being a subject of his Majesty George the Third, he was now a free citizen of the United States.

Rip, in fact, was no politician; the changes of states and empires made but little impression on him; but there was one species of despotism under which he had long groaned, and that was—petticoat government. Happily that was at an end; he had got his neck out of the yoke of matrimony, and could go in and out whenever he pleased, without dreading the tyranny of Dame Van Winkle. Whenever her name was mentioned, however, he shook his head, shrugged his shoulders, and cast up his eyes; which might pass either for an expression of resignation to his fate, or joy at his deliverance.

He used to tell his story to every stranger that arrived at Mr. Doolittle's hotel. He was observed, at first, to vary on some points every time he told it, which was, doubtless, owing to his having so recently awaked. It at last settled down precisely to the tale I have related, and not a man, woman, or child in the neighborhood, but knew it by heart. Some always pretended to doubt the reality of it, and insisted that Rip had been out of his head, and that this was one point on which he always remained flighty. The old Dutch inhabitants, however, almost universally gave it full credit. Even to this day they never hear a thunderstorm of a summer afternoon about the Catskills, but they say Henry Hudson and his crew are at their game of ninepins; and it is a common wish of all henpecked husbands in the neighborhood, when life hangs heavy on their hands, **32** that they might have a quieting draft out of Rip Van Winkle's flagon.

---

1. Our neighbor is a teacher.
   She lives across the street from us.
2. The "Legend of Sleepy Hollow" was also written by Washington Irving.
   It is a tale about a headless horseman.
3. I immediately fell in love with the dresser.
   The dresser was an old Victorian one.
   It belonged to my great aunt.

Student Activity 2. Write three original sentences in which you use adjective clauses.

---

31 Discussion Compare Rip's new lifestyle with his old one. Did his long sleep have positive or negative consequences for him? Explain your answer.

32 Critical Thinking and Reading Do you believe that other men sincerely wish to have the same experience that Rip had? What might Irving's purpose be in ending the story with this statement?

Reader's Response What might be some advantages of going to sleep and waking up twenty years later? Disadvantages? Explain.

Closure and Extension

(Questions begin on p. 146.)

ANSWERS TO THINKING ABOUT THE SELECTION
Recalling

1. Rip is a henpecked husband whose wife constantly nags him.
2. The people love Rip because he is gentle and always willing to help them with their work.
3. Rip is idle, careless, and dislikes all profitable labor.
4. He sees a group of odd-looking men dressed in old-fashioned clothes playing ninepins.
5. His once well-oiled gun is now rusty, the lock is falling off, and the stock is worm-eaten.
6. The people and dogs are unfamiliar to Rip. The people's clothes are of a different fashion. The village is larger and more populous, with rows of strange new houses and some old houses no longer standing. The names over the doors are strange, and his own house is abandoned and in state of ruin.

Interpreting

7. This suggests that a quarrelsome wife's nagging causes her husband to become mild-mannered, patient, and quiet, which are the qualities that would make a person popular with others.
8. Dame Van Winkle is a harsh woman who wants to get things done, while Rip is a simple, good-natured man who loves to be idle.
9. Rip's life resumes its old course of idleness after his long sleep. But now he has no wife to nag

(Answers begin on p. 145.)

him. Also, since he is twenty years older than before, he is not criticized for being lazy.

Applying

10. Answers will differ. Suggested Response: New people will be living there and the former residents will have gotten older, died, or moved away. The style of clothing will have changed. There will be new buildings, while some of the older buildings will have been torn down. Technology will have become more advanced, the cost of items will have altered, and there will be new political and social leaders.

ANSWERS TO ANALYZING LITERATURE

1. The American Revolutionary War has been fought, and America is now a free country governed by President George Washington rather than an English colony governed by King George III.
2. His wife has died.

ANSWERS TO CRITICAL THINKING AND READING

1. The Catskill Mountains and Hudson River are still there as in the past.
2. The gully leading up to the amphitheater has filled with water and become a mountain stream. The place where the ravine opened through the cliffs is now closed off by a wall of rocks over which the water cascades.
3. The village is larger and more populous, with rows of strange new houses and older houses no longer there. Also, the names of the houses' owners have changed.
4. Rip's home is abandoned and dilapidated.

ANSWERS TO UNDERSTANDING LANGUAGE

Answers may differ since dictionaries are not all uniform in their pronunciation and definitions. Suggested Responses:

1. **barometer** (be räm′ e ter) *n.* **1.** an instrument for measuring at-

---

THINKING ABOUT THE SELECTION

Recalling

1. What problems does Rip Van Winkle have with his wife?
2. How do the people in the village feel about Rip?
3. Describe "the great error" in Rip's character.
4. What does Rip see when he enters the amphitheater with the strange man carrying the keg?
5. When Rip awakes, what is the first sign that he has been asleep a very long time?
6. What changes does Rip discover in the village?

Interpreting

7. A sentence in the story says that a quarrelsome wife may be considered a blessing. What does this mean?
8. How do Dame Van Winkle's personality and Rip's personality differ?
9. Compare and contrast Rip's life after his long sleep with his earlier life.

Applying

10. Imagine that you have fallen into a long sleep like Rip's. What changes in your neighborhood and country do you think you would discover when you awoke?

ANALYZING LITERATURE

Recognizing the Passage of Time

Changes in appearance indicate that time has passed. When Rip awakes, such changes show vividly the advance of time. They are also linked with other kinds of change.

1. What historical and political changes have occurred during Rip's long sleep?
2. What change has occurred that will make Rip's life at home different from what it was before his long sleep?

CRITICAL THINKING AND READING

Comparing and Contrasting Settings

When you **compare** and **contrast** a setting at different times, you note similarities, or comparisons, and differences, or contrasts.

1. When Rip looks around after he awakes, what features of the natural world does he see that have not changed at all?
2. What differences does he see in the mountain setting?
3. How has the village changed?
4. How is his home different from what it was?

UNDERSTANDING LANGUAGE

Looking Up Words in a Dictionary

A dictionary provides several different kinds of information about a word. It gives the word's spelling, pronunciation, part of speech, and meanings. Some dictionaries also provide information about its history. Look up the following words from "Rip Van Winkle" in a dictionary. Be able to tell each word's meanings, part of speech, and pronunciation.

1. barometer
2. lattice
3. obsequious
4. pliant
5. malleable
6. tribulation

THINKING AND WRITING

Describing a Place Then and Now

Look at the "before" and "after" details you listed before you read the story. Use these details to write a composition in which you contrast how a place looked before it changed and how it looked after. When you revise, make sure your description would be clear even to a reader who never saw the place you are writing about.

---

mospheric pressure. **2.** anything that reflects or indicates change

2. **lattice** (lat′ is) *n.* **1.** an openwork structure of crossed strips or bars of wood, metal, etc., used as a screen, support, etc. **2.** something resembling or suggesting such a structure **3.** a door, gate shutter, trellis, etc. formed of such a structure *vt.* **1.** to arrange like a lattice; make a lattice of **2.** to furnish or cover with a lattice or latticework

3. **obsequious** (eb sē′ kwē es) *adj.* **1.** much too willing to serve or obey; fawning **2.** Archaic compliant; devoted; dutiful

4. **pliant** (plī′ ent) *adj.* **1.** easily bent; pliable **2.** adaptable

5. **malleable** (mal′ ē e b′l) *adj.* **1.** that can be hammered, pounded, or pressed into various shapes without breaking **2.** capable of being changed; adaptable

6. **tribulation** (trib ye lā′ shen) *n.* **1.** great misery or distress; deep sorrow **2.** something that causes suffering or distress; affliction; trial

Challenge What commentary on life is made by the fact that the Catskill Mountains and Hudson River look the same as they did twenty years before, while the things that people made looked so much different than they had in the past? Is twenty years a long time in nature? In a city?

Theme

THE FOUR LEAF CLOVER
Winslow Homer
The Detroit Institute of Arts

Humanities Note

Fine art, *The Four Leaf Clover*, 1873, Winslow Homer. The American painter Winslow Homer (1836–1910) was born in Boston. His formal training in art is insignificant; he was largely self-taught. Homer is best known for his genre, marine, and landscape paintings of the American Northeast. He remains one of America's foremost painters and illustrators.

The painting *The Four Leaf Clover* is a watercolor painted in the Hurley, New York, area. It is a charming outdoor study of a young girl gazing at a stem of clover. The sunlight pours down in the painting, and the colors glow with summer radiance. The window nearby provides an interesting background for the scene. The pleasant narrative quality of this painting is probably linked to the artist's years as an illustrator. Winslow Homer had a great love for portraying ordinary scenes such as this in a pleasant, direct fashion.

Focus

More About the Author Isaac Bashevis Singer is famous for his short stories, which are often inspired by Jewish and Polish folklore. Singer says that he must have a strong topic or theme in mind when he writes. Have students discuss the relationship between good writing and strong theme. Why is it important for a writer to begin with a clearly defined topic? How does it help to convey the author's message?

Literary Focus Often, the stated theme appears at the end of a story. This is particularly true with fables. In this story, the theme appears in more than one place. Tell the class some familiar fables, such as "The Tortoise and the Hare," and have them identify what the theme is and where it's placed in the story.

Look For Your less advanced students may find theme a difficult concept to grasp. It may be helpful to preview the Analyzing Literature questions on page 153 so that these questions can guide their reading.

Writing/Prior Knowledge Have students discuss the meaning of this quotation: "Never put off 'til tomorrow what you can do today." Then have them complete the freewriting assignment.

Vocabulary Have your less advanced students read these words aloud so that you can be sure they can pronounce them.

Spelling Tip Students will have less trouble spelling the word *industrious* if they spot the word *industry* in it.

Utzel and His Daughter, Poverty

Isaac Bashevis Singer (1904–   ), who was born in Poland, writes primarily in Yiddish, a language spoken by East European Jews and some of their descendants. Singer came to the United States in 1935 and earned his living by writing for Yiddish newspapers. As his novels and short stories were translated into English, he became famous for his accounts of Jewish life in Eastern Europe. In 1978 he won the Nobel Prize for literature. In "Utzel and His Daughter, Poverty," Singer entertains and teaches at the same time.

Stated Theme

Theme is the general idea about life that is revealed through the story. In stories with a **stated theme**, the writer or one of the characters tells you this idea directly. "Utzel and His Daughter, Poverty" is a story with a stated theme.

Look For

As you read this humorous story, look for statements that indicate the theme. Pay special attention to the motto Utzel hangs on his wall at the end of the story. How is the theme supported by the events of the story?

Writing

In the story you are about to read, Utzel puts off tasks he does not enjoy doing. Have you ever known of someone who put off a job or a chore even though this person knew it would have to be done eventually? Freewrite about what happened as a result of the delay.

Vocabulary

Knowing the following words will help you as you read "Utzel and His Daughter, Poverty."

fitting (fit' iŋ) *adj.*: Suitable; proper (p. 149)

reproached (ri prōcht') *v.*: Blamed; scolded (p. 149)

consternation (kän'stər nā' shən) *n.*: Sudden confusion and frustration (p. 150)

diligently (dil'ə jənt lē) *adv.*: With careful, steady effort (p. 152)

industrious (in dus'trē əs) *adj.*: Hard-working (p. 152)

148   *Short Stories*

Objectives

1 To identify the stated theme of a short story
2 To paraphrase the stated theme
3 To understand how to read dialogue
4 To explain why a certain motto is appropriate in a given situation

Support Material

Teaching Portfolio
Teacher Backup, p. 221
Grammar in Action Worksheet, *Paragraphing Dialogue*, p. 225
Usage and Mechanics Worksheet, p. 227
Vocabulary Check, p. 228
Critical Thinking and Reading Worksheet, *Paraphrasing*, p. 229

Language Worksheet, *Using Precise Words*, p. 231
Selection Test, p. 232

Utzel and His Daughter, Poverty

Isaac Bashevis Singer

Once there was a man named Utzel. He was very poor and even more lazy. Whenever anyone wanted to give him a job to do, his answer was always the same: "Not today."

"Why not today?" he was asked. And he always replied, "Why not tomorrow?"

Utzel lived in a cottage that had been built by his great-grandfather. The thatched roof needed mending, and although the holes let the rain in, they did not let the smoke from the stove out. Toadstools grew on the crooked walls and the floor had rotted away. There had been a time when mice lived there, but now there weren't any because there was nothing for them to eat. Utzel's wife had starved to death, but before she died she had given birth to a baby girl. The name Utzel gave his daughter was very fitting. He called her Poverty.

Utzel loved to sleep and each night he went to bed with the chickens. In the morning he would complain that he was tired from so much sleeping and so he went to sleep again. When he was not sleeping, he lay on his broken-down cot, yawning and complaining. He would say to his daughter, "Other people are lucky. They have money without working. I am cursed."

Utzel was a small man, but as his daughter, Poverty, grew, she spread out in all directions. She was tall, broad, and heavy. At fifteen she had to lower her head to get through the doorway. Her feet were the size of a man's and puffy with fat. The villagers maintained that the lazier Utzel got, the more Poverty grew.

Utzel loved nobody, was jealous of everybody. He even spoke with envy of cats, dogs, rabbits, and all creatures who didn't have to work for a living. Yes, Utzel hated everybody and everything, but he adored his daughter. He daydreamed that a rich young man would fall in love with her, marry her, and provide for his wife and his father-in-law. But not a young man in the village showed the slightest interest in Poverty. When her father reproached the girl for not making friends and not going out with young men, Poverty would say, "How can I go out in rags and bare feet?"

One day Utzel learned that a certain charitable society in the village loaned poor people money, which they could pay back in small sums over a long period. Lazy as he was, he made a great effort—got up, dressed, and went to the office of the society. "I would like to borrow five gulden,"[1] he said to the official in charge.

"What do you intend to do with the

---

1. **gulden** (gool'dən) *n.*: A coin that was once used in Germany, Austria, and other countries.

Utzel and His Daughter, Poverty   149

6 Discussion What's wrong with Utzel's counting on a future son-in-law to pay back his loan? How realistic is Utzel? Why is he so optimistic about Poverty's chances of marrying a wealthy young man?

7 Discussion What can you tell about Utzel's relationship with Poverty? In what ways is Utzel a good father? In what ways is he not?

8 Critical Thinking and Reading Can you figure out why Poverty's feet have grown again? Like Pinocchio's nose growing every time he tells a lie, Poverty's growing feet are a physical manifestation of an underlying problem.

9 Discussion Discuss Sandler's philosophy in terms of modern credit-card spending. Are people poorer with credit cards than they would be without, even though they might own more?

money?" he was asked. "We lend money only for useful purposes."

6 "I want to have a pair of shoes made for my daughter," Utzel explained. "If Poverty has shoes, she will go out with the young people of the village and some wealthy young man will surely fall in love with her. When they get married, I will be able to pay back the five gulden."

The official thought it over. The chances of anyone falling in love with Poverty were very small. Utzel, however, looked so miserable that the official decided to give him the loan. He asked Utzel to sign a promissory note and gave him five gulden.

Utzel had tried to order a pair of shoes for his daughter a few months before. Sandler the shoemaker had gone so far as to take Poverty's measurements, but the shoemaker had wanted his money in advance. From the charitable society Utzel went directly to the shoemaker and asked whether he still had Poverty's measurements.

"And supposing I do?" Sandler replied. "My price is five gulden and I still want my money in advance."

Utzel took out the five gulden and handed them to Sandler. The shoemaker opened a drawer and after some searching brought out the order for Poverty's shoes. He promised to deliver the new shoes in a week, on Friday.

7 Utzel, who wanted to surprise his daughter, did not tell her about the shoes. The following Friday, as he lay on his cot yawning and complaining, there was a knock on the door and Sandler came in carrying the new shoes. When Poverty saw the shoemaker with a pair of shiny new shoes in his hand, she cried out in joy. The shoemaker handed her the shoes and told her to try them on. But, alas, she could not get them on her puffy feet. In the months since the measure-**8** ments had been taken, Poverty's feet had be-

come even larger than they were before. Now the girl cried out in grief.

Utzel looked on in consternation. "How is it possible?" he asked. "I thought her feet stopped growing long ago."

For a while Sandler, too, stood there puzzled. Then he inquired, "Tell me, Utzel, where did you get the five gulden?" Utzel explained that he had borrowed the money from the charitable loan society and had given them a promissory note in return.

9 "So now you have a debt," exclaimed Sandler. "That makes you even poorer than you were a few months ago. Then you had nothing, but today you have five gulden less than nothing. And since you have grown

Grammar in Action

Dialogue adds interest and drama to a story. It makes the characters come alive and the story more natural and believable. With dialogue, paragraphs and quotation marks are used to show that someone is talking. When you write dialogue, begin a new paragraph each time there is a change of speaker. This alerts the reader that someone new is talking. Also, use quotation marks to enclose the exact words the speaker says. Notice how Isaac

Bashevis Singer in "Utzel and His Daughter, Poverty" uses paragraph indentation to indicate that someone is talking and quotation marks to indicate the exact words of the speaker.

"What do you intend to do with the money?" he was asked. "We lend money only for useful purposes."
"I want to have a pair of shoes made for my daughter," Utzel explained.

The paragraph indentations and quotation marks make this section of dialogue understandable. We know when someone is talking. Read the following paragraph to see the effect of omitting paragraphing and quotation marks. Would you know who is

speaking and what each speaker's exact words are if dialogue were written this way?

What do you intend to do with the money? he was asked. We lend money only for useful purposes. I want to have a pair of shoes made for my daughter, Utzel explained.

Student Activity 1. Using paragraph indentations and quotation marks, rewrite the following passage so that it is clear dialogue.

Mother, I want to go to the football game on Saturday. I'm sorry, but we have planned to visit the Snyders then and you have to come with us. That's not fair. I hardly know

them, and besides I can stay with Mary. She's going to the game.

Student Activity 2. Write your own brief dialogue of five or more lines using quotation marks and paragraphs to indicate who is speaking.

10

poorer, Poverty has grown bigger, and naturally her feet have grown with her. That is why the shoes don't fit. It is all clear to me now."

"What are we going to do?" Utzel asked in despair.

11

"There is only one way out for you," Sandler said. "Go to work. From borrowing one gets poorer and from work one gets richer. When you and your daughter work, she will have shoes that fit."

The idea of working did not appeal to either of them, but it was even worse to have new shoes and go around barefoot. Utzel and

12

Poverty both decided that immediately after the Sabbath they would look for work.

Utzel got a job as a water carrier. Poverty became a maid. For the first time in their lives, they worked diligently. They were kept so busy that they did not even think of the new shoes, until one Sabbath morning Poverty decided she'd try them on again. Lo and behold, her feet slipped easily into them. The new shoes fit.

At last Utzel and Poverty understood that all a man possesses he gains through work, and not by lying in bed and being idle. Even animals were industrious. Bees make honey, spiders spin webs, birds build nests, moles dig holes in the earth, squirrels store food for the winter. Before long Utzel got a better job. He rebuilt his house and bought some furniture. Poverty lost more weight. She had new clothes made and dressed prettily like the other girls of the village. Her looks improved, too, and a young man began to court her. His name was Mahir and he was the son of a wealthy merchant. Utzel's dream of a rich son-in-law came true, but by then he no longer needed to be taken care of.

Love for his daughter had saved Utzel. In his later years he became so respected he was elected a warden of that same charitable loan society from which he had borrowed five gulden.

On the wall of his office there hung the string with which Sandler had once measured Poverty's feet, and above it the framed motto: *Whatever you can do today, don't put off till tomorrow.*

13

14

15

10 Literary Focus Utzel is in debt and so his poverty, symbolized by his daughter Poverty, has become greater. Singer represents his subject in a humorous way in this story.

11 Reading Strategy Predict if what the shoemaker says will come true. How was Sandler able to figure this out?

12 Clarification The Sabbath is a day of rest in the Jewish religion. It lasts from sunset Friday evening until sunset Saturday. Orthodox Jews do not work, travel, or carry money on the Sabbath.

13 Discussion How does this represent a change in Utzel's thinking from the beginning of the story?

14 Discussion What do Utzel and Poverty learn from their experiences? What is the real value of honest labor?

15 Discussion What is the moral of the story and what does it mean? How is the final motto different from Utzel's original philosophy of life?

Enrichment Isaac Singer has written most of his stories in Yiddish, a language of the Jews that developed from several other languages, including German, Hebrew, Aramaic, French, and Italian. Yiddish uses the Hebrew alphabet. During World War II, many Yiddish writers and Yiddish-speaking people were killed. Singer is the first Yiddish writer to receive the Nobel prize for literature.

Reader's Response What important lesson does Utzel learn?

THINKING ABOUT THE SELECTION

Recalling

1. What is Utzel's daydream for his daughter?
2. Why does he want to buy shoes for Poverty?
3. Why are the shoes too small, even though Sandler the shoemaker took Poverty's measurements before making them?
4. What advice does Sandler give Utzel?
5. What does Utzel realize after he starts to work?

Interpreting

6. Why is it "fitting" that Utzel called his daughter Poverty?
7. The writer says that "the lazier Utzel got, the more Poverty grew." What could this statement indicate besides the fact that the girl grew physically larger?
8. What does the writer mean by saying, "Love for his daughter had saved Utzel"?

Applying

9. Why does a person become stronger by loving someone else?

ANALYZING LITERATURE

Identifying the Stated Theme

The **theme**, or central idea, of a story may be **stated** directly by the writer or one of the characters. In "Utzel and His Daughter, Poverty," there are several statements of the theme.

1. Find the place in the story where the character Sandler states the theme.
2. Find the place where the author, Isaac Bashevis Singer, states it.
3. How does the framed motto Utzel hangs on the wall also indicate the theme?

CRITICAL THINKING AND READING

Paraphrasing the Stated Theme

Paraphrasing a statement means putting it into your own words. By paraphrasing the stated theme, you will make sure that you really understand the story's point. You will gain more from your reading if you also think about this idea. It may turn out that you do not agree with what the writer is saying.

1. Paraphrase the stated theme of "Utzel and His Daughter, Poverty."
2. Explain why you agree or disagree with this idea.

SPEAKING AND LISTENING

Reading Dialogue in a Story

In a story, **dialogue** consists of the words characters say to each other. These words appear in quotation marks. To appreciate dialogue, you should try to imagine the way the different characters would talk. Sometimes a writer will tell you how a particular speech should sound by saying a character is "puzzled" or "happy" or "angry." However, you can also guess what characters sound like based on their personalities.

1. How do you imagine Utzel would speak through most of the story? Why?
2. With another person, read aloud the dialogue between Utzel and Sandler when Poverty first tries on her new shoes (page 150). Remember to use the writer's information about how these characters sound.

THINKING AND WRITING

Writing About a Motto

A **motto** is an expression that captures the goals or ideals of a person or group of people. At the end of the selection, Utzel chooses a motto for himself. Think about what this motto means and how it fits the way Utzel has changed. Draft a short essay explaining why you think it is or is not an appropriate motto for Utzel. Be sure to support your opinion with details from the story. Read over your essay, adding any details that would make your opinion more persuasive. Prepare a final draft and share it with your classmates.

else, a person puts the welfare of another first. This will cause the person to work harder, to share and to sacrifice for the loved one.

ANSWERS TO ANALYZING LITERATURE

1. Sandler states the theme when he says to Utzel, "Go to work. From borrowing one gets poorer and from work one gets richer."
2. The author says, "At last Utzel and Poverty understood that all a man possesses he gains through work and not by lying in bed and being idle."
3. Answers will differ. Suggested Response: When you put something off, you may never get to it. People who put things off do not accomplish as much as people who do things in a timely fashion.

ANSWERS TO CRITICAL THINKING AND READING

1. Answers will differ. Suggested Response: People should do today's work today rather than putting it off until tomorrow.
2. Answers will differ. Suggested Response: I agree because successful people are people of action who get things done on time.

ANSWERS TO SPEAKING AND LISTENING

1. Utzel would speak slowly, listlessly, angrily, and dejectedly because he sleeps much of the time, is lazy, complains a lot, hates and envies everyone, and feels nothing is going his way.

Challenge Based on what you perceive to be common flaws in people, write a motto that would have universal application.

THINKING AND WRITING

For help with this assignment, students can refer to Lesson 11 in the Handbook of Writing About Literature.

Publishing Student Writing Post the most convincing essay in the classroom. Have students add other relevant mottos to the class bulletin board as they find them throughout the year.

Closure and Extension

ANSWERS TO THINKING ABOUT THE SELECTION

Recalling

1. Utzel's daydream is that Poverty will marry a rich young man who will take care of him and his daughter.
2. Utzel wants shoes for Poverty so that she can find a husband.
3. The shoes are too small because as Utzel's poverty has grown so has Poverty. Her feet have grown again since the measurements were taken.
4. Sandler advises Utzel to get a job because as his poverty shrinks so will Poverty's feet.
5. Utzel realizes that what people have they gain through work, not idleness.

Interpreting

6. Poverty's name is appropriate because she was very poor.
7. It means that the less Utzel worked, the poorer they became.
8. Answers will differ. Suggested Response: Utzel was wasting his life in idleness until he felt compelled to do something for Poverty. Once he began working to pay back the loan for Poverty's shoes, he prospered.

Applying

9. Answers will differ. Suggested Response: Most students will respond that by loving someone

Focus

More About the Author Pearl Buck was the daughter of Presbyterian missionaries, who took her to China with them to open a mission. Buck was raised in China, learning to speak Chinese before English and attending Chinese schools until she was seventeen. She had a deep understanding and respect for everything Chinese and sought to make China understandable to her readers. Have students discuss the advantages and disadvantages for a writer who writes about a foreign country. Why might Buck have written more effectively about China than about the United States?

Literary Focus Point out to students that a theme is a general idea about life in a story but that a theme also applies to real-life situations. Have students think of a variety of real-life situations and identify the theme of each and the way it is exemplified.

Look For Your more advanced students may be able to think of common themes in literature. Have them list such common literary themes as "the evil person is eventually punished" or "the good person is tested and triumphs over adversity."

Writing/Prior Knowledge Have students discuss the meaning of the word *demon*. Then have them complete the freewriting assignment. For extra credit, ask them to use freewriting as the basis for a formal composition.

Vocabulary Have your less advanced students read the words aloud so that you can be sure they can pronounce them. These words may also give students some difficulty: *malicious, disconcerting* (p. 155); *quavering, deprecatingly* (p. 157); *extraordinary* (p. 159); *miraculously* (p. 160); *mortar* (p. 161); *hither,* and *thither* (p. 164).

154

The Old Demon

Implied Theme

Pearl Buck (1892–1973) was born in the United States, but her parents took her to China when she was still a baby. Altogether she lived in that country for nearly forty years and wrote about it in her stories, novels, plays, and essays. One of her novels about China, *The Good Earth,* was made into a successful motion picture. In 1938 Buck became the first American woman to win the Nobel Prize for literature. "The Old Demon" gives a picture of Chinese life in the late 1930's, when China was invaded and occupied by Japan.

Stories often communicate important ideas about life, called **themes**. However, authors do not always state these ideas directly. Sometimes the theme of a story is **implied**, and you must figure it out for yourself. In "The Old Demon," for example, the theme is revealed through the actions of the major character, Mrs. Wang.

Look For

In this story the world that Mrs. Wang has known for many years vanishes before her eyes. As you read, try to determine the theme of the story by noticing how Mrs. Wang behaves and what she values during this time of crisis.

Writing

In "The Old Demon" the river changes forever the world that Mrs. Wang knows. Recall a time when you experienced, or saw a film about, a violent natural force like a flood or a storm. What effects did this force bring about? Freewrite about this time. In what way could it be called a demon?

Vocabulary

Knowing the following words will help you as you read "The Old Demon."

coarse (kôrs) *adj.*: Inferior; crude; common (p. 158)
wheedle (hwē′d'l) *v.*: Persuade a person by flattery or coaxing (p. 158)
inert (in urt′) *adj.*: Without power to move (p. 159)
somberly (säm′bər lē) *adv.*: Gloomily; dully (p. 160)
tentatively (ten′tə tiv lē) *adv.*: Hesitantly; uncertainly (p. 163)
impetuous (im pech′oo wəs) *adj.*: Moving with great force or violence (p. 164)
resolutely (rez′ə loot′lē) *adv.*: With a firm purpose (p. 164)

Objectives

1 To recognize the implied theme of a short story
2 To summarize a story
3 To respond to the implied theme of a short story

Support Material

Teaching Portfolio
Teacher Backup, p. 235
Grammar in Action Worksheet, *Punctuating Direct Quotations,* p. 239
Grammar in Action Worksheet, *Recognizing Participial Phrases,* p. 241
Usage and Mechanics Worksheet, p. 243
Vocabulary Check, p. 244

Critical Thinking and Reading Worksheet, *Summarizing a Story,* p. 245
Language Worksheet, *Using Context Clues,* p. 246
Selection Test, p. 247
Art Transparency 5, *River Village in a Rainstorm* by Lu Wenying

The Old Demon

Pearl S. Buck

Old Mrs. Wang knew, of course, that there was a war. Everybody had known for a long time that there was war going on and that Japanese were killing Chinese. But still it was not real and no more than hearsay since none of the Wangs had been killed. The Village of Three Mile Wangs on the flat banks of the Yellow River, which was old Mrs. Wang's clan village, had never seen a Japanese. This was how they came to be talking about Japanese at all.

It was evening and early summer, and after her supper Mrs. Wang had climbed the dike steps, as she did every day, to see how high the river had risen. She was much more afraid of the river than of the Japanese. She knew what the river would do. And one by one the villagers had followed her up the dike, and now they stood staring down at the malicious yellow water, curling along like a lot of snakes, and biting at the high dike banks.

"I never saw it as high as this so early," Mrs. Wang said. She sat down on a bamboo stool that her grandson, Little Pig, had brought for her, and spat into the water.

"It's worse than the Japanese, this old devil of a river," Little Pig said recklessly.

"Fool!" Mrs. Wang said quickly. "The river god will hear you. Talk about something else."

So they had gone on talking about the Japanese. . . . How, for instance, asked Wang, the baker, who was old Mrs. Wang's nephew twice removed, would they know the Japanese when they saw them?

Mrs. Wang at this point said positively, "You'll know them. I once saw a foreigner. He was taller than the eaves of my house and he had mud-colored hair and eyes the color of a fish's eyes. Anyone who does not look like us—that is a Japanese."

Then Little Pig spoke up in his disconcerting way. "You can't see them, Grandmother. They hide up in the sky in airplanes."

Mrs. Wang did not answer immediately. Once she would have said positively, "I shall not believe in an airplane until I see it." But so many things had been true which she had not believed—the Empress, for instance, whom she had not believed dead, was dead. The Republic,[1] again, she had not believed in because she did not know what it was. She still did not know, but they had said for a long time there had been one. So now she merely stared quietly about the dike where

---

1. The Republic: China became a republic, a state run by elected representatives, in 1912. Before that time, China had been ruled by emperors and empresses. When the Republic ended in 1949, China was taken over by communists.

The Old Demon 155

Master Teacher Note Place Art Transparency 5, *River Village in a Rainstorm* by Lu Wen-ying, on the overhead projector. Point out that painting has been an established art form in China since about 300 B.C. Chinese paintings are produced by special brush strokes made with a bristle-hair brush. Many Chinese paintings depict landscapes with towering mountains, delicate trees, flowing water, and Chinese architecture. These paintings seek to convey the harmony between nature and the human spirit.

Have students study the painting and discuss the overall effect of the work. What feelings was the artist trying to convey in the painting? How do the washed-out colors and the streaks of gray enhance the feeling of rain? What might be the importance of rain to a village situated on the banks of a river? What would be some positive and negative aspects of living close to a river?

You might point out that some paintings, like works of literature, have themes. What might be the theme of this painting?

156 Short Stories

they all sat around her. It was very pleasant and cool, and she felt nothing mattered if the river did not rise to flood.

"I don't believe in the Japanese," she said flatly.

6 They laughed at her a little, but no one spoke. Someone lit her pipe—it was Little Pig's wife, who was her favorite, and she smoked it.

"Sing, Little Pig!" someone called.

So Little Pig began to sing an old song in a high quavering voice, and old Mrs. Wang listened and forgot the Japanese. The evening was beautiful, the sky so clear and still that the willows overhanging the dike were reflected even in the muddy water. Everything was at peace. The thirty-odd houses which made up the village straggled along beneath them. Nothing could break this peace. After all, the Japanese were only human beings.

"I doubt those airplanes," she said mildly to Little Pig when he stopped singing.

But without answering her, he went on to another song.

Year in and year out she had spent the summer evenings like this on the dike. The first time she was seventeen and a bride, and her husband had shouted to her to come out of the house and up the dike, and she had come, blushing and twisting her hands together, to hide among the women while the men roared at her and made jokes about her. All the same, they had liked her. "A pretty piece of meat in your bowl," they had said to her husband. "Feet a trifle big," he had answered deprecatingly. But she could see he was pleased, and so gradually her shyness went away.

He, poor man, had been drowned in a flood when he was still young. And it had taken her years to get him prayed out of Buddhist purgatory.[2] Finally she had grown tired of it, what with the child and the land all on her back, and so when the priest said coaxingly, "Another ten pieces of silver and he'll be out entirely," she asked, "What's he got in there yet?"

"Only his right hand," the priest said, encouraging her.

Well, then, her patience broke. Ten dollars! It would feed them for the winter. Besides, she had had to hire labor for her share of repairing the dike, too, so there would be no more floods.

"If it's only one hand, he can pull himself out," she said firmly.

She often wondered if he had, poor silly fellow. As like as not, she had often thought gloomily in the night, he was still lying there, waiting for her to do something about it. That was the sort of man he was. Well, some day, perhaps, when Little Pig's wife had had the first baby safely and she had a little extra, she might go back to finish him out of purgatory. There was no real hurry, though. . . .

"Grandmother, you must go in," Little Pig's wife's soft voice said. "There is a mist rising from the river now that the sun is gone."

"Yes, I suppose I must," old Mrs. Wang agreed. She gazed at the river a moment. The river—it was full of good and evil together. It would water the fields when it was curbed and checked, but then if an inch were allowed it, it crashed through like a soaring dragon. That was how her husband had been swept away—careless, he was, about his bit of the dike. He was always go-

---

2. Buddhist purgatory (boŏd′ist pʉr′ gə tôr′ē): Buddhism is a religion popular in China and other Asian countries. Some Buddhists believe in purgatory, a place where the souls of certain dead people must stay until they can be freed.

7
8
9

The Old Demon 157

6 Critical Thinking and Reading What conclusions can you draw about the relationship between Mrs. Wang and her family? How does her grandson's wife treat her? How old would you say Mrs. Wang is?

7 Discussion Why does the priest tell Mrs. Wang that her late husband's hand is still in purgatory?

8 Discussion Discuss Mrs. Wang's response to the priest. Is she a bad person or is this a sign of her growing independence and maturity? Explain your answer.

9 Discussion Does Little Pig's wife's concern for Mrs. Wang seem strange? What does this relationship tell you about Chinese society of the time?

10 Reading Strategy Mrs. Wang has always been a survivor. How do you think she would react if she met a Japanese soldier or had to defend her home against invaders?

11 Discussion What are these silver eggs dropping from the sky?

12 Clarification In ancient China, Chinese woman had their feet bound with bandages when they were children so that the feet would remain small. Small feet were considered beautiful, but this practice made if difficult for the women to walk.

13 Discussion What do you think Mr. Wang was like, based on Mrs. Wang's comment here and on other details you have read so far in the story?

ing to mend it, always going to pile more earth on top of it, and then in a night the river rose and broke through. He had run out of the house, and she had climbed on the roof with the child and had saved herself and it while he was drowned. Well, they had pushed the river back again behind its dikes, and it had stayed there this time. Every day she herself walked up and down the length of the dike for which the village was responsible and examined it. The men laughed and said, "If anything is wrong with the dikes, Granny will tell us."

It had never occurred to any of them to move the village away from the river. The Wangs had lived there for generations, and some had always escaped the floods and had fought the river more fiercely than ever afterward.

Little Pig suddenly stopped singing.

"The moon is coming up!" he cried. "That's not good. Airplanes come out on moonlight nights."

"Where do you learn all this about airplanes?" old Mrs. Wang exclaimed. "It is tiresome to me," she said, so severely that no one spoke. In this silence, leaning upon the arm of Little Pig's wife she descended slowly the earthen steps which led down into the village, using her long pipe in the other hand as a walking stick. Behind her the villagers came down, one by one, to bed. No one moved before she did, but none stayed long after her.

And in her own bed at last, behind the blue cotton mosquito curtains which Little Pig's wife fastened securely, she fell peacefully asleep. She had lain awake a little while thinking about the Japanese and wondering why they wanted to fight. Only very coarse persons wanted wars. In her mind she saw large coarse persons. If they came one must wheedle them, she thought, invite them to drink tea, and explain to them, reasonably—

only why should they come to a peaceful farming village . . . ?

So she was not in the least prepared for Little Pig's wife screaming at her that the Japanese had come. She sat up in bed muttering, "The tea bowls—the tea—"

"Grandmother, there's no time!" Little Pig's wife screamed. "They're here—they're here!"

"Where?" old Mrs. Wang cried, now awake.

"In the sky!" Little Pig's wife wailed.

They had all run out at that, into the clear early dawn, and gazed up. There, like wild geese flying in autumn, were great bird-like shapes.

"But what are they?" old Mrs. Wang cried.

And then, like a silver egg dropping, something drifted straight down and fell at the far end of the village in a field. A fountain of earth flew up, and they all ran to see it. There was a hole thirty feet across, as big as a pond. They were so astonished they could not speak, and then, before anyone could say anything, another and another egg began to fall and everybody was running, running . . .

Everybody, that is, but Mrs. Wang. When Little Pig's wife seized her hand to drag her along, old Mrs. Wang pulled away and sat down against the bank of the dike.

"I can't run," she remarked. "I haven't run in seventy years, since before my feet were bound. You go on. Where's Little Pig?" She looked around. Little Pig was already gone. "Like his grandfather," she remarked, "always the first to run."

But Little Pig's wife would not leave her, not, that is, until old Mrs. Wang reminded her that it was her duty.

"If Little Pig is dead," she said, "then it is necessary that his son be born alive." And

Grammar in Action

In fiction writing, **direct quotations** are the spoken words of the characters. Direct quotations require specific punctuation marks and capitalization. The punctuation marks and capitalization separate what is being said from the narration in a story. In the following sentences, Pearl S. Buck uses punctuation and capitalization to designate where spoken words begin and end.

"Go on—go on," she exclaimed.

"The moon is coming up!" he cried.

"If Little Pig is dead," she said, "then it is necessary that his son be born alive."

"You had better come out," she remarked. "I'll put some herb plaster on your side."

Use quotation marks to identify the exact words of the characters. The examples also show that you must use commas to separate dialogue from introductory, interrupting, and concluding expressions. Notice in the first and third examples that a comma is used even though the quotations are complete sentences. The exception to this rule, as shown in the second example, occurs when

when the girl still hesitated, she struck at her gently with her pipe. "Go on—go on," she exclaimed.

So unwillingly, because now they could scarcely hear each other speak for the roar of the dipping planes, Little Pig's wife went on with the others.

By now, although only a few minutes had passed, the village was in ruins and the straw roofs and wooden beams were blazing. Everybody was gone. As they passed they had shrieked at old Mrs. Wang to come on, and she had called back pleasantly:

"I'm coming—I'm coming!"

But she did not go. She sat quite alone watching now what was an extraordinary spectacle. For soon other planes came, from where she did not know, but they attacked the first ones. The sun came up over the fields of ripening wheat, and in the clear summery air the planes wheeled and darted and spat at each other. When this was over, she thought, she would go back into the village and see if anything was left. Here and there a wall stood, supporting a roof. She could not see her own house from here. But she was not unused to war. Once bandits had looted their village, and houses had been burned then, too. Well, now it had happened again. Burning houses one could see often, but not this darting silvery shining battle in the air. She understood none of it— not what those things were, nor how they stayed up in the sky. She simply sat, growing hungry, and watching.

"I'd like to see one close," she said aloud. And at that moment, as though in answer, one of them pointed suddenly downward, and, wheeling and twisting as though it were wounded, it fell head down in a field which Little Pig had ploughed only yesterday for soybeans. And in an instant the sky was empty again, and there was only this wounded thing on the ground and herself.

She hoisted herself carefully from the earth. At her age she need be afraid of nothing. She could, she decided, go and see what it was. So, leaning on her bamboo pipe, she made her way slowly across the fields. Behind her in the sudden stillness two or three village dogs appeared and followed, creeping close to her in their terror. When they drew near to the fallen plane, they barked furiously. Then she hit them with her pipe.

"Be quiet," she scolded, "there's already been noise enough to split my ears!"

She tapped the airplane.

"Metal," she told the dogs. "Silver, doubtless," she added. Melted up, it would make them all rich.

She walked around it, examining it closely. What made it fly? It seemed dead. Nothing moved or made a sound within it. Then, coming to the side to which it tipped, she saw a young man in it, slumped into a heap in a little seat. The dogs growled, but she struck at them again and they fell back.

"Are you dead?" she inquired politely.

The young man moved a little at her voice, but did not speak. She drew nearer and peered into the hole in which he sat. His side was bleeding.

"Wounded!" she exclaimed. She took his wrist. It was warm, but inert, and when she let it go, it dropped against the side of the hole. She stared at him. He had black hair and a dark skin like a Chinese and still he did not look like a Chinese.

"He must be a Southerner," she thought. Well, the chief thing was, he was alive.

"You had better come out," she remarked. "I'll put some herb plaster on your side."

The young man muttered something dully.

"What did you say?" she asked. But he did not say it again.

"I am still quite strong," she decided af-

The Old Demon   159

14 **Discussion** Why is Mrs. Wang more curious than afraid?

15 **Discussion** How is it possible that Mrs. Wang does not know that the wounded pilot is Japanese?

the sentence is exclamatory or interrogative. In that case the normal punctuation, an exclamation point or a question mark, is used.

Student Activity 1. Add the proper punctuation and capitalization to the following sentences.

1. Soon you will have to go home remarked Mother it is getting dark outside

2. Will you help me with my homework questioned Mark

3. The lilacs are blooming in the park exclaimed Martha and are filling the air with a heavenly scent

Student Activity 2. Write three original sentences containing direct quotations. Be sure to use the proper punctuation and capitalization.

16 Discussion Find other examples of Mrs. Wang's bravery in the story.

17 Clarification China is so huge that a number of different dialects are spoken. A Chinese person who speaks one dialect might not understand another.

ter a moment. So she reached in and seized him about the waist and pulled him out slowly, panting a good deal. Fortunately he was rather a little fellow and very light. When she had him on the ground, he seemed to find his feet; and he stood shakily and clung to her, and she held him up.

"Now if you can walk to my house," she said, "I'll see if it is there."

Then he said something, quite clearly. She listened and could not understand a word of it. She pulled away from him and stared.

"What's that?" she asked.

He pointed at the dogs. They were standing growling, their ruffs[3] up. Then he spoke again, and as he spoke he crumpled to the ground. The dogs fell on him, so that she had to beat them off with her hands.

"Get away!" she shouted. "Who told *you* to kill him?"

And then, when they had slunk back, she heaved him somehow onto her back; and, trembling, half carrying, half pulling him, she dragged him to the ruined village and laid him in the street while she went to find her house, taking the dogs with her.

Her house was quite gone. She found the place easily enough. This was where it should be, opposite the water gate into the dike. She had always watched that gate herself. Miraculously it was not injured now, nor was the dike broken. It would be easy enough to rebuild the house. Only, for the present, it was gone.

So she went back to the young man. He was lying as she had left him, propped against the dike, panting and very pale. He had opened his coat and he had a little bag from which he was taking out strips of cloth

---

3. **ruffs** (rufs) *n.*: Bands of fur around their necks.

and a bottle of something. And again he spoke, and again she understood nothing. Then he made signs and she saw it was water he wanted, so she took up a broken pot from one of many blown about the street, and, going up the dike, she filled it with river water and brought it down again and washed his wound, and she tore off the strips he made from the rolls of bandaging. He knew how to put the cloth over the gaping wound and he made signs to her, and she followed these signs. All the time he was trying to tell her something, but she could understand nothing.

"You must be from the South, sir," she said. It was easy to see that he had education. He looked very clever. "I have heard your language is different from ours." She laughed a little to put him at his ease, but he only stared at her somberly with dull eyes. So she said brightly, "Now if I could find something for us to eat, it would be nice."

He did not answer. Indeed he lay back, panting still more heavily, and stared into space as though she had not spoken.

18 "You would be better with food," she went on. "And so would I," she added. She was beginning to feel unbearably hungry.

It occurred to her that in Wang, the baker's, shop there might be some bread. Even if it were dusty with fallen mortar, it

The Old Demon 161

162

19 Discussion How is Mrs. Wang able to be so cheerful in the face of disaster? Do you think her life has prepared her for this crisis? Why?

20 Discussion Why is Mrs. Wang shocked to discover that the pilot is Japanese? Does this change the way she acts toward him?

would still be bread. She would go and see. But before she went she moved the soldier a little so that he lay in the edge of shadow cast by a willow tree that grew in the bank of the dike. Then she went to the baker's shop. The dogs were gone.

The baker's shop was, like everything else, in ruins. No one was there. At first she saw nothing but the mass of crumpled earthen walls. But then she remembered that the oven was just inside the door, and the door frame still stood erect, supporting one end of the roof. She stood in this frame, and, running her hand in underneath the fallen roof inside, she felt the wooden cover of the iron caldron. Under this there might be steamed bread. She worked her arm delicately and carefully in. It took quite a long time, but, even so, clouds of lime and dust almost choked her. Nevertheless she was right. She squeezed her hand under the cover and felt the firm smooth skin of the big steamed bread rolls, and one by one she drew out four.

19 "It's hard to kill an old thing like me," she remarked cheerfully to no one, and she began to eat one of the rolls as she walked back. If she had a bit of garlic and a bowl of tea—but one couldn't have everything in these times.

It was at this moment that she heard voices. When she came in sight of the soldier, she saw surrounding him a crowd of other soldiers, who had apparently come from nowhere. They were staring down at the wounded soldier, whose eyes were now closed.

20 "Where did you get this Japanese, Old Mother?" they shouted at her.

"What Japanese?" she asked, coming to them.

"This one!" they shouted.

"Is he a Japanese?" she cried in the greatest astonishment. "But he looks like us—his eyes are black, his skin—"

"Japanese!" one of them shouted at her.

"Well," she said quietly, "he dropped out of the sky."

"Give me that bread!" another shouted.

"Take it," she said, "all except this one for him."

"A Japanese monkey eat good bread?" the soldier shouted.

"I suppose he is hungry also," old Mrs. Wang replied. She began to dislike these men. But then, she had always disliked soldiers.

"I wish you would go away," she said. "What are you doing here? Our village has always been peaceful."

"It certainly looks very peaceful now," one of the men said, grinning, "as peaceful as a grave. Do you know who did that, Old Mother? The Japanese!"

"I suppose so," she agreed. Then she asked, "Why? That's what I don't understand."

"Why? Because they want our land, that's why!"

"Our land!" she repeated. "Why, they can't have our land!"

"Never!" they shouted.

But all this time while they were talking and chewing the bread they had divided among themselves, they were watching the eastern horizon.

"Why do you keep looking east?" old Mrs. Wang now asked.

"The Japanese are coming from there," the man replied who had taken the bread.

"Are you running away from them?" she asked, surprised.

"There are only a handful of us," he said apologetically. "We were left to guard a village—Pao An, in the county of—"

"I know that village," old Mrs. Wang in-

162   *Short Stories*

Grammar in Action

A **participle** is a form of a verb that acts as an adjective. For example, in the sentence "The screaming fireworks lit up the night," the word *screaming* is a participle. A **participial phrase** is a phrase made up of a participle and its modifiers and complements. In the sentence, "Screaming across the sky, the fireworks lit up the night," *screaming across the sky* is a participial phrase. It consists of a participle, *screaming,* and its modifier, *across the sky.* Notice how Pearl Buck uses participial phrases in these sentences:

But then she remembered that the oven was just inside the door, and the door frame still stood erect, *supporting one end of the roof.*

So she climbed the dike slowly, *getting very hot.*

In the first sentence, the participial phrase modifies the noun *door frame.* In the second sentence, the participial phrase modifies the pronoun *she.*

Compare Buck's sentences with the following shorter sentences.

But then she remembered that the oven was just inside the door, and the door frame still stood erect. It was supporting one end of the roof.

terrupted. "You needn't tell me. I was a girl there. How is the old Pao who keeps the tea-shop in the main street? He's my brother."

"Everybody is dead there," the man replied. "The Japanese have taken it—a great army of men came with their foreign guns and tanks, so what could we do?"

"Of course, only run," she agreed. Nevertheless she felt dazed and sick. So he was dead, that one brother she had left! She was now the last of her father's family.

But the soldiers were straggling away again leaving her alone.

"They'll be coming, those little black dwarfs," they were saying. "We'd best go on."

Nevertheless, one lingered a moment, the one who had taken the bread, to stare down at the young wounded man, who lay with his eyes shut, not having moved at all.

"Is he dead?" he inquired. Then, before Mrs. Wang could answer, he pulled a short knife out of his belt. "Dead or not, I'll give him a punch or two with this—"

But old Mrs Wang pushed his arm away.

"No, you won't," she said with authority. "If he is dead, then there is no use in sending him into purgatory all in pieces. I am a good Buddhist myself."

The man laughed. "Oh well, he is dead," he answered; and then, seeing his comrades already at a distance, he ran after them.

A Japanese, was he? Old Mrs. Wang, left alone with this inert figure, looked at him tentatively. He was very young, she could see, now that his eyes were closed. His hand, limp in unconsciousness, looked like a boy's hand, unformed and still growing. She felt his wrist but could discern no pulse. She leaned over him and held to his lips the half of her roll which she had not eaten.

"Eat," she said very loudly and distinctly. "Bread!"

But there was no answer. Evidently he

was dead. He must have died while she was getting the bread out of the oven.

There was nothing to do then but to finish the bread herself. And when that was done, she wondered if she ought not to follow after Little Pig and his wife and all the villagers. The sun was mounting and it was growing hot. If she were going, she had better go. But first she would climb the dike and see what the direction was. They had gone straight west, and as far as eye could look westward was a great plain. She might even see a good-sized crowd miles away. Anyway, she could see the next village, and they might all be there.

So she climbed the dike slowly, getting very hot. There was a slight breeze on top of the dike and it felt good. She was shocked to see the river very near the top of the dike. Why, it had risen in the last hour!

"You old demon!" she said severely. Let the river god hear it if he liked. He was evil, that he was—so to threaten flood when there had been all this other trouble.

She stooped and bathed her cheeks and her wrists. The water was quite cold, as though with fresh rains somewhere. Then she stood up and gazed around her. To the west there was nothing except in the far distance the soldiers still half-running, and beyond them the blur of the next village, which stood on a long rise of ground. She had better set out for that village. Doubtless Little Pig and his wife were there waiting for her.

Just as she was about to climb down and start out, she saw something on the eastern horizon. It was at first only an immense cloud of dust. But, as she stared at it, very quickly it became a lot of black dots and shining spots. Then she saw what it was. It was a lot of men—an army. Instantly she knew what army.

"That's the Japanese," she thought. Yes,

The Old Demon 163

21 Discussion Why do you think Mrs. Wang defends the Japanese pilot against the Chinese soldier?

22 Clarification The Chinese Buddhists worshiped many gods and appealed to them for help and mercy from the elements.

23 Reading Strategy Summarize the story up to this point, and predict what will happen to Mrs. Wang and the approaching Japanese army.

So she climbed the dike slowly. She was getting very hot. These shorter sentences are unnecessarily choppy and repetitive. Using participial phrases enable writers to connect related ideas in a single smooth sentence.

Student Activity 1. Find two more sentences from "Old Demon" in which Pearl Buck uses participial phrases. For each sentence, identify the participial phrase.

Student Activity 2. Using participial phrases, combine each pair of sentences to form a more effective sentence. Place the participial phrase directly before or after the word it modifies.
1. a. Mrs. Wang pulled the pilot from the wreckage of his plane.
   b. The pilot was bleeding from several wounds.
2. a. The Japanese army could be seen for miles.
   b. The Japanese army streamed across the plain.

24 Discussion Why does Mrs. Wang think that everyone has been killed except for herself, her grandson, and her grandson's wife? What impact has her brother's death had on her?

25 Critical Thinking and Reading What is Mrs. Wang thinking of doing? Why does the plan occur to her?

26 Enrichment Mrs. Wang's using the river to fight the Japanese has some basis in fact. In the early stages of China's war with Japan, General Chiang Kai-Shek, in order to stop the advancing Japanese army, dynamited the river's dikes, flooding a huge area and killing thousands of Japanese soldiers.

27 Literary Focus Mrs. Wang's last act in life is to defend her homeland the best way she can. How is her death consistent with the life she has led?

Reader's Response What do you think of Mrs. Wang's final act? Was it brave? Foolish? Sad? Explain your answer.

above them were the buzzing silver planes. They circled about, seeming to search for someone.

"I don't know who you're looking for," she muttered, "unless it's me and Little Pig and his wife. We're the only ones left. You've already killed my brother Pao."

She had almost forgotten that Pao was dead. Now she remembered it acutely. He had such a nice shop—always clean, and the tea good and the best meat dumplings to be had and the price always the same. Pao was a good man. Besides, what about his wife and his seven children? Doubtless they were all killed, too. Now these Japanese were looking for her. It occurred to her that on the dike she could easily be seen. So she clambered hastily down.

It was when she was about halfway down that she thought of the water gate. This old river—it had been a curse to them since time began. Why should it not make up a little now for all the wickedness it had done? It was plotting wickedness again, trying to steal over its banks. Well, why not? She wavered a moment. It was a pity, of course, that the young dead Japanese would be swept into the flood. He was a nice-looking boy, and she had saved him from being stabbed. It was not quite the same as saving his life, of course, but still it was a little the same. If he had been alive, he would have been saved. She went over to him and tugged at him until he lay well under the top of the bank. Then she went down again.

She knew perfectly how to open the water gate. Any child knew how to open the sluice for crops. But she knew also how to swing open the whole gate. The question was, could she open it quickly enough to get out of the way?

"I'm only one old woman," she muttered. She hesitated a second more. Well, it would

be a pity not to see what sort of a baby Little Pig's wife would have, but one could not see everything. She had seen a great deal in this life. There was an end to what one could see, anyway.

She glanced again to the east. There were the Japanese coming across the plain. They were a long clear line of black, dotted with thousands of glittering points. If she opened this gate, the impetuous water would roar toward them, rushing into the plains, rolling into a wide lake, drowning them, maybe. Certainly they could not keep on marching nearer and nearer to her, and to Little Pig and his wife who were waiting for her. Well, Little Pig and his wife—they would wonder about her—but they would never dream of this. It would make a good story— she would have enjoyed telling it.

She turned resolutely to the gate. Well, some people fought with airplanes and some with guns, but you could fight with a river, too, if it were a wicked one like this one. She wrenched out a huge wooden pin. It was slippery with silvery green moss. The rill of water burst into a strong jet. When she wrenched one more pin, the rest would give way themselves. She began pulling at it, and felt it slip a little from its hole.

"I might be able to get myself out of purgatory with this," she thought, "and maybe they'll let me have that old man of mine, too. What's a hand of his to all this? Then we'll—"

The pin slipped away suddenly, and the gate burst flat against her and knocked her breath away. She had only time to gasp, to the river:

"Come on, you old demon!"

Then she felt it seize her and lift her up to the sky. It was beneath her and around her. It rolled her joyfully hither and thither, and then, holding her close and enfolded, it went rushing against the enemy.

164   Short Stories

Closure and Extension

ANSWERS TO THINKING ABOUT THE SELECTION
Recalling

1. Mrs. Wang climbed up onto the roof of her house with her child to survive the flood.
2. She paid the priest for her husband to be prayed out of Buddhist purgatory.
3. The other people in the village run because the Japanese are bombing the village.
4. She stops the Chinese soldier from killing the Japanese pilot.
5. She pulls the pins of the water gate to flood the land and drown the advancing army.

Interpreting

6. Mrs. Wang protects and supports life by saving herself and her child from the flood, by checking the dike, by helping to repair the dike, by encouraging Little Pig's wife to

THINKING ABOUT THE SELECTION

Recalling

1. How did Mrs. Wang save herself and her child when her husband died?
2. What did she do for her husband after his death?
3. Why do the other people of her village run away?
4. How does she react when a soldier tries to kill the Japanese pilot?
5. How does she try to protect her land from the enemy?

Interpreting

6. In what ways is Mrs. Wang a person who protects and supports life?
7. In what ways does Mrs. Wang share some of the river's strength?
8. Explain the meaning of the story's title.

Applying

9. Although the Japanese pilot is an enemy, Mrs. Wang tries to help him. Do you think it is easier to fight an enemy you cannot see than one you can see? Explain your answer.

ANALYZING LITERATURE

Recognizing an Implied Theme

An **implied theme** is an idea about life that is suggested through a story. In "The Old Demon," the theme is suggested by the character of Mrs. Wang.

1. How does Mrs. Wang show that she values her family and her village?
2. What does her attempt to rescue the pilot reveal about her?
3. Which of the following statements best seems to express the implied theme of the story? Explain your answer.

a. Do not become involved with matters outside your family or community.
b. War is evil.
c. People should protect and care for each other.

4. How would you express the theme?

CRITICAL THINKING AND READING

Summarizing a Story

A **summary** of a story is a brief form of it containing the most important events in the order they occurred. By summarizing a story with many events like "The Old Demon," you can remember it more easily. Follow these steps in preparing a summary:

1. Reread the story
2. Decide which events are the most important
3. List these events in the order they occurred
4. Give a brief account of each one in your own words

Practice your summarizing skills on "The Old Demon."

1. Write a summary of the story.
2. When revising your summary, make sure it is brief but includes the key events.

THINKING AND WRITING

Responding to the Implied Theme

In "The Old Demon," the writer suggests that a person who protects and cares for others should be admired. List the reasons why you agree or disagree with this idea. Include examples to support your reasons. Then use your list to write a composition explaining your position. As you revise your work, check to see whether you have backed up your argument with good examples. Finally, share your composition with your classmates.

The Old Demon   165

---

flee without her, by caring for the Japanese soldier, and by opening the water gate to destroy the advancing Japanese army.

7. Like the river, Mrs. Wang is strong. She is listened to and respected by the village, she stays in spite of the bombing, she obtains food for herself and the Japanese pilot, she stands up to the Chinese soldier, and she gives her life to protect her people.

8. The title refers to both the Yellow River and Mrs. Wang. Mrs. Wang is an old woman of great strength who, like the river, is able to rise up and conquer her enemies. She became one with the river to vanquish the Japanese.

Applying

9. Answers will differ. Suggested Response: It is easier to fight an enemy you cannot see because it is easier to kill people you cannot see. Once you confront people, you recognize them as fellow human beings. Mrs. Wang had sympathy for the Japanese pilot but was able to fight the Japanese army.

ANSWERS TO ANALYZING LITERATURE

1. She gives her life to save her family and village.
2. Her attempt reveals that she is caring, compassionate, brave, resolute, and strong.
3. "People should protect and care for each other" best expresses the

implied theme. Mrs. Wang has protected and cared for her family and village all her life and makes the ultimate sacrifice for them in the end. She has led a noble life and has enriched the lives of others.

4. Answers will differ. Suggested Response: In order to make life more meaningful, people must care for and respect each other.

ANSWERS TO CRITICAL THINKING AND READING

1. Answers will differ. Suggested Response: Two forces threaten Mrs. Wang's village—the Yellow River and the Japanese. Although Mrs. Wang's grandson warns her about the Japanese, she doesn't believe him. But then the Japanese attack the village. Mrs. Wang is the only one to remain in the village and tries to save the life of a wounded Japanese pilot, even after she learns he is the enemy. When she sees the Japanese army approaching, she decides to use the river as a weapon to protect her family. She opens the water gate, sacrificing her life, to destroy the army.

2. Answers will differ accordingly.

Challenge How will Mrs. Wang be remembered in the village? Discuss the qualities that make a person a hero or heroine.

THINKING AND WRITING

For help with the assignment, students can refer to Lesson 11, "Writing About Theme," in the Handbook of Writing About Literature.

Writing Across the Curriculum

You might want to inform the social studies department that students are reading a story by Pearl Buck. Social studies teachers can help students to research Chinese history and traditions for a possible composition or extra-credit report.

GUIDE FOR READING

Humaweepi, the Warrior Priest

Leslie Marmon Silko (1948–   ), who was born in Albuquerque, New Mexico, was raised as a Pueblo Indian. Though her background is not entirely Pueblo, she identifies strongly with this tradition. She has explored its meaning in her well-known novel *Ceremony* (1977). Silko once said about the Laguna Pueblo reservation: "This place I am from is everything I am as a writer and a human being." "Humaweepi, the Warrior Priest" communicates Silko's strong feeling for the Southwest and for American Indian ways.

Key to Theme: Character

The way a character in a story grows or changes is often a key to the theme. Sometimes characters grow because they are helped by others. In "Humaweepi, the Warrior Priest" a Pueblo boy's uncle helps him to become a warrior priest by teaching him about nature and tribal traditions. By focusing on the boy's development, you can understand the implied theme of the story.

Look For

As you read "Humaweepi, the Warrior Priest," look for each of the lessons the uncle teaches the boy. What do these lessons reveal about life in general?

Writing

List some of the important skills you have learned from your parents or other adults. You can include knowledge you have gained simply by observing the way someone behaves.

Vocabulary

Knowing the following words will help you as you read "Humaweepi, the Warrior Priest."

clan (klan) *n.*: A group of people, usually relatives (p. 167)

crevasses (kri vas' əz) *n.*: Deep cracks (p. 168)

lacy (lā'sē) *adj.*: Having a delicate, open pattern, like lace (p. 168)

fragile (fraj''l) *adj.*: Delicate; easily broken (p. 168)

derive (di rīv') *v.*: To receive from someone or something (p. 169)

succulent (suk'yoo lənt) *adj.*: Juicy (p. 169)

triumphantly (trī um'fənt lē) *adv.*: Victoriously; successfully (p. 171)

166   *Short Stories*

from Humaweepi, the Warrior Priest

Leslie Marmon Silko

The old man didn't really teach him much; mostly they just lived. Occasionally Humaweepi would meet friends his own age who still lived with their families in the pueblo,[1] and they would ask him what he was doing; they seemed disappointed when he told them.

"That's nothing," they would say.

Once this had made Humaweepi sad and his uncle noticed. "Oh," he said when Humaweepi told him, "that shows you how little they know."

They returned to the pueblo for the ceremonials and special days. His uncle stayed in the kiva[2] with the other priests, and Humaweepi usually stayed with clan members because his mother and father had been very old when he was born and now they were gone. Sometimes during these stays, when the pueblo was full of the activity and excitement of the dances or the fiesta[3] when the Christians paraded out of the pueblo church carrying the saint, Humaweepi would wonder why he was living out in the hills with the old man. When he was twelve he thought he had it all figured out: the old man just wanted someone to live with him and help him with the goat and to chop wood and carry water. But it was peaceful in this place, and Humaweepi discovered that after all these years of sitting beside his uncle in the evenings, he knew the songs and chants for all the seasons, and he was beginning to learn the prayers for the trees and plants and animals. "Oh," Humaweepi said to himself, "I have been learning all this time and I didn't even know it."

Once the old man told Humaweepi to prepare for a long trip.

"Overnight?"

The old man nodded.

So Humaweepi got out a white cotton sack and started filling it with jerked venison,[4] piki bread,[5] and dried apples. But the old man shook his head sternly. It was late June then, so Humaweepi didn't bother to bring the blankets; he had learned to sleep on the ground like the old man did.

"Human beings are special," his uncle had told him once, "which means they can do anything. They can sleep on the ground like the doe and fawn."

And so Humaweepi had learned how to find the places in the scrub-oak thickets

---

1. pueblo (pweb′ lō) *n.*: A type of Native American village in the Southwest where families lived together in flat-roofed houses of stone or adobe.
2. kiva (kē′ və) *n.*: A large room in a pueblo dwelling used for religious or other purposes.
3. fiesta (fē eś tə) *n.*: A religious festival.

4. jerked venison: Deer meat that has been sliced into thin strips and dried in the sun to preserve it.
5. piki (pē′ kē) **bread:** Corn bread.

Humaweepi, the Warrior Priest 167

4 **Critical Thinking and Reading**
What does it mean to the old man to be a human being? What significance does he attach to being human? How can you tell?

5 **Discussion** What is the old man trying to teach Humaweepi by saying this?

where the deer had slept, where the dry oak leaves were arranged into nests. This is where he and his uncle slept, even in the autumn when the nights were cold and Humaweepi could hear the leaves snap in the middle of the night and drift to the ground.

Sometimes they carried food from home, but often they went without food or blankets. When Humaweepi asked him what they would eat, the old man had waved his hand at the sky and earth around them. "I am a human being, Humaweepi," he said: "I eat anything." On these trips they had gathered grass roots and washed them in little sandstone basins made by the wind to catch rain water. The roots had a rich, mealy taste. Then they left the desert below and climbed into the mesa[6] country, and the old man had

led Humaweepi to green leafy vines hanging from crevasses in the face of the sandstone cliffs. "Wild grapes," he said as he dropped some tiny dark-purple berries into Humaweepi's open palms. And in the high mountains there were wild iris roots and the bulbs from wild tulips which grew among the lacy ferns and green grass beside the mountain streams. They had gone out like this in each season. Summer and fall, and finally, spring and winter. "Winter isn't easy," the old man had said. "All the animals are hungry—not just you."

So this time, when his uncle shook his head at the food, Humaweepi left it behind as he had many times before. His uncle took the special leather pouch off the nail on the wall, and Humaweepi pulled his own buckskin bundle out from under his mattress. Inside he had a few objects of his own. A dried blossom. Fragile and yellow. A smooth pink

---

6. mesa (mā′ sə) *adj.*: Flat tableland with steep sides (usually a noun).

quartz crystal in the shape of a star. Tiny turquoise beads the color of a summer sky. And a black obsidian[7] arrowhead, shiny and sharp. They each had special meaning to him, and the old man had instructed him to assemble these things with special meaning. "Someday maybe you will derive strength from these things." That's what the old man had said.

They walked west toward the distant blue images of the mountain peaks. The water in the Rio Grande was still cold. Humaweepi was aware of the dampness on his feet: when he got back from the journey he decided he would make sandals for himself because it took hours for his boots to dry out again. His uncle wore old sandals woven from twisted yucca[8] fiber and they dried out almost immediately. The old man didn't approve of boots and shoes—bad for you, he said. In the winter he wore buckskin moccasins and in the warm months, these yucca sandals.

They walked all day, steadily, stopping occasionally when the old man found a flower or herb or stone that he wanted Humaweepi to see. And it seemed to Humaweepi that he had learned the names of everything, and he said so to his uncle.

The old man frowned and poked at a small blue flower with his walking stick. "That's what a priest must know," he said and walked rapidly then, pointing at stones and shrubs. "How old are you?" he demanded.

"Nineteen," Humaweepi answered.

"All your life," he said, "every day, I have been teaching you."

After that they walked along in silence, and Humaweepi began to feel anxious; all of a sudden he knew that something was going to happen on this journey. That night they reached the white sandstone cliffs at the foot of the mountain foothills. At the base of these cliffs were shallow overhangs with sandy floors. They slept in the sand under the rock overhang; in the night Humaweepi woke up to the call of a young owl; the sky was bright with stars and a half-moon. The smell of the night air made him shiver and he buried himself more deeply in the cliff sand.

In the morning they gathered tumbleweed sprouts that were succulent and tender. As they climbed the cliffs there were wild grapevines, and under the fallen leaves around the vine roots, the old man uncovered dried grapes shrunken into tiny sweet raisins. By noon they had reached the first of the mountain streams. There they washed and drank water and rested.

The old man frowned and pointed at Humaweepi's boots. "Take them off," he told Humaweepi; "leave them here until we come back."

So Humaweepi pulled off his cowboy boots and put them under a lichen-covered[9] boulder near a big oak tree where he could find them. Then Humaweepi relaxed, feeling the coolness of air on his bare feet. He watched his uncle, dozing in the sun with his back against a big pine. The old man's hair had been white and long ever since Humaweepi could remember; but the old face was changing, and Humaweepi could see the weariness there—a weariness not from their little journey but from a much longer time in this world. Someday he will die, Humaweepi was thinking. He will be gone and I will be by myself. I will have to do the things he did. I will have to take care of things.

Humaweepi had never seen the lake be-

---

7. obsidian (əb sid′ ē ən) *adj.*: Made of hard, black glass that comes from volcanoes (usually a noun).
8. yucca (yuk′ ə) *adj.*: Plants with stiff sword-shaped leaves and white flowers (usually a noun).

---

9. lichen (lī′ kən)-**covered:** Covered with small plants forming a crustlike growth.

Humaweepi, the Warrior Priest 169

6 **Discussion** How could Humaweepi some day "derive strength" from his special objects? What did the old man mean by that?

7 **Clarification** Priests performed public ceremonies for an entire group or village. They went through long periods of formal training.

8 **Reading Strategy** Summarize what you think the old man has been teaching Humaweepi all these years.

9 **Critical Thinking and Reading** What "things" will Humaweepi have to take care of after his uncle dies? How will he know what to do?

10 Enrichment The bear that lives in this part of the country is the grizzly. Because of its strength and speed, the bear became a symbol of power to the Indians and was worshiped as a god by many tribes.

11 Discussion Why did Humaweepi sing the bear song? What is the significance of the words? What conclusions can you draw about the role of the warrior priest from the song?

12 Discussion What was it that Humaweepi realized at the end of the bear song?

13 Critical Thinking and Reading What trip is Humaweepi describing to his friend? Do you think a great deal of time has passed since Humaweepi sang the bear song? Why or why not?

fore. It appeared suddenly as they reached the top of a hill covered with aspen trees. Humaweepi looked at his uncle and was going to ask him about the lake, but the old man was singing and feeding corn pollen from his leather pouch to the mountain winds. Humaweepi stared at the lake and listened to the songs. The songs were snowstorms with sounds as soft and cold as snowflakes; the songs were spring rain and wild ducks returning. Humaweepi could hear this; he could hear his uncle's voice become the night wind—high-pitched and whining in the trees. Time was lost and there was only the space, the depth, the distance of the lake surrounded by the mountain peaks.

When Humaweepi looked up from the lake he noticed that the sun had moved down into the western part of the sky. He looked around to find his uncle. The old man was below him, kneeling on the edge of the lake, touching a big gray boulder and singing softly. Humaweepi made his way down the narrow rocky trail to the edge of the lake. The water was crystal and clear like air; Humaweepi could see the golden rainbow colors of the trout that lived there. Finally the old man motioned for Humaweepi to come to him. He pointed at the gray boulder that lay half in the lake and half on the shore. It was then that Humaweepi saw what it was. The bear. Magic creature of the mountains, powerful ally to men. Humaweepi unrolled his buckskin bundle and picked up the tiny beads—sky-blue turquoise and coral that was dark red. He sang the bear song and stepped into the icy, clear water to lay the beads on bear's head, gray granite rock, resting above the lake, facing west.

"Bear
   resting in the mountains
   sleeping by the lake

Bear
   I come to you, a man,
   to ask you:
Stand beside us in our battles
   walk with us in peace.
Bear
   I ask you for your power
   I am the warrior priest
   I ask you for your power
   I am the warrior priest."

It wasn't until he had finished singing the song that Humaweepi realized what the words said. He turned his head toward the old man. He smiled at Humaweepi and nodded his head. Humaweepi nodded back.

Speaking to a friend, Humaweepi describes a trip he took with his uncle.

Humaweepi and his friend were silent for a long time. Finally Humaweepi said, "I'll tell you what my uncle told me, one winter, before he left. We took a trip to the mountain. It was early January, but the sun was warm and down here the snow was gone. We left early in the morning when the sky in the east was dark gray and the brightest star was still shining low in the western sky. I remember he didn't wear his ceremonial moccasins; he wore his old yucca sandals. I asked him about that.

"He said, 'Oh, you know the badger and the squirrel. Same shoes summer and winter,' but I think he was making that up, because when we got to the sandstone cliffs he buried the sandals in the sandy bottom of the cave where we slept and after that he walked on bare feet—up the cliff and along the mountain trail.

"There was snow on the shady side of the trees and big rocks, but the path we followed was in the sun and it was dry. I could hear

170   *Short Stories*

Grammar in Action

Concrete words are words that appeal to your senses. That is, they name or describe something that you can see, touch, smell, or hear. Because concrete words refer to things that are tangible and sensory, they are effective for description. In "Humaweepi, the Warrior Priest," the writer says that the uncle's songs were *snowstorms* with *sounds as soft and cold as snowflakes.*" The italicized words help you to see and feel the songs, as well as

hear them. Writers use concrete words to create vivid descriptions.

Notice how Leslie Marmon Silko uses concrete words to help you imagine how the sun and mountain air looked and felt to Humaweepi:

The *sun* felt *warm* on my body, *touching* me, but my *breath* still made *steam* in the *cold mountain air*.

The sentence appeals to the senses of sight and touch. The sun felt warm, *touching* Humaweepi, yet his breath *made steam* in the cold air. The author's use of concrete words helps you imagine the contrast between the warm sun and the cold air more vividly.

melting snow—the icy water trickling down into the little streams and the little streams flowing into the big stream in the canyon where yellow bee flowers grow all summer. The sun felt warm on my body, touching me, but my breath still made steam in the cold mountain air.

" 'Aren't your feet cold?' I asked him.

"He stopped and looked at me for a long time, then shook his head. 'Look at these old feet,' he said. 'Do you see any corns or bunions?'

"I shook my head.

" 'That's right,' he said, 'my feet are beautiful. No one has feet like these. Especially you people who wear shoes and boots. He walked on ahead before he said anything else. 'You have seen babies, haven't you?' he asked.

"I nodded, but I was wondering what this had to do with the old man's feet.

" 'Well, then you've noticed their grandmothers and their mothers, always worried about keeping the feet warm. But have you watched the babies? Do they care? No!' the old man said triumphantly, 'they do not care. They play outside on a cold winter day, no shoes, no jacket, because they aren't cold.' He hiked on, moving rapidly, excited by his own words; then he stopped at the stream. 'But human beings are what they are. It's not long before they are taught to be **14** cold and they cry for their shoes.'

"The old man started digging around the edge of a stream, using a crooked, dry branch to poke through the melting snow. 'Here,' he said as he gave me a fat, round root, 'try this.'

Humaweepi, the Warrior Priest **171**

Student Activity 1. Identify the concrete words in the following sentence from the story and explain the image that the words help create in your mind. Then substitute other concrete words to create a different impression of the uncle's voice.

"...he could hear his uncle's voice become the night wind—high-pitched and whining in the trees."

Student Activity 2. Write three original sentences in which you use concrete words. Before writing, think of the senses you want your reader to use and the images you want to create.

Critical Thinking and Reading
Why does the old man give a wolf cry? Why is it significant that Humaweepi thinks he hears a wolf's response to his uncle's cry? Do you think Humaweepi himself could do this?

Reader's Response What is the most important thing that Huma-weepi learns from his uncle? Support your answer.

"I squatted at the edge of the rushing, swirling water, full of mountain dirt, churning, and rolling—rich and brown and muddy with ice pieces flashing in the sun. I held the root motionless under the force of the stream water; the ice coldness of the water felt pure and clear as the ice that clung to the rocks in midstream. When I pulled my hand back it was stiff. I shook it and the root and lifted them high toward the sky.

"The old man laughed, and his mouth was full of the milky fibers of the root. He walked up the hill, away from the sound of the muddy stream surging through the snowbanks. At the top of the hill there was a grove of big aspens; it was colder, and the snow hadn't melted much.

" 'Your feet,' I said to him. 'They'll freeze.

"The snow was up to my ankles now. He was sitting on a fallen aspen, with his feet stretched out in front of him and his eyes half closed, facing into the sun.

" 'Does the wolf freeze his feet?' the old man asked me.

"I shook my head.

" 'Well then,' he said.

" 'But you aren't a wolf,' I started to say.

"The old man's eyes opened wide and then looked at me narrowly, sharply, squinting and shining. He gave a long, wailing, wolf cry with his head raised toward the winter sky.

"It was all white—pale white—the sky, the aspens bare white, smooth and white as the snow frozen on the ground. The wolf cry echoed off the rocky mountain slopes around us; in the distance, I thought I heard a wailing answer."

15

172   *Short Stories*

Closure and Extension

ANSWERS TO THINKING ABOUT THE SELECTION
Recalling

1. He thought his uncle just wanted someone to live with him and help him care for his goat, chop wood, and carry water.
2. His uncle taught him about life and nature and Indian tradition and ritual. He learned the songs and chants for all seasons and was learning the prayers for the trees, plants, and animals. He also learned how to find food and shelter in the forest.
3. He thinks that someday his uncle will die and he will have to as-

sume his duties and responsibilities.
4. Looking at Humaweepi narrowly and sharply, he gives a long, wailing wolf cry.

Interpreting

5. His uncle takes him on trips to teach him about nature, survival, and life in the wild.
6. Answers will differ. Suggested Response: Humaweepi wants the power that a bear possesses.

He wants the bear's strength, cunning, ferocity, speed, and sense of smell.
7. He and his uncle nod in acknowledgement of their mutual understanding of the bear song's meaning. Humaweepi is now a warrior priest.
8. Answers will differ. Students should choose three of the following: He can sleep on the ground, he eats natural foods from the forest, he knows the name of everything in nature, he

goes barefoot like the animals, he is respectful of nature.
9. Answers will differ. Suggested Response: The author does not mean the reader to take this at face value. The uncle was teaching Humaweepi continuously through the way they were living and through everything he said and did.

Applying

10. Answers will differ. Suggested Response: Humaweepi learned

THINKING ABOUT THE SELECTION

Recalling

1. When Humaweepi was twelve, why did he think his uncle wanted them to live together?
2. What kinds of things has Humaweepi learned from his uncle through the years?
3. What does Humaweepi think after seeing the weariness in his uncle's face?
4. On one of their trips, how does his uncle respond when Humaweepi tells the barefoot old man that he isn't a wolf?

Interpreting

5. Why does Humaweepi's uncle take him on trips?
6. In his song Humaweepi asks the "Bear" for its "power." What kind of "power" do you think he wants?
7. Why do Humaweepi and his uncle nod at each other when the song is over?
8. Give three examples showing that Humaweepi's uncle feels close to nature.
9. At the beginning of the story, the author writes, "The old man didn't really teach him much; mostly they just lived." Do you think the author means you to take this statement at face value? Explain your answer.

Applying

10. Compare and contrast Humaweepi's education with the way most people learn in school.

ANALYZING LITERATURE

Understanding Theme

The way a character grows is often a good clue to the theme of a story. In "Humaweepi, the Warrior Priest," the boy realizes that "sitting beside his uncle," he had "been learning all this time and . . . didn't even know it."

1. Briefly describe what Humaweepi learns from his uncle.

2. What evidence is there that the old man wants Humaweepi to take his place after he dies?
3. Choose one of the following ideas and explain why it best expresses the story's theme:
   a. Tradition is less important than freedom of expression.
   b. Young people learn about traditions from their elders.
   c. It is harmful to live apart from other people.
4. How would you express the theme of this story?

CRITICAL THINKING AND READING

Recognizing the Writer's Purpose

In this story the writer teaches you about Native American traditions, while presenting insights into life. Just as Humaweepi learns from his uncle almost without knowing it, you also learn about the Pueblo heritage.

1. Find two examples that show that Native Americans have a deep understanding of plants or animals.
2. What evidence is there that Native Americans believe there is a living spirit in things that might not seem alive to others?
3. How is a "warrior priest" different from and similar to other teachers or religious leaders?

THINKING AND WRITING

Responding to Theme

Imagine that Humaweepi's uncle suddenly arrives at your door. He wants to take you and your best friend on one of his trips to the mountains. You want to go on the trip but your friend is not as enthusiastic. List the reasons that would convince your friend to support the decision to go on the trip. Then use the list to write a persuasive note to your friend. When you are finished, revise the note to make sure it will work.

Humaweepi, the Warrior Priest 173

(Answers begin on p. 172)

knew how to find the place in which the deer had slept; they gathered grass roots, wild grapes, wild iris roots, wild tulip bulbs, and tumbleweed sprouts to eat; they used yucca fibers to make sandals; they knew the name of everything in nature; they knew the calls of different animals and birds and could imitate them.

2. They sang songs and chants for all seasons; they had prayers for the trees, plants, and animals; they felt they could derive strength from inanimate objects; they considered a gray boulder to be the bear, the magic creature of the mountains, and sang the bear song to it.
3. The warrior priest is different from other teachers or religious leaders because he helps people live with and in nature. He teaches that there is a living spirit to be respected in all things. His prayers are directed to natural forces, not to one supreme being. He uses no formal books or classes. A warrior priest is like other teachers or religious leaders in that he wants to pass on his tribe's rites and traditions. To do this, he makes himself a role model, a common teaching method.

Challenge Compare and contrast how people learn. Are good learning experiences always as indirect as Humaweepi's are? Could everyone learn this way? How does teaching technique depend on the subject being taught?

Writing Across the Curriculum You might want to have students research and report on life among the Pueblo Indians. If you do, perhaps inform the social studies department of this assignment. Social studies teachers might provide guidance for students in conducting their research.

through observation, experience, example, practice, and repetition as do students, to some extent, today. But Humaweepi had no formal classes or books, unlike students today.

ANSWERS TO ANALYZING LITERATURE

1. Humaweepi learns about plants, animals, and all of nature, how to live outdoors as the animals do, and the rites and customs of his tribe.

2. When Humaweepi says he knows the names of things in the forest, his uncle says that this is what a priest must know. He tells Humaweepi that he has been teaching him all his life. He has Humaweepi sing the bear song, which is the song of the warrior priest.
3. Young people learn about traditions from their elders. This best expresses the theme of the story because Humaweepi has learned how to be a warrior priest

by watching and listening to his uncle.
4. Answers will differ. Suggested Response: Through Humaweepi's development into a man, he realizes that his uncle has been shaping him into a warrior priest by his example.

ANSWERS TO CRITICAL THINKING AND READING

1. Answers will differ but should include two of the following: They

GUIDE FOR READING

Universal Theme

Look For

Writing

Vocabulary

Home

Gwendolyn Brooks (1917–   ) was born in Topeka, Kansas, and grew up in Chicago, Illinois. In 1950 she won the Pulitzer Prize for poetry, and she has received other honors for her writing. She once remarked on her work by saying, "I like to vivify [give life to] the universal fact . . . but the universal wears contemporary clothing very well." What Brooks meant by this is illustrated in "Home." The universal fact of people's attachment to their home is vividly depicted in this brief story of a black American family faced with the loss of theirs.

A **theme** is the central idea of a story, or the general idea about life that the story reveals. A **universal theme** is one that has meaning and importance for people all over the world. Usually such a theme will be implied rather than stated directly.

As you read "Home," ask yourself, "What does this home mean to the characters in this story? What universal truth does this story reveal about the importance of home to anyone, living anywhere?"

A house provides shelter, but a home provides much more. Freewrite about the meaning of the word *home.*

Knowing the following words will help you as you read "Home."
obstinate (äb′stə nit) *adj.*: Stubborn (p. 175)
emphatic (im fat′ik) *adj.*: Felt with emphasis; forceful; definite (p. 175)
staccato (stə kät′ō) *adj.*: Made up of sharp separate little elements (p. 176)
emerged (i murj′d) *v.*: Became visible (p. 176)

Home

Gwendolyn Brooks

What had been wanted was this always, this always to last, the talking softly on this porch, with the snake plant in the jardiniere[1] in the southwest corner, and the obstinate slip from Aunt Eppie's magnificent Michigan fern at the left side of the friendly door. Mama, Maud Martha and Helen rocked slowly in their rocking chairs, and looked at the late afternoon light on the lawn, and at the emphatic iron of the fence and at the poplar tree.

These things might soon be theirs no longer. Those shafts and pools of light, the tree, the graceful iron, might soon be viewed possessively by different eyes.

Papa was to have gone that noon, during his lunch hour, to the office of the Home Owners' Loan. If he had not succeeded in getting another extension, they would be leaving this house in which they had lived for more than fourteen years. There was little hope. The Home Owners' Loan was hard. They sat, making their plans.

"We'll be moving into a nice flat[2] somewhere," said Mama. "Somewhere on South Park, or Michigan, or in Washington Park Court." Those flats, as the girls and Mama knew well, were burdens on wages twice the size of Papa's. This was not mentioned now.

"They're much prettier than this old house," said Helen. "I have friends I'd just as soon not bring here. And I have other friends that wouldn't come down this far for anything, unless they were in a taxi."

Yesterday, Maud Martha would have attacked her. Tomorrow she might. Today she said nothing. She merely gazed at a little hopping robin in the tree, her tree, and tried to keep the fronts of her eyes dry.

HER WORLD
Philip Evergood
The Metropolitan Museum of Art

---

1. jardiniere (jär'd'n ir') *n.*: An ornamental bowl, pot, or stand for flowers or plants.
2. flat (flat) *n.*: An apartment.

175

"Well, I do know," said Mama, turning her hands over and over, "that I've been getting tireder and tireder of doing that firing.[3] From October to April, there's firing to be done."

"But lately we've been helping, Harry and I," said Maud Martha. "And sometimes in March and April and in October, and even in November, we could build a little fire in the fireplace. Sometimes the weather was just right for that."

She knew, from the way they looked at her, that this had been a mistake. They did not want to cry.

But she felt that the little line of white, somewhat ridged with smoked purple, and all that cream-shot saffron,[4] would never drift across any western sky except that in back of this house. The rain would drum with as sweet a dullness nowhere but here. The birds on South Park were mechanical birds, no better than the poor caught canaries in those "rich" women's sun parlors.

"It's just going to kill Papa!" burst out Maud Martha. "He loves this house! He *lives* for this house!"

"He lives for us," said Helen. "It's us he loves. He wouldn't want the house, except for us."

"And he'll have us," added Mama, "wherever."

"You know," Helen sighed, "if you want to know the truth, this is a relief. If this hadn't come up, we would have gone on, just dragged on, hanging out here forever."

"It might," allowed Mama, "be an act of God. God may just have reached down, and picked up the reins."

"Yes," Maud Martha cracked in, "that's what you always say—that God knows best."

Her mother looked at her quickly, decided the statement was not suspect, looked away.

Helen saw Papa coming. "There's Papa," said Helen.

They could not tell a thing from the way Papa was walking. It was that same dear little staccato walk, one shoulder down, then the other, then repeat, and repeat. They watched his progress. He passed the Kennedys', he passed the vacant lot, he passed Mrs. Blakemore's. They wanted to hurl themselves over the fence, into the street, and shake the truth out of his collar. He opened his gate—the gate—and still his stride and face told them nothing.

"Hello," he said.

Mama got up and followed him through the front door. The girls knew better than to go in too.

Presently Mama's head emerged. Her eyes were lamps turned on.

"It's all right," she exclaimed. "He got it. It's all over. Everything is all right."

The door slammed shut. Mama's footsteps hurried away.

"I think," said Helen, rocking rapidly, "I think I'll give a party. I haven't given a party since I was eleven. I'd like some of my friends to just casually see that we're homeowners."

---

3. **firing** (fīr′ iŋ) *n*.: Starting up and tending the fire in a stove or furnace.
4. **saffron:** (saf′ rən) An orange-yellow color.

THINKING ABOUT THE SELECTION

Recalling

1. What problem does the family face in "Home"?
2. What does Papa hope to do during his lunch hour to deal with this problem?
3. According to Helen, why does Papa want to keep the house?

Interpreting

4. How do Mama and the girls feel before Helen sees Papa returning?
5. How do Mama and the girls feel as they watch Papa approaching?
6. At the end Helen gets the idea of giving a party. What does this idea suggest about what she is feeling?

Applying

7. What are the conditions that would make moving to a new home a happy event?

ANALYZING LITERATURE

Understanding Universal Themes

A theme is **universal** when readers the world over can respond to it. "Home," for example, presents a black family living in Chicago sometime during this century. Yet the problem the family faces and the feelings these people have would be understood by people in China, South America, Italy, or anywhere else.

1. Find three passages in the story where love of home is revealed.
2. In your own words tell what idea the story suggests about love of home.
3. Why could people living anywhere respond to this idea?

CRITICAL THINKING AND READING

Reading Between the Lines

The expression *reading between the lines* means reading to grasp and understand what is not said directly. For example, consider this sentence from "Home": "The rain would drum with as sweet a dullness nowhere but here." In reality, the sound of rain is basically the same everywhere. But what is said "between the lines" is that Maud Martha is so attached to her home that she cannot imagine how another house can be as pleasant when it is raining. What can you read between the lines of the following sentences from "Home"?

1. "What had been wanted was this always, this always to last, the talking softly on this porch . . ."
2. "The birds on South Park were mechanical birds, no better than the poor caught canaries in those 'rich' women's sun parlors."

UNDERSTANDING LANGUAGE

Finding Synonyms

A **synonym** is a word that has the same or nearly the same meaning as another word. A dictionary or a thesaurus, which gives lists of synonyms for a word, can help you find synonyms. Using either of these books, find a synonym for each of the following words from "Home":

1. wages
2. gaze
3. hurl
4. stride
5. exclaim
6. presently

THINKING AND WRITING

Writing About Theme

One critic has identified a major theme in Gwendolyn Brooks's work as the need for stability, order, and beauty to keep life pleasant. Write a short composition explaining how "Home" reveals that these three qualities are necessary for a good life. Before you write your composition, take each one of these qualities and look for a passage in the story that suggests it is needed or wanted. (You may have to read between the lines to do this.) Then prepare your first draft. When you revise your composition, check that your statements all support your main point. Share your composition with your classmates.

Home 177

---

3. No matter where a person lives, he or she values home. This is a universal truth that applies to people around the world.

ANSWERS TO CRITICAL THINKING AND READING

1. They loved the life they have in this house. The time spent as a family on the porch is part of what they cherished in their home life.
2. Maud Martha is so attached to her home that she cannot imagine the birds on another street sounding as sweet as the ones on her street.

ANSWERS TO UNDERSTANDING LANGUAGE

1. earnings, salary, income
2. stare, look, watch
3. throw, project, pitch, toss, fling, cast
4. step, pace
5. cry out, shout
6. soon, shortly, eventually

Challenge Do you think the characters in this story would ever get used to a new house? How would they have adjusted if they had been forced to move? What might they have done to make the transition easier for themselves?

THINKING AND WRITING

For help with this assignment, students can refer to Lesson 11, "Writing About Theme," in the Handbook of Writing About Literature.

Publishing Student Writing You might display student compositions in the classroom. Have artistically inclined students illustrate some of the concepts of home expressed in the compositions. Display the artwork alongside the compositions illustrated.

Interpreting

4. They feel very sad, nostalgic, and close to tears.
5. They feel very anxious and on edge.
6. This suggests that Helen is so relieved and proud that she wants to celebrate.

Applying

7. Answers will differ. Suggested Response: Moving to a new home would be a happy occasion if the new house were in some way better than the old. For example, moving to a larger house or a better neighborhood would make moving a happy event.

ANSWERS TO ANALYZING LITERATURE

1. Answers will differ. Students should choose three of the following: "What had been wanted was this always . . ." "Those shafts and pools of light . . ." "She merely gazed at a little hopping robin . . ." "But she felt that the little line of white . . ." "Her eyes were lamps turned on." "It's all right . . . Everything is all right." "I think I'll give a party . . ."
2. Answers will differ. Suggested Response: People's homes are very important to them, as evidenced by the anxiety the characters feel when faced with the prospect of losing their home.

Focus

More About the Author Isaac Asimov not only is a prolific writer but also has been a professor of biochemistry at Boston University. He received his doctorate in biochemistry from Columbia University in New York. Ask students to discuss what satisfaction a scientist might derive from writing science fiction. In what way can popular success be a drawback for a serious scientist?

Literary Focus Science fiction often explores places, events, and characters that are out of the ordinary. Therefore, science fiction may provide the reader with new insights into everyday life through extraordinary impressions. Very often, all the events and characters' actions lead up to the science-fiction theme.

Look For Your less advanced students might be made aware of important details and the ways in which the characters act and react in the story. This will help them identify the theme and gain greater insights through the theme.

Writing/Prior Knowledge Have students discuss the meaning of this quotation: "The only thing we have to fear is fear itself." Then have them complete the freewriting assignment.

Vocabulary These words also may give students some difficulty: *transparent, gravitational* (p. 179); *hallucinations, planetary* (p. 180); *hyperspace, ruefully* (p. 182); *unfurled, diminished* (p. 183); *caricature, insubstantial* (p. 185); *manifestation* (p. 187); *ostentatiously* (p. 188); *speculative, animation* (p. 189); and *neurophysiologists* (p. 194). Be sure students know what these words mean as they read the story.

Hallucination

Isaac Asimov (1920–   ) was born in Russia and raised in Brooklyn, New York. He has written hundreds of books, many of which are science-fiction. Asimov's love of science fiction developed when he began reading the science-fiction magazines sold in his father's candy store. In a way this childhood reading can be considered the earliest inspiration for "Hallucination," a story in which Asimov probes the mysteries of communication between two worlds.

Theme in Science Fiction

The **theme** of a story is its central idea, or the general idea about life it reveals. In a science-fiction story, a science-fiction theme will often apply to life as we know it. Because the story is often set far away in space or time and the characters and events are strange and unusual, however, you are likely to see the theme in a new light—a way that makes it more vivid and memorable.

Look For

As you read "Hallucination," look for all that is said about the effects of fear on the human mind. Pay attention to how each character reacts to strange and unusual experiences. By keeping these details in mind and determining why Sam is able to communicate with the alien life form when others could not, you will come to understand the theme.

Writing

Fears may often prevent people from accomplishing goals or even from seeing situations as they really are. Think of four or five things that make people afraid. List them, and next to each one briefly tell how it gets in the way of doing or understanding something.

Vocabulary

Knowing the following words will help you as you read "Hallucination."

technology (tek näl′ə jē) *n.*: The ideas of science applied to practical problems (p. 179)
hexagonal (hek sag′ə n′l) *adj.*: Six-sided (p. 183)
concave (kän kāv′) *adj.*: Empty and curved like the inside of a hollow ball (p. 183)
billowed (bil′ōd) *v.*: Surged or

swelled (p. 184)
tethered (teth′ ərd) *v.*: Fastened with a rope or chain (p. 185)
insolent (in′sə lənt) *adj.*: Disrespectful (p. 188)
opaque (ō pāk′) *adj.*: Not letting light pass through (p. 190)

178   Short Stories

Objectives

1 To recognize the theme of a science-fiction short story
2 To understand the way a character reasons in a short story
3 To write a report about a science-fiction event

Support Material

Teaching Portfolio
Teacher Backup, p. 271
Grammar in Action Worksheet, *Agreement Between Subjects and Verbs,* p. 275
Grammar in Action Worksheet, *Commas and Coordinating Conjunctions,* p. 277
Grammar in Action Worksheet, *Using Sentence Fragments in Dialogue,* p. 279

Usage and Mechanics Worksheet, p. 281
Vocabulary Check, p. 282
Analyzing Literature Worksheet, *Recognizing Theme,* p. 283
Critical Thinking and Reading Worksheet, *Looking at Reasoning,* p. 284
Selection Test, p. 285

Hallucination [1]

Isaac Asimov

Sam Chase arrived on Energy Planet on his 15th birthday.

It was a great achievement, he had been told, to have been assigned there, but he wasn't at all sure he felt that at the moment.

It meant a three-year separation from Earth and from his family, while he continued a specialized education in the field, and that was a sobering thought. It was not the field of education in which he was interested, and he could not understand why Central Computer had assigned him to this project, and that was downright depressing.

He looked at the transparent Dome overhead. It was quite high, perhaps a thousand meters high, and it stretched in all directions farther than he could clearly see. He asked, "Is it true that this is the only dome on the planet, sir?"

Donald Gentry, to whom the question had been addressed, smiled. He was a large man, a little chubby, with dark brown, good-natured eyes, not much hair, and a short, graying beard.

He said, "The only one, Sam. It's quite large, though, and most of the housing facilities are underground, where you'll find no lack of space. Besides, once your basic training is done, you'll be spending most of your time in space. This is just our planetary base."

"I see, sir," said Sam, a little troubled.

Gentry said, "I am in charge of our basic trainees, so I have to study their records carefully. It seems to me that this assignment was not your first choice. Am I right?"

Sam hesitated, and then decided he didn't have much choice but to be honest about it. He said, "I'm not sure that I'll do as well as I would like to in gravitational engineering."

"Why not? Surely the Central Computer, which evaluated your scholastic record and your social and personal background, can be trusted in its judgments. And if you do well, it will be a great achievement for you; for right here, we are at the cutting edge of a new technology."

"I know that, sir," said Sam. "Back on Earth, everyone is very excited about it. No one before has ever tried to get close to a neutron star[1] and make use of its energy." [3]

"Yes?" Gentry asked. "I haven't been on Earth for two years. What else do they say about it? I understand there's considerable opposition."

His eyes probed the boy.

Sam shifted uneasily, aware he was being tested. He said, "There are people on Earth who say it's all too dangerous and might be a waste of money." [4]

"Do you believe that?"

"It might be so, but most new technologies have their dangers, and many are worth

---

1. **neutron star:** A collapsed star made up of many densely packed neutrons, or uncharged atomic particles.

Presentation

Motivation/Prior Knowledge Have students imagine that they have been sent to another planet to continue their education. Although this is a great opportunity, they have not been assigned to the project they were really interested in. What would their reaction be? Would they be more excited or disappointed? How might they turn their disappointment into accomplishment and prove themselves at the same time?

Purpose-Setting Question What role do hallucinations play in this story?

1 **Clarification** A hallucination is a mental state in which a person sees, hears, tastes, smells, or feels something that does not exist. Hallucinations may be a symptom of some mental or physical illness, but healthy people can also have hallucinations under certain circumstances.

2 **Discussion** In what ways is Sam mature for a 15-year-old boy? Do you think there could be a hidden reason for his being assigned to a project in which he had not expressed interest?

3 **Enrichment** Neutron stars are very dense and spin very rapidly. As they spin, they emit energy in the form of radio waves. Astronomers can detect these pulses of radio waves. They call the stars pulsars for this reason.

4 **Critical Thinking and Reading** Does Sam's statement remind you of anything you've heard about the actual space program? Do most people think space exploration is without value?

5 **Discussion** What might make you think that Sam should not have said this? Based on Gentry's reaction, do you think the Commander is sick?

6 **Critical Thinking and Reading** Now why do you think that Sam was sent to Energy Planet?

Humanities Note

To give students an idea of what a hallucination might look like, bring in some Marc Chagall reproductions. Chagall has been identified with Surrealism because of the fantastic and dreamlike elements in his work. We particularly recommend looking at his *Flying Over the Town*. Point out to students the hallucinogenic quality of this painting.

doing despite that. This one is, I think."

"Very good. What else do they say on Earth?"

"They say the Commander isn't well and that the project might fail without him." When Gentry didn't respond, Sam added, hastily, "That's what they say."

Gentry acted as though he didn't hear. He put his hand on Sam's shoulder and said, "Come, I've got to show you to your Corridor, introduce you to your roommate and explain what your initial duties will be." As they walked toward the elevator that would take them downward, he said, "What was your first choice of assignment, Chase?"

"Neurophysiology,[2] sir."

"Not a bad choice. Even today, the human brain continues to be a mystery. We know more about neutron stars than we do about the brain—as we found out when this project first began."

"Oh?"

"Indeed! At the start, various people at the base—it was much smaller and more primitive then—reported having experienced hallucinations. It never had any bad effect, and after a while, there were no further reports. We never found out the cause."

Sam stopped, and looked up and about again. "Was that why the Dome was built, Dr. Gentry?"

"No, not at all. We needed a place with a completely Earth-like environment, but we haven't isolated ourselves. People can go outside freely. There are no hallucinations being reported now."

Sam said, "The information I was given about Energy Planet is that there is no life on it except for plants and insects, and that they're harmless."

"That's right, but they're also inedible.

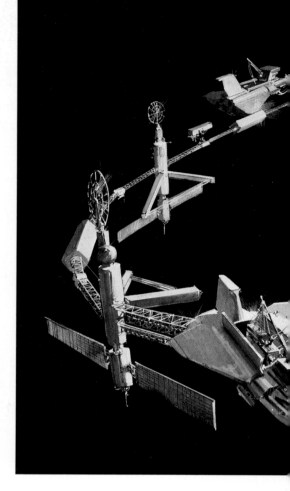

So we grow our own vegetables, and keep some small animals, right here under the Dome. Still, we've found nothing hallucinogenic about the planetary life."

"Anything unusual about the atmosphere, sir?"

Gentry looked down from his only slightly greater height and said, "Not at all. People have camped in the open overnight on occasion, and nothing has happened. It is a pleasant world. There are streams but

---

2. **neurophysiology** (noor′ ō fiz′ ē äl′ ə jē) *n.*: The study of the brain and nervous system.

180   *Short Stories*

Grammar in Action

When checking for **agreement between subjects and verbs,** sentences with inverted word order require the reader to look for the subject after the verb. Even though the subject comes after the verb, the subject and verb must still agree in number. Notice how the subjects and verbs in the following sentences agree, despite the unusual word order.

"What *was* your first *choice* of assignment, Chase?"
There *are* frequent light *rains,* and it is sometimes windy, but there *are* no *extremes* of heat and cold.

These examples show two of the most common uses of inverted word order. Questions are often presented with inverted word order, as shown in the first example. The second sentence contains two independent clauses beginning with *there,* which are almost always in inverted word order. Sentences beginning with the word *here* are often in inverted word order also. Knowing these cases will help you identify sentences with inverted word order, which will aid your checking of subject-verb agreement.

7 Thematic Idea Compare the atmosphere on Energy Planet with the atmosphere on the planet described in the story *"All Summer in a Day"* (page 107) by Ray Bradbury.

8 Critical Thinking and Reading Why does Sam seem doubtful here? Why does he assume a connection between the Commander's illness and hallucinations?

no fish, just algae[3] and water-insects. There is nothing to sting you or poison you. There are yellow berries that look delicious and taste terrible, but do no other harm. The weather's pretty nearly always good. There are frequent light rains, and it is sometimes windy, but there are no extremes of heat and cold."

3. **algae** (al′ jē) *n*.: Plants like seaweed that live in water or damp places.

"And no hallucinations anymore, Dr. Gentry?"

"You sound disappointed," said Gentry, smiling.

Sam took a chance. "Does the Commander's trouble have anything to do with the hallucinations, sir?"

The good nature vanished from Gentry's eyes. "What trouble do you refer to?"

Sam flushed, and they proceeded in silence.

Hallucination 181

Student Activity 1. Find three sentences where Asimov has inverted the word order. Copy each sentence on a piece of paper and underline the subject of each sentence once and the verb twice.

Student Activity 2. Find the subject in each of the following sentences, and write the correct verb next to it.

1. Where (is, are) Mary's purse?

2. There (was, were) a few pieces of candy left on the table.

3. When (was, were) the men from Venous supposed to arrive?

9 **Discussion** Do you think Robert's attitude is typical of the attitude on Energy Planet? What's wrong with this way of thinking?

10 **Discussion** Why does Sam keep coming back to this?

Sam found few others in the Corridor he had been assigned to, but Gentry had explained it was a busy time at the forward station, where the power system was being built in a ring around the neutron star, the tiny object less than 10 miles across, that had all the mass of a normal star, and a magnetic field of incredible power.

It was a magnetic field that would be tapped. Energy would be led away in enormous amounts, and yet it would all be a pinprick, less than a pinprick to the star's rotational energy,[4] which was the ultimate source. It would take billions of years to bleed off all that energy, and in that time, dozens of populated planets, fed the energy through hyperspace, would have all they needed for an indefinite time.

Sharing Sam's room was Robert Gillette, a dark-haired, unhappy-looking young man. After cautious greetings had been exchanged, Robert revealed that he was 16 and had been "grounded" with a broken arm, though the break didn't show because it had been pinned internally.

Robert said, ruefully, "It takes a while before you learn to handle things in space. They may not have weight, but they have inertia,[5] and you have to allow for that."

Sam said, "They always teach you that . . ." He was going to say that it was taught in fourth-grade science, but realized that would be insulting, and stopped himself.

Robert caught the implication, however, and flushed. He said, "It's easy to know it in your head. It doesn't mean you get the ·proper reflexes till you've practiced quite a bit. You'll find out."

---

4. rotational energy: Energy that comes from the star's rotation, or turning.
5. inertia (in ʉr′ shə) *n.*: The tendency of an object to remain at rest if it is at rest, or to remain moving if it is moving—unless it is disturbed by an outside force.

Sam asked, "Is it very complicated to get to go outside?"

"No, but why do you want to go?"

"Have you ever been outside?"

"Sure."

Sam took a chance. He asked, very casually, "Did you ever see one of these hallucinations they talk about?"

Robert said, "*Who* talk about?"

Sam didn't answer directly. He said, "A lot of people used to see them—but they don't anymore. Or so they say."

"So *who* say?"

Sam took another chance. "Or if they see them, they keep quiet about them."

Robert said, gruffly, "Listen, don't get interested in these—whatever they are. If you start telling yourself you see—uh-something, you might be sent back. You'll lose your chance at a good education and an important career."

Sam shrugged and sat down on the unused bunk. "All right for this to be my bed?"

"It's the only other bed here," said Robert. He paused and then, as though to let bygones be bygones, said, "I'll show you around later."

"Thanks," said Sam. "What kind of a guy is the Commander?"

"He's aces. He knows more about hyperspatial technology than anyone, and he's got pull with the Space Agency, so we get the money and equipment we need."

Sam opened his trunk and, with his back to Robert, said, casually, "I hear he's not well."

"Things get him down. We're behind schedule, there are cost overruns, and like that."

"Depression, huh? Any connection, you suppose, with . . . ?"

Robert stirred impatiently in his seat. "Say, why are you so interested in all this?"

"Energy physics[6] isn't really my deal. Coming here. . . ."

11 "Well, here's where you are, mister, and you better make up your mind to it, or you'll get sent home, and then you won't be anywhere—I'm going to the library."

Sam remained in the room alone—with his thoughts.

It was not at all difficult for Sam to get permission to leave the Dome.

The Corridor-Master nodded. "Fair enough, but you only get three hours, you know. And don't wander out of sight of the Dome. If we have to look for you, we'll find you, because you'll be wearing this," and he held out a transmitter, which Sam knew had been tuned to his own personal wavelength, one which had been assigned him at birth. "But if we have to go to that trouble, you won't be allowed out again for a pretty long time. And it won't look good on your record, either."

It won't look good on your record. Any reasonable career these days had to include experience and education in space, so it was an effective warning. No wonder people might have stopped reporting hallucinations, even if they saw them.

12 Even so, Sam was going to have to take his chance. After all, the Central Computer *couldn't* have sent him here just to do energy physics.

As far as looks were concerned, the planet might have been Earth—some part of Earth anyway, someplace where there were a few trees and low bushes and lots of tall grass.

There were no paths, and with his every cautious step, the grass swayed, and flying creatures whirred upward with a soft, hissing noise of wings.

One of them landed on his finger, and Sam looked at it curiously. It was very small and, therefore, hard to see in detail, but it seemed hexagonal, bulging above and concave below. There were many short, small legs so that when it moved it almost seemed to do so on tiny wheels. There were no signs of wings till it suddenly took off, and then four tiny, feathery objects unfurled.

What made the planet different from Earth, though, was the smell. It wasn't unpleasant; it was just different. The plants must have an entirely different chemistry[7] from those on Earth.

The smell diminished with time, however, as it saturated his nostrils. He found an exposed bit of rocky ledge he could sit on and considered the prospect. The sky was filled with lines of clouds, and the sun was periodically obscured, but the temperature was pleasant, and there was only a light wind. The air felt a bit damp.

Sam had brought a small hamper with two sandwiches, water and a canned drink.

He chewed away and thought: Why should there be hallucinations?

13 Surely, those accepted for a job as important as that of taming a neutron star would have been selected for mental stability. It would be surprising to have even one hallucinating, let alone a number of them. Was it a matter of chemical influences on the brain?

They would surely have checked that out.

Sam plucked a leaf, tore it in two and squeezed. He then put the torn edge to his

---

6. energy physics (fiz′ iks): Physics is the science that deals with the properties of matter and energy; energy physics would be a branch of this science that studies energy especially.

---

7. chemistry (kem′ is trē) *n.*: The chemical makeup and reaction of substances.

11 **Discussion** Why does Robert become hostile?

12 **Reading Strategy** Summarize the events of the story so far and predict what will happen to Sam on Energy Planet.

13 **Critical Thinking and Reading** Why do you think people have had hallucinations on Energy Planet? Speculate about possible causes based on what you already know about the planet.

nose cautiously, and took it away again. A very acrid, unpleasant smell. He tried a blade of grass. Much the same.

Was the smell enough? It hadn't made him feel dizzy or in any way peculiar.

14 He used a bit of his water to rinse off the fingers that had held the plants, then finished his sandwiches slowly, trying to see if anything else might be considered unnatural.

All that greenery. There ought to be animals eating it, not just insects—or whatever those little things might be, with the gentle sighing of their tiny feathery wings and the very soft crackle of their munching of leaves and stalks.

What if there were a cow, a big, fat cow, doing the munching? And with the last mouthful of his second sandwich, Sam's munching stopped.

There was a kind of smoke in the air between himself and a line of hedges. It waved, billowed and altered, a very thin smoke. He blinked his eyes, then shook his head, but it was still there.

He swallowed hastily, closed his lunch box and slung it over his shoulder by its strap. He stood up.

184   Short Stories

Grammar in Action

A compound sentence consists of two or more independent clauses. These clauses, of equal importance, are joined because the ideas expressed in them are closely related. One way to join the clauses in a compound sentence is with a **comma** and a **coordinating conjunction.** Using a comma and conjunction separates the two clauses without breaking the flow of thought. Furthermore, the conjunction shows the relationship between the clauses. Using a comma and conjunction to create compound sentences thus adds clarity and unity to writing. It can also heighten the drama of the situation. In the following sentences, notice how the coordinating conjunctions clarify the relationship between the independent clauses.

He blinked his eyes, then shook his head, *but* it was still there.

Sam could see the vegetation dimly through it, *and* when a gust of wind caught it, it moved a bit as though it were a tethered balloon.

In the first sentence, the coordinating conjunction *but* shows a contrasting relationship between the two independent clauses. In the second sentence, *and* reveals an equal relationship between the two clauses.

He felt no fear. He was only excited—and curious.

The smoke was growing thicker, and taking on a shape. Vaguely, it looked like a cow, a smoky, insubstantial shape that he could see through. Was it a hallucination? A creation of his mind? He had just been thinking of a cow.

Hallucination or not, he was going to investigate.

With determination, he stepped toward the cow outlined in smoke on the strange, far planet on which his education and career were to be advanced.

He was convinced there was nothing wrong with his mind. It was the "hallucination" that Dr. Gentry had mentioned, but it was no hallucination. Even as he pushed his way through the tall, rank, grass-like greenery, he noted the silence, and knew not only that it was no hallucination, but what it really *was*.

The smoke seemed to condense and grow darker, outlining the cow more sharply. It was as though the cow were being painted in the air.

Sam laughed, and shouted, "Stop! Stop! Don't use me; I don't know a cow well enough. I've only seen pictures. You're getting it all wrong."

It looked more like a caricature than a real animal, and, as he cried out, the outline wavered and thinned. The smoke remained, but it was as though an unseen hand had passed across the air to erase what had been written.

Then a new shape began to take form. At first, Sam couldn't quite make out what it was intended to represent, but it changed and sharpened quickly. He stared in surprise, his mouth hanging open and his hamper bumping emptily against his side.

The smoke was forming a human being. There was no mistake about it. It was forming accurately, as though it had a model it could imitate, and of course it did have one, for Sam was standing there.

It was becoming Sam, clothes and all, even the outline of the hamper and the strap over his shoulder. It was another Sam Chase.

It was still a little vague, wavering a bit, insubstantial, but it firmed as though it were correcting itself, and then, finally, it was steady.

It never became entirely solid. Sam could see the vegetation dimly through it, and when a gust of wind caught it, it moved a bit as though it were a tethered balloon.

But it was real. It was no creation of his mind. Sam was sure of that.

But he couldn't just stand there, simply facing it. Diffidently, he said, "Hello, there."

Somehow, he expected the Other Sam to speak too, and, indeed, its mouth opened and closed, but no sound came out. It might just have been imitating the motion of Sam's mouth.

Sam said, again, "Hello. Can you speak?"

There was no sound but his own voice, and yet there was a tickling in his mind, a conviction that they could communicate.

Sam frowned. What made him so sure of that? The thought seemed to pop into his mind.

He asked, "Is that what has appeared to other people—human people—my kind—on this world?"

No answering sound, but he was quite sure what the answer to this question was. This had appeared to other people, not necessarily in their own shape, but *something*. And it hadn't worked.

What made him so sure of *that*? Where did these convictions come from in answer to his questions?

Yes, of course, they *were* the answers to his questions. The Other Sam was putting thoughts into his mind. It was adjusting the

Hallucination 185

15 Discussion Why do you think Sam is unafraid? Would most people react this way? Why or why not?

16 Discussion What do you think is going on here? In what way is the smoke a form of communication?

17 Discussion How are Sam's questions being answered? What other examples of nonverbal communication can you think of? How is this similar and how is it different?

When joining independent clauses with a comma and a coordinating conjunction, be sure to use the proper conjunction to show the exact relationships between the clauses. The coordinating conjunctions *and, but, for, nor, or, so,* and *yet* each indicate a specific type of relationship.

Student Activity 1. Find three other compound sentences from "Hallucination" in which Asimov effectively uses a comma and a coordinating conjunction to join independent clauses.

Student Activity 2. Using a comma and a coordinating conjunction, combine each pair of sentences to form a compound sentence.

1. Sam went outside the dome. Sam only had one hour to explore the planet.
2. The planet was covered with green grass. The sun was pleasantly warm.
3. Sam thought he saw the form of a cow in the distance. The cow was distorted and billowing in the wind.

18 Discussion Why does Sam feel that he needs practice?

tiny electric currents in his brain cells so that the proper thoughts would arise.

He nodded thoughtfully at *that* thought, and the Other Sam must have caught the significance of the gesture, for it nodded too.

It had to be so. First a cow had formed, when Sam had thought of a cow, and then it had shifted when Sam had said the cow was imperfect. The Other Sam could grasp his thoughts somehow, and if it could grasp them, then it could modify them, too, perhaps.

Was this what telepathy[8] was like, then?

---

8. telepathy (tə lep′ ə thē) *n.*: Communication between minds by exchanging thoughts.

It was not like talking. It was having thoughts, except that the thoughts originated elsewhere and were not created entirely of one's own mental operations. But how could you tell your own thoughts from thoughts imposed from outside?

Sam knew the answer to that at once. Right now, he was unused to the process. He had never had practice. With time, as he grew more skilled at it, he would be able to tell one kind of thought from another without trouble.

In fact, he could do it now, if he thought about it. Wasn't he carrying on a conversation, in a way? He was wondering, and then knowing. The wondering was his own ques-

186 **Short Stories**

tion, the knowing was the Other Sam's answer. Of course it was.

There! The "of course it was," just now, was an answer.

"Not so fast, Other Sam," said Sam aloud. "Don't go too quickly. Give me a chance to sort things out, or I'll just get confused."

He sat down suddenly on the grass, which bent away from him in all directions.

The Other Sam slowly tried to sit down as well.

Sam laughed, "Your legs are bending in the wrong place."

That was corrected at once. The Other Sam sat down, but remained very stiff from the waist up.

"Relax," said Sam.

Slowly, the Other Sam slumped, flopping a bit to one side, then correcting that.

Sam was relieved. With the Other Sam so willing to follow his lead, he was sure goodwill was involved. It was! Exactly!

"No," said Sam. "I said, not so fast. Don't go by my thoughts. Let me speak out loud, even if you can't hear me. *Then* adjust my thoughts, so I'll know it's an adjustment. Do you understand?"

He waited a moment and was then sure the Other Sam understood.

Ah, the answer had come, but not right away. Good!

"Why do you appear to people?" asked Sam.

He stared earnestly at the Other Sam, and knew that the Other Sam wanted to communicate with people, but had not succeeded.

But then, no answer to that question had really been required. The answer was obvious. But, then, *why* had they failed?

He put it in words. "Why did you fail? You are successfully communicating with me."

Sam was beginning to learn how to understand the alien manifestation. It was as though his mind were adapting itself to a new technique of communication, just as it would adapt itself to a new language. Or was the Other Sam influencing Sam's mind and teaching him the method without Sam even knowing it was being done?

What Sam found himself doing was letting his mind empty itself of immediate thoughts. After he asked this question, he let his eyes focus on nothing and his eyelids droop, as though he were about to drop off to sleep, and then he knew the answer. There was a little clicking—or something—in his mind, a signal that something had been put in from outside.

He now knew, for instance, that the Other Sam's previous attempts at communication had failed because the people to whom it had appeared had been frightened. They had doubted their own sanity. And because they feared, their minds—tightened. Their minds would not receive. The attempts at communication diminished, though they had never entirely stopped.

"But you're communicating with me," said Sam.

Sam was different from all the rest. He had not been afraid.

"Couldn't you have made them not afraid first? Then talked to them?"

It wouldn't work. The fear-filled mind resisted all. An attempt to change might damage. It would be wrong to damage a thinking mind. There had been one such attempt, but it had not worked.

"What is it you are trying to communicate, Other Sam?"

A wish to be left alone. *Despair!*

Despair was more than a thought; it was an emotion; it was a frightening sensation. Sam felt despair wash over him intensely, heavily, and yet, it was not part of himself.

Hallucination 187

19 **Discussion** Why does Sam need to speak out loud even though the Other Sam is reading his thoughts?

20 **Critical Thinking and Reading** How is fear an impediment to good communication even under ordinary circumstances?

21 **Discussion** Would you characterize the inhabitants of Energy Planet as peaceful or hostile? How can you tell? Can you conclude who was involved in the communication attempt that failed?

22 **Thematic Idea** Compare the way the creatures of Energy Planet view their home with the way the characters in Gwendolyn Brooks's story "Home" (page 175) view theirs. How are the creatures similar to humans?

23 **Critical Thinking and Reading** Humans are seen as the aggressors by the creatures of Energy Planet. Is space exploration a scientific pursuit of knowledge or is it aggressive intrusion into other cultures? Explain your answer.

24 **Reading Strategy** Predict how Sam will solve the problem of saving the creatures of Energy Planet.

He felt despair on the surface of his mind, keenly, but underneath it, where his own mind was, he was free of it.

Sam said, wonderingly, "It seems to me as though you're giving up. Why? Are we interfering with you?"

22 Human beings had built the Dome, cleared a large area of all planetary life and substituted their own. And once the neutron star had its power station; once floods of energy moved outward through hyperspace to power-thirsty worlds; more power stations would be built and still more. Then what would happen to *Home?* (There must be a name for the planet that the Other Sam used, but the only thought Sam found in his mind was *Home* and, underneath that, the thought *ours—ours—ours.*)

This planet was the nearest convenient base to the neutron star. It would be flooded with more and more people, more and more Domes, and their home would be destroyed.

"But you could change our minds if you had to, even if you damaged a few, couldn't you?"

23 If they tried, people would find them dangerous. People would work out what was happening. Ships would approach, and from a distance, use weapons to destroy the life on Home, and then bring in People-life instead. This could be seen in the people's minds. People had a violent history; they would stop at nothing.

"But what can I do?" Sam asked. "I'm just an apprentice. I've just been here a few days. What can I do?"

Fear. Despair.

There were no thoughts that Sam could work out, just the numbing layer of fear and despair.

He felt moved. It was such a peaceful world. They threatened nobody. They didn't even hurt minds, although they had the ability to do so.

It wasn't their fault they were near a neu-

tron star. It wasn't their fault they were in the way of expanding humanity.

He said, "Let me think."

He thought, and there was the feeling of another mind watching. Sometimes his thoughts skipped forward, and he recognized a suggestion from outside.

There came the beginning of hope, Sam felt it, but wasn't certain.

He looked at the time-strip on his wrist and jumped a little. Far more time had passed than he had realized. His three hours were nearly up. "I must go back now," he said.

He opened his lunch hamper and removed the small thermos of water, drank from it thirstily, and emptied it. He placed the empty thermos under one arm. He removed the wrapping of the sandwich and stuffed it in his pocket.

The Other Sam wavered and turned smoky. The smoke thinned, dispersed and was gone.

Sam closed the hamper, swung it over his shoulder and turned toward the Dome.

24 His heart was hammering. Would he have the courage to go through with his plan? And if he did, would it work?

When Sam entered the Dome, the Corridor-Master was waiting for him, and said, as he looked ostentatiously at his own time-strip, "You shaved it rather fine, didn't you?"

Sam's lips tightened, and he tried not to sound insolent. "I had three hours, sir."

"And you took two hours and 58 minutes."

"That's less than three hours, sir."

"Hmm," the Corridor-Master was cold and unfriendly. "Dr. Gentry would like to see you."

"Yes, sir. What for?"

"He didn't tell me. But I don't like you cutting it that fine your first time out,

Chase. And I don't like your attitude, either, and I don't like an officer of the Dome wanting to see you. I'm just going to tell you once, Chase: If you're a trouble-maker, I won't want you in this Corridor. Do you understand?"

"Yes, Sir. But what trouble have I made?"

"We'll find that out soon enough."

Sam had not seen Donald Gentry since their one and only meeting when the young apprentice had reached the Dome. Gentry still seemed good-natured and kindly, and there was nothing in his voice to indicate anything else. He sat in a chair behind his desk, and Sam stood before it, his hamper still bumping his side.

Gentry said, "How are you getting along, Sam? Having an interesting time?"

"Yes, sir," said Sam.

"Still feeling you'd rather be doing something else, working somewhere else?"

Sam said, earnestly, "No, sir. This is a good place for me."

"Because you're interested in hallucinations?"

"Yes, sir."

"You've been asking others about it, haven't you?"

"It's an interesting subject to me, sir."

"Because you want to study the human brain?"

"Any brain, sir."

"And you've been wandering about outside the Dome, haven't you?"

"I was told it was permitted, sir."

"It is. But few apprentices take advantage of that so soon. Did you see anything interesting?"

Sam hesitated, then said, "Yes, sir."

"A hallucination?"

"No, sir." He said it quite positively.

Gentry stared at him for a few moments, and there was a kind of speculative harden-ing of his eyes. "Would you care to tell me what you did see? Honestly."

Sam hesitated again. Then he said, "I saw and spoke to an inhabitant of this planet, sir."

"An intelligent inhabitant, young man?"

"Yes, sir."

Gentry said, "Sam, we had reason to wonder about you when you came. The Central Computer's report on you did not match our needs, though it was favorable in many ways, so I took the opportunity to study you that first day. We kept our collective eye on you, and when you left to wander about the planet on your own, we kept you under observation."

"Sir," said Sam, indignantly, "that violates my right of privacy."

"Yes, it does, but this is a most vital project, and we are sometimes driven to bend the rules a little. We saw you talking with considerable animation for a substantial period of time."

"I just told you I was, sir."

"Yes, but you were talking to nothing; to empty air. You were experiencing a hallucination, Sam!"

Sam was speechless. A hallucination? It couldn't be a hallucination.

Less than half an hour ago, he had been speaking to the Other Sam; had been experiencing the thoughts of the Other Sam. He knew exactly what had happened then, and he was still the same Sam Chase he had been during that conversation and before. He put his elbow over his lunch hamper as though it were a connection with the sandwiches he had been eating when the Other Sam had appeared.

He said, with what was almost a stammer. "Sir—Dr. Gentry—it wasn't a hallucination. It was real."

Gentry shook his head. "My boy, I saw you talking with animation to nothing at all. I didn't hear what you said, but you were

Hallucination 189

25 **Discussion** Why has Sam changed his mind about being on Energy Planet?

26 **Discussion** What did Gentry observe Sam doing on the planet's surface? Do you think Sam's experience could have been a hallucination after all?

25

26

27 **Critical Thinking and Reading**
Why do you think more apprentices have not reported experiences like Sam's with the inhabitants of the planet?

28 **Discussion** How does Sam know what's wrong with the Commander and how he can be cured?

talking. Nothing else was there except plants. Nor was I the only one. There were two other witnesses, and we have it all on record."

"On record?"

"On a television cassette. Why should we lie to you, young man? This has happened before. At the start, it happened rather frequently. Now it happens only very rarely. For one thing, we tell the new apprentices of the hallucinations at the start, as I told you, and they generally avoid the planet until they are more acclimated, and then it doesn't happen to them."

"You mean you scare them," blurted out Sam, "so that it's not likely to happen. And they don't tell you if it does happen—but I wasn't scared."

Gentry shook his head. "I'm sorry you weren't, if that was what it would have taken to keep you from seeing things."

"I wasn't seeing things. At least, not things that weren't there."

"How do you intend to argue with a television cassette, which will show you staring at nothing?"

"Sir, what I saw was not opaque. It was smoky, actually; foggy, if you know what I mean."

"Yes, I do. It looked as a hallucination might look, not as reality. But the television set would have seen even smoke."

"Maybe not, sir. My mind must have been focused to see it more clearly. It was probably less clear to the camera than to me."

"It focused your mind, did it?" Gentry stood up, and he sounded rather sad. "That's an admission of hallucination. I'm really sorry, Sam, because you are clearly intelligent, and the Central Computer rated you highly—but we can't use you."

"Will you be sending me home, sir?"

"Yes, but why should that matter? You didn't particularly want to come here."

"I want to stay here *now*."

"But I'm afraid you cannot."

"You can't just send me home. Don't I get a hearing?"

"You certainly can, if you insist, but in that case, the proceedings will be official and will go on your record, so that you won't get another apprenticeship anywhere. As it is, if you are sent back unofficially, as better suited to an apprenticeship in neurophysiology, you might get that, and be better off, actually, than you are now."

"I don't want that. I want a hearing—before the Commander."

"Oh, no, not the Commander. He can't be bothered with that."

"It *must* be the Commander," said Sam, with desperate force, "or this project will fail."

"Unless the Commander gives you a hearing? Why do you say that? Come, you are forcing me to think that you are unstable in ways other than those involved with hallucinations."

"Sir," the words were tumbling out of Sam's mouth now. "The Commander is ill—they know that even on Earth—and if he gets too ill to work, this project will fail. I did not see a hallucination, and the proof is that I know why he is ill and how he can be cured."

"You're not helping yourself," said Gentry.

"If you send me away, I tell you the project will fail. Can it hurt to let me see the Commander? All I ask is five minutes."

"Five minutes? What if he refuses?"

"Ask him, sir. Tell him that I say the same thing that caused his depression can remove it."

"No, I don't think I'll tell him that. But I'll ask him if he'll see you."

The Commander was a thin man, not

Grammar in Action

If you carefully listen to a casual conversation, you will notice that people's speech is often grammatically incorrect. Often, people speak in **sentence fragments.** A sentence fragment is only part of a sentence. It lacks a subject, a predicate, or both, and it does not express a complete thought. For example:

Went outside the dome.
The insects in the air.

If that was what you saw.
Spoke with a cow.

If you are not sure whether a group of words is a sentence or a fragment, try reading them aloud. Often, hearing the words will help you decide.

Good writers avoid sentence fragments in formal writing. However, writers include sentence fragments when they are writing realistic dialogue in order to reflect the way people actually speak. Notice the fragments in the following dialogue from "Hallucination":

"On record?"
"On a television cassette. Why should we lie to you, young man? This has happened before."

very tall. His eyes were a deep blue, and they looked tired.

His voice was very soft, a little low-pitched and definitely weary.

"You're the one who saw the hallucination?"

"It was not a hallucination, Commander, it was real. So was the one you saw, Commander." (If that did not get him thrown out, Sam thought, he might have a chance. He felt his elbow tightening on his hamper again. He still had it with him.)

29 The Commander seemed to wince. "The one *I* saw?"

"Yes, Commander. It said it had hurt one person. They had to try with you because you were the Commander, and they—did damage."

The Commander ignored that and said, "Did you ever have any mental problems before you came here?"

"No, Commander. You can consult my Central Computer record."

Sam thought: *He* must have had problems, but they let it go because he's a genius and they had to have him.

Then he thought: Was that my own idea? Or had it been put there?

The Commander was speaking. Sam had almost missed it. He said, "What you saw can't be real. There is no intelligent life-form on this planet."

"Yes, sir. There is."

"Oh? And no one ever discovered it till you came here and did the job?" The Commander smiled very briefly. "I'm afraid I have no choice but to . . ."

"Wait, Commander," said Sam, in a strangled voice. "We know about the intelligent life-form. It's the insects, the little flying things."

30 "You say the insects are intelligent?"

"Not an individual insect by itself, but they fit together when they want to, like little jigsaws. They can do it in any way they want.

And when they do, their nervous systems fit together too, and build up. A lot of them *together* are intelligent."

The Commander's eyebrows lifted. "That's an interesting idea, anyway. Almost crazy enough to be true. How did you come to that conclusion, young man?"

"By observation, sir. Everywhere I walked, I disturbed the insects in the grass, and they flew about in all directions. But once the cow started to form, and I walked toward it, there was nothing to see or hear. The insects were gone. They had gathered together in front of me, and they weren't in the grass anymore. That's how I knew."

"You talked with a cow?"

"It was a cow at first, because that's what I thought of. But they had it wrong, so they switched and came together to form a human being—*me*."

"You?" And then, in a lower voice, "Well, that fits anyway."

"Did you see it that same way too, Commander?"

The Commander ignored that. "And when it shaped itself like you, it could talk as you did? Is that what you're telling me?"

"No, Commander. The talking was in my mind."

"Telepathy?"

"Sort of."

"And what did it say to you—or think to you?"

31 "It wanted us to refrain from disturbing this planet. It wanted us not to take it over." Sam was all but holding his breath. The interview had lasted more than five minutes already, and the Commander was making no move to put an end to it, to send him home.

"Quite impossible."

"Why, Commander?"

"Any other base will double and triple the expense. We're having enough trouble getting grants as it is. Fortunately, it is all a hallucination, young man, and the problem

Hallucination 191

---

29 Discussion What hint do you get here that what Sam is saying might be accurate?

30 Literary Focus Note how Asimov cleverly explains how the insects form intelligent life forms. The writers of science fiction must often create extraordinary yet believable new forms of life.

31 Literary Focus How do the wishes of the inhabitants of Energy Planet fit in with the story's theme?

When we speak to each other, we often use fragments to ask or to answer questions. The meaning is made clear by the context of the conversation, by the tone of voice, and by body language.

Student Activity 1. Find five other examples of sentence fragments in the dialogue of "Hallucination." Rewrite each example as a complete sentence.

Student Activity 2. Write a conversation between Sam and his roommate, Robert, in which Sam relates his experiences with the insects and the Commander. Use sentence fragments where appropriate to reflect the natural rhythm of conversation.

does not arise." He closed his eyes, then opened them and looked at Sam without really focusing on him. "I'm sorry, young man. You will be sent back—officially."

Sam gambled again. "We can't afford to ignore the insects, Commander. They have a lot to give us."

The Commander had raised his hand partway, as though about to give a signal. He paused long enough to say, "Really? What do they have that they can give us?"

"The one thing more important than energy, Commander. An understanding of the brain."

"How do you know that?"

"I can demonstrate it. I have them here." Sam seized his hamper and swung it forward onto the desk.

"What's that?"

32

Sam did not answer in words. He opened the hamper, and a softly whirring, smoky cloud appeared.

The Commander rose suddenly and cried out. He lifted his hand high, and an alarm bell sounded.

Through the door came Gentry, others behind him. Sam felt himself seized by the arms, and then a kind of stunned and motionless silence prevailed in the room.

The smoke was condensing, wavering, taking on the shape of a head; a thin head, with high cheekbones, a smooth forehead and receding hairline. It had the appearance of the Commander.

"I'm seeing things," croaked the Commander.

Sam said, "We're all seeing the same thing, aren't we?" He wriggled and was released.

Gentry said in a low voice, "Mass hysteria."[9]

---

9. mass hysteria (his ter' ē ə): An outbreak of excited feeling in a group of people, sometimes causing them to see things that are not there.

"No," said Sam, "it's real." He reached toward the Head in midair and brought back his finger with a tiny insect on it. He flicked it, and it could just barely be seen making its way back to its companions.

No one moved.

Sam said, "Head, do you see the problem with the Commander's mind?"

Sam had the brief vision of a snarl in an otherwise smooth curve, but it vanished and left nothing behind. It was not something that could be easily put into human thought. He hoped the others experienced that quick snarl. Yes, they had. He knew it.

The Commander said, "There is no problem . . ." and stopped.

Sam said, "Can you adjust it, Head?"

Of course, they could not. It was not right to invade a mind.

Sam said, "Commander, give permission."

The Commander put his hands to his eyes and muttered something Sam did not make out. Then he said, clearly, "It's a nightmare, but I've been in one since . . . Whatever must be done, I give permission."

33

Nothing happened.

Or nothing seemed to happen.

And then slowly, little by little, the Commander's face lit in a smile.

He said, just above a whisper. "Astonishing. I'm watching a sun rise. It's been cold night for so long, and now I feel the warmth again." His voice rose high. "I feel wonderful."

34

The Head deformed at that point, turned into a vague, pulsing fog, then formed a curving, narrowing arrow that sped into the hamper. Sam snapped it shut.

He asked, "Commander, have I your permission to restore these little insect-things to their own world?"

"Yes, yes," said the Commander, dismissing that with a wave of his hand. "Gentry, call a meeting. We've got to change all our plans."

35

---

32 Discussion How does Sam intend both to convince and to help the Commander? Why does he release the insects?

33 Discussion Why does the Commander give the insects permission to communicate with his mind?

34 Discussion How is the Commander cured?

35 Discussion Why is the Commander going to change all his plans? What influenced him to make that decision?

36 **Critical Thinking and Reading** Why is the study of the brain as important as the study of energy?

37 **Master Teacher Note** Students may be interested to know that a neutron star, the basic premise of the scientific aspect of the story, is the last stage in the life cycle of certain types of stars. You might want to bring in a science text and provide students with some interesting background information on the life cycles of stars. For example, a chunk of matter the size of a sugar cube from a neutron star would have a mass of about 100 million tons.

38 **Discussion** How did Sam conclude that he was sent to Energy Planet to study the so-called hallucinations?

39 **Discussion** How was Sam's faith in the Central Computer justified?

40 **Critical Thinking and Reading** This was not a case of faith in the usual sense but in a futuristic sense. How was Sam's faith different from what you usually think of as faith? What is Asimov's implied vision of the future?

Reader's Response How would you have felt if you were Sam and you saw the "cow" forming before your eyes? What would you have done?

Sam had been escorted outside the Dome by a solid guard and had then been confined to his quarters in the Corridor for the rest of the day.

It was late when Gentry entered, stared at him thoughtfully, and said, "That was an amazing demonstration of yours. The entire incident has been fed into the Central Computer, and we now have a double project, neutron star energy and neurophysiology. I doubt that there will be any question about pouring money into this project now. And we'll have a group of neurophysiologists arriving eventually. Until then you're going to be working with those little things, those insects, and you'll probably end up the most important person here."

Sam said, "But will we leave their world to them?"

Gentry said, "We'll have to if we expect to get anything out of them, won't we? The Commander thinks we're going to build elaborate settlements in orbit about this world and shift all operations to them except for a skeleton crew in this Dome to maintain direct contact with the insects—or whatever we'll decide to call them. It will cost a great deal of money, and take time and labor, but it's going to be worth it. No one will question that."

Sam said, "Good!"

Gentry stared at him again, longer and more thoughtfully than before.

"My boy," he said, "it seems that what happened came about because you did not fear the supposed hallucination. Your mind remained open, and that was the whole difference. Why was that? Why weren't you afraid?"

Sam flushed. "I'm not sure, sir. As I look back on it, though, it seemed to me I was puzzled as to why I was sent here. I had been doing my best to study neurophysiology through my computerized courses and I knew very little about astrophysics.[10] The Central Computer had my record, all of it, the full details of everything I had ever studied, and I couldn't imagine why I had been sent here.

"Then, when you first mentioned the hallucinations, I thought, 'That must be it. I was sent here to look into it.' I just made up my mind that was the thing I had to do. I had no *time* to be afraid, Dr. Gentry. I had a problem to solve, and I—I had faith in the Central Computer. It wouldn't have sent me here, if I weren't up to it."

Gentry shook his head. "I'm afraid I wouldn't have had that much faith in that machine. But they say faith can move mountains, and I guess it certainly did in this case."

---

10. astrophysics (as' trō fiz' iks) *n.*: The science of the physical properties of the stars, planets, and other heavenly bodies.

Closure and Extension

ANSWERS TO THINKING ABOUT THE SELECTION
Recalling

1. They're on Energy Planet to try to harness the energy of the neutron star.
2. Sam thinks of a cow and sees the shadowy image of a cow. He tells the image that it's not working and the smokelike substance forms a duplicate, but transparent, image of Sam. Sam then communicates mentally with his image and finds that the inhabitants of Energy Planet feel that the Earth people are ruining their planet.
3. The Other Sam communicates to Sam that it feels despair because it wants to be left alone.
4. Sam succeeds because he is not afraid.
5. Sam convinces the Commander by releasing the insectlike creatures of the planet, who cure the Commander of his depression.

THINKING ABOUT THE SELECTION
Recalling

1. Why are Sam, Dr. Gentry, and the Commander on Energy Planet?
2. Describe the strange encounter Sam has when he leaves the Dome.
3. What message does the "Other Sam" communicate to Sam?
4. Why does Sam succeed in communicating with the life form when others could not?
5. How does Sam convince the Commander not to send him back to Earth?
6. What changes will be made in the project as a result of all that Sam has done?

Interpreting

7. How is the intelligence of the life form different from human intelligence?
8. What conclusions does Sam come to about how the alien life form is communicating with him?

Applying

9. Gentry says to Sam, "My boy, it seems that what happened came about because you did not fear the supposed hallucination. Your mind remained open, and that was the whole difference." What real-life examples of openmindedness and courage can you think of that have allowed people to gain knowledge that they otherwise could not have gained?

ANALYZING LITERATURE
Recognizing Theme in Science Fiction

The **theme** of a story is its central idea. In "Hallucination" the theme is revealed through what the main characters come to understand about the strange events taking place on an alien planet. The strangeness of the plot, of the aliens, and of the setting is what makes the theme stand out sharply.

1. Compare and contrast Sam's reaction to the alien life form he encounters with that of the Commander.
2. What does the story suggest about dealing with strange and unusual events?
3. What do you think is the theme of "Hallucination"?

CRITICAL THINKING AND READING
Looking at Reasoning

Reasoning is thinking logically. The part of the story in which Sam meets the alien life form reveals sound reasoning at work. Because of the way Sam reasons, events ultimately turn out favorably for him and the others assigned to Energy Planet.

1. Why does Sam reason that the reported hallucinations are highly unlikely?
2. When the cow appears before Sam, why does he reason that it is not a hallucination?
3. How does Sam figure out the way that the life form communicates?

THINKING AND WRITING
Writing Science Fiction

Imagine that you have been sent to Energy Planet shortly after the events presented in "Hallucination." Your duty is to send back to Earth reports on any strange or dangerous beings you meet outside the Dome. In your explorations you encounter one such being, and now you are writing a report about your adventure for an Information Committee on Earth made up of your classmates. Before you write the report, be sure you have assembled enough details to convey a full and clear picture of your experience. When you revise your work, keep in mind the question "Based on the information in my report, will people on Earth be able to visualize, or see, what I have seen?"

(Answers begin on p. 194)

temporarily damaged by the aliens.
2. The story suggests that people need to be unafraid, courageous, and open-minded in dealing with strange and unusual events.
3. Answers will differ. Suggested Response: Being open-minded and unafraid allows people to learn and accomplish things that they otherwise could not.

ANSWERS TO CRITICAL THINKING AND READING

1. Sam reasons this way because he knows that the people chosen for this mission would have to be mentally stable and unlikely to have hallucinations. Therefore, he thought that the hallucinations were, in fact, another phenomenon that people did not understand.
2. He reasons that it is not a hallucination because it is more like the caricature of a cow than a real cow and because the insects have stopped flying out of the grass since the image began to form.
3. He figures out that the life form did not form a cow until he had thought of a cow and, thus, the life form must be able to read his mind. When the Other Sam appears, Sam realizes that the questions he is asking are being answered in his mind since there is no other way he could know the answers.

Challenge Have students describe what they would include in an Earth dome on a strange planet. Have them give reasons for their choices.

THINKING AND WRITING
Writing Across the Curriculum

You might want to have students research and report on space exploration and the possibility of life on other planets. If you do, perhaps inform the science department of this assignment. Science teachers might provide guidance for students in conducting their research.

---

6. A minimal staff will be kept on Energy Planet and elaborate settlements will be built only to orbit the planet.

Interpreting

7. The intelligence of the creatures is different from human intelligence in that the creatures communicate directly with their minds. Also, the creatures individually are not intelligent. They must fit together into large groups and combine their systems for intelligence.

8. Sam concludes that the alien life form is communicating with him through telepathy. The creatures adjust electric currents in his brain so that the desired thoughts will arise as long as the mind is receptive and unafraid.

Applying

9. Answers will differ. Suggested responses should include such people as Columbus, the Wright brothers, Marie Curie, Martin Luther King, and the astronauts.

Most students should see that any discovery in any field, from science to human relations, is made because of someone's courage and open-mindedness.

ANSWERS TO ANALYZING LITERATURE

1. Sam is excited by and curious about the alien life forms and, therefore, is receptive to their telepathic mode of communication. The Commander is afraid and resists and, therefore, his mind is

Focus

More About the Author Growing up in an immigrant family, William Saroyan knew poverty and prejudice as a young boy. However, his writing celebrates the capacity of the human spirit to find joy and beauty in life. What does this indicate about the author?

Literary Focus Point out that symbols can stand for more than one thing. Also, they are common in everyday life. For example, the lion is recognized as a symbol of courage and as a symbol of power. Tell students that they are going to read a story in which a bird is an important symbol.

Look For The title of a short story is often a clue to its meaning. As they read, you might have students think about the title and consider how it might relate to a theme.

Writing/Prior Knowledge For less advanced students, list words on the board that could have symbolic meanings. You might use flower, teddy bear, ring. Ask students what these objects might symbolize. Suggest they use this list to help get writing ideas.

Vocabulary You might have less advanced students work with more advanced students to create original sentences using the vocabulary words.

Spelling Tip Students might find it easier to remember how to spell *transformation* if they break it down into two parts: *trans* and *formation*.

196

The Hummingbird That Lived Through Winter

William Saroyan (1908–1981) was born in Fresno, California, and raised in the San Joaquin Valley. During his lifetime, Saroyan published short stories, plays, and novels. Among his better known works are *My Name is Aram, The Human Comedy,* and his Pulitzer-prize winning play, *The Time of Your Life.* Saroyan often wrote about his own childhood growing up among Armenian immigrants in Fresno. The following story is about an old Armenian immigrant and a hummingbird whose beauty the old man loves and cherishes.

Symbol

A **symbol** is anything that stands for or represents something beyond itself. An object that serves as a symbol has its own meaning, but it also represents an idea, a belief, a value, or a group of feelings. For example, a dove, perhaps because of its calm and unaggressive behavior, has become a symbol of peace. Because it is used as a weapon, a sword can be a symbol of war. Symbols can make ideas or feelings come alive in a vivid and concrete way.

Look For

The hummingbird that is rescued by the old man in "The Hummingbird That Lived Through Winter" is both a real animal and a symbol. Pay careful attention to what is said about it. Then form your own opinion about what it represents.

Writing

Symbols such as the American flag have public, widely recognized meanings. But symbols may also have private and personal meanings. For example, a seashell kept for years may serve as a symbol of a happy family vacation at the shore. List three or four objects that have special meanings for you. Alongside each, write down the meaning—the memories—it holds for you.

Vocabulary

Knowing the following words will help you as you read "The Hummingbird That Lived Through Winter."

pathetic (pə thet′ ik) *adj.*: Arousing pity, sorrow, and sympathy (p. 198)

transformation (trans′ fər mā′ shən) *n.*: A change in condition and outward appearance (p. 198)

196   Short Stories

Objectives

1 To understand symbols in literature
2 To recognize symbols in everyday life
3 To write a paragraph describing and explaining a symbol

Support Material

Teaching Portfolio
Teacher Backup, p. 287
Usage and Mechanics Worksheet, p. 291
Vocabulary Check, p. 292
Analyzing Literature Worksheet, *Understanding Symbols in Literature,* p. 293
Language Worksheet, *Antonyms,* p. 294
Selection Test, p. 295

The Hummingbird That Lived Through Winter

William Saroyan

There was a hummingbird once which in the wintertime did not leave our neighborhood in Fresno, California.

I'll tell you about it.

1 Across the street lived old Dikran, who was almost blind. He was past eighty and his wife was only a few years younger. They had a little house that was as neat inside as it was ordinary outside—except for old Dikran's garden, which was the best thing of its 2 kind in the world. Plants, bushes, trees—all strong, in sweet black moist earth whose guardian was old Dikran. All things from the sky loved this spot in our poor neighborhood, and old Dikran loved *them*.

3 One freezing Sunday, in the dead of winter, as I came home from Sunday School I saw old Dikran standing in the middle of the street trying to distinguish what was in his hand. Instead of going into our house to the fire, as I had wanted to do, I stood on the steps of the front porch and watched the old man. He would turn around and look upward at his trees and then back to the palm of his hand. He stood in the street at least two minutes and then at last he came to me. He held his hand out, and in Armenian[1] he said, "What is this in my hand?"

I looked.

"It is a hummingbird," I said half in English and half in Armenian. Hummingbird I said in English because I didn't know its name in Armenian.

"What is that?" old Dikran asked.

"The little bird," I said. "You know. The one that comes in the summer and stands in the air and then shoots away. The one with

---

1. Armenian (är mē′ nē ən) *adj.*: The language spoken in Armenia and by Armenian immigrants in other countries. Armenia is a region of southwestern Asia, now part of Turkey, Iran, and the Soviet Union.

The Hummingbird That Lived Through Winter 197

Presentation

Motivation/Prior Knowledge Have students imagine that they helped to revive an animal who seemed near death. How would they feel after they had succeeded? What thoughts and feelings would they associate with such animals in the future? Tell students that they are about to read about a young boy who helped save a hummingbird's life.

Purpose-Setting Question At the end of the story, what does the boy learn from the old man?

Master Teacher Note Students might more readily appreciate the story if they know some facts about hummingbirds before they begin. Explain that hummingbirds are the smallest birds known to man, about two inches in length. They have brightly colored plumage and live on the nectar of flowers. They move with extreme quickness, darting up and down, forward and backward, even hovering in midair with wings beating so quickly they make a humming sound that gives the bird its name. Indeed, hummingbirds are beautiful, delicate, and unique creatures. In the story, how might the hummingbird's unique qualities add to the narrator's feelings toward the frozen hummingbird?

1 **Clarification** Dikran is pronounced Dē′krän.

2 **Discussion** What does this description of Dikran's garden indicate about Dikran?

3 **Discussion** Notice that the setting is a "freezing Sunday," in the "dead of winter." What thoughts and associations does this description bring to mind? What mood does it evoke?

Thematic Idea In the short story, "The Trout," (page 113), a fish has symbolic significance similar to that of the hummingbird in this story. You may want to pair the two selections. You may also wish to pair this story with "The Legend of the Hummingbird," (page 589), a legend from Puerto Rico that explains the existence of hummingbirds.

Primary Source

The first description of the hummingbird as the boy saw it in Old Dikran's hand is an example of Saroyan's skillful use of vivid language to paint a picture for the reader. In his memoir, *Chance Meetings*, Saroyan writes, "I was especially concerned about noticing carefully people who did things like draw or paint, for it seemed to me that they were using a language which I was not sure wasn't better than the language of words." You might ask students to find examples of how Saroyan "paints" pictures with words. Point out in these descriptions the use of sensory words—words that appeal to the five senses.

198

---

4 the wings that beat so fast you can't see them. It's in your hand. It's dying."

"Come with me," the old man said. "I can't see, and the old lady's at church. I can feel its heart beating. Is it in a bad way? Look again, once."

5 I looked again. It was a sad thing to behold. This wonderful little creature of summertime in the big rough hand of the old peasant. Here it was in the cold of winter, absolutely helpless and pathetic, not suspended in a shaft of summer light, not the most alive thing in the the world, but the most helpless and heartbreaking.

"It's dying," I said.

The old man lifted his hand to his mouth and blew warm breath on the little thing in **6** his hand which he could not even see. "Stay now," he said in Armenian. "It is not long till summer. Stay, swift and lovely."

We went into the kitchen of his little house, and while he blew warm breath on the bird he told me what to do.

"Put a tablespoonful of honey over the gas fire and pour it into my hand, but be sure it is not too hot."

This was done.

After a moment the hummingbird began **7** to show signs of fresh life. The warmth of the room, the vapor of the warm honey—and, well, the will and love of the old man. Soon the old man could feel the change in his hand, and after a moment or two the hummingbird began to take little dabs of the honey.

8 "It will live," the old man announced. "Stay and watch."

The transformation was incredible. The old man kept his hand generously open, and I expected the helpless bird to shoot upward out of his hand, suspend itself in space, and scare the life out of me—which is exactly what happened. The new life of the little bird was magnificent. It spun about in the little

kitchen, going to the window, coming back to the heat, suspending, circling as if it were summertime and it had never felt better in its whole life.

The old man sat on the plain chair, blind but attentive. He listened carefully and tried to see, but of course he couldn't. He kept asking about the bird, how it seemed to be, whether it showed signs of weakening again, what its spirit was, and whether or not it appeared to be restless; and I kept describing **9** the bird to him.

When the bird was restless and wanted to go, the old man said, "Open the window and let it go."

"Will it live?" I asked.

"It is alive now and wants to go," he said. **10** "Open the window."

I opened the window, the hummingbird stirred about here and there, feeling the cold from the outside, suspended itself in the area of the open window, stirring this way and that, and then it was gone.

"Close the window," the old man said.

We talked a minute or two and then I went home.

The old man claimed the hummingbird lived through that winter, but I never knew for sure. I saw hummingbirds again when summer came, but I couldn't tell one from the other.

One day in the summer I asked the old man.

"Did it live?"

"The little bird?" he said.

"Yes," I said. "That we gave the honey to. You remember. The little bird that was dying in the winter. Did it live?"

"Look about you," the old man said. "Do **11** you see the bird?"

"I see humming*birds*," I said.

"Each of them is our bird," the old man said. "Each of them, each of them," he said swiftly and gently.

198   *Short Stories*

THINKING ABOUT THE SELECTION

Recalling

1. Describe "old Dikran." Tell both how he looks and what he is like.
2. What do the narrator and Dikran do to help the hummingbird? How does the hummingbird respond?
3. How does Dikran respond to the narrator's question about whether or not the hummingbird lived?

Interpreting

4. Old Dikran is described as the guardian of his garden. How is Dikran's garden different from the rest of the neighborhood?
5. What does Dikran mean by his final statement?

Applying

6. Sometimes we describe people as being really alive or full of life. Isn't every living person full of life? What do we mean by this expression? What people do you know who fit this description especially well?

ANALYZING LITERATURE

Understanding Symbols in Literature

An author may use a **symbol** to suggest the theme of a story. Usually, recognizing what the symbol is and what it represents helps you to understand the theme. In this story, the hummingbird is both an important part of the story and a symbol of something else.

1. Does Dikran believe that the hummingbird lived? Explain.
2. How does Dikran feel about nature and living creatures?
3. What does Dikran mean when he says, "Each of them is our bird"?
4. What does the hummingbird symbolize?
5. How does this symbol relate to the theme?

CRITICAL THINKING AND READING

Recognizing Symbols in Everyday Life

In everyday life we use symbols as a type of shorthand. They allow us to express meaning quickly without saying a word. For example, a red light is a kind of symbol meaning "Stop." We see it and we know what to do.

However, the meaning of a symbol can also be more complex and can have different meanings for different people. For example, the Statue of Liberty may mean political freedom to some, religious freedom to others, and economic opportunity to yet others. Moreover, it will arouse different feelings in different people.

1. Briefly explain what the following symbols generally represent.
   a. A flashing red light on a police car
   b. The Olympic Torch
   c. A raised hand with two fingers forming a V
   d. The Liberty Bell in Philadelphia
2. Choose another symbol and tell what feelings and ideas it suggests to you. Then choose a partner. Compare your responses with your partner's.

THINKING AND WRITING

Creating a Symbol

Imagine that you and a group of friends and acquaintances were stranded on a pleasant but uncharted island. Since you all expect to be there for a long time, the group has decided to draw up rules and laws for a society. You have been asked to create a symbol—a visual one—that will suggest what your society stands for, its goals, values, or ideals. First, think of the various things, living or nonliving, that might be appropriate symbols. Choose the best one. Write a paragraph that describes it, that explains its meaning, and that tells why it is a good symbol for the island society. Revise your paper to make sure your reasoning is clear.

The Hummingbird That Lived Through Winter 199

---

the human spirit can triumph. The hummingbird, like the human spirit, is beautiful and delicate but strong. It responds to love and caring and needs freedom.

The return of the hummingbirds after the winter symbolizes the triumph of the human spirit over the difficulties it encounters in life.

ANSWERS TO CRITICAL THINKING AND READING

1. Answers may differ. Suggested answers:
   a. an emergency
   b. sportsmanship
   c. peace, victory
   d. democracy, freedom
2. Students might suggest widely recognized symbols such as the Vietnam War Memorial in Washington, D.C., or the American flag. Alternatively, they might suggest personal symbols such as an article of clothing, a piece of furniture, or some other personal possession.

THINKING AND WRITING

For help with this assignment, students can refer to Lesson 11, "Writing About Theme," on page 803 of the Handbook of Writing About Literature.

Writing Across the Curriculum
A nation's flag is often symbolic of values or principles. For example, on the flag of the United States, the thirteen stars represent the thirteen original colonies, and the fifty stars represent the fifty states. Our flag represents our fight for freedom and democracy and the union of the separate states. You might work with a social studies teacher to research the symbolic meanings behind the designs and colors of the flags of other nations.

Applying

6. Answers may differ. Suggested Response: When we say a person is "really alive" or "full of life," we mean that the person appreciates the beauty and joy in life, and takes advantage of all that life has to offer.

ANSWERS TO ANALYZING LITERATURE

1. Answers may differ. Suggested Response: Dikran must have known that the hummingbird could not live. He has a wonderful garden visited by many birds, he knows how to save the hummingbird, and he knows the bird will need to be released. However, he probably believes that what the bird symbolizes does live.

2. Dikran loves things of nature and living creatures, he has a marvelous garden, and he loves "all things from the sky."
3. Dikran means that each time we see a hummingbird we are reminded that what the bird symbolized is still alive.
4. Answers may differ. Suggested Response: The hummingbird symbolizes the human spirit.
5. Answers may differ. Suggested Response: The theme of the story is that even in difficult times

199

More About The Author Kenyatta felt strongly about the injustice of the colonial system. The best lands were taken by Europeans, while Africans could barely survive on the poor lands left over. How might this attitude affect the ideas Kenyatta presents in his writing?

Literary Focus You might point out that this story is similar to a fable. A fable is a story that teaches a lesson or moral. Its characters and plot situations are symbols for other people and situations. Ask students to retell the fables they know, or read one, such as "The Fox and the Crow" on page 547, aloud to the class.

Look For You might have students pay particular attention to how the man's attitude toward the animals changes from the beginning of the story to the end.

Writing/Prior Knowledge To help students get started, ask them to recall expressions that compare a person with an animal —"He's a sly fox," or "She's a busy bee." Discuss how the behavior of an animal can be compared to the behavior of people.

Spelling Tip Knowing that *impartiality* means "not taking any side or *part*" will help students remember how to spell the word.

GUIDE FOR READING

Characters and Situations as Symbols

Look For

Writing

Vocabulary

The Gentlemen of the Jungle

Jomo Kenyatta (1891–1978) was the first president of Kenya, a country in east Africa, after it was granted independence. When Kenya was a colony of Great Britain, Kenyatta was a leader in the struggle for self-rule for his people. "Gentlemen of the Jungle" was included in his book, *Facing Mount Kenya* (1938), which is a study of his native people, the Gikuyu. According to Kenyatta, the story illation between the Gikuyu and the Europeans" during the time that Europe had colonized much of Africa.

A **symbol** is something that stands for or represents something beyond itself. Sometimes an entire story can have a symbolic meaning. In such a story, all of the characters and situations may stand for real people and real situations. In this way, the writer may use a seemingly simple story to present a real problem or to teach a lesson.

This story was written to illustrate the relationship between the native peoples of Africa and the Europeans who occupied African lands. Pay careful attention to the actions and statements of the man and the animals. Then form your own opinion about the ideas and feelings that the author is expressing through the story.

Think about other stories in which animals may have represented qualities or characteristics of humans. What animals represent what human characteristics? Brainstorm to develop a list of animals and the traits or characteristics they might represent. For example, you might choose an elephant to symbolize a long memory or a shark to represent meanness. Write down your list.

Knowing the following words will help you as you read "The Gentlemen of the Jungle."

turmoil (tur′ moil′) *n.*: Uproar; confusion (p. 201)
intricacy (in′ tri kə sē) *n.*: The quality of being hard to follow or understand (p. 202)
impartiality (im pär′ shē al′ i tē) *n.*: Fairness; not taking sides (p. 202)
endowed (en dou′d′) *v.*: Pro-

vided with some talent or quality (p. 202)
relevant (rel′ ə vənt) *adj.*: Relating to the matter at hand; to the point (p. 202)
unbiased (un′ bī′ əst) *adj.*: Without prejudice; fair (p. 202)
verdict (vur′ dikt) *n.*: A decision or judgment (p. 202)

Objectives

1 To interpret symbols in a short story
2 To recognize bias

Support Material

Teaching Portfolio
Teacher Backup, p. 297
Usage and Mechanics Worksheet, p. 301
Vocabulary Check, p. 302
Critical Thinking and Reading Worksheet, *Recognizing Bias*, p. 303
Language Worksheet, *Understanding Connotations*, p. 304
Selection Test, p. 305

The Gentlemen of the Jungle

Jomo Kenyatta

Once upon a time an elephant made a friendship with a man. One day a heavy thunderstorm broke out, the elephant went to his friend, who had a little hut at the edge of the forest, and said to him: "My dear good man, will you please let me put my trunk inside your hut to keep it out of this torrential rain?" The man, seeing what situation his friend was in, replied: "My dear good elephant, my hut is very small, but there is room for your trunk and myself. Please put your trunk in gently." The elephant thanked his friend, saying: "You have done me a good deed and one day I shall return your kindness." But what followed? As soon as the elephant put his trunk inside the hut, slowly he pushed his head inside, and finally flung the man out in the rain, and then lay down comfortably inside his friend's hut, saying: "My dear good friend, your skin is harder than mine, and as there is not enough room for both of us, you can afford to remain in the rain while I am protecting my delicate skin from the hailstorm."

The man, seeing what his friend had done to him, started to grumble; the animals in the nearby forest heard the noise and came to see what was the matter. All stood around listening to the heated argument between the man and his friend the elephant. In this turmoil the lion came along roaring, and said in a loud voice: "Don't you all know that I am the King of the Jungle! How dare anyone disturb the peace of my kingdom?" On hearing this the elephant, who was one of the high ministers in the jungle kingdom, replied in a soothing voice, and said: "My lord, there is no disturbance of the peace in your kingdom. I have only been having a little discussion with my friend here as to the possession of this hut which your lordship sees me occupying." The lion, who wanted to have "peace and tranquillity" in his kingdom, replied in a noble voice, saying: "I command my ministers to appoint a Commission of Enquiry to go thoroughly into this matter and report accordingly." He then turned to the man and said: "You have done well by establishing friendship with my people, especially with the elephant, who is one of my honorable ministers of state. Do not grumble anymore, your hut is not lost to you. Wait until the sitting of my Imperial Commission, and there you will be given plenty of opportunity to state your case. I am sure that you will be pleased with the findings of the Commission." The man was very pleased by these sweet words from the King of the Jungle, and innocently waited for his opportunity, in the belief that naturally the hut would be returned to him.

The elephant, obeying the command of his master, got busy with other ministers to appoint the Commission of Enquiry. The following elders of the jungle were appointed to sit in the Commission: (1) Mr. Rhinoceros; (2) Mr. Buffalo; (3) Mr. Alligator; (4) The Rt. Hon.[1] Mr. Fox to act as chairman; and (5) Mr. Leopard to act as Secretary to the Commission. On seeing the personnel, the man

---

1. Rt. Hon. Abbreviation for "Right Honorable." Used as a courtesy title or an official title for high governmental officials.

The Gentlemen of the Jungle   201

Master Teacher Note Discuss with the class the methods of Mohandas Gandhi who led the struggle for reforms and for the eventual independence for India from British rule. His methods were rooted in a commitment to nonviolence and included peaceful civil disobedience, labor strikes, and hunger strikes.

After they have finished reading the story, students might consider how a leader like Gandhi might have written the story differently.

Thematic Idea Because of its similarity to fables, you may wish to have students read this story in conjunction with the fables by Aesop and Thurber, (pages 545–553).

ESL Teaching Strategy Students might not be familiar with some of the names of animals in the story. You might want to make sure they know the meaning of the following words: *elephant, lion, rhinoceros, buffalo, alligator, fox, leopard, hyena.*

Presentation

Motivation/Prior Knowledge Ask students if they have ever read a book or seen a movie in which someone is being unfairly treated by another person or group. What were students feelings about this situation? How did the character try to correct the unfair treatment? Did the character succeed? Tell students that this story is about a person who is unfairly treated over and over again.

Purpose-Setting Question What group of people does the man in the story represent? What group of people do the animals represent?

1 Clarification This story has animal characters who have human character traits and can speak. What is an advantage in having an animal character portray human characteristics instead of using a human character?

2 Discussion What does the man's reply to the elephant indicate about the man?

3 Discussion Is a man's skin really harder than an elephant's? What does this statement indicate about the elephant?

4 Critical Thinking and Reading The elephant is one of the lion's ministers. How might this prove to be a disadvantage to the man? Who might the lion be inclined to favor in this dispute?

5 Discussion The lion's principal concern is that "peace and tranquillity" be maintained. What should be a more important concern for the King of the Jungle?

6 Reading Strategy What does this statement indicate about the lion's attitude toward the man? Ask students to predict what kind of treatment the man might receive from the Commission.

202

7 Literary Focus Based on the author's background and what they have read so far, have students discuss what groups of people the man and the animals might represent. What does this passage indicate about the people the animals represent?

8 Discussion The elephant is twisting the facts. What does this indicate about the elephant? How would you feel if you were the man?

9 Literary Focus Why was the space in the man's hut "unoccupied"? What might the "undeveloped" space symbolize?

10 Clarification Explain that the use of "conclusive" to describe the evidence is meant to contrast humorously with what the author really thinks.

11 Critical Thinking and Reading How might the composition of the Commission contribute to their not giving the man a fair hearing? What does their treatment of the man indicate about the attitude of the Commission toward him?

12 Clarification Explain to students that phrases such as "backwardness of your ideas," "sacred duty of protecting your interests," and "for your good" were typically used by people to justify the domination of others.

13 Discussion Do you agree that the man had "no alternative?" If not, what alternative did he have?

14 Reading Strategy The man decides he needs to "adopt an effective method of protection." What might this be?

protested and asked if it was not necessary to include in this Commission a member from his side. But he was told that it was impossible, since no one from his side was well enough educated to understand the intricacy of jungle law. Further, that there was nothing to fear, for the members of the Commission were all men of repute for their impartiality in justice, and as they were gentlemen chosen by God to look after the interests of races less adequately endowed with teeth and claws, he might rest assured that they would investigate the matter with the greatest care and report impartially.

The Commission sat to take the evidence. The Rt. Hon. Mr. Elephant was first called. He came along with a superior air, brushing his tusks with a sapling which Mrs. Elephant had provided, and in an authoritative voice said: "Gentlemen of the Jungle, there is no need for me to waste your valuable time in relating a story which I am sure you all know. I have always regarded it as my duty to protect the interests of my friends, and this appears to have caused the misunderstanding between myself and my friend here. He invited me to save his hut from being blown away by a hurricane. As the hurricane had gained access owing to the unoccupied space in the hut, I considered it necessary, in my friend's own interests, to turn the undeveloped space to a more economic use by sitting in it myself; a duty which any of you would undoubtedly have performed with equal readiness in similar circumstances."

After hearing the Rt. Hon. Mr. Elephant's conclusive evidence, the Commission called Mr. Hyena and other elders of the jungle, who all supported what Mr. Elephant had said. They then called the man, who began to give his own account of the dispute. But the Commission cut him short, saying: "My good man, please confine yourself to relevant issues. We have already heard the circumstances from various unbiased sources; all we wish you to tell us is whether the undeveloped space in your hut was occupied by anyone else before Mr. Elephant assumed his position?" The man began to say: "No, but—" But at this point the Commission declared that they had heard sufficient evidence from both sides and retired to consider their decision. After enjoying a delicious meal at the expense of the Rt. Hon. Mr. Elephant, they reached their verdict, called the man, and declared as follows: "In our opinion this dispute has arisen through a regrettable misunderstanding due to the backwardness of your ideas. We consider that Mr. Elephant has fulfilled his sacred duty of protecting your interests. As it is clearly for your good that the space should be put to its most economic use, and as you yourself have not reached the stage of expansion which would enable you to fill it, we consider it necessary to arrange a compromise to suit both parties. Mr. Elephant shall continue his occupation of your hut, but we give you permission to look for a site where you can build another hut more suited to your needs, and we will see that you are well protected."

The man, having no alternative, and fearing that his refusal might expose him to the teeth and claws of members of the Commission, did as they suggested. But no sooner had he built another hut than Mr. Rhinoceros charged in with his horn lowered and ordered the man to quit. A Royal Commission was again appointed to look into the matter, and the same finding was given. This procedure was repeated until Mr. Buffalo, Mr. Leopard, Mr. Hyena and the rest were all accommodated with new huts. Then the man decided that he must adopt an effective method of protection, since Commissions of Enquiry did not seem to be of any use to him. He sat down and said, *"Ng' enda thi ndagaga motegi,"* which literally means

202 Short Stories

Commentary

Kenya is an independent republic in East Africa. (You may want to locate Kenya on a map.) More than ninety percent of Kenya's population is African, yet from 1895 until 1963, it was ruled by Great Britain. Africans had little voice in the government. Most of the large plantations were owned by the British, and Africans worked as laborers on these farms. Only after many years of struggle, including violence and bloodshed, did Kenya become an independent nation in 1963. In what ways are the historical events in Kenya similar to the events in the story?

Closure and Extension

ANSWERS TO THINKING ABOUT THE SELECTION
Recalling

1. The elephant goes into the hut and throws the man out.
2. The Commission's explanation is that the elephant is acting in the man's interest by putting his hut

"there is nothing that treads on the earth that cannot be trapped," or in other words, you can fool people for a time, but not forever.

Early one morning, when the huts already occupied by the jungle lords were all beginning to decay and fall to pieces, he went out and built a bigger and better hut a little distance away. No sooner had Mr. Rhinoceros seen it than he came rushing in, only to find that Mr. Elephant was already inside, sound asleep. Mr. Leopard next came to the window, Mr. Lion, Mr. Fox and Mr. Buffalo entered the doors, while Mr. Hyena howled for a place in the shade and Mr. Alligator basked on the roof. Presently they all began disputing about their rights of penetration, and from disputing they came to fighting, and while they were all embroiled together the man set the hut on fire and burnt it to the ground, jungle lords and all. Then he went home, saying: "Peace is costly, but it's worth the expense," and lived happily ever after.

THINKING ABOUT THE SELECTION

Recalling

1. What does the elephant do after the man agrees to let him put his trunk in the hut?
2. What is the Commission's explanation for siding with the elephant in the dispute?
3. How does the man solve his problem with the animals?

Interpreting

4. In what ways is the Commission of Enquiry unfair? Explain your answer.
5. Why does the man finally decide that the Commission of Enquiry is of no use to him?
6. How did the man know what would happen when he built the final hut?

Applying

7. Imagine that your community were occupied or taken over by a foreign power. Discuss with your classmates the ways in which your daily life might change.

ANALYZING LITERATURE

Interpreting Symbols

To interpret the symbols in this story, it is important to know that the author was an African who believed that his native land should be ruled by its native people. At the time he wrote the story, much of Africa was controlled by European countries. The story's characters and situation illustrate the relationship between the Africans and the Europeans at that time.

1. For whom is the man a symbol?
2. For whom are the animals symbols?
3. What traits and characteristics are represented by the animals? By the man?
4. Do you think using symbols to tell a story makes the story's meaning clearer and more powerful? Why or why not?

CRITICAL THINKING AND READING

Recognizing Bias

Bias is a person's mental leaning for or against something. It is important for people who judge disputes between others to have no bias toward either party in the dispute. For example, if two youths have a dispute, then their fathers should not be allowed to decide who is right because each father's bias toward his own child would make it difficult for him to make a fair decision.

1. What bias does the Commission have?
2. What are some examples of their statements and actions that show this bias?

The Gentlemen of the Jungle 203

Putting It Together The material outlined on this page is a summary of the primary elements of the short story. Students have studied each of these elements separately in the Short Stories unit. The purpose of the Putting It Together process is to emphasize how each of the separate elements of the short story is dependent on and interwoven with the other elements. As students review these elements, have them consider how each affects the others. Students should read actively to consider how each of these elements contributes to the total effect of the story.

All the elements in a short story are tied into the plot. Characters' actions and emotions are determined by the conflict. The setting may influence the events. A theme is revealed through characters' actions and the outcome of the conflict.

Remind students that, as they read actively, they should be able to see how these elements of fiction produce an effective story.

For further practice with these elements, use the selection on page 311 in the Teaching Portfolio, "The Boy Who Drew Cats," which students can annotate themselves.

Teaching to Ability Levels If your **less advanced** students have difficulty comprehending any of these elements, you might have them review the instruction on the appropriate pages or look up the necessary terms in the Handbook of Literary Terms and Techniques.

The Short Story

An active reader looks at the elements of the short story and considers how a writer uses them to make the story effective. By asking and answering questions about these elements, the reader gains a better appreciation of the story.

Plot

Plot is the sequence of events of the story. The events center on a conflict that may be external (outside the character) or internal (inside the character). The conflict reaches a climax that is finally resolved at the end, sometimes through a surprising turn of events.

Characters

Characters are the people—and sometimes the animals—in a story. The main character is the most important character in the story. The minor characters take part in the story's events but are not as important. Characters can be flat or round, depending on what the story reveals about them. A character's motivation, or reasons for acting, often sets the story moving in a certain direction.

Setting

Setting is the time and place in which the action of the story occurs. Time involves not only a historical period (past, present, future) but also the year, season, and time of day. Place involves not only the specific region or country, but also the city, town, or even type of neighborhood. Setting can be merely the backdrop for the story, or it can play a major role in the development of the plot and the characters.

Theme

Theme is the general idea about life that the story communicates. It is the central idea of the story, the idea to which all the elements— plot, characters, setting—add up. In some stories, the theme is stated directly. More often, however, it is implied, that is, suggested by the details of the story.

The comments in the margin of the story that follows review for you the elements of the short story. They also show questions an active reader might ask about these elements while reading.

204   Short Stories

Objectives

1 To review a short story
2 To make inferences about conflict
3 To recognize the Greek root *demos*
4 To explain how to show internal conflict on a television program

Support Material

Teaching Portfolio
Teacher Backup, p. 307
Putting It Together, p. 311
Grammar in Action Worksheet, *Prepositional Phrases,* p. 315
Usage and Mechanics Worksheet, p. 317
Critical Thinking and Reading Worksheet, *Making Inferences,* p. 318

Language Worksheet, *Recognizing Root Words,* p. 319
Selection Test, p. 320

A Day's Wait

Ernest Hemingway

Title: The title refers to someone or something waiting for a day. How will this waiting affect the story?

He came into the room to shut the windows while we were still in bed and I saw he looked ill. He was shivering, his face was white, and he walked slowly as though it ached to move.

"What's the matter, Schatz?"[1]

"I've got a headache."

"You better go back to bed."

"No. I'm all right."

"You go to bed. I'll see you when I'm dressed."

But when I came downstairs he was dressed, sitting by the fire, looking a very sick and miserable boy of nine years. When I put my hand on his forehead I knew he had a fever.

"You go up to bed," I said, "you're sick."

"I'm all right," he said.

When the doctor came he took the boy's temperature.

"What is it?" I asked him.

"One hundred and two."

Downstairs, the doctor left three different medicines in different colored capsules with instructions for giving them. One was to bring down the fever, another a purgative, the third to overcome an acid condition. The germs of influenza can only exist in an acid condition, he explained. He seemed to know all about influenza and said there was nothing to worry about if the fever did not go above one hundred and four degrees. This was a light epidemic[2] of flu and there was no danger if you avoided pneumonia.

Character: The boy insists he is all right even though he looks ill. He does not complain easily.

Plot: The conflict of the story centers on the boy's illness. He seems seriously ill. Will he recover, or will he become sicker as the story progresses?

---

1. Schatz (shäts): A German term of affection, used here as a loving nickname.

2. epidemic (ep'ə dem' ik) *n.*: An outbreak of a contagious disease.

Presentation

Motivation/Prior Knowledge
Have students imagine that they have an internal conflict of some sort—perhaps a problem that they do not want to divulge for fear of upsetting family and friends. How would this problem affect their actions? How would they go about resolving the problem? Would they reveal what had been bothering them after the problem was resolved? Why or why not?

Purpose-Setting Question
What misunderstanding causes the boy to act the way he does?

Thematic Idea In "A Secret for Two," on page 45, a character shows courage by keeping a secret. You may want to pair the two selections.

Master Teacher Note You might have students look up the word *courage* in a thesaurus or in a dictionary that lists synonyms, and write down all the synonyms they find for the noun *courage*.

Suggest they keep all the possible synonyms for the word in mind as they read, and be prepared, at the end of the story, to discuss which word for courage would best fit the boy in the story.

Primary Source

In all his work, as in this story, Hemingway's characters are believable and realistic. Hemingway wrote, ". . . a writer should create living people; people not characters." (*Death in the Afternoon*, 1932). You might ask students to tell the difference between people and characters, and then ask them what makes the characters in this story believable as people.

Character: The boy seems unable to concentrate.

Character and Plot: Although the father is unconcerned about his son's illness, the boy is behaving strangely. Why?

Setting: The story takes place in a house in the country during the winter. The time of year has contributed to the boy's illness. Will it have any other effect on the story?

Back in the room I wrote the boy's temperature down and made a note of the time to give the various capsules.

"Do you want me to read to you?"

"All right. If you want to," said the boy. His face was very white and there were dark areas under his eyes. He lay still in the bed and seemed very detached from what was going on.

I read aloud from Howard Pyle's *Book of Pirates;* but I could see he was not following what I was reading.

"How do you feel, Schatz?" I asked him.

"Just the same, so far," he said.

I sat at the foot of the bed and read to myself while I waited for it to be time to give another capsule. It would have been natural for him to go to sleep, but when I looked up he was looking at the foot of the bed, looking very strangely.

"Why don't you try to go to sleep? I'll wake you up for the medicine."

"I'd rather stay awake."

After a while he said to me, "You don't have to stay in here with me, Papa, if it bothers you."

"It doesn't bother me."

"No, I mean you don't have to stay if it's going to bother you."

I thought perhaps he was a little lightheaded and after giving him the prescribed capsules at eleven o'clock I went out for a while. It was a bright, cold day, the ground covered with a sleet that had frozen so that it seemed as if all the bare trees, the bushes, the cut brush and all the grass and the bare ground had been varnished with ice. I took the young Irish setter for a little walk up the road and along a frozen creek, but it was difficult to stand or walk on the glassy surface and the red dog slipped and slithered and I fell twice, hard, once dropping my gun and having it slide away over the ice.

We flushed[3] a covey[4] of quail under a high clay bank with overhanging brush and I killed two as they went out of sight over the top of the bank. Some of the covey lit in trees but most of them scattered into brush piles and it was necessary to jump on the ice-coated mounds of brush several times be-

---

3. flushed (flusht) *v.*: Drove from hiding.
4. covey (kuv′ ē) *n.*: A small flock of birds.

Grammar in Action

One way in which writers add detail to their sentences is by using prepositional phrases. A **prepositional phrase** is a group of words that begins with a preposition and ends with a noun or pronoun. Prepositional phrases function as adjectives or as adverbs in sentences. Because prepositional phrases show relationships, they make your sentences clearer and more interesting. Notice how Ernest Hemingway uses prepositional phrases to make the following passage come alive:

We flushed a covey of quail under a high clay bank with overhanging brush and I killed two as they went out of sight over the top of the bank.

The following chart analyzes the prepositional phrases in Hemingway's sentence:

Prepositional Phrase	Function	Modifies
of quail	adjective	covey
under a high clay bank	adverb	flushed
with overhanging brush	adjective	bank
out of sight	adverb	went
over the top	adverb	went
of the bank	adjective	top

fore they would flush. Coming out while you were poised unsteadily on the icy, springy brush they made difficult shooting, and I killed two, missed five, and started back pleased to have found a covey close to the house and happy there were so many left to find on another day.

At the house they said the boy had refused to let anyone come into the room.

"You can't come in," he said. "You mustn't get what I have."

I went up to him and found him in exactly the position I had left him, white-faced, but with the tops of his cheeks flushed by the fever, staring still, as he had stared at the foot of the bed.

I took his temperature.

"What is it?"

"Something like a hundred," I said. It was one hundred and two and four tenths.

"It was a hundred and two," he said.

"Who said so?"

"The doctor."

"Your temperature is all right," I said. "It's nothing to worry about."

"I don't worry," he said, "but I can't keep from thinking."

"Don't think," I said. "Just take it easy."

"I'm taking it easy," he said and looked straight ahead. He was evidently holding tight on to himself about something.

"Take this with water."

"Do you think it will do any good?"

"Of course it will."

I sat down and opened the *Pirate* book and commenced to read, but I could see he was not following, so I stopped.

"About what time do you think I'm going to die?" he asked.

"What?"

"About how long will it be before I die?"

"You aren't going to die. What's the matter with you?"

"Oh, yes, I am. I heard him say a hundred and two."

"People don't die with a fever of one hundred and two. That's a silly way to talk."

"I know they do. At school in France the boys told me you can't live with forty-four degrees. I've got a hundred and two."

Plot: The boy is not acting himself. Why? Is it his illness or is it something else?

Character and Plot: The boy thinks he is going to die! So that is what is bothering him so much. Yet he faces this quietly and displays concern for others.

A Day's Wait   207

Cooperative Learning A group of students might work together to find all the specific words and phrases in the story that give the reader clues to a character's feelings or motivation. For example, the boy changes the phrase, "if it bothers you," to "if it's going to bother you" (page 206).

Speaking and Listening In this story, the boy's father reads him a story about pirates to try to occupy the boy while he is sick. Ask students if they remember any favorite stories they enjoyed having read to them when they were younger. Discuss with students what kinds of stories are particularly suited to reading aloud.

Suggest that students might enjoy preparing these stories to tell or read to first or second graders at another school.

Student Activity 1. Add prepositional phrases to the following sentences to make them more interesting. Include phrases that function as adjectives and phrases that function as adverbs.

1. The father went outside and hunted.
2. The boy did not want to see anyone.
3. The boy was relieved and cried easily the following day.

Student Activity 2. Write three original sentences using prepositional phrases to make each sentence more lively and colorful.

He had been waiting to die all day, ever since nine o'clock in the morning.

"You poor Schatz," I said. "Poor old Schatz. It's like miles and kilometers.[5] You aren't going to die. That's a different thermometer. On that thermometer thirty-seven is normal. On this kind it's ninety-eight."

"Are you sure?"

"Absolutely," I said. "It's like miles and kilometers. You know, like how many kilometers we make when we do seventy miles in the car?"

"Oh," he said.

But his gaze at the foot of the bed relaxed slowly. The hold over himself relaxed too, finally, and the next day it was very slack and he cried very easily at little things that were of no importance.

---

5. kilometers (ki läm′ ə tərz) *n.*: A kilometer is 1,000 meters or about 5/8 of a mile.

Ernest Hemingway (1899–1961), who was born in Oak Park, Illinois, is one of America's most famous writers. He received the Nobel Prize for his novels and short stories. Hemingway lived an adventurous life, participating in both World War I and World War II and spending much time hunting and fishing. Many of his books, like *A Farewell to Arms* and *The Old Man and the Sea*, are based on such experiences. Many of these stories dramatize the importance of courage in the face of life's problems. "A Day's Wait" is not about adventures like these, but deals with a quieter kind of courage.

208   Short Stories

THINKING ABOUT THE SELECTION

Recalling

1. Why does the boy think he will die?
2. Why does the boy's father not correct this mistake until the end of the story?
3. How does the father explain the mistake to his son?

Interpreting

4. What is the meaning of the story's title?
5. What conflicting feelings does the boy struggle with?
6. Describe two ways in which the boy shows courage or concern for others.
7. Why does the boy cry "very easily at little things" the next day?

Applying

8. In this story the boy shows a kind of quiet courage. What other characters in literature can you name who have shown quiet courage?

ANALYZING LITERATURE

Reviewing a Short Story

The elements of plot, character, setting, and theme work together to create a total effect. Think of all these elements and apply them to "A Day's Wait."

1. Give a brief summary of the story.
2. Describe the character of the boy.
3. What external conflict is present in the story? What internal conflict is present?
4. In what way does the setting—Europe—play an important role in this story?
5. What is the theme of the story?
6. What is the total effect of the story?

CRTITICAL THINKING AND READING

Making Inferences About Conflict

The boy in "A Day's Wait" experiences a conflict, but the struggle is within his mind. Because the conflict occurs in the boy's mind, you do not learn about it directly. Instead, you learn about it by making inferences based on clues from what the boy says and does.

The trick of finding clues to the boy's conflict is to search for statements and actions that seem out of place. Such unusual behavior indicates that the boy is responding to an inner conflict rather than to the actual situation around him. For example, one clue to the conflict is that the boy seems "very detached."

1. Find two other examples of unusual actions (not words) that indicate the boy is experiencing a conflict.
2. Find two examples of unusual statements that point to the boy's internal conflict.

UNDERSTANDING LANGUAGE

Recognizing the Greek Root *demos*

A **root** is the core of a word to which suffixes and prefixes can be added. Many English words have Greek roots. The word *epidemic*, for example, is made up of a Greek prefix (*epi-*) meaning "among" and a Greek root (*demos*) meaning "people."

Find the same root in the following words. Then look up each word in a dictionary. Finally, use it in a sentence.

1. democracy   2. democrat   3. pandemic

THINKING AND WRITING

Planning a Television Program

Imagine that your class is producing a program based on this story. As director, you have to write a memo telling the camera person how to show the boy's internal conflict. Brainstorm to think of different camera shots that would reveal the boy's inner struggle. Then use these ideas to write a one-page memo. Explain why each shot you have chosen would be effective. As you revise your memo, make sure that the camera person will be able to follow your directions.

fears build during the day and can be released only when the crisis is over.

ANSWERS TO CRITICAL THINKING AND READING

1. Answers will differ. The following are some examples of unusual actions: He was looking very strangely at the foot of the bed and not listening to his father's story. He wanted to stay awake rather than go to sleep.
2. Answers will differ. The following are some examples of unusual statements: "You don't have to stay if it's going to bother you." "You can't come in. You mustn't get what I have." "Do you think it will do any good?"

ANSWERS TO UNDERSTANDING LANGUAGE

1. *democracy* The meaning of the word should be one of the following: government in which people hold the power; a country or state with such a government; majority rule; the principle of equality of the common people, especially as the wielders of political power. Students' sentences will differ.
2. *democrat* The meaning of the word should be one of the following: a person who believes in and upholds government by the people; a person who believes in and practices the principle of equality. Students' sentences will differ.
3. *pandemic* The meaning of the word should be one of the following: prevalent over a whole area; universal; epidemic over a large region (said of a disease). Students' sentences will differ.

THINKING AND WRITING

Writing Across the Curriculum

Have a group of students interview a science teacher and a math teacher to learn their views on the metric system versus the system of measurement we use in the United States. Which system does each teacher prefer and why? Have students write up their interviews.

ANSWERS TO ANALYZING LITERATURE

1. Summaries should include the following details: The boy becomes ill. A doctor examines him and says the boy has influenza with a temperature of 102. For the rest of the day, the boy acts tense and listless. Finally, he tells his father that he believes he will die because he heard at school in France that a person with a temperature of 44 would die. His father explains to him that in France a different temperature scale is used. The boy had been worried and afraid but remained silent to avoid upsetting his father. Now he is relieved to know he will live.
2. Suggested Response: The boy is courageous, considerate, and loving. He does not complain; he keeps his fears to himself.
3. The external conflict is the father's misunderstanding of his son's behavior. The internal conflict is between the boy's fear of dying and his wish not to worry or upset others.
4. The central problem is the result of an American boy's misunderstanding of a European system of measurement.
5. The theme of the story is that sometimes a courageous person can suffer unnecessarily because of his or her courage.
6. The total effect of the story is a building up of emotion, and then a release, much as the boy's

Before reading FOCUS ON
READING, ask the students to
define the word *relationship*. Ask
them what kinds of relationships
are in short stories. Explain that
relationships are very important
in short stories and other types of
literature. Explain that this section will help them understand relationships better.

**ANSWERS (Time Order
Activity)**

Time order signal words: *when, first,
before, then, while, earlier, now*
1. Darzee's baby had been eaten by
   Nag.
2. Darzee was miserable.
3. Rikki-tikki-tavi met Darzee.
4. Nag appeared.
5. Rikki talked to the cobra and Nagaina tried to sneak up to attack.
6. Darzee warned Rikki
7. Rikki jumped into the air
8. Nagaina struck.
9. Rikki understood Darzee's fear.

**ANSWERS (Cause and
Effect Activity)**

Suggested Response: Since Nag
had eaten his baby, Darzee was
miserable. The cobra had almost
killed Rikki. Therefore, Rikki, the
mongoose, understood why the
tailorbird greatly feared these
snakes. Because Darzee had warned
Rikki earlier, the mongoose jumped
into the air and escaped the fatal
bite of Nagaina.

FOCUS ON READING

Understanding Relationships

Reading a short story actively involves understanding the relationships that exist between events in the plot, setting, and
characters. There are often clues in the story to help you see the connections. Understanding **time order, cause and effect,** and **comparison and contrast** relationships is important.

Time Order

Time order refers to the sequence of events in a story. Usually
events are arranged chronologically so that one follows another. Writers often include signal words to help you see the sequence of
events. Be aware of the following time-order signal words:

first	then	before	later	during	when
at last	next	after	earlier	finally	now

Activity

Read the following paragraph and jot down the time-order signal
words. Then list the events in the order in which they occurred.

When Rikki-Tikki-Tavi first met Darzee, the tailorbird was
miserable because Nag had eaten one of his babies. Before
Darzee could tell Rikki who Nag was, Nag appeared. Then
while Rikki was talking with the cobra, Nagaina tried to sneak
up and attack Rikki. Luckily an earlier warning by Darzee
prompted Rikki to jump as high in the air as he could, which
saved him from the fatal cobra bite. Now he knew why the
tailorbird so greatly feared the two snakes.

Cause and Effect

A **cause** is a reason for something happening. An **effect** is the
result of some action or cause. The cause always occurs first and
may produce many effects. The following signal words are often used
to indicate a cause-and-effect relationship:

as	thus	therefore	consequently	so that
for	since	as a result	in order that	because

There were three cause-and-effect relationships in the preceding
paragraph about Rikki-Tikki-Tavi.

Activity

Read the following sentences based on "Rikki-Tikki-Tavi."

Darzee was miserable because Nag had eaten his baby.
Because the cobras had almost killed Rikki, the mongoose
understood why the tailorbird greatly feared these snakes.

Note that the signal word *because* is used in each sentence to introduce the cause and that the cause can come at the beginning or end of the sentence.

Rewrite each sentence, using a different signal word and changing the order in which the cause-and-effect statements appear in the sentence. Then find the third cause-and-effect relationship in the paragraph and write it as a sentence.

Comparison and Contrast

Comparing involves finding ways that things are similar, while **contrasting** involves noting ways that they are different. By comparing and contrasting events, characters, themes, and other story elements, you gain greater insights and understanding. Words such as "both," "similar," and "just as much" indicate a comparison relationship. The following words are used to show contrasting relationships:

but	although	in contrast	on the contrary	whereas
yet	however	nevertheless	on the other hand	while

Activity

Make a chart to show how each of the animal characters in "Rikki-Tikki-Tavi" are alike and different. Write the following traits on the top of the chart: brave, shrewd, wicked, selfish, trustworthy, loving, fearful, sensible, curious, sly. Write the following names on the vertical side of the chart: Rikki, Darzee, Darzee's wife, Chuchundra, Nag, Nagaina, Karait. Make a checkerboard grid on the chart and check each box that applies to each character. Using the relationships that you noted in making the chart, write a paragraph comparing and contrasting the characters. Use the comparison and contrast signal words.

YOU THE WRITER

Guidelines for Evaluating Assignment 1

1. Does the composition begin with a description of the setting?
2. Does the description show specific objects that help create a single overall impression?
3. Does the description create a vivid picture of the setting?
4. Is the description free from grammar, usage, and mechanics errors?

Guidelines for Evaluating Assignment 2

1. Does the first sentence of the character sketch tell what kind of person the imaginary character is?
2. Does the student tell the kinds of things this person does during the course of the day?
3. Does the student enter into the character's mind and show what he or she is thinking?
4. Is there a physical description of appearance and apparel?
5. Is the character sketch free from grammar, usage, and mechanics errors?

Guidelines for Evaluating Assignment 3

1. Does the short story show the main character facing a problem?
2. Does the short story show the character taking a series of actions to solve the problem?
3. Does the character solve the problem in a surprising way?
4. Is the short story organized chronologically, and is it free from grammar, usage, and mechanics errors?

YOU THE WRITER

Assignment

1. The time and place where a story occurs is called the setting. Describe the setting of a short story you might write. Be sure this setting creates only a *single* overall impression.

    Prewriting. Brainstorm, listing specific objects in this setting. From this list, select the ones that best create the desired impression.

    Writing. First the first draft of a description of the setting. Show the specific objects that help create impression. Be sure to show them in sharp detail.

    Revising. When you revise, make sure you have created a vivid picture of the setting. Does your description create a unified impression?

Assignment

2. Authors make the characters in their stories seem real by showing (1) how they act, (2) how they speak, (3) how they look, and (4) how they think and feel. Write a character sketch of an imaginary character.

    Prewriting. Make a list of several different kinds of personalities. Then take one of these personalities and make another list of the kinds of things a character with this personality might do and say and think.

    Writing. Now write your character sketch. In the first sentence, tell what kind of person your imaginary character is. After you have done this, tell the kind of things this person does during the course of a day. Enter into this character's mind and show what he or she is thinking and feeling. Tell what he or she looks like and what he or she is wearing. Finally, let this person speak.

    Revising. When you revise your composition, check to see that you have identified your character's main personality traits.

Assignment

3. Write a short story in which a character faces a problem and acts to resolve the problem. Try to make the ending a surprise.

    Prewriting. Divide a sheet of paper into three columns. In the first column, make a list of problems a person might have. In the second column, list the solutions to these problems. In the third column, list the surprising ways in which these solutions might come about.

    Writing. Using the lists you have made, write your story. Show your main character facing the problem you have chosen. Then show this person taking a series of actions to overcome this problem against some sort of opposition. Finally, show the character solving the problem in a surprising way.

    Revising. When you revise your story, check to see that you have related events in chronological order.

YOU THE CRITIC

Assignment

1. The theme of coming of age is common in literature. Write an essay explaining how a character from a short story you have read comes of age.

   Prewriting.   What does it mean to pass from childhood to maturity? Freewrite, exploring how one character does just that.

   Writing.   Write the first draft of your essay. Relate events in chronological order. Remember to tell how the character is different at the end of the story.

   Revising.   Make sure you have included enough details to prove that this character has truly come of age.

Assignment

2. The theme of a short story is the insight into life it reveals. Write an essay interpreting the theme of one of the short stories in this unit. Then support your opinion by referring to specific characters and incidents in the story.

   Prewriting.   Freewrite about the short story and the characters. Ask yourself what these characters have learned during the course of the story. Then ask yourself what *you* have learned.

   Writing.   Now write the first draft of your essay. In your opening paragraph, state the theme. In the body explain how the short story reveals this insight into life. In the last line of the essay, restate the theme, but add a little twist to it, something to end the essay with flair.

   Revising.   As you revise your essay, check to see that you have fully interpreted the theme.

Assignment

3. Write an essay about how the author of one of the short stories in this unit prepares the reader in the early part of the story for things that will happen later.

   Prewriting.   Before you write, examine the second half of the story first. Focus on the surprises that occur in this part, for it is these surprises that the author must prepare the reader for. After you have examined the surprises in the second half of the story, scan through the first half of the story to see how the author prepared you for them.

   Writing.   Now write your essay. State your thesis or main idea in your introductory paragraph. In the body paragraphs, include a *brief* summary of the story, the surprises at the end, and the ways in which the author prepared you for these surprises.

   Revising.   As you revise your essay, make sure you have arranged your information in a logical order.

You the Critic   213

YOU THE CRITIC
Guidelines for Evaluating Assignment 1

1. Does the essay explain how the character has come of age?
2. Does the student explain how the character is different at the end of the story?
3. Has the student included enough details to prove that the character has truly come of age?
4. Is the essay in chronological order, and is it free from grammar, usage, and mechanics errors?

Guidelines for Evaluating Assignment 2

1. Does the opening paragraph of the essay state the theme of the short story?
2. Does the body explain how the short story reveals insights about life by using sufficient examples and details from the work?
3. Does the essay fully interpret the theme?
4. Does the essay conclude with a restatement of the theme and end with a flair?
5. Is the essay free from grammar, usage, and mechanics errors?

Guidelines for Evaluating Assignment 3

1. Does the student begin by stating a thesis about foreshadowing in the introductory paragraph?
2. Does the essay include a brief summary of the short story?
3. Are the surprises at the end clearly presented?
4. Has the student clearly explained how the author prepared the reader for the surprises by foreshadowing?
5. Is the essay logically arranged, and is it free from grammar, usage, and mechanics errors?

PARADE CURTAIN AFTER PICASSO
© David Hockney, 1980

DRAMA

The word *drama* leaves a thrill in the air. Hear the word and you immediately think of the excitement of the theater with live actors on the stage and a live audience offering its applause. Or you recall the pleasure of drama brought into your home through television or radio or into the cinema through movies.

Since drama is meant to be performed, when you read it, you must imagine how it would appear on the stage or screen, or, if it is a radio play, how it would sound over the radio or on a tape cassette. The story of the drama is told mainly through dialogue, or conversation between characters. From what the characters say, you discover what they are feeling and what they are like. In addition, stage directions describe how the characters would move or act before an audience. The sets are the re-creation of settings on the stage; the props, the physical objects the characters use; the costumes, the clothes the characters wear; and the sound effects, the planned noise that accompanies the play. Each of these devices helps create the world of the play on the stage.

Just as a short story may be divided into episodes, a short play may be divided into scenes. Just as a novel is divided into chapters, a full-length play is divided into acts.

In this unit you will encounter plays on a variety of topics and for a variety of media. You will read a stage play, a radio play, a television play, and even a full-length play based on a famous book.

Humanities Note

Fine art, *Parade Curtain After Picasso,* 1980, David Hockney. David Hockney, born in 1937, is Britain's best known contemporary painter, designer, and graphic artist. Educated at Bradford College of Art and the Royal College of Art in London, David Hockney first drew attention with his innovative "pop art" statements. Today he is known as a painter of difficult effects, such as sunlight on water in a pool, and for his remarkable stage and costume designs.

Parade Curtain After Picasso is a painting executed after Hockney successfully designed the staging of the work *Parade,* a salute to twentieth-century French musical theater, produced at the Metropolitan Opera in New York City. Stimulated by that experience, Hockney explored works of some of the artists who had inspired him with their stage designs, notably Picasso. In this work, Hockney utilizes some of the elements created by Picasso for the ballet curtain from the original *Parade* production. Hockney expands and explores the forms, textures, and colors of Picasso's great work. Using a wet-on-wet painting technique, Hockney creates a different, more organic, interpretation of Picasso's work which pays homage to that man's great genius.

Reading Actively Reading drama requires the student to visualize the action. The plays presented here are written for three different mediums. *Grandpa and the Statue* is a radio play, in which stage directions are given for music and evocative sounds. As students read, they should imagine hearing this play without actually seeing the characters or action. *The Dying Detective* and *A Christmas Carol: Scrooge and Marley* are stage plays, and have the standard stage directions. In these plays, the directions are lengthy and detailed because the setup on the stage is most important. *The Monsters Are Due on Maple Street* is a television play. The stage directions may contain terminology that is unfamiliar to students. Be sure students know what the camera is doing when it pans, for example. They should be aware that they are reading this play through a camera lens, in a sense.

Drama

Drama is a story told in dialogue by performers before an audience. When we think of drama, we think of stage plays and the exciting world of the theater—actors, costumes, stage sets, and lights. But drama includes more than the theater; television plays and radio plays are drama too. Even movies are a form of drama. In all of these kinds of drama, actors make a world come alive before an audience.

Plays are meant to be performed, but it is possible just to read a play. When you read a play, you can make it come alive by staging it in your imagination. The play you are reading is a script. It contains not only the words that the actors speak but also the stage directions the playwright provides to indicate how to put on the play. Stage directions tell what the stage should look like, what the characters wear, how they speak their lines, and where they move.

Stage directions use a particular vocabulary. *Right, left, up, down,* and *center* refer to areas of the stage as the actors see it. To help you visualize what is meant when a stage direction tells an actor to move down left, for example, picture the stage like this:

THE STAGE

Wings (offstage)   Wings (offstage)

Upstage Right	Upstage Center	Upstage Left
Right	Center	Left
Downstage Right	Downstage Center	Downstage Left

Curtain

Television plays and film scripts have their own kinds of directions; these are camera directions. *Fade in, fade out, long shot, close up* should make sense to you. *Pan* means "to move the camera to follow a moving object or to create a panoramic scene." When you read these directions, you know what character or actions get emphasized.

Just as you read short stories actively, you should also read drama actively. Reading actively includes trying to see the play in your mind while you continually question the meaning of what the actors are saying and doing.

Use the following strategies to help you read drama actively. These strategies will help you to enjoy and appreciate the plays in this unit.

Visualize   Use the directions and information supplied by the playwright to picture the stage and the characters in action. Hear their voices. Go beyond the stated words and actions to create the scene in your mind.

Question   As you meet the characters, ask yourself what each character is like. What situation does each character face? What motives and traits does each character reveal by his or her words and actions?

Predict   Building on the play's conflict and the characters' words and actions, predict what you think will happen. How will the conflict be resolved? What will become of each character?

Clarify   If a character's words or actions are not clear to you, stop and try to make sense of them. Look for answers to your questions and check your predictions.

Summarize   Pause occasionally to review what has happened. Put the characters' actions and words together. What is the story being told?

Pull It Together   Pull together all of the elements of the play. What does the play mean? Is it purely entertainment or is there a message? What does it say to you?

Using these strategies when you read drama will help you to be a more effective reader. You will be better able to understand the conflict of the play and its resolution and to apply your understanding to your world.

217

Reading Strategies Emphasize the reading strategies on this page. One strategy that is particularly useful when reading drama is to visualize the characters and action. Students should create each scene in their minds. They should use the stage directions to help them visualize the characters, hear the voices, and see the gestures in their minds. Doing this will make the plays come alive for students. Another valuable strategy is questioning the characters' words and actions. Why is a character behaving a certain way? What do his or her gestures suggest about what is really going on? Analyzing characters' motivations through their words and actions is an important part of reading drama actively.

More About the Author Arthur Miller often writes realistically about the conflict between the individual and society. In many of Miller's plays, it is this conflict that shapes the individual in either a positive or a negative way. Another one of Miller's common themes is how the ordinary person becomes a tragic hero. Ask students to discuss why a writer would choose to express his ideas in play form. What are the advantages and disadvantages of trying to convey feelings through characters' dialogue alone?

Literary Focus Explain to students that dialogue is what they do when they speak to friends, parents, and teachers every day. Every word they speak is dialogue. Suggest to students that they think about how the words would look on paper the next time they have a conversation with someone.

Look For Point out that, since this play was originally written for radio presentation, the stage directions also include sound effects, such as the creaking of a rocking chair, the rustling of paper, and the whistling of the wind. Stage directions appear throughout the play in italic type.

Writing/Prior Knowledge Have students discuss what part anticipation plays in visiting well-known tourist attractions. Then have them complete the freewriting assignment.

Vocabulary Most students will have no difficulty with these words. You might have them use each word in a sentence orally before reading the story.

Grandpa and the Statue

Arthur Miller (1915–   ) is one of America's most honored playwrights. After graduating from the University of Michigan, he returned to New York City, where he was born, and wrote radio plays. Most of his work, though, has been for the stage. His play *Death of a Salesman* is considered one of the greatest modern plays. Miller often writes about families, and the immigrant experience. The play you are about to read portrays a remarkable grandfather and shows the special meaning the Statue of Liberty comes to have for him.

Dialogue

Dialogue is talk between characters. In a play dialogue carries the plot forward and shows what the characters are like. In some plays it even establishes the setting: Characters can indicate by their words where they are and when something is happening. Because *Grandpa and the Statue* is a radio play, the dialogue is especially important.

Look For

Grandpa and the Statue was originally written to be presented on the radio. Since it is a radio play, as you read, pretend that you are only listening to it, not seeing it performed on the stage. Imagine the sound of the characters' voices. How would you read the lines? Notice the bracketed directions for music: They signal that the action is shifting from one place to another or from one time to another.

Writing

In this play the grandfather and grandson visit the Statue of Liberty. Think of a time you visited a special place that you had long looked forward to seeing. It might be a famous monument, a national park, a city, a professional-sports center, or any other place. Freewrite about what you expected before you made your trip and what you actually felt when you were there.

Vocabulary

Knowing the following words will help you as you read *Grandpa and the Statue*.

subscribed (səb skrībd') *v.*: Supported (p. 221)

peeved (pēvd) *v.*: Irritated (p. 221)

register (rej' is tər) *n.*: A record

containing a list of names (p. 222)

gleefully (glē' fə lē) *adj.*: Merry (p. 223)

218   Drama

Objectives

1 To analyze dialogue in a play
2 To make inferences about characters from dialogue
3 To recognize dialect
4 To write dialogue

Support Material

Teaching Portfolio
Teacher Backup, p. 341
Grammar in Action Worksheet, *Inverted Word Order*, p. 345
Usage and Mechanics Worksheet, p. 347
Vocabulary Check, p. 348
Analyzing Literature Worksheet, *The Purpose of Dialogue*, p. 349

Critical Thinking and Reading Worksheet, *Making Inferences About Characters*, p. 350
Selection Test, p. 352

Grandpa and the Statue

Arthur Miller

CHARACTERS

Announcer	Grandfather Monaghan	Jack	Girl
August	Child Monaghan	Mike	Young Man
Young Monaghan	George	Joe	Megaphone Voice
Sheean	Charley	Alf	Veteran

[*Music: Theme*]

ANNOUNCER. The scene is the fourth floor of a giant army hospital overlooking New York Harbor. A young man sitting in a wheel chair is looking out a window; just looking. After a while another young man in another wheel chair rolls over to him and both look.

[*Music out*]

AUGUST. You want to play some checkers with me, Monaghan?

MONAGHAN. Not right now.

AUGUST. Okay. [*Slight pause*] You don't want to go feeling blue, Monaghan.

MONAGHAN. I'm not blue.

AUGUST. All you do most days is sit here looking out this window.

MONAGHAN. What do you want me to do, jump rope?

AUGUST. No, but what do you get out of it?

MONAGHAN. It's a beautiful view. Some companies make millions of dollars just printing that view on postcards.

AUGUST. Yeh, but nobody keeps looking at a postcard six, seven hours a day.

MONAGHAN. I come from around here, it reminds me of things. My young days.

AUGUST. That's right, you're Brooklyn, aren't you?

MONAGHAN. My house is only about a mile away.

AUGUST. That so. Tell me, are you looking at just the water all the time? I'm curious. I don't get a kick out of this view.

MONAGHAN. There's the Statue of Liberty out there. Don't you see it?

AUGUST. Oh, that's it. Yeh, that's nice to look at.

MONAGHAN. I like it. Reminds me of a lot of laughs.

AUGUST. Laughs? The Statue of Liberty?

MONAGHAN. Yeh, my grandfather. He got all twisted up with the Statue of Liberty.

AUGUST. [*Laughs a little*] That so? What happened?

Grandpa and the Statue 219

Presentation

Motivation/Prior Knowledge Have students imagine that they are close to a relative who holds a unique and unpopular opinion. This relative has convinced students of his or her opinion, but the more they hear from other people, the more they begin to doubt their relative's opinion. How would you handle this situation? Would you want to examine the evidence yourself in order to form your own opinion? Would you then try to change your relative's mind?

Master Teacher Note Provide students with some background information on the Statue of Liberty, formally titled "Liberty Enlightening the World." Liberty is the largest statue ever made, measuring 151 feet from her sandals to the top of the torch she is holding. The statue is made of copper hammered over an iron framework, and stands on a granite and concrete pedestal. The French people donated about $250,000 for the construction of the statue, and the people of the United States gave about $280,000 for the pedestal. France gave the monument to the United States in 1884 as a symbol of friendship between the two countries and of the liberty that the citizens of both countries enjoy.

Purpose-Setting Question How does Grandfather Monaghan's distrust deny him participation in the statue's construction?

1 Critical Thinking and Reading What conclusions can you draw about the young men based on where they are as the play opens?

2 Discussion What do you think this is leading to? Will the subject of the play be the two young men or will it be something else? How can you tell?

PENNIES FOR THE PEDESTAL
The World, *April 3, 1885*
Courtesy of the New York Historical Society, New York City

MONAGHAN. Well. My grandfather was the stingiest man in Brooklyn. "Mercyless" Monaghan, they used to call him. He even used to save umbrella handles.

AUGUST. What for?

MONAGHAN. Just couldn't stand seeing anything go to waste. After a big windstorm there'd be a lot of broken umbrellas laying around in the streets.

AUGUST. Yeh?

MONAGHAN. He'd go around picking them up. In our house the closets were always full of umbrella handles. My grandma used to say that he would go across the Brooklyn Bridge on the trolley just because he could come back on the same nickel. See, if you stayed on the trolley they'd let you come back for the same nickel.

AUGUST. What'd he do, just go over and come back?

MONAGHAN. Yeh, it made him feel good. Savin' money. Two and a half cents.

AUGUST. So how'd he get twisted up with the Statue of Liberty?

MONAGHAN. Well, way back in 1887 around there they were living on Butler Street. Butler Street, Brooklyn, practically runs right down to the river. One day he's sitting on the front porch, reading a paper he borrowed from the neighbors, when along comes this man Jack Sheean who lived up the block.

[*Music: Sneak into above speech, then bridge, then out*]

SHEEAN. [*Slight brogue*] A good afternoon to you, Monaghan.

MONAGHAN. How're you, Sheean, how're ya?

SHEEAN. Fair, fair. And how's Mrs. Monaghan these days?

MONAGHAN. Warm. Same as everybody else in summer.

SHEEAN. I've come to talk to you about the fund, Monaghan.

MONAGHAN. What fund is that?

SHEEAN. The Statue of Liberty fund.

MONAGHAN. Oh, that.

SHEEAN. It's time we come to grips with the subject, Monaghan.

MONAGHAN. I'm not interested, Sheean.

SHEEAN. Now hold up on that a minute. Let me tell you the facts. This here Frenchman has gone and built a fine statue of Liberty. It costs the Lord knows how many millions to build. All they're askin' us to do is contribute enough to put up a base for the statue to stand on.

MONAGHAN. I'm not . . . !

SHEEAN. Before you answer me. People all over the whole United States are puttin' in for it. Butler Street is doin' the same. We'd like to hand up a flag on the corner saying—"Butler Street, Brooklyn, is one hundred percent behind the Statue of Liberty." And Butler Street *is* a hundred percent subscribed except for you. Now will you give us a dime, Monaghan? One dime and we can put up the flag. Now what do you say to that?

MONAGHAN. I'm not throwin' me good money away for somethin' I don't even know exists.

SHEEAN. Now what do you mean by that?

MONAGHAN. Have you seen this statue?

SHEEAN. No, but it's in a warehouse. And as soon as we get the money to build the pedestal they'll take it and put it up on that island in the river, and all the boats comin' in from the old country will see it there and it'll raise the hearts of the poor immigrants to see such a fine sight on their first look at this country.

MONAGHAN. And how do I know it's in this here warehouse at all?

SHEEAN. You read your paper, don't you? It's been in all the papers for the past year.

MONAGHAN. Ha, the papers? Last year I read in the paper that they were about to pave Butler Street and take out all the holes. Turn around and look at Butler Street, Mr. Sheean.

SHEEAN. All right. I'll do this: I'll take you to the warehouse and show you the statue. Will you give me a dime then?

MONAGHAN. Well . . . I'm not sayin' I would, and I'm not sayin' I wouldn't. But I'd be more *likely* if I saw the thing large as life, I would.

SHEEAN. [*Peeved*] All right, then. Come along.

[*Music up and down and out*]
[*Footsteps, in a warehouse . . . echo . . . they come to halt*]

Now then. Do you see the Statue of Liberty or don't you see it?

MONAGHAN. I see it all right, but it's all broke!

SHEEAN. *Broke!* They brought it from France on a boat. They had to take it apart, didn't they?

MONAGHAN. You got a secondhand statute, that's what you got, and I'm not payin' for new when they've shipped us something that's all smashed to pieces.

SHEEAN. Now just a minute, just a minute. Visualize what I'm about to tell you, Monaghan, get the picture of it. When this statue is put together it's going to stand ten stories high. Could they get a thing ten stories high into a four-story building such as this is? Use your good sense, now, Monaghan.

MONAGHAN. What's that over there?

SHEEAN. Where?

MONAGHAN. That tablet there in her hand. What's it say? July Eye Vee [IV] MDCCLXXVI . . . what . . . what's all that?

Grandpa and the Statue   221

---

5 Clarification Frédéric Auguste Bartholdi, a well-known French sculptor, designed the Statue of Liberty and supervised its construction.

6 Discussion Why is this project so important to Sheean and the other people on Butler Street?

7 Clarification The Statue of Liberty stands on Liberty Island facing the channel of New York harbor. It became a symbol of refuge for immigrants from many countries.

8 Discussion What is the purpose of these italicized words? Why do you not see them in other kinds of stories?

9 Clarification The statue was shipped from France in 214 separate crates.

10 **Discussion** What does Grandfather Monaghan object to about the statue? What is he missing about the significance of the date and what the statue represents?

11 **Discussion** Why does Grandfather Monaghan expect the statue to topple into the river? If he had known that the assembled statue would weigh 450,000 pounds, do you think he would still have said this?

12 **Liberary Focus** The stage direction here prefaces a flashback. The flashback is a literary device that allows characters in the present to transport the reader back to events that happened in the past.

SHEEAN. That means July 4, 1776. It's in Roman numbers. Very high class.

MONAGHAN. What's the good of it? If they're going to put a sign on her they ought to put it: Welcome All. That's it. Welcome All.

SHEEAN. They decided July 4, 1776, and July 4, 1776, it's going to be!

MONAGHAN. All right, then let them get their dime from somebody else!

SHEEAN. Monaghan!

MONAGHAN. No, sir! I'll tell you something. I didn't think there was a statue but there is. She's all broke, it's true, but she's here and maybe they can get her together. But even if they do, will you tell me what sort of a welcome to immigrants it'll be, to have a gigantic thing like that in the middle of the river and in her hand is July Eye Vee MCDVC . . . whatever it is?

SHEEAN. That's the date the country was made!

MONAGHAN. The divil with the date! A man comin' in from the sea wants a place to stay, not a date. When I come from the old country I git off at the dock and there's a feller says to me, "Would you care for a room for the night?" "I would that," I sez, and he sez, "All right then, follow me." He takes me to a rooming house. I no sooner sign me name on the register—which I was able to do even at that time—when I look around and the feller is gone clear away and took my valise in the bargain. A statue anyway can't move off so fast, but if she's going to welcome let her say welcome, not this MCDC. . . .

SHEEAN. All right, then, Monaghan. But all I can say is, you've laid a disgrace on the name of Butler Street. I'll put the dime in for ya.

MONAGHAN. Don't connect me with it! It's a swindle, is all it is. In the first place, it's

broke; in the second place, if they do put it up it'll come down with the first high wind that strikes it.

SHEEAN. The engineers say it'll last forever!

MONAGHAN. And I say it'll topple into the river in a high wind! Look at the inside of her. She's all hollow!

SHEEAN. I've heard everything now, Monaghan. Just about everything. Good-bye.

MONAGHAN. What do you mean, good-bye? How am I to get back to Butler Street from here?

SHEEAN. You've got legs to walk.

MONAGHAN. I'll remind you that I come on the trolley.

SHEEAN. And I'll remind you that I paid your fare and I'm not repeating the kindness.

MONAGHAN. Sheean? You've stranded me!

[*Music up and down*]

YOUNG MONAGHAN. That was grandpa. That's why I have to laugh every time I look at the statue now.

AUGUST. Did he ever put the dime in?

YOUNG MONAGHAN. Well—in a way. What happened was this: His daughters got married and finally my mom . . . put *me* out on Butler Street. I got to be pretty attached to grandpa. He'd even give me an umbrella handle and make a sword out of it for me. Naturally, I wasn't very old before he began working on me about the statue.

[*High wind*]

CHILD MONAGHAN. [*Softly, as though grandpa is in bed*] Grampa?

MONAGHAN. [*Awakened*] Heh? What are you doin' up?

CHILD MONAGHAN. Ssssh! Listen!

[*Wind rising up and fading. Rising higher and fading*]

MONAGHAN. [*Gleefully*] Aaaaaaaah! Yes, yes. This'll do it, boy. This'll do it! First thing in the morning we'll go down to the docks and I'll bet you me life that Mr. Sheean's statue is smashed down and layin' on the bottom of the bay. Go to sleep now, we'll have a look first thing.

[*Music up and down*]
[*Footsteps*]

CHILD MONAGHAN. If it fell down, all the people will get their dimes back, won't they, grampa? Slow down, I can't walk so fast.

MONAGHAN. Not only will they get their dimes back, but Mr. Sheean and the whole crew that engineered the collection are going to rot in jail. Now mark my words. Here, now, we'll take a short cut around this shed . . .

[*Footsteps continue a moment, then gradually . . . disappointedly they come to a halt*]

CHILD MONAGHAN. She's . . . she's still standing, grampa.

13 | **MONAGHAN.** She is that. [*Uncomprehending*] I don't understand it. That was a terrible wind last night. Terrible.

CHILD MONAGHAN. Maybe she's weaker though. Heh?

MONAGHAN. Why . . . sure, that must be it. I'll wager she's hangin' by a thread. [*Realizing*] Of course! That's why they put her out there in the water so when she falls down she won't be flattening out a lot of poor innocent people. Hey—feel that?

CHILD MONAGHAN. The wind! It's starting to blow again!

MONAGHAN. Sure, and look at the sky blackening over!

[*Wind rising*]

Feel it comin' up! Take your last look at the statue, boy. If I don't mistake me eyes she's takin' a small list to Jersey already!

[*Music up and down*]

YOUNG MONAGHAN. It was getting embarrassing for me on the block. I kept promising the other kids that when the next wind came the statue would come down. We even had a game. Four or five kids would stand in a semicircle around one kid who was the statue. The statue kid had to stand on his heels and look right in our eyes. Then we'd all take a deep breath and blow in his face. He'd fall down like a stick of wood. They all believed me and grampa . . . until one day. We were standing around throwing rocks at an old milk can . . .

[*Banging of rocks against milk can*]

GEORGE. [*Kid*] What're you doin?

CHILD MONAGHAN. What do we look like we're doin?

GEORGE. I'm going someplace tomorrow.

CHARLEY. [*Kid*] I know, church. Watch out, I'm throwin'.

[*Can being hit*]

GEORGE. I mean after church.

JACK. Where?

GEORGE. My old man's going to take me out on the Statue of Liberty boat.

[*Banging against can abruptly stops*]

CHILD MONAGHAN. You're not going out on the statue, though, are you?

GEORGE. Sure, that's where we're going.

CHILD MONAGHAN. But you're liable to get killed. Supposing there's a high wind tomorrow?

Grandpa and the Statue 223

13 Discussion What part does Grandfather Monaghan's miserliness play in his belief that the statue is going to be blown over by the wind?

14 Discussion Why is Child Monaghan becoming embarrassed? Why does he believe the statue will fall?

15 Discussion How true is what George says?

16 Discussion Why is Child Monaghan about to burst into tears?

17 Critical Thinking and Reading What do you suppose Child Monaghan is leading up to?

GEORGE. My old man says that statue couldn't fall down if all the wind in the world and John L. Sullivan[1] hit it at the same time.

CHILD MONAGHAN. Is that so?

15 **GEORGE.** Yeh, that's so. My old man says that the only reason your grandfather's saying that it's going to fall down is that he's ashamed he didn't put a dime in for the pedestal.

CHILD MONAGHAN. Is that so?

GEORGE. Yeh, that's so.

CHILD MONAGHAN. Well, you tell your old man that if he gets killed tomorrow not to come around to my grandfather and say he didn't warn him!

JACK. Hey, George, would your father take me along?

GEORGE. I'll ask him, maybe he—

CHILD MONAGHAN. What, are you crazy, Jack?

MIKE. Ask him if he'd take me too, will ya, George?

CHILD MONAGHAN. Mike, what's the matter with you?

JOE. Me too, George, I'll ask my mother for money.

CHILD MONAGHAN. Joe! Didn't you hear what my grampa said?

JOE. Well . . . I don't really believe that any more.

CHILD MONAGHAN. You don't be . . .

MIKE. Me neither.

---

1. **John L. Sullivan:** A famous American boxer (1858–1918).

224 Drama

JACK. I don't really think your grampa knows what he's talkin' about.

CHILD MONAGHAN. He don't, heh? [*Ready to weep*] Okay . . . Okay. [*Bursting out*] I just hope that wind blows tomorrow, boy! I just hope that wind blows! 16

[*Music up and down*]
[*Creaking of a rocking chair*]

MONAGHAN. Huh?

CHILD MONAGHAN. Can you stop rocking for a minute?

[*Rocking stops*]

Can you put down your paper?

[*Rustle of paper*]

I—I read the weather report for tomorrow.

MONAGHAN. The weather report . . .

CHILD MONAGHAN. Yeh. It says fair and cool.

MONAGHAN. What of it?

CHILD MONAGHAN. I was wondering. Supposing you and me we went on a boat tomorrow. You know, I see the water every day when I go down to the docks to play, but I never sat on it. I mean in a boat. 17

MONAGHAN. Oh. Well, we might take the ferry on the Jersey side. We might do that.

CHILD MONAGHAN. Yeh, but there's nothing to see in Jersey.

MONAGHAN. You can't go to Europe tomorrow.

CHILD MONAGHAN. No, but couldn't we go toward the ocean? Just . . . *toward* it?

MONAGHAN. Toward it. What—what is it on your mind, boy? What is it now?

CHILD MONAGHAN. Well, I . . .

MONAGHAN. Oh, you want to take the Staten Island ferry. Sure, that's in the direction of the sea.

CHILD MONAGHAN. No, grampa, not the Staten Island ferry.

MONAGHAN. You don't mean—[*Breaks off*] Boy!

CHILD MONAGHAN. All the kids are going tomorrow with Georgie's old man.

MONAGHAN. You don't believe me any more.

CHILD MONAGHAN. I do, grampa, but . . .

MONAGHAN. You don't. If you did you'd stay clear of the Statue of Liberty for love of your life!

CHILD MONAGHAN. But, grampa, when is it going to fall down? All I do is wait and wait.

MONAGHAN. [*With some uncertainty*] You've got to have faith.

CHILD MONAGHAN. But every kid in my class went to see it and now the ones that didn't are going tomorrow. And they all keep talking about it and all I do . . . Well, I can't keep telling them it's a swindle. I—I wish we could see it, grampa. It don't cost so much to go.

MONAGHAN. As long as you put it that way I'll have to admit I'm a bit curious meself as to how it's managed to stand upright so long. Tell you what I'll do. Barrin' wind, we'll chance it tomorrow.

CHILD MONAGHAN. Oh, gramp!

MONAGHAN. But! If anyone should ask you where we went you'll say—Staten Island. Are y' on?

CHILD MONAGHAN. Okay, sure. Staten Island.

MONAGHAN. [*Secretively*] We'll take the early boat, then. Mum's the word, now. For if old man Sheean hears that I went out there I'll have no peace from the thief the rest of m' life.

[*Music up and down*]

[*Boat whistles*]

CHILD MONAGHAN. Gee, it's nice ridin' on a boat, ain't it, grampa?

MONAGHAN. Never said there was anything wrong with the boat. Boat's all right. You're sure now that Georgie's father is takin' the kids in the afternoon.

CHILD MONAGHAN. Yeh, that's when they're going. Gee, look at those two sea gulls. Wee!—look at them swoop! They caught a fish!

MONAGHAN. What I can't understand is what all these people see in that statue that they'll keep a boat like this full makin' the trip, year in year out. To hear the newspapers talk, if the statue was gone we'd be at war with the nation that stole her the followin' mornin' early. All it is is a big high pile of French copper.

CHILD MONAGHAN. The teachers says it shows us that we got liberty.

MONAGHAN. Bah! If you've got liberty you don't need a statue to tell you you got it; and if you haven't got liberty no statue's going to do you any good tellin' you you got it. It was a criminal waste of the people's money. [*Quietly*] And just to prove it to you I'll ask this feller sitting right over there what he sees in it. You'll see what a madness the whole thing was. Say, mister?

ALF. Hey?

MONAGHAN. I beg your pardon. I'm a little strange here, and curious. Could you tell me why you're going to the Statue of Liberty?

ALF. Me? Well, I tell ya. I always wanted to take an ocean voyage. This is a pretty big boat—bigger than the ferries—so on Sundays, sometimes, I take the trip. It's better than nothing.

Grandpa and the Statue 225

18 Discussion How does Child Monaghan persuade his grandfather to take him to the statue? Why is Grandfather Monaghan really going?

19 Discussion What did the teacher mean by this?

20 Critical Thinking and Reading Do you agree with Grandfather Monaghan's opinion? Why or why not?

Humanities Note

Fine art, *The Wake of the Ferry II,* 1907, by John Sloan. John Sloan (1871–1951) was an American painter. Sloan began his art career as a newspaper illustrator for a Philadelphia newspaper. His paintings of scenes from the city life around him brought freshness and spontaneity to early twentieth-century American art.

The Wake of the Ferry II was probably inspired by Sloan's memory of the ferry rides he took each day to work when he lived in Philadelphia. The point of view is from the dark interior of the ferry looking out. The railing and a person are in silhouette against the water. The wake, churning behind the ferry, smooths out into the distance. Tugs and boats disappear into the mist and smoke of the scene. Painted in a broad Impressionistic style, this painting creates a mood of nostalgia and melancholy.

1. If you have ever taken a ferry ride, is this how it looked to you? How is it the same? How is it different?
2. If you have never taken a ferry ride, is this how you imagine it to be? Why or why not?

THE WAKE OF THE FERRY II, 1907
John Sloan
The Phillips Collection

226 Drama

Grammar in Action

In sentences with **normal word order,** the subject comes before the verb. Most sentences in English are in normal word order.

Sometimes, however, the verb comes before the subject in a sentence. This is called **inverted word order.** Inverted word order is found most often in questions. Arthur Miller uses inverted word order in the following questions:

"Do you feel her rockin'?"
"Well, what'd you think it was?"

Notice in both examples, the subject appears in the middle of a verb phrase.

Another situation when a sentence is usually in inverted word order is when the sentence begins with *here* or *there. There* is used as an adverb in the following example:

"There's a peanut stand!"

If you have trouble finding the subject in a sentence beginning with *here* and *there,* simply reword the sentence. If you have trouble finding the subject in a question, reword the sentence into a statement. In both cases the subject will appear in normal word order.

MONAGHAN. Thank you. [*To the kid*] So much for the great meaning of the statue, me boy. We'll talk to this lady standing at the rail. I just want you to understand why I didn't give Sheean me dime. Madam, would you be good enough to . . . Oh pardon me. [*To kid*] Better pass her by, she don't look so good. We'll ask that girl there. Young lady, if you'll pardon the curiosity of an old man . . . could you tell me in a few good words what it is about that statue that brings you out here?

GIRL. What statue?

MONAGHAN. Why, the Statue of Liberty up 'head. We're coming up to it.

GIRL. Statue of Liberty! Is this the Statue of Liberty boat?

MONAGHAN. Well, what'd you think it was?

GIRL. Oh, my! I'm supposed to be on the Staten Island ferry! Where's the ticket man? [*Going away*] Ticket man! Where's the ticket man?

CHILD MONAGHAN. Gee whiz, nobody seems to want to see the statue.

MONAGHAN. Just to prove it, let's see this fellow sitting on this bench here. Young man, say . . .

YOUNG MAN. I can tell you in one word. For four days I haven't had a minute's peace. My kids are screaming, my wife is yelling, upstairs they play the piano all day long. The only place I can find that's quiet is a statue. That statue is my sweetheart. Every Sunday I beat it out to the island and sit next to her, and she don't talk.

21 | **CHILD MONAGHAN.** I guess you were right, grampa. Nobody seems to think it means anything.

22 | **MONAGHAN.** Not only doesn't mean anything, but if they'd used the money to build an honest roomin' house on that island, the immigrants would have a place to spend the night, their valises wouldn't get robbed, and they—

MEGAPHONE VOICE. *Please keep your seats while the boat is docking. Statue of Liberty—all out in five minutes!*

CHILD MONAGHAN. Look down there, gramp! There's a peanut stand! Could I have some?

MONAGHAN. I feel the wind comin' up. I don't think we dare take the time.

[*Music up and down*]

CHILD MONAGHAN. Sssssseuuuuuww! Look how far you can see! Look at that ship way out in the ocean!

MONAGHAN. It is, it's quite a view. Don't let go of me hand now.

CHILD MONAGHAN. I betcha we could almost see California.

MONAGHAN. It's probably that grove of trees way out over there. They do say it's beyond Jersey.

CHILD MONAGHAN. Feels funny. We're standing right inside her head. Is that what you meant . . . July IV, MCD . . . ?

MONAGHAN. That's it. That tablet in her hand. Now shouldn't they have put Welcome All on it instead of that foreign language? Say! Do you feel her rockin'?

CHILD MONAGHAN. Yeah, she's moving a little bit. Listen, the wind!

[*Whistling of wind*]

MONAGHAN. We better get down, come on! This way!

CHILD MONAGHAN. No, the stairs are this way! Come on!

[*Running in echo. Then quick stop*]

Grandpa and the Statue 227

21 **Discussion** Did the Monaghans reach a legitimate conclusion after speaking to three people on the ferry?

22 **Discussion** Could Grandfather Monaghan be right? Would a rooming house have been a better project than a statue? Why or why not?

23 **Discussion** Can you really see California from the top of the statue? What does this comment reveal about Grandfather Monaghan?

Student Activity 1. Copy the following sentences and for each, underline the subject once and the verb or verbs twice.
1. Where is my red jacket?
2. There are three songs that I really like on the album.
3. How is Beatrice going to get to school?
4. Here is the book that you asked me to get you.

Student Activity 2. The following sentences are in normal word order. Rewrite them in inverted word order.
1. Your red sweater is here. (begin the sentence with *here*)
2. The movie was good. (rewrite the sentence as a question)

3. Alfonse did bring his football to the park. (Rewrite the sentence as a question.)
4. Twelve months are in a year. (Begin the sentence with *there*.)

24 Discussion In what way is it significant that a war veteran has visited the statue so many times?

25 Critical Thinking and Reading Why is the statue so important to the veteran? What does it stand for to him?

26 Discussion Why is Grandfather Monaghan upset and angry at Sheean?

27 Discussion What is it that Grandfather Monaghan finally understands?

28 Clarification The poem referred to here is "The New Colossus" by Emma Lazarus. It was inscribed on a tablet in the pedestal in 1903.

MONAGHAN. No, I told you they're the other way! Come!

VETERAN. [Calm, quiet voice] Don't get excited, pop. She'll stand.

MONAGHAN. She's swayin' awful.

VETERAN. That's all right. I been up here thirty, forty times. She gives with the wind, flexible. Enjoy the view, go on.

MONAGHAN. Did you say you've been up here forty times?

VETERAN. About that many.

MONAGHAN. What do you find here that's so interesting?

VETERAN. It calms my nerves.

MONAGHAN. Ah. It seems to me it would make you more nervous than you were.

VETERAN. No, not me. It kinda means something to me.

MONAGHAN. Might I ask what?

VETERAN. Well . . . I was in the Philippine War[2] . . . back in '98. Left my brother back there.

MONAGHAN. Oh, yes. Sorry I am to hear it. Young man, I suppose, eh?

VETERAN. Yeh. We were both young. This is his birthday today.

MONAGHAN. Oh, I understand.

VETERAN. Yeh, this statue is about the only stone he's got. In my mind I feel it is anyway. This statue kinda looks like what we believe. You know what I mean?

MONAGHAN. Looks like what we believe

. . . I . . . I never thought of it that way. I . . . I see what you mean. It does look that way. [Angrily] See now, boy? If Sheean had put it that way I'd a give him me dime. [Hurt] Now, why do you suppose he didn't tell me that? Come down now. I'm sorry, sir, we've got to get out of here.

[Music up and down]
[Footsteps under]

Hurry now, I want to get out of here. I feel terrible. I do, boy. That Sheean, that fool. Why didn't he tell me that? You'd think . . .

CHILD MONAGHAN. What does this say?

[Footsteps halt]

MONAGHAN. Why, it's just a tablet, I suppose. I'll try it with me spectacles, just a minute. Why, it's a poem, I believe . . . "Give me your tired, your poor, your huddled masses yearning to breathe free, the wretched refuse of your teeming shore. Send these, the homeless, tempest-tost to me, I lift . . . my lamp beside . . . the golden door!"[3] Oh, dear. [Ready to weep] It had Welcome All on it all the time. Why didn't Sheean tell me? I'd a given him a quarter! Boy . . . go over there and here's a nickel and buy yourself a bag of them peanuts.

CHILD MONAGHAN. [Astonished] Gramp!

MONAGHAN. Go on now, I want to study this a minute. And be sure the man gives you full count.

CHILD MONAGHAN. I'll be right back.

[Footsteps running away]

MONAGHAN. [To himself] "Give me your tired, your poor, your huddled masses . . . "

---

2. Philippine War: A brief conflict that took place between Spain and the United States in 1898 and is more frequently called the Spanish-American War.

3. "Give me your tired . . .": A quote from a poem about the statue written by the American poet Emma Lazarus (1849–1887) and engraved on the statue's pedestal.

THE UNVEILING OF THE STATUE OF LIBERTY
Edward Moran
Museum of the City of New York

Grandpa and the Statue 229

Humanities Note

Fine Art, *The Unveiling of the Statue of Liberty,* 1886, by Edward Moran. Edward Moran (1829–1901) was a British-born American marine painter. Moran came from a family of painters. Today he is remembered for his paintings of fisherman at work, harbors crowded with vessels, and lonely stretches of beach.

The painting, *The Unveiling of the Statue of Liberty,* was painted to commemorate festivities surrounding the placing of the statue in New York harbor. This is the second painting Moran did of this subject. The first, done ten years earlier, was a visualization of the statue in place and was used by the American Committee for fundraising. This painting is of a joyous scene with cannon smoke, waving flags, and a cheering crowd.

1. How would Monaghan have reacted to these festivities before visiting the statue?
2. How would Monaghan have reacted if he had first visited the statue?
3. Why has the statue caused so much celebration?

29 Discussion Why does Grandfather Monaghan press fifty cents into a crack in the pedestal? What does this indicate about his state of mind?

30 Critical Thinking and Reading How do you think most people feel about the Statue of Liberty? Why does the statue represent so much to so many?

Reader's Response What does the Statue of Liberty mean to you?

[*Music swells from a sneak to full, then under to background*]

YOUNG MONAGHAN. [*Soldier*] I ran over and got my peanuts and stood there cracking them open, looking around. And I happened to glance over to grampa. He had his nose right up to that bronze tablet, reading it. And then he reached into his pocket and kinda spied around over his eyeglasses to see if anybody was looking, and then he took out a coin and stuck it in a crack of cement over the tablet.

[*Coin falling onto concrete*]

It fell out and before he could pick it up I got a look at it. It was a half a buck. He picked it up and pressed it into the crack so it stuck. And then he came over to me and we went home. **29**

[*Music: Change to stronger, more forceful theme*]

That's why, when I look at her now through this window, I remember that time and that poem, and she really seems to say, Whoever you are, wherever you come from, Welcome All. Welcome Home. **30**

[*Music: Flare up to finish*]

THINKING ABOUT THE SELECTION
Recalling

1. Why does Grandfather refuse Sheean's request?
2. What does Grandfather predict will happen to the Statue after it is put up?
3. What does the veteran tell Grandfather that changes his mind about the Statue of Liberty?

Interpreting

4. What does the veteran mean by the words "This statue kinda looks like what we believe"?
5. Near the end of the play, why does Grandfather put the half dollar into the crack above the tablet?

6. In what way do you think Monaghan's memories of his grandfather's relationship with the Statue of Liberty have affected him?

Applying

7. Why do monuments sometimes hold special significance for Americans?

ANALYZING LITERATURE
Reading Dialogue

Dialogue is talk between characters. When reading the dialogue in a play, pay attention to what is said that advances the plot or that provides background information. Through the dia-

230   *Drama*

logue you must form pictures in your mind of the movements and gestures of the characters and the details of the setting. Above all, as you read dialogue, you must imagine what the characters sound like as they speak. Put simply, you have to create a little theater in your own mind.

Reread the first twenty-two lines of dialogue between Sheean and Grandfather (pages 220–221).

1. What conflict is revealed through the dialogue?
2. What impression of Grandfather do you get from these lines?
3. Which of the following phrases describes how Grandfather probably sounds when he speaks in the play?
   a. meek, mild, and easily led by others
   b. stubborn, defensive, ready to argue
   c. consistently nasty and unpleasant

CRITICAL THINKING AND READING
Making Inferences About Characters

You can make inferences about characters by imagining how they utter their lines—their tone of voice, their facial expressions, and the gestures that go with their words. For example, when Grandfather and young Monaghan go to look at the Statue of Liberty on a windy morning, Grandfather says, "Sure, and look at the sky blackening over! Feel it comin' up! Take your last look at the statue, boy. . . ." His tone of voice as he speaks these words is probably one of pleased excitement. His eyes are wide. He is straining to see any sign that the Statue is about to collapse. By picturing all of this, you can infer something about Grandfather's feelings. He desperately wants to be proved right in his opposition to the Statue of Liberty fund.

From each of the following lines, what can you infer about Grandfather's feelings?

1. "Not only will they get their dimes back, but Mr. Sheean and the whole crew that engineered the collection are going to rot in jail."
2. "Looks like what we believe . . . I . . . I never

thought of it that way. I . . . I see what you mean. It does look that way. See now, boy? If Sheean had put it that way I'd a give him me dime."

UNDERSTANDING LANGUAGE
Recognizing Dialect

Dialect is the special kind of speech used by a particular group of people or found in a particular region of a country. Unusual, even nonstandard expressions and pronunciations are two signs of dialect. Sheean's remark, "This here Frenchman has gone and built a fine statue of Liberty" is an example of the dialect of the working-class Irish people who came to America in the late nineteenth and early twentieth centuries.

1. Reread the dialogue between Grandfather and Sheean near the beginning of the play (pp. 220–222). What other examples of dialect can you find?
2. Reread Grandfather's speech beginning "Why, it's just a tablet . . ." near the end of the play. Find examples of dialect here.

THINKING AND WRITING
Writing Dialogue

Imagine that you are visiting the place you wrote about before reading the play. Grandfather Monaghan walks up to you, informs you that he sees nothing interesting or important about the place, and asks you what it means to you. Write a dialogue between you and Grandfather modeled on the dialogue in the play. Grandfather should be just as he is in the play. He asks questions and makes comments just as Arthur Miller's character would. You reply as if you, too, were a character in a play. By the end of the dialogue, Grandfather should come to understand your point of view. After you have finished your first draft, revise your dialogue, making sure it contains enough details to make Grandfather come alive. Finally, with one of your classmates in the role of Grandfather, act out your dialogue before your class.

Grandpa and the Statue 231

More About the Author Sir Arthur Conan Doyle was interested in many fields, including medicine, history, detective work, social causes, and the military. He used his broad-based knowledge to create the famous detective Sherlock Holmes and his faithful companion Dr. Watson. The characters are still so popular that there are Sherlock Holmes Societies in countries around the world. Michael and Mollie Hardwick are members of the Society in London. Ask students to discuss the popularity and longevity of certain fictional characters. Why do some fictional characters endure? How do they capture the public's imagination?

Literary Focus The playwright helps both the stage director and the reader by including brief stage directions and descriptions in between the dialogues. Point these out as they will help students visualize the settings and actions as they read the play.

Look For Your more advanced students might try elaborating on the description at the start of each scene. Students could use their imaginations to fill in missing details.

Writing/Prior Knowledge Have students discuss their ideas for staging either this play or another they have read. Then have them complete the freewriting assignment.

Vocabulary Have your less advanced students read these words aloud so that you can be sure they can pronounce them. It would be helpful for students to know the following words also: *hale* (p. 234); *contracted, contagious, practitioner, mediocre* (p. 236); *non-conductor* (p. 237); *methodical* (p. 238); and *dissimulation* (p. 244).

232

GUIDE FOR READING

The Dying Detective

Sir Arthur Conan Doyle (1859–1930) was born in Edinburgh, Scotland. While studying medicine there, he got to know Joseph Bell, a skillful surgeon who could diagnose a patient's occupation and character as well as disease. Bell was the model for Sherlock Holmes. Eventually, Doyle abandoned medicine to devote full time to writing. **Michael and Mollie Hardwick** are best-selling authors in England. Michael Hardwick is an expert on Sherlock Holmes and his creator. Mollie Hardwick has written numerous plays.

Staging

Staging a play means making it come to life on a stage. Staging includes acting, costumes, scenery, lighting, sound effects, and special effects. When you read a play, you should try your best to stage it in your imagination.

Look For

As you read *The Dying Detective,* read carefully the description at the start of each scene. Picture what you would see at a performance. Also, notice the stage directions. These statements in brackets will help you to picture the characters in action.

Writing

Think of a short story that you especially enjoyed and that you would make into a play. Make notes on how you would stage it. Your notes should answer these questions: In what place is the story set? What is the time of day? What objects should appear on stage, and how should they be arranged? What characters should be on stage at the start of the action? What do they look like? How are they dressed? What are they doing?

Vocabulary

Knowing the following words will help you as you read *The Dying Detective.*

masterful (mas′ tər fəl) *adj.*: Able to force one's will on others (p. 235)

incubation (in′ kyə bā′ shən) *n.*: The phase in a disease between the infection and the first appearance of symptoms (p. 236)

pathological (path′ ə läj′ i k′l) *adj.*: Due to, concerned with, or involving disease (p. 236)

complaint (kəm plānt′) *n.*: An illness (p. 236)

remonstrance (ri män′ strəns) *n.*: The act of protesting or pleading (p. 236)

implore (im plôr′) *v.*: Ask or beg earnestly (p. 238)

corroborate (kə räb′ ə rāt′) *v.*: Confirm, support (p. 243)

232   *Drama*

Objectives

1 To understand staging in a drama
2 To relate staging to dramatic purpose
3 To present a scene from a play
4 To write a memo specifying staging

Support Material

Teaching Portfolio
Teacher Backup, p. 355
Grammar in Action Worksheet, *Three Cases of Personal Pronouns,* p. 359
Usage and Mechanics Worksheet, p. 361
Vocabulary Check, p. 362
Analyzing Literature Worksheet, *Staging,* p. 363

Critical Thinking and Reading Worksheet, *Relating Staging to Dramatic Purpose,* p. 365
Selection Test, p. 367

The Dying Detective
from a story by Sir Arthur Conan Doyle
Michael and Mollie Hardwick

CHARACTERS, IN ORDER OF APPEARANCE

Mrs. Hudson
Dr. Watson
Sherlock Holmes
Culverton Smith: "A great yellow face, coarse-grained and greasy, with heavy double chin, and two sullen, menacing gray eyes which glared at me from under tufted and sandy brows . . ."
Inspector Morton: Middle-aged, tough, dressed in plain clothes.

Scene 1: Sherlock Holmes's bedroom, *afternoon*
Scene 2: The same, *dusk*
Scene 3: The same, *evening*

Scene 1

[SHERLOCK HOLMES'S *bedroom at 221B Baker Street. The essential features are: a bed with a large wooden head, placed crosswise on the stage, the head a foot or two from one side wall; a small table near the bed-head, on the audience's side, on which stand a carafe of water and a glass, and a tiny metal or ivory box; a window in the back wall, the curtains parted; and, under the window, a table or chest of drawers, on which stand a green wine bottle, some wine-glasses, a biscuit-barrel,[1] and a lamp. Of course, there may be further lamps and any amount of furnishing and clutter:* Holmes's *bedroom was adorned with pictures of celebrated criminals and littered with everything from tobacco pipes to revolver cartridges.*]

[*There is daylight outside the window.* SHERLOCK HOLMES *lies in the bed on his back, tucked up to the chin and evidently asleep. He is very pale.* MRS. HUDSON *enters followed by* DR. WATSON, *who is wearing his coat and hat and carrying his small medical bag.* MRS. HUDSON *pauses for a moment.*]

MRS. HUDSON. He's asleep, sir.

[*They approach the bed.* WATSON *comes round to the audience's side and looks down at* HOLMES *for a moment. He shakes his head gravely, then he and* MRS. HUDSON

---

1. **biscuit-barrel** (bis′ kit bar′ əl) *n.*: A British term for a container holding cookies or crackers.

The Dying Detective 233

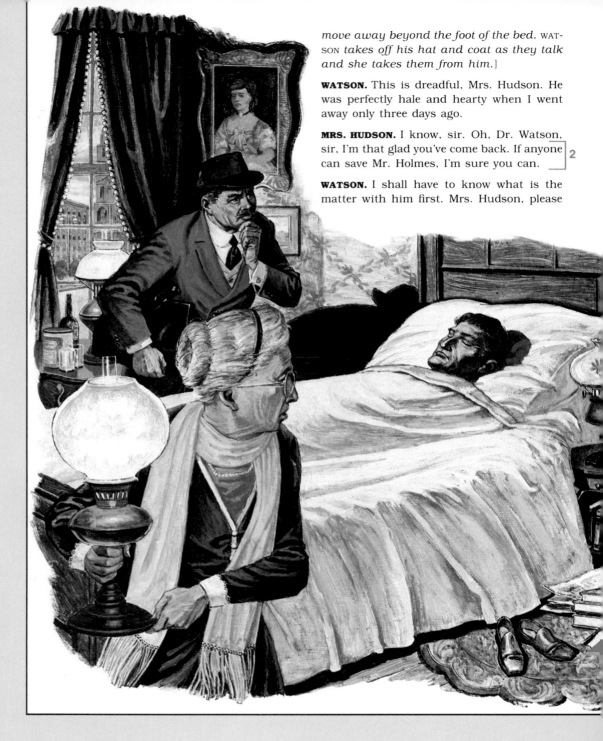

move away beyond the foot of the bed. WATSON *takes off his hat and coat as they talk and she takes them from him.*]

WATSON. This is dreadful, Mrs. Hudson. He was perfectly hale and hearty when I went away only three days ago.

MRS. HUDSON. I know, sir. Oh, Dr. Watson, sir, I'm that glad you've come back. If anyone can save Mr. Holmes, I'm sure you can. 2

WATSON. I shall have to know what is the matter with him first. Mrs. Hudson, please tell me, as quickly as you can, how it all came about.

MRS. HUDSON. Yes, sir. Mr. Holmes has been working lately on some case down near the river—Rotherhithe,[2] I think.

WATSON. Yes, yes. I know.

MRS. HUDSON. Well, you know what he is for coming in at all hours. I was just taking my lamp to go to my bed on Wednesday night when I heard a faint knocking at the street door. I . . . I found Mr. Holmes there. He could hardly stand. Just muttered to me to help him up to his bed here, and he's barely spoken since.

WATSON. Dear me!

MRS. HUDSON. Won't take food or drink. Just lies there, sleeping or staring in a wild sort of way.

WATSON. But, goodness gracious, Mrs. Hudson, why did you not send for another doctor in my absence?

---

2. Rotherhithe (räth′ ər hith)

MRS. HUDSON. Oh, I told him straightaway I was going to do that, sir. But he got so agitated—almost shouted that he wouldn't allow any doctor on the premises. You know how masterful he is, Dr. Watson.

WATSON. Indeed. But you could have telegraphed for me.

[MRS. HUDSON *appears embarrassed.*]

MRS. HUDSON. Well, sir . . .

WATSON. But you didn't. Why, Mrs. Hudson?

MRS. HUDSON. Sir, I don't like to tell you, but . . . well, Mr. Holmes said he wouldn't even have you to see him.

WATSON. What? This is monstrous! I, his oldest friend, and . . .

[HOLMES *groans and stirs slightly.*]

Ssh! He's waking. You go along, Mrs. Hudson, and leave this to me. Whether he likes it or not, I shall ensure that everything possible is done.

MRS. HUDSON. Thank you, sir. You'll ring if I can be of help.

[*She exits with* WATSON'S *things.* HOLMES *groans again and flings out an arm restlessly.* WATSON *comes to the audience's side of the bed and sits on it.*]

WATSON. Holmes? It's I—Watson.

HOLMES. [*Sighs*] Ahh! Well, Watson? We . . . we seem to have fallen on evil days.

WATSON. My dear fellow!

[*He moves to reach for* HOLMES'S *pulse.*]

HOLMES. [*Urgently*] No, no! Keep back!

WATSON. Eh?

HOLMES. Mustn't come near.

WATSON. Now, look here, Holmes . . . !

HOLMES. If you come near . . . order you out of the house.

The Dying Detective 235

3 Discussion Is this the way a sick person usually acts? What might Holmes's objection be to seeing a doctor?

4 Discussion Why would Holmes not want Watson, a doctor, to touch him? Does this make you suspicious?

5 **Critical Thinking and Reading** Considering that Holmes and Watson are such good friends, do you think Holmes might have a hidden motive for insulting Watson this way?

6 **Discussion** How do you know that Watson is a good friend to Holmes?

7 **Literary Focus** Part of the charm of the Sherlock Holmes series is the strain of subtle humor that runs through the stories. Since Conan Doyle was a doctor, he could easily have come up with the name of some real disease but chose instead to make up these absurd diseases.

WATSON. [*Defiantly*] Hah!

HOLMES. For your own sake, Watson. Contracted . . . a disease—from Sumatra.[3] Very little known, except that most deadly. Contagious by touch. So . . . must keep away.

WATSON. Utter rubbish. Holmes! Mrs. Hudson tells me she helped you to your bed. There's nothing the matter with her.

HOLMES. Period of . . . incubation. Only dangerous after two or three days. Deadly by now.

WATSON. Good heavens, do you suppose such a consideration weighs with me? Even if I weren't a doctor, d'you think it would stop me doing my duty to an old friend? Now, let's have a good look at you. [*He moves forward again.*]

HOLMES. [*Harshly*] I tell you to keep back!

WATSON. See here, Holmes . . .

HOLMES. If you will stay where you are, I will talk to you. If you will not, you can get out.

WATSON. Holmes! [*Recovering*] Holmes, you aren't yourself. You're sick and as helpless as a child. Whether you like it or not, I'm going to examine you and treat you.

HOLMES. [*Sneering*] If I'm to be forced to have a doctor, let him at least be someone I've some confidence in.

WATSON. Oh! You . . . After all these years, Holmes, you haven't . . . confidence in me?

HOLMES. In your friendship, Watson—yes. But facts are facts. As a medical man you're a mere general practitioner, of limited experience and mediocre qualifications.

WATSON. Well. . . ! Well, really!

---

3. **Sumatra** (soo mä′trə): A large island of Indonesia in the Pacific Ocean.

HOLMES. It is painful to say such things, but you leave me no choice.

WATSON. [*Coldly*] Thank you. I'll tell you this, Holmes. Such a remark, coming from you, merely serves to tell me what state your nerves are in. Still, if you insist that you have no confidence in me, I will not intrude my services. But what I shall do is to summon Sir Jasper Meek or Penrose Fisher, or any of the other best men in London.

HOLMES. [*Groans*] My . . . dear Watson. You mean well. But do you suppose they—any of them—know of the Tapanuli Fever?

WATSON. The Tap. . . ?

HOLMES. What do you yourself know of the Black Formosa Corruption?

WATSON. Tapanuli Fever? Black Formosa Corruption? I've never heard of either of 'em.

HOLMES. Nor have your colleagues. There are many problems of disease, many pathological possibilities, peculiar to the East. So I've learned during some of my recent researches. It was in the course of one of them that I contracted this complaint. I assure you, Watson, you can do nothing.

WATSON. Can't I? I happen to know, Holmes, that the greatest living authority on tropical disease, Dr. Ainstree, is in London just now.

HOLMES. [*Beseeching*] Watson!

WATSON. All remonstrance is useless. I am going this instant to fetch him.

[*He gets up.*]

HOLMES. [*A great cry*] No!

WATSON. Eh? Holmes . . . my dear fellow . . .

HOLMES. Watson, in the name of our old friendship, do as I ask.

WATSON. But . . .

HOLMES. You have only my own good at heart. Of course, I know that. You . . . you shall have your way. Only . . . give me time to . . . to collect my strength. What is the time now?

[WATSON *sits again and consults his watch.*]

WATSON. Four o'clock.

HOLMES. Then at six you can go.

WATSON. This is insanity!

HOLMES. Only two hours, Watson. I promise you may go then.

WATSON. Hang it, this is urgent, man!

HOLMES. I will see no one before six. I will not be examined. I shall resist!

WATSON. [*Sighing*] Oh, have it your own way, then. But I insist on staying with you in the meantime. You need an eye keeping on you, Holmes.

HOLMES. Very well, Watson. And now I must sleep. I feel exhausted. [*Drowsily*] I wonder how a battery feels when it pours electricity into a non-conductor?

WATSON. Eh?

HOLMES. [*Yawning*] At six, Watson, we resume our conversation. [*He lies back and closes his eyes.* WATSON *makes as though to move, but thinks better of it. He sits still, watching* HOLMES. *A slow black-out*]

Scene 2

[*The stage lights up again, though more dimly than before, to disclose the same scene. Twilight is apparent through the window.* HOLMES *lies motionless.* WATSON *sits as before, though with his head sagging, half asleep. His chin drops suddenly and he wakes with a jerk. He glances round, sees the twilight outside, and consults his watch. He yawns, flexes his arms,*

then proceeds to glance idly about him. His attention is caught by the little box on the bedside table. Stealthily, he reaches over and picks it up.]

HOLMES. [*Very loudly and urgently*] No! No, Watson, no!

WATSON. [*Startled*] Eh? What?

[HOLMES *starts up on to his elbow.*]

HOLMES. Put it down! Down this instant! Do as I say, Watson!

WATSON. Oh! All right, then. [*Putting the box down*]. Look here, Holmes, I really think . . .

HOLMES. I hate to have my things touched. You know perfectly well I do.

WATSON. Holmes . . . !

HOLMES. You fidget me beyond endurance. You, a doctor—you're enough to drive a patient into an asylum!

WATSON. Really!

HOLMES. Now, for heaven's sake, sit still, and let me have my rest.

WATSON. Holmes, it is almost six o'clock, and I refuse to delay another instant. [*He gets up determinedly.*]

HOLMES. Really? Watson, have you any change in your pocket?

WATSON. Yes.

HOLMES. Any silver?

WATSON. [*Fishing out his change*] A good deal.

HOLMES. How many half-crowns?

WATSON. Er, five.

HOLMES. [*Sighing*] Ah, too few, too few. However, such as they are, you can put them in your watch-pocket—and all the rest of your money in your left trouser-pocket. It will balance you so much better like that.

The Dying Detective   237

8 Discussion What other reasons might Holmes have for delaying Watson? Do you suspect that Holmes might have some larger plan in progress? Why or why not?

9 Discussion Would a dying man be this alert, strong, and emphatic?

10 Literary Focus Holmes's delirium is another touch of humor in the story.

238

11 Critical Thinking and Reading
What other purpose might a lamp burning in the window serve?

12 Discussion Based on this description, how much confidence do you have in the medical skills of Culverton Smith?

13 Enrichment When Conan Doyle finally did kill off Sherlock Holmes in his story *The Final Problem*, Holmes fans were in despair. The "death" of Holmes created such a furor that Conan Doyle's publisher prevailed upon him to bring Holmes back to life ten years later.

14 Critical Thinking and Reading
Why would Holmes ask a man with a grudge against him to save his life?

WATSON. Balance . . . ? Holmes, you're raving! This has gone too far . . . !

HOLMES. You will now light that lamp by the window, Watson, but you will be very careful that not for one instant shall it be more than at half flame.

WATSON. Oh, very well. [WATSON *goes to the lamp and strikes a match.*]

11

HOLMES. I implore you to be careful.

WATSON. [*As though humoring him*] Yes, Holmes.

[*He lights the lamp, carefully keeping the flame low. He moves to draw the curtains.*]

HOLMES. No, you need not draw the curtains.

[WATSON *leaves them and comes back round the bed.*]

So! Good. You may now go and fetch a specialist.

WATSON. Well, thank heaven for that.

HOLMES. His name is Mr. Culverton Smith, of 13 Lower Burke Street.

WATSON. [*Staring*] Eh?

HOLMES. Well, go on, man. You could hardly wait to fetch someone before.

WATSON. Yes, but . . . Culverton Smith? I've never heard the name!

12

HOLMES. Possibly not. It may surprise you to know that the one man who knows everything about this disease is not a medical man. He's a planter.

WATSON. A planter!

HOLMES. His plantation is far from medical aid. An outbreak of this disease there caused him to study it intensely. He's a very methodical man, and I asked you not to go before six because I knew you wouldn't find him in his study till then.

238 Drama

WATSON. Holmes, I . . . I never heard such a . . . !

HOLMES. You will tell him exactly how you have left me. A dying man. **13**

WATSON. No, Holmes!

HOLMES. At any rate, delirious. Yes, not dying, delirious. [*Chuckles*] No, I really can't think why the whole ocean bed isn't one solid mass of oysters.

WATSON. Oysters?

HOLMES. They're so prolific, you know.

WATSON. Great Heavens! Now, Holmes, you just lie quiet, and . . .

HOLMES. Strange how the mind controls the brain. Er, what was I saying, Watson?

WATSON. You were . . .

HOLMES. Ah, I remember. Culverton Smith. My life depends on him, Watson. But you will have to plead with him to come. There is no good feeling between us. He has . . . a grudge. I rely on you to soften him. Beg, Watson. Pray. But get him here by any means. **14**

WATSON. Very well. I'll bring him in a cab, if I have to carry him down to it.

HOLMES. You will do nothing of the sort. You will persuade him to come—and then return before him. [*Deliberately*] Make any excuse so as not to come with him. Don't forget that, Watson. You won't fail me. You never did fail me.

WATSON. That's all very well, Holmes, but . . .

HOLMES. [*Interrupting*] Then, shall the world be overrun by oysters? No doubt there are natural enemies which limit their increase. And yet . . . No, horrible, horrible!

WATSON. [*Grimly*] I'm going, Holmes. Say no more, I'm going!

Grammar in Action

Writers use pronouns to avoid constantly repeating nouns, thus adding variety and smoothness to their sentences. Personal pronouns change form according to their use in sentences. Use the **nominative case**—I, we, you, he, she, it, they—when a personal pronoun is used for the subject of a verb or for a predicate pronoun. Use the **objective case**—me, us, you, him, her, it, them—when a personal pronoun is used as a direct object, indirect object, or object of a preposition. Use the **possessive case**—my, mine, our, ours, you, yours, his, hers, its, their, theirs—to show ownership. Notice the use of personal pronouns in this example from *The Dying Detective.*

HOLMES. I implore you to be careful.
HOLMES. My life depends on him, Watson.

In the first sentence, the personal pronoun is used for the subject of the verb, therefore the nominative form, I, is used. In the second sentence, the possessive form, my, is used to show ownership, and the objective form, him, is used because it is the object of the preposition.

[He hurries out. HOLMES *remains propped up for a moment, staring after* WATSON, *then sinks back into a sleeping posture as the stage blacks out.*]

Scene 3

[*The stage lights up on the same scene.* HOLMES *lies still. It is now quite dark outside. After a moment* WATSON *bustles in, pulling off his coat. He pauses to hand it to* MRS. HUDSON, *who is behind him.*]

WATSON. Thank you, Mrs. Hudson. A gentleman will be calling very shortly. Kindly show him up here immediately.

MRS. HUDSON. Yes, sir.

[*She exits.* WATSON *approaches the bed.*]

HOLMES. [*Drowsily*] Watson?

WATSON. Yes, Holmes. How are you feeling?

HOLMES. Much the same, I fear. Is Culverton Smith coming?

WATSON. Should be here any minute. It took me some minutes to find a cab, and I almost expected him to have got here first.

HOLMES. Well done, my dear Watson.

WATSON. I must say, Holmes, I'm only doing this to humor you. Frankly, I didn't take to your planter friend at all.

HOLMES. Oh? How So?

WATSON. Rudeness itself. He almost showed me the door before I could give him your message. It wasn't until I mentioned the name, Sherlock Holmes . . .

15 **HOLMES.** Ah!

WATSON. Quite changed him—but I wouldn't say it was for the better.

HOLMES. Tell me what he said.

WATSON. Said you'd had some business dealings together, and that he respected your character and talents. Described you as an amateur of crime, in the way that he regards himself as an amateur of disease.

HOLMES. Quite typical—and surely, quite fair?

WATSON. Quite fair—if he hadn't put such sarcasm into saying it. No, Holmes, you said he bears you some grudge. Mark my words, as soon as he has left this house I insist upon calling a recognized specialist.

HOLMES. My dear Watson, you are the best of messengers. Thank you again.

WATSON. Not at all. Holmes, Holmes—let me help you without any of this nonsense. The whole of Great Britain will condemn me otherwise. Why, my cabmen both inquired anxiously after you; and so did Inspector Morton . . .

HOLMES. Morton? **16**

WATSON. Of the Yard. He was passing our door just now as I came in. Seemed extremely concerned.

HOLMES. Scotland Yard[4] concerned for me? How very touching! And now, Watson, you may disappear from the scene.

WATSON. Disappear! I shall do no such thing. I wish to be present when this Culverton Smith arrives. I wish to hear every word of this so-called medical expert's opinion.

HOLMES. [*Turning his head*] Yes, of course. Then I think you will just find room behind the head of the bed.

WATSON. What? Hide?

HOLMES. I have reason to suppose that his opinion will be much more frank and valuable if he imagines he is alone with me.

---

4. Scotland Yard: Headquarters of the London police, especially the detective bureau.

The Dying Detective 239

15 Discussion What impression do you form of Culverton Smith from Watson's description?

16 Critical Thinking and Reading Could it be more than coincidence that Inspector Morton was passing 221B Baker Street just as Watson returned from Smith's house? Why do you think the inspector is there?

Student Activity 1. Identify the case of the personal pronouns that are underlined in the following dialogue from *The Dying Detective.*

HOLMES. His plantation is far from medical aid. An outbreak of this disease there caused him to study it intensely. He's a very methodical man, and I asked you not to go before six because I knew you wouldn't find him in his study till then.

Student Activity 2. Complete each of the following sentences by writing the appropriate personal pronoun in the blank. Then indicate how each pronoun is used in the sentence.

1. _____ went fishing yesterday and didn't catch a thing.
2. Carla told _____ that the birthday party was next Saturday.
3. That black cat belongs to _____ .
4. It was Monica and _____ who went to the carnival with Dad and _____ .
5. _____ family went to _____ cousin's house to celebrate Thanksgiving.

17 Discussion What kind of friend is Dr. Watson? Do you think Holmes would be the type of person to make friends easily? Why or why not?

18 Reading Strategy Summarize what has happened so far in the story and predict what is going to happen next.

19 Literary Focus Holmes is being ironic here as he is saying one thing but meaning another.

20 Critical Thinking and Reading Why has Holmes called in someone whom he knows to be a murderer? Why did Smith come to Holme's bedside knowing that Holmes knows that he killed Victor Savage?

[*We hear the murmur of* MRS. HUDSON's *and* CULVERTON SMITH's *voices off-stage.*]

Listen! I hear him coming. Get behind the bed, Watson, and do not budge, whatever happens. *Whatever* happens, you understand?

17 | **WATSON.** Oh, all right, Holmes. Anything to please you. But I don't like this. Not at all.

18 | [*He goes behind the bed-head and conceals himself.* MRS. HUDSON *enters, looks round the room and then at* HOLMES. SMITH *enters behind her.*]

MRS. HUDSON. [*To* SMITH] Oh, Dr. Watson must have let himself out. No doubt he'll be back directly, sir.

SMITH. No matter, my good woman.

[MRS. HUDSON *bristles at this form of address.*]

You may leave me alone with your master.

MRS. HUDSON. As you wish—sir.

[*She sweeps out.* SMITH *advances slowly to the bed and stands at the foot, staring at the recumbent* HOLMES.]

SMITH. [*Almost to himself*] So, Holmes. It has come to this, then.

[HOLMES *stirs.* SMITH *chuckles and leans his arms on the bed-foot and his chin on them, continuing to watch* HOLMES.]

HOLMES. [*Weakly*] Watson? Who . . . ? Smith? Smith, is that you?

SMITH. [*Chuckles*]

HOLMES. I . . . I hardly dared hope you would come.

SMITH. I should imagine not. And yet, you see, I'm here. Coals of fire,[5] Holmes—coals of fire!

---

5. Coals of fire: A reference to a Biblical passage, Proverbs 25:21-22, about revenging oneself on an enemy.

HOLMES. Noble of you . . .

SMITH. Yes, isn't it?

19

HOLMES. I appreciate your special knowledge.

SMITH. Then you're the only man in London who does. Do you know what is the matter with you?

HOLMES. The same as young Victor—your cousin.

SMITH. Ah, then you recognize the symptoms. Well, then, it's a bad look-out for you. Victor was a strong, hearty young fellow—but a dead man on the fourth day. As you said at the time, it *was* rather surprising that he should contract an out-of-the-way Asiatic disease in the heart of London—a disease of which I have made such a very special study. [*Chuckles*] And now, you, Holmes. Singular coincidence, eh? Or are you going to start making accusations once again—about cause and effect and so on.

HOLMES. I . . . I knew you caused Victor Savage's death.

[SMITH *comes round the bed.*]

SMITH. [*Snarling*] Did you? Well, proving it is a different matter, Holmes. But what sort of a game is this, then—spreading lying reports about me one moment, then crawling to me for help the next?

20

HOLMES. [*Gasping*] Give . . . give me water. For . . . pity's sake, Smith. Water!

[SMITH *hesitates momentarily, then goes to the table and pours a glass from the carafe.*]

SMITH. You're precious near your end, my friend, but I don't want you to go till I've had a word with you.

[*He holds out the glass to* HOLMES *who struggles up feebly to take it and drinks.*]

HOLMES. [*Gulping water*] Ah! Thank . . . thank you. Please . . . do what you can for me. Only cure me, and I promise to forget.

SMITH. Forget what?

HOLMES. About Victor Savage's death. You as good as admitted just now that you had done it. I swear I will forget it.

SMITH. [*Laughs*] Forget it, remember it—do as you like. I don't see you in any witness-

21 Discussion How does Holmes get Smith to confess?

22 Discussion What is Holmes doing with Smith? Isn't his loss of memory rather sudden?

23 Discussion Were you surprised when Holmes sits up and asks Smith for his pipe? What had Holmes's plan been all along?

box, Holmes. Quite another shape of box, I assure you. But you must hear first how it came about.

HOLMES. Working amongst Chinese sailors. Down at the docks.

SMITH. Proud of your brains, aren't you? Think yourself smart? Well, you've met a smarter one this time.

[HOLMES *falls back, groaning loudly.*]

Getting painful, is it?

[HOLMES *cries out, writhing in agony.*]

SMITH. That's the way. Takes you as cramp, I fancy?

HOLMES. Cramp! Cramp!

SMITH. Well, you can still hear me. Now, can't you just remember any unusual incident—just about the time your symptoms began?

22 **HOLMES.** I . . . can't think. My mind is gone! Help me, Smith!

SMITH. Did nothing come to you through the post, for instance?

HOLMES. Post? Post?

SMITH. Yes. A little box, perhaps?

HOLMES. [*A shuddering groan*]

SMITH. [*Closer; deadly*] Listen! You *shall* hear me! Don't you remember a box—a little ivory box? [*He sees it on the table and holds it up.*] Yes, here it is on your bedside table. It came on Wednesday. You opened it—do you remember?

HOLMES. Box? Opened? Yes, yes! There was . . . sharp spring inside. Pricked my finger. Some sort of joke . . .

SMITH. It was no joke, Holmes. You fool! Who asked you to cross my path? If you'd only left me alone I would never have hurt you.

HOLMES. Box! Yes! Pricked finger. Poison!

SMITH. [*Triumphantly*] So you do remember.

242   *Drama*

Good, good! I'm glad indeed. Well, the box leaves this room in my pocket, and there's your last shred of evidence gone. [*He pockets it.*] But you have the truth now, Holmes. You can die knowing that I killed you. You knew too much about what happened to Victor Savage, so you must share his fate. Yes, Holmes, you are very near your end now. I think I shall sit here and watch you die. [*He sits on the bed.*]

HOLMES. [*Almost a whisper*] The . . . shadows . . . falling. Getting . . . so dark. I can't see. Smith! Smith, are you there? The light . . . for charity's sake, turn up the light!

[SMITH *laughs, gets up and goes to the light.*]

SMITH. Entering the valley of the shadow,[6] eh, Holmes? Yes, I'll turn up the light for you. I can watch your face more plainly, then. [*He turns the flame up full.*] There! Now, is there any *further* service I can render you?

HOLMES. [*In a clear, strong voice*] A match and my pipe, if you please.

[*He sits bolt upright.* SMITH *spins round to see him.*]

SMITH. Eh? What the devil's the meaning of this?

23

HOLMES. [*Cheerfully*] The best way of successfully acting a part is to *be* it. I give you my word that for three days I have neither tasted food nor drink until you were good enough to pour me out that glass of water. But it's the tobacco I find most irksome.

[*We hear the thud of footsteps running upstairs off-stage.*]

Hello, hello! Do I hear the step of a friend?

[INSPECTOR MORTON *hurries in.*]

---

6. valley of the shadow: A reference to death, based on Psalm 23 of the Bible, which mentions the "valley of the shadow of death."

MORTON. Mr. Holmes?

24 **HOLMES.** Inspector Morton, this is your man.

SMITH. What is the meaning of . . . ?

MORTON. Culverton Smith, I arrest you on the charge of the murder of one Victor Savage, and I must warn you that anything you say . . .

SMITH. You've got nothing on me? It's all a trick! A pack of lies!

[*He makes to escape.* MORTON *restrains him.*]

MORTON. Keep still, or you'll get yourself hurt!

SMITH. Get off me!

MORTON. Hold your hands out!

[*They struggle.* MORTON *gets out handcuffs and claps them on* SMITH's *wrists.*]

That'll do.

HOLMES. By the way, Inspector, you might add the attempted murder of one Sherlock Holmes to that charge. Oh, and you'll find a
25 small box in the pocket of your prisoner's coat. Pray, leave it on the table, here. Handle it gingerly, though. It may play its part at his trial.

[MORTON *retrieves the box and places it on the table.*]

SMITH. Trial! You'll be the one in the dock,[7] Holmes. Inspector, he asked me to come here. He was ill, and I was sorry for him, so
26 I came. Now he'll pretend I've said anything he cares to invent that will corroborate his insane suspicions. Well, you can lie as you like, Holmes. My word's as good as yours.

HOLMES. Good heavens! I'd completely forgot-
27 ten him!

MORTON. Forgotten who, sir?

---

7. dock (däk) *n.*: The place where the accused sits or stands in court.

HOLMES. Watson, my dear fellow! Do come out!

[WATSON *emerges with cramped groans.*]

I owe you a thousand apologies. To think that I should have overlooked you!

WATSON. It's all right, Holmes. Would have come out before, only you said, whatever happened, I wasn't to budge.

SMITH. What's all this about?

HOLMES. I needn't introduce you to my witness, my friend Dr. Watson. I understand you met somewhat earlier in the evening.

SMITH. You . . . you mean you had all this planned?

HOLMES. Of course. To the last detail. I think I may say it worked very well—with your as- 28 sistance, of course.

SMITH. Mine?

HOLMES. You saved an invalid trouble by giving my signal to Inspector Morton, waiting outside. You turned up the lamp.

[SMITH *and* WATSON *are equally flabbergasted.*]

MORTON. I'd better take him along now, sir. [*To* SMITH] Come on.

[*He bundles* SMITH *roughly toward the door.*]

We'll see you down at the Yard tomorrow, perhaps, Mr. Holmes?

HOLMES. Very well, Inspector. And many thanks.

WATSON. Goodbye, Inspector.

[MORTON *exits with* SMITH.]

[*Chuckles*] Well, Holmes?

HOLMES. Well, Watson, there's a bottle of claret over there—it is uncorked—and some biscuits in the barrel. If you'll be so kind, I'm badly in need of both.

[WATSON *goes to fetch them.*]

The Dying Detective 243

24 **Discussion** What had Inspector Morton been waiting for when Watson ran into him in the street?

25 **Discussion** How did Smith murder Savage and how had he tried to murder Holmes?

26 **Discussion** How convincing is Smith? Is his word as good as Holmes's?

27 **Discussion** What effect does Smith's denial of guilt have on Holmes?

28 **Reading Strategy** Summarize what Holmes's plan had been. Describe each character's part in the plan to catch Smith.

29 Discussion Why did Holmes not divulge his plan to Watson in advance?

30 Discussion What does Holmes really think of Watson's ability as a doctor? How was his behavior a measure of his respect for Watson?

31 Discussion Why had Smith killed Savage?

32 Critical Thinking and Reading How has this incident affected Holmes's and Watson's friendship? Do you think they'll act any differently toward each other in the future?

Reader's Response What aspect of Holmes's character do you find most admirable? Why?

WATSON. Certainly. You know, Holmes, all this seems a pretty, well, elaborate way to go about catching that fellow. I mean, taking in Mrs. Hudson—*and me*—like that. Scared us half to death.

HOLMES. It was very essential that I should make Mrs. Hudson believe in my condition. She was to convey it to you, and you to him.

WATSON. Well . . .

HOLMES. Pray do not be offended, my good Watson. You must admit that among your *many* talents, dissimulation scarcely finds a place. If you'd shared my secret, you would never have been able to impress Smith with the urgent necessity of coming to me. It was the vital point of the whole scheme. I knew his vindictive nature, and I was certain he would come to gloat over his handiwork.

[WATSON *returns with the bottle, glasses and barrel.*]

WATSON. But . . . but your appearance, Holmes. Your face! You really do look ghastly.

HOLMES. Three days of absolute fast does not improve one's beauty, Watson. However, as you know, my habits are irregular, and such a feat means less to me than to most men. For the rest, there is nothing that a sponge won't cure. Vaseline to produce the glistening forehead; belladonna[8] for the watering of the eyes; rouge over the cheekbones and crust of beeswax round one's lips . . .

WATSON. [*Chuckling*] And that babbling about oysters! [*He begins pouring the wine.*]

HOLMES. Yes. I've sometimes thought of writing a monograph on the subject of malingering.[9]

WATSON. But why wouldn't you let me near you? There was no risk of infection.

HOLMES. Whatever I may have said to the contrary in the grip of delirium, do you imagine that I have no respect for your medical talents? Could I imagine that you would be deceived by a dying man with no rise of pulse or temperature? At four yards' distance I *could* deceive you.

[WATSON *reaches for the box.*]

WATSON. This box, then . . .

HOLMES. No, Watson. I wouldn't touch it. You can just see, if you look at it sideways, where the sharp spring emerges as you open it. I dare say it was by some such device that poor young Savage was done to death. He stood between that monster and an inheritance, you know.

WATSON. Then it's true, Holmes! You . . . you might have been killed, too!

HOLMES. As you know, my correspondence is a varied one. I am somewhat on my guard against any packages which reach me. But I saw that by pretending he had succeeded in his design I might be enabled to surprise a confession from him. That pretense I think I may claim to have carried out with the thoroughness of a true artist.

WATSON. [*Warmly*] You certainly did, Holmes. Er, a biscuit? [*He holds out the barrel.*]

HOLMES. On second thought, Watson, no thank you. Let us preserve our appetite. By the time I have shaved and dressed, I fancy it will just be nice time for something nutritious at our little place in the Strand.[10]

[*They raise their glasses to one another and drink. The curtain falls.*]

---

8. belladonna (bel′ ə dän′ ə) *n.*: A poisonous European plant.
9. monograph on . . . malingering: A study on the subject of pretending to be ill in order to avoid work.

10. the Strand: London's main shopping and entertainment district; also, the name of a specific street within this district.

244 Drama

Closure and Extension

ANSWERS TO THINKING ABOUT THE SELECTION
Recalling

1. Holmes claims that the disease is highly contagious and that Watson is a mediocre doctor.
2. Holmes needs Watson to convince Smith that he is dying and that Smith must come to Baker Street. Therefore, Holmes must convince Watson that he is dying.
3. Smith reveals that he has killed Victor Savage and has tried to kill Holmes by sending him a poison box.
4. Holmes has Smith turn up the light to alert Inspector Morton that Smith had confessed and could be arrested.

Interpreting

5. Watson's hiding place was important because it allowed him to see and hear everything.
6. Holmes did not tell Watson because Watson is such a direct,

THINKING ABOUT THE SELECTION

Recalling

1. What reasons does Sherlock Holmes give for not letting Dr. Watson treat him?
2. How does this deception fit in with Holmes's plan to bring Culverton Smith to justice?
3. What criminal doings does Holmes trick Smith into revealing?
4. What is the real reason that Holmes asks Culverton Smith to turn up the light?

Interpreting

5. Explain the importance of Watson's hiding place in Holmes's plot against Smith.
6. Why did Holmes not tell Watson of his plan for proving Smith a murderer?
7. Explain the purpose of each of the various steps in Holmes's plot to trap Smith.

Applying

8. Compare and contrast Sherlock Holmes with another fictional detective or a detective from television or movies. How are Holmes's personality and methods similar or different?

ANALYZING LITERATURE

Understanding Staging

Two important aspects of **staging** are sets and props. A **set** is the arrangement of physical objects that make up scenery. In *The Dying Detective* only one set is needed because the scenery remains the same from start to finish. **Props** are the objects that actors use, often to advance the plot or reveal character.

1. Describe the set of "The Dying Detective."

2. How are the bed and the window important to the plot?
3. How are the box and the lamp important to it?

CRITICAL THINKING AND READING

Relating Staging to Dramatic Purpose

In a detective play such as *The Dying Detective,* the creation of suspense is important to the plot.

1. The setting of the play is confined to a single room. How does this single-room setting add to the suspense?
2. Picture Watson in his hiding place behind the bed. How does this use of staging add to the suspense?

SPEAKING AND LISTENING

Presenting a Scene from the Play

With your classmates and yourself in the roles of the characters, read *The Dying Detective* aloud in class. When you rehearse the reading, discuss how each role should be played. Evaluate one another's performance, and make suggestions for improvement.

THINKING AND WRITING

Writing About Staging

Imagine that you are the director for the drama club in your school. The club will be presenting a dramatic adaptation of the short story you have selected. Using the notes you made before reading this play, write a memo to the drama coach in which you describe in detail the staging you want. Specify the sets and props. Revise your memo. Is the description clear? Is it complete? Is the staging appropriate for the story?

---

honest, and simple person that he could never have persuaded Smith to come if he had known the plan.

7. Holmes first convinced Mrs. Hudson of his illness, who, in turn, alerted Watson. Holmes pretended to be delirious to ask Watson to do some seemingly irrational tasks. He pretended to be highly contagious so that Watson would not detect Holmes's normal pulse and temperature. He had Watson turn on the lamp in the win-

dow and had Smith turn it up to alert Inspector Morton. He pretended to have a loss of memory so that Smith would have to fill him in on the murder of Savage and on the way Smith intended to kill Holmes himself.

Applying

8. Answers will differ, but students may choose such detectives as Nancy Drew, Mike Hammer, Magnum, Simon Templar ("The Saint"), or Jane Marple.

ANSWERS TO ANALYZING LITERATURE

1. There is a bed with a large wooden headboard placed crosswise on the stage. There is a small table on the audience side near the bed's head. On the table are a carafe of water, a glass, and a small box. There is a window in the back wall with parted curtains. Under the window is a table or chest on which stands a green wine bottle, wine glasses, a tin of biscuits, and a lamp.

(Answers begin on p. 244)

2. The bed and window are important to the plot because Holmes must look like he's dying and so must be in bed, because Watson must hide behind the bed as a witness, and because Holmes must be able to summon Inspector Morton from the window.
3. The box and lamp are important because the box is how Smith intended to kill Holmes and the lamp is how Holmes intended to signal Morton.

ANSWERS TO CRITICAL THINKING AND READING

1. Answers will differ. Suggested Response: The single-room setting narrows the audience's focus and confines everyone's attention to Holmes and his visitors, thus heightening the suspense. Also, anything that is going to happen must happen in that one room, which creates a sense of anticipating and suspense.
2. Watson crouching behind the headboard adds to the suspense because the audience hopes he is hearing everything and fears he will be discovered by Smith.

Challenge Have students read the actual Conan Doyle story, *The Adventure of the Dying Detective,* and compare it with the Hardwicks' adaptation.

SPEAKING AND LISTENING

Because there are so few parts, in order to give all or most students a chance to read, you might reassign roles half way through the reading.

THINKING AND WRITING
Publishing Student Writing
Consider having students form groups to share and discuss their ideas for staging the play.

More About the Author Rod Serling began his career as a writer of realistic drama that commented on society. Television censorship forced him to turn to fantasy. Although his fantasies contained social commentary, they did not have the impact of his realistic dramas. Have students discuss the relationship between realistic drama and fantasy. Can fantasy ever present the biting social commentary that realistic drama can? What might fantasy allow a writer to do that could not be done in a standard drama?

Literary Focus Conflict is central to the plot of a drama. In fact, it is the conflict and its resolution that makes a play dramatic. Conflict is also central to real-life, daily situations. Identify some common examples of the fundamental kinds of conflict.

Look for As you explore the different kinds of conflict in the play, think about how they are like real-life conflicts and how they are different from real-life conflicts.

Writing/Prior Knowledge Have students identify the causes of the strange events in fantasies they have seen or read. Then have them complete the freewriting assignment.

Vocabulary It would be helpful for students to know the following words also: *nebulae, superstition, pan* (p. 247); *transfixed* (p. 248); *intelligible* (p. 249); *reflectively* (p. 250); *optimism, validity, antagonism,* (p. 251); *inexplicably, revelation, taut* (p. 252); *accusations, interjecting, overlapping, insomnia* (p. 253); *timorously* (p. 254); *idiosyncrasy* (p. 255); *materialized* (p. 256); *converging* (p. 258); *morass, silhouetted* (p. 259); and *variations* (p. 260).

The Monsters Are Due on Maple Street

Rod Serling (1924–1975) was born and raised in New York State. He is best known as the creator of the television series *The Twilight Zone*. In this series Serling often presented science-fiction plays that highlighted his views of life and society on this planet. *The Monsters Are Due on Maple Street* raises the question of whether the real monsters are up there or down here.

Conflict in Drama

Conflict, a struggle between opposing forces, is basic to drama. A play is usually based on one of the fundamental kinds of conflict. These include conflict between individuals, between an individual and society, between an individual and nature, and between an individual and himself or herself. Although one type of conflict will be central to a play, other types will often be present, too.

Look For

As you read this television play, notice the different kinds of conflict. Are characters in conflict with each other, with society, or with nature? Do certain characters seem torn apart, with one side of their personality warring against another side? Decide which type of conflict is the most important to the plot. Also, try to visualize how the various conflicts would appear when the play is broadcast on television.

Writing

The problems in this play start when strange happenings occur on Maple Street. Imagine that you and some friends are in a room in one of your homes. Strange things start to happen: Lights go on and off by themselves, chairs and tables move, weird noises are heard. Freewrite about the possible effects of such strange goings-on.

Vocabulary

Knowing the following words will help you as you read *The Monsters Are Due on Maple Street.*

flustered (flus′ tərd) *v.*: Made nervous (p. 249)

sluggishly (slug′ ish lē) *adv.*: As if lacking energy (p. 250)

assent (ə sent′) *n.*: Agreement (p. 250)

persistently (pər sist′ ənt lē) *adv.*: Firmly and steadily (p. 250)

defiant (di fi′ ənt) *adj.*: Boldly resisting (p. 251)

metamorphosis (met′ ə môr′ fə sis) *n.*: A change of form (p. 252)

scapegoat (skāp′ gōt′) *n.*: A person or group blamed for the mistakes or crimes of others (p. 256)

246   *Drama*

The Monsters Are Due on Maple Street

Rod Serling

CHARACTERS

Narrator
Figure One
Figure Two

Residents of Maple Street

Steve Brand	Charlie's Wife	Mrs. Goodman
Mrs. Brand	Tommy	Woman
Don Martin	Sally, Tommy's	Man One
Pete Van Horn	Mother	Man Two
Charlie	Les Goodman	

ACT I

[*Fade in on a shot of the night sky. The various nebulae and planet bodies stand out in sharp, sparkling relief, and the camera begins a slow pan across the Heavens.*]

NARRATOR'S VOICE. There is a fifth dimension beyond that which is known to man. It is a dimension as vast as space, and as timeless as infinity. It is the middle ground between light and shadow—between science and superstition. And it lies between the pit of man's fears and the summit of his knowledge. This is the dimension of imagination. It is an area which we call The Twilight Zone.

[*The camera has begun to pan down until it passes the horizon and is on a sign which reads "Maple Street." Pan down until we are shooting down at an angle toward the street below. It's a tree-lined, quiet residential American street, very typical of the small town. The houses have front porches on which people sit and swing on gliders, conversing across from house to house. Steve Brand polishes his car parked in front of his house. His neighbor, Don Martin, leans against the fender watching him. A Good Humor man rides a bicycle and is just in the process of stopping to sell some ice cream to a couple of kids. Two women gossip on the front lawn. Another man waters his lawn.*]

NARRATOR'S VOICE: Maple Street, U.S.A., late summer. A tree-lined little world of front

The Monsters Are Due on Maple Street 247

Motivation/Prior Knowledge Have students imagine that they live in a small, friendly town. They know all their neighbors, and they lead a simple, suburban life. Suddenly one day, strange events start to happen on the block and different people seem to be affected in different ways. Would they suspect one of their neighbors of causing the strange events? What would they say if their neighbors suspected them? Would the events bind the community together or tear it apart?

Thematic Idea Other selections that deal with fantasy and the unexplained include "The Third Wish," on page 3; "The Third Level," on page 127; "Rip Van Winkle," on page 133; "Hallucination," on page 179; "A Christmas Carol: Scrooge and Marley," on page 263 and "The Cremation of Sam McGee," on page 445.

Purpose-Setting Question How does fear change each of the characters in the play?

1 Discussion What do you think of the Narrator's definition of imagination?

2 Discussion What impression do you immediately form of Maple Street? What kind of street is it? Why might it make a good setting for a science-fiction story?

3 **Literary Focus** To create the feeling that these events are actually happening, the narrator pinpoints an exact time as if this were a documentary. Explain to students that a documentary shows real-life events with their exact times and places.

4 **Reading Strategy** What do you think the flash is? Predict what effect this event will have on the community.

porch gliders, hop scotch, the laughter of children, and the bell of an ice cream vendor.

[*There is a pause and the camera moves over to a shot of the Good Humor man and two small boys who are standing alongside, just buying ice cream.*]

NARRATOR'S VOICE. At the sound of the roar and the flash of light it will be precisely 6:43 P.M. on Maple Street.

[*At this moment one of the little boys, Tommy, looks up to listen to a sound of a tremendous screeching roar from overhead. A flash of light plays on both their faces and then it moves down the street past lawns and porches and rooftops and then disappears.*]

Various people leave their porches and stop what they're doing to stare up at the sky. Steve Brand, the man who's been pol-

ishing his car, now stands there transfixed, staring upwards. He looks at Don Martin, his neighbor from across the street.]

STEVE. What was that? A meteor?

DON. [*Nods*] That's what it looked like. I didn't hear any crash though, did you?

STEVE. [*Shakes his head*] Nope. I didn't hear anything except a roar.

MRS. BRAND. [*From her porch*] Steve? What was that?

STEVE. [*Raising his voice and looking toward porch*] Guess it was a meteor, honey. Came awful close, didn't it?

MRS. BRAND. Too close for my money! Much too close.

[*The camera pans across the various por-*

248 Drama

ches to people who stand there watching and talking in low tones.]

NARRATOR'S VOICE. Maple Street. Six-forty-four P.M. on a late September evening. [*A pause*] Maple Street in the last calm and reflective moment . . . before the monsters came!

[*The camera slowly pans across the porches again. We see a man screwing a light bulb on a front porch, then getting down off the stool to flick the switch and finding that nothing happens.*

Another man is working on an electric power mower. He plugs in the plug, flicks on the switch of the power mower, off and on, with nothing happening.

Through the window of a front porch, we see a woman pushing her finger back and forth on the dial hook. Her voice is indistinct and distant, but intelligible and repetitive.]

WOMAN. Operator, operator, something's wrong on the phone, operator!

[*Mrs. Brand comes out on the porch and calls to Steve.*]

MRS. BRAND. [*Calling*] Steve, the power's off. I had the soup on the stove and the stove just stopped working.

WOMAN. Same thing over here. I can't get anybody on the phone either. The phone seems to be dead.

[*We look down on the street as we hear the voices creep up from below, small, mildly disturbed voices highlighting these kinds of phrases:*]

VOICES.
Electricity's off.
Phone won't work.
Can't get a thing on the radio.
My power mower won't move, won't work at all.

Radio's gone dead!

[*Pete Van Horn, a tall, thin man, is seen standing in front of his house.*]

VAN HORN. I'll cut through the back yard . . . See if the power's still on on Floral Street. I'll be right back!

[*He walks past the side of his house and disappears into the back yard.*

The camera pans down slowly until we're looking at ten or eleven people standing around the street and overflowing to the curb and sidewalk. In the background is Steve Brand's car.]

STEVE. Doesn't make sense. Why should the power go off all of a sudden, and the phone line?

DON. Maybe some sort of an electrical storm or something.

CHARLIE. That don't seem likely. Sky's just as blue as anything. Not a cloud. No lightning. No thunder. No nothing. How could it be a storm?

WOMAN. I can't get a thing on the radio. Not even the portable.

[*The people again murmur softly in wonderment and question.*]

CHARLIE. Well, why don't you go downtown and check with the police, though they'll probably think we're crazy or something. A little power failure and right away we get all flustered and everything.

STEVE. It isn't just the power failure, Charlie. If it was, we'd still be able to get a broadcast on the portable.

[*There's a murmur of reaction to this. Steve looks from face to face and then over to his car.*]

STEVE. I'll run downtown. We'll get this all straightened out.

The Monsters Are Due on Maple Street 249

5 Discussion How does the Narrator build suspense here? What impact does his statement have on you?

6 Critical Thinking and Reading Do you think there is a logical explanation for all this? What may have caused all these things to stop working at the same time?

7 **Discussion** How is the idea of aliens introduced? At this point, do you believe aliens are causing the problems?

8 **Critical Thinking and Reading** Why do the adults stop to listen to Tommy? What do you learn from the stage directions about what Steve is really feeling?

[*He walks over to the car, gets in it, turns the key. Looking through the open car door, we see the crowd watching him from the other side. Steve starts the engine. It turns over sluggishly and then just stops dead. He tries it again and this time he can't get it to turn over. Then, very slowly and reflectively, he turns the key back to "off" and slowly gets out of the car.*

The people stare at Steve. He stands for a moment by the car, then walks toward the group.]

STEVE. I don't understand it. It was working fine before . . .

DON. Out of gas?

STEVE. [*Shakes his head*] I just had it filled up.

WOMAN. What's it mean?

CHARLIE. It's just as if . . . as if everything had stopped. [*Then he turns toward* STEVE.] We'd better walk downtown. [*Another murmur of assent at this.*]

STEVE. The two of us can go, Charlie. [*He turns to look back at the car.*] It couldn't be the meteor. A meteor couldn't do *this*.

[*He and Charlie exchange a look, then they start to walk away from the group.*

We see Tommy, a serious-faced fourteen-year-old in spectacles who stands a few feet away from the group. He is halfway between them and the two men, who start to walk down the sidewalk.]

7 **TOMMY.** Mr. Brand . . . you better not!

STEVE. Why not?

TOMMY. They don't want you to.

[*Steve and Charlie exchange a grin, and Steve looks back toward the boy.*]

STEVE. Who doesn't want us to?

250   Drama

TOMMY. [*Jerks his head in the general direction of the distant horizon*] Them!

STEVE. Them?

CHARLIE. Who are them?

TOMMY. [*Very intently*] Whoever was in that thing that came by overhead.

[*Steve knits his brows for a moment, cocking his head questioningly. His voice is intense.*]

STEVE. What?

TOMMY. Whoever was in that thing that came over. I don't think they want us to leave here.

[*Steve leaves Charlie and walks over to the boy. He kneels down in front of him. He forces his voice to remain gentle. He reaches out and holds the boy.*]

STEVE. What do you mean? What are you talking about?

TOMMY. They don't want us to leave. That's why they shut everything off.

STEVE. What makes you say that? Whatever gave you that idea?

WOMAN. [*From the crowd*] Now isn't that the craziest thing you ever heard?

TOMMY. [*Persistently but a little intimidated by the crowd*] It's always that way, in every story I ever read about a ship landing from outer space.

WOMAN. [*To the boy's mother, Sally, who stands on the fringe of the crowd*] From outer space, yet! Sally, you better get that boy of yours up to bed. He's been reading too many comic books or seeing too many movies or something.

SALLY. Tommy, come over here and stop that kind of talk.

STEVE. Go ahead, Tommy. We'll be right

8

Grammar in Action

Subjects and verbs must agree in number. It often helps to remember that with most nouns you add s to make the noun plural, whereas with most verbs you add s to make the verb singular. Notice that the subjects and verbs agree in number in the following sentences:

Steve and *Charlie exchange* a grin, and *Steve looks* back toward the boy.
He walks over to the car, *gets* in it, *turns* the key.

The first sentence is compound. Notice that the verb in the first clause does not have an s because the subject is plural, while the verb in the second clause does have an s because the subject is singular. The subject of the second sentence is singular, therefore, the series of verbs that follow all end with s.

back. And you'll see. That wasn't any ship or anything like it. That was just a . . . a meteor or something. Likely as not—[*He turns to the group, now trying to weight his words with an optimism he obviously doesn't feel but is desperately trying to instill in himself as well as the others.*] No doubt it did have something to do with all this power failure and the rest of it. Meteors can do some crazy things. Like sunspots.

9 **DON.** [*Picking up the cue*] Sure. That's the kind of thing—like sunspots. They raise Cain with[1] radio reception all over the world. And this thing being so close—why, there's no telling the sort of stuff it can do. [*He wets his lips, smiles nervously.*] Go ahead, Charlie. You and Steve go into town and see if that isn't what's causing it all.

[*Steve and Charlie again walk away from the group down the sidewalk. The people watch silently.*
Tommy stares at them, biting his lips, and finally calling out again.]

TOMMY. *Mr. Brand!*

[*The two men stop again. Tommy takes a step toward them.*]

TOMMY. Mr. Brand . . . please don't leave here.

[*Steve and Charlie stop once again and turn toward the boy. There's a murmur in the crowd, a murmur of irritation and concern as if the boy were bringing up fears that shouldn't be brought up; words which carried with them a strange kind of validity that came without logic but nonetheless registered and had meaning and effect. Again we hear a murmur of reaction from the crowd.*
Tommy is partly frightened and partly defiant as well.]

---

1. raise Cain with: Badly disturb.

TOMMY. You might not even be able to get to town. It was that way in the story. Nobody could leave. Nobody except—

STEVE. Except who?

TOMMY. Except the people they'd sent down ahead of them. They looked just like humans. And it wasn't until the ship landed that— **10**

[*The boy suddenly stops again, conscious of the parents staring at them and of the sudden hush of the crowd.*]

SALLY. [*In a whisper, sensing the antagonism of the crowd*] Tommy, please son . . . honey, don't talk that way—

MAN ONE. That kid shouldn't talk that way . . . and we shouldn't stand here listening to him. Why this is the craziest thing I ever heard of. The kid tells us a comic book plot and here we stand listening—

[*Steve walks toward the camera, stops by the boy.*]

STEVE. Go ahead, Tommy. What kind of story was this? What about the people that they sent out ahead?

TOMMY. That was the way they prepared things for the landing. They sent four people. A mother and a father and two kids who looked just like humans . . . but they weren't.

[*There's another silence as Steve looks toward the crowd and then toward Tommy. He wears a tight grin.*]

STEVE. Well, I guess what we'd better do then is to run a check on the neighborhood and see which ones of us are really human. **11**

[*There's laughter at this, but it's a laughter that comes from a desperate attempt to lighten the atmosphere. It's a release kind*

The Monsters Are Due on Maple Street 251

9 **Clarification** A meteor is commonly called a shooting or falling star. Such phenonema as precipitation, lightning, and rainbows are sometimes attributed to meteors. Sunspots are cooler areas on the surface of the sun that appear as dark spots. They are associated with magnetic disturbances in Earth's atmosphere.

10 **Literary Focus** The suspense becomes more urgent now with the suggestion that the monsters might look "just like humans." This concept sets the stage for the paranoia that will shortly engulf Maple Street.

11 **Critical Thinking and Reading** How much truth do you think there is in Steve's joke?

12 Discussion Discuss the importance of the stage directions in this play. Why are they so extensive and detailed?

13 Discussion Do you think it's significant that Les Goodman didn't come out to look at "that thing that flew overhead"? Does this make him an "oddball"?

14 Discussion Why does Don think that Goodman can explain the strange events on Maple Street? Do you think it's meaningful that the other male characters are identified by their first names while Les Goodman is identified by his surname? Why?

of laugh. The people look at one another in the middle of their laughter.]

CHARLIE. There must be somethin' better to do than stand around makin' bum jokes about it. [Rubs his jaw nervously] I wonder if Floral Street's got the same deal we got. [He looks past the houses.] Where is Pete Van Horn anyway? Didn't he get back yet?

[Suddenly there's the sound of a car's engine starting to turn over.
We look across the street toward the driveway of Les Goodman's house. He's at the wheel trying to start the car.]

SALLY. Can you get it started, Les? [He gets out of the car, shaking his head.]

GOODMAN. No dice.

[He walks toward the group. He stops suddenly as behind him, inexplicably and with a noise that inserts itself into the silence, the car engine starts up all by itself. Goodman whirls around to stare toward it.
The car idles roughly, smoke coming from the exhaust, the frame shaking gently.
Goodman's eyes go wide, and he runs over to his car.
The people stare toward the car.]

MAN ONE. He got the car started somehow. He got his car started!

[The camera pans along the faces of the people as they stare, somehow caught up by this revelation and somehow, illogically, wildly, frightened.]

WOMAN. How come his car just up and started like that?

SALLY. All by itself. He wasn't anywheres near it. It started all by itself.

[Don approaches the group, stops a few feet away to look toward Goodman's car and then back toward the group.]

DON. And he never did come out to look at that thing that flew overhead. He wasn't even interested. [He turns to the faces in the group, his face taut and serious.] Why? Why didn't he come out with the rest of us to look?

CHARLIE. He always was an oddball. Him and his whole family. Real oddball.

DON. What do you say we ask him?

[The group suddenly starts toward the house. In this brief fraction of a moment they take the first step toward performing a metamorphosis that changes people from a group into a mob. They begin to head purposefully across the street toward the house at the end. Steve stands in front of them. For a moment their fear almost turns their walk into a wild stampede, but Steve's voice, loud, incisive, and commanding, makes them stop.]

STEVE. Wait a minute . . . wait a minute! Let's not be a mob!

[The people stop as a group, seem to pause for a moment, and then much more quietly and slowly start to walk across the street. Goodman stands alone facing the people.]

GOODMAN. I just don't understand it. I tried to start it and it wouldn't start. You saw me. All of you saw me.

[And now, just as suddenly as the engine started, it stops and there's a long silence that is gradually intruded upon by the frightened murmuring of the people.]

GOODMAN. I don't understand. I swear . . . I don't understand. What's happening?

DON. Maybe you better tell us. Nothing's working on this street. Nothing. No lights, no power, no radio. [And then meaningfully] Nothing except one car—yours!

[*The people pick this up and now their murmuring becomes a loud chant filling the air with accusations and demands for action. Two of the men pass Don and head toward Goodman, who backs away, backing into his car and now at bay.*]

GOODMAN. Wait a minute now. You keep your distance—all of you. So I've got a car that starts by itself—well, that's a freak thing, I admit it. But does that make me some kind of a criminal or something? I don't know why the car works—it just does!

[*This stops the crowd momentarily and now Goodman, still backing away, goes toward his front porch. He goes up the steps and then stops to stand facing the mob.*

We see a long shot of Steve as he comes through the crowd.]

STEVE. [*Quietly*] We're all on a monster kick, Les. Seems that the general impression holds that maybe one family isn't what we think they are. Monsters from outer space or something. Different than us. Fifth columnists[2] from the vast beyond. [*He chuckles.*] You know anybody that might fit that description around here on Maple Street?

GOODMAN. What is this, a gag or something? This a practical joke or something?

[*We see a close-up of the porch light as it suddenly goes out. There's a murmur from the group.*]

GOODMAN. Now I suppose that's supposed to incriminate me! The light goes on and off. That really does it, doesn't it?

[*He looks around the faces of the people.*] I just don't understand this—[*He wets his lips, looking from face to face.*] Look, you all know me. We've lived here five years. Right

---

2. Fifth columnists: People who help an invading enemy from within their own country.

in this house. We're no different from any of the rest of you! We're no different at all. Really . . . this whole thing is just . . . just weird—

WOMAN. Well, if that's the case, Les Goodman, explain why—[*She stops suddenly, clamping her mouth shut.*]

GOODMAN. [*Softly*] Explain what?

STEVE. [*Interjecting*] Look, let's forget this—

CHARLIE. [*Overlapping him*] Go ahead, let her talk. What about it? Explain what?

WOMAN. [*A little reluctantly*] Well . . . sometimes I go to bed late at night. A couple of times . . . a couple of times I'd come out on the porch and I'd see Mr. Goodman here in the wee hours of the morning standing out in front of his house . . . looking up at the sky. [*She looks around the circle of faces.*] That's right, looking up at the sky as if . . . as if he were waiting for something. [*A pause*] As if he were looking for something.

[*There's a murmur of reaction from the crowd again.*

We cut suddenly to a group shot. As Goodman starts toward them, they back away frightened.]

GOODMAN. You know really . . . this is for laughs. You know what I'm guilty of? [*He laughs.*] I'm guilty of insomnia. Now what's the penalty for insomnia? [*At this point the laugh, the humor, leaves his voice.*] Did you hear what I said? I said it was insomnia. [*A pause as he looks around, then shouts.*] I said it was insomnia! You fools. You scared, frightened rabbits, you. You're sick people, do you know that? You're sick people—all of you! And you don't even know what you're starting because let me tell you . . . let me tell you—this thing you're starting—that

15 Critical Thinking and Reading How did this idea take hold among the neighbors? It began as a youngster's idea based on his science-fiction reading. Why is it now the "general impression"?

16 Critical Thinking and Reading How is Goodman's reaction typical of victims of prejudice?

17 Discussion How unusual is it for someone to stand outside early in the morning? Does this prove Goodman is an alien? Would this seem strange under different circumstances?

18 **Discussion** What does Good-man mean by this? What could his neighbors' thinking lead to?

19 **Discussion** What do the neighbors do to Goodman? Why is Sally uncomfortable with that?

20 **Enrichment** Tell students about Orson Welles's 1938 radio broadcast of H. G. Wells's *The War of the Worlds*. The actors were so convincing that people believed that the program was a live account of an actual invasion of Earth from outer space.

should frighten you. As God is my witness
18 . . . you're letting something begin here that's a nightmare!

ACT II

[*We see a medium shot of the Goodman entry hall at night. On the side table rests an unlit candle. Mrs. Goodman walks into the scene, a glass of milk in hand. She sets the milk down on the table, lights the candle with a match from a box on the table, picks up the glass of milk, and starts out of scene.*

Mrs. Goodman comes through her porch door, glass of milk in hand. The entry hall, with table and lit candle, can be seen behind her.

Outside, the camera slowly pans down the sidewalk, taking in little knots of people who stand around talking in low voices. At the end of each conversation they look toward Les Goodman's house. From the various houses we can see candlelight but no electricity, and there's an all-pervading quiet that blankets the whole area, disturbed only by the almost whispered voices of the people as they stand around. The camera pans over to one group where Charlie stands. He stares across at Goodman's house.

We see a long shot of the house. Two men stand across the street in almost sentry-like poses. Then we see a medium shot of a group of people.]

19 **SALLY.** [*A little timorously*] It just doesn't seem right, though, keeping watch on them. Why . . . he was right when he said he was one of our neighbors. Why, I've known Ethel Goodman ever since they moved in. We've been good friends—

CHARLIE. That don't prove a thing. Any guy who'd spend his time lookin' up at the sky early in the morning—well, there's something wrong with that kind of person. There's something that ain't legitimate. Maybe under normal circumstances we could let it go by, but these aren't normal circumstances. Why, look at this street! Nothin' but candles. Why, it's like goin' back into the dark ages or somethin'!

[*Steve walks down the steps of his porch, walks down the street over to Les Goodman's house, and then stops at the foot of the steps. Goodman stands there, his wife behind him, very frightened.*]

GOODMAN. Just stay right where you are, Steve. We don't want any trouble, but this time if anybody sets foot on my porch, that's what they're going to get—trouble!

STEVE. Look, Les—

GOODMAN. I've already explained to you people. I don't sleep very well at night sometimes. I get up and I take a walk and I look up at the sky. I look at the stars!

MRS. GOODMAN. That's exactly what he does. Why this whole thing, it's . . . it's some kind of madness or something.

20

STEVE. [*Nods grimly*] That's exactly what it is—some kind of madness.

CHARLIE'S VOICE. [*Shrill, from across the street*] You best watch who you're seen with, Steve! Until we get this all straightened out, you ain't exactly above suspicion yourself.

STEVE. [*Whirling around toward him*] Or you, Charlie. Or any of us, it seems. From age eight on up!

WOMAN. What I'd like to know is—what are we gonna do? Just stand around here all night?

CHARLIE. There's nothin' else we can do! [*He turns back looking toward Steve and Good-*

man again.] One of 'em'll tip their hand. They got to.

STEVE. [*Raising his voice*] There's something you can do, Charlie. You could go home and keep your mouth shut. You could quit strutting around like a self-appointed hanging judge and just climb into bed and forget it.

CHARLIE. You sound real anxious to have that happen, Steve. I think we better keep our eye on you too!

21 **DON.** [*As if he were taking the bit in his teeth, takes a hesitant step to the front*] I think everything might as well come out now. [*He turns toward Steve.*] Your wife's

done plenty of talking, Steve, about how odd you are!

CHARLIE. [*Picking this up, his eyes widening*] Go ahead, tell us what she's said.

[*We see a long shot of Steve as he walks toward them from across the street.*]

STEVE. Go ahead, what's my wife said? Let's get it all out. Let's pick out every idiosyncrasy of every single man, woman, and child on the street. And then we might as well set up some kind of kangaroo court.[1] How about a firing squad at dawn, Charlie, so we can

---

1. kangaroo court: An unofficial court that does not follow normal rules.

The Monsters Are Due on Maple Street 255

22 Discussion Why does Steve say this? Do his neighbors recognize the absurdity of his statements?

23 Enrichment Tell students about the Salem, Massachusetts, witch trials, which were precipitated by the accusations of children. Arthur Miller's play *The Crucible* depicts the atmosphere in Salem at the time and shows that people condemned each other to save themselves. Ask students if they can draw a parallel between the Salem witch trials and the characters' actions in this play.

24 Discussion What role has Tommy played in the community's hysteria?

get rid of all the suspects? Narrow them down. Make it easier for you.

DON. There's no need gettin' so upset, Steve. It's just that . . . well . . . Myra's talked about how there's been plenty of nights you spent hours down in your basement workin' on some kind of radio or something. Well, none of us have ever seen that radio—

[*By this time Steve has reached the group. He stands there defiantly close to them.*]

CHARLIE. Go ahead, Steve. What kind of "radio set" you workin' on? I never seen it. Neither has anyone else. Who you talk to on that radio set? And who talks to you?

22 **STEVE.** I'm surprised at you, Charlie. How come you're so dense all of a sudden? [*A pause*] Who do I talk to? I talk to monsters from outer space. I talk to three-headed green men who fly over here in what look like meteors.

[*Steve's wife steps down from the porch, bites her lip, calls out.*]

MRS. BRAND. Steve! Steve, please. [*Then looking around, frightened, she walks toward the group.*] It's just a ham radio set, that's all. I bought him a book on it myself. It's just a ham radio set. A lot of people have them. I can show it to you. It's right down in the basement.

STEVE. [*Whirls around toward her*] Show them nothing! If they want to look inside our house—let them get a search warrant.

CHARLIE. Look, buddy, you can't afford to—

23 **STEVE.** [*Interrupting*] Charlie, don't tell me what I can afford! And stop telling me who's dangerous and who isn't and who's safe and who's a menace. [*He turns to the group and shouts.*] And you're with him, too—all of you! You're standing here all set to crucify—all set to find a scapegoat—all desperate to point

some kind of a finger at a neighbor! Well now look, friends, the only thing that's gonna happen is that we'll eat each other up alive—

[*He stops abruptly as Charlie suddenly grabs his arm.*]

CHARLIE. [*In a hushed voice*] That's not the only thing that can happen to us.

[*Cut to a long shot looking down the street. A figure has suddenly materialized in the gloom and in the silence we can hear the clickety-clack of slow, measured footsteps on concrete as the figure walks slowly toward them. One of the women lets out a stifled cry. The young mother grabs her boy as do a couple of others.*]

TOMMY. [*Shouting, frightened*] It's the monster! It's the monster! **24**

[*Another woman lets out a wail and the people fall back in a group, staring toward the darkness and the approaching figure.*

We see a medium group shot of the people as they stand in the shadows watching. Don Martin joins them, carrying a shotgun. He holds it up.*]

DON. We may need this.

STEVE. A shotgun? [*He pulls it out of Don's hand.*] Good Lord—will anybody think a thought around here? Will you people wise up? What good would a shotgun do against—

[*Now Charlie pulls the gun from Steve's hand.*]

CHARLIE. No more talk, Steve. You're going to talk us into a grave! You'd let whatever's out there walk right over us, wouldn't yuh? Well, some of us won't!

[*He swings the gun around to point it toward the sidewalk.*

The dark figure continues to walk toward them.*]

256   Drama

Grammar in Action

To make their dialogue realistic, writers have their characters speak as real people speak. Because we use informal language in so much of our everyday conversation, dialogue is written to reflect this. Sentence fragments, slang words, and improper usage are all acceptable in dialogue. Another aspect of informal speech is the use of contractions—shortened forms of words and phrases. Notice how contractions make the following sentences more informal.

Carol is not going home as planned, she is going to the beach.
Carol isn't going home as planned, she's going to the beach.

To form a contraction, use an **apostrophe** to indicate the position of the missing letter or letters. Rod Serling uses contractions in the dialogue of *The Monsters Are Due on Maple Street.*

What kind of "radio set" you workin' on?
It's just a ham radioset, that's all.
And stop telling me who's dangerous and who isn't and who's safe and who's a menace.

Notice that the first contraction is a shortened form of the word

The group stands there, fearful, apprehensive, mothers clutching children, men standing in front of wives. Charlie slowly raises the gun. As the figure gets closer and closer he suddenly pulls the trigger. The sound of it explodes in the stillness. There is a long angle shot looking down at the figure, who suddenly lets out a small cry, stumbles forward onto his knees and then falls forward on his face. Don, Charlie, and Steve race forward over to him. Steve is there first and turns the man over. Now the crowd gathers around them.]

STEVE. [*Slowly looks up*] It's Pete Van Horn.

DON. [*In a hushed voice*] Pete Van Horn! He was just gonna go over to the next block to see if the power was on—

WOMAN. You killed him, Charlie. You shot him dead!

CHARLIE. [*Looks around at the circle of faces, his eyes frightened, his face contorted*] But . . . but I didn't know who he was. I certainly didn't know who he was. He comes walkin' out of the darkness—how am I supposed to know who he was? [*He grabs Steve.*] Steve—you know why I shot! How was I supposed to know he wasn't a monster or something? [*He grabs Don now.*] We're all scared of the same thing. I was just tryin' to . . . tryin' to protect my home, that's all! Look, all of you, that's all I was tryin' to do. [*He looks down wildly at the body.*] I didn't know it was somebody we knew! I didn't know—

[*There's a sudden hush and then an intake of breath. We see a medium shot of the living room window of Charlie's house. The window is not lit, but suddenly the house lights come on behind it.*]

WOMAN. [*In a very hushed voice*] Charlie . . . Charlie . . . the lights just went on in your house. Why did the lights just go on?

DON. What about it, Charlie? How come you're the only one with lights now?

GOODMAN. That's what I'd like to know.

[*A pause as they all stare toward Charlie.*]

GOODMAN. You were so quick to kill, Charlie, and you were so quick to tell us who we had to be careful of. Well, maybe you had to kill. Maybe Peter there was trying to tell us something. Maybe he'd found out something and came back to tell us who there was amongst us we should watch out for—

[*Charlie backs away from the group, his eyes wide with fright.*]

CHARLIE. No . . . no . . . it's nothing of the sort! I don't know why the lights are on. I swear I don't. Somebody's pulling a gag or something.

[*He bumps against Steve, who grabs him and whirls him around.*]

STEVE. A gag? A gag? Charlie, there's a dead man on the sidewalk and you killed him! Does this thing look like a gag to you?

[*Charlie breaks away and screams as he runs toward his house.*]

CHARLIE. No! No! Please!

[*A man breaks away from the crowd to chase Charlie.*

We see a long angle shot looking down as the man tackles Charlie and lands on top of him. The other people start to run toward them. Charlie is up on his feet, breaks away from the other man's grasp, lands a couple of desperate punches that push the man aside. Then he forces his way, fighting, through the crowd to once again break free, jumps up on his front porch. A rock thrown from the group smashes a window alongside of him, the broken glass flying past him. A couple of pieces cut him. He stands there perspiring, rumpled, blood

The Monsters Are Due on Maple Street **257**

25 Discussion Can Charlie justify his killing of Pete Van Horn? Are his excuses convincing?

26 Discussion Are you surprised when Goodman turns on Charlie? Why or why not?

working. The other contractions are shortened forms of two words. In each of the contractions, the apostrophe indicates the position of the missing letter or letters.

Student Activity 1. Find five other sentences from *The Monsters Are Due on Maple Street* that contain contractions. For each sentence, explain what word or words are being shortened.

Student Activity 2. Each of the following sentences contains one or more word groups that can be written as contractions. On a piece of paper, write each word group as a contraction.

1. But I did not know who he was, or what he had been doing.
2. I have already told you that I am not from around here.
3. They are getting nervous about the strange events.
4. What will we do when we have finished here?
5. Could we not try to go for help?

27

Discussion Does Charlie know who the monster is? Why does he swear that he does?

Critical Thinking and Reading Evaluate each neighbor's thinking and conclusion. Is someone an alien from outer space because his car started by itself or because he has an elaborate radio? What has caused these people to lose all sense of reason? Does this ever happen in real life? Explain your answer.

running down from a cut on the cheek. His wife breaks away from the group to throw herself into his arms. He buries his face against her. We can see the crowd converging on the porch now.]

VOICES.
It must have been him.
He's the one.
We got to get Charlie.

[*Another rock lands on the porch. Now Charlie pushes his wife behind him, facing the group.*]

27 **CHARLIE.** Look, look I swear to you . . . it isn't me . . . but I do know who it is . . . I swear to you, I do know who it is. I know who the monster is here. I know who it is that doesn't belong. I swear to you I know.

GOODMAN. [*Shouting*] What are you waiting for?

WOMAN. [*Shouting*] Come on, Charlie, come on.

MAN ONE. [*Shouting*] Who is it, Charlie, tell us!

DON. [*Pushing his way to the front of the crowd*] All right, Charlie, let's hear it!

[*Charlie's eyes dart around wildly.*]

CHARLIE. It's . . . it's . . .

MAN TWO. [*Screaming*] Go ahead, Charlie, tell us.

CHARLIE. It's . . . it's the kid. It's Tommy. He's the one!

[*There's a gasp from the crowd as we cut to a shot of Sally holding her son Tommy. The boy at first doesn't understand and then, realizing the eyes are all on him, buries his face against his mother.*]

SALLY. [*Backs away*] That's crazy! That's crazy! He's a little boy.

WOMAN. But he knew! He was the only one who knew! He told us all about it. Well, how did he know? How *could* he have known?

[*The various people take this up and repeat the question aloud.*]

VOICES.
How could he know?
Who told him?
Make the kid answer.

DON. It was Charlie who killed old man Van Horn.

WOMAN. But it was the kid here who knew what was going to happen all the time. He was the one who knew!

[*We see a close-up of Steve.*]

STEVE. Are you all gone crazy? [*Pause as he looks about*] Stop.

[*A fist crashes at Steve's face, staggering him back out of the frame of the picture.*

There are several close camera shots suggesting the coming of violence. A hand fires a rifle. A fist clenches. A hand grabs the hammer from Van Horn's body, etc. Meanwhile, we hear the following lines.]

DON. Charlie has to be the one—Where's my rifle—

WOMAN. Les Goodman's the one. His car started! Let's wreck it.

MRS. GOODMAN. What about Steve's radio—He's the one that called them—

28

MR. GOODMAN. Smash the radio. Get me a hammer. Get me something.
STEVE. Stop—Stop—

CHARLIE. Where's that kid—Let's get him.

MAN ONE. Get Steve—Get Charlie—They're working together.

[*The crowd starts to converge around the mother, who grabs the child and starts to run with him. The crowd starts to follow, at first walking fast, and then running after him.*

We see a full shot of the street as suddenly Charlie's lights go off and the lights in another house go on. They stay on for a moment, then from across the street other lights go on and then off again.]

MAN ONE. [*Shouting*] It isn't the kid . . . it's Bob Weaver's house.

WOMAN. It isn't Bob Weaver's house, it's Don Martin's place.

CHARLIE. I tell you it's the kid.

DON. It's Charlie. He's the one.

[*We move into a series of close-ups of various people as they shout, accuse, scream, interspersing these shots with shots of houses as the lights go on and off, and then slowly in the middle of this nightmarish morass of sight and sound the camera starts to pull away, until once again we've reached the opening shot looking at the Maple Street sign from high above.*

The camera continues to move away until we dissolve to a shot looking toward the metal side of a space craft, which sits shrouded in darkness. An open door throws out a beam of light from the illuminated interior. Two figures silhouetted against the bright lights appear. We get only a vague feeling of form, but nothing more explicit than that.]

29

29 Discussion How effective are the stage directions in helping you to visualize the action? What is the difference between stage directions written for a stage play and stage directions written for a television play? How does viewing the action through the eye of a camera affect your perceptions?

The Monsters Are Due on Maple Street 259

30 **Discussion** What is the aliens' plan for conquering Earth? Do you think Maple Street is typical?

31 **Critical Thinking and Reading** The Narrator's summation is typical of Serling's plays. How powerful a force is prejudice in the real world? What statement is Serling making here? What effect do today's fear, suspicion, and prejudice have on future generations?

Reader's Response Which do you think is more dangerous, guns and bombs or prejudice? Explain.

FIGURE ONE. Understand the procedure now? Just stop a few of their machines and radios and telephones and lawn mowers . . . throw them into darkness for a few hours, and then you just sit back and watch the pattern.

FIGURE TWO. And this pattern is always the same?

FIGURE ONE. With few variations. They pick the most dangerous enemy they can find . . . and it's themselves. And all we need do is sit back . . . and watch.

FIGURE TWO. Then I take it this place . . . this Maple Street . . . is not unique.

FIGURE ONE. [*Shaking his head*] By no means. Their world is full of Maple Streets. And we'll go from one to the other and let them destroy themselves. One to the other . . . one to the other . . . one to the other—

[*Now the camera pans up for a shot of the starry sky and over this we hear the Narrator's voice.*]

NARRATOR'S VOICE. The tools of conquest do not necessarily come with bombs and explosions and fallout. There are weapons that are simply thoughts, attitudes, prejudices—to be found only in the minds of men. For the record, prejudices can kill and suspicion can destroy and a thoughtless frightened search for a scapegoat has a fallout all its own for the children . . . and the children yet unborn. [*A pause*] And the pity of it is . . . that these things cannot be confined to . . . The Twilight Zone!

THINKING ABOUT THE SELECTION
Recalling

1. What are the first signs that something strange is happening on Maple Street?
2. What does Tommy think has happened?
3. Why do the people become suspicious of Les Goodman?
4. Why do they turn against Steve Brand?
5. Why does Charlie shoot Pete Van Horn?
6. What happens after the shooting?
7. What is the real cause of the strange occurrences on Maple Street?

Interpreting

8. Why does the group of friendly neighbors turn into a dangerous mob?
9. How does the appearance of the aliens at the end affect your view of the preceding action?
10. How do the events of the play prove the narrator's statement: "The tools of conquest do

260 Drama

Closure and Extension

ANSWERS TO THINKING ABOUT THE SELECTION
Recalling

1. The stove stops working at the Brand house. Other houses experience power failures, dead radios, and inoperative lawn mowers.
2. Tommy thinks aliens have invaded Earth.
3. People suspect Goodman when his car starts by itself.
4. They turn against Steve because he spends a lot of time working on a radio that no one has ever seen.
5. Charlie thinks Pete Van Horn is a monster.
6. People turn against Charlie.
7. The real cause is aliens from outer space, but the aliens merely caused some appliances to stop working and then sat back to watch the people destroy themselves.

Interpreting

8. The neighbors turn into a mob because they're afraid.
9. Answers will differ, but students should see that human beings destroy themselves through their own fear, prejudice, and hysteria. The preceding action seems even more horrible because the aliens were able to predict it so easily.
10. Answers will differ. Suggested Response: The events of the play prove that people can be conquered when their own fears are turned against themselves. Conventional weapons were unnecessary for the aliens to conquer Earth.
11. The humans are the real monsters.

Applying

12. Answers will differ. Suggested Response: Students will either say that they would have reacted like the characters or not. Students may think that they would remain calm and rational.

260

not necessarily come with bombs and explosions and fallout"?

11. Who are the real "monsters"?

Applying

12. How do you think you would have responded if you were one of the residents of Maple Street?

ANALYZING LITERATURE
Recognizing Conflict in Drama

Conflict is a struggle between opposing forces. Understanding the different conflicts present will help you better understand the play.

1. How does Serling's play show conflict between individuals?
2. How does the play show conflict between individuals and society?
3. What other conflict occurs in the play?
4. What is the central conflict of the play?

CRITICAL THINKING AND READING
Identifying Invalid Conclusions

A **valid conclusion** is based on strong evidence or sound reasoning. For example, when Don Martin says that an electrical storm may have caused the loss of power on Maple Street, Charlie forms a valid conclusion. He says, "That don't seem likely. Sky's just as blue as anything. Not a cloud. No lightning. No thunder. . . ." His conclusion is valid because it is based on evidence.

An **invalid** conclusion is not well founded. It is based on little or no evidence, on faulty evidence, or on poor thinking. For example, when phones, portable radios, and lawn mowers stop working, Charlie concludes that an electrical-power failure has occurred. But if that were so, portable radios operating on batteries or transistors would be working—and they are not. Charlie's thinking is not sound and his conclusion is invalid.

1. Analyze the crowd's conclusion that Les

Goodman is guilty of something. Why is their conclusion invalid? (What is wrong with their evidence and thinking?)
2. Point out two other similar invalid conclusions made about characters in the play. Explain why each is invalid.

UNDERSTANDING LANGUAGE
Recognizing Colloquial English

Colloquial English is the relaxed, informal English that people use in conversation. Playwrights often use colloquial English in dialogue to make their characters sound realistic. Steve Brand, for example, is speaking colloquial English in the following lines: "We're all on a monster kick, Les. Seems that the general impression holds that maybe one family isn't what we think they are. Monsters from outer space or something." (p. 253) Slang expressions ("kick"), loose grammar ("Seems that . . ."), and incomplete sentences ("Monsters from outer space or something.") are characteristics of colloquial English.

1. Find two or three examples of colloquial English in the dialogue of the play.
2. Reread the narrator's speech at the very end of the play (p. 260). Tell why you think it is or is not an example of colloquial English.
3. Why do you suppose colloquial English is more acceptable in speech than in writing?

THINKING AND WRITING
Extending the Play

Imagine that the producers of *The Monsters Are Due on Maple Street* have asked you to write an additional scene for the play. It will fit in right after the dialogue between the two figures near the end and before the narrator's concluding words. The setting is Maple Street on the following morning. Write a scene that shows the new situation there. When you revise your scene, make sure it follows naturally from all that happens before. Finally proofread your scene and prepare a final draft.

The Monsters Are Due on Maple Street 261

cause it is mob mentality based on fear and not on solid physical evidence.
2. Answers will differ. Suggested Response: Two other invalid conclusions are that Steve is an alien because he is a ham radio operator and that Tommy is an alien because he "knew" about the aliens from the start. The conclusion about Steve is invalid because many people are ham radio operators and he is, in all respects, a normal man. The conclusion about Tommy is invalid because Tommy didn't "know" anything. He merely drew some conclusions based on every story he ever read about a spaceship landing on Earth.

Challenge Think of some examples of prejudice in real life. Explain why certain people have a particular prejudice and identify the error in their thinking that leads to their invalid conclusion.

ANSWERS TO UNDERSTANDING LANGUAGE

1. There are numerous examples of colloquial English throughout the play. Mrs. Brand's speech at the bottom of page 248 is one example. Students should be able to explain why the examples they give are colloquial.
2. The speech is not an example of colloquial English. It does not contain slang expressions, loose grammar, or incomplete sentences.
3. Answers will differ. Suggested Response: Colloquial English is more acceptable in casual speech than in writing because, when people speak, they also communicate with gestures and tone of voice, as well as words. These additional ways of communicating allow people to be lax in their speech. Written communication must be more precise because the words are the only means of communication.

THINKING AND WRITING
Publishing Student Writing
Have students illustrate their new scenes and display the illustrations along with the scripts in the classroom.

ANSWERS TO ANALYZING LITERATURE

1. Serling's play shows conflict between individuals when neighbor turns against neighbor. Men who were friends become suspicious of one another and accuse each other of being alien and strange.
2. The play shows conflict between individuals and society in that certain neighbors establish criteria for what's normal behavior in order to judge other neighbors.

People are therefore in conflict with society's standards when they don't conform to what their neighbors define as normal.
3. Conflicts also occur within individuals as they try to overcome their fears.
4. Answers will differ, but students should see that the central conflict is between people and their own fears, suspicious, and attitudes.

ANSWERS TO CRITICAL THINKING AND READING

1. The crowd concludes Goodman is guilty because his car starts by itself and he has been seen standing in front of his house at odd hours looking at the sky. Neither of these things reflects negatively on Goodman. The so-called evidence is refuted by Goodman himself who doesn't know why his car started and who has insomnia. The crowd's thinking is wrong be-

Focus

More About the Author Charles Dickens was a social commentator on his times. Through his sensitive portrayals of the poor, Dickens drew attention to the social conditions that forced people to live in streets and children to work in factories. Discuss the relationship between the world Dickens depicted and our own society today.

Literary Focus Every story has a plot. Even the stories you tell your friends have plots. But exposition is another matter. Exposition is a literary device and is often missing from real-life siutations. In fact, in real life, you may frequently wonder why someone is acting a certain way but may never find out.

Look For As you become aware of the plot in Act I of the play, note how it carries the play along. The plot is the action. Also be aware of the revelation of Scrooge's past history. This revelation, or exposition, is the advantage literature gives you in understanding the characters in stories.

Writing/Prior Knowledge Have students discuss the feelings most people have during the holiday season, beginning with Thanksgiving. Explore how this time of year is different from the rest of the year. Then have them complete the freewriting assignment.

Vocabulary These words may also give students some difficulty: *covetous, gait* (p. 264); *bestow* (p. 265); *resolute* (p. 267); *endeavoring, surplus* (p. 268); *malcontent, insomniac* (p. 270); *forbearance, benevolence, penance, procuring* (p. 272); *reclamation* (p. 274); *stagnant* (p. 275); *withered* (p. 277); *burdensome, idol, aspirations, engrosses, fraught* (p. 279); and *remorse* (p. 280).

A Christmas Carol: Scrooge and Marley, Act I

Charles Dickens (1812–1870) was born in Portsmouth, England. He took upon himself the support of his family when he was twelve years old. For the rest of his life, he remembered what it was like to be poor. His sympathy for his fellow human beings is powerfully expressed in his story "A Christmas Carol." **Israel Horovitz** (1939–   ) has great respect for Dickens and this story. He has written, "I come to this work humbly, under the pressures of great respect for the Master: Charles Dickens."

Plot and Exposition

The **plot** of a play usually begins by introducing a conflict. The conflict rises to a climax, or high point of excitement or emotion. Then, as the play comes to a close, the excitement dies down, any unanswered questions about the story are answered, and the curtain falls.

Exposition is the revealing (exposing) of information needed to understand the action shown on stage. It often explains events that occurred before the start of the onstage events.

Look For

This play tells the story of a man who comes to learn sympathy for his fellow human beings. As you read Act I, notice how the plot develops in a way that makes you wonder what will happen to Scrooge. Also, notice the information given about events that occurred before Christmas 1843. How do these past events affect Scrooge?

Writing

Scrooge has become part of our everyday vocabulary. Brainstorm to list all the ideas that come to mind when you hear the word *Scrooge*.

Vocabulary

Knowing the following words will help you as you read *A Christmas Carol: Scrooge and Marley*.

implored (im plôrd') *v.*: Asked or begged earnestly (p. 265)
morose (mə rōs') *adj.*: Gloomy, ill-tempered (p. 266)
destitute (des' tə tōot') *adj.*: Living in complete poverty (p. 268)

misanthrope (mis' ən thrōp') *n.*: A person who hates or distrusts everyone (p. 270)
void (void) *n.*: Total emptiness (p. 270)
ponderous (pän' dər əs) *adj.*: Very heavy, bulky (p. 272)

262   Drama

Objectives

1 To understand the plot and exposition of a drama
2 To recognize foreshadowing
3 To understand Latin roots
4 To write a summary of a drama that could be read aloud for entertainment

Support Material

Teaching Portfolio
Teacher Backup, p. 383
Grammar in Action Worksheet, *Predicate Nouns*, p. 388
Grammar in Action Worksheet, *The Four Functions of Sentences*, p. 390
Usage and Mechanics Worksheet, p. 392
Vocabulary Check, p. 394

Analyzing Literature Worksheet, *Exposition in Drama*, p. 395
Critical Thinking and Reading Worksheet, *Foreshadowing*, p. 397
Selection Test, p. 398
Library of Video Classics: *A Christmas Carol*

A Christmas Carol: Scrooge and Marley

from *A Christmas Carol* by Charles Dickens

Israel Horovitz

THE PEOPLE OF THE PLAY

Jacob Marley, a specter
Ebenezer Scrooge, not yet
 dead, which is to say still alive
Bob Cratchit, Scrooge's clerk
Fred, Scrooge's nephew
Thin Do-Gooder
Portly Do-Gooder
Specters (Various), carrying money-
 boxes
The Ghost of Christmas Past
Four Jocund Travelers
A Band of Singers
A Band of Dancers
Little Boy Scrooge
Young Man Scrooge
Fan, Scrooge's little sister
The Schoolmaster
Schoolmates
Fezziwig, a fine and fair employer
Dick, young Scrooge's co-worker
Young Scrooge
A Fiddler
More Dancers
Scrooge's Lost Love
Scrooge's Lost Love's Daughter
Scrooge's Lost Love's Husband

The Ghost of Christmas
 Present
Some Bakers
Mrs. Cratchit, Bob Cratchit's wife
Belinda Cratchit, a daughter
Martha Cratchit, another
 daughter
Peter Cratchit, a son
Tiny Tim Cratchit, another son
Scrooge's Niece, Fred's wife
The Ghost of Christmas Fu-
 ture, a mute Phantom
Three Men of Business
Drunks, Scoundrels,
 Women of the Streets
A Charwoman
Mrs. Dilber
Joe, an old second-hand goods
 dealer
A Corpse, very like Scrooge
An Indebted Family
Adam, a young boy
A Poulterer
A Gentlewoman
Some More Men of Business

Presentation

Motivation/Prior Knowledge
Have students imagine that they work for a miserly and insensitive person. Not only is their employer cruel to them but they constantly witness inhumanity to others as well. Would they be able to work for such a person? Would they be able to recognize their employer's worth as a human being despite the treatment they receive? Would they be optimistic that this person might one day change for the better?

Master Teacher Note To give students a feeling for the sound of Dickens's play, obtain and play one of the following recordings of "A Christmas Carol": Tom Conti reading, Caedmon (CP-1657 cassette or TC-1657 disk). Ralph Richardson and Paul Scofield reading, Caedmon (CDL5-1135 cassette or TC-1135 disk). Frani Pettingell reading, Spoken Arts (SAC-7053 cassette or 728 disk). To give students the flavor of an English Christmas, you might play a recording entitled "On Christmas Night" (Argo, 2RG-5333), which is a collection of nineteenth-century carols sung by the choir of King's College, Cambridge.

Purpose-Setting Question What role does greed play in Act I of this play?

1 **Discussion** What advantages do you expect Marley to have as a narrator since he is dead?

2 **Discussion** What is your first impression of Scrooge?

THE PLACE OF THE PLAY

Various locations in and around the City of London, including Scrooge's Chambers and Offices; the Cratchit Home; Fred's Home; Scrooge's School; Fezziwig's Offices; Old Joe's Hide-a-Way.

THE TIME OF THE PLAY

The entire action of the play takes place on Christmas Eve, Christmas Day, and the morning after Christmas, 1843.

ACT I

Scene 1

[*Ghostly music in auditorium. A single spotlight on* JACOB MARLEY, D.C. *He is ancient; awful, dead-eyed. He speaks straight out to auditorium.*]

MARLEY. [*Cackle-voiced*] My name is Jacob Marley and I am dead. [*He laughs.*] Oh, no, there's no doubt that I am dead. The register of my burial was signed by the clergyman, the clerk, the undertaker . . . and by my chief mourner . . . Ebenezer Scrooge . . . [*Pause; remembers*] I am dead as a doornail.

[*A spotlight fades up, Stage Right, on* SCROOGE, *in his counting-house,[1] counting. Lettering on the window behind* SCROOGE *reads:* "SCROOGE AND MARLEY, LTD." *The spotlight is tight on* SCROOGE's *head and shoulders. We shall not yet see into the offices and setting. Ghostly music continues, under.* MARLEY *looks across at* SCROOGE; *pitifully. After a moment's pause*]

I present him to you: Ebenezer Scrooge . . . England's most tightfisted hand at the grindstone, Scrooge! a squeezing, wrench-ing, grasping, scraping, clutching, covetous, old sinner! secret, and self-contained, and solitary as an oyster. The cold within him freezes his old features, nips his pointed nose, shrivels his cheek, stiffens his gait; makes his eyes red, his thin lips blue; and speaks out shrewdly in his grating voice. Look at him. Look at him . . .

[SCROOGE *counts and mumbles.*]

SCROOGE. They owe me money and I will collect. I will have them jailed, if I have to. They owe me money and I will collect what is due me.

[MARLEY *moves towards* SCROOGE; *two steps. The spotlight stays with him.*]

MARLEY. [*Disgusted*] He and I were partners for I don't know how many years. Scrooge was my sole executor, my sole administrator, my sole assign, my sole residuary legatee,[2] my sole friend and my sole mourner. But Scrooge was not so cut up by the sad event of my death, but that he was an excellent man of business on the very day of my funeral, and solemnized[3] it with an undoubted

---

1. counting house: An office for keeping financial records and writing business letters.

2. my sole executor (ig zek′yə tər), **my sole administrator, my sole assign** (ə sin′), **my sole residuary legatee** (ri zij′ oo wer′ ē leg′ ə tē′): All legal terms.

3. solemnized (säl′ əm nīzd′) v. : Honored or remembered; Marley is being ironic.

Grammar in Action

When a noun, pronoun, or adjective follows a linking verb and tells something about the subject it is a **subject complement.** Nouns used as subject complements are called **predicate nouns.** To identify predicate nouns, first notice whether a sentence has a linking verb. The linking verb acts like an equals sign between the noun and the subject. Both the noun and the subject will refer to the same thing. It is important to remember that a predicate noun, like other complements, can never be the object of a preposition. Study the following examples from *A Christmas Carol: Scrooge and Marley.* The predicate nouns and are labeled.

> MARLEY. My name is Jacob Marley and I am dead.
> MARLEY. Scrooge was my sole executor . . .

Student Activity 1. Copy the following sentences onto a piece of paper and underline each predicate noun.

1. NEPHEW. You are a better Christian than I am, sir.
2. SCROOGE. It's not convenient, and it's not fair.
3. PAST. I am the Ghost of Christmas Past.
4. YOUNG SCROOGE. He is the best, best, the very and absolute best.

3 Discussion Why has Scrooge kept Marley's name on the window? How does Marley obviously feel about that?

bargain. [*Pauses again in disgust*] He never painted out my name from the window. There it stands, on the window and above the warehouse door: Scrooge and Marley.

3 Sometimes people new to our business call him Scrooge and sometimes they call him Marley. He answers to both names. It's all the same to him. And it's cheaper than painting in a new sign, isn't it? [*Pauses; moves closer to* SCROOGE] Nobody has ever stopped him in the street to say, with gladsome looks, "My dear Scrooge, how are you? When will you come to see me?" No beggars implored him to bestow a trifle, no children ever ask him what it is o'clock, no man or woman now, or ever in his life, not once, inquire the way to such and such a place. [MARLEY *stands next to* SCROOGE *now. They share, so it seems, a spotlight.*] But what does Scrooge care of any of this? It is the very thing he likes! To edge his way along the crowded paths of life, warning all human sympathy to keep its distance.

[*A ghostly bell rings in the distance.* MARLEY *moves away from* SCROOGE, *now, heading* D. *again. As he does, he "takes" the light:* SCROOGE *has disappeared into the black void beyond.* MARLEY *walks* D.C., *talking directly to the audience. Pauses*]

The bell tolls and I must take my leave. You must stay a while with Scrooge and watch him play out his scroogey life. It is now the story: the once-upon-a-time. Scrooge is busy in his counting-house. Where else? Christmas eve and Scrooge is busy in his counting-house. It is cold, bleak, biting weather outside: foggy withal: and, if you listen closely,

A Christmas Carol: Scrooge and Marley   265

5. WOMAN. Our contract is an old one.

Student Activity 2. Write five original sentences using a predicate noun in each.

4 **Discussion** How does Scrooge treat Cratchit?

5 **Critical Thinking and Reading** Discuss the relationship between wealth and happiness. Can people always "buy" happiness?

6 **Discussion** Contrast Scrooge's view of Christmas with his nephew's.

you can hear the people in the court go wheezing up and down, beating their hands upon their breasts, and stamping their feet upon the pavement stones to warm them . . .

[*The clocks outside strike three.*]

Only three! and quite dark outside already: it has not been light all day this day.

[*This ghostly bell rings in the distance again.* MARLEY *looks about him. Music in.* MARLEY *flies away.*] (N.B. *Marley's comings and goings should, from time to time, induce the explosion of the odd flash-pot.* I.H.)

Scene 2

[*Christmas music in, sung by a live chorus, full. At conclusion of song, sound fades under and into the distance. Lights up in set: offices of Scrooge and Marley, Ltd.* SCROOGE *sits at his desk, at work. Near him is a tiny fire. His door is open and in his line of vision, we see* SCROOGE'S *clerk,* BOB CRATCHIT, *who sits in a dismal tank of a cubicle, copying letters. Near* CRATCHIT *is a fire so tiny as to barely cast a light: perhaps it is one pitifully glowing coal?* CRATCHIT *rubs his hands together, puts on a white comforter[4] and tries to heat his hands around his candle.* SCROOGE'S NEPHEW *enters, unseen.*]

4 | **SCROOGE.** What are you doing, Cratchit? Acting cold, are you? Next, you'll be asking to replenish your coal from my coal-box, won't you? Well, save your breath, Cratchit! Unless you're prepared to find employ elsewhere!

NEPHEW. [*Cheerfully; surprising* SCROOGE] A merry Christmas to you, Uncle! God save you!

SCROOGE. Bah! Humbug![5]

---

4. comforter (kum′ fər tər) *n.*: A long, woolen scarf.
5. Humbug (hum′ bug′) *interj.*: Nonsense! (can also be used as a noun to mean nonsense or something done to cheat or deceive).

266   Drama

NEPHEW. Christmas a "humbug," Uncle? I'm sure you don't mean that.

SCROOGE. I do! Merry Christmas? What right do you have to be merry? What reason have you to be merry? You're poor enough!

NEPHEW. Come, then. What right have you to be dismal? What reason have you to be morose? You're rich enough.

SCROOGE. Bah! Humbug!

NEPHEW. Don't be cross, Uncle.

SCROOGE. What else can I be? Eh? When I live in a world of fools such as this? Merry Christmas? What's Christmastime to you but a time of paying bills without any money; a time for finding yourself a year older, but not an hour richer. If I could work my will, every idiot who goes about with "Merry Christmas" on his lips, should be boiled with his own pudding, and buried with a stake of holly through his heart. He should!

NEPHEW. Uncle!

SCROOGE. Nephew! You keep Christmas in your own way and let me keep it in mine.

NEPHEW. Keep it! But you don't keep it, Uncle.

SCROOGE. Let me leave it alone, then. Much good it has ever done you!

NEPHEW. There are many things from which I have derived good, by which I have not profited, I daresay. Christmas among the rest. But I am sure that I always thought of Christmas time, when it has come round— as a good time: the only time I know of, when men and women seem to open their shut-up hearts freely, and to think of people below them as if they really were fellow-passengers to the grave, and not another race of creatures bound on other journeys. And therefore, Uncle, though it has never put a scrap of gold or silver in my pocket, I believe that it *has* done me good, and that it *will* do me good; and I say, God bless it!

[*The* CLERK *in the tank applauds, looks at the furious* SCROOGE *and pokes out his tiny fire, as if in exchange for the moment of impropriety.* SCROOGE *yells at him.*]

SCROOGE. [*To the* CLERK] Let me hear another sound from *you* and you'll keep your Christmas by losing your situation. [*To the* NEPHEW] You're quite a powerful speaker, sir. I wonder you don't go into Parliament.[6]

NEPHEW. Don't be angry, Uncle. Come! Dine with us tomorrow.

SCROOGE. I'd rather see myself dead than see myself with your family!

NEPHEW. But, why? Why?

SCROOGE. Why did you get married?

NEPHEW. Because I fell in love.

SCROOGE. That, sir, is the only thing that you have said to me in your entire lifetime which is even more ridiculous than "Merry Christmas"! [*Turns from* NEPHEW] Good afternoon.

NEPHEW. Nay, Uncle, you never came to see me before I married either. Why give it as a reason for not coming now?

SCROOGE. Good afternoon, Nephew!

NEPHEW. I want nothing from you; I ask nothing of you; why cannot we be friends?

SCROOGE. Good afternoon!

NEPHEW. I am sorry with all my heart, to find you so resolute. But I have made the trial in homage to Christmas, and I'll keep my Christmas humor to the last. So A Merry Christmas, Uncle!

SCROOGE. Good afternoon!

NEPHEW. And A Happy New Year!

SCROOGE. Good afternoon!

NEPHEW. [*He stands facing* SCROOGE.] Uncle, you are the most . . . [*Pauses*] No, I shan't. My Christmas humor is intact . . . [*Pause*] God bless you, Uncle . . . [NEPHEW *turns and starts for the door; he stops at* CRATCHIT's *cage.*] Merry Christmas, Bob Cratchit . . .

CRATCHIT. Merry Christmas to you sir, and a very, very happy New Year . . .

SCROOGE. [*Calling across to them*] Oh, fine, a perfection, just fine . . . to see the perfect pair of you: husbands, with wives and children to support . . . my clerk there earning fifteen shillings a week . . . and the perfect pair of you, talking about a Merry Christmas! [*Pauses*] I'll retire to Bedlam![7]

NEPHEW. [*To* CRATCHIT] He's impossible!

CRATCHIT. Oh, mind him not, sir. He's getting on in years, and he's alone. He's noticed your visit. I'll wager your visit has warmed him.

NEPHEW. Him? Uncle Ebenezer Scrooge? *Warmed?* You are a better Christian than I am, sir.

CRATCHIT. [*Opening the door for* NEPHEW; *two* DO-GOODERS *will enter, as* NEPHEW *exits*] Good day to you, sir, and God bless.

NEPHEW. God bless . . . [*One man who enters is portly, the other is thin. Both are pleasant.*]

CRATCHIT. Can I help you, gentlemen?

---

6. Parliament (pär′ lə mənt): The national legislative body of Great Britain, in some ways like the American Congress.

---

7. Bedlam (bed′ ləm): A hospital in London for the mentally ill.

7 Critical Thinking and Reading How is Scrooge's nephew really feeling toward him? Why does he not show his anger toward his uncle?

8 Discussion What kind of man is Bob Cratchit? How is he able to work for Scrooge?

THIN MAN. [*Carrying papers and books; looks around* CRATCHIT *to* SCROOGE] Scrooge and Marley's, I believe. Have I the pleasure of addressing Mr. Scrooge, or Mr. Marley?

SCROOGE. Mr. Marley has been dead these seven years. He died seven years ago this very night.

PORTLY MAN. We have no doubt his liberality is well represented by his surviving partner . . . [*Offers his calling card*]

SCROOGE. [*Handing back the card; unlooked at*] . . . Good afternoon.

THIN MAN. This will take but a moment, sir . . .

PORTLY MAN. At this festive season of the year, Mr. Scrooge, it is more than usually desirable that we should make some slight provision for the poor and destitute, who suffer greatly at the present time. Many thousands are in want of common necessities; hundreds of thousands are in want of common comforts, sir.

9 **SCROOGE.** Are there no prisons?

PORTLY MAN. Plenty of prisons.

SCROOGE. And aren't the Union workhouses still in operation?

THIN MAN. They are. Still. I wish that I could say that they are not.

SCROOGE. The Treadmill[8] and the Poor Law[9] are in full vigor, then?

THIN MAN. Both very busy, sir.

---

8. **the Treadmill** (tred' mil'): A kind of mill wheel turned by the weight of persons treading steps arranged around it; this devise was used to punish prisoners in jails.

9. **the Poor Law:** A series of laws were passed in England from the 17th century on to help the poor; changes to the law in 1834 gave responsibility for this relief to the national government but did not provide much aid for the poor.

SCROOGE. Ohhh, I see. I was afraid, from what you said at first, that something had occurred to stop them from their useful course. [*Pauses*] I'm glad to hear it.

PORTLY MAN. Under the impression that they scarcely furnish Christian cheer of mind or body to the multitude, a few of us are endeavoring to raise a fund to buy the Poor some meat and drink, and means of warmth. We choose this time, because it is a time, of all others, when Want is keenly felt, and Abundance rejoices. [*Pen in hand; as well as notepad*] What shall I put you down for, sir?

SCROOGE. Nothing!

10

PORTLY MAN. You wish to be left anonymous?

SCROOGE. I wish to be left alone! [*Pauses; turns away; turns back to them*] Since you ask me what I wish, gentlemen, that is my answer. I help to support the establishments that I have mentioned: they cost enough: and those who are badly off must go there.

THIN MAN. Many can't go there; and many would rather die.

SCROOGE. If they would rather die, they had better do it, and decrease the surplus population. Besides—excuse me—I don't know that.

THIN MAN. But you might know it!

SCROOGE. It's not my business. It's enough for a man to understand his own business, and not to interfere with other people's. Mine occupies me constantly. Good afternoon, gentlemen! [*Scrooge turns his back on the gentlemen and returns to his desk.*]

PORTLY MAN. But, sir, Mr. Scrooge . . . think of the poor.

SCROOGE. [*Turns suddenly to them. Pauses*] Take your leave of my offices, sirs, while I am still smiling.

[*The* THIN MAN *looks at the* PORTLY MAN. *They are undone. They shrug. They move to door. Cratchit hops up to open it for them.*]

THIN MAN. Good day, sir . . . [*To* CRATCHIT] A merry Christmas to you, sir . . .

CRATCHIT. Yes. A Merry Christmas to both of you . . .

PORTLY MAN. Merry Christmas . . .

[CRATCHIT *silently squeezes something into the hand of the* THIN MAN.]

THIN MAN. What's this?

CRATCHIT. Shhhh . . .

[CRATCHIT *opens the door; wind and snow whistle into the room.*]

THIN MAN. Thank you, sir, thank you.

[CRATCHIT *closes the door and returns to his workplace.* SCROOGE *is at his own counting table. He talks to* CRATCHIT *without looking up.*]

SCROOGE. It's less of a time of year for being merry, and more a time of year for being loony . . . if you ask me.

CRATCHIT. Well, I don't know, sir . . .

[*The clock's bell strikes six o'clock.*]

Well, there it is, eh, six?

SCROOGE. Saved by six bells, are you?

CRATCHIT. I must be going home . . . [*He snuffs out his candle and puts on his hat.*] I hope you have a . . . very very lovely day tomorrow, sir . . .

SCROOGE. Hmmm. Oh, you'll be wanting the whole day tomorrow, I suppose?

11 **Discussion** What does Cratchit give the thin man? Why does he want it kept secret? Can he afford to do this? Why does he do it?

Humanities Note

In the photograph on this page, note the nineteenth-century dress of the characters. Is this how you visualized Scrooge and Marley? Why or why not? How might you change the look of the scene?

12 **Discussion** What does Scrooge think of doing to make up for giving Cratchit Christmas Day off?

13 **Literary Focus** Scrooge is so extreme in his negative thinking that he, at times, seems comical. Note other instances in the play in which Scrooge's vile behavior seems almost humorous or joking.

14 **Critical Thinking and Reading** Do you think there might be something in Scrooge's past that ruins Christmas for him? How do people become so unhappy? Could Scrooge's personality have formed overnight or did it take many years?

CRATCHIT. If quite convenient, sir.

SCROOGE. It's not convenient, and it's not fair. If I was to stop half-a-crown for it, you'd think yourself ill-used, I'll be bound?

[CRATCHIT *smiles faintly.*]

CRATCHIT. I don't know, sir . . .

12 SCROOGE. And yet, you don't think me ill-used, when I pay a day's wages for no work . . .

CRATCHIT. It's only but once a year . . .

SCROOGE. A poor excuse for picking a man's pocket every 25th of December! But I suppose you must have the whole day. Be here all the earlier the next morning!

CRATCHIT. Oh, I will, sir. I will. I promise you. And, sir . . .

SCROOGE. Don't say it, Cratchit.

CRATCHIT. But let me wish you a . . .

SCROOGE. Don't say it, Cratchit. I warn you . . .

CRATCHIT. Sir!

SCROOGE. Cratchit!

[CRATCHIT *opens the door.*]

CRATCHIT. All right, then, sir . . . well . . . [*Suddenly*] Merry Christmas, Mr. Scrooge!

[*And he runs out the door, shutting same behind him.* SCROOGE *moves to his desk; gathering his coat, hat, etc. A* BOY *appears at his window. . . .*]

BOY. [*Singing*] "Away in a manger . . ."

[SCROOGE *seizes his ruler and whacks at the image of the* BOY *outside. The* BOY *leaves.*]

SCROOGE. Bah! Humbug! Christmas! Bah! Humbug! [*He shuts out the light.*]

A note on the crossover, following Scene 2:

[SCROOGE *will walk alone to his rooms from his offices. As he makes a long slow cross of the stage, the scenery should change. Christmas music will be heard, various people will cross by* SCROOGE, *often smiling happily.*

There will be occasional pleasant greetings tossed at him.

SCROOGE, *in contrast to all, will grump and mumble. He will snap at passing boys, as might a horrid old hound.*

In short, SCROOGE's *sounds and movements will define him in contrast from all other people who cross the stage: he is the misanthrope, the malcontent, the miser. He is* SCROOGE.

13 *This statement of* SCROOGE's *character, by contrast to all other characters, should seem comical to the audience.*

During SCROOGE's *crossover to his rooms, snow should begin to fall. All passers-by will hold their faces to the sky, smiling, allowing snow to shower them lightly.* SCROOGE, *by contrast, will bat at the flakes with his walking-stick, as might an insomniac swat at a sleep-stopping, middle-of-the-night swarm of mosquitoes. He will comment on the blackness of the night, and, finally, reach his rooms and his encounter with the magical specter:* MARLEY, *his eternal mate.*]

Scene 3

SCROOGE. No light at all . . . no moon . . . *that* is what is at the center of a Christmas Eve: dead black: void . . . **14**

[SCROOGE *puts his key in the door's keyhole. He has reached his rooms now. The door knocker changes and is now* MARLEY's *face. A musical sound; quickly; ghostly.* MARLEY's *image is not at all angry, but looks at* SCROOGE *as did the old* MARLEY *look at* SCROOGE. *The hair is curiously stirred; eyes wide open, dead: absent of focus.* SCROOGE *stares wordlessly here. The face, before his very eyes, does deliquesce.[10] It is a knocker again.* SCROOGE *opens the door and checks the back of same, probably for* MARLEY'S *pigtail. Seeing nothing but screws and nuts,* SCROOGE *refuses the memory.*]

Pooh, pooh!

[*The sound of the door closing resounds throughout the house as thunder. Every room echoes the sound.* SCROOGE *fastens the door and walks across the hall to the stairs, trimming his candle as he goes; and then he goes slowly up the staircase. He checks each room: sitting room, bedroom, lumber-room. He looks under the sofa, under the table: nobody there. He fixes his evening gruel on the hob,[11] changes his jacket.* SCROOGE *sits near the tiny low-flamed fire, sipping his gruel. There are various pictures on the walls: all of them now show likenesses of* MARLEY. SCROOGE *blinks his eyes.*]

15 | Bah! Humbug!

[SCROOGE *walks in a circle about the room. The pictures change back into their natural images. He sits down at the table in front of the fire. A bell hangs overhead. It begins to ring, of its own accord. Slowly, surely, begins the ringing of every bell in the house. They continue ringing for nearly half a minute.* SCROOGE *is stunned by the phenomenon. The bells cease their ringing all at once. Deep below* SCROOGE, *in the basement of the house, there is the sound of clanking, of some enormous chain being dragged across the floors; and now up the stairs. We hear doors flying open.*]

---

10. deliquesce (del' ə kwes') *v.*: Melt away.
11. gruel (groo͞' əl) **on the hob** (häb): A thin broth warming on a ledge at the back or side of the fireplace.

Bah still! Humbug still! This is not happening! I won't believe it!

[MARLEY'S GHOST *enters the room. He is horrible to look at: pigtail, vest, suit as usual, but he drags an enormous chain now, to which is fastened cash-boxes, keys, padlocks, ledgers, deeds, and heavy purses fashioned of steel. He is transparent.* MARLEY *stands opposite the stricken* SCROOGE.]

How now! What do you want of me?

MARLEY. Much!

SCROOGE. Who are you?

MARLEY. Ask me who I *was.*

SCROOGE. Who *were* you then?

MARLEY. In life, I was your business partner: Jacob Marley.

SCROOGE. I see . . . can you sit down?

MARLEY. I can.

SCROOGE. Do it then.

MARLEY. I shall. [MARLEY *sits opposite* SCROOGE, *in the chair across the table, at the front of the fireplace.*] You don't believe in me.

SCROOGE. I don't.

MARLEY. Why do you doubt your senses?

SCROOGE. Because every little thing affects them. A slight disorder of the stomach makes them cheat. You may be an undigested bit of beef, a blot of mustard, a crumb of cheese, a fragment of an underdone potato. There's more of gravy than of grave about you, whatever you are! | 16

[*There is a silence between them.* SCROOGE *is made nervous by it. He picks up a toothpick.*]

Humbug! I tell you: humbug!

A Christmas Carol: Scrooge and Marley 271

15 Discussion How important are the stage directions in this play? Would the play be as good without them? Why or why not?

16 Discussion Why does Scrooge doubt seeing the ghost of Marley? What does he think is causing the vision?

17 Discussion How does Marley convince Scrooge that he is real?

18 Discussion Why is Marley condemned to wander the earth? Why does he drag a heavy chain?

19 Discussion What is Marley's message to Scrooge?

17 [MARLEY *opens his mouth and screams a ghosty, fearful scream. The scream echoes about each room of the house. Bats fly, cats screech, lightning flashes.* SCROOGE *stands and walks backwards against the wall.* MARLEY *stands and screams again. This time, he takes his head and lifts it from his shoulders. His head continues to scream.* MARLEY'S *face again appears on every picture in the room: all screaming.* SCROOGE, *on his knees before* MARLEY.]

Mercy! Dreadful apparition,¹² mercy! Why, O! why do you trouble me so?

MARLEY. Man of the worldly mind, do you believe in me, or not?

SCROOGE. I do. I must. But why do spirits such as you walk the earth? And why do they come to me?

18 **MARLEY.** It is required of every man that the spirit within him should walk abroad among his fellow-men, and travel far and wide; and if that spirit goes not forth in life, it is condemned to do so after death. [MARLEY *screams again; a tragic scream; from his ghosty bones.*] I wear the chain I forged in life. I made it link by link, and yard by yard. Is its pattern strange to *you?* Or would you know, you, Scrooge, the weight and length of the strong coil you bear yourself? It was full as heavy and long as this, seven Christmas Eves ago. You have labored on it, since. It is a ponderous chain.

[*Terrified that a chain will appear about his body,* SCROOGE *spins and waves the unwanted chain away. None, of course, appears. Sees* MARLEY *watching him dance about the room.* MARLEY *watches* SCROOGE; *silently.*]

SCROOGE. Jacob. Old Jacob Marley, tell me more. Speak comfort to me, Jacob . . .

───────────

12. apparition (ap′ ə rish′ ən) *n.*: Ghost.

272 Drama

MARLEY. I have none to give. Comfort comes from other regions, Ebenezer Scrooge, and is conveyed by other ministers, to other kinds of men. A very little more, is all that is permitted to me. I cannot rest, I cannot stay, I cannot linger anywhere . . . [*He moans again.*] my spirit never walked beyond our counting-house—mark me!—in life my spirit never roved beyond the narrow limits of our money-changing hole; and weary journeys lie before me!

SCROOGE. But you were always a good man of business, Jacob.

MARLEY. [*Screams word "business"; a flashpot explodes with him.*] BUSINESS!!! Mankind was my business. The common welfare was my business; charity, mercy, forbearance, benevolence, were, all, my business. [SCROOGE *is quaking.*] Hear me, Ebenezer Scrooge! My time is nearly gone.

SCROOGE. I will, but don't be hard upon me. And don't be flowery, Jacob! Pray!

MARLEY. How is it that I appear before you in a shape that you can see, I may not tell. I have sat invisible beside you many and many a day. That is no light part of my penance. I am here tonight to warn you that you have yet a chance and hope of escaping my fate. A chance and hope of my procuring, Ebenezer.

SCROOGE. You were always a good friend to me. Thank'ee!

MARLEY. You will be haunted by Three Spirits.

SCROOGE. Would that be the chance and hope you mentioned, Jacob?

MARLEY. It is.

SCROOGE. I think I'd rather not.

MARLEY. Without their visits, you cannot hope to shun the path I tread. Expect the first one tomorrow, when the bell tolls one.

19

Grammar in Action

Writers use different kinds of sentences to do different things. There are four types of sentences in English, and writers use them all. **Declarative sentences** are the most common type of sentences. They state an idea and end with a period:

The main character in this drama is Ebenezer Scrooge.

Interrogative sentences ask questions and end with a question mark:

What lesson will Scrooge learn from Marley's visit?

Imperative sentences are sentences that give suggestions or commands. They start with a verb and end with a period or an exclamation mark, depending on the force of the statement. The subject is usually not included but understood to be you:

Tell me more.
Come back here!

Exclamatory sentences convey strong emotions and always end with exclamation marks:

There's a Ghost in my bedroom!

Israel Horovitz uses all four sentence types in the play:

SCROOGE. Couldn't I take 'em all at once, and get it over, Jacob?

MARLEY. Expect the second on the next night at the same hour. The third upon the next night when the last stroke of twelve has ceased to vibrate. Look to see me no more. Others may, but you may not. And look that, for your own sake, you remember what has passed between us!

[MARLEY *places his head back upon his shoulders. He approaches the window and beckons to* SCROOGE *to watch. Outside the window, specters[13] fly by, carrying money-boxes and chains. They make a confused sound of lamentation.* MARLEY, *after listening a moment, joins into their mournful dirge. He leans to the window and floats out into the bleak, dark night. He is gone.*]

20

SCROOGE. [*Rushing to the window*] Jacob! No, Jacob! Don't leave me! I'm frightened!

[*He sees that* MARLEY *has gone. He looks outside. He pulls the shutter closed, so that the scene is blocked from his view. All sound stops. After a pause, he re-opens the shutter and all is quiet, as it should be on Christmas Eve. Carolers carol out of doors, in the distance.* SCROOGE *closes the shutter and walks down the stairs. He examines the door by which* MARLEY *first entered.*]

No one here at all! Did I imagine all that? Humbug! [*He looks about the room.*] I did imagine it. It only happened in my foulest dream-mind, didn't it? An undigested bit of . . .

[*Thunder and lightning in the room; suddenly*]

Sorry! Sorry!

[*There is silence again. The lights fade out.*]

------

13. specters (spek′ tərz) *n.*: Ghosts.

Scene 4

[*Christmas music, choral, "Hark the Herald Angels Sing," sung by an onstage choir of children, spotlighted,* D.C. *Above,* SCROOGE *in his bed, dead to the world, asleep, in his darkened room. It should appear that the choir is singing somewhere outside of the house, of course, and a use of scrim[14] is thus suggested. When the singing is ended, the choir should fade out of view and* MAR-LEY *should fade into view, in their place.*]

MARLEY. [*Directly to audience*] From this point forth . . . I shall be quite visible to you, but invisible to him. [*Smiles*] He will feel my presence, nevertheless, for, unless my senses fail me completely, we are—you and I—witness to the changing of a miser: that one, my partner in life, in business, and in eternity: that one: Scrooge. [*Moves to staircase, below* SCROOGE] See him now. He endeavors to pierce the darkness with his ferret eyes.[15] [*To audience*] See him, now. He listens for the hour.

21

[*The bells toll.* SCROOGE *is awakened and quakes as the hour approaches one o'clock, but the bells stop their sound at the hour of twelve.*]

SCROOGE. [*Astonished*] Midnight! Why this isn't possible. It was past two when I went to bed. An icicle must have gotten into the clock's works! I couldn't have slept through the whole day and far into another night. It isn't possible that anything has happened to the sun, and this is twelve at noon! [*He runs to window; unshutters same; it is night.*] Night, still. Quiet, normal for the season, cold. It is certainly not noon. I cannot in any way afford to lose my days. Securities come

------

14. scrim (skrim) *n.*: A light, semi-transparent curtain.
15. ferret eyes: A ferret is a small, weasellike animal used for hunting rabbits; this expression means to look persistently, the way a ferret hunts.

A Christmas Carol: Scrooge and Marley 273

20 Discussion What does Scrooge see when he looks out the window? Are Scrooge and Marley the only ones guilty of greed?

21 Critical Thinking and Reading Why is Marley an excellent narrator?

But you were always a good man of business, Jacob. (declarative)
And why do they come to me? (interrogative)
Don't leave me! (imperative)
No, Jacob! (exclamatory)

Student Activity 1. Look through the play and find two more examples of each of the four types of sentences. Write the eight sentences on a sheet of paper and exchange papers with a partner. Identify the sentence types of your partner's sentences and correct your papers together.

Student Activity 2. Write a brief dialogue between Scrooge and yourself, imagining that you are trying to convince him to believe in Christmas. Use at least one of each of the four sentence types in your dialogue.

22 **Critical Thinking and Reading** Explain the appearance of the Ghost of Christmas Past. Why does the ghost look as it does?

23 **Reading Strategy** Describe what has happened in the play so far, and predict what is going to happen to Scrooge.

due, promissory notes,[16] interest on investments: these are things that happen in the daylight! [*He returns to his bed.*] Was this a dream?

[MARLEY *appears in his room. He speaks to the audience.*]

MARLEY. You see? He does not, with faith, believe in me fully, even still! Whatever will it take to turn the faith of a miser from money to men?

SCROOGE. Another quarter and it'll be one and Marley's ghosty friends will come. [*Pauses; listens*] Where's the chime for one? [*Ding, dong*] A quarter *past* [*Repeats*] Half-past! [*Repeats*] A quarter to it! But where's the heavy bell of the hour one? This is a game in which I lose my senses! Perhaps, if I allowed myself another short doze . . .

MARLEY. . . . Doze, Ebenezer, doze.

[*A heavy bell thuds its one ring: dull and definitely one o'clock. There is a flash of light.* SCROOGE *sits up, in a sudden. A hand draws back the curtains by his bed. He sees it.*]

SCROOGE. A hand! Who owns it! Hello!

[*Ghosty music again, but of a new nature to the play. A strange figure stands before* SCROOGE—*like a child, yet at the same time like an old man: white hair, but unwrinkled skin, long, muscular arms, but delicate legs and feet. Wears white tunic; lustrous belt cinches waist. Branch of fresh green holly in its hand, but has its dress trimmed with fresh summer flowers. Clear jets of light spring from the crown of its head. Holds cap in hand. The Spirit is called* PAST.]

Are you the Spirit, sir, whose coming was foretold to me?

---

16. **promissory** (präm′ i sôr′ ē) **notes:** Written promises to pay someone a certain sum of money.

274 Drama

PAST. I am.

MARLEY. Does he take this to be a vision of his green grocer?

SCROOGE. Who, and what are you?

PAST. I am the Ghost of Christmas Past.

SCROOGE. Long past?

PAST. Your past.

SCROOGE. May I ask, please, sir, what business you have here with me?

PAST. Your welfare.

SCROOGE. Not to sound ungrateful, sir, and really, please do understand that I am plenty obliged for your concern, but, really, kind spirit, it would have done all the better for my welfare to have been left alone altogether, to have slept peacefully through this night.

PAST. Your reclamation, then. Take heed!

SCROOGE. My what?

PAST. [*Motioning to* SCROOGE *and taking his arm*] Rise! Fly with me! [*He leads* SCROOGE *to the window.*]

SCROOGE. [*Panicked*] Fly, but I am a mortal and cannot fly!

PAST. [*Pointing to his heart*] Bear but a touch of my hand *here* and you shall be upheld in more than this!

[SCROOGE *touches the* SPIRIT'*s heart and the lights dissolve into sparkly flickers. Lovely crystals of music are heard. The scene dissolves into another. Christmas music again*]

Scene 5

[SCROOGE *and the* GHOST OF CHRISTMAS PAST *walk together across an open stage. In the background, we see a field that is open; covered by a soft, downy snow: a country road.*]

24 **Critical Thinking and Reading** What effect does this scene have on Scrooge? How is Scrooge different here from the Scrooge who saw Marley's ghost?

25 **Discussion** Why is Scrooge crying?

SCROOGE. Good Heaven! I was bred in this place. I was a boy here!

[SCROOGE *freezes, staring at the field beyond.* MARLEY's *ghost appears beside him; takes* SCROOGE's *face in his hands, and turns his face to the audience.*]

MARLEY. You see this Scrooge: stricken by feeling. Conscious of a thousand odors floating in the air, each one connected with a thousand thoughts, and hopes, and joys, and care long, long forgotten. [*Pause*] This one—this Scrooge—before your very eyes, returns to life, among the living. [*To audience, sternly*] You'd best pay your most careful attention. I would suggest rapt.[17]

[*There is a small flash and puff of smoke and* MARLEY *is gone again.*]

---

17. rapt (rapt) *adj.*: Giving complete attention, totally carried away by something.

PAST. Your lip is trembling, Mr. Scrooge. And what is that upon your cheek?

SCROOGE. Upon my cheek? Nothing . . . a blemish on the skin from the eating of overmuch grease . . . nothing . . . [*Suddenly*] Kind Spirit of Christmas Past, lead me where you will, but *quickly!* To be stagnant in this place is, for me, *unbearable!*

PAST. You recollect the way?

SCROOGE. Remember it! I would know it blindfolded! My bridge, my church, my winding river! [*Staggers about, trying to see it all at once. He weeps again.*]

PAST. These are but shadows of things that have been. They have no consciousness of us.

[*Four jocund travelers enter, singing a Christmas song in four-part harmony—"God Rest Ye Merry Gentlemen."*]

A Christmas Carol: Scrooge and Marley 275

26 Discussion Why does the ghost mock Scrooge? Was there ever a time when Scrooge enjoyed Christmas?

27 Discussion What kind of childhood did Scrooge have? Could it account for the way he acts now?

28 Critical Thinking and Reading How can you tell that Scrooge is already a changed man?

29 Literary Focus This is just one of the many examples of exposition in this play. How does it help to clarify the character of Scrooge? Do you begin to understand Scrooge as you explore his past with him? What purpose do these flashbacks serve?

SCROOGE. Listen! I know these men! I know them! I remember the beauty of their song!

26 **PAST.** But, why do you remember it so happily? It is Merry Christmas that they say to one another! What is Merry Christmas to you, Mr. Scrooge? Out upon Merry Christmas, right? What good has Merry Christmas ever done you, Mr. Scrooge? . . .

SCROOGE. [*After a long pause*] None. No good. None . . . [*He bows his head.*]

PAST. Look, you, sir, a school ahead. The schoolroom is not quite deserted. A solitary child, neglected by his friends, is left there still.

[SCROOGE *falls to the ground; sobbing as he sees, and we see, a small boy, the young* SCROOGE, *sitting and weeping, bravely, alone at his desk: alone in a vast space, a void.*]

SCROOGE. I cannot look on him!

27 **PAST.** You must, Mr. Scrooge, you must.

SCROOGE. It's me. [*Pauses; weeps*] Poor boy. He lived inside his head . . . alone . . . [*Pauses; weeps*] poor boy. [*Pauses; stops his weeping*] I wish . . . [*Dries his eyes on his cuff*] ah! it's too late!

PAST. What is the matter?

28 **SCROOGE.** There was a boy singing a Christmas Carol outside my door last night. I should like to have given him something: that's all.

PAST. [*Smiles; waves his hand to* SCROOGE] Come. Let us see another Christmas.

[*Lights out on little boy. A flash of light. A puff of smoke. Lights up on older boy*]

SCROOGE. Look! Me, again! Older now! [*Realizes*] Oh, yes . . . still alone.

[*The boy—a slightly older* SCROOGE—*sits alone in a chair, reading. The door to the* room opens and a young girl enters. She is much, much younger than this slightly older SCROOGE. She is, say, six, and he is, say, twelve. Elder SCROOGE *and the* GHOST OF CHRISTMAS PAST *stand watching the scene, unseen.*]

FAN. Dear, dear brother, I have come to bring you home.

BOY. Home, little Fan?

FAN. Yes! Home, for good and all! Father is so much kinder than he ever used to be, and home's like heaven! He spoke so gently to me one dear night when I was going to bed that I was not afraid to ask him once more if you might come home; and he said "yes" . . . you **29** should; and sent me in a coach to bring you. And you're to be a man and are never to come back here, but first, we're to be together all the Christmas long, and have the merriest time in the world.

BOY. You are quite a woman, little Fan!

[*Laughing; she drags at* BOY, *causing him to stumble to the door with her. Suddenly we hear a mean and terrible voice in the hallway. Off. It is the* SCHOOLMASTER.]

SCHOOLMASTER. Bring down Master Scrooge's travel box at once! He is to travel!

FAN. Who is that, Ebenezer?

BOY. O! Quiet, Fan. It is the Schoolmaster, himself!

[*The door bursts open and into the room bursts with it the* SCHOOLMASTER.]

SCHOOLMASTER. Master Scrooge?

BOY. Oh, Schoolmaster. I'd like you to meet my little sister, Fan, sir . . .

[*Two boys struggle on with* SCROOGE's *trunk.*]

FAN. Pleased, sir . . . [*She curtsies.*]

SCHOOLMASTER. You are to travel, Master Scrooge.

SCROOGE. Yes, sir. I know sir . . .

[*All start to exit, but* FAN *grabs the coattail of the mean old* SCHOOLMASTER.]

BOY. Fan!

SCHOOLMASTER. What's this?

FAN. Pardon, sir, but I believe that you've forgotten to say your goodbye to my brother, Ebenezer, who stands still now awaiting it . . . [*She smiles, curtsies, lowers her eyes.*] pardon, sir.

SCHOOLMASTER. [*Amazed*] I . . . uh . . . harumph . . . uhh . . . well, then . . . [*Outstretches hand*] Goodbye, Scrooge.

BOY. Uh, well, goodbye, Schoolmaster . . .

[*Lights fade out on all but* BOY *looking at* FAN; *and* SCROOGE *and* PAST *looking at them.*]

SCROOGE. Oh, my dear, dear little sister, Fan . . . how I loved her.

30 **PAST.** Always a delicate creature, whom a breath might have withered, but she had a large heart . . .

SCROOGE. So she had.

PAST. She died a woman, and had, as I think, children.

31 **SCROOGE.** One child.

PAST. True. Your nephew.

SCROOGE. Yes.

PAST. Fine, then. We move on, Mr. Scrooge. That warehouse, there? Do you know it?

SCROOGE. Know it? Wasn't I apprenticed[18] there?

---

18. apprenticed (ə pren' tist) *v.*: Receiving financial support and instruction in a trade in return for work.

PAST. We'll have a look.

[*They enter the warehouse. The lights crossfade with them, coming up on an old man in Welsh wig:* FEZZIWIG.]

SCROOGE. Why, it's old Fezziwig! Bless his heart; it's Fezziwig, alive again!

[FEZZIWIG *sits behind a large, high desk, counting. He lays down his pen; looks at the clock: seven bells sound.*]

Quittin' time . . .

FEZZIWIG. Quittin' time . . . [*He takes off his waistcoat and laughs; calls off*] Yo ho, Ebenezer! Dick!

[DICK WILKINS *and* EBENEZER SCROOGE—*a young man version—enter the room.* DICK *and* EBENEZER *are* FEZZIWIG's *apprentices.*]

SCROOGE. Dick Wilkins, to be sure! My fellow-'prentice! Bless my soul, yes. There he is. He was very much attached to me, was Dick. Poor Dick! Dear, dear!

FEZZIWIG. Yo ho, my boys. No more work tonight. Christmas Eve, Dick. Christmas, Ebenezer!

[*They stand at attention in front of* FEZZIWIG; *laughing*] **32**

Hilli-ho! Clear away, and let's have lots of room here! Hilli-ho, Dick! Chirrup, Ebenezer!

[*The young men clear the room, sweep the floor, straighten the pictures, trim the lamps, etc. The space is clear now. A fiddler enters, fiddling.*]

Hi-ho, Matthew! Fiddle away . . . where are my daughters?

[*The* FIDDLER *plays. Three young daughters of* FEZZIWIG *enter followed by six young male suitors. They are dancing to the music. All employees come in: workers, clerks, housemaids, cousins, the baker, etc.*

A Christmas Carol: Scrooge and Marley   **277**

30 **Critical Thinking and Reading** If Scrooge loved his sister so much, why is he so hostile toward her son, his only nephew?

31 **Thematic Idea** Compare the way Scrooge acts with the way the grandfather acts in the story "A Season of Acceptance" on page 197. In what other ways are the stories similar?

32 **Discussion** What kind of boss was Fezziwig? What effect did his personality have on his workers?

33 Literary Focus The Ghost of Christmas Past is being ironic. That is, the ghost is saying one thing but meaning the opposite.

34 Critical Thinking and Reading What happened to the vow young Scrooge made? Do you think most people keep the vows they make to themselves when they are young? Why or why not?

All dance. Full number wanted here. Throughout the dance, food is brought into the feast. It is "eaten" in dance, by the dancers. EBENEZER *dances with all three of the daughters, as does* DICK. *They compete for the daughters, happily, in the dance.* FEZZIWIG *dances with his daughters.* FEZZIWIG *dances with* DICK *and* EBENEZER. *The music changes:* MRS. FEZZIWIG *enters. She lovingly scolds her husband. They dance. She dances with* EBENEZER, *lifting him and throwing him about. She is enormously fat. When the dance is ended, they all dance off, floating away, as does the music.* SCROOGE *and the* GHOST OF CHRISTMAS PAST *stand alone now. The music is gone.*]

33 **PAST.** It was a small matter, that Fezziwig made those silly folks so full of gratitude.

SCROOGE. Small!

PAST. Shhh!

[*Lights up on* DICK *and* EBENEZER]

DICK. We are blessed, Ebenezer, truly, to have such a master as Mr. Fezziwig!

YOUNG SCROOGE. He is the best, best, the very and absolute best! If ever I own a firm of my own, I shall treat my apprentices with the same dignity and the same grace. We have learned a wonderful lesson from the master, Dick! **34**

DICK. Ah, that's a fact, Ebenezer. That's a fact!

PAST. Was it not a small matter, really? He spent but a few pounds[19] of his mortal money on your small party. Three or four

---

19. pounds (poŭndz) *n.*: A common type of money used in Great Britain.

pounds, perhaps. Is that so much that he deserves such praise as you and Dick so lavish now?

SCROOGE. It isn't that! It isn't that, Spirit. Fezziwig had the power to make us happy or unhappy; to make our service light or burdensome; a pleasure or a toil. The happiness he gave is quite as great as if it cost him a fortune.

PAST. What is the matter?

SCROOGE. Nothing particular.

PAST. Something, I think.

SCROOGE. No, no. I should like to be able to say a word or two to my clerk just now! That's all!

[EBENEZER *enters the room and shuts down all the lamps. He stretches and yawns. The* GHOST OF CHRISTMAS PAST *turns to* SCROOGE; *all of a sudden.*]

PAST. My time grows short! Quick!

[*In a flash of light,* EBENEZER *is gone, and in his place stands an* OLDER SCROOGE, *this one a man in the prime of his life. Beside him stands a young woman in a mourning dress. She is crying. She speaks to the man, with hostility.*]

WOMAN. It matters little . . . to you, very little. Another idol has displaced me.

MAN. What idol has displaced you?

WOMAN. A golden one.

MAN. This is an even-handed dealing of the world. There is nothing on which it is so hard as poverty; and there is nothing it professes to condemn with such severity as the pursuit of wealth!

WOMAN. You fear the world too much. Have I not seen your nobler aspirations fall off one by one, until the master-passion, Gain, engrosses you? Have I not?

SCROOGE. No!

MAN. What then? Even if I have grown so much wiser, what then? Have I changed towards you?

WOMAN. No . . .

MAN. Am I?

WOMAN. Our contract is an old one. It was made when we were both poor and content to be so. You *are* changed. When it was made, you were another man.

MAN. I was not another man: I was a boy.

WOMAN. Your own feeling tells you that you were not what you are. I am. That which promised happiness when we were one in heart is fraught with misery now that we are two . . .

SCROOGE. No!

WOMAN. How often and how keenly I have thought of this, I will not say. It is enough that I *have* thought of it, and can release you . . .

SCROOGE. [*Quietly*] Don't release me, madame . . .

MAN. Have I ever sought release?

WOMAN. In words. No. Never.

MAN. In what then?

WOMAN. In a changed nature; in an altered spirit. In everything that made my love of any worth or value in your sight. If this has never been between us, tell me, would you seek me out and try to win me now? Ah, no!

SCROOGE. Ah, yes!

MAN. You think not?

WOMAN. I would gladly think otherwise if I could, heaven knows! But if you were free today, tomorrow, yesterday, can even I believe

A Christmas Carol: Scrooge and Marley 279

35 **Discussion** Why must Scrooge explain this to the ghost? Is Scrooge beginning to understand the power of kindness?

36 **Critical Thinking and Reading** What do you think Scrooge wants to say to Cratchit right now?

37 **Discussion** Why does Scrooge's fiancée leave him? Why had he changed?

38 **Discussion** In what ways had Scrooge changed since he met this woman?

that you would choose a dowerless girl[20]—you who in your very confidence with her weigh everything by Gain; or, choosing her, do I not know that your repentance and regret would surely follow? I do; and I release you. With a full heart, for the love of him you once were.

SCROOGE. Please, I . . . I . . .

MAN. Please, I . . . I . . .

WOMAN. Please. You may—the memory of what is past half makes me hope you will—have pain in this. A very, very brief time, and you will dismiss the memory of it, as an unprofitable dream, from which it happened well that you awoke. May you be happy in the life that you have chosen for yourself . . .

SCROOGE. No!

39 **WOMAN.** Yourself . . . alone . . .

SCROOGE. No!

WOMAN. Goodbye, Ebenezer . . .

SCROOGE. Don't let her go!

MAN. Goodbye.

SCROOGE. No!

[*She exits.* SCROOGE *goes to younger man: himself.*]

40 You fool! Mindless loon! You fool!

MAN. [*To exited woman*] Fool. Mindless loon. Fool . . .

SCROOGE. Don't say that! Spirit, remove me from this place.

PAST. I have told you these were shadows of the things that have been. They are what they are. Do not blame me, Mr. Scrooge.

SCROOGE. Remove me! I cannot bear it!

---

20. **a dowerless** (dou′ ər les) **girl:** A girl without a dowery, the property or wealth a woman brought to her husband at marriage.

[*The faces of all who appeared in this scene are now projected for a moment around the stage: enormous, flimsy, silent.*]

Leave me! Take me back! Haunt me no longer!

[*There is a sudden flash of light: a flare. The* GHOST OF CHRISTMAS PAST *is gone.* SCROOGE *is, for the moment, alone onstage. His bed is turned down, across the stage. A small candle burns now in* SCROOGE'S *hand. There is a child's cap in his other hand. He slowly crosses the stage to his bed, to sleep.* MARLEY *appears behind* SCROOGE, *who continues his long, elderly cross to bed.* MARLEY *speaks directly to the audience.*]

MARLEY. Scrooge must sleep now. He must surrender to the irresistible drowsiness caused by the recognition of what was. [*Pauses*] The cap he carries is from ten lives past: his boyhood cap . . . donned atop a hopeful hairy head . . . askew, perhaps, or at a rakish angle. Doffed now in honor of regret.[21] Perhaps even too heavy to carry in his present state of weak remorse . . .

[SCROOGE *drops the cap. He lies atop his bed. He sleeps. To audience*]

He sleeps. For him, there's even more trouble ahead. [*Smiles*] For you? The play house tells me there's hot cider, as should be your anticipation for the specter Christmas Present and Future, for I promise you both. [*Smiles again*] So, I pray you hurry back to your seats refreshed and ready for a miser—to turn his coat of gray into a blazen Christmas holly-red.

41

[*A flash of lightning. A clap of thunder. Bats fly. Ghosty music.* MARLEY *is gone.*]

---

21. **donned . . . regret:** To *don* and *doff* a hat means to put it on and take it off; *askew* means "crooked," and *at a rakish angle* means "having a dashing or jaunty look."

THINKING ABOUT THE SELECTION

Recalling

1. What relationship did Scrooge and Marley have in the past?
2. For what purpose does scrooge's nephew come to see Scrooge?
3. What expression of Scrooge's sums up his attitude toward Christmas? Why?
4. How does Scrooge respond to the Thin Man and the Portly Man's request for money?
5. How does he respond to Cratchit's request for Christmas Day off?
6. What scenes of Scrooge's past life are revealed by the Ghost of Christmas Past?

Interpreting

7. How do the scenes of Scrooge's past reveal a change in him?
8. How does Scrooge react to each of these scenes?

Applying

9. Do you think people who are like Scrooge are ever really happy? Why or why not?

ANALYZING LITERATURE

Understanding Plot and Exposition

The **plot** of a play is the sequence of its incidents and events. The first part of the plot is called the **exposition**. Here the opening situation is established, major characters are introduced, and the central problem of the play is made clear. Also, here earlier events are revealed.

Once the opening situation is established, the plot of the play develops until the climax is reached. The part of the play that builds up to the climax is called the rising action.

1. Describe the situation established in Scene 1 of *A Christmas Carol: Scrooge and Marley.*
2. What earlier events are disclosed here?
3. What problem does Scrooge have?
4. As you were reading Act I, what thoughts or questions did you have about how the story would turn out?

CRITICAL THINKING AND READING

Recognizing Foreshadowing

Foreshadowing is the use of hints or clues to suggest future events. For example, in his speech at the end of Act I, Marley says of Scrooge: "For him, there's even more trouble ahead." When reading or viewing a play, you should be alert to such hints or clues.

1. Early in Scene 5, Scrooge says to the Ghost of Christmas Past, "There was a boy singing a Christmas Carol outside my door last night. I should like to have given him something . . ." How might this statement be a hint of a future development?
2. Find one other example of foreshadowing present in Act I.

UNDERSTANDING LANGUAGE

Understanding Latin Roots

A **root** is the part of a word that contains its basic meaning. Many words in English come from Latin roots. For example, when Marley describes Scrooge as "solitary as an oyster," he is using a word—*solitary*—that comes from the Latin root -*solus*-, meaning "alone." Look up the following words, which contain the same root, in a dictionary. Tell what each means.

1. solely
2. soliloquy
3. solitude
4. soloist

THINKING AND WRITING

Retelling *A Christmas Carol*

Imagine that you are going to entertain a group of young children by telling them the story of *A Christmas Carol,* Act I. Write a summary of the five scenes that you have just read so that if it were read aloud it would be a lively, easy-to-follow story that your young readers would understand and enjoy. Revise your summary to make sure it contains the important events.

A Christmas Carol: Scrooge and Marley 281

(Answers begin on p. 280.)

ANSWERS TO ANALYZING LITERATURE

1. Scene I establishes Marley's identity past and present and Scrooge's miserable nature. The atmosphere inside the office is as cold and bleak as the weather outside.
2. It is revealed that Scrooge conducted business on the day of Marley's funeral.
3. Scrooge is miserly, greedy, and cold-hearted.
4. Answers will differ, but students should respond that they wondered what caused Scrooge to act as he did and if he could change.

ANSWERS TO CRITICAL THINKING AND READING

1. It might mean that Scrooge is capable of feeling again and could become a warm and generous person.
2. Another example of foreshadowing is when Scrooge says to the ghost, "I should like to be able to say a word or two to my clerk just now!"

ANSWERS TO UNDERSTANDING LANGUAGE

1. Solely means (1) without another or others; alone (2) only, exclusively, merely, or altogether
2. Soliloquy means (1) an act or instance of talking to oneself (2) lines in a drama in which a character reveals his thoughts to the audience but not to the other characters, by speaking as if to himself
3. Solitude means (1) the state of being solitary, or alone; seclusion, isolation, or remoteness (2) a lonely or secluded place
4. Soloist means a person who performs a solo.

4. Scrooge responds that he supports the prisons and the workhouses and will not "aid" the poor further.
5. He tells Cratchit that it's unfair to have to pay him for a day off and tells him to be in the office early on the twenty-sixth.
6. Scrooge sees himself as a student, as an apprentice at Fezziwig's, at boarding school with his sister, and at his last meeting with his fiancée.

Interpreting

7. Scrooge has been a happy man at Fezziwig's. He had loved his sister, Fan, and his fiancée before being engulfed by greed.
8. Scrooge reacts emotionally to each scene and regrets much of his past and present.

Applying

9. Answers will differ. Suggested Response: People like Scrooge cannot be happy because they shut themselves off from other people, alienate themselves from people who love them, and find something negative to say about everything.

Challenge Think about other stories you've read lately. How did the main character's past in each story contribute to the present person? In what ways were the characters shaped by their pasts?

Literary Focus Different actors interpret their characters in different ways. You may prefer one interpretation to another when actually watching a performance because it comes closer to the way you visualized the character. One interpretation may also be preferable to another because it better elucidates the theme of the play.

Look For Your less advanced students may benefit from making a list of the character traits that Scrooge exhibited in Act I. Then, in a second column, students can note in Act II how each character trait changes for the better.

Writing/Prior Knowledge Have students discuss the validity of this old saying: "You can't teach an old dog new tricks." Then have them complete the freewriting assignment.

Vocabulary Have your less advanced students read the words aloud so that you can be sure they can pronounce them. These words may also give students some difficulty: *seething* (p. 283); *scabbard* (p. 284); *odious* (p. 288); *consequence* (p. 290); *phantom* (p. 291); *waning* (p. 292); *scoundrels, slovenly, defiantly* (p. 293); *obscene, parallel* (p. 295); *undulates, intercourse* (p. 297) *sealingwax* (p. 300); *endeavor, scuttle* (p. 301); and *borough* (p. 302). Be sure students know what these words mean as they read the story.

Spelling Tip Point out the double *l* in *dispelled*.

A Christmas Carol:
Scrooge and Marley, Act II

Character and Theme

A **character** in a play is portrayed, in part, by what he or she says in the dialogue. If the play is performed onstage, then the acting will greatly affect the portrayal. The actor's facial expressions, gestures, movements, speaking style, and so on, will make the character come alive. To understand a character when you are reading a play, therefore, imagine an actor performing the lines.

The **theme** of a play is its central idea, or insight into life. One way to arrive at the theme of a play is to notice how the main character changes. If you can explain why the main character changes for the better, or for the worse, you probably are very close to understanding the theme.

Look For

As you read Act II, notice how Scrooge reacts to the scenes presented by the Ghosts of Christmas Present and Christmas Future. In what way does he change? Why does he change? What does the change suggest about the theme of the play?

Writing

Write the heading What Makes People Change? on a piece of paper. Beneath it list six experiences that you think could lead to a big change in a person's life and behavior. Discuss your list with your classmates.

Vocabulary

Knowing the following words will help you as you read Act II of *A Christmas Carol: Scrooge and Marley.*

astonish (ə stän′ ish) *v.*: Amaze (p. 283)

compulsion (kəm pul′ shən) *n.*: A driving, irresistible force (p. 285)

severe (sə vir′) *adj.*: Harsh (p. 285)

meager (mē′ gər) *adj.*: Of poor quality, small in amount (p. 286)

threadbare (thred′ ber) *adj.*: Worn, shabby (p. 287)

audible (ô′ də b'l) *adj.*: Loud enough to be heard (p. 291)

gnarled (närld) *adj.*: Knotty and twisted (p. 291)

dispelled (dis peld′) *v.*: Scattered and driven away, made to vanish (p. 297)

Objectives

1 To connect character and theme
2 To support an opinion of a character
3 To write a review of a play

Support Material

Teaching Portfolio

Teacher Backup, p. 401

Grammar in Action Worksheet, *Ellipses,* p. 404

Grammar in Action Worksheet, *Agreement Between Pronouns and Antecedents,* p. 406

Usage and Mechanics Worksheet, p. 408

Vocabulary Check, p. 409

Critical Thinking and Reading Worksheet, *Supporting an Opinion of a Character,* p. 410

Language Worksheet, *Synonyms and Antonyms,* p. 412

Selection Test, p. 413

Art Transparency 7, *View of Heath Street, Hampstead, by Night,* John Atkinson Grimshaw

ACT II

Scene 1

[*Lights. Choral music is sung. Curtain.* SCROOGE, *in bed, sleeping, in spotlight. We cannot yet see the interior of his room.* MARLEY, *opposite, in spotlight equal to* SCROOGE'S. MARLEY *laughs. He tosses his hand in the air and a flame shoots from it, magically, into the air. There is a thunder clap, and then another; a lightning flash, and then another. Ghostly music plays under. Colors change.* MARLEY'S *spotlight has gone out and now reappears, with* MARLEY *in it, standing next to the bed and the sleeping* SCROOGE. MARLEY *addresses the audience directly.*]

MARLEY. Hear this snoring Scrooge! Sleeping to escape the nightmare that is his waking day. What shall I bring to him now? I'm afraid nothing would astonish old Scrooge now. Not after what he's seen. Not a baby boy, not a rhinoceros, nor anything in between would astonish Ebenezer Scrooge just now. I can think of nothing . . . [*Suddenly*] that's it! Nothing! [*He speaks confidentially.*] I'll have the clock strike one and, when he awakes expecting my second messenger, there will be no one . . . nothing. Then I'll have the bell strike twelve. And then one again . . . and then nothing. Nothing . . . [*Laughs*] nothing will . . . astonish him. I think it will work.

[*The bell tolls one.* SCROOGE *leaps awake.*]

SCROOGE. One! One! This is it: time! [*Looks about the room*] Nothing!

[*The bell tolls midnight.*]

Midnight! How can this be? I'm sleeping backwards.

[*One again*]

Good heavens! One again! I'm sleeping back and forth! [*A pause.* SCROOGE *looks about.*] Nothing! Absolutely nothing!

[*Suddenly, thunder and lightning.* MARLEY *laughs and disappears. The room shakes and glows. There is suddenly springlike music.* SCROOGE *makes a run for the door.*]

MARLEY. Scrooge!

SCROOGE. What?

MARLEY. Stay you put!

SCROOGE. Just checking to see if anyone is in here.

[*Lights and thunder again: more music.* MARLEY *is of a sudden gone. In his place sits the* GHOST OF CHRISTMAS PRESENT—*to be called in the stage directions of the play,* PRESENT—*center of room. Heaped up on the floor, to form a kind of throne, are turkeys, geese, game, poultry, brawn, great joints of meat, suckling pigs, long wreaths of sausages, mince-pies, plum puddings, barrels of oysters, red hot chestnuts, cherry-cheeked apples, juicy oranges, luscious pears, immense twelfth cakes, and seething bowls of punch, that make the chamber dim with their delicious steam. Upon this throne sits* PRESENT, *glorious to see. He bears a torch, shaped as a Horn of Plenty.[1]* SCROOGE *hops out of the door, and then peeks back again into his bedroom.* PRESENT *calls to* SCROOGE.]

PRESENT. Ebenezer Scrooge. Come in, come in! Come in and know me better!

SCROOGE. Hello. How should I call you?

PRESENT. I am the Ghost of Christmas Present. Look upon me.

---

1. Horn of Plenty: A horn overflowing with fruits, flowers, and grain, standing for wealth and abundance.

3 Critical Thinking and Reading
What is the ghost really asking Scrooge? Who are the younger members of his family?

[PRESENT *is wearing a simple green robe. The walls around the room are now covered in greenery, as well. The room seems to be a perfect grove now: leaves of holly, mistletoe and ivy reflect the stage lights. Suddenly, there is a mighty roar of flame in the fireplace and now the hearth burns with a lavish, warming fire. There is an ancient scabbard girdling the* GHOST's *middle, but without sword. The sheath is gone to rust.*]

You have never seen the like of me before?

SCROOGE. Never.

PRESENT. You have never walked forth with younger members of my family; my elder brothers born on Christmases past. **3**

284   *Drama*

Grammar in Action

A **personal pronoun must agree with its antecedent** in both person and number. Person tells whether the pronoun refers to the person speaking (first person), the person spoken to (second person), or the person, place, or thing spoken about (third person). Number indicates whether the pronoun is singular or plural. The following passage by Israel Horovitz illustrates the correct use of pronoun-antecedent agreement:

These *revelers,* Mr. Scrooge, carry *their* own dinners to *their* jobs, where they will work to bake the meals the *rich men and women* of this city will eat as *their* Christmas dinners.

The pronouns used in this sentence agree with their antecedents in both person and number. The antecedents *revelers* and *rich men and women* are both third-person and plural. Therefore, the pronouns used in their places; *their, their, they, their* are also third-person and plural.

SCROOGE. I don't think I have. I'm afraid I've not. Have you had many brothers, Spirit?

PRESENT. More than eighteen hundred.

SCROOGE. A tremendous family to provide for! [PRESENT *stands*] Spirit, conduct me where you will. I went forth last night on compulsion, and learnt a lesson which is working now. Tonight, if you have aught to teach me, let me profit by it.

PRESENT. Touch my robe.

[SCROOGE *walks cautiously to* PRESENT *and touches his robe. When he does, lightning flashes, thunder claps, music plays. Blackout*]

Scene 2

[*PROLOGUE:* MARLEY *stands spotlit, L. He speaks directly to the audience.*]

MARLEY. My ghostly friend now leads my living partner through the city's streets.

[*Lights up on* SCROOGE *and* PRESENT]

See them there and hear the music people make when the weather is severe, as it is now.

[*Winter music. Choral group behind scrim, sings. When the song is done and the stage is re-set, the lights will fade up on a row of shops, behind the singers. The choral group will hum the song they have just completed now and mill about the streets,[2] carrying their dinners to the bakers' shops and restaurants. They will, perhaps, sing about being poor at Christmastime, whatever.*]

PRESENT. These revelers, Mr. Scrooge, carry their own dinners to their jobs, where they will work to bake the meals the rich men and women of this city will eat as their Christmas dinners. Generous people these . . . to care for the others, so . . .

[PRESENT *walks among the choral group and a sparkling incense[3] falls from his torch on to their baskets, as he pulls the covers off of the baskets. Some of the choral group become angry with each other.*]

MAN #1. Hey, you, watch where you're going.

MAN #2. Watch it yourself, mate!

[PRESENT *sprinkles them directly, they change.*]

MAN #1. I pray go in ahead of me. It's Christmas. You be first!

MAN #2. No, no, I must insist that YOU be first!

MAN #1. All right, I shall be, and gratefully so.

MAN #2. The pleasure is equally mine, for being able to watch you pass, smiling.

MAN #1. I would find it a shame to quarrel on Christmas Day . . .

MAN #2. As would I.

MAN #1. Merry Christmas then, friend!

MAN #2. And a Merry Christmas straight back to you!

[*Church bells toll. The choral group enter the buildings: the shops and restaurants; they exit the stage, shutting their doors closed behind them. All sound stops.* SCROOGE *and* PRESENT *are alone again.*]

SCROOGE. What is it you sprinkle from your torch?

PRESENT. Kindness.

---

2. **mill about the streets:** Walk around aimlessly.

3. **incense** (in′ sens) *n.:* Any of various substances that produce a pleasant odor when burned.

A Christmas Carol: Scrooge and Marley 285

---

4 Discussion Compare and contrast Scrooge's reaction to this ghost with his reaction to the Ghost of Christmas Past. Has Scrooge become more receptive? Why?

5 Literary Focus As this is the Ghost of Christmas Present, Scrooge is actually walking the same streets he walks every day. But on this walk he will notice things that he has, for some time, chosen to ignore.

Student Activity 1. Rewrite each of the following sentences, filling in the blank with an appropriate pronoun.

1. Each dog had to pull _____ sled over the Arctic trail.

2. Neither Tom nor Dick studied for _____ tests.

3. Jane and Sally went to _____ grandmother's house over Christmas vacation.

Student Activity 2. Write three original sentences in which you have pronouns and antecedents in agreement.

6 **Discussion** Why do the very poor need kindness the most?

7 **Discussion** How can you tell that Scrooge has not yet been completely changed? What does the ghost think of Cratchit's large family?

SCROOGE. Do you sprinkle your kindness on any particular people or on all people?

PRESENT. To any person kindly given. And to the very poor most of all.

SCROOGE. Why to the very poor most?

PRESENT. Because the very poor need it most. Touch my heart . . . here, Mr. Scrooge. We have another journey.

[SCROOGE *touches the* GHOST's *heart and music plays, lights change color, lightning flashes, thunder claps. A choral group appears on the street, singing Christmas carols.*]

Scene 3

[MARLEY *stands spotlit in front of a scrim on which is painted the exterior of* CRATCHIT's *four-roomed house. There is a flash and a clap and* MARLEY *is gone. The lights shift color again, the scrim flies away, and we are in the interior of the* CRATCHIT *family home.* SCROOGE *is there, with the* SPIRIT (PRESENT), *watching* MRS. CRATCHIT *set the table, with the help of* BELINDA CRATCHIT *and* PETER CRATCHIT, *a baby, pokes a fork into the mashed potatoes on his highchair's tray. He also chews on his shirt collar.*]

SCROOGE. What is this place, Spirit?

PRESENT. This is the home of your employee, Mr. Scrooge. Don't you know it?

SCROOGE. Do you mean Cratchit, Spirit? Do you mean this is Cratchit's home?

PRESENT. None other.

SCROOGE. These children are his?

PRESENT. There are more to come presently.

SCROOGE. On his meager earnings! What foolishness!

PRESENT. Foolishness, is it?

286 Drama

SCROOGE. Wouldn't you say so? Fifteen shillings[4] a week's what he gets!

PRESENT. I would say that he gets the pleasure of his family, fifteen times a week times the number of hours a day! Wait, Mr. Scrooge. Wait, listen and watch. You might actually learn something . . .

MRS. CRATCHIT. What has ever got your precious father then? And your brother, Tiny Tim? And Martha warn't as late last Christmas by half an hour!

[MARTHA *opens the door, speaking to her mother as she does.*]

MARTHA. Here's Martha, now, Mother! [*She laughs. The* CRATCHIT CHILDREN *squeal with delight.*]

BELINDA. It's Martha, Mother! Here's Martha!

PETER. Marthmama, Marthmama! Hullo!

BELINDA. Hurrah! Martha! Martha! There's such an enormous goose for us, Martha!

MRS. CRATCHIT. Why, bless your heart alive, my dear, how late you are!

MARTHA. We'd a great deal of work to finish up last night, and had to clear away this morning, Mother.

MRS. CRATCHIT. Well, never mind so long as you are come. Sit ye down before the fire, my dear, and have a warm, Lord bless ye!

BELINDA. No, no! There's Father coming. Hide, Martha, hide!

[MARTHA *giggles and hides herself.*]

MARTHA. Where? Here?

PETER. *Hide, hide!*

BELINDA. Not there! *THERE!*

---

4. **fifteen shillings:** A small amount of money for a week's work.

[MARTHA *is hidden.* BOB CRATCHIT *enters, carrying* TINY TIM *atop his shoulder. He wears a threadbare and fringeless comforter hanging down in front of him.* TINY TIM *carries small crutches and his small legs are bound in an iron frame brace.*]

BOB and **TINY TIM.** Merry Christmas.

BOB. Merry Christmas my love, Merry Christmas Peter, Merry Christmas Belinda. Why, where is Martha?

MRS. CRATCHIT. Not coming.

BOB. Not coming? Not coming upon Christmas Day?

MARTHA. [*Pokes head out*] Ohhh, poor Father. Don't be disappointed.

BOB. What's this?

MARTHA. 'Tis I!

BOB. Martha! [*They embrace.*]

TINY TIM. Martha! Martha!

MARTHA. Tiny Tim!

[TINY TIM *is placed in* MARTHA's *arms.* BELINDA *and* PETER *rush him offstage.*]

BELINDA. Come, brother! You must come hear the pudding singing in the copper.

TINY TIM. The pudding? What flavor have we?

PETER. Plum! Plum!

TINY TIM! Oh, Mother! I love plum!

[*The children exit the stage, giggling.*]

MRS. CRATCHIT. And how did little Tim behave?

BOB. As good as gold, and even better. Somehow he gets thoughtful sitting by himself so much, and thinks the strangest things you ever heard. He told me, coming home, that he hoped people saw him in the church, because he was a cripple, and it might be pleasant to them to remember upon Christmas Day, who made lame beggars walk and blind men see. [*Pauses*] He has the oddest ideas sometimes, but he seems all the while to be growing stronger and more hearty . . . one would never know. [*Hears* TIM's *crutch on floor outside door*]

PETER. The goose has arrived to be eaten!

BELINDA. Oh, mama, mama, it's beautiful.

MARTHA. It's a perfect goose, Mother!

TINY TIM. To this Christmas goose, Mother and Father I say . . . [*Yells*] Hurrah! Hurrah!

OTHER CHILDREN. [*Copying* TIM] Hurrah! Hurrah!

[*The family sits round the table.* BOB *and* MRS. CRATCHIT *serve the trimmings, quickly. All sit; all bow heads; all pray.*]

BOB. Thank you, dear Lord, for your many gifts . . . our dear children; our wonderful meal; our love for one another; and the warmth of our small fire— [*Looks up at all*] A merry Christmas to us, my dear. God bless us!

ALL. [*Except* TIM] Merry Christmas! God bless us!

TINY TIM. [*In a short silence*] God bless us every one.

[*All freeze. Spotlight on* PRESENT *and* SCROOGE]

SCROOGE. Spirit, tell me if Tiny Tim will live.

PRESENT. I see a vacant seat . . . in the poor chimney corner, and a crutch without an owner, carefully preserved. If these shadows remain unaltered by the future, the child will die.

SCROOGE. No, no, kind Spirit! Say he will be spared!

A Christmas Carol: Scrooge and Marley   287

8 Critical Thinking and Reading
What kind of child is Tim? Is he growing stronger and heartier every day? Why does Bob say this?

9 Critical Thinking and Reading
What might save Tiny Tim?

10 Discussion Does this phrase "surplus population" sound familiar? Who is the ghost quoting?

11 Discussion How is Bob able to toast Scrooge? What does Mrs. Cratchit think of Scrooge?

PRESENT. If these shadows remain unaltered by the future, none other of my race will find
10 him here. What then? If he be like to die, he had better do it, and decrease the surplus population.

[SCROOGE *bows his head. We hear* BOB's *voice speak* SCROOGE'S *name.*]

BOB. Mr. Scrooge . . .

SCROOGE. Huh? What's that? Who calls?

11 **BOB.** [*His glass raised in a toast*] I'll give you Mr. Scrooge, the Founder of the Feast!

SCROOGE. Me, Bob? You toast *me*?

PRESENT. Save your breath, Mr. Scrooge. You can't be seen or heard.

MRS. CRATCHIT. The Founder of the Feast, indeed! I wish I had him here, that miser Scrooge. I'd give him a piece of my mind to feast upon, and I hope he'd have a good appetite for it!

BOB. My dear! Christmas Day!

MRS. CRATCHIT. It should be Christmas Day, I am sure, on which one drinks the health of such an odious, stingy, unfeeling man as Mr. Scrooge . . .

SCROOGE. Oh, Spirit, must I? . . .

288 Drama

MRS. CRATCHIT. You know he is, Robert! Nobody knows it better than you do, poor fellow!

BOB. This is Christmas Day, and I should like to drink to the health of the man who employs me and allows me to earn my living and our support and that man is Ebenezer Scrooge . . .

MRS. CRATCHIT. I'll drink to his health for your sake and the day's, but not for his sake . . . a Merry Christmas and a Happy New Year to you, Mr. Scrooge, wherever you may be this day!

SCROOGE. Just here, kind madam . . . out of sight, out of sight . . .

BOB. Thank you, my dear. Thank you.

SCROOGE. Thank *you*, Bob . . . and Mrs. Cratchit, too. No one else is toasting me, . . . not now . . . not ever. Of that I am sure . . .

BOB. Children . . .

ALL. Merry Christmas to Mr. Scrooge.

BOB. I'll pay you sixpence, Tim, for my favorite song.

TINY TIM. Oh, Father, I'd so love to sing it, but not for pay. This Christmas goose—this feast—you and Mother, my brother and sisters close with me: that's my pay—

BOB. Martha, will you play the notes on the lute,[5] for Tiny Tim's song.

BELINDA. May I sing, too, Father?

BOB. We'll all sing.

[*They sing a song about a tiny child lost in the snow—probably from Wordsworth's poem.* TIM *sings the lead vocal; all chime in for the chorus. Their song fades under, as* THE GHOST OF CHRISTMAS PRESENT *speaks.*]

---

5. lute (lo̅o̅t) *n.*: An old-fashioned stringed instrument like a guitar.

PRESENT. Mark my words, Ebenezer Scrooge. I do not present the Cratchits to you because they are a handsome, or brilliant family. They are not handsome. They are not brilliant. They are not well-dressed, or tasteful to the times. Their shoes are not even waterproofed by virtue of money or cleverness spent. So when the pavement is wet, so are the insides of their shoes and the tops of their toes. These are the Cratchits, Mr. Scrooge. They are not highly special. They are happy, grateful, pleased with one another, contented with the time and how it passes. They don't sing very well, do they? But, nonetheless, they do sing . . . [*Pauses*] think of that, Scrooge. Fifteen shillings a week and they do sing . . . hear their song until its end.

SCROOGE. I am listening.

[*The chorus sings full volume now, until . . . the song ends here.*]

Spirit, it must be time for us to take our leave. I feel in my heart that it is . . . that I must think on that which I have seen here . . .

PRESENT. Touch my robe again . . .

[SCROOGE *touches* PRESENT'S *robe. The lights fade out on the* CRATCHITS, *who sit, frozen, at the table.* SCROOGE *and* PRESENT *in a spotlight now. Thunder, lightning, smoke. They are gone.*]

Scene 4

[MARLEY *appears D.L. in single spotlight. A storm brews. Thunder and lightning.* SCROOGE *and* PRESENT *"fly" past, U. The storm continues, furiously, and, now and again,* SCROOGE *and* PRESENT *will zip past in their travels.* MARLEY *will speak straight out to the audience.*]

A Christmas Carol: Scrooge and Marley **289**

12 **Critical Thinking and Reading**
What lesson can Tiny Tim teach Scrooge?

13 **Critical Thinking and Reading**
Contrast the values in the Cratchit family with Scrooge's values.

14 **Discussion** What point does Scrooge's nephew make about who suffers the most from Scrooge's attitude?

15 **Discussion** Why does Fred continue to invite Scrooge for Christmas each year?

MARLEY. The Ghost of Christmas Present, my co-worker in this attempt to turn a miser, flies about now with that very miser, Scrooge, from street to street, and he points out partygoers on their way to Christmas parties. If one were to judge from the numbers of people on their way to friendly gatherings, one might think that no one was left at home to give anyone welcome . . . but that's not the case, is it? Every home is expecting company and . . . [*He laughs.*] Scrooge is amazed.

[SCROOGE *and* PRESENT *zip past again. The lights fade up around them. We are in the* NEPHEW's *home, in the living room,* PRESENT *and* SCROOGE *stand watching the* NEPHEW: FRED *and his wife, fixing the fire.*]

SCROOGE. What is this place? We've moved from the mines!

PRESENT. You do not recognize them?

SCROOGE. It is my nephew! . . . and the one he married . . .

[MARLEY *waves his hand and there is a lightning flash. He disappears.*]

FRED. It strikes me as sooooo funny, to think of what he said . . . that Christmas was a humbug, as I live! He believed it!

WIFE. More shame for him, Fred!

FRED. Well, he's a comical old fellow, that's the truth.

WIFE. I have no patience with him.

14 **FRED.** Oh, I have! I am sorry for him; I couldn't be angry with him if I tried. Who suffers by his ill whims? Himself, always . . .

SCROOGE. It's me they talk of, isn't it, Spirit?

FRED. Here, wife, consider this. Uncle Scrooge takes it into his head to dislike us, and he won't come and dine with us. What's the consequence?

WIFE. Oh . . . you're sweet to say what I think you're about to say, too, Fred . . .

FRED. What's the consequence? He don't lose much of a dinner by it, I can tell you that!

WIFE. Ooooooo, Fred! Indeed, I think he loses a very good dinner . . . ask my sisters, or your bachelor friend, Topper . . . ask any of them. They'll tell you what old Scrooge, your uncle, missed: a dandy meal!

FRED. Well, that's something of a relief, wife. Glad to hear it! [*He hugs his wife. They laugh. They kiss.*] The truth is, he misses much yet. I mean to give him the same chance every year, whether he likes it or not, for I pity him. Nay, he is my only uncle and I feel for the old miser . . . but, I tell you, wife: I see my dear and perfect mother's face on his own wizened cheeks and brow: brother and sister they were, and I cannot erase that from each view of him I take . . . 15

WIFE. I understand what you say, Fred, and I am with you in your yearly asking. But he never will accept, you know. He never will.

FRED. Well, true, wife. Uncle may rail at Christmas till he dies. I think I shook him some with my visit yesterday . . . [*Laughing*] I refused to grow angry . . . no matter how nasty he became . . . [*Whoops*] It was HE who grew angry, wife! [*They both laugh now.*]

SCROOGE. What he says is true, Spirit . . .

FRED and **WIFE.** Bah, humbug!

FRED. [*Embracing his wife*] There is much laughter in our marriage, wife. It pleases me. You please me . . .

WIFE. And you please me, Fred. You are a good man . . . [*They embrace.*] Come now. We must have a look at the meal . . . our guests will soon arrive . . . my sisters, Topper . . .

FRED. A toast first . . . [*He hands her a glass.*] A toast to Uncle Scrooge . . . [*Fills their glasses*]

WIFE. A toast to him?

FRED. Uncle Scrooge has given us plenty of merriment. I am sure, and it would be ungrateful not to drink to his health. And I say . . . *Uncle Scrooge!*

WIFE. [*Laughing*] You're a proper loon,[6] Fred . . . and I'm a proper wife to you . . . [*She raises her glass.*] Uncle Scrooge! [*They drink. They embrace. They kiss.*]

SCROOGE. Spirit, please, make me visible! Make me audible! I want to talk with my nephew and my niece!

[*Calls out to them. The lights that light the room and* FRED *and wife fade out.* SCROOGE *and* PRESENT *are alone, spotlit.*]

PRESENT. These shadows are gone to you now, Mr. Scrooge. You may return to them later tonight in your dreams. [*Pauses*] My time grows short, Ebenezer Scrooge. Look you on me! Do you see how I've aged?

SCROOGE. Your hair has gone gray! Your skin, wrinkled! Are spirits' lives so short?

PRESENT. My stay upon this globe is very brief. It ends tonight.

SCROOGE. Tonight?

PRESENT. At midnight. The time is drawing near!

―――――――
6. a proper loon: A silly person.

[*Clock strikes 11:45.*]

Hear those chimes? In a quarter hour, my life will have been spent! Look, Scrooge, man. Look you here.

[*Two gnarled baby dolls are taken from* PRESENT's *skirts.*]

SCROOGE. Who are they?

PRESENT. They are Man's children, and they cling to me, appealing from their fathers. The boy is Ignorance; the girl is Want. Beware them both, and all of their degree, but most of all beware this boy, for I see that written on his brow which is doom, unless the writing be erased. [*He stretches out his arm. His voice is now amplified: loudly and oddly.*]

SCROOGE. Have they no refuge or resource?

PRESENT. Are there no prisons? Are there no workhouses? [*Twelve chimes*] Are there no prisons? Are there no workhouses?

[*A* PHANTOM, *hooded, appears in dim light, D., opposite.*]

Are there no prisons? Are there no workhouses?

[PRESENT *begins to deliquesce.* SCROOGE *calls after him.*]

SCROOGE. Spirit, I'm frightened! Don't leave me! Spirit!

PRESENT. Prisons? Workhouses? Prisons? Workhouses . . .

[*He is gone.* SCROOGE *is alone now with the* PHANTOM, *who is, of course, the* GHOST OF CHRISTMAS FUTURE. *The* PHANTOM *is shrouded in black. Only its outstretched hand is visible from under his ghostly garment.*]

16 Discussion Compare this toast to the Cratchits' toast to Scrooge. How are the toasts alike and how are they different?

17 Critical Thinking and Reading What is the significance of the Ghost of Christmas Present aging in so short a time?

18 Discussion What do this boy and girl represent? Why should Scrooge beware of the boy even more than the girl?

19 Discussion What effect do Scrooge's own words have on him now?

20 Discussion Why is Scrooge now willing to accompany the ghost even though he fears the Ghost of the Future even more that he feared the other two? Do the ghostly visits seem to be working?

21 Reading Strategy Predict what Scrooge will see in his future. Do you think he'll become a changed man? Will he be able to change the future?

22 Discussion Whose funeral are the businessmen talking about? What is their attitude toward the deceased?

SCROOGE. Who are you, Phantom? Oh, yes, I think I know you! You are, are you not, the Spirit of Christmas Yet to Come? [*No reply*] And you are about to show me the shadows of the things that have not yet happened, but will happen in time before us. Is that not so, Spirit?

[*The* PHANTOM *allows* SCROOGE *a look at his face. No other reply wanted here. A nervous giggle here*]

20 Oh, Ghost of the Future, I fear you more than any Specter I have seen! But, as I know that your purpose is to do me good and as I hope to live to be another man from what I was, I am prepared to bear you company.

[FUTURE *does not reply, but for a stiff arm, hand and finger set, pointing forward.*]

21 Lead on, then, lead on. The night is waning fast, and it is precious time to me. Lead on, Spirit!

[FUTURE *moves away from* SCROOGE *in the same rhythm and motion employed at its arrival.* SCROOGE *falls into the same pattern, a considerable space apart from the* SPIRIT. *In the space between them,* MARLEY *appears. He looks to* FUTURE *and then to* SCROOGE. *He claps his hands. Thunder and lightning. Three* BUSINESSMEN *appear, spotlighted singularly: One is D.L.; One is D.R.; One is U.C. Thus, six points of the stage should now be spotted in light.* MARLEY *will watch this scene from his position,* C. SCROOGE *and* FUTURE *are R. and L. of C.*]

FIRST BUSINESSMAN. Oh, no, I don't know much about it either way, I only know he's dead.

SECOND BUSINESSMAN. When did he die?

FIRST BUSINESSMAN. Last night, I believe.

SECOND BUSINESSMAN. Why, what was the matter with him? I thought he'd never die, really . . .

FIRST BUSINESSMAN. [*Yawning*] Goodness knows, goodness knows . . .

THIRD BUSINESSMAN. What has he done with his money?

SECOND BUSINESSMAN. I haven't heard. Have you?

FIRST BUSINESSMAN. Left it to his Company, perhaps. Money to money; you know the expression . . .

THIRD BUSINESSMAN. He hasn't left it to *me*. That's all I know . . .

22

FIRST BUSINESSMAN. [*Laughing*] Nor to me . . . [*Looks at* SECOND BUSINESSMAN] You, then? You got his money???

SECOND BUSINESSMAN. [*Laughing*] Me, me, his money? Nooooo! [*They all laugh.*]

THIRD BUSINESSMAN. It's likely to be a cheap funeral, for upon my life, I don't know of a living soul who'd care to venture to it. Suppose we make up a party and volunteer?

SECOND BUSINESSMAN. I don't mind going if a lunch is provided, but I must be fed, if I make one.

FIRST BUSINESSMAN. Well, I am the most disinterested among you, for I never wear black gloves, and I never eat lunch. But I'll offer to go, if anybody else will. When I come to think of it, I'm not all sure that I wasn't his most particular friend; for we used to stop and speak whenever we met. Well, then . . . bye, bye!

SECOND BUSINESSMAN. Bye, bye . . .

THIRD BUSINESSMAN. Bye, bye . . .

[*They glide offstage in three separate directions. Their lights follow them.*]

SCROOGE. Spirit, why did you show me this? Why do you show me businessmen from my streets as they take the death of Jacob Marley. That is a thing past. You are *future*!

[JACOB MARLEY *laughs a long, deep laugh. There is a thunder clap and lightning flash, and he is gone.* SCROOGE *faces* FUTURE, *alone on stage now.* FUTURE *wordlessly stretches out his arm-hand-and-finger-set, pointing into the distance, U. There, above them, Scoundrels "fly" by, half-dressed and slovenly. When this scene has passed, a woman enters the playing area. She is almost at once followed by a second woman; and then a man in faded black; and then, suddenly, an old man, who smokes a pipe. The old man scares the other three. They laugh, anxious.*]

FIRST WOMAN. Look here, old Joe, here's a chance! If we haven't all three met here without meaning it!

OLD JOE. You couldn't have met in a better place. Come into the parlor. You were made free of it long ago, you know; and the other two an't strangers [*He stands; shuts a door. Shrieking*] We're all suitable to our calling. We're well matched. Come into the parlor. Come into the parlor . . .

[*They follow him D.* SCROOGE *and* FUTURE *are now in their midst, watching; silent. A truck comes in on which is set a small wall with fireplace and a screen of rags, etc. All props for the scene.*]

Let me just rake this fire over a bit . . .

[*He does. He trims his lamp with the stem of his pipe. The* FIRST WOMAN *throws a large bundle on to the floor. She sits beside it, crosslegged; defiantly.*]

FIRST WOMAN. What odds then? What odds, Mrs. Dilber? Every person has a right to take care of themselves. HE always did!

MRS. DILBER. That's true indeed! No man more so!

FIRST WOMAN. Why, then, don't stand staring as if you was afraid, woman! Who's the wiser? We're not going to pick holes in each other's coats, I suppose?

MRS. DILBER. No, indeed! We should hope not!

FIRST WOMAN. Very well, then! That's enough. Who's the worse for the loss of a few things like these? Not a dead man, I suppose?

MRS. DILBER. [*Laughing*] No, indeed!

FIRST WOMAN. If he wanted to keep 'em after he was dead, the wicked old screw, why wasn't he natural in his lifetime? If he had been, he'd have had somebody to look after him when he was struck with Death, instead of lying gasping out his last there, alone by himself.

MRS. DILBER. It's the truest word that was ever spoke. It's a judgment on him.

FIRST WOMAN. I wish it were a heavier one, and it should have been, you may depend on it, if I could have laid my hands on anything else. Open that bundle, old Joe, and let me know the value of it. Speak out plain. I'm not afraid to be the first, nor afraid for them to see it. We knew pretty well that we were helping ourselves, before we met here, I believe. It's no sin. Open the bundle, Joe.

FIRST MAN. No, no, my dear! I won't think of letting you being the first to show what you've . . . earned . . . earned from this. I throw in mine. [*He takes a bundle from his shoulder, turns it upside down, and emp-*

A Christmas Carol: Scrooge and Marley   293

23 **Critical Thinking and Reading** Why doesn't Scrooge realize that it's his own death the ghost is showing him?

24 **Discussion** What are Joe and the two women doing? Who are they? Why didn't anyone stop them?

ties its contents out on to the floor.] It's not very extensive, see . . . seals . . . a pencil case . . . sleeve buttons . . .

MRS. DILBER. Nice sleeve buttons, though . . .

FIRST MAN. Not bad, not bad . . . a brooch there . . .

OLD JOE. Not really valuable, I'm afraid . . .

FIRST MAN. How much, old Joe?

OLD JOE. [*Writing on the wall with chalk*] A pitiful lot, really. Ten and six and not a sixpence more!

FIRST MAN. You're not serious!

OLD JOE. That's your account and I wouldn't give another sixpence if I was to be boiled for not doing it. Who's next?

MRS. DILBER. Me! [*Dumps out contents of her bundle*] Sheets, towels, silver spoons, silver sugar-tongs . . . some boots . . .

OLD JOE. [*Writing on wall*] I always give too much to the ladies. It's a weakness of mine and that's the way I ruin myself. Here's your total comin' up . . . two pounds-ten . . . if you asked me for another penny, and made it an open question, I'd repent of being so liberal and knock off half-a-crown.

FIRST WOMAN. And now do MY bundle, Joe.

OLD JOE. [*Kneeling to open knots on her bundle*] So many knots, madam . . . [*He drags out large curtains; dark*] What do you call this? Bed curtains!

FIRST WOMAN. [*Laughing*] Ah, yes, bed curtains!

OLD JOE. You don't mean to say you took 'em down, rings and all, with him lying there?

FIRST WOMAN. Yes, I did, why not?

OLD JOE. You were born to make your fortune and you'll certainly do it.

FIRST WOMAN. I certainly shan't hold my hand, when I can get anything in it by reaching it out, for the sake of such a man as he was, I promise you, Joe. Don't drop that lamp oil on those blankets, now!

OLD JOE. His blankets?

FIRST WOMAN. Whose else's do you think? He isn't likely to catch cold without 'em, I daresay.

OLD JOE. I hope that he didn't die of anything catching? Eh?

FIRST WOMAN. Don't you be afraid of that. I ain't so fond of his company that I'd loiter about him for such things if he did. Ah! You may look through that shirt till your eyes ache, but you won't find a hole in it, nor a threadbare place. It's the best he had, and a fine one, too. They'd have wasted it, if it hadn't been for me.

OLD JOE. What do you mean "They'd have wasted it?"

FIRST WOMAN. Putting it on him to be buried in, to be sure. Somebody was fool enough to do it, but I took it off again . . . [*She laughs, as do they all, nervously.*] If calico[7] an't good enough for such a purpose, it isn't good enough then for anything. It's quite as becoming to the body. He can't look uglier than he did in that one!

SCROOGE. [*A low-pitched moan emits from his mouth; from the bones.*] [*OOOOOOOoo oooOOOOOooooOOOOOOOOooooOOOOO OooooOO!*]

OLD JOE. One pound six for the lot. [*He produces a small flannel bag filled with*

---

7. **calico** (kal′ ə kō) *n.*: A coarse and cheap cloth.

Grammar in Action

Ellipsis is a punctuation mark of three dots (. . .). It is used by writers in special situations to indicate the omission of a word or words. The ellipsis is used to show an interruption or pause in thought, to show a character's thought jumping from one subject to another without completing the first, to show a character's forgetfulness, or to show a voice trailing off.

Notice how Israel Horovitz uses the ellipsis in the dialogue of "A Christmas Carol: Scrooge and Marley":

FIRST MAN. It's not very extensive, see . . . seals . . . a pencil case . . . sleeve buttons . . .
MRS. DILBER. Nice sleeve buttons, though . . .
FIRST MAN. Not bad, not bad . . . a brooch there . . .
OLD JOE. Not really valuable, I'm afraid . . .

The special purpose for using the ellipsis is to capture the flavor and rhythm of conversation or thought. In the examples above we know by the ellipses that the characters' voices are trailing off and that they are pausing in midsentence. However, excessive use of the ellipsis can indicate a lack of understanding of its use, or indicate laziness on the part of the writer.

money. He divvies it out. He continues to pass around the money as he speaks. All are laughing.] That's the end of it, you see! He frightened every one away from him while he was alive, to profit us when he was dead! Hah ha ha!

ALL. HAHAHAHAhahahahahahah!

SCROOGE. OOOoooOOOoooOOOoooOOOooo OOoooOOoooOOOooo! [*He screams at them.*] Obscene demons! Why not market the corpse itself, as sell its trimming??? [*Suddenly*] Oh, Spirit, I see it, I see it! This unhappy man—this stripped-bare corpse . . . could very well be my own. My life holds parallel! My life ends that way now!

[SCROOGE *backs into something in the dark behind his spotlight.* SCROOGE *looks at* FUTURE, *who points to the corpse.* SCROOGE *pulls back the blanket. The corpse is, of course,* SCROOGE, *who screams. He falls aside the bed; weeping.*]

Spirit, this is a fearful place. In leaving it, I shall not leave its lesson, trust me. Let us go!

[FUTURE *points to the corpse.*]

Spirit, let me see some tenderness connected with a death, or that dark chamber, which we just left now, Spirit, will be forever present to me.

[FUTURE *spreads his robes again. Thunder and lightning. Lights up, U., in the Cratchit home setting.* MRS. CRATCHIT *and her daughters, sewing*]

TINY TIM'S VOICE. [*Off*] And He took a child and set him in the midst of them.

SCROOGE. [*Looking about the room; to* FUTURE] Huh? Who spoke? Who said that?

MRS. CRATCHIT. [*Puts down her sewing*] The color hurts my eyes. [*Rubs her eyes*] That's

better. My eyes grow weak sewing by candlelight. I shouldn't want to show your father weak eyes when he comes home . . . not for the world! It must be near his time . . .

PETER. [*In corner, reading. Looks up from book*] Past it, rather. But I think he's been walking a bit slower than usual these last few evenings, Mother.

MRS. CRATCHIT. I have known him walk with . . . [*Pauses*] I have know him walk with Tiny Tim upon his shoulder and very fast indeed.

PETER. So have I, Mother! Often!

DAUGHTER. So have I.

MRS. CRATCHIT. But he was very light to carry and his father loved him so, that it was not trouble—no trouble.

[BOB, *at door*]

And there is your father at the door.

[BOB CRATCHIT *enters. He wears a comforter. He is cold, forlorn.*]

PETER. Father!

BOB. Hello, wife, children . . .

[*The daughter weeps; turns away from* CRATCHIT.]

Children! How good to see you all! And you, wife. And look at this sewing! I've no doubt, with all your industry, we'll have a quilt to set down upon our knees in church on Sunday!

MRS. CRATCHIT. You made the arrangements today, then, Robert, for the . . . service . . . to be on Sunday.

BOB. The funeral. Oh, well, yes, yes, I did. I wish you could have gone. It would have done you good to see how green a place it is. But you'll see it often, I promised him that I

A Christmas Carol: Scrooge and Marley 295

26 Critical Thinking and Reading Although Scrooge sees parallel between himself and the corpse, he doesn't realize it's himself until he pulls back the blanket. Describe the feelings Scrooge must have had when he recognized himself.

27 Discussion Whose funeral are Bob and his wife talking about?

Student Activity One. Find five other uses of the ellipsis in "A Christmas Carol: Scrooge and Marley." Read each example aloud to see how the ellipsis adds to the natural flow of the dialogue.

Student Activity 2. An interior monologue is the thoughts of a character. Make up an interior dialogue for Scrooge in which he argues in his mind between remaining a mean miser or changing into a more thoughtful, kind man. Use the ellipsis to indicate when his thoughts jump from one idea to another.

28 Discussion What lesson have the Cratchits learned from Tiny Tim?

29 Critical Thinking and Reading What leads you to suspect that Scrooge intends to change his behavior?

would walk there on Sunday, after the service. [*Suddenly*] My little, little child! My little child!

ALL CHILDREN. [*Hugging him*] Oh, Father . . .

BOB. [*He stands*] Forgive me. I saw Mr. Scrooge's nephew, who you know I'd just met once before, and he was so wonderful to me, wife . . . he is the most pleasant-spoken gentleman I've ever met . . . he said "I am heartily sorry for it and heartily sorry for your good wife. If I can be of service to you in any way, here's where I live." And he gave me this card.

PETER. Let me see it!

BOB. And he looked me straight in the eye, wife, and said, meaningfully, "I pray you'll come to me, Mr. Cratchit, if you need some help. I pray you do." Now it wasn't for the sake of anything that he might be able to do for us, so much as for his kind way. It seemed as if he had known our Tiny Tim and felt with us.

MRS. CRATCHIT. I'm sure that he's a good soul.

BOB. You would be surer of it, my dear, if you saw and spoke to him. I shouldn't be at all surprised, if he got Peter a situation.

MRS. CRATCHIT. Only hear that, Peter!

MARTHA. And then, Peter will be keeping company with someone and setting up for himself!

PETER. Get along with you!

BOB. It's just as likely as not, one of these days, though there's plenty of time for that, my dear. But however and whenever we part from one another, I am sure we shall none of us forget poor Tiny Tim—shall we?—or this first parting that was among us?

ALL CHILDREN. Never, Father, never!

BOB. And when we recollect how patient and mild he was, we shall not quarrel easily among ourselves, and forget poor Tiny Tim in doing it.

ALL CHILDREN. No, Father, never!

LITTLE BOB. I am very happy, I am, I am, I am very happy.

[BOB *kisses his little son, as does* MRS. CRATCHIT, *as do the other children. The family is set now in one sculptural embrace. The lighting fades to a gentle pool of light, tight on them.*]

SCROOGE. Specter, something informs me that our parting moment is at hand. I know it, but I know not how I know it.

[FUTURE *points to the other side of the stage. Lights out on Cratchits.* FUTURE *moves slowing, gliding.* SCROOGE *follows.* FUTURE *points opposite.* FUTURE *leads* SCROOGE *to a wall and a tombstone. He points to the stone.*]

Am I that man those ghoulish parasites[8] so gloated over? [*Pauses*] Before I draw nearer to that stone to which you point, answer me one question. Are these the shadows of things that will be, or the shadows of things that MAY be, only?

[FUTURE *points to the gravestone.* MARLEY *appears in light well U. He points to grave as well. Gravestone turns front and grows to ten feet high. Words upon it: EBENEZER SCROOGE. Much smoke billows now from the grave. Choral music here.* SCROOGE *stands looking up at gravestone.* FUTURE *does not at all reply in mortals' words, but*

---

8. ghoulish parasites (gōōl' ish par' ə sits): The man and women who stole and divided Scrooge's goods after he died.

points once more to the gravestone. The stone undulates and glows. Music plays, beckoning SCROOGE. SCROOGE reeling in terror]

Oh, no, Spirit! Oh, no, no!

[FUTURE's *finger still pointing*]

Spirit! Hear me! I am not the man I was. I will not be the man I would have been but for this intercourse. Why show me this, if I am past all hope?

[FUTURE *considers* SCROOGE's *logic. His hand wavers.*]

Oh, Good Spirit, I see by your wavering hand that your good nature intercedes for me and pities me. Assure me that I yet may change these shadows that you have shown me by an altered life!

[FUTURE's *hand trembles; pointing has stopped.*]

30 I will honor Christmas in my heart and try to keep it all the year. I will live in the Past, the Present, and the Future. The Spirits of all Three shall strive within me. I will not shut out the lessons that they teach. Oh, tell me that I may sponge away the writing that is upon this stone!

[SCROOGE *makes a desperate stab at grabbing* FUTURE's *hand. He holds it firm for a moment, but* FUTURE, *stronger than* SCROOGE, *pulls away.* SCROOGE *is on his knees, praying.*]

Spirit, dear Spirit, I am praying before you. Give me a sign that all is possible. Give me a sign that all hope for me is not lost. Oh, Spirit, kind Spirit, I beseech thee: give me a sign . . .

31 [FUTURE *deliquesces, slowly, gently. The* PHANTOM's *hood and robe drop gracefully to*

the ground in a small heap. Music in. There is nothing in them. They are mortal cloth. The Spirit is elsewhere. SCROOGE *has his sign.* SCROOGE *is alone. Tableau. The lights fade to black.*]

Scene 5

[*The end of it.* MARLEY, *spotlighted, opposite* SCROOGE, *in his bed, spotlighted.* MARLEY *speaks to audience, directly.*]

MARLEY. [*He smiles at* SCROOGE.] The firm of Scrooge and Marley is doubly blessed; two misers turned; one, alas, in Death, too late; but the other miser turned in Time's penultimate nick.[9] Look you on my friend, Ebenezer Scrooge . . .

SCROOGE. [*Scrambling out of bed; reeling in delight*] I will live in the Past, in the Present, and in the Future! The Spirits of all Three shall strive within me!

MARLEY. [*He points and moves closer to* SCROOGE's *bed.*] Yes, Ebenezer, the bedpost is your own. Believe it! Yes, Ebenezer, the room is your own. Believe it!

32 **SCROOGE.** Oh, Jacob Marley! Wherever you are, Jacob, know ye that I praise you for this! I praise you . . . and heaven . . . and Christmastime! [*Kneels facing away from* MARLEY] I say it to ye on my knees, old Jacob, on my knees! [*He touches his bed curtains.*] Not torn down. My bed curtains are not at all torn down! Rings and all, here they are! They are here: I am here: the shadows of things that would have been, may now be dispelled. They will be, Jacob! I know they will be! [*He chooses clothing for the day. He tries different pieces of clothing and settles,*

---

9. in Time's penultimate nick: Just at the last moment.

30 **Discussion** What vow does Scrooge make now? Do you think he'll keep it? Why or why not?

31 **Discussion** What sign does Scrooge receive from the ghost? Of what is it a sign?

32 **Discussion** What is Scrooge's reaction when he finds himself back in his bedroom?

33 Critical Thinking and Reading
Contrast the new Scrooge with the old Scrooge in Act I of this play. Would the old Scrooge have acted this way? Why not?

perhaps, on a dress suit, plus a cape of the bed clothing: something of color.] I am light as a feather, I am happy as an angel, I am as merry as a schoolboy. [Yells out window and then out to audience] Merry Christmas to everybody! Merry Christmas to everybody! A Happy New Year to all the world! Hallo here! Whoop! Whoop! Hallo! Hallo! I don't know what day of the month it is! I don't care! I don't know anything! I'm quite a baby! I don't care! I don't care a fig! I'd much rather be a baby than be an old wreck like me or Marley! (Sorry, Jacob, wherever ye be!) Hallo! Hallo there!

298 Drama

[*Church bells chime in Christmas Day. A small boy, named* ADAM, *is seen now D.R., as a light fades up on him.*]

Hey, you boy! What's today? What day of the year is it?

ADAM. Today, sir? Why, it's Christmas Day!

SCROOGE. It's Christmas Day, is it? Whoop! Well, I haven't missed it after all, have I? The Spirits did all they did in one night. They can do anything they like, right? Of course they can! Of course they can!

ADAM. Excuse me, sir?

SCROOGE. Huh? Oh, yes, of course, what's your name, lad?

[SCROOGE *and* ADAM *will play their scene from their own spotlights.*]

ADAM. Adam, sir.

SCROOGE. Adam! What a fine, strong name! Do you know the poulterer's[10] in the next street but one, at the corner?

ADAM. I certainly should hope I know him, sir!

SCROOGE. A remarkable boy! An intelligent boy! Do you know whether the poulterer's have sold the prize turkey that was hanging up there? I don't mean the little prize turkey, Adam, I mean the big one!

ADAM. What, do you mean the one they've got that's as big as me?

SCROOGE. I mean, the turkey the size of Adam: that's the bird!

ADAM. It's hanging there now, sir.

SCROOGE. It is? Go and buy it! No, no, I am absolutely in earnest. Go and buy it and tell 'em to bring it here, so that I may give them

---

10. **poulterer's** (pōl′ tər ərz) *n.:* A British word for a store that sells chickens, turkeys, and geese.

the directions to where I want it delivered, as a gift. Come back here with the man, Adam, and I'll give you a shilling. Come back here with him in less than five minutes, and I'll give you half-a-crown!

ADAM. Oh, my sir! Don't let my brother in on this.

[ADAM *runs offstage.* MARLEY *smiles.*]

MARLEY. An act of kindness is like the first green grape of summer: one leads to another and another and another. It would take a queer man indeed to not follow an act of kindness with an act of kindness. One simply whets the tongue for more . . . the taste of kindness is too too sweet. Gifts—goods— are lifeless. But the gift of goodness one feels in the giving is full of life. It . . . is . . . a . . . wonder.

[*Pauses; moves closer to* SCROOGE, *who is totally occupied with his dressing and arranging of his room and his day. He is making lists, etc.* MARLEY *reaches out to* SCROOGE.]

ADAM. [*Calling, off*] I'm here! I'm here!

[ADAM *runs on with a man, who carries an enormous turkey.*]

Here I am, sir. Three minutes flat! A world record! I've got the poultryman and he's got the poultry! [*He pants, out of breath.*] I have earned my prize, sir, if I live . . .

[*He holds his heart, playacting.* SCROOGE *goes to him and embraces him.*]

SCROOGE. You are truly a champion, Adam . . .

MAN. Here's the bird you ordered, sir . . .

SCROOGE. *Oh, my, MY!!!* Look at the size of that turkey, will you! He never could have stood upon his legs, that bird! He would have snapped them off in a minute, like

A Christmas Carol: Scrooge and Marley 299

34 **Critical Thinking and Reading**
List some of the ways in which Scrooge has changed.

35 **Critical Thinking and Reading**
Evaluate Marley's speech. How true do you think it is and why?

sticks of sealingwax! Why you'll never be able to carry that bird to Camden-Town. I'll give you money for a cab . . .

MAN. Camden-Town's where it's goin', sir?

SCROOGE. Oh, I didn't tell you? Yes, I've written the precise address down just here on this . . . [*Hands paper to him*] Bob Cratchit's house. Now he's not to know who sends him this. Do you understand me? Not a word . . . [*Handing out money and chuckling*]

MAN. I understand, sir, not a word.

SCROOGE. Good. There you go then . . . this is for the turkey . . . [*Chuckle*] and this is for the taxi. [*Chuckle*] . . . and this is for your world-record run, Adam . . .

ADAM. But I don't have change for that, sir.

SCROOGE. Then keep it, my lad. It's Christmas!

ADAM. [*He kisses* SCROOGE's *cheek, quickly.*] Thank you, sir. Merry, Merry Christmas! [*He runs off.*]

MAN. And you've given me a bit overmuch here, too, sir . . .

SCROOGE. Of course I have, sir. It's Christmas!

MAN. Oh, well, thanking you, sir. I'll have this bird to Mr. Cratchit and his family in no time, sir. Don't you worry none about that. Merry Christmas to you, sir, and a very happy New Year, too . . .

[*The man exits.* SCROOGE *walks in a large circle about the stage, which is now gently lit. A chorus sings Christmas music far in the distance. Bells chime as well, far in the distance. A gentlewoman enters and passes.* SCROOGE *is on the streets now.*]

SCROOGE. Merry Christmas, madam . . .

WOMAN. Merry Christmas, sir . . .

[*The portly businessman from the first act enters.*]

SCROOGE. Merry Christmas, sir.

PORTLY MAN. Merry Christmas, sir.

SCROOGE. Oh, you! My dear sir! How do you do? I do hope that you succeeded yesterday! It was very kind of you. A Merry Christmas.

PORTLY MAN. Mr. Scrooge?

SCROOGE. Yes, Scrooge is my name though I'm afraid you may not find it very pleasant. Allow me to ask your pardon. And will you have the goodness to— [*He whispers into the man's ear.*]

PORTLY MAN. Lord bless me! My dear Mr. Scrooge, are you *serious!?!*

SCROOGE. If you please. Not a farthing[11] less. A great many back payments are included in it, I assure you. Will you do me that favor?

PORTLY MAN. My dear sir, I don't know what to say to such munifi—

SCROOGE. [*Cutting him off*] Don't say anything, please. Come and see me. Will you?

PORTLY MAN. I will! I will! Oh I will, Mr. Scrooge! It will be my pleasure!

SCROOGE. Thank'ee, I am much obliged to you. I thank you fifty times. Bless you!

[*Portly man passes offstage, perhaps by moving backwards.* SCROOGE *now comes to the room of his* NEPHEW *and* NIECE. *He stops at the door, begins to knock on it, loses his courage, tries again, loses his courage again, tries again, fails again, and then backs off and runs at the door, causing a tremendous bump against it. The* NEPHEW

---

11. farthing (fär' thiŋ) *n.*: A small British coin.

and NIECE *are startled.* SCROOGE, *poking head into room*]

Fred!

NEPHEW. Why, bless my soul! Who's that?

NEPHEW and **NIECE.** [*Together*] How now? Who goes?

SCROOGE. It's I. Your Uncle Scrooge.

NIECE. Dear heart alive!

SCROOGE. I have come to dinner. May I come in, Fred?

NEPHEW. *May you come in???!!!* With such pleasure for me you may, Uncle!!! What a treat!

NIECE. What a treat, Uncle Scrooge! Come in, come in!

[*They embrace a shocked and delighted* SCROOGE. FRED *calls into the other room.*]

37

NEPHEW. Come in here, everybody, and meet my Uncle Scrooge! He's come for our Christmas party!

[*Music in. Lighting here indicates that day has gone to night and gone to day again. It is early, early morning.* SCROOGE *walks alone from the party, exhausted, to his offices, opposite side of the stage. He opens his offices. The offices are as they were at the start of the play.* SCROOGE *seats himself with his door wide open so that he can see into the tank, as he awaits.* CRATCHIT, *who enters, head down, full of guilt.* CRATCHIT *starts writing almost before he sits.*]

38

SCROOGE. What do you mean by coming in here at this time of day, a full eighteen minutes late, Mr. Cratchit? Hallo, sir? Do you hear me?

BOB. I am very sorry, sir. I *am* behind my time.

SCROOGE. You are? Yes, I certainly think you are. Step this way, sir, if you please . . .

BOB. It's only but once a year, sir . . . it shall not be repeated. I was making rather merry yesterday and into the night . . .

SCROOGE. Now, I'll tell you what, Cratchit. I am not going to stand this sort of thing any longer. And therefore . . .

[*He stands and pokes his finger into* BOB'S *chest.*]

39

I am . . . about . . . to . . . raise . . . your salary.

BOB. Oh, no, sir, I . . . [*Realizes*] what did you say, sir?

SCROOGE. A Merry Christmas, Bob . . . [*He claps* BOB'S *back.*] A merrier Christmas, Bob, my good fellow! than I have given you for many a year. I'll raise your salary and endeavor to assist your struggling family and we will discuss your affairs this very afternoon over a bowl of smoking bishop.[12] Bob! Make up the fires and buy another coal scuttle before you dot another i, Bob. It's too cold in this place! We need warmth and cheer, Bob Cratchit! Do you hear me? DO . . . YOU . . . HEAR . . . ME?

[BOB CRATCHIT *stands, smiles at* SCROOGE. BOB CRATCHIT *faints. Blackout. As the main lights black out, a spotlight appears on* SCROOGE. C. *Another on* MARLEY. *He talks directly to the audience.*]

40

MARLEY. Scrooge was better than his word. He did it all and infinitely more; and to Tiny Tim, who did NOT die, he was a second father. He became as good a friend, as good a master, as good a man, as the good old city

---

12. **smoking bishop:** A hot, sweet, orange-flavored drink.

37 Discussion How do Scrooge's nephew and niece react to Scrooge's appearance at their home? Why is Scrooge surprised?

38 Discussion Why is Scrooge making fun of himself?

39 Critical Thinking and Reading What would the old Scrooge have said to Cratchit? Why is Bob shocked?

40 Discussion Why does Bob faint?

41 Critical Thinking and Reading
How do you think Scrooge celebrated Christmas from then on? Is this a noble goal for everyone to aspire to? Explain.

Reader's Response What was the most important lesson Scrooge learned about Christmas?

knew, or any other good old city, town, or borough in the good old world. And it was always said of him that he knew how to keep Christmas well, if any man alive possessed the knowledge. [*Pauses*] May that be truly said of us, and all of us. And so, as Tiny Tim observed . . .

41

TINY TIM. [*Atop* SCROOGE's *shoulder*] God Bless Us, Every One . . .

[*Lights up on chorus, singing final Christmas Song.* SCROOGE *and* MARLEY *and all spirits and other characters of the play join in. When the song is over, the lights fade to black.*]

302   *Drama*

Closure and Extension

ANSWERS TO THINKING ABOUT THE SELECTION
Recalling

1. The Ghost of Christmas Present foretells Tim's death.
2. Scrooge wants to be made visible so he can talk to them.
3. He promises to honor Christmas and keep the spirit of Christmas all year.
4. The Ghost of Christmas Future shows Scrooge (1) businessmen talking disinterestedly about Scrooge's funeral, (2) thieves dividing up Scrooge's stolen possessions, (3) the Cratchit family mourning the death of Tiny Tim, and (4) his own gravestone.
5. Scrooge becomes a good friend to the Cratchits and celebrates Christmas in the right spirit every year.

Interpreting

6. Cratchit is willing to toast Scrooge as his employer and out of simple

THINKING ABOUT THE SELECTION
Recalling

1. What fate does the Ghost of Christmas Present foretell for Tiny Tim?
2. What does Scrooge ask of the Ghost of Christmas Present while observing Fred and his wife?
3. What promise does Scrooge make to the Ghost of Christmas Present at the end of Scene 4?
4. What four sights does the Ghost of Christmas Future show Scrooge?
5. How does Scrooge live up to his promise in the final scene?

Interpreting

6. Compare and contrast the attitudes of Cratchit and his wife toward Scrooge when they toast him.
7. What does this difference in attitudes indicate about each of these characters?
8. What does Scrooge mean when he says, "I will live in the Past, the Present, and the Future"?
9. The name Scrooge has come to stand for anyone who is miserly and heartless. Explain why the name as it is usually used would not fit Scrooge as he is at the end of the play.

Applying

10. Charles Dickens lived in the nineteenth century. Do you think the message of his play applies to our world today?

ANALYZING LITERATURE
Connecting Character and Theme

Theme is the central idea or insight about life revealed in a work of literature. Because the character of Scrooge is of central importance to the play, understanding why he changes will help you understand the theme.

1. Find three places in Act II where Scrooge's reactions show him changing for the better.
2. In general, why does Scrooge change for the better over the course of Act II?
3. Using your answer to the preceding question, write a brief statement of the theme.

CRITICAL THINKING AND READING
Supporting an Opinion of a Character

Although an opinion cannot be proven true or false, a sound opinion is one that is supported by facts or details. For instance, to support an opinion that Scrooge is willing to change, you could mention his statement to the Ghost of Christmas Present (early in Act II) "Tonight, if you have aught to teach me, let me profit by it."

1. In Act II, Scene 3, Scrooge observes the Cratchits at home. What does Scrooge say that could support the opinion that he is developing feelings of kindness or compassion?
2. Write a one-sentence description of Scrooge as he is at the end of the play. Support your statement with two details from the final scene.

THINKING AND WRITING
Writing a Review of a Play

A review of a play does two things. First, it gives the reader a clear idea of what the play is about. Second, it tells why the reviewer liked or did not like the play. Write a review of A Christmas Carol: Scrooge and Marley. To prepare for the writing, first list those details of the story you will use to give students who will read the play next an idea of what it is about. Then jot down your thoughts on why you liked or did not like the play. When you revise your first draft, make sure that your review would be fair and useful to someone who was considering whether or not to read the play.

A Christmas Carol: Scrooge and Marley   303

cause he is shown the error of his ways, because he has seen the awful results of his cruel behavior, and because he wants to alter his own dismal fate.
3. Answers will differ. Suggested Response: People should be kind to one another not just for the sake of others but for their own sakes as well.

ANSWERS TO CRITICAL THINKING AND READING

1. Scrooge says to the spirit, "Say he will be spared!" while observing Tiny Tim.
2. Answers will differ. Suggested Response: Scrooge is a happy man because he now knows the value of kindness and the satisfaction of helping others. Two details that support this are (1) that Scrooge attends his nephew's Christmas party and (2) that he sends the Cratchits a turkey and gives Bob a raise.

Challenge How do you think most people would change if they could see their futures? In what ways might people become better? Do people ever change on their own without a dramatic experience to motivate them? Why or why not?

THINKING AND WRITING
Publishing Student Writing
Make a class booklet of reviews. Perhaps have students work in small groups to produce a review of A Christmas Carol: Scrooge and Marley. Then, as students read other plays and stories, they can form groups, write reviews, and add them to the booklet. Review the booklet with the students at the end of the year to see how, or if, their opinions have changed.

good will. Mrs. Cratchit doesn't want to toast Scrooge because she thinks he's miserly and mean, but does so out of good will for her husband.
7. It indicates that Bob is more charitable and forgiving than his wife who is more realistic and practical.
8. Scrooge means that he will remember the past, live correctly in the present, and remember that his behavior in the present will affect his future.

9. It would not fit because, by the end of the play, Scrooge has become loving, generous, and kind.

Applying
10. Answers will differ. Suggested Response: The message of the play is timeless and universal and so applies even to our world today. The most important goal for people is to be kind to one another. This is an especially meaningful message in our materialistic society.

ANSWERS TO ANALYZING LITERATURE

1. Answers will differ. Suggested Response: Scrooge is changing for the better when he (1) is willing to accompany the Ghost of Christmas Present, (2) wants to speak to his niece and nephew, and (3) is eager to accompany the Ghost of Christmas Future in order to change.
2. Answers will differ. Suggested Response: Scrooge changes be-

SEMANTIC MAPPING

After the students have read and discussed semantic mapping, expand the map by having the class suggest additional material. If you reproduce the map on page 305 on a transparency before the activity, you will save time and have it for next year.

Mapping

One good way to understand and remember what you read is to make a semantic map of the material. **Semantic mapping** is an easy method of organizing information in graphic form. It is an excellent study technique that helps you to see how things are related to one another and provides a graphic pattern that is easy to remember.

To make a semantic map, you first have to decide what is the important information in the material you read. What material do you want to organize? You may want to make a map that organizes the story elements such as plot, setting, and characters. You might choose to concentrate on plotting the character traits of one or more characters. After you have chosen your information, you need to determine what are the main ideas and pertinent details. Next decide what type of diagram is best suited to organizing this information. Now create your map. Once your map is constructed, begin filling it in with information you remember from your reading. First fill in all the information you can recall without referring back to the material. Then skim to find information you couldn't recall and to check your facts. After skimming, fill in any blanks.

To help you understand what a semantic map is like, look at the following map that was constructed to show how some of the story elements in *A Christmas Carol: Scrooge and Marley* relate to one another.

Notice that this map is very much like an outline because everything is organized into main ideas or headings and details or subheadings and everything is written as concisely as possible. "Who" refers to characters and includes only the major characters in the play. You could have expanded this map by listing two or three character traits under each character's name. "What" lists the main events in the plot, including those that occurred in the climax and conclusion. "Where" lists only the city in which the action takes place, but you could have included all of the various places Scrooge went.

Guidelines

- Select important information to organize.
- Identify the main ideas and pertinent details.
- Determine appropriate map shape.
- Construct map.
- Fill in map from memory.
- Fill in gaps by skimming material.

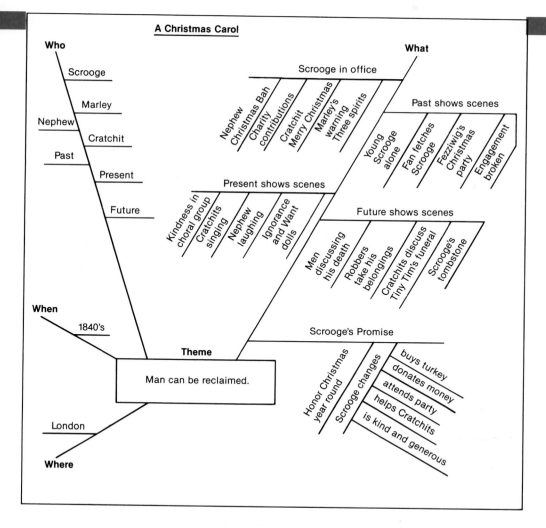

A Christmas Carol

Who
- Scrooge
- Marley
- Nephew
- Cratchit
- Past
- Present
- Future

What

Scrooge in office
- Nephew
- Christmas Bah
- Charity contributions
- Cratchit
- Merry Christmas
- Marley's warning
- Three spirits

Past shows scenes
- Young Scrooge alone
- Fan fetches Scrooge
- Fezziwig's Christmas party
- Engagement broken

Present shows scenes
- Kindness in choral group
- Cratchits singing
- Nephew laughing
- Ignorance and Want dolls

Future shows scenes
- Men discussing his death
- Robbers take his belongings
- Cratchits discuss Tiny Tim's funeral
- Scrooge's tombstone

When
- 1840's

Theme
Man can be reclaimed.

Scrooge's Promise
- Honor Christmas year round
- Scrooge changes
  - buys turkey
  - donates money
  - attends party
  - helps Cratchits
  - is kind and generous

Where
- London

Activity

Now you are going to create your own map. Brainstorm with your classmates to list the character traits that would apply to Scrooge in all the different periods in his life. Brainstorm some more to decide how you could organize these traits so that your map would show how he changed throughout the play. You will need to group the traits that refer to what he was like in the past in one group, in the present in another, and in the future in a third. Make your map. When you have created and filled in your map, compare it with those of your classmates.

Focus on Reading 305

The writing assignments on page 306 have students write creatively, while those on page 307 have them think about drama and write critically.

YOU THE WRITER
Guidelines for Evaluating Assignment 1

1. Has the student written a summary of a play which has both kinds of conflicts?
2. Does the student tell something about the characters involved in the conflict and show their methods of confrontation?
3. Does the student show the main character having doubts and then resolving the problem?
4. Has the student focused on the way one person's actions cause the other person's response?
5. Is the essay free from grammar, usage, and mechanics errors?

Guidelines for Evaluating Assignment 2

1. Does the scene focus on the conflict between two people and present the basic facts about the people and their situation?
2. Does the scene show them becoming more seriously involved in the conflict?
3. Is the scene written entirely in dialogue and stage directions, which make the characters seem as if they are talking to one another?
4. Is the scene free from grammar, usage, and mechanics errors?

Guidelines for Evaluating Assignment 3

1. Does the introductory paragraph explain what the student is to do: Write a composition explaining the physical ways he or she shows emotions?
2. Do the body paragraphs describe each feeling and explain two ways the feeling might be expressed physically?
3. Do the sentences have a mature ring to them, which might have resulted from sentence combining?
4. Is the essay free from grammar, usage, and mechanics errors?

Assignment

1. Among the most common types of conflict are (1) a conflict between two people, and (2) a conflict a person has within his or her own mind. Write a summary of a play which has both types of conflicts.

Prewriting. Before you write, think of the kinds of things that bring people into conflict. Then imagine a person coming into conflict with another person for one of these reasons. What might this person say and do? What might the other person say and do in response? Think of a surprising way in which he or she might resolve the problem.

Writing. As you write, tell something about the characters involved in the conflict. Show the two people confronting each other. Then show the main character taking action to resolve the problem.

Revising. When you revise, tighten up the plot by focusing on the way one person's actions cause the other person's response, and how this person's response causes the other person's next action.

Assignment

2. Write a brief scene that (1) introduces a conflict between two people, and (2) presents the basic facts about these people and the situation they are in—their relationship, ages, jobs, etc. Write this scene entirely in dialogue and stage directions.

Prewriting. Before you write, make an outline with the following categories: (1) how the conflict begins, (2) how it gets worse, (3) reasons for the conflict, (4) the personalities of the two characters.

Writing. Now write the scene. As you write, focus on the conflict between the two people. Show the characters bringing up the subject about which they have a conflict. Then show them getting more serious about it—perhaps after trying to avoid it for a while. Finally, show them confronting each other directly about it.

Revising. When you revise, check to see that the characters sound as if they're talking to each other.

Assignment

3. Write a composition explaining how you would show each of the following feelings in physical ways: anger, sorrow, grief, joy, weariness. Provide *two* physical expressions for each feeling.

Prewriting. Before you write, think of the ways different parts of the body might show each feeling. How can you show anger with your face? With your hands? With your feet? How can you show joy with your legs? With your fingers? With your entire body?

Writing. In your introductory paragraph, explain what you are about to do. In your body paragraphs, describe the feelings you are discussing one at a time. Then tell how you would express these feelings in physical ways.

Revising. Combine your sentences. Sentences that are combined in the right way have a mature ring to them.

Assignment

1. Choose a character from one of the plays who has changed in some way. Write an essay in which you tell (1) what this character was like before the change, (2) what made this character change, and (3) the effect of his or her change.

    Prewriting. As you scan the play, ask yourself what this character was like before the change, what made him or her change, and what effect his or her change had.

    Writing. Start your essay by identifying the character who changes and the play in which this person appears. Tell what kind of change this person undergoes, what this person was like before the change, what made him or her change, and what effects his or her change had. Sum up what you have said and end with an interesting quotation.

    Revising. When you revise, ask yourself these questions: Have I mentioned the names of the characters I wrote about? Have I described in enough detail the situations these characters are in? Have I connected my evidence so there are no logical gaps?

Assignment

2. A play review is an essay that briefly tells what a play is about and then indicates how the author of the review feels about the play. Write a review of one of the plays in this unit.

    Prewriting. Before you write, make notes about your reactions to the characters and the plot.

    Writing. Start by giving your overall opinion of the play. Then describe the plot and the characters (but don't tell the ending!). Next tell what you liked and disliked about the play. Cite specific characters and events and describe your reactions to them in specific terms. Conclude by telling whether you recommend this play.

    Revising. When you revise, be sure your descriptions of the plot and characters and your reactions are as specific as possible.

Assignment

3. Write an essay in which you show that one of the characters learns something he or she didn't know before. Then show that this character's new way of looking at things led to a dramatic turnaround in the plot.

    Prewriting. Select a play. Jot down notes about what a character learns.

    Writing. Now write your essay. Describe the situation as it was before the character made the discovery. Then describe the discovery and how it came about. Next tell how the discovery led to a reversal in the plot. Finally, summarize.

    Revising. When you revise, make sure you have shown both the discovery and the reversal.

You the Critic   *307*

1. Does the essay begin by identifying the character who changes, the play in which this person appears, and what kind of change this person experiences?
2. Does the body of the essay tell what this person was like before the change, what made him or her change, and what effect the change had on the story and other characters?
3. Does the conclusion summarize what the student said and end with an interesting last sentence, perhaps a quote from the play?
4. Is there sufficient, well-organized detail?
5. Is the essay free from grammar, usage, and mechanics errors?

*Guidelines for Evaluating
Assignment 2*

1. Does the beginning of the review give the student's overall opinion of the drama?
2. Does the student specifically and clearly describe the characters and the plot without telling the ending?
3. Has the student supported his or her likes and dislikes with examples from the play?
4. Has the student included a recommendation to see or avoid the play?
5. Is the review free from grammar, usage, and mechanics errors?

*Guidelines for Evaluating
Assignment 3*

1. Has the student described the situation as it was before the character learns something he or she did not know?
2. Is there a description of the discovery and how it came about?
3. Is there an explanation how the discovery led to a reversal in plot?
4. Is there a summary of the major points of the essay with a satisfactory concluding sentence?
5. Is the essay free from grammar, usage, and mechanics errors?

RECLINING WOMAN, 1952
John Robinson

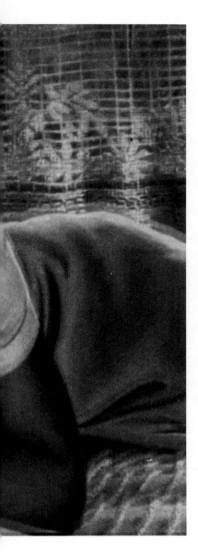

NONFICTION

Many people who love reading believe that the most interesting literature being written today is nonfiction. Nonfiction does not deal with imaginary people or events but with real life. The characters are real people and the events are actual happenings. If a work of nonfiction is concerned mainly with ideas or opinions, they are ideas or opinions taken from real life.

The world of nonfiction is a wide one. It includes true stories of people's lives and experiences. It includes thoughtful writings that instruct, persuade, or inform you. It includes diaries, speeches, letters, and magazine articles. Nonfiction is created by men and women who use words well. What they write has clarity, liveliness, interest, and style. When you read the nonfiction in this unit, try to notice these qualities. They contribute much to your reading enjoyment.

Humanities Note

Fine art, *Reclining Woman,* John Robinson. This sensitive and compelling portrait of a young black woman, entitled *Reclining Woman,* was painted in 1952 by the American painter John Robinson. The composition gains drama by the foreshortening of the figure and by the interesting point of view. The details of the room, the ribbed spread, the worn blanket, and the lace curtains lend textural interest to the composition and frame the figure. The beauty of the woman's features is rendered with skill and grace. This portrait is evocative and wistful; it fills the viewer with curiosity about the life being glimpsed.

Reading Actively Based on research into the ways good readers get meaning from works of literature, the strategies outlined on this page will help students become active and comprehensive readers. This systematic approach leads students to interact with the text they are reading by questioning, predicting, clarifying, and summarizing.

The strategies for active reading of nonfiction are similar to those outlined on page 2 for reading fiction actively. The primary difference concerns the author's purpose. Instead of questioning characters' motives, students should question the author's purpose for writing the essay. They should look for main ideas in the body of the essay that support the purpose.

Consider having students read this selection aloud. Oral reading would allow you to have students share their questions, predictions, clarifications, and summarizations, as well as other thoughts. It would also provide the opportunity for students to comment on the annotations.

For further practice with the process, use the selection in the Teaching Portfolio, an excerpt from *Rascal,* by Sterling North, page 336, which students can annotate themselves. Encourage students to continue to use these strategies when reading the other nonfiction selections.

Teaching to Ability Levels Your less advanced students may need additional individual attention in working with this active reading process.

Nonfiction

Some people seem to gain more from their reading of nonfiction than others. Why? Most likely, they gain more because they read with an active mind. To read nonfiction successfully, you must interact with the information the author presents. Ask questions about this information and make predictions about where the information is leading. Pause to answer your questions and to check your predictions. At appropriate points, stop to summarize the information you have received so far.

Use the following strategies to help you read actively.

Question

Ask questions about the information the author presents. What does the author reveal about the topic? Determine whether the author's conclusions seem based on the information given. In addition, question the author's purpose for writing.

Predict

Think about what you already know about the topic. Make predictions about the conclusions you think the author will reach based on this information. As you read, you will find out whether your predictions are accurate.

Clarify

As you read, try to find the answers to your questions and check the accuracy of your predictions. In this way, you will monitor, or guide, your own reading and so gain the fullest understanding of the information presented.

Summarize

Every now and then, pause to summarize, or review, the information the author has presented so far. What important points has the author made? How has the author supported this information?

Pull It Together

Determine the main idea of the entire selection. What did you find out about the topic? How do you feel about the topic?

On the facing page is a model showing how an active reader might read an essay.

Objectives

1 To learn how to read non-fiction actively
2 To understand essays about people
3 To understand the main idea
4 To appreciate vivid adjectives
5 To write about a remembered person

Support Material

Teaching Portfolio
Teacher Backup, p. 425
Reading Actively, from *Rascal,* p. 429
Grammar in Action Worksheet, *Using Transitions,* p. 431
Usage and Mechanics Work sheet, p. 433
Critical Thinking and Reading Worksheet, *Understanding the Main Idea,* p. 434

Language Worksheet, *Appreciating Vivid Verbs,* p. 435
Selection Test, p. 436
Art Transparency 8, *Maudell Sleet's Magic Garden,* by Romare Bearden

from In Search of Our Mothers' Gardens

Alice Walker

Questions: What is the meaning of the title? What is the author's purpose for writing this essay?

My mother made all the clothes we wore, even my brothers' overalls. She made all the towels and sheets we used. She spent the summers canning vegetables and fruits. She spent the winter evenings making quilts enough to cover all our beds.

During the "working" day, she labored beside—not behind—my father in the fields. Her day began before sunup, and did not end until late at night. There was never a moment for her to sit down, undisturbed, to unravel her own private thoughts; never a time free from interruption—by work or the noisy inquiries of her many children. And yet, it is to my mother—and all our mothers who were not famous—that I went in search of the secret of what has fed that muzzled[1] and often mutilated,[2] but vibrant,[3] creative spirit that the black woman has inherited, and that pops out in wild and unlikely places to this day.

Clarification: The author's purpose is to uncover the secret of the black woman's creative spirit.

But when, you will ask, did my overworked mother have time to know or care about feeding the creative spirit?

The answer is so simple that many of us have spent years discovering it. We have constantly looked high, when we should have looked high—and low.

Question: Why should they have looked low?

For example: in the Smithsonian Institution[4] in Washington, D.C., there hangs a quilt unlike any other in the world. In fanciful,[5] inspired, and yet simple and identifiable figures,

---

1. muzzled (muz' 'ld) *adj.*: Prevented from expressing itself.
2. mutilated (myōot' 'l at' id) *adj.*: Damaged or injured.
3. vibrant (vī' brənt) *adj.*: Lively and energetic.
4. Smithsonian Institution: A group of museums with exhibits in the fields of science, art, and history.
5. fanciful (fan' si fəl) *adj.*: Playfully imaginative.

Presentation

Motivation/Prior Knowledge You might lead the class in a discussion of how the memories of loved ones affect people's lives. Ask for student volunteers to share some fond memories of people they love. How have these people affected their lives? What have they learned from these memories?

Thematic Idea Other selections that are tributes to writers' mothers are "The Courage That My Mother Had," on page 492, and "My Mother Pieced Quilts," on page 494.

Purpose-Setting Question How has Alice Walker's mother affected her creative spirit?

Master Teacher Note Students should and will have their own reactions to the selection. Remind them that they should try to formulate their own questions, predictions, clarifications, and summarizations as they are reading. By paying attention to the annotations that are provided, as well as their own responses, students will gain a better understanding of the selection.

Clarification: This anecdote explains why they should have looked low. Here an anonymous poor black woman has created a priceless quilt.

Prediction: Walker will go on to explain how her mother has created works of art.

it portrays the story of the Crucifixion.[6] It is considered rare, beyond price. Though it follows no known pattern of quilt-making, and though it is made of bits and pieces of worthless rags, it is obviously the work of a person of powerful imagination and deep spiritual feeling. Below this quilt I saw a note that says it was made by "an anonymous[7] Black woman in Alabama, a hundred years ago."

If we could locate this "anonymous" black woman from Alabama, she would turn out to be one of our grandmothers—an artist who left her mark in the only materials she could afford, and in the only medium her position in society allowed her to use.

And so our mothers and grandmothers have, more often than not anonymously, handed on the creative spark, the seed of the flower they themselves never hoped to see: or like a sealed letter they could not plainly read.

And so it is, certainly, with my own mother. Unlike "Ma" Rainey's songs,[8] which retained their creator's name even while blasting forth from Bessie Smith's mouth,[9] no song or poem will bear my mother's name. Yet so many of the stories that I write, that we all write, are my mother's stories. Only recently did I fully realize this: that through years of listening to my mother's stories of her life, I have absorbed not only the stories themselves, but something of the manner in which she spoke, something of the urgency that involves the knowledge that her stories—like her life—must be recorded. It is probably for this reason that so much of what I have written is about characters whose counterparts in real life are so much older than I am.

But the telling of these stories, which came from my mother's lips as naturally as breathing, was not the only way my mother showed herself as an artist. For stories, too, were subject to being distracted, to dying without conclusion. Dinners must be started, and cotton must be gathered before the big rains. The artist that was and is my mother showed itself to me only after many years. This is what I finally noticed:

---

6. the Crucifixion (krōō′ sə fik′ shən): Jesus Christ's suffering and death on the cross.
7. anonymous (ə nän′ ə məs) *adj*.: With no name known.
8. "Ma" Rainey's songs: Gertrude ("Ma") Rainey, one of America's first blues singers, lived during the early years of this century.
9. Bessie Smith's mouth: Bessie Smith was a well-known blues singer (1898?–1937) who knew and learned from "Ma" Rainey.

Grammar in Action

Transitions are words that help connect ideas while showing the logical order of the ideas. One effective use of transitional words is to connect or emphasize comparisons and contrasts. Through the use of comparisons and contrasts a writer can present ideas more vividly and dramatically. In the following passage, Alice Walker uses transitions to emphasize her comparisons and contrasts:

Unlike "Ma" Rainey's songs, which retained their creator's name even *while* blasting forth from Besse Smith's mouth, no song or poem will bear my mother's name. *Yet* so many of the stories that I write, that we all write, are my mother's stories.

Notice how smoothly Walker's ideas flow. By using the transitional words *unlike, while,* and *yet* to express comparisons and contrasts, the writer makes her mother's stories seem extremely important.

Like Mem, a character in *The Third Life of Grange Copeland*,[10] my mother adorned with flowers whatever shabby house we were forced to live in. And not just your typical straggly[11] country stand of zinnias, either. She planted ambitious gardens—and still does—with over fifty different varieties of plants that bloom profusely from early March until late November. Before she left home for the fields, she watered her flowers, chopped up the grass, and laid out new beds. When she returned from the fields she might divide clumps of bulbs, dig a cold pit,[12] uproot and replant roses, or prune branches from her taller bushes or trees—until night came and it was too dark to see.

Question: Is this the garden mentioned in the title?

Whatever she planted grew as if by magic, and her fame as a grower of flowers spread over three counties. Because of her creativity with her flowers, even my memories of poverty are seen through a screen of blooms—sunflowers, petunias, roses, dahlias, forsythia, spirea, delphiniums, verbena . . . and on and on.

Clarification: This is why the garden is important. It screened the reality of poverty.

And I remember people coming to my mother's yard to be given cuttings from her flowers; I hear again the praise showered on her because whatever rocky soil she landed on, she

---

10. *The Third Life of Grange Copeland:* The title of a novel by Alice Walker.
11. straggly (strag′ lē) *adj.*: Spread out in an irregular way.
12. cold pit: A hole in which seedlings are planted at the beginning of the spring.

from *In Search of Our Mother's Gardens*   313

Student Activity 1. Find three other sentences where Walker uses transitional words to point out a comparison or contrast. Identify the transitional words and explain how they emphasize the comparison or contrast.

Student Activity 2. Using some of the transitional words listed below, write three original sentences in which you compare or contrast something.

though	like	similarly	whereas
although	but	nevertheless	instead
however	yet	in contrast	likewise

Summary: Walker's mother has displayed her artistry through the telling of stories and through the creation of her garden.

Clarification: Here is another reason the garden is important. It has taught Walker respect for the possibilities of life.

turned into a garden. A garden so brilliant with colors, so original in its design, so magnificent with life and creativity, that to this day people drive by our house in Georgia—perfect strangers and imperfect strangers—and ask to stand or walk among my mother's art.

I notice that it is only when my mother is working in her flowers that she is radiant, almost to the point of being invisible—except as Creator: hand and eye. She is involved in work her soul must have. Ordering the universe in the image of her personal conception of Beauty.

Her face, as she prepares the Art that is her gift, is a legacy[13] of respect she leaves to me, for all that illuminates and cherishes life. She has handed down respect for the possibilities—and the will to grasp them.

For her, so hindered and intruded upon in so many ways, being an artist has still been a daily part of her life. This ability to hold on, even in very simple ways, is work black women have done for a very long time.

This poem is not enough, but it is something, for the woman who literally covered the holes in our walls with sunflowers:

> They were women then
> My mama's generation
> Husky of voice—Stout of
> Step
> With fists as well as
> Hands
> How they battered down
> Doors
> And ironed
> Starched white
> Shirts
> How they led
> Armies
> Headragged[14] Generals
> Across mined[15]
> Fields

---

13. legacy (leg′ ə sē) *n.*: Something handed down by a parent or an ancestor.
14. headragged (hed′ rag'd) *adj.*: With head wrapped around by a rag or kerchief.
15. mined (mīnd) *adj.*: Filled with buried explosives that are set to go off when stepped on.

Booby-trapped[16]
Kitchens
To discover books
Desks
A place for us
How they knew what we
Must know
Without knowing a page
Of it
Themselves.

Guided by my heritage of a love of beauty and a respect for strength—in search of my mother's garden, I found my own.

Question: What does Walker mean by this statement?

And perhaps in Africa over two hundred years ago, there was just such a mother; perhaps she painted vivid and daring decorations in oranges and yellows and greens on the walls of her hut; perhaps she sang—in a voice like Roberta Flack's[17]—*sweetly* over the compounds of her village; perhaps she wove the most stunning mats or told the most ingenious[18] stories of all the village storytellers. Perhaps she was herself a poet—though only her daughter's name is signed to the poems that we know.

Perhaps Phillis Wheatley's[19] mother was also an artist.

Perhaps in more than Phillis Wheatley's biological life is her mother's signature made clear.

Pulling It Together: In searching for the secret of her mother's creative spirit, Walker has discovered her own wellspring of creativity.

---

16. booby-trapped (boo′ bē trapt) *adj.*: With bombs or mines hidden and set to go off when someone touches or lifts an object.
17. Roberta Flack's: Roberta Flack is a contemporary black singer.
18. ingenious (in jēn′ yəs) *adj.*: Clever and inventive.
19. Phillis Wheatley's: Phillis Wheatley (1753?–1784) was a poet, considered the first important black writer in America.

Alice Walker (1944–   ), who was born in Eatonton, Georgia, is a black writer concerned with social injustice. A poet, novelist, biographer, and essayist, Walker has written widely about the experiences of women and black individuals and families. Her novel *The Color Purple*, which was made into a movie, was awarded a Pulitzer Prize in 1983. A major influence on Walker's life and writing has been her mother. She dedicated her novel *The Third Life of Grange Copeland* "for my mother, who made a way out of no way."

from *In Search of Our Mother's Gardens*   315

Reader's Response Do you agree with the author that our skills and creativity are passed on to us from our parents? Why or why not?

Closure and Extension

Questions begin on page 316

ANSWERS TO THINKING ABOUT THE SELECTION
Recalling

1. Alice Walker sets out to discover what has contributed to the creative spirit of black woman.
2. Walker's mother revealed herself as an artist in the ambitious and successful gardens she created and in the stories she told.
3. The legacies that Walker's mother has left her are the respect and love of beauty, a respect for strength, and the will to grasp at the possibilities of life.

Interpreting

4. Walker means that the source of the creative spirit in black women can be found as much in average, anonymous women, such as the creator of the quilt hanging in the Smithsonian Institution, as it can in well-known black, female artists.
5. Answers will differ. Suggested Response: The poem is a fitting tribute because it describes the strength with which these women faced the difficulties of their lives and how they cared and provided knowledge for their children.
6. Walker means that in searching for the essence of the creative spirit within her mother, she found the source of her own creativity.
7. Walker uses "Our" in the title because she feels that the essence of her mother's creative spirit is identical in all women. Therefore a

More About the Author Much of Alice Walker's work is drawn from her experiences in life. Born to a family of sharecroppers in Georgia, Walker had to work her way through college. She has also worked for welfare rights and helped with voter registration. Her travels have taken her from Kenya and Uganda to the Soviet Union. How might some of these experiences have helped her with the ideas expressed in this essay?

(Answers begin on p. 315.)

search for her mother's source of creative energy is a search for women's creative spirit.

Applying

8. Answers will differ. Students might discuss mannerisms, attitudes, physical characteristics, and creative traits which they possess and which were or are in evidence in their parents and grandparents.

ANSWERS TO ANALYZING LITERATURE

1. Walker presents her mother as a unique individual when describing the work she did for the family, her gardening, and her story-telling skills. She is presented as representative of black women in general when Walker credits her as the source of her own creative essence.
2. Answers will differ. Suggested Response: Walker's attitude toward her mother is one of admiration, respect, and love.

ANSWERS TO CRITICAL THINKING AND READING

1. "And yet, it is to my mother—and all our mothers who were not famous—that I went in search of the secret of what had fed that muzzled and often mutilated, but vibrant, creative spirit that the black woman had inherited, and that pops out in wild and unlikely places to this day." Suggested Restatement: Walker is striving to discover the source of her mother's creative spirit, which was hampered by the constraints of a large family and a limited income, but which shone forth in several ways.
2. The anecdote clarifies the main idea by giving an example of an average, anonymous black woman who could have been anyone's ancestor, who had little opportunity or materials, yet created a work of art.
3. Other details that support the main idea are: Walker's mother's garden, her story telling abilities, the supposition of a mother living in Africa over two hundred years ago who was also an artist, and the possibility that Phyllis Wheatley's mother was also an artist.
4. "Guided by my heritage of a

THINKING ABOUT THE SELECTION
Recalling

1. What does Walker set out to discover?
2. In what two ways did Walker's mother reveal herself as an artist?
3. What legacies, or gifts, has Walker's mother given her daughter?

Interpreting

4. What does Walker mean when she writes, "We have constantly looked high, when we should have looked high—and low"?
5. Do you think Walker's poem is a fitting tribute to her mother? Explain your answer.
6. Explain the following statement: "In search of my mother's garden, I found my own."
7. Why does Walker call this selection "In Search of *Our* Mothers' Gardens" instead of "In Search of *My* Mother's Garden"?

Applying

8. In what way are the signatures of our parents and grandparents made clear through us?

ANALYZING LITERATURE
Understanding Essays About People

An essay is a work of nonfiction. One common topic for the essay is a remembered person. Often an essay about a remembered person contains anecdotes, or little stories, that reveal what the person is like. However, such an essay presents not only a vivid portrait of the subject but also explains the subject's importance to the writer. In this way, the essay reveals both the subject and the writer.

1. In what way does Walker present her mother as a unique individual? In what way does she present her as representative of black women in general?
2. How would you describe Walker's attitude toward her mother?

CRITICAL THINKING AND READING
Understanding the Main Idea

The **main idea** is the most important idea the writer presents. In the essay the main idea is often expressed in a thesis statement near the beginning. The rest of the essay contains information that supports or clarifies the main idea.

1. Look again at the first two paragraphs. Which sentence expresses the main idea? Restate the main idea in your own words.
2. How does the anecdote of the quilt hanging in the Smithsonian Institute clarify the main idea?
3. Find one other detail that supports the main idea.
4. Find the sentence near the end of the selection that again expresses the main idea. Restate this sentence in your own words.

UNDERSTANDING LANGUAGE
Appreciating Vivid Adjectives

Essays about people often contain vivid adjectives. For example, in this essay, Walker describes her mother's creative spirit as "muzzled and often mutilated, but vibrant."

1. Why is *muzzled* an appropriate adjective to describe the creative spirit of black women?
2. Why is *mutilated* an appropriate word?
3. Why is *vibrant* appropriate?

THINKING AND WRITING
Writing About a Remembered Person

List people who have been important in your life. Choose the person you think you can describe most fully. Next, list everything you can remember about this person, such as appearance, traits, quirks. Select details you would include in an essay. Write a first draft telling your best friend why this person is significant to you. When you review your essay, make sure you have included enough details to support your main idea. Prepare a final draft and share it with your classmates.

love of beauty and a respect for strength—in search of my mother's garden, I found my own." Suggested Restatement: While searching for her mother's source of creative spirit, Alice Walker discovered that her own source was the same.

Challenge Can this main idea be applied to all women? Have students discuss this question and support there answers with examples.

ANSWERS TO UNDERSTANDING LANGUAGE

1. Suggested Response: *muzzled* is an appropriate adjective because, in general, black women have not had the same opportunities to express themselves as other people.
2. Suggested Response: *mutilated* is an appropriate word because the creative spirit in black women has sometimes been crippled or changed due to the difficult lives they have led.

3. Suggested Response: *vibrant* is appropriate because it accurately describes the creative spirit of black women as lively and energetic, despite the hardships of their lives.

THINKING AND WRITING
Publishing Student Writing Ask for student volunteers to read their essays aloud for the class. Have the rest of the class make inferences as to whether the subject is a relative or a friend.

Biographies and Personal Accounts

SELF PORTRAIT, 1934
Malvin Johnson
National Museum of American Art

Humanities Note

Fine art, *Self Portrait,* 1934, Malvin Grey Johnson. Malvin Grey Johnson (1896–1934) was an Afro-American painter born in Northboro, North Carolina. Johnson studied art at the National Academy of Design in New York City under F. C. Jones. His seemingly simple paintings, organized around figures, recorded everyday life and its rituals. Malvin Johnson's early death was a great loss to the Harlem Renaissance, a movement of black art and literature, of which he was an important member.

His *Self Portrait* has the intense stare common to most self portrayals. The contrast of his head with the stylized heads of the African masks behind him speaks of his African heritage. He has simplified the shapes in this composition without succumbing to abstraction. This very personal statement maintains the charm that was attractive to his public. Today Malvin Johnson's paintings are exhibited in the collections of the nation's leading museums.

Eugenie Clark and the Sleeping Sharks

Margery Facklam (1927–   ) has been fascinated by the animal kingdom since she was a child. She pursued this interest by working as a volunteer at the Buffalo Zoo, in Buffalo, New York, and later she became the zoo's Educational Coordinator. She has also written a number of books about people involved with nature. In this biographical sketch, she tells about a scientist whose lifelong study of sharks has earned her the nickname of the "shark lady."

More About the Author Margery Facklam has worked at a science museum, an aquarium, and a zoo. She has been a teacher. She loves both teaching and writing but prefers writing because it offers a wider, more eager audience. If you knew a certain subject very well, would you choose to teach it or write about it?

Literary Focus You might wish to tell your students that many of the biographies being written today offer much the same kind of appeal as a good novel. In fact, biographies may at present be the most popular of all the literary genres. Certainly, they rival fiction for popularity. Ask your class if they are likely to prefer an interesting story about a real person to an interesting fictional work.

Look For Remind students that active reading will increase their enjoyment of this selection. What interesting scientific information is presented? What information about Dr. Clark might young readers want to remember as they plan their own careers?

Writing/Prior Knowledge You might quote John Ruskin's remark in *The Two Paths* that "No human being, however great, or powerful, was ever so free as a fish." Encourage students to discuss this statement, and then direct them to the writing exercise.

Vocabulary You might encourage your **less advanced** students to write a list of some of the more difficult words (with definitions) they encounter in this selection. **More advanced** students might be encouraged to use context clues to figure out the meanings of difficult words.

Biography

A **biography** is an account of a person's life written by someone else. Biographies often focus on the achievements of the people they describe. They also tell you about the difficulties these people had to overcome in order to reach their goals. An author usually chooses as the subject of the biography someone who has achieved something significant. Subjects of biographies may include baseball stars, political leaders, poets, kings and queens, generals, and scientists. "Eugenie Clark and the Sleeping Sharks," for example, is about a scientist with an unusual interest.

Look For

As you read, look for the facts about sharks and their behavior that Dr. Clark has discovered. What aspects of Clark's life make her a good subject for a biography?

Writing

Think about sharks you have seen on film or at an aquarium. Write about the way they looked and behaved and how you reacted to them.

Vocabulary

Knowing the following words will help you as you read "Eugenie Clark and the Sleeping Sharks."

assortment (ə sôrt′ mənt) *n.*: A group or collection of different kinds of things (p. 319)

repellent (ri pel′ ənt) *n.*: Something that pushes away (p. 319)

oozed (o͞ozd) *v.*: Flowed or leaked slowly (p. 319)

commotion (kə mō′ shən) *n.*: Noisy reaction; confusion (p. 322)

elusive (i lo͞o′ siv) *adj.*: Hard to find (p. 322)

diligently (dil′ ə jənt lē) *adv.*: With hard work; carefully (p. 325)

maneuver (mə no͞o′ vər) *n.*: A planned movement or procedure (p. 326)

Objectives

1 To understand what a biography is
2 To learn about the scientific method
3 To analyze the word part *-logy*
4 To write a biography

Support Material

Teaching Portfolio
Teacher Backup, p. 439
Grammar in Action Worksheet, *Identifying Infinitive Phrases,* p. 442
Usage and Mechanics Worksheet, p. 444
Vocabulary Check, p. 445
Analyzing Literature Worksheet, *Understanding Biography,* p. 446
Critical Thinking and Reading Worksheet, *Learning the Scientific Method,* p. 447
Selection Test, p. 448

Eugenie Clark
and the Sleeping Sharks
Margery Facklam

Sunlight sparkled on bright blue-green water as a small boat dropped anchor. Three divers wearing black wet suits adjusted their scuba gear. One diver leaned over the side of the boat and peered into the water. It was so clear he could see the rainbow assortment of fishes swimming around the coral reef.[1]

"Sharks below," he called.

"No problem," a second diver answered calmly. "Use this," she said, handing cans of shark repellent to the others.

When they had sprayed themselves all over with the repellent, the divers put on their masks and flipped backward out of the boat into the warm water. Two tiger sharks began to circle the divers. Silently they picked up speed to attack, but as they closed in on the swimmers, they slammed on invisible brakes. Suddenly their mouths seemed to be frozen open. They shook their heads as though trying to get rid of something. And the divers went about exploring the coral reef, unconcerned about the sharks.

So far, that scene is only make-believe. There is no shark repellent that really keeps sharks away, but there may be soon because Dr. Eugenie Clark was curious about a little fish called the Moses sole.

In 1960, Eugenie was netting fish in the Red Sea when she came across the fish known scientifically as *Pardachirus;* local fishermen called it the Moses sole. When she touched the fish, a milky substance oozed from the pores along its fins. It was slippery, and her fingers felt tingly and tight, the way they might feel if they fell asleep.

The Moses sole is a flatfish, like the flounder you buy at the market, and it got its name from a traditional story told in Israel. According to the legend, when Moses parted the Red Sea, this little fish was caught in the middle and split in half. Each half became a sole.

Eugenie is an ichthyologist,[2] a scientist who studies fish. She was working at the Marine Laboratory at the Hebrew University in Elat, Israel, when she decided to find out more about the sole's poison. A scientist had reported the poisonous substance in 1871, but no one had studied it further. When Eugenie tested it on sea urchins, starfish, and reef fishes, she found that small doses killed these creatures quickly. She began to wonder how it would work on larger fishes, especially sharks.

Three reef whitetip sharks lived in a tank at the laboratory, and they ate anything

---

1. coral reef: A ridge near the surface of the water made of countless skeletons of tiny ocean animals.

2. ichthyologist (ik′ thē äl′ ə jist)

Eugenie Clark and the Sleeping Sharks   319

Presentation

Motivation/Prior Knowledge Suggest that students imagine they have the opportunity to experiment safely with sharks. What would they like to discover? What kinds of experimental activities would they carry out?

Master Teacher Note Because sharks are so fascinating to many young readers, having your students discuss sharks will further motivate them to read this selection attentively. You might also give a brief description of the scientific method (see page 327) and mention that in the selection students will read about how an actual scientist uses it.

Purpose-Setting Question What can you learn from this account of Dr. Clark that you can make use of in your own lives?

1 Critical Thinking and Reading Point out that this nonfiction selection begins with several paragraphs of fiction, a "make-believe" scene. Why might a writer of a true-life story use fiction in this way?

2 Discussion What do you learn from this paragraph about how a scientist thinks and works?

3 **Discussion** What personal quality helpful to a scientist is indicated here?

4 **Critical Thinking and Reading** Why does Facklam mention three kinds of shark repellent that do *not* work all the time? What is the topic sentence of this paragraph?

dropped into the water. One day as Eugenie was experimenting with the fish, she found one small Moses sole that had not been completely "milked" of its poison. She put a string through its gills, which did not hurt it, and lowered the fish into the shark's tank. The moment the sole touched the water, the sharks swept toward it with mouths open wide. But when they got within a few feet of the fish on the string, the sharks' jaws seemed to be frozen open. They dashed away, shaking their heads as though trying to get rid of something awful. For six hours Eugenie watched the sharks approach the sole, and the reactions were the same each time the sharks swam near the poisonous fish.

The use of this poison as a shark repellent was an exciting idea. So far everything invented to keep sharks away has not worked on all sharks all the time. Streams of air bubbles used as a barrier along beaches eventually attracted sharks, who seemed to enjoy the feeling of the bubbles as they swam through them. Different dyes that swimmers can release in the water only hide the swimmer from the shark temporarily but cannot keep a really hungry shark away. Lifeboats on ships and Navy planes are sometimes equipped with plastic bags large enough to hold a person. Stranded in the water, the person inflates the top ring and crawls into the tubelike bag. A shark cannot follow the scent of a human inside this bag, nor can it see kicking legs or blood from a wound. But such bags are not carried as regular equipment by swimmers at an ocean beach. A substance that can be sprayed on, the way mosquito repellent is, would be perfect.

But before Eugenie could experiment further on the Moses sole, she had to leave the Elat laboratory, and other work claimed her attention for many years. It wasn't until 1974 that she was able to collect some of the fish and test the shark-stopping poison. After dozens of experiments in tanks and in the sea, a final test was arranged to find out how free-swimming sharks reacted to the live Moses sole.

An eighty-foot shark line, with ten shorter lines dropping from it, was stretched close to the rocky Israeli coastline three feet underwater at a point where a ledge dropped off to a depth of one thousand feet. Each of the ten dropper lines was baited with parrot fish, groupers, nonpoisonous flatfish, and the Moses sole. As Eugenie, her fourteen-year-old son, and other assistants snorkeled[3] quietly along the underwater ledge and watched the sharks approach the bait at dawn or sunset, they saw the poison at work.

One by one the fish were gulped down by hungry sharks, but the Moses sole remained untouched. When Eugenie wiped the skin of a Moses sole with alcohol to remove the poison and tossed the fish into the water, a shark would instantly eat it. It was an excit-

---

3. snorkeled (snôr′ k'ld) v.: Swam underwater using a snorkel, or breathing tube, that extends above the surface of the water.

ing discovery—a substance that could really stop a shark. Further work is being done now to make a chemical compound like the poison of the Moses sole that can be used as a reliable commercial shark repellent.

Eugenie knew she wanted to be an ichthyologist long before she knew the word meant "someone who studies fish." Her father died when she was very small, and she lived in New York City with her mother. When her mother had to work on Saturdays, Eugenie went to the old aquarium in Battery Park at the tip of Manhattan. The hours went quickly for her as she watched the colorful reef fishes and the graceful sea turtles. It wasn't long before she had her own collection of guppies and swordtail platys, and she became the youngest member of the Queens County Aquarium Society. She learned to keep careful records of her fish and their scientific names.

All during elementary school and high school, her mother encouraged her in her new interest. When she went to Hunter College in New York for a degree in biology, Mrs. Clark, aware of the limited job possibilities for women, suggested that Eugenie add typing and shorthand to her studies. But Eugenie never had the time or interest to do it. When she graduated from Hunter College during World War II, there were not many jobs for biologists, so she worked for a while at the Celanese Corporation as a chemist and attended graduate school at night.

She wrote later on, "In the field of science, a Ph.D. degree is handy to have although not absolutely necessary. One of the most brilliant and accomplished ichthyologists in the country never went to college, although later he became a university professor. But a person without a formal education has a more difficult time proving his worth, especially when applying for a position. A Ph.D. among your qualifications helps start

5
6
7

5 **Discussion** Do you think Facklam's experiment is a complete and proven success? Can you think of further work that needs to be done?

6 **Literary Focus** Notice that Facklam waits until this point to present a chronological survey of Dr. Clark's life. Why didn't Facklam place this material right at the beginning of her account?

7 **Clarification** Ph.D. is the abbreviation for Doctor of Philosophy, a high academic degree conferred by a college or university.

8 **Critical Thinking and Reading**
What do you think is the point of this paragraph?

9 **Discussion** What would be a more glamorous part of being a scientist?

things out on the right foot. I hoped to get this degree . . . my career had enough other disadvantages for a woman."

In 1947, the U.S. Fish and Wildlife Service was planning a survey of the Philippine Island area for possible fisheries. They needed a person who knew fish and chemistry. Eugenie was qualified. She applied for the job and got it.

8 "Several people were surprised that a girl had been hired for the job. Then it was called to someone's attention in Washington that I was the only female scientist on the program. Some commotion followed. I got as far as Hawaii, but my passport was mysteriously delayed because, they told me, the FBI had to check my Oriental [Eugenie's mother is Japanese] origin and connections. As far as I know they are still checking. They never did tell me I was cleared. After weeks of waiting, I accepted my fate and handed in my resignation to waiting hands. They hired a man in my place."

Being stranded in Hawaii was no hardship for Eugenie. For an ichthyologist, the freedom to dive among the fascinating fishes around the Hawaiian volcanic reefs[4] was as satisfying as being a cat free to roll in a meadow of catnip. But even that ended. She said later, "The longer you put off graduate studies, the harder it is to find the time and enthusiasm to go back to school." So she went back.

It takes years of study and research to complete a Ph.D. Very often the original research requires going into the field to learn about the subject firsthand.

"Women scientists have to buck some difficulties when it comes to field work," said Eugenie, "but I had one decided advantage. A man in my position often has a family to

support and is not free to travel. I was independent and free to go anywhere and do anything I liked, and there was only my own neck to risk."

Eugenie went many places. She learned to dive while studying at Scripps Institute of Oceanography in California. She used her diving skills constantly in Micronesia in the Pacific Ocean, where she collected the *plectognaths* she was studying. These are small fish that live mostly in tropical waters near coral reefs. They include the triggerfish, porcupine fish, puffer, filefish, and boxfish.

One of her research fellowships took her to the Red Sea, where she found the Moses sole and collected the elusive garden eels that burrow in the ocean bottom. They are long, smooth fish that sway gently with the water currents as they feed upon small ocean creatures.

9 In Cairo, Egypt, Eugenie married a doctor she had met during her studies in the United States. When they returned to the States, Eugenie began the less glamorous part of being a scientist—sorting through notes and writing the scientific results of things she had found. And she began to raise a family.

In 1955, she was delighted to be asked to start a marine laboratory in Florida. Her husband was ready to open a medical office, and he agreed that Florida would be a good place to live. With their first two children, they moved to Florida's west coast, and Eugenie became the director of the Cape Haze Marine Laboratory. At first the laboratory was only a small wooden building, twelve by twenty feet, built on skids[5] so it could be moved if the first site did not work out. There was a dock and a boat for collecting.

---

4. volcanic reefs: Reefs built up on sunken volcanoes.

5. skids (skidz) *n.*: Planks or logs on which a heavy object can be slid.

Grammar in Action

An *infinitive* is the form of a verb that comes after the word *to;* it acts as a noun, adjective, or adverb. When an infinitive has modifiers or a complement, it is called an **infinitive phrase.** Using infinitives or infinitive phrases is an effective way to present ideas and add variety to your sentence structure. In the following passage, Margery Facklam uses infinitives and infinitive phrases to present information.

A man in my position often has a family *to support* and is not free *to travel.* I was independent and free *to go anywhere* and [to] *do anything I liked,. . . .*

Notice that the first sentence contains infinitives, whereas the second sentence has infinitive phrases.

When you use several infinitives in a series, you must make sure that you use the same form of the verb each time. Sometimes writers are careless and use the *ing* form of the verb instead of the infinitive form. Read the following passage to note the confusion that can arise when the wrong form of the verb is used.

Eugenie decided her first job should be to collect and identify all the local fishes.

The day after she arrived, she received a phone call from a doctor who needed shark livers for cancer research. She checked with the man who was going to handle the boat, and even before supplies were unpacked, they were in the shark-hunting business.

There are about 250 different sharks in the world, ranging in size from the 24-inch dogfish studied in biology classes to the 60-foot giant whale shark that eats plankton[6] and is so gentle that divers have hung onto its fins for a short ride. In between are the man-eaters we hear horror stories about. All the sharks belong to a group of fishes called cartilaginous. They have skeletons made not of bone but of cartilage, that bendable tissue our ears and noses are made of. And all the sharks are torpedo-shaped predators. They have many sets of razor-sharp teeth that they can fold back into a nonbiting position or thrust forward, ready to slice easily into prey. When a tooth is lost, another moves into place quite quickly.

The shark's always-staring eyes give it an evil appearance. It cannot blink or close its eyes for sleep, but it has a membrane that can cover the eye for protection.

Eugenie and her assistant began collecting some of the eighteen species of sharks found off the west coast of Florida. As she dissected hammerhead, nurse, lemon, and sand sharks on the dock, her children, neighbors, and children of visiting scientists watched. Sometimes she gave them jobs to do—measuring parts of the intestines, washing out a shark stomach, or hosing the dock after the dissection. Some of the sharks brought in on lines survived, and Eugenie wanted to know as much about the live ani-

mals as she knew about the organs she was weighing and measuring.

A stockaded pen, forty by seventy feet, was built next to the dock to hold the live sharks. A tiger shark, named Hazel, and a reddish color nurse shark, named Rosy, were two of the first guests in the pen, and a new problem arose. Nosy visitors, ignoring signs and fences, poked around and teased the animals. Eugenie was worried that both people and sharks would be hurt. When several of the sharks were killed by trespassers, Eugenie began to talk to groups in the community, especially at schools. She explained what sharks eat and how they live. Whenever people know about an animal, they fear it less. Soon the newspapers labeled her the "shark lady." It is a name that has stayed with her in spite of all her research with other sea creatures.

It wasn't long before Eugenie was involved in finding out how sharks learn. She enjoyed working with the live sharks day after day and getting to know the individual personalities of the animals.

When she set up experiments in which sharks would have to hit a target to receive the reward of food, one scientist warned her, "Don't be discouraged. It may take months." But he was wrong. The sharks learned quickly. When two lemon sharks learned that they could press an empty target and get food for it, Eugenie thought up harder problems for them to solve.

She trained them to swim to the end of the seventy-foot pen to pick up food after they pressed the target; and the female shark, who usually hung back and waited for the male to go first, quickly learned that if she circled the food drop area, she could pick up the male's reward while he was still at the target.

Eugenie stopped the tests during the winter months when the sharks lost interest

10

11

---

6. **plankton** (plaŋk' tən) *n.*: Very small animal and plant life that floats or drifts in the water.

Eugenie Clark and the Sleeping Sharks　323

10 **Critical Thinking and Reading** If these two paragraphs were left out of the selection, the paragraph above and the paragraph below would still fit together. Why do you think Facklam included this material on sharks?

11 **Discussion** Do you see any practical purpose for Dr. Clark's efforts? Why might she be so interested in finding out how sharks learn? Should a scientist sometimes conduct experiments just to satisfy his or her curiosity?

A man in my position often has a family to support and is not free traveling. I was independent and free to go anywhere and doing anything I liked.

Student Activity 1. Identify the infinitives in the following sentences. Revise any sentence where the wrong form of the verb is used.

1. I like to play tennis and riding horses.

2. That music is difficult to play.

3. Mrs. Evans is the woman to ask about jobs.

Student Activity 2. Write three original sentences in which you use infinitives or infinitive phrases.

in food, but she found that the sharks remembered everything they had learned when spring training began. She moved on to more complicated learning. She used targets of different sizes, shapes, and designs, and she found that sharks of the same species, like other animals, have great individual differences. Some are smarter than others.

Scientists from all over the world visited the Cape Haze laboratory, studying everything from parasites[7] on sharks to microscopic life on algae. By the time Eugenie had been the laboratory's director for ten years, she had four children who enjoyed diving and helping her underwater explorations.

When Eugenie heard that there were "sleeping" sharks a diver could swim right up to, she was determined to find out more about them. With her daughter, Aya, and some research assistants, she went to Mexico's beautiful Isla Mujeres[8] off the tip of the Yucatan Peninsula.[9] There, in the warm, clear underwater caves, she found the great, sleek sharks of the requiem[10] family—the notorious man-eaters. They were lying on the floor of the caves, looking half-asleep even though their open, staring eyes watched the divers swim toward them.

12 Ordinarily, these sharks must keep moving. They swim constantly in order to keep the oxygen-rich water flowing through their mouths and out over the gills. When they rest on the bottom, they must pump water over the gills, and that takes more energy than leisurely swimming. But in the caves the sharks were motionless. Even with di-

vers churning up water and sand, and even with the glare of photographers' lights, the sharks acted as though they were tranquilized.

Eugenie and her team measured the depth and temperature of the water in the cave. They mapped the water currents by dropping dyes in the water and following their paths. They took water and rock samples for chemical analysis. And they noticed

---

7. **parasites** (par′ ə sīts) n.: Animals that live on other organisms in order to get food, protection, or both. Often, parasites harm the organisms on which they live.
8. **Isla Mujeres** (ēs′ lä mōō her′ is)
9. **Yucatán** (yōō′ kä tän′) **Peninsula:** A projection of land, located mostly in southeast Mexico, that separates the Caribbean Sea from the Gulf of Mexico.
10. **requiem** (rek′ wē əm)

how clean the sharks looked compared to those caught by local fishermen. These cave sharks were not infested with the parasites found on most sharks.

They watched the "shark's faithful housekeeper," the small remora fish, as it worked around the eyes and mouths and into the gill slits of the resting sharks. The remora is a fish whose dorsal fin has evolved into a kind of suction disk on the top of its head. It can hitch a ride on a shark, sea turtle, whale, or even a ship by means of this suction disk. The remora picks up pieces of food dropped by its host. In the caves, however, these remoras worked diligently. Could it be that these "sleeping" sharks gathered in the caves for a health treatment? Were the caves cleaning stations?"

Eugenie discovered fresh water seeping into the caves, diluting the sea water. There

Eugenie Clark and the Sleeping Sharks   325

Closure and Extension

ANSWERS TO THINKING ABOUT THE SELECTION
Recalling

1. First, testing the poison on various small fishes indicated that it was deadly. Second, when a Moses sole was lowered into a shark tank, it repelled the sharks.

2. Three devices to keep sharks away are a stream of air bubbles, a dye to hide swimmers, and a tubelike bag for a person to climb into. Sharks eventually become attracted to the bubbles. The dye works only temporarily and will not repel a very hungry shark. The bag is impractical—swimmers do not carry such things with them when they go swimming.

3. A series of lines were baited with various fish, including a Moses

---

13 Critical Thinking and Reading Has Dr. Clark drawn any definite conclusions about the "sleeping" sharks? What do these paragraphs suggest about how scientists think?

14 Discussion What question occurs to Dr. Clark when she observes the egg-bearing females? How much and what kind of work are needed to arrive at an answer? What do you think makes Dr. Clark's discovery exciting?

Challenge How might another scientist differ from Dr. Clark in experimenting with fish? Do you think, for example, that it might not be better for a scientist to begin with a definite practical problem that needs solving, rather than with curiosity about an unusual observation? Explain why.

Reader's Response What do you admire most about Eugenie Clark? Why?

---

was less salt in the caves than in the open ocean. She remembered that when she was a kid she would put her saltwater fish into fresh water for a little while so that the parasites would drop off. Perhaps the same thing was happening with the sharks. Maybe these eighteen-foot tiger and reef sharks were intelligent enough to seek comfort in the caves.

Eugenie had taught sharks to ring a bell and push targets for meals and to distinguish right from wrong targets at the Florida laboratory. "Surely," she said, "they are capable of learning that in water of below-normal salinity, a condition they apparently must sense, annoying parasites loosen their grip."

The sharks may not know the water is less salty, but they know it feels good, so they go there. There are three such caves known around Mexico. Recently, some underwater caves full of sharks were reported around Japan. So many divers swarmed into the caves, catching sharks by the hundreds for food, that by the time Eugenie got to Japan to see them, the sharks had learned it was not safe to go to that cleaning station. Another cave was discovered near Japan, but Eugenie and other scientists are keeping its location secret to protect the sharks.

When asked about her life as a scientist, Eugenie said, "Being a scientist and a woman has some advantages, some disadvantages. It balances out. It takes some time to prove yourself initially, but then you get more credit than a man when you do accomplish something. For example, I am a diver, and when I dive into a cave with sharks it seems to be much more amazing than when a man does it."

The "shark lady" publicity has followed Eugenie, and no matter what she does, people think of her as the spear-carrying shark hunter. But she said, "I get just as excited about the garden eels in the Red Sea. Per-

haps the discovery that thrilled me the most was the first hermaphroditic vertebrate,[11] a fish that changes sex."

Looking for an excuse to go swimming one hot July day, Eugenie decided to take a census of the fish around a certain coral reef near the Cape Haze laboratory. She watched a tiny grouper fish, called *Serranus*. There were dozens of females swollen with eggs that would have to be laid and fertilized. But she could not find any males. No matter how long she followed some of these fish or what time of day she watched, no males appeared.

For a year she found no answers. But after many dives and long hours in the lab looking at fish under the microscope and watching live fish in lab tanks, she finally solved the mystery. *Serranus* is an hermaphrodite—an animal with both male and female parts. There are a few vertebrates that start life as one sex and turn into another, functioning as both in a lifetime, but never at the same time. *Serranus* turned out to be the first vertebrate found in which every individual could function at the same time as a male and female, able to fertilize itself. It seems, however, that this self-fertilization is used only in an emergency when a mate is not available. It was an exciting discovery that will probably lead to other investigations.

Eugenie Clark obviously loves what she does. "If from my research mankind gains some practical application or benefit, this is added delight and satisfaction to my work," she said. "But this is not what drives me to study late into the night or to watch a fish on the bottom making some strange maneuver until all the air in my scuba tank is gone and I hold my breath for those last few seconds."

---

11. vertebrate (vər′ tə brāt′): An animal with a backbone.

---

sole. Sharks ate all the fish except the sole. However, the sole was eaten once its poison was removed.

4. As a child, Dr. Clark spent hours at an aquarium. She had her own collection of tropical fish. She became the youngest member of the Queens County Aquarium Society. She kept careful records of her fish and their scientific names.

5. Dr. Clark lost a job with the Fish and Wildlife Service because she was the only woman in the pro-

gram. However, as an independent woman, she was free to travel and take risks.

6. She discovered that the fresh water of the caves and the remora fish removed parasites from the sharks. The sharks probably went to the caves because the waters felt good.

Interpreting

7. Dr. Clark is persevering, imaginative, observant, enthusiastic, dedicated, hardworking, inquisitive,

curious, innovative, and undiscouraged.

8. Her response reveals that she deals with problems in a reasonable, sensible way. She responded similarly to the loss of her Fish and Wildlife Service job: she used her time in Hawaii wisely and then furthered her education.

Applying

9. Suggested Response: It is assumed that people with a formal education possess knowledge

THINKING ABOUT THE SELECTION

Recalling

1. What two events led Dr. Clark to think that the poison from the Moses sole might be used as a shark repellent?
2. According to this article, what are three devices used to keep sharks away?
3. Describe the experiment Clark set up in 1974 to test the effectiveness of the poison from the Moses sole.
4. Find two ways in which Clark as a child displayed interest in the study of fish.
5. How did Clark's being a woman work against her goal to become a scientist? In what ways did it serve as an advantage?
6. What did Clark discover about the "sleeping" sharks?

Interpreting

7. What qualities of a good scientist does Clark display?
8. What does Clark's response to the killing of her sharks by trespassers reveal about her?

Applying

9. Clark said, "But a person without a formal education has a more difficult time proving his worth, especially when applying for a position." Why do you think this is so?

ANALYZING LITERATURE

Understanding Biography

A **biography** is an account of a person's life written by someone else.

1. Is Eugenie Clark a good subject for a biography? Why or why not?
2. How do you think the author wants you to feel about her subject—Dr. Clark?

CRITICAL THINKING AND READING

Learning About the Scientific Method

The term **scientific method** refers to the systematic way in which scientists try to solve a problem. The basic steps in this method are:

a. Stating the problem to be solved
b. Gathering information about the problem
c. Making a hypothesis, which is a possible explanation that can be tested
d. Performing experiments to test the hypothesis
e. Reaching a conclusion

With these steps in mind, look again at the passage on the "sleeping" sharks.

1. What problem was Dr. Clark trying to solve?
2. Show how she followed the second and third steps of the scientific method.
3. Think of an experiment that would test her hypothesis.

UNDERSTANDING LANGUAGE

Analyzing the Word Part *-logy*

The word *ichthyology* is made up of two parts: *ichthyo,* which comes from the Greek word for "fish," and *-logy,* which means a science or field of study. You will find the word part *-logy* in many scientific terms.

The following names of sciences all contain the word part *-logy.* Look up each one in a dictionary and use it in a sentence that explains the field of study.

1. seismology   2. geology   3. psychology

THINKING AND WRITING

Writing a Biography

Imagine that you want to make a television documentary about a person's life. You must convince the producers that your choice is a good one. Brainstorm to decide on a subject, and list some of the unusual or exciting events in this person's life. Then write a short biography of this person that will persuade the producers to use your idea. When you revise your biography, make sure you have included information about the difficulties that this person overcame.

Eugenie Clark and the Sleeping Sharks   327

---

and that their knowledge and intellectual abilities are, at least to a degree, indicated by their grades and academic degrees.

ANSWERS TO ANALYZING LITERATURE

1. Suggested Response: Dr. Clark is a good subject for a biography because she is interesting as a person and significant as a scientist.
2. Suggested Response: The author wants the reader to admire Dr. Clark. She portrays Dr. Clark over-

coming obstacles. She includes incidents that reveal her intelligence, persistence, dedication, hard work, compassion, and other virtues.

ANSWERS TO CRITICAL THINKING AND READING

1. Dr. Clark was trying to determine why the "sleeping" sharks gathered in the caves.
2. She followed the second step by measuring the temperature and depth of the water, by mapping currents, by analyzing water and rock samples, by comparing the cave sharks with others for parasite infestation, by studying the remoras' activity, and by noting the presence of fresh water. She

---

(Answers begin on p.326)

followed the third step by forming the hypothesis that the sharks went to the caves for comfort and to be cleaned.

3. Answers will differ. However, one experiment might be to capture and transport some of the "sleeping" sharks to underwater caves without any fresh water present and then study their behavior and degree of parasite infestation.

ANSWERS TO UNDERSTANDING LANGUAGE

Answers will differ. Suggested Responses:

1. Seismology is the study of earthquakes and the mechanical properties of the earth.
2. Geology is the scientific study of the origin, history, and structure of the earth.
3. Psychology is the study of mental processes and behavior.

THINKING AND WRITING

Publishing Student Writing You might divide your class into groups and have each group of students discuss one another's short biographies. The groups might concentrate on evaluating the persons written about as subjects for the documentary.

Challenge The word *vocation* is based on the Latin verb *vocare,* meaning "to call." What is the difference between a calling and a job? Do you think Dr. Clark considers her work a vocation or a job? Why is it easier to work long hours at a vocation than at a job?

Writing Across the Curriculum Work with a science teacher to obtain "Sharks," a National Geographic PBS special. Midway through this tape, Eugenie Clark talks about her work and takes viewers on an underwater dive to see the "sleeping" sharks. Have students compare their impressions of Dr. Clark from the written biography and from seeing her at work on tape.

More About the Author Russell Baker's *Observer* column for the *The New York Times* established his reputation as a political satirist. Later, he wrote about a variety of subjects, such as tax reform, trendiness, inflation, and urban fear; and his articles earned him a Pulitzer Prize. In *Growing Up,* Baker suggests that the cruelties of family life stem more from cultural forces than from personal viciousness. If you were going to write a column for a newspaper or magazine, what are some of the subjects you would write about?

Literary Focus You might explain to your **more advanced** students that many of the best autobiographies are valued less because of the life of the autobiographer than because of the thoughts and ideas presented or the way the autobiography captures the history of a place and time.

Look For You might point out that while an adult can look back on his or her childhood and see the humor that was present, the child living through those years would have seldom felt humor.

Writing/Prior Knowledge If you can relate some experience of your own early years and point out the humor you now see in it, you will help the students warm up to the writing assignment.

Vocabulary You might tell your students that *gumption* is the most important word in the selection and that it appears more than once. After students have finished the selection, have them think about this word and decide how its meaning has grown from the way Baker used it.

GUIDE FOR READING

Autobiography

Look For

Writing

Vocabulary

No Gumption

Russell Baker (1925–   ) grew up in Virginia and New Jersey. When he was in the seventh grade, he decided to become a writer since "making up stories must surely be almost as much fun as reading them." As it turned out, he became a reporter rather than a fiction writer. He has won awards both for his newspaper column and for *Growing Up*, a book about his life. In this selection from his autobiography, you will learn about his failure in the business world—at a very young age!

An **autobiography** is a person's own account of his or her life. Like biographies, autobiographies often focus on conflicts and struggles. However, an autobiography can reveal more about its subject's thoughts and feelings because the writer and the subject are the same person.

As you read "No Gumption," try to understand the problems that Baker faced at this time in his childhood. Think about how he makes you see the humorous side of his childhood woes.

In this section from his autobiography, Russell Baker tells about how he once tried to sell newspapers. Perhaps like Baker you once tried to sell something. If not, imagine yourself in this type of situation— selling lemonade on the corner or raffle tickets door-to-door, for example. Freewrite about the experience, describing the product and telling whether or not you were successful. Try to capture the humorous aspects of the situation.

Knowing the following words will help you as you read "No Gumption."

gumption (gump' s·hən) *n.*: Courage and enterprise (p. 329)

appraisal (ə prā' z'l) *n.*: Judgment of something's or someone's quality (p. 329)

paupers (pô' pərz) *n.*: People who are very poor (p. 329)

interrogations (in ter' ə gā' s·hənz) *n.*: Situations where a

person is formally questioned (p. 330)

crucial krōō' s·həl) *adj.*: Of great importance (p. 331)

accessible (ak ses' ə b'l) *adj.*: Easy to get (p. 331)

aptitude (ap' tə tōōd') *n.*: Talent; ability (p. 332)

maxims (mak' simz) *n.*: Wise sayings (p. 334)

328   *Nonfiction*

Objectives

1 To understand autobiography
2 To compare and contrast characters
3 To write an autobiographical sketch

Support Material

Teaching Portfolio

Teacher Backup, p. 451
Grammar in Action Worksheet, *Using Semicolons,* p. 454
Usage and Mechanics Worksheet, p. 456
Vocabulary Check, p. 457
Analyzing Literature Worksheet, *Understanding Autobiography,* p. 459
Critical Thinking and Reading

Worksheet, *Comparing and Contrasting Characters,* p. 460
Selection Test, p. 461
Art Transparency 9, *Self-Portrait,* by Paul Gauguin

No Gumption

Russell Baker

I began working in journalism when I was eight years old. It was my mother's idea. She wanted me to "make something" of myself and, after a level-headed appraisal of my strengths, decided I had better start young if I was to have any chance of keeping up with the competition.

The flaw in my character which she had already spotted was lack of "gumption." My idea of a perfect afternoon was lying in front of the radio rereading my favorite Big Little Book,[1] *Dick Tracy Meets Stooge Viller.* My mother despised inactivity. Seeing me having a good time in repose, she was powerless to hide her disgust. "You've got no more gumption than a bump on a log," she said. "Get out in the kitchen and help Doris do those dirty dishes."

My sister Doris, though two years younger than I, had enough gumption for a dozen people. She positively enjoyed washing dishes, making beds, and cleaning the house. When she was only seven she could carry a piece of short-weighted cheese back to the A&P, threaten the manager with legal action, and come back triumphantly with the full quarter-pound we'd paid for and a few ounces extra thrown in for forgiveness. Doris could have made something of herself if she hadn't been a girl. Because of this defect, however, the best she could hope for was a career as a nurse or schoolteacher, the only work that capable females were considered up to in those days.

This must have saddened my mother, this twist of fate that had allocated all the gumption to the daughter and left her with a son who was content with Dick Tracy and Stooge Viller. If disappointed, though, she wasted no energy on self-pity. She would make me make something of myself whether I wanted to or not. "The Lord helps those who help themselves," she said. That was the way her mind worked.

She was realistic about the difficulty. Having sized up the material the Lord had given her to mold, she didn't overestimate what she could do with it. She didn't insist that I grow up to be President of the United States.

Fifty years ago parents still asked boys if they wanted to grow up to be President, and asked it not jokingly but seriously. Many parents who were hardly more than paupers still believed their sons could do it. Abraham Lincoln had done it. We were only sixty-five years from Lincoln. Many a grandfather who walked among us could remember Lincoln's

---

1. **Big Little Book:** A small, inexpensive, illustrated book that often portrayed the adventures of comic strip heroes like Dick Tracy.

No Gumption 329

Presentation

Motivation/Prior Knowledge Ask students to describe the kind of incidents they expect to read about in an autobiographical selection with the title "No Gumption."

Master Teacher Note Since the selection deals in part with young Baker's attempts to sell *The Saturday Evening Post,* you might bring in and allow your students to peruse any copies from the 1930's that you or a librarian can find. The pictures will help the class get an idea of what life in America was like in Baker's youth.

Purpose-Setting Question How would you feel if you had to go out and sell magazines at a time when few people had money for them?

1 **Enrichment** Journalism is the collecting, writing, and distributing of news to the public. The term, however, may also cover any kind of writing for newspapers or magazines.

2 **Discussion** What impression of Russell's mother do you get from this remark?

3 **Enrichment** In 1932, the attitude toward girls and women expressed here was not at all unusual. Would people today have similar ideas about females?

Master Teacher Note You might point out that autobiographies should reveal different aspects of the writer's character to be unbiased. To help with this discussion, place Art Transparency 9, *Self-Portrait* by Paul Gauguin, on the overhead projector. Have students study the painting and discuss what different aspects of the artist's personality are revealed. What might be some of the meanings of the items pictured along with the artist? Why did he include a halo, as well as a snake?

Thematic Idea Another selection that is humorous and at least purportedly autobiographical is Thurber's "The Night the Bed Fell," page 363.

time. Men of grandfatherly age were the worst for asking if you wanted to grow up to be President. A surprising number of little boys said yes and meant it.

I was asked many times myself. No, I would say, I didn't want to grow up to be President. My mother was present during one of these interrogations. An elderly uncle, having posed the usual question and exposed my lack of interest in the Presidency, asked, "Well, what *do* you want to be when you grow up?"

I loved to pick through trash piles and collect empty bottles, tin cans with pretty labels, and discarded magazines. The most de-

sirable job on earth sprang instantly to mind. "I want to be a garbage man," I said.

My uncle smiled, but my mother had seen the first distressing evidence of a bump budding on a log. "Have a little gumption, Russell," she said. Her calling me Russell was a signal of unhappiness. When she approved of me I was always "Buddy."

When I turned eight years old she decided that the job of starting me on the road toward making something of myself could no longer be safely delayed. "Buddy," she said one day, "I want you to come home right after school this afternoon. Somebody's coming and I want you to meet him."

When I burst in that afternoon she was in conference in the parlor with an executive of the Curtis Publishing Company. She introduced me. He bent low from the waist and shook my hand. Was it true as my mother had told him, he asked, that I longed for the opportunity to conquer the world of business?

My mother replied that I was blessed with a rare determination to make something of myself.

"That's right," I whispered.

"But have you got the grit, the character, the never-say-quit spirit it takes to succeed in business?"

My mother said I certainly did.

"That's right," I said.

He eyed me silently for a long pause, as though weighing whether I could be trusted to keep his confidence, then spoke man-to-man. Before taking a crucial step, he said, he wanted to advise me that working for the Curtis Publishing Company placed enormous responsibility on a young man. It was one of the great companies of America. Perhaps the greatest publishing house in the world. I had heard, no doubt, of the *Saturday Evening Post*?

Heard of it? My mother said that everyone in our house had heard of the *Saturday Post* and that I, in fact, read it with religious devotion.

Then doubtless, he said, we were also familiar with those two monthly pillars of the magazine world, the *Ladies Home Journal* and the *Country Gentleman*.

Indeed we were familiar with them, said my mother.

Representing the *Saturday Evening Post* was one of the weightiest honors that could be bestowed in the world of business, he said. He was personally proud of being a part of that great corporation.

My mother said he had every right to be.

Again he studied me as though debating whether I was worthy of a knighthood. Finally: "Are you trustworthy?"

My mother said I was the soul of honesty.

"That's right," I said.

The caller smiled for the first time. He told me I was a lucky young man. He admired my spunk. Too many young men thought life was all play. Those young men would not go far in this world. Only a young man willing to work and save and keep his face washed and his hair neatly combed could hope to come out on top in a world such as ours. Did I truly and sincerely believe that I was such a young man?

"He certainly does," said my mother.

"That's right," I said.

He said he had been so impressed by what he had seen of me that he was going to make me a representative of the Curtis Publishing Company. On the following Tuesday, he said, thirty freshly printed copies of the *Saturday Evening Post* would be delivered at our door. I would place these magazines, still damp with the ink of the presses, in a handsome canvas bag, sling it over my shoulder, and set forth through the streets to bring the best in journalism, fiction, and cartoons to the American public.

He had brought the canvas bag with him. He presented it with reverence fit for a chasuble.[2] He showed me how to drape the sling over my left shoulder and across the chest so that the pouch lay easily accessible to my right hand, allowing the best in journalism, fiction, and cartoons to be swiftly extracted and sold to a citizenry whose happiness and security depended upon us soldiers of the free press.

The following Tuesday I raced home from school, put the canvas bag over my

---

2. chasuble (chaz' yoob'l) *n*.: A sleeveless outer garment worn by priests.

6 **Discussion** Several times when the executive asks Russell a question, Mrs. Baker answers for her son, and Russell adds, "That's right." What impression of Mrs. Baker do you get? What do you think Russell is feeling during this interview?

7 **Literary Focus** Even though Baker is writing about a particular episode in his life, he steps away from the present to provide background information. How does this information add to your understanding of Russell's situation? Why do you think Baker discusses Uncle Allen?

8 **Critical Thinking and Reading** Background information such as this can change your view of characters or events. How does this paragraph affect your understanding of Russell's mother? Why is she so eager for Russell to succeed in business? Do you feel differently about her now? Explain.

shoulder, dumped the magazines in, and, tilting to the left to balance their weight on my right hip, embarked on the highway of journalism.

We lived in Belleville, New Jersey, a commuter town at the northern fringe of Newark. It was 1932, the bleakest year of the Depression. My father had died two years before, leaving us with a few pieces of Sears, Roebuck furniture and not much else, and my mother had taken Doris and me to live with one of her younger brothers. This was my Uncle Allen. Uncle Allen had made something of himself by 1932. As salesman for a soft-drink bottler in Newark, he had an income of $30 a week; wore pearl-gray spats,[3] detachable collars, and a three-piece suit; was happily married; and took in threadbare relatives.

With my load of magazines I headed toward Belleville Avenue. That's where the people were. There were two filling stations at the intersection with Union Avenue, as well as an A&P, a fruit stand, a bakery, a barber shop, Zuccarelli's drugstore, and a diner shaped like a railroad car. For several hours I made myself highly visible, shifting position now and then from corner to corner, from shop window to shop window, to make sure everyone could see the heavy black lettering on the canvas bag that said *The Saturday Evening Post.* When the angle of the light indicated it was suppertime, I walked back to the house.

"How many did you sell, Buddy?" my mother asked.

"None,"

"Where did you go?"

"The corner of Belleville and Union Avenues."

---

3. **spats** (spats) *n.*: Pieces of cloth or leather that cover the upper part of the shoe or ankle.

"What did you do?"

"Stood on the corner waiting for somebody to buy a *Saturday Evening Post.*"

"You just stood there?"

"Didn't sell a single one."

"For God's sake, Russell!"

Uncle Allen intervened. "I've been thinking about it for some time," he said, "and I've about decided to take the *Post* regularly. Put me down as a regular customer." I handed him a magazine and he paid me a nickel. It was the first nickel I earned.

Afterwards my mother instructed me in salesmanship. I would have to ring doorbells, address adults with charming self-confidence, and break down resistance with a sales talk pointing out that no one, no matter how poor, could afford to be without the *Saturday Evening Post* in the home.

I told my mother I'd changed my mind about wanting to succeed in the magazine business.

"If you think I'm going to raise a good-for-nothing," she replied, "you've got another think coming." She told me to hit the streets with the canvas bag and start ringing doorbells the instant school was out next day. When I objected that I didn't feel any aptitude for salesmanship, she asked how I'd like to lend her my leather belt so she could whack some sense into me. I bowed to superior will and entered journalism with a heavy heart.

My mother and I had fought this battle almost as long as I could remember. It probably started even before memory began, when I was a country child in northern Virginia and my mother, dissatisfied with my father's plain workman's life, determined that I would not grow up like him and his people, with calluses on their hands, overalls on their backs, and fourth-grade educations in their heads. She had fancier ideas of life's

Grammar in Action

One use of **semicolons** is to avoid confusion in a sentence that already contains several commas. A semicolon indicates a pause that is stronger than that of a comma, yet weaker than that of a period. Notice how effectively Russell Baker uses semicolons to avoid confusion between ideas.

As salesman for a soft-drink bottler in Newark, he had an income of $30 a week; wore pearl-gray spats, detachable collars, and a three-piece suit; was happily married; and took in threadbare relatives.

By using semicolons, Baker separates descriptions of his uncle. Compare the example with the following sentence to see how confusing the description would be if only commas were used.

As a salesman for a soft-drink bottler in Newark, he had an income of $30 a week, wore pearl-gray spats, detachable collars, and a three-piece suit, was happily married, and took in threadbare relatives.

possibilities. Introducing me to the *Saturday Evening Post*, she was trying to wean me as early as possible from my father's world where men left with lunch pails at sunup, worked with their hands until the grime ate into the pores, and died with a few sticks of mail-order furniture as their legacy. In my mother's vision of the better life there were desks and white collars, well-pressed suits, evenings of reading and lively talk, and perhaps—if a man were very, very lucky and hit the jackpot, really made something important of himself—perhaps there might be a fantastic salary of $5,000 a year to support a big house and a Buick with a rumble seat[4] and a vacation in Atlantic City.

And so I set forth with my sack of magazines. I was afraid of the dogs that snarled behind the doors of potential buyers. I was timid about ringing the doorbells of strangers, relieved when no one came to the door, and scared when someone did. Despite my mother's instructions, I could not deliver an engaging sales pitch. When a door opened I simply asked, "Want to buy a *Saturday Evening Post*?" In Belleville few persons did. It was a town of 30,000 people, and most weeks I rang a fair majority of its doorbells. But I rarely sold my thirty copies. Some weeks I canvassed the entire town for six days and still had four or five unsold magazines on Monday evening; then I dreaded the coming of Tuesday morning, when a batch of thirty fresh *Saturday Evening Posts* was due at the front door.

"Better get out there and sell the rest of those magazines tonight," my mother would say.

I usually posted myself then at a busy intersection where a traffic light controlled commuter flow from Newark. When the light turned red I stood on the curb and shouted my sales pitch at the motorists.

"Want to buy a *Saturday Evening Post*?"

One rainy night when car windows were sealed against me I came back soaked and with not a single sale to report. My mother beckoned to Doris.

"Go back down there with Buddy and show him how to sell these magazines," she said.

Brimming with zest, Doris, who was then seven years old, returned with me to the corner. She took a magazine from the bag, and when the light turned red she

---

4. **rumble seat:** In early automobiles, an open seat in the rear of the car that could be folded shut.

9 **Discussion** What do you think of Russell's method of selling?

No Gumption 333

Student Activity 1. Copy each sentence, adding semicolons where they should be used.

1. I want a hamburger with lettuce, tomato, and pickles a pizza with cheese, sausage, and mushrooms and a sandwich with rye bread, roast beef, and cheese.

2. On her trip Mary went to Portland, Maine Gloucester, Massachusetts and Newport, Rhode Island.

3. I want you to meet Jane, my sister Cathy, my next door neighbor and Carrie, my tennis partner.

Student Activity 2. Write three original sentences where you use semicolons to avoid confusion.

10 Discussion Why is Doris more successful than Russell at selling magazines?

11 Enrichment Maxims are brief, easily remembered sayings that contain good advice. Probably the most famous writer of maxims is François, Duc de La Rochefoucauld (1613–1680). One of his maxims is "Nothing is given so profusely as advice." Does Mrs. Baker give too much advice?

12 Discussion Why does Russell believe that writing is the best career for him? Do you suppose that writing is as easy and pleasant a career as Russell thinks it is?

Challenge What do you think are the special difficulties of selling a product or service? What are the rewards of success in this line of work? What personal qualities and abilities do you think a good salesperson must have?

Reader's Response Would you describe this selection as humorous? Sad? Heartwarming? Can it be described in some other way? Support your answer.

strode to the nearest car and banged her small fist against the closed window. The driver, probably startled at what he took to be a midget assaulting his car, lowered the window to stare, and Doris thrust a *Saturday Evening Post* at him.

"You need this magazine," she piped, "and it only costs a nickel."

Her salesmanship was irresistible. Before the light changed half a dozen times she disposed of the entire batch. I didn't feel humiliated. To the contrary. I was so happy I decided to give her a treat. Leading her to the vegetable store on Belleville Avenue, I bought three apples, which cost a nickel, and gave her one.

"You shouldn't waste money," she said.

"Eat your apple." I bit into mine.

"You shouldn't eat before supper," she said. "It'll spoil your appetite."

Back at the house that evening, she dutifully reported me for wasting a nickel. Instead of a scolding, I was rewarded with a pat on the back for having the good sense to buy fruit instead of candy. My mother reached into her bottomless supply of maxims and told Doris, "An apple a day keeps the doctor away."

By the time I was ten I had learned all my mother's maxims by heart. Asking to stay up past normal bedtime, I knew that a refusal would be explained with, "Early to bed and early to rise, makes a man healthy, wealthy, and wise." If I whimpered about having to get up early in the morning, I could depend on her to say, "The early bird gets the worm."

The one I most despised was, "If at first you don't succeed, try, try again." This was the battle cry with which she constantly sent me back into the hopeless struggle whenever I moaned that I had rung every doorbell in town and knew there wasn't a single potential buyer left in Belleville that week. After listening to my explanation, she handed me the canvas bag and said, "If at first you don't succeed . . ."

Three years in that job, which I would gladly have quit after the first day except for her insistence, produced at least one valuable result. My mother finally concluded that I would never make something of myself by pursuing a life in business and started considering careers that demanded less competitive zeal.

One evening when I was eleven I brought home a short "composition" on my summer vacation which the teacher had graded with an A. Reading it with her own schoolteacher's eye, my mother agreed that it was top-drawer seventh grade prose and complimented me. Nothing more was said about it immediately, but a new idea had taken life in her mind. Halfway through supper she suddenly interrupted the conversation.

"Buddy," she said, "maybe you could be a writer."

I clasped the idea to my heart. I had never met a writer, had shown no previous urge to write, and hadn't a notion how to become a writer, but I loved stories and thought that making up stories must surely be almost as much fun as reading them. Best of all, though, and what really gladdened my heart, was the ease of the writer's life. Writers did not have to trudge through the town peddling from canvas bags, defending themselves against angry dogs, being rejected by surly strangers. Writers did not have to ring doorbells. So far as I could make out, what writers did couldn't even be classified as work.

I was enchanted. Writers didn't have to have any gumption at all. I did not dare tell anybody for fear of being laughed at in the schoolyard, but secretly I decided that what I'd like to be when I grew up was a writer.

THINKING ABOUT THE SELECTION
Recalling

1. According to Russell's mother, what is the flaw in his character?
2. How does she try to repair this flaw when he is eight?
3. How does Russell feel about selling magazines?
4. What does his mother conclude after he has worked at his job for three years?
5. What is his mother's new plan for his career?

Interpreting

6. What qualities prevent him from being a good salesman? How might these same qualities help him in his chosen career?
7. How does Baker show a sense of humor in the way that he writes about this part of his life? Do you think he thought the situation humorous at the time the events were happening to him? Find evidence to support your answer.
8. How does Baker's sense of humor make you feel about him?

Applying

9. How does the description of Doris in the third paragraph show the different expectations people had for boys and for girls? Have these expectations changed since the time that this selection takes place? Support your answer.

ANALYZING LITERATURE
Understanding Autobiography

A person's account of his or her own life is called an **autobiography**. Such accounts include not only the facts of the writers' lives but their thoughts and feelings as well. In "No Gumption," Russell Baker gives you first-hand information about what happened when his mother tried to make him into a successful salesman at the age of eight.

1. What is the main problem that Baker faces during this part of his life?

2. Find a passage where he reveals his thoughts or feelings about this problem.
3. Would his account have been as humorous if he had written it as a boy? Why or why not?
4. Why is it that the passage of time can make events that seemed terrible when they happened now seem humorous?
5. How might the account of these events be different if Doris had written it?

CRITICAL THINKING AND READING
Comparing and Contrasting Characters

Comparing characters means seeing how they are similar. **Contrasting** them means finding how they are different. Although the main character of an autobiography is the writer, other characters will appear also. By comparing and contrasting these characters with the writer, you can gain a better idea of his or her personality.

1. How do Russell's and Doris's attitudes toward household chores differ?
2. Why was Doris better at selling magazines?
3. How does the incident where Russell buys an apple reveal a difference between them?
4. In what ways are both Doris and Russell admirable?

THINKING AND WRITING
Writing an Autobiographical Sketch

You have just started writing to a student your age in another country. Now that you have agreed to exchange letters, you want to tell this student something about your life. Think of a problem you faced when you were in kindergarten or first grade that now seems humorous to you. Before writing about this incident in a letter, list the most interesting and amusing parts of the story. Then turn this list into a humorous autobiographical sketch. When you revise your letter, make sure your description is clear and humorous. Then proofread your letter and prepare a final draft.

No Gumption 335

ers should find Baker a likable and sympathetic man because of his sense of humor.

Applying

9. The description shows that girls were expected to perform domestic chores and that nursing and teaching were the only careers considered to be suitable for them. Expectations have, of course, changed. Women are now doctors, lawyers, and business executives; and they do many of the same jobs that men do.

Closure and Extension

More About the Author Ernesto Galarza brought to his writing his experiences as a young immigrant in Sacramento, California, as a cannery worker, and as a teacher and principal. He was greatly concerned with the problems of Mexican-Americans and especially with the economic and social difficulties of farm workers. Why do you think writing ability might be valuable to someone who wants to do something about social problems?

Literary Focus You might explain to your students that the narrator of an autobiography brings a certain viewpoint to events. Just as a student seated at one side of a classroom sees the teacher somewhat differently from a student seated at the other side, so the narrator of an autobiography sees people and events in his or her own unique way.

Look For Have your students imagine that they are entering the first grade in a school in a foreign country. What emotions would they feel when they first arrive at school?

Writing/Prior Knowledge Ask for volunteers to mention experiences they had in this situation. Hearing about a few such experiences will help the class get started on the writing exercise.

Vocabulary You might mention that the vocabulary of the selection, while not especially difficult, indicates how thoroughly Galarza mastered his second language, English.

GUIDE FOR READING

from Barrio Boy

Ernesto Galarza (1905–1984) was born in the Mexican town of Jalcocotán. When his family resettled in California, they struggled to make ends meet. Ernesto was a good student. He eventually became a gifted teacher and writer. *Barrio Boy,* his most successful book, tells the story of his childhood in California. In this section from *Barrio Boy,* he tells of the frightening experience of attending school for the first time in a new country.

The Narrator in Autobiography

The **narrator** of a work is the person who tells the story. In an autobiography, the narrator is the writer telling you about his or her life. Ernesto Galarza, for example, is the narrator of *Barrio Boy.* Like most writers of autobiography, he refers to himself as "I" and tells you his thoughts and feelings about people and events.

Look For

As you read this section from *Barrio Boy,* put yourself in Ernesto's shoes. See the school, the students, and the teacher as they must have appeared to the young boy from Mexico. This will help you understand more fully his thoughts and feelings.

Writing

Everyone is a stranger at some time in life. Think about a time when you were a stranger. It could be when you moved to a new block, your first day at a new school, or your first day at a new camp, for example. Freewrite about your experiences.

Vocabulary

Knowing the following words will help you as you read this excerpt from *Barrio Boy.*

barrio (bär' ē ō) *n.*: Part of a town or city where most of the people are Hispanic (p. 337)
menace (men' is) *n.*: Danger; threat (p. 337)
formidable (fôr' mə də b'l) *adj.*: Impressive (p. 338)
mobilized (mō' bə līzd') *v.*: Put into motion (p. 338)
interpreter (in tur' prə tər) *n.*: Someone who translates from

one language into another (p. 338)
radiant (rā' dē ənt) *adj.*: Shining brightly (p. 338)
consultations (kän' s'l tā' shənz) *n.*: Discussions (p. 338)
persistently (pər sis' tənt lē) *adv.*: Constantly (p. 338)
grieving (grēv' iŋ) *v.*: Feeling sorrow for a loss (p. 339)

Objectives

1 To understand the narrator in autobiography
2 To understand stereotypes
3 To learn words from Spanish
4 To write about a school experience

Support Material

Teaching Portfolio
Teacher Backup, p. 463
Grammar in Action Worksheet, *Recognizing Personal Pronouns,* p. 466
Usage and Mechanics Worksheet, p. 468
Vocabulary Check, p. 469
Analyzing Literature Worksheet, *Thinking About the Narrator,* p. 471

Critical Thinking and Reading Worksheet, *Understanding Stereotypes,* p. 472
Selection Test, p. 473

from **Barrio Boy**

Ernesto Galarza

My mother and I walked south on Fifth Street one morning to the corner of Q Street and turned right. Half of the block was occupied by the Lincoln School. It was a three-story wooden building, with two wings that gave it the shape of a double-T connected by a central hall. It was a new building, painted yellow, with a shingled roof that was not like the red tile of the school in Mazatlán. I noticed other differences, none of them very reassuring.

We walked up the wide staircase hand in hand and through the door, which closed by itself. A mechanical contraption screwed to the top shut it behind us quietly.

Up to this point the adventure of enrolling me in the school had been carefully rehearsed. Mrs. Dodson had told us how to find it and we had circled it several times on our walks. Friends in the *barrio* explained that the director was called a principal, and that it was a lady and not a man. They assured us that there was always a person at the school who could speak Spanish.

Exactly as we had been told, there was a sign on the door in both Spanish and English: "Principal." We crossed the hall and entered the office of Miss Nettie Hopley.

Miss Hopley was at a roll-top desk to one side, sitting in a swivel chair that moved on wheels. There was a sofa against the opposite wall, flanked by two windows and a door that opened on a small balcony. Chairs were set around a table and framed pictures hung on the walls of a man with long white hair and another with a sad face and a black beard.

The principal half turned in the swivel chair to look at us over the pinch glasses crossed on the ridge of her nose. To do this she had to duck her head slightly as if she were about to step through a low doorway.

What Miss Hopley said to us we did not know but we saw in her eyes a warm welcome and when she took off her glasses and straightened up she smiled wholeheartedly, like Mrs. Dodson. We were, of course, saying nothing, only catching the friendliness of her voice and the sparkle in her eyes while she said words we did not understand. She signaled us to the table. Almost tiptoeing across the office, I maneuvered myself to keep my mother between me and the gringo lady. In a matter of seconds I had to decide whether she was a possible friend or a menace. We sat down.

from Barrio Boy 337

Presentation

Motivation/Prior Knowledge Ask your students to tell what they know or have heard about life in a barrio. How is it different from life in a community where there are no immigrants?

Master Teacher Note The full title of Galarza's autobiography is *Barrio Boy: The Story of a Boy's Acculturation.* Explain that *acculturation* means conditioning a person to the patterns or customs of a culture. Ask students to imagine what is involved in conditioning a child to a foreign culture.

Purpose-Setting Question What qualities in the principal, Miss Hopley, and the teacher, Miss Ryan, help Ernesto to succeed in his new school?

1 **Enrichment** Mazatlán is a seaport in western Mexico. Its chief exports are metal ores, hides, tobacco, and shrimp.

2 **Enrichment** *Gringo* is the Latin-American term for a foreigner, especially an English-speaking one. It has overtones of dislike or hostility. What are young Ernesto's feelings at this moment? Do you think he dislikes Miss Hopley? Why or why not?

3 **Discussion** What details in this paragraph indicate that the narrator's viewpoint is that of a child? What makes Ernesto decide that he likes Miss Hopley?

4 **Crical Thinking and Reading** Galarza does not tell the reader what he thought of Miss Ryan as a teacher. What opinion of her does he probably want you to form?

5 **Discussion** What difficulties or problems might Miss Ryan face in managing her class while providing these "private lessons"?

3 Then Miss Hopley did a formidable thing. She stood up. Had she been standing when we entered she would have seemed tall. But rising from her chair she soared. And what she carried up and up with her was a buxom superstructure,[1] firm shoulders, a straight sharp nose, full cheeks slightly molded by a curved line along the nostrils, thin lips that moved like steel springs, and a high forehead topped by hair gathered in a bun. Miss Hopley was not a giant in body but when she mobilized it to a standing position she seemed a match for giants. I decided I liked her.

She strode to a door in the far corner of the office, opened it and called a name. A boy of about ten years appeared in the doorway. He sat down at one end of the table. He was brown like us, a plump kid with shiny black hair combed straight back, neat, cool, and faintly obnoxious.

Miss Hopley joined us with a large book and some papers in her hand. She, too, sat down and the questions and answers began by way of our interpreter. My name was Ernesto. My mother's name was Henriqueta. My birth certificate was in San Blas. Here was my last report card from the Escuela Municipal Numero 3 para Varones of Mazatlán,[2] and so forth. Miss Hopley put things down in the book and my mother signed a card.

As long as the questions continued, Doña[3] Henriqueta could stay and I was secure. Now that they were over, Miss Hopley saw her to the door, dismissed our inter-

---

1. **buxom superstructure:** Full figure.
2. **Escuela Municipal Numero 3 para Varones of Mazatlán** (es kwä lə mōō nē sē päl nōō′me rô träs pärä vä rō′nas mä sät län′): Municipal School Number 3 for Boys of Mazatlán.
3. **doña** (dô′ nyä): A Spanish title of respect meaning "lady" or "madam".

preter and without further ado took me by the hand and strode down the hall to Miss Ryan's first grade.

Miss Ryan took me to a seat at the front of the room, into which I shrank—the better to survey her. She was, to skinny, somewhat runty me, of a withering height when she patrolled the class. And when I least expected it, there she was, crouching by my desk, her blond radiant face level with mine, her voice patiently maneuvering me over the awful idiocies of the English language.

4 During the next few weeks Miss Ryan overcame my fears of tall, energetic teachers as she bent over my desk to help me with a word in the pre-primer. Step by step, she loosened me and my classmates from the safe anchorage of the desks for recitations at the blackboard and consultations at her desk. Frequently she burst into happy announcements to the whole class. "Ito can read a sentence," and small Japanese Ito, squint-eyed and shy, slowly read aloud while the class listened in wonder: "Come, Skipper, come. Come and run." The Korean, Portuguese, Italian, and Polish first graders had similar moments of glory, no less shining than mine the day I conquered "butterfly," which I had been persistently pronouncing in standard Spanish as boo-ter-flee. "Children," Miss Ryan called for attention. "Ernesto has learned how to pronounce *butterfly!*" And I proved it with a perfect imitation of Miss Ryan. From that celebrated success, I was soon able to match Ito's progress as a sentence reader with "Come, butterfly, come fly with me."

5 Like Ito and several other first graders who did not know English, I received private lessons from Miss Ryan in the closet, a narrow hall off the classroom with a door at each end. Next to one of these doors Miss Ryan placed a large chair for herself and a small one for me. Keeping an eye on the class

Grammar in Action

A **pronoun** is a word used in place of a noun or a group of words acting as a noun. Pronouns allow you to avoid using the same noun repeatedly. The most commonly used pronouns are **personal pronouns.** Using the proper case, number, and person of personal pronouns is essential to insure that the sentence makes sense and sounds right. In the following passage, Ernesto Galarza's use of personal pronouns makes the sentence flow and keeps the meaning clear:

And when *I* least expected *it*, there *she* was, crouching by *my* desk, *her* blond radiant face level with *mine*, *her* voice patiently maneuvering *me* over the awful idiocies of the English language.

Galarza uses the first-person, singular pronouns *I*, *my*, *mine*, and *me* to refer to himself. He uses the third-person, singular pronouns *she* and *her* to refer to his teacher. The third-person, singular pronoun *it* refers to the teacher's coming to help him. He uses these personal pronouns to tie this passage to earlier passages and thus add unity to the selection.

Compare Galarza's sentence to the following one in which only nouns have been used.

6 Critical Thinking and Reading
How can a young boy's falling in love with his teacher enable him to graduate with honors? Is this statement meant to be taken seriously, humorously, or both?

through the open door she read with me about sheep in the meadow and a frightened chicken going to see the king, coaching me out of my phonetic ruts in words like *pasture*, *bow-wow-wow*, *hay*, and *pretty*, which to my Mexican ear and eye had so many unnecessary sounds and letters. She made me watch her lips and then close my eyes as she repeated words I found hard to read. When we came to know each other better, I tried interrupting to tell Miss Ryan how we said it in Spanish. It didn't work. She only said "oh" and went on with *pasture*, *bow-wow-wow*, and *pretty*. It was as if in that closet we were both discovering together the secrets of the English language and grieving together over the tragedies of Bo-Peep. The main reason I was graduated with honors from the first grade was that I had fallen in love with Miss Ryan. Her radiant, no-nonsense character made us either afraid not to love her or love her so we would not be afraid, I am not sure which. It was not only that we sensed she was with it, but also that she was with us.

Like the first grade, the rest of the Lincoln School was a sampling of the lower part of town where many races made their home.

from *Barrio Boy* 339

And when Ernesto least expected Miss Ryan to come, there Miss Ryan was, crouching by Ernesto's desk, Miss Ryan's blond radiant face level with Ernesto's, Miss Ryan's voice patiently maneuvering Ernesto over the awful idiocies of the English language.

Student Activity 1. Find three other sentences where Galarza uses personal pronouns. Identify the pronouns in each sentence and tell how each pronoun is used in the sentence.

Student Activity 2. Rewrite the sentences below, correcting errors in pronoun usage.

1. Jamie told Rhonda and I about the party.

2. Mary, Ronny, and me told her that her could go with us.

3. Us girls don't have to take the test.

Critical Thinking and Reading
What is the main idea of this paragraph? What two sentences express this idea in different words? What message or lesson might the author be communicating to those involved professionally with immigrants? Do you agree with this message?

Challenge What arguments could be made against what Galarza is implying in the final paragraph?

Reader's Response What do you think would be the most difficult aspect of adjusting to life in a new country with a new language and unfamiliar culture? Explain.

My pals in the second grade were Kazushi, whose parents spoke only Japanese; Matti, a skinny Italian boy; and Manuel, a fat Portuguese who would never get into a fight but wrestled you to the ground and just sat on you. Our assortment of nationalities included Koreans, Yugoslavs, Poles, Irish, and home-grown Americans.

At Lincoln, making us into Americans did not mean scrubbing away what made us originally foreign. The teachers called us as our parents did, or as close as they could pronounce our names in Spanish or Japanese. No one was ever scolded or punished for speaking in his native tongue on the playground. Matti told the class about his mother's down quilt, which she had made in Italy with the fine feathers of a thousand geese. Encarnación acted out how boys learned to fish in the Philippines. I astounded the third grade with the story of my travels on a stagecoach, which nobody else in the class had seen except in the museum at Sutter's Fort. After a visit to the Crocker Art Gallery and its collection of heroic paintings of the golden age of California, someone showed a silk scroll with a Chinese painting. Miss Hopley herself had a way of expressing wonder over these matters before a class, her eyes wide open until they popped slightly. It was easy for me to feel that becoming a proud American, as she said we should, did not mean feeling ashamed of being a Mexican.

7

THINKING ABOUT THE SELECTION

Recalling

1. Why is Ernesto nervous at the start of this selection?
2. How does Miss Hopley reassure him?
3. Why is he afraid of Miss Ryan at first?
4. How does Miss Ryan make Ernesto and his classmates feel successful?

Interpreting

5. Explain the writer's statement that Miss Ryan was both "with it" and "with us."
6. What is the main problem that Ernesto faces during this part of his life?
7. What is the meaning of the title?

Applying

8. What qualities does a person need in order to make someone feel at home in a strange situation?
9. How would you make foreign students feel more at home in a school?

ANALYZING LITERATURE

Thinking About the Narrator

The **narrator** of a work is the person who tells the story. The narrator of an autobiography is the author. However, the narrator often tells about a different time in life. In this selection, the older, maturer Ernesto Galarza, tells about the young boy Ernesto.

Closure and Extension

ANSWERS TO THINKING ABOUT THE SELECTION
Recalling

1. He is nervous because he is going to an American school for the first time.
2. Her eyes display a warm welcome, and she smiles wholeheartedly.
3. Miss Ryan is tall and energetic, and she crouches by his desk unexpectedly. Also, she is a stranger and a figure of authority.
4. She helps them individually and praises them publicly.

Interpreting

5. She was "with it" in the sense that she knew what was going on and taught well. She was "with us" in that she cared about the students.
6. Ernesto's main problem is learning English.
7. The title means that Galarza's account will focus on a boy who is a foreigner and who must struggle to be at home in a different culture.

Applying

8. Suggested Response: A person needs to be understanding, sensitive, patient, resourceful, friendly, and respectful. Students may, of course, think of other relevant qualities.
9. Answers will differ; however, students might mention such ac-

Narrators of autobiographies, like Ernesto Galarza, refer to themselves as "I" and tell you their thoughts and feelings about the events of their lives. In this selection from *Barrio Boy,* Galarza focuses on the problems he faced and overcame as a new, Spanish-speaking student in an American school.

1. Find three places where Galarza refers to himself as "I."
2. Identify two passages where Galarza reports his thoughts or feelings.
3. Most readers probably feel glad when Galarza overcomes his problems. Why might readers be less involved if Galarza himself were not the narrator?
4. In what ways do you think the narrator Ernesto Galarza is different from the young boy Ernesto? Find evidence to support your answer.

CRITICAL THINKING AND READING
Understanding Stereotypes

A **stereotype** is a negative idea about the traits or behavior of a group of people. This idea does not let you see the individuals of that group for who they are. For example, Ernesto feels threatened by "tall, energetic teachers." Since Miss Ryan is a member of this group, he is afraid of her. However, as he begins to know her, he realizes that his stereotype was wrong.

1. Judging by Galarza's experience, what is the best way to overcome stereotypes?

2. Galarza comments that, "At Lincoln, making us into Americans did not mean scrubbing away what made us originally foreign." What does he mean by this statement?

UNDERSTANDING LANGUAGE
Learning Words from Spanish

Ernesto Galarza spoke Spanish before he learned English. In this selection, he uses a Spanish word that has become part of the English language. *Barrio* means "part of a town or city where most of the people are Hispanic."

Look up the following words in a dictionary and use each in a sentence.
1. rodeo 2. arroyo 3. lariat 4. taco

THINKING AND WRITING
Writing About a School Experience

Imagine that a young friend of yours is about to go to a new school. You want to encourage that person. To do so, write an account of your own first time in a strange situation. Look back at the writing assignment you did before reading this selection. Turn that description into an autobiographical sketch that your young friend will enjoy. When you revise the sketch, make sure you have used the word "I" when talking about yourself, just as Galarza does. Proofread your account and share it with your classmates.

from Barrio Boy 341

(Answers begin on p. 340)

he adjusted to American life. Ernesto the boy is fearful, struggling with a new language, and not yet at home in his new culture.

Challenge It has been said that the most important freedom is the freedom to choose one's attitudes. How does this relate to "Barrio Boy"?

ANSWERS TO CRITICAL THINKING AND READING
1. The best way is to find out more about a person as an individual, rather than as a representative of a group.
2. He means that at Lincoln the teachers did not attempt to cut students off from their backgrounds and cultures. They recognized that one could be an American while preserving one's cultural heritage.

ANSWERS TO UNDERSTANDING LANGUAGE
1. rodeo: A cattle roundup; a public competition featuring cowboy skills. (Bronco riding is my favorite rodeo event.)
2. arroyo: A gully cut by a stream that is now dry; a stream. (They placed their sleeping bags in the arroyo.)
3. lariat: A lasso; a rope used for capturing or tethering animals. (He kept his lariat on his saddle horn.)
4. taco: A crispy, thin cake of cornmeal or flour containing a filling such as ground meat or cheese. (Mom made a large batch of tacos for the guests.)

---

tions as extending invitations, showing interest in the foreign student's culture, helping him or her with language problems, and, in general, being friendly.

Challenge How does the phrase "meeting someone right where they are" relate to Ernesto's situation?

ANSWERS TO ANALYZING LITERATURE

1. He refers to himself as "I" in many places. For example, on the first page of the selection (337), he does so twice in the first paragraph and twice in the last.
2. Galarza says:, "I liked her [Miss Hopley]," (page 338); "As long as the questions continued...I was secure," (page 338); "...I had fallen in love with Miss Ryan," (page 339); "It was easy for me

to feel that becoming a proud American...did not mean feeling ashamed of being a Mexican," (page 340);
3. If Galarza were not the narrator, the account would be less personal. Readers would not feel that they were in touch with his thoughts, feelings, and point of view. Hence, they would feel less involved.
4. The narrator-author is a successful writer whose well-written account is itself evidence of how well

Writing Across the Curriculum You might ask a colleague in the social studies department to suggest some research-paper topics dealing with Hispanic Americans. You might encourage your **more advanced** students to write a paper for extra-credit.

More About the Author Jade Snow Wong is one of the first Chinese-American writers. Her literary interest in the problems faced by young Chinese growing up in America stems from the conflicts that she experienced between Chinese and American cultures. You might ask your students to discuss why Wong's writings, because of her background, must be considered valuable to American literature.

Literary Focus You might point out that the effect produced by this point of view in an autobiography is unusual. Suggest that, as they read through the selection, they keep in mind that it is Jade Snow Wong who is always referring to herself as "she." How would they describe the effect this method produces? What are its advantages or disadvantages?

Look For Encourage your students, especially the **less advanced** ones, to think of Wong's autobiography as illustrating the way to success in almost any field of endeavor. What lessons can they apply to their own hopes and efforts?

Writing/Prior Knowledge If a volunteer presents orally the steps that he or she follows, you can then question the student on any aspect that requires further explanation. Then point out to the class that any such explanation must be full and complete so that every reader can follow it.

Vocabulary Students who are **less advanced** may need help in pronouncing these words. When reading through or discussing this selection, you might select passages for an exercise in understanding word meanings through context clues.

GUIDE FOR READING

A Time of Beginnings

Jade Snow Wong (1922–   ) grew up in San Francisco's China-town. As a girl, she tried to learn American customs while her parents followed a traditional Chinese way of life. Wong tells about this period of her life in her popular autobiography *Fifth Chinese Daughter* (1950). In 1975, she published the story of her adult life in *No Chinese Stranger*. "A Time of Beginnings," which comes from that later book, describes how she fought against odds to become an artist and a businesswoman.

Third-Person Narrative in Autobiography

While in most autobiographies the writers refer to themselves as "I," Jade Snow Wong refers to herself by name or as "she." This method of writing is called **third-person narrative.** Wong explains this un-usual practice in the introduction to her autobiography, telling readers about the importance of modesty in the Chinese tradition. According to this tradition, it is "unnecessary to sign works of art and unbecom-ing to talk at length using 'I' or 'me.' "

Look For

As you read "A Time of Beginnings," look for the many problems that Wong must overcome to achieve success in her chosen field. What is it about Wong's character that helps her overcome these obstacles?

Writing

In this selection Jade Snow Wong explains how she succeeded as a potter. Think about something that you do well. It could be anything from building a model airplane to cooking a meal. How would you ex-plain what you do to someone else? List the important points you would include in your explanation.

Vocabulary

Knowing the following words will help you as you read "A Time of Be-ginnings."

ironically (ī rän' i k'l lē) *adv.*: In a way different from what is ex-pected (p. 343)

prevalent (prev' ə lənt) *adj.*: Widely accepted (p. 343)

utilizing (yōōt''l īz' iŋ) *v.*: Using (p. 343)

catastrophe (kə tas' trə fē) *n.*: Sudden disaster or misfortune (p. 345)

immeasurably (i mezh' ər əb' lē) *adv.*: Extremely; very (p. 345)

comparable (käm' pər ə b'l) *adj.*: Similar (p. 345)

liability (lī' ə bil' ə tē) *n.*: Disad-vantage (p. 345)

aesthetically (es thet' ik lē) *adv.*: From an artistic point of view (p. 347)

342   *Nonfiction*

Support Material

Teaching Portfolio
Teacher Backup, p. 475
Grammar in Action Worksheet, *Recognizing Antonyms,* p. 479
Usage and Mechanics Work-sheet, p. 481
Vocabulary Check, p. 482
Critical Thinking and Reading Worksheet, *Distinguishing De-tails,* p. 484

Language Worksheet, *Jargon,* p. 485
Selection Test, p. 486

A Time of Beginnings

Jade Snow Wong

After Jade Snow began working in Mr. Fong's window, which confined her clay spatters, her activity revealed for the first time to Chinatown residents an art which had distinguished Chinese culture. Ironically, it was not until she was at college that she became fascinated with Tang and Sung Dynasty[1] achievements in clay, a thousand years ago.

Her ability to master pottery made her father happy, for Grandfather Wong believed that a person who could work with his hands would never starve. When Father Wong was young, Grandfather made him learn how to hand-pierce and stitch slipper soles, and how to knot Chinese button heads, both indispensable in clothing. But to Mother Wong, the merits of making pottery escaped her—to see her college-educated daughter up to her elbows in clay, and more clay flying around as she worked in public view, was strangely unladylike. As for Chinatown merchants, they laughed openly at her, "Here comes the girl who plays with mud. How many bowls could you sell today?" Probably they thought: Here is a college graduate foolish enough to dirty her hands.

It has been the traditional belief from Asia to the Middle East, with Japan the exception, that scholars do not soil their hands and that a person studied literature in order to escape hard work. (This attitude is still prevalent in most Asian countries outside of the People's Republic of China and Japan.)

From the first, the local Chinese were not Jade Snow's patrons. The thinness and whiteness of porcelains imported from China and ornate decorations which came into vogue during the late Ching Dynasty[2] satisfied their tastes. They could not understand why "silly Americans" paid dollars for a hand-thrown bowl[3] utilizing crude California colored clays, not much different from the inexpensive peasant ware of China. That the Jade Snow Wong bowl went back to an older tradition of understated beauty was not apparent. They could see only that she wouldn't apply a dragon or a hundred flowers.

Many years later when Jade Snow met another atypical artist, a scholar and calligrapher[4] born and educated in China, he was to say to her, "I shudder if the majority of people look at my brush work and say it is pretty, for then I know it is ordinary and I have failed. If they say they do not understand it, or even that it is ugly, I am happy, for I have succeeded."

---

1. Tang and Sung (soong) **Dynasty:** A dynasty is a succession of rulers who belong to the same family. The period of the Tang Dynasty was 618–906 and that of the Sung Dynasty 960–1279.

2. Ching Dynasty: This dynasty lasted from 1644 to 1912.

3. hand-thrown bowl: A bowl shaped by hand on a potter's wheel, which spins the clay around.

4. calligrapher (kə lig′ rə fər) n.: Someone skilled in the art of beautiful handwriting.

However, there were enough numbers of the American public who bought Jade Snow's pottery to support her modestly. The store window was a temporary experiment which proved what she needed to know. In the meantime, her aging father, who was fearful that their home and factory might be in a redevelopment area, made a down payment with lifetime savings to purchase a small white wooden building with six rentable apartments at the perimeter of Chinatown. Jade Snow agreed to rent the two tiny empty ground-floor storefronts which he did not yet need, one for a display room, with supplies and packing center at its rear, the other for the potter's wheel, kiln,[5] glazing

booth,[6] compressor,[7] and other equipment. Now, instead of paying Mr. Fong a commission on gross sales, she had bills to pay. Instead of sitting in a window, she worked with doors thrown open to the street.

Creativeness was 90 percent hard work and 10 percent inspiration. It was learning from errors, either from her lack of foresight or because of the errors of others. The first firing[8] in an unfamiliar new gas kiln brought crushing disappointment when the wares blew up into tiny pieces. In another firing,

5

---

5. **kiln** (kiln) n.: An oven to bake pottery.

6. **glazing booth:** A place to apply glaze, a glassy finish, to pottery.
7. **compressor:** (kəm pres′ ər): A machine for compressing air or gas.
8. **firing** (fir′ iŋ) n.: The application of heat to harden or glaze pottery.

344   *Nonfiction*

Grammar in Action

An **antonym** is a word that means the opposite of another word. By using antonyms, writers can present vivid and specific contrasts, which make their ideas more colorful and memorable.

In the following passage, Jade Snow Wong uses antonyms to point up and intensify the problems she encounters in her work.

A piece she worked on *diligently* could *disappoint*. Another made *casually* had been enhanced successively until it *delighted.*

Wong uses two sets of antonyms in her two sentences: *Diligently* and *casually; disappoint* and *delight.* Through her use of these antonyms, Wong vividly conveys her frustration over the unpredictability of her work.

Student Activity 1. Find two passages from "A Time of Beginnings" in which Wong uses antonyms well. Explain why you think the use of antonyms in these sentences is effective.

glaze results were uneven black and dark green, for the chemical supply house had mistakenly labeled five pounds of black copper oxide as black iron oxide. One morning there was a personal catastrophe. Unaware of a slow leak all night from the partially opened gas cock, she lit a match at the kiln. An explosion injured both hands, which took weeks to heal.

The day-to-day work of potterymaking tested her deepest discipline. A "wedged" ball of clay (prepared by kneading) would be "thrown" (shaped) on the potter's wheel, then dried overnight and trimmed, sometimes decorated with Chinese brush or bamboo tools. It took about a hundred thoroughly dried pieces to fill a kiln for the first firing that transformed fragile mud walls into hard bisque ware.[9] Glazes, like clays the results of countless experiments, were then applied to each piece. A second twelve-hour firing followed, with the temperatures raised hour by hour up to the final maturing point of somewhere around 2,000 degrees Fahrenheit. Then the kiln was turned off for twenty-four hours of cooling. Breakage was a potential hazard at every stage; each step might measure short in technical and artistic accomplishment. A piece she worked on diligently could disappoint. Another made casually had been enhanced successively until it delighted. One piece in ten might be of exhibition quality, half might be salable, and the others would be flawed "seconds" she would discard.

Yet Jade Snow never wavered from her belief that if moments in time could result in a thing of beauty that others could share, those moments were immeasurably satisfying. She owned two perfect Sung tea bowls. Without copying, she tried to make her pottery "stand up" in strength and grace to that standard.

It became routine to work past midnight without days off. Hand work could not be rushed; failures had to be replaced, and a host of other unanticipated business chores suddenly manifested themselves. She had kept comparable hours when she worked all through college to meet her expenses. Again, the hope of reaching valued goals was her spur. If she should fail, then she could accept what tradition dictated for most Chinese daughters—to be a wife, daughter-in-law, and mother. But unlike her college, the American business world was not dedicated to helping her. Because she was pioneering in a new venture, her identity was a liability. Her brains and hands were her only assets. How could she convert that liability? How could she differ from other struggling potters?

To enlarge her production base, she experimented with enamels[10] on copper forms conceived in the fluid shapes of her pottery, layering jewel tones for brilliant effects. They differed from the earth tints of clay and attracted a new clientele. With another kiln and new equipment, she made functional forms, believing that fine things should become part of the user's everyday life. The best results were submitted to exhibitions. Some juries rejected them, some accepted, and others awarded prizes.

To reach a market larger than San Francisco, she wrote to store buyers around the country, and, encouraged, she called on them. Traveling to strange cities far across the United States, as a rare Oriental woman alone in hotel dining rooms, she developed strong nerves against curious stares. That trip produced orders. Stipulated delivery and

---

9. bisque (bisk) **ware:** Unglazed pottery.

10. enamels (i nam′′ls) *n.*: Glassy colored substances used as coatings on metal, glass, and pottery.

---

6 Critical Thinking and Reading After you read this paragraph, explain in your own words how Wong's discipline was tested.

7 Discussion *Imitation* means copying a model. *Emulation* means trying to equal or surpass the excellence of a model. Which does Wong believe in?

8 Critical Thinking and Reading Compare and contrast Wong's experiences in college and business. How were they similar? How were they different? A liability is something that works to one's disadvantage. An asset is something valuable or helpful. How was her identity a liability?

9 Discussion How is Wong making progress in her career? What problems is progress bringing?

Student Activity 2. Complete the following sentences with clauses that include antonyms of other words in the sentence.

1. My friend Jody is extremely tall, while. . . .

2. The air in the room was beastly hot, yet. . . .

3. In the land of Nod, some children were roly-poly fat, but then. . . .

cancellation dates made it necessary to hire first one and then more helpers who had to be trained, checked, kept busy and happy.

The strains increased. So did the bills, and she borrowed in small amounts from her sympathetic father, who said, "A hundred dollars is easy to come by, but the first thousand is very, very tricky. Look at the ideograph[11] for hundred—solidly square. Look at it for thousand—pointed, slippery. The ancients knew this long ago." When hundreds were not enough, tactful Western friends offered help. Oldest Brother, noticing her worries and struggles, sniffed scornfully. "You'll be out of business in a year."

She had learned to accept family criticism in silence, but she was too deeply involved to give up. Money was a worry, but creating was exciting and satisfying. These were lonely years. Jade Snow's single-minded pursuit did not allow her pleasant interludes with friends. To start a kiln at dawn, then watch till its critical maturing moment, which could happen any time between early evening and midnight or later (when gas pressure was low, it took until the next dawn), kept her from social engagements.

Then, gradually, signs indicated that she was working in the right direction. The first was a letter from the Metropolitan Museum of Art in New York, where the Eleventh Ceramic National Syracuse Show had been sent. The curator wrote, "We think the green, gold and ivory enamel bowl a skillful piece of workmanship and are anxious to add it to our collections." They referred to a ten-inch shallow bowl which Jade Snow had made.

A reviewer in *Art Digest* wrote, "In plain enamels without applied design, Jade Snow Wong of San Francisco seemed to this critic to top the list."

Recognition brought further recognition. National decorating magazines featured her enamels, and in the same year, 1947, the Museum of Modern Art installed an exhibit by Mies Van der Rohe[12] which displayed 100 objects of fine design costing less than $100. A note introducing this exhibit read, "Every so often the Museum of Modern Art selects and exhibits soundly designed objects available to American purchasers in the belief that this will encourage more people to use beautiful things in their everyday life. . . ."

---

11. ideograph (id′ē ə graf′) *n.*: A symbol that stands for a thing or idea without expressing the sounds that make up its name.

12. Mies Van der Rohe (mēz′ van dər rō′ə): Ludwig Mies Van der Rohe (1886–1969) was a German-born American architect.

Two of Jade Snow's enamels, a dinner plate in Chinese red and a dessert plate in grayish gold, were included in the exhibition, which subsequently went to Europe.

So it did not seem unusual to receive an interviewer from *Mademoiselle,* but it was indeed unexpected to receive one of the magazine's ten awards for 1948 to women outstanding in ten different fields. They invited Jade Snow to fly to New York to claim her silver medal.

The more deeply one delves into a field, the more one realizes limitations. When Bernard Leach, the famous English potter, accepted an invitation from Mills College to teach a special course, Jade Snow attended. Another summer, Charles Merritt came from Alfred University's staff to give a course in precise glaze chemistry. Again, she commuted to Oakland. She became friends with these two unusual teachers. Both agreed that in pottery making, one never found a final answer. A mass-produced bathtub may be a technical triumph; yet a chemically balanced glaze on a pot can be aesthetically dull. Some of the most pleasing glaze effects could never be duplicated, for they were the combination of scrapings from the glaze booth. Like the waves of the sea, no two pieces of pottery art can be identical.

After three years of downs, then ups, the business promised to survive. Debts had been cleared. A small staff could handle routine duties. A steady clientele of San Franciscans came to her out-of-the-way shop. A beginning had been made.

A Time of Beginnings **347**

11 **Discussion** Since Wong is by now a successful artist, why is she going back to school? What does the first sentence of this paragraph mean?

12 **Critical Thinking and Reading** Tell why you think the following would or would not be a better concluding sentence: *Her career was now in full swing, and she was truly a success.*

Thematic Ideas Another selection that deals with the theme of women overcoming gender-based difficulties is "Eugenie Clark and the Sleeping Sharks" on page 319. "A Time of Beginnings" can be compared with "Barrio Boy" for the theme of conflict between one's ethnic culture and mainstream American culture.

Reader's Response What aspect of the author's personality do you believe was the greatest help in making her a success? Support your answer.

Closure and Extension

ANSWERS TO THINKING ABOUT THE SELECTION
Recalling

1. Her father was pleased, since he valued the ability to work with one's hands. Her mother thought Wong's work was unladylike and unsuitable for a college graduate.
2. She defied traditional Chinese ways by working with her hands even though she was college-educated. She defied traditional expectations for a woman by not being a wife, daughter-in-law, and mother.
3. The appearance of the ideographs supported his belief that a hundred dollars is easy to come by but that the first thousand is hard.

Interpreting

4. Suggested Response: You can infer that she possesses determination, persistence, and genuine talent and that these qualities eventually reap rewards. Other incidents that support this inference include these: her pieces being exhibited by various museums; her work receiving critical praise from art critics; receiving an award for her achievements from *Mademoiselle* magazine.
5. Being Chinese and female did not bring her support or encouragement. Her brains and hands were her only assets inasmuch as only they could enable her to succeed, since the opinion and expectations of others were unfavorable.
6. The last line expresses her humility while indicating that Wong will probably succeed, since the start-up period for a career in art is the most difficult.

Applying

7. Answers will differ; however, students should see that such a sacrifice is worth making if the goal is valued highly enough.
8. An artistic success is one that meets one's own high standards or generally accepted artistic standards. It may have nothing to do with public approval. A popular success is one that pleases a

---

THINKING ABOUT THE SELECTION
Recalling

1. How did Wong's father and mother differ in their reactions to her work as a potter?
2. How did Wong defy traditional Chinese ways? How did she defy the traditional expectations of the time for women?
3. The ideograph for hundred is 百 and for thousand is 千 . According to Wong's father, what is the significance of these ideographs?

Interpreting

4. What do you infer about Wong from her success in reaching a market beyond San Francisco? What other incidents support this inference?
5. In what way was Wong's identity a liability? In what way were her brains and hands her only assets?
6. Explain the significance of the last line.

Applying

7. Jade Snow Wong says that her work did not allow her to spend much time with friends. Do you think it worth making such a sacrifice to reach a goal? Why or why not?
8. Another artist says to Wong, "I shudder if the majority of people look at my brush work and say it is pretty, for then I know it is ordinary and I have failed." What is the difference between an artistic success and a popular success? Can a person be both? Support your answer.

ANALYZING LITERATURE
Understanding Third-Person Narrative

This autobiography is unusual because Jade Snow Wong uses **third-person narrative,** referring to herself as "she" rather than "I." In keeping with the Chinese tradition of modesty, she records her struggles and successes as a potter as if she were talking about someone else.

1. Look at the paragraph beginning, "It became routine . . . ," on page 345. Reread it, changing every *she* to *I* and every *her* to *my*.
2. Compare and contrast your version of the paragraph with the original.
3. Wong uses third-person narrative so it will not seem that she is boasting. What else in her account shows her modesty?

CRITICAL THINKING AND READING
Distinguishing Details

Autobiographies contain both objective and subjective details. An **objective detail** is a description of an event or object in the world outside the writer's mind. For example, when Jade Snow Wong says that she received an award from *Mademoiselle* in 1948, this is an objective detail. A **subjective detail** is a description of the writer's thoughts or feelings or opinions and judgments. Wong's statement that "creating was exciting and satisfying" is a subjective detail.

Find three objective details Wong gives about herself. Find three subjective details.

THINKING AND WRITING
Writing a Third-Person Sketch

Imagine that you are doing the task you wrote about before reading this selection. Suddenly you have the power to actually leave your body and watch yourself at work. Write a description of the way you look from your new perspective. Include in this description not only what your hands and body are doing but also your ideas and feelings. To help you with your writing, use the list you made for the earlier writing assignment. When you revise what you have written, make sure you have referred to yourself by name or as "he" or "she," just as Jade Snow Wong does.

---

great many people, regardless of artistic quality. Suggested Response: A person can be, or achieve, both, though doing so is rare. Answers will vary as to why such a double success is or is not possible.

ANSWERS TO ANALYZING LITERATURE

1. The students will be changing the paragraph from a third-person to a first-person point of view.

2. Answers will differ, but students should notice the change of tone. The revised version will seem more personal and self-revealing, but it will lose the tone of reserve and modesty in the original. Of course, the biographical information remains the same.
3. She records her accomplishments in a matter-of-fact tone. Also, here successes are revealed primarily through reporting what others have expressed about her work.

ANSWERS TO CRITICAL THINKING AND READING

Answers will differ. Make sure students can explain why the details they choose are objective or subjective.

Essays for Enjoyment

ICED COFFEE
Fairfield Porter
Private Collection

Humanities Note

Fine art, *Iced Coffee,* 1966, Fairfield Porter. Fairfield Porter (1907–1975) studied art history at Harvard University and art at the Art Students League in New York City. Although Porter traveled extensively through Europe, the United States, and Canada, he preferred to live in New England and devoted his art to the study of the effect of the northeastern light on color. His style of art remained representational despite the trend in American art toward Abstract Expressionism. The Impressionists and the Fauves, particularly the French artist Vuillard, had a significant influence on Porter's painting.

In the picture *Iced Coffee,* Porter has presented a pleasant, domestic summer scene typical of an intimist painter. In painting the slant of direct sunlight on the man's face, the diffused light on the porch, and the brightness of the summer meadow outside, Porter displays an Impressionist's interest in study of the effect of light on color. The scene is fresh, unposed, and painted in simple direct strokes. The painting is evocative of the warmth and pleasure of a relaxing summer afternoon.

Master Teacher Note Place Art Transparency 10, *The Cup of Tea* by Andre Derain, on the overhead projector. The painting is of a woman who was reading a book and drinking tea and now seems lost in deep thought. You might point out that the purpose of many essays is to provoke thought from the reader. Have students study the painting and discuss what the woman might be thinking about. Is it a memory or something she has read in the book? What emotions is she feeling?

Focus

More About the Author You might tell students that James Herriot's work has been extremely popular—his first book, *All Creatures Great and Small*, served as the basis for a television series. Some critics, however, have questioned whether his work will continue to be well received if he keeps writing in the same way. Ask students whether a writer should avoid repeating a type of essay or story that he or she does well.

Literary Focus For less advanced students, you may want to reinforce the differences between a narrative essay, a short story, and an autobiographical sketch.

You might also consider telling students that "human interest" stories appearing in newspapers are a type of narrative essay. Lead them to see that such news stories center around a person—or animal, in some cases—whose experience readers may find particularly touching. Have students recount human interest stories they have read in a newspaper, witnessed themselves, or heard.

Look For You might want to discuss with students the idea that an animal can have a personality. Ask them, for instance, to describe the personality of their own or their friends' pets. Since an animal cannot talk, how does it display its personality?

Writing/Prior Knowledge As a preparation for this assignment, you may want to have students discuss the most intelligent, affectionate, or independent animals they have known.

Vocabulary Have less advanced students read aloud the words and definitions. Ask more advanced students to look up in a thesaurus synonyms for the adverb *surreptitiously*.

Cat on the Go

James Herriot (1916–   ) was born James Alfred Wight in Scotland. However, he uses the name Herriot when writing about his experiences as a veterinarian in Yorkshire, an English county. Herriot's books are famous for their lively descriptions of the characters he met, both animal and human. "Cat on the Go," which comes from his book *All Things Wise and Wonderful,* describes a cat that loves to go visiting.

Narrative Essay

An **essay** is a kind of musing, or thinking, upon a subject. It takes the form of a brief and personal discussion of any topic that a writer wants to consider. A **narrative essay** explores the subject by telling a true story. This type of essay may remind you of an autobiographical sketch. In an autobiography, however, the writer is always the central character, while a narrative essay may focus on a character other than the writer. The narrative essay "Cat on the Go," for instance, centers on the actions of Oscar, a friendly and restless cat.

Look For

As you read, pay close attention to the cat's personality. Look for how his personality gives you clues to the secret of his disappearances.

Writing

Oscar is a most unusual cat. Write about an animal you have known that stood out from others of its kind. What made this animal special?

Vocabulary

Knowing the following words will help you as you read "Cat on the Go."

grotesquely (grō tesk′ lē) *adv.*: In a strange or distorted way (p. 351)

emaciated (i mā′ s·hē āt′ əd) *adj.*: Extremely thin; starving (p. 351)

sieve (siv) *n.*: Utensil with many tiny openings; strainer (p. 353)

inevitable (in ev′ ə tə b′l) *adj.*: Certain to happen (p. 353)

sauntered (sôn′ tərd) *v.*: Strolled (p. 354)

distraught (dis trôt′) *adj.*: Extremely upset (p. 355)

despondent (di spän′ dənt) *adj.*: Lacking hope; depressed (p. 355)

intrigued (in trēgd′) *v.*: Fascinated (p. 356)

consolation (kän′ sə lā′ s·hən) *n.*: Comfort (p. 359)

surreptitiously (sur′ əp tish′ əs lē) *adv.*: Secretly (p. 360)

Objectives

1 To understand the features of the narrative essay
2 To learn how to consider other perspectives
3 To learn how to recognize British English
4 To create a television program based on a narrative essay

Support Material

Teaching Portfolio
Teacher Backup, p. 489
Grammar in Action Worksheets, *Using Contractions,* p. 493; *Combining Sentences,* p. 495
Usage and Mechanics Worksheet, p. 497
Vocabulary Check, p. 498
Critical Thinking and Reading Worksheet, *Considering Another Perspective,* p. 500

Language Worksheet, *Recognizing British English,* p. 501
Selection Test, p. 502

Cat on the Go

James Herriot

One winter evening Tristan shouted up the stairs from the passage far below.

"Jim! Jim!"

I went out and stuck my head over the bannisters. "What is it, Triss?"

"Sorry to bother you, Jim, but could you come down for a minute?" The upturned face had an anxious look.

I went down the long flights of steps two at a time and when I arrived slightly breathless on the ground floor Tristan beckoned me through to the consulting room at the back of the house. A teenage girl was standing by the table, her hand resting on a stained roll of blanket.

"It's a cat," Tristan said. He pulled back a fold of the blanket and I looked down at a large, deeply striped tabby. At least he would have been large if he had had any flesh on his bones, but ribs and pelvis stood out painfully through the fur and as I passed my hand over the motionless body I could feel only a thin covering of skin.

Tristan cleared his throat. "There's something else, Jim."

I looked at him curiously. For once he didn't seem to have a joke in him. I watched as he gently lifted one of the cat's hind legs and rolled the abdomen into view. There was a gash on the ventral surface[1] through which a coiled cluster of intestines spilled grotesquely onto the cloth. I was still shocked and staring when the girl spoke.

"I saw this cat sittin' in the dark, down Brown's yard. I thought 'e looked skinny, like, and a bit quiet and I bent down to give 'im a pat. Then I saw 'e was badly hurt and I went home for a blanket and brought 'im round to you."

"That was kind of you," I said. "Have you any idea who he belongs to?"

The girl shook her head. "No, he looks like a stray to me."

"He does indeed." I dragged my eyes away from the terrible wound. "You're Marjorie Simpson, aren't you?"

"Yes."

"I know your Dad well. He's our postman."

"That's right." She gave a half smile then her lips trembled.

"Well, I reckon I'd better leave 'im with you. You'll be going to put him out of his misery. There's nothing anybody can do about . . . about that?"

I shrugged and shook my head. The girl's eyes filled with tears, she stretched out a hand and touched the emaciated animal then turned and walked quickly to the door.

"Thanks again, Marjorie," I called after the retreating back. "And don't worry—we'll look after him."

In the silence that followed, Tristan and I looked down at the shattered animal. Under the surgery lamp it was all too easy to

---

1. **ventral** (ven' trəl) **surface:** The surface near or on the belly.

Presentation

Motivation/Prior Knowledge Ask students if they have ever seen an injured animal—in the city, on a farm, or out in the woods. Have them describe this experience. Tell them that, in the essay they are about to read, James Herriot is brought a badly injured stray cat and must decide very quickly what action to take.

Purpose-Setting Question How would you describe this cat's personality in your own words?

1 Master Teacher Note You might want to discuss with students the idea that narrative essays, like short stories, are often based on the resolution of problems or conflicts. Ask students to look for the way in which Herriot keeps their interest in the narrative by introducing and resolving problems. As one problem is resolved, another takes its place—until the final resolution at the end of the essay.

2 Discussion How does Herriot capture your interest at the very start of the essay?

3 Discussion What does Herriot's remark reveal about Tristan's personality? What does Tristan's unusual behavior indicate about the situation?

4 Enrichment The story Herriot tells in his essay takes place in Yorkshire, an English county, and some of the characters speak in the dialect of that region. One feature of this dialect is the dropping of the letter *h* in words like *he* and *him*.

Herriot imitates this dialect to give readers the flavor of the place.

5 Literary Focus What problem does Herriot face?

Thematic Ideas Stories you might want to use with this selection are "Rikki-tikki-tavi," page 13; "A Secret for Two," page 45; "Last Cover," page 57; "Luke Baldwin's Vow," page 95; and "A Season of Acceptance," page 197. The first story is about a mongoose who has a strong personality. The other stories deal with animals who become close with humans.

6 Enrichment Located in the north of England, Yorkshire is the largest English county. Parts of Yorkshire have a great deal of industry, such as textile mills, chemical plants, and coal mines. Other parts of the county are known for dairy farming, grain cultivation, and sheep raising. The photograph on page 352 conveys the flavor of a Yorkshire village.

7 Discussion What does the cat's purring reveal about his nature?

8 Literary Focus In a narrative essay, writers sometimes digress to add background information. How does Herriot's insertion of this little story give the essay a more personal quality?

see. He had almost been disemboweled[2] and the pile of intestines was covered in dirt and mud.

"What d'you think did this?" Tristan said at length. "Has he been run over?"

"Maybe," I replied. "Could be anything. An attack by a big dog or somebody could have kicked him or struck him." All things were possible with cats because some people seemed to regard them as fair game for any cruelty.

Tristan nodded. "Anyway, whatever happened, he must have been on the verge of starvation. He's a skeleton. I bet he's wandered miles from home."

"Ah well," I sighed. "There's only one thing to do. Those guts are perforated in several places. It's hopeless."

---

2. disemboweled (dis′ im bou′ əld) v.: Lost its intestines.

352 Nonfiction

Tristan didn't say anything but he whistled under his breath and drew the tip of his forefinger again and again across the furry cheek. And, unbelievably, from somewhere in the scraggy chest a gentle purring arose.

The young man looked at me, round eyed. "My God, do you hear that?"

"Yes . . . amazing in that condition. He's a good-natured cat."

Tristan, head bowed, continued his stroking. I knew how he felt because, although he preserved a cheerfully hard-boiled attitude to our patients he couldn't kid me about one thing; he had a soft spot for cats. Even now, when we are both around the sixty mark, he often talks to me about the cat he has had for many years. It is a typical relationship—they tease each other unmercifully—but it is based on real affection.

"It's no good, Triss," I said gently. "It's got to be done." I reached for the syringe but

Grammar in Action

Contractions are shortened forms of words or phrases. An apostrophe is used in a contraction to show the position of a missing letter or letters. Use contractions in writing to capture the informal tone of conversation. In the following passage, James Herriot uses contractions to convey dialogue in a realistic fashion:

"*I'm* afraid so, Helen," I said. "*We've* done our best for him but I honestly *don't* think he has much chance."

Notice how the use of contractions in Herriot's dialogue captures the informal tone used by most people when they speak. Compare this passage with the following one. What effect does the omission of contractions have on the tone of the dialogue?

"I am afraid so, Helen," I said. "We have done our best for him but I honestly do not think he has much chance."

Remember that you should not use contractions in formal writing.

Student Activity 1. Write each of the following word groups as contractions.

something in me rebelled against plunging a needle into that mutilated body. Instead I pulled a fold of the blanket over the cat's head.

"Pour a little ether onto the cloth," I said. "He'll just sleep away."

Wordlessly, Tristan unscrewed the cap of the ether bottle and poised it above the head. Then from under the shapeless heap of blanket we heard it again; the deep purring which increased in volume till it boomed in our ears like a distant motorcycle.

Tristan was like a man turned to stone, hand gripping the bottle rigidly, eyes staring down at the mound of cloth from which the purring rose in waves of warm friendly sound.

At last he looked up at me and gulped. "I don't fancy this much, Jim. Can't we do something?"

"You mean, put that lot back?"

"Yes."

"But the bowels are damaged—they're like a sieve in parts."

"We could stitch them, couldn't we?"

I lifted the blanket and looked again. "Honestly, Triss, I wouldn't know where to start. And the whole thing is filthy."

He didn't say anything, but continued to look at me steadily. And I didn't need much persuading. I had no more desire to pour ether onto that comradely purring than he had.

"Come on, then," I said. "We'll have a go."

With the oxygen bubbling and the cat's head in the anesthetic mask we washed the whole prolapse³ with warm saline.⁴ We did it again and again but it was impossible to remove every fragment of caked dirt. Then we started the painfully slow business of stitching the many holes in the tiny intestines,

and here I was glad of Tristan's nimble fingers which seemed better able to manipulate the small round-bodied needles than mine.

Two hours and yards of catgut⁵ later, we dusted the patched up peritoneal⁶ surface with sulfanilamide⁷ and pushed the entire mass back into the abdomen. When I had sutured muscle layers and skin everything looked tidy but I had a nasty feeling of sweeping undesirable things under the carpet. The extensive damage, all that contamination—peritonitis⁸ was inevitable.

"He's alive, anyway, Triss," I said as we began to wash the instruments. "We'll put him onto sulfapyridine and keep our fingers crossed." There were still no antibiotics at that time but the new drug was a big advance.

The door opened and Helen came in. "You've been a long time, Jim." She walked over to the table and looked down at the sleeping cat. "What a poor skinny little thing. He's all bones."

"You should have seen him when he came in." Tristan switched off the sterilizer and screwed shut the valve on the anesthetic machine. "He looks a lot better now."

She stroked the little animal for a moment. "Is he badly injured?"

"I'm afraid so, Helen," I said. "We've done our best for him but I honestly don't think he has much chance."

"What a shame. And he's pretty, too. Four white feet and all those unusual colors." With her finger she traced the faint bands of auburn and copper-gold among the gray and black.

---

5. catgut (kat′ gut′) n.: A tough string or thread used in surgery.
6. peritoneal (per′ it 'n ē′ əl) adj.: Having to do with the membrane that lines the abdomen.
7. sulfanilamide (sul′ fə nil′ ə mīd) n.: Sulfa drugs were used to treat infections before penicillin was discovered and other antibiotics were created.
8. peritonitis (per′ it 'n īt′ əs) n.: Inflammation of the abdominal lining.

---

3. prolapse (prō′ laps) n.: An internal organ—here, the intestines—that has fallen out of place.
4. saline (sā′ līn) n.: A salt solution.

Cat on the Go 353

---

9 Literary Focus Writers of narrative essays often heighten the suspense to keep readers interested. How does Herriot build suspense in this paragraph?

10 Reading Strategy At this point, you might want to ask students to predict what will happen next.

11 Discussion Why do you think Herriot includes technical details about the operation, even though they may seem unpleasant to some readers?

12 Enrichment Sulfa drugs were the first that effectively battled many types of infection resulting from bacteria. These drugs were widely used from the late 1930's to the mid-1940's and saved many lives during World War II. They usually worked by keeping bacteria from multiplying, so that the body's normal defenses could kill them.

13 Critical Reading and Thinking How might this story have begun if Helen were telling it rather than her husband?

14 Discussion How does this description of the cat make you want to find out more about him?

---

1. I will	4. it is	7. I would	10. where is
2. could not	5. will not	8. they will	11. they will
3. who is	6. you are	9. do not	12. who is

3. Are you not happy with the trip that he is planning for our class?

Student Activity 2. The following sentences contain word groups that could be used as contractions. Rewrite these word groups as contractions.

1. Where is the book you are taking to class?

2. I would love to meet the man who is going on the mountain climbing expedition.

Tristan laughed. "Yes, I think that chap has a ginger Tom somewhere in his ancestry."

Helen smiled, too, but absently, and I noticed a broody look about her. She hurried out to the stock room and returned with an empty box.

"Yes . . . yes . . ." she said thoughtfully. "I can make a bed in this box for him and he'll sleep in our room, Jim."

"He will?"

"Yes, he must be warm, mustn't he?"

"Of course."

Later, in the darkness of our bed-sitter,[9] I looked from my pillow at a cozy scene. Sam in his basket on one side of the flickering fire and the cat cushioned and blanketed in his box on the other.

As I floated off into sleep it was good to know that my patient was so comfortable, but I wondered if he would be alive in the morning. . . .

I knew he was alive at 7:30 a.m. because my wife was already up and talking to him. I trailed across the room in my pajamas and the cat and I looked at each other. I rubbed him under the chin and he opened his mouth in a rusty miaow. But he didn't try to move.

"Helen," I said. "This little thing is tied together inside with catgut. He'll have to live on fluids for a week and even then he probably won't make it. If he stays up here you'll be spooning milk into him umpteen times a day."

"Okay, okay." She had that broody look again.

It wasn't only milk she spooned into him over the next few days. Beef essence, strained broth and a succession of sophisticated baby foods found their way down his

---

9. **bed-sitter:** A British term for a one-room apartment.

throat at regular intervals. One lunch time I found Helen kneeling by the box.

"We shall call him Oscar," she said.

"You mean we're keeping him?"

"Yes."

I am fond of cats but we already had a dog in our cramped quarters and I could see difficulties. Still I decided to let it go.

"Why Oscar?"

"I don't know." Helen tipped a few drops of chop gravy onto the little red tongue and watched intently as he swallowed.

One of the things I like about women is their mystery, the unfathomable part of them, and I didn't press the matter further. But I was pleased at the way things were going. I had been giving the sulfapyridine every six hours and taking the temperature night and morning, expecting all the time to encounter the roaring fever, the vomiting and the tense abdomen of peritonitis. But it never happened.

It was as though Oscar's animal instinct told him he had to move as little as possible because he lay absolutely still day after day and looked up at us—and purred.

His purr became part of our lives and when he eventually left his bed, sauntered through to our kitchen and began to sample Sam's dinner of meat and biscuit it was a moment of triumph. And I didn't spoil it by wondering if he was ready for solid food; I felt he knew.

From then on it was sheer joy to watch the furry scarecrow fill out and grow strong, and as he ate and ate and the flesh spread over his bones the true beauty of his coat showed in the glossy medley of auburn, black and gold. We had a handsome cat on our hands.

Once Oscar had fully recovered, Tristan was a regular visitor.

He probably felt, and rightly, that he, more than I, had saved Oscar's life in the first place and he used to play with him for long periods. His favorite ploy was to push his leg round the corner of the table and withdraw it repeatedly just as the cat pawed at it.

19 Oscar was justifiably irritated by this teasing but showed his character by lying in wait for Tristan one night and biting him smartly[10] in the ankle before he could start his tricks.

From my own point of view Oscar added many things to our menage.[11] Sam was delighted with him and the two soon became firm friends, Helen adored him and each evening I thought afresh that a nice cat washing his face by the hearth gave extra comfort to a room.

Oscar had been established as one of the family for several weeks when I came in from a late call to find Helen waiting for me with a stricken face.

"What's happened?" I asked.

20 "It's Oscar—he's gone!"

"Gone? What do you mean?"

"Oh, Jim, I think he's run away."

I stared at her. "He wouldn't do that. He often goes down to the garden at night. Are you sure he isn't there?"

"Absolutely. I've searched right into the yard. I've even had a walk round the town. And remember." Her chin quivered. "He . . . he ran away from somewhere before."

I looked at my watch. "Ten o'clock. Yes, that is strange. He shouldn't be out at this time."

As I spoke the front door bell jangled. I galloped down the stairs and as I rounded the corner in the passage I could see Mrs. Heslington, the vicar's[12] wife, through the glass. I threw open the door. She was holding Oscar in her arms.

10. **smartly** (smärt′ lē) *adv.*: Sharply.
11. **menage** (mə näzh′) *n.*: Household.
12. **vicar's** (vik′ ərz) *n.*: A vicar is a parish priest.

"I believe this is your cat, Mr. Herriot," she said.

"It is indeed, Mrs. Heslington. Where did you find him?"

She smiled. "Well it was rather odd. We were having a meeting of the Mothers' Union at the church house and we noticed the cat sitting there in the room."

"Just sitting . . .?"

"Yes, as though he were listening to what we were saying and enjoying it all. It was unusual. When the meeting ended I thought I'd better bring him along to you."

"I'm most grateful, Mrs. Heslington." I snatched Oscar and tucked him under my arm. "My wife is distraught—she thought he was lost."

21 It was a little mystery. Why should he suddenly take off like that? But since he showed no change in his manner over the ensuing week we put it out of our minds.

Then one evening a man brought in a dog for a distemper[13] inoculation and left the front door open. When I went up to our flat I found that Oscar had disappeared again. This time Helen and I scoured the marketplace and side alleys in vain and when we returned at half past nine we were both despondent. It was nearly eleven and we were thinking of bed when the doorbell rang.

It was Oscar again, this time resting on the ample stomach of Jack Newbould. Jack was a gardener at one of the big houses. He hiccuped gently and gave me a huge benevolent smile. "Brought your cat, Mr. Herriot."

"Gosh, thanks, Jack!" I said, scooping up Oscar gratefully. "Where the devil did you find him?"

"Well, s'matter o' fact 'e sort of found me."

"What do you mean?"

13. **distemper** (dis tem′ pər) *n.*: An infectious virus disease of young dogs.

19 Discussion How does Oscar's behavior show "his character"?

20 Literary Focus Notice how Herriot maintains your interest in the narrative by introducing a new problem now that Oscar has recovered.

21 Discussion What do you think is the solution to the "little mystery"?

22 Enrichment Notice that Jack Newbould speaks in dialect, just as Marjorie Simpson did. Some examples are: "tha knows" for *you know;* "t'lads" for *the lads;* "'isself" for *himself.*

23 Reading Strategy You might want to ask students to summarize Oscar's three escapades.

24 Discussion Why do Herriot and his wife feel relieved by their insight into Oscar's behavior?

25 Literary Focus How does Herriot give his writing the personal flavor that all good essays have?

22 Jack closed his eyes for a few moments before articulating carefully. "Thish is a big night, tha knows, Mr. Herriot. Darts championship. Lots of t'lads round at t'Dog and Gun—lotsh and lotsh of 'em. Big gatherin'."

"And our cat was there?"

"Aye, he were there, all right. Sitting among t'lads. Shpent t'whole evenin' with us."

"Just sat there, eh?"

"That 'e did." Jack giggled reminiscently. "By gaw 'e enjoyed 'isself. Ah gave 'em a drop out of me own glass and once or twice ah thought 'e was going to have a go at chuckin' a dart. He's some cat." He laughed again.

As I bore Oscar upstairs I was deep in thought. What was going on here? These sudden desertions were upsetting Helen and I felt they could get on my nerves in time.

I didn't have long to wait till the next one. Three nights later he was missing again. This time Helen and I didn't bother to search—we just waited.

He was back earlier than usual. I heard the door bell at nine o'clock. It was the elderly Miss Simpson peering through the glass. And she wasn't holding Oscar—he was prowling on the mat waiting to come in.

Miss Simpson watched with interest as the cat stalked inside and made for the stairs. "Ah, good, I'm so glad he's come home safely. I knew he was your cat and I've been intrigued by his behavior all evening."

"Where . . . may I ask?"

"Oh, at the Women's Institute. He came in shortly after we started and stayed there till the end."

"Really? What exactly was your program, Miss Simpson?"

"Well, there was a bit of committee stuff, then a short talk with lantern slides by Mr. Walters from the water company and we finished with a cake-making competition."

"Yes . . . yes . . . and what did Oscar do?"

She laughed. "Mixed with the company, apparently enjoyed the slides and showed great interest in the cakes."

"I see. And you didn't bring him home?"

23 "No, he made his own way here. As you know, I have to pass your house and I merely rang your bell to make sure you knew he had arrived."

"I'm obliged to you, Miss Simpson. We were a little worried."

I mounted the stairs in record time. Helen was sitting with the cat on her knee and she looked up as I burst in.

"I know about Oscar now," I said.

"Know what?"

"Why he goes on these nightly outings. He's not running away—he's visiting."

"Visiting?"

"Yes," I said. "Don't you see? He likes getting around, he loves people, especially in groups, and he's interested in what they do. He's a natural mixer."

Helen looked down at the attractive mound of fur curled on her lap. "Of course . . . that's it . . . he's a socialite!"

"Exactly, a high stepper!"

"A cat-about-town!"

It all afforded us some innocent laughter and Oscar sat up and looked at us with evident pleasure, adding his own throbbing purr to the merriment. But for Helen and me there was a lot of relief behind it; ever since **24** our cat had started his excursions there had been the gnawing fear that we would lose him, and now we felt secure.

25 From that night our delight in him increased. There was endless joy in watching this facet of his character unfolding. He did the social round meticulously, taking in most of the activities of the town. He became a familiar figure at whist drives,[14] jumble

---

14. whist (hwist) **drives:** Attempts to raise money for charities and other purposes by playing the card game whist.

sales,[15] school concerts and scout bazaars. Most of the time he was made welcome, but was twice ejected from meetings of the Rural District Council who did not seem to relish the idea of a cat sitting in on their deliberations.

At first I was apprehensive about his making his way through the streets but I watched him once or twice and saw that he looked both ways before tripping daintily across. Clearly he had excellent traffic sense and this made me feel that his original injury had not been caused by a car.

Taking it all in all, Helen and I felt that it was a kind stroke of fortune which had brought Oscar to us. He was a warm and cherished part of our home life. He added to our happiness.

When the blow fell it was totally unexpected.

I was finishing the evening surgery.[16] I looked round the door and saw only a man and two little boys.

"Next, please," I said.

The man stood up. He had no animal with him. He was middle-aged, with the rough weathered face of a farm worker. He twirled a cloth cap nervously in his hands.

"Mr. Herriot?" he said.

---

15. jumble sales: A British term for sales of contributed articles to raise money for charity.

16. surgery (sur′ jər ē) *n.*: A British term for "office hours."

Cat on the Go 357

26 **Discussion** What qualities make Oscar an especially unusual animal?

27 **Literary Focus** Notice how, once again, Herriot maintains the interest level of his narrative by introducing a problem, just when events seem to be going smoothly.

28 Discussion How do you think the man feels about his mission?

29 Discussion Why does Herriot react so strongly to what the man has said?

30 Discussion What type of person does Sep Gibbons seem to be?

31 Discussion Are you surprised by Helen's willingness to give Oscar to the Gibbons family? Explain.

"Yes, what can I do for you?"

He swallowed and looked me straight in the eyes. "Ah think you've got ma cat."

"What?"

"Ah lost ma cat a bit since." He cleared his throat. "We used to live at Missdon but ah got a job as plowman to Mr. Horne of Wederly. It was after we moved to Wederly that t'cat went missin'. Ah reckon he was tryin to find 'is way back to his old home."

"Wederly? That's on the other side of Brawton—over thirty miles away."

"Aye, ah knaw, but cats is funny things."

"But what makes you think I've got him?"

28 He twisted the cap around a bit more. "There's a cousin o' mine lives in Darrowby and ah heard tell from 'im about this cat that goes around to meetin's. I 'ad to come. We've been huntin' everywhere."

"Tell me," I said. "This cat you lost. What did he look like?"

"Gray and black and sort o' gingery. Right bonny[17] 'e was. And 'e was allus goin' out to gatherin's."

29 A cold hand clutched at my heart. "You'd better come upstairs. Bring the boys with you."

Helen was putting some coal on the fire of the bed-sitter.

"Helen," I said. "This is Mr.—er—I'm sorry, I don't know your name."

"Gibbons, Sep Gibbons. They called me Septimus because ah was the seventh in family and it looks like ah'm goin' t'same way 'cause we've got six already. These are our two youngest." The two boys, obvious twins of about eight, looked up at us solemnly.

I wished my heart would stop hammering. "Mr. Gibbons thinks Oscar is his. He lost his cat some time ago."

My wife put down her little shovel. "Oh . . . oh . . . I see." She stood very still for a

moment then smiled faintly. "Do sit down. Oscar's in the kitchen, I'll bring him through."

She went out and reappeared with the cat in her arms. She hadn't got through the door before the little boys gave tongue.

"Tiger!" they cried. "Oh, Tiger, Tiger!"

The man's face seemed lit from within. He walked quickly across the floor and ran his big work-roughened hand along the fur.

"Hullo, awd lad," he said, and turned to me with a radiant smile. "It's 'im, Mr. Herriot. It's 'im awright, and don't 'e look well!"

"You call him Tiger, eh?" I said.

"Aye," he replied happily. "It's them gingery stripes. The kids called 'im that. They were brokenhearted when we lost 'im."

As the two little boys rolled on the floor our Oscar rolled with them, pawing playfully, purring with delight.

30 Sep Gibbons sat down again. "That's the way 'e allus went on wi' the family. They used to play with 'im for hours. By gaw we did miss 'im. He were a right favorite."

I looked at the broken nails on the edge of the cap, at the decent, honest, uncomplicated Yorkshire[18] face so like the many I had grown to like and respect. Farm men like him got thirty shillings a week in those days and it was reflected in the threadbare jacket, the cracked, shiny boots and the obvious hand-me-downs of the boys.

But all three were scrubbed and tidy, the man's face like a red beacon, the children's knees gleaming and their hair carefully slicked across their foreheads. They looked like nice people to me. I didn't know what to say.

31 Helen said it for me. "Well, Mr. Gibbons." Her tone had an unnatural brightness. "You'd better take him."

---

17. **bonny** (bän' ē) *adj.*: Pretty.

18. **Yorkshire:** A former county of northern England.

Grammar in Action

As writers revise, they use various methods of **sentence combining.** Instead of writing a series of short, choppy sentences containing only one idea, writers combine sentences with related ideas. Notice the following sets of sentences, which are short and choppy:

I shrugged my head. I shook my head.

I bore Oscar upstairs. I was deep in thought.

I could see Mrs. Heslington through the glass. She was the vicar's wife.

He did the social round meticulously. He took in most of the activities of the town.

Now look at some of the methods James Herriot uses to combine these sentences:

I shrugged *and shook* my head.
(one sentence changed to part of a compound verb)

As I bore Oscar upstairs, I was deep in thought.
(one sentence changed to a prepositional phrase)

I could see Mrs. Heslington, *the vicar's wife,* through the glass.

The man hesitated. "Now then, are ye sure, Missis Herriot?"

"Yes . . . yes, I'm sure. He was your cat first."

"Aye, but some folks 'ud say finders keepers or summat like that. Ah didn't come 'ere to demand 'im back or owt of t'sort."

"I know you didn't, Mr. Gibbons, but you've had him all those years and you've searched for him so hard. We couldn't possibly keep him from you."

He nodded quickly. "Well, that's right good of ye." He paused for a moment, his face serious, then he stooped and picked Oscar up. "We'll have to be off if we're goin' to catch the eight o'clock bus."

Helen reached forward, cupped the cat's head in her hands and looked at him steadily for a few seconds. Then she patted the boys' heads. "You'll take good care of him, won't you?"

"Aye, missis, thank ye, we will that." The two small faces looked up at her and smiled.

"I'll see you down the stairs, Mr. Gibbons," I said.

On the descent I tickled the furry cheek resting on the man's shoulder and heard for the last time the rich purring. On the front door step we shook hands and they set off down the street. As they rounded the corner of Trengate they stopped and waved, and I waved back at the man, the two children and the cat's head looking back at me over the shoulder.

32 It was my habit at that time in my life to mount the stairs two or three at a time but on this occasion I trailed upwards like an old man, slightly breathless, throat tight, eyes prickling.

I cursed myself for a sentimental fool but as I reached our door I found a flash of consolation. Helen had taken it remarkably well. She had nursed that cat and grown deeply attached to him, and I'd have thought an unforeseen calamity like this would have upset her terribly. But no, she had behaved calmly and rationally.

It was up to me to do as well. I adjusted my features into the semblance of a cheerful smile and marched into the room.

33 Helen had pulled a chair close to the table and was slumped face down against the wood. One arm cradled her head while the other was stretched in front of her as her body shook with an utterly abandoned weeping.

I had never seen her like this and I was appalled. I tried to say something comforting but nothing stemmed the flow of racking sobs.

Feeling helpless and inadequate I could only sit close to her and stroke the back of her head. Maybe I could have said something if I hadn't felt just about as bad myself.

You get over these things in time. After all, we told ourselves, it wasn't as though Oscar had died or got lost again—he had gone to a good family who would look after him. In fact he had really gone home.

34 And of course, we still had our much-loved Sam, although he didn't help in the early stages by sniffing disconsolately where Oscar's bed used to lie then collapsing on the rug with a long lugubrious sigh.

35 There was one other thing, too. I had a little notion forming in my mind, an idea which I would spring on Helen when the time was right. It was about a month after that shattering night and we were coming out of the cinema at Brawton at the end of our half day. I looked at my watch.

"Only eight o'clock," I said. "How about going to see Oscar?"

Helen looked at me in surprise. "You mean—drive on to Wederly?"

"Yes, it's only about five miles."

A smile crept slowly across her face. "That would be lovely. But do you think they would mind?"

Cat on the Go 359

(one sentence changed to an appositive)

He did the social round meticulously, *taking in most of the activities of the town.*

(one sentence changed to a participial phrase)

Student Activity 1. Rewrite the following long sentences into short, simple sentences.

1. Tristan, head bowed, continued his stroking.
2. Then one evening a man brought in a dog for a distemper inoculation and left the front door open.
3. I heard the door bell ring at nine o'clock.
4. It was as though Oscar's animal instinct told him he had to move as little as possible because he lay absolutely still day after day and looked up at us—and purred.

Student Activity 2. Combine the following sentences using any method you choose.

1. Helen reached forward. She cupped the cat's face in her hand.
2. All three were tidy. They looked like nice people to me.
3. One arm cradled her head. The other was stretched in front of her. Her body shook with weeping.

360

36 Discussion What does the kitchen-living room reveal about the financial means of the Gibbons family?

37 Discussion How do Sep and his wife greet the Herriots?

38 Discussion How does Oscar show once again that he is more than just an ordinary cat?

39 Literary Focus Narrative essays, like short stories, often end with the resolution of a problem. How is the final problem in this narrative essay—the Herriots' loss of Oscar—resolved?

40 Discussion Why do you think Herriot chose to end his essay with this paragraph?

Reader's Response What do you like best about Oscar's character? Why?

"The Gibbons? No, I'm sure they wouldn't. Let's go."

Wederly was a big village and the plowman's cottage was at the far end a few yards beyond the Methodist chapel. I pushed open the garden gate and we walked down the path.

A busy-looking little woman answered my knock. She was drying her hands on a striped towel.

"Mrs. Gibbons?" I said.

"Aye, that's me."

"I'm James Herriot—and this is my wife."

Her eyes widened uncomprehendingly. Clearly the name meant nothing to her.

"We had your cat for a while," I added.

Suddenly she grinned and waved her towel at us. "Oh aye, ah remember now. Sep told me about you. Come in, come in!"

36 The big kitchen-living room was a tableau[19] of life with six children and thirty shillings a week. Battered furniture, rows of much-mended washing on a pulley, black cooking range and a general air of chaos.

37 Sep got up from his place by the fire, put down his newspaper, took off a pair of steel-rimmed spectacles and shook hands.

He waved Helen to a sagging armchair. "Well, it's right nice to see you. Ah've often spoke of ye to t'missis."

His wife hung up her towel. "Yes, and I'm glad to meet ye both. I'll get some tea in a minnit."

She laughed and dragged a bucket of muddy water into a corner. "I've been washin' football jerseys. Them lads just handed them to me tonight—as if I haven't enough to do."

As she ran the water into the kettle I peeped surreptitiously around me and I no-

───────────

19. tableau (tab′ lō) *n.*: A dramatic scene or picture.

ticed Helen doing the same. But we searched in vain. There was no sign of a cat. Surely he couldn't have run away again? With a growing feeling of dismay I realized that my little scheme could backfire devastatingly.

It wasn't until the tea had been made and poured that I dared to raise the subject.

"How—" I asked diffidently. "How is—er—Tiger?"

"Oh, he's grand," the little woman replied briskly. She glanced up at the clock on the mantelpiece. "He should be back any time now, then you'll be able to see 'im."

As she spoke, Sep raised a finger. "Ah think ah can hear 'im now."

38 He walked over and opened the door and our Oscar strode in with all his old grace and majesty. He took one look at Helen and leaped onto her lap. With a cry of delight she put down her cup and stroked the beautiful fur as the cat arched himself against her hand and the familiar purr echoed round the room.

"He knows me," she murmured. "He knows me."

Sep nodded and smiled. "He does that. You were good to 'im. He'll never forget ye, and we won't either, will we mother?"

39 "No, we won't, Mrs. Herriot," his wife said as she applied butter to a slice of gingerbread. "That was a kind thing ye did for us and I 'ope you'll come and see us all whenever you're near."

"Well, thank you," I said. "We'd love to—we're often in Brawton."

I went over and tickled Oscar's chin, then I turned again to Mrs. Gibbons. "By the way, it's after nine o'clock. Where has he been till now?"

She poised her butter knife and looked into space.

40 "Let's see, now," she said. "It's Thursday, isn't it? Ah yes, it's 'is night for the Yoga class."

Closure and Extension

ANSWERS TO THINKING ABOUT THE SELECTION
Recalling

1. It is wounded somehow and cannot return home.
2. Herriot attends to the cat's injury and his wife nurses the cat back to health.
3. He goes to various social functions in town—a meeting of the Mothers' Union at the church house; a dart championship at a pub; and a meeting at the Women's Institute.
4. They discover that he is a "'natural mixer'" who loves to be with people.
5. The first owners heard from a cousin that the Herriots' cat liked to go to meetings. Since their lost cat behaved in the same way, they visited Herriot on the chance that his cat might be theirs.

Interpreting

6. The purring seems to indicate the cat's good nature and leads them to try to save him.
7. Suggested Response: She sees that the man and his children love the cat, that they are decent people, and that they have a right to him as the original owners.
8. The cat is very good-natured and loves to be with people.

Applying

9. Student' answers will differ. Suggested Response: Pets make a home seem warmer and more

THINKING ABOUT THE SELECTION

Recalling

1. What happens to the cat during one of its trips from the Gibbonses' home?
2. Explain how Herriot and his wife help the cat.
3. Where does the cat go each time it wanders off from the Herriots' apartment?
4. What do Herriot and his wife discover about the cat that makes them laugh?
5. Explain how the cat is reunited with his first owners.

Interpreting

6. What is the effect of the injured cat's purring on Herriot and Tristan?
7. Why does Helen decide to give the cat up rather than claim "finders keepers"?
8. What qualities make this cat special?

Applying

9. Why do you think that many people enjoy having pets?

ANALYZING LITERATURE

Understanding the Narrative Essay

An **essay** is a brief and personal discussion of any topic that a writer wants to consider. A **narrative essay** considers the topic by telling a true story. In "Cat on the Go," Herriot gives a strong personal flavor to his narrative by telling you his thoughts and feelings. He writes about the healing cat, for example, ". . . it was sheer joy to watch the furry scarecrow fill out. . . ."

1. What is the topic of this narrative essay? What is Herriot's attitude toward the topic?
2. Identify three passages where Herriot tells you his thoughts or feelings about the topic.
3. How does Herriot's enjoyment of the cat increase your interest in the essay?
4. Compare and contrast reading a narrative essay and hearing a friend tell a story.

CRITICAL THINKING AND READING

Considering Another Perspective

This story is told from the point of view of James Herriot. That is why the sequence of events begins when Herriot first hears about the injured cat from Tristan. If the story had been told by Septimus Gibbons, however, it would have had a different shape.

1. How might the story have begun if Mr. Gibbons were telling it?
2. Which events in Herriot's story might *not* have been included in Gibbons' story?
3. Would Gibbons' story have ended in the same way? Why?

UNDERSTANDING LANGUAGE

Recognizing British English

Although the English language is used in Great Britain and America, it is not exactly the same in both countries. For example, James Herriot, a British writer, refers to "jumble sales." Americans, however, would use the phrase *rummage sales* to describe "sales of contributed articles to raise money for charity." Other British terms that appear in the story are *bed-sitter* and *surgery* (see footnotes 9 and 16).

Look up the following British terms in a dictionary—the abbreviation *Brit.* usually appears next to the British meaning—and use each in a sentence.

1. petrol   2. lorry   3. bonnet

THINKING AND WRITING

Creating a Television Program

This essay has actually been made into a television program. Pretend that you were the writer hired to create this show. The producer has told you, however, that there is not enough time to include every episode. List the episodes that you think *must* appear in the program. Then write a memo to the producer defending your list. When you revise the memo, make sure it is convincing.

Cat on the Go   361

More About the Author As a young man, James Thurber imitated the humorous paragraphs written by an editorialist for an Ohio newspaper. His work was also influenced by comic strips and movies. What might be key influences for a young comic writer starting out today?

Literary Focus You might point out to students that mistaken ideas often lead to humorous situations in everyday life. Ask students what humorous situation might result, for instance, if they dialed a wrong number and began talking to a stranger as if he or she were their best friend.

Look For You might want to clarify the idea of a "crotchet" for **less advanced** students. Tell them that crotchets, though strange, are usually harmless. An example of a crotchet would be the strange notion that it is necessary to wear a hat at all times, indoors or outdoors, to avoid catching a cold. Have students think of other, equally silly crotchets.

Writing/Prior Knowledge Consider dividing the class into small groups and having students tell their stories to other group members before completing the assignment.

Vocabulary Have **more advanced** students look up the origin of all the vocabulary words and determine how many of them come from Latin.

The Night the Bed Fell

James Thurber (1894–1961) lost the vision in one eye due to a childhood accident; however, he did not allow this disability to slow him down. He worked as a newspaper reporter and later wrote humorous pieces for *The New Yorker,* a famous magazine. In addition to being a talented writer, Thurber was a cartoonist. His amusing line drawings often accompany his writing. "The Night the Bed Fell," like many of his essays, describes the funny goings-on in his family.

Humorous Essay

A **humorous essay** is a brief work of nonfiction that is meant to amuse you. Many of James Thurber's humorous essays, like "The Night the Bed Fell," are about his lovable but silly relatives. During the night that Thurber tells about in this essay, each family member, including Thurber himself, has a different and mistaken idea of what is going on. The result is total confusion for the characters and a great deal of fun for the reader.

Look For

As you read, look for Thurber's descriptions of the "crotchets," or peculiar ideas, of his relatives. Be aware of how Briggs's unusual notions, in particular, add to the confusion of the night's events. Think about how all these peculiarities work together to make you laugh.

Writing

Thurber tells how a simple event snowballs into an outrageous episode. Recall a time when you took part in an event with an amusing outcome. Describe the people who were involved, and make a list of the main things that happened. Make sure your description shows what made the event humorous.

Vocabulary

Knowing the following words will help you as you read "The Night the Bed Fell."

ominous (äm′ə nəs) *adj.*: Threatening (p. 363)

allay (ə lā′) *v.*: Put to rest; calm (p. 363)

fortitude (fôr′ tə tōōd′) *n.*: Firm courage (p. 364)

perilous (per′ əl əs) *adj.*: Dangerous (p. 364)

deluge (del′ yōōj) *n.*: A great flood or rush of anything (p. 365)

pungent (pun′ jənt) *adj.*: Sharp-smelling (p. 365)

extricate (eks′ trə kāt′) *v.*: Set free; disentangle (p. 365)

culprit (kul′ prit) *n.*: Guilty person (p. 366)

362 Nonfiction

Objectives

1 To understand the features of the humorous essay
2 To identify exaggeration in humorous essays
3 To create a humorous essay

Support Material

Teaching Portfolio
Teacher Backup, p. 505
Grammar in Action Worksheet, *Using Pronouns,* p. 508
Usage and Mechanics Worksheet, p. 510
Vocabulary Check, p. 511
Critical Thinking and Reading Worksheet, *Identifying Exaggeration,* p. 513

Language Worksheet, *Formal Language,* p. 514
Selection Test, p. 515

The Night the Bed Fell

James Thurber

I suppose that the high-water mark of my youth in Columbus, Ohio, was the night the bed fell on my father. It makes a better recitation (unless, as some friends of mine have said, one has heard it five or six times) than it does a piece of writing, for it is almost necessary to throw furniture around, shake doors, and bark like a dog, to lend the proper atmosphere and verisimilitude[1] to what is admittedly a somewhat incredible tale. Still, it did take place.

It happened, then, that my father had decided to sleep in the attic one night, to be away where he could think. My mother opposed the notion strongly because, she said, the old wooden bed up there was unsafe: it was wobbly and the heavy headboard would crash down on father's head in case the bed fell, and kill him. There was no dissuading him, however, and at a quarter past ten he closed the attic door behind him and went up the narrow twisting stairs. We later heard ominous creakings as he crawled into bed. Grandfather, who usually slept in the attic bed when he was with us, had disappeared some days before. On these occasions he was usually gone six or eight days and returned growling and out of temper, with the news that the Federal Union[2] was run by a passel of blockheads and that the Army of the Potomac[3] didn't have a chance.

We had visiting us at this time a nervous first cousin of mine named Briggs Beall, who believed that he was likely to cease breathing when he was asleep. It was his feeling that if he were not awakened every hour during the night, he might die of suffocation. He had been accustomed to setting an alarm clock to ring at intervals until morning, but I persuaded him to abandon this. He slept in my room and I told him that I was such a light sleeper that if anybody quit breathing in the same room with me, I would wake instantly. He tested me the first night—which I had suspected he would—by holding his breath after my regular breathing had convinced him I was asleep. I was not asleep, however, and called to him. This seemed to allay his fears a little, but he took the precaution of putting a glass of spirits of camphor[4] on a little table at the head of his bed. In case I didn't arouse him until he was almost gone, he said, he would sniff the camphor, a powerful reviver. Briggs was not the only member of his family who had his crotchets.[5] Old Aunt Melissa Beall (who could whistle like a man, with two fingers in her mouth) suffered under the premonition that she was destined to die on South High Street, because she had been born on South High Street and married on South High Street. Then there was Aunt Sarah Shoaf, who never went to bed at night without the

---

1. **verisimilitude** (ver′ ə si mil′ə tōōd′) *n*.: The appearance of being true or real.
2. **Federal Union:** The Northern side during the Civil War. He is under the illusion that the Civil War has not yet ended.
3. **Army of the Potomac:** One of the Northern armies during the Civil War.

4. **spirits of camphor:** A liquid with a powerful odor.
5. **crotchets** (kräch′ its) *n*.: Peculiar or stubborn ideas.

The Night the Bed Fell   363

Presentation

Motivation/Prior Knowledge Ask students if they were ever half-awakened from sleep by a loud noise or disturbance and, for a while, were too dazed to understand what was happening. Have them describe their experiences. Then tell them that this is exactly what happens to the narrator of this humorous story.

Purpose-Setting Question How does a single event touch off a chain reaction that produces total confusion?

1 **Master Teacher Note** You might suggest to students that they will appreciate this essay more if they clearly understand the locations and movements of Thurber and his family members during this hilarious night. Advise students to draw a plan of the house, as Thurber describes it, showing each person's bedroom. Then they can indicate key events by means of little captions, and they can illustrate people's movements by means of arrows. It is not necessary to draw each of the characters—this will just be a schematic diagram.

When students have finished reading the essay, they can compare and, if necessary, correct their diagrams. You may even want to pair less advanced students with more advanced students to facilitate this process.

2 **Discussion** How does Thurber capture your attention and make you eager to keep reading?

3 **Reading Strategy** How does this detail, which is also mentioned in the title, provide a clue about what will happen?

Thematic Ideas Other selections that deal humorously with family situations are Shirley Jackson's story "The Sneaker Crisis," pages 67–73, and Russell Baker's autobiographical sketch "No Gumption," pages 329–334. Jackson's story in particular is similar to this selection, in that the chaotic events in a loving but eccentric family generate the comedy.

4 Reading Strategy What do these "crotchets" reveal about the author's family? Have students predict, based on this information, how the family might react to the bed falling.

5 Literary Focus In this essay, the humor results from the mistaken ideas of the characters. Why do you think it is so important for readers *not* to be mistaken about where people are located and what is really going on?

6 Enrichment Thurber co-authored a humorous play, *The Male Animal* (1940). He also acted in *A Thurber Carnival*, a collection of his witty scenes and sketches, when it appeared on Broadway just before his death. Thurber was blind by that time, but he played himself in a skit about a publishing company that kept sending him unwanted books.

Thurber's theatrical sense is evident in this essay. For example, he is clearly setting up the cot as an important prop, just as he established the camphor bottle as a prop on page 363. You might explain to students that a prop, short for property, is "a movable article that is part of the setting for a play and often is important in the stage action."

You might ask students to speculate what role this prop will play in the action. You might also ask them to consider whether this essay could be easily adapted for the stage.

Copyright © 1933, 1961 James Thurber
From My Life and Hard Times, published by Harper & Row

fear that a burglar was going to get in and blow chloroform[6] under her door through a tube. To avert this calamity—for she was in greater dread of anesthetics than of losing her household goods—she always piled her money, silverware, and other valuables in a neat stack just outside her bedroom, with a note reading: "This is all I have. Please take it and do not use your chloroform, as this is all I have." Aunt Gracie Shoaf also had a burglar phobia, but she met it with more fortitude. She was confident that burglars had been getting into her house every night for forty years. The fact that she never missed

---

6. chloroform (klôr′ə fôrm′) *n.*: A substance used at one time as an anesthetic, or pain-killer, during operations because it can cause a person to pass out.

any thing was to her no proof to the contrary. She always claimed that she scared them off before they could take anything, by throwing shoes down the hallway. When she went to bed she piled, where she could get at them handily, all the shoes there were about her house. Five minutes after she had turned off the light, she would sit up in bed and say "Hark!" Her husband, who had learned to ignore the whole situation as long ago as 1903, would either be sound asleep or pretend to be sound asleep. In either case he would not respond to her tugging and pulling, so that presently she would arise, tiptoe to the door, open it slightly and heave a shoe down the hall in one direction, and its mate down the hall in the other direction. Some nights she threw them all, some nights only a couple of pair.

But I am straying from the remarkable incidents that took place during the night that the bed fell on father. By midnight we were all in bed. The layout of the rooms and the disposition[7] of their occupants is important to an understanding of what later occurred. In the front room upstairs (just under father's attic bedroom) were my mother and my brother Herman, who sometimes sang in his sleep, usually "Marching Through Georgia" or "Onward, Christian Soldiers." Briggs Beall and myself were in a room adjoining this one. My brother Roy was in a room across the hall from ours. Our bull terrier, Rex, slept in the hall.

My bed was an army cot, one of those affairs which are made wide enough to sleep on comfortably only by putting up, flat with the middle section, the two sides which ordinarily hang down like the sideboards of a drop-leaf table. When these sides are up, it is perilous to roll too far toward the edge, for

4

5

6

---

7. disposition (dis′ pə zish′ ən) *n.*: Arrangement.

Grammar in Action

One reason that writers use a **pronoun** instead of a noun or group of nouns is to avoid dull repetition—they don't want to repeat the same noun or nouns over and over. Using the appropriate pronoun avoids repetition and adds clarity and smoothness to writing. In the following passage, James Thurber's use of pronouns makes Briggs's actions perfectly clear and hence keeps the humor intact:

With a low moan, *he* grasped the glass of camphor at the head of *his* bed and instead of sniffing *it* poured *it* over *himself.*

Thurber has made the action clear through the proper use of pronouns. For example, if the pronoun *him* had been used rather than *himself,* the reader would have thought that Briggs had poured the camphor over someone else. Thurber used the reflexive pronoun *himself.* Reflexive pronouns refer to a preceding noun or pronoun and are formed by adding *self* or *selves* to personal pronouns. Make sure you always use the proper pronoun in your writing so that your intended meaning is clear.

then the cot is likely to tip completely over, bringing the whole bed down on top of one, with a tremendous banging crash. This, in fact, is precisely what happened about two o'clock in the morning. (It was my mother who, in recalling the scene later, first referred to it as "the night the bed fell on your father.")

Always a deep sleeper, slow to arouse (I had lied to Briggs), I was at first unconscious of what had happened when the iron cot rolled me onto the floor and toppled over on me. It left me still warmly bundled up and unhurt, for the bed rested above me like a canopy. Hence I did not wake up, only reached the edge of consciousness and went back. The racket, however, instantly awakened my mother, in the next room, who came to the immediate conclusion that her worst dread was realized: the big wooden bed upstairs had fallen on father. She therefore screamed, "Let's go to your poor father!" It was this shout, rather than the noise of my cot falling, that awakened Herman, in the same room with her. He thought that mother had become, for no apparent reason, hysterical. "You're all right, Mamma!" he shouted, trying to calm her. They exchanged shout for shout for perhaps ten seconds:

"Let's go to your poor father!" and "You're all right!" That woke up Briggs. By this time I was conscious of what was going on, in a vague way, but did not yet realize that I was under my bed instead of on it. Briggs, awakening in the midst of loud shouts of fear and apprehension, came to the quick conclusion that he was suffocating and that we were all trying to "bring him out." With a low moan, he grasped the glass of camphor at the head of his bed and instead of sniffing it poured it over himself. The room reeked of camphor. "Ugf, ahfg," choked Briggs, like a drowning man, for he had almost succeeded in stopping his breath under the deluge of pungent spirits. He leaped out of bed and groped toward the open window, but he came up against one that was closed. With his hand, he beat out the glass, and I could hear it crash and tinkle on the alleyway below. It was at this juncture that I, in trying to get up, had the uncanny sensation of feeling my bed above me! Foggy with sleep, I now suspected, in my turn, that the whole uproar was being made in a frantic endeavor to extricate me from what must be an unheard-of and perilous situation. "Get me out of this!"

Copyright © 1933, 1961 James Thurber
From My Life and Hard Times, published by Harper & Row

The Night the Bed Fell 365

9 **Discussion** What is funny about the idea that Thurber's father was the very last one to awaken?

10 **Discussion** How is Thurber's mother's fear a key to the whole situation?

11 **Reading Strategy** Summarize the chain reaction of events, explaining how one thing led to another.

Reader's Response What was the funniest part of this story? Why?

I bawled. "Get me out!" I think I had the nightmarish belief that I was entombed in a mine. "Gugh," gasped Briggs, floundering in his camphor.

By this time my mother, still shouting, pursued by Herman, still shouting, was trying to open the door to the attic, in order to go up and get my father's body out of the wreckage. The door was stuck, however, and wouldn't yield. Her frantic pulls on it only added to the general banging and confusion. Roy and the dog were now up, the one shouting questions, the other barking.

9 Father, farthest away and soundest sleeper of all, had by this time been awakened by the battering on the attic door. He decided that the house was on fire. "I'm coming, I'm coming!" he wailed in a slow, sleepy voice—it took him many minutes to regain full consciousness. My mother, still believing 10 he was caught under the bed, detected in his "I'm coming!" the mournful, resigned note of one who is preparing to meet his Maker. "He's dying!" she shouted.

"I'm all right!" Briggs yelled to reassure her. "I'm all right!" He still believed that it was his own closeness to death that was worrying mother. I found at last the light switch in my room, unlocked the door, and Briggs and I joined the others at the attic door. The dog, who never did like Briggs, jumped for him—assuming that he was the culprit in whatever was going on—and Roy had to throw Rex and hold him. We could hear father crawling out of bed upstairs. Roy pulled the attic door open, with a mighty jerk, and father came down the stairs, sleepy and irritable but safe and sound. My mother began to weep when she saw him. Rex began to howl. "What in the name of heaven is going on here?" asked father.

The situation was finally put together like a gigantic jigsaw puzzle. Father caught 11 a cold from prowling around in his bare feet but there were no other bad results. "I'm glad," said mother, who always looked on the bright side of things, "that your grandfather wasn't here."

366 Nonfiction

Closure and Extension

ANSWERS TO THINKING ABOUT THE SELECTION
Recalling

1. His father wanted to sleep in the attic so he could get away to think. However, his mother was afraid that the bed in the attic would collapse and kill him.
2. Briggs believed that he would suf- focate while he slept, unless he was awakened at intervals during the night.
3. Thurber's mother and brother Herman slept in the front room upstairs, under the attic bedroom. Thurber and Briggs were in a room adjoining his mother's bedroom. Thurber's brother Roy was in a room across the hall from Thurber, and the dog slept in the hall. The placement of the rooms helps explain how the chain of events occurred.
4. Thurber does not awaken. His mother awakens and begins shouting. Herman awakens and shouts to calm his mother. Briggs awakens and pours the camphor on himself, leaps out of bed, and smashes the window. Thurber awakens and begins to shout. His mother runs to the attic door, with Herman following, and pulls on it. Roy and the dog awaken. Thurber's father awakens and calls out. Thurber's mother begins shouting that her husband is dying. Briggs shouts that he is all right. Thurber

THINKING ABOUT THE SELECTION

Recalling

1. How does a difference of opinion between Thurber's parents set the stage for the events of the night?
2. What is Briggs's crotchet, or peculiar idea?
3. Describe the layout of the rooms and their placement or grouping. Why is their placement important to the plot of the story?
4. In chronological, or time, order, list the actions that occur after Thurber's cot collapses.

Interpreting

5. Why does Thurber introduce the essay with a description of some of his relatives?
6. Identify the moment at which the events reach their climax.
7. What evidence is there that Thurber felt affection for his family?

Applying

8. Would you like to have known the Thurber family? Why or why not?

ANALYZING LITERATURE

Understanding the Humorous Essay

A **humorous essay** is a brief work of nonfiction that is meant to amuse you. In "The Night the Bed Fell" much of the humor comes from the contrast between what is really happening and what the characters think is happening. For example, Thurber's mother believes that her husband lies crushed in the wreckage of his bed when he is really safely asleep.

1. Contrast what actual happens when the bed falls and what each character thinks is happening.
2. Would the essay be as funny if you were as confused about what happened as the characters are? Why?
3. At the beginning of the essay, Thurber writes, "It makes a better recitation . . . than it does a piece of writing, for it is almost necessary to throw furniture around, shake doors, and bark like a dog, to lend the proper atmosphere and verisimilitude to what is admittedly a somewhat incredible tale." Do you think such theatrics would make this funny tale even funnier? Why or why not?

CRITICAL THINKING AND READING

Identifying Exaggeration

Writers of humorous essays often **exaggerate,** or enlarge, their descriptions to make them funnier. In "The Night the Bed Fell," for example, Thurber says that Briggs poured a "deluge of pungent spirits" on himself. Of course, we know that Briggs did not really *flood* himself with camphor. The contrast between what is really happening and the exaggerated description is humorous.

In each of the following passages, point out what is exaggerated and explain the contrast between the exaggeration and the reality.

1. " 'Get me out of this!' I bawled. 'Get me out!' I think I had the nightmarish belief that I was entombed in a mine."
2. ". . . Herman, still shouting, was trying to open the door to the attic, in order to go up and get my father's body out of the wreckage."

THINKING AND WRITING

Creating a Humorous Essay

Recall the amusing events that you listed before reading the essay. Use this list to tell the story aloud to different friends. Each time you tell it, try to make it funnier by exaggerating one of the events. When you have perfected your narrative, write a humorous essay based on it. In revising the essay, make sure you have included the exaggerations that worked best when you told the story aloud. You may include humorous drawings, as Thurber did. When you are finished, share your essay with your classmates.

The Night the Bed Fell 367

(Answers begin on p. 366)

Herman thinks she has become hysterical for no reason and tries to calm her. Briggs hears people shouting and thinks that he is suffocating. Thurber wakes up under the cot and thinks he is in a mine. Thurber's father hears the general noise and thinks that the house is on fire. Thurber's mother hears her husband shout " 'I'm coming!' " and thinks he is dying. Briggs thinks that Thurber's mother is shouting because he is suffocating and tries to calm her. The dog thinks that Briggs has caused this whole mess and jumps him.

2. Students' answers will differ. Suggested Response: Most students will realize that a reader can best appreciate the humor of the events by being aware of the characters' mistaken impressions and the truth.
3. Students' answers will differ. Suggested Response: Students should support their answers with reasonable arguments. For instance, one approach might be to assert that such theatrics would have to be performed skillfully to work.

ANSWERS TO CRITICAL THINKING AND READING

1. Although he is only underneath his cot, Thurber wildly exaggerates his situation and believes he is "entombed in a mine."
2. Herman's belief that his father is in the wreckage of the bed is an exaggeration. His father is perfectly fine and has only been awakened by the noise everyone is making.

THINKING AND WRITING

Publishing Student Writing
You might want to divide the class into small groups so that students can practice telling their stories before they write them down.

After students have completed the assignment, ask for volunteers to read their humorous essays to the class.

---

and Briggs join the others. The dog jumps Briggs. Thurber's father finally emerges.

Interpreting

5. Suggested Response: His description of these relatives provides further illustrations of family crotchets and sets a humorous tone for what follows.
6. The climax occurs when Roy pulls open the door and Thurber's father emerges.

7. Suggested Response: Thurber makes gentle and affectionate fun of his family. He does not ridicule them. Their foibles and mistakes seem silly and lovable.

Applying

8. Students' answers will differ. Suggested Response: Many students will probably say that they would have liked to know the Thurber family, because the family members were lovable and silly. Also, it seems as if there was never a dull moment around the Thurber household.

Challenge Suppose Thurber's grandfather were there that night. What might have been his role in the confusing events?

ANSWERS TO ANALYZING LITERATURE

1. Thurber's cot falls, but his mother thinks the attic bed has fallen on her husband. When she calls out,

More About the Author Tell students that Marjorie Kinnan Rawlings gave up a career in journalism to move to a farm in the tiny, remote town of Cross Creek, Florida. Have students compare and contrast the country and the city as places for a writer to live. What advantages and disadvantages would each have?

Literary Focus You might want to dramatize the importance of description by having students vividly describe their trip to school that morning. Encourage them to appeal to as many senses as possible: Did you buy and eat any food? What did it taste like? What sounds did you hear? Did you see anything unusual?

Look For Suggest that students allow the writer's descriptions to paint pictures in their imagination as they read. Encourage them to read a descriptive passage again if it does not convey a clear picture the first time.

Writing/Prior Knowledge Review with students the importance of vivid words in a good description. Tell them that a general verb, like *move,* does not help a reader see an action as well as a more specific verb, like *wriggle, lope,* or *glide.*

Divide the class into small groups in preparation for this assignment. Have each group brainstorm to think of vivid words to describe snakes. Then ask each student to write his or her description.

Vocabulary Have less advanced students read these words aloud so that they know how to pronounce them. Ask more advanced students to look up the meaning of the prefix *trans* in the word *translucent.* Then have them find five other words in which this prefix appears and explain how the meaning of the prefix contributes to the meaning of each word.

GUIDE FOR READING

Rattlesnake Hunt

Marjorie Kinnan Rawlings (1896–1953) was born in Washington, D.C., but later moved to rural Florida, where "Rattlesnake Hunt" is set. There at Cross Creek she wrote about the world around her, and eventually, she became famous for her novels describing life in that part of the country. *The Yearling* (1938), for example, an American classic, was made into a successful film. Animals often play a major part in her work. As you will see, she was even fascinated by such creatures as rattlesnakes.

Description in an Essay

When writers describe people or scenes, they use language that appeals to your senses so that their descriptions come alive for you. For example, a writer describing a beach might tell about the surf that roars like an express train and the sand that feels powdery and warm. Good descriptions are just as important in essays as in other types of writing. You will be less likely to pay attention to what an essay writer says if you cannot see in your mind the people and places being discussed. In "Rattlesnake Hunt," Marjorie Kinnan Rawlings gives a vivid description of a desolate area in Florida where rattlesnakes live.

Look For

As you read "Rattlesnake Hunt," let the writer's skillful descriptions help you visualize the rattlers and their environment. To which of your senses do her descriptions appeal?

Writing

Have you ever seen a snake in the woods or watched one at the zoo or on a television program? Describe the snake's appearance and the reaction you had when you saw it.

Vocabulary

Knowing the following words will help you as you read "Rattlesnake Hunt."

data (dāt′ ə) *n.:* Information (p. 369)

desolate (des′ ə lit) *adj.:* Lonely; solitary (p. 369)

conventional (kən ven′ shən'l) *adj.:* Ordinary; usual (p. 370)

translucent (trans lo͞o′ s'nt) *adj.:* Clear (p. 370)

arid (ar′ id) *adj.:* Dry and barren (p. 370)

mortality (môr tal′ ə tē) *n.:* Having to die someday (p. 371)

preferable (pref′ ər ə b'l) *adj.:* More desirable (p. 371)

camouflaged (kam′ ə fläzhd′) *v.:* Disguised (p. 371)

Objectives

1 To understand description in essays
2 To separate fact from opinion in an essay
3 To write a vivid description

Support Material

Teaching Portfolio
Teacher Backup, p. 517
Grammar in Action Worksheet, *Recognizing Compound-Complex Sentences,* p. 521
Usage and Mechanics Worksheet, p. 523
Vocabulary Check, p. 524
Analyzing Literature Worksheet, *Understanding Description in Essays,* p. 526

Critical Thinking and Reading Worksheet, *Separating Fact from Opinion,* p. 527
Selection Test, p. 528

Rattlesnake Hunt

Marjorie Kinnan Rawlings

Ross Allen, a young Florida herpetologist,[1] invited me to join him on a hunt in the upper Everglades[2]—for rattlesnakes. Ross and I drove to Arcadia in his coupé[3] on a warm January day.

I said, "How will you bring back the rattlesnakes?"

"In the back of my car."

My courage was not adequate to inquire whether they were thrown in loose and might be expected to appear between our feet. Actually, a large portable box of heavy close-meshed wire made a safe cage. Ross wanted me to write an article about his work and on our way to the unhappy hunting grounds I took notes on a mass of data that he had accumulated in years of herpetological research. The scientific and dispassionate detachment of the material and the man made a desirable approach to rattlesnake territory. As I had discovered with the insects and varmints,[4] it is difficult to be afraid of anything about which enough is known, and Ross' facts were fresh from the laboratory.

The hunting ground was Big Prairie, south of Arcadia and west of the northern tip of Lake Okeechobee. Big Prairie is a deso-

late cattle country, half marsh, half pasture, with islands of palm trees and cypress and oaks. At that time of year the cattlemen and Indians were burning the country, on the theory that the young fresh wire grass that springs up from the roots after a fire is the best cattle forage. Ross planned to hunt his rattlers in the forefront of the fires. They lived in winter, he said, in gopher holes, coming out in the midday warmth to forage, and would move ahead of the flames and be easily taken. We joined forces with a big man named Will, his snake-hunting companion of the territory, and set out in early morning, after a long rough drive over deep-rutted roads into the open wilds.

I hope never in my life to be so frightened as I was in those first few hours. I kept on Ross' footsteps, I moved when he moved,

---

1. herpetologist (hûr′ pə täl′ ə jist) *n.*: Someone who studies reptiles and amphibians.
2. Everglades: A large region of swampland in southern Florida, about 100 miles long and 50–75 miles wide.
3. coupé (ko̅o̅ pā′) *n.*: A small, two-door automobile.
4. varmints (vär′ mənts) *n.*: Animals regarded as troublesome.

Rattlesnake Hunt 369

Thematic Ideas Another selection you might want to use with "Rattlesnake Hunt" is the essay "Eugenie Clark and the Sleeping Sharks," pages 319–326. Both essays are similar in describing a woman contending with a dangerous type of animal. Eugenie Clark, however, is an expert about sharks, while Rawlings knew precious little about rattlers.

Finally, you might want to use Theodore Roethke's poem "The Bat," page 472, with this selection. The poem contains an excellent, and humorous, description of an animal that makes some people as uncomfortable as snakes do.

Presentation

Motivation/Prior Knowledge Ask students to imagine they are going on a rattlesnake hunt. Have them describe the feelings they would experience and the preparations they would undertake. Then tell them that, in this essay, Rawlings recounts what happened when she hunted rattlers for the first time.

Purpose-Setting Question What vivid words does Rawlings use to make descriptions come alive?

1 Master Teacher Note Suggest to students that writers who tell about overcoming their own fears often include a turning point in their narrative—a moment when they gain a new perspective on what has frightened them. Have students look for the turning point in this essay. Ask them to consider how this moment changes the way Rawlings tells her story.

2 Enrichment The Everglades are one of the largest swamplands in the world. Among the animals found there, in addition to rattlesnakes, are alligators, crocodiles, manatees, giant turtles, and many types of swampbird. No humans lived there until the middle of the nineteenth century, when Seminole Indians fleeing from soldiers hid in the swamps.

3 Discussion What is the writer's attitude toward this hunt?

4 Discussion Do you agree that knowledge of an animal's way of life will make you less afraid of it? Explain.

5 Enrichment You might have students look at the picture of a rattlesnake on this page. Ask them how this picture could help them to identify a rattler in the wild.

6 Discussion How does Ross's plan for the hunt reveal his scientific frame of mind?

7 **Literary Focus** You might tell students that writers try to use vivid adjectives to help readers imagine what they are describing. Review the meaning of adjective for **less advanced** students—"a word that modifies a noun"—and give them several examples (red, cold, windy, and so forth). Ask students to find the vivid adjectives that Rawlings uses in this passage.

8 **Discussion** Can you think of an experiment that would determine whether the snakes come to the truck to be near other snakes or to be in its shade?

sometimes jolting into him when I thought he might leave me behind. He does not use the forked stick of conventional snake hunting, but a steel prong, shaped like an L, at the end of a long stout stick. He hunted casually, calling my attention to the varying vegetation, to hawks overhead, to a pair of the rare whooping cranes that flapped over us. In mid-morning he stopped short, dropped his stick, and brought up a five-foot rattlesnake draped limply over the steel L. It seemed to me that I should drop in my tracks.

"They're not active at this season," he said quietly. "A snake takes on the temperature of its surroundings. They can't stand too much heat for that reason, and when the weather is cool, as now, they're sluggish."

The sun was bright overhead, the sky a translucent blue, and it seemed to me that it was warm enough for any snake to do as it willed. The sweat poured down my back. Ross dropped the rattler in a crocus sack[5] and Will carried it. By noon, he had caught four. I felt faint and ill. We stopped by a pond and went swimming. The region was flat, the horizon limitless, and as I came out of the cool blue water I expected to find myself surrounded by a ring of rattlers. There were only Ross and Will, opening the lunch basket. I could not eat. Will went back and drove his truck closer, for Ross expected the hunting to be better in the afternoon. The hunting was much better. When we went back to the truck to deposit two more rattlers in the wire cage, there was a rattlesnake lying under the truck.

Ross said, "Whenever I leave my car or truck with snakes already in it, other rattlers always appear. I don't know whether this is because they scent or sense the presence of other snakes, or whether in this arid area

------
5. **crocus sack:** A term used in the southern United States for a burlap bag.

they come to the car for shade in the heat of the day."

The problem was scientific, but I had no interest.

That night Ross and Will and I camped out in the vast spaces of the Everglades prairies. We got water from an abandoned well and cooked supper under buttonwood bushes by a flowing stream. The camp fire blazed cheerfully under the stars and a new moon lifted in the sky. Will told tall tales of the cattlemen and the Indians and we were at peace.

Ross said, "We couldn't have a better night for catching water snakes."

After the rattlers, water snakes seemed innocuous enough. We worked along the edge of the stream and here Ross did not use his L-shaped steel. He reached under rocks and along the edge of the water and brought out harmless reptiles with his hands. I had said nothing to him of my fears, but he un-

Grammar in Action

One effective way to add variety to your sentences is to use **compound-complex sentences.** As the name suggests, this sentence structure is the combination of a compound sentence and a complex sentence. That is, it is made up of two or more independent clauses and one or more subordinate clauses. Writers use compound-complex sentences to show the relationship between information that is of equal importance and other information which is unequal in importance. Notice how effec-

tively Marjorie Kinnan Rawlings uses a compound-complex sentence to make the action come alive.

> When it was at a safe distance *he walked within its range of vision,* which he had proved to be no higher than a man's knee, and *the snake whirled and drew back in an attitude of fighting defense.*

The two independent clauses of the sentence are *italicized.* They are of equal importance. The relationship between these main ideas and the less important information is indicated by placing the less important information in subordinate clauses. Using the structure of the compound-complex sentence allows Rawlings to connect her ideas in such a way that a vivid picture of the action is produced.

derstood them. He brought a small dark snake from under a willow root.

"Wouldn't you like to hold it?" he asked. "People think snakes are cold and clammy, but they aren't. Take it in your hands. You'll see that it is warm."

Again, because I was ashamed, I took the snake in my hands. It was not cold, it was not clammy, and it lay trustingly in my hands, a thing that lived and breathed and had mortality[6] like the rest of us. I felt an upsurgence of spirit.

The next day was magnificent. The air was crystal, the sky was aquamarine, and the far horizon of palms and oaks lay against the sky. I felt a new boldness and followed Ross bravely. He was making the rounds of the gopher holes. The rattlers came out in the mid-morning warmth and were never far away. He could tell by their trails whether

9

10

11

12

---

6. had mortality: Would die.

one had come out or was still in the hole. Sometimes the two men dug the snake out. At times it was down so long and winding a tunnel that the digging was hopeless. Then they blocked the entrance and went on to other holes. In an hour or so they made the original rounds, unblocking the holes. The rattler in every case came out hurriedly, as though anything were preferable to being shut in. All the time Ross talked to me, telling me the scientific facts he had discovered about the habits of the rattlers.

"They pay no attention to a man standing perfectly still," he said, and proved it by letting Will unblock a hole while he stood at the entrance as the snake came out. It was exciting to watch the snake crawl slowly beside and past the man's legs. When it was at a safe distance he walked within its range of vision, which he had proved to be no higher than a man's knee, and the snake whirled and drew back in an attitude[7] of fighting defense. The rattler strikes only for paralyzing and killing its food, and for defense.

"It is a slow and heavy snake," Ross said. "It lies in wait on a small game trail and strikes the rat or rabbit passing by. It waits a few minutes, then follows along the trail, coming to the small animal, now dead or dying. It noses it from all sides, making sure that it is its own kill, and that it is dead and ready for swallowing."

A rattler will lie quietly without revealing itself if a man passes by and it thinks it is not seen. It slips away without fighting if given the chance. Only Ross' sharp eyes sometimes picked out the gray and yellow diamond pattern, camouflaged among the grasses. In the cool of the morning, chilled by the January air, the snakes showed no fight. They could be looped up limply over the steel L and dropped in a sack or up into

13

---

7. attitude: (at' ə tōod') *n.*: In this case, a position or posture of the body.

Rattlesnake Hunt   371

---

9 **Enrichment** Suggest that students look at the picture on pages 370 and 371. Ask them to describe this landscape. You might also ask them whether they can identify any of the trees or other plant life that Rawlings mentions on page 369.

10 **Enrichment** A snake's body is covered by scales that are dry rather than moist or clammy. This scaly skin is divided into a layer of dead cells at the top and growing cells underneath. From time to time, a snake will shed it outer layer of dead cells in a process called molting.

11 **Discussion** Why does Rawlings feel "an upsurgence of spirit"?

12 **Discussion** Contrast Rawlings's new attitude with her feelings on the previous day.

13 **Reading Strategy** You might want to have students summarize what they have learned about rattlesnakes.

Student Activity 1. Find three sentences from "Rattlesnake Hunt" in which Rawlings uses compound-complex sentences. Identify the independent and subordinate clauses in each sentence.

Student Activity 2. Combine the following sentences into one compound-complex sentence.

A rattlesnake's rattle is made up of a set of horny pieces.
These pieces are loosely joined together.
A rattlesnake shakes this rattle.
It makes a clear sound.

Student Activity 3. Write two original compound-complex sentences.

14 **Reading Strategy** Ask students to predict what Rawlings will do after discovering this rattlesnake.

15 **Discussion** You might want to tell students that the ability to make jokes about frightening or repelling subjects is often called "grim humor." Where else in the essay has Rawlings displayed this kind of humor? How does her humor make you feel more sympathetic toward her?

16 **Discussion** Do you think that Ross has proved himself to be a good teacher? Explain.

17 **Discussion** Do you think Rawlings is correct in her prediction? Why or why not?

Reader's Response What is your definition of courage?

the wire cage on the back of Will's truck. As the sun mounted in the sky and warmed the moist Everglades earth, the snakes were warmed too, and Ross warned that it was time to go more cautiously. Yet having learned that it was we who were the aggressors; that immobility meant complete safety; that the snakes, for all their lightning flash in striking, were inaccurate in their aim, with limited vision; having watched again and again the liquid grace of movement, the beauty of pattern, suddenly I understood that I was drinking in freely the magnificent sweep of the horizon, with no fear of what might be at the moment under my feet. I went off hunting by myself, and though I found no snakes, I should have known what to do.

The sun was dropping low in the west. Masses of white cloud hung above the flat marshy plain and seemed to be tangled in the tops of distant palms and cypresses. The sky turned orange, then saffron.[8] I walked leisurely back toward the truck. In the distance I could see Ross and Will making their way in too. The season was more advanced than at the Creek, two hundred miles to the north, and I noticed that spring flowers were blooming among the lumpy hummocks.[9] I **14** leaned over to pick a white violet. There was a rattlesnake under the violet.

15 If this had happened the week before, if it had happened the day before, I think I should have lain down and died on top of the rattlesnake, with no need of being struck and poisoned. The snake did not coil, but lifted its head and whirred its rattles lightly. I stepped back slowly and put the violet in a buttonhole. I reached forward and laid the steel L across the snake's neck, just back of the blunt head. I called to Ross:

---

8. **saffron** (saf′ rən) adj.: Orange-yellow.
9. **hummocks** (hum′ əks) n.: Areas of fertile, wooded land, higher than the surrounding swamp.

372 *Nonfiction*

"I've got one."

He strolled toward me.

"Well, pick it up," he said.

I released it and slipped the L under the middle of the thick body.

"Go put it in the box."

He went ahead of me and lifted the top of the wire cage. I made the truck with the rattler, but when I reached up the six feet to drop it in the cage, it slipped off the stick and dropped on Ross' feet. It made no effort to strike.

"Pick it up again," he said. "If you'll pin it down lightly and reach just back of its head with your hand, as you've seen me do, you can drop it in more easily."

I pinned it and leaned over.

"I'm awfully sorry," I said, "but you're pushing me a little too fast."

He grinned. I lifted it on the stick and again as I had it at head height, it slipped off, down Ross' boots and on top of his feet. He stood as still as a stump. I dropped the snake on his feet for the third time. It **16** seemed to me that the most patient of rattlers might in time resent being hauled up and down, and for all the man's quiet certainty that in standing motionless there was no danger, would strike at whatever was nearest, and that would be Ross.

I said, "I'm just not man enough to keep this up any longer," and he laughed and reached down with his smooth quickness and lifted the snake back of the head and dropped it in the cage. It slid in among its mates and settled in a corner. The hunt was over and we drove back over the uneven trail to Will's village and left him and went on to Arcadia and home. Our catch for the two days was thirty-two rattlers.

I said to Ross, "I believe that tomorrow I **17** could have picked up that snake."

Back at the Creek, I felt a new lightness. I had done battle with a great fear, and the victory was mine.

Closure and Extension

ANSWERS TO THINKING ABOUT THE SELECTION
Recalling

1. Ross Allen wanted her to write about his work.
2. "Big Prairie is a desolate cattle country, half marsh, half pasture, with islands of palm trees and cypress and oaks."
3. She stays close to Ross, only moving when he moves. Later, she feels faint and ill, and she has no appetite.
4. The following are some of the facts about rattlesnakes that students can learn from this essay— they take on the temperature of their surroundings and therefore cannot stand too much heat and are sluggish in cold weather; they won't bother a person who is standing still; they strike only to paralyze and kill their food, and for defense; they strike quickly but are inaccurate in their aim.

THINKING ABOUT THE SELECTION
Recalling

1. Why does Rawlings go on the rattlesnake hunt?
2. Describe the area to which she, Will, and Ross travel.
3. How does she show her fear of rattlesnakes?
4. Tell two facts she learns about rattlers.
5. How does she show that she has partly overcome her fear.

Interpreting

6. Why do Rawlings' feelings about snakes change when she holds one?
7. How do experience and knowledge influence her feelings about rattlers?
8. What reason can you suggest for rattlers having a "gray and yellow diamond pattern"?
9. At the end of the selection, why does Rawlings feel "a new lightness"? Is the victory truly hers?

Applying

10. Why does knowledge often drive away fear?

ANALYZING LITERATURE
Understanding Description in Essays

Descriptive passages include lively language and details that appeal to your senses. In this essay, for example, Rawlings writes: "Masses of white cloud . . . seemed to be tangled in the tops of distant palms and cypresses. The sky turned orange, then saffron." She helps you to see this scene by using many colors in her description: white, orange, and saffron. By using the verb "tangled," she gives you a vivid picture of the way the clouds look in the trees.

1. Find two other passages where Rawlings tells you the color of what she describes.
2. At the start of the essay, she writes: "In midmorning he . . . brought up a five-foot rattlesnake draped limply over the steel L." Would this description have been better or worse if she had written "hanging" instead of "draped limply"? Why?

CRITICAL THINKING AND READING
Separating Fact from Opinion

A **fact** is something that can be proven, while an **opinion** is a person's belief or impression. Rawlings' statement that "The sweat poured down my back," is a fact. However, when she says, " 'I believe that tomorrow I could have picked up that snake,' " she is stating an opinion.

As you read essays, you should be able to separate fact from opinion. Indicate which of the following passages from this essay are facts and which are opinions.

1. "Our catch for the two days was thirty-two rattlers."
2. "It seemed to me that the most patient of rattlers might in time resent being hauled up and down. . . ."
3. "We stopped by a pond and went swimming."
4. "If this had happened the week before, . . . I think I should have lain down and died on top of the rattlesnake. . . ."

THINKING AND WRITING
Writing a Description

The year is 2020. A distant planet has just entered into radio communication with Earth. The people of this planet are eager to discover what kind of animals exist here. Choose a type of animal that you have often observed and list its important qualities. Then use your list to write a description of it that will satisfy the curiosity of these extraterrestrial creatures. In revising your work, make sure your description gives them a clear picture of the animal you have chosen.

Rattlesnake Hunt   373

(Answers begin on p. 372)

Challenge What should you do if you encounter a rattlesnake on a trail in the woods? Choose the best response and explain your choice.

a. Assault it with a large stick.
b. Try to step around it.
c. Stand still and then, very slowly, back away.

ANSWERS TO ANALYZING LITERATURE

1. Suggested Response: Students may choose two of the following passages—"The sun was bright overhead, the sky a translucent blue. . . ." (p. 370); ". . . as I came out of the cool blue water. . . ." (p. 370); ". . . the sky was aquamarine. . . ." (p. 371); "Only Ross' sharp eyes sometimes picked out the gray and yellow diamond pattern. . . ." (p. 371); "I leaned over to pick a white violet." (p. 372)
2. Suggested Response: The description would have been worse. The words that she does use are more specific and clearly convey that the snake is harmless.

ANSWERS TO CRITICAL THINKING AND READING

1. Fact   3. Fact
2. Opinion   4. Opinion

THINKING AND WRITING
Publishing Student Writing
You might want to bind the essays together and entitle them: Report for the Extraterrestrials.

Writing Across the Curriculum
Have students research and report on rattlesnakes or any other kind of poisonous snake. You might want to inform the science department about this assignment, so that science teachers can provide guidance and perhaps extra credit for students.

---

5. She goes off hunting by herself.

Interpreting

6. Suggested Response: She realizes that snakes are not cold and clammy, and she sees that it lies trustingly in her hands. Most important, she realizes that snakes are mortal creatures, too.
7. Suggested Response: Her experience and knowledge make her less afraid of rattlesnakes. She is therefore more at ease about meeting them.

8. Suggested Response: This pattern may serve as camouflage, helping them blend in with their environment.
9. Suggested Response: She feels "a new lightness" because she has overcome her fear. Especially insightful students will realize that the victory belongs partly to Ross, her teacher.

Applying

10. Students' answers will differ. Suggested Response: Much fear is due to the unknown. Lack of knowledge often leads us to imagine horrible things. When we know more about a subject, we often realize that what we have imagined is not true.

More About the Author Tell students that James Dickey often writes about the need for people to be more in tune with nature, the way our primitive ancestors were. Ask students how living in cities, or even small towns, may distance people from nature and make them feel less part of the natural world.

Literary Focus You may want to stress the idea that there are several types of explanation. For instance, you can give someone directions for assembling a model airplane or finding a certain building in a city. This type of explanation is very definite and precise.

Another type of explanation, however, involves telling someone about the value of a subject in which you are interested. You may give this type of explanation to a friend who asks you why you collect stamps or listen to a certain kind of music. Dickey's suggestions about how to approach poetry fall under this category of explanation.

Look For Consider telling students that, after they finish each section of the essay, they may want to reread the first few sentences in that section to make sure they remember the main point.

Writing/Prior Knowledge You might divide the class into small groups and have students discuss the various forms of ice they have seen—icicles, trees coated with ice, ice on a lake, and so forth—before they begin the assignment.

Vocabulary Have less advanced students read these words aloud and quiz each other on their meanings.

How to Enjoy Poetry

James Dickey (1923–   ) was born in Atlanta, Georgia, and attended Vanderbilt University. As a young man, he was a football player and a motorcycle enthusiast. Although these interests are not usually associated with poetry, Dickey is one of America's best-known poets. He is also famous for his novel *Deliverance* (1970), which was made into a film. In this selection, he demonstrates that poetry was not "invented as a school subject" and explains how to enjoy poetry as only a writer can.

Expository Essay

The purpose of an **expository essay** is to explain a subject or give information about it. You may have seen magazine articles with titles such as "How to Build Your Vocabulary" or "How to Operate a Computer." These articles explaining a process are expository essays. However, unlike many "How-to" articles, "How to Enjoy Poetry" does not give you rules that you *must* follow to achieve a goal. Instead, its purpose is to explain the value of poetry and offer suggestions for appreciating it.

Look For

Expository essays often contain key ideas. As you read "How to Enjoy Poetry," look for the **bold print** headings and use them as guideposts. The first sentence after each heading usually contains a key idea.

Writing

Dickey writes of the ice cube, "what more mysterious and beautiful *interior* of something has there ever been?" Look closely at an ice cube. Freewrite about what you see.

Vocabulary

Knowing the following words will help you as you read "How to Enjoy Poetry."

emblems (em′ bləmz) *n.*: Signs; symbols (p. 376)
encounter (in koun′ tər) *n.*: Meeting (p. 376)
compelling (kəm pel′ iŋ) *adj.*: Having a powerful effect (p. 377)
prose (prōz) *n.*: Nonpoetic language (p. 377)

definitive (di fin′ ə tiv) *adj.*: Final; the last word (p. 377)
inevitability (in ev′ ə tə b′l′ i tē) *n.*: Certainty (p. 377)
interacts (in′ tər akts′) *v.*: Affects and is affected by (p. 378)
vital (vīt′'l) *adj.*: Essential to life; living (p. 378)

Objectives

1 To understand the features of the expository essay
2 To experiment with a writer's suggestion
3 To recognize the Latin root *Vita-*
4 To write an expository essay

Support Material

Teaching Portfolio
Teacher Backup, p. 531
Grammar in Action Worksheet, *Identifying Indefinate Pronouns,* p. 534
Usage and Mechanics Worksheet, p. 536
Vocabulary Check, p. 537
Critical Thinking and Reading Worksheet, *Experimenting With a Suggestion,* p. 538

Language Worksheet, *Latin and Greek Roots for the Word Life,* p. 539
Selection Test, p. 540

How to Enjoy Poetry

James Dickey

What is poetry? And why has it been around so long? Many have suspected that it was invented as a school subject, because you have to take exams on it. But that is not what poetry is or why it is still around. That's not what it feels like, either. When you really feel it, a new part of you happens, or an old part is renewed, with surprise and delight at being what it is.

Where Poetry Is Coming From

From the beginning, people have known that words and things, words and actions, words and feelings, go together, and that they can go together in thousands of different ways, according to who is using them. Some ways go shallow, and some go deep.

Your Connection
with Other Imaginations

The first thing to understand about poetry is that it comes to you from outside you, in books or in words, but that for it to live, something from within you must come to it and meet it and complete it. Your response with your own mind and body and memory and emotions gives the poem its ability to work its magic; if you give to it, it will give to you, and give plenty.

When you read, don't let the poet write down to you; read up to him. Reach for him from your gut out, and the heart and muscles will come into it, too.

Which Sun? Whose Stars?

The sun is new every day, the ancient philosopher Heraclitus[1] said. The sun of poetry is new every day, too, because it is seen in different ways by different people who have lived under it, lived with it, responded to it. Their lives are different from yours, but by means of the special spell that poetry brings to the *fact* of the sun—everybody's sun; yours, too—you can come into possession of many suns: as many as men and women have ever been able to imagine. Poetry makes possible the deepest kind of personal possession of the world.

The most beautiful constellation in the winter sky is Orion,[2] which ancient poets thought looked like a hunter, up there, moving across heaven with his dog Sirius.[3] What is this hunter made out of stars hunting for? What does he mean? Who owns him, if

---

1. Heraclitus (her′ ə klīt′ əs): A Greek philosopher who lived about 500 B.C.
2. Orion (ō rī′ ən)
3. Sirius (sir′ ē əs)

How to Enjoy Poetry 375

Humanities Note

Fine art, *The Starry Night*, 1889, by Vincent Van Gogh (1853–1890). Although he sold only one painting during his lifetime, Van Gogh is now one of the most famous artists of all time. He had a brief and tragic life, producing many of his greatest paintings in a few short years.

1. How does the night sky contrast with the village?
2. What is unusual about the way that Van Gogh has painted the sky?
3. What feelings does this painting call up in you?
4. Dickey says that a poet in some way "owns" what he or she describes. In Dickey's sense of the word, does Van Gogh "own" the night sky? Explain.

5 **Discussion** Why do you think that Dickey suggests your encounter with poetry "should bypass all classrooms, all textbooks, courses, examinations, and libraries"?

THE STARRY NIGHT, 1889
Vincent van Gogh
The Museum of Modern Art

anybody? The poet Aldous Huxley[4] felt that he did, and so, in Aldous Huxley's universe of personal emotion, he did.

> Up from among the emblems of the
>   wind into its heart of power,
> The Huntsman climbs, and all his
>   living stars
> Are bright, and all are mine.

---

4. Aldous Huxley: An English poet, essayist, and novelist (1894–1963).

Where to Start

The beginning of your true encounter with poetry should be simple. It should bypass all classrooms, all textbooks, courses, examinations, and libraries and go straight to the things that make your own existence exist: to your body and nerves and blood and muscles. Find your own way—a secret way that just maybe you don't know yet—to open yourself as wide as you can and as deep as you can to the moment, the *now* of your own existence and the endless mystery of it, and

5

Grammar in Action

Indefinite pronouns refer to people, places, or things, often without specifying which ones. That is, indefinite pronouns do not require specific antecedents. When an indefinite pronoun is used as a subject, the verb must agree with it in number. Many indefinite pronouns can agree with either a singular or a plural verb. The choice depends upon the meaning given to the pronoun. In the following passage, James Dickey quotes a verse from an Aldous Huxley poem in which the indefinite pronoun is plural.

The Huntsman climbs, and all his living stars
Are bright, and *all are* mine.

Dickey repeats the word *all,* first as an adjective of *stars* then as an indefinite pronoun. Using the plural form of the verbs, the poet makes sure that his readers know *all* refers to *stars.* A careful writer must make sure that indefinite pronouns used as subjects agree with their verbs to get across the intended meaning.

Student Activity 1. Find another sentence where Dickey uses an indefinite pronoun as a subject. Explain whether it is singular or plural.

perhaps at the same time to one other thing that is not you, but is out there: a handful of gravel is a good place to start. So is an ice cube—what more mysterious and beautiful *interior* of something has there ever been?

As for me, I like the sun, the source of all living things, and on certain days very good-feeling, too. "Start with the sun," D. H. Lawrence[5] said, "and everything will slowly, slowly happen." Good advice. And a lot *will* happen.

What is more fascinating than a rock, if you really feel it and *look* at it, or more interesting than a leaf?

> Horses, I mean; butterflies, whales;
> Mosses, and stars; and gravelly
> Rivers, and fruit.

> Oceans, I mean; black valleys; corn;
> Brambles, and cliffs; rock, dirt, dust,
> ice . . .

Go back and read this list—it is quite a list, Mark Van Doren's[6] list!—item by item. Slowly. Let each of these things call up an image out of your own life.

Think and feel. What moss do you see? Which horse? What field of corn? What brambles are *your* brambles? Which river is most yours?

The Poem's Way of Going

Part of the spell of poetry is in the rhythm of language, used by poets who understand how powerful a factor rhythm can be, how compelling and unforgettable. Almost anything put into rhythm and rhyme is more memorable than the same thing said in prose. Why this is, no one knows completely, though the answer is surely rooted far down in the biology by means of which we exist; in the circulation of the blood that goes forth from the heart and comes back, and in the repetition of breathing. Croesus[7] was a rich Greek king, back in the sixth century before Christ, but this tombstone was not his:

> No Croesus lies in the grave you see;
> I was a poor laborer, and this suits
> me.

That is plain-spoken and definitive. You believe it, and the rhyme helps you believe it and keep it.

Some Things You'll Find Out

Writing poetry is a lot like a contest with yourself, and if you like sports and games and competitions of all kinds, you might like to try writing some. Why not?

The possibilities of rhyme are great. Some of the best fun is in making up your own limericks.[8] There's no reason you can't invent limericks about anything that comes to your mind. No reason. Try it.

The problem is to find three words that rhyme and fit into a meaning. "There was a young man from . . ." *Where* was he from? What situation was he in? How can these things fit into the limerick form—a form everybody knows—so that the rhymes "pay off," and give that sense of completion and inevitability that is so deliciously memorable that nothing else is like it?

---

5. **D. H. Lawrence:** An English poet and novelist (1885–1930).
6. **Mark Van Doren:** An American poet, teacher, and critic (1894–1972).

---

7. **Croesus** (krē′ səs)
8. **limericks** (lim′ ər iks) *n.*: Nonsense poems of five lines.

How to Enjoy Poetry 377

6 **Discussion** How does the way that Dickey advises you to read a poem differ from the way that you would read an article in a newspaper?

7 **Discussion** How might Dickey answer a person who argued that using rhythm and rhyme to express one's thoughts in poetry is not as *natural* as writing out ideas in plain prose?

8 **Discussion** How might writing poetry resemble a sport or game?

9 **Enrichment** You might want to read students the limericks by Oliver Herford on page 529. You can also read them the following limerick by Edward Lear.

"There was an Old Man of Coblenz,/The length of whose legs was immense./He went with one prance/from Turkey to France,/That surprising Old Man of Coblenz."

For **less advanced** students, you may want to emphasize that the first, second, and fifth lines have three beats, while the third and fourth lines have two beats. Read one of the limericks stressing this rhythmic pattern.

Students who are **more advanced** might enjoy reading more poetry by Edward Lear in *The Nonsense Books of Edward Lear* (New York: The New American Library, 1964).

Student Activity 2. Choose the correct verb from the choices in parentheses and write it on your paper.

1. Most of the milk (is, are) sour.

2. Some of us (has, have) never ridden on a ferris wheel.

3. All of the players (was, were) asked to turn in their jerseys.

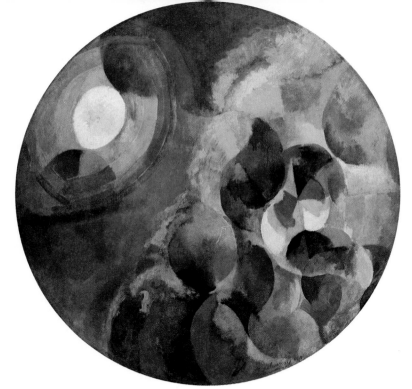

SIMULTANEOUS CONTRASTS: SUN AND MOON, 1913
Robert Delaunay
The Museum of Modern Art

How It Goes with You

The more your encounter with poetry deepens, the more your experience of your own life will deepen, and you will begin to see things by means of words, and words by means of things.

You will come to understand the world as it interacts with words, as it can be re-created by words, by rhythms and by images.

You'll understand that this condition is one charged with vital possibilities. You will pick up meaning more quickly—and you will *create* meaning, too, for yourself and for others.

Connections between things will exist for you in ways that they never did before. They will shine with unexpectedness, wide-openness, and you will go toward them, on your own path. "Then . . ." as Dante[9] says, ". . . Then will your feet be filled with good desire." You will know this is happening the first time you say, of something you never would have noticed before, "Well, would you look at *that*! Who'd 'a thunk it?" (Pause, full of new light)

"*I* thunk it!"

10

---

9. Dante (dän' tā): An Italian poet (1265–1321) whose most famous work is *The Divine Comedy.*

378   *Nonfiction*

THINKING ABOUT THE SELECTION

Recalling

1. According to James Dickey, how can you get the most from a poem?
2. How can poetry help you to own "many suns"?
3. Why are rhythm and rhyme important to poetry?
4. How is poetry "like a contest with yourself"?

Interpreting

5. What does Dickey mean when he writes, "when you read, don't let the poet write down to you; read up to him"? Why would reading this way increase your enjoyment?
6. Why do you think Dickey relates rhythm in poetry to biology?
7. What does he mean by asking you "to open yourself as wide as you can and as deep as you can to the moment. . . ."?

Applying

8. Dickey says you can enjoy poetry more by focusing on yourself and also on "one other thing that is not you." Which "other thing" would you choose? Why?

ANALYZING LITERATURE

Understanding the Expository Essay

The purpose of an **expository essay** is to explain a subject rather than present a story. In "How to Enjoy Poetry," James Dickey explains why poetry is valuable not as a school subject but as a response to life. He also offers suggestions for getting the most from poems.

1. What key idea does Dickey offer under the heading "Your connection with other imaginations"? What key idea does he offer under the heading "Which sun? Whose stars?"
2. Identify three suggestions that he offers for increasing your enjoyment of poetry.
3. Which suggestion do you find most helpful? Why?

CRITICAL THINKING AND READING

Experimenting with a Suggestion

In the section of this essay entitled "Where to Start," Dickey suggests reading a list of things in a poem and responding to each item.

1. Choose three items from the list in the poem.
2. Freewrite about the picture that each of these items calls up in you.
3. Has writing about these items given you a better appreciation of the lines from the poem? Why or why not?

UNDERSTANDING LANGUAGE

Recognizing the Latin Root *Vita-*

One of the words in this essay is *vital*, which means "living" or "essential to life." The Latin root *vita-*, which is the source of this word, means "life." This root is also part of other English words whose meaning is related to "life."

Write the meaning of each of the following *vita*- words or phrases. If you do not know what the word means, try to figure out the meaning and check your answer in a dictionary. Then use each word in a sentence.

1. vitality
2. vitamin
3. vitalize
4. vital signs

THINKING AND WRITING

Writing an Expository Essay

Imagine that a friend has moved to another city and you have told him or her about a new hobby you have taken up. This hobby can be anything you really like doing. Your friend wants to know about your hobby and to understand why you enjoy it so much. List the key aspects of your hobby and the reasons why it is fun. Then use this list to write a letter to your friend explaining what you do and why you enjoy it. In revising your letter, put yourself in your friend's place. Make sure that he or she will understand the value of what you do.

How to Enjoy Poetry   379

(Answers begin on p. 378)

3. Students' answers will differ. There is no correct answer and responses should be evaluated based on the accompanying explanations. However, most students will realize that, by responding to the poem more fully, they have gained a better appreciation of it.

ANSWERS TO UNDERSTANDING LANGUAGE

1. vitality—a principle regarded as the source of life in living organisms; power to live; power to endure or survive; energy
2. vitamin—substances found in foods that are important for the functioning of the body
3. vitalize—give life to; make lively
4. vital signs—indicators of the efficient functioning of the body, such as pulse, temperature, and so forth

THINKING AND WRITING
Publishing Student Writing
You might want to have students actually send their letters to a friend or relative.

Writing Across the Curriculum
You may want to have students exercise their powers of perception by keeping a scientific journal. This journal might contain observations of a pet, the growth of a plant, or anything similar. Consider informing the science department of this assignment, so that science teachers can provide guidance for students.

Applying
8. Students' answers will differ. Suggested Response: Make sure that students give an adequate justification for their choice.

ANSWERS TO ANALYZING LITERATURE
1. Suggested Response: Your Connection with Other Imaginations— To make poetry live, you must respond to it with every part of yourself. Which Sun? Whose Stars?—Through poetry, you can understand the world from many different perspectives and therefore your experience will be richer.
2. Suggested Response: Students may choose any three of the following suggestions—Respond to a poem with every part of yourself; be as open as possible to your own existence and to that of one other thing; read the list in Mark Van Doren's poem and try to imagine each item he names; be aware of the rhyme and rhythm in a poem; try writing a limerick as a kind of contest with yourself.
3. Students' answers will differ. Evaluate each answer based on the adequacy of the explanation offered.

ANSWERS TO CRITICAL THINKING AND READING
1. Suggested Response: Students should choose three of the items mentioned in the poem.
2. Students' answers will differ. Encourage students to use vivid language that appeals to the senses.

Challenge Read poems that have not been assigned in class and try to follow some of Dickey's suggestions for appreciating them. Keep a written account of the results of your efforts.

More About the Author Tell students that the television commentator Walter Cronkite has said that Andrew Rooney is "Everyman, articulating all the frustrations with modern life that the rest of us Everymen . . . suffer with silence or mumbled oaths." Ask students what qualities in a writer or television commentator would make him or her seem like an average person. Why would a writer or television personality want to make this type of impression on readers or viewers?

Literary Focus Consider suggesting to students that a persuasive essay is only a more formal example of everyday situations in which people try to persuade each other to accept a certain idea or act in a certain way. Ask students, for instance, what arguments they would use to convince their best friend to see a certain movie.

You might ask **more advanced** students to distinguish between arguments they would use if their friend were very reluctant and arguments they would use if their friend seemed willing to be convinced.

Look For You may want to tell students that, by forming an opinion of a writer's main point, they will become more actively involved in reading the essay. As a result, they will think more carefully about the writer's arguments.

Writing/Prior Knowledge Consider dividing the class into small groups so that students can tell group members about their attempt at persuasion before describing it in writing.

Vocabulary Ask **more advanced** students to look up *deterioration* —the noun form of the vocabulary word *deteriorated*—in the thesaurus.

GUIDE FOR READING

Letter Writing

Andrew A. Rooney (1919–   ) received a bronze star for his service in the Air Force during World War II, and among his many books are *Air Gunner* and *The Fortunes of War*. He has also been a newspaper columnist for the *New York Herald Tribune*. Rooney, however, is probably best known for his work in television. He received television's highest award, the Emmy, and he appears often on the CBS show *60 Minutes*. In the essay "Letter Writing," he expresses himself as strongly in writing as he usually does on the air.

Persuasive Essay

A **persuasive essay** is a brief work of nonfiction in which a writer tries to convince you to accept a certain idea or view or to act a certain way. Writers usually offer arguments, or reasons, to support their position. In "Letter Writing," for example, Andrew A. Rooney states his opinion about personal letters at the start of his essay. Then he presents a variety of arguments to back up this idea.

Look For

Rooney states his main point in the first paragraph. React to this idea. Form an opinion of it. Then, as you read the essay, ask yourself whether Rooney's arguments are convincing and whether they cause you to agree with him.

Writing

Recall a time when you had to persuade someone that you were right. Tell what the discussion was about, how you tried to convince this person, and whether you were successful. If you were not, what might you have done to ensure your success?

Vocabulary

Knowing the following words will help you as you read "Letter Writing."

conspiring (kən spir' iŋ) *v.*: Combining; working together (p. 381)
deteriorated (di tir' ē ə rāt' id) *v.*: Became worse (p. 381)
provisional (prə vizh' ə n'l) *adj.*: Temporary, depending on future events (p. 381)

bias (bī' əs) *n.*: Preference; learning; prejudice (p. 383)
retrospect (ret' rə spekt') *n.*: A looking back on the past (p. 383)

Objectives

1 To understand the features of the persuasive essay
2 To understand contrasts
3 To debate a premise
4 To write a persuasive essay

Support Material

Teaching Portfolio
Teacher Backup, p. 543
Grammar in Action Worksheet, *Writing a Friendly Letter,* p. 547
Usage and Mechanics Worksheet, p. 549
Vocabulary Check, p. 550
Analyzing Literature Worksheet, *Understanding the Persuasive Essay,* p. 551
Critical Thinking and Reading

Worksheet, *Understanding Contrasts,* p. 552
Selection Test, p. 553

Letter Writing

Andrew A. Rooney

There ought to be a five-cent stamp for personal letters. Letter writing is one of the good things about a civilized society, and it should be encouraged. It's a shame that everything is conspiring against letter writing. Our whole postal system has deteriorated to the point where mail is no fun at all. The excitement we used to feel about the arrival of the mailman is gone.

It costs twenty-two cents for a regular stamp now. That's a terrible number, and you don't dare buy a roll of twenty-two-cent stamps because you know it's going to change before you get used to it and certainly before you use up a roll.

I object to the fact that it costs me more to send a letter to a friend than it costs some fly-by-night real estate operator to send me a phony brochure in the mail telling me I'm the provisional winner of a $10,000 sweepstakes. I don't like strangers knocking on my door trying to sell me something, and I don't want my mail cluttered with advertising. If anyone wants to accuse me of feeling that way because I make a living from the advertising found in newspapers and on television, go ahead and accuse me of it. It isn't true.

I don't get five good, genuine, personal letters a year. The time is coming when the letter written with pen and ink and sent as a personal message from one person to another will be as much of a rarity as the gold pocket watch carried on a chain. It's a shame.

There is something special about a personal letter. It's better than a phone call, no matter what the telephone company says. A phone call disappears into the air as soon as the receiver is put back on the hook. A good letter can last a lifetime.

Some of my most precious possessions are letters that have been written to me sometime in the past. I don't have a single memorable phone call stored in a box in my attic or basement. I've never thrown away a good letter and, like any real treasure, I don't even have to look at them to enjoy having them. I *know* I have them. The telephone calls come and go. They make no permanent impression on me and have no place in my memory.

A personal letter is a good thing because you say things you can't say in a crowd and might not even say to the person face to face. If you feel like it, a letter allows you to take yourself and your thoughts more seriously than you would dare take them in conversation. And you can say things without interruption.

Presentation

Motivation/Prior Knowledge You may want to ask students if they have ever received a letter that they considered important enough to save. Have them describe the type of letter it was. Then tell them that the author of this essay believes very strongly in the value of personal letters.

Purpose-Setting Question What is Rooney's main point and how does he support it?

1 **Master Teacher Note** You might want to tell students that a useful technique in reading persuasive essays is to think of all the arguments opposed to what the writer is saying. It may even be helpful for students to pretend that Rooney is in a debate. Every time he presents one of his arguments, students might try to imagine what the debater for the other side would say. Tell students that this technique will enable them to think more critically about a writer's ideas.

2 **Enrichment** Students may be interested to hear that the pony express, which began in 1860, carried mail a distance of 2,000 miles—from Missouri to California—in about eight days. Riders faced many hardships and often had to travel through dangerous territory. No wonder a personal letter carried this way was precious to someone who received it!

3 **Discussion** Where does Rooney use strong, colloquial language? Why do you think he uses words like these?

4 **Discussion** Why do you think that Rooney often uses short sentences?

5 **Discussion** How does Rooney introduce a personal quality into his essay? Why might such a personal touch make the essay more persuasive?

Thematic Ideas Other essays that you might want to read with this selection are "How to Enjoy Poetry," pages 375–378, and "Winslow Homer: America's Greatest Painter," pages 395–398. Each of these essays has a persuasive component.

Other selections in which persuasion plays a part are the fable "The Fox and the Crow," page 547, and the Ashanti tale "All Stories Are Anansi's," pages 611–612. In each of these little stories, the art of persuasion is practiced by a trickster.

Fine art, *Girl Writing*, by Milton Avery (1893–1965). Avery's works were abstract at a time when most American painters were working in a realistic vein. He is considered one of the fore-runners of the American Abstract Expressionist painters of the 1950's.

1. Why do you think the painter has not chosen to include a great many realistic details?
2. What do you think the girl is writing? Explain.
3. What mood does this painting create?
4. Do you think this painting goes well with the essay? Why or why not?

GIRL WRITING
Milton Avery
The Phillips Collection

Grammar in Action

A **friendly letter** is written to communicate to friends, relatives, or aquaintances. The basic form of a friendly letter consists of five parts: the heading, the salutation, the body, the closing, and the signature.

Write the *heading* at the top of the letter. It should contain your address and the date.

The *salutation* greets the reader. You might write, "Dear Tony," or "Hello," or "Greetings." What you write depends on whom you are writing to.

The *body* is the main part of the friendly letter. It should contain everything you want to say. The body can be as short or as long as you wish to make it.

The *closing* signals the end of the letter. You might say "Sincerely yours," or "Love," or "Take it easy." As in the salutation, what you say depends on whom you are writing to.

Finish your letter with your *signature*.

When you are ready to mail your letter, prepare an envelope. Write the complete address in the letter in the center of the envelope and your complete return address in the upper left-hand corner.

Student Activity. Write a friendly letter to a real or imaginary friend or relative. Be sure to use the proper form for a friendly letter and prepare an envelope to sent it in.

A good letter is, in many ways, the exact opposite of a political speech. A politician addressing a crowd has to talk so broadly and generally about the issues in order not to offend any one of the thousands of people listening that he usually ends up saying nothing. A letter can be specific, and if the writer has some bias or prejudice, he can even reveal his true self by letting this show. Writing a friend, you shouldn't have to be careful. Abraham Lincoln's letter to his stepbrother telling him he wasn't going to loan him the eighty dollars he asked for tells you more about Abraham Lincoln than the Gettysburg Address does.

Some of our best history has come that way, from personal letters of famous people that scholars have dug up. You get a better idea of what someone is really like from a personal letter they weren't expecting you to read than you get from a carefully considered public statement they've made. We say real things in letters.

There are several reasons why we aren't writing many personal letters. We don't write letters with news of the family because we already have that by telephone; we don't write secrets because we're all so aware that they may fall into the wrong hands and end up in print; and we don't write awkward love letters much anymore because we're afraid of sounding silly. Love letters were almost always silly, but only in retrospect. The moment it is opened and read, a love letter is never silly. That's the other good thing about a personal letter. If you know each other well, it doesn't have to make absolute sense to anyone else.

Personal letters should go for a five-cent stamp.

6 **Enrichment** You may want to bring to class a book such as *Treasury of the World's Great Letters: From Ancient Days to Our Own Time,* edited by Lincoln M. Schuster (New York: Simon & Schuster, 1960). Read excerpts from some of these letters aloud to students and ask what they reveal about the writer's personality.

7 **Discussion** What methods of communication may take the place of the telephone some day? Do you think such future inventions will make letter writing obsolete? Explain.

8 **Reading Strategy** Ask students to summarize Rooney's key arguments.

Reader's Response Has the author's argument persuaded you to write more personal letters? Why or why not?

Closure and Extension

(Questions begin on p. 384)

ANSWERS TO THINKING ABOUT THE SELECTION
Recalling

1. "Letter writing is one of the good things about a civilized society, and it should be encouraged."
2. Three of the arguments that Rooney uses are the following: it now costs more to send personal letters than it does to send advertisements; a letter allows you to say things without interruption; personal letters from people in history have great value.
3. A letter is the opposite of a speech because it can be specific and reveal bias or prejudice while a speech must be broad and general.
4. We use the telephone for family news. We are afraid of writing secrets in a personal letter because the wrong person may see them. We do not write love letters because they may seem silly.

Interpreting

5. Answers will differ. Suggested Response: When you write a letter, you have time to think about what you want to say. That you are making a permanent record of your thoughts may encourage you to take the communication more seriously.

    Whether or not students agree, they should support their arguments.
6. Suggested Response: When you are writing and receiving such

letters, you are deeply involved with your feelings. These letters may seem silly afterward, when your emotions have cooled.

Applying

7. Students' answers will differ. Suggested Response: Students who prefer a phone call may argue that this method of communication is more direct and immediate. Students who prefer receiving letters may feel that they are a more permanent record and can become prized possessions.

ANSWERS TO ANALYZING LITERATURE

1. Suggested Response: The idea that personal letters should require only a five-cent stamp is a catchy way to call attention to the main point, that letter writing should be encouraged. He repeats this proposal at the beginning and end of the essay so that readers will remember it.
2. Answers will differ. Suggested Response: Most students will probably choose two of the following arguments—a letter is more permanent than a phone call; a letter allows you to express yourself without interruption; letters can reveal a writer's deepest thoughts and feelings; letters written by famous people have great value.
3. Answers will differ. Suggested Response: Students who argued that letters are more permanent will probably say that they can be read over and over again. Those who argued that a letter allows you to express yourself without interruption might say that there is less chance of forgetting what you wanted to say. Students who argued that a letter allows you to express your deepest thoughts will probably say that many people are too embarrassed to express such thoughts in conversation. Students who argued that letters by famous people are valuable may argue that such letters provide a valuable resource for historians.

ANSWERS TO CRITICAL THINKING AND READING

1. He says that a phone call is over once you hang up the receiver, but a personal letter can be reread any number of times.

THINKING ABOUT THE SELECTION

Recalling

1. Rooney clearly states his thesis, or main idea, at the beginning of the essay. What is it?
2. Tell three of the arguments that Rooney uses to support this idea.
3. Explain why he thinks "A good letter is . . . the exact opposite of a political speech."
4. According to Rooney, why do people no longer write personal letters?

Interpreting

5. What does Rooney mean by saying that you can "take . . . your thoughts more seriously" in a letter than in a conversation? Do you agree with this? Why or why not?
6. What does he mean when he says that love letters are silly "only in retrospect" and not when received?

Applying

7. Would you rather get a letter or a phone call from a friend in a distant city. Why?

ANALYZING LITERATURE

Understanding the Persuasive Essay

A **persuasive essay** is a brief work of nonfiction in which a writer tries to convince you to accept a certain idea or view or to act a certain way. In "Letter Writing," for example, Andrew Rooney argues that personal letters should require only a five-cent stamp.

1. Why does he discuss the cost of personal letters at the start and end of the essay?
2. Identify two of his arguments that you think are especially persuasive.
3. Explain why the arguments you have chosen are convincing.

CRITICAL THINKING AND READING

Understanding Contrasts

Contrasting means showing differences. Writers often use this technique to indicate how

384   Nonfiction

an idea or approach they favor is better than others. For example, Andrew Rooney points up the value of personal letters by contrasting them with other types of communication. Explain how he uses each of the following contrasts to show that letters are superior.
1. Personal letters versus telephone calls
2. Personal letters versus political speeches

SPEAKING AND LISTENING

Debating a Premise

A **premise** is a statement that can be **debated,** meaning that reasons can be given for and against it. For example, the following statement from the essay can be taken as a premise for debate: . . . "a personal letter [is] better than a phone call. . . ."

Your teacher will divide you into two debating teams and a group that will judge the debate. One team will argue for the premise and the other against it.

Brainstorm for arguments. Then choose a speaker to present your case. If you are a judge, rate the two speakers on a scale of 1 (worst) to 5 (best) in the following categories: quality of evidence; organization; speaking skill.

THINKING AND WRITING

Writing a Persuasive Essay

Imagine that your school is running a contest. The prize is a free day to visit a park or a museum, see a sports event, or attend a concert. To win you must convince the panel of teachers that what you choose to do is educational. First select the activity that you would like to pursue. Then list the educational advantages of this activity. Use your list to write a persuasive essay that will win you a free day. In revising the essay, put yourself in the panel's place. Stress the arguments that will be the most convincing to them.

2. He says that a political speech is so general that it "usually ends up saying nothing." In a personal letter, the writer can be specific and reveal his or her biases.

SPEAKING AND LISTENING
You might want to let shyer students be judges.

THINKING AND WRITING
Publishing Student Writing Challenge Imagine that you are a member of a writer's organization and, you want to encourage people to write personal letters. A local television station has agreed to give you a one-minute commercial. Brainstorm to think of a commercial that would catch people's attention and persuade them that letter writing is important. Then write a memo to the station manager describing your commercial. In revising your memo, be sure that your com-

mercial will be attention-getting and convincing.

Writing Across the Curriculum
Have students research and report on the letters of Abraham Lincoln, or any other important figure in American history. Consider notifying the social studies department about this assignment, so that social studies teachers can provide guidance for students.

Essays in the Content Areas

THE LIBRARY
J. Lawrence
National Museum of American Art
The Smithsonian Institution

More About the Author Isaac Asimov early discovered that he was an able and entertaining explainer of difficult subjects. He has said that explaining complex matters not only excites him but also enables him to clarify them to his own mind. Ask your students whether any of them have ever succeeded in explaining something difficult to a friend. How did they feel after doing so?

Skills Focus To illustrate outlining, as well as to ease the students into the selection, you might present the following outline of the "Not-a-Number."
I. Infinity
  A. No limits to addition—can always say *that number plus 1*
  B. Series of integers is infinite
    1. Negative numbers are infinite
    2. Positive imaginaries (+1i, +2i, +3i . . .) are infinite
    3. Even or odd numbers are infinite
    4. Any series of integers is infinite

Look For Point out that finding the main idea keeps a reader from getting confused by details and increases comprehension.

Writing/Prior Knowledge You might start this exercise with an example: Imagine purchasing a quart of milk by handing a clerk a five-dollar bill. Without a system of counting, how would you get change?

Vocabulary The vocabulary of the selection should present few problems. Your **less advanced** students, however, should be strongly encouraged to read slowly and carefully, and to reread a paragraph or section if they have any difficulty with basic comprehension.

386

GUIDE FOR READING

Endlessness

Isaac Asimov (1920–   ) was born in Russia and grew up in Brooklyn. He has a Ph.D. in biochemistry, a subject he taught at Boston University from 1949 to 1958, when he turned to full-time writing. It is said that since 1969 he has written a book a month. His nonfiction works, such as the essay you are about to read, are admirable for making scientific and technological subjects understandable to the general reader. In this essay, he explores the subject of endlessness. What does it mean for something to be without end?

Outlining

Outlining means organizing the content of a piece of writing to show the main ideas and supporting details. An outline might look as follows:
  I. First main topic
    A. First subtopic
      1. First supporting idea or detail
      2. Second supporting idea or detail
    B. Second subtopic
  II. Second main topic {The outline continues in the same way.}
  By dividing an essay into its main ideas and supporting details, you will understand and remember more of what you read.

Look For

As you read "Endlessness," pick out the main mathematical ideas of each of the four parts of the essay. Also, try to decide why other material is included—to explain, to illustrate, to clarify, or to achieve some other purpose.

Writing

Imagine a world without mathematics. Freewrite about the changes that would occur in your everyday life.

Vocabulary

Knowing the following words will help you as you read "Endlessness."
succession (sək sesh′ ən) *n.*: The act of coming after another in order (p. 388)
clamoring (klam′ ər iŋ) *v.*: Loudly demanding (p. 388)
expectantly (ik spek′ tənt lē) *adv.*: In a way that shows eager waiting (p. 389)
conceivable (kən sē′ və b'l) *adj.*: Imaginable (p. 389)
denumerable (di n o͞o′ mər ə b'l) *adj.*: Countable—said of a set whose elements can be put in one-to-one correspondence with the natural integers (p. 389)

Objectives
1 To practice outlining
2 To understand inductive reasoning
3 To understand mathematical terms
4 To write about mathematics

Support Material

Teaching Portfolio
Teacher Backup, p. 555
Grammar in Action Worksheet, *Using Transitions,* p. 559
Usage and Mechanics Worksheet, p. 561
Vocabulary Check, p. 562
Reading in the Content Areas Worksheet, *Outlining,* p. 563
Critical Thinking and Reading Worksheet, *Inductive Reasoning,* p. 564

Selection Test, p. 565
Art Transparency 11, *Numbers 0 to 9,* by Jasper Johns

Endlessness

Isaac Asimov

The "Not-a-Number"

Anyone thinking about numbers must come to the conclusion that there are a great many of them, and feel at a loss to express just how many. In poetry, one could make use of some simile: "as many as the sands of the sea"; "as numerous as the stars that shine and twinkle in the Milky Way."

To the mathematician, however, similes are of no use. To him, it merely seems that the integers are formed by beginning with one, adding one to that for the next number, and one to that for the next number, and so on. Since the mathematical rules do not set any limits to addition (*any* two numbers may be added) there can be no end to this process. After all, however large a number is named—*however* large—though it stretch in a line of small figures from here to the farthest star, it is always possible to say "that number plus one" and have a still higher number.

The series of integers, if written in order, 1, 2, 3 . . . is "infinite," a word coming from Latin words meaning "no end." Consequently, when we can write the series of numbers thus: 1, 2, 3 . . . , we mean "1, 2, 3, and so on endlessly."

In the same way if we consider the negative numbers, −1, −2, −3, and so on, we can see that they too go on forever and can be written: −1, −2, −3 . . . Similarly, the series of positive imaginaries may be written as +1i, +2i, +3i . . . , and the negative imaginaries as −1i, −2i, −3i . . .

Now let's consider another kind of series of integers. Let's think of the even numbers: 2, 4, 6, 8, and so on. How many even numbers are there?

One way of arguing this question would be to say: Well, the integers can be divided into odd numbers and even numbers alternately, so that in the first ten numbers there are five odds and five evens, in the first hundred numbers there are fifty odds and fifty evens, and so on. This sort of thing would go on no matter how many integers are taken. Therefore, the total number of even integers is half the total number of all integers.

But this is not so. The number of integers is infinite, and one cannot talk of "a half of infinity."

Instead, consider the even integers this way. The series 2, 4, 6, 8 . . . can continue endlessly. There is no "largest even number" any more than there is a "largest number." For though you name an even number written in small numerals from here to the farthest star, it is always possible to say "that number plus two." Hence the series of even numbers should be written: 2, 4, 6 . . .

In the same way, odd numbers are 1, 3, 5 . . . ; the series of numbers, counting by fives , are 5, 10, 15. . . ; and the series of numbers counting by millions are 1000000, 2000000, 3000000 . . . All these series of integers are endless and that is all that infinity (or an infinite number) means.

Counting Without Counting

But this may not satisfy you. Surely, you may be thinking, even though the series of even numbers is endless and the series of all

Endlessness 387

387

Presentation

Motivation/Prior Knowledge You might write the word *infinity* on the board and ask the class what ideas or impressions the word calls up. You might then ask if something can be infinitely small. Tell them that Asimov's selection will give them new insights into the notion of infinity and endlessness.

Master Teacher Note Perhaps your best teaching strategy, especially with **less advanced** students, will be to relate each self-contained section of the essay to the word *infinity*. You might frequently ask such questions as *How does this section help explain what infinity is?* and *What idea about infinity do you think Asimov is leading up to?*

Purpose-Setting Question Does this essay change any of your ideas about reality? If it does, describe the change in your thinking.

1 **Clarification** Write a large number on the board; for example, 178,000,000,000,000 (one hundred and seventy-eight trillion). Ask, "Who can make this a larger number? How?" Point out that changing the last "0" to "1" would suffice.

2 **Reading Strategy** To check comprehension of this paragraph and the preceding four present this problem: A friend says, "If you count from 1 to 10 there are ten numbers, but only five even numbers—half as many. So if you keep counting there will always be half as many even numbers as even plus odd numbers. That's common sense." How would you prove him wrong?

Master Teacher Note You might set the tone for this essay by leading the class in a discussion about numbers. Show students Art Transparency 11, *Numbers 0 to 9* by Jasper Johns, on the overhead projector. Ask them to identify all of the numbers in the painting. What other unusual uses for numbers are there? What difficulties would we face if we had no concept of numbers?

ORPHEAN ELEGY 1, 1978
Bridget Riley
Rowan Gallery

integers is endless, the fact still remains that there are only half as many even numbers as there are all integers, and that there are only a millionth as many even-million numbers. It stands to reason!

(Never trust an argument *only* because it stands to reason. It stands to reason that if a man is facing north, his back is toward the south. However, if he's standing at the South Pole and is facing north, his back is also toward the north.)

Well, then, let's settle the matter by finding out how many even numbers there are compared with all the integers. How, if the quantity is endless? Why, we'll count.

Let's first see what we mean by counting. In the ordinary meaning of the word, we count objects by assigning each one a number in succession. This object is number one, that is number two, the other is number three, and so on. When we finish, if the last object was assigned number ten, then there are ten objects.

But can we count without numbers? So used are we to numbers for the purpose, that this sounds as though I were asking, Can we count without counting?—and yet we can. | 3

Suppose you have a number of lollipops (you don't know how many) and a crowd of clamoring children (you don't know how many). You distribute the lollipops, one to a child, and when you are finished, all the children have lollipops and you still have additional lollipops in your hand. Obviously, then, even without counting in the ordinary

Grammar in Action

Transitions are words that help make smooth, clear connections between ideas while pointing out the logical relationship between the ideas. Writers use transitions to denote spatial order, chronological order, order of importance, comparison and contrast order, or other logical orders. Notice how Isaac Asimov's use of transitions adds unity and clarity to the following passage:

But if, . . . each child had a lollipop, and there were no children left unsatisfied and no lollipops left in your hand, *then* you would know . . . that the number of children was equal to the number of lollipops.

Through his initial transition, Asimov alerts the reader that a contrasting idea is being presented; his next transition helps the reader see the chronological order of the ideas. By using transitions, he connects his ideas and makes clear their relationship.

Student Activity 1. Find six different transitions in the selection and tell whether each points out chronological order, spatial order, order of importance, comparison and contrast order, or another logical order.

fashion, you know there were more lollipops than children. If, on the other hand, you ran out of lollipops while some children still stood expectantly waiting, you would know there were more children than lollipops.

But if, at the conclusion of the distribution, each child had a lollipop, and there were no children left unsatisfied and no lollipops left in your hand, then you would know beyond the shadow of a doubt, and without ever having counted in the usual fashion, that the number of children was equal to the number of lollipops.

This way of counting, then, which consists of lining up two series (one of children and one of lollipops; or one of all integers and one of even numbers) will tell you whether the two series are equal or unequal; and, if unequal, which is the larger.

Suppose we line up the series of all integers and all even numbers, then, as follows:

$$1\ 2\ 3\ 4\ 5\ 6\ 7\ 8\ 9\ 10\ .\ .\ .$$
$$\updownarrow\ \updownarrow\ \updownarrow\ \updownarrow\ \updownarrow\ \updownarrow\ \updownarrow\ \updownarrow\ \updownarrow\ \updownarrow$$
$$2\ 4\ 6\ 8\ 10\ 12\ 14\ 16\ 18\ 20\ .\ .\ .$$

As you see there is an even number for every conceivable integer, and you can obtain the even number by simply doubling the integer. No matter how far you go, no integer need be omitted and no even number is missing. (Every child, in other words, is being satisfied with a lollipop.) At no point, no matter how far you go, will you find an integer for which you can't write an even number, and each integer (no matter how many you've gone through) has a different even number attached to it.

Does this mean that there are exactly as many even numbers as there are integers all together? Well, the phrase "as many" doesn't really have the usual everyday meaning when we're talking about things that are endless. Instead it is more proper to say that the series of even numbers is "in one-to-one corre-

4

spondence" with the series of all integers; meaning that the even numbers can be lined up systematically with the integers so that there is one of the first series for every one of the second and vice versa.

You can also set up a series of numbers counting by millions and compare it with the series of all integers in the same way. For every integer there's an even-million number obtained by multiplying the integer by a million. For 1 there's 1000000, for 6 there's 6000000, for 2873 there's 2873000000 and so on. So there are "as many" numbers counting by a million as there are integers altogether. Or, at least, the two series are in one-to-one correspondence. Any series of numbers that is in one-to-one correspondence with the series of integers is said to be "denumerable." And the set of integers is also called "denumerable."

5

The Infinite in a Nutshell

6

Of course, the "infinite" gives one a notion of vastness and foreverness. It may even seem to you to have no usefulness.

However, even if we concerned ourselves only with small numbers, notions of "infinity" would crop up. For instance, suppose we were to divide 1 by $\frac{1}{10}$. Remembering the reciprocal rule, this is the same as 1×10 and therefore $1 \div \frac{1}{10} = 10$. Similarly, $1 \div \frac{1}{100} = 100$, and $1 \div \frac{1}{1000} = 1000$.

In fact, the smaller you make your divisor, the larger your quotient becomes.

Indeed, when you divide 1 (or any number) by a series of numbers that grow smaller and smaller, then the quotient grows larger and larger, and as the divisor grows endlessly small, the answer grows endlessly large.

7

Endlessness 389

4 **Literary Focus** Analogies involving simple, everyday matters are an excellent way to explain the unfamiliar or abstract, as in mathematical writing. Lead students to understand this expository method by asking, "Why was Asimov talking about lollipops? How does it relate to his main point—and what is the main point?"

5 **Critical Thinking and Reading** Ask, "Do these sentences introduce a new idea, or do they simply illustrate an idea already presented?" (The latter) You might then ask your **more advanced** students to restate the idea being illustrated ("that the series of even numbers is in one-to-one correspondence with the series of all integers").

6 **Reading Strategy** Suggest that students think about this section title. What does "Nutshell" suggest? What might this part of the essay be about?

7 **Discussion** Does this paragraph give you any hint of an answer to the preceding question?

Student Activity 2. Copy the following paragraph, filling in the blanks with the appropriate transitions from those listed below.

| before | first | while | also | until |
| after | finally | soon | then | |

Making sloppy joes is easy when you use a canned sauce. _____, you brown one pound of ground meat in a skillet. _____ it is browned, pour off any grease that accumulated as you cooked it. _____ stir in one can of sloppy joe sauce. Allow this mixture to simmer for five minutes. _____ it is simmering, warm hamburger buns in the oven or microwave oven. _____, spread the sloppy joe mixture on the buns for a delectable treat.

8 Challenge Ask for volunteers to explain, using fractions, the concept *endlessly small*.

9 Discussion Why does Asimov include these remarks about 0? Do they relate to anything said earlier? ("Surely, smallness has an end at zero"—which Asimov rejects.)

10 Challenge Ask students to respond to this challenge: "Infinity is big. How can there be infinite smallness? How can there be *both* infinite smallness and infinite largeness?" You can help your **less advanced** students by asking, "What did we learn that we can do to any whole number, however small, or any fraction, however small?"

However, what, you may wonder, is meant by "endlessly small"? Surely smallness has an end at zero. Ah, but smallness may be expressed in the form of a fraction. Thus $\frac{1}{10}$ is a small number, $\frac{1}{100}$ is smaller, $\frac{1}{1000}$ is smaller still. There is no limit to the smallness as you increase the number of zeros to $\frac{1}{100000000000000000}$ . . . for no matter how far you increase it you never quite reach zero.

We may therefore also say: When you divide 1 (or any number) by a series of numbers that grows larger and larger, then the quotient grows smaller and smaller, and as the divisor grows endlessly large, the answer grows endlessly small.

Note, however, that we can never divide any number by 0. This operation is excluded from mathematics. And for a very good reason. What number, for instance, would be the quotient if we tried to divide 6, say, by 0? We would have $\frac{6}{0}=$? In other words, what number *times* zero comes out 6? There is no such number, since every number times 0 is 0. So we can never divide any number by 0.

The interval between any two numbers, say between 1 and 2, can be divided into any number of fractions by breaking it up into millionths, or trillionths, and each trillionth into trillionths and so on. This can be done for any smaller interval, such as that between $\frac{1}{4}$ and $\frac{1}{2}$ or between 0.0000000 and 0.0000001.

And yet mathematicians have managed to show that all conceivable fractions (that is, all rational numbers) can be arranged in such a way that a one-to-one correspondence can be set up with the series of integers. For every integer there will be a fraction, and vice versa, with no integers left out and no fractions left out. The series of all possible fractions is therefore denumerable.

Closer and Closer and Closer . . .

Consider a series of fractions like this: $\frac{1}{2}, \frac{1}{4}, \frac{1}{8}, \frac{1}{16}, \frac{1}{32}, \frac{1}{64}, \frac{1}{128}, \frac{1}{256}, \frac{1}{512},$ and so on endlessly.

Notice that each fraction is one-half the size of the preceding fraction, since the denominator doubles each time. (After all, if you take any of the fractions in the series, say $\frac{1}{128}$, and divide it by 2, that is the same as multiplying it by $\frac{1}{2}$, and $\frac{1}{128} \times \frac{1}{2} = \frac{1}{256}$, the denominator doubling.)

Although the fractions get continually smaller, the series can be considered endless because no matter how small the fractions get, it is always possible to multiply the denominator by 2 and get a still smaller fraction and the next in the series. Furthermore, the fractions never quite reach zero because the denominator can get larger endlessly and it is only if an end could be reached (which it can't) that the fraction could reach zero.

The question is, What is the sum of all those fractions? It might seem that the sum of an endless series of numbers must be endlessly large ("it stands to reason") but let's start adding, anyway.

First $\frac{1}{2}$ plus $\frac{1}{4}$ is $\frac{3}{4}$. Add $\frac{1}{8}$ and the sum is $\frac{7}{8}$; add $\frac{1}{16}$ and the sum is $\frac{15}{16}$; and $\frac{1}{32}$ and the sum is $\frac{31}{32}$, and so on.

Notice that after the first two terms of the series are added, the sum is $\frac{3}{4}$ which is only $\frac{1}{4}$ short of 1. Addition of the third term

390 *Nonfiction*

REYTEY, 1968
Victor Vasarely
Solomon R. Guggenheim Museum

gives a sum that is only $\frac{1}{8}$ short of 1. The next term gives a sum that is only $\frac{1}{16}$ short of 1, then $\frac{1}{32}$, $\frac{1}{64}$, and so on.

In other words, as you sum up more and more terms of that series of fractions, you get closer and closer to 1, as close as you want, to within a millionth of one, a trillionth of one, a trillionth of a trillionth of one. You get closer and closer and closer and closer to 1, but you *never quite reach 1.*

Mathematicians express this by saying that the sum of the endless series of fractions $\frac{1}{2}$, $\frac{1}{4}$, $\frac{1}{8}$ . . . "approaches 1 as a limit."

This is an example of a "converging series," that is, a series with an endless number of members but with a total sum that approaches an ordinary number (a "finite" number) as a limit.

The Greeks discovered such converging series but were so impressed with the endlessness of the terms of the series that they did not realize that the sum might not be endless. Consequently, a Greek named Zeno[1] set up a number of problems called "paradoxes"[2] which seemed to disprove things that were obviously true. He "disproved," for instance, that motion was possible. These paradoxes were famous for thousands of

---

1. Zeno (zē′ no)
2. paradoxes (par′ ə däks′ iz) *n.*: Statements that seem to contain opposite meanings or to be unbelievable.

Endlessness 391

Humanities Note

Fine art, *Reytey,* 1968, by Victor Vasarely. Vasarely (1908–   ) was born in Hungary. He was a commercial artist until the 1940's, when he decided to paint. He is known for the complex color gradations of his paintings and for technical proficiency, which probably derives from his commercial-art work.

1. How would you describe the effect, or effects, of this painting?
2. Does your response, or the way you see it, change while you are looking at it?
3. Which of the two paintings that accompany "Endlessness" do you prefer? Why?

11 Challenge In math the term *converging* means "approaching a definite limit." If you were asked to explain in your own words what a converging series is, what would you say? What is the meaning of the section title?

12 Enrichment Zeno of Elea (490 B.C.?–430 B.C.?) tried to prove that motion, change, and plurality (the existence of numerous different things) are impossible. He devised four paradoxes concerning motion. In one of them he argues that a runner can never reach the end of a race course: the runner completes half the course, then half of the remaining half, half of the remaining quarter, and so on, never quite reaching the end. Philosophers and scientists still grapple with Zeno's paradoxes.

13 Challenge Before reading further, you might invite **more advanced** students to suggest how they would establish this paradox.

14 Discussion Might it be possible to disprove Zeno's paradox without using mathematics?

Challenge Ask your **more advanced** students if any of them can disprove Asimov and reestablish Zeno.

Reader's Response What was the most interesting information you learned from "Endlessness"? Why?

years, but all vanished as soon as the truth about converging series was realized.

Zeno's most famous paradox is called "Achilles[3] and the Tortoise." Achilles was a Homeric[4] hero renowned for his swiftness, and a tortoise is an animal renowned for its slowness. Nevertheless, Zeno set out to demonstrate that in a race in which the tortoise is given a head start, Achilles could never overtake the tortoise.

Suppose, for instance, that Achilles can run ten times as fast as the tortoise and that the tortoise is given a hundred-yard head start. In a few racing strides, Achilles wipes out that hundred-yard handicap, but in that time, the tortoise, traveling at one-tenth Achilles's speed (pretty darned fast for a tortoise), has moved on ten yards. Achilles next makes up that ten yards, but in that time the tortoise has moved one yard further. Achilles covers that one yard, and the tortoise has traveled an additional tenth of a yard. Achilles—

But you see how it is. Achilles keeps advancing, but so does the tortoise, and Achilles never catches up. Furthermore, since you could argue the same way, however small the tortoise's head start—one foot or one inch—Achilles could never make up any head start, however small. And this means that motion is impossible.

Of course, you know that Achilles *could* overtake the tortoise and motion *is* possible. Zeno's "proof" is therefore a paradox.

Now, then, what's wrong with Zeno's proof? Let's see. Suppose Achilles could run

ten yards per second and the tortoise one yard per second. Achilles makes up the original hundred-yard head start in 10 seconds during which time the tortoise travels ten yards. Achilles makes up the ten yards in 1 second, during which time the tortoise travels one yard. Achilles makes up the one yard in 0.1 second during which time the tortoise travels a tenth of a yard.

In other words, the time taken for Achilles to cover each of the successive head starts of the turtle forms a series that looks like this: 10, 1, 0.1, 0.01, 0.001, 0.0001, 0.00001, and so on.

How much time does it take for Achilles to make up all the head starts? Since there are an endless number of terms in this Zeno series, Zeno assumed the total sum was infinite. He did not realize that some series of endless numbers of terms "converge" and have a finite sum.

For instance, the sum of the first two terms in the Zeno series above is 11; the sum of the first three is 11.1; of the first four, 11.11; of the first five, 11.111 and so on. As you see, if you add up all the endless series of terms, you get an endless decimal as the sum; 11.1111111111111111111 . . . and so on forever.

But if you work out the decimal equivalent of the number $11\frac{1}{9}$, you find that it also is the endlessly repeating decimal 11.1111111111111111111111111 . . . and so on forever.

The sum of the Zeno series is therefore $11\frac{1}{9}$ seconds and that is the time in which Achilles will overtake and pass the tortoise even though he has to work his way through an endless series of continually smaller head starts that the tortoise maintains. He *will* overtake the tortoise after all; motion *is* possible, and we can all relax.

---

3. Achilles (ə kil′ ēz): A legendary Greek hero who fought in the Trojan War, which the Greeks waged against the city of Troy in Asia Minor about 3,000 years ago.
4. Homeric (hō mer′ ik) *adj.*: The Greek poet Homer is said to have lived during the 8th century B.C. He wrote two epic poems, the *Iliad* and the *Odyssey*, about the Trojan War and the events that occurred afterward.

Closure and Extension

3. It seemed to disprove that motion is possible.

ANSWERS TO THINKING ABOUT THE SELECTION
Recalling

1. Infinity means a series of numbers that has no end.
2. A converging series is a series with an endless number of members but with a total sum that approaches an ordinary number as a limit.

THINKING ABOUT THE SELECTION

Recalling

1. In mathematics, what does infinity mean?
2. What is a converging series?
3. What did Zeno's paradox seem to disprove?
4. How does Asimov disprove Zeno's paradox?

Interpreting

5. What does Asimov mean by "counting without counting"?
6. How does Asimov use fractions to demonstrate the concept of the "endlessly small"?

Applying

7. What new ideas about infinity do you now have as a result of reading "Endlessness"?

READING IN THE CONTENT AREAS

Outlining

Outlining means organizing the content of a piece of writing to show the main ideas and supporting details. For example, the following is an outline of the first part of "Endlessness."

   I. Infinity
      A. Poet—can use simile to show it
      B. Mathematician—cannot use simile
         1. No limits to addition
         2. Any series of integers is infinite—can always be added to

Make an outline of the next part of the essay, headed "Counting Without Counting."

CRITICAL THINKING AND READING

Explaining Mathematics Inductively

Inductive reasoning means drawing a general conclusion from particular facts or cases. In "Endlessness," Asimov uses inductive reasoning to explain the general concepts with which his essay is concerned. For example, in the first part he wishes to explain the general concept that the total number of even integers is infinite, like the total number of all integers. He does so by reasoning from a particular case.

> The series 2, 4, 6, 8 . . . can continue endlessly . . . [because] it is always possible to say "that [even] number plus two."

1. How does Asimov use inductive reasoning to show that the series of fractions 1/2, 1/4, 1/8 . . . will never reach zero?
2. How does he use inductive reasoning to show that the sum total of all fractions in this series will never quite reach one?

UNDERSTANDING LANGUAGE

Understanding Mathematical Terms

Mathematical terms need to be understood exactly. When you come upon an unfamiliar term, try to figure out its meaning from the way it is used—from its context. When, for example, Asimov says that "the smaller you make your divisor, the larger your quotient becomes," the context helps to make clear what "divisor" and "quotient" mean. He says, "Similarly $1 \div 1/100 = 100$, and $1 \div 1/1000 = 1000$." This context clue suggests that a divisor is a number by which another number is divided and a quotient is the result obtained by the division. If, however, you cannot figure out from context what a math term means, you should consult a math book.

1. What is the difference between an integer and a number?
2. What is a paradox? What is an example of a paradox?

THINKING AND WRITING

Writing About Mathematics

Imagine that you are visiting a planet that has not discovered counting. Write an essay explaining the concept of counting to the people living on the planet. Revise your essay to make sure your explanation is clear.

Endlessness 393

(Answers begin on p. 392.)

  B. 1 2 3 4 5
      2 4 6 8 10
 II. An even number exists for every conceivable integer.
   A. At no point can an integer be found for which you can't write an even number.
   B. Series of even numbers is in one-to-one correspondence with series of all integers.
   C. Other series of numbers (e.g., counting by millions) can be in one-to-one correspondence with series of all integers (any such series is called *denumerable*).

ANSWERS TO CRITICAL THINKING AND READING

1. He uses particular facts—a series of fractions that can be made endlessly small by doubling the denominator—to arrive at a general conclusion: that such a series will never reach an end at zero.
2. He again uses particular facts—the sum of the fractions $\frac{1}{2}$, $\frac{1}{4}$, $\frac{1}{8}$...—to arrive at the general conclusion that such a series can only approach 1 as a limit but can never reach it.

ANSWERS TO UNDERSTANDING LANGUAGE

1. An integer is a positive or negative whole number or zero; for example $+1$, -1, or 0. A number is generally defined as any *real number;* for example, $+1$, -1, 0, $\frac{1}{2}$, or $.5$. The term *number* excludes only imaginary numbers. An integer, therefore, is one type of number.
2. As used in Asimov's essay, a paradox is a problem consisting of a statement that contradicts, or declares false, what is obviously true. The statement that motion is impossible is a paradox.

---

4. He disproved it by showing that the series of time measurements Zeno used was a converging series with a maximum absolute value, such as $11\frac{1}{9}$ seconds when Asimov's figures are used.

Interpreting

5. "Counting without counting" means lining up two series of numbers to determine if either series is greater than, less than, or equal to the other series.
6. He shows that smallness may be expressed fractionally and that any fraction can be made endlessly small because its divisor can be made endlessly large. Therefore, the concept of the endlessly small is established.

Applying

7. Answers will differ, but students should at least see that the concept of infinity applies not only to a series of ever larger numbers but also to a series of ever smaller numbers and to a converging series.

ANSWERS TO READING IN THE CONTENT AREAS

Student outlines may differ. The following, however, is one possible outline.

  I. Counting without counting = lining up two series to determine whether they are equal or unequal.
    A. Children
      Lollipops

THINKING AND WRITING

Publishing Student Writing Having students read their essays aloud should be both interesting and entertaining. Have listening students record at least one noteworthy feature of each essay.

Focus

More About the Author You might mention to your students that the term *Renaissance man* could be applied to H. N. Levitt. This term denotes a man who is accomplished in different areas of life. For Levitt, these areas include military life, education, the theater, painting, and art criticism. Consider having your class discuss whether it is better to strive for excellence in one area of life or to seek excellence in several different areas.

Skills Focus Suggest that your students look at the title, then at the paintings on page 396 and page 398 and form their own questions. Have volunteers tell the class what questions they would hope Levitt's essay will answer.

Look For It would be helpful to all your students, but especially to your **less advanced** ones, to show how these questions can be used to draw out most of the information in an actual news story from a local newspaper.

Writing/Prior Knowledge Help your class with this exercise by asking for volunteers to give their immediate reactions to the paintings.

Vocabulary You might want to introduce students to the term *realism,* the representation of life as an artist believes it really is. Explain that Homer's most famous paintings are usually classified as realistic.

Winslow Homer: America's Greatest Painter

H. N. Levitt (1920–   ) was born and raised in New York City. During World War II he was a naval officer. After the war, he pursued a career as a playwright and college professor of drama. However, he has always loved the visual arts too. He learned how to paint with watercolors at a well-known art school, and he has written many magazine articles about painters. In this article he tells why he considers Winslow Homer "America's Greatest Painter."

Setting a Purpose for Reading

A **purpose** is a reason for doing something. You can learn more from any work of nonfiction if you set a purpose for your reading before you start. One strategy for setting a goal is to imagine that you are a newspaper reporter gathering information for a story. Reading "Winslow Homer: America's Greatest Painter" as a reporter, for instance, you would use the journalistic formula *who? what? when? where? why?* and *how?* You might wonder *who* Winslow Homer was, *what* he did, *when* and *where* he lived, *how* he worked, and *why* he is considered a great painter.

Your information about Homer will not be complete, however, unless you look at his paintings (pages 396 and 398). Glancing at them before you begin will give you a general sense of his art.

Look For

As you read look for answers to the questions *who? what? when? where?* and *why?* in regard to Winslow Homer.

Writing

Before starting, look at Homer's paintings on pages 396 and 398. Choose one. Study it carefully and freewrite about it. You might want to consider the subjects he paints, the colors he uses, and the feelings he communicates.

Vocabulary

Knowing the following words will help you as you read "Winslow Homer: America's Greatest Painter."

cantankerous (kan taŋ′ kər əs) *adj.*: Bad-tempered (p. 395)

subtle (sut′ 'l) *adj.*: Delicately skillful or clever (p. 395)

brutality (brōō tal′ ə tē) *n.*: Violence; harshness (p. 396)

vanquished (vaŋ′ kwisht) *n.*: The person defeated (usually a verb) (p. 397)

serenity (sə ren′ ə tē) *n.*: Calmness (p. 397)

subservient (səb sur′ vē ənt) *adj.*: Inferior (p. 398)

Objectives

1 To set a purpose for reading
2 To evaluate art criticism
3 To learn about art terms
4 To write about a painting

Support Material

Teaching Portfolio

Teacher Backup, p. 567

Grammar in Action Worksheet, *Recognizing the Three Degrees of Comparison,* p. 571

Usage and Mechanics Worksheet, p. 573

Vocabulary Check, p. 574

Reading in the Content Areas Worksheet, *Setting a Purpose for Reading,* p. 575

Language Worksheet, *Learning About Art Terms,* p. 576

Selection Test, p. 577

Art Transparency 12, *The Turtle Pond,* by Winslow Homer

Winslow Homer: America's Greatest Painter

H. N. Levitt

His oil paintings and watercolors are in all major American museums and collections today. But even when Winslow Homer was alive, they called him America's greatest painter.

That wasn't all they said about him. They also called him crusty, bad-tempered, cantankerous, grouchy, sour as a crab, and surly as a bear. He was all those things, and more.

His brother's wife—and Winslow's only female friend—thought Homer the most courteous gentleman she ever knew. She said he knew what he wanted in life, and he went about getting it without any fuss or feathers.

When it came to painting, he took five lessons, decided that was enough, then went on to become a self-taught genius.

Homer was born into a middle-class family on Feb. 24, 1836. The family lived near the harbor in Boston, so Homer's earliest memories were of ships, sailors, fishermen and the sea.

When he was six, the family moved to Cambridge, directly across the street from Harvard College. Sometimes Winslow's dad would suggest that the boy consider attending Harvard someday. But it was no use. All young Winslow wanted to do was fish and draw.

After a while, the family realized there was something special about Winslow, because that's all he would do—fish and draw, day in and day out, all year long.

But even if Homer had wanted to go to college, there would have been no money for it. When Homer was 13, his dad sold all and left to make his fortune in the California gold rush. He came back a few years later empty-handed.

But the family remained close. And once they realized how important art was to Homer, they encouraged it. In fact, his brothers secretly bought up his paintings at early exhibitions so he wouldn't get discouraged if no one else bought them. Those two brothers remained his best friends all his life.

When the Civil War broke out in 1861, Homer was a young artist already on his way to fame. As a freelance illustrator for *Harper's Weekly*, America's most important news magazine, he was considered one of the country's finest wood-block engravers.

In those days, an artist would cut illustrations into a wood block, which was then inked in black and printed on sheets of paper. Techniques like subtle shadowing and distant perspective were hard to achieve, but Homer's illustrations were unusually lively and strong.

Harper's Weekly offered Homer a good

PRISONERS FROM THE FRONT, 1866
Winslow Homer
The Metropolitan Museum of Art

job, and he could have remained a weekly illustrator all his life. But he wanted to work
for no one but himself, so he turned the offer
down.

Homer left New York to paint the war.
He joined Gen. George McClellan's Army of
the Potomac[1] as a freelance artist-correspon-
dent. He painted scenes at the siege of Yorktown[2] and did many drawings of Abraham
Lincoln, the tall, gaunt, serious president
who was desperately trying to keep the
Union together.

In a few short years, Homer's Civil War
paintings brought him fame at home and
abroad. He painted war as no other artist
ever had. He emphasized not brutality but
rather scenes of loneliness, camp life, endless waiting, and even horseplay on the
battlefield.

Homer was a Yankee,[3] but he showed
equal concern for soldiers from both the
North and South. His paintings did not glo-
rify war; they seemed to cry out for it to end.

His *Prisoners from the Front* made a rep-

---

1. Gen. George McClellan's Army of the Potomac:
McClellan served for a time as the general in chief of
the Union Army during the Civil War. The Union
Army in the East was known as the Army of the
Potomac.

2. Yorktown: Yorktown, Virginia, which Gen.
McClellan occupied on May 4, 1862.

3. Yankee: Here, a native or inhabitant of a
Northern state.

396 Nonfiction

utation overnight. This one painting, done in Homer's honest, realistic style, showed the common humanity that linked North and South, victor and vanquished, Americans all. Homer's war paintings give us the best record we have of how the Civil War soldier actually looked and acted.

After the war, railroads and new industries changed America from a rural to an industrial society almost overnight. But Homer paid no attention. He went back to painting the things he liked: country scenes, farmers, beautiful women in fashionable clothes, and kids at play.

He never painted kids with the gushy sentimentalism of other American painters. And he didn't look down on young people. His paintings showed what was then a typical American upbeat attitude marked by humor and innocence. The public loved it.

And then something strange happened. Homer stopped painting. For three years, his brushes sat idle. He left his studio for Europe, but avoided the art world in Paris. Instead, he went to Tynemouth, England, a small fishing port on the North Sea.

It was there, at Tynemouth, that Winslow Homer witnessed the fierce, day-to-day struggle of men and women against the sea. Their hard, bitter, dangerous lives made him think critically about his own life and work.

After that, women, children and country life appeared less often in his paintings. What replaced them was the harsh existence of men of the sea. These heroic people became, in his mind, the best examples of mankind. That's apparent in his famous painting *The Life Line.* To Homer, the sea had lost its serenity and had become a powerful force of nature.

Homer began painting larger pictures too, and his style became more bold and powerful. Some complained that his paintings now looked unfinished. But he didn't care. Nice finishing touches were no longer important.

Besides the sea and its people, Homer started painting scenes of the American wilderness. He did big, masculine pictures of hunting and fishing, canoeing the rapids, sitting around the campfire and trekking over rugged trails.

He painted large oils, but he also painted many watercolors. By the time he had hit his stride, he had become America's first great watercolor painter. It was he who developed the technique of using the white, unpainted paper as sparkling highlight.

Then, at 48, when he was selling just about everything he painted, he did another about-face.

He surprised his family, friends and fellow artists by turning his back on the city and the world of art. He packed up and left to spend the rest of his life—27 years—as a hermit on a rocky cliff overlooking the sea in Prouts Neck, Maine.

In typical, cantankerous, Yankee fashion, when asked how he could leave New York, the scene of his success, he said, "I left New York to escape jury duty."

In a more serious mood, he told his brother that his new, lonely life was the only setting in which he could do his work in peace, free from visitors and publicity seekers.

Winslow Homer finally came to love his life. It was at Prouts Neck that he finished one of his great masterpieces, *The Gulf Stream,* in 1899.

This painting showed a black man marooned in a broken-masted boat circled by sharks in the Gulf Stream.[4] It was an immediate sensation, but only one of a long series

---

4. Gulf Stream: The warm ocean current flowing from the Gulf of Mexico along the East Coast of the United States.

Winslow Homer: America's Greatest Painter 397

4 **Literary Focus** An essay concerned with art will normally attempt to describe and characterize individual works as well as entire bodies of work. Have students look at *Prisoners From the Front* in the light of Levitt's comment on it, and then evaluate the comment in the light of the painting. Do they agree with the comment? How would they characterize the painting in a sentence or two?

5 **Literary Focus** Point out that a sharp change in a person's—and especially an artist's—life and career is of special interest. Levitt focuses on just such a change in these paragraphs. Have students clarify just what the change was. How much of this change is explained? What is the explanation? What is not explained?

6 **Literary Focus** Levitt focuses again on a change in Homer's life. Have students state the change in their own words and explain it.

Student Activity 1. Find three examples from "Winslow Homer: America's Greatest Painter" where Levitt uses degrees of comparison. Identify which degree of comparison is used for each example.

Student Activity 2. Revise each sentence to correct the errors in degree.

1. When we measured them, we found that Frank was more big than Robert.

2. She was the best behaved child of the two.

3. It was the worse disaster in twenty years.

THE GULF STREAM, 1899
Winslow Homer
The Metropolitan Museum of Art

of oils and watercolors that Homer painted of American blacks. This was at a time when blacks were usually depicted as minstrel singers and servants, or in other subservient poses.

In his last years, Homer made another big change. Instead of painting scenes of men struggling against the sea and wilderness, he started painting the sea and wilderness alone.

Like a stubborn tree growing out of a rock, he stood on his lonely cliff and painted the sea, forever untamed and uncontrolled by man.

In 1910, just before he died, he wrote in a letter, "All is lovely outside my house and inside my house and myself." Winslow Homer was a simple, modest, unsentimental man—the kind of American we Americans like.

THINKING ABOUT THE SELECTION

Recalling

1. What scenes were part of Homer's first memories?
2. How did his family know there was "something special" about him?
3. In what way did the Civil War change Homer's life? What other turning points did he have in his life?
4. Why are Homer's Civil War paintings unusual? How did *Prisoners From the Front* affect his reputation?
5. How did his work change after he lived in Tynemouth, England?
6. Why did he leave New York City for Maine?

Interpreting

7. What do you think might have caused Homer to stop painting for three years?
8. How did Homer show his self-reliance and independent spirit throughout his life?
9. What does the author's last statement indicate about American values? Do you agree that these are values most Americans share? Support your answer.

Applying

10. Why do you think artists must have the ability to surprise the public?

READING IN THE CONTENT AREAS

Setting a Purpose for Reading

One way to set a purpose for reading is to pretend to be a reporter gathering information about a subject. After using this method with this essay about Winslow Homer, you should have the answers to the usual reporter's questions: Who? What? When? Where? Why? and How?

1. Who was Winslow Homer?
2. What did he do?
3. When and where did he work?
4. How did he work?
5. Why is he considered a great painter?

CRITICAL THINKING AND READING

Evaluating the Writer's Opinions

The writer, H. N. Levitt, comments specifically on the Homer paintings that accompany this essay. He says, for example, that *Prisoners From the Front* (page 396) is "honest" and "realistic," showing the "common humanity" of soldiers from both sides. You can evaluate the writer's opinions by looking carefully at the picture yourself.

1. Describe what is happening in the scene, identifying the soldiers from each side.
2. Consider whether the scene is "realistic." What leads you to think that Homer either changed it or painted it realistically?

UNDERSTANDING LANGUAGE

Learning About Art Terms

In discussing Winslow Homer and his work, the writer uses special words from the visual arts. Look up each of the following terms in the dictionary and explain how it relates to painting or drawing.

1. perspective
2. watercolor
3. shadowing
4. studio

THINKING AND WRITING

Writing About a Painting

Imagine that you are an editor putting together a book of Winslow Homer's paintings for junior high school students. You have been assigned to write several paragraphs to accompany *The Gulf Stream*. Before starting, review what H. N. Levitt said about Homer's career in general and this work in particular. Then look at the picture closely. List its important qualities. For instance, you might want to mention the drama of the scene, the portrayal of a black man, and the way Homer has painted the ocean. Consider whether the painting has a theme—an idea that it communicates. When revising, check your writing for clarity.

Winslow Homer: America's Greatest Painter 399

(Answers begin on p. 398.)

Applying

10. Suggested Response: Surprise attracts public attention and forestalls indifference.

ANSWERS TO READING IN THE CONTENT AREAS

1. He was a great American painter.
2. He was an illustrator, an engraver, and a painter of oils and watercolors.
3. He worked during the late nineteenth and early twentieth centuries in the northeastern region of the United States and, for a time, in England.
4. Answers will differ, though students should see that independence of approach and manner characterized his entire career.
5. He is considered great because of his honesty and realism, his originality, and of course his technical excellence.

ANSWERS TO CRITICAL THINKING AND READING

1. Union soldiers have captured Confederate soldiers. The three on the left are the Confederate captives; the one in the middle with a rifle is a Union soldier; on the right is a Union officer.
2. Suggested Response: The scene is realistic. The soldiers' expressions, the discarded weapons, the horses—all seem part of a scene Homer witnessed.

ANSWERS TO UNDERSTANDING LANGUAGE

1. perspective: The art of depicting subjects on a flat surface so that they appear to have depth and distance.
2. watercolor: The art of painting in watercolors or a painting done in watercolors.
3. shadowing: The technique of darkening an area in a drawing or painting.
4. studio: A room where an artist works.

to England, where he observed the harsh life of men and women struggling against the sea. He started to paint what he observed there. The next turning point came when he moved to Maine and his painting began to reflect his life there. Finally, in his last years, he started painting the sea and the wilderness without depicting people.

4. His Civil War paintings are unusual because he emphasized not brutality but scenes of loneliness, camp life, endless waiting, and horseplay. *Prisoners From the Front* established Homer's reputation as an accomplished painter.
5. He began to depict the harsh life of men and women battling the sea.
6. He felt that a lonely life there was necessary for his work.

Interpreting

7. Answers will differ, but one answer is that he was unsure what he wanted to do with his life and needed time to think about the direction his life should take.
8. He did not follow the ways of others. He lived and painted where and as he wished.
9. The statement reveals that Americans value modesty and simplicity and disdain vanity, conceit, affectation, and ornamentation. Student answers will differ, as will the reasons given.

THINKING AND WRITING

For help with this assignment, students can refer to Lesson 2, "Drafting and Revising," in the Handbook of Writing About Literature.

Focus

More About the Author Maxwell Nurnberg wrote a dozen books and numerous articles on language. All of his writings were intended to promote the cause of good English, and all are as humorous and lighthearted as they are informative. During the 1940's, he was the moderator of a radio series, *What's the Good Word*? He also wrote a well-received play inspired by his teaching experiences, *Chalk Dust*. Ask your students to suggest reasons why someone who took language so seriously should choose to write about it humorously.

Skills Focus You might want to emphasize that slow, intensive reading, with pauses for questions, is in fact a most efficient way to read. What the students gain in absorption and retention more than compensates for the time spent reading in this way. You might also have your students close their books, and then ask a few to distinguish between scanning and skimming.

Look For Allow students a few minutes to skim the selection. Then ask them to tell you what the general idea of it was.

Writing/Prior Knowledge You can help students get started by writing on the board some expression that struck you yourself. Then tell them what you found interesting about it.

Vocabulary The word *unique* is frequently misused—as when people say "very unique" or "slightly unique," or otherwise qualify the word. Point out that a thing is either unique or not unique. You might also explain that this word derives from *unus,* Latin for "one." Ask if any student can think of something that is truly unique in the strict sense of the word.

The Mystery and Wonder of Words

Maxwell Nurnberg (1897–1984) was born in Poland but lived much of his life in New York City. He was a brilliant student of language and, afterward, a much-respected teacher of it. For thirty-six years, he taught English in a New York City high school. Later, he was a professor of English at New York University and a lecturer at Brooklyn College. The title of the following essay, "The Mystery and Wonder of Words," reflects Nurnberg's lifelong fascination with language.

Varying Rates of Reading

Vary your reading rate with the kind of material you are reading. Usually choose among three kinds of reading: slow intensive reading, rapid skimming, and rapid scanning. **Reading intensively** means reading carefully and slowly. It involves stopping after each paragraph or brief section and asking yourself, "What have I just read?" **Scanning** means running your eyes over a page rapidly until you find specific information you are looking for. **Skimming** means reading quickly to get a general idea of what a book or selection is about.

Look For

Skim Nurnberg's essay to get an overview of it. Then read it intensively, pausing frequently to question yourself on what you have read. When you are answering the questions that follow the selection, going back to the article and scanning it may prove helpful.

Writing

Like the author, have you, too, been fascinated by language? Think of a word or expression you may have heard at some time that caused you to stop and think about it. What was the word or expression? What struck you about it as odd or interesting? Write about the thoughts that occurred to you about it.

Vocabulary

Knowing the following words will help you as you read "The Mystery and Wonder of Words."

convey (kən vā′) *v.*: Make known (p. 401)

aeons (ē′ ənz) *n.*: Very long periods of time (p. 401)

equivalent (i kwiv′ ə lənt) *n.*: A thing similar to another thing (p. 401)

distinctions (dis tiŋk′ shənz) *n.*: Differences of meaning (p. 403)

unique (yo͞o nēk′) *adj.*: Having no like or equal (p. 403)

amends (ə mendz′) *n.*: Things given or done to make up for injury or loss (p. 404)

Objectives

1 To learn when to use different rates of reading
2 To distinguish fact from speculation
3 To write a speculative story about the origins of an interjection

Support Material

Teaching Portfolio
Teacher Backup, p. 579
Grammar in Action Worksheet, *Making Subjects and Verbs Agree,* p. 583
Usage and Mechanics Worksheet, p. 585
Vocabulary Check, p. 586
Critical Thinking and Reading Worksheet, *Distinguishing Fact From Speculation,* p. 587

Language Worksheet, *Punctuating Interjections,* p. 588
Selection Test, p. 589

The Mystery and Wonder of Words

Maxwell Nurnberg

1 *How long a time lies in one little word!*
WILLIAM SHAKESPEARE: *King Richard II*

Millions of years ago, there were no words. There was no language. The first human beings, like animals, were probably able to make only those sounds that expressed the simplest feelings. They must have made sounds like the bark of a dog to convey excitement or like the purr of a cat to show contentment. Man was very much like Tennyson's

2 *An infant crying in the night;*
An infant crying for the light,
And with no language but a cry.

3 These sounds and cries nature gave to man as she gave him hands. Man's hands, however, were not by themselves powerful enough to conquer the earth and get from it everything that was needed. Therefore, he had to invent tools made out of wood and stone to extend the power of his hands.

In the same way man had somehow to create or invent words, tools made from sounds, to extend his power of communication with others, to share with them some of the ideas that lay imprisoned in his brain.

One day, aeons ago, it is possible that an early ancestor of ours, running barefoot on the forest floor, suddenly happened to step on a sharp stone. Undoubtedly he uttered a startled, piercing cry of pain—the primitive equivalent of a word like *Ouch!* He was probably frightened by his outburst, yet somehow excited by it too.

Imagine him later that day back in his cave. Remembering the sharpness of the pain, he was eager to let the others know all about his experience. As he acted out his story for them with gestures, he came to his **4** startled outcry. Having a sense of the dramatic, he pointed to the sole of his injured foot and, to make his story more vivid, let out the same piercing sound he had made at the time of his accident.

The story was an instant success. He was made to tell it over and over again, the others joining in when he came to the "sound effect." After frequent repetitions we can see how the sound became a word that they could now all use. And it probably had many meanings. Depending on the particular gesture that accompanied it, the word could mean "pain" or "wound" or "blood" or "sharp stone" or even "sole of a foot"!

How do we know all this? We don't. Through the years, students of language have developed many theories, pure guesses. This is my guess.

However, at this point science can step in to help us with part of the story of lan-

The Mystery and Wonder of Words *401*

OWHI IN SAN PAO, 1951
Stuart Davis
The Whitney Museum of American Art

guage. For there is a theory which says, "Ontogeny[1] recapitulates phylogeny."[2] Simply stated, it tells us that the individual, especially in his earliest stages, goes through a development similar to those stages that the human race has gone through. If, therefore, we study how a little child's language develops, it may give us some idea of how language itself developed.

Let us take the case of Ellen. She was a big-city child, surrounded constantly by passing automobiles and trucks. Therefore, the first word she learned—it was really a sentence—was *It's a car*. She would call attention to each passing vehicle proudly with *It's a car*.

On her first day in the country, she saw an ant crawl by. Her pudgy little finger shot out and triumphantly she announced, "It's a

---

1. **ontogeny** (än täj′ ə nē) *n.*: The life cycle of a single organism or individual.
2. **phylogeny** (fī läj′ ə nē) *n.*: The development of a species or group.

car." For Ellen, anything that moved was a car. No distinctions or refinements were made. *It's-a-car* was a general word to describe any moving object.

In the same way, the *ouch* word of our earliest ancestors was a general word and often covered a lot of ground. Later, much later, more specific words were developed. *Ouch* remained the word for a cry of pain and other words were found for stone and sharp and pain and wound and blood and sole that had specific, unique meanings. Today, Webster's Third New International Dictionary contains 450,000 separate entries. And there exist in the world today about 2,500 languages!

In his play *Prometheus*[3] *Bound*, Robert Lowell[4] has Prometheus say:

"Before I made men talk and write with words, knowledge dropped like a dry stick into the fire of their memories, fed that fading blaze an instant, then died without leaving an ash behind."

It is written words that have made man's memories live on in others and have fed the flame of knowledge which lighted the avenues to all of man's serious thinking and his great achievements.

For example, you press a button and where there was darkness before there is now light. You press another button and you shoot up eighty floors, almost to the top of the Empire State Building. You turn a dial in your living room and you are present at an event taking place thousands of miles away. These miracles, which have taken millions of years to achieve, are taken for granted by all of us.

In the same way, we take for granted another miracle—the words we speak, read, and write so naturally and effortlessly. Let's take a very simple example. Every morning, wherever English is spoken, people sit down to what they call breakfast. Few of us ever think of the word as meaning more than merely some fruit juice, a cereal or egg, toast, and a hot drink. Yet if you look closely at the word, you see that it means that you are "breaking your fast," eating for the first time since the evening before.

You *don* (do on) your clothes before sitting down to breakfast and you may *doff* (do off) your hat when you say goodbye. But what are you saying when you say goodbye? In Shakespeare's plays you will find that characters, on leaving one another, sometimes say, "God be wi' ye!" (God be with you!) Now say *God be wi' ye* fast. Faster. Faster still. In a few seconds you have covered hundreds of years and you have arrived at the modern *goodbye*. Thus whenever you say goodbye you are really saying "God be with you."

In most modern languages of Western Europe the formal words of farewell have God in them. The French say *Adieu*[5]; so do the Germans and Austrians, though they pronounce it a little differently. The Spaniards say, *Adios*[6] and the Italians, *Addio*.[7] All of these words come from the Latin word for a god, *deus*,[8] which comes from the Greek *theos*,[9] which comes from—but that's another story.

You may eat breakfast with, or say goodbye to, a *companion*. Let's not take that word for granted. Let's look into it. *Compan-*

---

3. **Prometheus** (prə mē' thē əs): In Greek mythology, a titan who stole fire from heaven for the benefit of mankind. To punish him, Zeus chained him to a rock, where a vulture attacked him each day.
4. **Robert Lowell** (1917–1977): American poet and dramatist.

5. **Adieu:** Pronounced ə dyoo'.
6. **Adios:** Pronounced a dē ōs'.
7. **Addio:** Pronounced a dē' o.
8. **deus:** Pronounced dā oos.
9. **theos:** Pronounced thē' əs.

The Mystery and Wonder of Words 403

6 Critical Thinking and Reading What point is Nurnberg making here? Suggest that the example, or "case," of Ellen provides a clue.

7 Discussion In these three paragraphs the author discusses a number of words, both English and foreign. How does he analyze the English words, and what does he discover about them? What does he reveal about the foreign words for farewell?

Student Activity 1. Find three other sentences where Nurnberg separates the subject and verb by a prepositional phrase. Identify the subject and verb in each sentence and tell whether they are singular or plural.

Student Activity 2. On your paper write the verb in parentheses that agrees in number with the subject.

1. Many people in our country (thinks, think) jogging is a good way to keep fit.

2. Few of us ever (dreams, dream) of climbing the highest mountains in the world.

3. The life cycle of butterflies (is, are) fascinating and (seems, seem) unbelievably complex.

THE PARIS BIT, 1959
Stuart Davis
The Whitney Museum of American Art

ion has the structure of most English words of three syllables or more: a prefix, *com*; a root, *pan*; a suffix, *ion*.

You have seen the prefix *com* in words like *combine, combat* (fight *with*), *compose* (put *together*), and you probably know that *com* is a prefix meaning "with" or "together." The suffix *ion* shows that the word is a noun.

But what does the all-important middle part *pan* mean? It comes from a Latin word *panis*, appearing in French as *pain* (pronounced "paa" with a nasal twist at the end), in Spanish as *pan*, and in Italian as *pane* (pronounced "pah-nay") and it means "bread." Is there a better way to describe a companion than to say that he is one with whom we share our bread?

You probably know that the word *alphabet* is made up of the first two Greek letters—*alpha* and *beta*. But do you know that the word atone really means "at one"? If you atone, if you make amends, for something you have done, you feel "at one" again with whomever you may have offended.

If all you know about a word is its spelling and its meaning, you sometimes don't know the half of it. As a matter of fact, you don't know the most interesting half of it. You don't know who its parents are, who its relatives are, what country it was born in, or what picture may be hidden somewhere within it. By the way, the word *infant* comes from Latin *in*, "not," plus *fant*, "speaking." Strictly speaking, therefore, you are no longer an infant when you begin to speak.

404   *Nonfiction*

Reader's Response If you had to choose one word and find its origins, which word would you choose? Why?

THINKING ABOUT THE SELECTION
Recalling

1. Why did human beings invent words?
2. Why is the word *breakfast* used for morning meals?
3. What earlier expression is the basis of the word *goodbye*?
4. When you look into the word parts (prefix, root, and suffix) that make up *companion,* what underlying meaning is revealed?

Interpreting

5. Explain the opening quotation from Shakespeare—"How long a time lies in one little word!" In what way could this quotation be considered a summary of the entire essay?
6. What is the similarity between the invention of words and the invention of tools?
7. What point does Nurnberg make by his analysis of such words as *breakfast, goodbye,* and *companion*?
8. According to Nurnberg, why are you "no longer an infant when you begin to speak"?

Applying

9. Henry Ward Beecher once wrote, "All words are pegs to hang ideas on." What is the meaning of this quotation? Do you think Nurnberg would agree with its main idea? Why or why not?

READING IN THE CONTENT AREAS
Varying Rates of Reading

Slow, careful, intensive reading, rapid skimming, and rapid scanning are three useful ways of reading depending on what you are reading and why you are reading it.

Think of all the different kinds of reading you do. Then answer the following questions.

1. For what kinds of reading can you appropriately use skimming?

2. What kinds of material would you scan?
3. What kinds of material would you read intensively?

CRITICAL THINKING AND READING
Distinguishing Fact from Speculation

A statement of **fact** is a statement that can be proved true or false. A **speculation** is a reasonable guess. For example, when Nurnberg says that a certain dictionary contains 450,000 separate entries, he is making a statement of fact. When he says that the first humans "must have made sounds like the bark of a dog to convey excitement," he is speculating.

Tell whether each of the following statements is a statement of fact or a speculation.
1. ". . . the *ouch* word of our earliest ancestors was a general word and often covered a lot of ground."
2. "All of these words [*Adieu, Adios, Addio*] come from the Latin word for a god, *deus.*"

THINKING AND WRITING
Speculating About Words

Early in his essay, Nurnberg tells a little story in which he speculates about how an interjection —a word that expresses sudden excitement or strong feeling—like *ouch* may have originated. Choose another injection—*aha, oops, psst, ugh,* or some other—and imagine the situation in which it might have first been used. Tell a brief story to express your speculation about how the word originated.

Before you write, take the time to imagine what was taking place that led someone to use the interjection. What other characters were there? What was the setting? When you revise, check that your story is a believable account of how your interjection was born.

The Mystery and Wonder of Words 405

6. Both words and tools are an extension of human power.
7. His point is that common words of today evolved over a very long time and that they contain meanings that a superficial understanding would not reveal.
8. The word parts of *infant* mean "not speaking." That is why Nurnberg believes you are no longer an infant when you start to speak.

Applying

9. Answers will differ, but the quotation may mean that words exist to express previously existing ideas. Nurnberg might agree, since he gives examples of words that came to be in order to express something a speaker thought or felt.

ANSWERS TO READING IN THE CONTENT AREAS

1. Answers will differ, but students should see that skimming is appropriate for pleasure reading, for previewing a chapter in a textbook, for newspaper reading, and the like.
2. Answers will differ, but students might mention such material as telephone directories, menus, indexes and tables of contents, and certain news stories.
3. Reading intensively is suitable for serious fiction and nonfiction, including textbooks and other kinds of study material.

ANSWERS TO CRITICAL THINKING AND READING

1. speculation
2. fact

THINKING AND WRITING

Publishing Student Writing
These essays should prove enjoyable if shared among your students. Encourage students to read their stories aloud.

Closure and Extension

ANSWERS TO THINKING ABOUT THE SELECTION
Recalling

1. They invented words to increase their ability to communicate with others.
2. The word *breakfast* indicates that you are "breaking your fast" from the previous evening.

3. The expression *God be with you* is the basis of the word *goodbye*.
4. The underlying meaning is that a companion is one with whom we share our bread.

Interpreting

5. The quotation shows that words have histories that may be centuries old. The quotation sums up the main idea implied in Nurnberg's analyses of individual words and in his other remarks on language.

405

More About the Author Edwin Way Teale's four-volume series, *The American Seasons,* required fifteen years of work and 75,000 miles of travel. The fourth volume, *Wandering Through Winter,* won a Pulitzer Prize. Meticulous research both in the field and in libraries went into his books, which strive to depict the colors, forms, and sounds of nature. Ask your class what kind of nature book would issue from a combination of library and field research. Why might such a book surpass a book based on just one kind of research?

Literary Focus People often say, "I'll make a mental note of that." They mean that they will try to remember something. Explain that information, thoughts, records of various kinds, and so on, need to be recorded or else they will not be preserved. Stress the value of journals not only as a way developing powers of written expression but also as a good habit and a form of intellectual discipline.

Look For You can point out that the literary freedom allowed in the writing of a journal makes it appropriate to blend objective observations or information and subjective feelings and responses.

Writing/Prior Knowledge The poet Alexander Pope wrote, "All nature is but art, unknown to thee." Your **more advanced** students can discuss the meaning of this statement before starting on the writing exercise. Carefully observing nature will reveal its resemblance to man-made works.

Vocabulary Less advanced students may find some of the language of the excerpts difficult. You may therefore wish to read passages in class and have students attempt to use context clues to arrive at the meanings of the more difficult words.

406

GUIDE FOR READING

from Circle of the Seasons

Edwin Way Teale (1899–1980) was born and raised in Joliet, Illinois. Up to the age of sixteen, he spent his summers at his grandparents' farm in Indiana, close to Lake Michigan. Here he developed a fascination with plants and animals that lasted all his life. He became a naturalist and a Pulitzer Prize-winning author of nature books. The journal entries that follow are remarkable for their perceptiveness and thoughtfulness. They will show you how much nature can teach a sensitive observer.

Journal Writing

Journal writing is a way of recording events as they happen. Because a journal is personal, it usually includes a writer's thoughts, feelings, and insights as well as objective details. Many scientists keep journals as a record of observations and experiments. They can thereby keep track of their work. They can also use a journal to record information for future projects. Others, like Teale, treat journals as a place to do their best writing. Ultimately, such journals are published as books for the public.

Look For

As you read the excerpts from *Circle of the Seasons,* notice how Teale blends close and careful observations of nature with his own thoughts and scientific reflections.

Writing

Freewrite about your observations of a specific aspect of nature in or near your neighborhood. Include whatever thoughts, questions, or feelings occur to you as you write down your observations.

Vocabulary

Knowing the following words will help you as you read the excerpts from *Circle of the Seasons.*
susceptible (sə sep′ tə b'l) *adj.*: Easily affected by (p. 407)
apt (apt) *adj.*: Inclined; likely (p. 407)
invariable (in ver′ ē ə b'l) *adj.*: Not changing, uniform (p. 407)
opalescent (ō′ pə les′ 'nt) *adj.*: Showing a play of colors (p. 408)

406   Nonfiction

Objectives

1 To understand journal writing
2 To distinguish observation from inference
3 To write a journal entry

Support Material

Teaching Portfolio
Teacher Backup, p. 591
Usage and Mechanics Worksheet, p. 594
Vocabulary Check, p. 595
Critical Thinking and Reading Worksheet, *Observing and Inferring,* p. 596
Language Worksheet, *Building Words From Latin Roots,* p. 597
Selection Test, p. 598

from Circle of the Seasons

Edwin Way Teale

The following are excerpts from a journal that Edwin Way Teale kept for every day of a year. Scientists often use journals with dated entries as an ongoing record of their observations or experiments.

January 11

POISON IVY BERRIES. To the cedar woods at sunset. An overwintering catbird is feeding on the purple berries of the cat-briars and the gray berries of the poison ivy. Cows eat poison ivy leaves with immunity; birds eat the berries without ill effects. Only human beings, and only some human beings at that, are susceptible, through an allergy, to the torments of ivy poisoning. Yet those of us who fall victims, through this peculiarity in our own systems, are apt to bewail the presence of poison ivy in the world and to consider it an enemy lying in wait for our approach. Why was poison ivy put in the world?

The catbird, feeding in the quiet of this winter sunset, finding nourishment in the berries, supplies at least one of the answers. On the shifting sand of Fire Island,[1] there is another answer. There, the remarkably adaptive ivy, able to grow on barren sand as well as in swamps, anchors down the windblown earth. Each form of life, plant as well as animal, has its part to play. Whether the results delight or outrage man is no concern of nature's. Man plays, to be sure, a leading role in the drama of life. But he still is only a part of a cast that includes many, many actors.

January 24

THE WHITENESS OF THE SNOW. Looking across the white fields today, I am reminded that an invariable rule of nature is that nothing is invariable. "As like as two peas in a pod" is an exact statement of nature's way. For no two peas in a pod are ever exactly alike. Nature does not plagiarize herself, repeat herself. Her powers of innovation are boundless. No two hills or ants or oranges or sheep or snowflakes are identical. Ten thousand seem alike because we do not see them clearly enough, because our senses are too dull or inadequate or inaccurate to detect the differences.

And so it is with one of the oldest similes in the world: "As white as the snow." The whiteness of the snow is infinitely varied. In fact, its whiteness is produced by elements that are not white at all. The individual crystals that go into the make-up of a snowflake are transparent and colorless when they are created far up in the sky. They are like clear glass. It is when they are grouped together in flakes, when they lie in untold millions in a drift, that they appear white.

What is the explanation of this paradox? It is the same answer that explains how a transparent window pane when it is broken and powdered appears white while the intact pane is colorless. Both the infinite number of crystals that make up the snowdrift and

---

1. **Fire Island:** A long, narrow, sandy island off the south shore of Long Island, New York.

from *Circle of the Seasons*   407

the vast number of particles that comprise the powdered glass have so many facets that they reflect all the rays of light in all directions. Put all the rays of the spectrum together and you have white just as when you take all the rays of the spectrum away you have black. It is the numberless crystals in the piled-up snow that turn it into a mound of the purest white.

Yet even this "purest white" has many subtle variations. The famous New York advertising photographer, H. I. Williams, once told me of his surprise in noting the differences in the whites recorded by his color camera. They all looked alike to his eyes. But the sensitive color film showed that some were tinged with blues or yellows or reds and some were pearly and opalescent. The white of a billiard ball, of a sheet of writing paper, of a dress shirt, of a tablecloth all were different. Probably no two tablecloths are exactly the same in whiteness, although our eyes are unable to detect the difference.

Similarly, it is likely that no two snowbanks are identical in the whiteness of their exterior. Their surroundings, the time of day, the conditions of the sky all contribute to their tinting. Even our eyes can note the blue in the shadows of trees stretching across the drifts and the pink glow of sunset spreading over an expanse of snow. But under the noonday sun, except when soot or mud has stained them or when old drifts have been discolored by deposits from the air, the whiteness of the snow remains all the same to our eyes—the purest white we know.

April 4

WORLD'S MOST VALUABLE ANIMAL. A long soaking rain before daybreak. And all along the way, when I walk for the morning papers, I find earthworms here and there stranded on the inhospitable cement of the sidewalk. Appearing naked and bewildered, they are in imminent danger of the early bird or of drying out in the sun-warmed air. This is the time of year when my morning walk is slowed by stops to put earthworms back on the ground where they belong. People probably wonder what treasure I am finding when they see me stoop so often!

And, in a way, I am dealing in treasure.

The pelt of a silver fox may sell for hundreds of dollars. The legs of a racehorse may be insured for a quarter of a million. Yet neither the silver fox nor the racehorse is the world's most valuable animal. This is the earthworm—a creature without fur and without legs; a creature that has neither paws nor eyes nor ears; a humble burrower, nature's plowman.

As frost has left the topsoil, earthworms have worked upward. They have begun once more their invaluable activity of plowing, pulverizing, aerating, fertilizing, leveling and thinning the soil. As many as 5,000 earthworms may plow through the earth of a single acre. During spring and summer and fall, they may bring as much as eighteen tons of new earth to the surface.

This labor is achieved with curious but effective equipment. Instead of legs, the earthworm employs hundreds of stiff bristles. Each body segment, except the first and last, is equipped with eight of these bristle-hooks. They are used to grip the soil on all sides and they explain the tugging of the robin when it seeks to drag an earthworm from the ground.

Underground, the earthworm pushes or literally eats its way through the soil. Its mouth, functioning like a suction pump, draws earth into its body. There it is pulverized and organic particles are digested. The rest is deposited as castings[2] at the mouth of the burrow. In its surface feeding, during

---

2. castings: (kas' tiŋz) n.: Waste material.

the hours of darkness, the creature usually anchors its tail in its burrow and then, elongating its body, moves in a circle like a tethered calf in its search for bits of decayed leaves.

At such times, it is warned of danger by curious senses, amazingly keen. Although it has no eyes, its skin is so sensitive to light that it warns the worm when dawn is break-

ing. Although it has no ears, it is so sensitive to earth vibrations that it is alarmed by the footfall of even an approaching shrew.[3]

This is the earthworm, that humble and invaluable creature I see so frequently along my way this morning.

---

3. shrew: (shr$\overline{oo}$) *n.*: A small, slender, mouselike animal with soft, brown fur and a long pointed snout.

THINKING ABOUT THE SELECTION

Recalling

1. What are Teale's answers to the question "Why was poison ivy put in the world?"
2. Explain the different tintings of color in snow.

Interpreting

3. Why is the earthworm "nature's plowman"?
4. What is the meaning of Teale's remark that humans are only part of the drama of life?
5. How strong is his argument for the idea that the earthworm is the most valuable animal?

Applying

6. In the first entry, Teale points out the value of poison ivy. What are some other aspects of nature he might have written about in a similar way?

READING IN THE CONTENT AREAS

Journal Writing

Journal writing can be a way of learning. It can stimulate a writer's thinking so that he or she sees meaning in the events recorded.
1. What is the specific observation that begins the January 24th entry?
2. What rule of nature does this observation lead Teale to recall?

CRITICAL THINKING AND READING

Observing and Inferring

Observing is the act of noting and recording facts and events. For example, when Teal notes and records that poison ivy anchors down the windblown earth on Fire Island, he is making an observation. **Inferring** means drawing a conclusion—often from observations. For example, after observing that the catbird is nourished by poison-ivy berries and earth is anchored down by the ivy, Teale makes the inference that "Each form of life . . . has its part to play."

Tell why you think that the following statement is an observation or an inference: "Yet neither the silver fox nor the racehorse is the world's most valuable animal."

THINKING AND WRITING

Writing a Journal Entry

Using your freewriting as a starting point, write an entry modeled on any one of the three by Teale. Include any inferences or other thoughts that come to you. When you revise your entry, make sure your observation is presented in a way that will be clear to any reader. Compare your entry with those written by others in your class.

from *Circle of the Seasons*   409

from These Were the Sioux

Mari Sandoz (1901–1966) was born in Nebraska but learned English only when she entered school; her Swiss parents spoke German at home. Sandoz worked as a teacher and a proofreader in a newspaper office before she became a successful writer. Influenced by her childhood on a frontier farm, she wrote many books about the American West. She was especially fascinated by the history and customs of Native Americans. In this excerpt from *These Were the Sioux*, she describes the upbringing of Sioux children.

Taking Notes

Taking notes is an excellent technique for remembering the most important information from your reading. Before you even start to take notes, however, you will find it helpful to skim through the selection to gain a general idea of it. Then you can read the piece more slowly, listing the main points. It is not necessary to use complete sentences in your list. Also, you can make note-taking easier by eliminating articles (*a, an, the*) and using abbreviations. As you read, pay special attention to words that indicate main ideas—*in conclusion, most important, the causes of,* and similar phrases. Finally, you may want to review your notes after writing them so they stay in your memory.

Look For

Mari Sandoz knew about the Indian way of life from her own experience on the frontier. As you read her essay about the Sioux, pick out the main ideas she wants to convey.

Writing

Imagine that you have been given the responsibility of caring for a young friend or relative for a weekend. Tell what you would do to teach or entertain this child.

Vocabulary

Knowing the following words will help you as you read "These Were the Sioux."

favoritism (fā′ vər it iz′m) *n.*: Showing special kindness (p. 412)

rites (rīts) *n.*: Religious observances (p. 412)

usurped (yōō surpt′) *v.*: Took without right (p. 413)

tepid (tep′ id) *adj.*: Not warm or cold; lukewarm (p. 413)

enticing (in tīs′ iŋ) *adj.*: Tempting (p. 413)

regalia (ri gāl′ yə) *n.*: Splendid clothes and decorations (p. 414)

judicious (jōō dish′ əs) *adj.*: Wise (p. 414)

latent (lāt′′nt) *adj.*: Hidden and not fully developed (p. 414)

410   *Nonfiction*

from These Were the Sioux

Mari Sandoz

By the time I was seven or eight I had begun to sense a special kind of individual responsibility among the Sioux, not only for oneself but for the family, the band, the whole tribe. Then one morning I saw something of the start of this. A small girl from the camp across the road came tapping shyly at our door, motioning to me.

"Ahh, I have a brother too now," she whispered, her dark eyes on the baby astride my hip. "He is just born."

I pushed the oatmeal back on the stove, glanced toward the stable where Mother was milking our cow and hurried across the road as fast as I could, my brother bobbing on my side. I slowed up at the smoky old canvas tipi, shy, too, now, but I did peer into the dusky interior where an Indian woman bent over the new baby on her lap. At the noise of our excitement, the tiny red-brown face began to pucker up tighter, but the mother caught the little nose gently between her thumb and forefinger and with her palm over the mouth, stopped the crying. When the baby began to twist for breath, she let go a little, but only a little, and at the first sign of another cry, she shut off the air again, crooning a soft little song as she did this, a growing song of the Plains Indians, to make the boy straight-limbed and strong of body and heart as the grandson of Bad Arm must be.

I watched the mother enviously. Our babies always cried, and so I had to ride them on my hip, but I knew that none of our small Indian friends made more than a whimper at the greatest hurt, even falling from the high limb of a tree. Now I saw what an old woman had tried to explain to me. During the newborn minutes, that newborn hour, Indian children, boy and girl, were taught the first and greatest lesson of their lives: that no one could be permitted to endanger the people by even one cry to guide a roving enemy to the village or to spoil a hunt that could mean the loss of the winter meat for a whole band or even a small tribe. In return the child would soon discover that all the community felt an equal responsibility toward him. Every fire became like that of his parents, welcoming the exploring, the sleepy or injured toddler. Every pot would have a little extra for a hungry boy, and every ear was open to young sorrow, young joys and aspirations. I also knew that never, in the natural events of this small boy's life, would he be touched by a punishing adult hand. If he grew up like the Sioux of the old hunting days he would be made equal to the demands of his expanding world without any physical restriction beyond the confines of the cradleboard.[1] I still remember the closed, distant faces of the Sioux when I was whipped for staying out to watch the *heyoka*[2] in the thunderstorm, and at other whippings as well.

---

1. cradleboard (krā' d'l bôrd) *n.*: A board for carrying a baby.

2. heyoka (hā ō' kə) *n.*: An Indian who made others laugh by doing things backward, for example, wearing warm clothes in summer and hardly any clothes in winter; dreaming of thunder was one qualification for becoming a *heyoka*.

from *These Were the Sioux* 411

Presentation

Motivation/Prior Knowledge Tell your students that the Sioux tribe included such great chiefs as Sitting Bull and Crazy Horse, and that the Sioux made up the majority of the fighters against General Custer at the battle of the Little Big Horn. In the selection from *These Were the Sioux*, students will learn how young members of the tribe were trained to be strong, resourceful, and self-sufficient.

Master Teacher Note *Son of the Morning Star* by Evan S. Connell is a brilliant study of Custer and his "last stand." It also contains a great deal of fascinating information about the Sioux. Reading or summarizing some of the more interesting sections—particularly those about Crazy Horse and the battle of the Little Big Horn—will whet your students' appetite to learn more about the Sioux. Ask your students what they may already know or have read about this people.

Purpose-Setting Question How did the upbringing of a young Sioux differ from the way boys and girls are brought up today?

1 **Discussion** The main idea here —that Sioux had a special kind of individual responsibility—will be developed further. Ask students to restate this idea in their own words.

2 **Skills Focus** Ask your class to pick out the main points of this long paragraph. Allow them time to sift through the details until they see that these ideas are (1) that no Sioux could be permitted to endanger the people, (2) that the community felt responsible for each individual, and (3) that corporal punishment was disdained.

Humanities Note

Fine art, *Chee-a-ka-tchee, Wife of Not-to-Way*, 1830–39, by George Catlin. Catlin (1796–1872) was an American artist who is famous for his paintings and drawings of Native Americans. His paintings are not only notable art but also a remarkable visual record of Indian life before the advent of the camera.

The cradleboard shown in this painting is no doubt very similar to the one Sandoz refers to in the selection. The woman, however, is not a Sioux; she is the wife of an Iroquois chief. Give students a few moments to look the painting over.

1. What kind of life do you think this woman led?
2. What kind of life might the baby have led?
3. What is suggested about the relationship between mother and child in this painting?

3 **Skills Focus** The provision of a second father and mother in order to avoid overprotection and favoritism is the main idea here. All of the details amplify it. Ask students to find the idea. If they seem to be having trouble doing so, ask them, "What is this paragraph about? What do all the details relate to?" To help **less advanced** students, suggest that they reread the first few sentences of the paragraph on page 412. Ask, "What practice is explained here and in the next two paragraphs?"

CHEE-A-KA-TCHEE, WIFE OF NOT-TO-WAY, 1830–39
George Catlin
National Museum of American Art
The Smithsonian Institution

In the old days our Sioux neighbors still had their traditional set of precautions against immaturities and resentments among their young people. They avoided overprotecting the young and saved the eldest son from the mother's favoritism that could destroy the parents as well as the boy. By custom every son and daughter, too, was provided with a second father and mother at birth—usually friends of the blood parents, or some relatives outside of the immediate family. The second father of a boy was often selected partly for excellence as hunter, war- rior, horse catcher, band historian, holy man who listened and advised, or medicine man—either healer or one learned in rites and ceremonials. Still earlier the man might have been a maker of arrows, spears or shields, an outstanding runner or gifted in decoying and snaring animals. His wife, the second mother, was preferably known as warmhearted, and fond of boys around the tipi, the lodge. Sometimes the youth showed a special and unexpected talent as he grew and then a third father might be selected, one gifted in this new bent. Or if the puberty

3

412 *Nonfiction*

Grammar in Action

An **adverb clause** is a subordinate clause that modifies a verb, an adjective, or an adverb. Writers use adverb clauses to answer any of the following questions about the words they modify: *Where? When? In what manner? To what extent? Under what condition?* or *Why?* Also, using adverb clauses adds variety to the sentence structure and thus makes the writing more interesting and lively. In the following passage, Mari Sandoz uses adverb clauses.

Every Indian child had to keep himself afloat awhile *if he slipped off into deep water,* [if he] *was caught in a cloudburst or in a river accident while the people were fleeing from enemies or a buffalo stampede.*

By using an appropriate subordinating conjunction to begin her adverb clauses, Sandoz shows precisely the connection that exists between the clauses. The first two adverb clauses modify the verb and answer the question *Under what conditions?* The third adverb clause modifies the word *caught* and answers the question *When?*

dream was of thunder, a *heyoka* might be added as a sort of uncle.

The second mother took over much of the small boy's care so he would never shame his blood mother by trailing at her moccasin heel, never bring the scornful whisper, "Little husband! Little husband!" as he usurped another's place in her attention and affection. The Indians understood the anger and resentment that could grow up in the most tolerant, fortitudinous man if his wife preferred the son over the husband, used the boy against him, brought him humiliation in the village circle.

In the second mother's lodge the boy could tease and laugh in a way improper in his own home. He could talk freely, so long as it was respectful. And when a boy like Young One across the road went to war, whether in the old days against the Pawnees or the Crows, or later, to the Pacific or Korea,[3] the women of his second home could show emotion and cry out, "Be careful, our brother!" and "Be careful, our son!"

By the time Young One was six weeks old he was little trouble to anyone, either in the cradleboard propped against a tipi pole or riding a mother's back while she went about her work. He would be up there some of the time until he was a year old or more, out of harm's way, seeing all the world from the high place and unpossessed by the mother's eyes. Before Young One was two months old it was decided he must swim, "before he forget it," the older mother told us, by signs. I took my baby brother down to see this. The woman carried Young One into a quieter spot along the riverbank and with her hands under the chest and belly, she eased the boy into the shallow, tepid water until it came up

---

3. **the Pacific or Korea:** World War II (1939–1945), fought on the Pacific Ocean and elsewhere, or the Korean War (1950–1953).

around him. Then, suddenly, his sturdy legs began to kick and his arms to flail out. The next time he lasted a little longer, and by the third or fourth time the woman could take her hands away for a bit while he held his head up and dog paddled for himself.

Winter babies, boys or girls, who couldn't be taught to swim early, were thrown into ponds or river holes in the spring by the father, the impact calculated to revive the fading urge to swim. Every Indian child had to keep himself afloat awhile if he slipped off into deep water, was caught in a cloudburst or in a river accident while the people were fleeing from enemies or a buffalo stampede.

The young Indian learned to make his own decisions, take the responsibility for his actions at an incredibly early age. When the baby began to crawl no one cried, "No, no!" and dragged him back from the enticing red of the tipi fire coals. Instead, his mother or anyone near watched only that he did not burn up. "One must learn from the bite of the fire to let it alone," he was told when he jerked his hand back, whimpering a little, and with tear-wet face brought his burnt finger to whoever was near for the soothing. The boy's eyes would not turn in anger toward the mother or other grownup who might have pulled him back, frustrated his natural desire to test, to explore. His anger was against the pretty coals, plainly the source of his pain. He would creep back another time but more warily, and soon he would discover where warmth became burning.

From birth the young Sioux was in the midst of the adult world. There was only one room in the lodge, and only one out-of-doors. Back when he was small his cradleboard often hung on a tipi pole or a meat rack, the wind swaying him drowsily, while the children played and raced and sang around him and one of his mothers or frequently several

from These Were the Sioux 413

4 **Literary Focus** The requirement that infants swim is developed at length here. These two paragraphs should be treated as the preceding three were, so that students will grasp the main idea and see that all the details that follow serve to develop it.

Student Activity 1. Find three sentences where Sandoz uses adverb clauses. Identify the adverb clause and the word each modifies.

Student Activity 2. Using adverb clauses, combine each group of sentences to form a more effective sentence.

1. You have charged five dollars for your pup.
   The new owner will be afraid to return it.
   It will look like he is hard up for money.

2. We go to the store.
   I look at all the games and books.
   Mother is in a hurry.
   She has some pressing commitment to take care of afterwards.

women worked nearby, busy with the meat or the hides or perhaps beading the regalia of the men.

But the little Sioux had to learn some use of his legs this summer. He spent more and more time on the ground, perhaps on a robe or soft grass but often alone, free to discover his body now and begin to get his discipline in the natural way, as he must be free to take his ideals and aspirations from the precepts and examples of those around him.

When the thrust of the boy's growing legs took on insistence, one of the fathers or perhaps an uncle lay on his back and held the baby erect for a short walk up his stomach and chest, laughing hard at the sturdy push of the legs, shouting that this was a warrior son, this was a great and powerful hunter. Perhaps the man was a young war chief, or, if older, just out of the evening council circle where any toddler could approach the headmen unhindered. He could see them smoking quietly, deliberating the common problems of today and tomorrow or planning ceremonials and hunts, perhaps selecting the warrior society to police the village for the next moon, and protect it from disturbances inside and out. The boy could hear the crier, always some old and very judicious and respected man, hurry through the camp with any news or with warnings of danger, or of a hunt coming up, perhaps carrying invitation sticks to a feast or a celebration, or proclaiming the council's decisions. And they were decisions, not orders, for no Sioux could tell anyone what to do. The only position a Sioux inherited was his membership in the tribe. He became a leader, a chief because some were willing to follow him and retained his position only as long as the following remained.

The young Sioux rode early. Sometimes before he could walk he was carried behind his father, clinging to the rawhide string of the man's breechclout.[4] He learned to climb up the foreleg of an old mare like a tree, mounting on the right side as the grown Indians all did, the man with the bow in his left hand when he leaped on, out of the way, and leaving the right hand free to draw the bowstring fast.

From back before he understood the words or the wisdom, the young Sioux heard the hero tales of his people told around the evening fires, but in his early years he learned most from the other children. They took joy in showing him all their knowledge, and in practicing the latent parent lying deep in everyone, eager to care for any small creature or being around. But he learned much, perhaps most, from the scorn and laughter of these peers, and from another boy's fist in his face. Eventually he discovered how to avoid some of the laughing, and the blows, or to fend them off.

When Bad Arm, the man who had once carried me home from the plum thicket, was asked if there wasn't injustice in this discipline by children he drew on his old pipe awhile. All life was injustice, he thought. Lightning found the good man and the bad; sickness carried no respect for virtue, and luck flitted around like the spring butterfly. "It is good to learn this in the days of the mother's milk. Discipline from the young comes as from the earth and is accepted like hunger and weariness and the bite of winter cold. Coming so, it hatches no anger against the grown-up ones, no anger and hatred to sit in the heart like an arrow pointed to shoot both ways."

So the young Sioux learned from his peers, learned from their companionship, their goodness and the power of their ridicule, the same ridicule he saw used against

---

4. breechclout (brĕch′ klout′) *n*.: A piece of cloth worn about the body at the hips.

SIOUX ENCAMPMENT, 1874–1884
Jules Tavernier
Laurie Platt Winfrey, Inc.

Humanities Note

Fine art, *Sioux Encampment*, circa 1874–84, by Jules Tavernier. Tavernier (1844–1889) was a French-born American painter and illustrator. Working for magazines, he was sent to the West to record the countryside. *Sioux Encampment* is one of a series of paintings he did for *Harper's Weekly*. It is a skillfully painted view of Native Americans and teepees set in a beautifully rendered landscape.

1. What impression of Sioux life do you get from this painting?
2. How would living in this encampment differ from living in a typical American home of today?

7 **Reading Strategy** In this and the succeeding paragraphs, a great deal of information is presented about the Sioux. Review scanning with your students, and suggest that they scan these paragraphs to get a general idea of what each one is about—of how each paragraph focuses on a different area of Sioux life. Such scanning will make it easier to see main ideas.

those in highest position sometimes, for even great war leaders bowed in humiliation before concentrated laughter. And he saw men and women of his people walk in dignity through the village circle, the peaceful, orderly village where normally one heard no quarreling in tipi or outside.

"It is better to use ridicule early—to keep the young on the good road," Bad Arm and the *heyoka* agreed, telling me that in this, had I been a Sioux, I should have had a real place, for ridicule from the girls and the women stings like the yellow-striped hornet.

In the old buffalo days the very young Sioux learned to snare and track small animals, even the rabbit, with his trick of doubling back on his trail, teaching the hunter to use his eyes while other creatures taught him to sharpen his nose and his ears. As the boy grew he was drawn into the hunting games as he was those of the village: prairie ball, running and jumping contests, tag, snow snake in the winter, and always wrestling and horse racing, the boys riding sometimes so small they seemed like some four-footed creature clinging to the mane and back. Young One would have seen the men pile their wagers in goods at the betting stake before the horses were whipped home with dust and whooping. He would have learned to ride in a dead run while hanging to the far side of his pony with a moccasin toe over the back, a hand twisted into the mane, ready for war. He would have been along on raids against enemy horse herds as

from *These Were the Sioux* 415

8 Discussion After questioning your students on what the main idea of this paragraph is, ask them to compare and contrast the passage from childhood to adolescence for the Sioux and the same passage in our own society.

Reader's Response What do you admire most about the way the Sioux raise their young? Why?

a young white man might study his father's methods of raiding a competitor's customers.

As the boy grew he ran with his village kind as young antelope run together. He teased the girls, grabbed bits of meat from the drying racks when he was hungry. He went to watch the older youths and young men stand in their courting blankets at this tipi or that one for a few words with the young daughter and could hardly wait until he, too, was a man. He imitated the warriors and ran their errands, hoping to be asked out on a raid, as was done for promising boys, particularly by the war society of a father or an uncle, much as a white youth would be eased toward his father's fraternity, and often with little more bloodshed. Except in a few tribal struggles for hunting grounds, Plains Indian fights were scarcely more dangerous than a hard-fought football game. The first-class coup—striking an enemy with the hand, the bow or the coup stick without harming him—was the highest war achievement, more important than any scalp.

Occasionally the boy was taken out on night guard of the village and the horse herds, or to scout the region for unauthorized war parties trying to slip away, endangering themselves and perhaps the village with avenging attacks. An Indian who gave up the right to cry at birth because it would bring enemies upon the people must not do the same thing by rash and foolish acts later.

Understanding of the regular ceremonials and rituals came gradually to the young Sioux. Eventually he realized what old Contrary told us through the interpretation of his teenage granddaughter, who cheerfully turned all the *heyoka* said around to its rightful meaning. The Sioux camp of any size was always set in a circle because all sacred things were round—the sun, the moon, the earth horizon, as one could plainly see. Even the tipis were round, and their openings as well as that of the whole camp always faced the east, to welcome and honor the light that brought the day and the springtime. But the simplest and perhaps the most profound ritual that the young Sioux saw was the most common. The first puff of the pipe at a smoking and the first morsel of food at a meal were always offered to the Great Powers—the earth, the sky and the four directions, which included everything that lay within their arms. All things were a part of these Powers, brothers in them, and anyone could understand what a brother was.

After his seventh birthday the Sioux boy never addressed his blood mother or sister directly again, speaking to them only through a third person. When he showed signs of coming manhood he was prepared for his puberty fasting by men close to the family, including some wise and holy one. There were also holy women among the Sioux, advising and officiating in many of the rites with both men and women but not for the puberty fasting, which was the youth's orientation into maleness. When he was ready the boy was escorted to some far barren hill and left there in breechclout and moccasins against the sun of day, the cold of night, without food or water. The ordeal was to strip away every superficiality, all the things of the flesh, to prepare for a dreaming, a vision from the Powers. Usually by the third or fourth day the youth had dreamed and was brought down, gaunt and weak. He was given a few drops of water at a time and some food, but slowly, and after he was restored a little, and bathed and feasted, his advisors and the holy man tried to interpret the vision that was to guide him in this manhood he was now entering.

8

THINKING ABOUT THE SELECTION

Recalling

1. What was "the first and greatest lesson" for the Sioux?
2. How did the Sioux feel about punishing children?
3. What custom protected children from favoritism?
4. How did the young learn from their peers?
5. How were boys trained to be warriors?
6. Why did young boys fast on a "far . . . hill"?

Interpreting

7. Why would a young Sioux learn to feel responsible for the whole tribe?
8. What can you infer from this essay about the qualities that the Sioux valued?

Applying

9. Explain whether or not the Sioux methods of child-rearing would work today, outside of the Sioux tribe.

READING IN THE CONTENT AREA

Taking Notes

Taking notes will help you to remember the important ideas in your reading. First you should skim through the piece. Then you should read it slowly, listing the main ideas and using words or phrases rather than complete sentences. The following notes, for example, cover the first four paragraphs.

At early age—senses Sioux have special feeling for family and tribe
Sioux mother stops baby's breathing to prevent crying—noise could bring enemies, chase away game
Benefits: children cared for by whole tribe, not physically punished

1. Skim through the rest of the essay and then take notes on it.
2. Compare your notes with the essay, making sure you have recorded the main ideas.

CRITICAL THINKING AND READING

Understanding Cause and Effect

A **cause** is what brings about a result, or **effect.** The writer of this essay tells you, for example, that a Sioux mother gently stops her baby's breathing when it cries. This action (cause) results in the baby's learning not to cry (effect).

On a separate piece of paper, write the missing cause.
1. *Cause*: ? *Effect*: The eldest son is protected from his mother's favoritism.
2. *Cause*: ? *Effect*: The Sioux are expert riders.

UNDERSTANDING LANGUAGE

Signaling Cause and Effect

The following words are among those that signal a cause-and-effect relationship: *because, since, therefore, consequently,* and *as a result*. For example, you can say, "The mother gently stopped her baby's breath when he cried; *consequently,* he learned not to cry." Or you can say, "The baby learned not to cry *because* his mother gently stopped his breath when he cried."

Connect the following statements with a word or phrase signaling cause and effect.
1. Every Indian knew how to swim. Indian babies were thrown into the water.
2. A child burned his hand on a hot coal. He crept back to the coal more carefully.

THINKING AND WRITING

Writing an Article About a Sioux Visitor

Imagine that a Sioux boy or girl from many years ago suddenly appears in your house. List some of the ways in which he or she would react to modern life. Then use the list to write a magazine article describing this miraculous visit. When revising your article, refer to "These Were the Sioux" to check that your portrait of a young Indian is accurate.

from *These Were the Sioux* 417

Applying

9. Answers will differ, but most students should see that the kind of outdoor communal living found among the Sioux, as well as other peculiarities of this tribe, would make many of their child-rearing practices impossible in modern American society. However, avoidance of corporal punishment, an emphasis on physical development, training in customs and traditions, peer influence, and some other distinctive features of Sioux child-rearing certainly could be adapted to our own society.

ANSWERS TO READING IN THE CONTENT AREAS

Student note-taking will differ from one student to another, but the main ideas noted should include many of the following (however they may be phrased): precautions against overprotection, early training in swimming, early training in decision-making, exposure to the ways and values of the community, early training in horsemanship, peer training, early hunting, initiation into ceremonies and rituals, passage into adolescence.

ANSWERS TO CRITICAL THINKING AND READING

1. *Cause:* The eldest son is provided with a second father and mother.
2. *Cause:* The young Sioux learned to ride early.

ANSWERS TO UNDERSTANDING LANGUAGE

Answers will differ in wording, but the following are typical correct answers.
1. Every Indian knew how to swim, because Indian babies were thrown into the water.
2. A child burned his hand on a hot coal. Consequently, he crept back to the coal more carefully.

THINKING AND WRITING

Writing Across the Curriculum
You may wish to have students research and report on the Sioux or another tribe. If you do, perhaps inform the social studies department of this assignment. Social studies teachers might provide guidance for students in conducting research. 417

Closure and Extension

ANSWERS TO THINKING ABOUT THE SELECTION

Recalling

1. The lesson was that no one could be permitted to endanger the people by an outcry.
2. The Sioux frowned on punishing children.
3. The custom of providing each child with a second father and mother protected children from favoritism.
4. They learned from the scorn, laughter, and assaults of their peers. In time, youngsters would learn how to avoid such abuse.
5. If promising, they were invited to go along on a raid or to take part in night guards or scouting expeditions.
6. Fasting on a far hill was part of a young boy's passage into manhood.

Interpreting

7. From birth, the young Sioux was taught to do nothing to endanger the tribe, and in return the whole tribe demonstrated responsibility for the child. Youngsters were freely exposed to all the customs and traditions of the tribe.
8. Answers will differ, but students should mention at least some of the following qualities: loyalty, independence, courage, hospitality, physical strength, respect, and piety.

Putting It Together The purpose
of Putting It Together is to emphasize how techniques, ideas,
and structure interrelate to produce the overall effect of the
selection. By following the systematic approach outlined in the
annotations, students will enhance their understanding of the
elements of nonfiction and increase their comprehension.
They should also read actively to
form their own questions and
opinions about the purpose,
techniques, support, and arrangement of the selection.

Remind students that, as
they read actively, they should
be able to see how separate
elements of nonfiction interrelate
to produce an effective essay.

For further practice with
these elements, use the selection in the Teaching Portfolio
"Hope Buyukmihci and the
Keepers of the Stream" by Margery Facklam, on page 486,
which students can annotate
themselves.

Teaching to Ability Levels If
your less advanced students
have difficulty comprehending
any of these elements, you might
have them review the instruction
on the appropriate pages or look
up the necessary terms in the
Handbook of Literary Terms and
Techniques on page 832.

PUTTING IT TOGETHER

Nonfiction

Nonfiction is different from fiction in that it deals with real people
and real events. Usually a nonfiction writer sets out with a certain purpose and intended audience in mind. A reader can gain a full appreciation of nonfiction by examining the techniques the writer uses to accomplish this purpose, the support the writer uses to back up or clarify
the main idea, and the way the writer arranges this supporting information.

Purpose

Purpose is the author's reason for writing. A writer usually has
both a general purpose and a specific purpose. The general purpose
may be to explain or inform, to describe, or to persuade. The specific
purpose is the main point the writer wants to make about the topic.
Often this main point is stated in a thesis statement.

Techniques

Techniques are the tools the writer uses to accomplish the purpose. For example, the writer may use figurative language to vividly
describe the subject or emotive language to arouse your feelings and
so persuade you to do something.

Support

Support is the information the writer uses to back up or clarify the
main idea. Support may take the form of facts and opinions or of reasons and examples. It may take the form of incidents or even of descriptive details.

Arrangement

The writer arranges the support material to best accomplish the
purpose. The information may be arranged according to chronological order, spatial order, or order of importance.

On the following pages is an essay with annotations in the margin
showing details an active reader might notice while reading.

Objectives

1 To understand how tech-
   niques and ideas work together in nonfiction
2 To understand an essay
   describing an event
3 To separate fact and opinion
4 To describe an event

Support Material

Teaching Portfolio
Teacher Backup, p. 613
Putting It Together, "Hope Buy-
ukmihci and the Keepers of the
Stream," by Margery Facklam,
p. 616
Grammar in Action Worksheet,
Recognizing Vivid Verbs, p. 618
Usage and Mechanics Work-
sheet, p. 620

Critical Thinking and Reading
Worksheet, *Separating Fact
From Opinion,* p. 621
Language Worksheet, *Homo-
phones,* p. 622
Selection Test, p. 623

Morning— "The Bird Perched for Flight"

Anne Morrow Lindbergh

We wake to the alarm at four thirty and leave our motel at five fifteen. The three astronauts must be already climbing into their seats at the top of their "thirty-six-story" rocket, poised for flight. The pilgrimage[1] of sightseers has started to the Cape.[2] Already the buses have left and lines of cars are on the roads. It is dark, a little chilly, with a sky full of stars. As we approach the Cape we see again the rocket and its launching tower from far off over the lagoon. It is still illumined with searchlights, but last night's vision has vanished. It is no longer tender or biological but simply a machine, the newest and most perfected creation of a scientific age—hard, weighty metal.

We watch the launching with some of the astronauts and their families, from a site near the Vehicle Assembly Building. Our cars are parked on a slight rise of ground. People get out, walk about restlessly, set up cameras and adjust their binoculars. The launch pad is about three miles away, near the beach. We look across Florida marsh grass and palmettos.[3] A cabbage palm[4] stands up black against a shadowy sky, just left of the rocket and its launching tower. As dawn flushes the horizon, an egret rises and lazily glides across the flats between us and the pad. It is a still morning. Ducks call from nearby inlets. Vapor trails of a high-flying plane turn pink in an almost cloudless sky. Stars pale in the blue.

---

1. pilgrimage (pil' gram ij) *n.*: A long journey to a place of interest.
2. the Cape: Cape Canaveral, a sandy stretch of land that juts into the Atlantic Ocean from an island off the eastern coast of Florida. For many years, it has been an important site for rocket launchings. At the time this piece was written, it was called Cape Kennedy in honor of John F. Kennedy, 35th president of the United States (1961–1963).
3. palmettos (pal met' ōz) *n.*: Palm trees with fan-shaped leaves.
4. cabbage palm (kab' ij päm) *n.*: A palm tree with a bud that can be eaten as a vegetable.

Purpose: The title provides a clue to the writer's main idea. What "bird" will this essay be about? What point will the author make about this "bird"?

Purpose: The author's general purpose seems to be to describe an event. What is this event?

Techniques: The author uses specific words and sensory details to create vivid word pictures. What specific words do you find? What details appeal to your senses?

Presentation

Motivation/Prior Knowledge Discuss with the class their impressions of watching a spacecraft lift off. If students have never witnessed this on television or in person, have them imagine what it might be like. What thoughts do they have about this sight? How much power might be needed to accomplish this? Would they ever want to ride in a spacecraft?

Master Teacher Note To give students a better idea about what a lift-off is like, you might show them some of the many pictures taken of various spacecraft blasting off from Cape Canaveral. What makes the photos so dramatic and impressive?

Thematic Idea Selections that deal with space travel are the short stories, "All Summer in a Day," by Ray Bradbury, on page 107, and Isaac Asimov's "Hallucination," on page 179. In these two stories, the use of sensory language to produce vivid images is similar to language used in this essay.

Purpose-Setting Question What is the author's attitude toward the object she is describing?

Arrangement: The details are arranged in chronological order. How does this arrangement help build suspense?

Techniques: Notice again the sensory details. Why do these details increase the suspense?

Purpose: We still do not know the author's specific purpose. Perhaps it has something to do with her feeling as if she is going to cry. Why would she feel this way?

With the morning light, Apollo 8[5] and its launching tower become clearer, harder, and more defined. One can see the details of installation. The dark sections on the smooth sides of the rocket, marking its stages, cut up the single fluid line. Vapor steams furiously off its side. No longer stark and simple, this morning the rocket is complicated, mechanical, earthbound. Too weighty for flight, one feels.

People stop talking, stand in front of their cars, and raise binoculars to their eyes. We peer nervously at the launch site and then at our wrist watches. Radio voices blare unnaturally loud from car windows. "Now only thirty minutes to launch time . . . fifteen minutes . . . six minutes . . . thirty seconds to go . . . twenty . . . T minus fifteen . . . fourteen . . . thirteen . . . twelve . . . eleven . . . ten . . . nine . . . Ignition!"

A jet of steam shoots from the pad below the rocket. "Ahhhh!" The crowd gasps, almost in unison. Now great flames spurt, leap, belch out across the horizon. Clouds of smoke billow up on either side of the rocket, completely hiding its base. From the midst of this holocaust,[6] the rocket begins to rise—slowly, as in a dream, so slowly it seems to hang suspended on the cloud of fire and smoke. It's impossible—it can't rise. Yes, it rises, but heavily, as if the giant weight is pulled by an invisible hand out of the atmosphere, like the lead on a plumb line[7] from the depths of the sea. Slowly it rises and—because of our distance—silently, as in a dream.

Suddenly the noise breaks, jumps across our three separating miles—a shattering roar of explosions, a trip hammer over one's head, under one's feet, through one's body. The earth shakes; cars rattle; vibrations beat in the chest. A roll of thunder, prolonged, prolonged, prolonged.

I drop the binoculars and put my hands to my ears, holding my head to keep it steady. My throat tightens—am I going to cry?—my eyes are fixed on the rocket, mesmerized[8] by its slow ascent.

---

5. Apollo (ə päl′ ō) **8:** This spacecraft, carrying astronauts Frank Borman, William A. Anders, and James A. Lovell, Jr., orbited the moon 10 times. Apollo was the Greek god of music, prophecy, poetry, and medicine.

6. holocaust (häl′ ə kôst′) *n.*: In ancient times, an offering burned to the gods; the author is reminded of such offerings by the flames shooting from the rocket.

7. plumb (plum) **line:** A line weighted with lead at one end to measure the depth of water.

8. mesmerized (mez′ mər īzd′) *v.*: Hypnotized.

Grammar in Action

Vivid verbs are words that present a lively, clear picture. Vivid verbs are vigorous and specific. Authors use vivid verbs to make the action come alive. Notice how Anne Morrow Lindbergh uses vivid verbs to dramatize and bring to life the launching of the rocket.

Now great flames, *spurt, leap, belch out* across the horizon.

By using a series of vivid verbs, Lindbergh makes you see the scene in all its intensity. To see the effect of using vivid verbs compare her sentence with the following one.

Now great flames shoot forth, jump, throw out across the horizon.

Student Activity 1. Replace the italicized word in each sentence with a more specific, lively verb.

1. At the bell, the two boxers *moved* out of their corners.

2. Frightened by the noise, the child *walked* over to his mother.

3. Angrily, Michael *threw* the ball to his brother.

Enrichment The United States space program began in 1959 and in a relatively short time, it has accomplished a great deal. On May 5, 1961, Alan Shepard, Jr., became the first American to travel in space. John H. Glenn was the first American to orbit the earth on February 20, 1962. In 1965, Edward H. White II was the first man from the United States to walk in space. The crew of the Apollo 8 mission were the first humans to travel around a celestial body other than the earth when they orbited the moon ten times from December 21 to December 27, 1968. On July 20, 1969, Neil Armstrong and Edwin Aldrin, Jr., became the first persons to walk on the moon. There were five other moon landings from 1969 to 1972. Since that time, the United States has launched a space station (1973), undertaken a joint space mission with the Soviet Union (1975), and launched the first reusable manned spacecraft (1981).

The foreground is now full of birds; a great flock of ducks, herons, small birds, rise pell-mell from the marshes at the noise. Fluttering in alarm and confusion, they scatter in all directions as if it were the end of the world. In the seconds I take to look at them, the rocket has left the tower.

It is up and away, a comet boring through the sky, no longer the vulnerable untried child, no longer the earth-bound machine, or the weight at the end of a line, but sheer terrifying force, blasting upward on its own titanic[9] power.

It has gone miles into the sky. It is blurred by a cloud. No, it has made its own cloud—a huge vapor trail, which hides it. Out of the cloud something falls, cartwheeling down, smoking. "The first-stage cutoff," someone says. Where is the rocket itself?

Techniques: Notice the contrast between the natural world and the world of rockets and machinery. How does this contrast make you feel about this takeoff?

---

9. titanic (tī tan′ ik) *adj.*: Having great size, strength, or power. In Greek mythology, the Titans were a race of giants who were defeated by the gods.

Morning—"The Bird Perched for Flight"   421

Student Activity 2. Using vivid, specific words, write a paragraph describing some exciting event you watched in person or on television. Make the action come alive through your choice of verbs.

There, above the cloud now, reappears the rocket, only a very bright star, diminishing every second. Soon out of sight, off to lunar space.

One looks earthward again. It is curiously still and empty. A cloud of brown smoke hangs motionless on the horizon. Its long shadow reaches us across the grass. The launch pad is empty. The abandoned launching tower is being sprayed with jets of water to cool it down. It steams in the bright morning air. Still dazed, people stumble into cars and start the slow, jammed trek back to town. The monotone[10] of radio voices continues. One clings to this last thread of contact with something incredibly beautiful that has vanished.

"Where are they—where are they now?" In eleven minutes we get word. They are in earth orbit. They "look good" in the laconic[11] space talk that comes down from over a hundred miles above earth. And one realizes again that it is the men above all that matter, the individuals who man the machine, give it heart, sight, speech, intelligence, and direction; and the men on earth who are backing them up, monitoring[12] their every move, even to their heartbeats. This is not sheer power, it is power under control of man.

We drive slowly back to town. Above us the white vapor trail of the rocket is being scattered by wind into feathery shapes of herons' wings—the only mark in the sky of the morning's launching.

Purpose and Support: Here the author states her specific purpose. What is it? Which details support her main idea?

Pulling It Together: The author views the launching as a triumph for human beings. However, once the event is over, little trace of it is left in the natural world.

---

10. monotone (män′ ə tōn) *n.*: A single, unchanging tone.
11. laconic (lə kän′ ik) *adj.*: Using few words.
12. monitoring (män′ə tər′ iŋ) *v.*: Watching or keeping track of.

Anne Morrow Lindbergh (1906–   ) is especially well equipped to write about flight. The wife of Charles Lindbergh, the first pilot to fly solo across the Atlantic, she herself is also a licensed pilot. In fact, she accompanied her famous husband as a copilot on a 40,000-mile flight across five continents. Her many books and articles on flight have received wide praise. In this selection from *Earth Shine,* she describes the takeoff of Apollo 8.

422   *Nonfiction*

Closure and Extension

ANSWERS TO THINKING ABOUT THE SELECTION
Recalling

1. Lindbergh leaves the motel early in the morning so she will be in time to see the spacecraft lift off.
2. Apollo 8 appears harder and more defined than it did the night before. It seems complicated, mechanical, and earthbound. It leads her to feel that the craft is too weighty for flight.
3. The people awaiting the launch lead her to feel nervous.

Interpreting

4. Answers will differ. Suggested Response: Lindbergh compares the rocket to a "vulnerable untried child" before it takes off because its appearance the night before gave the impression of a tender, almost animate object. Also, there are no test flights for the space-

THINKING ABOUT THE SELECTION
Recalling

1. Why does Lindbergh leave her motel room at five fifteen in the morning?
2. How does Apollo 8 look in the morning light? What does its appearance lead her to feel?
3. How do the people awaiting the launch lead her to feel?

Interpreting

4. Why does Lindbergh compare the rocket before blastoff to a "vulnerable untried child"?
5. Why does she call it "sheer terrifying force" immediately after takeoff?
6. When the rocket ascends, the birds scatter, "as if it were the end of the world." In what way does the rocket's takeoff signal the end of a world?

Applying

7. Do you consider the astronauts heroes? Explain your answer.

ANALYZING LITERATURE
Understanding an Essay

A common topic for an essay is a description of an event. Often this type of essay is written by a person who lived through the event, and so gives you first-hand information about it. Through the use of descriptive language, the author helps you visualize what has happened and imagine you are there experiencing the event for yourself. In most essays of this type, however, the author also shows you why this event is significant.

1. Find three descriptive details that give you an especially good picture of the sightseers. What impression do you form of the sightseers?
2. Find three descriptive details that give you an especially good picture of the site near the Vehicle Assembly Building. What impression do you form of the site?
3. Find three descriptive details that give you an especially good picture of the rocket. What impression do you form of the rocket?
4. What significance does Lindbergh see in the Apollo 8 takeoff?

CRITICAL THINKING AND READING
Separating Fact and Opinion

A **fact** can be proved true or false. For example, the following statement is a fact: Apollo 8 was launched in December 1968. An **opinion** expresses attitudes, evaluations, judgments, or even predicts the future. It cannot be proved true or false. For example, the following statement is an opinion: The rocket looked beautiful in the cold morning light. Writers will often include both facts and opinions in an essay describing an event.

Read the following sentences. Decide which contain facts and which contain opinions.

1. "[The rocket] is still illumined with searchlights. . . ."
2. "[The rocket] is no longer tender . . ."
3. "The launch pad is about three miles away, near the beach."
4. "And one realizes again that it is the men above all who matter, the individuals who man the machine . . ."

THINKING AND WRITING
Describing an Event

In this essay Lindbergh describes an historical event—the launching of Apollo 8. List all of the historical events you have lived through—for example, the election of a president, the disaster of the shuttle *Challenger*. From this list, select the event you would like to write about. Then freewrite about this event, exploring all your thoughts and feelings. Use your freewriting as a source of ideas for your first draft of an essay describing this event. When you revise your essay, make sure that your descriptions are clear and that you have shown the significance of the events. Prepare a final draft and share it with your classmates.

Morning—"The Bird Perched for Flight" 423

(Answers begin on p. 422.)

the launch site and then at (their) wrist watches"; "still dazed, people stumble into cars..." after the launch is over. The sightseers are regular people who are awed by the magnificent and powerful sight of the rocket launch.
2. Answers will differ. Three details that describe the site are these: it is on a slight rise of ground, it is three miles away from the launch pad, and it is separated from it by a marshy area.
3. Answers will differ. Three details that describe the rocket are these: It is "a machine, the newest and most perfected creation of a scientific age—hard, weighty metal"; "the rocket is complicated, mechanical, earthbound. Too weighty for flight"; and it is "a comet boring through the sky, no longer the vulnerable untried child, no longer the earth-bound machine, or the weight at the end of a line, but sheer terrifying force, blasting upward on its own titanic power."
4. Answers will differ. Suggested Response: The effect of comparing the natural world to the world of rocketry is a contrast between the mechanical, man-made force of rocketry and the force of nature. It puts rocketry into perspective because, despite its awesome display of power and technology, it is small and fleeting compared with the forces of the natural world.

---

craft, so before the actual liftoff it is literally untried, and therefore vulnerable.
5. Suggested Response: She calls it a "sheer terrifying force" because this vividly describes her impression of the sight and noise the rocket's ignition and thrust.
6. Suggested Response: The ascent of the rocket signals the end of the world in terms of the history of men bound to this planet. It signals the beginning of the new world which is man's exploration of space.

Applying
7. Answers will differ. If students do consider astronauts heroes, they might include ideas such as: how modern heroes differ from the traditional heroes of the past, how astronauts are isolated in a sense when they are performing their missions, how they capture the imagination of people as heroes in the past did, or how they risk their lives for the good of society. If students do not consider astronauts heroes, the reason may be that

they compare them directly to the traditional heroes of the past, or they may find the accomplishments and skills of astronauts to be unworthy of the status of hero.

ANSWERS TO ANALYZING LITERATURE

1. Answers will differ. Three details that describe the sightseers are these: a "pilgrimage of sightseers"; they "peer nervously at

ANSWERS TO CRITICAL THINKING AND READING

1. fact
2. opinion
3. fact
4. opinion

Understanding Persuasive Techniques

Authors often use **persuasive techniques** in nonfiction to try to convince readers to accept their opinions or to take some action. Understanding the persuasive techniques writers use will help you determine whether or not you should agree with the writer.

Stated Position

When reading persuasive writing, you must first identify the stated position that the writer wants you to accept. This position will be stated in the topic sentence and should be expressed simply and clearly so that it is easy to understand. Any terms that you may not know should be defined so that you have a clear idea of what the writer is proposing. This stated position is an opinion that the author holds and that can be debated. It is not a fact because there is nothing to debate about a fact.

Look at the following sentences:

Winslow Homer is a nineteenth-century American painter.
I like Winslow Homer's paintings.
Winslow Homer should be called America's greatest painter.

Neither the first nor second sentence would be an acceptable stated position. The first is a fact that cannot be disputed, while the second is merely an opinion that tells how someone feels. It cannot be debated. The third sentence, on the other hand, is a good topic sentence because it is stating an opinion that may or may not be accepted. Facts can be used to support or dispute it.

Major Points

Another effective persuasive technique is to restate the major points. Writers often restate their position at the conclusion of their essay. Therefore, looking for ideas that are repeated will help you locate the writer's stated position and major points.

To understand persuasive writing, you must identify the facts the author uses to back up his or her position. Evaluate them in terms of their quality and quantity. The following criteria will help you evaluate them. The supporting facts should be accurate, logical, and relevant to the argument. They should be introduced in an appropriate order. For instance, if you were trying to convince someone that Winslow Homer should be considered America's greatest painter, you probably would discuss the contributions that he made to painting in the order in which he made them, as this would be the easiest order to follow.

By using examples, descriptions, and comparisons to support facts, the writer makes the argument stronger. For example, a description of one of Homer's paintings could illustrate his techniques and accomplishments and thus clarify and strengthen the argument. A comparison of the types of scenes Homer and others painted of the Civil War would reveal the unique talent Homer possessed. Giving an example of people's reactions to Homer's work could also add weight to the argument.

Finally, the more facts a writer includes to support the stated position, the more convincing is the argument. Check that there are sufficient supporting facts or reasons to make a strong argument.

Guidelines

- Identify the writer's stated position. It should appear as the topic sentence and be an opinion that can be debated.
- Make sure you understand the stated position.
- Identify the major points that support the author's position.
- Evaluate these points insofar as they are
  accurate, logical, and relevant
  introduced in an appropriate order
  clarified through examples, descriptions, and the use of
    strong comparisons
  sufficient in number to make a strong argument

Activity

Reread "Letter Writing" by Andrew A. Rooney and use it to answer the following questions.

1. What is the stated position of the author? Is this position clearly expressed? Give reasons to support your answer?
2. Has the writer used repetition to emphasize his stated position? Where?
3. List the facts the author uses to back up his position.
4. Are these facts presented in an appropriate order? Explain your answer.
5. Are these facts accurate, logical, and relevant? Explain your answer.
6. Does the author use examples to back up his facts? If so, give examples.
7. Does the author use comparisons to clarify and make his supporting facts more convincing? If so, give examples.

1. The author's clearly stated position is that personal letters should need only a five-cent stamp. Rooney clearly states his position in the first and last sentence of the essay.
2. He repeats his thesis statement in the last line.
3. His facts: a personal letter costs more than advertising now; Rooney receives few personal letters now; a letter can be saved.
4. The facts are logically presented. He moves from costs to why letters are special to the historical importance of letters.
5. The facts are accurate, logical, and relevant because they all support the thesis.
6. Rooney uses examples such as Lincoln's letter to his son.
7. He uses comparisons when he contrasts letters with politicians' speeches.

The writing assignments on page 426 have students write creatively, while those on page 427 have them think about the essays and write critically.

YOU THE WRITER
Guidelines for Evaluating Assignment 1

1. Does the student use chronological order to write about an incident?
2. Has the student given the reader a sense of the setting?
3. Has the student used transitions to help the reader understand the order in which things occurred?
4. Is the essay free from grammar, usage, and mechanics errors?

Guidelines for Evaluating Assignment 2

1. Has the student narrowed the topic to enable him or her to write a specific description and explanation?
2. Are any specialized words defined?
3. Are the student's ideas in a reasonable order, which has been created by connecting expressions?
4. Is the essay free from grammar, usage, and mechanics errors?

Guidelines for Evaluating Assignment 3

1. Does the description of the person show him or her doing something?
2. Are the idea clusters placed where they fit naturally?
3. Are the details sharp and specific?
4. Is the essay free from grammar, usage, and mechanics errors?

YOU THE WRITER

Assignment

1. Write a personal narrative describing an incident. This incident may be funny, sad, exciting, scary, and so on.

Prewriting. Before you write, select an incident and freewrite about it.

Writing. Write your narrative. Tell what happened in chronological order. Try to give a sense of the place where this incident occurred. Was it quiet or noisy there? Was the weather hot or cold?

Revising. When you revise, check to see that your reader will understand the order in which events occurred. To help the reader, you might want to use time words like, "Later, . . ." or "Soon . . ."

Assignment

2. Write an essay about something you are interested in—a hobby, a sport, a favorite vacation spot. Include a description of your interest and your reactions.

Prewriting. Once you have chosen the subject, narrow it. For example, if you are going to write about baseball, narrow down your topic to hitting or playing second base. Then begin to cluster. Jot down ideas and feelings about the topic, connecting the ones that seem to go together.

Writing. Now write your essay. Follow your notes, but also pay attention to new ideas that come into your mind. Did you leave out any facts or impressions that you now want to include? If so, include them now—in the place where they fit most naturally. Explain any specialized terms you use.

Revising. Check to see that your ideas are in a reasonable order. Does one idea flow into the next one smoothly? You can make your ideas flow smoothly by using connecting expressions.

Assignment

3. Details are especially important in capturing the look, the spirit, the essence of a person. Write an essay in which you describe a person. Be sure to tell hard, sharp details about this person.

Prewriting. Jot down as many things about this person as you can think of: his or her appearance, gestures, activities, habits, way of speaking, ideas, and so on. Then cluster these details.

Writing. Now write your essay. Show your character *doing* something, maybe going about his or her daily routine. As he or she goes from one thing to another, insert your idea clusters in places where they fit naturally. For example, you might show how the character dresses as he or she leaves the house in the morning.

Revising. Make sure the images in your essay are clear by checking to see that the details are sharp and specific. Remember, good writing is the art of the particular.

426 Nonfiction

YOU THE CRITIC

Assignment

1. Choose an essay that you found especially interesting. Then write an essay in which you state the main idea of this essay and then show which devices the author used to support his or her main idea.

Prewriting. Write down the main idea the essay communicated. List the ways in which the author supported his or her ideas.

Writing. Now write your essay. State your main idea. In your body paragraphs, identify the ways in which the author supports the main idea, providing specific examples of each way you identify.

Revising. When you revise, check to see that your essay is well organized.

Assignment

2. Write an essay explaining what you can tell about the author of one of the essays based on his or her writing. Discuss the author's interests, personality, attitudes, beliefs, and so on.

Prewriting. Reread the essay you are going to write about. Read it for its explicit message, the points the author makes about the subject he or she is discussing. Read it also for its implicit message, the kinds of things the author is saying between the lines.

Writing. Write your first draft. Discuss the things you deduced about the author from the explicit message of the essay. Next discuss the things you deduced about the author from reading between the lines. Finally draw conclusions about the author.

Revising. Check to see that you have included enough information to give the reader a clear impression of the author. Also check to see that the evidence supports your conclusions.

Assignment

3. Write an essay about *two* essays, one that instructs more than it entertains and one that entertains more than it instructs. Explain what you learned in the instructional essay and what you found interesting in the entertaining essay.

Prewriting. Ask yourself which essay provided you with the most information about things you didn't know before. Ask yourself which essay you found the most entertaining. Now make a list of the things you have learned from the informative essay and a list of the things you found interesting in the entertaining essay.

Writing. Write your essay, organizing it in the following way: Start by stating your main idea. Then discuss the things you learned from the informative essay. Next discuss the things you found interesting in the entertaining essay. Finally sum up your major points.

Revising. When you revise, cut out unnecessary words and sentences, for these clutter up your essay and prevent your important ideas from shining through.

You the Critic   427

Guidelines for Evaluating Assignment 1

1. Does the student state his or her main idea about the essay chosen?
2. Does the body of the essay identify the ways in which the author supports the main idea, providing specific examples?
3. Is the essay well-organized?
4. Is the essay free from grammar, usage, and mechanics errors?

Guidelines for Evaluating Assignment 2

1. Does the essay explain what the student discovered about the author from the explicit essay?
2. Does the essay explain what the student deduced about the author from reading between the lines?
3. Has the student included enough information to give the reader a clear impression of the author without making any incorrect conclusions?
4. Is the essay free from grammar, usage, and mechanics errors?

Guidelines for Evaluating Assignment 3

1. Does the essay begin with a thesis about an informative essay and an entertaining essay?
2. Does the essay present what the student learned from the informative essay and what he or she found interesting in the entertaining essay?
3. Does the essay conclude with a summary of the student's major points?
4. Are unnecessary words and sentences eliminated from the essay?
5. Is the essay free from grammar, usage, and mechanics errors?

Humanities Note

Fine art, *Springtime Fantasy* by Adolphe Faugeron. *Springtime Fantasy* was painted by the French artist Adolphe Faugeron (b. 1866). It was inspired by a painting done by the great French Barbizon School artist, Jean François Millet, in 1868. In celebration of Millet's composition, Faugeron painted this landscape with the same reverence for nature, realistic style and admiration for the French countryside. This delightful convocation of the elements of a spring landscape is a fitting evocation of poetic images.

SPRINGTIME FANTASY
Adolphe Faugeron
Three Lions

POETRY

Poetry is language that says more than ordinary language and says it with fewer words and in less space. Poets use language in a special way. Like other writers, poets choose words for their sense, but they also choose words for what they hint at or suggest, for the way they sound, and for the word pictures they create. Ordinary language makes sense. Poetry makes sense—and sound, and rhythm and music, and vision.

Short stories, essays, newspaper articles, your schoolbooks, and so on, are written in prose. Poetry is usually written in verse. Verse is language with a definite rhythm, or beat. It is usually arranged in columns down the page. Sometimes these columns of lines are divided into units called stanzas. Lines of verse often (but not always) rhyme. Although you could say that poetry is what is written in verse, it is always more than rhythm and rhyme. Poetry, as a great poet said, is the most memorable kind of language.

You may want to explain to students that this process is similar to the one they would use in reading fiction. The special requirements of poetry, however, call for a few key differences in approach.

Since poetry tends to be more musical than prose, it is important to read a poem slowly and read it several times—aloud as well as silently. You may also want to tell students that the music of a poem often reinforces its meaning. A poem about a peaceful place, for instance, will usually have calm and peaceful rhythms too.

Another strategy that you might want to highlight for students is paraphrasing. In its intensity, poetry can sometimes be intimidating. When students are able to put a poem into their own words, they will feel more at home with it. Caution them, however, that a paraphrase is not a substitute for a poem. Show them that, while paraphrasing is a useful technique, it also drains away a poem's music.

After discussing each strategy with students, you may want to read "The Village Blacksmith" with them and show how these approaches work in action. Tell them that the annotations accompanying the poem are only a sample and that their own questions might be different.

For further practice with the process, use the selection in the Teaching Portfolio, "To Be of Use," by Marge Piercy, on page 506, which students can annotate themselves. Encourage them to continue to use these strategies when reading other poems.

READING ACTIVELY

Poetry

Reading poetry is an act of discovery. Active readers ask questions about the use of words and clarify the intended use of language. They listen for the music of the poem. They stop to summarize and to paraphrase the poem's meaning. Finally, they pull together all the elements of the poem and add to it themselves. Use the following strategies to help you read a poem actively.

Question   The poet Samuel Coleridge defined poetry as "the best words in the best order." As you read, ask questions about the effect of the words. Think about the vivid images, or word pictures. What do they make you see? What do they make you feel?

Clarify   Poems are often filled with figurative language—that is, language that says one thing but means another. As you read poetry, stop to clarify—to ask if the words mean exactly what they say. If the words suggest something beyond their basic literal meaning, perhaps the poet is using them figuratively or intends a more imaginative meaning.

Listen   Poetry has a musical quality. To fully enjoy it, listen to the music created by the use of rhythm and rhyme. Look for the effect of the repetition of sounds, words, and phrases. Also remember that the end of a sentence in poetry is not necessarily the end of a line. Let punctuation marks guide your reading.

Summarize   Some poems tell a story. When you read, stop at appropriate points in the story to summarize what has happened so far.

Paraphrase   Ask what the poem means, and then put this meaning into your own words. You do not truly own, or understand, a poem until you can express its meaning in your own words.

Pull It Together   A poem consists of words, images, rhythms, and meaning. However, as James Dickey says in "How to Enjoy Poetry" (page 375), "for a poem to live, something from within you must come to it and meet it and complete it." After you have read a poem, bring all the elements together. What did the poem say to you?

Objectives

1 To learn how to read poetry actively
2 To understand theme in poetry
3 To understand a poet's purpose
4 To interpret similes
5 To write about work

Support Material

Teaching Portfolio
Teacher Backup, p. 641
Grammar in Action Worksheet, *Recognizing Specific Nouns,* p. 644
Reading Actively, "Dusting," by Julia Alvarez, p. 646
Usage and Mechanics Worksheet, p. 647
Critical Thinking and Reading

Worksheet, *Understanding the Poet's Purpose,* p. 648
Language Worksheet, *Interpreting Similes,* p. 649
Selection Test, p. 650
Art Transparency 13, *The Village Smithy,* by Konstantin Rodko

Library of Video Classics, *Poets and Poetry*

The Village Blacksmith

Henry Wadsworth Longfellow

Under a spreading chestnut tree
   The village smithy[1] stands;
The smith, a mighty man is he,
   With large and sinewy[2] hands;
5 And the muscles of his brawny arms
   Are strong as iron bands.

His hair is crisp,[3] and black, and long,
   His face is like the tan;
His brow is wet with honest sweat,
10   He earns whate'er he can,
And looks the whole world in the face,
   For he owes not any man.

Week in, week out, from morn till night,
   You can hear his bellows[4] blow;
15 You can hear him swing his heavy sledge,[5]
   With measured beat and slow,
Like a sexton[6] ringing the village bell,
   When the evening sun is low.

And children coming home from school
20   Look in at the open door;
They love to see the flaming forge,
   And hear the bellows roar,
And catch the burning sparks that fly
   Like chaff from a threshing floor.

Question: What picture of the blacksmith do these words create? Which words are particularly effective? What feelings toward the blacksmith do the words arouse?

Clarify: The poet is using figurative language when he compares the blacksmith to a sexton.

Question: In what special way are the blacksmith and a sexton alike? What does this simile suggest about the blacksmith?

Listen: The poem has a slightly irregular rhythm. Read the lines aloud and tap out the pattern of stressed and unstressed syllables. The rhyme scheme is abcbdb. Which words rhyme?

---

1. smithy (smith' ē) *n.*: The workshop of a blacksmith.
2. sinewy (sin' yōō wē) *adj.*: Tough and strong.
3. crisp (krisp) *adj.*: In this case, it means closely curled and wiry.
4. bellows (bel' ōz) *n.*: A device for quickening the fire by blowing air on it.
5. sledge (slej) *n.*: Sledgehammer, a long, heavy hammer, usually held with both hands.
6. sexton (seks' tən) *n.*: A church official in charge of ringing the bells.

The Village Blacksmith   431

Presentation

Motivation/Prior Knowledge Asking students to imagine the job that they would most like to do when they graduate from school. Tell them that Longfellow wrote "The Village Blacksmith" to honor a type of work that was important in his day.

Thematic Idea Another selection that you might use with this one is "A Time of Beginnings," page 343. In this essay, Jade Snow Wong demonstrates that she shares the same ideas about hard work that Longfellow expresses in "The Village Blacksmith."

Purpose-Setting Question What values do you think Longfellow is trying to teach in this poem?

Master Teacher Note By encouraging students to interact with the text, you will help them to become active readers. Questioning and clarifying are strategies that students may have already used in reading fiction.

Listening is an activity that is particularly suited to poetry, with its rich texture of sounds. Students will gain more from a poem by noticing sound devices, reading aloud the passages in which they are used, and considering the relation of sound to meaning.

Paraphrasing is also a strategy that is especially appropriate for poetry. You may want to have students paraphrase shorter poems in their entirety. For longer poems, you can ask students to paraphrase difficult passages or key thematic statements.

As students first work with this process, you may have to coach them on how to formulate good questions, or how to relate sound to meaning, and on how to construct paraphrases.

Reading Strategy Remind students that the annotations accompanying "The Village Blacksmith" are samples and that their own questions about the test may differ from the ones here.

Discussion What qualities does the blacksmith have in common with the tree that was mentioned at the start of the poem?

432   *Poetry*

Grammar in Action

Poets prefer words that are specific, precise, and concrete. In "The Village Blacksmith," for example, Longfellow chooses specific nouns rather than general nouns to convey his images.

GENERAL NOUNS	SPECIFIC NOUNS
tree	chestnut tree
metal	iron bands
tool	bellows
person	sexton

Why use a general noun when a specific one packs so much more emotional punch? These specific nouns conjure detailed images. Even their sounds are richer. When you write, try to think of specific nouns in order to make your writing more precise and interesting. Use a dictionary or a thesaurus to find specific nouns when you are writing poetry or prose.

Student Activity 1. For each pair of nouns, decide which word is more specific and explain why.

1. a. dog
   b. cocker spaniel
2. a. 'Where the Red Fern Grows"
   b. novel

25 He goes on Sunday to the church,
    And sits among his boys;
He hears the parson pray and preach,
    He hears his daughter's voice,
Singing in the village choir,
30   And it makes his heart rejoice.

It sounds to him like her mother's voice,
    Singing in Paradise!
He needs must think of her once more,
    How in the grave she lies;
35 And with his hard, rough hand he wipes
    A tear out of his eyes.

Toiling—rejoicing—sorrowing,
    Onward through life he goes;
Each morning sees some task begin,
40   Each evening sees it close;
Something attempted, something done,
    Has earned a night's repose.

Thanks, thanks to thee, my worthy friend,
    For the lesson thou hast taught!
45 Thus at the flaming forge of life
    Our fortunes must be wrought;
Thus on its sounding anvil shaped
    Each burning deed and thought.

Summarize: A hard-working blacksmith takes pleasure in hearing his daughter sing in the church choir, for her singing recalls to him his now-dead wife, and so brings a tear to his eye.

Listen: Three words end in *-ing*. What effect does this repetition create?

Paraphrase: The blacksmith's philosophy is that hard work has great value. The completion of a task earns one a good night's sleep.

Listen: Three words begin with the letter *f*. What effect does the repetition of this initial sound create?

Pull It Together: There is a lesson to be found in the blacksmith's life. The poet praises his ethic of hard work. However, he also points out that although the blacksmith has been hardened by life, his heart is still tender—he is kind to the village children and sheds a tear for his now-dead wife.

Henry Wadsworth Longfellow (1807–1882) was born in Maine. After graduating from Bowdoin College, he traveled in Europe, but returned to become a professor of languages at Bowdoin and later at Harvard. Longfellow is associated with a group of poets known as the Fireside Poets, since their work often attracted a family audience that would read the poems aloud while sitting around the fireplace. In many of his poems, Longfellow strove to portray the myths and values of the still-young nation. After the publication of his second book of poems, which included "The Village Blacksmith," he became recognized as one of the major poets in the United States.

The Village Blacksmith 433

3. a. dwelling
   b. shack
4. a. hurricane
   b. storm

Student Activity 2. Find a more specific noun for each of the following general nouns, then use the specific noun in a sentence.

laborer   house   animal
vehicle   relative   job

Student Activity 3. Collect specific nouns on slips of paper in a box in your classroom. Grab a handful of nouns to inspire an original poem.

Closure and Extension

ANSWERS TO THINKING ABOUT THE SELECTION
Recalling

1. He is not in debt and does not depend on anyone else for his living.
2. It reminds him of his wife's voice.
3. He begins a task in the morning and finishes it at night.

Interpreting

4. Suggested Response: Among the details that indicate he is honest and hard-working are his "honest sweat" and the fact that he works "from morn till night."
5. Suggested Response: His tear indicates that he loved his wife very much and still feels her loss.

Applying

6. Suggested Response: The blacksmith would probably agree, because he works very hard and seems to be content with what he does.

ANSWERS TO ANALYZING LITERATURE

1. Lines 37–42 reveal the blacksmith's philosophy of life.
2. Suggested Response: He goes through life working hard and feeling joy and sorrow. By accomplishing some task each day, he earns his rest at night.
3. Suggested Response: The last stanza indicates that the poet agrees with the blacksmith's philosophy. In that stanza, the poet holds the blacksmith up as an example for others to follow.

ANSWERS TO CRITICAL THINKING AND READING

1. Suggested Response: Lines 10–12 indicate that the blacksmith is to be admired for earning his own living and for not owing money to anyone.
2. Suggested Response: Lines 35–6 indicate that the blacksmith's tender feelings for his wife are admirable.
3. Suggested Response: In the second stanza, Longfellow seems to praise the blacksmith because "His brow is wet with honest

THINKING ABOUT THE SELECTION
Recalling

1. Why is the blacksmith able to look the whole world in the face?
2. Why does his daughter's voice make his heart rejoice?
3. How does the blacksmith begin and end each day?

Interpreting

4. Which details tell you that the blacksmith is an honest, hard-working man?
5. What does the tear in his eye indicate about him?

Applying

6. President Theodore Roosevelt once said in a Labor Day address: "Far and away the best prize that life offers is the chance to work hard at work worth doing." Do you think the village blacksmith would agree or disagree with this sentiment? Explain your answer.

ANALYZING LITERATURE
Understanding Theme in Poetry

Theme is the insight into life revealed by the poem. Sometimes the theme is stated directly. To fully understand it, paraphrase it, or express it in your own words.
1. Which lines reveal the blacksmith's philosophy of life?
2. Paraphrase these lines.
3. Which details indicate that the poet agrees with the blacksmith's philosophy of life?

CRITICAL THINKING AND READING
Understanding the Poet's Purpose

When Longfellow wrote in the mid-nineteenth century, the United States was still a rather young country. One of his purposes for writing was to present myths for the new land and to portray the values of our native American culture.
1. Which details in the poem show the American culture during the nineteenth century valued independence?
2. Which details show that it valued sentiment, or tender feelings?
3. Which details show that it valued hard work?
4. Do you think views toward work in the later part of the twentieth century are different from those during Longfellow's time? Explain your answer.

UNDERSTANDING LANGUAGE
Interpreting Similes

A simile is a comparison between two basically unlike things. A simile makes its comparison by using the word like or as. By using a simile, a poet can make a point in a vivid way. For example: "And the muscles of his brawny arms/Are strong as iron bands." By comparing the muscles of the blacksmith's arms to iron bands, the poet emphasizes the muscles' strength.
1. What simile do you find in lines 15–18? What point does the poet make through the use of this simile?
2. What simile do you find in lines 23–24? What point does the poet make through the use of this simile?

THINKING AND WRITING
Writing About Work

Think of someone you know who enjoys his or her work. What does this person do? Why does this person take pleasure from the job? Write a short poem telling about a day in the work life of this person. Use similes to help you make your points. Revise your poem to make sure its meaning is clear. Prepare a final draft, and read it aloud to your classmates.

sweat." In the seventh stanza, he seems to praise the man for earning his rest at night by accomplishing some task each day.
4. Answers will differ. Suggested Response: Students may say that hard work is still valued but that some people are bored with jobs that are dull and repetitive. Especially insightful students may note that manual labor is not as respected today as it seems to have been in Longfellow's time.

Challenge Explain why independence and hard work might have been especially valued in the United States at the time Longfellow wrote.

ANSWERS TO UNDERSTANDING LANGUAGE

1. The blacksmith swinging his hammer is compared to the sexton ringing the churchbell. Suggested Response: The poet uses the simile to show his respect for the blacksmith's work by associating it with church and religion.

2. The sparks that leap from the forge are compared to the chaff, or husks, that are separated from wheat in threshing. Suggested Response: The poet uses this simile to point up that the blacksmith's work is just as valuable as threshing.

THINKING AND WRITING

Publishing Student Writing You might want to have students practice reading their poem to a small group before they present it to the class.

Narrative Poetry

THE BOY
Thomas Hart Benton
© Three Lions

Humanities Note

Fine art, *The Boy,* 1950, by Thomas Hart Benton. Thomas Hart Benton (1889–1975) an American Regionalist painter, attended the Art Institute of Chicago and the Academie Julien in Paris. His true education, he felt, began after Paris when he spent several years roaming the United States, working at odd jobs and painting. During this period he became an advocate of the American Midwest. By portraying scenes of the simple rural folk, living out life's tragedies and joys, he helped change the focus of American painting from Manhattan to the heartland.

The Boy narrates a rural farewell. In it, Benton used his peculiar technique, wherein he painted from a clay model of his subject, rather than from life. This resulted in his unique style, which has a sculpted, high relief quality. The repetition of curves in the figures, the landscape, and the rutted country road give movement to the composition. The string of telephone poles, like so many exclamation points, unifies the picture, which has a narrative quality. Thomas Hart Benton painted scenes such as this with love and enthusiasm for his subject.

The Highwayman

Alfred Noyes (1880–1958) was both a poet and critic. He was born in Staffordshire, England, although he lived for many years in the United States and taught at Princeton University. Noyes often wrote about legendary figures from English history, such as Robin Hood and Sir Francis Drake. He wrote "The Highwayman," his best-known poem, about an outlaw and his love, while visiting Bagshot Heath. The poem may have been inspired by the fact that this region of England had once been terrorized by outlaws.

Narrative Poetry

Narrative poetry is poetry that tells a story. Narrative poems have a special appeal. They present dramatic events in a vivid way, using some of the same elements as short stories: plot, characters, and dialogue, for example. Some narrative poems, like "The Highwayman," use words and phrases that are repeated throughout the work. These repetitions help to create a songlike rhythm and focus your attention on important details of the story.

Look For

While reading "The Highwayman," look for the words and phrases that are repeated. Decide why the poet might have wanted to emphasize these words and phrases. How does the repetition help create a romantic picture of the outlaw?

Writing

A highwayman was an outlaw who robbed travelers. Recall a famous outlaw you have heard or read about. List some of the details you remember about this outlaw's legend. Which of these details made the outlaw seem a romantic, or dashing figure?

Vocabulary

Knowing the following words will help you as you read "The Highwayman."

torrent (tôr′ ənt) *n.*: Flood (p. 437)

moor (moor) *n.*: Open, rolling land with swamps (p. 437)

breeches (brich′ iz) *n.*: Trousers that reach to or just below the knee (p. 437)

cascade (kas kād′) *n.*: Waterfall or anything tumbling like water (p. 439)

tawny (tô′ nē) *adj.*: Yellowish brown (p. 440)

strive (strīv) *v.*: Struggle (p. 441)

brandished (bran′ dishd) *v.*: Waved in a threatening way (p. 442)

The Highwayman

Alfred Noyes

Part One

The wind was a torrent of darkness among the gusty trees.
The moon was a ghostly galleon[1] tossed upon cloudy seas.
The road was a ribbon of moonlight over the purple moor,
And the highwayman came riding—
5   Riding—riding—
The highwayman came riding, up to the old inn door.

He'd a French cocked-hat on his forehead, a bunch of lace at
  his chin,
A coat of the claret velvet, and breeches of brown doeskin.
They fitted with never a wrinkle. His boots were up to the
  thigh.
10 And he rode with a jeweled twinkle,
   His pistol butts a-twinkle,
His rapier hilt[2] a-twinkle, under the jeweled sky.

Over the cobbles he clattered and clashed in the dark innyard.
He tapped with his whip on the shutters, but all was locked
  and barred.
15 He whistled a tune to the window, and who should be waiting
  there
But the landlord's black-eyed daughter,
   Bess, the landlord's daughter,
Plaiting[3] a dark red love knot into her long black hair.

And dark in the dark old innyard a stable wicket[4] creaked
20 Where Tim the ostler[5] listened. His face was white and peaked.
His eyes were hollows of madness, his hair like moldy hay,
But he loved the landlord's daughter,
   The landlord's red-lipped daughter.
Dumb as a dog he listened, and he heard the robber say—

---

1. galleon (gal' ē ən) *n*.: A large Spanish sailing ship.
2. rapier (rā' pē ər) **hilt:** The large cup-shaped handle of a rapier,
which is a type of sword.
3. plaiting (plăt' iŋ) *n*.: Braiding.
4. stable wicket (stā' b'l wik' it): A small door or gate to a stable.
5. ostler (äs' lər) *n*.: Someone who takes care of horses at an inn
or stable.

The Highwayman   437

Master Teacher Note As students read "The Highwayman," they might consider whether the poet based his account on fact or legend. In reality, highwaymen were notorious bandits who ambushed travelers along rural roads. Ask students to name famous highwaymen; for example, Robin Hood, Pancho Villa, Zorro, and Jesse James. What can they recall about the legends surrounding these highwaymen? Which details in the lives of these highwaymen seem to be factual and which appear to be legendary? Then you might ask **more advanced** students to try to separate factual from legendary details as they read this poem.

Thematic Idea You might want to have students read two other narrative poems—"Annabel Lee," p. 455, and "Oranges," p. 459—and compare the relationships depicted in them with the relationship between Bess and the highwayman. Students may want to consider, for example, the outcomes—or predicted outcomes—of these relationships and the signs of devotion displayed by the various characters.

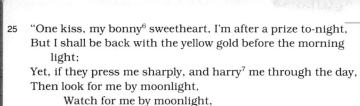

25   "One kiss, my bonny[6] sweetheart, I'm after a prize to-night,
But I shall be back with the yellow gold before the morning
     light;
Yet, if they press me sharply, and harry[7] me through the day,
Then look for me by moonlight,
     Watch for me by moonlight,
30 I'll come to thee by moonlight, though hell should bar the
     way."

He rose upright in the stirrups. He scarce could reach her
     hand,
But she loosened her hair in the casement.[8] His face burnt
     like a brand[9]
As the black cascade of perfume came tumbling over his
     breast;
And he kissed its waves in the moonlight,
35   (O, sweet black waves in the moonlight!)
Then he tugged at his rein in the moonlight, and galloped
     away to the west.

---

6. bonny (bän′ ē) *adj.*: Scottish for pretty.
7. harry (har′ ē) *v.*: To disturb by constant attacks.
8. casement (kās′ mənt) *n.*: A window frame that opens on hinges.
9. brand (brand) *n.*: A piece of burning wood.

6 Literary Focus Why do you think that the poet stresses the word *moonlight* in lines 28–30 and 34–36? What, for instance, does moonlight add to the scene that sunlight would not?

7 Literary Focus In a narrative poem, the dialogue often plays an important role in pointing up character traits and hinting at future events. You might ask students how the highwayman's speech reveals his character and hints at the coming events.

8 Reading Strategy You might have students summarize the events of the first part of the poem.

9 **Discussion** Point out to students that the red coats of the soldiers mark just one of many references to the color red in the poem. Ask them to find other references and to speculate why the poet emphasized this color.

10 **Discussion** How does the poet build suspense?

11 **Discussion** Where does the poet refer to blood in describing Bess's struggle to warn the highwayman? How does this red imagery add to the vividness of the scene?

Part Two

He did not come in the dawning. He did not come at noon;
And out of the tawny sunset, before the rise of the moon,
When the road was a gypsy's ribbon, looping the purple moor,
40   A redcoat troop came marching—   9
      Marching—marching—
King George's men[10] came marching, up to the old inn door.

They said no word to the landlord. They drank his ale instead.
But they gagged his daughter, and bound her, to the foot of
   her narrow bed.
45   Two of them knelt at her casement, with muskets at their
   side!
There was death at every window;
    And hell at one dark window;
For Bess could see, through her casement, the road that *he*
   would ride.
    10

They had tied her up to attention, with many a sniggering
   jest.[11]
50   They had bound a musket beside her, with the muzzle
   beneath her breast!
"Now, keep good watch!" and they kissed her. She heard the
   doomed man say—
Look for me by moonlight;
    Watch for me by moonlight;
I'll come to thee by moonlight, though hell should bar the
   way!

55   She twisted her hands behind her; but all the knots held
   good!
She writhed her hands till her fingers were wet with sweat or
   blood!   11
They stretched and strained in the darkness, and the hours
   crawled by like years,
Till, now, on the stroke of midnight,
    Cold, on the stroke of midnight,
60   The tip of one finger touched it! The trigger at least was hers!

The tip of one finger touched it. She strove no more for the
   rest.

———

10. **King George's men:** Soldiers serving King George of England.
11. **sniggering** (snig′ ər iŋ) **jest:** Sly joke.

440   Poetry

Grammar in Action

Exclamation marks are used to punctuate statements showing strong feelings. Exclamation marks can be used after exclamatory sentences, imperative sentences, and interjections. Exclamatory sentences are statements that show strong emotion. Imperative sentences are urgent, forceful commands. Interjections are words or phrases that express strong emotions. Mature writers use exclamation marks to add drama and excitement to their writing. In the following passage, Alfred Noyes uses exclamation marks to heighten the suspense:

Tlot-tlot, in the frosty silence! *Tlot-tlot*, in the echoing night!

Noyes accentuates the drama of the situation by repeating the pattern of words and ending each phrase with an exclamation mark. The punctuation adds to the tension.

   Skilled writers realize that they must use the exclamation mark sparingly. Overuse of the exclamation mark would diminish its effect.

Student Activity 1. Find three sentences from "The Highwayman" in which Noyes uses exclamation marks. Explain why you think the author used exclamation marks in these sentences.

Up, she stood up to attention, with the muzzle beneath her
     breast.
She would not risk their hearing; she would not strive again;
For the road lay bare in the moonlight;
65   Blank and bare in the moonlight;
And the blood of her veins, in the moonlight, throbbed to her
     love's refrain.

Tlot-tlot; tlot-tlot! Had they heard it? The horsehoofs ringing
     clear;
Tlot-tlot, tlot-tlot, in the distance? Were they deaf that they did
     not hear?
Down the ribbon of moonlight, over the brow of the hill,
70 The highwayman came riding—   **12**
          Riding—riding—
The redcoats looked to their priming![12] She stood up, straight
     and still.

Tlot-tlot, in the frosty silence! *Tlot-tlot,* in the echoing night!
Nearer he came and nearer. Her face was like a light.

――――――
12. priming (prī′ miŋ) *n.*: The explosive used to set off the charge
in a gun.

12 Discussion How does the repetition of the sound of the horsehoofs create suspense?

Student Activity 2. Add exclamation marks where appropriate in
the following statements.

1. Hooray We beat Bridgeville

2. Martha, get in here now

3. Hurry I'm losing my grip on the rope

13 Literary Focus You might point out to students that Bess does not say a single word in the poem. Ask them why her struggle to reach the trigger is all the more effective because it takes place in silence. You might also ask them why her gesture of loosening her hair is as eloquent as many fine words.

14 Discussion Ask students if they think that Bess's self-sacrifice is believable. Can they think of any examples of such selfless love in today's world?

15 Discussion Why does the highwayman return?

16 Critical Thinking and Reading Why do you think that the poet divided the sequence of events into two parts? Why do you think that he ended the first section with the highwayman's parting from Bess?

Reader's Response In this poem, why do we sympathize with the Highwayman even though he is an outlaw?

Humanities Note

Tell students that many works of literature describe a person's sacrifice for a loved one. In Charles Dickens's *Tale of Two Cities,* for example, Sydney Carton allows himself to be guillotined in order to save the husband of a woman he loves. (You might want to encourage **less advanced** students to read the easier edition of this novel, available from Amsco.)

Ask students why self-sacrifice is such a powerful theme.

Enrichment Ask students to discuss the meaning of the term *highway robbery.* Have them speculate about the origin of the term.

75   Her eyes grew wide for a moment; she drew one last deep
          breath,
     Then her finger moved in the moonlight,
               Her musket shattered the moonlight,
     Shattered her breast in the moonlight and warned him—with
          her death.

     He turned. He spurred to the west; he did not know who stood
80   Bowed, with her head o'er the musket, drenched with her own
          blood!
     Not till the dawn he heard it, and his face grew gray to hear
     How Bess, the landlord's daughter,
               The landlord's black-eyed daughter,
     Had watched for her love in the moonlight, and died in the
          darkness there.

85   Back, he spurred like a madman, shouting a curse to the sky,
     With the white road smoking behind him and his rapier
          brandished high.
     Blood-red were his spurs in the golden noon; wine-red was his
          velvet coat;
     When they shot him down on the highway,
               Down like a dog on the highway,
90   And he lay in his blood on the highway, with a bunch of lace
          at his throat.

     .   .   .   .

     And still of a winter's night, they say, when the wind is in
          the trees,
     When the moon is a ghostly galleon tossed upon cloudy
          seas,
     When the road is a ribbon of moonlight over the purple moor,
     A highwayman comes riding—
95   *Riding—riding—*
     A highwayman comes riding, up to the old inn door.

     Over the cobbles he clatters and clangs in the dark innyard.
     He taps with his whip on the shutters, but all is locked and
          barred.
     He whistles a tune to the window, and who should be
          waiting there
100 *But the landlord's black-eyed daughter,*
               Bess, the landlord's daughter,
     Plaiting a dark red love knot into her long black hair.

Closure and Extension

ANSWERS TO THINKING ABOUT THE SELECTION
Recalling

1. He plans to rob some gold and return before morning. If the soldiers pursue him, however, he will return the next night.
2. Without speaking to the landlord, they gag Bess and tie her to the foot of her bed. They tie a musket next to her, laughing at her and

THINKING ABOUT THE SELECTION

Recalling

1. Explain the highwayman's plans. (Lines 25–30)
2. Describe the Redcoats' actions at the inn. (Lines 43–51)
3. How does Bess warn the highwayman of the soldier's presence? (Lines 75–80)
4. What happens to the highwayman when he returns the day after Bess's warning?

Interpreting

5. How do the soldiers learn of the highwayman's plans to return to the inn?
6. Find three details that make the highwayman appear a romantic, or dashing figure.
7. Find each mention of the color *red* in this poem. How does the repetition of this color add to the romantic quality of the poem?
8. How does the setting add to this quality?
9. Would this poem have been as effective if it had ended at line 90? Explain your answer.

Applying

10. What is it about outlaws that has made people romanticize them—or has made their lives seem romantic and glamorous?

ANALYZING LITERATURE

Understanding Narrative Poetry

Narrative poetry tells a story, using elements like plot, character, and setting. In "The Highwayman," for example, the two main characters are the outlaw and Bess. Using strong rhythm and repeated words, the poet tells how the love between Bess and the outlaw leads to their deaths.

1. Describe the two main characters.
2. How is the conflict resolved?
3. Where and when does most of the action take place?
4. How do the poem's rhythms and repetitions add to the drama of the story?

CRITICAL THINKING AND READING

Following the Sequence of Events

A storyteller creates an effect by the order in which he or she chooses to **sequence,** or arrange, the events. Noyes tells "The Highwayman" in **chronological sequence,** describing events in the order they occur.

1. List the important events of the poem in chronological sequence.
2. Would the poem be as effective if the sequence were changed and you knew right away what would happen? Why or why not?

SPEAKING AND LISTENING

Reading with Expression

Reading with expression means using your voice to bring out the meaning of a work. You can best practice this type of reading in small groups. Choose one of the following passages to read aloud: lines 1–18; lines 37–54; lines 91–102. Read your chosen passage several times to your group. Try varying the speed with which you say different words and phrases. Also, you may choose to say some phrases in a louder, or a softer, voice. In some places, you might want to stop at the end of a line, while in others you may want to continue smoothly from one line to the next.

THINKING AND WRITING

Summarizing a Narrative Poem

Summarizing a story means retelling it briefly in the correct order, giving only the essential details. Imagine that you are creating a movie based on this poem. In order to go ahead with your plans, you need a summary of the action. Look again at the list that you made of the poem's events. Turn this list into a summary of the story, adding only the most important details. In revising, make sure that your summary is brief but complete.

The Highwayman 443

(Answers begin on p. 442.)

ANSWERS TO ANALYZING LITERATURE

1. The highwayman is a stylish and daring outlaw. Bess, the landlord's daughter, is a beautiful young woman with long black hair, dark eyes, and red lips. She is also brave and faithful.
2. The soldiers kill the outlaw after Tim betrays him.
3. Most of the action takes place at an English inn, during two nights.
4. The galloping rhythms carry the action onward. The repetitions highlight dramatic details, like the moonlight and the shining pistol butts.

ANSWERS TO CRITICAL THINKING AND READING

1. The highwayman visits Bess; Tim overhears them; the highwayman promises to return to her; the soldiers come to the inn the next day at sunset; they tie up Bess and wait in ambush for the outlaw; Bess shoots herself to warn him; at dawn the next day, the highwayman hears what happened; he rides back and is shot down on the highway.
2. Suggested Response: No. There would be less suspense.

Challenge What is the poet's attitude toward the highwayman? Support your answer with evidence from the poem.

SPEAKING AND LISTENING
Provide sufficient class time for this activity. Since some students might be shy, you might start the assignment by asking for student volunteers.

THINKING AND WRITING
Publishing Student Writing You might want to have each student tape his or her summary to a larger sheet of colored paper and decorate the paper with scenes from the proposed movie.

---

pretending that she is a soldier. Then they wait in ambush at the windows for the highwayman to return.
3. She fires the musket, killing herself. He hears the shot and realizes that something is wrong.
4. He is shot down on the highway.

Interpreting

5. They are told by Tim.
6. Suggested Response: His fancy dress, his weapons, his apparent scorn for danger, his appearances by moonlight, and his love for Bess.
7. Red is mentioned or suggested in the following lines: 8, 18, 23, 32, 40, 56, 66, 72, 80, 87, 90, and 102. The associations of this color with love and death heighten the romantic quality of the poem.
8. The moonlight and wind create an eerie, mysterious atmosphere that adds to the romantic quality of the poem.
9. Suggested Response: No. The last two stanzas make it seem as if the love between Bess and the highwayman is so strong that it continues when they are ghosts.

Applying

10. Students' answers will differ. However, outlaws might seem glamorous because they take risks, play for high stakes, and violate the rules that others follow.

More About the Author Many of Robert Service's most popular poems describe life in the Yukon, a Canadian territory east of Alaska, during the 1890's gold rush. Ask students what place in today's world would provide equally exciting subject matter.

Literary Focus Ask students to discuss the part that rhythm plays in their favorite kinds of music. You may even want to bring in a record, like the Beatles' "Yellow Submarine," and have the students tap out the rhythm. Tell students that rhythm is as important in poetry as it is in music.

Look For To help students hear the rhythm, consider reading the first stanza aloud to them, emphasizing the accented syllables. Tell them that this way of reading is useful in pointing up the rhythm of the poem. Advise them, however, that when they give a formal reading of a poem, they should read the words as they would naturally speak them.

Writing/Prior Knowledge After students read the writing assignment, you might divide them into small groups and have them brainstorm to think of all the words they associate with the cold. Write these words on the chalkboard. You may want the students to consult a thesaurus to find additional words. Then have them complete the freewriting assignment using any words from the list that are helpful.

Vocabulary Have more advanced students look up the history of the word *ghastly,* tracing its relationship to the word *ghost* and the Old English word *gast,* meaning "soul, spirit, demon."

The Cremation of Sam McGee

Robert Service (1874–1958) was a Canadian poet who grew up in Glasgow, Scotland. He moved to Canada at the age of twenty and was hired by a bank in 1905. When the bank transferred him to a branch in the Yukon, Service began to write lively poems about the trappers and prospectors he met there. These poems were an immediate success. Soon he was able to leave the bank and concentrate on writing. In "The Cremation of Sam McGee," Service creates a memorable character with an intense hatred of the cold.

Rhythm

Rhythm is the sound pattern created by combining stressed and unstressed syllables. In the following lines from "The Cremation of Sam McGee," for example, the stressed syllables (marked ′) receive more emphasis than the unstressed ones (marked ˘):

Aňd Ĭ looḱed ăt iť, aňd Ĭ thouǵht ă bít, aňd Ĭ looḱed ăt mў fróz̆en chúm;
Thĕn "Hére," saĭd Í, wiťh ă súddĕn crý, "iš mў cré-mă-tór-ĕum."

The same general pattern of stressed and unstressed syllables continues throughout the poem. Other poems have different rhythms, and sometimes a poem's rhythm may change from line to line.

Look For

"The Cremation of Sam McGee" is a poem with a strong, thumping rhythm. Look for the drumbeat of the stressed syllables as you read. You may even want to tap out this rhythm with your fingers. What effect does the rhythm have on the poem?

Writing

A character in this poem, Sam McGee, does not like cold. Remember a time when, for one reason or another, you felt very cold. Write about the situation, telling how bitter cold it was.

Vocabulary

Knowing the following words will help you as you read "The Cremation of Sam McGee."

whimper (hwim′ pər) *v.*: Make low, crying sounds; complain (p. 445)
cremated (krē′ māt id) *v.*: Burned to ashes (p. 445)
ghastly (gast′ lē) *adj.*: Ghostlike; frightful (p. 446)
brawn (brôn) *n.*: Physical strength (p. 446)

stern (stʉrn) *adj.*: Strict; unyielding (p. 446)
loathed (lōt̸hd) *v.*: Hated (p. 446)
scowled (skould) *v.*: Frowned (p. 447)
grisly (griz′ lē) *adj.*: Horrible (p. 447)

Objectives

1 To understand the part that rhythm plays in poetry
2 To evaluate the effects of rhythm in poetry
3 To practice choral reading
4 To imitate the rhythm of a poem

Support Material

Teaching Portfolio
Teacher Backup, p. 665
Usage and Mechanics Worksheet, p. 668
Vocabulary Check, p. 669
Analyzing Literature Worksheet, *Understand Rhythm,* p. 670
Speaking and Listening Worksheet, *Practicing Choral Reading,* p. 671
Selection Test, p. 673

The Cremation of Sam McGee

Robert Service

There are strange things done in the midnight sun[1]
    By the men who moil[2] for gold;
The Arctic trails have their secret tales
    That would make your blood run cold;
5 The Northern Lights have seen queer sights,
    But the queerest they ever did see
Was that night on the marge[3] of Lake Lebarge
    I cremated Sam McGee.

Now Sam McGee was from Tennessee, where the cotton
    blooms and blows.
10 Why he left his home in the South to roam 'round the Pole,
    God only knows.
He was always cold, but the land of gold seemed to hold
    him like a spell;
Though he'd often say in his homely way that "he'd sooner
    live in hell."

On a Christmas Day we were mushing[4] our way over the
    Dawson trail.
Talk of your cold! through the parka's fold it stabbed like a
    driven nail.
15 If our eyes we'd close, then the lashes froze till sometimes
    we couldn't see;
It wasn't much fun, but the only one to whimper was Sam
    McGee.

And that very night, as we lay packed tight in our robes
    beneath the snow,
And the dogs were fed, and the stars o'erhead were dancing
    heel and toe,

---

1. the midnight sun: The sun visible at midnight in the arctic or
antarctic regions during the summer.
2. moil (moil) *v.*: To toil and slave.
3. marge (märj) *n.*: A poetic word for the shore of the lake.
4. mushing (mush' iŋ) *v.*: Traveling by foot over snow, usually with
a dog sled. "Mush" is a command to sled dogs to start or go faster.

The Cremation of Sam McGee   445

5 **Literary Focus** Point out to students that the second accented syllable in each line rhymes with the fourth. In line 21, for example, "low" rhymes with "no." Ask students to find other examples of this rhyme. Then ask them what effect this rhyme has on the poem's rhythm.

6 **Reading Strategy** Have the students identify how the poet prepared readers for this last request in the previous description of Sam.

7 **Language** Tell students that the word *ghastly* is usually associated with "the horror aroused by the sight or suggestion of death."

8 **Discussion** Have students discuss why a promise might take on special importance in a frontier environment like the Yukon at the turn of the century.

9 **Reading Strategy** Ask students to predict how the narrator might resolve his dilemma.

He turned to me, and "Cap," says he, "I'll cash in[5] this trip, I guess;

20 And if I do, I'm asking that you won't refuse my last request."

Well, he seemed so low that I couldn't say no; then he says with a sort of moan:　　5

"It's the cursèd cold, and it's got right hold till I'm chilled clean through to the bone.

Yet 'tain't being dead—it's my awful dread of the icy grave that pains;

So I want you to swear that, foul or fair, you'll cremate my last remains."　　6

25 A pal's last need is a thing to heed, so I swore I would not fail;

And we started on at the streak of dawn; but God! he looked ghastly pale.　　7

He crouched on the sleigh, and he raved all day of his home in Tennessee;

And before nightfall a corpse was all that was left of Sam McGee.

There wasn't a breath in that land of death, and I hurried, horror-driven,

30 With a corpse half hid that I couldn't get rid, because of a promise given;

It was lashed to the sleigh, and it seemed to say: "You may tax your brawn and brains,

But you promised true, and it's up to you to cremate those last remains."

Now a promise made is a debt unpaid, and the trail has its own stern code.　　8

In the days to come, though my lips were dumb, in my heart how I cursed that load.　　9

35 In the long, long night, by the lone firelight, while the huskies,[6] round in a ring,

Howled out their woes to the homeless snows—O God! how I loathed the thing.

And every day that quiet clay seemed to heavy and heavier grow;

---

5. cash in: A slang expression meaning "die."
6. huskies (hus′ kēs) *n.*: Strong dogs used for pulling sleds over the snow.

And on I went, though the dogs were spent and the grub
    was getting low;
The trail was bad, and I felt half mad, but I swore I would
    not give in;
40 And I'd often sing to the hateful thing, and it hearkened
    with a grin.

Till I came to the marge of Lake Lebarge, and a derelict[7]
    there lay;
It was jammed in the ice, but I saw in a trice it was called
    the "Alice May."
And I looked at it, and I thought a bit, and I looked at my
    frozen chum;
Then "Here," said I, with a sudden cry, "is my cre-ma-tor-
    eum."

45 Some planks I tore from the cabin floor, and I lit the boiler
    fire;
Some coal I found that was lying around, and I heaped the
    fuel higher;
The flames just soared, and the furnace roared—such a
    blaze you seldom see;
And I burrowed a hole in the glowing coal, and I stuffed in
    Sam McGee.

Then I made a hike, for I didn't like to hear him sizzle so;
50 And the heavens scowled, and the huskies howled, and the
    wind began to blow.
It was icy cold, but the hot sweat rolled down my cheeks,
    and I don't know why;
And the greasy smoke in an inky cloak went streaking
    down the sky.

I do not know how long in the snow I wrestled with grisly
    fear;
But the stars came out and they danced about ere again I
    ventured near;
55 I was sick with dread, but I bravely said: "I'll just take a
    peep inside.
I guess he's cooked, and it's time I looked"; . . . then the
    door I opened wide.

---

7. derelict (der′ ə likt′) *n.*: An abandoned ship.

The Cremation of Sam McGee   447

10 **Master Teacher Note** You might
point out that the poet makes use
of many fantastic details. Review
with students the difference between realistic and fantastic details. A realistic detail is true to
life, while a fantastic detail could
never have really happened.
Have students find the fantastic
detail in line 40. Then ask them to
look for other fantastic details as
they read.

11 **Discussion** Why do you think the
narrator is sweating even though
it is "icy cold"?

12 **Reading Strategy** Ask students
to predict what the narrator will
see when he opens the door. Will
the scene that confronts him be
realistic or fantastic?

13 Discussion You might want to have students look at the illustration on page 448. Ask them who the man is and why there is a fire in the background. Then you might challenge them to think of an illustration that would be equally good, or better.

Reader's Response Did you find this to be a humorous poem? Why or why not?

And there sat Sam, looking cool and calm, in the heart of
    the furnace roar;
And he wore a smile you could see a mile, and he said:
    "Please close that door.
It's fine in here, but I greatly fear you'll let in the cold and
    storm—
60   Since I left Plumtree, down in Tennessee, it's the first time
    I've been warm."

There are strange things done in the midnight sun
*   By the men who moil for gold;*
The Arctic trails have their secret tales
*   That would make your blood run cold;*
65   *The Northern Lights have seen queer sights,*
*   But the queerest they ever did see*
Was that night on the marge of Lake Lebarge
*   I cremated Sam McGee.*

13

448   *Poetry*

Closure and Extension

ANSWERS TO THINKING ABOUT THE SELECTION
Recalling

1. Sam McGee comes from Tennessee. He does not want to go home because he is searching for gold.
2. He asks the narrator to cremate his last remains.
3. The code of the trail requires a man to keep his promises.

4. The narrator uses an abandoned ship stuck in the ice as his crematoreum. He tears planks from the cabin floor and gets coal to make a fire in the furnace. Then he places Sam McGee's body in the furnace.
5. He finds Sam alive and smiling. Sam asks him to close the door because it is drafty.

Interpreting

6. Sam dislikes the cold and is afraid of being buried in an icy grave,

but the narrator is strong-minded and better able to bear the freezing weather.
7. Sam may have been acting when he claimed he was going to die on this trip. Also, he may have only been pretending when the narrator thought he died.

Applying

8. Students' answers will differ; however, most will realize that, since a promise is a commitment to do

THINKING ABOUT THE SELECTION
Recalling

1. Where did Sam McGee come from? Why doesn't he go home? (Lines 8–11)
2. What does Sam ask the narrator to promise? (Lines 21–24)
3. Why does the narrator try to keep his promise, even though he curses the load? (Lines 29–36)
4. How is the narrator to keep his promise? (Lines 41–48)
5. Describe what the narrator finds when he opens the furnace door? (Lines 53–61)

Interpreting

6. Compare and contrast Sam and the narrator.
7. In what way is the ending of this poem an elaborate practical joke? Explain the details that suggest Sam was playing a trick on his pal in order to get warm.

Applying

8. Do you agree with the narrator that "a promise made is a debt unpaid"? Why or why not?

ANALYZING LITERATURE
Understanding Rhythm

Rhythm is the pattern of stressed and unstressed syllables in the lines of a poem. Many poems have the same rhythmic pattern in each line.

1. Tap out the pattern of stressed and unstressed syllables in line 43. Find three other lines with this exact same rhythm.
2. How does the rhythm of line 44 differ from that of line 43? Find three other lines with the exact same rhythm as line 44.
3. What conclusion do you draw about the rhythmic pattern of this poem?

CRITICAL THINKING AND READING
Evaluating the Effects of Rhythm

Like a drumbeat, the pattern of stressed syllables in poetry can produce different moods: excitement, peace, sadness, for example. In evaluating the effects of rhythm, compare a passage from a poem with a similar passage written as a paragraph.

1. Use your own words to summarize lines 57–60 of the poem in a paragraph.
2. Read your own words and the lines of poetry out loud.
3. Compare and contrast the mood of the poetry with that of your paragraph.

SPEAKING AND LISTENING
Practicing Choral Reading

Choral reading refers to the reading aloud of a poem by a group of people. Your teacher can divide the class in half and each group can prepare a choral reading of this poem for the other group. Remember that in a choral reading, some parts of the poem can be read by everyone. However, other parts, like Sam McGee's words, can be read by a single person.

Each group may also act as an audience for the other group. After hearing a choral reading, the audience can offer comments and suggestions for improvement.

THINKING AND WRITING
Patterning the Rhythm of a Poem

Imagine the narrator's reactions to Sam's trick. Freewrite about what you think the narrator said to Sam after he saw him looking cool and calm in the heart of the roaring furnace. Then use your freewriting as the basis for writing a new stanza for this poem. Using the same rhythmic pattern, write a stanza telling the narrator's reactions. Review your stanza, reading it aloud and tapping out the rhythm. Finally, prepare a proofread draft and read it to your classmates.

The Cremation of Sam McGee 449

(Answers begin on p. 448.)

drama and jaunty humor that are missing from their paraphrases.

Challenge The phrase "grim humor" refers to laughter about a subject that is usually thought of as unpleasant or repelling. How does the poet display grim humor in this poem?

SPEAKING AND LISTENING
Provide sufficient class time for this activity. You might want to allow shyer students to be audience members rather than readers.

THINKING AND WRITING
Publishing Student Writing
You can publish students' work by displaying it on the class bulletin board, along with appropriate illustrations or cutouts from magazines showing arctic scenes.

Writing Across the Curriculum
You might want to have students research and report on the gold rush in the Yukon Territory at the turn of the century. You might inform the social studies department of this assignment. Social studies teachers might provide guidance for students' research.

Challenge Imagine that the premise, or basic idea, of this story were reversed. Instead of being a man from the South exploring the Yukon, for instance, Sam is a man from the Yukon exploring the tropics. Also, instead of longing for the warmth of Tennessee, Sam longs for the arctic cold.

In two or three paragraphs, tell how this new story would differ from the one that Service recounts.

something, breaking a promise is like not paying a debt. Of course, sometimes circumstances make it impossible to keep a promise.

ANSWERS TO ANALYZING LITERATURE

1. The following lines have the same rhythm as line 43: 21, 33, 34, and 51. (Note that, in answering this and the following question, students must choose lines that correspond exactly to the designated line. It is incorrect to choose a line that merely has the same number of beats. Obviously, this task is challenging.)
2. The following lines have the same rhythm as line 44: 9, 25, 38, 45, 47, 56, and 59.
3. While the poem has a recognizable beat (based on the many anapestic feet: unaccented, unaccented, accented), individual lines show a variety of rhythmic patterns.

ANSWERS TO CRITICAL THINKING AND READING

1. Suggested Response: Sam is sitting calmly in the middle of the blazing furnace. Smiling, he tells the narrator to close the door because a draft is blowing in. He says this is the first time he has felt warm since he left his home in Tennessee.
2. Students may work with a partner.
3. Most students should notice that the rhythm of the poem adds

Literary Focus Point out to students that they were probably exposed to rhyme long before they studied poetry as a school subject. Young children hear nursery rhymes, for instance, and advertisements sometimes make use of rhyme. Have students speculate why rhyme is so appealing.

You might want to go over the different types of rhyme for **less advanced** students. Write on the chalkboard: "crumbs-bubblegum, mustard-custard." You might have students determine what sounds rhyme in each pair. Identify the first pair as a half rhyme and the second as an exact rhyme. Tell students that they will find both kinds of rhyme in this poem and that most of the rhymes will be end rhymes.

Look For Have students brainstorm for examples of end rhyme, exact rhyme, and half rhyme.

Writing/Prior Knowledge You might first have students mention types of household chores that they like to avoid. They can choose one of these and humorously exaggerate the consequences of *not* doing this task. Then have them choose another chore to write about.

Vocabulary Point out to students that a number of the vocabulary words—such as *withered, curdled,* and *rancid*—relate to spoiled food. Have students look up these words in a thesaurus and find synonyms for them.

450

GUIDE FOR READING

Sarah Cynthia Sylvia Stout Would Not Take the Garbage Out

Shel Silverstein (1932–) was born in Chicago, Illinois, and grew up hoping to be a dancer or a baseball player someday. Instead, his artistic talents led him to become one of America's most popular writers and cartoonists. Illustrated with his own drawings, his poetry books, such as *Where the Sidewalk Ends,* are enjoyed by young and old alike. In the poem you are about to read, he humorously tells the outrageous results of Sarah Cynthia Sylvia Stout's refusal to take the garbage out.

Rhyme

Rhyme is the repetition of a sound in two or more words or phrases. The common type of rhyme that occurs at the end of lines is called **end rhyme**. However, rhyme can occur within a line as well. Some rhymes are **exact rhymes,** like *peas* and *cheese*. The sounds of these words are exactly alike, except for the consonants at the beginning. Other rhymes are **half rhymes**—words whose sounds are similar but not identical, like *pans* and *hams*.

Rhyme is important for several reasons. You soon begin to listen for it, and the expectation of hearing sounds repeated keeps you interested in a poem. Also, a poet can vary the **rhyme scheme,** or pattern of rhymes, to focus your attention on a particular passage.

Look For

Listen for the rhymes as you read this poem. Notice how the rhymes make the poem even more humorous.

Writing

This poem is about a chore that was left undone. Have you ever forgotten or put off doing a chore? Let your mind roam freely. Exaggerate the results of leaving the job undone.

Vocabulary

Knowing the following words will help you as you read "Sarah Cynthia Sylvia Stout Would Not Take the Garbage Out."

scour (skour) v.: To clean by rubbing vigorously (p. 451)
candy (kan' dē) v.: To coat with sugar (p. 451)
rinds (rīnds) n. Tough outer layers or skins (p. 451)
withered (with' ərd) adj.: Dried up (p. 451)

curdled (kʉr' d'ld) adj.: Thickened; clotted (p. 452)
rancid (ran' sid) adj.: Spoiled and bad-smelling (p. 452)
relate (ri lāt') v.: Tell (p. 452)

450 *Poetry*

Objectives

1 To understand the part that rhyme plays in poetry
2 To evaluate the effect of rhyme
3 To appreciate specific words
4 To write a rhymed poem

Support Material

Teaching Portfolio
Teacher Backup, p. 675
Usage and Mechanics Worksheet, p. 678
Vocabulary Check, p. 679
Analyzing Literature Worksheet, *Understanding Rhyme,* p. 680
Language Worksheet, *Appreciating Specific Words,* p. 681
Selection Test, p. 682

Sarah Cynthia Sylvia Stout Would Not Take the Garbage Out [1]

Shel Silverstein

Sarah Cynthia Sylvia Stout
Would not take the garbage out!
She'd scour the pots and scrape the pans,
Candy the yams and spice the hams,
5 And though her daddy would scream and shout,
She simply would not take the garbage out.
And so it piled up to the ceilings:
Coffee grounds, potato peelings,
Brown bananas, rotten peas,
10 Chunks of sour cottage cheese.
It filled the can, it covered the floor,
It cracked the window and blocked the door
With bacon rinds and chicken bones,
Drippy ends of ice cream cones,
15 Prune pits, peach pits, orange peel,
Gloppy glumps of cold oatmeal,
Pizza crusts and withered greens,
Soggy beans and tangerines,
Crusts of black burned buttered toast,
20 Gristly bits of beefy roasts . . .
The garbage rolled on down the hall,
It raised the roof, it broke the wall . . .
Greasy napkins, cookie crumbs,
Globs of gooey bubblegum,
25 Cellophane from green baloney,
Rubbery blubbery macaroni,
Peanut butter, caked and dry,

[2]

Presentation

Motivation/Prior Knowledge
Ask students to describe the quantity of garbage that a large city can produce in one day. Tell them that the poem they will read shows, in a humorous way, how that amount of garbage, and more, accumulates because one girl decides not to take the garbage out.

Master Teacher Note Read this poem aloud for students. You might try reading it faster and slower, emphasizing different passages. Ask students which reading best brings out the humor of the poem.

You might ask students to consider why this reading works better than the others.

Thematic Ideas Have students compare and contrast Sarah's behavior with that of Utzel and Poverty in the story "Utzel and His Daughter, Poverty," p. 149. In each case, the characters get into trouble by refusing to do distasteful tasks. Silverstein is making fun of stories with a moral, however, while Singer seems to be serious about his moral, even though he includes humorous touches.

You might want to have students compare and contrast the humor in this poem with that in "The Cremation of Sam McGee," p. 445. Silverstein relies more on exaggeration, but both poets include fantastic details.

Purpose-Setting Question How does the poet use exaggeration to make his poem humorous?

1 **Discussion** Why is Sarah's name humorous? What does her last name reveal about her?

2 **Discussion** What devices other than rhyme does the poet use to keep his long list from getting boring?

3 **Literary Focus** Why do you think the poet uses the same two rhymes at the end of the poem as he did at the beginning?

You may want to encourage **more advanced** students to research poems with patterns of rhymes different from the couplets that Silverstein uses through most of this poem.

Reader's Response What do you think happened to Sarah Cynthia Sylvia Stout?

Humanities Note

Tell students that the young hero of Mark Twain's novel *Tom Sawyer* (1876) finds a clever way of avoiding an unpleasant chore. He pretends that he is having so much fun whitewashing a fence that all his friends pay him to be allowed to help.

You might suggest to students that they would enjoy reading this fictional account of a young boy's life in a nineteenth-century American town. Many of Tom Sawyer's adventures are based on Mark Twain's own boyhood experiences in Hannibal, Missouri.

Curdled milk and crusts of pie,
Moldy melons, dried up mustard,
30 Eggshells mixed with lemon custard,
Cold french fries and rancid meat,
Yellow lumps of Cream of Wheat.
At last the garbage reached so high
That finally it touched the sky.
35 And all the neighbors moved away,
And none of her friends would come to play.
And finally Sarah Cynthia Stout said,
"OK, I'll take the garbage out!"
But then, of course, it was too late
40 The garbage reached across the state,
From New York to the Golden Gate
And there, in the garbage she did hate,
Poor Sarah met an awful fate,
That I cannot right now relate
45 Because the hour is much too late.
But children, remember Sarah Stout
And always take the garbage out! 3

THINKING ABOUT THE SELECTION

Recalling

1. Name four chores that Sarah Cynthia Sylvia Stout does.
2. However, what chore does she absolutely refuse to do?
3. Find the lines that tell the reactions of her neighbors and friends. What do they do as a result of the situation?

Interpreting

4. At what point does the poem become unrealistic? What is the effect of the poet's use of exaggeration?

5. What reason might the poet have—besides the fact that it is "late"—for not telling you what happened to Sarah?
6. What do you think was Sarah's "awful fate"?
7. The poet parodies, or humorously imitates, the type of story told to teach a lesson. How do you know the poet does not mean for you to take this lesson seriously?

Applying

8. Shel Silverstein's poems are recognized for their ability to make people laugh. Discuss with your classmates what makes something funny.

ANALYZING LITERATURE
Understanding Rhyme

The repetition of sounds in two or more words, called **rhyme,** is a key element of poetry. In "Sarah Cynthia Sylvia Stout Would Not Take the Garbage Out," the poet uses rhymes that add humor as they seem to pile up just as the garbage does.

1. Are the rhymes at the end of lines 25 and 26 exact rhymes or half rhymes?
2. Find one example of a rhyme in the middle, rather than at the end, of a line.
3. How might the poem be different if most of the rhyming words did not come right after each other?

CRITICAL THINKING AND READING
Evaluating the Effect of Rhyme

Rhyme sets up an expectation that keeps you alert. The list of discarded items in this poem, for example, might become boring without the delightful rhymes. Also, a change in the rhyme scheme can be very dramatic, marking a turning point in the poem. Most of the pairs of lines in this poem have end rhymes, but the pattern is broken at one point.

1. Identify the two lines in the poem that do *not* rhyme.
2. What important event in the story occurs at this point?
3. What is the effect of the sudden lack of rhyme?
4. Why do you think that the poet used the same

rhyme seven times in a row after the break in rhyme?

UNDERSTANDING LANGUAGE
Appreciating Specific Words

Specific words are words that appeal to the senses because they refer to particular things. For example, the word *animal* is not very specific, but the word *giraffe* is. Poets usually try to use specific words so that you can vividly picture what they are talking about.

1. Which of the following words from the poem are general and which are specific:
   a. bacon rinds   c. garbage
   b. chicken bones
2. Find at least ten other specific words.
3. What is the effect of having so many specific words in this poem?

THINKING AND WRITING
Writing a Rhymed Poem

Can you write a rhymed poem that will make your classmates laugh? Look again at your description of an undone job, and list the humorous aspects of the situation. Like Shel Silverstein, you may want to use exaggeration to increase the humor. Then turn your description and list into a funny, rhymed poem about the results of an undone job. After revising your poem, read it to some classmates to see whether they think it is amusing.

ridiculous situations are humorous.

ANSWERS TO ANALYZING LITERATURE

1. They are exact rhymes.
2. The following lines have internal rhymes: 1, 4, 18, 26.
3. Answers may vary, but students might note that the immediate rhymes accelerate the pace of the poem, thereby adding to the humor.

ANSWERS TO CRITICAL THINKING AND READING

1. These two lines are 37 and 38.
2. She agrees to take the garbage out.
3. It breaks the pattern, adding to the drama of Sarah's sudden change of mind.
4. Answers will differ, but insightful students will realize that these seven rhymes seem to pile up, just as the garbage does, contributing to the drama of the poem's conclusion.

ANSWERS TO UNDERSTANDING LANGUAGE

1. a. Specific   c. General
   b. Specific
2. Answers will differ, but students should refer to any ten specific items of garbage mentioned in the poem.
3. Answers will differ, but students should realize that the poet's use of many specific words makes the poem much more vivid. You can readily picture what the poet is describing.

THINKING AND WRITING

For help with this assignment, students can refer to Lesson 18, "Writing a Poem," in the Handbook of Writing About Literature.

Publishing Student Writing You might have each student bind his or her poem into a booklet that can be displayed on a bulletin board.

Closure and Extension

ANSWERS TO THINKING ABOUT THE SELECTION
Recalling

1. She scours the pots, scrapes the pans, candies the yams, and spices the hams.
2. She refuses to take the garbage out.

3. Her neighbors move away, and none of her friends would play with her. (Lines 35–36)

Interpreting

4. The poem becomes unrealistic when the garbage cracks the window and blocks the door. Exaggeration makes the poem humorous.
5. Though answers will differ, students might indicate that it is more effective to leave her fate to the

reader's imagination.
6. Though answers will differ, most students will say that she is lost in the garbage in some strange way.
7. Answers will differ, but most students will indicate that the exaggerations and the humorous tone of the poem are clues.

Applying

8. Though answers will differ, many students will say that absurd or

More About the Author Edgar Allan Poe's life was filled with trouble and tragedy. As a result of quarrels with John Allan, for example, he was not able to graduate from college or complete his course at the U.S. Military Academy. Later, he was devastated when his wife died of tuberculosis. Some critics have argued that an artist must suffer deeply in order to produce excellent work. Ask students to comment on this opinion.

Literary Focus Ask students to list the reasons why they might repeat a word or phrase in recounting a story to a friend. Tell them that poets use repetition for many of the same reasons—emphasizing a particular detail, focusing their audience's attention, and adding to the drama of a tale. In addition, poets use repetition to create moods and various musical effects. Tell them that Poe's repetitions contribute to his poem's haunting melody.

Ask students to look for repetition in the lyrics of popular songs and to speculate about the purpose of it.

Look For Tell students that, in music, the word *melody* refers to a memorable sequence of sounds. Similarly, a melody in poetry is a pleasing series of sounds. Ask students to think of a series of words with harmonious sounds. Also ask why the name Annabel Lee is melodious.

Writing/Prior Knowledge Point out to students before they write that the face of a person they love may seem more attractive than that of a movie star. The appeal of a face can depend as much on the beholder's feelings as on conventional ideas of beauty.

Vocabulary Have less advanced students pronounce the words and read aloud the definitions.

454

GUIDE FOR READING

Annabel Lee

Edgar Allan Poe (1809–1849) was born in Boston, the son of two actors who died before his third birthday. He was raised in the United States and England by John Allan, with whom he had a troubled relationship. Poe's adult life was difficult, too. He earned only a meager living from his writings. Still, during his short life he wrote poems and stories that have made him one of the best-known American authors. A critic has called his verse "easy but unforgettable," and "Annabel Lee" with its strange story and haunting melody is both.

Repetition in Poetry

Repetition is the use of a word or group of words more than once in a poem. Like rhyme, which is itself a form of repetition, this technique creates a variety of effects. In a quiet poem, for example, repetition creates a feeling of peacefulness, like the lapping waves of a calm sea. It can also create excitement and suspense in a poem with galloping rhythms, such as "The Highwayman." Still another use of repetition is to focus attention on important words and phrases. By employing several forms of repetition in "Annabel Lee," Poe creates a pattern of word-sounds very much like music.

Look For

While reading "Annabel Lee," look for repeated words and phrases and consider the effect they create. How do they help create a haunting melody?

Writing

In this poem Poe is haunted by the memory of "the beautiful Annabel Lee." Think of the most beautiful or handsome face that you have ever seen. It could be the face of a friend or of someone you saw in a movie, on television, or in a painting. Write a description of this face.

Vocabulary

Knowing the following words will help you as you read "Annabel Lee."
coveted (kuv′ it əd) *v.*: Envied (p. 456)
sepulcher (sep′ 'l kər) *n.*: Grave; tomb (p. 456)
demons (dē′ mənz) *n.*: Evil spirits (p. 456)
beams (bēmz) *v.*: Shines brightly (p. 456)

454 *Poetry*

Annabel Lee

Edgar Allan Poe

It was many and many a year ago,
    In a kingdom by the sea.
That a maiden there lived whom you may know
    By the name of Annabel Lee;—
5 And this maiden she lived with no other thought
    Than to love and be loved by me.

She was a child and *I* was a child,
    In this kingdom by the sea.

Annabel Lee 455

Presentation

Motivation/Prior Knowledge
Tell students that Poe was deeply in love with his young wife, who died of tuberculosis in 1847. Ask them to imagine some of his feelings about her death. Tell them that many critics believe that "Annabel Lee" is Poe's response to this tragic event.

You might also want to read the poem aloud to students so they can hear its haunting music, or play for students the excellent recording by Joan Baez of this poem. It is included in her album *Joan* (Vanguard #79240), 1967.

Thematic Idea You might want to have students compare and contrast the narrator's response to the death of a loved one with the blacksmith's response in "The Village Blacksmith," page 431.

Purpose-Setting Question What mood or moods does this poem call up in you?

Master Teacher Note Tell students that one measure of the success of a poem, or any work of art, is its ability to suggest a world different from the everyday world we know. Although this newly created world may seem strange, it still has a reality of its own. Ask students to keep this idea in mind and to decide whether Poe has created such a world in "Annabel Lee."

1 **Discussion** What details in the first stanza make the poem seem like a fairy tale?

You might want to ask **more advanced** students to consider why a poet would want to create such an effect.

Humanities Note

Fine art, *Belgium,* by James Edward MacDonald. MacDonald (1873–1932) was a Canadian landscape painter. Showing an early interest in art, he was apprenticed at a lithography company at the age of fourteen. (Lithography involves printing designs from a flat stone or metal plate.)

You might want to ask students whether this picture creates a world of its own.
1. What is the mood that this world calls up in a viewer?
2. What elements in the picture contribute to this mood?
3. Remember this mood while reading "Annabel Lee." Is it in keeping with the feelings that the poem inspires?

2 **Discussion** Why do you think the poet gives so little information about the setting, saying only that it is a "kingdom by the sea"?

3 **Discussion** What can you infer about the narrator's relationship to Annabel Lee's "highborn kinsmen"?

4 **Literary Focus** Point out to students that rhyme is also a form of repetition. Indicate that many of the same words—*sea, Lee, me* —appear again and again as rhymes. Ask them what effect these rhymes have.

You might want to have **less advanced** students find all the rhymes in the poem. It is not necessary, however, to have them write out a formal rhyme scheme.

5 **Discussion** What predictions can you make about the future course of the narrator's life?

Reader's Response What thoughts and feelings does this poem evoke in your imagination.

But we loved with a love that was more than love—
10   I and my Annabel Lee—
With a love that the wingèd seraphs[1] of Heaven
    Coveted her and me.

And this was the reason that, long ago,
    In this kingdom by the sea,
15 A wind blew out of a cloud by night
    Chilling my Annabel Lee;
So that her highborn kinsmen[2] came
    And bore her away from me,
To shut her up in a sepulcher
20   In this kingdom by the sea.

The angels, not half so happy in Heaven,
    Went envying her and me:—
Yes! that was the reason (as all men know,
    In this kingdom by the sea)
25 That the wind came out of a cloud, chilling
    And killing my Annabel Lee.

But our love it was stronger by far than the love
    Of those who were older than we—
    Of many far wiser than we—
30 And neither the angels in Heaven above
    Nor the demons down under the sea,
Can ever dissever[3] my soul from the soul
    Of the beautiful Annabel Lee:—

For the moon never beams without bringing me dreams
35 Of the beautiful Annabel Lee;
And the stars never rise but I see the bright eyes
    Of the beautiful Annabel Lee;
And so, all the nighttide,[4] I lie down by the side
Of my darling, my darling, my life and my bride,
40   In her sepulcher there by the sea—
    In her tomb by the side of the sea.

---

1. **seraphs** (ser' əfs) *n.*: Angels.
2. **highborn kinsmen:** Relatives of noble birth.
3. **dissever** (di sev' ər) *v.*: Separate.
4. **nighttide** (nīt' tīd') *n.*: An old-fashioned way of saying nighttime.

THINKING ABOUT THE SELECTION

Recalling

1. Where do the events in this poem take place?
2. At what stage of life was the narrator of the poem when he fell in love?
3. What caused Annabel Lee's death?
4. Why can neither the angels nor the demons separate the narrator's soul from that of Annabel Lee? (Lines 27–33)
5. What does the narrator do "all the nighttide"? (Lines 34–41)

Interpreting

6. How can a love be "more than love"? (Lines 9–10)
7. How would you describe the love between the narrator and Annabel Lee.
8. Describe the narrator's mood.

Applying

9. The poet Countee Cullen once wrote, "Never love with all your heart,/It only ends in aching." Do you think the narrator of Annabel Lee would agree? Why or why not?

ANALYZING LITERATURE

Understanding Repetition in Poetry

Poets sometimes use certain words and phrases over and over in the same poem. This technique, called **repetition,** can make a poem seem almost like a piece of music. Poe's "Annabel Lee," in particular, seems to be woven together from repeated word-sounds.

1. Not including the title, how many times does the name Annabel Lee appear in the poem?
2. What line in the first stanza is repeated, almost exactly, in the next three stanzas?.
3. Which adjective describing Annabel Lee is repeated three times in the poem?
4. How does the use of repetition help create a haunting melody?

CRITICAL THINKING AND READING

Evaluating the Effects of Repetition

A poet can use repetition for several reasons. It can help create a peaceful or disturbing rhythm in a poem. Also, by stressing certain words and phrases, it can show you that these are clues to the poem's meaning.

1. Is the rhythm created by the repetitions in this poem disturbing or restful? Give reasons for your answer.
2. Why do you think the writer repeats the name "Annabel Lee" so many times?
3. Why do you think he stresses the setting of the poem by repeating the word "sea"?

UNDERSTANDING LANGUAGE

Appreciating Old-Fashioned Words

Old-fashioned words are words that are no longer a part of everyday speech. Poets sometimes use them to create a mood. In "Annabel Lee," for example, Poe uses several old-fashioned words. Words like "seraph," "kinsman," and "nighttide" convey an old-time, romantic flavor.

Identify the old-fashioned word in each of the following pairs and look it up in a dictionary. Then use each word in a sentence.

1. galleon, ship
2. sky, firmament
3. horse, steed
4. garments, clothes

THINKING AND WRITING

Writing About a Narrative Poem

Write a letter to a friend explaining why you did or did not enjoy this poem. In your letter retell the story of the poem. Then explain the effect created by the use of repetition. As you revise your letter, make sure you have supported your opinion of the poem with details from it. Finally, proofread your letter and prepare a final draft.

Annabel Lee 457

2. Line 2 is repeated almost exactly.
3. The adjective "beautiful" is repeated three times.
4. Answers may differ, but students should indicate that the repetitions lead you to pay less attention to the sense of words than to their rhythm and sound. Also, the repeated rhyme-words weave a pleasing, almost hypnotic, pattern of sounds.

Challenge Ask students what instruments they would use if they were setting this poem to music. Have them give reasons for each choice.

ANSWERS TO CRITICAL THINKING AND READING

1. Answers will differ; however, students should realize that the rhythm is restful because the repeated words and phrases are melodic. Also, the rhythm seems to imitate the regular and repeated lapping of waves on a shore rather than, for example, the galloping of a horse (as in "The Highwayman").
2. Her name is repeated to stress the writer's intense love and devotion.
3. Answers will differ, but students might indicate that the poet wants to suggest the lapping waves of a calm sea. Especially insightful students may realize that he sets the poem at the shore because, in a sense, he is standing on the shores of life looking toward death.

ANSWERS TO UNDERSTANDING LANGUAGE

The old-fashioned words are:
1. galleon
2. firmament
3. steed
4. garments

THINKING AND WRITING

For help with this assignment, students can refer to Lesson 13, "Writing About a Poem," in the Handbook of Writing About Literature.

Publishing Student Writing You might want to ask students to send their letter about Poe to a friend.

_____
457

Closure and Extension

ANSWERS TO THINKING ABOUT THE SELECTION

Recalling

1. The events take place in a kingdom by the sea.
2. He fell in love as a child, but he tells about these events as a man.
3. The angels were jealous of their love and sent a wind to kill Annabel Lee.
4. Neither the angels nor the demons can separate their souls because their love is so strong.
5. He lies down by the side of Annabel Lee.

Interpreting

6. Most students will realize that the narrator is exaggerating to indicate the strength of their love.
7. Students' answers will vary. Most should indicate, however, that the narrator is asserting the superiority of the love between him and Annabel Lee to the love between older and supposedly wiser, individuals.
8. The narrator is sad, haunted, and filled with longing for Annabel Lee.

Applying

9. He would probably not agree. He has obviously loved with all his heart and does not regret it.

ANSWERS TO ANALYZING LITERATURE

1. Her name appears seven times.

GUIDE FOR READING

Oranges

Gary Soto (1952–   ) is a Mexican American, or Chicano, who grew up in the San Joaquin Valley in California. His first book of poetry, *The Elements of San Joaquin* (1977), describes the lives of migrant workers in that part of the country. Soto himself had worked in the fields as a migrant laborer, moving from farm to farm to harvest seasonal crops. One critic said that his poetry has "a lean, simple style." This description certainly is true of the poem "Oranges," a poem about the magic of an early love.

The Speaker in a Narrative Poem

When a narrative poem is told by a character in the story, we call that character the **speaker**. This speaker refers to himself or herself as "I." It is important to remember, however, that the "I" telling the story is not the poet. The speaker is an imaginary person whom the poet has invented, just like a first-person narrator in a short story. In "Oranges," for example, the speaker is a character remembering "The first time" he "walked/With a girl."

Look For

As you read "Oranges," look for details about the speaker. Decide what he is like and why the time he describes holds such magic memories for him.

Writing

Recall when you spent some time with someone you liked very much. Tell about the first moments of that experience. Or if you prefer, write a description of the first moments of an imaginary experience.

Vocabulary

Knowing the following words will help you as you read "Oranges."
rouge (ro͞ozh) *n.*: A reddish cosmetic used to color the cheeks (p. 459)
tiered (tird) *v.*: Stacked in rows (p. 459)
bleachers (blēch′ ərz) *n.*:

Benches stacked in rows for spectators at sporting events (p. 459)
hissing (his′ iŋ) *v.*: Making a sound like a prolonged *s* (p. 459)

Oranges

Gary Soto

The first time I walked
With a girl, I was twelve,
Cold, and weighted down
With two oranges in my jacket.
5   December. Frost cracking
Beneath my steps, my breath
Before me, then gone,
As I walked toward
Her house, the one whose
10 Porchlight burned yellow
Night and day, in any weather.
A dog barked at me, until
She came out pulling
At her gloves, face bright
15 With rouge. I smiled,
Touched her shoulder, and led
Her down the street, across
A used car lot and a line
Of newly planted trees,
20 Until we were breathing
Before a drug store. We
Entered, the tiny bell
Bringing a saleslady
Down a narrow aisle of goods.
25 I turned to the candies
Tiered like bleachers,
And asked what she wanted—
Light in her eyes, a smile
Starting at the corners

30 Of her mouth. I fingered
A nickel in my pocket,
And when she lifted a chocolate
That cost a dime,
I didn't say anything.
35 I took the nickel from
My pocket, then an orange,
And set them quietly on
The counter. When I looked up,
The lady's eyes met mine,
40 And held them, knowing
Very well what it was all
About.

        Outside,
A few cars hissing past,
45 Fog hanging like old
Coats between the trees.
I took my girl's hand
In mine for two blocks,
Then released it to let
50 Her unwrap the chocolate.
I peeled my orange
That was so bright against
The gray of December
That, from some distance,
55 Someone might have thought
I was making a fire in my hands.

Oranges   459

Closure and Extension

ANSWERS TO THINKING ABOUT THE SELECTION
Recalling

1. He is a twelve-year-old boy. At the start of the poem, he is on his way to his first date and is carrying two oranges in his jacket pocket.
2. Her face is bright with rouge and she is putting on her gloves.
3. He does not have enough money for the candy.
4. He peels his orange.

Interpreting

5. He likes her. He displays his feelings by spending all his money for her candy and holding her hand as they walk.
6. The saleslady knew that he did not have enough money and took an orange to make up for the missing nickel.
7. He brought two oranges and gave one to the saleslady.
8. The orange represents his warm feeling for the girl.
9. Suggested Answer: "The gray of December" is associated with bleakness and desolation, while the orange symbolizes his strong feelings. His feelings seem even stronger against the backdrop of the gray weather.

Applying

10. Students' answers will differ, but most will indicate that a first date is an exciting experience. You are entering into a new type of relationship with someone you like.

ANSWERS TO ANALYZING LITERATURE

1. The poem is less personal and more objective.
2. Students' answers will vary, but many will realize that a poem about a personal experience is more intense when there is a first-person speaker.

ANSWERS TO CRITICAL THINKING AND READING

1. The saleslady is helpful and understanding.

460

THINKING ABOUT THE SELECTION
Recalling

1. Describe the speaker of this poem at the time this event took place.
2. Describe the girl when she first comes out of her house.
3. Why does the speaker try to pay for the candy with a nickel and an orange?
4. What is the last action of the speaker in the poem?

Interpreting

5. How does the speaker feel about the girl? Give evidence to support your answer.
6. What does the speaker mean when he says the saleslady knew "Very well what it was all/About"?
7. Why does the narrator still have the orange at the end of the poem?
8. What has the orange come to represent, or stand for, to the speaker?
9. What does the speaker mean when he describes his orange as "so bright against/The gray of December"?

Applying

10. Why is a first date such an important event in a person's life?

ANALYZING LITERATURE
Understanding the Speaker

A narrative poem can be told by a **speaker** who takes part in the story and refers to himself or herself as "I." The speaker is an invented character, not the poet talking to you directly.

You can perform an experiment to see the difference between a narrative poem told by a speaker and one told by the poet. Read "Oranges" again, and every time you see "I" change it in your mind to "he." Also, each time you see "we," change it to "they." When you have made

these changes, the poem will no longer have a speaker.

1. How is the poem different without a speaker?
2. Does the poem seem better to you with or without a speaker? Give reasons for your answer.

CRITICAL THINKING AND READING
Making Inferences About a Speaker

An **inference** is a reasonable conclusion you make based on stated information. In a poem like "Oranges," the poet does not tell you about the speaker directly. However, you can infer a great deal about the speaker from the way he talks, the details on which he focuses, and others' reactions to him. Your inferences will help you form an idea of his personality.

1. How does the saleslady act toward him?
2. How does his girlfriend act toward him?
3. The speaker seems to put special emphasis on the detail about the orange at the end of the poem. Why do you think this is so?
4. Does the speaker boast about this experience, or does he seem to be modest? Give reasons for your answer.
5. Based on all these clues, give a brief summary of the speaker's personality.

THINKING AND WRITING
Adding to a Narrative Poem

Every story involving two or more people has two or more different sides to it. Up to this point, we have heard only the boy's voice. How do you think the girl's side of the story would sound? Brainstorm to think of how she might talk differently from the boy. Which details of this story would she describe? Also, would she use short lines of poetry, as the boy does, or longer ones? Turn your ideas into another version of the story, using the girl as a speaker. When you revise your work, ask yourself whether the way you have written the poem is true to the girl's personality.

2. His girlfriend is enthusiastic and affectionate.
3. The orange becomes a symbol of his warm feelings.
4. He seems to be modest, because he simply states what happened and uses the orange as a symbol of his warm feelings rather than expressing them directly.
5. Student's answers will vary, but most should see that he is honest, affectionate, caring, considerate, and confident.

Challenge Imagine what the saleslady thinks after she accepts the orange and nickel and watches the young couple leave the store.

THINKING AND WRITING

Publishing Student Writing Display the poems on a bulletin board by placing Soto's poem in the center with students' poems surrounding it.

Figurative Language and Imagery

WATERFALL NO. III, IAO VALLEY
Georgia O'Keeffe, 1939
Art Resource

Humanities Note

Fine art, *Waterfall No. III,* 1939, by Georgia O'Keeffe. Georgia O'Keeffe (1887–1986) was one of the most notable American artists of her generation. Born in Wisconsin, she decided at the age of ten that she wanted to become an artist. Her formal art education was acquired at the Art Institute of Chicago and the Art Students League in New York City, under William Meritt Chase. She worked as a commercial artist and taught art in various places before she decided to dedicate her life to painting. Her work was discovered by Alfred Stieglitz, a major exhibitor of art in New York City, whom she later married.

Georgia O'Keeffe was an early abstract painter known for her enlarged, poetic abstractions of natural forms. The clean lines and massive simple forms of *Waterfall No. III, Ino Valley,* count for much of its power. The mountain gorge is bisected by the thin white ribbon of the waterfall which disappears and reappears as a winding stream in the foreground. The severity of the subject is relieved by the clouds of mist swathing the hilltops. Although simplified in form, this painting evokes the essence of a majestic scene of nature.

Robert Herrick was extremely well educated in the literature of ancient Greeks and Romans, and wrote for readers with a similar educational background. Many of his poems imitate classical poetry in both content and style. You might have your class discuss whether it is better for an artist to be completely original or to use great works of the past as models for his or her own work.

More About the Author Robert P. Tristam Coffin had an exceptional academic background. He graduated from college with the highest honors; he earned a master's degree from Princeton; he studied at Oxford as a Rhodes scholar. You might discuss with your students whether a great deal of education is necessary for writing poetry.

More About the Author Carl Sandburg also worked as a delivery boy, a bootblack, a bottlewasher, a firefighter, a truck driver, and a house painter. Ask your class how working at a great number of different jobs can be beneficial to a writer.

GUIDE FOR READING

Upon Mistress Susanna Southwell, Her Feet

Robert Herrick (1591–1674) was born in London and as a boy was apprenticed to a goldsmith there. He later became a minister, serving for more than thirty years at a remote country church. Herrick published just one book, a collection of 1,400 short poems, but these were good enough to establish Herrick as one of the finest English poets. In "Upon Mistress Susanna Southwell, Her Feet" he creates a vivid picture with a few skillfully chosen phrases.

The Pheasant

Robert P. Tristram Coffin (1892–1955) lived in New England, where his family had settled about 300 years earlier. Coffin wrote that he "grew up on a Maine saltwater farm . . . among lighthouses and barns and boats, tides and fogs and apples and hired men." He won many prizes for his poetry and wrote other types of books as well: biographies, novels, and collections of essays. Coffin's sharp eye for natural details brought him acclaim. He demonstrates his powers of observation in "The Pheasant."

Fog

Carl Sandburg (1878–1967) was born in Galesburg, Illinois, the son of Swedish immigrants. He was unique in winning the Pulitzer Prize for both poetry and history. Sandburg often wrote about the rough-and-tumble everyday world. By the time his first book appeared in 1916, Sandburg had been a farm worker, a stagehand, a railroad worker, a soldier, and a cook, among other things. He was working as a newspaper reporter when he wrote "Fog," a poem he jotted down one day while waiting to interview a Chicago judge.

462　*Poetry*

Objectives
1 To understand simile
2 To understand metaphor
3 To evaluate the effect of a metaphor
4 To undenrstand extended metaphor
5 To write a poem with an extended metaphor

Support Material
Teaching Portfolio
Teacher Backup, p. 705
Usage and Mechanics Worksheet, p. 709
Vocabulary Check, p. 710
Analyzing Literature Worksheet, *Understanding Figurative Language*, p. 711
Language Worksheet, *Appreciating Vivid Verbs*, p. 712
Selection Test, p. 713

Art Transparency 15, *Fog Horns*, by Arthur Dove

Figurative Language

Figurative language is language that is not meant literally, or exactly as the dictionary definition of the words would indicate. One important type of figurative language is simile. A **simile** uses the connecting words *like* or *as* to point up a similar quality in two generally unlike things. For example: The man's bright dinner jacket looks *like* an unfurled flag. The dinner jacket and the flag are unlike in many ways, but they are similar in being bright and showy.

A **metaphor** also indicates a similar quality in two generally unlike things. However, metaphors do not use the words *like* or *as*. The simplest way to create a metaphor is to say that two dissimilar things are the same. For example, you can turn the simile describing the dinner jacket into a metaphor by saying this: The man's bright dinner jacket is an unfurled flag. You can also create a metaphor by speaking about one thing in terms of another. For example: The crowd *floods* into the open area, *swirls* around, and *collects* in *small pools* of people. In this metaphor, the italicized words describe the crowd as if it were water.

An **extended metaphor** is a metaphor that continues past a single phrase or sentence. You might begin such a metaphor by saying, "The tornado is a dragon, gobbling up the houses." Then you could extend the metaphor by continuing to describe the tornado as a dragon.

Look For

As you read the following poems, look for similes, metaphors, and extended metaphors. How does the use of figurative language help create vivid word pictures?

Writing

The poems you are about to read use figurative language to create vivid word pictures. Recall the first time you met someone who later became your friend. Using similes or metaphors, create a vivid word picture of that person.

Vocabulary

Knowing the following words will help you as you read these poems.
scorn (skôrn) *n.*: Strong dislike for someone or something thought to be inferior (p. 466)
hymn (him) *n.*: A song of praise (p. 466)

meek (mēk) *adj.*: Patient and mild (p. 466)
haunches (hônch′ iz) *n.*: An animal's lower back and legs (p. 468)

Guide for Reading 463

Motivation/Prior Knowledge
Ask your students if they have ever found their attention captured by a small detail of, for example, a pet—such as an unusual marking or eye color. Ask the class for other examples of interesting little details. You might then ask them to discuss why a writer might choose to write about such details rather than a large-scale subject.

Purpose-Setting Question Why does the poem begin with two short lines, then present a longer line, then a still longer line, and finally end with a shorter line? (Answer: The structure imitates the gradual emergence and withdrawal of the young lady's feet.)

Master Teacher Note Herrick wrote hundreds of exquisite little lyrics similar in content and scope to the poem printed here. It would take a small amount of time to read several of these simple, readily understood lyrics to your students and thereby give them a better appreciation of one of the best "miniaturists" in English. You might also have your class compare and contrast Herrick's poem with an appropriate haiku.

Critical Thinking and Reading In what way is the sound of the words and rhythm of the verses appropriate to the subject? Why is the *e* sound of *pretty, feet, creep,* and *Bo-peep* effective?

Humanities Note

Fine Art: *Little Goody Two Shoes,* a woodcut by John Newbery. John Newbery was an eighteenth century British seller of books and patent medicines who plied his wares in St. Paul's churchyard, in London. He also wrote and published some of the very first books exclusively for children. He sold these books

Upon Mistress Susanna Southwell, Her Feet

Robert Herrick

Her pretty feet
   Like snails did creep
A little out, and then,
As if they started at Bo-peep,[1]
5 Did soon draw in again.

---

1. started at Bo-peep: Were playing a game of Bo-peep, an old-fashioned name for peekaboo.

LITTLE GOODY TWO SHOES
John Newbery
New York Public Library

464 *Poetry*

merely for the cost of the binding and defrayed some of his expense by advertising his patent medicines within the covers. This generosity coupled with his genuine concern to educate and amuse children won him a description in Goldsmith's *The Vicar of Wakefield* as the "philantrophic bookseller."

Little Goody Two Shoes is a woodcut illustration that appeared in a 1766 edition of a Newbery book by the same title. One of the first children's books ever published, it is notable for its good humor and natural style. This woodcut of a demure young lady in a laced up bodice and cap is unique for its time in that it was an image children could identify with. These little books were very popular and many including *Little Goody Two Shoes,* were reprinted in America.

1. What aspects of the woodcut give it a playful quality?
2. In what ways are Little Goody Two Shoes and Miss Susanna Southwell alike?

THINKING ABOUT THE SELECTION

Recalling

1. Without using figurative langauge, describe what Mistress Susanna Southwell's feet do in this poem.

Interpreting

2. Do you think it appropriate that the poet describes the feet as playing peekaboo? Why or why not?
3. How do you think the poet feels about Mistress Susanna Southwell? Find evidence to support your answer.

Applying

4. Use a simile to describe the way your own feet move.

ANALYZING LITERATURE

Understanding Simile

In a **simile,** a writer compares two apparently different things by using the connecting words *like* or *as*. Similes help you to see the world in a new way by suggesting surprising comparisons that you might not have made yourself.

1. How are Mistress Susanna Southwell's feet like snails?
2. Do you think this simile is an effective one? Why or why not?
3. How would the effect of this poem be different if the poet had compared Susanna's feet to tortoises?

Closure and Extension

ANSWERS TO THINKING ABOUT THE SELECTION
Recalling

1. Suggested Response: Her feet appear from under the hem of her dress, then withdraw and are once again out of sight.

Interpreting

2. Suggested Response: Yes, the peekaboo image is appropriate, because it suggests something small quickly appearing and then hiding again.
3. He probably feels fondness for the young lady. He describes her feet as "pretty," and the tone of the poem is gentle and good-humored.

Applying

4. Answers will differ. Suggested Response: For large, slow-moving feet, "Like two glaciers"; for small, quick feet, "Like two frisky kittens."

ANSWERS TO ANALYZING LITERATURE

1. Like snails, her feet are tiny; they do not move far or fast; they withdraw from sight.
2. Suggested Response: The simile is effective. It presents a clear image that suggests what the speaker sees and his gentle, affectionate response to the sight.
3. Tortoises would suggest something large and heavy. Hence, the effect would be mocking or sarcastic humor.

Challenge Think of another simile the writer could have used to describe Susanna Southwell's feet. What would be the effect of this simile?

Upon Mistress Susanna Southwell, Her Feet 465

465

Motivation/Prior Knowledge
Ask your students to think of an animal—perhaps one they saw in a zoo or in a wildlife documentary—whose beauty very much impressed them. What kind of animal was it? How would they describe its beauty?

Master Teacher Note Before reading "The Pheasant," you might further motivate your students by displaying some of John James Audubon's paintings of birds (from *Birds of America,* Macmillan, 1947). You might point out how Audubon tried to capture the living beauty of birds, and then ask your class to notice how Coffin tried to express the beauty of the pheasant in life and in death.

You might also compare Audubon's painting of a pheasant with that of Roger Tory Peterson on page 467.

Purpose-Setting Question The speaker never directly states his feelings about what he is describing. What do you think his feelings are?

1 Discussion What aspect of the pheasant's appearance does this line describe?

2 Literary Focus *Thunder* is a metaphor. Ask the class what it stands for. You might also clarify the context: A hunter has fired a shotgun or rifle at the bird.

3 Discussion Here, as in previous lines (4, 8, 9, 11, and 12), human feelings are attributed to the pheasant. You might ask your students to describe the effect of this use of human traits.

Reader's Response Is this poem a protest against hunting? Give reasons for your opinion.

The Pheasant

Robert P. Tristram Coffin

A pheasant cock sprang into view,
A living jewel, up he flew.

His wings laid hold on empty space,
1 Scorn bulged his eyeballs out with grace.

5 He was a hymn from tail to beak
With not a tender note or meek.

2 Then the gun let out its thunder,
The bird descended struck with wonder.

He ran a little, then, amazed,
10 Settled with his head upraised.

The fierceness flowed out of his eyes
And left them meek and large and wise.

3 Gentleness relaxed his head,
He lay in jeweled feathers, dead.

THINKING ABOUT THE SELECTION
Recalling

1. Summarize the action of this poem without using figurative language.

Interpreting

2. What is the meaning of lines 5–6?
3. What is the meaning of lines 7–8?
4. Compare and contrast the description of the bird in lines 1–6 with that in lines 9–14.
5. How do you think the poet wants you to feel about the event in this poem? Find evidence to support your answer.

Applying

6. Coffin describes the pheasant as "a hymn from tail to beak." What other creatures do you think fit this description? Explain your answer.

ANALYZING LITERATURE
Understanding Metaphor

Poets use **metaphors** to compare apparently unlike things. However, a metaphor identifies the two things being compared more closely than a

Closure and Extension

ANSWERS TO THINKING ABOUT THE SELECTION
Recalling

1. A beautiful pheasant cock springs up and flies through the air. It is shot, falls to earth, runs a little, and dies.

Interpreting

2. The pheasant was beautiful, but not in a soft, gentle way.

3. The bird was shot and fell to earth.
4. In lines 1–6, the living beauty of the bird is emphasized. The speaker describes the pheasant as if it were scornful and without tenderness or meekness. In lines 9–14, the shot bird loses its fierceness and becomes gentle. Its beauty is dead beauty.
5. Suggested Response: The poet probably wants the reader to be saddened by the shooting of the bird. The emphasis on the bird's beauty and strong personality suggest that the poet wants the

RING NECKED PHEASANT, 1977
Roger Tory Peterson
Courtesy of the artist and Mill Pond Press, Inc.

Humanities Note
Fine art, *Ring Necked Pheasant,* 1977, by Roger Tory Peterson. Peterson (1908–   ) is an American ornithologist, artist, and writer. He has been on the board of directors of the Audubon Society and was art director for the National Wildlife Federation.

His pen-and-ink drawing *Ring Necked Pheasant* is precise in detail. It is typical of the drawings that have earned him the nickname the "modern Audubon." Such work not only shows his love for birds but has contributed to the knowledge of bird-watchers.

1. What seems to you most striking about the appearance of the pheasant?
2. What details of the pheasant would suggest "a living jewel"?
3. How did the artist create the suggestion of living, active creatures?

simile. For example, instead of saying that the pheasant is *like* a jewel, the poet simply calls it "a living jewel."

1. What quality or qualities do the pheasant and the jewel share?
2. Where is this metaphor of the pheasant as a jewel repeated later in the poem? Do you think this repetition adds to the effectiveness of the poem? Why or why not?
3. What other metaphor does the poet use to describe the pheasant?
4. In what essential way are a hymn and a jewel alike?

CRITICAL THINKING AND READING
Evaluating the Effect of a Metaphor

You can evaluate the effect of a metaphor by replacing it with a description that does not use figurative language and then comparing the two passages. Here, for example, are a metaphor from "The Pheasant" and a description expressing a similar idea:

Metaphor: "A living jewel, up he flew."
Description: Brightly colored, up he flew.

1. Compare and contrast these two lines.
2. Which do you find more effective? Explain your answer.

The Pheasant 467

reader to regret the loss of such an impressive creature.

Applying
6. Suggested Responses: Tigers, leopards, eagles, greyhounds, and other beautiful, graceful animals might be mentioned. A person could see the beauty of a hymn in all such creatures.

ANSWERS TO ANALYZING LITERATURE
1. They share the beauty of glistening color and graceful lines.
2. The metaphor is repeated in line 14. The repetition is effective, because it reemphasizes the beauty of the bird while pointing up the contrast between its living beauty and its dead beauty.
3. He uses the metaphor of the hymn.
4. A hymn and a jewel are both beautiful.

ANSWERS TO CRITICAL THINKING AND READING
1. Both lines express the same idea, but the metaphor expresses the idea in an image.
2. Answers will differ. Suggested Response: The metaphor is more effective because it is more vivid and appeals to the reader's sense of sight.

Fog
Carl Sandburg

1
The fog comes
on little cat feet.

2
It sits looking
over harbor and city
5 on silent haunches
and then moves on.

THINKING ABOUT THE SELECTION
Recalling

1. Being as specific as possible, describe the setting of this poem.
2. Describe the three things the fog does.

Interpreting

3. What impression does this poem create of the fog?
4. What is the effect of the writer's use of short lines?

Applying

5. Many poets have written poems about fog. What is it about this type of weather that makes it a good subject for a poem?

468   Poetry

ANALYZING LITERATURE
Understanding Extended Metaphor

An **extended metaphor** develops beyond a single sentence or phrase. Once a poet has shown that two apparently unlike things are similar, it is fascinating to see how long the comparison can be continued. An extended metaphor can go on for several lines, or even many pages.

1. To what does the writer compare the fog?
2. What qualities of the fog does the writer emphasize with this comparison?
3. How would the poem have been different if the poet had compared the fog to a velvet blanket?

THINKING AND WRITING

Writing an Extended Metaphor

Sandburg created an effective poem by comparing the fog to a cat. Of what animal does the fog remind you? For example, does it remind you of a warm puppy or of a brown cow? Let your imagination roam freely. What qualities does the fog share with this animal? Using an extended metaphor, write a poem describing the fog. Read over your poem to make sure you have carried your metaphor through the poem. Prepare a final draft and place it on a bulletin board with your classmates' fog poems.

3. Had the fog been compared to a velvet blanket, the image of the fog would have seemed heavier and thicker. At the very least, different qualities of fog would have been expressed.

Writing Across the Curriculum
Consider having students work in groups to prepare a scientific explanation of fog. You might inform the science department of this assignment, as science teachers could guide students and perhaps give them credit for their work. Once students have finished, they can compare their scientific explanations with Sandburg's figurative description.

GUIDE FOR READING

The Bat

Theodore Roethke (1908–1963) was one of the best-known American poets writing after World War II. He won many awards for his work, including the Bollingen Prize, the Pulitzer Prize, and the National Book Award. In addition, he earned a reputation as a college teacher who challenged and inspired his students. Roethke was born and grew up in Saginaw, Michigan, where his father was a florist. As a boy, Roethke loved to play in and around the family greenhouse. These experiences gave him a feeling of kinship with nature that he never lost. In "The Bat" he writes with knowledge and humor about one of nature's more unusual creatures.

The Pasture

Robert Frost (1875–1963) is associated with New England, but he was born and spent his early years in San Francisco. When his father died, the family returned to its New England roots. Frost remained in that region for most of his life, making his living for a while as a farmer and part-time teacher. He was not well known as a writer until his first book of poetry, *A Boy's Will* (1913), appeared in Great Britain. Then, almost overnight, he became famous for his poems about New England people and landscapes. He won the Pulitzer Prize four times, more than any other poet. Frost used poetic forms that some writers thought old-fashioned. However, by combining these forms with the rhythms of everyday speech, he created highly original poems. "The Pasture" contains an invitation that makes you want to experience the joys of nature with the poet.

470   *Poetry*

Images in Poetry

Images are the pictures that poets create with their words. As you read a poem, you can see these images in your mind's eye. Poets use lively and specific words so that you can see their images more clearly. In "The Pasture," for instance, Robert Frost says a small calf is so young that "It totters" when its mother "licks it with her tongue." By using the specific verb "totters," Frost paints a picture of the scene that is easy to visualize.

Look For

As you read "The Bat" and "The Pasture" look for the specific words the poets use to create vivid word pictures.

Writing

Picture an animal that fascinates you. It can be a pet, or an animal that you have seen in a zoo or on film. Freewrite about the qualities of this animal that interest you the most.

Vocabulary

Knowing the following words will help you as you read these poems.

amiss (ə mis′) *adv.*: In a wrong way; improper (p. 472)

totters (tät′ ərz) *v.*: Rocks or shakes as if about to fall; is unsteady (p. 473)

Literary Focus Though not a poet, the great novelist Joseph Conrad once described his artistic purpose as to make the reader "see." Point out that images in poetry serve just this purpose. You might ask your students to discuss why poets and other writers so often try to paint pictures in words.

Look For You might point out to your **less advanced** students that seeing clearly in their imaginations what the poet is writing about is a clue that the words are especially specific.

Writing/Prior Knowledge You can help the class get started by having them mention a few animals that capture their imaginations. Write the animals' names on the board, and ask students to offer brief descriptive phrases that capture the animals' distinctive appearance.

Teaching to Ability Levels To help your **less advanced** students grasp the concept of imagery, you might challenge them to find the most clear and vivid word pictures in "The Bat" and "The Pasture."

Vocabulary You might mention that though *shan't,* in "the Pasture," sounds quaint, the word is simply the contraction of *shall not.* Both poems are good examples of how effective simple and direct words can be.

Motivation/Prior Knowledge
Ask students to volunteer all that they know or have heard about bats. Have they ever seen one up close? How are bats portrayed in films? What have students read or heard about bats' living habits?

Master Teacher Note You might wish to tell your class a little about bats. All species of bats can see, though some see poorly. Bats help preserve ecological balance by devouring large numbers of insects. Some oriental artists represent bats as signs of good luck, happiness, and long life. You might ask whether any of this information contradicts impressions about bats that the students may have had.

Thematic Idea Two other poems that present vivid descriptions of animals are "The Pheasant," p. 466, and "Seal," p. 475.

Purpose-Setting Question What seem to be the speaker's feelings about bats?

1 Discussion In what sense is the bat cousin to the mouse?

2 Literary Focus Line 3 presents a good example of imagery. The metaphor introduced by *hat* makes the image striking.

3 Discussion What does the poet mean by "mice with wings"? Why does he speak of "a human face"?

Closure and Extension

The Bat
Theodore Roethke

1 By day the bat is cousin to the mouse.
He likes the attic of an aging house.

2 His fingers make a hat about his head.
His pulse beat is so slow we think him dead.

5 He loops in crazy figures half the night
Among the trees that face the corner light.

But when he brushes up against a screen,
We are afraid of what our eyes have seen:

For something is amiss or out of place
3 10 When mice with wings can wear a human face.

THINKING ABOUT THE SELECTION
Recalling

1. Where does the bat spend the daytime?
2. What does the bat do at night?

Interpreting

3. Contrast the description of the bat in lines 3 and 4 with that in lines 5 and 6.
4. What details make the picture that the poet paints in line 10 so strange?

Applying

5. What is it about animals like bats and snakes that makes people both curious and afraid?

ANALYZING LITERATURE
Understanding Images

Images are pictures in words. By choosing lively and specific language, poets invite you to see the world in a fresh and original way. In "The Bat," for example, Roethke creates a vivid picture when he says that this creature's "fingers make a hat about his head."

1. Describe the picture that Roethke paints in lines 5 and 6.
2. Why do you think Roethke saved the image in line 10 for the end of the poem?

THINKING AND WRITING
Writing a Poem About an Animal

Use your freewriting about a fascinating animal to write a brief poem. Organize the lines in groups of two, as Roethke does. When you revise your poem, replace general words with lively and specific ones. You might want to read your poem to several classmates when you are finished and ask them whether your images are clear. Then, based on your classmates' comments, prepare a final draft.

ANSWERS TO THINKING ABOUT THE SELECTION
Recalling

1. The bat spends the daytime in the attic of an old house.
2. The bat flies in "loops" at night.

Interpreting

3. In lines 3 and 4, the bat is described as asleep, almost lifeless in appearance. In lines 5 and 6, he is awake and wildly active.
4. The odd combination of *mice, wings,* and *human face* make the picture strange.

Applying

5. Answers will differ. Suggested Response: Perhaps the strange ap-

pearance of such creatures strikes fear in people's hearts even while it arouses their curiosity.

ANSWERS TO ANALYZING LITERATURE

1. The picture is of the bat flying in loops in the dark. It is visible because of the lamppost light.
2. The image in line 10 sums up the strange, weird appearance of the

bat. It is therefore an appropriate climax to the poem.

THINKING AND WRITING

For help with this assignment, refer students to Lesson 18, "Writing a Poem," in the Handbook of Writing About Literature.

The Pasture

Robert Frost

I'm going out to clean the pasture spring;
I'll only stop to rake the leaves away
(And wait to watch the water clear, I may):
I shan't be gone long.—You come too. ⌐1

5 I'm going out to fetch the little calf
That's standing by the mother. It's so young
It totters when she licks it with her tongue.
I shan't be gone long.—You come too. ⌐2

THINKING ABOUT THE SELECTION

Recalling

1. What two chores is the speaker going to do?
2. What invitation does the speaker offer? What effect does this invitation have on you?

Interpreting

3. Although the speaker is going out to perform chores, he makes them sound attractive and inviting. What images make you feel like accompanying the speaker?

4. Why do you think the poet enclosed line 3 in parentheses?
5. Based on information in the poem, do you think the speaker is a grown man or a boy? Find evidence to support your answer.

Applying

6. An Indian holy book states: "What is work? and What is not work? are questions that perplex the wisest of men." Do you think the speaker in this poem considers the chores work? Find evidence to support your answer. How do you define work?

The Pasture   473

More About the Author William Jay Smith has been a member of the Vermont legislature. You might ask your students if they ever thought of poets as practicing politicians. When some say that they have not, you might take the opportunity to dispel the stereotype of the poet as a being too sensitive for the real world. Point out that poets have been monarchs, soldiers, criminals, and corporate executives, among other occupations.

Literary Focus Point out that poems printed in shapes that suggest their subjects are not unique to the twentieth century although the spread of typewriters and modern printing methods made the writing of concrete poems more feasible. Ask students to think of other kinds of writing in which the words were arranged to suggest a definite shape.

Look For You might point out that the appearance of "Seal" draws the reader's eye down the page in a swerving movement. Ask the students how such eye-movement affects their response as they read.

Writing/Prior Knowledge Suggest that your students concentrate on the physical aspects of the activity that they freewrite about.

Vocabulary You might point out that the vocabulary of the poem includes a great many words that describe physical movement and appearances.

Spelling Tip Write the word *swerve* on the board. Ask students to list other words that begin with the sound spelled by *sw*: *sway, swim, sweat,* etc.

Seal

William Jay Smith (1918–   ) was born in Winnfield, Louisiana. He has led a busy life—teaching college, writing poetry and essays, translating Russian and French poetry, and even serving in the Vermont state legislature for three years. His most successful writing has been his poetry for young people. When you read "Seal," you will see why. Lively and amusing, it shows that poetry can be pure and simple fun.

Concrete Poetry

Concrete poetry is poetry that is meant to be seen on the page, as well as heard like an ordinary poem. In a concrete poem, the words are arranged into a shape, often one that looks like the subject. The term *concrete* refers to the shape's being a specific, or concrete, representation of something.

Look For

Look at the shape formed by the words in "Seal." Does it remind you of anything? When you have read the poem, see if you can explain how the shape added to your reading experience. What would be lost if "Seal" were written as a single straight column of words?

Writing

The activities the seal performs are described vividly in the poem you are about to read. Freewrite about some physical activity that you enjoy. It might be running, swimming, skating, or riding a bike. Try to describe the activity in a way that suggests the fun you get out of it.

Vocabulary

Knowing the following words will help you as you read "Seal."
feed (fēd) *n.*: The tiny particles that minnows feed on (p. 475)
swerve (swɜrv) *n.*: A curving motion (p. 475)
quicksilver (kwik′ sil′ vər) *n.*: Quick, changeable, unpredictable; like the chemical element mercury, which is silver-white and flows easily (p. 475)

Objectives

1 To understand concrete poetry
2 To write a concrete poem

Support Material

Teaching Portfolio
Teacher Backup, p. 725
Usage and Mechanics Worksheet, p. 728
Vocabulary Check, p. 729
Critical Thinking and Reading Worksheet, *Writing About Animals,* p. 730
Language Worksheet, *Recognizing Words That Are Both Nouns and Verbs,* p. 731
Selection Test, p. 732

Seal

William Jay Smith

1

    See how he dives
        From the rocks with a zoom!
      See how he darts
        Through his watery room
    5 Past crabs and eels
      And green seaweed,
      Past fluffs of sandy
      Minnow feed!
    See how he swims

2

    10 With a swerve and a twist,
     A flip of the flipper,
     A flick of the wrist!
    Quicksilver-quick,
    Softer than spray,
15 Down he plunges
  And sweeps away;
Before you can think,
Before you can utter
Words like "Dill pickle"
20 Or "Apple butter,"
  Back up he swims
   Past Sting Ray and Shark,
  Out with a zoom,
  A whoop, a bark;
    25 Before you can say
      Whatever you wish,

3

        He plops at your side
        With a mouthful of fish!

THINKING ABOUT THE SELECTION

Recalling

1. In a sentence or two, summarize "Seal."

Interpreting

2. Describe the setting of the poem. Give evidence to support your answer.
3. How would you describe the spirit, or mood, of the poem? Find at least three words that help create this mood.

Applying

4. If you saw seals in an aquarium, how might this poem affect your response to them?

ANALYZING LITERATURE

Understanding Concrete Poetry

Concrete poems are often lighthearted. When the words of a poem are arranged in a shape that imitates the subject or suggests something about it, the effect is usually playful.

1. How would the effect of "Seal" be changed if the poem did not have its unusual shape?
2. The lines of "Seal" are very short. What connection might there be between the shortness of the lines and the shape of the poem?
3. After reading the poem aloud, tell which of the following words or phrases best describes its rhythm: (a) slow and relaxed; (b) quick and lively; (c) powerful.

THINKING AND WRITING

Writing a Concrete Poem

Use the freewriting you did as a starting point for writing a concrete poem. First decide on a suitable shape. It should be one that resembles, or suggests something about, your subject. Though you need not use rhyme, try to write lines that have a definite rhythm. When you revise, think of the effect you are trying to achieve. You should do your best to make everything about your poem contribute to that effect.

Seal 475

Focus

More About the Author Taniguchi Buson's fame is as much due to his painting as to his poetry. He was greatly influenced by Chinese literature. He often painted figures found in Chinese literature but depicted them in settings based on the landscape around Kyoto. What do you think is the special value of art and literature produced in a culture very different from one's own?

More About the Author The earliest haiku were comic in style and simple to write. Otsuji's essays on the writing of haiku contributed to the development of haiku as a more serious art form with a theoretical basis. If a person performs an activity well, such as a sport or an art, why might it be desirable to think and even write about it?

More About the Author Kyorai was a follower of Bashō. Critics have pointed out that though he lacked his master's genius, Kyorai reached the highest level of mastery through dedicated, diligent effort. Bashō himself said, "In solidness of content, no one can equal Kyorai." If a person cannot have both, is it better to have inborn talent or the ability to work hard and with dedication?

More About the Author Matsuo-Bashō once said, "Whoever would achieve artistic excellence must follow along with nature and take the four seasons to be his friends . . . must follow along with nature and return to nature." What do you think the world of nature can teach an artist?

Haiku

Taniguchi Buson (1715–1783) was a Japanese poet whose poems many Japanese of today know by heart. He was also a painter, and his sharp eye for detail no doubt helped him compose poems whose focus is on small things that express a great deal.

Otsuji (? –1772) wrote many essays about the art of writing haiku. He believed that a poet should view human life as part of the larger world of nature. He also felt that in the best haiku, emotions should be suggested, not expressed directly.

Kyorai (1651–1704) was the son of a physician to a royal Japanese family. He sought to write poems in which every word was necessary and none could be changed without destroying the poem's meaning.

Matsuo-Bashō (1644–1694) was born near Kyoto, Japan. In many of his haiku, he presents a scene in which a vivid or momentary feature stands out against an unchanging background. He can present a whole landscape or an entire season by describing just a few key details.

476 *Poetry*

Haiku

Haiku is a form of poetry that originated in Japan. A haiku has three lines; the first and third lines have five syllables each; the second line has seven. A haiku usually depicts a scene in nature and often implies a strong feeling. In a good haiku, a mere handful of words will make you see an entire scene and will convey a universal feeling, such as fear, surprise, regret, hope, or mystery.

Look For

As you read and reread each of these little poems, try to put yourself in the poet's place. Try to see and hear what he saw and felt. Ask yourself, "What was the poet experiencing?" Remember that in a haiku every word counts.

Writing

Think of a simple scene in nature that is vivid in your memory. It should be one that is like a sharp, clear unforgettable snapshot. Describe in writing what this mental photograph shows. If you can make this brief description express a feeling without your saying directly what the feeling is, you will be writing the way haiku poets write.

Vocabulary

In haiku simple words are used to create vivid images. Although you may think you know the meaning of each word, pause over each one and think about what it implies.

Literary Focus Point out that the rigidity of the haiku form makes it difficult to write. Great skill is needed to say what one wants to say and create the effect one wants to create in seventeen syllables with a strict division of five-seven-five.

Look For Encourage your students to reread the haiku at least a few times and attempt to adopt the poet's point of view. You might tell them that the art of haiku is largely the art of leaving out details and leaving feelings unexpressed. It is up to the reader to sense or imagine what is left out or unexpressed.

Writing/Prior Knowledge To help your students get started, bring in collections of nature photographs. You might suggest that your students try to recall scenes similar to the ones that you display.

Vocabulary At some point in your reading of the haiku, you might ask students to substitute words for those found in the poems. You might then discuss the effects of the substitutions.

Motivation/Prior Knowledge
You might have your students read or summarize the nature scenes they described. Other students might comment on the feelings these descriptions suggested to them.

Master Teacher Note Haiku, as well as other forms of Oriental poetry, has had a great influence on the development of modern poetry in England and America. From Ezra Pound and the Imagists down to the present day, poets have learned the virtues of precision, clarity, and objectivity from the Chinese and Japanese masters. You might ask your students whether they find haiku more appealing or less appealing than the other poems in the Figurative Language and Imagery section.

Purpose-Setting Question What feeling or emotion does each haiku communicate?

1 Critical Thinking and Reading
The ellipses indicate that something has been left out. What might it be?

2 Discussion For what reason might the speaker have called into the forest?

3 Discussion Why did the speaker call "Who's there?" to the wind?

Three Haiku

translated from the Japanese by Harry Behn

1   Deep in a windless
    wood, not one leaf dares to move. . . .
    Something is afraid.
    Buson

2   Into a forest
    I called. . . . The voice in reply
    was no voice I knew.
    Otsuji

3   I called to the wind,
    "Who's there?" . . . Whoever it was
    still knocks at my gate.
    Kyorai

THINKING ABOUT THE SELECTION

Recalling

1. Describe the real-life scene or situation that is the basis of each haiku.

Interpreting

2. In the haiku by Buson, what might be the "something" that is afraid?
3. Whose voice do you think replies to the poet in the haiku by Otsuji?
4. In the haiku by Kyorai, how might the continual knocking at the gate be explained?

Applying

5. Tell why you would, or would not, use the haiku form if you wanted to write a poem expressing strong personal feelings about something.

ANALYZING LITERATURE

Understanding Haiku

A haiku has three lines. The first and third lines have five syllables each; the second line has seven. One reason that readers enjoy haiku is that a single poem can be interpreted in different ways, and it is interesting to compare and discuss different interpretations.

1. Review your classmates' answers to Question 2, under Thinking About the Selection. Which seem to you good answers, though different from yours?
2. What was the basis for your answer to Question 3, under Thinking About the Selection.
3. Some readers think that the haiku by Kyorai is meant to be humorous. What reasons might be given for this interpretation?

ANSWERS TO THINKING ABOUT THE SELECTION
Recalling

1. In Buson's haiku, the speaker is in a quiet wood where all is still. He senses fear. In Otsuji's haiku, the speaker calls out into a forest. He

478

hears a reply—possibly an echo—but cannot recognize the voice. In Kyorai's haiku, the speaker hears what sounds like a person in the wind. Whether or not it is just the wind, he fails to discover. His gate knocks, possibly because of the wind.

Interpreting

2. The "something" that is afraid might be a creature of the woods, or it might be the speaker.

3. Answers will differ, but the voice that replies might be the speaker's own, distorted in an echo.
4. The knocking at the gate might be caused by the wind.

Applying

5. Answers will differ. Some students might use haiku if they wished to express feelings indirectly. Others might reasonably think the form is too restrictive for full self-expression.

ANSWERS TO ANALYZING LITERATURE

1. Students might be asked to explain why they agreed or disagreed with their classmates' answers.
2. Encourage each student to explain as fully as possible his or her reasons for the answer.
3. Humor could result from the speaker's being fooled by the sound of the wind into thinking that a person is there.

Three Haiku

Bashō

translated by Daniel C. Buchanan

On sweet plum blossoms
The sun rises suddenly.
Look, a mountain path! **1**

Has spring come indeed?
On that nameless mountain lie **2**
Thin layers of mist.

Temple bells die out.
The fragrant blossoms remain.
A perfect evening! **3**

RAVENS IN MOONLIGHT, 1882
Gengyo
Omni Photo Communications

Presentation

Motivation/Prior Knowledge
Ask students to recall moments when they suddenly noticed a change in nature—a change in weather, in cloud formations, or the like. Did their feelings change in response to what they observed?

Master Teacher Note Bashō's poetry is renowned for its quiet, thoughtful spirit, its mysterious beauty, and its sensitiveness of perception. After reading his three poems, you might ask your students to express their sense of the kind of personality Bashō might have had.

Purpose-Setting Question
What feelings do Bashō's poems express that are different from those of the three preceding haiku?

1 Discussion What is the tone of this line?

2 Discussion Why might the speaker doubt that spring has come?

3 Critical Thinking and Reading Do you think the poem offers enough information to make clear why the speaker feels that the evening is perfect? Explain your answer.

Reader's Response Of the six haiku, which did you like best? Why?

Humanities Note

Fine Art, *Ravens in Moonlight,* by Gengyo. Gengyo (1817–1880) was a Japanese painter and designer. He specialized in work done for "accessories," such as fans, book covers, and privately commissioned highly decorated prints. *Ravens in Moonlight* is a fan print. It was meant to be mounted as a flat, round fan on a stick. The full-moon scene is typically Oriental. The variety in the positions of the birds lends a dynamic, lifelike quality to the general stillness of the composition.

1. Describe the mood, or atmosphere, of the print.
2. In what way is this example of Japanese visual art similar in spirit or style to haiku? In what way is it different?
3. Tell why you think the print is or is not a suitable illustration for the haiku on the page.

Closure and Extension

ANSWERS TO THINKING ABOUT THE SELECTION
Recalling

1. In the first haiku, he sees sunlight on plum blossoms and notices a mountain path. In the second, he notices mist on a mountain and therefore wonders if good weather has really arrived. In the third, he hears the last sounds of temple bells, but notices that pleasant-smelling blossoms have not faded with the bells.

Interpreting

2. He expresses surprise because he had not noticed the path before the sun rose.
3. He is probably uncertain that spring has come because the sight of mist on the mountain suggests the dreary weather of winter.
4. He may feel that the evening is perfect because the beauty of nature seems to outlast the sounds of humanity.

Applying

5. Answers will differ. You may wish to concentrate less on which poem a student chose than on his or her reasons for choosing it.

THINKING AND WRITING

Publishing Student Writing
Students might enjoy a haiku bulletin board. Consider having students illustrate their haiku (or find illustrations). Display the haiku with their illustrations.

THINKING ABOUT THE SELECTION

Recalling

1. In your own words tell what the poet has noticed or observed in each haiku.

Interpreting

2. Why does the poet express surprise in the first haiku?
3. In the second haiku, why is he uncertain that spring has come?
4. In the third haiku, why do you think he feels that the evening is perfect?

Applying

5. Reread the biography of Bashō. Then decide which one of these three haiku best illustrates what is said there about his poetry. Why did you pick the poem you did rather than either of the other two?

THINKING AND WRITING

Writing a Haiku

Write a haiku based on the description you wrote before you read these haiku. Remember the correct form: the first and third lines have five syllables each; the second has seven. As you rewrite and revise your haiku, be sure that every word counts. Let the scene or moment you describe suggest your feelings about it. When you are satisfied that you have said all you can in seventeen syllables, share your haiku with your classmates.

Lyric Poetry

YOUNG GIRLS AT THE PIANO
Pierre Auguste Renoir
Joslyn Art Museum

Humanities Note

Fine art, *Two Girls at the Piano,* 1873, Pierre Renoir. Pierre August Renoir (1841–1919) was one of the most famous artists of the French Impressionist School of painting. His formal art training is sparse, beginning with a short career as a china painter and a few classes in Paris. His was a natural talent that grew and developed as he worked and through association with other artists. Renoir was a prolific painter who did many studies of women and children. He often used family and friends as models for these paintings. In true Impressionist fashion, all of these portraits were studies of the effects of light on the human form.

The painting *Two Girls at the Piano* is a pleasant scene of the type that recurs in his work. The diffused light causes the harmonious pastel colors of the painting to glow. The repeated curves of the composition always lead the eye back to the focal point, the faces of the two girls. Although this is a conventional scene of privilege and comfort, it is painted in a masterly Impressionist style that is in no way ordinary.

More About the Author James Stephens was living in Paris during World War I. He could not write, however, because he felt that this usually festive city was sad and dull. Stephens therefore returned to Dublin, Ireland. You might want to ask students to consider the effect of a writer's environment on his or her work. What do students consider an ideal place to write?

More About the Author Mary O'Neill, like many other authors, began her career as a copywriter for an advertising agency. You might want to have students comment on the similarities and differences between writing poetry and writing advertising copy.

More About the Author Vachel Lindsay traveled across the United States to gain firsthand experience of the country and its people. Students might enjoy commenting on the differences between knowing a subject through books and knowing it through personal experience. Ask them to think of instances when each of these ways of knowing would help a poet.

GUIDE FOR READING

Washed in Silver

James Stephens (1880–1950) was a poet and storyteller who grew up in a poor neighborhood of Dublin, Ireland. As a young man, he worked for a lawyer, but in his free time he read all he could about Irish legends and fairy tales. His books include *The Crock of Gold* (1912), which is an imaginative novel, and *Songs from the Clay* (1915), a volume of poems. Stephens had a wonderful speaking voice and gave many readings of his poetry. "Washed in Silver" captures the magical quality of Irish legends.

Feelings About Words

Mary O'Neill (1908–   ) began writing to entertain her family as she grew up in a small town near Cleveland, Ohio. She kept her interest in writing even while making a career in advertising. When her own children grew up, she published many stories and poems for young people. One of her best-loved books is *Words, Words, Words* (1966). Her fascination with words is clearly seen in her poem "Feelings About Words."

The Flower-Fed Buffaloes

Vachel Lindsay (1879–1931) believed that poetry was most exciting when it was heard. He often traveled through the countryside reading his poems aloud and receiving shelter and food in return. One of his books, in fact, is called *Rhymes to Be Traded for Bread* (1912). Lindsay used strong rhythms in his poetry and often wrote about popular figures like baseball players and movie stars. In "The Flower-Fed Buffaloes," repeated words and phrases add to both the rhythm and the meaning.

Objectives

1 To understand the features of lyric poetry
2 To understand connotation
3 To appreciate vivid verbs
4 To write about a lyric poem

Support Material

Teaching Portfolio
Teacher Backup, p. 745
Usage and Mechanics Worksheet, p. 750
Vocabulary Check, p. 751
Critical Thinking and Reading Worksheet, *Understanding Connotation and Denotation*, p. 752
Language Worksheet, *Appreciating Vivid Verbs*, p. 753

Selection Test, p. 754
Art Transparency 17, *Indians Simulating Buffalo,* by Frederic Remington

Lyric Poetry

A **lyric poem** is the expression of a poet's personal thoughts and feelings in vivid and musical language. In ancient times, lyric poetry was actually sung to the music of a stringed instrument known as a lyre. That is why such poetry was called *lyr*-ic and why we still refer to the words of songs as *lyrics*. While most lyric poems are no longer set to music, they still tend to be brief and melodic like songs.

Any subject that calls up a poet's thoughts and feelings is suitable for a lyric poem. James Stephens, for example, describes the "silvery radiance" of moonlight, while Vachel Lindsay imagines the mighty buffaloes that "trundle around the hills no more."

Lyric poetry can take many forms, with different patterns of rhyme and rhythm. Most lyric poems, however, include vivid language that is filled with energy. Such lively words help you remember a poet's thoughts and feelings.

Look For

As you read the following lyric poems, look for the vivid language that these poets use to express their thoughts and feelings. Listen for the musical quality of the poems. How does this musical quality help convey the meaning of the poems?

Writing

Think about the songs you like the best. What is it about the lyrics that makes you remember them? Brainstorm with your classmates to list the qualities of lyrics that make them memorable.

Vocabulary

Knowing the following words will help you as you read these poems.

squat (skwät) *adj.*: Short and heavy (p. 487)

glint (glint) *v.*: Gleam, flash, or glitter (p. 487)

saunter (sôn′ tər) *v.*: Walk about idly; stroll (p. 487)

preen (prēn) *v.*: Dress up; show pride in one's appearance (p. 487)

pomp (pämp) *n.*: An impressive show or display (p. 487)

trundle (trun′ d'l) *v.*: Move on wheels or as if on wheels (p. 488)

Guide for Reading 483

Motivation/Prior Knowledge
You might ask students if they can remember seeing a city or country scene by moonlight. Ask them to describe the feelings that this type of light calls up and the visual effects it creates. Encourage them to use vivid language in their descriptions.

Purpose-Setting Question
What feelings do the poet's descriptions inspire in you?

Thematic Idea A moonlit setting plays an important role in the narrative poem "The Highwayman," pages 437–42. Consider having students compare and contrast the moods that Noyes and Stephens create with their descriptions of moonlight.

You might also want to have **more advanced** students compare and contrast the metaphors that these two poets use to describe the moon. Students can then analyze how these metaphors contribute to the feelings that these two poems call up in readers.

1 Master Teacher Note You might want to play for students the first movement of Beethoven's "Moonlight Sonata" in order to create a mood for reading the poem. Have students listen to the music for a few minutes with their eyes closed. Then ask them what scenes the music leads them to imagine.

After they have read the poem, you can ask them to compare and contrast its mood with that of the music or that of Eliot Porter's photograph on this page, *Coastline*.

2 Literary Focus Lyric poets often choose vivid verbs to make their thoughts and feelings memorable. You might ask students why the verb *spills* is more lively in this context than the verb *shines* would be.

Washed in Silver

James Stephens

Gleaming in silver are the hills!
Blazing in silver is the sea!

And a silvery radiance spills
Where the moon drives royally!

5 Clad in silver tissue, I
March magnificently by!

3 Discussion What is the effect of the poem's rhythm on its meaning? For your **less advanced** students, you might review accented and unaccented syllables in poetry. You might read the poem aloud, exaggerating the accented syllables. Advise students, however, that this is not the way one usually reads poetry aloud for an audience.

You might have **more advanced** students consider why the poet begins lines 1 and 2 with an accented syllable and lines 3 and 4 with an anapestic foot (two unaccented syllables and an accented syllable). Students might also consider why lines 5 and 6 are made up of trochaic feet (accented syllable, unaccented syllable). How, for instance, does this type of rhythm imitate a march?

THINKING ABOUT THE SELECTION

Recalling

1. Briefly describe what the poet sees.
2. What is the poet doing?

Interpreting

3. What does the poet mean by saying he is "Clad in silver tissue"?
4. Explain the poem's title.

Applying

5. Light is important in this lyric. How do different kinds of light affect people's moods?

ANALYZING LITERATURE

Understanding Lyric Poetry

A **lyric poem** expresses a poet's emotions and thoughts in language that is lively and musical. Most lyrics also contain vivid words that communicate the poet's feelings in a memorable way. As an example, at the end of "Washed in Silver," Stephens declares: ". . . I / March magnificently by!" With this bold phrase he communicates feelings of triumph and delight.

1. In songs, words and phrases are often repeated. How many times does the word *silver* appear in this poem? What effect does the repetition of this word have on the poem?
2. What picture does the vivid phrase "the moon drives royally" bring to your mind? Why do you think Stephens uses this phrase rather than "the moon shines in the sky"?
3. What feelings do you think the poet wants to communicate about the landscape bathed in moonlight?

Washed in Silver　485

Humanities Note

Photograph, *Coastline,* by Eliot Porter (1901–　　). Porter graduated from Harvard University Medical School but gave up medicine to pursue photography. Starting as a photographer of birds, he has become famous for his sensitive pictures of natural landscapes.

1. Why do you think Porter chose this section of the shore as a subject?
2. What is the quality of light in the photograph?
3. How does the mood of the photography compare with that of "Washed in Silver"?

Motivation/Prior Knowledge
You may want to tell students that, in addition to having definitions, words suggest images and feelings. For example, the word *lace* may remind one person of a lace curtain in the house of a loved grandparent. Of course, this word may call up different associations for others. You might have students mention some of the feelings and images they associate with the word *dance*. Then tell them that the poem they will be reading describes the feelings that the poet has about various words.

Thematic Idea Another selection that you might want to teach with this poem is Maxwell Nurnberg's essay "The Mystery and Wonder of Words." pages 401–04. Nurnberg's essay will give students an insight into the link between the history of a word and its connotative meanings.

Purpose-Setting Question Are your feelings about the words in the poem the same as the poet's?

Humanities Note

Fine art, *Dominant Curve,* April 1936, by Wassily Kandinski (1866–1944). Kandinski was the first artist to paint pictures without a recognizable subject. He believed that painting should be as abstract as music.

You might want to tell students that this picture was painted before "Feelings About Words" was written and with its bright colors and geometric shapes, is similar to others by this artist.
1. What colors and shapes do you see in this painting?
2. Why do you think that Kandinski chose the title *Dominant Curve?*
3. What feelings does the painting inspire in you?
4. Do you think that the painting goes with the poem? Explain.

DOMINANT CURVE, APRIL 1936
Wassily Kandinski
Solomon R. Guggenheim Museum

1 # Feelings About Words

Mary O'Neill

Some words clink
As ice in drink.
Some move with grace
A dance, a lace.
5   Some sound thin:

1 **Master Teacher Note** Consider having each student set up a chart called *Word Associations.* The categories along the top might include: *Color, Type of Music, Image,* and *Feeling.* You might ask students to list the color, music, image, and feeling they associate with each word you mention. By having students discuss these associations, you can demonstrate to them that some of these associations are private and some are shared.

Ask **more advanced** students to consider whether the poet's feelings about the words she mentions are probably shared by most of her readers.

2

Wail, scream and pin.
Some words are squat:
A mug, a pot,
And some are plump,
10 Fat, round and dump.
Some words are light:
Drift, lift and bright.
A few are small:
A, is and all.

3

15 And some are thick,
Glue, paste and brick.
Some words are sad:
"I never had . . ."
And others gay:
20 Joy, spin and play.
Some words are sick:
Stab, scratch and nick.
Some words are hot:
Fire, flame and shot.
25 Some words are sharp,
Sword, point and carp.
And some alert:
Glint, glance and flirt.
Some words are lazy:
30 Saunter, hazy.
And some words preen:
Pride, pomp and queen.
Some words are quick,
A jerk, a flick.
35 Some words are slow:
Lag, stop and grow,
While others poke
As ox with yoke.
Some words can fly—
40 There's wind, there's high;
And some words cry:

4

"Goodbye . . .
Goodbye . . ."

THINKING ABOUT THE SELECTION
Recalling

1. O'Neill calls some words "squat" and others "light." What examples does she give of each kind of word?
2. Name three other adjectives she uses to describe words. What examples does she give of each of these types of words?

Interpreting

3. Why is *flick* a good example of a quick word?
4. Why is *goodbye* a word that cries?
5. Why does O'Neill call this poem "Feelings About Words"? What are her feelings about words?

Applying

6. Look at the painting by Wassily Kandinski on page 486. In what way is a poet's love of words similar to an artist's love of color and form?

CRITICAL THINKING AND READING
Understanding Connotation

Connotation refers to the feelings and associations words stir up in us. O'Neill explores the connotations of different words. For example, she says that *saunter* gives her a lazy feeling. When you read *saunter,* you, like her, may picture someone who moves in a lazy fashion.

When people use words to persuade you to buy or do things, they often rely on connotation. A company selling a new kind of soap, for instance, will choose a name that suggests cleanliness—like Rainwater or Springtime.

1. O'Neill lists words that suggest grace to her. List four words that suggest grace to you.
2. List four words that suggest sadness to you.
3. List four words that suggest gaiety to you.
4. A car manufacturer once hired the poet Marianne Moore to think of names for its latest models. Do you think it was a good idea to choose a poet for this job? Why or why not?

Feelings About Words   487

---

2 Discussion Why do you think the poet chose to use short lines for her poem?

3 Discussion You might ask **less advanced** students to identify the pattern of rhymes in the poem. Where does this pattern change? **More advanced** students might want to comment on possible reasons for this change.

4 Discussion Are there any other words that you would have liked to see the poet mention? Explain.

Reader's Response Does this poem change the way you feel about words? Why or why not?

Closure and Extension

ANSWERS TO THINKING ABOUT THE SELECTION
Recalling

1. The words "mug" and "pot" are "squat," while "Drift, lift and bright" are "light."

2. Students may choose any three of the following groups: "thin—"Wail, scream, and pin"; "plump"—"Fat, round and dump"; "small"—"A, is and all"; "thick"—"Glue, paste and brick"; "sad"—"'I never had . . .'"; "gay"—"Joy, spin and play"; "sick"—"Stab, scratch and nick"; "hot"—"Fire, flame and shot"; "sharp"—"Sword, point, and carp"; "alert"—"Glint, glance and flirt"; "lazy"—"Saunter, hazy"; "quick"—"A jerk, a flick"; "slow"—"Lag, stop and grow."

Interpreting

3. It refers to a quick movement and, since the word has only one syllable, it sounds quick.
4. Many people do cry when they say goodbye.
5. Answers will differ, but most students should realize that the poet is expressing some of her feelings about words. She obviously has varied feelings, depending on the word. In general, however, she seems to take delight in the associations and feelings that words call up.

Applying

6. Answers will differ, but students might indicate that the painter and poet both seem to enjoy the suggestiveness of words.

ANSWERS TO CRITICAL THINKING AND READING

1. Answers will differ. Suggested Responses: *easy, smooth, practiced,* or any other words that suggest "grace" through their meaning, sound, or both.
2. Answers will differ. Suggested Responses: *blues, grief, sorrowfulness,* or any other words that suggest "sadness" through their meaning, sound, or both.
3. Answers will differ. Suggested Responses: *cheerfulness, happiness, rejoicing,* or any other words that suggest "gaiety" through their meaning, sound, or both.
4. Answers will differ. Suggested Response: Students might indicate that a poet would be good at choosing names because he or she would be sensitive to the feelings that words call up.

487

Presentation

Motivation/Prior Knowledge
You might tell students that buffaloes used to roam the plains in herds of a million or more. Sometimes these herds extended further than the eye could see. During the nineteenth century, many of these animals were killed off by white hunters. Tell students that this poem is a kind of lament for the vanished buffalo herds.

Thematic Idea Another selection you might want to teach with this poem is Leslie Marmon Silko's story "Humaweepi, the Warrior Priest," page 167. This story indicates that, despite Lindsay's eulogy for the Blackfeet and Pawnees, native American values still exist and have relevance in the contemporary world.

Purpose-Setting Question What feelings does the poet have about the vanished buffaloes?

Master Teacher Note You might want students to discuss some of the causes for the disappearance of the buffalo herds from the plains. Place Art Transparency 17, *Indians Simulating Buffalo* by Frederic Remington, on the overhead projector. Point out the group of covered wagons in the background. Is this group the reason for the Indians' disguise? Are the Indians avoiding detection or are they hunting for buffalo? Is there a connection between the settlers moving west and the disappearance of the buffalo herds?

1 Master Teacher Note You might ask students to offer definitions of the word *progress.* Then ask them to give examples of progress in their environment. What changes might progress bring about in the next ten years? You might suggest to them that progress can involve losses as well as gains, although the losses are sometimes harder to see. Then

The Flower-Fed Buffaloes

Vachel Lindsay

1
The flower-fed buffaloes of the spring
In the days of long ago,
Ranged where the locomotives sing
And the prairie flowers lie low:—
5 The tossing, blooming, perfumed grass
Is swept away by the wheat,

2
Wheels and wheels and wheels spin by
In the spring that still is sweet.
But the flower-fed buffaloes of the spring
10 Left us, long ago.
They gore no more, they bellow no more,
They trundle around the hills no more:—
With the Blackfeet, lying low,
With the Pawnees,[1] lying low,

3 15 Lying low.

---

1. Blackfeet, Pawnees: The names of groups of native Americans who hunted buffalo.

THINKING ABOUT THE SELECTION

Recalling

1. According to the poem, in what ways has the prairie scene changed?
2. What has brought about this change?
3. With whom does Lindsay associate the buffaloes at the end of the poem? How are they alike?

Interpreting

4. Why does the poet describe the buffaloes as "flower-fed"? What is the effect of this image?

5. How does the repetition of the words "no more" in lines 11 and 12 emphasize the poem's meaning?
6. What is the implication of the words "lying low" in lines 13–15?
7. What does this poem suggest about progress?

Applying

8. The writer G. K. Chesterton defines progress as "leaving things behind us" and growth as "leaving things inside us." What do these definitions mean? What do you think is the difference between progress and growth?

488 *Poetry*

tell them that this poem is about such losses.

You might ask **more advanced** students to find examples of progress in this poem.

2 Discussion Why do you think the poet repeats so many words and phrases? What is the effect, for instance, of repeating the word *wheels* in line 7?

3 Discussion Why do you think the poet made the last line especially short?

Closure and Extension

ANSWERS TO THINKING ABOUT THE SELECTION
Recalling

1. The buffaloes disappeared with the coming of the trains, and wheat replaced the grass.
2. The change was brought about by people moving west, creating a transportation network and cultivating the land.
3. He associates the buffaloes with

THE BUFFALO TRAIL, 1867–68
Albert Bierstadt
Museum of Fine Arts, Boston

UNDERSTANDING LANGUAGE

Appreciating Vivid Verbs

Poets and other writers use vivid, specific verbs to help you picture the actions they are describing. In "The Flower-Fed Buffaloes," Vachel Lindsay uses verbs like "bellow," and "trundle" to bring to life the vanished buffalo herds. Notice that the verb "trundle," for instance, is much more vivid and specific than the general verb *move*.

Replace the italicized word in each sentence with a more lively verb.

1. The lion *walked* through the jungle.
2. The airplane *traveled* down the runway.
3. The runner *went* around the track.

THINKING AND WRITING

Writing About a Lyric Poem

Imagine that your friend is going to give a public reading of "The Flower-Fed Buffaloes" and has asked for your help. List the important points that he or she should keep in mind while reading this poem aloud. Remember to consider where a reader's voice should be loud or soft. Also think about where a reader should pause or continue at the end of a line. Turn your list into a note to your friend that will help make the reading a success. When revising this note, make sure your friend will understand your instructions. Proofread your note and prepare a final draft.

The Flower-Fed Buffaloes 489

(Answers continued from p.488.)

More About the Author In her later poetry, Edna St. Vincent Millay turned from private concerns to such public issues as the causes of World War II. You might ask students if any of the events they read about in the newspaper would make a good subject for a poem.

More About the Author While it took Teresa Paloma Acosta only about an hour to write this poem, she had been working on it in the back of her mind for a long time. Ask students how it is possible for a poet to compose part or all of a poem subconsciously.

GUIDE FOR READING

The Courage That My Mother Had

Edna St. Vincent Millay (1892–1950) was born and raised in Rockland, Maine. Millay revealed her poetic talent very early, writing "Renascence," one of her most famous poems, when she was only nineteen years old. She published her first book of poetry while still only in her mid-20's and quickly became a well-known poet. In 1923, she won a Pulitzer Prize for three of her works. Millay had a special fondness for the sonnet, a fourteen-line poem with a regular rhythm and pattern of rhymes. She published a collection of her sonnets in 1941. In "The Courage That My Mother Had," as in many of her lyric poems, she expresses strong emotions and intense feelings.

My Mother Pieced Quilts

Teresa Palomo Acosta (1949–   ) grew up in Texas. She became a journalist after studying at the University of Texas and Columbia University. As a girl, Acosta listened to her grandfather's stories about his childhood in Mexico and his life as a cowboy. These stories inspired her to begin reading literature. She wrote "My Mother Pieced Quilts" as an assignment for a university class. This poem was later read at the University of Southern California, during the first national festival of Chicano literature and art (1973). In "My Mother Pieced Quilts," Acosta follows in her grandfather's and mother's footsteps as a recorder of family history.

490   Poetry

Objectives

1 To understand the features of figurative and literal language
2 To paraphrase a poem
3 To appreciate concrete language in a poem
4 To write a lyric poem

Support Material

Teaching Portfolio
Teacher Backup, p. 757
Usage and Mechanics Worksheet, p. 761
Vocabulary Check, p. 762
Analyzing Literature Worksheet, *Understanding Figurative Language,* p. 763
Language Worksheet, *Appreciating Concrete Language,* p. 764
Selection Test, p. 765

Figurative and Literal Language

Figurative language is language used with meaning beyond the usual dictionary definitions. It is the highly imaginative use of words. This type of language is often based on vivid comparisons that can help to change your usual way of seeing the world. By comparing a snowflake to a soldier, for instance, a writer can surprise you into looking at a snowstorm in a new way. Suddenly the bits of white may resemble an army retreating or attacking. This perception may lead you to see other aspects of a winter scene with fresh eyes.

Literal language refers to language that does not go beyond the dictionary definitions of the words. A literal description of a snowfall, for example, might include the ideas that each snowflake has six sides and that each falls at a certain rate of speed. Poets often weave literal and figurative language together in their work. This combination ensures that their poems will be both understandable and surprising.

Look For

As you read the following two poems, look for the ways these poets skillfully combine literal and figurative language to express their thoughts and emotions. Identify passages in each poem where the poet shifts from one kind of language to another.

Writing

The two poems you are about to read express strong positive feelings about courageous women. Freewrite about the meaning of courage.

Vocabulary

Knowing the following words will help you as you read these two poems.

quarried (kwôr′ ēd) *v.*: Carved out of the ground (p. 492)
brooch (brōch) *n.*: A large ornamental pin worn on a dress (p. 492)
somber (säm′ bər) *adj.*: Dark and solemn (p. 495)
mosaic (mō zā′ ik) *adj.*: Made of different pieces combined to form a whole (p. 495)

testimonies (tes′ tə mō′ nēz) *n.*: Statements or declarations (p. 495)
muslin (muz′ lin) *n.*: A plain, strong kind of cotton (p. 496)

Literary Focus You might point out to students that people use figurative language in everyday conversation. Two examples are: 1) My heart was in my mouth, and 2) She went on a wild goose chase.

Ask students if they can add to this list.

You may also want to emphasize that the dictionary meaning of words does not change when they are used figuratively. The point for students to keep in mind is that figurative language is highly imaginative and often based on comparisons. When they call a search a wild goose chase, for instance, they are comparing it to the nearly impossible task of seizing such a bird.

Look For You might tell students that literal, or factual, language helps us to understand what the poet is talking about. They might read a poem, for instance, in which a woman is cutting wood. Part of the poem, therefore, might be a literal description of this activity. The poet may also use figurative language in comparing the flashing ax-head to a star. The literal description roots the poem in reality, while the figurative language takes us beyond what seems familiar.

Writing/Prior Knowledge You might tell students that Anaïs Nin once wrote that "Life shrinks or expands in proportion to one's courage." Have them discuss the meaning of this statement before they begin writing.

Vocabulary Ask less advanced students to pronounce the words and read aloud their meanings.

Spelling Tip Write the words *quarry, quarried* on the board. Point out to students that when a word ends in *y*, usually we change the *y* to *i* when adding -*ed*.

The Courage That My Mother Had

Edna St. Vincent Millay

> The courage that my mother had
> Went with her, and is with her still:
> Rock from New England quarried;
> Now granite in a granite hill.
>
> 5 The golden brooch my mother wore
> She left behind for me to wear;
> I have no thing I treasure more:
> Yet, it is something I could spare.
>
> Oh, if instead she'd left to me
> 10 The thing she took into the grave!—
> That courage like a rock, which she
> Has no more need of, and I have.

1
2
3
4

THINKING ABOUT THE SELECTION

Recalling

1. What quality does the speaker wish for?
2. What would the speaker give up to have this quality?

Interpreting

3. Explain lines 3–4.
4. Why is a rock an effective metaphor for a courageous woman? How is courage also like granite?
5. What do lines 3–4 suggest about the importance of the mother's New England heritage?
6. In your own words, describe the feeling that the speaker expresses in this lyric poem.

Applying

7. The speaker implies that courage is a quality you either have or do not have. Do you think that a person could learn to be more courageous? Why or why not?

ANALYZING LITERATURE

Understanding Figurative Language

The poet uses both figurative language and literal language to express her strong feelings about her mother. For example, both literal and figurative language appear in the first stanza.

492   Poetry

PORTRAIT OF HENRIETTE
Andrew Wyeth
Courtesy of the San Antonio Museum Association

(Answers continued from p. 492.)

Humanities Note
Fine art, *Portrait of Henrietta*, Andrew Wyeth (1917–   ). Allen S. Weller, a critic, has called Wyeth "the most popular American painter of his time." One reason for his popularity is the accessibility of his work. In his portraits, Wyeth frequently depicts his family, friends, and neighbors.

1. What do you imagine the woman in the painting is thinking?
2. What might she be looking at?
3. Has the artist given you any clues to her personality? Explain.
4. How might this picture relate to the theme of courage in Millay's poem?

ANSWERS TO CRITICAL THINKING AND READING

1. Students' paraphrases will differ. Suggested Response:
   When my mother died, she left me her golden brooch to wear. Though I treasure it more than anything else I have, I could still do without it. What I really wish she had given me was her courage, which reminds me of a rock. Instead, it is buried with her. She, however, no longer needs it, while I need it very much.
2. Students' answers will differ. Suggested Response: The figurative language, even when it is preserved in the paraphrase, is not as direct and immediate. Also, the shifts between literal and figurative language are not as dramatic. Other elements that contribute to the liveliness of the poem, and are missing in the paraphrase, are rhythm and rhyme.

Challenge Write a poem in which the mother is somehow able to answer her daughter. What would she say to her? What feelings would her words communicate?

---

1. Where in this stanza does the poet shift from a literal to a figurative description?
2. In which line of the third stanza does the poet start using figurative language again?
3. How would the poem be different if it were written entirely in literal language?

CRITICAL THINKING AND READING

Paraphrasing a Poem

   Paraphrasing a poem means briefly restating it in your own words. Often you can clarify a difficult poem by paraphrasing it. However, you should realize that a paraphrase does not include many of the qualities that make a poem exciting. The following is a paraphrase of the first stanza of "The Courage That My Mother Had."

   When my mother died, she took her courage with her. In its strength, that courage reminded me of New England granite. Now the granite of her courage is buried with her in the hill, just as real granite is buried.

1. Paraphrase the other two stanzas.
2. Why is the poem more exciting than the paraphrase?

The Courage That My Mother Had   493

Interpreting
3. Her mother's courage is like New England rock. Now that her mother is dead, it is buried with her like granite in a hill of granite.
4. A rock is strong and can be a firm support. Since granite is one of the hardest types of rock, it is an especially suitable symbol for courage.
5. These lines suggest that she gained her strength and courage from her New England heritage.

6. Students' answers will differ. Suggested Response: She expresses admiration for her mother's courage, as well as an almost desperate longing for it.

Applying
7. Students' answers will differ; however, most will see that a person can learn to be more courageous. Courage is not a trait over which you have no control, like the color of your eyes. It is a quality that can be cultivated.

ANSWERS TO ANALYZING LITERATURE

1. Lines 1 and 2 are literal, while lines 3 and 4 are figurative.
2. She starts using figurative language again in line 11.
3. Students' answers will differ. Suggested Response: Without the comparison of courage to a rock, the poem would be less vivid.

Presentation

Motivation/Prior Knowledge
You might tell students that folk art is art that is practiced and handed on by people. It differs from fine art in that it is not usually identified with a particular artist or exhibited in a museum.

Quilt-making has been a folk art practiced in America since colonial times. Tell students that crazy quilts are quilts made from pieces of cloth of various colors, patterns, shapes, and sizes. Refer them to the picture on page 495 for an example of such a quilt, and ask them why the term *crazy quilt* is appropriate. For additional examples of quilts and other folk art products, you might want to obtain a copy of the book *Young America—A Folk-Art History,* published by Hudson Hills Press.

Tell students that, in the poem they are about to read, a crazy quilt serves as a kind of family record.

Purpose-Setting Question What feelings about her mother does the poet reveal in describing the quilts her mother made?

Thematic Idea You might have students compare the mother in this poem with Alice Walker's mother in "In Search of Our Mothers' Gardens," page 311. Both of these women triumph over circumstances to produce their works of art. Both of them also become positive models for their daughters.

1 **Master Teacher Note** Consider telling students that one definition of the term *symbol* is "an object that takes on special meanings or associations for a person." Examples might be a lucky rabbit's foot worn by a high school quarterback during a big game or a seashell that reminds a girl of an enjoyable visit to the beach.

Ask students if they have

any objects that have become symbolic for them. Have them describe the object and explain the special meaning it has taken on.

Tell them that the quilts described in this poem are also symbolic. Ask them to consider the special meaning that these quilts have for the poet.

My Mother Pieced Quilts

Teresa Palomo Acosta

1
they were just meant as covers
in winter
as weapons
against pounding january winds

2
5 but it was just that every morning I awoke to these
october ripened canvases
passed my hand across their cloth faces
and began to wonder how you pieced
all these together
10 these strips of gentle communion cotton and flannel
        nightgowns
wedding organdies[1]
dime store velvets

how you shaped patterns square and oblong and round
positioned
15 balanced
then cemented them
with your thread
a steel needle
a thimble

3
20 how the thread darted in and out
galloping along the frayed edges, tucking them in
as you did us at night
oh how you stretched and turned and re-arranged
your michigan spring faded curtain pieces
25 my father's santa fe[2] work shirt
the summer denims, the tweeds of fall

in the evening you sat at your canvas
—our cracked linoleum floor the drawing board

---

1. organdies (ôr' gən dēz) *n.*: Thin, crisp cotton fabrics used for items like dresses and curtains.
2. Santa Fe (san' ta fā'): The capital of New Mexico.

2 **Discussion** Why do the quilts become for the poet more than just a protection against the "january winds"?

3 **Discussion** How does the care the mother takes with the quilts show itself in other ways as well?

4 **Discussion** How do the quilts become a record of family history?

5 **Discussion** Explain why the poet compares her mother to a "caravan master."

6 **Discussion** Why does the poet call the different pieces of cloth "testimonies"?

me lounging on your arm
30   and you staking out the plan:
whether to put the lilac purple of easter against the red
      plaid of winter-going
into-spring
whether to mix a yellow with blue and white and paint the
corpus christi[3] noon when my father held your hand
35   whether to shape a five-point star from the
somber black silk you wore to grandmother's funeral

you were the river current
carrying the roaring notes
forming them into pictures of a little boy reclining
40   a swallow flying
you were the caravan master at the reins
driving your threaded needle artillery across the mosaic
      cloth bridges
delivering yourself in separate testimonies.

---

3. Corpus Christi (kor' pəs kris' tē): A city in southeast Texas.

My Mother Pieced Quilts   495

Closure and Extension

ANSWERS TO THINKING ABOUT THE SELECTION
Recalling

1. They were meant to keep the family warm in their beds.
2. They were made from the family's clothing and curtains that were no longer used.

Interpreting

3. The quilts were weapons against the cold that attacked the family members. The mother has battled death and sickness and fought to keep her family together.
4. She is comparing her mother to an artist who paints pictures on canvases.
5. They reflect family history because the materials in them are associated with important family events.
6. Students' answers may differ. Most students will realize that when the poet says she "began to wonder how you pieced all these together," she is referring to the family as well as the quilts. Also, the poet's comparison of her mother to a "river current/carrying the roaring notes" and a "caravan master" indicate the mother's key role in keeping the family together.

Applying

7. Students' answers will differ. Most students, however, will see that these two women are similar in their courage. Of course, we know far more about the mother in this poem.

Challenge Imagine that someone has questioned the poet's decision not to use capital letters or periods. Write a response to this criticism, defending the poet's choice and explaining how the lack of capital letters and periods contributes to the meaning of the poem.

---

oh mother you plunged me sobbing and laughing
45 into our past
into the river crossing at five
into the spinach fields
into the plainview[4] cotton rows
into tuberculosis wards
50 into braids and muslin dresses
sewn hard and taut to withstand the thrashings of twenty-
    five years

stretched out they lay
armed/ready/shouting/celebrating

knotted with love
55 the quilts sing on

---

4. Plainview: A town in Texas.

THINKING ABOUT THE SELECTION
Recalling

1. What were the quilts meant to do?
2. What kinds of materials went into the quilts?

Interpreting

3. Like the quilts themselves, the poem is "pieced . . . together" from literal and figurative language. In what way were the quilts weapons? What battles has the mother fought?
4. To what is the speaker comparing her mother by using the word *canvases* in line 6?
5. How do the quilts reflect family history?
6. The speaker wonders how her mother was able to shape and cement the pieces of cloth to form a quilt. Find evidence that shows she also wonders how her mother was able to shape and cement the family.

Applying

7. Compare the mother in this poem with the mother in Millay's poem.

496   Poetry

UNDERSTANDING LANGUAGE
Appreciating Concrete Language

Concrete language is specific language. In "My Mother Pieced Quilts," the poet names many specific kinds of cloth rather than simply using a general term like *material*.

1. Identify two types of material named in the second stanza.
2. Find two types of fabric mentioned in the fourth stanza.
3. How does the poet relate a type of material to her family's history?

THINKING AND WRITING
Writing a Lyric Poem

Write a lyric poem about a courageous person. First brainstorm to list details that reveal this person's courage. Then shape these details into a poem expressing your feelings about this courageous person. Revise your poem to improve its musical quality. Prepare a final draft and share it with your classmates.

ANSWERS TO UNDERSTANDING LANGUAGE

1. Two other types of material named in the stanza are "communion cotton" and "dime store velvets."
2. Students may choose two from the following types of fabric mentioned in the fourth stanza: "michigan spring faded curtain pieces"; "santa fe work shirt"; "summer denims"; and "tweeds of fall."

3. Students may choose from the following examples in which the poet uses words or phrases related to family history to describe a piece of material—"gentle communion cotton"; "wedding organdies"; "michigan spring faded curtain pieces"; "father's santa fe work shirt"; and "somber black silk you wore to grandmother's funeral."

THINKING AND WRITING

For help with this assignment, students can refer to Lesson 18, "Writing a Poem," in the Handbook of Writing About Literature.

Publishing Student Writing You might want to consider publishing students' poems in a class booklet called *Poems About Courage.*

The Changing Seasons

BATCHEWANA WOOD, ALGOMA
J. E. H. MacDonald
Art Gallery of Ontario, Toronto

The Changing Seasons 497

Humanities Note

Fine art, *Batchewana Wood, Algoma,* James MacDonald. James Edward Hervy MacDonald (1873–1932) was a Canadian painter. He became a member of the "Group of Seven," a band of Canadian nationalist artists whose radical works brought about revolutionary changes in Canadian art trends. The group strove to portray the essence of their country's wild northern landscape. They achieved this in a fresh rugged impressionistic style that was totally new to Canadian art.

The painting entitled *Batchewana Wood, Algoma,* was done in the wild Algoma region east of Lake Superior. MacDonald and a few other artists from the "Group" traveled north in a converted boxcar that was shunted onto sidings and used as a base of operations for autumn painting trips. MacDonald was enthusiastic about the Algoma landscape and often painted the autumn panorama from the tracks of the Algoma Central Railroad. In this painting the autumn woods are painted with fresh directness, pure color, and an exuberance of brush stroke. The brilliance of the leaves contrasts favorably with the solid form of the rocks. The whole is simplified almost to the point of abstraction and filled with a pure, clean light. Although this is a carefully thought out, complete work or art, it retains the charm of a quick sketch. This spontaneity is a trademark of this great landscape artist and lover of nature.

In Just—

E. E. Cummings (1894–1962) was born in Cambridge, Massachusetts. Cummings graduated from Harvard University in 1915. He served in World War I as an ambulance driver. After the war, he worked as a painter and a poet. So successful a poet was he, that unlike many other poets, he was able to earn his living through his poetry. Individual liberty is a deeply rooted tradition in New England, and Cummings's life and writings are stamped with it. It is most clearly seen in the unusual way his poems are printed and in their strikingly original language. If you have not read any of Cummings's poems before, you will find "In just—" a unique reading experience, and probably a delightful one.

Winter

Nikki Giovanni (1943–   ) was born in Knoxville, Tennessee, and grew up in Cincinnati, Ohio. She has received numerous awards and honors, among them a National Book Award nomination and election to the Ohio Women's Hall of Fame. Much of her poetry expresses the feelings and experiences of the black-American community. She has also written about the joys and closeness of black family life. In "Winter," Giovanni writes about a universal subject, the first signs of the coming of winter.

Stopping by Woods on a Snowy Evening

Robert Frost (1875–1963) lived in rural New England for most of his life. As a result, Frost's poetry presents a full picture of nature and of country life in New Hampshire, Vermont, and other parts of New England. Frost won the Pulitzer Prize four times. His poems that describe and comment on a rural scene or event are among his most popular, and among these "Stopping by Woods on a Snowy Evening" is one of his best. If the poem seems to draw you into the scene described, it is partly because the scene is one that Frost knew well from real life.

Sensory Language

Sensory language is language that appeals to your senses. Poets as well as other writers frequently include details that appeal to your sense of sight, hearing, touch, taste, or smell.

To convey her impression of the heat of summer, the poet Hilda Doolittle (known as H. D.) wrote these lines in her poem "Garden":

> Fruit cannot drop
> Through this thick air;
> Fruit cannot fall into heat
> That presses up and blunts
> The points of pears,
> And rounds the grapes.

The sensory language here helps you almost see and feel the heavy, almost visible heat.

Look For

As you read the following poems, notice the clear word pictures they contain—the language that appeals to your sense of sight. Find examples of language that appeal to your sense of hearing and even to your sense of touch.

Writing

The poems you are about to read describe the changing seasons. Which one of the four seasons—spring, summer, fall, or winter—can you see most clearly in your imagination? Choose one, and list those sights, sounds, smells, and physical feelings that it brings to mind.

Vocabulary

Knowing the following words will help you as you read these poems.

wee (wē) *adj.*: Very small, tiny (p. 500)

burrow (bur′ ō) *v.*: To dig a hole or tunnel, especially for shelter (p. 502)

downy (doun′ ē) *adj.*: Soft and fluffy, like soft, fine feathers (p. 504)

Literary Focus Help less advanced students recognize the words that appeal to the senses. You might ask them to tell the sense to which each such word appeals.

Look For To help your less advanced students understand sensory language, present a situation, such as a day with a temperature of 90 degrees and humidity of 95 percent. Ask students for details that would describe this situation. As they give details, list them on the chalkboard in chart form with a column for details that appeal to each sense. For example, details might be that skin feels sticky (sense of touch) and ice cream melts (sight, taste, touch).

Writing/Prior Knowledge To get less advanced students started, write the names of the seasons on the board, and for each season have the students suggest a few associated sights and sounds.

Vocabulary You may wish to let the class know that "In Just—" will include a couple of interesting made-up words, *mud-luscious* and *puddle-wonderful*. Students could be asked to tell what sights, sounds, or feelings these words make them imagine.

in Just-

E. E. Cummings

in Just-
spring   when the world is mud-
luscious the little
lame balloonman

5 whistles   far   and wee

and eddieandbill come
running from marbles and
piracies and it's
spring

10 when the world is puddle-wonderful

the queer
old balloonman whistles
far   and   wee
and bettyandisbel come dancing

15 from hop-scotch and jump-rope and

it's
spring
and
     the

20   goat-footed[1]

balloonMan   whistles
far
and
wee

---

1. goat-footed: Like the Greek god Pan, who had the legs of a goat and was associated with fields, forests, and wild animals.

THINKING ABOUT THE SELECTION

Recalling

1. What event does this poem describe?

Interpreting

2. From whose point of view—a child's or adult's—is spring described? Which words seem especially appropriate for this group?
3. What is the effect of the poet's writing "eddieandbill" and "bettyandisbel" instead of "Eddie and Bill" and "Betty and Isbel"?
4. In what way does the arrangement of lines on the page mimic the way the people in the poem move?
5. Look at the adjectives used to describe the balloon man. How does the description of him change as the poem progresses?
6. The balloonman is associated with Pan, the goat-footed Greek god of woods and fields. What connection might there be between the balloonman's whistling and the children's running and dancing?

7. Why does the poet call this poem "in Just-," instead of "In Spring"?

Applying

8. What is it about spring that often makes us want to abandon our chores to play?

ANALYZING LITERATURE

Understanding Sensory Language

Sensory language is language that appeals to your senses. Poets frequently use such language to give you a vivid impression of the physical world. Cummings creates words that boldly appeal to your senses.

1. To which of your senses do the words "mud-luscious" and "puddle-wonderful" appeal?
2. The poet created these words by joining a noun and an adjective. In what way do these words capture the spirit of the poem?
3. Using the poet's technique of joining a noun and an adjective, create three words you think would be appropriate for describing spring.

in Just- 501

Winter

Winter

Nikki Giovanni

1
  Frogs burrow the mud
  snails bury themselves

2
  and I air my quilts
  preparing for the cold

5 Dogs grow more hair
  mothers make oatmeal
  and little boys and girls
  take Father John's Medicine[1]

  Bears store fat
10 chipmunks gather nuts
  and I collect books
  For the coming winter

---

1. Father John's Medicine: An old-fashioned cough syrup.

THINKING ABOUT THE SELECTION

Recalling

1. How does each animal mentioned prepare for winter?
2. What two things does the speaker do to prepare for winter?

Interpreting

3. In what way is the airing of quilts (line 3) a sign that winter is coming?

4. In what way does the collecting of books (line 11) suggest the approach of winter?
5. In what way does this poem suggest that people and animals are alike?

Applying

6. If you were asked to write an additional stanza for "Winter," what details might you include that fit in with those of the four stanzas Giovanni wrote?

502   *Poetry*

Presentation

Motivation/Prior Knowledge Ask your students to think of events and occurrences that signal the beginning of a new season.

Master Teacher Note Some modern poets avoid punctuation in order to give their poems a lean, stripped-down look. They rely on meaning and line divisions alone to keep the sense of their sentences clear. You might ask your students to point out what is unusual about the way the poem is written. When someone mentions the absence of punctuation, you can have the class suggest reasons for it. If necessary, you can mention the practice of some poets to omit punctuation they consider unnecessary.

Purpose-Setting Question What feelings about the coming of winter does the speaker seem to have?

Thematic Idea Point out that "Winter" may be both compared and contrasted with "in Just—." Both deal with a season, but in style, tone, and detail are quite different.

1 **Literary Focus** You may either point out or lead students to discover that this poem relies on simple and concrete nouns and verbs, such as "Frogs burrow" and "chipmunks gather nuts," that enable the reader to see the animals and people performing their activities.

2 **Critical Thinking and Reading** Ask students to imagine the poem with conventional punctuation. Would its effect be different? Have students give reasons for their answers.

Grammar in Action

Examples, details, and facts are often used to support the main idea. A writer can use one of these, or all three, to develop the main idea. In the following lines, Nikki Giovanni effectively uses examples to suggest the approach of winter:

  Frogs burrow the mud
  snails bury themselves
  and I air my quilts
  preparing for the cold

1. Frogs and snails go into the ground; dogs grow hair; bears get fatter; chipmunks store up nuts.
2. She airs her quilts and collects books.

Interpreting

3. The airing of quilts indicates that she will need warmer bed coverings in winter.
4. She expects to be indoors during the cold months and will spend time reading.
5. Both people and animals anticipate seasonal change by preparing for it.

Applying

6. Answers will differ. Acceptable answers will consist of any details that show people or animals performing tasks with an eye to the upcoming winter—for example, collecting firewood or getting winter clothes out of storage.

THINKING AND WRITING

For help with this assignment, students can refer to Lesson 18, "Writing a Poem," in the Handbook of Writing About Literature.

Publishing Student Writing You might encourage your students to illustrate their poems with drawings or color illustrations. The illustrated poems could be mounted for display.

THINKING AND WRITING

Writing a Poem

Write a poem in which you describe the activities you think of in connection with any one of the seasons where you live. Before writing, think about and then list the details that express your idea of the coming of the season you chose.

Although the details of your poem will be different from Giovanni's, follow the pattern she used. Write three four-line stanzas. Keep the lines short. Let some of the details be about nature and other people, and other details be about you.

Revise your poem and share it with your classmates.

Winter 503

Each example intensifies the reader's understanding of what winter is like. By using the same sentence structure in the first three lines (subject-verb-direct object), Giovanni emphasizes the unity of her examples.

Student Activity. Identify the examples, details, or facts in each of the following passages.

1. My backyard is beautiful in the springtime. The daffodils' jaunty, bright, yellow heads are fluttering in the breeze. Pink, white and red tulips march in a row beside the blooming pachysandra. And all the trees are sporting budding leaves, light green as they emerge.

2. Winter sports include ice hockey, basketball, wrestling, figure and speed-skating, skiing, and tobaganing.

3. Dolphins are extremely intelligent animals. They can be trained to leap through the air to catch a fish and to jump through a loop. Their intelligence is often ranked between that of the dog and that of the chimpanzee.

Presentation

Motivation/Prior Knowledge
You might have a class discussion that centers around the idea of how appealing certain places are—how tempting it can be to "hide out" in them and take a break from one's responsibilities.

Master Teacher Note Lead your more advanced students to look for the subtle double contrast in the poem: between the speaker, who stops to contemplate the beauty of the woods, and the horse, who thinks such stopping a "mistake," and between the speaker and the owner of the woods, who resides elsewhere.

Purpose-Setting Question What feelings lie just below the surface of the words?

1 Discussion Who gains more from property, an owner who is absent or a person who, though not possessing it, enjoys or appreciates it?

2 Clarification The horse-drawn wagon will seem less quaint if you point out that this poem was first published in 1923.

Master Teacher Note When students have finished reading the poem, place Art Transparency 18, *Bringing in the Christmas Tree* by Konstantin Rodko, on the overhead projector. Have students compare Frost's attitude towards the forest and nature with the artist's attitude conveyed in the painting. What are the similarities? What are the differences? How does the poem paint a picture in the reader's mind?

Reader's Response What mood does this poem evoke? Why?

Stopping by Woods on a Snowy Evening
Robert Frost

1
Whose woods these are I think I know.
His house is in the village, though;
He will not see me stopping here
To watch his woods fill up with snow.

5   My little horse must think it queer
To stop without a farmhouse near
Between the woods and frozen lake
The darkest evening of the year.

2
10   He gives his harness bells a shake
To ask if there is some mistake.
The only other sound's the sweep
Of easy wind and downy flake.

The woods are lovely, dark, and deep,
But I have promises to keep,
15   And miles to go before I sleep,
And miles to go before I sleep.

THINKING ABOUT THE SELECTION
Recalling

1. Describe the setting—both the time and the place—of the poem.
2. Why has the speaker stopped by the woods?
3. What is the horse's reaction to the pause in their journey?

Interpreting

4. What is the significance of the word *darkest* in line 8?

5. What does the speaker mean when he says that he has "promises to keep"?
6. What associations and feelings are stirred up by the word *sleep*? What might this word mean in this poem?

Applying

7. This is one of the most popular poems by one of America's best-loved poets. Why do you think it appeals to so many readers?

504   Poetry

SPEAKING AND LISTENING
Reading a Lyric Poem

When you read a poem like "Stopping by Woods on a Snowy Evening"—a poem with rhythm and rhyme—you should be careful not to read it in a singsong way. For example, do not overemphasize the beat of the lines, and do not pause for the same length of time whenever you reach the end of a line.

The right way to read such a poem is to read the words with natural pronunciation and let the rhythm take care of itself. If there is no punctuation at the end of a line, read on, without a pause, to the first word of the next line. With these hints in mind, read Frost's poem aloud to your classmates.

THINKING AND WRITING
Writing About a Poem

"Stopping by Woods on a Snowy Evening," like most poems, can be understood on many levels. Write an explanation for your classmates of what you think the poem might mean. Start by making notes on why the speaker feels he must move on, where you think he might be going, and what promises he must keep. You might think of the situation as a mystery to be solved. Draft your ideas into a paragraph. End your paragraph with a summary statement about the meaning of the poem. Revise your draft, checking that what you have said is clear and sensible. Proofread it and prepare a final draft. Then share your interpretation of the poem with your classmates.

Stopping by Woods on a Snowy Evening   505

Closure and Extension
ANSWERS TO THINKING ABOUT THE SELECTION
Recalling

1. It is a dark night in winter. The speaker is in a horse-drawn wagon on a road with a frozen lake on one side, dark woods on the other. Snow is falling.
2. He has stopped to watch the woods fill up with snow.
3. The horse thinks the pause "queer"—a mistake.

Interpreting

4. *Darkest* suggests the very depth of winter and connotes coldness, bleakness, oblivion.
5. The speaker means that he cannot stay where he is; he has responsibilities elsewhere.
6. *Sleep* connotes death, oblivion, escape from living. In this poem, it may symbolize death as an escape or release from "promises."

Applying

7. Suggested Response: Its appeal is partly due to its beautiful simplicity and clarity, partly due to its lyrical and pictorial appeal, and partly due to the universal feelings it touches upon.

Challenge What effect does the repetition of the last line have on the reader?

THINKING AND WRITING

For help with this assignment, students can refer to Lesson 13, "Writing About a Poem," in the Handbook of Writing About Literature.

More About the Author An editor's suggestion caused Phyllis McGinley to change from writing sad, serious poetry to the light-hearted verse for which she is famous. Her first book of verse poked fun at the fads and trivia of city life. Ask students to think of a subject they might someday write a story or poem about. Then ask whether they would approach this subject seriously or humorously. Then ask why they would take this approach. You might suggest that they think about whether the subject of "Season at the Shore" could be treated in a serious poem.

More About the Author James Whitcomb Riley's work as a house and sign painter and as a traveling vendor of patent medicines acquainted him with the rural types and dialect that appear in his verse. When reciting his verse, he would accompany himself on a banjo. Have students discuss the advantages and disadvantages of writing in a dialect used only in a limited area of the country.

GUIDE FOR READING

Season at the Shore

Phyllis McGinley (1905–1978) was born in Ontario, Oregon. She is most famous for her lighthearted, humorous poetry, for which she won a Pulitzer Prize in 1961. McGinley, who wrote with humor and affection about ordinary life, once summed up the viewpoint of her work by saying, "Cheerfulness was always breaking in." In "Season at the Shore," she takes her cheerfulness and humor to the beach for a romp on the sand.

When the Frost Is on the Punkin

James Whitcomb Riley (1849–1916) was born in Indiana. He wrote so many poems in the dialect, or country speech, of his native state that he has come to be known as "the Hoosier poet." He knew the land and the people of Indiana very well, and he used his knowledge to write poems that are still a source of local pride. "When the Frost Is on the Punkin" is both a colorful picture of an Indiana farm such as Riley would have known and a lively tune in the dialect that was for him a kind of music. Reading it aloud will add to your enjoyment of the language.

Objectives

1 To understand the use of alliteration in a poem
2 To write a poem in which alliteration is used
3 To understand the use of onomatopoeia in a poem
4 To write a travel article in which alliteration and onomatopoeia are used

Support Material

Teaching Portfolio
Teacher Backup, p. 781
Grammar in Action Worksheets, *Using Prepositional Phrases,* p. 786; *Recognizing Dialect,* p. 788
Usage and Mechanics Worksheet, p. 790
Vocabulary Check, p. 791
Analyzing Literature Worksheet, *Understanding Alliteration and*

Onomatopoeia, p. 792
Language Worksheet, *Understanding Dialect,* p. 793
Selection Test, p. 794

Sound Devices

Sound devices are a poet's way of making language more expressive and musical. Two of the most frequently used of these devices are alliteration and onomatopoeia. **Alliteration** is the repetition of the same consonant sounds at the beginning of words. For example, in "Season at the Shore" McGinley writes, "*s*and in the *s*andwiches *s*pread for luncheon." Here the consonant sound *s* is repeated.

Onomatopoeia is the use of a word that imitates or suggests the sound of what the word refers to. For example, in "When the Frost Is on the Punkin" Riley writes, "And you hear the kyouck and gobble of the struttin' turkey-cock." Here "kyouck" and "gobble" suggest the sounds a turkey makes.

Look For

As you read "Season at the Shore," notice the frequent use of alliteration. What consonant sound occurs most often, and why do you think McGinley used this sound rather than another? What examples of onomatopoeia can you find in "When the Frost Is on the Punkin"? In what way does the use of onomatopoeia add to the poem's effectiveness?

Writing

Try using alliteration and onomatopoeia yourself. Imagine that you are visiting a zoo or animal preserve—or even traveling on foot through a jungle. Think of some of the animal sounds you might hear. Write down phrases you would use if you were going to describe these sounds in a report or magazine article. Use alliteration and onomatopoeia to make these descriptive phrases vivid and forceful. For example, the lion *r*oaring *r*egally, or Grrrr, roared the big cats.

Vocabulary

Knowing the following words will help you as you read "Season at the Shore" and "When the Frost Is on the Punkin."

adhesive (əd hē′ siv) *adj.*: Sticking (p. 508)

sibling (sib′ liŋ) *n.*: Brother or sister (p. 508)

odious (ō′ dē əs) *adj.*: Disgusting, offensive (p. 508)

gaiters (gāt′ ərz) *n.*: Coverings for the legs extending from the instep to the ankle or knee (p. 508)

stubble (stub′ ′l) *n.*: Short stumps of corn or grain (p. 513)

Literary Focus To introduce sound devices such as alliteration and onomatopoeia, read a few lines of verse in which they are used. You might alter such verses to remove the devices and ask students to discuss the difference between the verses with sound devices and those without. For example, the following lines from Shakespeare contain both alliteration and onomatopoeia:

Hark, hark! I hear
The strain of strutting
    chanticleer
Cry, "Cock-adoodle-doo!"

Compare these lines with the following:

Listen! I hear
The cry of strutting
    chanticleer
As he greets the dawn.

You could then point out that in the revision much of the vigor and music of the original is lost.

Look For Consider helping your **less advanced** students to find examples of the sound devices. For example, you might point out the *s* sound in line 5 of "Season at the Shore" and the "buzzin'" of the bees" in line 12 of "When the Frost Is on the Punkin." Encourage your **more advanced** students to tell how such devices affect their response to the poems.

Writing/Prior Knowledge Use a couple of words or sounds (*meow, woof*) that illustrate some animal sounds. Then have the class suggest others. Help the class to describe some common phenomenon—e.g., rain or thunder—in a sentence in which alliteration is used.

Vocabulary Help your **less advanced** students pronounce these words.

Season at the Shore
Phyllis McGinley

Oh, not by sun and not by cloud
And not by whippoorwill, crying loud,
And not by the pricking of my thumbs,
Do I know the way that the summer comes.
5 Yet here on this seagull-haunted strand,[1]
Here is an omen I understand—
Sand:

Sand on the beaches,
    Sand at the door,
10 Sand that screeches
    On the new-swept floor;
In the shower, sand for the foot to crunch on;
Sand in the sandwiches spread for luncheon;
Sand adhesive to son and sibling,
15 From wallet sifting, from pockets dribbling;
Sand by the beaker
    Nightly shed
From odious sneaker;
    Sand in bed;
20 Sahara[2] always in my seaside shanty
Like the sand in the voice
Of J. Durante.[3]

Winter is mittens, winter is gaiters
Steaming on various radiators.
25 Autumn is leaves that bog the broom.
Spring is mud in the living room
Or skates in places one scarcely planned.
But what is summer, her seal and hand?
Sand:

30 Sand in the closets,
    Sand on the stair,

---

1. **strand** (strand) *n.*: The ocean shore.
2. **Sahara** (sə har′ ə): A large desert in North Africa.
3. **J. Durante** (də ran′ tē): Jimmy Durante (1893–1980), an American comedian with a husky, scraping voice.

Grammar in Action

A **prepositional phrase** is a group of words that begins with a preposition and ends with a noun or pronoun. An effective way to present and emphasize ideas, especially in a description, is through a series of prepositional phrases. Notice how Phyllis McGinley uses a series of prepositional phrases to convey the feeling and prevasiveness of sand.

    Sand adhesive *to son and sibling,*
    From wallet sifting, from pockets dribbling

By writing one prepositional phrase after another, McGinley emphasizes and intensifies what sand is like in the summer. The entire second stanza of the poem is one smooth, flowing sentence made up predominantly of prepositional phrases that emphasize how sand pervades everything at the shore.

Student Activity 1. Identify the prepositional phrases in the following passage.

The weary dog climbed over the rocks, up the mountain-side, across the pass, down the steep ridge, through the valley, past the deserted cabin, and on toward the mountain looming ahead.

Student Activity 2. Write a four-line poem in which you describe something using a series of prepositional phrases. The poem does not have to rhyme.

4 **Discussion** What is the effect of introducing Biblical language and tone and then returning to the word *sand*?

Desert deposits
    In the parlor chair;
Sand in the halls like the halls of ocean;
35 Sand in the soap and the sun-tan lotion;
Stirred in the porridge, tossed in the greens,
Poured from the bottoms of rolled-up jeans;
    In the elmy street,
      On the lawny acre;
40   Glued to the seat
      Of the Studebaker;[4]
Wrapped in the folds of the *Wall Street Journal;*[5]
Damp sand, dry sand,
Sand eternal.
45 When I shake my garments at the Lord's command,
What will I scatter in the Promised Land?
Sand.

---

4. Studebaker: A car that is no longer made.
5. Wall Street Journal: A well-known financial newspaper.

THINKING ABOUT THE SELECTION

Recalling

1. What word is repeated more frequently than any other throughout the poem?
2. The poet thinks of sand as the "seal and hand" of summer. What things does she think of as standing for winter, autumn, and spring?

Interpreting

3. The poet includes a great number of images—word pictures—of sand in different places. What effect does the accumulation, or piling up, of details have on the poem? How is this effect reinforced by the repetition of the word *sand*?
4. To what senses does the poet appeal?
5. What is the poet's attitude toward sand?
6. Interpret, or explain the meaning of, the last three lines.
7. Why is "Season at the Shore" a better title for this poem than "Day at the Shore"?

Applying

8. What would you choose as the one thing that best represents summer? Why would this be your choice?

ANALYZING LITERATURE

Understanding Alliteration

Alliteration is the repetition of the same consonant sound at the beginning of words. This sound device can reinforce meaning as well as contribute to the "music" of a poem. The line "Sand adhesive to son and sibling," in which the *s* sound is repeated, is a more effective line in McGinley's poem than a line such as "Sand adhesive to daughter and brother" would have been. Why?

1. Find three or four other examples of alliteration in which the *s* sound is repeated.
2. Why is this sound especially appropriate to the poem?
3. Find an example of alliteration in which some other consonant sound is repeated.

THINKING AND WRITING

Writing a Poem with Alliteration

Write a four-line poem (it need not rhyme) in which you use alliteration. You may use one of the following subjects and the suggested consonant sound for alliteration, or you may choose another subject.

The winter wind (*w*, as in *wail, whoosh, wild*)
A snake (*s*, as in *slither, slimy, silent*)
A guitar (*p*, as in *pluck, play, pick*)
The rain (*d*, as in *downpour, damp, dreary*)

When you revise, first check that your poem says what you want to say about the subject. Then see if you can replace any words to add alliteration to your poem.

Read your poem to some of your classmates and listen to those they wrote.

Closure and Extension

ANSWERS TO THINKING ABOUT THE SELECTION
Recalling

1. The word *sand* is repeated.
2. Mittens and gaiters stand for winter. Leaves stand for autumn. Mud and skates stand for spring.

Interpreting

3. The accumulation of details suggests the pervasiveness of sand. Repeating the word *sand* emphasizes the effect.
4. The alliteration appeals to the ear. The many images appeal to the eye. Lines 12–13 and 35–36 appeal to the sense of touch and taste.
5. Suggested Response: Her attitude might be described as amused frustration.
6. Even in the hereafter, she will have sand with her.
7. The word *season* implies an entire summer spent with sand.

Applying

8. Suggested Response: sunshine, lakes, boats, lemonade.

ANSWERS TO ANALYZING LITERATURE

1. Other examples are found in lines 8–13, lines 20, 27, 28, 35.
2. The *s* sound imitates the sound of sand.
3. In line 25, *b* is repeated in "bog the broom." In line 32, *d* is repeated in "Desert deposits."

THINKING AND WRITING

For help with this assignment, students can refer to Lesson 18, "Writing a Poem," in the Handbook of Writing About Literature.

Publishing Student Writing You might collect these poems into a volume of some kind. Have the students suggest possible titles —with alliteration in them—for this volume.

Motivation/Prior Knowledge
Ask students to recall a time
when it felt great to be outdoors
in stimulating weather. What
sights, sounds, and sensations
naturally come to mind when
they think of this time?

Master Teacher Note Before
your students begin to examine
the poem closely, treat them to a
brisk and lively reading of it. Suggest that they just listen and try to
catch the spirit and rhythm of the
poem.

Purpose-Setting Question What
impression of fall does the poem
give you?

1 Clarification Remind students
that the setting is an Indiana
farm.

2 Discussion What is "hallylooyer"
in standard English? What is the
"rooster's hallylooyer"?

When the Frost Is on the Punkin

James Whitcomb Riley

When the frost is on the punkin and the fodder's
    in the shock,[1]
And you hear the kyouck and gobble of the
    struttin' turkey-cock,
And the clackin' of the guineys,[2] and the cluckin' of
    the hens,
And the rooster's hallylooyer as he tiptoes on the
    fence;
5 O, it's then's the times a feller is a-feelin' at his
    best,
With the risin' sun to greet him from a night of
    peaceful rest,
As he leaves the house, bareheaded, and goes out
    to feed the stock,[3]
When the frost is on the punkin and the fodder's
    in the shock.

They's something kindo' harty-like about the
    atmusfere
10 When the heat of summer's over and the coolin' fall
    is here—
Of course we miss the flowers, and the blossums on
    the trees,
And the mumble of the hummin'-birds and buzzin'
    of the bees;
But the air's so appetizin'; and the landscape
    through the haze
Of a crisp and sunny morning of the airly[4] autumn
    days
15 Is a pictur' that no painter has the colorin' to mock[5]—

---

1. the fodder's in the shock: The corn or hay used to feed the
animals is stacked in piles, or shocks.
2. guineys (gin' ēs) guineas *n.*: Fowls with a featherless head,
rounded body, and dark feathers spotted with white.
3. stock (stäk) *n.*: Short for livestock, the domestic animals kept on
a farm.
4. airly (er' lē): Early.
5. mock (mäk) *v.*: Copy.

Grammar in Action

Writers use **dialect** to capture the flavor of a particular area or
people. Dialect is the form of language that is specific to a
particular region or group and different from what most people
consider to be standard English.

    A dialect can have its own ways of pronouncing words as
well as words unique to that area or people. A particular dialect
may also have its own rules of grammar. For example, notice the
pronunciations and the ungrammatical usage in the following
lines from "When the Frost Is on the Punkin":

When the frost is on the punkin and the fodder's
  in the shock.

The husky, rusty russel of the tossels[6] of the corn,
And the raspin' of the tangled leaves, as golden as
  the morn;
The stubble in the furries[7]—kindo' lonesome-like,
  but still
20 A-preachin' sermuns to us of the barns they growed
  to fill;
The strawstack in the medder,[8] and the reaper in the
  shed;
The hosses in theyr stalls below—the clover
  overhead!—
O, it sets my hart a-clickin' like the tickin' of a
  clock,
When the frost is on the punkin and the fodder's
  in the shock!

25 Then your apples all is getherd, and the ones a
  feller keeps
Is poured around the celler-floor in red and yeller
  heaps;
And your cider-makin' 's over, and your wimmern-folks
  is through
With ther mince[9] and apple-butter, and theyr souse[10] and
  sausage, too! . . .
I don't know how to tell it—but ef sich a thing
  could be
30 As the Angels wantin' boardin', and they'd call
  around on *me*—
I'd want to 'commodate 'em[11]—all the whole-indurin'
  flock—
When the frost is on the punkin and the fodder's
  in the shock!

3 **Reading Strategy** Help students
paraphrase these lines.

4 **Discussion** What is the speaker
implying about his feelings?

5 **Discussion** What do you think
the speaker is unsure of being
able to express?

Reader's Response Do you
think the dialect adds to the
poem? Why or why not?

----

6. **tossels:** Tassels, which are silky, threadlike tufts at the tip of
an ear of corn.
7. **furries** (fŭr' ēs) *n.:* Furrows, which are narrow grooves cut in
the ground by a plow.
8. **medder** (med' ar): Meadow.
9. **mince** (mins) *n.:* Mincemeat, a mixture of chopped apples,
spices, and sometimes meat, used as a pie filling.
10. **souse** (sous) *n.:* A pickled food.
11. **'commodate** (käm' ə dāt') **'em:** Accommodate them, or give
them food and a place to stay.

When the Frost Is on the Punkin 513

"And the rooster's hallylooyer as he tiptoes on the fence;
O, it's then's the times a feller is a-feelin' at his best . . ."
"Then your apples all is getherd, and the ones a feller
keeps
Is poured around the celler-floor in red and yeller heaps;"

Student Activity 1. Rewrite each of the examples above following the rules of standard grammar and spelling. Compare your
rewritten sentences with the originals. Which sentences are more
appropriate for the poem?

Student Activity 2. Write a conversation between two people
using dialect of a particular area. First, choose an area with
whose dialect you are familiar. Then write the dialogue. Read the
finished dialogue aloud with a partner.

Closure and Extension

ANSWERS TO THINKING ABOUT THE SELECTION
Recalling

1. The details include the frost on the punkin, the piles of feed, and the sounds of the various fowl.
2. He likes the invigorating atmosphere, clean air, and beautiful landscape.
3. The sounds made by the corn tassles and leaves, the sounds made by the wind blowing across the stubble in the fields and everything on the farm being in its proper place all set the author's heart "a-clickin'."

Interpreting

4. Fall on the farm is so beautiful that any living being would be happy to live there.
5. Fall delights his senses, lifts his spirits, stirs his heart, and appeals to his sense of beauty.
6. The speaker lives and works on a farm. He may not be sophisticated, but he is responsive to the beauties of his environment.
7. The poet probably decided to use dialect to show how a person who lives on an Indiana farm expresses his feelings about his surroundings.

Applying

8. Suggested Response: The theme of natural beauty and people's responsiveness to it is a timeless and universal one.

ANSWERS TO ANALYZING LITERATURE

1. The examples are "clackin'" and "hallylooyer."
2. In stanza 2, onomatopoeia is found in line 12 ("mumble" and "buzzin'"). In stanza 3, it is found in lines 17 and 18 ("husky', rusty russel" and "raspin'") and in line 23 ("a-clickin'").
3. Answers will differ. Students should support their responses.
4. They appeal to the ear.
5. It is concrete, vivid, sensuous, and forceful.

THINKING ABOUT THE SELECTION
Recalling

1. In the first stanza, what details suggest "the times a feller is a-feelin' at his best"?
2. In the second stanza, what does the speaker especially like about the atmosphere and landscape of fall?
3. Summarize in your own words what sets the speaker's heart "a-clickin' " in stanza three.

Interpreting

4. What is the meaning or point of the last four lines of the poem?
5. Summarize the speaker's feelings about fall, "when the frost is on the punkin."
6. What can you conclude about the speaker and his way of life?
7. This poem is written in dialect rather than standard English. Why might the poet have decided to write it this way?

Applying

8. Although this poem is set in rural Indiana, it has long appealed to readers all over the country. Why do you think its appeal is so widespread?

ANALYZING LITERATURE
Understanding Onomatopoeia

Onomatopoeia is the use of a word that imitates or suggests the sound of what the word refers to. The word "cluckin'," for example, in the phrase "the cluckin' of the hens," suggests the sound hens make. This device adds vividness to a poet's descriptions of sound.

1. Besides "kyouck," "gobble," and "cluckin'," what other examples of onomatopoeia can you find in the first stanza?
2. Find two examples in each of the next two stanzas.
3. Of the examples you found, which seems to you most effective?
4. To which of your senses do these uses of onomatopoeia appeal?
5. Why is onomatopoeia so effective in poetry?

THINKING AND WRITING
Writing a Travel Article

Write an article for your school newspaper or literary magazine about an imaginary trip you took to a zoo, an animal preserve, or a jungle. Using the phrases you wrote before reading these poems, describe the memorable sounds you heard. Use alliteration and onomatopoeia to make your descriptions vivid. When you revise your article, see if you can use more vivid words and phrases to make your description even more clear to someone who may never have heard the sounds you are writing about.

THINKING AND WRITING

Publishing Students Writing
Consider having students break into groups and read their descriptions to their group.

People in Their Variety

SNAPSHOT AT THE BEACH, 1891
Three Lions

Fine art, *Snapshot at the Beach,* 1891. In 1861 the idea was conceived of using a postcard as a cheaper and faster means of communicating by mail. Soon afterward the decorative "picture" postcard made its appearance. Originally intended as a souvenir of a place or resort, these cards were soon being sent as greetings from these places. At the turn of the century the craze for collecting postcards had become a national pastime. This encouraged the manufacture of them on thousands of subjects. The process of getting a postcard made was simple. A photograph or drawing was sent to a postcard printing firm with an order; this firm returned the art and the finished cards within a few weeks. If color was required, the cards were sent to a second firm who hand colored the picture before returning it to the customer.

Snapshot at the Beach is a comic view from one of these postcards. It was probably commissioned by a resort or hotel and sold to visitors as souvenirs. These picture postcards are a delightful source of historical information as well as a unique form of folk art.

GUIDE FOR READING

Mother to Son

Langston Hughes (1902–1967) was born in Joplin, Missouri, and later lived in different parts of the country. He is most associated with Harlem, an area in New York City. Many of his poems, including "Mother to Son," use the rhythms of black music, especially jazz and blues. These poems present memorable, and sometimes powerful, portraits of black life. Often, as in "Mother to Son," they center on a character with a distinctive and forceful voice.

A Song of Greatness

The **Chippewa Indians** lived at one time on the shores of Lake Superior. Today, about 30,000 Chippewa live on reservations in the Midwest and West. "A Song of Greatness" recalls the Chippewa past when battles were fought and heroes were made.

    Mary Austin (1868–1934) lived most of her life in the southwest, where she studied the ways of native Americans.

I'm Nobody

Emily Dickinson (1830–1886) hardly ever traveled outside Amherst, Massachusetts, where she was born. When she died, she had written about 1,175 poems, but only seven had been published—anonymously. "I'm Nobody" reflects her life. She was a private person. But it does not reflect her destiny. Today, her fame is worldwide and her admirers are without number.

Life

Naomi Long Madgett (1923–   ) was born in Norfolk, Virginia, but has lived for much of her adult life in Detroit, Michigan. She retired from Eastern Michigan University in 1984 after sixteen years of teaching in the English Department. She has said, "I would rather be a good poet than anything else I can imagine." Her desire to write good poetry has led to seven collections of poetry and the appearance of poems in hundreds of anthologies. In "Life," Madgett uses a striking comparison to convey an idea about the way people live.

516   Poetry

Martin Luther King

Raymond Richard Patterson (1929–) was born in New York City. Patterson has been a teacher for thirty years, both at the high school and at the college level. His poetry has appeared in poetry anthologies and in his own collection of poetry, *Twenty-six Ways of Looking at a Black Man and Other poems.* "From Our Past" was the title of a weekly column on black history that Patterson wrote for several newspapers. "Martin Luther King" is also about history, paying tribute to a great man from America's past.

Tone

Tone in poetry is the poet's or speaker's attitude toward the subject, toward the reader, or toward himself or herself. It can often be described by such words as *serious, amused, sad, cheerful, proud,* or *mocking.* Tone comes from all the elements of a poem: the subject, what is said about it, the connotations of words, the rhythm, the figures of speech, and so on.

Look For

To understand the tone of a poem, read it as if you were the speaker uttering the words in real life. How you would describe your feelings as you were reading. Describe in a word or phrase the tone of each of the following poems.

Writing

Tone is the attitude shown through our words or our actions. Imagine that you are greeting the following people at a party: first, someone you have not seen in a very long time and are surprised and happy to see; second, someone you like who recently lost a much-loved pet; next, someone you dislike but wish to greet politely; and last, your best friend whom you see every day. Describe how you would greet each person. Do so in a way that shows the tone of your greetings. Include your words, the way you would speak the words, and any gestures you would use.

Vocabulary

Knowing the following words will help you as you read these poems.

esteemed (ə stēmd') *v.*: Respected, held in high regard (p. 520)

banish (ban' ish) *v.*: Send into exile (p. 521)

bog (bäg) *n.*: A small marsh or swamp (p. 521)

beset (bē set') *v.*: Covered; set thickly with (p. 523)

profound (prō found') *adj.*: Deeply or intensely felt (p. 523)

Guide for Reading   517

Motivation/Prior Knowledge
You might have students remember a piece of valued advice that they received from a parent or another adult. Have them explain why this advice was so helpful. Tell them that they are going to read a poem in which a mother gives important advice to her son.

Purpose-Setting Question Do you think this poem can be understood and appreciated by people of all ages and backgrounds? Explain.

Thematic Idea Other poems that deal with the relationship between a mother and a child are "The Courage That My Mother Had," page 492, and "My Mother Pieced Quilts," pages 494–6.

1 Enrichment You might want to tell students that Langston Hughes took part in an important cultural movement called the Harlem Renaissance. With the migration of southern blacks to northern cities at the turn of the century, the New York City community of Harlem became a cultural center for blacks. During the 1920's, there was a flowering of the arts—music, painting, and literature—in this community. Black writers also wanted to express the thoughts and feelings of those who lived in Harlem and other black communities in America.

More advanced students may want to read additional poems by Hughes in the following collections: *The Weary Blues* (1926); *The Dream Keeper* (1932); *Fields of Wonder* (1947); and *Montage of a Dream Deferred* (1951).

2 Discussion Why do you think the poet has the mother use a metaphor to describe her life? Is it likely that such a woman would have chosen this metaphor? Explain.

518

Mother to Son

Langston Hughes

Well, son, I'll tell you:
Life for me ain't been no crystal stair.
It's had tacks in it,
And splinters,
5   And boards torn up,
And places with no carpet on the floor—
Bare.
But all the time
I'se been a-climbin' on,
10   And reachin' landin's,
And turnin' corners,
And sometimes goin' in the dark
Where there ain't been no light.
So boy, don't you turn back.
15   Don't you set down on the steps
'Cause you finds it's kinder hard.
Don't you fall now—
For I'se still goin', honey,
I'se still climbin',
20   And life for me ain't been no crystal stair.

THINKING ABOUT THE SELECTION

Recalling

1. What does the mother tell the boy her life has not been?
2. What advice does she give him?

Interpreting

3. The mother uses an extended metaphor to describe her life. What do the details in lines 3–7 suggest about this life?

4. What is the mother saying about her life in lines 8–13?
5. What is she telling her son in lines 14–17 about how to live?

Applying

6. Since our earliest days, Americans have valued stick-to-itiveness, or perseverance. What is it about our early history that would have made these traits desirable?

3 Discussion What other metaphor can you think of to describe the progress of a life?

4 Discussion What do the woman's words reveal about her personality?

5 Clarification You might tell students that the mother in this poem speaks in dialect. Examples from this poem include: " 'Cause" instead of *because;* "you finds" instead of *you find;* "kinder" instead of *kind of.*

Tell students that poets include dialect in their poems when they want a speech to seem realistic.

You might ask students to find other examples of dialect in this poem. How would the poem be different if it did not contain any dialect?

6 Master Teacher Note Tell students that a poem in which one character speaks to a silent listener is called a dramatic monologue. This type of poem is dramatic because you can almost imagine the character speaking these lines on a stage. The poem is a *mono*logue rather than a *dia*logue because only one character speaks.

Ask **less advanced** students to think of a suitable setting for

ORGANDY COLLAR, 1936
Edmund Archer
Whitney Museum of American Art

ANALYZING LITERATURE

Understanding Tone

Tone is the basic attitude expressed in a poem. It is like the emotional coloring you give your words in conversation by the way you use your voice. Just think, for example, of the different way you can say the one word *Hello*!

1. How would you describe the tone of the first sentence (lines 1–7) of the poem?

2. How is the tone different in the next sentence (lines 8–13)?

3. Which of the following descriptions best fits the tone of the entire poem? Give reasons for your choice.

   a. Exhausted and hopeless
   b. Weary, yet strong and determined
   c. Lively and humorous
   d. Sorrowful and gloomy

Mother to Son 519

---

this monologue. Are the mother and son indoors or outdoors? If they are indoors, what does the room look like? Are the characters seated or standing?

More advanced students might enjoy speculating about the events that could have led up to this monologue. What might the son have said to prompt this speech? What will the boy say after his mother has finished speaking?

Humanities Note

Fine art, *Organdy Collar*, 1936, Edmund Archer (1904–). Archer is best known for his sensitive portraits, like this one of a mature black woman.

1. What personality traits has the artist revealed in his portrait?
2. Do you think this woman would make a good mother? Explain.

3. What is the mood of this picture? Is it the same as that of the poem?

Motivation/Prior Knowledge
Consider bringing to class reproductions of paintings of Native
Americans by artists like Seth
Eastman, George Catlin, and
Charles B. King. You can find
such reproductions in *Treasures
from the National Museum of
American Art,* edited by William
Kloss (Smithsonian Institution,
1986). Tell students that they will
be reading a poem in which a
young Native American expresses the thoughts inspired in him
by stories about great warriors of
the past.

Purpose-Setting Question
Which words in this poem are
clues to its tone?

1 **Master Teacher Note** You might
want to discuss with students the
idea that young people in any
society need adult models. Ask
them why models are important
and what qualities they admire
most in an adult. Have them
compare and contrast the way
that young native Americans
learned about models with the
way that young people in our
society learn about them.

Closure and Extension

**ANSWERS TO THINKING
ABOUT THE SELECTION**
Recalling

1. The speaker is referring to heroes
of the past.

Interpreting

2. Suggested Response: The "great
ones" are probably famous warriors, chiefs, and medicine men.
3. The speaker is not an adult, because he says that he will "do
mightily" in the future.
4. Suggested Response: The speaker is confident in his ability to
achieve great things.

A Song of Greatness

Chippewa Traditional
Mary Austin

When I hear the old men
Telling of heroes,
Telling of great deeds
Of ancient days—
5 When I hear that telling,
Then I think within me
I, too, am one of these.

When I hear the people
Praising great ones,
10 Then I know that I too—
Shall be esteemed:
I, too, when my time comes
Shall do mightily.

THINKING ABOUT THE SELECTION
Recalling

1. To whom is the speaker referring when he
says in line 7, "I, too, am one of these"?

Interpreting

2. Who might the "great ones" (line 9) be?
3. What is your impression of the speaker?
4. What makes the speaker think that he shall
"be esteemed" and "do mightily"?

Applying

5. How does the attitude of young people today
toward heroes of the past compare with the attitude of the speaker in this poem?

CRITICAL THINKING AND READING
Comparing and Contrasting Tone

Tone is the speaker's attitude toward his or
her subject. For example, the tone may be sorrowful or pleased, angry or accepting. You will find
it easier to grasp the tone of a poem by comparing
and contrasting it with the tone of another poem,
especially one with a similar subject or point of
view.
1. Describe the tone of "A Song of Greatness."
2. If you have not already done so, read the preceding poem, "Mother to Son." How are the
subjects of "Mother to Son" and "A Song of
Greatness" similar?
3. Finally, compare and contrast the tone of "A
Song of Greatness" with the tone of "Mother to
Son."

Applying

5. Suggested Response: Most
young people today are more likely to look up to contemporary heroes, such as sports figures, en-
tertainers, or characters portrayed in television shows.

Challenge Choose a hero of
yours and tell why you admire
him or her.

**ANSWERS TO CRITICAL
THINKING AND READING**

1. Suggested Response: The tone is
optimistic, confident, and earnest.
2. Suggested Response: Each
poem is about the importance of
taking a positive attitude toward
life.
3. Suggested Response: The tone of
each speaker is positive; however,
the mother is weary but determined while the young native
American is more optimistic. He

seems confident that he will
achieve great things, while she
seems satisfied to overcome the
obstacles in her way.

I'm Nobody

Emily Dickinson

I'm Nobody! Who are you?
Are you—Nobody—too?
Then there's a pair of us!
Don't tell! they'd banish us—you know!

5   How dreary—to be—Somebody!
How public—like a Frog—
To tell your name—the livelong June—
To an admiring Bog!

THINKING ABOUT THE SELECTION

Recalling

1. What does the speaker believe will happen if it is discovered that they are "nobodies"?
2. What is it like to be a "Somebody"?

Interpreting

3. What does the word "Nobody" mean in this poem?
4. How does the speaker feel about discovering another nobody?
5. What does the word "public" suggest?
6. To what does the speaker compare being public?
7. What might the admiring bog stand for?

Applying

8. What is your opinion of the speaker's preference for being a nobody to being a somebody?

CRITICAL THINKING AND READING

Paraphrasing a Poem

Paraphrasing a poem means restating it in your own words. It is an excellent way of seeing through hard words, unusual sentence structures, and figurative language in order to come to a basic meaning of the poem.

The following lines are from a poem called "Solitude," by Alexander Pope. Notice how the paraphrase that follows them restates the meaning of the lines in simpler language.

> Happy the man whose wish and care
> A few paternal acres bound,
> Content to breathe his native air
>   In his own ground.

Paraphrase: A man is fortunate if everything he wants or worries about lies within the land he lives on. He is fortunate if he's happy at home and doesn't desire to travel.

Once you have paraphrased a poem, you can then reread it with greater understanding and enjoyment.

Write a paraphrase of "I'm Nobody." Be sure to restate the poem in your own words in a way that makes clear all that the poem is expressing.

I'm Nobody   521

Motivation/Prior Knowledge
You might ask students if they have ever seen a pocketwatch. If not, describe one to them and explain that they were much more popular before wrist-watches were invented. Tell students they are about to read a poem in which a pocketwatch is used as a metaphor.

Purpose-Setting Question What is the poet's attitude toward life in this poem?

Thematic Idea This poem could be interpreted as having a pessimistic tone. You might want to contrast it with "Mother to Son," on page 518. This poem uses a different metaphor to create a tone of perseverance. "Martin Luther King," page 523, also presents a striking contrast to "Life" in both tone and theme.

1 Literary Focus What does the word *but* mean in this line? How does it affect the tone of the whole poem?

2 Discussion Whom does the infant represent?

Reader's Response How does this poem make you feel? Explain.

Closure and Extension

ANSWERS TO THINKING ABOUT THE SELECTION
Recalling

1. Life is compared to a pocket-watch.

Interpreting

2. Suggested Response: To an infant, everything in life is new and full of wonder.
3. Answers will differ. Suggested Response: The keeper is a a very old man because he represents a power that has existed for eternity —perhaps fate or the power of life.

Life

Naomi Long Madgett

Life is but a toy that swings on a bright gold chain
Ticking for a little while
To amuse a fascinated infant,
Until the keeper, a very old man,
5   Becomes tired of the game
And lets the watch run down.

THINKING ABOUT THE SELECTION

Recalling

1. To what is life compared in line 1?

Interpreting

2. Why is life amusing to the "fascinated infant"?
3. Why is "the keeper" a very old man?
4. What does the speaker mean by "the game" in line 5?
5. What happens when the keeper "lets the watch run down"?
6. In your own words, explain the meaning of this poem.

Applying

7. Like Naomi Long Madgett, many writers have used metaphors, or figurative comparisons, to describe life. For example, you probably know the expression, "Life is a bowl of cherries." Working with your classmates, make a list of common metaphors describing life. Discuss the attitude toward life expressed in each.

UNDERSTANDING LANGUAGE

Appreciating Vivid Adjectives

Poets use **vivid adjectives** to give their audience a precise mental image of the people, places, or things they are describing. For example, in line 1 the poet describes a "bright gold chain." The adjectives "bright" and "gold" give the reader a concrete picture of the chain.
1. Find two other vivid adjectives in the poem.
2. Write five sentences of your own using vivid adjectives to describe any nouns or pronouns.

522   *Poetry*

4. The literal meaning of "the game" is playing with the watch. The figurative meaning is a person's life-time.
5. Answers may differ. Suggested Response: When the watch runs down, a person's life runs out.
6. Answers will differ. Responses should include the idea that life is fascinating when we are young. As we get older, life becomes less fascinating and slowly winds down as we approach death.

Applying

7. Responses might include a bed of roses, a race to the finish, a game, a mountain, a fleeting melody.

ANSWERS TO UNDERSTANDING LANGUAGE

1. fascinated; very old
2. Answers will differ. Students should try not to use ordinary, over-used adjectives.

Challenge You could interpret the tone of the poem as pessimistic. Can you interpret the poem in any other way?

Martin Luther King

Raymond Richard Patterson

He came upon an age
Beset by grief, by rage—

His love so deep, so wide,
He could not turn aside.

5　His passion, so profound,
He would not turn around.

He taught this suffering Earth
The measure of Man's worth.

He showed what Man can be
10　Before death sets him free.

THINKING ABOUT THE SELECTION

Recalling

1. What two emotions did King possess that would not let him turn back?
2. What does the speaker say that King taught us?

Interpreting

3. What tone does the speaker use in this poem?
4. What is meant by the "measure of Man's worth" in line 8?
5. To what might the speaker be referring when describing the "age" as "Beset by grief, by rage—" and the earth as "suffering"?
6. What does the speaker mean by lines 9–10?

Applying

7. Martin Luther King was killed in 1968, working for what he believed in—equal rights for all people in the United States. What makes people who die for what they believe in especially admirable? Do you consider such people heroes? Why or why not?

THINKING AND WRITING

Writing to Express Tone

Write a paragraph, in the same tone as "Martin Luther King," about a person whom you admire. You might choose to write about a famous actor, athlete, or politician, or you might choose a friend, a relative, or a parent. First, freewrite about why you believe the person is worthy of admiration. As you write your first draft, you might include an example of your subject's actions or behavior that supports your reasons for admiring him or her. Let a classmate read your draft and offer suggestions. Then revise your paragraph and prepare a final draft.

Presentation

Motivation/Prior Knowledge You might ask students what knowledge or impressions they have of Martin Luther King. Tell students they are going to read a poem about Martin Luther King.

Purpose-Setting Question According to this poem, what made King different from other people?

Master Teacher Note Have students list what qualities make a person a hero. Encourage them to consider qualities in addition to physical bravery, such as integrity, compassion, and foresight. After reading the poem, students can use this list to answer the question, "Was Martin Luther King a hero?"

1 **Discussion** What did Martin Luther King love?

2 **Discussion** What was it from which he "could not turn aside"?

3 **Discussion** What was his passion?

4 **Discussion** From what would King not turn around?

5 **Discussion** From what does death set a person free?

Reader's Response Do you think most people are capable of the kind of heroism described in this poem? Why or why not?

Closure and Extension

ANSWERS TO THINKING ABOUT THE SELECTION

Recalling

1. He possessed love and passion.
2. The speaker says that King taught us that human beings should be measured by their worth, not by their skin.

Interpreting

3. Suggested Response: The tone is one of reverence and admiration.

4. Suggested Response: By "The measure of man's worth," the speaker means how good human beings can be.
5. Answers will differ. Suggested Response: The speaker is referring to prejudice and hatred that has caused grief, anger, and suffering in recent times.
6. Answers may differ. Suggested Response: The speaker might mean that King's life is an example of the great and heroic things people can accomplish.

Applying

7. Answers will differ. Students might discuss the idea that giving your life is the ultimate sacrifice and is especially admirable because most people consider their lives the most precious thing they have. They are considered heroes when the ideas they sacrifice their lives for are admirable.

THINKING AND WRITING

For help with this assignment, students can refer to Lesson 20, "Writing a Personal Essay," on page 829 in the Handbook of Writing About Literature.

523

Literary Focus You might want to point out to students that humor in everyday life also arises from exaggeration, surprise, and the bringing together of unrelated things. Have students recall humorous events or situations in which one or more of these elements was present.

You might also ask students to paraphrase the Ogden Nash poem, eliminating the rhythm and rhyme, to verify that the prose summary will be far less humorous.

Look For Consider reviewing with students the way to scan a poem for its rhythm. Write on the chalkboard the following lines from "The Cremation of Sam McGee," page 447: "I was sick with dread, but I bravely said: 'I'll just take a peep inside./I guess he's cooked, and it's time I looked'; . . . then the door I opened wide." Tell students that the symbol ˘ stands for an unaccented syllable and the symbol ´ indicates an accented syllable.

Read the lines aloud for students, stressing the accented syllables.

You might want to ask **more advanced** students to scan every line of "Father William."

Writing/Prior Knowledge Consider dividing the class into small groups to prepare for this assignment. Have each group visualize the interview. For instance, what might this distinguished adult be wearing? What might he or she

GUIDE FOR READING

Father William

Lewis Carroll (1832–1898) is the pen name of Charles Lutwidge Dodgson, who was born in Cheshire, England. Under his real name he wrote mathematical works, but as Lewis Carroll he wrote two of the most famous books for children of all time, *Alice in Wonderland* and *Through the Looking Glass*. His outward life was very quiet and uneventful, but in works like "Father William" he found escape from his serious work into a delightfully zany, topsy-turvy world that still amuses children old and young.

Humor

Humor in poetry can arise from a number of sources, such as surprise, exaggeration, or the bringing together of unrelated things. The majority of funny poems, however, have two things in common, rhythm and rhyme. These devices often make language more lively and sharp. This more spirited language makes humorous situations even more humorous. For example, here is a little poem by Ogden Nash called "The Porcupine."

> Any hound a porcupine nudges
> Can't be blamed for harboring grudges.
> I know one hound that laughed all winter
> At a porcupine that sat on a splinter.

Take away the rhythm and rhyme and the humor vanishes.

Look For

As you read "Father William," listen to the rhymes and catch the beat of the lines. By doing so you will find this funny poem even funnier. What do you feel is especially funny about it?

Writing

Imagine that you are interviewing a distinguished-looking adult about his or her career, interests, or way of life. For each question you ask, you get a reply that is absolutely ridiculous. Write down the questions you might ask and the zany replies that would follow.

Vocabulary

Knowing the following words will help you as you read "Father William."

incessantly (in ses' 'nt lē) *adv.*: Without stopping (p. 525)
sage (sāj) *n.*: A very wise man (p. 526)
supple (sup' 'l) *adj.*: Flexible (p. 526)

shilling (shil' iŋ) *n.*: A British coin. In Carroll's day, a shilling had much more monetary value than it has today. (p. 526)

do for a living? Students may also enjoy developing the first few questions and ridiculous answers with their group before they complete the assignment on their own.

Vocabulary Have less advanced students read aloud the words and definitions.

Because *shilling* is a vocabulary word, **more advanced** students may enjoy researching the

terms for monetary units used in different nations. Dictionaries sometimes list this information in chart form near the term *monetary*.

Spelling Tip Point out the double *s* in *incessantly*.

Objectives

1 To understand the features of humorous poetry
2 To write a humorous poem

Father William

Lewis Carroll

1
"You are old, Father William," the young man said,
   "And your hair has become very white;
And yet you incessantly stand on your head—
   Do you think, at your age, it is right?"

2
5   "In my youth," Father William replied to his son,
   "I feared it might injure the brain;
But, now that I'm perfectly sure I have none,
   Why, I do it again and again."

3
   "You are old," said the youth, "as I mentioned before.
10   And have grown most uncommonly[1] fat;
Yet you turned a back-somersault in at the door—
   Pray, what is the reason of that?"

YOU ARE OLD FATHER WILLIAM, 1865
Sir John Tenniel
The Granger Collection

Support Material

Teaching Portfolio
Teacher Backup, p. 809
Usage and Mechanics Worksheet, p. 812
Vocabulary Check, p. 813
Analyzing Literature Worksheet, *Understanding Humor in Poetry*, p. 814
Language Worksheet, *Punctuating Dialogue*, p. 815
Selection Test, p. 816

4 Discussion Which of these two characters is more appealing? Explain.

Humanities Note

Illustrations for "Father William," by John Tenniel (1820–1914). Tenniel was a well-known English cartoonist and illustrator. He illustrated Carroll's two most famous books, *Alice's Adventures in Wonderland* (1865) and *Through the Looking Glass* (1871). These two illustrations appeared in the former book.

1. To which passage in the poem does each illustration relate?
2. How do the illustrations reveal the personalities of the characters?
3. What details contribute to the humor in these illustrations?
4. Choose any passage of the poem and explain how you would illustrate it.

5 Clarification "'Don't give yourself airs'" means "Don't act in a snobby, pretentious way."

6 Master Teacher Note You may want to tell students that poets structure their work by setting up patterns. One such pattern is the arrangement of accented syllables in each line. Another is the placement of rhymes. In this poem, still another pattern is the alternation of question and response. Have **less advanced** students trace this pattern through the poem. How many lines are devoted to each question and each answer? Also, how does the poet change the pattern slightly in the last stanza?

Ask **more advanced** students how the poet creates a sense of surprise within the predictable pattern of question and response. How might the poem be different if it did not contain any surprises?

"In my youth," said the sage, as he shook his gray locks,
  "I kept all my limbs very supple
15 By the use of this ointment—one shilling the box—
  Allow me to sell you a couple?"

"You are old," said the youth, "and your jaws are too weak
  For anything tougher than suet;[2]
Yet you finished the goose, with the bones and the beak—
20 Pray, how did you manage to do it?"

4   "In my youth," said his father, "I took to the law,
  And argued each case with my wife;
And the muscular strength, which it gave to my jaw
  Has lasted the rest of my life."

  1. uncommonly (un käm′ ən lē) *adv.*: Remarkably.
  2. suet (soo′ it) *n.*: Fat used in cooking.

YOU ARE OLD FATHER WILLIAM, 1865
Sir John Tenniel
The Granger Collection

Closure and Extension

ANSWERS TO THINKING ABOUT THE SELECTION
Recalling

1. Now that he knows he does not have a brain, he is no longer afraid of standing on his head.
2. He has kept his limbs supple by using a certain ointment.
3. He strengthened his jaw by arguing about law cases with his wife.

25　"You are old," said the youth, "one would hardly suppose
　　　　That your eye was as steady as ever;
　　　Yet you balanced an eel on the end of your nose—
　　　　What made you so awfully clever?"

　　　"I have answered three questions, and that is enough,"
30　　　　Said his father. "Don't give yourself airs!
　　　Do you think I can listen all day to such stuff?
　　　　Be off, or I'll kick you downstairs!"

THINKING ABOUT THE SELECTION

Recalling

1. What reason does Father William give for incessantly standing on his head?
2. What enables him to do back-somersaults?
3. How did he develop jaws strong enough to devour a goose, including the bones and beak?
4. Why does he refuse to answer his son's question about balancing an eel on his nose?

Interpreting

5. What is it about Father William's physical condition that makes his behavior so absurd?
6. Which one of his zany activities struck you as the funniest? Explain.

Applying

7. Why do people like to laugh? Why do they enjoy telling utterly ridiculous stories?

ANALYZING LITERATURE

Understanding Humor in Poetry

Rhythm and rhyme are important aids to humorous poets, but they are not in themselves funny. The more common sources of humor include surprise, exaggeration, and bringing together unrelated things. For example, being elderly is not humorous, and neither (most of the time) is standing on one's head. But being elderly and standing on one's head is funny because we usually associate standing on one's head with children. Such humor is based on bringing together unrelated things.

1. First rewrite any one of the pairs of stanzas in which a question is asked and then answered. Remove the rhythm and rhyme, but do not change the meaning. How is the humor affected by the changes you made?
2. Next find in "Father William" an example of humor based on surprise or the unexpected.
3. Find an example of humor based on exaggeration.

THINKING AND WRITING

Writing a Humorous Poem

Using the questions and answers you wrote for your imaginary interview, write a humorous poem in dialogue with questions and replies. Your poem need not be as long as Carroll's, but it should be funny.

When you revise, read your poem to a friend to see if it is funny. Share your poem with your classmates.

Father William 527

---

serves some elements of surprise and exaggeration. Without rhythm and rhyme, however, the passage seems flatter and less humorous.

2. Students' answers will differ. Suggested Response: Students may choose any of the following examples of the unexpected—Father William's standing on his head; his saying that he has no brain; his turning a back-somersault even though he is old and fat; his trying to sell the youth his ointment; his finishing "the goose, with the bones and the beak," even though his jaws are weak; the reason he gives for his jaws being strong—arguing law cases with his wife; his balancing an eel on his nose; and his sudden threat to kick his son downstairs.

3. Students' answers will differ. Suggested Response: Students may choose any of the following examples of exaggeration—All of the activities cited above as examples of surprise are also examples of exaggeration, except perhaps for Father William's offering to sell his son the ointment.

THINKING AND WRITING

For help with this assignment, students can refer to Lesson 18, "Writing a Poem," in the Handbook of Writing About Literature.

Publishing Student Writing Ask volunteers to read their humorous poems to the class and display students' work on the bulletin board.

Challenge Rewrite this poem as a television skit for a comedy show, using the same idea—a young man interviewing a distinguished, older man and receiving ridiculous replies. Make sure, however, that the setting and dialogue are modern.

---

4. He says that three questions are enough and that his son is giving himself airs.

Interpreting

5. He is old and fat, and he has weak jaws. Also, his vision has probably gotten worse.
6. Students' answers will differ. Make sure that they choose something that Father William has actually done and that they give reasons for their answers.

Applying

7. Students' answers will differ. Suggested Response: Laughing makes people forget their worries. Sometimes it is a strain to be dignified or serious. Telling utterly ridiculous stories enables people to relax and be silly.

ANSWERS TO ANALYZING LITERATURE

1. Students' answers will differ. Suggested Response: The last two stanzas can be paraphrased as follows: The youth said to Father William, "You are old and your vision is probably worse than it used to be. However, you were able to balance an eel on the tip of your nose. How did you get to be so clever?" His father replied, "I have already answered three of your questions, and I am not answering any others. Don't be so pretentious. Do you think I can listen to your nonsense all day? Get lost, or I'll boot you down the staircase."

The paraphrase still pre-

More About the Author After some of Oliver Herford's poems were repeatedly rejected by a magazine, he resubmitted them along with the following note: "Sir: Your office boy has been continually rejecting these masterpieces. Kindly see that they receive the attention of the editor." The editor responded by accepting several of the poems. Ask students how a sense of humor can help a writer in dealing with discouraging situations.

Literary Focus You might want to tell students that some people believe that the source of the term *limerick* is the chorus of an old song that mentioned the city of Limerick, Ireland. This chorus had the same rhythmic pattern as that used in limericks.

You may want to encourage students to bring in their favorite limericks. Each student can then compile these, along with the ones written in class, in a limerick book.

Look For You might want to encourage students to think of limericks as jokes, with the punch line coming at the end. Like jokes, they are much funnier when told aloud and shared with others.

Writing/Prior Knowledge Consider dividing the class into small groups to do this assignment.

Vocabulary Encourage **more advanced** students to use one or more of the vocabulary words in the limericks they write.

Spelling Tip Point out that the words *scale* and *quail* rhyme. However, the sound /āl/ in scale is spelled *ale* and in quail is spelled *ail*.

Two Limericks

Oliver Herford (1863–1935) was born in England but lived from childhood on in the United States. Once, passing a schoolhouse at night, he imagined the typical school day that lay ahead for the teacher and pupils. He entered the school and covered the chalkboard with drawings of animals. Next day, the teachers and pupils were as amused as they were surprised. This incident reveals two qualities of Herford's, his sense of humor and his fondness for animals as subjects. You will find both in his limericks.

Limericks

A **limerick** is a poem of five lines. The first, second, and fifth lines have three rhythmic beats and rhyme with one another. The third and fourth lines have two beats, and they also rhyme. Using letters to represent the different rhyme sounds, you can describe the rhyme pattern of a limeric as *aabba*. Limericks are always lighthearted, humorous poems.

Look For

As you read Herford's limericks, notice how they fit the pattern of rhythm and rhyme described above. Enjoy the humor more by reading these poems aloud.

Writing

To prepare for writing your own limericks, write the line *There once was a boy* (or *girl*) named . . . (supply a name). Then list a number of words that rhyme with the name and that could be used in funny statements about the boy or girl named. Since limericks have two rhyme sounds, make a second list of rhyme words.

Vocabulary

Knowing the following words will help you as you read Herford's two limericks.

dote (dōt) *v.*: To be extremely fond (p. 529)

scale (skāl) *n.*: A series of musical tones (p. 529)

quail (kwāl) *v.*: Draw back in fear (p. 529)

Objectives

1 To understand the form of a limerick
2 To write a limerick

Support Material

Teaching Portfolio
Teacher Backup, p. 819
Usage and Mechanics Worksheet, p. 822
Vocabulary Check, p. 823
Critical Thinking and Reading Worksheet, *Using Context to Choose the Meaning of the Word,* p. 824

Language Worksheet, *Appreciating Words From Place Names,* p. 825
Selection Test, p. 826

Two Limericks

Oliver Herford

1   Said the Lion: "On music I dote,
But something is wrong with my throat.
    When I practice a scale,
2   The listeners quail,
And flee at the very first note!"

A puppy whose hair was so flowing
There really was no means of knowing
    Which end was his head,
    Once stopped me and said,
"Please, sir, am I coming or going?"

THINKING ABOUT THE SELECTION

Recalling

1. What activity does the lion say he performs?
2. How do his listeners respond?
3. Describe the puppy in the second limerick.

Interpreting

4. What is the lion really doing?
5. Why is the puppy's question funny?

Applying

6. Why do you think that the limerick form is never used for serious poetry?

ANALYZING LITERATURE

Understanding Limericks

A **limerick** has short lines, a swift, catchy rhythm, and heavily stressed rhymes. There are three beats in the first, second, and fifth lines, which rhyme, and two beats in the third and fourth lines, which also rhyme.

The following is a limerick about limericks. See if you can paraphrase it—restate it in your own words—to discover what it says about why limericks are amusing. (The word "conceits" in line 4 means "imaginative or clever ideas.")

Well, it's partly the shape of the thing
That gives the old limerick wing;
    These accordion pleats
    Full of airy conceits
Take it up like a kite on a string.

THINKING AND WRITING

Writing a Limerick

Using the opening line and the list of rhymes you have written, write a limerick of your own. When you revise, make sure that you did not damage the sense of your lines while getting them to rhyme. Also, check that your lines have the correct rhythm. Share your limerick with those of your classmates.

Two Limericks   529

Closure and Extension

ANSWERS TO THINKING ABOUT THE SELECTION

Recalling

1. He practices a musical scale.
2. His listeners shrink back in fear and run away.
3. His hair is "so flowing" that you cannot tell which end is his head.

Interpreting

4. The lion is really roaring.
5. The puppy does not know his front end from his back. He therefore does not know whether he is " 'coming or going.' "

Applying

6. Suggested Response: The heavily stressed rhymes and the jaunty rhythm would not go well with a serious subject.

ANSWERS TO ANALYZING LITERATURE

Suggested Response: It is partly the form of the limerick that makes it work. The tightly packed form, when filled with imaginative and clever ideas, takes off just like a kite in the wind.

THINKING AND WRITING

Publishing Student Writing

Have each student collect his or her limericks in a limerick book.

You might also want students to publish a newspaper called *The Daily Limerick,* made up entirely of limericks.

Presentation

Motivation/Prior Knowledge You might ask students to think of ideas and good first lines for humorous limericks about the following subjects: 1) a lion and 2) a puppy with long hair. Then tell them that they can compare their ideas and lines with Herford's limericks about these subjects.

Thematic Ideas Another selection to teach with these limericks is James Dickey's essay, "How to Enjoy Poetry," pages 375–8. Dickey mentions limericks specifically and encourages students to write them. He approaches poetry as an enjoyable game or contest rather than a required school subject.

Purpose-Setting Question How does the last line of each limerick add a humorous twist to the story?

1 **Enrichment** Tell students that limericks get their jaunty, humorous rhythm from a combination of two unaccented syllables followed by an accented syllable.

2 **Clarification** Point out that lines 3 and 4, which contain only two beats each, are indented.

Challenge Divide the class into small groups and have these groups battle with each other in a Limerick War. Students who do not want to participate can serve as judges.

Each group must write a limerick on a certain subject (or starting with a certain line) within a given time limit. Students who are judges can help you determine whether the poem that each group submits is a true limerick.

Putting It Together When students read poetry, they should be able to recognize the elements of poetry and how they function in a poem. This lesson reviews these elements, using the poem "Miracles" as a model.

You may want first to review the elements, using the points suggested on this page. Then you can read the poem "Miracles" with students, discussing the annotations.

For further practice with these elements, use the selection in the Teaching Portfolio, "Salute to a City Tree," by Margaret Tsuda on page 676, which students can annotate themselves. Encourage students to continue to look for these elements when reading other poems.

Master Teacher Note Review with students the idea that poetry is language at its most concentrated and intense. Suggest to them that, for this very reason, it is appropriate to read a poem several times, both quietly and aloud.

■ PUTTING IT TOGETHER ■

Poetry

Poetry is hard to categorize, although you probably know a poem when you see one. It can deal with any subject matter, take a variety of forms, use imagery and figurative language, and apply one or more of many sound devices. In addition, a poem often has a theme, or insight into life. To fully appreciate a poem, put the elements of it together.

Types of Poetry

There are several types of poetry. The most common are narrative poetry and lyric poetry. Narrative poetry tells a story. Lyric poetry expresses strong personal feelings about the subject.

Figurative Language

Figurative language consists of words used with meanings beyond their usual dictionary meanings. Three common types of figurative language are simile, metaphor, and extended metaphor. A simile is a comparison between two essentially unlike objects that uses the word *like* or *as* to make this comparison. A metaphor is like a simile, but it does not use the word like or as. An extended metaphor is carried through from the beginning to the end of the poem.

Imagery

Imagery is the use of vivid language to create word pictures. Usually these word pictures appeal to the senses and arouse strong feelings.

Sound Devices

The music of poetry is created by **sound devices.** Four common sound devices are rhythm, rhyme, alliteration, and onomatopoeia. Rhythm is the pattern of stressed and unstressed lines in a poem. Rhyme is the matching of sounds at the ends of words. Alliteration is the repetition of initial consonant sounds, and onomatopoeia is the creation of words to imitate sounds.

Theme

Many poems suggest an insight into life. As you read, ask yourself what general truth does the poem reveal to you.

Objectives

1 To appreciate a poem by putting the elements of it together
2 To understand free verse
3 To understand the process of categorizing and the role it plays in poetry
4 To build new words
5 To write a poem about miracles

Support Material

Teaching Portfolio
Teacher Backup, p. 829
Putting It Together, "Salute to a City Tree," by Margaret Tsuda, p. 832
Usage and Mechanics Worksheet, p. 833
Critical Thinking and Reading Worksheet, *Categorizing,* p. 834

Language Worksheet, *Building New Words,* p. 835
Selection Test, p. 836

GOOD FORTUNE, 1939
René Magritte
Museum Boymans-Van Beuningen, Rotterdam

Miracles

Walt Whitman

Why, who makes much of a miracle?
As to me I know of nothing else but miracles,
Whether I walk the streets of Manhattan,
Or dart my sight over the roofs of houses toward the sky,
5 Or wade with naked feet along the beach just in the edge of
   the water,

> **Theme:** The title provides a clue to the theme. What does the title suggest about the theme of this poem?

> **Sound:** This poem is written in free verse. It has no set pattern of stressed and unstressed syllables. Do the words at the end of lines rhyme? Are the lines of equal length? What effect is created by the use of free verse?

Miracles 531

Presentation

Motivation/Prior Knowledge You may want to ask students to define the word *miracle* and to give an example of one. Then tell them that they might find Whitman's approach to this topic, in his poem "Miracles," somewhat surprising.

Thematic Idea You may want to use James Dickey's essay "How to Enjoy Poetry," page 375, with this poem. Like Whitman, Dickey encourages readers to see the miraculous in everyday objects and occurrences.

Purpose-Setting Question How did the poet combine elements of the poem to create a unified effect?

Humanities Note

Fine art, *Good Fortune,* 1939, by René Magritte. Magritte (1898–1967) was a Belgian artist known for his surrealistic style. In his paintings, ordinary objects appear in unusual contexts and combinations.
1. What are the ordinary details included in this painting?
2. What is unusual about the combination of these details?
3. How does this painting relate to the theme of "Miracles"?

Master Teacher Note You may want to read the poem aloud to students without pausing and then go through it with them, discussing each of the annotations.

Reading Strategy You might suggest to students that a title is like a sign on a highway. It orients readers and tells them what is coming. This title indicates that the poem will deal with "Miracles"—remarkable, or possibly even supernatural, events.

Imagery: Notice the vivid imagery in these lines. Which words and phrases appeal to your senses?

Theme: These two lines provide a clue to the theme. In what way do all these details form a whole? In what way do they remain distinct.

Types of Poetry: This is a lyric poem. What strong feelings does the poem express?

Theme: The answer to the question provides a clue to the theme. What is the answer?

Pulling It Together: The poet sees miracles in the world around him. Both events in everyday life and in nature are so remarkable that they seem miraculous.

Or stand under trees in the woods,
Or talk by day with any one I love . . .
Or sit at table at dinner with the rest,
Or look at strangers opposite me riding in the car,
10 Or watch honeybees busy around the hive of a summer
      forenoon[1]
Or animals feeding in the fields,
Or birds, or the wonderfulness of insects in the air,
Or the wonderfulness of the sundown, or of stars shining
      so quiet and bright,
Or the exquisite[2] delicate thin curve of the new moon in
      spring;
15 These with the rest, one and all, are to me miracles,
The whole referring, yet each distinct[3] and in its place.

To me every hour of the light and dark is a miracle,
Every cubic inch of space is a miracle,
Every square yard of the surface of the earth is spread with
      the same,
20 Every foot of the interior swarms[4] with the same.

To me the sea is a continual miracle,
The fishes that swim—the rocks—the motion of the waves—
      the ships with men in them,
What stranger miracles are there?

---

1. **forenoon** (fôr' nōōn) *n.*: Morning.
2. **exquisite** (eks' kwi zit) *adj.*: Very beautiful, especially in a delicate way.
3. **distinct** (dis tiŋkt') *adj.*: Separate and different.
4. **swarms** (swôrmz) *v.*: Is filled or crowded.

Walt Whitman (1819–1892) was born on Long Island but lived most of his life in Brooklyn, New York. He worked at many occupations—printer, carpenter, teacher, newspaper reporter—and praised the value of the common person in many of his poems. Called the father of modern poetry, most of his poems are highly original, using free verse to capture the various rhythms and moods of American life. They are collected in *Leaves of Grass*.

532   *Poetry*

THINKING ABOUT THE SELECTION

Recalling

1. What is a miracle? What is the first question the speaker asks about miracles?
2. Find at least ten events the speaker considers miracles.
3. What is the second question about miracles the speaker asks?

Interpreting

4. In what way is talking with a person you know a miracle?
5. In what way is the sea a continual miracle?
6. Think about the answer to the speaker's second question. How would you express the theme of the poem?

Applying

7. List at least five events you consider miracles.

ANALYZING LITERATURE

Understanding Free Verse

Free verse is poetry that has no regular rhythmic pattern and no regular rhyme scheme. Usually, free verse uses the sounds and rhythms of natural speech to create its own unique musical quality. One way free verse creates rhythm is by using a similar word-order pattern from line to line.

1. What do you notice about word order in lines 4–14?
2. What do you notice about word order in lines 17–22?
3. What effect is created by the similar structure of the lines?

CRITICAL THINKING AND READING

Categorizing

A category is a group of related items. When you form categories, you put things that are sim-

ilar in the same group. For example, you might arrange the clothes in your closet into two groups: school clothes and play clothes. You might arrange the supplies you bring home into categories: for example, things that need to go directly into the refrigerator, canned goods, and cleaning supplies.

Arrange the events the speaker mentions in "Miracles" in groups.

1. Which events fit into the category "City Experiences"?
2. Which fit into the category "Wonders of the Natural World"?
3. Which fit into the category "Communicating with Others"?

UNDERSTANDING LANGUAGE

Building New Words

A miracle is so amazing that it causes you to wonder. The word *wonder* is at the root of many words that are probably already in your vocabulary. Define each of the words below based on the word *wonder*. Then use each word in a sentence.

1. wonderful
2. wonderment
3. wonderland
4. wonderworker
5. wondrous

THINKING AND WRITING

Writing a Poem About Miracles

Look over the list you created of things you consider miracles. Brainstorm with your classmates to add to this list. Then, using free verse, write a poem about miracles in everyday life. Revise your poem to be sure you have included enough details that appeal to the senses. Create a final draft, and share it with your classmates.

Miracles 533

---

sponse: The sea is a miracle because it is a source of life and motion, as well as a means by which humans can travel.

6. Suggested Response: The most common events and sights are miracles, if viewed with a sense of wonder.

Applying
7. Answers will differ. Suggested Response: Students will probably choose everyday events—a sunset, the growth of a small brother

or sister, and so forth—that they have viewed with a sense of wonder.

Challenge What problems does a poet face in convincing readers that everyday events and sights are miracles?

ANSWERS TO ANALYZING LITERATURE

1. Suggested Response: Lines 4–14 all begin with the word "Or." Es-

pecially insightful students may notice that, in lines 4–10, this word is followed by a verb, while in lines 11–14, it is followed by a noun or a noun described by adjectives.

2. Suggested Response: The poet begins all of these lines except the last with the phrase "To me" or the word "Every."

3. Suggested Response: The repeated words create a pattern that you come to expect, just as rhyme does. Especially insightful students may notice that the lists or-

---

(Answers begin on p. 532.)

ganized by these repeated words build to an emotional climax.

ANSWERS TO CRITICAL THINKING AND READING

1. Suggested Response: "City Experiences" would include walking "the streets of Manhattan," looking over rooftops, and looking at strangers in a streetcar.
2. Suggested Response: "Wonders of the Natural World" would include wading in the water; standing in the woods; watching bees, animals, birds, insects, sundown, stars, and the moon; the surface and interior of the earth; and the sea.
3. Suggested Response: "Communicating with Others" would include talking with a loved one, sitting with people at dinner, and looking at strangers in a streetcar.

ANSWERS TO UNDERSTANDING LANGUAGE

1. *wonderful:* Causing wonder, marvelous.
2. *wonderment:* State or expression of wonder, amazement.
3. *wonderland:* Imaginary land full of wonders.
4. *wonderworker:* Someone who performs wonderful works or miracles.
5. *wonderous:* Wonderful.

THINKING AND WRITING
Publishing Student Writing
Consider dividing the class into small groups and having students read their poems to their group rather than the class as a whole.

Writing Across the Curriculum
Have students research and report on miracles of modern science. Students might choose such topics as atomic energy, communications satellites, radio telescopes, genetic engineering, computers, or superconductors. Consider informing the science department of this assignment, so that science teachers can help students find resource materials.

Making Inferences

Reading a poem requires careful reading and thinking because it is usually made up of very few words. Making inferences, or educated guesses, about what the poet is saying is often necessary to understand the poem. An **inference** is a conclusion based on evidence such as facts or clues provided by the author. Another form of evidence is the reader's background knowledge and experience. Both types of evidence must be carefully weighed to determine if they support the inference that is being made.

Setting

Inferences can help you understand the setting, characters, plot, words or phrases, and major ideas in a poem. Think about "The Highwayman." What is the setting at the beginning of this poem? The answer would be an extremely windy, cloudy, moonlit night in an area of the country that is desolate except for an old inn. How do you arrive at this conclusion? First, the words "torrent" and "gusty" indicate that the wind is blowing violently. "Ghostly" indicates that the moon is pale, while "cloudy seas" refer to the many clouds in the sky. Because a moor is considered a wasteland, this would indicate that the area was desolate except for the old inn.

Character

By making inferences, or "reading between the lines," you can gain insights into the characters. What can you infer about the highwayman? First you can infer that he makes a dashing, handsome, romantic figure because of the clothes he wears and his twinkling pistol butts and sword handle. Next you can infer that he is going to commit a robbery tonight because a highwayman is a robber and he says that he is "after a prize to-night." Then you can guess that he deeply loves Bess because he became so emotional when her hair cascaded over him that his face became fiery red, because his face grew gray when he learned of her plight, and because he is willing to risk his life for her. His actions as a robber and in seeking to avenge Bess's death indicate that he is daring and courageous.

Plot

Incidents in the plot become more understandable when you make inferences. For instance, how do you know who informed the soldiers that the highwayman would be returning to the inn? Look at the clues in the poem. Tim, who loved Bess himself, overheard the highwayman tell Bess he would return. Tim's eyes are described as "hollows of madness," which makes you think that he is crazy. Saying that he listened "dumb as a dog" suggests that he is not very intelligent. Your background knowledge would make you realize that someone who is dim-witted and mad would inform the authorities about the highwayman to get rid of a rival. Because there is no one else in the poem with a reason to inform on the highwayman, you can infer that Tim is the one who did it.

Activity

Read the following excerpt from Henry Wadsworth Longfellow's poem "The Building of the Ship." Then answer the questions.

Thou, too, sail on, O Ship of State!
Sail on, O Union, strong and great!
Humanity with all its fears,
With all its hopes of future years,
Is hanging breathless on thy fate!
We know what Master laid thy keel,
What Workmen wrought thy ribs of steel,
Who made each mast, and sail, and rope,
What anvils rang, what hammers beat,
In what a forge and what a heat
Were shaped the anchors of thy hope!
Fear not each sudden sound and shock,
'Tis of the wave and not the rock;
'Tis but the flapping of the sail,
And not a rent made by a gale!
In spite of rock and tempest's roar,
In spite of false lights on the shore,
Sail on, nor fear to breast the sea!
Our hearts, our hopes, are all with thee,
Our hearts, our hopes, our prayers, our tears,
Our faith, triumphant o'er our fears,

1. What is the "Ship of State"? Support your answer.
2. Why is humanity "hanging breathless" on the ship's fate? Give evidence to support your answer.
3. Why does the speaker say to "fear not each sudden sound and shock"? Give evidence to support your answer.
4. What might be the "rock and tempest's roar"?
5. What might be the "false lights on the shore"?
6. Why should the ship sail on? Support your answer.

Focus on Reading 535

The writing assignments on page 536 have students write creatively, while those on page 537 have them think about the poetry and write critically.

YOU THE WRITER
Guidelines for Evaluating Assignment 1

1. Is the poem about a familiar place?
2. Are five objects in this place compared to five other things?
3. Are the comparisons vivid, fresh, and original?
4. Is the poem free from grammar, usage, and mechanics errors?

Guidelines for Evaluating Assignment 2

1. Is the poem about personified objects in an outdoor setting?
2. Does the student give these personified objects individual personalities?
3. Is there dialogue between these "people" that demonstrates their individual styles?
4. Is the poem free from grammar, usage, and mechanics errors?

Guidelines for Evaluating Assignment 3

1. Does the mood poem include objects associated with that mood?
2. Does the student use rhyme in the poem?
3. Are there comparisons and images in the poem?
4. Is the poem free from grammar, usage, and mechanics errors?

YOU THE WRITER

Assignment

1. The ability to compare one thing to another is essential to the art of poetry. Write a short poem about a place you are familiar with—your room, the street you live on, a nearby woods or field, and so on. In your poem, compare five objects in this place to five other things.

Prewriting. Choose carefully the place about which you are going to write. Be sure it contains lots of interesting objects, objects that suggest comparisons. Then picture it in your imagination. Letting your mind relax, scan it carefully, noting all the objects it contains. Jot down all the ideas that come into your mind.

Writing. Now write your poem. Remember to include five vivid comparisons.

Revising. When you revise, make sure your comparisons are original, fresh, and vivid.

Assignment

2. Write a poem about the people of a specific outdoors place—only these "people" will be *personified objects*. Have the objects in this place think, feel, talk, and act like people.

Prewriting. Imagine an outdoors place close to home. What objects do you picture in this place? Pretend they are people. What would these objects be thinking, feeling, doing, and saying if they were human beings? How, for example, does the sand at the water's edge feel about being pounded all day by the ocean's "fist"? What do the rocks say when people aren't around?

Writing. Now write about "The People in the _____." Make one of these people cranky, another thoughtful, a third silly and loud. Let them talk to each other, each in his or her individual style.

Revising. When you revise, examine the places where the "people" talk to each other to see that you have punctuated the dialogue correctly.

Assignment

3. Write a poem that creates a certain feeling or mood. Include objects associated with this mood.

Prewriting. Before you write, decide on the mood you want to create. Jot down the feelings associated with this mood. Then connect the feelings that seem to go together. Look for physical things that "stand for" these feelings. Cobwebs, for example, "stand for" dusty and old. Fresh snow "stands for" winter and peace.

Writing. Write your poem. Make the lines in your poem rhyme. Use comparisons—similes, metaphors, personification. Finally, use lots of images.

Revising. When you revise, check to see that each of your objects really does help create the mood you want it to create. Prepare a final draft of your poem and share it with your classmates.

YOU THE CRITIC

Assignment

1. Some of the poems you have read are about specific characters. Choose two of these characters, each from a different poem, and then write an essay comparing and contrasting them.

Prewriting. Choose the two characters. Prepare a chart showing their similarities and their differences.

Writing. Now write your essay. Be sure to mention the names of the characters and the poems they are found in. Show how the two characters are similar and how they are different.

Revising. When you revise, make sure you have included a sufficient number of details from the poems to back up your points.

Assignment

2. A *central* image in a poem is one that dominates the poem, that is, ideas and feelings connected with this image are found in most of the lines of the poem. Write an essay about *two* poems with central images. Identify the central image in each and show how it helps the poet develop and clarify his or her feelings and ideas.

Prewriting. When you have selected two poems with central images, make notes about how these images are expressed throughout the poem.

Writing. Now write your essay. Treat each poem separately. For each poem (1) tell what the central image is, perhaps citing the line where it first appears. Then (2) show that words, ideas, and feelings connected with this image are found throughout the poem. Cite some of the lines that contain references to the central image.

Revising. When you revise, ask yourself these questions: (1) Did you identify the central image in each poem? (2) Did you show the ways in which the central image helps develop the meaning?

Assignment

3. An American poet has proclaimed as his motto: "No ideas except in things." By this he means that the best way for a poet to communicate his or her ideas is through concrete physical things. Choose *two* poems from this section and discuss the ways in which these poems follow the motto, "No ideas except in things."

Prewriting. Before you write, scan the poems in this section to find the two you intend to write about. Jot down lines that use concrete objects to portray ideas.

Writing. Now write your essay. Present your material one poem at a time. Cite several lines—or parts of lines—from each poem which express ideas through concrete things. Explain how each poem supports the motto.

Revising. When you revise, check to see that you have blended your citations from the poems smoothly into your essay.

You the Critic 537

Humanities Note

Fine art, *Classical Fable* by Thomas McKnight. The American painter and printmaker Thomas McKnight was born in 1941. He was educated at Wesleyan University in Connecticut and Columbia University in New York City. McKnight is best known for his work in serigraphy, which is the production of creative silkscreen prints. The print *Classical Fable* is a serigraph which shows the sharp images and smooth, intense colors that can be obtained with the silkscreen process. Thomas McKnight's debt to naive art is apparent in this print. His childlike interpretation of the figures on the temple steps and the landscape of this imaginary land give this print a pleasing, sentimental appeal. Utilizing symbols from ancient Greek culture—columned temples, archaic ships, draped clothing, and statues—he evokes a world that exists only fables, myths, and legends.

FABLES, MYTHS, AND LEGENDS

Gods and goddesses, talking animals, strange and wondrous events—these are some of the subjects of fables, myths, and legends. All such stories are very old. They come to us from the distant past. Although different writers retell these stories in print, most of them originated long before reading and writing began. They have survived by being handed down by word of mouth from generation to generation. Taken together, fables, myths, and legends make up what is known as the oral tradition of literature.

Why have these old tales survived through the centuries? One reason is that they are about subjects that people love to read or hear about. Superhuman characters and marvelous events always make for entertaining stories. Another reason is that these tales say so much about human nature and the world. In fact, they represent some of the earliest efforts of the human race to explain the world. Reading fables, myths, and legends should be both a pleasurable and rewarding experience.

CLASSICAL FABLE, 1986
Thomas McKnight
Chalk & Vermilion

539

■READING ACTIVELY■

Fables, Myths, and Legends

Background

Fables, myths, legends, and folk tales are among the oldest forms of literature. Fables are short stories that teach moral lessons. The characters are usually animals who have human speech and characteristics. Usually associated with Greeks and Romans, myths are anonymous stories, usually involving gods and goddesses, that convey cultural ideals and beliefs, or explain natural occurrences such as lightning and volcanoes. Legends are also very old stories handed down through generations. Many are believed to have a historical basis. Although subjects of legends may have been actual people, the stories are fictitious and tend to emphasize traits admired by the cultures that created them. Folk tales are similar to myths but they are usually about ordinary people instead of gods. All cultures have their own traditions of such highly imaginative stories. They explain natural events, teach moral lessons, and emphasize behaviors, attitudes, and ideals admired by the people who create them.

Reading Strategies

As you read through this unit, you will find differences from other forms of literature that you should be aware of. For example, the characters in fables are animals, yet they speak and behave like humans. The myths, legends, and folktales contain names that you might have difficulty pronouncing and places you may never have heard of. Many of the events in myths are fantastic and even superhuman.

Have an open mind as you read the selections in this unit; accept what is presented and try to learn as much as you can about other people and cultures. You will find that, although the tales were created long ago and in different cultures, they convey ideas and attitudes common to people today. Finally, as you read, interact with the literature by using the active reading strategies: question, predict, clarify, summarize, and pull together.

Themes

You will encounter the following themes in the *Fables, Myths, and Legends* unit.
- The importance of conforming to the ideals and values of society
- The need to explain the unexplainable
- The strength and value of friendship and love
- The need for justice and truth
- The journey to personal fulfillment

540   *Fables, Myths, and Legends*

CHARIOT OF THE MOON
Frederic E. Church
The Cooper-Hewitt Museum

Characters

Become familiar with the following characters before you read the *Fables, Myths, and Legends* unit.

Greek and Roman Myths
(In parentheses you will find the Roman form of the name.)

Zeus (Jupiter)—king of the gods
Hera (Juno)—queen of the gods
Poseidon (Neptune)—god of the sea
Hades (Pluto)—god of the underworld
Apollo (Apollo)—god of the sun
Athena (Minerva)—goddess of wisdom
Aphrodite (Venus)—goddess of love
Hermes (Mercury)—messenger of the gods
Demeter (Ceres)—goddess of agriculture
Persephone—daughter of Demeter and wife of Hades
Prometheus—a Titan who stole the secret of fire from the gods
Phaëthon—son of Apollo who tried, unsuccessfully, to drive his father's chariot
Baucis and Philemon—husband and wife who were rewarded by the gods for their hospitality to strangers
Icarus—son of Daedalus who refused to listen to his father
Daedalus—man who built wings for his son and himself to escape from prison
Narcissus—handsome youth who loved his own image too much
Echo—nymph who was punished by Hera for tricking her and who loved Narcissus

Myths, Legends, and Folktales from Around the World

Alida—daughter of an Indian chief who loved Taroo
Taroo—youth who fell in love with Alida, member of an enemy tribe
Ojeeg—great hunter who vanquished the Ice Man
The Ice Man (Peboan)—the spirit of winter
Popocatepetl—great warrior who loved Ixtlaccihuatl
Ixtlaccihuatl—daughter of the Emperor, who loved Popocatepetl
Anansi—a cunning and intelligent spider

542   *Fables, Myths, and Legends*

Fables

THE BLUE HORSE
Franz Marc
© *Three Lions*

Fables 543

Humanities Note

Fine art, *The Blue Horse,* 1907, by Franz Marc. The German Expressionist painter Franz Marc (1880–1916) was educated in art at the Munich Academy. His painting evolved from poetic impressions of nature to intense mystic studies of animal symbolism. Marc felt the animal form and nature to be purer in spirit than that of the human. He explored the essence of the animal form and became more and more abstract as his art matured. His career as a painter abruptly ended with his death at Verdun during World War I.

A favorite subject of Marc's was the horse, an animal considered sacred by ancient Germans. The painting *The Blue Horse* was produced during the period when Marc was experimenting with Impressionistic handling of single animals. Marc felt the color blue was symbolic of masculinity and robust spiritedness. By using blue for this painting, he reinforced the strength of the gigantic curves of the neck and limbs of the horse. The graceful animal fills the picture plane furthering the powerful visual impact. Franz Marc sought to paint the magical essence of animal spirit. In this case he has succeeded in capturing the wild strength and innocent beauty of the horse.

More About the Author Aesop was reputed to be a slave in Greece in the sixth century B.C. However, some scholars doubt he was an actual person. Ask the class if they believe that slaves would be given the freedom to write, and why Aesop was given this unique privilege.

Literary Focus Point out that the writer of a fable wants to teach a lesson about life. Other forms of literature often seek to do this in a less obvious way. Ask the class to name a song or a television program that seems designed to teach a lesson.

Look For If a real animal said something, you would be amazed. Yet in a fable like the "The Fox and the Crow," we accept the idea of animals conversing. Explain that this is because talking animals are a common literary device, as old as Aesop and as up to date as Disney. It allows writers to present ideas that might not be accepted so readily if they came from a human character.

Writing/Prior Knowledge Certain animals are associated with particular human traits. Elephants, for example, are thought of as wise. Ask students to name animals associated with human traits. Then have them complete the assignment.

Vocabulary Have your less advanced students read these words aloud. Then select individual students to use each one in a sentence.

Teaching to Ability Levels Reminding the class that the authorship of Aesop's fables is in doubt, ask your more advanced students to consider whether "The Town Mouse and the Country Mouse" and "The Fox and the Crow" seem to be the work of the same writer.

544

The Town Mouse and the Country Mouse
The Fox and the Crow

Aesop (ē′ śäp) (about 620–560 B.C.) was an ancient Greek whose name was associated with a collection of wise tales about animals. Little is known about him, except that he was a slave who was later freed by his master. Actually many of Aesop's tales or fables were based on tales told long before his birth. Many of them were also rewritten by others after his death. They are fun to read and contain good advice.

Fables

A **fable** is a brief tale, in prose or verse, that teaches a lesson called a **moral**. Often this moral appears as a wise saying at the end of the tale. In Aesop's fables, the characters are animals who act like human beings and often illustrate human failings and weaknesses. However, other writers use human characters in their fables or even plants and objects that talk and behave like humans.

Look For

As you read these entertaining fables, look for the ways in which the animals act like humans. Also, identify the human failings that some of the charaters illustrate. How does the way the characters act point to a moral?

Writing

Imagine that you are planning to write a fable in which pairs of animal characters will represent the following pairs of qualities: courage and cowardice, wisdom and foolishness, loyalty and faithlessness. Decide on an animal for each quality and briefly explain your choice.

Vocabulary

Knowing the following words will help you as you read these fables.

heartily (härt′l ē) adv.: Warmly; completely (p. 545)
fare (fer) n.: Food (p. 545)
glossy (glôs′ ē) adj.: Smooth and shiny (p. 547)
surpass (sər pas′) v.: Be superior to (p. 547)

flatterers (flat′ ər ərz) n.: Those who praise a person insincerely in order to gain something for themselves (p. 547)

544   Fables, Myths, and Legends

Objectives

1 To understand fables
2 To write a fable

Support Material

Teaching Portfolio
Teacher Backup, p. 857
Usage and Mechanics Worksheet, p. 860
Vocabulary Check, p. 861
Analyzing Literature Worksheet, *Understanding Fables,* p. 862
Language Worksheet, *Word Analogies,* p. 863
Selection Test, p. 864

The Town Mouse and the Country Mouse

Aesop

Now you must know that a Town Mouse once upon a time went on a visit to his cousin in the country. He was rough and ready, this cousin, but he loved his town friend and made him heartily welcome. Beans and bacon, cheese and bread were all he had to offer, but he offered them freely.

1 The Town Mouse rather turned up his long nose at this country fare, and said: "I cannot understand, Cousin, how you can put up with such poor food as this, but of course 2 you cannot expect anything better in the country; come you with me and I will show you how to live. When you have been in town 3 a week you will wonder how you could ever have stood a country life."

No sooner said than done: the two mice

Presentation

Motivation/Prior Knowledge Ask students to discuss places they have visited that were, like the country mouse's trip to the city, a "mixed blessing."

Master Teacher Note These fables come from ancient Greece. Have the class look up ancient Greece in an encyclopedia or other reference book to find out something about what life was like there. Ask the class to consider how the Greek love of philosophizing might have encouraged Aesop's master to indulge his slave's desire to compose fables like these.

Purpose-Setting Question Do the characters in these fables act in ways that people really act, based on your experience?

1 **Clarification** The expression "to turn up one's nose" means to show a strong dislike for someone or something.

2 **Discussion** What do you think of the Town Mouse from the first thing he says?

3 **Reading Strategy** In promising his country cousin that he will prefer life in town, the Town Mouse is assuming that the Country Mouse shares his point of view. Have students predict whether or not the Country Mouse will prefer the town.

4 **Critical Thinking and Reading**
What word in this paragraph indicates that the Town Mouse's home is not really his, but someone else's?

5 **Discussion** You might indicate to **more advanced** students that irony is a contrast between what is stated and what is read. What is ironic about the Country Mouse's reference to the dogs' growling as "music"?

Speaking and Listening Have three students read the fable aloud to the class, one as narrator, the other two taking the parts of the Town Mouse and the Country Mouse. Encourage them to emphasize the difference between the two mice by saying their parts in distinctly different ways.

Reader's Response Do you relate better to the Town Mouse or the Country Mouse? Why?

Closure and Extension

ANSWERS TO THINKING ABOUT THE SELECTION
Recalling

1. The food is simple in the country, and there is little to choose from.
2. The fact that the house in which the Town Mouse lives contains two large dogs disturbs the Country Mouse.

Interpreting

3. The Town Mouse is more demanding and is willing to accept a degree of danger in his life. The Country Mouse has simpler wants and prefers safer surroundings.
4. Answers will differ. Some students may think that the Town Mouse is a snob, and like his country cousin better. Others may think the Country Mouse leads a boring life and sympathize more with the Town Mouse.

set off for the town and arrived at the Town Mouse's residence late at night. "You will want some refreshment after our long journey," said the polite Town Mouse, and took his friend into the grand dining room. There 4 they found the remains of a fine feast, and soon the two mice were eating up jellies and cakes and all that was nice. Suddenly they heard growling and barking.

"What is that?" said the Country Mouse.

"It is only the dogs of the house," answered the other.

5 "Only!" said the Country Mouse. "I do not like that music at my dinner."

Just at that moment the door flew open, in came two huge mastiffs,[1] and the two mice had to scamper down and run off.

"Good-by, Cousin," said the Country Mouse.

"What! going so soon?" said the other.

"Yes," he replied:

*"Better beans and bacon in peace
than cakes and ale in fear."*

---

1. mastiffs (mas' tifs) *n.*: Large, powerful, smooth-coated dogs with hanging lips and drooping ears. They were used for hunting and as watchdogs.

THINKING ABOUT THE SELECTION
Recalling

1. What disturbs the Town Mouse about his meal in the country?
2. What disturbs the Country Mouse about his meal in town?

Interpreting

3. Compare and contrast the two mice. Explain what traits each mouse represents.
4. Which mouse do you feel more sympathy for? Explain your answer.

Applying

5. Why might a fable with animal characters teach a lesson better than a tale with human characters?

ANALYZING LITERATURE
Understanding Fables

A **fable** is a brief tale, in prose or verse, that teaches a lesson called a **moral.** In "The Town Mouse and the Country Mouse" each of the characters has a different approach to life. The moral suggests that the Country Mouse's point of view is better.

1. What is the moral of this fable?
2. Express the moral in your own words.
3. Explain why you agree or disagree with the moral.

THINKING AND WRITING
Writing a Fable

Write a fable with a moral that is the opposite of Aesop's lesson. The moral of your fable must be: *Better an interesting life with danger than a safe life that is dull.* Think of two contrasting animal characters for your fable. They can be animals of the same species, like the two mice, or different animals. Write a fable placing these characters in a modern setting. In revising your work, make sure that your tale really teaches the new moral. When you are finished, share your fable with your classmates.

546   *Fables, Myths, and Legends*

Applying

5. Suggested Response: A fable with animal characters may teach a lesson better than one with human characters because the reader may respond to it more freely. This is due to the fact that the characters, being animals, are unlike the reader in a fundamental way. This can make readers less defensive about the story and its moral.

ANSWERS TO ANALYZING LITERATURE

1. The moral of the fable is "Better beans and bacon in peace than cakes and ale in fear."
2. Another way of saying this is that it is difficult to enjoy things that involve danger.
3. Answers will differ, depending on whether an individual student prizes safety or excitement.

THINKING AND WRITING

Publishing Student Writing Students would probably enjoy sharing their fables. Perhaps you could post them on the bulletin board along with any illustrations students draw to accompany them.

546

The Fox and the Crow

Aesop

A Fox once saw a Crow fly off with a piece of cheese in its beak and settle on a branch of a tree. "That's for me, as I am a Fox," said Master Reynard,[1] and he walked up to the foot of the tree.

"Good day, Mistress Crow," he cried. "How well you are looking today: how glossy your feathers; how bright your eye. I feel sure your voice must surpass that of other birds, just as your figure does; let me hear but one song from you that I may greet you as the Queen of Birds."

The Crow lifted up her head and began to caw her best, but the moment she opened her mouth the piece of cheese fell to the ground, only to be snapped up by Master Fox. "That will do," said he. "That was all I wanted. In exchange for your cheese I will give you a piece of advice for the future—

"Do not trust flatterers."

---

1. Master Reynard (ren' ərd): The fox in the medieval beast epic *Reynard the Fox*; therefore, a proper name for the fox in other stories.

THINKING ABOUT THE SELECTION

Recalling

1. How does the Crow lose the cheese?

Interpreting

2. What character traits do the Fox and the Crow represent?
3. How do the actions of these two animals support the moral?
4. The seventeenth-century Frenchman Jean La Fontaine rewrote many of Aesop's fables and stamped them with his own style. He expressed the moral of "The Fox and the Crow" as follows: Learn that every flatterer/Lives at the flattered listener's cost. Compare this version of the moral with Aesop's. How would you rewrite the moral to stamp it with your own style?

Applying

5. What is it about human nature that allows flattery to do its work?

Closure and Extension

ANSWERS TO THINKING ABOUT THE SELECTION

Recalling

1. The Crow drops the cheese when she begins to sing at the Fox's request.

Interpreting

2. The Fox represents cunning, the Crow vanity.
3. The Fox's flattery is not sincere, and being taken in by it costs the Crow her cheese.
4. LaFontaine's moral is stated in a more elegant and complicated way, but essentially means the same as Aesop's more direct statement. Student's rewritten versions will differ.

Applying

5. Suggested Response: Flattery often works because we all like to hear good things said about ourselves, even if they are somewhat far-fetched.

Challenge How might the Crow have reacted differently to the Fox if she had asked herself what his motive was in praising her?

Focus

More About the Author Many of James Thurber's writings are wry parables about the pressures of modern life and the foibles of modern man. Ask students to find elements in the fable that show it to be the work of a modern writer.

Literary Focus A satire is usually written because its writer has a strong feeling about something. What human weakness does Thurber wish to criticize in his retelling of the fable?

Look for Have your **more advanced students** look for signs Thurber gives you that he is retelling an old tale.

Writing/Prior Knowledge Have students discuss the meaning of the expression, "To err is human." Then have them complete the freewriting assignment.

Vocabulary Choose students to use the words in a sentence to show that they understand their meanings.

The Fox and the Crow

James Thurber (1894–1961) admired the work of famous writers, but he was also influenced by comic strips and movies. In fact, a successful movie was made from his best-known short story, "The Secret Life of Walter Mitty." Thurber showed an awareness of human weaknesses in his stories, plays, and essays. However, he revealed these faults with humor and understanding. In "The Fox and the Crow," he rewrites an old fable to poke fun at a common flaw.

Satire

Satire is writing that uses laughter and wit to criticize or ridicule human weaknesses. This type of writing appears in various literary forms. In some cases, the humor of satire is bitter and harsh, while in others it is warm and affectionate. Thurber's satire in "The Fox and the Crow" is the more gentle type.

Look For

As you read Thurber's version of "The Fox and the Crow," look for the various ways in which Thurber has changed this traditional fable. Also, compare and contrast Thurber's moral with Aesop's. What does Thurber's moral tell you about the modern world?

Writing

Think of a foolish way of behaving that you have observed both in yourself and in others. This behavior should not be a serious fault, just a minor weakness that might seem amusing. Describe this behavior in a way that gently makes fun of it.

Vocabulary

Knowing the following words will help you as you read "The Fox and the Crow."

warblers (wôr′ blərz) *n.*: Song-birds (p. 549)
unique (yo͞o nēk′) *adj.*: Highly unusual or rare (p. 549)
cunning (kun′ iŋ) *adj.*: Sly; crafty (p. 550)

arrogantly (ar′ə gənt lē) *adv.*: Proudly; self-importantly (p. 550)
appeased (ə pēzd′) *v.*: Satisfied (p. 550)
forlornly (fər lôrn′ lē) *adv.*: Hopelessly; miserably (p. 550)

Objectives

1 To understand satire
2 To recognize satire in a boast
3 To find homophones
4 To compare and contrast fables

Support Material

Teaching Portfolio
Teacher Backup, p. 867
Usage and Mechanics Work-
  sheet, p. 870
Vocabulary Check, p. 871
Analyzing Literature Worksheet,
  Understanding Satire, p. 872
Critical Thinking and Reading
  Worksheet, *Recognizing Satires
  in Foolish Boasts,* p. 873
Selection Test, p. 874

The Fox
and the Crow

James Thurber

Original art by James Thurber
© 1956 by James Thurber

A crow, perched in a tree with a piece of cheese in his beak, attracted the eye and nose of a fox. "If you can sing as prettily as you sit," said the fox, "then you are the prettiest singer within my scent and sight." The fox had read somewhere, and somewhere, and somewhere else, that praising the voice of a crow with a cheese in his beak would make him drop the cheese and sing. But this is not what happened to this particular crow in this particular case.

"They say you are sly and they say you are crazy," said the crow, having carefully removed the cheese from his beak with the claws of one foot, "but you must be nearsighted as well. Warblers wear gay hats and colored jackets and bright vests, and they are a dollar a hundred. I wear black and I am unique." He began nibbling the cheese, dropping not a single crumb.

"I am sure you are," said the fox, who was neither crazy nor nearsighted, but sly. "I

The Fox and the Crow 549

Presentation

Motivation/Prior Knowledge Ask the class to describe the personality of someone who praises himself. Why does he? Why is such a person vulnerable to deception and hurt? Have the class compare the boaster in this fable with the flattery victim in Aesop's.

Purpose-Setting Question What is the result of the crow's bragging?

1 Discussion The tone in Thurber's opening paragraph is clever and ironic. Is this the tone we expect to find in a fable, judging from Aesop's?

2 Discussion Why does the crow carefully remove the cheese with his claws?

3 Discussion Why does the crow say that the fox must be nearsighted?

550

4 Discussion Why does Thurber use the old-fashioned words "fain" and "tarry"?

5 Enrichment The "lion's share" refers to the greater part in any allotment, especially the part given to the higher-ranking person. This phrase comes from another fable by Aesop in which a lion, a donkey, and a fox go hunting with the understanding that they will divide equally any prey. They catch a stag, and the donkey divides it exactly; however, the lion becomes enraged feeling that because of his stature and dignity, he deserves a greater part. He flies at the donkey and kills him. The fox then craftily redivides the prey, taking only a small bite for himself and giving the rest to the lion. Thus, the larger share of something has become known as "the lion's share."

6 Discussion What old-fashioned words can you find in Thurber's statement of the fable's moral?

Critical Thinking and Reading Have the class compare the boaster in this fable with the flattery victim in Aesop's. What are the likenesses or differences in their characters?

Master Teacher Note Thurber is as famous for his cartoons as for his writing. Have students look at his cartoon on page 549 and describe his special brand of humor.

Reader's Response Why is it important to feel good about oneself?

recognize you, now that I look more closely, as the most famed and talented of all birds, and I fain[1] would hear you tell about yourself, but I am hungry and must go."

"Tarry[2] awhile," said the crow quicky, "and share my lunch with me." Whereupon he tossed the cunning fox the lion's share of the cheese, and began to tell about himself. "A ship that sails without a crow's nest[3] sails to doom," he said. "Bars may come and bars may go, but crow bars last forever. I am the pioneer of flight, I am the map maker. Last, but never least, my flight is known to scientists and engineers, geometrists and scholars, as the shortest distance between two points. Any two points," he concluded arrogantly.

"Oh, every two points, I am sure," said the fox. "And thank you for the lion's share of what I know you could not spare." And with this he trotted away into the woods, his appetite appeased, leaving the hungry crow perched forlornly in the tree.

MORAL: *'Twas true in Aesop's time, and La Fontaine's,[4] and now, no one else can praise thee quite so well as thou.*

---

1. fain (fān) *adv.*: An old-fashioned way of saying "gladly."

2. tarry (tar' ē) *v.*: An old-fashioned way of saying "wait."

3. crow's nest: A small, partly enclosed platform near the top of a ship's mast where the lookout stands.

---

4. La Fontaine (la' fōn ten'): A French poet and writer of fables.

THINKING ABOUT THE SELECTION

Recalling

1. Why does the fox praise the crow's voice?
2. How does the crow answer the fox?
3. What does the fox say to make the crow share his lunch?

Interpreting

4. What evidence shows that the fox knows Aesop's fable about the fox and the crow?
5. How does the fox show the ability to solve new problems as they arise?
6. Explain the moral of this fable. How do the actions of these two animals support the moral?

Applying

7. Why are some people willing to give up valuable possessions just to have the opportunity to brag?

ANALYZING LITERATURE

Understanding Satire

Satire is writing that uses laughter and wit to criticize or ridicule human weaknesses. In "The Fox and the Crow" the animal characters of the fable stand for human beings. Thurber directs most of his satire at the type of person represented by the crow.

1. What weakness in human personality is Thurber satirizing?
2. How does the fox's rapid departure make the crow's long speech seem ridiculous?
3. What details suggest that Thurber's satire is more gentle than angry?

CRITICAL THINKING AND READING

Recognizing Satire in Foolish Boasts

In satire, writers include many details to point out the foolishness of the characters they are criticizing. One type of detail is a foolish boast. For in-

stance, Thurber's crow brags to the fox, " 'I wear black and I am unique.' " You can picture him puffing himself up proudly as he speaks.

Find four other foolish boasts the crow makes. Explain each of these boasts.

UNDERSTANDING LANGUAGE

Finding Homophones

A **homophone** is a word that sounds like another word but has a different spelling and meaning from that word. For example, the words *piece* and *peace* are homophones. Some word-analogy tests require you to identify the first pair of words as homophones and complete the second pair with a homophone. For example:

pair : pear : : so :_____

The word sew completes the second pair.

The third word in each word analogy below is from "The Fox and the Crow." Complete each analogy with a homophone.

1. new : knew : : eye :_____
2. cash : cache : : claws :_____
3. not : knot : : scent :_____
4. there : their : : sail :_____
5. wood : would : : time :_____

THINKING AND WRITING

Comparing and Contrasting Fables

Comparing two things means showing how they are similar. **Contrasting** them means showing how they are different. List the ways in which Thurber's fable and Aesop's are similar and different. Consider the personalities of the fox and crow in each fable, the tricks that each fox uses, and the two morals. Then turn your list into a composition. Devote one paragraph to showing the similarities between the fables and one to showing the differences. When revising make sure you have shown how the two fables are both similar and different. Finally, share your writing with your classmates.

The Fox and the Crow 551

Closure and Extension

ANSWERS TO THINKING ABOUT THE SELECTION

Recalling

1. The fox praises the crow in the hope of making him drop his cheese.
2. The crow tells the fox he must be nearsighted to think he is "pretty."
3. The fox threatens to leave, and the

crow throws him a large piece of cheese to keep him from going.

Interpreting

4. The writer says that the fox had read about a similar situation.
5. When this crow does not react like the crow in Aesop's fable, the fox tries a different tactic, knowing the crow will want to talk about himself.
6. The moral is that no one will praise you as well as you can praise

yourself. The crow proves this by launching into an absurdly grandiose description of himself.

Applying

7. Answers will differ. Suggested Response: Some people are willing to give up valuable possessions in order to brag because their vanity is stronger than their desire for those possessions.

ANSWERS TO ANALYZING LITERATURE

1. Thurber is satirizing boastfulness.
2. The fox's rapid departure shows that he was listening to the crow only for as long as it took him to eat the cheese.
3. Thurber shows that his satire is more gentle than angry by the whimsical details he includes, such as having the animals use old-fashioned language, having the crow praise himself in a comical way, and expressing the moral in playful couplet.

ANSWERS TO CRITICAL THINKING AND READING

The crow makes the following boasts:
a. "a ship that sails without a crow's nest sails to doom," meaning that any good ship has a lookout point called the "crow's nest" from which to watch for dangerous things ahead.
b. "bars may come and bars may go, but crow bars last forever," meaning that crow bars are hard to destroy because they are made of iron.
c. "I am the pioneer of flight," suggests that humans got the idea of flight from watching birds.
d. "I am the map maker," apparently is a reference to the fact that maps provide a "bird's eye view."
e. "my flight is known . . . as the shortest distance between two points" refers to the expression "as the crow flies," meaning a straight line from one geographical point to another.

ANSWERS TO UNDERSTANDING LANGUAGE

1. I
2. clause
3. sent
4. sale
5. thyme

THINKING AND WRITING

For help with this assignment, students can refer to lesson 16, "Writing a Comparative Evaluation," in the Handbook of Writing About Literature.

More About the Author Explain to the class that Louis Untermeyer, the poet who wrote this poem, preferred poetry that rhymes and is arranged in regular stanzas to the free verse written by most modern American poets. Ask students which kind of poem they like better, giving reasons for their preferences.

Literary Focus Suggest that students notice how the boy's tendency to "cry wolf," that is, to lie about nonexistent danger, gets him trouble.

Look for Your less advanced students might be better able to recognize the details that support the advice if they read the moral first.

Writing/Prior Knowledge Trust is a delicate thing. It takes a long time to develop, but it can be easily lost. Ask members of the class to discuss instances in which they won a person's (or an animal's) trust. Then have them complete the freewriting assignment.

The Boy and the Wolf

Louis Untermeyer (1885–1977) read so many books as a teenager that he had three cards from his local library—two of them in the names of other family members. Untermeyer went on to produce books at almost the same speed that he read them. Besides writing poetry, fiction, and essays, he edited several well-known poetry anthologies. In 1956, he was awarded the Gold Medal of the Poetry Society of America. "The Boy and the Wolf" is his poetic version of a fable by Aesop.

A Fable and a Common Expression

"The Boy and the Wolf" is such a popular fable that it is the source of a commonly used expression: "Don't cry wolf!" The meaning of that expression will become clear to you as you read Untermeyer's version of the fable.

Look For

As you read "The Boy and the Wolf," look for the details that support the practical advice given in the lesson.

Writing

"The Boy and the Wolf" is about a boy who lies so much that people no longer trust him. Recall a book you have read or a television program you have seen in which one of the characters got into trouble for lying. Tell why this character lied and what happened to him or her as a result.

Vocabulary

Knowing the following words will help you as you read "The Boy and the Wolf."

despised (di spīzd') *v.*: Looked down on, disliked intensely (p. 553)

flock (fläk') *n.*: Group of sheep (p. 553)

heed (hēd) *n.*: Attention (p. 553)

552 *Fables, Myths, and Legends*

Objectives
1 To understand a common expression
2 To read a fable aloud
3 To complete word analogies
4 To write a fable in verse

Support Material

Teaching Portfolio
Teacher Backup, p. 877
Usage and Mechanics Worksheet, p. 880
Vocabulary Check, p. 881
Analyzing Literature Worksheet, *Understanding a Common Expression*, p. 882
Critical Thinking and Reading Worksheet, *Predicting Probable Future Actions*, p. 883

Selection Test, p. 884
Art Transparency 19, *Boy and the Wolf*, by Ben Shahn

The Boy and the Wolf

from **the Greek of Aesop**

Louis Untermeyer

A boy employed to guard the sheep
Despised his work. He liked to sleep.
And when a lamb was lost, he'd shout,
"Wolf! Wolf! The wolves are all about!"

The neighbors searched from noon till nine,
But of the beast there was no sign.
Yet "Wolf!" he cried next morning when
The villagers came out again.

One evening around six o'clock
A real wolf fell upon the flock.
"Wolf!" yelled the boy. "A wolf indeed!"
But no one paid him any heed.

Although he screamed to wake the dead,
"He's fooled us every time," they said,
And let the hungry wolf enjoy
His feast of mutton,[1] lamb—and boy.

THE MORAL'S this: The man who's wise
Does not defend himself with lies.
Liars are not believed, forsooth,[2]
Even when liars tell the truth.

---

1. **mutton** (mut' n) *n.*: Sheep.
2. **forsooth** (fər sooth') *adv.*: No doubt.

Presentation

Motivation/Prior Knowledge Have the class consider the problems of the perpetual liar. Why does such a person forfeit his right to credibility—even at a time when he may be entitled to it?

Purpose-Setting Question What problem does the boy in this story make for himself?

1 Discussion The writer mentions several times of day in the poem. They are not crucial to the story, but they make it convincing. Why do such details help us to believe a story really happened?

2 Discussion Like Thurber, Untermeyer uses an old-fashioned word in his statement of the moral ("forsooth"). How is his use of it different from Thurber's?

Discussion Unlike the other three fables in this unit, Untermeyer's is in verse. Ask the class whether they prefer fables in prose or verse and to explain the reasons for their preferences.

Master Teacher Note The fable from which Untermeyer derived his poem not only comes from a different language; it was written in a different alphabet. Have the class find the Greek alphabet in a dictionary under "alphabet." Help them find letters that resemble those in the Roman alphabet and those that are different. What English word is suggested by putting the names of the first two letters of the Greek alphabet together?

Master Teacher Note The theme presented in "The Boy and the Wolf" can be found in other works of art as well as in literature. To show an example, use Art Transparency 19, *Boy and the Wolf,* by Ben Shahn. Place the transparency on the overhead projector and have students study it carefully. Why are the two people standing apart and wearing masks? What might they be saying to each other? What feelings are evoked by the bare trees and the bleak landscape?

Reader's Response How do you think the villagers felt when they discovered the true fate of the boy? Explain.

Closure and Extension

ANSWERS TO THINKING ABOUT THE SELECTION
Recalling

1. The first two lines tell you that the boy often sleeps when he should be watching his sheep.
2. The people did not come because they thought the boy was trying to fool them again as he had in the past.

Interpreting

3. The boy cried "Wolf!" to conceal the fact that he had fallen asleep and allowed the sheep to wander off. He wanted people to think that a wolf had eaten it.
4. The last two lines mean that someone who has a reputation for lying will not be believed, even if he or she stops lying and tells the truth.

Applying

5. Suggested Response: The writer meant that truth helps trust to continue and to grow, while lying destroys it.

ANSWERS TO ANALYZING LITERATURE

1. The expression "Don't cry wolf" means not to say that danger is present when it is not.
2. Answers will differ. Suggested Response: A person who frequently pretends to be hurt while playing baseball may not be believed if he or she is really hurt one day.

ANSWERS TO UNDERSTANDING LANGUAGE

Several responses may be correct. The following are among the acceptable answers.
1. hate
2. evening
3. satiated
4. prudent

Challenge The boy in the fable lied to cover up a mistake. What are some other motives people have for lying?

THINKING ABOUT THE SELECTION
Recalling

1. What key fact do you learn about the boy in the first two lines?
2. Why did the people not come when a real wolf threatened the flock?

Interpreting

3. Why did the boy cry "Wolf!" whenever he lost a lamb?
4. Explain the last two lines of the poem?

Applying

5. A writer has compared trust among people to a plant that is watered by the truth but uprooted by lies. Explain what the writer meant by this observation.

ANALYZING LITERATURE
Understanding a Common Expression

"The Boy and the Wolf" is the source of a common expression in our language: "Don't cry wolf!" This fable shows you how a boy who did "cry wolf" once too often brought about his own downfall.
1. What do we mean by the expression, "Don't cry wolf"?
2. Describe a modern situation to which this expression could apply.

SPEAKING AND LISTENING
Reading a Fable Aloud

Since this fable is in poetic form, you can read it aloud the way you would read any poem. Do not pause at the end of a line unless there is a period or a comma. Pause briefly at a comma, and stop longer at a period. Above all, remember not to read in a singsong voice. A poem should sound as natural as ordinary speech.
1. Practice reading the fable aloud to one or two classmates.
2. Ask your classmates to comment on your reading, and use their suggestions to improve your presentation.

UNDERSTANDING LANGUAGE
Completing Word Analogies

Some word-analogy tests require you to identify whether the words in the first pair are synonyms or antonyms and to complete the second pair appropriately. For example:

employ : hire : : toil :_____

Since the first two words are synonyms, you should complete the second pair with a synonym: work.

awake : asleep : : truth :_____

Since the first two words are antonyms, you should complete the second pair with an antonym: lie.

Complete each of the word analogies below.
1. guard : watch : : despise :_____
2. lost : found : : morning :_____
3. real : false : : hungry :_____
4. fool : trick : : wise :_____

THINKING AND WRITING
Writing a Fable in Verse

You have thought about a modern situation to which this fable's moral would apply. Write a brief prose description of this situation. Then turn your description into a fable in verse, like Untermeyer's. However, you do not have to use rhymes or four-line stanzas. As you revise your poem, be sure you have included a moral at the end.

Greek and Roman Myths

HECTOR AND ANDROMACHE
Giorgio de Chirico
Scala/Art Resource

Humanities Note

Fine art, *Hector and Andromache* by Giorgio de Chirico. Georgio de Chirico (1888–1978) was an Italian painter who began his artistic career painting traditional land and seascapes. Travel through Germany and Italy in 1906–9 opened his eyes to the rapid changes in art and technology that were taking place in the world. This new awareness influenced his first characteristic work in 1910, which founded the movement of Metaphysical Painting (imaginary and abstract images influenced by the metaphysical philosophers of the day). Chirico's paintings had a profound influence on the Surrealist movement and on the art of Picasso and other leading modern artists of the early twentieth century.

Hector and Andromache is a painting of complicated composition with inexplicable perspective, strange architectural elements, and two mannequins to represent the characters in its title. This impersonality creates an unnatural meaning, which in turn arouses feelings of anxiety in the viewer. Nevertheless, the classical subjects still have their universal appeal.

Focus

More About the Myth The Greeks invented gods and goddesses to explain the forces of the natural world that affected their lives. Demeter, the goddess of the harvest, was one of their chief divinities, depicted in art, in literature, even in household decoration. Discuss with the class why she would be such an important goddess in an agricultural society like that of the Greeks.

Literary Focus Although they can be fun to read, myths were not devised to entertain. They were a serious effort to understand the world. You might point out to students that myths are a feature of societies throughout the world, from Iceland to Polynesia, and that figures like Demeter often have close parallels in other cultures, although the divinity elsewhere may have a different name.

Look For Your less advanced students may have some difficulty distinguishing between emotions and actions. Ask them to explain how Demeter's emotions are those of a human mother, while her actions—devastating the world's vegetation, for instance—are superhuman.

Writing/Prior Knowledge The change of seasons affects people today, just as it did in the ancient world. Ask students to discuss how they feel when spring begins. What do they like about spring? What activities do they look forward to at that time of the year?

Vocabulary Have your more advanced students look up the derivation of each of the words to determine how many of them, like those in the Understanding Language activity, have Latin roots.

Demeter and Persephone

The ancient Greeks often thought of **Demeter** (di mēt′ ər) and her daughter **Persephone** (pər sef′ ənē) as a pair, calling them the Two Goddesses. Farmers honored and worshiped Demeter during the planting and harvesting of corn, as important a crop in the ancient world as it is today. The Greek poet Homer described Demeter as "blonde," giving her the color of ripened corn.

Anne Terry White (1896–   ), the reteller of this myth, was a teacher and has written many books for young people.

Myth

A **myth** is an ancient story about gods or heroes created to express beliefs or explain natural events. Among the matters that myths explain are how the world began, why the sun travels across the sky, and how humans gained fire. Since myths are stories, these mythical explanations of nature are both lively and imaginative. Therefore, they have lasted for generations.

Greek and Roman myths have had the greatest influence on our own culture. For hundreds of years, writers have retold these stories in the English language. "Demeter and Persephone" has been especially popular because it explains the rhythms of nature in terms of human emotions.

Look For

Although the characters in this myth are gods and goddesses, they experience the same feelings as humans do. Look for these feelings and the events they cause.

Writing

Imagine that you come from a planet where the season is always winter. You are visiting the earth for the first time, just as the spring is beginning. Freewrite about your reaction to this new experience.

Vocabulary

Knowing the following words will help you as you read "Demeter and Persephone."

asunder (ə sun′ dər) *adv.*: Into parts or pieces (p. 557)

realm (relm) *n.*: Kingdom (p. 557)

defies (di fīz′) *v.*: Boldly opposes or resists (p. 557)

monarch (män′ ərk) *n.*: Ruler; king or queen (p. 557)

dominions (də min′ yənz) *n.*: Region over which he ruled (p. 558)

intervene (in′ tər vēn′) *v.*: Step into a situation (p. 558)

abode (ə bōd′) *n.*: Home (p. 560)

556   *Fables, Myths, and Legends*

Demeter and Persephone

Anne Terry White

Deep under Mt. Aetna, the gods had buried alive a number of fearful, fire-breathing giants. The monsters heaved and struggled to get free. And so mightily did they shake the earth that Pluto, the king of the underworld, was alarmed.

"They may tear the rocks asunder and leave the realm of the dead open to the light of day," he thought. And mounting his golden chariot, he went up to see what damage had been done.

Now the goddess of love and beauty, fair Aphrodite,[1] was sitting on a mountainside playing with her son, Eros.[2] She saw Pluto as he drove around with his coal-black horses and she said:

"My son, there is one who defies your power and mine. Quick! Take up your darts! Send an arrow into the breast of that dark monarch. Let him, too, feel the pangs of love. Why should he alone escape them?"

At his mother's words, Eros leaped lightly to his feet. He chose from his quiver[3] his sharpest and truest arrow, fitted it to his bow, drew the string, and shot straight into Pluto's heart.

The grim King had seen fair maids enough in the gloomy underworld over which he ruled. But never had his heart been touched. Now an unaccustomed warmth stole through his veins. His stern eyes softened. Before him was a blossoming valley, and along its edge a charming girl was gathering flowers. She was Persephone, daughter of Demeter, goddess of the harvest. She had strayed from her companions, and now that her basket overflowed with blossoms, she was filling her apron with lilies and violets. The god looked at Persephone

Demeter and Persephone   557

---

1. Aphrodite (af′ rə dīt′ ē)
2. Eros (er′ äs): In Greek mythology, the god of love, identified by the Romans with Cupid.
3. quiver (kwiv′ ər) *n.*: A case for arrows.

3 Critical Thinking and Reading From the description here, ask the class whether they think this myth might have been used to explain a widespread crop failure that ancient science could not account for.

4 Discussion Why does Zeus finally decide to intervene in Persephone's disappearance?

and loved her at once. With one sweep of his arm he caught her up and drove swiftly away.

"Mother!" she screamed, while the flowers fell from her apron and strewed the ground. "Mother!"

And she called on her companions by name. But already they were out of sight, so fast did Pluto urge the horses on. In a few moments they were at the River Cyane.[4] Persephone struggled, her loosened girdle[5] fell to the ground, but the god held her tight. He struck the bank with his trident.[6] The earth opened, and darkness swallowed them all—horses, chariot, Pluto, and weeping Persephone.

From end to end of the earth Demeter sought her daughter. But none could tell her where Persephone was. At last, worn out and despairing, the goddess returned to Sicily. She stood by the River Cyane, where Pluto had cleft[7] the earth and gone down into his own dominions.

Now a river nymph[8] had seen him carry off his prize. She wanted to tell Demeter where her daughter was, but fear of Pluto kept her dumb. Yet she had picked up the girdle Persephone had dropped, and this the nymph wafted[9] on the waves to the feet of Demeter.

The goddess knew then that her daughter was gone indeed, but she did not suspect Pluto of carrying her off. She laid the blame on the innocent land.

"Ungrateful soil!" she said. "I made you fertile. I clothed you in grass and nourishing grain, and this is how you reward me. No more shall you enjoy my favors!"

_____

4. River Cyane (sī′ an): A river in Sicily, an island just south of Italy.
5. girdle (gər′ d'l) _n._: A belt or sash for the waist.
6. trident (trīd′ 'nt) _n._: A spear with three points.
7. cleft (kleft) _v._: Split or opened.
8. river nymph (nimf): A goddess living in a river.
9. wafted (wäft′ 'd) _v._: Carried.

558 *Fables, Myths, and Legends*

That year was the most cruel mankind had ever known. Nothing prospered, nothing grew. The cattle died, the seed would not come up, men and oxen toiled in vain. There was too much sun. There was too much rain. Thistles[10] and weeds were the only things that grew. It seemed that all mankind would die of hunger.

"This cannot go on," said mighty Zeus. "I see that I must intervene." And one by one he sent the gods and goddesses to plead with Demeter.

But she had the same answer for all: "Not till I see my daughter shall the earth bear fruit again."

Zeus, of course, knew well where Persephone was. He did not like to take from his brother the one joyful thing in his life, but he saw that he must if the race of man was to be preserved. So he called Hermes[11] to him and said:

"Descend to the underworld, my son. Bid Pluto release his bride. Provided she has not tasted food in the realm of the dead, she may return to her mother forever."

Down sped Hermes on his winged feet, and there in the dim palace of the king, he found Persephone by Pluto's side. She was pale and joyless. Not all the glittering treasures of the underworld could bring a smile to her lips.

"You have no flowers here," she would say to her husband when he pressed gems upon her. "Jewels have no fragrance. I do not want them."

When she saw Hermes and heard his message, her heart leaped within her. Her cheeks grew rosy and her eyes sparkled, for she knew that Pluto would not dare to disobey his brother's command. She sprang up,

_____

10. thistles (this′ 'lz) _n._: Stubborn, weedy plants with sharp leaves and usually purplish flowers.
11. Hermes (hʉr′ mēz): A god who served as a messenger.

Grammar in Action

Because the personalities of ancient Greeks are unfamiliar to modern audiences, writers of myths identify gods and people as they tell their stories. To do this, Anne Terry White often uses **appositives.** An appositive is a noun or pronoun placed after another noun or pronoun to identify, rename, or explain the preceding word. An **appositive phrase** is a noun or pronoun with modifiers that acts as an appositive. For example,

The goddess of love and beauty, *fair Aphrodite,* was sitting on a mountainside.

She was Persephone, *daughter of Demeter, goddess of the harvest.*

In the first example, the phrase *fair Aphrodite* is the appositive that identifies *the goddess of love and beauty.* The second example contains two appositives, both of which rename and identify *Persephone.* Notice that appositives are set off by commas.

Student Activity 1. Find two other examples of identifying appositives in "Demeter and Persephone."

Demeter and Persephone 559

Student Activity 2. Supply appositives in the following sentences. Use the footnotes in this story as sources of information.

1. Aphrodite loved her son Eros, _____ , and played with him on the mountainside.
2. Zeus sent for Hermes, _____ .
3. Pluto struck the bank with his trident, _____ .
4. _____ , a simple pomegranate was Persephone's downfall.

Student Activity 3. Write three other sentences about the Greek gods and goddesses using and punctuating appositives correctly.

Margin notes (left column)

5 Discussion What has Persephone done that will prevent her permanently leaving the underworld?

6 Reading Strategy Ask your less advanced students to explain what happens to Persephone in the myth in their own words.

7 Literary Focus What explanation for the changing seasons does the myth offer?

Master Teacher Note The story of Demeter has been retold by many modern authors. You might ask several interested students to read other versions (the one in Edith Hamilton's *Mythology*, for instance) and report to the class about how they differ from this one.

Reader's Response For whom do you feel more sorry, Persephone or Pluto? Explain.

Main text

ready to go at once. Only one thing troubled her—that she could not leave the underworld forever. For she had accepted a pomegranate[12] from Pluto and sucked the sweet pulp from four of the seeds.

With a heavy heart Pluto made ready his golden car.[13] He helped Persephone in while Hermes took up the reins.

"Dear wife," said the King, and his voice trembled as he spoke, "think kindly of me, I pray you. For indeed I love you truly. It will be lonely here these eight months you are away. And if you think mine is a gloomy palace to return to, at least remember that your husband is great among the immortals. So fare you well—and get your fill of flowers!"

Straight to the temple of Demeter at Eleusis, Hermes drove the black horses. The goddess heard the chariot wheels and, as a deer bounds over the hills, she ran out swiftly to meet her daughter. Persephone flew to her mother's arms. And the sad tale of each turned into joy in the telling.

So it is to this day. One third of the year Persephone spends in the gloomy abode of Pluto—one month for each seed that she tasted. Then Nature dies, the leaves fall, the earth stops bringing forth. In spring Persephone returns, and with her come the flowers, followed by summer's fruitfulness and the rich harvest of fall.

12. **pomegranate** (päm′ gran′ it) *n.*: A round fruit with a red, leathery rind and many seeds.
13. **car** (kär) *n.*: chariot.

THINKING ABOUT THE SELECTION

Recalling

1. Who is Pluto? Who is Demeter? Who is Persephone?
2. What motivates Pluto to take Persephone to his kingdom?
3. What does Demeter think has happened to Persephone? Why does she make the earth infertile?
4. How is the situation saved?
5. Why is Persephone unable to leave the underworld forever?

6. How does nature change as Persephone moves between the earth and the underworld?

Interpreting

7. Why is Persephone unhappy in the underworld?
8. Why is Pluto referred to as "the grim King"? How do you know that he truly loves Persephone?
9. Evaluate the judgment of the gods in regard to Persephone's fate. Do you think it just? Why or why not?

Closure and Extension

responsible for her daughter's disappearance. She wreaks vengeance on the land by making it infertile.

ANSWERS TO THINKING ABOUT THE SELECTION
Recalling

1. Pluto is the king of the underworld. Demeter is the goddess of the harvest. Persephone is her daughter.
2. Pluto falls in love because he is struck by one of Eros's arrows.
3. Demeter thinks the land itself is

4. The situation is saved when Zeus sends Hermes to rescue Persephone.
5. Persephone cannot leave the underworld permanently because she has eaten food there.
6. When Persephone goes to the underworld, vegetation dies (in autumn and winter); when she returns it flourishes (in spring and summer).

Interpreting

7. Persephone is unhappy because there are no flowers in the underworld.
8. Pluto is called "the Grim King" because he rules the land of the dead. He proves his love for Persephone by letting her return to her mother for eight months of every year.
9. Suggested Response: The gods' judgment in regard to Persephone seems harsh because she is an innocent victim, in effect,

Applying

10. Why do you think the return of spring would be so important to ancient Greeks and Romans?
11. Create a celebration in honor of the returning spring. Briefly describe what you would have people wear, say, and do.

ANALYZING LITERATURE
Appreciating Myth

A myth is an ancient story about gods or heroes created to express beliefs or explain natural events. Often in myths the explanation of natural events has its roots in the powerful emotions of the gods and goddesses involved. The story of "Demeter and Persephone," for example, explains why "the earth stops bringing forth" in the fall and winter but blooms again in the spring.

1. Identify the feelings that Pluto experiences during the course of the story.
2. What emotions do Persephone and Demeter experience in this myth?
3. How do the powerful emotions of these three characters account for the change in seasons?
4. Why do you think that the emotions expressed in this myth have touched people for thousands of years?

CRITICAL THINKING AND READING
Contrasting Science and Myth

Science and myth explain natural events in different ways. While a scientific explanation contains facts and theories, a myth offers a highly imaginative story as an explanation. For example, a scientific account of lightning would mention the discharge of electricity. A myth, however, might tell a story about an angry god hurling a spear.

1. In what way can myths reveal truths about life?
2. Which do you think reveals truths about life more vividly—myths or science? Which reveals truths more accurately?
3. Which explanations do you think make a greater impact on our hearts and minds? Explain your answer.

UNDERSTANDING LANGUAGE
Analyzing Words with the Root *mors*

A **prefix** is the part of a word that goes in front of its **root,** or core. The word *immortal,* which appears in "Demeter and Persephone," consists of the prefix *im-* ("not") and the root *mortal* ("a being that dies"). A god is immortal while a human being is mortal. Both of these words come from the Latin word *mors,* which means "death." The following words also contain this Latin root. Look up each in a dictionary and explain how it relates to the idea of death.

1. morgue   3. morbid   5. murder
2. mortician   4. mortuary

THINKING AND WRITING
Writing a Myth

Imagine a society that uses myth rather than science to explain dramatic and destructive earthquakes. Briefly outline the lively story about gods or heroes that this society might have devised. For instance, the story might involve giants battling under the earth, a god stamping with her foot, or anything you can imagine. Then, using your outline, write the myth in greater detail. In revising your myth, make sure the characters, like those in "Demeter and Persephone," express strong emotions. When you are finished, share your myth with your classmates.

Demeter and Persephone   561

(Answers begin on p. 560.)

Challenge Ask the class to find out, using the library, what the harvest goddess is called in five other cultures around the world.

ANSWERS TO CRITICAL THINKING AND READING

1. Myths can reveal truths about life by showing how human beings think and feel and how they interact.
2. While science may express natural truths more accurately, many people might feel that myths express them more vividly.
3. Answers will differ. The appeal of mythological or scientific explanations depends on the person involved. An intuitive, imaginative person will prefer myth; more rational personalities will feel more at home with science.

ANSWERS TO UNDERSTANDING LANGUAGE

1. A morgue is a place where bodies of people found dead are kept for identification and arrangement for burial.
2. A mortician is a funeral director, one who arranges funeral ceremonies for the dead.
3. *Morbid* refers to an unhealthy preoccupation with matters dealing with death.
4. A mortuary is a place where dead bodies are kept before burial or cremation.
5. Murder is the unlawful killing of a person.

THINKING AND WRITING
Publishing Student Writing
Ask students to choose which of the myths written by the class they like best. Then ask interested students to draw scenes from the myth which can be displayed on the bulletin board along with the story itself.

---

of the trick Aphrodite played on Pluto.

Applying
10. In the time before central heating and refrigeration, the return of spring meant a chance to be warm again and to eat fresh food.
11. Suggested Response: Any good spring celebration needs to be held outdoors. One way of celebrating the spring would be for people to put flowers in their hair as a way of participating in the

return of leaves and flowers to the land.

ANSWERS TO ANALYZING LITERATURE
1. During the course of the story, Pluto feels alarm, love, and sadness.
2. Persephone feels happiness, terror, unhappiness, then relief and happiness again. Demeter feels sorrow, anger, and joy.
3. According to the myth, these divine emotions account for the

change of seasons. When Persephone returns to her loving husband, Pluto, in the underworld, Demeter grieves and vegetation withers. When Persephone returns to earth, her mother's joy brings life back to the fields.
4. The emotions in the myth have held their appeal for thousands of years because they involve one of the most fundamental human feelings: the profound, even fierce, love of mother for child.

More About the Myth The figure of Prometheus has inspired many writers, artists, and composers, including Beethoven and Shelley. Ask students to explain why he is a far more appealing figure than any of the Olympian gods.

Literary Focus Explain to the class that conflict is at the heart of most good stories. Conflict is fascinating because readers want to see which of the opposing sides will win. Tell the class they are about to read a story about a conflict between two characters with superhuman powers.

Look For Explain that conflicts are often caused by two people having different viewpoints. For example, if one sister likes music and the other, sports, trying to choose which television program to watch may produce a conflict. Ask students to think of conflicts they have been aware of recently.

Writing/Prior Knowledge Ask students to describe their conception of what human life was like before people learned how to build a fire. Where did people live? What kind of food would they have had to rely on if they lacked good weapons? In what other ways was life more difficult? Then have the class complete the freewriting assignment.

Vocabulary Ask your **more advanced** students to write the opening paragraph of a story set at some earlier period in history using all of the vocabulary words. Have them set the scene as dramatically as they can.

GUIDE FOR READING

Prometheus the Fire-Bringer

Many ancient cultures have myths about gods or heroes who first taught humans to build fire or to plant crops. These stories show the importance that early people placed on this type of knowledge. It seemed so miraculous that it must have come from heaven! In Greek mythology **Prometheus** (prə mē′ thē əs) stole fire from the gods and taught humans to build fire.

Jeremy Ingalls (1911–   ) has included her version of the Prometheus myth in her *Book of Legends*.

Conflict in Myth

A **conflict** is a struggle between opposing sides or forces. In "Prometheus the Fire-Bringer," there is a conflict between Zeus, the king of the gods, and the race of humans he has created. The Titan Prometheus makes this struggle more equal by taking the side of the humans.

Look For

Like people, the Greek gods can show many different character traits. As you read this myth, look for the contrast between the personalities of Zeus and his adviser Prometheus. How does this contrast lead to a serious conflict? What is the effect of this conflict?

Writing

If fire can seem mysterious today, it must have seemed even more mysterious to humans of long ago. Imagine that you have been transported back to those times. You are sitting near a campfire at night, staring into the dancing yellow and red flames. Freewrite about this experience.

Vocabulary

Knowing the following words will help you as you read "Prometheus the Fire-Bringer."

councilor (koun′ sə lər) *n.*: Adviser (p. 563)
ominous (äm′ ə nəs) *adj.*: Threatening (p. 564)
hearth (härth) *n.*: Stone or brick floor of a fireplace (p. 566)

deftly (deft′ lē) *adv.*: Skillfully (p. 568)
kindling (kin′ dliŋ) *n.*: Bits of dry wood for starting a fire (p. 568)
gravely (grāv′ lē) *adv.*: With great seriousness (p. 568)

Objectives

1 To understand conflict in a myth
2 To evaluate the reasons for a conflict
3 To understand the adjective *promethean*
4 To predict the outcome of a conflict

Support Material

Teaching Portfolio
Teacher Backup, p. 899
Grammar in Action Worksheet, *Identifying Particles and Participial Phrases,* p. 903
Usage and Mechanics Worksheet, p. 905
Vocabulary Check, p. 906
Analyzing Literature Worksheet, *Understanding Conflict in Myths,* p. 907

Critical Thinking and Reading Worksheet, *Evaluating the Reasons for a Conflict,* p. 908
Selection Test, p. 909

Prometheus the Fire-Bringer

Jeremy Ingalls

Fire itself and the civilized life which fire makes possible—these were the gifts of Prometheus to the men of ancient times. Prometheus himself was not of the oldest race of men. He was not alive in the first age of mankind.

Ancient writers tell us there were three ages of men on earth before the fourth age in which we are now living. Each of the previous ages ended in terrible disasters which destroyed a large part of the human race. A raging fire ended the first age of the world. At the end of the second and of the third age, vast floods engulfed plains and mountains. According to the oldest poets these misfortunes were punishments the gods visited upon men for their wickedness and wrongdoing.

The story of Prometheus, remembered by the Greeks and set down in their books, tells of the days when Zeus[1] was king of the world and Prometheus was his chief councilor. From their ancestors they and their companions upon Mount Olympus had inherited the secrets of fire, of rain, of farming and metalworking. This knowledge gave them a power so great that they appeared as gods to the men who served them.

After the flood which destroyed many of the men of the second age, Zeus, with the help of Prometheus, had bred a new race of men in Arcadia.[2] But Zeus did not find life on earth so simple for men and gods as it had been in earlier times.

---

1. Zeus (zōōs)
2. Arcadia (är kā′ dē ə): A beautiful region of ancient Greece.

When Cronus,[3] the father of Zeus, had ruled the earth, summer had been the only season. Great land masses toward the north had barred all the icy winds. The age of Cronus was an age of contentment. No man had needed to work for food or clothes or a house to shelter him.

After the first flood, the land masses were broken. Winter winds blew upon countries which before had known only summer.

The race of gods did not suffer. They warmed their houses, having the secret of

---

3. Cronus (krō′ nəs)

Prometheus the Fire-Bringer   563

4 Discussion Why does Zeus dislike the human race and want to destroy it?

5 Reading Strategy How does Prometheus's response to Zeus suggest that he may do something to try to help the humans?

6 Critical Thinking and Reading How does the description of Prometheus's voice suggest the strength of his feelings?

fire. And the women of the race were weavers of cloth, so that the gods were clothed and defended from the north wind.

But winter was a harsh season for the men and women who did not live on the gods' mountain. Without defense from the cold, they huddled with the animals. They complained against the gods, whom they must serve for what little comfort they might find of food and warmth. They scarcely believed the stories which their ancestors had handed down to them of a time when men had lived in endless summer weather, when men were friends and favorites of the gods.

Men became rebels and grumblers. For this reason Zeus, seeing winter coming on again, determined to destroy the people of Arcadia. Then Prometheus, his chief councilor, sought to save this third race of man from destruction.

"They quarrel among themselves," said Zeus angrily. "They start trouble in the fields. We must train up a new race of men who will learn more quickly what it means to serve the gods."

Zeus was walking across the bronze floor of his mountain palace. A tremendous, tall figure of a man he was, the king-god Zeus. But he who stood beside him, Prometheus of the family of Titans,[4] was even taller.

"Worthless," Zeus was saying as if to himself. "Worthless," he repeated again, "the whole race. They complain of the winters. They are too weak a race for the climate of these times. Why should we continue to struggle with them? Better to be rid of them, every man and woman of the troublesome tribe."

"And then?" inquired Prometheus. "What if you create a new race to provide manpower for the farms and the bigger buildings? That race, too, will rebel while they can see and envy our knowledge and our power."

"Even so, I will destroy these Arcadians," insisted Zeus stubbornly. "Men are our creatures. Let them learn to serve us, to do our will."

"Up here on your mountain," observed Prometheus thoughtfully, "you make men and destroy them. But what about the men themselves? How can they learn wisdom when, time after time, you visit them with destruction?"

"You have too much sympathy for them," answered Zeus in a sharp voice. "I believe you love these huddling, sheepish men."

"They have minds and hearts," replied Prometheus warmly, "and a courage that is worth admiring. They wish to live even as the gods wish to live. Don't we feed ourselves on nectar and ambrosia[5] every day to preserve our lives?"

Prometheus was speaking rapidly. His voice was deep. "This is your way," he went on. "You won't look ahead. You won't be patient. You won't give men a chance to learn how to live. Over and over again, with floods or with cracking red thunderbolts, you destroy them."

"I have let you live, Prometheus," said Zeus in an ominous tone, "to advise me when you can. You are my cousin. But I am not your child to be scolded." Zeus was smiling, but there was thunder behind the smile.

Silently Prometheus turned away. Leaving the marble-columned hall, he went out among the gardens of Olympus, the gods' mountain. The last roses were fading before the time of winter winds and rain.

This was not the first time Prometheus

---

4. Titans (tīt' 'nz): Giant gods who were defeated by the Olympian gods.

5. nectar (nek' tər) **and ambrosia** (am brō' zhə): The drink and food of the gods; by feeding on these substances, the gods were able to live forever.

had heard thunder in the voice of Zeus. Prometheus knew that someday Zeus would turn against him, betray him, and punish him. Prometheus the Titan had the gift of reading the future. He could foresee the fate hidden and waiting for him and for others and even for Zeus himself.

Climbing among the upper gardens, Prometheus stopped at last beside an ancient, twisted ash tree. Leaning against its trunk, he looked toward the south. Beyond the last canal, the last steep sea wall, he could see the ocean. He looked far out toward that last shining circle of water. Then, with his head bent, he sat down on the tree roots bulging in thick knots above the ground.

It would be hard to tell you all the thoughts in the mind of the Titan— thoughts that coiled and twined like a nest of dragons. In his mighty brain were long memories of the past and far-reaching prophecies of what was to come.

He thought most often of the future, but the talk with Zeus just now had brought the past before him once again. He remembered once more the terrible war in which Zeus had seized the kingship of the gods. He thought of the exile and imprisonment of Cronus, the father of Zeus. He remembered the Titans, his people, now chained in the black pit of Tartarus.[6]

The great god Cronus himself, who had given peace to gods and men, where was he now? And the mighty-headed Titans, the magnificent engineers, builders of bridges and temples, where were they? All of them fallen, helpless, as good as dead.

Zeus had triumphed. Of the Titans, only two now walked the upper earth—he, Prometheus, and Epimetheus,[7] his brother.

---

6. **Tartarus** (tär′ tər əs): A dark pit beneath Hades (hā′ dēz), the home of the dead, which itself was under the earth.

7. **Epimetheus** (ə′ pi mē′ thē əs)

And now, even now, Zeus was not content. It was not enough for his glory, it seemed, to have dethroned his own father, not enough to have driven the race of Titans from the houses of the gods. Now Zeus was plotting to kill the race of men.

Prometheus had endured the war against the Titans, his own people. He had even given help to Zeus. Having seen what was to come, he had thought, "Since Zeus must win, I'll guide him. I'll control his fierce anger and his greed for power."

But Prometheus could not submit to this latest plot of Zeus. He would use all his wits to save the men of Arcadia from destruction.

Why were they to be destroyed? Because they were cold and full of fears, huddled together in caves like animals. It was well enough in the warm months. They worked willingly in the fields of the gods and reared the horses and bulls and guarded the sheep. But when the cold days came, they grumbled against Olympus. They grumbled because they must eat and hunt like the animals and had no hoof nor claw nor heavy fur for protection.

What did they need? What protection would be better than hoof or claw? Prometheus knew. It was fire they needed—fire to cook with, to warm them, to harden metal for weapons. With fire they could frighten the wolf and the bear and the mountain lion.

Why did they lack the gift of fire? Prometheus knew that too. He knew how jealously the gods sat guard about their flame.

More than once he had told Zeus the need men had of fire. He knew why Zeus would not consent to teach men this secret of the gods. The gift of fire to men would be a gift of power. Hardened in the fire, the spears which men might make to chase the mountain lion might also, in time, be hurled against the gods. With fire would come comfort and time to think while the

7 **Literary Focus** How does this suggest that there have been previous conflicts between Zeus and Prometheus?

8 **Discussion** What is Prometheus's motive in cooperating with Zeus, his former opponent?

Prometheus the Fire-Bringer 565

9 flames leaped up the walls of hidden caves. Men who had time to think would have time to question the laws of the gods. Among men who asked questions disorder might breed, and rebellion stronger than any mere squabble in the fields.

"But men are worth the gift of fire," thought Prometheus, sitting against the roots of his favorite ash tree. He could see ahead dimly into that time to come when gods would lose their power. And he, Prometheus, through his love for men, must help to bring on that time.

Prometheus did not hesitate. By the fall of night his plans were accomplished. As the sun went down, his tall figure appeared upon a sea beach. Above the sands a hundred caves, long ago deserted by the waters of the ocean, sheltered families of Arcadians. To them the Titan was bringing this very night the secret of the gods.

He came along the pebble line of high water. In his hand he carried a yellow reed.

This curious yellow stalk was made of metal, the most precious of the metals of the gods. From it the metalworkers molded rare and delicate shapes. From it they made the reedlike and hollow stalks which carried in wisps of fennel[8] straw, coals from the gods' ever-burning fire. The gods who knew the sources of flame never built new fires in the sight of men. Going abroad on journeys, they took from their central hearth a smoldering coal.

Prometheus had left Olympus as one upon a journey. He alone knew he was not going to visit the home of Poseidon,[9] Zeus's brother, lord of the sea—nor going into India nor into the cold north. He was going only as far as the nearest sea beach.

---

8. **fennel** (fen' 'l): A tall herb.
9. **Poseidon** (pō sī' d'n)

He knew that, though he was going only to the sea beach, he was in truth starting upon a journey. He knew the hatred of Zeus would follow him. He knew that now he, Prometheus, could never return to the house of the gods. From this night he must live his life among the men he wished to save.

While the stars came out, bright as they are on nights when winter will soon come on, Prometheus gathered together a heap of driftwood. Opening the metal stalk, he set the flame of the gods in the waiting fuel.

Eating into the wood, the fire leaped up, fanned in the night breeze. Prometheus sat down beside the fire he had made. He was not long alone.

Shadowy figures appeared at the mouths of caves. One by one, men, women, and children crept toward the blaze. The night was cold. North winds had blown that day. The winds had blown on the lands of men, even as they had blown on the head of Zeus in his palace above them. Now in the night they came, the people of men, to the warmth of the beckoning fire.

Hundreds there were of them now. Those nearest the tall fire-bringer, the Titan, were talking with him. They knew him well. It was not the first time Prometheus had come to talk with them. But never before had he come late, alone, and lighted a fire against the dark.

It was not the first time men had seen a fire or felt its warmth. More than once a god, walking the earth, had set a fire, lit from the coals he carried secretly. Men reverenced the slender magic wands with which, it seemed, the gods could call up flame. But never before had they stood so near a fire nor seen the firewand.

Now men might hold in their own hands the mysterious yellow rod. They said "Look" and "See" and, fingering the metal, "How

Grammar in Action

A **participle** is a form of a verb that is used as an adjective. For example, the word *sizzling* in the sentence "The sizzling hamburger fell from the grill" is a participle. A **participial phrase** is a phrase made up of a participle and its modifiers and complements. If you change the above sentence to read "Sizzling from the heat of the coals, the hamburger fell from the grill," then *sizzling* becomes a part of a participial phrase. The participle *sizzling* and the participial phrase *sizzling from the heat of the coals* modify the noun, hamburger.

Notice how Jeremy Ingalls uses participial phrases in the following sentence.

Eating into the wood, the fire leaped up, *fanned in the night breeze.*

Ingalls uses both present and past participles in this sentence. You can recognize the difference by their endings. All present participles, such as the example *eating,* end in *-ing.* Most past participles, like the example *fanned,* end in *-d,* or *-ed.* Using both types of participles show the fire in an active and passive role. The fire is actively doing something as well as having something done to it.

wonderfully the gods can mold what is hard in the hands."

For a while Prometheus let them talk. He watched with pleasure the gleam of firelight in their shining eyes. Then quietly he took the metal stalk from the man who held it. With a swift gesture he threw it into the heap of burning wood.

The people groaned. The fire-wrought metal crumpled against the heat. The metal which carried well a single coal melted in the blazing fire.

10

The people murmured among themselves, "Hasn't he taken away the secret now? Hasn't he destroyed before our eyes the source of fire?"

Patiently, silently they waited. A few asked questions but got no answers. The cold wind cut them as the last of the burning driftwood grayed and blackened in the sand.

10 **Critical Thinking and Reading**
What misunderstanding makes the people despair when Prometheus throws the metal stalk into the fire?

Student Activity 1. Find three examples where Ingalls uses participial phrases. Identify the word each phrase modifies and tell whether the participle is in the present or past tense.

Student Activity 2. Write a sentence for three of the participial phrases that follow.
1. climbing up the mountain
2. crowded into the dirty railroad car
3. tossed by the wind
4. shouting to her friend across the street

While the embers crumbled away, Prometheus rose, calling with him a few of the
men who had asked him questions. Watching, they saw him scrape a hollow pit. Wondering, they followed his every movement,
his hands holding a bronze knife, shaving
chips of wood, taking from the fold of his
cloak handfuls of bark and straw.

Next he set in his pit a chunk of ashwood, flat and firm, notched cleanly on one
side. Beneath and around this notch he laid
in bark and straw. Into the notch he set a
pointed branch, slender, hard-tipped, and
firm. Then slowly he swung the branch in
his palms, twirled it in a steady rhythm, boring, drilling more and more rapidly with his
skilled and powerful hands.

The wood grew warm. The dust ground
from the ash block heated to smoldering.
The straw caught. Light sputtered from the
pit. Small sparks glowed, flew up, went out.
Tugged by the night wind, smoke curled
from the dry straw, from the bark, from the
wood shavings fed gently from the heap Prometheus had made ready to his hand. At
last, more suddenly than the eye could follow, out of the pit in the sand rose the living
flame.

Deftly Prometheus removed the ash
block, added heavier kindling. Last of all, the
driftwood yielded to the strengthening fire.
He knelt beside it a while, breathing upon it,
guarding, urging the blaze. At last he rose,
stood back, folded his arms. As if considering a thought, half sorrow, half pleasure, he
looked up at the glare of fire invading the
night sky.

Whispers and murmuring first, then
cries, then shouting. Men ran to scoop new
hollows in the sand. They begged Prometheus' knife. The children, running from the
beach to the caves and fields, hurried back
with fists crammed full of straw and withered leaves.

The people of the caves were breathless
with excitement. Here was no secret. The
fire-wand did not breed the fire as they had
thought. No nameless power of the gods bred
the flame.

The hard, pale ashwood passed from
hand to hand as men struggled to light their
own fires. They despaired at first. New
sparks flew up and died. Or the hands were
weak, too weak to drill the flame. But at last
came triumph. A dozen fires sprang up.
Women and children ran with laden arms to
feed each growing blaze.

The gods, from their distant houses, saw
the glow. There to the south it shone, fighting against the starlight, the glare in the
sky. Was it the end of the world? Would the
terrible fire consume the earth again?

Hermes,[10] the messenger, came at last
with an answer to all their questions.

"Great Zeus," said Hermes gravely in the
assembly of the gods, "Prometheus, your
cousin, stands in the midst of those rising
fires. He took coals from the central hearth
as for a journey."

"So?" asked Zeus, nodding his head.
Then, as if he were holding an argument
with himself, he continued, saying, "But
then? What then? The fire will die. It is not
a crime for a god or for a Titan to light a fire
for himself on a cold evening."

11

"But that fire will not die," interrupted
Hermes. "That fire is not the fire of gods and
Titans. Prometheus has taught men the
source of fire. Those fires are their own, the
fires of men. They've drilled flame out of hard
wood with their own hands."

Then the gods knew the end of the world
was not yet come upon them. But they knew,
and Zeus most of all, that it might be their
own great power that was burning away in
the fires of men.

12

---

10. Hermes (hʉr′ mēz).

Closure and Extension

**ANSWERS TO THINKING
ABOUT THE SELECTION**
Recalling

1. The age of Cronus was a period
   of contentment, when summer
   was the only season. According
   to the myth, there have been four
   ages of human beings.
2. Humans are unhappy because
   they have no protection against
   the winters. They show their un-

THINKING ABOUT THE SELECTION

Recalling

1. What was the earth like during the age of Cronus, the father of Zeus? How many ages of human beings has there been?
2. Why are humans unhappy under the rule of Zeus? How do they show their unhappiness?
3. How does Zeus want to solve the problem?
4. What does Prometheus say about this plan?
5. How will the gift of fire help humans?

Interpreting

6. In Greek, Prometheus means "forethought," or the ability to plan. Why is this a fitting name for the Titan?
7. Why does Prometheus feel "half sorrow, half pleasure" after building a fire for humans?
8. How will the gift of fire mark a change in the relationship between humans and gods?

Applying

9. Imagine that someone from a more advanced civilization could visit earth. We already know how to use fire, but what other important gift could this being bring to us?

ANALYZING LITERATURE

Understanding Conflict in Myth

A **conflict** is a struggle between opposing sides or forces. In this myth Prometheus opposes the plans of Zeus, who wants to destroy the human race.

1. Why is there a conflict between Zeus and human beings?
2. How is the conflict between Prometheus and Zeus resolved in this myth?
3. Do you think this resolution is final, or will the conflict continue? Explain.

CRITICAL THINKING AND READING

Evaluating the Reasons for a Conflict

Conflicts between gods seem more awesome than struggles between humans. However, gods oppose each other for many of the same reasons that humans do. Whether on Mount Olympus or earth, conflicts can result from differences in personality and background.

1. Compare and contrast the personalities of Zeus and Prometheus.
2. How might the fact that Prometheus is a Titan and not an Olympian god influence his attitude toward Zeus?
3. Show how their disagreement about humans arises from differences in their personalities and backgrounds.
4. Why do you think Prometheus disobeys Zeus?

UNDERSTANDING LANGUAGE

Interpreting the Adjective *Promethean*

As a result of this myth, the adjective *Promethean* has become part of our language. The general meaning of this word is "about or like Prometheus."

1. Recall what you know about Prometheus's personality and actions. Based on this knowledge, what kind of person or deed would you call Promethean?
2. Look up the word in a dictionary to see whether the definition you have arrived at is correct.

THINKING AND WRITING

Predicting the Outcome of a Conflict

Imagine that you have written a successful screenplay based on this version of the Prometheus myth. So many people have seen your movie that the producer wants to make a sequel called "Prometheus II." Briefly outline some of the events that would occur where this story leaves off. Would Zeus punish Prometheus? If so, what kind of punishment would he devise? How would the conflict be resolved? Use your outline to write a letter to the producer describing the plot of the new movie. As you revise this letter, make sure that moviegoers will be satisfied by the way you have resolved the conflict.

(Answers begin on p. 568.)

ANSWERS TO ANALYZING LITERATURE

1. The human beings resent the fact that their only warmth and comfort comes from the gods.
2. The conflict between Prometheus and Zeus is resolved when Prometheus takes action on the humans' behalf.
3. The end of the myth suggests that the conflict will continue, because Zeus understands that the actions of Prometheus have changed the balance of power between humans and the gods.

ANSWERS TO CRITICAL THINKING AND READING

1. Zeus is impulsive and quick to anger, while Prometheus is thoughtful and sympathetic toward others.
2. As a remnant of the conquered race of Titans, Prometheus probably feels hostility toward Zeus.
3. Zeus is one of the Olympian gods who have triumphed over the Titans, and therefore he believes that force is the proper way to settle a conflict. As part of a conquered race, Prometheus can sympathize with the woeful state of mankind.
4. Prometheus disobeys Zeus in order to prevent his pointless destruction of the human race.

ANSWERS TO UNDERSTANDING LANGUAGE

1. Suggested Response: Based on the myth, a reader might think *Promethean* would mean able to see into the future.
2. Actually the word means "boldly creative or original."

THINKING AND WRITING

Publishing Student Writing

Have students volunteer to read their letters aloud. Class members can decide which plot idea they like best.

happiness by complaining about the gods.

3. Zeus wants to destroy the human race.
4. Prometheus says it is pointless to destroy the human race because any new race will act the same way.
5. The gift of fire will help humans stay warm, cook, and make weapons for hunting.

Interpreting

6. His name is fitting because Prometheus can see future events.
7. Prometheus feels pleasure because he knows the good fire will do for man, but he feels sorrow because he also knows it will produce a further conflict with Zeus.
8. The gift of fire gives human beings a power only the gods had had before. It will enable a new race of more civilized humans to develop.

Applying

9. Answers will differ. Suggested Response: A more advanced civilization that came to earth now could bring such practical gifts as a cure for disease or a way of alleviating physical pain. It might also bring an even more powerful gift, such as a way of fostering human understanding to prevent war and other violence among people.

Focus

More About the Myth According to another Greek myth, Apollo once killed a dragon at Delphi. That site became one of the most visited places in the ancient world. People came there from all over the Mediterranean because the woman priest at Delphi, called the oracle, was believed to foretell the future. Discuss with the class the power someone would have if others believed that they could predict the future.

Literary Focus Hubris is a common human weakness and a common literary theme. Explain to the class that Phaëthon has a long line of literary counterparts, from the builders of the Tower of Babel in the *Bible* to Ahab in *Moby Dick*. Point out that the danger of hubris is that it lures people into acting beyond their capacities.

Look For You might explain that what distinguishes hubris from an appropriate pleasure in one's abilities and achievements is that hubris is excessive. Ask students to look for the point at which Phaëthon's confidence in his ability becomes excessive.

Writing/Prior Knowledge It is often hard to imagine how dangerous or difficult a new experience will be. Ask students to describe an experience of theirs that was much harder than they had expected. Then have them complete the freewriting assignment.

Vocabulary Have students use each word in a sentence to show that they understand its meaning.

Phaëthon, Son of Apollo

Apollo (ə päl′ ō) was the son of Zeus and Leto. He is portrayed in Greek art as a handsome and athletic young man. He was known as the god of poetry and music, and he was often shown carrying the ancient stringed instrument called a lyre. He was also associated with the life-giving power of the sun, as you will see in this myth.

    Olivia E. Coolidge (1908–   ), the modern teller of this myth, has written many books for young people about history and ancient legends.

Character in Myth: Hubris

Hubris is a Greek word meaning excessive pride or arrogance. The ancient Greeks believed very strongly in the separation between mortal humans and immortal gods. A human being who boasted of god-like powers was guilty of hubris and would almost certainly be punished. In "Phaëthon, Son of Apollo," you will see what happens to a young man who reaches too high.

Look For

Phaëthon (fā′ ə thən) displays his hubris in many ways. Look for evidence of his excessive pride in both his words and deeds. Also, look for clues that hint at the outcome.

Writing

At the end of this myth, Phaëthon is taken on a wild ride as he tries to steer the chariot of the sun. Recall the most dangerous carnival ride that you have ever been on or seen and freewrite about it.

Vocabulary

Knowing the following words will help you as you read "Phaëthon, Son of Apollo."

mortal (môr′ t'l) *n.*: A being who must eventually die (p. 571)
rash (rash) *adj.*: Reckless (p. 571)
deference (def′ ər əns) *n.*: Respect (p. 571)
implored (im plôrd′) *v.*: Begged (p. 571)
dissuade (di swād′) *v.*: Advise someone against an action (p. 572)

anointed (ə noint′ əd) *v.*: Rubbed oil or ointment on (p. 572)
precipitous (pri sip′ ə təs) *adj.*: Very steep (p. 573)
amber (am′ bər) *n.*: A yellowish or brownish substance that comes from certain trees (p. 574)

Objectives

1 To understand a myth involving hubris
2 To recognize clues to the outcome of a myth
3 To understand the history of the words *Olympian* and *Olympic games*
4 To create a modern myth

Support Material

Teaching Portfolio
Teacher Backup, p. 911
Grammar in Action Worksheet, *Finding Compound Adjectives,* p. 915
Usage and Mechanics Worksheet, p. 917
Vocabulary Check, p. 918
Analyzing Literature Worksheet, *Understanding Hubris,* p. 920
Critical Thinking and Reading

Worksheet, *Recognizing Clues to the Outcome of a Myth,* p. 921
Selection Test, p. 922

Phaëthon, Son of Apollo

Olivia E. Coolidge

Though Apollo always honored the memory of Daphne she was not his only love. Another was a mortal, Clymene,[1] by whom he had a son named Phaëthon. Phaëthon grew up with his mother, who, since she was mortal, could not dwell in the halls of Olympus[2] or in the palace of the sun. She lived not far from the East in the land of Ethiopia, and as her son grew up, she would point to the place where Eos,[3] goddess of the dawn, lighted up the sky and tell him that there his father dwelt. Phaëthon loved to boast of his divine father as he saw the golden chariot riding high through the air. He would remind his comrades of other sons of gods and mortal women who, by virtue of their great deeds, had themselves become gods at last. He must always be first in everything, and in most things this was easy, since he was in truth stronger, swifter, and more daring than the others. Even if he were not victorious, Phaëthon always claimed to be first in honor. He could never bear to be beaten, even if he must risk his life in some rash way to win.

Most of the princes of Ethiopia willingly paid Phaëthon honor, since they admired him greatly for his fire and beauty. There was one boy, however, Epaphos,[4] who was rumored to be a child of Zeus himself. Since this was not certainly proved, Phaëthon chose to disbelieve it and to demand from Epaphos the deference that he obtained from all others. Epaphos was proud too, and one day he lost his temper with Phaëthon and turned on him, saying, "You are a fool to believe all that your mother tells you. You are all swelled up with false ideas about your father."

Crimson with rage, the lad rushed home to his mother and demanded that she prove to him the truth of the story that she had often told. "Give me some proof," he implored her, "with which I can answer this insult of Epaphos. It is a matter of life and death to me, for if I cannot, I shall die of shame."

"I swear to you," replied his mother solemnly, "by the bright orb of the sun itself that you are his son. If I swear falsely, may I never look on the sun again, but die before the next time he mounts the heavens. More than this I cannot do, but you, my child, can go to the eastern palace of Phoebus[5] Apollo— it lies not far away—and there speak with the god himself."

The son of Clymene leaped up with joy at his mother's words. The palace of Apollo was indeed not far. It stood just below the eastern horizon, its tall pillars glistening with bronze and gold. Above these it was white with gleaming ivory, and the great doors were flashing silver, embossed with pictures of earth, sky, and sea, and the gods that

---

1. **Clymene** (klim′ ə nē)
2. **Olympus** (ō lim′ pas): A mountain in Northern Greece that was known as the home of the gods.
3. **Eos** (ē äs)
4. **Epaphos** (ep′ ə fəs)

---

5. **Phoebus** (fē′ bəs): Means "bright one" in Greek.

Phaëthon, Son of Apollo 571

4 Discussion What pleases Apollo about Phaëthon?

5 Discussion What warning does Apollo give Phaëthon that would have discouraged a more sensible person from trying to drive the chariot?

6 Clarification The "Hours" were the three goddesses of the seasons, associated with growth and decay.

7 Discussion Point out that Phaëthon thought strength was all he needed to drive the chariot. However, his inability to do so results not only from insufficient strength but also from another lack. What else does Phaëthon lack that causes his problem?

dwelt therein. Up the steep hill and the bright steps climbed Phaëthon, passing unafraid through the silver doors, and stood in the presence of the sun. Here at last he was forced to turn away his face, for Phoebus sat in state on his golden throne. It gleamed with emeralds and precious stones, while on the head of the god was a brilliant diamond crown upon which no eye could look undazzled.

Phaëthon hid his face, but the god had recognized his son, and he spoke kindly, asking him why he had come. Then Phaëthon plucked up courage and said, "I come to ask you if you are indeed my father. If you are so, I beg you to give me some proof of it so that all may recognize me as Phoebus' son."

4 The god smiled, being well pleased with his son's beauty and daring. He took off his crown so that Phaëthon could look at him, and coming down from his throne, he put his arms around the boy, and said, "You are indeed my son and Clymene's, and worthy to be called so. Ask of me whatever thing you wish to prove your origin to men, and you shall have it."

Phaëthon swayed for a moment and was dizzy with excitement at the touch of the god. His heart leaped; the blood rushed into his face. Now he felt that he was truly divine, unlike other men, and he did not wish to be counted with men any more. He looked up for a moment at his radiant father. "Let me drive the chariot of the sun across the heavens for one day," he said.

5 Apollo frowned and shook his head. "I cannot break my promise, but I will dissuade you if I can," he answered. "How can you drive my chariot, whose horses need a strong hand on the reins? The climb is too steep for you. The immense height will make you dizzy. The swift streams of air in the upper heaven will sweep you off your course. Even the immortal gods could not drive my chariot. How then can you? Be wise and make some other choice."

The pride of Phaëthon was stubborn, for he thought the god was merely trying to frighten him. Besides, if he could guide the sun's chariot, would he not have proved his right to be divine rather than mortal? For that he would risk his life. Indeed, once he had seen Apollo's splendor, he did not wish to go back and live among men. Therefore, he insisted on his right until Apollo had to give way.

6 When the father saw that nothing else would satisfy the boy, he bade the Hours bring forth his chariot and yoke the horses. The chariot was of gold and had two gold-rimmed wheels with spokes of silver. In it there was room for one man to stand and hold the reins. Around the front and sides of it ran a rail, but the back was open. At the end of a long pole there were yokes for the four horses. The pole was of gold and shone with precious jewels: the golden topaz, the bright diamond, the green emerald, and the flashing ruby. While the Hours were yoking the swift, pawing horses, rosy-fingered Dawn hastened to the gates of heaven to draw them open. Meanwhile Apollo anointed his son's face with a magic ointment, that he might be able to bear the heat of the fire-breathing horses and the golden chariot. At last Phaëthon mounted the chariot and grasped the reins, the barriers were let down, and the horses shot up into the air.

7 At first the fiery horses sped forward up the accustomed trail, but behind them the chariot was too light without the weight of the immortal god. It bounded from side to side and was dashed up and down. Phaëthon was too frightened and too dizzy to pull the reins, nor would he have known anyway whether he was on the usual path. As soon

Grammar in Action

The world of mythology is a world in which the impossible often happens. Consequently, writers of myths must make their readers picture vivid experiences in rich detail. To do so, writers such as Olivia E. Coolidge use rich, vivid adjectives, some of which are actually combinations of two or more words. These **compound adjectives** often convey more than one physical characteristic:

> . . . *rosy-fingered* Dawn hastened to the gates of heaven to draw them open. [conveys both color and personification]

> . . . he might be able to bear the heat of the *fire-breathing* horses and the golden chariot. [conveys both action and image]

> . . . dried fishes were left baking upon the *white-hot* sands. [conveys both color and temperature]

The hyphen in these adjectives shows that the two words function together as one part of speech.

Student Activity 1. Use each of the following compound adjectives in a sentence that might appear in a myth. What characteristics are reflected in each?

much-needed
teeth-gnashing

golden-haired
sword-carrying

as the horses felt that there was no hand controlling them, they soared up, up with fiery speed into the heavens till the earth grew pale and cold beneath them. Phaëthon shut his eyes, trembling at the dizzy, precipitous height. Then the horses dropped down, more swiftly than a falling stone, flinging themselves madly from side to side in panic because they were masterless. Phaëthon dropped the reins entirely and clung with all his might to the chariot rail. Meanwhile as they came near the earth, it dried up and cracked apart. Meadows were reduced to white ashes, cornfields smoked and

THE FALL OF PHAËTHON
Peter Paul Rubens

Phaëthon, Son of Apollo 573

Humanities Note

Fine art, *The Fall of Phaëthon,* by Peter Paul Rubens. Rubens (1577–1640) is considered the greatest Flemish painter of the 1600's. Along with being an accomplished artist, Rubens was a scholar and a respected diplomat.

Rubens studied painting first in Antwerp and then in Italy. He returned to Antwerp and became the court painter to the Brussels court of Archduke Albert. After the death of his first wife, Rubens accepted diplomatic assignments which took him to Spain and England, where he was eventually knighted by King Charles I. He gradually withdrew from political life after his second marriage.

Rubens did many portraits of noblemen as well as paintings for churches during his life. Later, he painted many landscape scenes. His paintings are noted for their intensity of emotion, wide range of color, and large scale. His style was influenced by ancient Roman sculpture and the paintings and sculptures of Italian Renaissance artists such as those of Michelangelo.

1. How do the positions of the horses and of Phaëthon indicate motion and falling?
2. How does the artist convey intense emotion in the painting?

icy-cold
thousand-year-old

mud-caked
forest-like

Student Activity 2. Create three more compound adjectives and use them in sentences about possible mythological events.

574

8 Discussion The description of the destruction caused by the chariot suggests the damage a falling meteor might produce. Ask the class whether they think the myth might have been devised to explain such an occurrence.

9 Discussion Why does Zeus take action against Phaëthon?

10 Discussion What happens to Clymene and her daughters at the end of the myth?

Reader's Response Do you feel sorry for Phaëthon? Why or why not?

8 shriveled, cities perished in flame. Far and wide on the wooded mountains the forests were ablaze, and even the snowclad Alps were bare and dry. Rivers steamed and dried to dust. The great North African plain was scorched until it became the desert that it is today. Even the sea shrank back to pools and caves, until dried fishes were left baking upon the white-hot sands. At last the great earth mother called upon Zeus to save her from utter destruction, and Zeus hurled **9** a mighty thunderbolt at the unhappy Phaëthon, who was still crouched in the chariot, clinging desperately to the rail. The dart cast

him out, and he fell flaming in a long trail through the air. The chariot broke in pieces at the mighty blow, and the maddened horses rushed snorting back to the stable of their master, Apollo.

Unhappy Clymene and her daughters wandered over the whole earth seeking the body of the boy they loved so well. When they found him, they took him and buried him. Over his grave they wept and could not be comforted. At last the gods in pity for their grief changed them into poplar trees, which weep with tears of amber in memory of Phaëthon. **10**

THINKING ABOUT THE SELECTION

Recalling

1. Why does Phaëthon go to Apollo's palace?
2. Why does Apollo urge Phaëthon to make a wish different from his first one?
3. What is Phaëthon's secret reason for his request?
4. What is the result of this request?
5. What natural features are explained in this myth?

Interpreting

6. Why do you think Phaëthon feels that he had to "always be first in everything"?
7. How does Phaëthon display his pride with his

classmates? How does he display it with Apollo?
8. How might this story have been different if Phaëthon had resembled his father less?

Applying

9. Given Phaëthon's choice, tell what you would have requested from Apollo. Explain the reasons for your decision.

ANALYZING LITERATURE

Understanding Hubris

Hubris means excessive pride or arrogance. In this myth, Phaëthon shows hubris by wanting

Closure and Extension
ANSWERS TO THINKING ABOUT THE SELECTION
Recalling

1. Phaëthon wants proof that Apollo is his father.
2. Apollo knows that Phaëthon will be unable to control the chariot.
3. He hopes to prove that he is not mortal, but divine.
4. The chariot ravages the earth as it passes over it, and Phaëthon is killed by a thunderbolt from Zeus.

to become an immortal. However, his attempt to assume his father's godlike powers threatens the earth and causes his own death.

1. Why do you think Phaëthon could not stand to be an ordinary human being?
2. Was Phaëthon's hubris his own fault or was it the result of the fact that he *was* the son of a god? Explain.
3. Was the punishment that Phaëthon received too harsh? Why or why not?
4. What lesson does this myth suggest?

CRITICAL THINKING AND READING
Recognizing Clues to the Outcome

Throughout this myth there are clues that Phaëthon's behavior may lead to disaster. You can find these hints by looking for remarks he makes or feelings he experiences that seem exaggerated or too intense. These indicate how desperate he is to prove that he is immortal.

1. Find two examples where Phaëthon feels that he would risk his life to get his way.
2. Why is his reaction to Apollo's embrace a clue to the coming disaster?

UNDERSTANDING LANGUAGE
Understanding Word Histories

Olympus is the highest mountain in Greece. The ancient Greeks imagined that the gods lived on top of this mountain in a great palace surrounded by swirling clouds. As you learn in this myth, mortals "could not dwell in the halls of Olympus." The word *Olympian* has come to be used as an adjective meaning "majestic" or "celestial."

1. Aside from Mount Olympus and the Greek gods themselves, what kind of place or person would you describe with the adjective *Olympian*?
2. What were the Olympic games in ancient Greece?
3. What are they today?

THINKING AND WRITING
Creating a Modern Myth

You and your literary agent have decided that the story of Phaëthon would make a wonderful best-selling novel. However, readers will not buy your book unless the story is up to date. Brainstorm to gather ideas for putting this myth into a modern setting. Phaëthon's father, for instance, cannot be a god, but he could be the president of a billion-dollar company. In this modern setting, perhaps Phaëthon wants to fly his father's corporate jet. Present your best ideas in a letter to your agent explaining the modern situation and setting for your novel. Then revise the letter to make sure your agent will be convinced that the book will sell.

Phaëthon, Son of Apollo 575

5. The myth explains the lack of forests on the Alps and the deserts of North Africa as having been caused by the chariot's passing close to them.

Interpreting
6. He hopes to prove his right to become a god.
7. He demands that his classmates defer to him. With Apollo, he acts proud in insisting on driving the chariot.
8. Perhaps Apollo would not have made such a rash promise to him if Phaëthon's appearance had not impressed him so.

Applying
9. Answers will differ. Suggested Response: It would have been better for Phaëthon to ask for some proof of his divine origin that did not involve him in such great risks. In that way, Phaëthon could have lived to enjoy his position as the son of a god.

ANSWERS TO ANALYZING LITERATURE

1. Phaëthon felt superior to other people.
2. Phaëthon's hubris may have been caused by his being the son of a god. Apollo initially seems pleased with his son's daring, suggesting that this is a godlike quality.
3. Suggested Response: Phaëthon's punishment seems too harsh because it gives him no chance to learn from his mistake.

(Answers begin on p. 574.)

4. The myth suggests that hubris is wrong and can be dangerous.

Challenge Ask students to describe a situation from current events, sports, or entertainment where someone's excessive pride caused problems. How was that situation like or unlike Phaëthon's?

ANSWERS TO CRITICAL THINKING AND READING
1. The opening paragraph states that Phaëthon would sometimes risk his life rather than be beaten in any contest. When Phaëthon confronts his mother, he says he will die of shame if he cannot prove his divine origin. When he has the chance to drive Apollo's chariot, Phaëthon is again willing to risk his life.
2. He feels that he is divine and no longer wants to live among men. This suggests that he may do something rash.

ANSWERS TO UNDERSTANDING LANGUAGE
1. The adjective *Olympian* can also be used to describe people or attitudes that seem lofty or distant from ordinary human life.
2. The ancient Olympic games were a Greek religious festival.
3. Today they are an international athletic competition.

Writing Across the Curriculum Have students research the reestablishment of the Olympic games in modern times. You might want to tell the social studies teacher about this assignment. Social studies teachers might give students guidance and credit.

575

Baucis and Philemon

Because myths have been retold so often, they exist in many different versions. One of the best known collections of myths is the *Metamorphoses,* by the Roman poet **Ovid** (äv′ id) (43 B.C.–A.D. 17). This long poem, whose title means "changes," contains many accounts of supernatural magical changes caused by the gods.

Edith Hamilton (1867–1963) used Ovid's poem as a source for her version of "Baucis and Philemon." She was famous for her books on ancient Greece and Rome.

**Myths:
Lessons
in Living**

Myths served many purposes. Although they tended to concentrate on explaining the origins of natural phenomena, often they also taught lessons. While stories about the gods and heroes explained such matters as how a certain flower or tree came to exist or how the sun traveled across the sky each day, myths also taught people how to live their lives. In "Baucis and Philemon," for instance, a devoted couple who treat guests kindly are rewarded by the gods for their behavior.

Look For

Look for the many ways in which Baucis (bô′ sis) and Philemon (fi lē′ mən) make their guests feel welcome. How do the gods show their appreciation?

Writing

Through the myths of a people, we learn what they value. The ancient Greeks and Romans valued hospitality. Recall an enjoyable visit you made to the home of a friend or relative. Tell how your host made you feel at ease.

Vocabulary

Knowing the following words will help you as you read "Baucis and Philemon."

immeasurable (i mezh′ ər ə b′l) *adj.*: So great it cannot be measured (p. 577)

pious (pī′ əs) *adj.*: Good; virtuous (p. 577)

shrewdest (shrōōd′ əst) *adj.*: Cleverest (p. 577)

insolently (in′ sə lənt lē) *adv.*: Rudely; disrespectfully (p. 577)

snug (snug) *adj.*: Cozy; comfortable (p. 577)

bustled (bus′′ ld) *v.*: Hurried (p. 577)

quavering (kwā′ vər iŋ) *adj.*: Shaking (p. 578)

despises (di spīz′ əz) *v.*: Looks down on with scorn (p. 578)

576   *Fables, Myths, and Legends*

Baucis and Philemon

Edith Hamilton

In the Phrygian[1] hill-country there were once two trees which all the peasants near and far pointed out as a great marvel, and no wonder, for one was an oak and the other a linden, yet they grew from a single trunk. The story of how this came about is a proof of the immeasurable power of the gods, and also of the way they reward the humble and the pious.

Sometimes when Jupiter[2] was tired of eating ambrosia and drinking nectar[3] up in Olympus and even a little weary of listening to Apollo's lyre and watching the Graces[4] dance, he would come down to the earth, disguise himself as a mortal and go looking for adventures. His favorite companion on these tours was Mercury,[5] the most entertaining of all the gods, the shrewdest and the most resourceful. On this particular trip Jupiter had determined to find out how hospitable the people of Phrygia were. Hospitality was, of course, very important to him, since all guests, all who seek shelter in a strange land, were under his especial protection.

The two gods, accordingly, took on the appearance of poor wayfarers and wandered through the land, knocking at each lowly hut or great house they came to and asking for food and a place to rest in. Not one would admit them; every time they were dismissed insolently and the door barred against them. They made trial of hundreds; all treated them in the same way. At last they came upon a little hovel of the humblest sort, poorer than any they had yet found, with a roof made only of reeds. But here, when they knocked, the door was opened wide and a cheerful voice bade them enter. They had to stoop to pass through the low entrance, but once inside they found themselves in a snug and very clean room, where a kindly-faced old man and woman welcomed them in the friendliest fashion and bustled about to make them comfortable.

The old man set a bench near the fire and told them to stretch out on it and rest their tired limbs, and the old woman threw a soft covering over it. Her name was Baucis, she told the strangers, and her husband was called Philemon. They had lived in that cottage all their married life and had always been happy. "We are poor folk," she said, "but poverty isn't so bad when you're willing to own up to it, and a contented spirit is a great help, too." All the while she was talking, she was busy doing things for them. The coals under the ashes on the dark hearth she fanned to life until a cheerful fire was burning. Over this she hung a little kettle full of water and just as it began to boil her husband came in with a fine cabbage he

---

1. **Phrygian** (frĭj′ ē ən): Phrygia was an ancient country in Asia.
2. **Jupiter** (jōō′ pə tər): King of the gods in Roman Mythology, like Zeus in Greek Mythology.
3. **ambrosia** (am brō′ zhə) . . . **nectar:** The food and drink of the gods that enabled them to live forever.
4. **the Graces:** Three sister goddesses who were associated with pleasure, charm, and beauty.
5. **Mercury** (mʉr′ kyoo rē): The messenger of the gods in Roman Mythology, like Hermes in Greek Mythology.

Baucis and Philemon 577

4 Clarification Wine turns to vinegar when it gets old. The implication here, perhaps, is that the couple seldom drink their wine, but have brought out some especially for their guests.

5 Discussion What is the first evidence Baucis and Philemon have that there is something unusual about their visitors?

6 Discussion How does Philemon's attitude towards his guest change here?

7 Discussion How does the speed with which Baucis and Philemon decide on a wish show the closeness that exists between them?

8 Discussion How do the couple's last words reflect what is most important to them?

9 Critical Thinking and Reading How does the response of other people show that Baucis and Philemon's actions are admired by the community as a whole?

Reader's Response Do you think that the gods' punishment of the people of Phyrgia was fair? Why or why not?

had got from the garden. Into the kettle it went, with a piece of the pork which was hanging from one of the beams. While this cooked Baucis set the table with her trembling old hands. One table-leg was too short, but she propped it up with a bit of broken dish. On the board she placed olives and radishes and several eggs which she had roasted in the ashes. By this time the cabbage and bacon were done, and the old man pushed two rickety couches up to the table and bade his guests recline and eat.

Presently he brought them cups of beechwood and an earthenware mixing bowl which held some wine very like vinegar, plentifully diluted with water. Philemon, however, was clearly proud and happy at being able to add such cheer to the supper and he kept on the watch to refill each cup as soon as it was emptied. The two old folks were so pleased and excited by the success of their hospitality that only very slowly a strange thing dawned upon them. The mixing bowl kept full. No matter how many cups were poured out from it, the level of the wine stayed the same, up to the brim. As they saw this wonder each looked in terror at the other, and dropping their eyes they prayed silently. Then in quavering voices and trembling all over they begged their guests to pardon the poor refreshments they had offered. "We have a goose," the old man said, "which we ought to have given your lordships. But if you will only wait, it shall be done at once." To catch the goose, however, proved beyond their powers. They tried in vain until they were worn out, while Jupiter and Mercury watched them greatly entertained.

But when both Philemon and Baucis had had to give up the chase panting and exhausted, the gods felt that the time had come for them to take action. They were really very kind. "You have been hosts to gods," they said, "and you shall have your reward. This wicked country which despises the poor stranger will be bitterly punished, but not you." They then escorted the two out of the hut and told them to look around them. To their amazement all they saw was water. The whole countryside had disappeared. A great lake surrounded them. Their neighbors had not been good to the old couple; nevertheless standing there they wept for them. But of a sudden their tears were dried by an overwhelming wonder. Before their eyes the tiny, lowly hut which had been their home for so long was turned into a stately pillared temple of whitest marble with a golden roof.

"Good people," Jupiter said, "ask whatever you want and you shall have your wish." The old people exchanged a hurried whisper, then Philemon spoke. "Let us be your priests, guarding this temple for you—and oh, since we have lived so long together, let neither of us ever have to live alone. Grant that we may die together."

The gods assented, well pleased with the two. A long time they served in that grand building, and the story does not say whether they ever missed their little cozy room with its cheerful hearth. But one day standing before the marble and golden magnificence they fell to talking about that former life, which had been so hard and yet so happy. By now both were in extreme old age. Suddenly, as they exchanged memories each saw the other putting forth leaves. Then bark was growing around them. They had time only to cry, "Farewell, dear companion." As the words passed their lips they became trees, but still they were together. The linden and the oak grew from one trunk.

From far and wide people came to admire the wonder, and always wreaths of flowers hung on the branches in honor of the pious and faithful pair.

THINKING ABOUT THE SELECTION

Recalling

1. What is special about the oak and linden mentioned in the opening paragraph?
2. Why does Jupiter disguise himself as a poor traveler to visit Phrygia?
3. How do most of the people greet him and Mercury? How do Baucis and Philemon treat them differently?
4. How do the gods reward Baucis and Philemon? How do they treat the other Phrygians?
5. What transformation, or changes, do Baucis and Philemon undergo?

Interpreting

6. Find two details that make the scene inside the little cottage come alive.
7. Why is it accurate to say that Baucis and Philemon are rewarded *twice* by the gods?

Applying

8. How would you make a guest feel comfortable in your home?

ANALYZING LITERATURE

Understanding Lessons in Myth

Myths were not only meant to entertain people or explain facts of nature. Sometimes these stories also contained lessons about the way to live. In this story, the gods reward Baucis and Philemon. You can therefore deduce what the myth is teaching by examining the couple's behavior and attitudes.

1. What does Baucis and Philemon's treatment of the two strangers reveal about them?
2. What do the two requests they make of the gods reveal about the couple?
3. What lessons is the myth teaching by holding up Baucis and Philemon as models of behavior?

CRITICAL THINKING AND READING

Learning About a Culture from Its Myths

You can learn what a culture values by examining its myths. The story of Baucis and Philemon indicates that the ancient Greeks and Romans valued hospitality.

1. How does Jupiter expect people to treat unexpected and unknown guests?
2. Why do you think hospitality was so important to the ancient Greeks and Romans?
3. Is hospitality as important in our society today? Why or why not?

UNDERSTANDING LANGUAGE

Analyzing Words with the Root *Phil*

The meaning of *Philemon* in Greek is "affectionate." This name contains the root *phil,* which means "love of." The Greek root *phil* (or *philo,* or *phile*) appears in many English words. Look up the following words in a dictionary, and write their meanings. Note how the definitions relate to the concept of love. Use each word in a sentence: 1. philosophy; 2. philanthrophy; 3. philharmonic; 4. Anglophile

THINKING AND WRITING

Writing Dialogue for a Myth

Dialogue is the words that characters speak to each other. Edith Hamilton includes only a few of the words that the characters would say. Imagine that you must make up more dialogue for a dramatized version of this myth to be presented before your classmates. Focus on the conversation that the characters have around the dinner table. Read the myth again to make sure you understand the sequence of events. Then write the dialogue. When revising this dialogue make sure it will not sound old-fashioned. Also, check to see that each character's words are in keeping with his or her personality.

Baucis and Philemon 579

Focus

More About the Myth This retelling of the myth blames Daedalus' imprisonment on King Minos's capriciousness, but other versions cite a more specific reason. They say Daedalus helped Ariadne, the king's daughter, elope with Theseus, the slayer of the minotaur. The King was then so angry that he ordered Daedalus and his son imprisoned.

Literary Focus Point out that writers use several ways to reveal a character's traits: his or her actions and thoughts, as well as what other characters say and think about them. Ask students to identify which of these ways of revealing character traits are used in this myth to tell what kind of person Icarus is.

Look For You might ask students to compare Icarus with Phaëthon as they read. How are their fates similar? How are their personalities different?

Writing/Prior Knowledge Ask those students who have flown in an airplane to describe what their first flight was like. Were they frightened or pleased and excited? Then have the class complete the free-writing assignment.

Vocabulary Ask students to write a short paragraph describing something that happened to them recently using at least four of the vocabulary words.

Icarus and Daedalus

The name Daedalus (ded′ 'l əs) means "artful craftsman" in Greek, and Daedalus deserved his name. According to legend, he learned his craftsmanship from the gods themselves. Not only did he design buildings, machines, and weapons for various Greek kings, but he also made wonderful toys for their children. His son, Icarus (ik′ ə rəs), is remembered for the fateful flight recounted in this myth.

Josephine Preston Peabody (1874–1922), who wrote this version of the myth, was best known for her poetry and plays.

Characters in Myth

Like people in real life or characters in fiction, the gods and heroes in myths have different ways of thinking and acting. Prometheus, for instance, is concerned about the results of his deeds, while Zeus is more stubborn and emotional. Hades is dark and forbidding, like his underworld kingdom, but Apollo loves the light.

You can understand the characters in myths by paying attention to what the storyteller says about them. You can also learn about them by observing what they say and do themselves. In "Icarus and Daedalus," you will meet a father and son who are quite different from each other.

Look For

In this myth, Daedalus invents wings that enable him and Icarus to fly. Look for the differences in the ways that these two characters respond to the experience of flight. What does this difference tell you about each character?

Writing

Have you ever wanted to fly—not in an airplane, but as a human being with wings? Imagine that you could drift in an updraft of air like a hawk or fly for great distances like a migrating bird. Describe the sensation of flying as you imagine it. For instance, what would you see and hear, and what would the wind feel like against your body?

Vocabulary

Knowing the following words will help you as you read "Icarus and Daedalus."

cunning (kun′ iŋ) *adj.*: Skillful; clever (p. 581)

veered (vird) *v.*: Changed directions (p. 581)

fledgling (flej′ liŋ) *n.*: Young bird (p. 581)

rash (rash) *adj.*: Reckless (p. 581)

vacancy (vā′ kən sē) *n.*: Emptiness (p. 581)

sustained (sə stānd′) *v.*: Supported (p. 582)

580   *Fables, Myths, and Legends*

Objectives

1 To understand the characters in a myth
2 To compare and contrast characters in a myth
3 To create a dramatic monologue
4 To write a newspaper story about the characters in a myth

Support Material

Teaching Portfolio
Teacher Backup, p. 935
Usage and Mechanics Worksheet, p. 938
Vocabulary Check, p. 939
Critical Thinking and Reading Worksheet, *Comparing and Contrasting Characters in a Myth,* p. 940
Language Worksheet, *Choosing the Meaning That Fits the Context,* p. 941
Selection Test, p. 942
Art Transparency 20, *Icarus,* by Henri Matisse

Icarus and Daedalus

Josephine Preston Peabody

Among all those mortals who grew so wise that they learned the secrets of the gods, none was more cunning than Daedalus.

1 He once built, for King Minos of Crete,[1] a wonderful Labyrinth[2] of winding ways so cunningly tangled up and twisted around that, once inside, you could never find your way out again without a magic clue. But the king's favor veered with the wind, and one day he had his master architect imprisoned in a tower. Daedalus managed to escape from his cell; but it seemed impossible to leave the island, since every ship that came or went was well guarded by order of the king.

2 At length, watching the sea-gulls in the air—the only creatures that were sure of liberty—he thought of a plan for himself and his young son Icarus, who was captive with him.

Little by little, he gathered a store of feathers great and small. He fastened these together with thread, moulded them in with wax, and so fashioned two great wings like those of a bird. When they were done, Daedalus fitted them to his own shoulders, and after one or two efforts, he found that by waving his arms he could winnow[3] the air and cleave it, as a swimmer does the sea. He 3 held himself aloft, wavered this way and that with the wind, and at last, like a great fledgling, he learned to fly.

Without delay, he fell to work on a pair of wings for the boy Icarus, and taught him carefully how to use them, bidding him beware of rash adventures among the stars. "Remember," said the father, "never to fly 4 very low or very high, for the fogs about the earth would weigh you down, but the blaze of the sun will surely melt your feathers apart if you go too near."

5 For Icarus, these cautions went in at one ear and out by the other. Who could remember to be careful when he was to fly for the first time? Are birds careful? Not they! And not an idea remained in the boy's head but the one joy of escape.

The day came, and the fair wind that was to set them free. The father bird put on his wings, and, while the light urged them to be gone, he waited to see that all was well with Icarus, for the two could not fly hand in hand. Up they rose, the boy after his father. The hateful ground of Crete sank beneath them; and the country folk, who caught a glimpse of them when they were high above the treetops, took it for a vision of the gods— Apollo, perhaps, with Cupid after him.

6 At first there was a terror in the joy. The wide vacancy of the air dazed them—a glance downward made their brains reel. But when a great wind filled their wings, and Icarus

---

1. King Minos (mī′ nəs) **of Crete:** King Minos was a son of the god Zeus. Crete is a Greek island in the eastern Mediterranean sea, southeast of Greece.
2. Labyrinth (lab′ ə rint͟h′)
3. winnow (win′ ō) *v.*: Beat as with wings.

Icarus and Daedalus   581

Motivation/Prior Knowledge Ask students to describe a situation in which they "overdid" something. What were the results of their actions?

Purpose-Setting Question How do the different fates of Daedalus and his son suggest that inventiveness can have both positive and negative results?

Thematic Idea Another selection that shows impulsiveness like that of Icarus is the short story, "The Luckiest Time of All," page 75. How are the results of impulsiveness different in the story?

1 **Enrichment** Some parks or gardens have hedgerow mazes that are similar to the labyrinth described in the myth. Ask students who have been in such a maze tell what the experience was like.

2 **Discussion** How does Daedalus get the idea of an escape?

3 **Discussion** What details does the author use to make human flight believable? What ordinary human activities does she compare it to?

4 **Discussion** How does Daedalus' warning to his son give the story added suspense?

5 **Discussion** How does Icarus react to his father's warnings?

6 **Critical Thinking and Reading** How does Icarus' reaction to flying for the first time differ from his father's?

DAEDALUS AND ICARUS
Albrecht Dürer

felt himself sustained, like a halcyon bird[4] in the hollow of a wave, like a child uplifted by his mother, he forgot everything in the world but joy. He forgot Crete and the other islands that he had passed over: he saw but vaguely that wingèd thing in the distance before him that was his father Daedalus. He longed for one draft of flight to quench the thirst of his captivity: he stretched out his arms to the sky and made towards the highest heavens.

Alas for him! Warmer and warmer grew the air. Those arms, that had seemed to uphold him, relaxed. His wings wavered, drooped. He fluttered his young hands vainly—he was falling—and in that terror he remembered. The heat of the sun had melted the wax from his wings; the feathers were falling, one by one, like snowflakes; and there was none to help.

He fell like a leaf tossed down the wind, down, down, with one cry that overtook Daedalus far away. When he returned, and sought high and low for his poor boy, he saw nothing but the birdlike feathers afloat on the water, and he knew that Icarus was drowned.

The nearest island he named Icaria, in memory of the child; but he, in heavy grief, went to the temple of Apollo in Sicily, and there hung up his wings as an offering. Never again did he attempt to fly.

---

4. halcyon (hal' sē ən) **bird** *n.:* A legendary bird, identified with the kingfisher, which could calm the sea by resting on it.

582 *Fables, Myths, and Legends*

THINKING ABOUT THE SELECTION

Recalling

1. Why does Daedalus want to leave Crete?
2. How does Daedalus plan to escape?
3. Paraphrase the warning he gives to Icarus.
4. Why does Icarus fall from the sky?

Interpreting

5. Do you think that Daedalus was punished by the gods for daring an unusual deed? Explain.
6. Do you think Icarus was punished for disobeying his father? Explain.
7. What lesson does this myth teach?

Applying

8. Why do you think humans have always wanted to fly like birds?

ANALYZING CHARACTER

Understanding Characters in Myth

Like novels and short stories, myths present a variety of characters. In "Icarus and Daedalus," you learn about a famous father and son through what the storyteller says about them and what they do themselves.

1. Where does the storyteller inform you that Daedalus is "cunning"? In what ways does Daedalus display his cunning?
2. What does Daedalus reveal about himself in his words to his son?
3. At what point in the story does the storyteller hint that Icarus will disobey his father?
4. What does the boy's flying too close to the sun tell you about him?
5. Do you think Icarus's behavior is typical of that of most young people? Why or why not?

CRITICAL THINKING AND READING

Comparing and Contrasting Characters

Comparing means finding similarities. **Contrasting** means showing differences. By comparing and contrasting Icarus and Daedalus, you can learn even more about them.

1. Find evidence to show that the father and son both are eager to escape the island.
2. How are the two similar in their first reaction to the experience of flying?
3. How are they different in the ways they adapt to this new experience?
4. Explain whether the contrast between them results more from the difference in their ages or from their differing personalities.

SPEAKING AND LISTENING

Creating a Dramatic Monologue

A **dramatic monologue** is a poem in which a fictional character expresses his or her thoughts and feelings to an imaginary listener. Write a dramatic monologue in which Icarus tells about the escape. Include his thoughts and feelings about each important event. For instance, how did he feel as he saw his father making the wings, or what did he think when his father warned him about flight? The poem does not have to rhyme. After you have finished your peom, share it with classmates. Ask them to help you think about ways to revise your monologue so that it sounds like Icarus talking.

THINKING AND WRITING

Writing About Characters in Myth

Imagine that you are a reporter for an Athenian newspaper. You suddenly hear that an old man who just died on one of the Greek islands was Icarus. It turns out that he survived his fall into the sea and lived for many years, hiding his identity. Write a story for your newspaper with the following headline: The Secret Life of Icarus. In the story, tell what happened to Icarus after his fall. Explain such matters as how he survived the accident, whether he felt sorry for what he did, why he never contacted his father, and whether he married. As you revise your account, make sure it will be interesting enough to sell newspapers.

(Answers begin on p. 582.)

first time, partly because experience has not yet taught them to be careful.

ANSWERS TO CRITICAL THINKING AND READING

1. Their willingness to try such a desperate measure as human flight shows both characters are eager to leave the island.
2. Both are dazed by flight at first.
3. Daedalus is able to maintain his self-control and keep himself at a safe height, while Icarus forgets everything else in the thrill of flying.
4. Answers will differ. Suggested Response: The difference in the two characters seems genuinely representative of the difference between the young and the old. Most older men would display Daedalus's caution, many young men would be as impulsive as Icarus.

SPEAKING AND LISTENING

To help students begin, have them put themselves in the mind of Icarus and list his thoughts. Remind students to prepare their monologues using "I" as Icarus. When students have prepared their monologues, have them deliver them to the class.

THINKING AND WRITING

For help with this assignment, students can refer to Lesson 9, "Writing About Character," in the Handbook of Writing About Literature.

Writing Across the Curriculum

We all know why birds and airplanes fly: because they have wings. But exactly *how* do wings make flight possible? Ask students to write a brief paragraph explaining how they think a wing functions, without looking the question up in a reference book. (You might give them the clue that it works in the same way as a boat's sail.) Then have them look up the subject in an encyclopedia to see if they have guessed correctly. You might want to inform the science teachers about this assignment. Science teachers might provide additional guidance for students.

6. Icarus seems to have been punished for disobeying his father, but perhaps his father should have foreseen that an impulsive young man would be too excited by flight to pay attention to how high he was going.
7. The myth teaches that there are limits to human activity, and that human endeavors that ignore these limits risk disaster.

Applying

8. Answers will differ. Suggested Response: The allure of flight is the freedom flight seems to offer. Birds travel at a speed greater than that of the fastest runner. For these reasons, flying has always seemed like the ultimate form of movement to humans.

ANSWERS TO ANALYZING LITERATURE

1. The storyteller says that Daedalus was "cunning" in the first sentence of the story. Daedalus displays his cunning by building the Labyrinth, and then by building wings for himself and Icarus.
2. Daedalus's words reveal his knowledge and cautiousness.
3. The storyteller suggests Icarus will not heed these warnings by saying they went "in at one ear and out by the other."
4. Icarus shows that he is excitable and impulsive.
5. Suggested Response: Many young people get "carried away" like Icarus, partly because of the excitement of doing things for the

More About the Myth Narcissus was the son of the river god Cephisus. Perhaps this makes it appropriate that he should meet his fate beside a body of water. You might read Ovid's version of this story to the class from Horace Gregory's translation and ask students to compare his telling the story to MacPherson's.

Literary Focus Point out that we live in a world of constant change over which we have little control. We grow up, grow old, and die while seasons come and go around us. Because of this, one of the most enduring human fantasies is of changes outside the natural pattern, often instantaneous ones, rather than the gradual ones more common in nature. For example, a child who loves to swim might want to become a fish so that he can always be swimming. Ask students to describe changes they have fantasized about.

Look For Show students a picture of a narcissus flower. Ask students to consider whether being changed into this flower is a change Narcissus would have liked or disliked, explaining the reasons for their opinions.

Writing/Prior Knowledge Point out to students that metamorphosis is a common theme in literature. Sometimes things change into something similar, as when the puppet boy Pinocchio becomes a real boy. Sometimes the change is more drastic, as in the case of the Kafka character who wakes up and discovers that he has been changed into an insect. Ask students to discuss stories they have read that involve metamorphosis.

Vocabulary Have your **more advanced** students find antonyms for the three adjectives in the vocabulary list and then use each of the six words in a separate sentence to show that they know what each one means.

Narcissus

The story of the handsome youth Narcissus (när sis′ əs) has been retold for hundreds of years. This popular Greek myth has also inspired many painters, who have shown Narcissus staring enchanted at his own reflection in the water.

   Jay MacPherson (1931–   ), the author of this version of the myth, has lived most of her life in Canada and is best known for her poetry.

Metamorphosis

Metamorphosis means change from one form into another. In the imaginative world of myths, both gods and mortals can experience this type of change. The sea-god Proteus, for example, has the power to transform himself into any shape he chooses. Also, the gods can change humans into other forms. At the end of "Phaëthon, Son of Apollo," the gods take pity on the grief of Clymene and her daughters and change them into poplar trees. In "Narcissus," you will read about another metamorphosis.

Look For

Identify the metamorphosis that occurs in this myth. Look for the resemblance between the character and the thing into which he changes.

Writing

Metamorphosis is not limited to myths. Many remarkable changes take place in the world around you. Have you ever watched a caterpillar develop into a butterfly, or a person grow from a small baby to a school-age child? Freewrite about an "everyday" metamorphosis that you have witnessed.

Vocabulary

Knowing the following words will help you as you read "Narcissus."
courted (kôrt′ əd) v.: Tried to win someone's love (p. 585)
marred (märd) v.: Disturbed (p. 585)
deluded (di lōōd′ əd) v.: Fooled; misled (p. 585)
disdained (dis dānd′) adj.: Scorned; regarded as unworthy (p. 585)
unrequited (un ri kwīt′ əd) adj.: Unreturned (p. 585)
haggard (hag′ ərd) adj.: Looking worn from grief or illness (p. 586)
lament (lə ment′) v.: Express deep sorrow for; mourn (p. 586)

584   *Fables, Myths, and Legends*

Narcissus

Jay MacPherson

1   As beautiful as Adonis[1] was the ill-fated Narcissus, who from his childhood was loved by all who saw him but whose pride would let him love no one in return. At last one of those who had hopelessly courted him

2   turned and cursed him, exclaiming: "May he suffer as we have suffered! May he too love in vain!" The avenging goddess Nemesis[2] heard and approved this prayer.

3   There was nearby a clear pool, with shining silvery waters. No shepherd had ever come there, nor beast nor bird nor falling branch marred its surface: the grass grew fresh and green around it, and the sheltering woods kept it always cool from the midday sun.

  Here once came Narcissus, heated and tired from the chase, and lay down by the pool to drink. As he bent over the water, his eyes met the eyes of another young man, gazing up at him from the depth of the pool. Deluded by his reflection, Narcissus fell in love with the beauty that was his own. Without thought of food or rest he lay beside the pool addressing cries and pleas to the image, whose lips moved as he spoke but whose reply he could never catch. Echo came by, the most constant of his disdained lovers. She

4   was a nymph who had once angered Hera, the wife of Zeus, by talking too much, and in consequence was deprived of the use of her tongue for ordinary conversation: all she could do was repeat the last words of others. Seeing Narcissus lying there, she pleaded with him in his own words. "I will die unless you pity me," cried Narcissus to his beloved. "Pity me," cried Echo as vainly to hers. Nar-

5   cissus never raised his eyes to her at all, though she remained day after day beside him on the bank, pleading as well as she was able. At last she pined away, withering and wasting with unrequited love, till nothing was left of her but her voice, which the trav-

NARCISO ALLA FONTE
Caravaggio
Scala/Art Resource

---

1. Adonis (ə dän′is): A handsome young man loved by Aphrodite, the goddess of love.
2. Nemesis (nem′ ə sis)

Humanities Note

Detail, *Narciso Alla Fonta* by Caravaggio. Michelangelo Merisi, known as Caravaggio (1571–1610) was an Italian painter of the Renaissance. Apprenticed at the age of twelve to a rigid academic painter, Caravaggio learned the mechanics of being an artist. Independently he developed his own painting style. Unlike his contemporaries, Caravaggio painted only from live models or from nature; he never used the work of another artist as a model. This practice resulted in clear, very realistic, and intense renderings of his subjects.

  Narcissus was painted in the years 1598–1600. This detail shows Narcissus dressed in contemporary rather than classical clothing. As he leans foward to see his image in the pool, the reflection duplicates his figure in reverse. In this painting, as in all of his works, Caravaggio relies on his strong personal style to emphasize his artistic statement.
1. What emotion is shown on the face of Narcissus?
2. What features might suggest a resembance to a flower?

Literary Focus What does Narcissus become at the end of the myth?

Reader's Response Do you think the punishment of Narcissus was fair and just? How about Echo? Explain your answers.

Closure and Extension

ANSWERS TO THINKING ABOUT THE SELECTION
Recalling

1. He is unable to return any woman's love.
2. He falls in love with his own reflection in a pool.
3. Echo angered Hera by talking too much. Hera gets revenge by making Echo unable to utter words of her own; she can only repeat what others say.
4. Echo repeats the words "pity me," which are said by Narcissus.
5. Echo withers into a disembodied voice; Narcissus is turned into a flower.

Interpreting

6. Narcissus' punishment suits him in that he falls hopelessly in love with the person he has thought most of all the time: himself.
7. The myth explains the origin of the flower narcissus and of the natural phenomenon of echoes.

Applying

8. Suggested Response: There is a little of Narcissus in everyone. In fact, learning to like oneself is important in any personality's development. However, as the myth shows, too much self-love can be dangerous and self-defeating.

ANSWERS TO ANALYZING LITERATURE

1. It is appropriate that Narcissus becomes a flower because in doing so he becomes as beautiful as he believed himself to be.
2. If Narcissus simply died, without turning into a flower, the myth would have no connection to the present. As it is, it suggests a magical origin for a real plant.

---

eler still hears calling unexpectedly in woods and waste places.

As for the cruel Narcissus, he fared no better. The face that looked back at him from the water became pale, thin and haggard, till at last poor Echo caught and repeated his last "Farewell!" But when she came with the other nymphs to lament over his body, it was nowhere to be found. Instead, over the pool bent a new flower, white with a yellow center, which they called by his name. From this flower the Furies, the avengers of guilt, twist garlands to bind their hateful brows.

THINKING ABOUT THE SELECTION

Recalling

1. What does Narcissus do that causes him to be cursed?
2. How does Narcissus finally fall in love?
3. Why has Echo incurred the wrath of Hera? How does Hera get her revenge?
4. What does Echo do while Narcissus lies gazing at the object of his love?
5. How are Echo and Narcissus changed at the end of the myth?

Interpreting

6. How is what happens to Narcissus a fitting punishment for his pride?
7. What are two facts of nature explained by this myth?

Applying

8. Do you think there is a little bit of Narcissus in each of us? Explain.

ANALYZING LITERATURE

Understanding Metamorphosis

Metamorphosis refers to a change from one form to another. In this myth, Narcissus experiences such a change.
1. Why is it appropriate that Narcissus becomes a flower?
2. Explain how the story would be different if Narcissus simply died, without undergoing a magical change.

586   Fables, Myths, and Legends

UNDERSTANDING LANGUAGE

Understanding Word Origins

The English word *narcissism,* which refers to a certain way of thinking and acting, is based on the name Narcissus. You can therefore infer that narcissism is related to the way that Narcissus thinks and behaves in this myth.
1. What do you think the word *narcissism* means?
2. Look up the word in a dictionary to check your answer.
3. Write a sentence using the word.

THINKING AND WRITING

Writing Sketches About Metamorphosis

Imagine that the American Mythological Society has offered a $150 award for the best article entitled Metamorphosis: The Inside Story. Most myths contain descriptions of metamorphosis from the outside. However, the Society wants you to describe what it actually feels like to undergo a magical change. Think of a transformation that you can describe. For instance, what would it be like to change into a flower, like Narcissus, or into a sportscar, a mountain, or anything else? Imagine that you are experiencing the metamorphosis and describe it in vivid terms. When revising your article make sure it is both unusual and convincing enough to win the award.

Challenge Narcissus can perceive nothing but his own image. Echo can respond to the outside world, but cannot express herself. Ask students to explain how these two characters complement each other by focusing on the way each one acts as they sit at the side of the pool.

ANSWERS TO UNDERSTANDING LANGUAGE

1. Suggested Response: *Narcissism* means "loving oneself."
2. A dictionary definition of *narcissism* is "excessive admiration of oneself."
3. John's narcissism prevented him from being my good friend.

THINKING AND WRITING

Publishing Student Writing Have three students volunteer to judge the sketches about metamorphosis and choose the most imaginative one. Then have its author read it aloud to the class.

Myths, Legends, and Folktales from Around the World

THE SLEEPING GYPSY, 1897
Henri Rousseau
The Museum of Modern Art, New York

Humanities Note

Fine art, *Sleeping Gypsy*, 1897, by Henri Rousseau. Henri Rousseau (1844–1910), a French primitive painter, worked for most of his life as a customs clerk in Paris. This earned him the nickname "le Douanier" by which he is sometimes called. With no formal training Henri Rousseau began painting steadily at the age of forty. He produced portraits of shopkeepers and neighborhood people in addition to scenes of exotic fantasy. His style is described as primitive or naive because it produced simple renderings that concentrated entirely on what Rousseau had to say without the interference of academic rules of technique and method. Rousseau and his art were beloved of the Parisian avant garde. Through their championship he attained some recognition in his lifetime.

A simple and unsophisticated man, Henri Rousseau produced the art of true innocence. *Sleeping Gypsy* is one of Rousseau's best known works. The naiveté of concept and execution of this painting is compensated for by the imagination of the scene. A sleeping figure is approached by a lion who is at once cute and menacing. The viewer wonders what will happen: will the man awaken and tame the beast or will he be devoured? It is exactly the sort of anxious situation one would encounter in a restless dream. The palette of Henri Rousseau is bright and jewellike. His deceptively childlike images hold more than the viewer first suspects.

Focus

More About the Legend The Borinquen, or Arawak, Indians were the first Indians whom Christopher Columbus met in the West Indies in 1492. All of the various tribes of Borinquens were farmers who lived in large villages of up to 3,000 inhabitants. The Borinquen tribes were constantly at war with the Carib tribe. Do you think it would have been possible for a romance to occur between a Borinquen and a Carib? How would the rest of the people in both tribes have reacted to such a romance?

Literary Focus If students are having difficulty understanding the concept of universal theme, point out that the theme of this Puerto Rican legend is the same as that of William Shakespeare's well-known play, *Romeo and Juliet,* written in England in 1595. Because this theme is common to two completely separate cultures and times, it is universal. Ask your students to think of other stories that present the theme of forbidden love.

Look For You might have more advanced students look for details in the legend that give clues about the culture of the Borinquen Indians.

Writing/Prior Knowledge If some students have trouble thinking of a secret place, you might suggest that they write about a place, such as a tree house, that was not secret but was special.

Vocabulary The word in this vocabulary section should not be difficult for students to understand or pronounce.

The Legend of the Hummingbird

Puerto Rico (pwer′ tə rē′ kō) is a commonwealth of the United States located about 1,000 miles southeast of Florida. The earliest inhabitants of the island were the **Borinquen** Indians, from whom this legend comes. Some Puerto Ricans today can still trace their origins to this now vanished tribe.

Pura Belpre (poo′ rä bel′ prā) (1899–1982), who retells this legend, was born in Puerto Rico and moved to New York City as a young woman. She wrote a number of books based on Puerto Rican folklore.

Legend: Universal Theme

A **universal theme** is an idea or situation that has been common to many different groups throughout history. Such themes appear often in legends and folk tales. One repeated theme involves the problems that young people face when their love goes against the wishes of their families or society. In this legend, the daughter of an Indian chief invites danger by falling in love with a young man from an enemy tribe.

Look For

As you read, visualize the "small pool" where the two young Indians meet. Why do you think the story takes place there, rather than in a village or town? What happens to the two young lovers?

Writing

The two young Indians in this legend meet at a beautiful and secret pool "far up in the hills." Remember a secret place that you went to or heard about when you were a child. Describe this place and tell why it was special for you.

Vocabulary

Knowing the following word will help you as you read "The Legend of the Hummingbird."
dreaded (dred′ əd) *adj.:* Feared (p. 589)

Objectives

1 To understand a universal theme
2 To recognize clues to outcomes
3 To complete verbal analogues
4 To write a legend

Support Material

Teaching Portfolio
Teacher Backup, p. 955
Usage and Mechanics Worksheet, p. 958
Vocabulary Check, p. 959
Analyzing Literature Worksheet, *Understanding Universal Themes,* p. 960
Critical Thinking and Reading Worksheet, *Recognizing Clues to Outcomes,* p. 961
Selection Test, p. 962

The Legend of the Hummingbird

from **Puerto Rico**

Pura Belpré

Between the towns of Cayey and Cidra, far up in the hills, there was once a small pool fed by a waterfall that tumbled down the side of the mountain. The pool was surrounded by pomarosa trees, and the Indians used to call it Pomarosa Pool. It was the favorite place of Alida, the daughter of an Indian chief, a man of power and wealth among the people of the hills.

One day, when Alida had come to the pool to rest after a long walk, a young Indian came there to pick some fruit from the trees. Alida was surprised, for he was not of her tribe. Yet he said he was no stranger to the pool. This was where he had first seen Alida, and he had often returned since then to pick fruit, hoping to see her again.

He told her about himself to make her feel at home. He confessed, with honesty and frankness, that he was a member of the dreaded Carib tribe[1] that had so often attacked the island of Borinquen.[2] As a young boy, he had been left behind after one of those raids, and he had stayed on the island ever since.

Alida listened closely to his story, and the two became friends. They met again in the days that followed, and their friendship grew stronger. Alida admired the young man's courage in living among his enemies. She learned to call him by his Carib name, Taroo, and he called her Alida, just as her own people did. Before long, their friendship had turned into love.

Their meetings by the pool were always brief. Alida was afraid their secret might be discovered, and careful though she was, there came a day when someone saw them and told her father. Alida was forbidden to visit the Pomarosa Pool, and to put an end to her romance with the stranger, her father decided to marry her to a man of his own choosing. Preparations for the wedding started at once.

Alida was torn with grief, and one evening she cried out to her god: "O Yukiyú, help me! Kill me or do what you will with me, but do not let me marry this man whom I do not love!"

And the great god Yukiyú took pity on her and changed her into a delicate red flower.

Meanwhile Taroo, knowing nothing of Alida's sorrow, still waited for her by the Pomarosa Pool. Day after day he waited. Sometimes he stayed there until a mantle of stars was spread across the sky.

---

1. Carib (kar′ ib) **tribe:** Native Americans who formerly inhabited the Southwest Indies and the northern coast of South America.
2. Borinquen (bō′ rēn ken′): Puerto Rico.

The Legend of the Hummingbird　589

Presentation

Motivation/Prior Knowledge You might lead the class in a discussion about the theme of young people who are in love against the wishes of their families. What happens in such relationships?

Thematic Idea Other selections in which characters are transformed by gods or goddesses into animals or plants are "Baucis and Philemon," on page 577, and "Narcissus," on page 585.

Purpose-Setting Question How does this legend explain the behavior of a hummingbird?

1 Reading Strategy You might have students question who the strange youth is and what he wants. Where did he come from? Why does he want to see Alida?

2 Critical Thinking and Reading What does the young Indian's story indicate about his character? How did he survive alone on the island among his enemies? In what way might the fact that he is a member of an enemy tribe by a clue to the outcome of the legend?

3 Literary Focus You might point out to students that Alida's father's reaction to her relationship with Taroo establishes the universal theme of young love in the face of opposition from elders. How will the father's solution end their relationship?

4 Discussion Did Alida do a wise thing by asking for any fate, including death, to avoid marrying a man she did not love? Explain your answer. What other actions could she have taken?

Master Teacher Note To give students an idea of what Puerto Rico is like, you might show them photographs of the landscape of the island. How would the landscape have helped Taroo to hide from his enemies? What kinds of fruit might he have been picking at the pool where he met Alida?

One night the moon took pity on him. "Taroo," she called from her place high above the stars. "O Taroo, wait no longer for Alida! Your secret was made known, and Alida was to be married to a man of her father's choosing. In her grief she called to her god, Yukiyú; he heard her plea for help and changed her into a red flower."

"Ahee, ahee!" cried Taroo. "O moon, what is the name of the red flower?"

"Only Yukiyú knows that," the moon replied.

Then Taroo called out: "O Yukiyú, god of my Alida, help me too! Help me to find her!"

And just as the great god had heard Alida's plea, he listened now to Taroo and decided to help him. There by the Pomarosa Pool, before the moon and the silent stars, the great god changed Taroo into a small many-colored bird.

"Fly, Colibrí, and find your love among the flowers," he said.

Off went the Colibrí, flying swiftly, and as he flew his wings made a sweet humming sound.

In the morning the Indians saw a new bird darting about among the flowers swift as an arrow and brilliant as a jewel. They heard the humming of its wings, and in amazement they saw it hover in the air over every blossom, kissing the petals of the flowers with its long slender bill. They liked the new bird with the music in its wings, and they called it Hummingbird.

Ever since then the little many-colored bird has hovered over every flower he finds, but returns most often to the flowers that are red. He is still looking, always looking, for the one red flower that will be his lost Alida. He has not found her yet.

590   *Fables, Myths, and Legends*

THINKING ABOUT THE SELECTION

Recalling

1. Where does the stranger that Alida meets at the pool come from?
2. What relationship develops between Alida and the stranger?
3. How does Alida's father try to end it?
4. What happens to the two young lovers?

Interpreting

5. What does this legend tell you about the enduring quality of love?
6. Which facts of nature does this legend explain?

Applying

7. A proverb says: Love finds hidden paths. How does this legend prove the proverb?

ANALYZING LITERATURE

Understanding a Universal Theme

A **universal theme** is an idea or situation common to many different groups throughout history. Such themes appear often in literature and folklore. In *Romeo and Juliet,* for instance, William Shakespeare writes about the problems that young people face when they fall in love. "The Legend of the Hummingbird" deals with the same universal theme. Like Romeo and Juliet, Taroo and Alida encounter serious difficulties.

1. What problems might they have faced even if Alida's family accepted Taroo?
2. Why do you think that Alida's father did not approve of her romance?
3. Would the lovers have been happier if Yukiyú did not change them? Why or why not?

CRITICAL THINKING AND READING

Recognizing Clues to Outcomes

As you read this legend, you can find clues in the story to what will happen. You can become better at finding such clues by not only understanding events but also thinking where they might lead. For instance, the fact that Alida and Taroo become friends so quickly suggests that they may fall in love as well.

1. Find two clues indicating that Alida's father may not accept her romance.
2. How is the title a clue to what will happen when Alida becomes a flower?

UNDERSTANDING LANGUAGE

Completing Verbal Analogies

A **verbal analogy** is a comparison of relationships between words. For example, *wealth* is related to *riches* in the same way that *happiness* is related to *joy*. Each of the following word pairs consists of synonyms. In the following examples, choose the lettered pair of words that expresses the same relationship as that between the capitalized pair.

1. MANTLE:CAPE::
a. pill:bottle
b. arrow:target
c. car:tire
d. employee:worker

2. FEARED:DREADED::
a. sold:bought
b. helped:aided
c. threw:caught
d. sang:ate

THINKING AND WRITING

Writing a Legend

Many legends tell about real people but exaggerate their achievements. Imagine that you have been arguing with a friend about who is the greatest baseball player, television actor, or any other performer. List some of the accomplishments of the person you have chosen, and then exaggerate the items you have listed. Using one of the items on your list, write a legend about this person. Remember that a legend is in the form of a story. As you revise your legend, make sure it will persuade your friend that you are right.

The Legend of the Hummingbird 591

(Answers begin on p. 590.)

could not ever have been happy as they were because they continued to be separated. Students may also answer positively, supporting their answer by saying that it was possible that the two would have found a way to be together as humans, or that time would have made them forget each other.

Challenge What are other universal themes in myths, legend, or fairy tales? Students might suggest themes such as: "Crime doesn't pay," "Good things will happen to those who do good unto others," or "Virtue is rewarded."

ANSWERS TO CRITICAL THINKING AND READING

1. Two clues indicating that her father may not accept Alida's romance are that Taroo is a member of a dreaded enemy tribe and that Alida tries to keep the visits a secret.
2. The title is a clue because it indicates that the legend is an explanation of the hummingbird's origin and behavior, which includes feeding on flowers' nectar. The title hints to the reader that Taroo will become a hummingbird once the reader has learned that Alida becomes a flower.

ANSWERS TO UNDERSTANDING LANGUAGE

1. d
2. b

THINKING AND WRITING

Publishing Student Writing You might want to put students' legends on the class bulletin board, along with original art depicting these modern legends. Students could decide on a name for the display, such as "Living Legends," "Legendary Figures of _____ Class," or "The Wall of Legends."

---

says that love can be so enduring that people will do anything to remain true and to be with those they love. No obstacles are too large for two people who love each other very much.

6. This legend explains the origin of the hummingbird, and why it looks and acts as it does.

Applying

7. This legend proves the proverb because, although the two young Indians were forbidden to see each other, they found a "hidden path," namely their transformation into a flower and a hummingbird.

ANSWERS TO ANALYZING LITERATURE

1. Answers will differ. Suggested Responses: continual mistrust between Alida's family and the tribe; adapting to a different way of life; possible differences in religion and other beliefs; and the possibility of Alida's family and tribe being attacked by Taroo's former tribe.

2. Suggested Response: Alida's father did not approve of her romance because he did not trust anyone from the enemy tribe. He did not know any of the enemy personally, did not understand them, and knew only their aggressive attacks.

3. Answers will differ. Students may respond negatively and support their answer by saying that the two

Focus

More About the Legend The Micmac Indians hunted bear, moose, and other game during the winter. They used the pelts from these animals as clothing to stay warm. Another legendary figure of the Micmac tribe was a powerful being named Glooscap, who, among other things, shaped the landscape of the area where the tribe lived. Why do you think it was important for a tribe such as the Micmacs, which lived in an area in the north, to have a legend about the spirit of winter?

Literary Focus You might point out to students that all of the events in the legend are related to the development of the conflict. The conflict also helps maintain readers' interest. These factors prompt readers to want to continue to find out how the struggle involving the hero of the story will be resolved.

Look For You might have more advanced students look for the way in which the ice king is described and portrayed. Does this description agree or disagree with the students' own images of winter?

Writing/Prior Knowledge You might have students illustrate the costume of the king or queen of winter, based on their freewriting.

Vocabulary All but one of these vocabulary words is a verb. You might have less advanced students decide whether each verb is in past or present tense and then have them write down its other tenses.

Ojeeg, the Hunter, and the Ice Man

This tale comes from the **Micmac** (mik′ mak) Indians, who live in eastern Canada. Years ago, this tribe hunted, fished, and gathered clams for food. During the cold Canadian winter, they traveled by means of wooden toboggans and snowshoes. They kept themselves warm in tepees covered with birchbark or animal skins.

Dorothy de Wit (1916–1980) retells this Micmac tale in her book *The Talking Stone: An Anthology of Native American Tales and Legends* (1979).

Conflict in Legend

A **conflict** is a struggle between opposing sides or forces. Conflict plays an important role in legend, just as it does in short stories and novels. One difference, however, is that a legend may present a struggle between a hero with special powers and a supernatural being. In this Indian legend, the hero Ojeeg battles with old man Peboan, the powerful spirit of winter. Their weapons are not bows or guns, but the forces of ice and fire.

Look For

Look for the many details in this legend that re-create the warmth of a fire or the cold of a bitter winter. These details make the conflict between ice and fire seem even more vivid.

Writing

Imagine that you are designing a costume for a person who will represent the king or queen of the winter. Freewrite about this costume. Tell what colors, materials, and designs you would use to make this outfit represent the winter in an impressive way.

Vocabulary

Knowing the following words will help you as you read "Ojeeg, the Hunter, and the Ice Man."

vanquish (vaŋ′ kwish) *v.*: Overcome (p. 593)

pummeled (pum″ ld) *v.*: Hit with repeated blows (p. 594)

extracted (ik strakt′ əd) *v.*: Obtained by drawing out (p. 594)

rendered (ren′ dərd) *v.*: Melted down (p. 594)

flaunted (flônt′ əd) *v.*: Displayed; showed off (p. 594)

shuddered (shud′ ərd) *v.*: Shook (p. 596)

grizzled (griz″ ld) *adj.*: Gray (p. 596)

flit (flit) *v.*: Fly lightly and rapidly (p. 596)

Objectives

1 To understand conflict
2 To evaluate a personification
3 To present a readers' theater
4 To create a personification

Support Material

Teaching Portfolio
Teacher Backup, p. 965
Grammar in Action Worksheet, *Understanding Verb Tense*, p. 969
Usage and Mechanics Worksheet, p. 971
Vocabulary Check, p. 972
Analyzing Literature Worksheet, *Understanding Conflict in a Legend*, p. 973

Critical Thinking and Reading Worksheet, *Evaluating Personification*, p. 974
Selection Test, p. 975

Ojeeg, the Hunter, and the Ice Man

from **the Micmac (Canada)**

Dorothy de Wit

On the shores of a large body of water, near the great evergreen forests of the north, there lived a hunter with his wife and young son. Their wigwam[1] stood by itself, far from the village, and they were very content, for Ojeeg was skilled with his arrows and brought as much game and furs to his wife as they had need of! The little boy would have been happy, indeed, if the snow had not been so deep or the winters so long. He did not miss companions to play with, for his father showed him the tracks of the grouse[2] and the squirrels. He pointed out the white coats of the rabbits and the weasel, and he trained him to use his bow carefully so that he would not waste his arrows.

But the cold grew more bitter as the long winter months dragged on. One day the boy saw a squirrel running around a stump, looking vainly for buried nuts, for the snow was too deep. Finally, the squirrel rested on his bushy tail, and as the boy came toward him, he said, "I am hungry, and there is no food to be found anywhere! Aren't you, too, tired of this ice and cold?"

"I am," said the hunter's son. "But what can we do against the power of the Ice Man? We are weak; he is cruel and strong!"

"You can cry! You can howl with hunger!" replied the squirrel. "Your father is a great hunter. He has strong power, and maybe he can vanquish the Ice Man if he sees your grief. Cry, cry, small brother! It may help!"

That night the young boy came into the wigwam, threw down his bow and arrows, and huddled beside the fire, sobbing. He would not answer his mother when she questioned him, and he would not stop crying. When his father came home, the boy's cries grew even louder, and nothing would make him stop, until at last the hunter asked, "Is it perhaps that you are lonely? That you do not like the snow and the cold?" At that the boy nodded his head. "Then," said the father, "I shall see if I have the power to change it."

He went out the next day on his snowshoes.[3] Long he traveled by the frozen water till he came to a narrow place that was

---

1. wigwam (wig′ wäm) *n.*: A shelter with a rounded top made by certain Native American groups.
2. grouse (grous) *n.*: A group of game birds.

3. snowshoes (snō′ shōōz′) *n.*: Racket-shaped pieces of wood crisscrossed with strips of leather, worn on the feet to prevent sinking in deep snow.

Ojeeg, the Hunter, and the Ice Man 593

Motivation/Prior Knowledge Ask students to imagine what it might be like to meet a being who is a living form of winter. What would it look like? How would it act? Would it be scary or friendly?

Master Teacher Note To give the students a better idea about personification, you might ask them what the human forms of the seasons of spring, summer, and fall might look like. What would their ages be? Would they be male or female? How would they be dressed? How would they behave?

Thematic Idea Selections in which animal characters are given human qualities are "Rikki-tikki-tavi," on page 13, and "The Pheasant," on page 466. In "Fog," on page 468, the subject is personified in animal terms.

Purpose-Setting Question How is the ice king, who makes winter, portrayed in this legend?

1 Discussion What details from this paragraph give clues about the culture of the Micmac tribe?

2 Critical Thinking and Reading The squirrel is personified as having the human quality of speech. Ask students if they have ever given human qualities to animals, such as dogs or cats, imagining that the animals could have human thoughts or speech.

3 Literary Focus The conflict is now established between the hunter and the cold, long winter. What special qualities do you think the hunter has that make him think he can do something about winter?

4 **Critical Thinking and Reading**
What human qualities are given
to the character of the ice king?
How does his challenge increase
your interest in the story?

5 **Discussion** The hunter has
proven his great power, yet he
works diligently throughout the
summer to prepare for the hard
winter ahead. What does this indicate about the hunter's character? What characteristics do the
Micmacs seem to admire, based
on this character?

choked with huge blocks of ice. He took his
sharp knife and a stone chisel, and he began
to dig away at the chunks. Many hours he
chipped and hacked and pummeled the ice,
and in the end he heard the barricade crack!
The ice began to move, and a part of it broke
off and jostled and bumped around until
more cracks appeared. The whole mass of ice
began to float slowly away. The hunter rested
and wiped the sweat from his face. Then he
heard the voice of Peboan, the ice king,
piercing the air: "You have won for now, my
son! You are strong indeed, and your Manito
power[4] is great! But I shall gain the final victory, for next year I will return, and I will
bring even more snow! The North Wind will
blow more fiercely, and the trees will break
with the weight of the ice I will pile on their
branches! The waters will freeze so that no
matter how many warriors cross them, not a
crack will appear. Then you will see, grandson, who is the master of winter!"

The hunter returned to his wigwam. The
snows were melting, and green was returning to the earth. Sweet sap rose in the maple
trees, and his little son shouted with joy! But
the hunter remembered the threat which the
ice king had made: "Next winter will be
worse—much worse!"

So he set himself to cutting wood and
piling it in great stacks; he gathered the
resin[5] from the pine trees and formed it into
great lumps. From the game which he
brought home he extracted much fat, and
this he rendered and stored in large oil pots.
Baskets of evergreen cones and thick logs he
stored up also. Then, when the maple and
the oak flaunted their red and yellow ban-

___
4. Manito (man′ ə tō′) **power:** Power that comes
from nature spirits.
5. resin (rez′ ′n) *n.:* A sticky brownish or yellowish
substance that comes from evergreen trees.

ners at the dark hemlocks, he went somewhat apart from his own lodging and built a
small, very tight new wigwam. He left his
wife warm skins and food in quantity; then,
with supplies for himself, he began stacking
them, and the firewood, the resin lumps, the
oil pots, and the baskets of cones, within his
new lodging.

When the first snowfall whitened the
ground, he bade his wife and son have courage and went to the new wigwam. He laced
the skins tightly and closed the opening
securely. With food and water at
hand and warm furs to cover
him, he built a
very small

Grammar in Action

The **tense** of a **verb** is important because it tells the reader when
the action is taking place or when something exists. Verbs have
six tenses: present, past, future, present perfect, past perfect,
and future perfect. In the following passage, Dorothy de Wit
makes the reader aware of the times of the action by changing
the tenses of her verbs:

But the hunter *remembered* the threat which the ice king
had made: "Next winter *will be* worse—much worse!"

De Wit uses the past, past perfect, and future tenses of verbs.
The past perfect tense shows the relationship between two things
that happened in the past. The action of a past perfect verb
precedes another past action. In this case, *had made* indicates
that the ice king's threat occurred before the hunter remembered.
The future tense, *will be,* indicates an action yet to come.

Student Activity 1. Write the correct tense of the verb in parentheses. Use either the past, future, or past perfect form of the
verb. Remember that you will have to use a helping verb with the
last two forms.

1. "Jim *(have)* a tough time winning the race," *(remark)* Gerald, after he *(glance)* over the times posted for the trial heats.

2. Mother, seeing the books that Mary *(set)* on the table earlier in the day, *(exclaim),* "I wonder if she *(learn)* to put things away!"

Student Activity 2. Write three original sentences, each containing a verb in the past tense, one in the future, and one in the past perfect.

fire in the center of the fire hole and sat down to wait for Peboan.

6 Discussion Is this description of Peboan the way you imagined the ice king to look? What qualities does he seem to represent, based on this appearance? Why does the hunter refer to him as "Grandfather"?

7 Literary Focus The events of the legend are building to the climax, the point where the conflict is resolved. The ice king seems to be losing his power. How did Peboan's boasting get him into trouble?

8 Discussion The conflict has been resolved, yet it is clear that the ice king will return next year. Based on what you know about Peboan's character, do you think that the winter will be much easier next year?

9 Discussion What natural object is explained at the end of this legend?

Reader's Response What do you admire most about Ojeeg? Why?

fire in the center of the fire hole and sat down to wait for Peboan.

At first the frost was light, and the snow melted quickly. At night the wind did not rise much, and the hunter thought, "Perhaps I have frightened old Peboan away! He will see that it is not so easy to win over me!" But as the winter deepened, the tent poles rattled more, the skins shuddered a bit, and it took more fire to warm the wigwam. Still, Peboan did not come. The hunter heard the great owl swoop through the trees at night. He heard weasels and rabbits move through the snow, and once the heavy footfall of a moose crashed through the drifts. The cold became intense.

Then, suddenly one night, the skins across the door opening were torn away and a gust of North Wind almost blew the fire apart! Peboan stood there, grizzled and bent. His face was lined and cruel, and his long beard hung with icicles. "I have come as I said I would," he shouted.

The hunter rose swiftly, tied up the door skins, and put more wood on the fire. A chill ran through him—the ice king's power was very great! "Grandfather, be seated at my fire. You are my guest here!" he said. The old one sat far from the fire and watched him.

"My power is great! I blow my breath—the streams stand still; the waters are stiff and hard like rock crystal!"

The hunter shivered and put another log on the fire. "The snow covers the land when I shake my head; trees are without any leaves, and their branches break with the weight of my ice!"

The hunter added some cones, and the flames leaped up. "No birds fly now, for they have gone far away. Only the hardy ones flit around, and they are hungry."

The hunter added more wood to the fire, for the air in the wigwam was becoming bitter cold, and frost hung on his eyebrows and nose. "The animals hide away and sleep through the long cold." Peboan laughed grimly as he saw the man draw his fur closer around him.

"Even the hunters do not leave their lodges. The children curl deep into their blankets for warmth and cry with hunger."

Then Ojeeg pulled out the resin lumps; first one, then another he tossed into the coals, and they burned hotly. Peboan shook his white head and moved as far away from the heat as he could. When the hunter saw that, he added yet another clutch of pitch and more logs. Sweat began to roll down the wrinkled face; the ice king huddled close to the wall of the wigwam; his icy garments began to melt.

Ojeeg took up the pots of oil and poured them onto the fire. The flames burned orange and red and blue! They licked at the old man's long robe, at his ice-covered feet, at his snowy mantle, and the Ice Man cried out in pain, "Enough, enough! I have seen your power, Ojeeg! Take back your fire and heat! Stifle your flames!" But the hunter only built up the fire higher, and the Ice Man became smaller and smaller, till at last he melted into a pool of water which ran over the ground and out, under the wigwam opening. When he saw that, Ojeeg, the hunter, untied the skins and looked out. The Ice Man was gone completely! Beyond his doorway the ground was brown and soft with pine needles, he could hear running water, and birds flew through the treetops. How long had he been in his wigwam? The spring was at hand!

Ojeeg put out his fire and ran toward his wife and son, who had come out and stood waiting to welcome him! The ice king would not make so long a visit next year! Only the white flowers of the snowdrop, fragile and small, remained to mark where Peboan had left his footprints!

Closure and Extension

ANSWERS TO THINKING ABOUT THE SELECTION
Recalling

1. The hunter decides to make the snow and ice go away because his son does not like the cold and snow.
2. Peboan is grizzled and bent, his

face lined and cruel, and his beard hung with icicles. He has the power to make streams stand still by turning them to ice; to cover the land with snow; and to strip the trees of their leaves, and break their branches with the weight of his ice. He drives birds, animals, and even hunters into shelter to get away from the cold.
3. The ice king vanishes because the hunter builds up his fire to create tremendous heat, which melts the ice man into water.

Interpreting

4. Suggested Response: You knew that the hunter is a powerful hero because when the squirrel tells the boy that his father might be able to do something about the ice king, the hunter agrees to try. The hunter also succeeds in defeating the ice king twice.
5. Ojeeg influences the way that seasons change by breaking up Peboan's ice block, which starts the thawing process of spring. When the hunter melts down Peboan the

next winter, the hastening of spring is advanced again.
6. Suggested Response: The Micmacs thought of ice as having godlike powers because they lived in an area in the north that has extremely long, cold winters. These winters probably produced great amounts of ice on the water. The ice probably remained for a long time. The ice also influenced every aspect of their lives and the lives of the animals which lived in the region.

THINKING ABOUT THE SELECTION

Recalling

1. Why does the hunter decide to make the snow and cold go away?
2. Describe Peboan when he appears at the wigwam. What powers does he have?
3. Why does the ice king vanish?

Interpreting

4. How do you know that the hunter is a hero, with more power than an ordinary person?
5. How does Ojeeg influence the way that seasons change?
6. Why do you think the Micmacs thought of ice as having godlike powers?

Applying

7. Explain what you learn about the Micmac tribe from reading this legend.

ANALYZING LITERATURE

Understanding Conflict in a Legend

A **conflict** is a struggle between opposing sides or forces. Sometimes tales and legends present conflicts by giving a supernatural twist to a real situation. For instance, the Micmac had to fight against the cold in the northern woods. Their legend of Ojeeg and the Ice Man dramatizes that struggle by telling about a battle between a hero and a magical ice king.

1. How does Ojeeg win the first fight?
2. What is his plan to win again?
3. When does it seem that Ojeeg might lose?
4. What does he do to make Peboan retreat?
5. Is Ojeeg's victory total? Explain.

CRITICAL THINKING AND READING

Evaluating a Personification

A **personification** is a figure of speech that gives human qualities to an idea, an object, or an aspect of nature. In this legend, Peboan is a per-

sonification. Although he is magical, he represents the winter in human form. You can judge whether he is a suitable ice king by looking closely at his traits.

1. Why do you think he is personified as a grizzled old man rather than a boy or a young woman?
2. Why is his face "lined and cruel"?
3. Is Peboan a suitable personification of winter? Why or why not?
4. If you wanted to personify winter, what kind of person would you use?

SPEAKING AND LISTENING

Presenting a Readers Theater

A **readers theater** is a dramatic reading of a piece of literature. Work with your classmates to give a readers theater presentation of "Ojeeg, the Hunter and the Ice Man." Some of the students in your class can speak the words the characters actually say, while others can narrate the rest of the story.

As you read, try to imitate the way your character would speak. If you have the part of the ice king, for example, remember that he is a "grizzled and bent" old man. You can also design costumes for the characters to make the presentation more effective.

THINKING AND WRITING

Creating a Personification

Imagine that an advertising agency is offering a prize for the best personification of winter. The agency will use the character created by the winner in a campaign to promote ski resorts. This character must therefore convey a positive image of the winter season. List the qualities that such a personification should have. Using your list, write a letter to the agency explaining your concept. As you revise your letter, make sure it will convince the agency, and you will win the prize.

Ojeeg, the Hunter, and the Ice Man 597

(Answers begin on p. 596.)

Peboan and caused the beginning of spring, but winter is not gone forever and will return the following year.

ANSWERS TO CRITICAL THINKING AND READING

1. Suggested Response: Peboan is portrayed as an old man because winter seems to be at the end of the cycle of the seasons, just as old age is at the end of the cycle of human life.
2. Suggested Response: Peboan's face is lined and cruel because the harsh, cold conditions of the winter seem cruel to people and also age them more rapidly than the other seasons.
3. Answers will differ. Suggested Response: Peboan is a suitable personification of winter because his appearance and behavior reflect the feelings and experiences of people who live in areas where the winter is long and harsh.
4. Answers will differ. Students should support their answers.

Challenge How would you personify winter, based on the effect of that season on your life?

Speaking and Listening If more students want to get involved with this, have them do a reader's theater presentation of "The Legend of the Hummingbird" on page 589 as well. You might want to have the class present one or both legends to other classes or to a school assembly.

Writing Across the Curriculum You might want to have students research and report on the process that creates snow in the atmosphere or the reason that ice forms from water. It might be helpful for students assigned to either of these topics to receive assistance from science teachers. You could inform the science department if you use either of these assignments.

Applying

7. Students might mention the effect of winter on the animals and people; the preparations the Micmacs make for the winter; their means of travel during the winter; their glorification of the hunter; the Micmacs' attitude toward winter; the structures that they live in; the Micmac family structure; and what they hunt.

ANSWERS TO ANALYZING LITERATURE

1. Ojeeg wins the first fight by using strength and perseverance to chip and pound away the ice that is blocking up the water.
2. His plan to win again is to make complete and thorough preparations for the coming winter. He works very hard all summer gathering different kinds of fuel to keep his fire burning fiercely enough to vanquish Peboan.
3. It seems that the hunter might

lose, just before he throws resin lumps onto the fire, when the air in his wigwam becomes intensely cold and frost gathers on his eyebrows and nose.
4. The hunter throws on more logs, pine cones, and then pours oil on the fire, which generates so much heat that Peboan begins to melt and has to retreat.
5. Ojeeg's victory is not complete, because the legend ends stating that winter would not be as long the next year. Ojeeg has beaten

Focus

More About the Legend The city depicted in this legend, Tenochti-tlan, was the largest city of the Aztec Empire, as well as its capital. When the Spanish arrived, the population of the city may have been 100,000 or more. The city was built on an island in the middle of Lake Texcoco, with causeways linking it to the mainland. What might have been some of the advantages and disadvantages of building the city on an island?

Literary Focus A character's motivation can be an idea, a feeling, or an experience. For example, a character can be motivated by love to marry someone. A character can be motivated by the idea of equality to fight against those who seek domination. The experience of coming close to death because of carelessness can motivate a character to change his or her life. Motivation is often a combination of any or all of these things. The characters in this legend are motivated primarily by their feelings.

Look For Your less advanced students may have difficulty identifying the motives of the characters. It may be helpful to preview the Analyzing Literature questions on page 605.

Writing/Prior Knowledge You might have your more advanced students write about a story where a feeling, experience, or emotion other than love is key to a character's motivation.

Vocabulary You could have your more advanced students write an original sentence for each of the vocabulary words.

Popocatepetl and Ixtlaccihuatl

This folk legend comes to us from the **Aztec** Indians, who controlled a great empire in Mexico about 500 years ago. Some of their cities were even larger than European cities of that era. The Spanish destroyed this empire in 1521, but the influence of Aztec culture has continued in art, language, and food.

    Juliet Piggott (1924–   ), whose version of this tale appears in her book *Mexican Folk Tales,* has also written about Japanese history and folklore.

Motivation in Legend

The term **motivation** refers to the reasons that people act as they do. Like characters in fiction, those in legends have reasons or motives for their behavior. In "The Legend of the Hummingbird," for instance, Alida's motive for praying to her god is her wish to avoid marrying someone other than Taroo.

A storyteller may reveal the characters' motives or let you figure them out for yourself. In "Popocatepetl and Ixtlaccihuatl" the storyteller uses both of these methods.

Look For

As you read this legend, look for the motives that influence the actions of each character. Often the storyteller will tell you directly what these motives are.

Writing

The two main characters in this legend are strongly motivated by love for each other. Freewrite about a story you have read or a film you have seen in which love was a key motivation. Tell how this motive affected the characters' actions.

Vocabulary

Knowing the following words will help you as you read "Popocatepetl and Ixtlaccihuatl."

besieged (bi sēj′′d) *v.*: Surrounded (p. 601)
decreed (di krēd′) *v.*: Officially ordered (p. 601)
relished (rel′ isht) *v.*: Especially enjoyed (p. 601)
brandishing (bran′ dish iŋ) *v.*: Waving in a menacing way (p. 602)

unanimous (yōo nan′ə məs) *adj.*: Based on complete agreement (p. 602)
refute (ri fyōot′) *v.*: To prove someone wrong (p. 602)
routed (rout′ əd) *v.*: Completely defeated (p. 604)
edifice (ed′ə fis) *n.*: Large structure (p. 604)

Objectives

1 To understand motivation
2 To identify imaginative details
3 To use synonyms as context clues
4 To write about a legend

Support Material

Teaching Portfolio
Teacher Backup, p. 977
Grammar in Action Worksheet, *Recognizing Specific Nouns and Specific Adjectives,* p. 981
Usage and Mechanics Worksheet, p. 983
Vocabulary Check, p. 984
Analyzing Literature Worksheet, *Understanding Motivation in a Legend,* p. 985

Language Worksheet, *Using Synonyms,* p. 986
Selection Test, p. 987

Popocatepetl and Ixtlaccihuatl

from **Mexico**

Juliet Piggott

Before the Spaniards came to Mexico and marched on the Aztec capital of Tenochtitlan[1] there were two volcanoes to the southeast of that city. The Spaniards destroyed much of Tenochtitlan and built another city in its place and called it Mexico City. It is known by that name still, and the pass through which the Spaniards came to the ancient Tenochtitlan is still there, as are the volcanoes on each side of that pass. Their names have not been changed. The one to the north is Ixtlaccihuatl[2] and the one on the south of the pass is Popocatepetl.[3] Both are snowcapped and beautiful, Popocatepetl being the taller of the two. That name means Smoking Mountain. In Aztec days it gushed forth smoke and, on occasion, it does so still. It erupted too in Aztec days and has done so again since the Spaniards came. Ixtlaccihuatl means The White Woman, for its peak was, and still is, white.

Perhaps Ixtlaccihuatl and Popocatepetl were there in the highest part of the Valley of Mexico in the days when the earth was very young, in the days when the new people were just learning to eat and grow corn. The Aztecs claimed the volcanoes as their own, for they possessed a legend about them and their creation, and they believed that legend to be true.

There was once an Aztec Emperor in Tenochtitlan. He was very powerful. Some thought he was wise as well, whilst others doubted his wisdom. He was both a ruler and a warrior and he kept at bay those tribes living in and beyond the mountains surrounding the Valley of Mexico, with its huge lake called Texcoco[4] in which Tenochtitlan was built. His power was absolute and the splendor in which he lived was very great.

It is not known for how many years the Emperor ruled in Tenochtitlan, but it is known that he lived to a great age. However, it was not until he was in his middle years that his wife gave him an heir, a girl. The Emperor and Empress loved the princess very much and she was their only child. She was a dutiful daughter and learned all she could from her father about the art of ruling, for she knew that when he died she would reign in his stead in Tenochtitlan.

Her name was Ixtlaccihuatl. Her parents

---

1. Tenochtitlan (te nŏch′ tē tlän′): The Spanish conquered the Aztec capital in 1521.
2. Ixtlaccihuatl (ēs′ tä sē′ wät′l)
3. Popocatepetl (pŏ̂ pŏ̂′ kä tē′ pet′l)

4. Texcoco (tä skŏ′ kō)

Popocatepetl and Ixtlaccihuatl 599

Presentation

Motivation/Prior Knowledge You might lead the class in a discussion of the stories students freewrote about in the Writing activity. You could discuss why love is often a strong influence on people and in what ways love motivates people. Why do people attempt things they would not do otherwise, either heroic or foolish, as a result of love?

Master Teacher Note It might be helpful to show students photographs of the two volcanoes that are the subject of this selection. The snow-covered peaks of Ixtlaccihuatl actually resemble a reclining woman. Popocatepetl, which often emits clouds of smoke and gas, is one of the highest peaks in North America at 17,887 feet. You might find photographs of these two volcanoes in the World Book encyclopedia, or a reference book on volcanoes.

Thematic Idea Another selection that deals with the theme of a tragic end to love is "The Highwayman" on page 437.

Purpose-Setting Question How does the motive of jealousy affect this legend?

1 **Discussion** Why did the Aztecs claim that, because they had a legend about them, the volcanoes were their own?

2 **Literary Focus** Are the daughter's motivations for being dutiful and learning all that she can revealed directly or indirectly?

ERUPTING VOLCANO, 1943
Dr. Atl (Gerardo Murillo)
Laurie Platt Winfrey, Inc.

and her friends called her Ixtla. She had a pleasant disposition and, as a result, she had many friends. The great palace where she lived with the Emperor and Empress rang with their laughter when they came to the parties her parents gave for her. As well as being a delightful companion Ixtla was also very pretty, even beautiful.

Her childhood was happy and she was content enough when she became a young woman. But by then she was fully aware of the great responsibilities which would be

hers when her father died and she became serious and studious and did not enjoy parties as much as she had done when younger.

Another reason for her being so serious was that she was in love. This in itself was a joyous thing, but the Emperor forbade her to marry. He wanted her to reign and rule alone when he died, for he trusted no one, not even his wife, to rule as he did except his much loved only child, Ixtla. This was why there were some who doubted the wisdom of the Emperor for, by not allowing his heiress

3

to marry, he showed a selfishness and short-sightedness towards his daughter and his empire which many considered was not truly wise. An emperor, they felt, who was not truly wise could not also be truly great. Or even truly powerful.

The man with whom Ixtla was in love was also in love with her. Had they been allowed to marry their state could have been doubly joyous. His name was Popocatepetl and Ixtla and his friends all called him Popo. He was a warrior in the service of the Emperor, tall and strong, with a capacity for gentleness, and very brave. He and Ixtla loved each other very much and while they were content and even happy when they were together, true joy was not theirs because the Emperor continued to insist that Ixtla should not be married when the time came for her to take on her father's responsibilities.

This unfortunate but moderately happy relationship between Ixtla and Popo continued for several years, the couple pleading with the Emperor at regular intervals and the Emperor remaining constantly adamant. Popo loved Ixtla no less for her father's stubbornness and she loved him no less while she studied, as her father demanded she should do, the art of ruling in preparation for her reign.

When the Emperor became very old he also became ill. In his feebleness he channeled all his failing energies towards instructing Ixtla in statecraft, for he was no longer able to exercise that craft himself. So it was that his enemies, the tribes who lived in the mountains and beyond, realized that the great Emperor in Tenochtitlan was great no longer, for he was only teaching his daughter to rule and not ruling himself.

The tribesmen came nearer and nearer to Tenochtitlan until the city was besieged. At last the Emperor realized himself that he was great no longer, that his power was nearly gone and that his domain was in dire peril.

Warrior though he long had been, he was now too old and too ill to lead his fighting men into battle. At last he understood that, unless his enemies were frustrated in their efforts to enter and lay waste to Tenochtitlan, not only would he no longer be Emperor but his daughter would never be Empress.

Instead of appointing one of his warriors to lead the rest into battle on his behalf, he offered a bribe to all of them. Perhaps it was that his wisdom, if wisdom he had, had forsaken him, or perhaps he acted from fear. Or perhaps he simply changed his mind. But the bribe he offered to whichever warrior succeeded in lifting the siege of Tenochtitlan and defeating the enemies in and around the Valley of Mexico was both the hand of his daughter and the equal right to reign and rule, with her, in Tenochtitlan. Furthermore, he decreed that directly he learned that his enemies had been defeated he would instantly cease to be Emperor himself. Ixtla would not have to wait until her father died to become Empress and, if her father should die of his illness or old age before his enemies were vanquished, he further decreed that he who overcame the surrounding enemies should marry the princess whether he, the Emperor, lived or not.

Ixtla was fearful when she heard of her father's bribe to his warriors, for the only one whom she had any wish to marry was Popo and she wanted to marry him, and only him, very much indeed.

The warriors, however, were glad when they heard of the decree: there was not one of them who would not have been glad to have the princess as his wife and they all relished the chance of becoming Emperor.

And so the warriors went to war at their

4 Discussion Do you agree or disagree with this statement? Support your answer. Do you think that the same is true for leaders today?

5 Reading Strategy You might have students question what the outcome of this conflict will be.

6 Critical Thinking and Reading You could ask students what details of this legend might be based on actual history and what details might be imaginative. Is it important to include both kinds of details in a legend? Why or why not?

7 Literary Focus You might point out that the author offers several possible motivations for the Emperor's bribe to his warriors. Which motivation is probably the correct one? Might his decision have been a combination of all these factors?

8 Discussion Do you think that the Emperor's offer was a wise one? Support your answer. How might this motivate the warriors?

9 **Reading Strategy** You could have students summarize what they have read about Popo. Are they surprised that he emerged as the best leader? They might question how the Emperor will react when he discovers this.

10 **Discussion** What causes people to be jealous of others? Why do people often wish harm to those they are jealous of?

11 **Reading Strategy** You might have students predict how Ixtla will react to the news of Popo's supposed death.

ruler's behest, and each fought trebly[5] hard for each was fighting not only for the safety of Tenochtitlan and the surrounding valley, but for the delightful bride and for the right to be the Emperor himself.

Even though the warriors fought with great skill and even though each one exhibited a courage he did not know he possessed, the war was a long one. The Emperor's enemies were firmly entrenched around Lake Texcoco and Tenochtitlan by the time the warriors were sent to war, and as battle followed battle the final outcome was uncertain.

The warriors took a variety of weapons with them; wooden clubs edged with sharp blades of obsidian,[6] obsidian machetes,[7] javelins which they hurled at their enemies from troughed throwing boards, bows and arrows, slings and spears set with obsidian fragments, and lances, too. Many of them carried shields woven from wicker[8] and covered in tough hide and most wore armor made of thick quilted cotton soaked in brine.

The war was long and fierce. Most of the warriors fought together and in unison, but some fought alone. As time went on natural leaders emerged and, of these, undoubtedly Popo was the best. Finally it was he, brandishing his club and shield, who led the great charge of running warriors across the valley, with their enemies fleeing before them to the safety of the coastal plains and jungles beyond the mountains.

9 The warriors acclaimed Popo as the man most responsible for the victory and, weary though they all were, they set off for Tenoch-

---

5. trebly (tre′ blē) *adv.*: Three times as much, triply.
6. obsidian (əb sid′ ē ən) *n.*: A hard, usually dark-colored or black, volcanic glass.
7. machetes (mə shet′ ēs) *n.*: Large, heavy-bladed knives.
8. wicker (wik′ ər) *n.*: A thin, flexible twig.

titlan to report to the Emperor and for Popo to claim Ixtla as his wife at last.

But a few of those warriors were jealous of Popo. Since they knew none of them could rightly claim the victory for himself (the decision among the Emperor's fighting men that Popo was responsible for the victory had been unanimous), they wanted to spoil for him and for Ixtla the delights which the Emperor had promised. **10**

These few men slipped away from the rest at night and made their way to Tenochtitlan ahead of all the others. They reached the capital two days later, having traveled without sleep all the way, and quickly let it be known that, although the Emperor's warriors had been successful against his enemies, the warrior Popo had been killed in battle.

It was a foolish and cruel lie which those warriors told their Emperor, and they told it for no reason other than that they were jealous of Popo.

When the Emperor heard this he demanded that Popo's body be brought to him so that he might arrange a fitting burial. He **11** knew the man his daughter had loved would have died courageously. The jealous warriors looked at one another and said nothing. Then one of them told the Emperor that Popo had been killed on the edge of Lake Texcoco and that his body had fallen into the water and no man had been able to retrieve it. The Emperor was saddened to hear this.

After a little while he demanded to be told which of his warriors had been responsible for the victory but none of the fighting men before him dared claim the successful outcome of the war for himself, for each knew the others would refute him. So they were silent. This puzzled the Emperor and he decided to wait for the main body of his warriors to return and not to press the few

Grammar in Action

Specific nouns and adjectives name or describe clearly and precisely things that can be seen and imagined. Using specific nouns and adjectives make it easy for the reader to picture what is being described and thus remember it. In the following passage Juliet Piggott uses a series of specific nouns and adjectives to describe and emphasize the variety of weapons the warriors took with them:

The warriors took a variety of weapons with them; *wooden clubs* edged with *sharp blades* of *obsidian, obsidian machetes, javelins* which they hurled at their enemies from *troughed throwing boards, bows* and *arrows, slings* and *spears* set with *obsidian fragments,* and *lances,* too.

Using a series of specific nouns and adjectives allows Piggott to present a vivid picture of the warriors' diverse weapons. Compare the examples with the following sentence to see how much meaning is lost when precise nouns and adjectives are not used:

QUETZALCOATL
Laurie Platt Winfrey, Inc.

Humanities Note

Fine art, *Quetzalcoatl,* from a Mixtec manuscript (c. 1500). The Mixtec Indians lived in northern Mexico and were noted for their painting skills. This image is a representation of Quetzalcoatl from Mixtec mythology. Quetzalcoatl, the Feathered Serpent, was worshipped as the god of knowledge and civilization.

1. How does its appearance compare with the reasons that the god is worshipped?
2. Why would such a god be important to the people who lived in the city of Tenochtitlan?

12 Discussion Why is it unwise for the Emperor to speak to Ixtla about her new husband just after she learns about the loss of Popo?

who had brought the news of the victory and of Popo's death.

Then the Emperor sent for his wife and his daughter and told them their enemies had been overcome. The Empress was thoroughly excited and relieved at the news. Ixtla was only apprehensive. The Emperor, seeing her anxious face, told her quickly that Popo was dead. He went on to say that the warrior's body had been lost in the waters of Lake Texcoco, and again it was as though his wisdom had left him, for he spoke at some length of his not being able to tell Ixtla who her husband would be and who would **12** become Emperor when the main body of warriors returned to Tenochtitlan.

Popocatepetl and Ixtlaccihuatl 603

The warriors took a variety of weapons with them; clubs, knives, spears, bows and arrows, slings, spears, and lances, too.

Student Activity 1. Complete the following sentences with a series of specific nouns and adjectives.

1. If I had wanted to, I could have been a. . . .

2. Planning a vacation is such fun, for you can go to the. . . .

3. Some of may favorite games are. . . .

Student Activity 2. Write three original sentences in which you use a series of specific nouns and adjectives.

13 Literary Focus The motivation or reason for Ixtla's sickness is only guessed at by the author. You might ask students what they think might be the cause of her sickness. Are students familiar with any other books or movies where a similar event occurred?

14 Discussion What do you think about the actions Popo took after he found out about Ixtla?

Enrichment To give students an idea of what life was like for Aztecs who lived in the city of Tenochtitlan, you might show them some photos of Aztec artifacts or some artists' depictions of the city based on excavations and anthropological research. Included in the December, 1980, *National Geographic* magazine is an extensive article on Aztec civilization and culture.

Reader's Response Do you think that Popo's actions following the news of Ixtla's death were wise and just? Explain.

But Ixtla heard nothing of what he told her, only that her beloved Popo was dead. She went to her room and lay down. Her mother followed her and saw at once she was very ill. Witch doctors were sent for, but they could not help the princess, and neither could her parents. Her illness had no name, unless it was the illness of a broken heart. Princess Ixtlaccihuatl did not wish to live if Popocatepetl was dead, and so she died herself.

The day after her death Popo returned to Tenochtitlan with all the other surviving warriors. They went straight to the palace and, with much cheering, told the Emperor that his enemies had been routed and that Popo was the undoubted victor of the conflict.

The Emperor praised his warriors and pronounced Popo to be the new Emperor in his place. When the young man asked first to see Ixtla, begging that they should be married at once before being jointly proclaimed Emperor and Empress, the Emperor had to tell Popo of Ixtla's death, and how it had happened.

Popo spoke not a word.

He gestured the assembled warriors to follow him and together they sought out the few jealous men who had given the false news of his death to the Emperor. With the army of warriors watching, Popo killed each one of them in single combat with his obsidian studded club. No one tried to stop him.

That task accomplished Popo returned to the palace and, still without speaking and still wearing his stiff cotton armor, went to Ixtla's room. He gently lifted her body and carried it out of the palace and out of the city, and no one tried to stop him doing that either. All the warriors followed him in silence.

When he had walked some miles he gestured to them again and they built a huge pile of stones in the shape of a pyramid. They all worked together and they worked fast while Popo stood and watched, holding the body of the princess in his arms. By sunset the mighty edifice was finished. Popo climbed it alone, carrying Ixtla's corpse with him. There, at the very top, under a heap of stones, he buried the young woman he had loved so well and for so long, and who had died for the love of him.

That night Popo slept alone at the top of the pyramid by Ixtla's grave. In the morning he came down and spoke for the first time since the Emperor had told him the princess was dead. He told the warriors to build another pyramid, a little to the southeast of the one which held Ixtla's body and to build it higher than the other.

He told them too to tell the Emperor on his behalf that he, Popocatepetl, would never reign and rule in Tenochtitlan. He would keep watch over the grave of the Princess Ixtlaccihuatl for the rest of his life.

The messages to the Emperor were the last words Popo ever spoke. Well before the evening the second mighty pile of stones was built. Popo climbed it and stood at the top, taking a torch of resinous pine wood with him.

And when he reached to top he lit the torch and the warriors below saw the white smoke rise against the blue sky, and they watched as the sun began to set and the smoke turned pink and then a deep red, the color of blood.

So Popocatepetl stood there, holding the torch in memory of Ixtlaccihuatl, for the rest of his days.

The snows came and, as the years went by, the pyramids of stone became high white-capped mountains. Even now the one called Popocatepetl emits smoke in memory of the princess whose body lies in the mountain which bears her name.

Closure and Extension

ANSWERS TO THINKING ABOUT THE SELECTION
Recalling

1. The couple cannot marry because the Emperor does not trust anyone but Ixtla to rule after his death.

2. The Emperor shows his selfishness by not letting his daughter get married, and then by offering her hand in marriage to whomever would defeat the tribesmen. The effect of his selfishness is that he continues to rule into old age, and enemies of the city, realizing he is weak, gather and attack. Another effect is that the warriors who do not want Popo to win the bribe lie and say that Popo has died in the fighting. This leads to the death of Ixtla.

3. He offers Ixtla and his throne to his warriors because he is aware of the danger that the city faces and wants them to fight harder than ever before.

4. Several warriors, jealous of the fact that Popo is going to become the Emperor and marry Ixtla, inform the Emperor that Popo has died in the fighting. When Ixtla discovers this, she becomes ill and dies.

5. Popo refuses to rule because he wants to stand watch over the pyramid grave of Ixtla for the rest of his life.

Interpreting

6. Answers will differ. Suggested responses include: the Emperor was

THINKING ABOUT THE SELECTION

Recalling

1. Why are Ixtla and Popo unable to marry?
2. How does the emperor show his selfishness? What effect does his selfishness have on the safety of his kingdom?
3. Why does the emperor offer Ixtla and his throne as a bribe to his warriors?
4. What leads to Ixtla's death at the end of the war?
5. Why does Popo refuse to rule in Tenochtitlan?

Interpreting

6. Is the emperor a wise man? Why or why not?
7. On the basis of this legend, what traits do you think the Aztecs admired?

Applying

8. What traits do you think are necessary in a leader?

ANALYZING LITERATURE

Understanding Motivation in Legend

The term **motivation** refers to the reasons people act as they do. In "Popocatepetl and Ixtlaccihuatl" the storyteller often explains the characters' **motives,** or reasons for acting.

1. Which event is caused by selfishness?
2. Which is caused by jealousy?
3. Which are caused by love?
4. What do you think this legend indicates about the power of love?

CRITICAL THINKING AND READING

Identifying Imaginative Details

Legends are traditional tales passed down over the generations. Often they are based on the lives of people who actually once lived. However, legends are not history. The events they tell about have been filtered through a people's imagination and enlarged upon.

1. Which events in this legend might have been based on historical events?
2. Which events are highly imaginative and probably not based on historical events?

UNDERSTANDING LANGUAGE

Using Synonyms as Context Clues

The **context** of a word means the words that surround it. You can often find clues to a word you do not know by looking for synonyms in the context. In "Popocatepetl and Ixtlaccihuatl" for instance, you learn that when Ixtla grew up "she became serious and studious." You can figure out the meaning of *studious* if you know the definition of its **synonym,** *serious*. (Both words can mean "thoughtful.")

Find the meaning of the following *italicized* words using clues in the context. Check your answers in a dictionary.

1. " . . . the Emperor remaining constantly *adamant*. Popo loved Ixtla no less for her father's stubbornness. . . . "
2. "Most of the warriors fought together and in *unison*."

THINKING AND WRITING

Writing About a Legend

Imagine you are either Ixtla, Popo, or one of the jealous soldiers. Tell this story from this character's point of view. First list the details you would emphasize in your retelling of the myth. Arrange these details in chronological order. Then write your first draft. Revise your tale, making sure you have stayed in character. Prepare a final draft and share it with your classmates.

Ixtla's death and its cause: He kills the warriors, has one pyramid built for Ixtla and one for himself, and he remains on his pyramid for the rest of his life, overlooking the grave of Ixtla.

4. Suggested Response: This legend indicates that the power of love is stronger than life itself. It also indicates that people in love can die of a broken heart and that they will sacrifice anything for their loved ones.

ANSWERS TO CRITICAL THINKING AND READING

1. Events that might have been based on historical events are the Emperor not allowing his daughter to marry, the daughter's love for the great warrior, the war with the surrounding tribes, and the victory of the war being the responsibility of one great warrior.
2. The events that are highly imaginative and probably not based on historical facts are the building of the monuments for Popo and Ixtla, Popo's lifelong vigil over Ixtla's grave, and the transformation of these pyramids into the two volcanoes.

ANSWERS TO UNDERSTANDING LANGUAGE

1. adamant: not giving in, unyielding
2. unison: complete agreement

THINKING AND WRITING

Publishing Student Writing Ask for student volunteers to read their stories aloud, especially stories seen through the eyes of different characters. These reading will give the class the opportunity to hear the legend from many different points of view. Have the class note at least one important difference in each character's point of view.

---

wise because he taught his daughter everything he knew about ruling. He also motivated his warriors by offering his title and helped avert defeat. He was unwise because he did not let his daughter marry the man she loved and did not trust anyone except her to rule. He also spoke about another husband just after telling her about the death of Popo.

7. Answers should include the traits of strength, loyalty, honor, love, wisdom, and leadership.

Applying

8. Answers will differ but may include the traits of strength, wisdom, understanding, willingness to sacrifice, and assertiveness.

Challenge Do you think that Popo's actions at the end of the legend were those of a good leader? Should he have accepted the title of Emperor because of his skills and for the good of the people? Explain.

ANSWERS TO ANALYZING LITERATURE

1. One of the events caused by selfishness is the attack on the city by hostile tribesmen because of the Emperor's refusal to step down as ruler.
2. One of the events caused by jealousy is the death of Ixtla after warriors told the Emperor that Popo had died in the fighting.
3. The events caused by love are Popo's actions when he discovers

Focus

More About the Folk Tale This tale reflects a moral bind that many of the peasants of China were caught in. Although all people attempted to live by high moral standards, including unselfish behavior, the reality of life for the peasant was a struggle for survival. Therefore, moral considerations were sometimes difficult to live up to. This tale presents this dilemma in a humorous fashion. Why is it more difficult for a peasant to live by a strict code than for an immortal being?

Literary Focus Folk tales are the most popular type of stories in the world and have been told for thousands of years. Because they originally were spread by word of mouth, folk tales changed gradually with telling, and different versions of the same tales emerged. Usually, these tales tell about an average person.

Look For Remind students that people enjoy hearing about an average person who cleverly outwits a bigger, stronger, or supernatural being. You might have them look for this kind of incident in the story.

Writing/Prior Knowledge If students have difficulty thinking up magical powers, you might suggest the power to become invisible, the power to fly, the power to grant wishes, the power to read minds, the power to change form, and the power to make magical potions.

Vocabulary Have less advanced students pronounce the vocabulary words aloud so that you can be sure that they can read them.

The Pointing Finger

Chinese literature is one of the great literatures of the world. Poems and tales have been produced in China for nearly 3,000 years. For most of China's history, literature, such as the folk tale you are about to read, has had an important place in people's lives.

Carol Kendall (1917–　　) has written two collections of Chinese tales. Translating Chinese is a special interest of hers. **Yao-wen Li** (1924–　　) was born and raised in pre-Communist China and now lives in Kansas.

Folk Tale

A **folk tale** is a story made up by the common people of a country. It is handed down by word of mouth for many generations. Folk tales are especially interesting for what they imply about the values and beliefs of the people who create them.

Look For

As you read "The Pointing Finger," think about why this tale has lasted so long. What have many generations of Chinese people found interesting and enjoyable about it?

Writing

Magical powers are used in this tale. If you were writing or telling a story about someone with such powers, which ones would you choose? List and briefly describe three or four of them. Then choose one and tell how your character would use it for some useful purpose.

Vocabulary

Knowing the following words will help you as you read "The Pointing Finger."

tedious (tē′ dē əs) *adj.*: Long and boring (p. 607)

taint (tānt) *n.*: A trace (p. 607)

avarice (av′ ər is) *n.*: Greed for riches (p. 607)

proffered (präf′ ərd) *v.*: Offered (p. 607)

cupidity (kyōō pid′ ə tē) *n.*: Strong desire for wealth (p. 607)

Objectives

1 To understand a folk tale
2 To evaluate generalizations
3 To match meaning with context
4 To summarize a folk tale

Support Material

Teaching Portfolio
Teacher Backup, p. 989
Usage and Mechanics Worksheet, p. 992
Vocabulary Check, p. 993
Analyzing Literature Worksheet, *Understanding a Folk Tale,* p. 994
Language Worksheet, *Matching Meaning With Context,* p. 995
Selection Test, p. 996

The Pointing Finger

from **China**

Carol Kendall and Yao-wen Li

Even P'eng-lai has its tedious days, and when time hung heavy over that fairy mountain isle in the Eastern Sea, the Eight Immortals who dwelt there remembered and talked of their previous existence as mortals on earth. Upon occasion they took disguises and transported themselves from P'eng-lai to their old world to nose about in human affairs in the hope of discovering improvements in human nature. On the whole, however, they found the mortals of today to have the same shortcomings and the same longcomings as those of yesterday.

It came about that one of the Immortals, on such a nosing-about expedition, was seeking an unselfish man. He vowed that when he found a man without the taint of greed in his heart, he would make of him an Immortal on the spot and transport him to P'eng-lai Mountain forthwith.[1]

His test for avarice was simple. Upon meeting a foot-traveler in lane or road, he would turn a pebble into gold by pointing his finger at it. He would then offer the golden pebble to the traveler.

The first person he met accepted the pebble eagerly, but then, turning it over and over between his fingers, his eyes beginning to gleam and glint, he said, "Can you do the same thing again? To those?" and he pointed at a small heap of stones at their feet.

The Immortal shook his head sadly and went on.

The second person looked at the proffered golden pebble long and thoughtfully. "Ah," he finally said, his eyes narrowed in calculation, "but this is a fine thing you would give me. It will feed my family for a year, and feed them well, but what then? Back to rice water and elm bark? That would be a cruelty. How could I face their tears and laments? Kind sir, as it is such an effortless task for you, perhaps you could turn your finger toward something a little larger, like, for example"—and he pointed at a boulder as big as himself beside the road—"that bit of stone?"

All along the way the story was the same, until the Immortal despaired of finding human beings whose cupidity did not outweigh their gratitude. After many a weary mile's walking, he came upon a man of middle years stumping along the lane and, greeting him, said, "I should like to make you a present." He pointed his finger at a stone, and it turned into gold before their eyes.

The man studied the gleaming chunk of stone, his head canted[2] to one side. "What sort of trick is that?" he asked with a frown.

---

1. forthwith (fôrth′ with′) *adv.*: At once.

2. canted (kant′d) *v.*: Tilted.

The Pointing Finger   607

Master Teacher Note The desire of humans to transform ordinary items into gold is reflected in other cultures' folklore as well. Examples of this include European folk tales such as "Rumpelstiltskin," in which gold is spun from flax, and "Jack and the Beanstalk," in which one of the characters is a goose that lays golden eggs. In Greek mythology, there is the story of Midas, who turned all that he touched into gold. Are students familiar with other tales that have this element? Why have people always been obsessed with gold?

Thematic Idea Another selection that includes a test of selfishness through magical means is "The Third Wish," on page 3, by Joan Aiken.

Presentation

Motivation/Prior Knowledge Have students imagine that a mysterious stranger stopped them on the street, pointed at a pebble which immediately turned to gold, and offered the gold pebble to them. Would they accept the gift? What powers must the stranger possess to perform such a feat? Would they be suspicious that the transformation was a trick?

Purpose-Setting Question How is the immortal being surprised in the end?

1 Literary Focus Although most folk tales do not recount supernatural occurrences, they often do have magical events. How are these immortals similar to the gods and godesses of Greek myths?

2 Critical Thinking and Reading You might point out to students that this is a generalization. Do the immortals mean that all humans have the same short-comings as those from the past? Why is this statement incorrect?

3 Discussion Do you think that this test is fair? How would the average person react to such an offer?

4 Discussion What does this statement indicate about the life this man and his family lead? Do you agree with his reasoning? Basing your judgment on the fact that the family eats rice water and elm bark, do you think that he is being greedy to ask for more gold?

5 Literary Focus This man is the hero of the tale and represents the average, ordinary person. Would most people react similarly to the immortal's gift?

Discussion Do you think that it is fair for the immortal to continue to tempt the man as part of the test?

7 Enrichment Man's desire to change ordinary objects into gold was not expressed only in folk tales. For hundreds of years up to about 1700, alchemists attempted to transform less costly metals, such as lead, into gold. Although they failed, their study of chemical substances eventually led to the science of chemistry.

8 Literary Focus This statement is humorous and endears the man to the listeners of the story. He has cleverly surprised the immortal and shown that he has the same desires as any ordinary person.

Reader's Response Do you think the immortals' test for greed is a fair one? Why or why not?

"No trick," said the Immortal. "Pick it up. Or would you prefer a larger stone?" He pointed his finger at a small rock, and it instantly blossomed gold. "Take it, brother. It is yours. I give it to you."

The man thought a while, then slowly shook his head. "No-o-o. Not that it's not a very clever trick, and a pretty sight to see."

With growing excitement the Immortal pointed at a larger rock and a larger, until their eyes were dazzled by the glint of gold all round them, but each time the man shook his head, and each time the shake became more decisive. Had he found his unselfish man at last? Should he transform him this instant into an Immortal and carry him back to P'eng-lai?

"But every human being desires *something*," the Immortal said, all but convinced that this was untrue. "Tell me what it is you want!"

"Your finger," said the man.

608   *Fables, Myths, and Legends*

THINKING ABOUT THE SELECTION

Recalling

1. What is the Immortal seeking on earth?
2. What test does he use for this purpose?
3. What does the test reveal?

Interpreting

4. In what way does the third man seem at first different from the first two?
5. Why does the Immortal grow more and more excited as he speaks with the third man?
6. What is suggested by the very last sentence?

Applying

7. What does this story imply about the values or beliefs of the people who told it?

ANALYZING LITERATURE

Understanding a Folk Tale

Folk tales are part of our oral tradition. They are created by ordinary people and preserved by word of mouth. The tale is passed down from one generation to the next for many years, even centuries. Usually, if a folk tale is at last written down, it is because someone felt it ought to be preserved so that people of other lands can enjoy it.

1. In what way does "The Pointing Finger" remind you of other folk tales?
2. This folk tale is several hundred years old. Why do you think it has lasted so long?

CRITICAL THINKING AND READING

Evaluating Generalizations

A **generalization** is an idea or statement that covers a great many specific cases. For example, near the end of "The Pointing Finger" the Immortal says, "But every human being desires something." This is a generalization because the statement covers all human beings.

Generalizations need to be evaluated for their truth. To evaluate a generalization, look at the evi-

dence. Does it indicate that the statement is solidly grounded in facts? Are there no exceptions—specific cases that do not fit the statement?

1. Evaluate the generalization that "every human being desires something."
2. Tell why it would or would not have been reasonable for the Immortal to make the generalization that all humans are greedy.

UNDERSTANDING LANGUAGE

Matching Meaning with Context

Many English words have more than one meaning. Often it is only the context that suggests which one of a word's meanings a writer intends. For example, the word *immortal* is frequently used to mean a person who has gained lasting fame. But in "The Pointing Finger," this word means an undying, godlike person.

What is the meaning in context of the italicized words below?

1. " 'Ah,' [the second person] finally said, his eyes narrowed in *calculation*."
2. "[The Immortal] came upon a man of *middle* years . . . "
3. "[The Immortals] found the mortals of today to have the same shortcomings and the same *longcomings* as those of yesterday."

THINKING AND WRITING

Summarizing a Folk Tale

Summarizing a folk tale means retelling it in shortened form. Summarize "The Pointing Finger." Before you write, think about the several events that make up the story. Think about the characters' motives and purposes. When you write your summary, make clear not only what happens but also why it happens. When you revise, check your summary against the folk tale. Did you cover all the main incidents? Did you make clear why things happen as they do?

The Pointing Finger 609

Focus

More About the Folk Tale For several hundred years, thousands of people from West Africa were transported to the Western Hemisphere as slaves. These people brought their folk traditions along with them, including tales of the spider, Anansi. As they passed the tales along to other generations, the tales changed gradually to reflect conditions and problems in the New World. These stories continue to be popular today, not only in West Africa, but also in the Caribbean. What might be some of the topics of Anansi stories today in the Caribbean?

Literary Focus For thousands of years, humans have relied on their brains to overcome bigger and stronger animals and to solve the problems of survival. This necessity has contributed to the popularity of the trickster character. Also, humans enjoy stories in which the underdog triumphs.

Look For If less advanced students are having trouble with the idea of a trickster, you might have them preview the Analyzing Literature questions on page 613. These will help guide them in their reading.

Writing/Prior Knowledge Remind students that the animal they choose should be perceived as weak and inferior to traditionally dominant animals.

Vocabulary You might have less advanced students pronounce each word aloud and give their own definition of it.

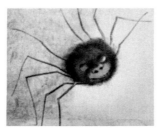

Folk Tales: The Trickster

Look For

Writing

Vocabulary

All Stories Are Anansi's

This folk tale comes from the **Ashanti** (ə shän′ tē), who ruled a large empire in West Africa during the 1700's and 1800's. Today, the Ashanti are an important people in the West African country of Ghana. They have made key contributions to farming, mining, and forestry. The Ashanti have also earned a reputation as skillful weavers.

Harold Courlander (1908–　) received a Guggenheim fellowship for work on African culture and has written versions of folk tales from many nations.

Like fables, many folk tales contain animals that talk and behave like humans. One of the best-loved animal characters in folk tales is the **trickster,** who relies on brains rather than strength or speed. The trickster is usually able to outwit bigger and stronger animals. For many North American Indians, the coyote played the role of the shrewd trickster. In African folklore, however, the slyest creature is often Kwaku Anansi (kwä′ kōō ə nän′ sē), the spider.

As you read, look for the ways in which Anansi appeals to the fears or vanity of his victims in order to fool them.

Choose a type of animal that you think would make a good trickster. Write a description of this animal. In your description, explain the reasons for your choice.

Knowing the following words will help you as you read "All Stories Are Anansi's."

yearned (yɜrnd) *v.*: Wanted very much (p. 611)
gourd (gôrd) *n.*: Fruit of a certain kind of plant; the dried, hollowed-shell of this fruit is used as a drinking cup or dipper (p. 611)
acknowledge (ək näl′ ij) *v.*: To recognize and admit (p. 612)

610   *Fables, Myths, and Legends*

All Stories Are Anansi's

from the Ashanti (Ghana)
Harold Courlander

1   In the beginning, all tales and stories belonged to Nyame,[1] the Sky God. But Kwaku Anansi, the spider, yearned to be the owner of all the stories known in the world, and he went to Nyame and offered to buy them.

    The Sky God said: "I am willing to sell the stories, but the price is high. Many people have come to me offering to buy, but the price was too high for them. Rich and powerful families have not been able to pay. Do you think you can do it?"

    Anansi replied to the Sky God: "I can do it. What is the price?"

2   "My price is three things," the Sky God said. "I must first have Mmoboro,[2] the hornets. I must then have Onini,[3] the great python. I must then have Osebo,[4] the leopard. For these things I will sell you the right to tell all stories."

    Anansi said: "I will bring them."

3   He went home and made his plans. He first cut a gourd from a vine and made a small hole in it. He took a large calabash[5] and filled it with water. He went to the tree where the hornets lived. He poured some of the water over himself, so that he was dripping. He threw some water over the hornets, so that they too were dripping. Then he put the calabash on his head, as though to protect himself from a storm, and called out to the hornets: "Are you foolish people? Why do you stay in the rain that is falling?"

    The hornets answered: "Where shall we go?"

    "Go here, in this dry gourd," Anansi told them.

    The hornets thanked him and flew into the gourd through the small hole. When the last of them had entered, Anansi plugged the hole with a ball of grass, saying: "Oh, yes, but you are really foolish people!"

    He took the gourd full of hornets to Nyame, the Sky God. The Sky God accepted them. He said: "There are two more things."

    Anansi returned to the forest and cut a long bamboo pole and some strong vines. Then he walked toward the house of Onini, the python, talking to himself. He said: "My wife is stupid. I say he is longer and stronger. My wife says he is shorter and weaker. I give him more respect. She gives him less respect. Is she right or am I right? I am right, he is longer. I am right, he is stronger."

    When Onini, the python, heard Anansi talking to himself, he said: "Why are you arguing this way with yourself?"

---

1. Nyame (nē ä′ mē)
2. Mmoboro (mō bô′ rō)
3. Onini (ō nē′ nē)
4. Osebo (ō sā′ bō)
5. calabash (kal′ ə bash′) *n.*: A large fruit that is dried and made into a bowl or cup.

"All Stories Are Anansi's" in *The Hat-Shaking Dance And Other Ashanti Tales from Ghana,* by Harold Courlander with Albert Kofi Prempeh. Harcourt Brace Jovanovich. Reprinted by permission of Harold Courlander. © 1957, 1985 by Harold Courlander.

All Stories Are Anansi's   611

4 Discussion Anansi claims to give the python more respect than his wife when guessing the python's size and strength. Why does this make it easier for him to trick the python?

5 Discussion How is the way Anansi tricked the leopard different from the way he tricked the other animals?

Reader's Response Which of Anansi's three tricks did you find the most clever? Why?

The spider replied: "Ah, I have had a dispute with my wife. She says you are shorter and weaker than this bamboo pole. I say you are longer and stronger."

Onini said: "It's useless and silly to argue when you can find out the truth. Bring the pole and we will measure."

So Anansi laid the pole on the ground, and the python came and stretched himself out beside it.

"You seem a little short," Anansi said.

The python stretched further.

"A little more," Anansi said.

"I can stretch no more," Onini said.

"When you stretch at one end, you get shorter at the other end," Anansi said. "Let me tie you at the front so you don't slip."

4 He tied Onini's head to the pole. Then he went to the other end and tied the tail to the pole. He wrapped the vine all around Onini, until the python couldn't move.

"Onini," Anansi said, "it turns out that my wife was right and I was wrong. You are shorter than the pole and weaker. My opinion wasn't as good as my wife's. But you were even more foolish than I, and you are now my prisoner."

Anansi carried the python to Nyame, the Sky God, who said: "There is one thing more."

Osebo, the leopard, was next. Anansi went into the forest and dug a deep pit where the leopard was accustomed to walk. He covered it with small branches and leaves and put dust on it, so that it was impossible to tell where the pit was. Anansi went away and hid. When Osebo came prowling in the black of night, he stepped into the trap Anansi had prepared and fell to the bottom. Anansi heard the sound of the leopard falling, and he said: "Ah, Osebo, you are half-foolish!"

When morning came, Anansi went to the pit and saw the leopard there.

"Osebo," he asked, "what are you doing in this hole?"

"I have fallen into a trap," Osebo said. "Help me out."

"I would gladly help you," Anansi said. "But I'm sure that if I bring you out, I will have no thanks for it. You will get hungry, and later on you will be wanting to eat me and my children."

"I swear it won't happen!" Osebo said.

"Very well. Since you swear it, I will take you out." Anansi said.

He bent a tall green tree toward the ground, so that its top was over the pit, and he tied it that way. Then he tied a rope to the top of the tree and dropped the other end of it into the pit.

"Tie this to your tail," he said.

Osebo tied the rope to his tail.

"Is it well tied?" Anansi asked.

"Yes, it is well tied," the leopard said.

"In that case," Anansi said, "you are not merely half-foolish, you are all-foolish."

And he took his knife and cut the other rope, the one that held the tree bowed to the ground. The tree straightened up with a snap, pulling Osebo out of the hole. He hung in the air head downward, twisting and turning. And while he hung this way, Anansi killed him with his weapons. **5**

Then he took the body of the leopard and carried it to Nyame, the Sky God, saying: "Here is the third thing. Now I have paid the price."

Nyame said to him: "Kwaku Anansi, great warriors and chiefs have tried, but they have been unable to do it. You have done it. Therefore, I will give you the stories. From this day onward, all stories belong to you. Whenever a man tells a story, he must acknowledge that it is Anansi's tale."

In this way Anansi, the spider, became the owner of all stories that are told. To Anansi all these tales belong.

612   Fables, Myths, and Legends

ANSWERS TO THINKING ABOUT THE SELECTION
Recalling

1. Anansi wants ownership of all stories and tales. Nyame's price is three things: the hornets, the great python, and the leopard.

2. Anansi captures the hornets by convincing them that there is a rain storm. He then offers the protection of a dry gourd with a small

THINKING ABOUT THE SELECTION

Recalling

1. What does Anansi want from Nyame? What is Nyame's price?
2. How does Anansi capture the hornets, the python, and the leopard?

Interpreting

3. Why do you think Anansi values so highly what Nyame owns?
4. What is Anansi's attitude toward the other animals?
5. Why is Anansi able to do what great warriors and chiefs have tried to do but have been unable to do?

Applying

6. Why do you think people enjoy folk tales in which animals behave like humans?

ANALYZING LITERATURE

Understanding the Trickster in Folklore

The trickster is a character in folklore, usually an animal, who relies on brains rather than strength or speed to accomplish his or her goals. In "All Stories Are Anansi's," the spider fools animals that could easily defeat him in a contest of strength.

1. What qualities does Anansi display?
2. How does each of these qualities help him succeed?
3. Why do you think the trickster has been such a popular character in folklore?
4. Modern versions of the trickster appear in liter-ature and movies. For example, Captain Kirk of *Star Trek* displays many of the trickster's characteristics. What other figures can be considered tricksters? Explain your choices.

CRITICAL THINKING AND READING

Making Inferences About Characters

An **inference** is a conclusion based on evidence. You can make inferences about animal characters in folk tales just as you would about a character in a short story or novel. In "All Stories Are Anansi's," the trickster helps you to make inferences about the other animals by pointing up their weaknesses.

1. What can you infer about the hornets based on their response to Anansi's warning?
2. What do you infer about the python when he keeps stretching to make himself as long as the pole?
3. Why must a trickster be able to make inferences about other animals?

THINKING AND WRITING

Writing a Folk Tale

Write your own folk tale modeled on the Anansi story. You might start with the animal trickster you wrote about before reading this tale. Give him or her some goal to be achieved by trickery. Create three animal characters your trickster must deceive. When you revise your tale, try to increase the cleverness of the tricks. You might also try to make your tale convey an idea or teach a lesson. Share your folk tale with your classmates.

All Stories Are Anansi's   613

(Answers begin on p. 612.)

feelings, and events, but from a different perspective. Also, it's easier to laugh at shortcomings and traits that humans might recognize in themselves when these traits are seen in represented by animals.

ANSWERS TO ANALYZING LITERATURE

1. Anansi displays the qualities of intelligence, resourcefulness, and cleverness.
2. They help him succeed by enabling him to devise clever plans to capture the animals by utilizing his own strengths.
3. The trickster has been a popular character in folklore because he is more representative of the average person, who does not have extraordinary powers of strength or magic to help solve problems. People also enjoy seeing an underdog succeed in a conflict.
4. There are many examples of modern versions of the trickster. Students should choose characters who outwit their opponents by using their intelligence instead of physical strength.

ANSWERS TO CRITICAL THINKING AND READING

1. You can infer that the hornets were easily frightened by rain and that they were not very smart because they flew into the gourd Anansi offered for protection.
2. You can infer that the python was vain and easily tricked by an appeal to his looks and strength.
3. The trickster must be able to make inferences about other animals in order to devise plans that will succeed in tricking them. Correct inferences enable the trickster to devise plans appealing to a specific fear or vanity that the animals possess.

---

opening in the top. When all of the hornets are inside the gourd, he seals the small hole. The python is convinced that he is helping to settle a quarrel over his actual size and strength. Anansi then captures the python by getting him to stretch out next to a bamboo pole and tying him securely to it. The leopard is captured after he falls into a well-concealed pit. Anansi pretends to help him tie a rope to his tail. The other end of the rope is attached to a bent over tree, so when the tree straightens, the leopard is pulled from the pit and dangles in the air by his tail.

Interpreting

3. Suggested Response: Anansi values the stories and legends that Nyame owns because owning them is prestigious. Many people tell the stories, and Anansi desires the attention that will come to him when a person who tells a tale gives him credit for ownership.

4. Anansi views the other animals as foolish and easily misled.
5. He is able to do what other warriors and chiefs have not been able to do because he uses his intelligence, instead of physical powers, to devise clever ways to capture the animals.

Applying

6. Suggested Response: People enjoy hearing tales about animals that behave like humans, because the stories portray familiar actions,

---

Writing Across the Curriculum
You might want students to research and report on some of the trickster stories from Native American folklore. If you do, you could inform the social studies department. Social studies teachers might assist students in their research.

More About the Legend Before the arrival of French colonists in the 1800's, Vietnam was primarily an agricultural society. People organized themselves along strong family ties in which the family's interests were held above all else.

Literary Focus Symbols are used to replace long explanations. They can be found in many places. A white flag symbolizes surrender, and road signs often use symbols such as arrows, shapes, and colors to symbolize directions and cautions. Putting your hand over your heart when you recite the Pledge of Allegiance symbolizes your sincerity.

Look For If your **less advanced** students have difficulty identifying the symbols, you might have them preview Analyzing Literature on page 619.

Writing/Prior Knowledge If students have difficulty thinking of ideas, you might suggest they base their game on one they are familiar with, or utilize common parts of games such as a playing board, dice, or playing cards.

Vocabulary Have **more advanced** students write an original sentence for each of the vocabulary words.

GUIDE FOR READING

The Little Lizard's Sorrow

Vietnam is a tropical country in Southeast Asia. The most popular form of literature in Vietnam is poetry, and poets are greatly respected there. This land also has a deeply rooted tradition of folk tales, of which "The Little Lizard's Sorrow" is an excellent example.

Mai Vo-Dinh (1933–), who translated the tale, was born in Vietnam. He came to live in the United States in 1960. He is not only a writer and translator of Vietnamese literature but also a painter and illustrator of books.

Symbols in Folk Tales

A **symbol** is an object that stands for an idea but also has its own existence. A dove, for example, is a symbol of peace. Symbols are frequently used in folk tales to express an idea in a concrete and memorable way.

Look For

As you read "The Little Lizard's Sorrow," look for those objects that seem to seem to have special meanings. Figure out what those special meanings might be.

Writing

Many interesting stories have been written in which games are of central importance. Make up a game in which a player can win or lose something that really matters. Describe the object of the game and its rules.

Vocabulary

Knowing the following words will help you as you read "The Little Lizard's Sorrow."

emitting (i mit′ iŋ) v.: Sending out or uttering (p. 615)

gaunt (gônt) adj.: Thin and bony (p. 615)

pauper (pô′ pər) n.: An extremely poor person (p. 615)

chortle (chor′ t'l) v.: Make an amused chuckling or snorting sound (p. 616)

domestic (də mes′ tik) n.: A servant for the home (p. 616)

harassed (hə rast′) v.: Troubled (p. 618)

614   Fables, Myths, and Legends

Support Material

Teaching Portfolio
Teacher Backup, p. 1009
Usage and Mechanics Worksheet, p. 1013
Vocabulary Check, p. 1014
Analyzing Literature Worksheet, *Understanding Symbols,* p. 1015
Critical Thinking and Reading Worksheet, *Making Generaliza-*
tions, p. 1016
Selection Test, p. 1017

The Little Lizard's Sorrow

from **Vietnam**

Translated by **Mai Vo-Dinh**

There is in Vietnam a certain species of small lizard only three inches long with webbed feet and a short, round head. They are often seen indoors, running swiftly upside down on the ceiling or along the walls, emitting little snapping cries that sound like "Tssst . . . tssst!" Suppose that you drop an egg on the kitchen floor; the kind of sound you would make then, with the tip of your tongue between your teeth, is like the cry of these harmless, funny little lizards. Sounds of mild sorrow, of genuine shock but somehow humorous regret that seem to say, "Oh, if only I had been . . . If only I had known . . . Oh, what a pity, what a pity . . . Tssst! Tssst!"

There was once a very rich man whose house was immense and filled with treasures. His land was so extensive that, as the Vietnamese say, "Cranes fly over it with outstretched wings," for cranes only do so over very long distances. Wealth breeding vanity, one of the rich man's greatest pleasures was beating other rich men at a game he himself had invented. One player would announce one of his rare possessions, the other would counter the challenge by saying that he, too—if he really did—owned such a treasure.

"A stable of fifty buffalos," one man would say. The other would reply, "Yes, I also have fifty of them." It was then his turn to announce, "I sleep in an all-teak[1] bed encrusted with mother-of-pearl."[2] The first player would lose if he slept on cherry planks![3]

One day, a stranger came to the rich man's house. Judging from his appearance, the gatekeeper did not doubt that the visitor was a madman. He wanted, he said, to play the famous game with the mansion's master. Yet dressed in clothes that looked as if they had been mended hundreds of times, and wearing broken straw sandals, the stranger appeared to be anything but a wealthy man. Moreover, his face was gaunt and pale as if he had not had a good meal in days. But there was such proud, quiet dignity to the stranger that the servant did not dare shut the gates in his face. Instead, he meekly went to inform his master of the unlikely visitor's presence. Intrigued, the man ordered that the pauper be ushered in.

Trying to conceal his curiosity and sur-

---

1. teak (tēk) *n.*: Yellowish-brown wood used for furniture.
2. mother-of-pearl *n.*: The hard, pearly inside of certain seashells.
3. cherry planks *n.*: Wood from a cherry tree.

The Little Lizard's Sorrow   615

Presentation

Motivation/Prior Knowledge
Have students imagine that they have agreed to play a simple game in which the winner gains something from the loser that is very important to each of them. Would they want to play for such important stakes? Would they play better or worse under such conditions? Is a game worth losing something you truly care about?

Purpose-Setting Question How does the opening paragraph fit in with the rest of the story?

1 **Literary Focus** The first paragraph is separated from the rest of the story, which emphasizes its importance. You might have students question how this paragraph relates to the rest of the story. Why is the lizard described this way? How does the description fit in with the title?

2 **Discussion** Here is another example of Vietnamese folklore in the form of a saying. The crane is used because it is a common bird in Vietnam. Sayings from our own folklore that mention birds include "Twenty miles as the crow flies," and "Don't count your chickens before they are hatched." Why are crows and chickens appropriate in American folklore?

3 **Discussion** Do you think this would be a fun game to play? What does the game indicate about the players?

4 **Reading Strategy** Have students summarize the appearance of the stranger in comparison with the rich man. You might have them predict how the mysterious nature of his visit might affect the rich man.

Thematic Idea Other selections that involve trickster figures using cunning to obtain their goals are "All Stories are Anansi's," on page 611, and the two fables entitled "The Fox and the Crow," on pages 547 and 549.

5 Discussion Do you agree with the stranger's statement? Have you ever played a game just for fun and with no consequences for the winner and loser?

6 Discussion Do you think that his two conditions are fair? Does he seem to have as much to lose as the rich man? What about the stranger's attitude makes him seem mysterious?

prise, the rich man offered his visitor the very best chair and served him hot, perfumed tea.

"Well, stranger, is it true that you have deigned[4] to come here to play a game of riches with me?" he began inquiringly.

The visitor was apparently unimpressed by the rich surroundings, giving them only a passing, casual look. Perfectly at ease, sipping his tea from the rare porcelain cup, he answered in a quiet though self-assured voice, "Yes, sir, that is if you, too, so wish."

"Naturally, naturally," the rich man raised his hand in a sweeping motion. "But, may I ask, with your permission, where you reside and what is your honorable occupation?"

The stranger gave a little chortle, visibly amused. "Sir, would you gain any to know about these? I came here simply to play your game; only, I have two conditions, if you are so generous as to allow them."

"By all means! Pray, tell me what they are," the rich man readily inquired.

5 The visitor sat farther back on the brocaded chair, his voice soft and confidential. "Well, here they are. A game is no fun if the winner does not win anything and the loser does not lose anything. Therefore I would suggest that if I win I would take everything in your possession—your lands, your stables, your servants, your house and everything contained in it. But if you win—" Here the stranger paused, his eyes narrowed ever **6** so slightly, full of humorous malice, "If you win, you would become the owner of everything that belongs to me." The stranger paused again. "And what belongs to me, sir, you will have no idea of. I am one of the most fortunate men alive, sir. . . . And besides that," he added with a knowing look, "I

4, deigned (dānd) *v.*: Graciously agreed to do something beneath him.

would remain in this house to serve you as a domestic the rest of my life."

For a long moment, the rich man sat back in silence. Another long moment went by, then the rich man spoke: "That's agreed. But, please tell me your other condition."

Eyes dreamy, the stranger looked out of the window. "My second condition, sir, is not so much a condition as a request. I hope you would not mind giving me, a visitor, an edge over you. May I be allowed to ask the first question?"

The rich man thought for a long second, then said, "That is also agreed. Let's begin."

"Do I really understand that you have agreed to both my conditions?" the stranger asked thoughtfully.

Something in the visitor's manner and voice hurt the rich man's pride. He was ready to stake his very life on this game that he himself had created. There was no way out. "Yes," he said. "Yes, indeed I have. Now tell me, please, what do you have that I have not got?" The stranger smiled. Reaching to his feet, he took up his traveling bag, a coarse cotton square tied together by the

four ends. Opening it slowly, ceremoniously, he took out an object and handed it to his host without a word. It was an empty half of a coconut shell, old and chipped, the kind poor people use as a container to drink water from.

"A coconut-shell cup!" the rich man exclaimed. One could not know whether he was merely amused or completely shattered.

"Yes, sir, a coconut-shell cup. A *chipped* shell cup. I use it to drink from on my wanderings. I am a wanderer," the visitor said quietly.

Holding the shell between his thumb and his forefinger and looking as if he had never seen such an object before, the rich man interrupted, "But, but you don't mean that I do not have a thing like this?"

Master Teacher Note You might want to lead the class in a discussion about games that people play in which the stakes are important. Many forms of gambling are card games that are played for money. Professional sports are also played for money, but participants are paid whether they win or lose. What are some other games that have important things at stake?

"No, sir, you have not. How could you?" the stranger replied.

Turning the residence upside down, the man and his servants discovered odds and ends of one thousand and one kinds, but they were unable to produce a drinking cup made from a coconut shell. In the servants' quarters, however, they found a few such utensils, but they were all brand new, not chipped. One could imagine that the servants of such a wealthy man would not deign to drink from a chipped cup. Even a beggar would throw it away. . . .

"You see, sir," the stranger said to the rich man once they were again seated across the tea table, "you see, I am a wanderer, as I have said. I am a free man. This cup here is several years old and my only possession besides these poor clothes I have on. If you do not think me too immodest, I would venture that I treasure it more than you do all of your collections of fine china. But, from this day, I am the owner and lone master of all that belongs to you. . . ."

Having taken possession of the rich man's land, houses, herds and all

his other treasures, the stranger began to give them away to the poor and needy people. Then, one day, taking up his old cotton bag, he left the village and no one ever saw him again.

As for the dispossessed rich man, it is believed that he died of grief and regret and was transformed into this small lizard. Curiously, one sees him scurrying about only indoors. Running up and down the walls, crossing the ceiling, staring at people and furniture, he never stops his "Tssst, Tssst." Vietnamese children, in particular, are very fond of him for he looks so harassed, so funny.

But, oh, such sorrow, such regret, such self-pity.

618   *Fables, Myths, and Legends*

THINKING ABOUT THE SELECTION

Recalling

1. Describe the game the rich man plays with other rich men.
2. Why does the servant not send the miserable-looking visitor away?
3. What two conditions for the game does the stranger request?
4. How does he defeat the rich man?
5. What does he do with his possessions?
6. What happens to the rich man at the end of the story?

Interpreting

7. Why does the stranger describe himself as one of the most fortunate men alive? Do you agree with this opinion? Why or why not?
8. Why does he treasure his coconut-shell cup more than the rich man treasures his china?
9. Why do you think the rich man is changed into a lizard rather than some other animal?
10. In what way does this folk tale teach a lesson in living?

Applying

11. J. Brotherton once wrote: "My riches consist not in the extent of my possessions but in the fewness of my wants." Would the stranger agree or disagree with him? Explain your answer.

ANALYZING LITERATURE

Understanding Symbols in Folk Tales

When some object—whether living or nonliving—seems to stand out as especially important in a folk tale, it is probably a **symbol**. In "The Little Lizard's Sorrow," the lizard and the coconut-shell cup are two such objects.

1. What human feelings are associated with the little lizard at the beginning and the end of the tale?
2. What, therefore, might the lizard symbolize?
3. What is said about the coconut-shell cup that suggests its importance to the stranger?
4. What might it symbolize?

UNDERSTANDING LANGUAGE

Recognizing the Root *mit*

Many English words are built on the Latin root *mit,* which is also spelled *miss.* It means "send." In the folk tale, the little lizard is described as "emitting little snapping cries . . ." Here "emitting" means "sending out." Recognizing this root and knowing what it means will help you to understand some unfamiliar words you may meet in your reading. Figure out what each of the following italicized words mean. Then check a dictionary to see if you were right.

1. Since I accidently paid too much for the game, the store *remitted* three dollars to me.
2. Try to *commit* these safety rules to memory.
3. The *transmission* of radio waves is often affected by weather conditions.

THINKING AND WRITING

Writing a Folk Tale with a Symbol

Using your description of the game you made up before reading this tale, write a folk tale modeled on "The Little Lizard's Sorrow." Include an object that symbolizes some important idea you wish to express. When you revise your work, check that your symbol fits in well with the rest of the story and helps to reveal its meaning. Share your folk tale with your classmates.

The Little Lizard's Sorrow 619

tions should include the fact that the stranger had very few possessions, and yet he considered himself one of the most fortunate men alive, and that he considered himself free because of his lack of possessions.

Challenge Compare and contrast the stranger to the character Anansi from "All Stories are Anansi's," on page 611. Does the stranger fit the description of a trickster?

ANSWERS TO ANALYZING LITERATURE

1. The feelings associated with the lizard are humor, grief, regret, shock, and self-pity.
2. Answers will differ. Suggested Response: The lizard represents the experience of regretting an unfortunate incident or a missed opportunity, and the pointless self-pitying that often accompanies this.
3. The stranger says that his cup is more valuable to him than all of the expensive china is to the rich man.
4. Suggested Response: The cup represents objects of true value to people, not ornaments but objects that add something to people's lives.

ANSWERS TO UNDERSTANDING LANGUAGE

1. remitted: gave back, refunded
2. commit: memorize, learn by heart
3. transmission: sending out

THINKING AND WRITING

Publishing Student Writing Ask for student volunteers to explain their games to the class. The class might try to play one or more of the games, and write down what they think the symbol of each game is.

Because of this he is free of all the responsibilities and cares that go along with having wealth and possessions. He considers himself fortunate because he does not need these things to be happy. Students answers will differ, but they should support answers with examples from the story or from their own experiences.

8. The stranger treasures his coconut shell more than the rich man treasures fine china, because it is his only possession and means more to him as a result. He is poor and would have more difficulty replacing his cup than the rich man would have replacing his china. Finally, the rich man has so many possessions that they lose their individual value to him.

9. Suggested Response: He is changed into a lizard because of the noise the lizard makes, which seems to reflect grief and regret. Also, the lizard is a small, harmless creature that seems funny and somewhat pathetic.

10. Suggested Response: This folktale suggests that people should value possessions for their true value and how they benefit their lives, and that they should not accumulate things simply for the sake of accumulation and vanity.

Applying

11. The stranger would agree with Brotherton's statement. Explana-

Write the following generalizations on the board or on a transparency:

There are 63 boys and 52 girls in the seventh grade. Therefore, most of the students in my class are boys.

My seventh-grade class has more boys than girls. Therefore, all seventh grade classes have more boys than girls.

Ask the students what they think of these generalizations. Discuss their answers but do not confirm their correct responses. After you have read and discussed Making Generalizations, let them identify which generalization is valid and which is hasty.

FOCUS ON READING

Making Generalizations

One way to increase your understanding of what you read and to get deeper meanings from it is to make generalizations. A generalization is a general statement or rule that is drawn from specific facts. It is a conclusion that is true for a number of different cases or situations.

**Sound
Generalizations**

Louis Untermeyer in his adaptation of "The Boy and the Wolf" makes a sound generalization when he concludes that "Liars are not believed, forsooth, even when liars tell the truth." This is a generalization drawn from the facts that occurred in the fable. The boy had cried, "Wolf!" two different times when there really was no wolf about. The villagers had responded to his cry each time and searched for the wolf. However, when they realized none was around, they lost faith in the boy and considered him a liar. Therefore, when he cried wolf because there really was a wolf, none of the villagers would come. He was not believed because he had lied to them in the past. This is a sound generalization because the facts support it and it is generally true. People usually do not trust liars.

It is important to evaluate a generalization by determining if the facts do support it and if it applies to a number of other situations or cases besides the one you are considering. Be aware that a generalization does not have to apply to all cases.

**Hasty
Generalizations**

Sometimes a generalization is drawn from insufficient facts or evidence. When this happens, it is called a **hasty generalization**. For instance, if you had drawn the conclusion that "Boys who watch sheep do not tell the truth" from "The Boy and the Wolf" fable, you would have made a hasty generalization. You have only one instance of a boy who watched sheep who did not tell the truth. There are insufficient facts to draw this conclusion.

Sometimes a hasty generalization is too broad for the facts it supports. For instance, the boy in the fable despised his work and liked to sleep. Therefore, when a lamb was lost, he shouted, "Wolf!" to get the villagers to come. If you had said, "All people who dislike their work lie," you would have drawn a generalization that is too broad. You do not have a sufficient number of cases to base this on; you have only one instance of a boy who disliked his work and lied. Avoid using words such as "all," "never," "must," and "definitely" because these kinds of words do not allow for any exceptions to the general rule.

620   *Fables, Myths, and Legends*

Guidelines

- Make sure you understand the main idea and supporting details of the material.
- Make sure the conclusions you draw are adequately supported by facts or evidence.
- Make sure the generalization you draw applies to many different cases or situations.
- Make sure you do not use words such as "always" or "must," which do not allow for any exceptions and which make the generalization too broad.

Activity

Read each of the following statements. Identify whether each is a sound generalization or a hasty generalization.

1. The fables "The Fox and the Crow" and "The Town Mouse and the Country Mouse" were written by Aesop. Aesop is a Greek. Therefore, all fables were written by Greeks.
2. Liars never tell the truth.
3. People sometimes lie to get out of doing work.
4. Boys are not to be trusted with sheep.
5. Some fables were written by Greeks.

Activity

Read each set of statements below. Then make a generalization that is based on the set.

1. "The Fox and the Crow" is a fable about animals. "The Town Mouse and the Country Mouse" is a fable about animals. Aesop wrote many other fables about animals.
2. "Narcissus" is a myth that explains how the narcissus flower got its name. "Phaëthon, Son of Apollo" is a myth that explains how the North African plain became a desert and why the poplar trees weep tears of amber. "Popocatepetl and Ixtlaccihuatl" explains the existence of these two volcanoes.
3. "Popocatepetl and Ixtlaccihuatl" is a Mexican legend. "The Legend of the Hummingbird" is a Puerto Rican legend. "Ojeeg, the Hunter, and the Ice Man" is a Micmac legend.

Focus on Reading   621

The writing assignments on page 622 have students write creatively, while those on page 623 have them think about the fables, myths, and legends and write critically.

YOU THE WRITER
Guidelines for Evaluating Assignment 1

1. Does the student follow the basics of good storytelling (problem, action, solution, surprise) in the fable?
2. Does the student show rather than tell about the animals' thoughts, actions, and interactions?
3. Does the fable end with a moral?
4. Is the fable free from grammar, usage, and mechanics errors?

Guidelines for Evaluating Assignment 2

1. Does the student focus on the conflict between characters in writing the myth?
2. Is the mythic explanation for the natural phenomenon revealed through the conflict?
3. Is there a surprising resolution?
4. Is the myth free from grammar, usage, and mechanics errors?

Guidelines for Evaluating Assignment 3

1. Has the student chosen a person from American history to use as the subject for the legend, and is the legend consistent with the way he or she actually behaved in history?
2. Are the characters presented as being larger than life as they are in oral tradition?
3. Is there dialogue that reflects the way they think?
4. Is the legend free from grammar, usage, and mechanics errors?

YOU THE WRITER

Assignment

1. Write a fable that contains animals who act like human beings.

Prewriting. Make a list of morals, or clever sayings. You might work with a small group of students to create this list. Choose the moral about which you intend to write your fable. Choose an animal. Prepare a story chart in which you give the animal a problem, show it acting to solve the problem, and have it succeed or fail in solving the problem.

Writing. Now write your fable. Since showing is more dramatic than telling, show the characters in your story doing things: thinking, talking, acting. Bring them into conflict with each other. End your fable with your moral.

Revising. When you revise, check to see that you have followed the basics of good storytelling. Have you punctuated the speech of your characters accurately?

Assignment

2. Write a myth that explains one of the following: a. Why grass is green; b. Why there are stars in the sky; c. Why it must be cold in order for it to snow.

Prewriting. Relax and let your imagination roam. You may know the historical and scientific explanations for the topics listed above, but forget them and think up imaginative, mythical reasons for each. Remember, a good story is built around a conflict, so bring two people, or two giants, or two supernatural characters, or any mixture of the above, into conflict with each other.

Writing. When you write, focus on the conflict between the characters. Let the mythic explanation for your topic be revealed through the conflict.

Revising. When you revise, check to see that your story has a strong conflict and a surprising resolution. Also, is your explanation of the topic original, maybe even ingenious?

Assignment

3. Choose a person from American history, either someone from the past or someone still alive. Then write a legend about him or her.

Prewriting. Before you write, jot down information about the life of the character you intend to write about. Then confront your character with a problem. Freewrite about the outcome.

Writing. When narrating your legend, try to capture the oral style legends are told in. Make the hero's opponent and everything else in the story larger than life. Let the characters talk to each other, and be sure that what they say and the way they say it reflect the way they think.

Revising. Check to see that your hero's character and actions are consistent with the way he or she behaved.

622   *Fables, Myths, and Legends*

YOU THE CRITIC

Assignment

1. Choose one fable from this section and write an essay in which you tell what lesson the fable teaches, cite words from the fable that tell what the lesson is, and indicate what made the fable effective.

    Prewriting. Before you read, freewrite about the moral of the fable you have chosen.

    Writing. Now write your essay. Start by stating your main idea. Then support your main idea by referring to specific characters and incidents in the fable.

    Revising. Make sure you have clearly stated the moral of the fable and shown why the fable was effective.

Assignment

2. Choose three selections from this section and write an essay explaining how they show that the peoples of the world are similar to modern citizens of the United States in some ways and different from us in other ways.

    Prewriting. Before you write, scan through the selections in this section. Draw up a list of similarities and differences.

    Writing. Using the list of similarities and differences you have drawn up, write your essay. After stating your main idea, tell about the similarities you have found, using specific references from the selections you have chosen and from life in the United States today. Next tell about the differences, again using specific references. Conclude your essay by restating the main-idea sentence.

    Revising. When you revise, make sure you have supported your main idea. Combine as many sentences as possible.

Assignment

3. Folk tales and legends often reflect the qualities that are admired by a certain society. For example, people who live in extremely cold climates might write about heroes who confront the Ice Demon and win. Select a legend or folk tale and write an essay discussing how it reflects qualities admired by the particular culture.

    Prewriting. Freewrite about the main character. Explore the qualities this character displayed.

    Writing. Write the first draft of an essay discussing the qualities the main character displayed. Speculate about why this culture may have admired these qualities. Be sure to use specific examples.

    Revising. Make sure you have provided adequate support for your main idea.

You the Critic   623

YOU THE CRITIC
Guidelines for Evaluating Assignment 1

1. Does the essay explain what lesson the fable teaches?
2. Has the student cited words from the fable that tell what the lesson is?
3. Has the student indicated what there is about each story that makes the fable effective?
4. Is the main idea supported by references to the fable?
5. Is the essay free from grammar, usage, and mechanics errors?

Guidelines for Evaluating Assignment 2

1. Does the essay show how the peoples of the world are similar to modern citizens of the United States?
2. Does the essay show how the peoples of the world are different from us in other ways?
3. Is the main idea supported by these similarities and differences, and is it restated in the conclusion?
4. Have sentences been combined to help the essay have a professional sound?
5. Is the essay free from grammar, usage, and mechanics errors?

Guidelines for Evaluating Assignment 3

1. Does the student discuss the qualities the main character displays?
2. Does the student suggest why the culture may have admired these qualities?
3. Has the student provided a sufficient number of examples and incidents to support his or her main idea, and has the student organized the support in a logical order?
4. Is the essay free from grammar, usage, and mechanics errors?

Humanities Note

Fine art, *On the Trail,* 1892, by Winslow Homer. The American artist Winslow Homer (1836–1910) is best known for his superior landscape, marine, and genre paintings. His formal training consisted of a two-year apprenticeship to a lithographer and a few months of art lessons. He began his career as an illustrator. His skill in drawing and his keen powers of observation quickly won him fame in this field. He continued to illustrate and to paint and is remembered as one of America's leading artists.

The painting *On the Trail* was done in the Adirondack region of New York. This painting was executed in watercolor, a medium Homer found easily portable for quick sketches. The paint is applied in an uncomplicated manner, washes of green and brown for the underbrush, dabs of color for leaves, and sketchily painted tree branches. The hunter and his dogs seem poised in that breathless moment before the quarry is flushed. For all of its simplicity and easy, this is a carefully composed and organized painting that justly shows Winslow Homer's complete mastery of the watercolor technique.

ON THE TRAIL
Winslow Homer
National Gallery of Art, Washington, D.C.

THE NOVEL

Like a short story, a novel is fiction. It is made up from an author's imagination, and it has the basic elements of fiction: plot, character, setting, and theme. The most obvious difference between a short story and a novel is length. A novel is longer—often much longer—than a short story. Because of its length, there are other differences, too. A novel often includes more characters than a short story. The plot may be more complicated. The setting may include a number of different places, and the time of the action may extend over months, years, and even decades. Most important, the total effect of a novel is different from that of a short story. A good short story makes a single, sharp impression on the reader. The effect of a novel, on the other hand, is like traveling to and getting to know a new part of the world. You get impression after impression, and you learn more and more about the people and their lives. At last, you feel that you have entered into that part of the world and that it has become part of you.

625

Where the Red Fern Grows

Background

This novel is set in the area of the country that the author, Wilson Rawls, knows best—the beautiful hills and river bottoms of the Ozark mountains in eastern Oklahoma. This land is characterized by its many streams and river valleys. The soil is very fertile, ideal for farming, and the wooded areas support a wide variety of animal life, including deer, opossums, raccoons, foxes, and squirrels. Rawls spent much of his time in these woods with the family hound dog. In fact, Rawls told his first stories to his dog.

Reading Strategies

As you read the novel, you will discover that it presents different advantages and problems from shorter works of fiction. Some advantages to the extended length of a novel are that the characters develop more fully and realistically, the plot can be more complex, more than one theme can be presented, and themes can be developed more fully than in shorter fiction. One of the problems is that unlike short stories, which are usually read in one sitting, the extended nature of a novel requires that it be read at intervals over a longer period of time. Because of this, readers sometimes forget portions of what they have read previously. It might help if you summarize what you have learned after you finish reading each portion of the novel. When you are ready to continue later, review the events and characters from the previous section. Finally, as you read, interact with the literature by using the active reading strategies: question, predict, clarify, summarize, and pull together.

Themes

You will encounter the following themes:
- The passage from youth to maturity
- The rewards of hard work and diligence
- The achievements gained through love and understanding
- The need to work together to achieve common goals

Characters

Become familiar with the following characters before you read:
Billy—the teenager who develops a close relationship with his two hound dogs
Papa—Billy's father, who is beginning to treat him like a man
Mama—Billy's mother, who tries to help him with all his problems
Grandpa—Billy's grandfather, who is Billy's good friend and advisor
Little Ann—Billy's female hound, the smaller and smarter dog
Old Dan—Billy's male hound, who is bigger and stronger

626   *The Novel*

Enrichment Introduce the novel to students as a piece of fiction longer than a short story. Because of their length, novels can explore human nature and experience in depth. Novelists can arrange events, times, characters, and places in a variety of ways. Perhaps students can identify some of the different ways in which novelists can present their ideas. For example, a writer may use a fictional time and place in which to set a story. In some novels, one of the characters tells the story. In others, an outside observer narrates.

Reading Actively Encourage students to become novel readers. The novel is, after all, the most popular form of literature. The novel appeals to people for many reasons. People read novels to escape the monotony of everyday life; they read to be informed and to be challenged; they read to gain new insights into familiar subjects and to learn about new subjects.

There are many ways to interest students in the novel. There are book clubs for young people, such as Read and TAB, which recommend age-appropriate novels for students. Encourage students to attend book fairs, and perhaps organize one in your own school or classroom. For teaching additional novels to your students, consider the Prentice Hall *Study Guides,* which analyze the plot, characters, and theme of each novel on a chapter-by-chapter basis.

Where the Red Fern Grows

HUNTER IN THE ADIRONDACKS, 1892 (detail)
Winslow Homer
Courtesy of the Harvard University
Art Museums

Humanities Note

Fine art, *Hunter in the Adirondacks,* 1892, Winslow Homer. Winslow Homer (1836–1910) was first exposed to painting through observation of his mother's accomplished flower paintings. His natural talent emerged in his illustrations and paintings. Winslow Homer is remembered for his landscape, marine, and genre paintings of the American northeast.

Hunter in the Adirondacks is a watercolor. Homer often left New York City to go on hunting and fishing trips in the Adirondack region of New York State. These trips inspired many watercolors—quick sketches of woodland scenes—of which this painting is an example. In his watercolors as in all his paintings, Homer captures the feeling of the moment—here, the hunter's anticipation of his success.

Reading Strategy You might need to review the active reading strategies before beginning *Where the Red Fern Grows.* Students may use any or all of the strategies while reading the novel. Summarizing the action at intervals and questioning to be sure that students have not forgotten what they have previously read are helpful strategies for young readers.

Focus

More About the Author Wilson Rawls had little formal education and, although he always wrote, his shame about his lack of grammar and vocabulary skills led him to burn the manuscripts of his five books. It was not until 1959, at the age of forty-six, that he became a full-time writer. What qualities are required to persevere for so long to fulfill a dream?

Literary Focus It is important for students to get to know and understand characters, to imagine them as real people. They will not be interested in the story if the characters are not genuine. You might want to explain to them that just as they get to know what their friends are like through their actions, speech, and appearance, so they get to know characters in a book.

Look For You might consider having your students write down Billy's traits as they read about them. Doing so might help them in answering some of the questions on page 665.

Writing/Prior Knowledge You might lead the class in a discussion of goal setting and achieving, eliciting examples from the students. You might suggest that **less advanced** students list the steps they took in achieving their goal before they begin writing. The list might help them to develop the assignment in a logical progression.

Vocabulary Have more advanced students write an original sentence for each vocabulary word.

Where the Red Fern Grows, Chapters 1–7

Wilson Rawls (1913–   ) was born and raised in Oklahoma. He wrote stories throughout his life but felt that his lack of education prevented him from producing anything that was worthy of being published. It was not until 1959 that he, with the encouragement and help of his wife, rewrote a previously destroyed manuscript for his first novel, *Where the Red Fern Grows*. In this novel, Rawls draws upon his experiences as a youth exploring the hills and rivers around his home with his only companion at the time, an old hound dog.

Character

Characters are the people in a novel. As in a short story, characters have traits that make them seem like real people. However, because a novel is longer than a short story, characters may be developed more fully—they can change or grow over time. You can see how a character develops and grows as the novel progresses.

The main character in *Where the Red Fern Grows* is a boy named Billy. Billy is also the narrator of the story. You first meet him as a man, who then tells the story of his childhood. Because the story is told by Billy, you learn about the events as he sees them or makes them happen. Therefore, you learn about his qualities "from the inside out," that is, through what he says and what he does. You learn about the other characters only as they relate to Billy or as he thinks about them.

Look For

As you read Chapters 1–7, you will get to know the main character, Billy. What are the major traits of his character? What does he do or say that shows these traits?

Writing

In the opening chapters of *Where the Red Fern Grows,* Billy sets a goal for himself, which he works extremely hard to achieve. Have you ever set a goal that you had to plan for and work hard to achieve? Describe the steps you took to reach your goal.

Vocabulary

Knowing the following words will help you as you read Chapters 1–7 of *Where the Red Fern Grows*.

quavering (kwā′ vər iŋ) *v.*: Shaking or trembling (p. 637)

riffle (rif′ ′l) *n.*: A shallow area in a stream (p. 639)

winced (wins′ ′d) *v.*: Drew back

slightly, twisting the face, as in pain or alarm (p. 640)

runt (runt) *n.*: The smallest animal of a litter (p. 647)

628   *The Novel*

Objectives

1 To understand character in a novel
2 To make inferences about characters
3 To understand word origins
4 To write about a character

Support Material

Teaching Portfolio
Teacher Backup, p. 1035
Grammar in Action Worksheets, *Recognizing Compound Nouns,* p. 1042; *Using Action Verbs,* p. 1044; *Varying Sentence Openers,* p. 1046; *Understanding Subordinate Conjunctions,* p. 1048
Usage and Mechanics Worksheet, p. 1050

Vocabulary Check, p. 1051
Analyzing Literature Worksheet, *Understanding Character,* p. 1052
Language Worksheet, *Native American Words in English,* p. 1053
Selection Test, p. 1054
Library of Video Classics: *Where the Red Fern Grows*

Where the Red Fern Grows

Wilson Rawls

Chapter 1

When I left my office that beautiful spring day, I had no idea what was in store for me. To begin with, everything was too perfect for anything unusual to happen. It was one of those days when a man feels good, feels like speaking to his neighbor, is glad to live in a country like ours, and proud of his government. You know what I mean, one of those rare days when everything is right and nothing is wrong.

I was walking along whistling when I heard the dogfight. At first I paid no attention to it. After all it wasn't anything to get excited about, just another dogfight in a residential section.

As the sound of the fight grew nearer, I could tell there were quite a few dogs mixed up in it. They boiled out of an alley, turned, and headed straight toward me. Not wanting to get bitten or run over, I moved over to the edge of the sidewalk.

I could see that all the dogs were fighting one. About twenty-five feet from me they caught him and down he went. I felt sorry for the unfortunate one. I knew if something wasn't done quickly the sanitation department would have to pick up a dead dog.

I was trying to make up my mind to help when I got a surprise. Up out of that snarling, growling, slashing mass reared an old redbone hound.[1] For a second I saw him. I caught my breath. I couldn't believe what I had seen.

Twisting and slashing, he fought his way through the pack and backed up under the low branches of a hedge. Growling and snarling, they formed a half-moon circle around him. A big bird dog, bolder than the others, darted in. The hedge shook as he tangled with the hound. He came out so fast he fell over backwards. I saw that his right ear was split wide open. It was too much for him and he took off down the street, squalling like a scalded cat.

A big ugly cur tried his luck. He didn't get off so easy. He came out with his left shoulder laid open to the bone. He sat down on his rear and let the world know that he had been hurt.

By this time, my fighting blood was boiling. It's hard for a man to stand and watch an old hound fight against such odds, especially if that man has memories in his heart like I had in mine. I had seen the time when an old hound like that had given his life so that I might live.

Taking off my coat, I waded in. My yelling and scolding didn't have much effect, but the swinging coat did. The dogs scattered and left.

Down on my knees, I peered back under the hedge. The hound was still mad. He growled at me and showed his teeth. I knew it wasn't his nature to fight a man.

In a soft voice, I started talking to him. "Come on, boy," I said. "It's all right. I'm your friend. Come on now."

---

1. **redbone hound:** A medium-sized, fast, dark red or red and tan hound used especially for hunting coon.

2 Clarification A check line, also called a check rein, is a narrow strip of leather attached to a bridle of a single horse or the harness for a team of horses. It is used to control and direct.

3 Discussion What events awaken the memories to which the narrator is referring?

The fighting fire slowly left his eyes. He bowed his head and his long, red tail started thumping the ground. I kept coaxing. On his stomach, an inch at a time, he came to me and laid his head in my hand.

I almost cried at what I saw. His coat was dirty and mud-caked. His skin was stretched drum-tight over his bony frame. The knotty joints of his hips and shoulders stood out a good three inches from his body. I could tell he was starved.

I couldn't figure it out. He didn't belong in town. He was far out of place with the boxers, poodles, bird dogs, and other breeds of town dogs. He belonged in the country. He was a hunting hound.

I raised one of his paws. There I read the story. The pads were worn down slick as the rind on an apple. I knew he had come a long way, and no doubt had a long way to go. Around his neck was a crude collar. On closer inspection, I saw it had been made from a piece of check-line leather. Two holes had been punched in each end and the ends were laced together with bailing wire.

As I turned the collar with my finger, I saw something else. There, scratched deep in the tough leather, was the name "Buddie." I guessed that the crude, scribbly letters had probably been written by a little boy.

It's strange indeed how memories can lie dormant in a man's mind for so many years. Yet those memories can be awakened and brought forth fresh and new, just by something you've seen, or something you've heard, or the sight of an old familiar face.

What I saw in the warm gray eyes of the friendly old hound brought back wonderful memories. To show my gratitude, I took hold of his collar and said, "Come on, boy, let's go home and get something to eat."

He seemed to understand that he had found a friend. He came willingly.

I gave him a bath and rubbed all the

630   *The Novel*

soreness from his muscles. He drank quarts of warm milk and ate all the meat I had in the house. I hurried down to the store and bought more. He ate until he was satisfied.

He slept all that night and most of the next day. Late in the afternoon he grew restless. I told him I understood, and as soon as it was dark, he could be on his way. I figured he had a much better chance if he left town at night.

That evening, a little after sundown, I opened the back gate. He walked out, stopped, turned around, and looked at me. He thanked me by wagging his tail.

With tears in my eyes, I said, "You're more than welcome, old fellow. In fact, you could've stayed here as long as you wanted to."

He whined and licked my hand.

I was wondering which way he would go. With one final whimper he turned and headed east. I couldn't help smiling as I watched him trot down the alley. I noticed the way his hind quarters shifted over to the right, never in line with the front, yet always in perfect rhythm. His long ears flopped up and down, keeping time with the jogging motion of his body. Yes, they were all there, the unmistakable marks of a hunting hound.

Where the alley emptied into the street, he stopped and looked back. I waved my hand.

As I watched him disappear in the twilight shadows, I whispered these words: "Good-bye, old fellow. Good luck, and good hunting!"

I didn't have to let him go. I could have kept him in my back yard, but to pen up a dog like that is a sin. It would have broken his heart. The will to live would have slowly left his body.

I had no idea where he had come from or where he was going. Perhaps it wasn't too far, or maybe it was a long, long way. I tried to make myself believe that his home was in the Ozark Mountains somewhere in Missouri, or Oklahoma. It wasn't impossible even though it was a long way from the Snake River Valley in Idaho. **4**

I figured something drastic must have happened in his life, as it is very unusual for a hound to be traveling all alone. Perhaps he had been stolen, or maybe he had been sold for some much-needed money. Whatever it was that had interrupted his life, he was trying to straighten it out. He was going home to the master he loved, and with the help of God, he would make it.

4 Clarification The distance from the Snake River Valley in Idaho to the Ozark Mountains is more than 1000 miles.

To him it made no difference how long the road, or how rough or rocky. His old red feet would keep jogging along, on and on, mile after mile. There would be no crying or giving up. When his feet grew tired and weary, he would curl up in the weeds and rest. Water from a rain puddle or a mountain stream would quench his thirst and cool his hot dry throat. Food found along the highway, or the offerings from a friendly hand would ease the pangs of hunger. Through the rains, the snows, or the desert heat, he would jog along, never looking back.

5 Some morning he would be found curled up on the front porch. The long journey would be over. He would be home. There would be a lot of tail-wagging and a few whimpering cries. His warm moist tongue would caress the hand of his master. All would be forgiven. Once again the lights would shine in his dog's world. His heart would be happy.

After my friend had disappeared in the darkness, I stood and stared at the empty alley. A strange feeling came over me. At first I thought I was lonely or sad, but I realized that wasn't it at all. The feeling was a wonderful one.

Although the old hound had no way of knowing it, he had stirred memories, and what priceless treasures they were. Memories of my boyhood days, an old K. C. Baking Powder can, and two little red hounds. Memories of a wonderful love, unselfish devotion, and death in its saddest form.

As I turned to enter my yard I started to lock the gate, and then I thought, "No, I'll leave it open. He might come back."

I was about halfway to the house when a cool breeze drifted down from the rugged Tetons.[2] It had a bite in it and goose pimples jumped out on my skin. I stopped at the

woodshed and picked up several sticks of wood.

I didn't turn on any lights on entering the house. The dark, quiet atmosphere was a perfect setting for the mood I was in. I built a fire in the fireplace and pulled up my favorite rocker.

As I sat there in the silence, the fire grew larger. It crackled and popped. Firelight shadows began to shimmer and dance around the room. The warm, comfortable heat felt good.

I struck a match to light my pipe. As I did, two beautiful cups gleamed from the mantel. I held the match up so I could get a better look. There they were, sitting side by side. One was large with long, upright handles that stood out like wings on a mourning dove. The highly polished surface gleamed and glistened with a golden sheen. The other was smaller and made of silver. It was neat and trim, and sparkled like a white star in the heavens.

I got up and took them down. There was a story in those cups—a story that went back more than a half century.

As I caressed the smooth surfaces, my mind drifted back through the years, back to my boyhood days. How wonderful the memories were. Piece by piece the story unfolded.

Chapter 2

I suppose there's a time in practically every young boy's life when he's affected by that wonderful disease of puppy love. I don't mean the kind a boy has for the pretty little girl that lives down the road. I mean the real kind, the kind that has four small feet and a wiggly tail, and sharp little teeth that can gnaw on a boy's finger; the kind a boy can romp and play with, even eat and sleep with.

I was ten years old when I first became infected with this terrible disease. I'm sure no boy in the world had it worse than I did.

---

2. Tetons (tē′ tänz): A range of the Rocky Mountains in northwest Wyoming and southeast Idaho.

Grammar In Action

To be as specific as possible and sometimes, to create a personalized word, Wilson Rawls often uses nouns that are really the combination of two words. These **compound nouns** give Rawls' sentences a unique flavor and capture the texture of the Ozarks and the people's dialect.

I stopped at the *woodshed* and picked up several sticks.

The ones that fascinated me the most were the baby-like tracks of a *river coon.*

If my *dog-wanting* had been that of an ordinary boy, I'm sure my mother and father would have gotten me a puppy . . .

In these three examples, two words combine to function as one noun. In the first example, the two words *wood* and *shed* have actually been combined into one word. In the second, the words are separate though they function as one. In the third example, the hyphen shows that the two parts are really one word. Can you see how closely the two parts in each example are related? *River* does not describe *coon,* it is a part of the name of the creature. Think about the two parts of your own name; it is another example of a compound noun.

It's not easy for a young boy to want a dog and not be able to have one. It starts gnawing on his heart, and gets all mixed up in his dreams. It gets worse and worse, until finally it becomes almost unbearable.

If my dog-wanting had been that of an ordinary boy, I'm sure my mother and father would have gotten me a puppy, but my wants were different. I didn't want just one dog. I wanted two, and not just any kind of a dog. They had to be a special kind and a special breed.

I had to have some dogs. I went to my father and had a talk with him. He scratched his head and thought it over.

"Well, Billy," he said, "I heard that Old Man Hatfield's collie is going to have pups. I'm sure I can get one of them for you."

He may as well have poured cold water on me. "Papa," I said. "I don't want an old collie dog. I want hounds—coon hounds—and I want two of them."

I could tell by the look on his face that he wanted to help me, but couldn't.

He said, "Billy, those kind of dogs cost money, and that's something we don't have right now. Maybe some day when we can afford it, you can have them, but not right now."

I didn't give up. After my talk with Papa, I went to Mama. I fared no better there. Right off she said I was too young to be hunting with hounds. Besides, a hunter needed a gun, and that was one thing I couldn't have, not until I was twenty-one anyway.

I couldn't understand it. There I was sitting right in the middle of the finest hunting country in the world and I didn't even have a dog.

Our home was in a beautiful valley far back in the rugged Ozarks. The country was new and sparsely settled. The land we lived on was Cherokee land, allotted to my mother because of the Cherokee blood that flowed in her veins. It lay in a strip from the foothills of the mountains to the banks of the Illinois River in northeastern Oklahoma.

The land was rich, black, and fertile. Papa said it would grow hair on a crosscut saw. He was the first man to stick the cold steel point of a turning plow into the virgin soil.

Mama had picked the spot for our log house. It nestled at the edge of the foothills in the mouth of a small canyon, and was surrounded by a grove of huge red oaks. Behind our house one could see miles and miles of the mighty Ozarks. In the spring the aromatic scent of wild flowers, redbuds, papaws, and dogwoods, drifting on the wind currents, spread over the valley and around our home.

Below our fields, twisting and winding, ran the clear blue waters of the Illinois River. The banks were cool and shady. The rich bottom land near the river was studded with tall sycamores, birches, and box elders.

To a ten-year-old country boy it was the most beautiful place in the whole wide world, and I took advantage of it all. I roamed the hills and the river bottoms. I knew every game trail in the thick canebrakes,[3] and every animal track that was pressed in the mud along the riverbanks.

The ones that fascinated me the most were the baby-like tracks of a river coon. I'd lie for hours examining them. Before leaving, I'd take a switch and sweep them all away. These I called my "trail looks." The next day I'd hurry back, and sure enough, nine times out of ten, there in the clean-swept ground I would again find the tracks of a ringtail coon.

I knew he had passed over the trail during the night. I could close my eyes and almost see him, humped up and waddling

---

3. canebrakes (kān′ brākz) *n.*: Dense growths of cane plants.

Where the Red Fern Grows 633

6

6 **Enrichment** The original territory of the Cherokee Indians was an area of the southeastern United States that centered in northwestern Georgia. In 1838, 15,000 Cherokee people were driven from their homes and forced to march to the Oklahoma territory, where they settled. From the 1890's on, Indians increasingly accepted allotments of land, which they owned individually.

Student Activity 1. Use each of these compound nouns in a sentence about *Where the Red Fern Grows*.

dogfight
hind quarters
Ozark Mountains
goose pimples

crosscut saw
bird dogs
K.C. Baking Powder
box elders

Student Activity 2. List five other compound nouns that you can think of. Use each one in a sentence about *Where the Red Fern Grows*.

7 Literary Focus It might be helpful to point out that whatever students learn about Billy's parents, they learn through Billy himself. What does this passage reveal about Billy's parents? What does it indicate about Billy's character? What are his parents' feelings concerning his desire for hound dogs?

along, fishing under the banks with his delicate little paws for crawfish, frogs, and minnows.

I was a hunter from the time I could walk. I caught lizards on the rail fences, rats in the corn crib, and frogs in the little creek that ran through the fields. I was a young Daniel Boone.

As the days passed, the dog-wanting disease grew worse. I began to see dogs in my sleep. I went back to my father and mother. It was the same old story. Good hounds cost money, and they just didn't have it.

My dog-wanting became so bad I began to lose weight and my food didn't taste good any more. Mama noticed this and she had a talk with Papa.

"You're going to have to do something," she said. "I never saw a boy grieve like that. It's not right, not right at all."

"I know," said Papa, "and I feel just as badly as you do, but what can I do? You know we don't have that kind of money."

"I don't care," said Mama. "You've got to do something. I can't stand to see him cry like that. Besides he's getting to be a problem. I can't get my work done. He follows me around all day long begging for hounds."

"I offered to get him a dog," said Papa, "but he doesn't want just any kind of dog. He wants hounds, and they cost money. Do you know what the Parker boys paid for those two hounds they bought? Seventy-five dollars! If I had that much money, I'd buy another mule. I sure do need one."

7 I had overheard this conversation from another room. At first it made me feel pretty good. At least I was getting to be a problem. Then I didn't feel so good. I knew my mother and father were poor and didn't have any money. I began to feel sorry for them and myself.

After thinking it over, I figured out a way to help. Even though it was a great sacrifice,

I told Papa I had decided I didn't want two hounds. One would be enough. I saw the hurt in his eyes. It made me feel like someone was squeezing water out of my heart.

Papa set me on his lap and we had a good talk. He told me how hard times were, and that it looked like a man couldn't get a fair price for anything he raised. Some of the farmers had quit farming and were cutting railroad ties so they could feed their families. If things didn't get better, that's what he'd have to do. He said he'd give anything if he could get some good hounds for me, but there didn't seem to be any way he could right then.

I went off to bed with my heart all torn up in little pieces, and cried myself to sleep.

The next day Papa had to go to the store. Late that evening I saw him coming back. As fast as I could, I ran to meet him, expecting a sack of candy. Instead he handed me three small steel traps.

If Santa Claus himself had come down out of the mountains, reindeer and all, I would not have been more pleased. I jumped up and down, and cried a whole bucketful of tears. I hugged him and told him what a wonderful papa he was.

He showed me how to set them by mashing the spring down with my foot, and how to work the trigger. I took them to bed with me that night.

The next morning I started trapping around the barn. The first thing I caught was Samie, our house cat. If this didn't cause a commotion! I didn't intend to catch him. I was trying to catch a rat, but somehow he came nosing around and got in my trap.

My sisters started bawling and yelling for Mama. She came running, wanting to know what in the world was going on. None of us had to tell her. Samie told her with his spitting and squalling.

He was mad. He couldn't understand what that thing was that was biting his foot, and he was making an awful fuss about it. His tail was as big as a wet corncob and every hair on his small body was sticking straight up. He spit and yowled and dared anyone to get close to him.

My sisters yelled their fool heads off, all the time saying, "Poor Samie! Poor Samie!"

Mama shushed them up and told me to go get the forked stick from under the clothesline. I ran and got it.

Mama was the best helper a boy ever had. She put the forked end over Samie's neck and pinned him to the ground.

It was bad enough for the trap to be biting his foot, but to have his neck pinned down that way was too much. He threw a fit. I never heard such a racket in all my life.

It wasn't long until everything on the place was all spooked up. The chickens started cackling and flew way up on the hillside. Daisy, our milk cow, all but tore the barn lot up and refused to give any milk that night. Sloppy Ann, our hog, started running in circles, squealing and grunting.

Samie wiggled and twisted. He yowled and spit, but it didn't do him any good. Mama was good and stout. She held him down, tight to the ground. I ran in and put my foot on the trap spring, mashed it down, and released his foot. With one loud squall, he scooted under the barn.

After it was all over, Mama said, "I don't think you'll have any more trouble with that cat. I think he has learned his lesson."

How wrong Mama was. Samie was one of those nosy kind of cats. He would lie up on the red oak limbs and watch every move I made.

I found some slick little trails out in our garden down under some tall hollyhocks. Thinking they were game trails, and not knowing they were Samie's favorite hunting trails, I set my traps. Samie couldn't understand what I was doing out there, messing around his hunting territory. He went to investigate.

It wasn't long until I had him limping with all four feet. Every time Papa saw Samie lying around in the warm sun with his feet wrapped up in turpentine rags, he would laugh until big tears rolled down his cheeks.

Mama had another talk with Papa. She said he was going to have to say something to me, because if I caught that cat one more time, it would drive her out of her mind.

Papa told me to be a little more careful where I set my traps.

"Papa," I said, "I don't want to catch Samie, but he's the craziest cat I ever saw. He sees everything I do, and just has to go sniffing around."

Papa looked over at Samie. He was lying all sprawled out in the sunshine with all four paws bandaged and sticking straight up. His long tail was swishing this way and that.

"You see, Papa," I said, "he's watching me right now, just waiting for me to set my traps."

Papa walked off toward the barn. I heard him laughing fit to kill.

It finally got too tough for Samie. He left home. Oh, he came in once in a while, all long and lean looking, but he never was the same friendly cat any more. He was nervous and wouldn't let anyone pet him. He would gobble down his milk and then scoot for the timber.

Once I decided to make friends with him because I felt bad about catching him in my traps. I reached out my hand to rub his back. He swelled up like a sitting hen. His eyeballs got all green, and he growled way down deep. He spat at me, and drew back his paw like he was going to knock my head off. I decided I'd better leave him alone.

In no time at all I cleaned out the rats.

8 **Discussion** What does Billy mean by this statement? Have you ever had this experience? Based on what you have read about his character, what do you think Billy will do?

9 **Critical Thinking and Reading** What inferences can you make about Billy based on this action? What inferences can you make about his mother based on how she reacts to him?

Then something bad happened. I caught one of Mama's prize hens. I got one of those "young man peach tree" switchings over that.

Papa told me to go down in the cane-brakes back of our fields and trap. This opened up all kinds of new wonders. I caught opossums, skunks, rabbits, and squirrels.

Papa showed me how to skin my game. In neat little rows I tacked the hides on the smokehouse wall. I'd stand for hours and ad-mire my magnificent trophies.

There was only one thing wrong. I didn't have a big coonskin to add to my collection. I couldn't trap old Mister Ringtail. He was too smart for me. He'd steal the bait from the traps, spring the triggers, and sometimes even turn them over.

Once I found a small stick standing up-right in one of my traps. I showed it to Papa. He laughed and said the stick must have fallen from a tree. It made no difference what Papa said. I was firmly convinced that a smart old coon had deliberately poked that stick in my trap.

8 The traps helped my dog-wanting con-siderably, but like a new toy, the newness wore off and I was right back where I started from. Only this time it was worse, much worse. I had been exposed to the feel of wild-life.

I started pestering Mama again. She said, "Oh, no! Not that again. I thought you'd be satisfied with the traps. No, Billy, I don't want to hear any more about hounds."

I knew Mama meant what she said. This broke my heart. I decided I'd leave home. I sneaked out a quart jar of peaches, some cold corn bread, and a few onions, and started up the hollow back of our house. I had it all figured out. I'd go away off to some big town, get a hundred dogs, and bring them all back with me.

I made it all right until I heard a timber wolf howl. This stopped my home-leaving.

When the hunting season opened that fall, something happened that was almost more than I could stand. I was lying in bed one night trying to figure out a way I could get some dogs when I heard the deep baying of a coon hound. I got up and opened my window. It came again. The deep voice rang loud and clear in the frosty night. Now and then I could hear the hunter whooping to him.

The hound hunted all night. He quit when the roosters started crowing at day-break. The hunter and the hound weren't the only ones awake that night. I stayed up and listened to them until the last tones of the hound's voice died away in the daylight hours.

9 That morning I was determined to have some hounds. I went again to Mama. This time I tried bribery. I told her if she'd get me a hunting dog, I'd save the money I earned from my furs, and buy her a new dress and a boxful of pretty hats.

That time I saw tears in her eyes. It made me feel all empty inside and I cried a little, too. By the time she was through kissing me and talking to me, I was sure I didn't need any dogs at all. I couldn't stand to see Mama cry.

The next night I heard the hound again. I tried to cover my head with a pillow to shut out the sound. It was no use. His voice seemed to bore its way through the pillow and ring in my ears. I had to get up and again go to the window. I'm sure if that coon hunter had known that he was slowly killing a ten-year-old boy, he would have put a muz-zle on his hound.

Sleep was out of the question. Even on nights when I couldn't hear the hound, I couldn't sleep. I was afraid if I did, he would come and I would miss hearing him.

636   *The Novel*

Grammar in Action

There are two types of verbs, *action verbs*, such as *think, drive, slide, eat,* and linking verbs such as *is, appear, seem.* Writers use *action verbs* to express their ideas vividly and forcefully. Although there are some sentences where linking verbs are required to show the proper relationship, action verbs generally state ideas more effectively. In the following passage, Wilson Rawls uses action verbs to make his ideas direct and forceful.

The traps *helped* my dog-wanting considerably, but like a new toy, the newness *wore* off. . . .

Compare Rawls's sentence with the following one, which substi-tutes linking verbs for action verbs. Notice how dull and wordy it is.

The traps *were* a considerable help to me for my dog-wanting, but like a new toy, the newness *seemed* to lose its effect. . . .

Student Activity 1. Rewrite the following sentences. Make the verbs action verbs.

By the time hunting season was over, I was a nervous wreck. My eyes were red and bloodshot. I had lost weight and was as thin as a bean pole. Mama checked me over. She looked at my tongue and turned back one of my eyelids.

"If I didn't know better," she said, "I'd swear you weren't sleeping well. Are you?"

"Why, Mama," I said, "I go to bed, don't I? What does a boy go to bed for if it isn't to sleep?"

By the little wrinkles that bunched up on her forehead, I could tell that Mama wasn't satisfied. Papa came in during one of these inspections. Mama told him she was worried about my health.

"Aw," he said, "there's nothing wrong with him. It's just because he's been cooped up all winter. A boy needs sunshine, and exercise. He's almost eleven now, and I'm going to let him help me in the fields this summer. That will put the muscles back on him."

I thought this was wonderful. I'd finally grown up to be a man. I was going to help Papa with the farm.

Chapter 3

The dog-wanting disease never did leave me altogether. With the new work I was doing, helping Papa, it just kind of burned itself down and left a big sore on my heart. Every time I'd see a coon track down in our fields, or along the riverbanks, the old sore would get all festered up and start hurting again.

Just when I had given up all hope of ever owning a good hound, something wonderful happened. The good Lord figured I had hurt enough, and it was time to lend a helping hand.

It all started one day while I was hoeing corn down in our field close to the river.

Across the river, a party of fishermen had been camped for several days. I heard the old Maxwell car as it snorted and chugged its way out of the bottoms.[4] I knew they were leaving. Throwing down my hoe, I ran down to the river and waded across at a place called the Shannon Ford. I hurried to the camp ground.

It was always a pleasure to prowl where fishermen had camped. I usually could find things: a fish line, or a forgotten fish pole. On one occasion, I found a beautiful knife stuck in the bark of a sycamore tree, forgotten by a careless fisherman. But on that day, I found the greatest of treasures, a sportsman's magazine, discarded by the campers. It was a real treasure for a country boy. Because of that magazine, my entire life was changed.

I sat down on an old sycamore log, and started thumbing through the leaves. On the back pages of the magazine, I came to the "For Sale" section—"Dogs for Sale"—every kind of dog. I read on and on. They had dogs I had never heard of, names I couldn't make out. Far down in the right-hand corner, I found an ad that took my breath away. In small letters, it read: "Registered redbone coon hound pups—twenty-five dollars each."

The advertisement was from a kennel in Kentucky. I read it over and over. By the time I had memorized the ad, I was seeing dogs, hearing dogs, and even feeling them. The magazine was forgotten. I was lost in thought. The brain of an eleven-year-old boy can dream some fantastic dreams.

How wonderful it would be if I could have two of those pups. Every boy in the country but me had a good hound or two. But fifty dollars—how could I ever get fifty dollars? I

---

4. **bottoms** (bät′ əmz) *n*.: Bottom land, or low land through which a river flows.

Where the Red Fern Grows 637

Literary Focus You might point out the difference in the ways Billy's mother and father react to him. What does this statement indicate about Billy's father?

11 **Discussion** Have the students discuss how this magazine and the ad might be the reason for a great change in Billy's life.

---

1. We were late in arriving at Grandmother's house.

2. Spring was early in coming this year.

3. The boy seemed to lose interest in the game.

Student Activity 2. Write three original sentences using forceful, lively action verbs.

knew I couldn't expect help from Mama and Papa.

I remembered a passage from the Bible my mother had read to us: "God helps those who help themselves." I thought of the words. I mulled them over in my mind. I decided I'd ask God to help me. There on the banks of the Illinois River, in the cool shade of the tall white sycamores, I asked God to help me get two hound pups. It wasn't much of a prayer, but it did come right from the heart.

When I left the campground of the fishermen, it was late. As I walked along, I could feel the hard bulge of the magazine jammed deep in the pocket of my overalls. The beautiful silence that follows the setting sun had settled over the river bottoms. The coolness of the rich, black soil felt good to my bare feet.

It was the time of day when all furried things come to life. A big swamp rabbit hopped out on the trail, sat on his haunches, stared at me, and then scampered away. A mother gray squirrel ran out on the limb of a bur oak tree. She barked a warning to the four furry balls behind her. They melted from sight in the thick green. A silent gray shadow drifted down from the top of a tall sycamore. There was a squeal and a beating of wings. I heard the tinkle of a bell in the distance ahead. I knew it was Daisy, our milk cow. I'd have to start her on the way home.

12 I took the magazine from my pocket and again I read the ad. Slowly a plan began to form. I'd save the money. I could sell stuff to the fishermen: crawfish, minnows, and fresh vegetables. In berry season, I could sell all the berries I could pick at my grandfather's store. I could trap in the winter. The more I planned, the more real it became. There was the way to get those pups—save my money.

I could almost feel the pups in my hands.

I planned the little doghouse, and where to put it. Collars I could make myself. Then the thought came, "What could I name them?" I tried name after name, voicing them out loud. None seemed to fit. Well, there would be plenty of time for names.

Right now there was something more important—fifty dollars—a fabulous sum—a fortune—far more money than I had ever seen. Somehow, some way, I was determined to have it. I had twenty-three cents—a dime I had earned running errands for my grandpa, and thirteen cents a fisherman had given me for a can of worms.

The next morning I went to the trash pile behind the barn. I was looking for a can—my bank. I picked up several, but they didn't seem to be what I wanted. Then I saw it, an old K. C. Baking Powder can. It was perfect, long and slender, with a good tight lid. I took it down to the creek and scrubbed it with sand until it was bright and new-looking.

I dropped the twenty-three cents in the can. The coins looked so small lying there on the shiny bottom, but to me it was a good start. With my finger, I tried to measure how full it would be with fifty dollars in it.

Next, I went to the barn and up in the loft. Far back over the hay and up under the eaves, I hid my can. I had a start toward making my dreams come true—twenty-three cents. I had a good bank, safe from the rats and from the rain and snow.

All through that summer I worked like a beaver. In the small creek that wormed its way down through our fields, I caught crawfish with my bare hands. I trapped minnows with an old screen-wire trap I made myself, baited with yellow cornbread from my mother's kitchen. These were sold to the fishermen, along with fresh vegetables and roasting ears. I tore my way through the blackberry patches until my hands and feet were scratched raw and red from the thorns.

I tramped the hills seeking out the huckleberry bushes. My grandfather paid me ten cents a bucket for my berries.

Once Grandpa asked me what I did with the money I earned. I told him I was saving it to buy some hunting dogs. I asked him if he would order them for me when I had saved enough. He said he would. I asked him not to say anything to my father. He promised me he wouldn't. I'm sure Grandpa paid little attention to my plans.

That winter I trapped harder than ever with the three little traps I owned. Grandpa sold my hides to fur buyers who came to his store all through the fur season. Prices were cheap: fifteen cents for a large opossum hide, twenty-five for a good skunk hide.

Little by little, the nickels and dimes added up. The old K. C. Baking Powder can grew heavy. I would heft its weight in the palm of my hand. With a straw, I'd measure from the lip of the can to the money. As the months went by, the straws grew shorter and shorter.

The next summer I followed the same routine.

"Would you like to buy some crawfish or minnows? Maybe you'd like some fresh vegetables or roasting ears."

The fishermen were wonderful, as true sportsmen are. They seemed to sense the ur-

13 Discussion How do young people today earn money? In what ways is the bank that Billy uses different from the way people save their money today?

14 **Literary Focus** You could point out that Billy's character is also revealed through his actions. Ask students what characteristics are revealed by his actions described in the last few paragraphs.

15 **Discussion** Why does the barn seem this way to Billy?

gency in my voice and always bought my wares. However, many was the time I'd find my vegetables left in the abandoned camp.

There never was a set price. Anything they offered was good enough for me.

14 A year passed. I was twelve. I was over the halfway mark. I had twenty-seven dollars and forty-six cents. My spirits soared. I worked harder.

Another year crawled slowly by, and then the great day came. The long hard grind was over. I had it—my fifty dollars! I cried as I counted it over and over.

15 As I set the can back in the shadowy eaves of the barn, it seemed to glow with a radiant whiteness I had never seen before. Perhaps it was all imagination. I don't know.

Lying back in the soft hay, I folded my hands behind my head, closed my eyes, and let my mind wander back over the two long years. I thought of the fishermen, the blackberry patches, and the huckleberry hills. I thought of the prayer I had said when I asked God to help me get two hound pups. I knew He had surely helped, for He had given me the heart, courage, and determination.

Early the next morning, with the can jammed deep in the pocket of my overalls, I flew to the store. As I trotted along, I whistled and sang. I felt as big as the tallest mountain in the Ozarks.

Arriving at my destination, I saw two wagons were tied up at the hitching rack. I knew some farmers had come to the store, so I waited until they left. As I walked in, I saw my grandfather behind the counter. Tugging and pulling, I worked the can out of my pocket and dumped it out in front of him and looked up.

Grandpa was dumbfounded. He tried to say something, but it wouldn't come out. He looked at me, and he looked at the pile of coins. Finally, in a voice much louder than

he ordinarily used, he asked, "Where did you get all this?"

"I told you, Grandpa," I said, "I was saving my money so I could buy two hound pups, and I did. You said you would order them for me. I've got the money and now I want you to order them."

Grandpa stared at me over his glasses, and then back at the money.

"How long have you been saving this?" he asked.

"A long time, Grandpa," I said.

"How long?" he asked.

I told him, "Two years."

His mouth flew open and in a loud voice he said, "Two years!"

I nodded my head.

The way my grandfather stared at me made me uneasy. I was on needles and pins. Taking his eyes from me, he glanced back at the money. He saw the faded yellow piece of paper sticking out from the coins. He worked it out, asking as he did, "What's this?"

I told him it was the ad, telling where to order my dogs.

He read it, turned it over, and glanced at the other side.

I saw the astonishment leave his eyes and the friendly-old-grandfather look come back. I felt much better.

Dropping the paper back on the money, he turned, picked up an old turkey-feather duster, and started dusting where there was no dust. He kept glancing at me out of the corner of his eye as he walked slowly down to the other end of the store, dusting here and there.

He put the duster down, came from behind the counter, and walked up to me. Laying a friendly old work-calloused hand on my head, he changed the conversation altogether, saying, "Son, you need a haircut."

I told him I didn't mind. I didn't like my

640   *The Novel*

hair short; flies and mosquitoes bothered me.

He glanced down at my bare feet and asked, "How come your feet are cut and scratched like that?"

I told him it was pretty tough picking blackberries barefoot.

He nodded his head.

It was too much for my grandfather. He turned and walked away. I saw the glasses come off, and the old red handkerchief come out. I heard the good excuse of blowing his nose. He stood for several seconds with his back toward me. When he turned around, I noticed his eyes were moist.

In a quavering voice, he said, "Well, Son, it's your money. You worked for it, and you worked hard. You got it honestly, and you want some dogs. We're going to get those dogs."

He walked over and picked up the ad again, asking, "Is this two years old, too?"

I nodded.

"Well," he said, "the first thing we have to do is write this outfit. There may not even be a place like this in Kentucky any more. After all, a lot of things can happen in two years."

Seeing that I was worried, he said, "Now you go on home. I'll write to these kennels and I'll let you know when I get an answer. If we can't get the dogs there, we can get them someplace else. And I don't think, if I were you, I'd let my Pa know anything about this right now. I happen to know he wants to buy that red mule from Old Man Potter."

I told him I wouldn't, and turned to leave the store.

As I reached the door, my grandfather said in a loud voice, "Say, it's been a long time since you've had any candy, hasn't it?"

I nodded my head.

He asked, "How long?"

I told him, "A long time."

"Well," he said, "we'll have to do something about that."

Walking over behind the counter, he reached out and got a sack. I noticed it wasn't one of the nickel sacks. It was one of the quarter kind.

My eyes never left my grandfather's hand. Time after time, it dipped in and out of the candy counter: peppermint sticks, jawbreakers, horehound, and gumdrops. The sack bulged. So did my eyes.

Handing the sack to me, he said, "Here. First big coon you catch with those dogs, you can pay me back."

I told him I would.

On my way home, with a jawbreaker in one side of my mouth and a piece of horehound in the other, I skipped and hopped, making half an effort to try to whistle and sing, and couldn't for the candy. I had the finest grandpa in the world and I was the happiest boy in the world.

I wanted to share my happiness with my sisters but decided not to say anything about ordering the pups.

Arriving home, I dumped the sack of candy out on the bed. Six little hands helped themselves. I was well repaid by the love and adoration I saw in the wide blue eyes of my three little sisters.

Chapter 4

Day after day, I flew to the store. Grandpa would shake his head. Then on a Monday, as I entered the store, I sensed a change in him. He was in high spirits, talking and laughing with half a dozen farmers. Every time I caught his eye, he would smile and wink at me. I thought the farmers would never leave, but finally the store was empty.

Grandpa told me the letter had come. The kennels were still there, and they had

16

16 **Critical Thinking and Reading**
What inference can you make about Grandpa from his actions?

Where the Red Fern Grows 641

dogs for sale. He said he had made the mail buggy wait while he made out the order. And, another thing, the dog market had gone downhill. The price of dogs had dropped five dollars. He handed me a ten-dollar bill.

"Now, there's still one stump in the way," he said. "The mail buggy can't carry things like dogs, so they'll come as far as the depot at Tahlequah,[5] but you'll get the notice here because I ordered them in your name."

I thanked my grandfather with all my heart and asked him how long I'd have to wait for the notice.

He said, "I don't know, but it shouldn't take more than a couple of weeks."

I asked how I was going to get my dogs out from Tahlequah.

"Well, there's always someone going in," he said, "and you could ride in with them."

That evening the silence of our supper was interrupted when I asked my father this question: "Papa, how far is it to Kentucky?"

I may as well have exploded a bomb. For an instant there was complete silence, and then my oldest sister giggled. The two little ones stared at me.

With a half-hearted laugh, my father said, "Well, now, I don't know, but it's a pretty good ways. What do you want to know for? Thinking of taking a trip to Kentucky?"

"No," I said. "I just wondered."

My youngest sister giggled and asked, "Can I go with you?"

I glared at her.

Mama broke into the conversation, "I declare, what kind of a question is that? How far is it to Kentucky? I don't know what's gotten into that mind of yours lately. You go around like you were lost, and you're losing weight. You're as skinny as a rail, and look

---

5. Tahlequah (tal' ə kwô): A town in eastern Oklahoma.

at that hair. Just last Sunday they had a haircutting over at Tom Rolland's place, but you couldn't go. You had to go prowling around the river and the woods."

I told Mama that I'd get a haircut next time they had a cutting. And I just heard some fellows talking about Kentucky up at the store, and wondered how far away it was. Much to my relief, the conversation was ended.

The days dragged by. A week passed and still no word about my dogs. Terrible thoughts ran through my mind. Maybe my dogs were lost; the train had a wreck; someone stole my money; or perhaps the mailman lost my order. Then, at the end of the second week, the notice came.

My grandfather told me that he had talked to Jim Hodges that day. He was going into town in about a week and I could ride in with him to pick up my dogs. Again I thanked my grandfather.

I started for home. Walking along in deep thought, I decided it was time to tell my father the whole story. I fully intended to tell him that evening. I tried several times, but somehow I couldn't. I wasn't scared of him, for he never whipped me. He was always kind and gentle, but for some reason, I don't know why, I just couldn't tell him.

That night, snuggled deep in the soft folds of a feather bed, I lay thinking. I had waited so long for my dogs, and I so desperately wanted to see them and hold them. I didn't want to wait a whole week.

In a flash I made up my mind. Very quietly I got up and put on my clothes. I sneaked into the kitchen and got one of Mama's precious flour sacks. In it I put six eggs, some leftover corn bread, a little salt, and a few matches. Next I went to the smokehouse and cut off a piece of salt pork. I stopped at the barn and picked up a gunny sack. I put the flour sack inside the gunny

Commentary: Tahlequah

When the Cherokee people resettled in the Oklahoma Territory in 1838–1839, they established the **Cherokee Nation,** whose capital was Tahlequah. The Cherokee Nation had a republican form of government, with a constitution providing for an elected chief, a senate, and a house of representatives.

Tahlequah was chosen for the capital because it is centrally located in what was then the Cherokee Nation. Throughout the middle of the nineteenth century Tahlequah was the center of culture and industry for the Cherokee people. Schools and churches were established, newspapers were published, and businesses developed.

In the late 1800's, the United States Congress abolished the tribal government and many of the Cherokee people began to accept individual allotments of land, which had previously been communally owned by the tribe. Billy's family, because his mother has Cherokee blood, lives on one such allotment of land near Tahlequah.

sack. This I rolled up and crammed lengthwise in the bib of my overalls.

I was on my way. I was going after my dogs.

Tahlequah was a small country town with a population of about eight hundred. By the road it was thirty-two miles away, but as the crow flies, it was only twenty miles. I went as the crow flies, straight through the hills.

Although I had never been to town in my life, I knew what direction to take. Tahlequah and the railroad lay on the other side of the river from our place. I had the Frisco Railroad on my right, and the Illinois River on my left. Not far from where the railroad crossed the river lay the town of Tahlequah. I knew if I bore to the right I would find the railroad, and if I bore to the left I had the river to guide me.

Sometime that night, I crossed the river on a riffle somewhere in the Dripping Springs country. Coming out of the river bottoms, I scatted up a long hogback ridge, and broke out on top in the flats. In a mile-eating trot, I moved along. I had the wind of a deer, the muscles of a country boy, a heart full of dog love, and a strong determination. I wasn't scared of the darkness, or the mountains, for I was raised in those mountains.

On and on, mile after mile, I moved along. I saw faint gray streaks appear in the east. I knew daylight was close. My bare feet were getting sore from the flint rocks and saw briers.[6] I stopped beside a mountain stream, soaked my feet in the cool water, rested for a spell, and then started on.

After leaving the mountain stream, my pace was much slower. The muscles of my legs were getting stiff. Feeling the pangs of hunger gnawing at my stomach, I decided I

---

6. saw briers (sô brī′ ərz) n: Prickly plants.

would stop and eat at the next stream I found. Then I remembered I had forgotten to include a can in which to boil my eggs.

I stopped and built a small fire. Cutting off a nice thick slab of salt pork, I roasted it, and with a piece of cold corn bread made a sandwich. Putting out my fire, I was on my way again. I ate as I trotted along. I felt much better.

I came into Tahlequah from the northeast. At the outskirts of town, I hid my flour sack and provisions, keeping the gunny sack. I walked into town.

I was scared of Tahlequah and the people. I had never seen such a big town and so many people. There was store after store, some of them two stories high. The wagon yard had wagons on top of wagons; teams, buggies, and horses.

Two young ladies about my age stopped, stared at me, and then giggled. My blood boiled, but I could understand. After all, I had three sisters. They couldn't help it because they were womenfolks. I went on.

I saw a big man coming up the street. The bright shiny star on his vest looked as big as a bucket. I saw the long, black gun at his side and I froze in my tracks. I'd heard of sheriffs and marshals, but had never seen one. Stories repeated about them in the mountains told how fast they were with a gun, and how many men they had killed.

The closer he came, the more frightened I got. I knew it was the end for me. I could just see him aiming his big, black gun and shooting me between the eyes. It seemed like a miracle that he passed by, hardly glancing at me. Breathing a sigh, I walked on, seeing the wonders of the world.

Passing a large store window, I stopped and stared. There in the window was the most wonderful sight I had ever seen; everything under the sun; overalls, jackets, bolts of beautiful cloth, new harnesses, collars,

18

18 **Discussion** Why are most people nervous when they are experiencing a situation like this that is strange or unfamiliar to them?

Where the Red Fern Grows 643

19 Literary Focus You might want students to reread the passage in which Billy sees the reflection of himself for the first time. It reveals a great deal about him. Ask what his appearance reveals about his character. How might his appearance mislead people who don't know him? What does this passage reveal about how and where he was brought up?

20 Enrichment To reinforce the significance of the fifty dollars that Billy saved, you could point out that Billy received change from ten dollars for all of the items that he purchased. About how much might those items cost today?

bridles; and then my eyes did pop open. There were several guns and one of them had two barrels. I couldn't believe it—two barrels. I had seen several guns, but never one with two barrels.

Then I saw something else. The sun was just right, and the plate glass was a perfect mirror. I saw the full reflection of myself for the first time in my life.

I could see that I did look a little odd. My straw-colored hair was long and shaggy, and was bushed out like a corn tassel that had been hit by a wind. I tried to smooth it down with my hands. This helped some but not much. What it needed was a good combing and I had no comb.

My overalls were patched and faded but they were clean. My shirt had pulled out. I tucked it back in.

I took one look at my bare feet and winced. They were as brown as dead sycamore leaves. The spider-web pattern of raw, red scratches looked odd in the saddle-brown skin. I thought, "Well, I won't have to pick any more blackberries and the scratches will soon go away."

I pumped up one of my arms and thought surely the muscle was going to pop right through my thin blue shirt. I stuck out my tongue. It was as red as pokeberry juice and anything that color was supposed to be healthy.

After making a few faces at myself, I put my thumbs in my ears and was making mule ears when two old women came by. They stopped and stared at me. I stared back. As they turned to go on their way, I heard one of them say something to the other. The words were hard to catch, but I did hear one word: "Wild." As I said before, they couldn't help it, they were womenfolks.

As I turned to leave, my eyes again fell on the overalls and the bolts of cloth. I thought of my mother, father, and sisters. Here was an opportunity to make amends for leaving home without telling anyone.

I entered the store. I bought a pair of overalls for Papa. After telling the storekeeper how big my mother and sisters were, I bought several yards of cloth. I also bought a large sack of candy.

Glancing down at my bare feet, the storekeeper said, "I have some good shoes."

I told him I didn't need any shoes.

He asked if that would be all.

I nodded.

He added up the bill. I handed him my ten dollars. He gave me my change.

After wrapping up the bundles, he helped me put them in my sack. Lifting it to my shoulder, I turned and left the store.

Out on the street, I picked out a friendly-looking old man and asked him where the depot was. He told me to go down to the last street and turn right, go as far as I could, and I couldn't miss it. I thanked him and started on my way.

Leaving the main part of town, I started up a long street through the residential section. I had never seen so many beautiful houses, and they were all different colors. The lawns were neat and clean and looked like green carpets. I saw a man pushing some kind of a mowing machine. I stopped to watch the whirling blades. He gawked at me. I hurried on.

I heard a lot of shouting and laughing ahead of me. Not wanting to miss anything, I walked a little faster. I saw what was making the noise. More kids than I had ever seen were playing around a big red brick building. I thought some rich man lived there and was giving a party for his children. Walking up to the edge of the playground, I stopped to watch.

The boys and girls were about my age, and were as thick as flies around a sorghum mill. They were milling, running, and jumping. Teeter-totters and swings were loaded down with them. Everyone was laughing and having a big time.

Over against the building, a large blue pipe ran up on an angle from the ground. A few feet from the top there was a bend in it. The pipe seemed to go into the building. Boys were crawling into its dark mouth. I counted nine of them. One boy stood about six feet from the opening with a stick in his hand.

Staring goggle-eyed, trying to figure out what they were doing, I got a surprise. Out of the hollow pipe spurted a boy. He sailed through the air and lit on his feet. The boy with the stick marked the ground where he landed. All nine of them came shooting out, one behind the other. As each boy landed, a new mark was scratched.

They ganged around looking at the lines. There was a lot of loud talking, pointing, and arguing. Then all lines were erased and a new scorekeeper was picked out. The others crawled back into the pipe.

I figured out how the game was played. After climbing to the top of the slide, the boys turned around and sat down. One at a time, they came flying down and out, feet first. The one that shot out the farthest was the winner. I thought how wonderful it would be if I could slide down just one time.

One boy, spying me standing on the corner, came over. Looking me up and down, he asked, "Do you go to school here?"

I said, "School?"

He said, "Sure. School. What did you think it was?"

"Oh. No, I don't go to school here."

"Do you go to Jefferson?"

"No. I don't go there either."

"Don't you go to school at all?"

"Sure I go to school."

"Where?"

"At home."

"You go to school at home?"

I nodded.

"What grade are you in?"

I said I wasn't in any grade.

Puzzled, he said, "You go to school at home, and don't know what grade you're in. Who teaches you?"

"My mother."

"What does she teach you?"

I said, "Reading, writing, and arithmetic, and I bet I'm just as good at it as you are."

He asked, "Don't you have any shoes?"

I said, "Sure, I have shoes."

"Why aren't you wearing them?"

"I don't wear shoes until it gets cold."

He laughed and asked where I lived.

I said, "Back in the hills."

He said, "Oh, you're a hillbilly."

He ran back to the mob. I saw him pointing at me and talking to several boys. They started my way, yelling, "Hillbilly, hillbilly."

Just before they reached me, a bell started ringing. Turning, they ran to the front of the building, lined up in two long lines, and marching like little tin soldiers disappeared inside the school.

The playground was silent. I was all alone, and felt lonely and sad.

I heard a noise on my right. I didn't have to turn around to recognize what it was. Someone was using a hoe. I'd know that sound if I heard it on a dark night. It was a little old white-headed woman working in a flower bed.

Looking again at the long, blue pipe, I thought, "There's no one around. Maybe I could have one slide anyway."

I eased over and looked up into the dark hollow. It looked scary, but I thought of all the other boys I had seen crawl into it. I could see the last mark on the ground, and thought, "I bet I can beat that."

Laying my sack down, I started climbing

21

21 Discussion What does Billy's reaction to the lawn mower and the school indicate about his background? Why do the other boys taunt him?

You might point out to students that Billy is making an inference about the stationmaster's character based on his behavior. As mentioned in the Critical Thinking and Reading section on page 665, readers can also make inferences about characters based on their actions, words and thoughts.

up. The farther I went, the darker and more scary it got. Just as I reached the top, my feet slipped. Down I sailed. All the way down I tried to grab on to something, but there was nothing to grab.

I'm sure some great champions had slid out of that pipe, and no doubt more than one world record had been broken, but if someone had been there when I came out, I know the record I set would stand today in all its glory.

I came out just like I went in, feet first and belly down. My legs were spread out like a bean-shooter stalk. Arms flailing the air, I zoomed out and up. I seemed to hang suspended in air at the peak of my climb. I could see the hard-packed ground far below.

As I started down, I shut my eyes tight and gritted my teeth. This didn't seem to help. With a splattering sound, I landed. I felt the air whoosh out between my teeth. I tried to scream, but had no wind left to make a sound.

After bouncing a couple of times, I finally settled down to earth. I lay spread-eagled for a few seconds, and then slowly got to my knees.

Hearing loud laughter, I looked around. It was the little old lady with the hoe in her hand. She hollered and asked how I liked it. Without answering, I grabbed up my gunny sack and left. Far up the street, I looked back. The little old lady was sitting down, rocking with laughter.

I couldn't understand these town people. If they weren't staring at a fellow, they were laughing at him.

Chapter 5

On arriving at the depot, my nerve failed me. I was afraid to go in. I didn't know what I was scared of, but I was scared.

Before going around to the front, I peeked in a window. The stationmaster was

in his office looking at some papers. He was wearing a funny little cap that had no top in it. He looked friendly enough but I still couldn't muster up enough courage to go in.

I cocked my ear to see if I could hear puppies crying, but could hear nothing. A bird started chirping. It was a yellow canary in a cage. The stationmaster walked over and gave it some water. I thought, "Anyone that is kind to birds surely wouldn't be mean to a boy."

With my courage built up I walked around to the front and eased myself past the office. He glanced at me and turned back to the papers. I walked clear around the depot and again walked slowly past the office. Glancing from the corner of my eye, I saw the stationmaster looking at me and smiling. He opened the door and came out on the platform. I stopped and leaned against the building.

Yawning and stretching his arms, he said, "It sure is hot today. It doesn't look like it's ever going to rain."

I looked up at the sky and said, "Yes, sir. It is hot and we sure could do with a good rain. We need one bad up where I come from."

He asked me where I lived.

I told him, "Up the river a ways."

"You know," he said, "I have some puppies in there for a boy that lives up on the river. His name is Billy Colman. I know his dad, but never have seen the boy. I figured he would be in after them today."

On hearing this remark, my heart jumped clear up in my throat. I thought surely it was going to hop right out on the depot platform. I looked up and tried to tell him who I was, but something went wrong. When the words finally came out they sounded like the squeaky old pulley on our well when Mama drew up a bucket of water.

I could see a twinkle in the stationmaster's eyes. He came over and laid his hand on

Commentary: Autobiographical Elements of the Story

Where the Red Fern Grows has several parallels with Wilson Rawls' life. Like Billy, Wilson Rawls was born and spent part of his youth in a small Ozark town on the Illinois River north of Tahlequah. Wilson enjoyed roaming the countryside with his hound dog as Billy does with Dan and Ann. Later in his youth, Rawls' family, like Billy's family, moved to Tahlequah.

Another parallel to Billy's life was Wilson Rawls' lack of formal education when he grew up. It was partly for this reason that Rawls struggled for years with his writing until 1959, when he finally had this novel published. His perserverence and belief in himself is reflected in Billy's grit and determination. Both believe that hard work and faith will eventually bring success.

You might explain that many writers write about characters and situations from their own experiences. The reason they do so is that in order to make the literature come to life, writers must draw from real experiences and people. What they know best are people and experiences from their own lives.

my shoulder. In a friendly voice he said, "So you're Billy Colman. How is your dad?"

I told him Papa was fine and handed him the slip my grandpa had given me.

"They sure are fine-looking pups." he said. "You'll have to go around to the freight door."

I'm sure my feet never touched the ground as I flew around the building. He unlocked the door, and I stepped in, looking for my dogs. I couldn't see anything but boxes, barrels, old trunks, and some rolls of barbed wire.

The kindly stationmaster walked over to one of the boxes.

"Do you want box and all?" he asked.

I told him I didn't want the box. All I wanted was the dogs.

"How are you going to carry them?"' he asked. "I think they're a little too young to follow."

I held out my gunny sack.

He looked at me and looked at the sack. Chuckling, he said, "Well, I guess dogs can be carried that way same as anything else, but we'll have to cut a couple of holes to stick their heads through so that they won't smother."

Getting a claw hammer, he started tearing off the top of the box. As nails gave way and boards splintered, I heard several puppy whimpers. I didn't walk over. I just stood and waited.

After what seemed like hours, the box was open. He reached in, lifted the pups out, and set them down on the floor.

"Well, there they are," he said. "What do you think of them?"

I didn't answer. I couldn't. All I could do was stare at them.

They seemed to be blinded by the light and kept blinking their eyes. One sat down on his little rear and started crying. The other one was waddling around and whimpering.

I wanted so much to step over and pick them up. Several times I tried to move my feet, but they seemed to be nailed to the floor. I knew the pups were mine, all mine, yet I couldn't move. My heart started acting like a drunk grasshopper. I tried to swallow and couldn't. My Adam's apple wouldn't work.

One pup started my way. I held my breath. On he came until I felt a scratchy little foot on mine. The other pup followed. A warm puppy tongue caressed my sore foot.

I heard the stationmaster say, "They already know you."

I knelt down and gathered them in my arms. I buried my face between their wiggling bodies and cried. The stationmaster, sensing something more than just two dogs and a boy, waited in silence. | 23

Rising with the two pups held close to my chest, I asked if I owed anything.

He said, "There is a small feed bill but I'll take care of it. It's not much anyway."

Taking his knife he cut two slits in the sack. He put the pups in it and worked their heads through the holes. As he handed the sack to me, he said, "Well, there you are. Good-bye and good hunting!"

Walking down the street toward town, I thought, "Now, maybe the people won't stare at me when they see what I've got. After all, not every boy owns two good hounds." | 24

Turning the corner onto the main street, I threw out my chest.

I hadn't gone far before I realized that the reception I got wasn't what I thought it would be. People began to stop and stare, some even snickered. I couldn't understand why they were staring. Surely it couldn't be at the two beautiful hound pups sticking out of the gunny sack.

Thinking that maybe I had a hole in the seat of my britches, I looked over to my reflection in a plate glass window. I craned my neck for a better view of my rear. I could see

Where the Red Fern Grows 647

23 **Literary Focus** Ask students to describe Billy's actions when he sees his dogs for the first time. Is his reaction understandable? What is the "something more than just two dogs and a boy" that causes the stationmaster to wait in silence? What do these actions reveal about Billy's character?

24 **Reading Strategy** Billy will have to walk through town again. The students might predict how the people of the town, based on their previous actions, will react to Billy.

25 Discussion Why do the women treat Billy this way? Is his reaction understandable under the circumstances? Why do the people laugh at him?

a patch there all right, and a few threadbare spots, but no whiteness was showing through. I figured that the people were just jealous because they didn't have two good hounds.

I saw a drunk coming. He was staggering all over the street. Just as he was passing me I heard him stop. As I looked back I saw he was staring wide-eyed at my sack. Closing his eyes, he rubbed them with his hands. Opening them again he stared. Shaking his head, he staggered on down the street.

All around people began to roar with laughter. Someone shouted, "What's the matter, John? You seeing things today?"

I hurried on, wanting to get away from the stares and the snickers.

It wouldn't have happened in a hundred years, but there they came. The same two old women I had met before. We stopped and had another glaring fight.

One said, "I declare."

The other one snorted, "Well, I never."

My face burned. I couldn't take any more. After all, a man can stand so much and no more. In a loud voice, I said, "You may have these people fooled with those expensive-looking feathers in your hats, but I know what they are. They're goose feathers painted with iodine."

One started to say something, but her words were drowned out by the roaring laughter from all around. Gathering up their long skirts, they swished on down the street.

648

All around me people began to shout questions and laugh. One wanted to know if I had the mother in the sack. Storekeepers stepped out and gawked. I could see the end of the street, but it looked as if it were a hundred miles away. My face was as red as a fox's tail. I ducked my head, tightened my grip on the sack, and walked on.

I don't know where they came from, but like chickens coming home to roost, they flocked around me. Most of them were about my age. Some were a little bigger, some smaller. They ganged around me, screaming and yelling. They started clapping their hands and chanting, "The dog boy has come to town. The dog boy has come to town."

My heart burst. Tears came rolling. The day I had waited for so long had turned black and ugly.

The leader of the gang was about my size. He had a dirty freckled face and his two front teeth were missing. I suppose he had lost them in a back alley fight. His shock of yellow sunburnt hair bobbed up and down as he skipped and jumped to the rhythm of the "dog boy" song. He wore a pair of cowboy boots. They were two sizes too big for him, no doubt handed down by an older brother.

He stomped on my right foot. I looked down and saw a drop of blood ooze out from under the broken nail. It hurt like the dickens but I gritted my teeth and walked on.

Freckle-face pulled the ear of my little girl pup. I heard her painful cry. That was too much. I hadn't worked two long hard years for my pups to have some freckle-face punk pull their ears.

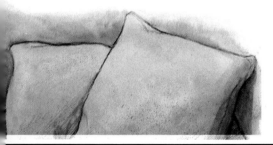

Swinging the sack from my shoulder, I walked over and set it down in a doorway. As I turned around to face the mob, I doubled up my fist, and took a Jack Dempsey[7] stance.

Freckle-face said, "So you want to fight." He came in swinging.

I reached way back in Arkansas somewhere. By the time my fist had traveled all the way down to the Cherokee Strip, there was a lot of power behind it.

Smack on the end of Freck's nose it exploded. With a loud grunt he sat down in the dusty street. Grabbing his nose in both hands, he started rocking and moaning. I saw the blood squeeze out between his fingers.

Another one sailed in. He didn't want to fight. He wanted to wrestle. He stuck a finger in my mouth. I ground down. Shaking his hand and yelling like the hoot owls were after him, he ran across the street.

Another one bored in. I aimed for his eye, but my aim was a little low. It caught him in the Adam's apple. A sick look came over his face. Bending over, croaking like a bullfrog that had been caught by a water moccasin, he started going around in a circle.

But there were too many of them. By sheer weight and numbers, they pulled me down. I managed to twist over on my stomach and buried my face in my arms. I could feel them beating and kicking my body.

All at once the beating stopped. I heard loud cries from the gang. Turning over on my back, I was just in time to see the big marshal plant a number-twelve boot in the seat of the last kid. I just knew I was next. I wondered if he'd kick me while I was down.

I lay where I was. He started toward me. I closed my eyes. I felt a hand as big as an

---

7. Jack Dempsey (demp' sē): William Harrison ("Jack") Dempsey (1895–1983), an American heavyweight boxer.

Where the Red Fern Grows 649

26 **Discussion** Based on Billy's description of him, what impression do you have of the character of Freckle-face? Does his behavior toward Billy match your impression?

27 **Discussion** Why is Billy afraid of the Sheriff?

28 **Discussion** To what stories might Billy be referring? What are some of the impressions you have of marshals and sheriffs?

27 anvil clamp on my shoulder. I thought, "He's going to stand me up, and then knock me down."

He raised me to a sitting position. His deep friendly voice said, "Are you all right, son?"

I opened my eyes. There was a smile on his wide rugged face. In a choking voice, I said, "Yes, sir. I'm all right."

He helped me to my feet. His big hands started brushing the dust from my clothes.

"Those kids are pretty tough, son," he said, "but they're really not bad. They'll grow up some day."

"Marshal," I said, "I wouldn't have fought them, but they pulled my pup's ears."

He looked over to my sack. One pup had worked its way almost out through the hole. The other one's head and two little paws were sticking out. Both of them were whimpering.

A smile spread all over the big marshal's face. "So that's what started the fight," he said.

Walking over, he knelt down and started petting the pups. "They're fine-looking dogs," he said. "Where did you get them?"

I told him I had ordered them from Kentucky.

"What did they cost you?" he asked.

"Forty dollars," I said.

He asked if my father had bought them for me.

"No," I said. "I bought them myself."

He asked me where I got the money.

"I worked and saved it," I said.

"It takes a long time to save forty dollars," he said.

"Yes," I said. "It took me two years."

"Two years!" he exclaimed.

I saw an outraged look come over the marshal's face. Reaching up, he pushed his hat back. He glanced up and down the street. I heard him mutter, "There's not a one in that bunch with that kind of grit."

Picking up my sack, I said, "Thanks for helping me out. I guess I'd better be heading for home."

He asked where I lived.

I said, "Up the river a way."

"Well, you've got time for a bottle of pop before you go, haven't you?"

I started to say "No," but looking at his big friendly smile, I smiled back and said, "I guess I have."

Walking into a general store, the marshal went over to a large red box and pulled back the lid. He asked what kind I wanted. I'd never had a bottle of pop in my life, and didn't know what to say.

Seeing my hesitation, he said, "This strawberry looks pretty good."

I said that would be fine.

28 The cool pop felt wonderful to my hot dry throat. My dark little world had brightened up again. I had my pups, and had found a wonderful friend. I knew that the stories I had heard about marshals weren't true. Never again would I be scared when I saw one.

Back out on the street, I shook hands with the marshal, saying as I did, "If you're ever up in my part of the country come over and see me. You can find our place by asking at my grandfather's store."

"Store?" he asked. "Why, the only store upriver is about thirty miles from here."

"Yes," I said, "that's my grandpa's place."

He asked if I was afoot.

"Yes," I said.

"You won't make it tonight," he said. "Will you?"

"No," I said. "I intend to camp out somewhere."

I saw he was bothered.

"I'll be all right," I said. "I'm not scared of the mountains."

He looked at me and at my pups. Taking

650   *The Novel*

Grammar in Action

One method writers use to vary their sentences is to use **different sentence openers**. Sentences can begin with subjects, adjectives and adverbs, phrases, and clauses. Varying sentence openers makes writing more readable and lively. Notice how Wilson Rawls varies his sentence openers to produce an interesting, fast-moving paragraph.

After the bed was made I built a fire. *In a can of water* from the mountain stream, I boiled three eggs. *Next,* I boiled half of the remaining salt pork. *Cutting the meat up in small pieces,* I fed it to my pups. *Each* of us had a piece of candy for dessert. *My pups* enjoyed the candy. *With their needle-sharp teeth,* they gnawed and worried with it until it was melted away.

Rawls writes a lively, engaging paragraph by intermingling prepositional and participial phrases, nouns and pronouns used as subjects, and an adverb as sentence openers.

off his hat, he scratched his head. Chuckling deep down in his barrel-like chest, he said, "Yes, I guess you will be all right. Well, good-bye and good luck! If you're ever in town again look me up."

From far down the street, I looked back. The marshal was still standing where I had left him. He waved his hand. I waved back.

On the outskirts of town, I stopped and picked up a can and my provisions.

I hadn't gone far before I realized that I had undertaken a tough job. The sack became heavier and heavier.

For a while my pups cried and whimpered. They had long since pulled their heads back in the sack. I would peek in at them every once in a while. They were doing all right. Curled up into two little round balls on my bundles, they were fast asleep.

Deep in the heart of the Sparrow Hawk Mountains, night overtook me. There, in a cave with a stream close by, I put up for the night.

Taking my pups and bundles from the gunny sack, I used it to gather leaves to make us a bed. My pups followed me on every trip, whimpering and crying, tumbling and falling over sticks and rocks.

After the bed was made I built a fire. In a can of water from the mountain stream, I boiled three eggs. Next, I boiled half of the remaining salt pork. Cutting the meat up in small pieces, I fed it to my pups. Each of us had a piece of candy for dessert. My pups enjoyed the candy. With their needle-sharp teeth, they gnawed and worried with it until it was melted away.

29 While they were busy playing, I dragged up several large timbers and built a fire which would last for hours. In a short time the cave grew warm and comfortable from the heat. The leaves were soft, and felt good to my tired body and sore feet. As I lay stretched out, my pups crawled all over me.

I played with them. They would waddle up to the front of the cave, look at the fire, and come scampering back to roll and play in the soft leaves.

I noticed the boy dog was much larger than the girl dog. He was a deeper red in color. His chest was broad and solid. His puppy muscles knotted and rippled under the velvety skin. He was different in every way. He would go closer to the fire. I saw right away he was bold and aggressive.

Once he went around the fire and ventured out into the darkness. I waited to see if he would come back. He came wobbling to the mouth of the cave, but hesitated there. He made several attempts to come back, but the flames were leaping higher by the minute. The space between the fire and the wall of the cave was much hotter than when he had ventured out. Whimpering and crying, he kept trying to get around the fire. I said not a word; just watched.

Puppy though he was, he did something which brought a smile to my face. Getting as close as he could to the side of the cave, he turned his rear to the fire. Hopping sideways, yipping at every jump, he made it through the heat and sailed into the pile of leaves. He had had enough. Curling up in a ball close to me, he went to sleep.

The girl pup was small and timid. Her legs and body were short. Her head was small and delicate. She must have been a runt in the litter. I didn't have to look twice to see that what she lacked in power, she made up in brains. She was a much smarter dog than the boy dog, more sure of herself, more cautious. I knew when the trail became tough, she would be the one to unravel it.

30 I knew I had a wonderful combination. In my dogs, I had not only the power, but the brains along with it.

I was a tired boy. My legs were stiff, and my feet sore and throbbing. My shoulders

Where the Red Fern Grows 651

29 **Literary Focus** Billy's absence of fear and his ability to take care of himself outdoors reveal another aspect of his character. What is revealed by his preparations and his absence of fear?

30 **Discussion** Why are Billy's dogs "a wonderful combination"? On what does Billy base this judgment?

Student Activity 1. Rewrite the following paragraph, varying the sentence openers. You may have to combine sentences, rearrange words, and add words, phrases, and clauses to do this.

Raccoons are fascinating, intelligent animals. They come equipped with black-brown tail rings, a grizzled coat, and a black mask. They are often thought of as masked bandits. This is an apt name for them. They rob nests and garbage cans. Their fingers are very nimble. They can pry off tightly fitting garbage can lids.

Student Activity 2. Write an original paragraph in which you use different openers for most of your sentences.

were red and raw from the weight of the sack. I covered my pups up in the leaves and moved my body as close to them as I could. I knew as night wore on, and the fire died down, the chill would come. Tired but happy, I fell asleep.

Along in the silent hours of night, I was awakened. I opened my eyes, but didn't move. I lay and listened, trying to figure out what it was that had aroused me. At first I thought one of my pups had awakened me by moving and whimpering. I discarded this thought for I could see that they were both fast asleep. I decided it was my imagination working.

My fire had burned down, leaving only a glowing red body of coals. The cave was dark and silent. Chill from the night had crept in. I was on the point of getting up to rebuild my fire, when I heard what had awakened me. At first I thought it was a woman screaming. I listened. My heart began to pound. I could feel the strain all over my body as nerves grew tighter and tighter.

It came again, closer this time. The high pitch of the scream shattered the silence of the quiet night. The sound seemed to be all around us. It screamed its way into the cave and rang like a blacksmith's anvil against the rock walls. The blood froze in my veins. I was terrified. Although I had never heard one, I knew what it was. It was the scream of a mountain lion.

The big cat screamed again. Leaves boiled and stirred where my pups were. In the reflection of the glowing coals, I could see that one was sitting up. It was the boy dog. A leaf had become entangled in the fuzzy hair of a floppy ear. The ear flicked. The leaf dropped.

Again the hellish scream rang out over the mountains. Leaves flew as my pup left the bed. I jumped up and tried to call him back.

Reaching the mouth of the cave, he

stopped. Raising his small red head high in the air, he bawled his challenge to the devil cat. The bawl must have scared him as much as it startled me. He came tearing back. The tiny hairs on his back were standing on end.

My father had told me lions were scared of fire. I started throwing on more wood. I was glad I'd dragged up a good supply while making camp.

Hearing a noise from the bed, I looked back. The girl pup, hearing the commotion, had gotten up and joined the boy dog. They were sitting side by side with their bodies stiff and rigid. Their beady little eyes bored into the darkness beyond the cave. The moist tips of their little black noses wiggled and twisted as if trying to catch a scent.

What I saw in my pups gave me courage. My knees quit shaking and my heart stopped pounding.

I figured the lion had scented my pups. The more I thought about anything harming them, the madder I got. I was ready to die for my dogs.

Every time the big cat screamed, the boy dog would run to the mouth of the cave and bawl back at him. I started whooping and throwing rocks down the mountainside, hoping to scare the lion away. Through the long hours of the night, I kept this up.

The lion prowled around us, screaming and growling; first on the right, and then on the left, and above and below. In the wee hours of morning, he gave up and left to stalk other parts of the mountains. I'm sure he thought he didn't stand a chance against two vicious hounds and a big hunter.

Chapter 6

After the terrifying night, the bright morning sun was a welcome sight. I fixed breakfast and soon we were on our way. I tried to get the pups to follow me, so as to lighten my load. They would for a way, and then, sitting down on their rears, they would cry and whimper. Back in the sack they would go, with their heads sticking out of the holes and their long ears flopping. I moved on.

About midday I entered country I knew. I wasn't far from home. I dropped down out of the mountains into the bottoms far above the place I had crossed the river on my way to town.

Staying on the left of the river, I followed its course past several campgrounds, but didn't stop until I came to the one where I had found the magazine. Here I took the pups out of the sack and sat down in the warm sand.

As the afternoon wore on, I sat there deep in thought. I was trying to think what I was going to tell my mother and father. I could think of nothing. Finally I decided I would just tell them the truth, and with the help of the new overalls, cloth, and candy, I would weather the storm.

My pups were having a big time playing. With their little front paws locked around each other, they were growling, rolling, and chewing on one another. They looked so cute, I laughed out loud.

While I was watching their romping, the thought came, "I haven't named them."

I went over the list of names. For him, I tried "Red," "Bugle," "Lead," name after name as before. For her, I tried "Susie," "Mabel," "Queen," all kinds of girl names. None seemed to fit.

Still mumbling names over and over, I glanced up. There, carved in the white bark of a sycamore tree, was a large heart. In the center of the heart were two names, "Dan" and "Ann." The name Dan was a little larger than Ann. It was wide and bold. The scar stood out more. The name Ann was small, neat, and even. I stared unbelieving—for there were my names. They were perfect.

I walked over and picked up my pups. Looking at him, I said, "Your name is Dan. I'll call you Old Dan." Looking at her, I said, "Your name, little girl, is Ann. I'll call you Little Ann."

It was then I realized it was all too perfect. Here in this fishermen's camp, I had found the magazine and the ad. I looked over at the old sycamore log. There I had asked God to help me get two hound pups. There were the pups, rolling and playing in the warm sand. I thought of the old K. C. Baking Powder can, and the fishermen. How freely they had given their nickels and dimes.

I looked up again to the names carved in the tree. Yes, it was all there like a large puzzle. Piece by piece, each fit perfectly until the puzzle was complete. It could not have happened without the help of an unseen power.

I stayed at the campground until dark. I knew I had to go home but I put it off as long as I could. The crying of the pups, telling me they were hungry, made up my mind for me. I knew the time had come for me to face my mother and father.

I sacked up my dogs and waded the river. As I came out of the bottoms, I could see the lamplight glow from the windows of our home. One of the small yellow squares darkened for an instant. Someone had walked across the floor. I wondered who it was. I heard Daisy, our milk cow, moo. I was thinking so hard of what I would say, it startled me for a second.

Reaching the gate to our house, I stopped. I had never thought our home very pretty, but that night it looked different. It looked clean and neat and peaceful, nestled there in the foothills of the Ozarks. Yes, on that night I was proud of our home.

My bare feet made no noise as I crossed the porch. With my free hand, I reached and pulled the leather that worked the latch. Slowly the door swung inward.

I couldn't see my father or sisters. They

Where the Red Fern Grows 653

32 Discussion Why is Billy afraid to face his mother and father?

32

33 Discussion Billy states that his mother's reaction to his gift "was something I will never forget." Why is giving so special?

were too far to the right of me, but my mother was directly in front of the door, sitting in her old cane-bottom rocker, knitting.

She looked up. I saw all the worry and grief leave her eyes. Her head bowed down. The knitting in her hands came up to cover her face. I stepped inside the room. I wanted to run to her and comfort her and tell her how sorry I was for all the worry and grief I had caused her.

The booming voice of my father shook me from my trance.

He said, "Well, what have you got there?"

Laughing, he got up from his chair and came over to me. He reached and took the sack from my shoulder.

"When we started looking for you," he said, "I went to the store and your grandpa told me all about it. It wasn't too hard to figure out what you had done, but you should have told us."

I ran to my mother and, dropping to my knees, I buried my face in her lap.

As Mama patted my head, I heard her say in a quavering voice, "Oh, why didn't you tell us? Why?"

I couldn't answer.

Between sobs, I heard the squeals of delight from my sisters as they fondled my pups.

I heard my father say, "What's this other stuff you've got?"

Without raising my head from my mother's lap, in a choking voice I said, "One is for you, one is for Mama, and the other is for the girls."

I heard the snapping of string and the rattle of paper. The oh's and ah's from my sisters were wonderful to hear.

Papa came over to Mama. Laying the cloth on the arm of her chair, he said, "Well, you've been wanting a new dress. Here is enough cloth to make half a dozen dresses."

Realizing that everything was forgiven, I stood up and dried my eyes. Papa was

pleased with his new overalls. My sisters forgot the pups for the candy. The light that was shining from my mother's eyes, as she fingered the cheap cotton cloth, was something I will never forget.

Mama warmed some milk for the pups. They drank until their little tummies were tight and round.

As I ate, Papa sat down at the table and started talking man-talk to me. He asked, "How are things in town?"

I told him it was boiling with people. The wagon yard was full of wagons and teams.

He asked if I had seen anyone I knew.

I told him I hadn't, but the stationmaster had asked about him.

He asked me where I had spent the night.

I told him about the cave in the Sparrow Hawk Mountains.

He said that must have been the one called "Robber's Cave."

My youngest sister piped up, "Did you stay all night with some robbers?"

My oldest sister said, "Silly, that was a long time ago. There aren't any robbers there now."

The other one put her nickel's worth in, "Weren't you scared?"

"No," I said, "I wasn't scared of staying in the cave, but I heard a mountain lion scream and it scared me half to death."

"Aw, they won't bother you," Papa said. "You had a fire, didn't you?"

I said, "Yes."

He said, "They'll never bother you unless they are wounded or cornered, but if they are, you had better look out."

Papa asked me how I liked town.

I said I didn't like it at all, and wouldn't live there even if they gave it to me.

With a querying look on his face, he said, "I'm afraid I don't understand. I thought you always wanted to go to town."

"I did," I said, "but I don't any more. I don't like the people there and couldn't understand them."

"What was wrong with them?" he asked.

I told him how they had stared at me, and had even laughed and made fun of me.

34 Reading Strategy You may wish to have students compare this statement to their own experiences. Do students agree or disagree with Papa? They should support their opinions with facts.

35 Discussion Why does the schoolhouse impress Billy and his sisters so much? You might try to find a picture of a school similar to the one described by Billy and show it to the class. Might there still be one-room schoolhouses today?

He said, "Aw, I don't think they were making fun of you, were they?"

"Yes, they were," I said, "and to beat it all, the boys jumped on me and knocked me down in the dirt. If it hadn't been for the marshal, I would have taken a beating."

Papa said, "So you met the marshal. What did you think of him?"

I told him he was a nice man. He had bought me a bottle of soda pop.

At the mention of soda pop, the blue eyes of my sisters opened wide. They started firing questions at me, wanting to know what color it was, and what it tasted like. I told them it was strawberry and it bubbled and tickled when I drank it, and it made me burp.

The eager questions of my three little sisters had had an effect on my father and mother.

Papa said, "Billy, I don't want you to feel badly about the people in town. I don't think they were poking fun at you, anyway not like you think they were."

"Maybe they weren't," I said, "but I still don't want to ever live in town. It's too crowded and you couldn't get a breath of fresh air."

In a sober voice my father said, "Some day you may have to live in town. Your mother and I don't intend to live in these hills all our lives. It's no place to raise a family. A man's children should have an education. They should get out and see the world and meet people."

"I don't see why we have to move to town to get an education," I said. "Hasn't Mama taught us how to read and write?"

34 "There's more to an education than just reading and writing," Papa said. "Much more."

I asked him when he thought we'd be moving to town.

"Well, it'll be some time yet," he said. "We don't have the money now, but I'm hoping some day we will."

From the stove where she was heating salt water for my feet, Mama said in a low voice, "I'll pray every day and night for that day to come. I don't want you children to grow up without an education, not even knowing what a bottle of soda pop is, or ever seeing the inside of a schoolhouse. I don't think I could stand that. I'll just keep praying and some day the good Lord may answer my prayer."

I told my mother I had seen the schoolhouse in town. Again I had to answer a thousand questions for my sisters. I told them it was made of red brick and was bigger than Grandpa's store, a lot bigger. There must have been at least a thousand kids going to school there. **35**

I told all about the teeter-totters, the swings made out of log chains, the funny-looking pipe that ran up the side of the building, and how I had climbed up in it and slid out like the other kids. I didn't tell them how I came out.

"I think that was a fire escape," Papa said.

"Fire escape!" I said. "It looked like a slide to me."

"Did you notice where it made that bend up at the top?" he asked.

I nodded my head.

"Well, inside the school there's a door," he said. "If the school gets on fire, they open the door. The children jump in the pipe and slide out to safety."

"Boy, that's a keen way of getting out of a fire," I said.

"Well, it's getting late," Papa said. "We'll talk about this some other time. We'd better get to bed as we have a lot of work to do tomorrow."

656   *The Novel*

Grammar in Action

Rawls' sentences are often simple and short, but sometimes he combines sentences that are closely related. When Rawls combines sentences with related but unequal ideas, he uses **subordinating conjunctions** to show the relationship between the two ideas. Some of the most common subordinating conjunctions are:

after	before	while
although	since	before
as	although	so that
because	unless	whenever

Notice how Rawls uses such conjunctions to combine two shorter sentences and to show how they are related. The conjunctions can appear at the beginning of the sentence or in the middle.

When we started looking for you, I went to the store and your grandpa told me all about it.

As the afternoon wore on, I sat there deep in thought.

My pups were put in the corncrib for the night. I covered them with shucks and kissed them good night.

The next day was a busy one for me. With the hampering help of my sisters I made the little doghouse.

Papa cut the ends off his check lines and gave them to me for collars. With painstaking care, deep in the tough leather I scratched the name "Old Dan" on one and "Little Ann" on the other. With a nail and a rock two holes were punched in each end of the straps. I put them around their small necks and laced the ends together with baling wire.

That evening I had a talk with my mother. I told her about praying for the two pups, about the magazine and the plans I had made. I told her how hard I had tried to find names for them and how strange it was finding them carved in the bark of a sycamore tree.

With a smile on her face, she asked, "Do you believe God heard your prayer and helped you?"

"Yes, Mama," I said. "I know He did and I'll always be thankful."

Chapter 7

It seems that the worries and wants of a young boy never cease. Now that I had my pups another obstacle had cropped up. This one looked absolutely impossible. I had to have a coonskin so I could train them.

With my three little traps and a bulldogged determination, I set out to trap Mister Ringtail. For three solid weeks I practically lived on the river. I tried every trick I knew. It was no use. I just couldn't catch the wily old coons.

In desperation I went to my grandfather. He smiled as he listened to my tale of woe.

"Well, we'll have to do something about that," he said. "To train those dogs right, you'll need that coon hide, that's for sure. Now you watch the store while I go over to my tool shed. I'll be right back."

After what seemed like an eternity, I saw him coming. He was carrying a brace and bit,[8] that was all.

With a mischievous little smile on his face, he said, "You wouldn't think a fellow could catch a coon with this brace and bit, would you?"

I thought he was kidding me and it made me feel bad. "Why, Grandpa," I said, "you couldn't catch a coon in a jillion years with that thing. You just don't have any idea how smart they are."

"Yes, you can," he said. "You bet your boots you can. Why, when I was a boy I caught coons on top of coons with one of these things."

I saw Grandpa was serious and I got interested.

He laid the brace down on the counter, picked up a small paper sack, and filled it about half-full of horseshoe nails.

"Now you do everything exactly as I tell you," he said, "and you'll catch that coon."

"Yes, sir, Grandpa," I said, "I will. I'll do anything to catch one of them."

"Now the first thing you'll need is some bright objects," he said. "The best thing is bright shiny tin. Cut out some little round pieces, a little smaller than this bit. Do you understand?"

I nodded my head.

"Now," he said, "you go down along the river where there are a lot of coon tracks. Find a good solid log close by and bore a hole down about six inches. Drop one of the

---

8. brace and bit *n.*: A tool for boring, consisting of a drill (bit) turned by cranking a handle (brace).

I hadn't gone far **before** I realized that the reception I got wasn't what I thought it would be.

In each example, the subordinate conjunction indicates that the clause that follows is dependent on the main clause for its meaning. The subordinate clause does not make sense by itself.

Student Activity 1. Use a subordinating conjunction from the list above to combine the following pairs of sentences.

1. I put my thumbs in my ears to make mule ears. Two old women came by.
2. The boys climbed to the top of the slide. They turned around and sat down.

3. Someday you'll have to live in town. We don't intend to live in these hills forever.

Student Activity 2. Write three original sentences about *Where the Red Fern Grows* using subordinating conjunctions.

bright pieces of tin down in the hole, and be sure it's laying right on the bottom."

I was all ears. I didn't want to miss one word my grandfather said. Now and then I would glance at him to see if he was kidding me.

In a serious voice, he went on talking. "Now pay close attention," he said, "because this is the main part of the trap."

With eyes as big as a hoot owl's, I looked and listened.

He took four of the horseshoe nails from the sack. With the thumb and forefinger of his left hand he made a small "o" about the size of the bit, which was an inch and a half in diameter.

"Now, we'll say this is the hole you bored in the log," he said. "About an inch apart, drive these nails in on a slant opposite each other."

Holding one of the nails in his right hand, he showed me the right angle.

"The ends of the nails will enter the hole about halfway between the top and the piece of tin," he continued. "Leave an opening between the sharp points big enough for a coon to get his paw through."

He asked me if I understood.

Again I nodded my head and moved a little closer to him.

"How is that going to catch a coon, Grandpa?" I asked.

"It'll catch him all right," he said, "and it won't fail. You see a coon is a curious little animal. Anything that is bright and shiny attracts him. He will reach in and pick it up. When his paw closes on the bright object it balls up, and when he starts to pull it from the hole, the sharp ends of the nails will gouge into his paw and he's caught."

He looked over at me.

"Well, what do you think of it?" he asked.

I closed my eyes and in my mind I could see the funnel-like entrance of the hole, and the sharp slanting points of the nails. I could see the coon reaching in for the shiny piece of metal. Naturally his paw would be much larger when closed than it was when he reached in. It would be impossible for it to pass the sharp nails.

It was all looking pretty good to me and I was on the point of saying so, when it hit me. Why, all the coon had to do was open his paw, drop the object, and he was free. It all blew up then and there. I just knew my grandfather was playing a joke on me.

I stepped back and almost cried as I said, "Grandpa, you're kidding me. That kind of a trap couldn't catch a coon. Why all he'd have to do is open his paw, drop the piece of tin, and he could pull it from the hole."

Grandpa started roaring with laughter. This did make me feel bad. With tears in my eyes, I started for the door.

"Wait a minute," Grandpa said. "I'm not kidding you. Oh, I know I like to have my jokes, same as any man, but I meant every word I said."

I turned around and looked at him. He had stopped laughing and there was a hurt expression on his face.

"I wasn't laughing at you," he said. "I was laughing more at myself than you. I just wanted to see if you were smart enough to see that there was a way the coon could free himself."

"A fellow wouldn't have to be very smart to see that," I said.

Grandpa started talking seriously again. "You know," he said, "a coon has more than one peculiarity about him. When I was a boy I had a pet coon. By watching him, I saw and learned a lot of things.

"He had a den in an old hollow tree in our front yard. I don't know the number of

Primary Source: Wilson Rawls

Wilson Rawls has spoken to many children in visits to schools. He always brings a manuscript of *Where the Red Fern Grows* with him to show to students. "I want to stress to them," he explains, "how important it is to learn to spell, punctuate, and mainly how important it is for them to stay in school."

"Children are always asking me what advice I can give them on trying to be a writer," Rawls told *Contemporary Authors*, (and) "I always tell them to do a lot of reading, read and study creative writing, then start writing and keep writing. Someday they will make it if they don't give up."

times I'd have to climb that tree and get my mother's scissors, buttons, needles, and thimble from his den. Why, he'd even carry out our knives, forks, and spoons. Anything that was bright and shiny, he took to his den."

Grandpa stopped talking for a few minutes. I could see a faraway look in his eyes. Once again he was living in those long-ago days. I waited in silence for him to go on with his story.

"One of the most peculiar things about that coon," he said, "was his front feet. Once he wrapped those little paws around something he would never let go.

"My mother had an old churn. It was one of those kinds with a small hole in the lid for the dasher. When she would get through churning, she would take the dasher out to wash it. That crazy coon would climb up on top of the churn, poke his little front paw through the hole, and get a fistful of butter. The hole was small, and when he closed his paw, he couldn't get it back out. All he had to do was open it, drop the butter, and he would be free, but do you think he would? No, sir. He would carry that churn lid all over the house, squalling and growling. Why, it took everyone in the house to free him. I'd have to wrap him up in a gunny sack or an old coat and pry his claws loose from the butter. Seeing this time after time is what gave me the idea for this trap. Once he reaches in and gets hold of that tin, he's caught, because he will never open his paw."

With my confidence restored, it all sounded pretty good to me and I was anxious to try out this wonderful plan. I thanked him and, taking the brace and nails, I left the store.

By the time I reached home it was too late in the day to start making my traps. That night I talked the idea over with Papa.

"I've heard of coons being caught that way," he said, "but I never paid much attention to it. Your grandfather should know, though, for he was quite a coon hunter when he was a boy."

"From what he told me," I said, "it never fails."

Papa asked if I wanted him to help make my traps.

"No," I said, "I think I can do it myself."

I didn't sleep too well that night. I bored holes, drove nails, and fought coons practically all night.

Early the next morning I went to the trash pile. As I stirred around in the rusty old cans, I thought of another time I had searched for a can. Finally I found the one I wanted. It was bright and shiny.

Everything was going along just fine until Mama caught me cutting out the circles of tin with her scissors. I always swore she could find the biggest switches of any woman in the Ozarks. That time she overdid it. I was almost to the river before the stinging stopped.

It wasn't hard to find places for my traps. All along the river large sycamore logs lay partly submerged in the clear blue water. On one where I could see the muddy little tracks of the ringtails, I bored a hole, dropped in a piece of tin, and drove my nails.

On down the river I went, making my traps. I stopped when I ran out of nails. Altogether I had fourteen traps.

That night Papa asked me how I was making out.

"Oh, all right," I said. "I've got fourteen of them made."

He laughed and said, "Well, you can't ever tell. You may catch one."

The next morning I was up with the chickens. I took my pups with me as I just knew I'd have a big ringtail trapped and I wanted them to see it. I was a disappointed boy when I peeked out of a canebrake at my last trap and didn't see a coon. All the way home I tried to figure out what I had done wrong.

I went to Papa. He put his thinking cap on and thought the situation over. "Maybe you left too much scent around when you made those traps," he said. "If you did, it'll take a while for it to go away. Now I wouldn't get too impatient. I'm pretty sure you'll catch one sooner or later."

36

Papa's words perked me up just like air does a deflated inner tube. He was right. I had simply left too much scent around my traps. All I had to do was wait until it disappeared and I'd have my coon hide.

Morning after morning it was the same old disappointment; no coon. When a week had gone by and still no results from my traps, I gave up. What little patience I had was completely gone. I was firmly convinced that coons didn't walk on sycamore logs any more, and bright shiny objects had about as much effect on them as a coon hound would.

One morning I didn't get up to run my trap line. I stayed in bed. What was the use? It was just a waste of time.

When the family sat down to breakfast, I heard my oldest sister say, "Mama, isn't Billy going to get up for breakfast?"

"Why, is he in his room?" Mama asked. "I didn't know. I thought he was down looking at his traps."

I heard Papa say, "I'll go wake him up."

He came to the door and said, "You'd better get up, Billy. Breakfast is ready."

"I don't want any breakfast," I said. "I'm not hungry."

Papa took one look at me and saw I had a bad case of the ringtail blues. He came over and sat down on the bed.

"What's the matter?" he asked. "You having coon trouble?"

"Grandpa lied to me, Papa," I said. "I should've known better. Who ever heard of anyone catching a coon with a brace and bit and a few horseshoe nails."

"I wouldn't say that," Papa said. "I don't think your grandpa deliberately lied to you. Besides, I've heard of coons being caught that way."

"Well, I don't think I've done anything wrong," I said. "I've done everything exactly as he said, and I haven't caught one yet."

"I still think it's that scent," Papa said. "You know, someone told me, or I read it somewhere, that it takes about a week for scent to die away. How long has it been since you made those traps?"

"It's been over a week," I said.

"Well, the way I figure, it's about time for you to catch one. Yes, sir, I wouldn't be surprised if you came in with one any day now."

After Papa had left the room I lay thinking of what he had said. "Any day now." I got up and hurried into my clothes.

As soon as I was finished with breakfast, I called my pups and lit out for the river.

The first trap was empty. So was the second one. That old feeling of doubt came over me again. I thought, "It's no use. I'll never catch one and I so need the skin to train my pups."

On the way to my third trap I had to walk through a thick stand of wild cane. It was tough going and my pups started whimpering. I stopped and picked them up.

"We'll be out of this in a few minutes," I said, "and then you'll be all right."

I came plowing out of the matted mass and was right on the trap before I realized it. I was met by a loud squall. I was so surprised I dropped the pups. There he was, my first coon.

He was humped up on the sycamore log, growling and showing his teeth. He kept jerking his front paw, which was jammed

37 Critical Thinking and Reading
Why do the dogs attack the raccoon even though they are still puppies and have not yet been trained? What can you infer about their characters based on these actions?

deep in the hole I had bored. He was trapped by his own curiosity.

I couldn't move and I felt like my wind had been cut off. I kept hearing a noise but couldn't make out what it was. The movement of the boy pup shook me from my trance. The unidentified sound was his bawling. He was trying to climb up on the log and get to the coon.

I yelled at him and darted in to get hold of his collar. On seeing my movement, the coon let out another squall. It scared me half to death. I froze in my tracks and started yelling again at my pup.

The girl pup worked around behind the coon and climbed up on the log. I screamed at her. She paid no attention to me.

Digging his sharp little claws in the bark, the boy pup made it to the top. He didn't hesitate. Straight down that sycamore log he charged. With teeth bared, the coon waited. When my pup was about two feet from him, he made a lunge. The coon just seemed to pull my pup up under his stomach and went to work with tooth and claw.

The girl pup saved him. Like a cat in a corncrib, she sneaked in from behind and sank her needle-sharp teeth in the coon's back.

It was too much for Old Ringy. He turned the boy pup loose, turned around, and slapped her clear off the log. She came running to me, yelping her head off. I grabbed her up in my arms and looked for the boy pup. When the coon had turned him loose, he too had fallen off the log. He was trying to

Where the Red Fern Grows 661

get back to the coon. I darted in and grabbed him by the hind leg.

With a pup under each arm and running as fast as I could, I lit out for the house. Coming out of the bottoms into a fresh-plowed field I set my pups down so I could get a little more speed. I started yelling as soon as I came in sight of the house.

Mama came flying out with my sisters right behind her. Papa was out by the barn harnessing his team. Mama yelled something to him about a snake. He dropped the harness, jumped over the rail fence, and in a long lope started for me.

Mama reached me first. She grabbed me and shouted, "Where did it bite you?"

"Bite me?" I said. "Why Mama, I'm not bit. I've got him, Mama. I've got him."

"Got what?" Mama asked.

"A big coon," I said. "The biggest one in the river bottoms. He's this big, Mama." I made a circle with my arms as big as a twenty-gallon keg.

Mama just groaned way down deep and covered her face with her hands. Some big tears squeezed out between her fingers. Almost in a whisper, I heard her say, "Thank God; I thought you were snake-bitten."

My sisters, seeing Mama crying, puckered up and started bawling.

"He needs a whipping," the oldest one said, "that's what he needs, scaring Mama that way."

Something busted loose inside me and I cried a little, too.

"I didn't mean to scare Mama," I sniffed. "I just wanted everyone to know I caught a coon."

Up until this time Papa hadn't said a word. He just stood looking on.

"Here now," he said, "let's have none of this crying. He didn't mean to scare anyone."

Taking his handkerchief from his pocket, he stepped over to Mama, put his arm around her, and started drying her eyes.

Mama poked her head around him and glared at me. "Billy Colman," she shouted, "if you ever scare me like that again, I'll take a switch and wear you to a frazzle."

This hurt my feelings and I really did get tuned up. "Everyone's mad at me," I said, "and I haven't done anything but catch the biggest coon on the river."

Mama came over. "I'm sorry," she said. "I didn't mean to be cross, but you did scare me. I thought a rattlesnake had bitten you."

"Now that that's all settled," Papa said, "we had better go get that coon." Looking at Mama, he said, "Why don't you and the girls go with us. I don't think it'll take long."

Mama looked at me, smiled, and turned to the girls. "Would you like to go?" she asked.

Their only answer was a lot of squealing and jumping up and down.

On the way, Mama noticed some blood on my shirt. She stopped me and started looking me over.

"Where did that come from?" she asked. "Did that coon bite you?"

"No, Mama," I said. "I didn't get close enough for him to bite me."

With a worried look on her face, she jerked out my shirt. "You don't seem to be scratched anywhere," she said.

"Maybe this is where it came from," Papa said.

He reached down and picked up my boy pup. His little black nose was split wide open and was bleeding.

I saw a relieved look come over Mama's face.

Looking at me, she started shaking her head. "I don't know," she said. "I just don't know."

"Did that coon get hold of this pup?" Papa asked.

"He sure did, Papa," I said, "but it wasn't the coon's fault. If it hadn't been for Little Ann, he'd have eaten him up."

I told how my dogs had tied into the coon.

Papa laughed as he fondled my pup. "This dog is going to be a coon hound," he said, " and I mean a good one."

The coon started squalling as soon as we came in sight.

"My goodness," Mama said, "you wouldn't think anything so small would be so vicious."

Papa picked up a club. "Now everybody stand back out of the way," he said. "This won't take long."

My pups were wanting to get to the coon so badly that they were hard to hold. I had to squeeze them up tight to keep them from jumping right out of my arms.

My sisters, with eyes as big as blue marbles, got behind Mama and peeked around her.

Papa whacked the coon a good one across the head. He let out a loud squall, growled, and showed his teeth. He tried hard to get to Papa but the trap held him.

The girls buried their faces in Mama's dress and started bawling. Mama turned her back on the fight. I heard her say, "I wish we hadn't come. Poor thing."

Papa whacked him again and it was all over.

It was too much for Mama and the girls. They left. I heard the tall cane rattling as they ran for the house.

After the coon was killed, I walked over. Papa was trying to get the coon's paw from the trap. He couldn't do it. Taking a pair of pliers from his pocket, he said, "It's a good thing I had these along or we would have had to cut his foot off."

After Papa had pulled the nails, he lifted the coon's paw from the hole. There, clamped firmly in it, was the bright piece of tin.

In a low voice Papa said, "Well, I'll be darned. All he had to do was open it up and

he was free, but he wouldn't do it. Your grandfather was right."

A sorrowful look came over Papa's face as he ran his fingers through the soft, yellow hair. "Billy," he said, "I want you to take a hammer and pull the nails from every one of those traps. It's summertime now and their fur isn't any good. Besides, I don't think this is very sportsmanlike. The coon doesn't have a chance. It's all right this time. You needed this one, but from now on I want you to catch them with your dogs. That way they have a fifty-fifty chance."

"I will, Papa," I said. "That's what I intended to do."

While we were skinning the coon, Papa asked me when I was going to start training my dogs.

"I don't know," I said. "Do you think they're too young?"

"No, I don't think so," he said. "I've heard that the younger they are the better it is."

"Well, in that case," I said, "I'll start tomorrow."

With the help of my oldest sister, we started giving my pups their first lessons. She would hold their collars while I made trails with the hide for them to follow.

I'd climb trees that leaned out over the river, jump out into the water, swim to the other side, and make trails up and down the bank. With a long pole and wire, I'd drag the hide on top of rail fences, swing it through the air, and let it touch the ground twenty or thirty feet away. I did everything with that hide a coon would do and probably a lot of things a coon couldn't do.

It was a beautiful sight to see my pups work those trails. At first they were awkward and didn't know what to do, but they would never quit trying.

Old Dan would get so eager and excited, he would overrun a trail. Where it twisted or turned, he would run straight on, bawling

38 Literary Focus What does this statement indicate about the character of Papa?

39 Discussion How does Billy know so much about the habits of raccoons?

Discussion You might want to ask your students if any of them has or has had a similar relationship with a pet. Do animals seem to understand and communicate in their own way? Why is this experience so special?

Reader's Response What quality do you admire most about Billy? Why?

Closure and Extension

ANSWERS TO THINKING ABOUT THE SELECTION
Recalling

1. Billy's home is set in the hills of the Ozark Mountains. He lives on a small farm between a river and some foothills. Billy's family consists of his mother, who has Cherokee blood and worries about Billy; his father, who is beginning to treat him like a man; and his three sisters.

2. At first, Billy asks his parents, then he begs, and then he tries to bribe them to get the dogs. This does not work because the hounds are far too expensive for their budget. Billy then decides to save the money to pay for the dogs himself.

3. Students should describe three of the following incidents. He sees items in the store and his reflection for the first time. He encounters two ladies who refer to him as "wild." He sees the children at the school, tries the slide, and lands on his stomach. The people in town laugh, yell, and stare at him as he makes his way out of town. He has a fight with the group of boys that is broken up by the marshall, who buys him his first bottle of soda pop. He spends the night in the cave and is scared by the mountain lion.

4. The first step Billy takes is his attempt to get a raccoon hide. He tries on his own and then goes to his grandfather for advice. Following this advice, he catches a raccoon and uses its hide to leave a trail of scent for his dogs to follow. He teaches them everything he knows about

up a storm. It didn't take him long to realize that a smart old coon didn't always run in a straight line.

Little Ann never overran a trail. She would wiggle and twist, cry and whine, and pretty soon she would figure it out.

At first they were afraid of water. I never would admit it even to myself. I always said that they just didn't like to get wet. They would follow the trail to the stream and stop. Sitting down on their rears, they would cry and beg for help. With a pup under each arm, I'd wade out into the stream and set them down in the cool water. Nine times out of ten, one pup would swim one way and the other one would go just the opposite way. I had a time with this part of their training, but my persistence had no bounds.

It wasn't long until they loved the water. Old Dan would jump as far out as he could and practically knock the river dry. Little Ann would ease herself in and swim like a muskrat for the opposite shore.

I taught my dogs every trick I knew and any new ones I heard about. I taught them how to split up on a riverbank to search for the hidden trail, because it was impossible to tell where a coon would come out of the water. Sometimes he might swim downstream and other times he might swim upstream. Maybe he would come back to the bank he had just left, or he would cross over to the other side. Perhaps he would stop in the middle of the stream on an old drift.

Sometimes he would come out of the water by catching the dangling limbs of a leaning birch and climbing up, never touching the bank. Or he could come out on the same trail he used to go in, and backtrack. He would sometimes crawl up under an undermined bank or into an old muskrat den.

One of the favorite tricks of a smart old ringtail is the treebarking trick. This he accomplished by running far up on the side of a tree and using his stout legs for leverage,

springing twenty or thirty feet away before touching the ground. Dumb hounds trail up to the tree and start bawling treed. I taught my dogs to circle for a good hundred yards to be sure he was still in the tree before bawling.

In order to learn more about coon hunting, I'd hang around my grandfather's store and listen to the stories told by the coon hunters. Some of the tales I heard were long and tall, but I believed them all.

I could always tell when Grandpa was kidding me by the twinkle in his eyes. He told me how a coon could climb right up the fog and disappear in the stars, and how he could leap on a horse's back and run him over your dogs. I didn't care, for I loved to hear the tall tales. Anything that had a coon hair in it I believed completely.

All through that summer and into the late fall the training went on. Although I was worn down to a frazzle, I was a happy boy. I figured I was ready for the ringtails.

Late one evening, tired and exhausted, I sat down by a big sycamore and called my dogs to me. "It's all over," I said. "There'll be no more lessons. I've worked hard and I've done my best. From now on it's all up to you. Hunting season is just a few days away and I'm going to let you rest for I want you to be in good shape the night it opens."

It was wonderful indeed how I could have heart-to-heart talks with my dogs and they always seemed to understand. Each question I asked was answered in their own doggish way.

Although they couldn't talk in my terms, they had a language of their own that was easy to understand. Sometimes I would see the answer in their eyes, and again it would be in the friendly wagging of their tails. Other times I could hear the answer in a low whine or feel it in the soft caress of a warm flicking tongue. In some way, they would always answer.

40

the tricks raccoons use to evade hunters. He also teaches them how to swim and to split up, when necessary, in their search.

Interpreting

5. The events of the first chapter bring back memories of the narrator's childhood because the dog he saves is the same breed as the two he owned. The dog's collar is made of the same material as the collars that his dogs had worn. The dog seemed to be

on a long journey to rejoin its master. This display of loyalty and love was identical to the devotion that his dogs once displayed.

6. The dogs are important to Billy because he has been brought up in the country and has been fascinated by wildlife and hunting since he was very young. It is also possible that, because he is the only boy, he wants to have companions in his activities.

7. Billy feels proud that his father wants him to work in the fields. It

means that his father is beginning to think of and treat him like a man, not a boy.

8. Billy's relationship with his grandfather is a special one. Billy goes to his grandfather when he has a problem and Grandfather always seems to know just what to do and say. Billy often trusts Grandfather with secrets. Above all, Grandfather is a friend of Billy's in a way that his father, who must also discipline him, cannot be.

9. Billy's mother often worries about him. When he returns from Tahle-

THINKING ABOUT THE SELECTION

Recalling

1. Describe Billy's home and family.
2. In what ways does Billy attempt to get the dogs he wants?
3. Describe three incidents that occur on Billy's trip to and from Tahlequah.
4. What steps does Billy take to train his dogs?

Interpreting

5. How do the events in Chapter 1 bring back the memories of the narrator's childhood?
6. Why are dogs so important to Billy?
7. How does Billy feel about working in the fields with his father for the first time?
8. Describe Billy's relationship with his grandfather.
9. Contrast the ways that Billy's mother and father treat him, particularly when he returns from his trip to get his dogs.

Applying

10. When Billy is in town, some people stare and laugh at him, and others try to beat him up. Why do people often act negatively toward those who seem different?

ANALYZING LITERATURE

Understanding Character

You find out about Billy's character and the characters of others by what Billy sees, thinks, or does and by what others say to him.

1. Name two of Billy's character traits.
2. What does Billy's decision to walk twenty miles to Tahlequah rather than wait a week for his dogs reveal about his character?
3. Why do Grandfather and the sheriff react as they do when Billy tells them what he did to get the dogs?

CRITICAL THINKING AND READING

Making Inferences About Characters

An **inference** is a conclusion that you draw from stated information. In a novel, a writer pre-sents a character's actions, words, and thoughts. From this given information, you can make infer-ences about the characters. For example, Billy works hard and saves his money for two years. You can infer from these actions that he is very persistent and highly motivated.

1. What statements made by other characters support this inference?
2. What can you infer about Billy's character from his actions toward his family when he returns home from Tahlequah?

UNDERSTANDING LANGUAGE

Discovering Word Origins

American English contains thousands of words that have interesting origins. Many of these words are borrowed from other languages, includ-ing the languages of the Native Americans. For example, the origin of the proper noun *Oklahoma* is two words from the Choctaw Indian language: *okla,* meaning "people," and *homma,* meaning "red."

Look up in a dictionary the following proper nouns from the novel. Find the language from which each word comes and its original meaning.

1. Missouri   3. Kentucky   5. Arkansas
2. Cherokee   4. Ozark

THINKING AND WRITING

Writing About Character

Imagine that you are Billy's grandfather and you are writing a letter to a friend describing your grandson. Tell your friend about the time that Billy came into the store with a can of money and asked you to help him get the dogs. First make a list of character traits that describe Billy as Grand-father sees him. Then write the letter, including examples of Billy's actions that show his charac-ter traits.

As you revise, be sure you have given specific examples.

(Answers begin on p. 664.)

Challenge Does Billy seem to be the kind of person you would like to know? Why or why not?

ANSWERS TO CRITICAL THINKING AND READING

1. This inference is supported by these statements: the Sheriff's statement referring to the boys of the town: "There's not a one in that bunch with that kind of grit"; the description of the way Grandpa said, "Two years!" when he found out about Billy's efforts and his pledge that "We're going to get those dogs."
2. You can infer that Billy is caring and concerned.

Challenge More advanced stu-dents could make inferences about the characters of Grand-pa, Mama, Papa, and the two dogs based on their actions and words.

ANSWERS TO UNDERSTANDING LANGUAGE

1. Derived from the Algonquian lan-guage, literally meaning people of the big canoes.
2. Probably derived from a tribal name in the Choctaw language meaning "cave people."
3. Derived from the Iroquoian lan-guage meaning "level land, plain."
4. Derived from the French words *aux Arcs* meaning "to the (region of the) Arc (Arkansa) Indians."
5. Derived from French, which de-rived it from a Siouan Tribal name, meaning "downstream people."

Writing Across the Curriculum
Students might report on the his-tory of Oklahoma. This informa-tion would give them a better idea of the setting of the Ozark Mountains, the history of the Cherokees and other tribes in the state, and the way of life for farm-ers during the 1920's. You could inform the social studies depart-ment of this assignment. Social studies teachers could assist with suggestions for research and companion assignments.

---

quah, Billy can tell that he has caused her grief and concern. In contrast, his father laughs and is unconcerned when he returns. He has a "man-talk" with Billy about his trip. Father is begin-ning to treat him as an equal.

Applying

10. Answers will differ but might in-clude the idea that people often react negatively toward those who seem different because they are afraid of anything that they are not familiar with. They react by making fun of the unfa-miliar person. This creates a sense of superiority and eases their fear of the unfamiliar peo-ple.

ANSWERS TO ANALYZING LITERATURE

1. Billy's character traits include per-serverence, kindness, stubborn-ness, a capacity for hard work, curiosity, courage, loyalty, self-sufficiency.

2. His decision to walk instead of wait to go to Talhequah reveals that Billy is impatient, independ-ent, and confident in his ability to go through the mountains.
3. Grandfather and the Sheriff react this way because they appreciate the great effort Billy made to save the amount of money that he did for the dogs. They know that most people his age would not be so strong-willed in their efforts.

Literary Focus You could use the first chapters to illustrate the elements of plot. The episode develops around a conflict between Billy's desire to have two hound dogs to hunt with and his parents' inability to pay for them. The events build to the climax that occurs when Billy has bought his puppies, returns home, and is unsure how his parents will react, despite the fact that he paid for the dogs with money he made working on his own. The conflict is resolved when his parents accept the dogs and approve of Billy's actions.

Look For More advanced students might also identify the climax of each episode. For **less advanced** students, you might point out that the conflict that runs throughout the four chapters is the numerous problems Billy and the dogs must solve while hunting raccoons. This pointer might help them to identify the individual conflicts of each chapter.

Writing/Prior Knowledge If less advanced students are having trouble with this assignment, it might be helpful to preview the first paragraph of the Critical Thinking and Reading section on page 697 to give them an example of a problem-solving approach.

Vocabulary To make sure that they understand the vocabulary, you could have **less advanced** students pronounce each word aloud.

Where the Red Fern Grows, Chapters 8–11

Plot in a Novel

Plot is the sequence of related events in a story or novel. These events develop around a conflict, which is a struggle between opposing sides. The plot usually develops in a pattern, in which the events rise to a climax, or point of highest interest. The conflict is then resolved.

In a novel, the plot develops over a longer period of time, often through episodes. An **episode** is a narrative incident complete in itself, including its own conflict, climax, and resolution. For example, the incident in which Billy travels into town and returns with his puppies is one episode. The separate plot episodes are unified by common characters and a common theme.

Look For

There are four episodes in Chapters 8–11. Look for them as you read. Each episode has its own conflict. What problem must Billy overcome to resolve the conflict in each episode?

Writing

In this novel, Billy encounters many problems, which he always manages to solve. Think of a time when you worked, alone or with a friend, to solve a difficult problem. Write down your problem-solving approach. Review the cause of the problem and the steps you took to solve it. What were the results of your efforts?

Vocabulary

Knowing the following words will help you as you read Chapters 8–11 of *Where the Red Fern Grows*.

baying (bā′ iŋ) *v.*: Long, deep barking (p. 668)

momentum (mō men′ təm) *n.*: The increasing force of a moving object (p. 681)

nonchalantly (nän′ shə länt′ lē) *adv.*: In a casual way (p. 683)

belligerent (bə lij′ ər ənt) *adj.*: Showing a readiness to fight (p. 685)

slough (slou) *n.*: A swamp, bog, or marsh that is part of an inlet or backwater (p. 687)

Objectives

1 To understand the elements of plot
2 To solve problems logically
3 To write a news article

Support Material

Teaching Portfolio
Teacher Backup, p. 1057
Grammar in Action Worksheets, *Finding, Present Participles*, p. 1063; *Understanding Infinitives*, p. 1065; *Identifying Transitions*, p. 1067; *Using Specific Words*, p. 1069
Usage and Mechanics Worksheet, p. 1071
Vocabulary Check, p. 1072

Critical Thinking and Reading Worksheet, *Solving Problems*, p. 1073
Language Worksheet, *Using Similes*, p. 1074
Selection Test, p. 1075

Chapter 8

The day hunting season opened, I was as nervous as Samie, our house cat. Part of that seemingly endless day was spent getting things ready for the coming night.

I cleaned my lantern and filled it full of oil. With hog lard I greased my boots until they were as soft as a hummingbird's nest. I was grinding my ax when Papa came around.

He smiled as he said, "This is the big night, isn't it?"

"It sure is, Papa," I said, "and I've waited a long time for it."

"Yes, I know," he said. "I've been thinking—there's not too much to do around here during the hunting season. I'm pretty sure I can take care of things, so you just go ahead and hunt all you want to."

"Thanks, Papa," I said. "I guess I'll be out pretty late at night, and I'll probably have to do a lot of sleeping in the daytime."

Papa started frowning. "You know," he said, "your mother doesn't like this hunting of yours very much. She's worried about you being out all by yourself."

"I can't see why Mama has to worry," I said. "Haven't I been roaming the woods ever since I was big enough to walk, and I'm almost fourteen now."

"I know," said Papa. "It's all right with me, but women are a little different than men. They worry more."

"Now just to be on the safe side, I think it would be a good idea for you to tell us where you'll be hunting. Then if anything happens, we'll know where to look."

I told him I would, but I didn't think anything was going to happen.

After Papa had left, I started thinking. "He doesn't even talk to me like I was a boy any more. He talks to me like I was a man." These wonderful thoughts made me feel just about as big as our old red mule.

I had a good talk with my dogs. "I've waited almost three years for this night," I said, "and it hasn't been easy. I've taught you everything I know and I want you to do your best."

Little Ann acted like she understood. She whined and saved me a wash job on my face. Old Dan may have, but he didn't act like it. He just lay there in the sunshine, all stretched out and limber as a rag.

During supper Mama asked me where I was going to hunt.

"I'm not going far," I said, "just down on the river."

I could tell Mama was worried and it didn't make me feel too good.

"Billy," she said, "I don't approve of this hunting, but it looks like I can't say no; not after all you've been through, getting your dogs, and all that training."

"Aw, he'll be all right," Papa said. "Besides, he's getting to be a good-size man now."

"Man!" Mama exclaimed. "Why, he's still just a little boy."

"You can't keep him a little boy always," Papa said. "He's got to grow up some day."

"I know," Mama said, "but I don't like it, not at all, and I can't help worrying."

"Mama, please don't worry about me," I said. "I'll be all right. Why, I've been all over these hills, you know that."

"I know," she said, "but that was in the daytime. I never worried too much when it was daylight, but at night, that's different. It'll be dark and anything could happen."

"There won't be anything happening," I said. "I promise I'll be careful."

Mama got up from the table saying, "Well, it's like I said, I can't say no and I can't help worrying. I'll pray every night you're out."

The way Mama had me feeling, I didn't know whether to go hunting or not. Papa must have sensed how I felt. "It's dark now,"

Where the Red Fern Grows 667

he said, "and I understand those coons start stirring pretty early. You had better be going, hadn't you?"

While Mama was bundling me up, Papa lit my lantern. He handed it to me, saying, "I'd like to see a big coonskin on the smokehouse wall in the morning."

The whole family followed me out on the porch. There we all got a surprise. My dogs were sitting on the steps, waiting for me.

I heard Papa laugh. "Why, they know you're going hunting," he said, "know it as well as anything."

"Well, I never," said Mama. "Do you really think they do? It does look like they do. Why, just look at them."

Little Ann started wiggling and twisting. Old Dan trotted out to the gate, stopped, turned around, and looked at me.

"Sure they know Billy's going hunting," piped the little one, "and I know why."

"How do you know so much, silly?" asked the oldest one.

"Because I told Little Ann, that's why," she said, "and she told Old Dan. That's how they know."

We all had to laugh at her.

The last thing I heard as I left the house was the voice of my mother. "Be careful, Billy," she said, "and don't stay out late."

It was a beautiful night, still and frosty. A big grinning Ozark moon had the countryside bathed in a soft yellow glow. The starlit heaven reminded me of a large blue umbrella, outspread and with the handle broken off.

Just before I reached the timber, I called my dogs to me. "Now the trail will be a little different tonight," I whispered. "It won't be a hide dragged on the ground. It'll be the real thing, so remember everything I taught you and I'm depending on you. Just put one up a tree and I'll do the rest."

I turned them loose, saying, "Go get 'em."

They streaked for the timber.

By the time I had reached the river, every nerve in my body was drawn up as tight as a fiddlestring. Big-eyed and with ears open, I walked on, stopping now and then to listen. **3** The way I was slipping along anyone would have thought I was trying to slip up on a coon myself.

I had never seen a night so peaceful and still. All around me tall sycamores gleamed like white streamers in the moonlight. A prowling skunk came wobbling up the riverbank. He stopped when he saw me. I smiled at the fox-fire glow of his small, beady, red eyes. He turned and disappeared in the underbrush. I heard a sharp snap and a feathery rustle in some brush close by. A small rodent started squealing in agony. A night hawk had found his supper.

Across the river and from far back in the rugged mountains I heard the baying of a hound. I wondered if it was the same one I had heard from my window on those nights so long ago.

Although my eyes were seeing the wonders of the night, my ears were ever alert, listening for the sound of my hounds telling me they had found a trail.

I was expecting one of them to bawl, but when it came it startled me. The deep tones of Old Dan's voice jarred the silence around me. I dropped my ax and almost dropped my lantern. A strange feeling came over me. I took a deep breath and threw back my head to give the call of the hunter, but something went wrong. My throat felt like it had been tied in a knot. I swallowed a couple of times and the knot disappeared.

As loud as I could, I whooped, "Who-e-e-e. Get him, Dan. Get him."

Little Ann came in. The bell-like tones of her voice made shivers run up and down my spine. I whooped to her. "Who-e-e-e. Tell it to him, little girl. Tell it to him."

This was what I had prayed for, worked and sweated for, my own little hounds bawling on the trail of a river coon. I don't know why I cried, but I did. While the tears rolled, I whooped again and again.

They straightened the trail out and headed down river. I took off after them as fast as I could run.

A mile downstream the coon pulled his first trick. I could tell by my dogs' voices that they had lost the trail. When I came to them they were out on an old drift, sniffing around. 4

The coon had pulled a simple trick. He had run out on the drift, leaped into the water, and crossed the river. To an experienced coon hound, the crude trick would have been nothing at all, but my dogs were just big, awkward pups, trailing their first live coon.

I stood and watched, wondering if they

4 **Clarification** A drift is a heap of sand or gravel, along with dead tree limbs and other debris, accumulated in the river or along the shore by the force of the river's current.

would remember the training I had given them. Now and then I would whoop, urging them on.

Old Dan was having a fit. He whined and he bawled. He whimpered and cried. He came to me and reared up, begging for help.

"I'm not going to help you," I scolded, "and you're not going to find him out on that drift. If you would just remember some of the training I gave you, you could find the trail. Now go find that coon."

He ran back out on the drift and started searching.

Little Ann came to me. I could see the pleading in her warm gray eyes. "I'm ashamed of you, little girl," I said. "I thought you had more sense than this. If you let him fool you this easily, you'll never be a coon dog."

She whined, turned, and trotted downstream to search again for the lost trail.

5 I couldn't understand. Had all the training I had given them been useless? I knew if I waded the river they would follow me. Once on the other side, it would be easy for them to find the trail. I didn't want it that way. I wanted them to figure it out by themselves. The more I thought about it, the more disgusted I became. I sat down and buried my face in my arms.

Out on the drift, Old Dan started whining. It made me angry and I got up to scold him again.

I couldn't understand his actions. He was running along the edge of the drift, whimpering and staring downriver. I looked that way. I could see something swimming for the opposite shore. At first I thought it was a muskrat. In the middle of the stream, where the moonlight was the brightest, I got a good look. It was Little Ann.

With a loud whoop, I told her how proud I was. My little girl had remembered her training.

She came out on a gravel bar, shook the water from her body, and disappeared in the thick timber. Minutes later, she let me know she had found the trail. Before the tones of her voice had died away, Old Dan plowed into the water. He was so eager to join her I could hear him whining as he swam.

As soon as his feet touched bottom in the shallows, he started bawling and lunging. White sheets of water, knocked high in the moonlight by his churning feet, gleamed like thousands of tiny white stars.

He came out of the river onto a sand bar. In his eagerness, his feet slipped in the loose sand and down he went. He came out of his roll, running and bawling. Ahead of him was a log jam. He sailed over it and disappeared down the riverbank. Seconds later I heard his deep voice blend with the sharp cries of Little Ann.

At that moment no boy in the world could have been more proud of his dogs than I was. Never again would I doubt them.

I was hurrying along, looking for a shallow riffle so I could wade across, when the voices of my dogs stopped. I waited and listened. They opened again on my side of the stream. The coon had crossed back over.

I couldn't help smiling. I knew that never again would a ringtail fool them by swimming the river.

The next trick the old fellow pulled was dandy. He climbed a large water oak standing about ten feet from the river and simply disappeared.

I got there in time to see my dogs swimming for the opposite shore. For half an hour they worked that bank. Not finding the trail, they swam back. I stood and watched them. They practically tore the riverbank to pieces looking for the trail.

Old Dan knew the coon had climbed the water oak. He went back, reared up on it, and bawled a few times.

"There's no use in doing that, boy," I said. "I know he climbed it, but he's not

Grammar in Action

As you read through *Where the Red Fern Grows,* you will notice an abundance of of **present participles,** forms of verbs ending in *-ing.* A present participle is a *verbal,* a verb that is used in a sentence not as a verb but as another part of speech. Present participles can be used in several different ways:

He *was running* along the edge of the drift. In this sentence, *running* is combined with the helping verb *was* to form a verb phrase.

As soon as his feet touched bottom in the shallows, he started *bawling* and *lunging.*
Bawling and lunging act as a compound direct object in this sentence.

I knew that never again would a ringtail fool them by *swimming* the river.
Swimming acts as the object of the preposition in this sentence.

. . . it had reminded me of a mother hen *hovering* over her young in a rainstorm.
In this sentence, *hovering* acts as an adjective describing the hen.

there now. Maybe it's like Grandpa said, he just climbed right on out through the top and disappeared in the stars."

My dogs didn't know it, but I was pretty well convinced that that was what the coon had done.

They wouldn't give up. Once again they crossed over to the other shore. It was no use. The coon hadn't touched that bank. They came back. Old Dan went up the river and Little Ann worked downstream.

An hour and a half later they gave up and came to me begging for help. I knelt down between their wet bodies. While I scratched and petted them, I let them know that I still loved them.

"I'm not mad," I said. "I know you did your best. If that coon can fool both of us, then we're just beat. We'll go someplace else to hunt. He's not the only coon in these bottoms."

Just as I picked up my ax and lantern, Little Ann let out a bawl and tore out down the riverbank. Old Dan, with a bewildered look on his face, stood for a moment looking after her. Then, raising his head high in the air, he made my eardrums ring with his deep voice. I could hear the underbrush popping as he ran to join her.

I couldn't figure out what had taken place. Surely Little Ann had heard or seen something. I could tell by their voices that whatever it was they were after, they were close enough to see it and were probably running by sight.

6 The animal left the bottoms and headed for the mountains. Whatever it was, it must have realized my dogs were crowding it too closely. At the edge of the foothills it turned and came back toward the river.

I was still trying to figure out what was going on, when I realized that on striking the river the animal had again turned and was coming straight toward me. I set my lantern down and tightened my grip on the ax.

I was standing my ground quite well when visions of bears, lions, and all kinds of other animals started flashing across my mind. I jumped behind a big sycamore and was trying hard to press my body into the tree when a big coon came tearing by. Twenty-five yards behind him came my dogs, running side by side. I saw them clearly when they passed me, bawling every time their feet touched the ground.

After seeing that there was nothing to be scared of, once again I was the fearless hunter, screaming and yelling as loud as I could, "Get him, boy, get him."

I tore out after them. The trails I knew so well were forgotten. I took off straight through the brush. I was tearing my way through some elders when the voices of my dogs stopped.

Holding my breath, I stood still and waited. Then it came, the long-drawn-out bawl of the tree bark. My little hounds had done it. They had treed their first coon.

When I came to them and saw what they had done I was speechless. I groaned and closed my eyes. I didn't want to believe it. There were a lot of big sycamores in the bottoms but the one in which my dogs had treed was the giant of them all.

While prowling the woods, I had seen the big tree many times. I had always stopped and admired it. Like a king in his own domain, it towered far above the smaller trees.

It had taken me quite a while to find a name suitable for the big sycamore. For a while I had called it "the chicken tree." In some ways it had reminded me of a mother hen hovering over her young in a rainstorm. Its huge limbs spread out over the small birch, ash, box elder, and water oak as if it alone were their protector.

Next, I named it "the giant." That name didn't last long. Mama told us children a story about a big giant that lived in the mountains and ate little children that were

Where the Red Fern Grows 671

6 Enrichment You might want to give students some information about raccoons. Raccoons are furry animals with bushy, ringed tails and a band of black fur across their eyes that looks like a mask. Have them look at the picture on page 661. The animals that Billy is hunting in this story, northern raccoons, live throughout the United States, Central America, and Canada. They grow to a length of thirty to thirty-eight inches, including their tails. They weigh from twelve to twenty-five pounds. Raccoons have long, flexible fingers with sharp claws. They use their hands to find food and can handle objects with great skill. Their food includes a wide variety of small animals, nuts, seeds, and fruit. Raccoons usually hunt at night and remain in their dens during the day. In wooded areas, such as the one in the novel, their dens are usually in trees, stumps, hollow logs, or abandoned muskrat dens.

Student Activity 1. Find six other examples of present participles in *Where the Red Fern Grows*. Explain how each functions in the sentence.

Student Activity 2. Use each of these present participles in an original sentence about Billy and his pups. Try to use them in a variety of ways: *chasing, caring, worrying, training, obeying.*

7 Reading Strategy Billy is again displaying the characteristics of loyalty and willingness to work hard to achieve his goal. You might want to ask students to summarize the actions and behaviors from the previous chapters that also portray these traits.

lost. Right away I started looking for another name.

One day, while lying in the warm sun staring at its magnificent beauty, I found the perfect name. From that day on, it was called "the big tree." I named the bottoms around it "the big tree bottoms."

Walking around it, and using the moon as a light, I started looking for the coon. High up in the top I saw a hollow in the end of a broken limb. I figured that that was the coon's den.

I could climb almost any tree I had ever seen but I knew I could never climb the big sycamore and it would take days to chop it down.

There had been very little hope from the beginning, but on seeing the hollow I gave up. "Come on," I said to my dogs. "There's nothing I can do. We'll go someplace else and find another coon."

I turned to walk away. My hounds made no move to follow. They started whining. Old Dan reared up, placed his front paws on the trunk, and started bawling.

"I know he's there," I said, "but there's nothing I can do. I can't climb it. Why it's sixty feet up to the first limb and it would take me a month to cut it down."

Again I turned and started on my way.

Little Ann came to me. She reared up and started licking my hands. Swallowing the knot in my throat, I said, "I'm sorry, little girl. I want him just as badly as you do, but there's no way I can get him."

She ran back to the tree and started digging in the soft ground close to the roots.

"Come on now," I said in a gruff voice. "You're both acting silly. You know I'd get the coon for you if I could but I can't."

With a whipped-dog look on her face and with her tail between her legs, Little Ann came over. She wouldn't even look at me. Old Dan walked slowly around behind the tree and hid himself. He peeped around the big trunk and looked at me. The message I read in his friendly eyes tore at my heart. He seemed to be saying, "You told us to put one in a tree and you would do the rest."

With tears in my eyes, I looked again at the big sycamore. A wave of anger came over me. Gritting my teeth, I said, "I don't care how big you are, I'm not going to let my dogs down. I told them if they put a coon in a tree I would do the rest and I'm going to. I'm going to cut you down. I don't care if it takes me a whole year."

I walked over and sank my ax as deep as I could in the smooth white bark. My dogs threw a fit. Little Ann started turning in circles. I could hear her pleased whimpering cry. Old Dan bawled and started gnawing on the big tree's trunk.

At first it was easy. My ax was sharp and the chips flew. Two hours later things were different. My arms felt like two dead grapevines, and my back felt like someone had pulled a plug out of one end of it and drained all the sap out.

While taking a breather, I saw I was making more progress than I thought I would. The cut I had started was a foot deep, but I still had a long way to go.

Sitting on their rears, my dogs waited and watched. I smiled at the look on their faces. Every time I stopped chopping they would come over. While Little Ann washed the sweat from my face, Old Dan would inspect my work. He seemed to be pleased with what he saw for he always wagged his tail.

Along about daylight I got my second wind and I really did make the chips fly. This burst of energy cost me dearly. By sunup I was so stiff I could hardly move. My hands and arms were numb. My back screamed with pain. I could go no further. Sitting down, I leaned back against the big tree and fell asleep.

Little Ann woke me up by washing my face. I groaned with the torture of getting to my feet. Every muscle in my body seemed to be tied in a knot. I was thinking of going down to the river to wash my face in the cool water when I heard a loud whoop. I recognized my father's voice. I whooped to let him know where I was.

Papa was riding our red mule. After he rode up, he just sat there and looked me over. He glanced at my dogs and at the big sycamore. I saw the worry leave his face. He straightened his shoulders, pursed his lips, and blew out a little air. He reminded me of someone who had just dropped a heavy load.

In a slow, calm voice, he asked, "Are you all right, Billy?"

"Yes, Papa," I said. "Oh, I'm a little tired and sleepy, otherwise I'm fine."

He slid from the mule's back and came over. "Your mother's worried" he said. "When you didn't come in, we didn't know what had happened. You should've come home."

I didn't know what to say. I bowed my head and looked at the ground. I was trying hard to choke back the tears when I felt his hand on my shoulder.

"I'm not scolding," he said. "We just thought maybe you had an accident or something."

I looked up and saw a smile on his face.

He turned and looked again at the tree. "Say," he said, "this is the sycamore you call 'the big tree,' isn't it?"

I nodded my head.

"Is there a coon in it?" he asked.

"There sure is, Papa," I said. "He's in that hollow limb. See—that one way up there. That's why I couldn't come home. I was afraid he'd get away."

"Maybe you just think he's there," Papa said. "I believe I'd make sure before I'd cut down a tree that big."

"Oh, he's there all right," I said. "My dogs weren't ten feet behind him when he went up it."

"Why are you so determined to get this coon?" Papa asked. "Couldn't you go somewhere else and tree one? Maybe the tree would be a smaller one."

"I thought about that, Papa," I said, "but I made a bargain with my dogs. I told them that if they would put one in a tree, I'd do the rest. Well, they fulfilled their part of the bargain. Now it's up to me to do my part, and I'm going to, Papa. I'm going to cut it down. I don't care if it takes me a year."

Papa laughed and said, "Oh, I don't think it'll take that long, but it will take a while. I tell you what I'll do. You take the mule and go get some breakfast. I'll chop on it until you get back."

"No, Papa," I said. "I don't want any help. I want to cut it down all by myself. You see, if someone helps me, I wouldn't feel like I kept my part of the agreement."

An astonished look came over my father's face. "Why, Billy," he said, "you can't stay down here without anything to eat and no sleep. Besides, it'll take at least two days to cut that tree down and that's hard work."

"Please, Papa," I begged, "don't make me quit. I just have to get that coon. If I don't, my dogs won't ever believe in me again."

Papa didn't know what to tell me. He scratched his head, looked over to my dogs and back at me. He started walking around. I waited for him to make up his mind. He finally reached a decision.

"Well, all right," he said. "If that's the way you want it, I'm for it even if it is only an agreement between you and your dogs. If a man's word isn't any good, he's no good himself.

"Now I have to get back and tell your mother that you're all right. It's a cinch that you can't do that kind of work on an empty

Where the Red Fern Grows 673

8 Discussion What does this statement reveal about Billy's character? Do you agree that if Papa helps, he would not be keeping his part of the agreement? Why is it so important for him to honor the agreement, even though it was with his dogs?

9 Discussion Do you agree with this statement? Why or why not? What does this indicate about Papa's character?

stomach, so I'll send your oldest sister down with a lunch bucket."

With tears in my eyes, I said, "Tell Mama I'm sorry for not coming home last night."

"Don't you worry about your mother," he said, as he climbed on the mule's back. "I'll take care of her. Another thing, I have to make a trip to the store today and I'll talk this over with your grandfather. He may be able to help some way."

After Papa left, things were a little different. The tree didn't look as big, and my ax wasn't as heavy. I even managed to sing a little as I chopped away.

When my sister came with the lunch bucket, I could have kissed her, but I didn't. She took one look at the big tree and her blue eyes got as big as a guinea's egg.

"You're crazy," she gasped, "absolutely crazy. Why, it'll take a month to cut that tree down, and all for an old coon."

I was so busy with the fresh side pork, fried eggs, and hot biscuits, I didn't pay much attention to her. After all, she was a girl, and girls don't think like boys do.

She raved on. "You can't possibly cut it down today, and what are you going to do when it gets dark?"

"I'm going to keep right on chopping," I said. "I stayed with it last night, didn't I? Well, I'll stay till it's cut down. I don't care how long it takes."

My sister got upset. She looked at me, threw back her small head, and looked up to the top of the big sycamore. "You're as crazy as a bedbug," she said. "Why, I never heard of such a thing."

She stepped over in front of me and very seriously asked if she could look in my eyes.

"Look in my eyes?" I said. "What do you want to do that for? I'm not sick."

"Yes, you are, Billy," she said, "very sick. Mama said when Old Man Johnson went crazy, his eyes turned green. I want to see if yours have."

This was too much. "If you don't get out of here," I shouted, "you're going to be red instead of green, and I mean that."

I grabbed up a stick and started toward her. Of course, I wouldn't have hit her for anything.

This scared her and she started for the house. I heard her saying something about an old coon as she disappeared in the underbrush.

Down in the bottom of my lunch bucket I found a neat little package of scraps for my dogs. While they were eating I walked down to a spring and filled the bucket with cool water.

The food did wonders for me. My strength came back. I spit on my hands and, whistling a coon hunter's tune, I started making the chips fly.

The cut grew so big I could have laid down in it. I moved over to another side and started a new one. Once while I was taking a rest, Old Dan came over to inspect my work. He hopped up in the cut and sniffed around.

"You had better get out of there," I said. "If that tree takes a notion to fall, it'll mash you flatter than a tadpole's tail."

With a "no care" look on his friendly face, he gave me a hurry-up signal with a wag of his tail.

Little Ann had dug a bed in a pile of dead leaves. She looked as if she were asleep but I knew she wasn't. Every time I stopped swinging the ax, she would raise her head and look at me.

Chapter 9

By late evening the happy tune I had been whistling was forgotten. My back throbbed like a stone bruise. The muscles in my legs and arms started quivering and jerking. I couldn't gulp enough air to cool the burning heat in my lungs. My strength was gone. I could go no further.

I sat down and called my dogs to me.

Grammar in Action

Writers such as Wilson Rawls use a variety of grammatical constructions in their writing. One such construction is the use of the **infinitive,** the principal form of a verb. The infinitive comes after the word *to* and can act as a noun, an adjective, or an adverb. Notice how Rawls uses infinitives as different parts of speech:

To work like that a fellow needs plenty of rest and food in his stomach. [noun: subject of sentence]

If that tree takes a notion *to fall,* it'll mash you flatter than a tadpole's tail. [adjective: describes *notion*]

She whined, turned, and trotted downstream **to search** again for the lost trail. [adverb: describes *trotted*]

It may be enough at this point that students recognize infinitives in sentences and that they can distinguish them from prepositional phrases beginning with *to.*

Student Activity 1. Locate the infinitives in the following sentences. Remember that infinitive are verbs acting as other parts of speech.

1. Billy begs, "I just want to get that coon."

With tears in my eyes, I told them that I just couldn't cut the big tree down.

I was trying hard to make them understand when I heard someone coming. It was Grandpa in his buggy.

I'm sure no one in the world can understand a young boy like his grandfather can. He drove up with a twinkle in his eyes and a smile on his whiskery old face.

"Hello! How are you gettin' along?" he boomed.

"Not so good, Grandpa," I said. "I don't think I can cut it down. It's just too big. I guess I'll have to give up."

"Give up!" Grandpa barked. "Now I don't want to hear you say that. No, sir, that's the last thing I want to hear. Don't ever start anything you can't finish."

"I don't want to give up, Grandpa," I said, "but it's just too big and my strength's gone. I'm give out."

"Course you are," he said. "You've been going at it wrong. To do work like that a fellow needs plenty of rest and food in his stomach."

"How am I going to get that, Grandpa?" I asked. "I can't leave the tree. If I do, the coon will get away."

"No, he won't," Grandpa said. "That's what I came down here for. I'll show you how to keep that coon in the tree."

He walked around the big sycamore, looking up. He whistled and said, "Boy, this is a big one all right."

"Yes, it is, Grandpa," I said. "It's the biggest one in the river bottoms."

Grandpa started chuckling. "That's all right," he said. "The bigger they are the harder they fall."

"How are you going to make the coon stay in the tree, Grandpa?" I asked.

With a proud look on his face, he said, "That's another one of my coon-hunting tricks; learned it when I was a boy. We'll keep him there all right. Oh, I don't mean we can keep him there for always, but he'll stay for four or five days. That is, until he gets so hungry he just has to come down."

"I don't need that much time," I said. "I'm pretty sure I can have it down by tomorrow night."

Grandpa looked at the cut. "I don't know," he said. "Even though it is halfway down, you must remember you've been cutting on it half of one night and one day. You might make it, but it's going to take a lot of chopping."

"If I get a good night's sleep," I said, "and a couple of meals under my belt, I can do a lot of chopping."

Grandpa laughed. "Speaking of meals," he said, "your ma is having chicken and dumplings for supper. Now we don't want to miss that, so let's get busy."

"What do you want me to do, Grandpa?" I asked.

"Well, let's see," he said. "First thing we'll need is some sticks about five feet long. Take your ax, go over in that canebrake, and get us six of them."

I hurried to do what Grandpa wanted, all the time wondering what in the world he was going to do. How could he keep the coon in the tree?

When I came back, he was taking some old clothes from the buggy. "Take this stocking cap," he said. "Fill it about half-full of grass and leaves."

While I was doing this, Grandpa walked over and started looking up in the tree. "You're pretty sure he's in that hollow limb, are you?" he asked.

"He's there all right, Grandpa," I said. "There's no other place he could be. I've looked all over it and there's no other hollow anywhere."

"Well, in that case," Grandpa said, "we'd better put our man along about here."

"What man, Grandpa?" I asked in surprise.

Where the Red Fern Grows　675

11 **Reading Strategy** Based on what they have read about Grandpa, have students predict the outcome of his visit to Billy.

2. Billy wants to give gifts to his family to make up for his being away so long.

3. Billy says to his father, "I want to cut it down all by myself."

Student Activity 2. Use the following infinitives in sentences of your own about Billy and his pups: *to wonder, to turn around, to carry, to understand, to prowl.*

Student Activity 3. Find three other examples of infinitives in this part of *Where the Red Fern Grows.*

12 Discussion What else are scare-crows used for? Do you think a scarecrow will work with the rac-coon?

"The one we're going to make," he said. "To us it'll be a scarecrow, but to that coon it'll be a man."

Knowing too well how smart coons were, right away I began to lose confidence. "I don't see how anything like that can keep a coon in a tree," I said.

"It'll keep him there all right," Grandpa said. "Like I told you before, they're curious little devils. He'll poke his head out of that hole, see this man standing here, and he won't dare come down. It'll take him four or five days to figure out that it isn't a real honest-to-goodness man. By that time it'll be too late. You'll have his hide tacked on the smokehouse wall."

The more I thought about it, the more I believed it, and then there was that serious look on Grandpa's face. That was all it took. I was firmly convinced.

I started laughing. The more I thought about it, the funnier it got. Great big laughing tears rolled down my cheek.

"What's so funny?" Grandpa asked. "Don't you believe it'll work?"

"Sure it'll work, Grandpa," I said. "I know it will. I was just thinking—those coons aren't half as smart as they think they are, are they?"

We both had a good laugh at this.

With the sticks and some baling wire, Grandpa made a frame that looked almost like a gingerbread man. On this he put an old pair of pants and a red sweater. We stuffed the loose flabby clothes with grass and leaves. He wired the stocking-cap head in place and stepped back to inspect his work.

"Well, what do you think of it?" he asked.

"If it had a face," I said, "you couldn't tell it from a real man."

"We can fix that," Grandpa chuckled.

He took a stick and dug some black grease from one of the hub caps on the

676   *The Novel*

buggy. I stood and watched while he applied his artistic touch. In the stocking-cap head he made two mean-looking eyes, a crooked nose, and the ugliest mouth I had ever seen.

"Well, what do you think of that?" he asked. "Looks pretty good, huh?"

Laughing fit to kill, and talking all at the same time, I told him that I wouldn't blame the coon if he stayed in the tree until Gabriel blew his horn.

"He won't stay that long," Grandpa chuckled, "but he'll stay long enough for you to cut that tree down."

"That's all I want," I said.

"We'd better be going," Grandpa said. "It's getting late and we don't want to miss that supper."

I was so stiff and sore he had to help me to the buggy seat.

I called to my dogs. Little Ann came, but not willingly. Old Dan refused to leave the tree.

"Come on, boy," I coaxed. "Let's go home and get something to eat. We'll come back tomorrow."

He bowed his head and looked the other way.

"Come on," I scolded, "we can't sit here all night."

This hurt his feelings. He walked around behind the big sycamore and hid.

"Well, I'll be darned," Grandpa said as he

13 **Discussion** You might want to have students reread this paragraph and discuss what Grandpa is talking about. Do they agree with Grandpa's statement? Do Americans have a lot of determination and will power? When in history have they proven this? Are there activities other than chopping down trees that might help people? If so, what would they be?

jumped down from the buggy. "He knows that coon's there and he doesn't want to leave it. You've got a coon hound there and I mean a good one."

He picked Old Dan up in his arms and set him in the buggy.

All the way home I had to hold on to his collar to keep him from jumping out and going back to the tree.

13 As our buggy wound its way up through the bottoms, Grandpa started talking. "You know, Billy," he said, "about this tree-chopping of yours, I think it's all right. In fact, I think it would be a good thing if all young boys had to cut down a big tree like that once in their life. It does something for them. It gives them determination and will-power. That's a good thing for a man to have. It goes a long way in his life. The American people have a lot of it. They have proved that, all down through history, but they could do with a lot more of it."

I couldn't see this determination and will-power that Grandpa was talking about very clearly. All I could see was a big syca-more tree, a lot of chopping, and the hide of a ringtail coon that I was determined to have.

As we reached the house, Mama came out. Right away she started checking me over. "Are you all right?" she asked.

"Sure, Mama," I said. "What makes you think something's wrong with me?"

"Well, I didn't know," she said. "The way you acted when you got down from the buggy, I thought maybe you were hurt."

"Aw, he's just a little sore and stiff from all that chopping," Grandpa said, "but he'll be all right. That'll soon go away."

After Mama saw that there were no broken bones, or legs choppped off, she smiled and said, "I never know anymore. I guess I'll just have to get used to it."

Papa hollered from the porch, "Come on in. We've been waiting supper on you."

"We're having chicken and dumplings,"

Mama beamed, "and I cooked them especially for you."

During the meal I told Grandpa I didn't think that the coon in the big tree was the same one my dogs had been trailing at first.

"What makes you think that?" he asked.

I told how the coon had fooled us and how Little Ann had seen or heard this other coon. I figured he had just walked up on my dogs before he realized it.

A smile spread all over Grandpa's face. Chuckling, he said, "It does look that way, but it wasn't. No, Billy, it was the same coon. They're much too smart to ever walk up on a hound like that. He pulled a trick and it was a good one. In fact, it'll fool nine out of ten dogs."

"Well, what did he do, Grandpa?" I asked. "I'm pretty sure he didn't cross the river, so how did he work it?"

Grandpa pushed the dishes back and, using his fork as a pencil, he drew an imaginary line on the tablecloth. "It's called the backtracking trick," he said. "Here's how he worked it. He climbed that water oak but he only went up about fifteen or twenty feet. He then turned around and came down in his same tracks. He backtracked on his original trail for a way. When he heard your dogs coming he leaped far up on the side of the nearest tree and climbed up. He was in that tree all the time your dogs were searching for the lost trail. After everything had quieted down, he figured that they had given up. That's when he came down and that's when Little Ann either heard or saw him."

Pointing the fork at me, Grandpa said very seriously, "You mark my word, Billy, in no time at all that Little Ann will know every trick a coon can pull."

"You know, Grandpa," I said, "she wouldn't bark treed at the water oak like Old Dan did."

"Course she wouldn't," he said. "She knew he wasn't there."

678   *The Novel*

"Why, I never heard of such a thing," Mama said. "I'd no idea coons were that smart. Why, for all anyone knows he may not be in the big tree at all. Maybe he pulled another trick. It'd be a shame if Billy cut it down and found there was no coon in it."

"Oh, he's there, Mama," I hastily replied. "I know he is. They were right on his tail when he went up. Besides, Little Ann was bawling her head off when I came to them."

"Of course he's there," Grandpa said. "They were crowding him too closely. He didn't have time to pull another trick."

Grandpa left soon after supper, saying to me, "I'll be back down in a few days and I want to see that coon hide."

I thanked him for helping me and walked out to the buggy with him.

14 "Oh, I almost forgot," he said. "I heard there was a fad back in the New England states. Seems like everyone is going crazy over coonskin coats. Now if this is true, I look for the price of coon hides to take a jump."

I was happy to hear this and told my father what Grandpa had said. Papa laughed and said, "Well, if you can keep the coons out of those big sycamores, you might make a little money."

Before I went to bed, Mama made me take a hot bath. Then she rubbed me all over with some liniment that burned like fire and **15** smelled like a civet cat.

It seemed like I had barely closed my eyes when Mama woke me up. "Breakfast is about ready, Billy," she said.

I was so stiff and sore I had trouble putting my clothes on. Mama helped me.

"Maybe you'd better let that coon go," she said. "I don't think he's worth all of this."

"I can't do that, Mama," I said. "I've gone too far now."

Papa came in from the barn. "What's the matter?" he asked. "You a little stiff?"

"A little stiff!" Mama exclaimed. "Why he could hardly put his clothes on."

"Aw, he'll be all right," Papa said. "If I know anything about swinging an ax, it won't be long before he's as limber as a rag."

Mama just shook her head and started putting our breakfast on the table.

While we were eating, Papa said, "You know I woke up several times last night and each time I was sure I heard a hound bawling. It sounded like Old Dan."

I quit the table on the run and headed for my doghouse. I didn't have to go all the way. Little Ann met me on the porch. I asked her where Old Dan was and called his name. He was nowhere around.

Little Ann started acting strangely. She whined and stared toward the river bottoms. She ran out to the gate, came back, and reared up on me.

Mama and Papa came out on the porch.

"He's not here," I said. "I think he has gone back to the tree."

"I don't think he'd do that, would he?" Mama said. "Maybe he's around someplace. Have you looked in the doghouse?"

I ran and looked. He wasn't there.

"Everybody be quiet and listen," I said.

I walked out beyond the gate a little ways and whooped as loud as I could. My voice rang like a bell in the still, frosty morning. Before the echo had died away the deep "Ou-u-u-u" of Old Dan rolled out of the river bottoms.

"He's there," I said. "He wanted to make sure the coon stayed in the tree. You see, Mama, why I have to get that coon. I can't let him down."

"Well, I never in all my life," she said. "I had no idea a dog loved to hunt that much. Yes, Billy, I can see now, and I want you to get him. I don't care if you have to cut down every tree in those bottoms. I want you to get that coon for those dogs."

"I'm going to get him, Mama," I said,

Where the Red Fern Grows 679

14 Clarification During the 1920's it was very popular to wear raccoon furs, especially as overcoats.

15 Clarification A civet cat is a nocturnal, spotted cat found in Africa, India, Malaysia, and South China. It is noted for the strong, musklike smell it secretes, which is used in some perfumes.

"and I'm going to get him today if I possibly can."

Papa laughed and said, "Looks like there wasn't any use in building that scarecrow. All you had to do was tell Old Dan to stay and watch the tree."

I left the house in a run. Now and then I would stop and whoop. Each time I was answered by the deep voice of Old Dan.

Little Ann ran ahead of me. By the time I reached the big tree, their voices were making the bottoms ring.

When I came tearing out of the underbrush, Old Dan threw a fit. He tried to climb the sycamore. He would back way off, then, bawling and running as fast as he could, he would claw his way far up on its side.

Little Ann, not to be outdone, reared up and placed her small front paws on the smooth white bark. She told the ringtail coon that she knew he was there.

After they had quieted down, I called Old Dan to me. "I'm proud of you, boy," I said. "It takes a good dog to stay with a tree all night, but there wasn't any need in you coming back. The coon wouldn't have gotten away. That's why we built the scarecrow."

Little Ann came over and started rolling in the leaves. The way I was feeling toward her, I couldn't even smile at her playful mood. "Of course you feel good," I said in an irritated voice, "and it's no wonder, you had a good night's sleep in a nice warm doghouse, but Old Dan didn't. He was down here in the cold all by himself, watching the tree. The way you're acting, I don't believe you care if the coon gets away or not."

I would have said more but just then I noticed something. I walked over for a better look. There, scratched deep in the soft leaves were two little beds. One was smaller than the other. Looking at Little Ann, I read the answer in her warm gray eyes.

Old Dan hadn't been alone when he had gone back to the tree. She too had gone along. There was no doubt that in the early morning she had come home to get me.

There was a lump in my throat as I said, "I'm sorry, little girl, I should've known."

The first half-hour was torture. At each swing of the ax my arms felt like they were being torn from their sockets. I gritted my teeth and kept hacking away. My body felt like it did the time my sister rolled me down the hill in a barrel.

As Papa had said, in a little while the warm heat from the hard work limbered me up. I remembered what my father did when he was swinging an ax. At the completion of each swing, he always said, "Ha!" I tried it. Ker-wham. "Ha!" Ker-wham. "Ha!" I don't know if it helped or not, but I was willing to try anything if it would hurry the job.

Several times before noon I had to stop and rake my chips out of the way. I noticed that they weren't the big, even, solid chips like my father made when he was chopping. They were small and seemed to crumble up and come all to pieces. Neither were the cuts neat and even. They were ragged and looked more like the work of beavers. But I wasn't interested in any beautiful tree-chopping. All I wanted was to hear the big sycamore start popping.

Along in the middle of the afternoon, I felt a stinging in one of my hands. When I saw it was a blister I almost cried. At first there was only one. Then two. One after another they rose up on my hands like small white marbles. They filled up and turned a pale pinkish color. When one would burst, it was all I could do to keep from screaming. I tore my handkerchief in half and wrapped my hands. This helped for a while, but when the cloth began to stick to the raw flesh I knew it was the end.

Crying my heart out, I called my dogs to me and showed them my hands. "I can't do it," I said. "I've tried, but I just can't cut it down. I can't hold the ax any longer."

Commentary: Dogs and Humans

The relationship between Billy and his dogs revolves around hunting. This is the activity that first brought humans and dogs together more than 12,000 years ago. It has been theorized that this relationship began when wolves were attracted to humans by the scraps of meat and bones that were left over from humans' meals. Gradually, some wolves became assimilated into the lives of the human family or village unit. Years of domestication and breeding gradually changed the animals from wild wolves to dogs capable of taking an active role in hunting. This relationship, based on the mutual need to hunt, has remained unchanged ever since.

Humans use breeding, mating two different types of dogs to combine the best characteristics of each, to produce dogs for specific purposes. Dan and Ann are Redbone hounds, which were probably bred from bloodhounds and an ancient Irish hound. This breed of dogs is noted for its excellent sense of smell, its endurance and toughness, and its pleasing bark. Although they specialize in racoon hunting, redbone hounds are also noted for hunting cougars and other wild cats.

Little Ann whined and started licking my sore hands. Old Dan seemed to understand. He showed his sympathy by nuzzling me with his head.

Brokenhearted, I started for home. As I turned, from the corner of my eye I saw Grandpa's scarecrow. It seemed to be laughing at me. I looked over to the big sycamore. It lacked so little being cut down. A small wedge of solid wood was all that was holding it up. I let my eyes follow the smooth white trunk up to the huge spreading limbs.

Sobbing, I said, "You think you have won, but you haven't. Although I can't get the coon, neither can you live, because I have cut off your breath of life." And then I thought, "Why kill the big tree and not accomplish anything?" I began to feel bad.

Kneeling down between my dogs, I cried and prayed. "Please God, give me the strength to finish the job. I don't want to leave the big tree like that. Please help me finish the job."

I was trying to rewrap my hands so I could go back to work when I heard a low droning sound. I stood up and looked around. I could still hear the noise but couldn't locate it. I looked up. High in the top of the big sycamore a breeze had started the limbs to swaying. A shudder ran through the huge trunk.

I looked over to my right at a big black gum tree. Not one limb was moving. On its branches a few dead leaves hung silent and still. One dropped and floated lazily toward the ground.

Over on my left stood a large hackberry. I looked up to its top. It was as still as a fence post.

Another gust of wind caught in the top of the big tree. It started popping and snapping. I knew it was going to fall. Grabbing my dogs by their collars, I backed off to safety.

I held my breath. The top of the big syca- more rocked and swayed. There was a loud crack that seemed to come from deep inside the heavy trunk. Fascinated, I stood and watched the giant of the bottoms. It seemed to be fighting so hard to keep standing. Several times I thought it would fall, but in a miraculous way it would pull itself back into perfect balance.

The wind itself seemed to be angry at the big tree's stubborn resistance. It growled and moaned as it pushed harder against the wavering top. With one final grinding, creaking sigh, the big sycamore started down. It picked up momentum as the heavy weight of the overbalanced top dove for the ground. A small ash was smothered by its huge bulk. There was a lightning-like crack as its trunk snapped.

In its downward plunge, the huge limbs stripped the branches from the smaller trees. A log-sized one knifed through the top of a water oak. Splintered limbs flew skyward and rained out over the bottoms. With a cyclone roar, the big tree crashed to the ground, and then silence settled over the bottoms.

Out of the broken, twisted, tangled mass streaked a brown furry ball. I turned my dogs loose and started screaming at the top of my voice, "Get him, Dan, get him."

In his eagerness, Old Dan ran head on into a bur oak tree. He sat down and with his deep voice told the river bottoms that he had been hurt.

It was Little Ann who caught the coon. I heard the ringtail squall when she grabbed him. Scared half to death, I snatched up a club and ran to help her.

The coon was all over her. He climbed up on her head, growling, slashing, ripping, and tearing. Yelping with pain, she shook him off and he streaked for the river. I thought surely he was going to get away. At the very edge of the river's bank, she caught him again.

Where the Red Fern Grows 681

Dogs have been bred to do all kinds of work. Some have been bred to guard, some to pull sleds and carts, and some to shepherd livestock. More recently, as people's needs for dogs have changed, dogs have been bred and trained for more modern duties. Dogs are used to assist handicapped people, to search for victims in areas devastated by earthquakes and other natural disasters, and even to provide companionship for humans.

The positive relationship between humans and dogs has continued without break throughout our history. Dogs' friendship and loyalty are given without question or condition. Because of this, dogs are among the most well-loved and popular of domestic animals.

Discuss humans' relationship with dogs. Have students tell about their own dogs, or tell dog stories they have heard. What qualities do dogs have? How do these qualities appeal to humans? What is the link between these qualities and humans' love of dogs?

16 **Literary Focus** The climax of this episode, the point where the conflict is resolved, is reached here. All of the action has developed around Billy's and the dogs' hunt for the raccoon. You could point this out to **less advanced** students. Why do you think Billy feels sorrow?

17 **Discussion** Why does Billy apologize to the tree? Why do people sometimes attach special meaning to things such as trees, rocks, or rabbit's feet?

I was trying hard to get in a lick with my club but couldn't for fear of hitting Little Ann. Through the tears in my eyes I saw the red blurry form of Old Dan sail into the fight. He was a mad hound. His anger at the bur oak tree was taken out on the coon.

16 They stretched Old Ringy out between them and pinned him to the ground. It was savage and brutal. I could hear the dying squalls of the coon and the deep growls of Old Dan. In a short time it was all over.

With sorrow in my heart, I stood and watched while my dogs worried the lifeless body. Little Ann was satisfied first. I had to scold Old Dan to make him stop.

17 Carrying the coon by a hind leg, I walked back to the big tree for my ax. Before leaving for home, I stood and looked at the fallen sycamore. I should have felt proud over the job I had done, but for some reason I couldn't. I knew I would miss the giant of the bottoms, for it had played a wonderful part in my life. I thought of the hours I had whiled away staring at its beauty and how hard it had been finding the right name for it.

"I'm sorry," I said. "I didn't want to cut you down, but I had to. I hope you can understand."

I was a proud boy as I walked along in the twilight of the evening. I felt so good even my sore hands had stopped hurting. What boy wouldn't have been proud? Hadn't my little hounds treed and killed their first coon? Along about then I decided I was a full-fledged coon hunter.

Nearing our house, I saw the whole family had come out on the porch. My sisters came running, staring wide-eyed at the dead coon.

Laughing, Papa said, "Well, I see you got him."

"I sure did, Papa," I said. I held the coon up for all to see. Mama took one look at the lifeless body and winced.

"Billy," she said, "when I heard that big tree fall, it scared me half to death. I didn't know but what it had fallen on you."

"Aw, Mama," I said, "I was safe. Why, I backed way off to one side. It couldn't have fallen on me."

Mama just shook her head. "I don't know," she said. "Sometimes I wonder if all mothers have to go through this."

"Come on," Papa said, "I'll help you skin it."

While we were tacking the hide on the smokehouse wall, I asked Papa if he had noticed any wind blowing that evening.

He thought a bit and said, "No, I don't believe I did. I've been out all day and I'm pretty sure I haven't noticed any wind. Why did you ask?"

"Oh, I don't know, Papa," I said, "but I thought something strange happened down in the bottoms this afternoon."

"I'm afraid I don't understand," said Papa. "What do you mean, 'something strange happened'?"

I told him about how my hands had gotten so sore I couldn't chop any more, and how I had asked for strength to finish the job.

"Well, what's so strange about that?" he asked.

"I don't know," I said, "but I didn't chop the big tree down. The wind blew it over."

"Why that's nothing," Papa said. "I've seen that happen a lot of times."

"It wasn't just the wind," I said. "It was the way it blew. It didn't touch another tree in the bottoms. I know because I looked around. The big tree was the only one touched by the wind. Do you think God heard my prayer? Do you think He helped me?"

Papa looked at the ground and scratched his head. In a sober voice, he said, "I don't know, Billy. I'm afraid I can't answer that. You must remember the big sycamore was the tallest tree in the bottoms. Maybe it was up there high enough to catch the wind where the others couldn't. No, I'm afraid I can't help you there. You'll have to decide for yourself."

It wasn't hard for me to decide. I was firmly convinced that I had been helped.

Chapter 10

Mama made me a cap out of my first coon hide. I was as proud of it as Papa would've been if someone had given him a dozen Missouri mules. Mama said afterwards that she wished she hadn't made it for me because, in some way, wearing that cap must've affected my mind. I went coon crazy.

I was out after the ringtails every night. About the only time I didn't go hunting was when the weather was bad, and even then Mama all but had to hog-tie me.

What wonderful nights they were, running like a deer through the thick timber of the bottoms, tearing my way through stands of wild cane, climbing over drifts, and jumping logs, running, screaming, and yelling, "Who-e-e-e, get him, boy, get him," following the voices of my little hounds.

It wasn't too hard for a smart old coon to fool Old Dan, but there were none that prowled the riverbanks that could fool my Little Ann.

As Grandpa had predicted, the price of coonskins jumped sky-high. A good-size hide was worth from four to ten dollars, depending on the grade and quality.

I kept the side of our smokehouse plastered with hides. Of course I would spread them out a little to cover more space. I always stretched them on the side facing the road, never on the back side. I wanted everyone in the country to see them.

The money earned from my furs was **18** turned over to my father. I didn't care about it. I had what I wanted—my dogs. I supposed that Papa was saving it for something because I never saw anything new turn up around our home, but, like any young boy, I wasn't bothered by it and I asked no questions.

My whole life was wrapped up in my dogs. Everywhere I went they went along. There was only one place I didn't want them to go with me and that was to Grandpa's store. Other dogs were always there, and it seemed as if they all wanted to jump on Old Dan.

It got so about the only time I went to see my grandfather was when I had a bundle of fur to take to the store. This was always a problem. In every way I could, I would try to slip away from my dogs. Sometimes I swore that they could read my mind. It made no difference what I tried; I couldn't fool them.

One time I was sure I had outsmarted them. The day before I was to make one of my trips I took my furs out to the barn and hid them. The next morning I hung around the house for a while, and then nonchalantly whistled my way out to the barn. I climbed up in the loft and peeked through a crack. I could see them lying in front of their doghouse. They weren't even looking my way.

Taking my furs, I sneaked out through a back door and, walking like a tomcat, I made it to the timber. I climbed a small dogwood tree and looked back. They were still there and didn't seem to know what I'd done.

Feeling just about as smart as Sherlock Holmes, I headed for the store. I was walking along singing my lungs out when they came tearing out of the underbrush, wiggling and twisting, and tickled to death to be with me. At first I was mad but one look at dancing Little Ann and all was forgiven. I sat down on my bundle of fur and laughed till I hurt all over. I could scold them a little, but I could no more have whipped one of them than I could have kissed a girl. After all, a boy just doesn't whip his dogs.

Where the Red Fern Grows 683

18 Reading Strategy You might have students predict what Papa is doing with the money that Billy earns. This is a good example of *foreshadowing,* the use of clues by a writer to prepare the reader for future developments in a narrative. This is a clue to the ending of the novel, when Billy discovers that the money he earned was saved so that the family would be able to move into town and the children could obtain a good education. Why is the narrator referring to this if he did not think about it at the time?

19 Reading Strategy This is another example of foreshadowing. You might want to point out that when Billy's question to Grandpa is not answered, it serves to raise the reader's curiosity. Why is Grandpa writing everything down? Does his refusal to answer make you want to keep reading to find out?

20 Discussion What does Billy mean when he says coon hunters did not lie, they "stretched things a little"? Is it all right to "stretch" things? Why or why not?

19   Grandpa always counted my furs carefully and marked something down on a piece of paper. I'd never seen him do this with other hunters and it got the best of my curiosity. One day while he was writing I asked him, "Why do you do that, Grandpa?" He looked at me over his glasses and said kind of sharp, "Never mind. I have my reasons."

When Grandpa talked to me like that I didn't push things any further. Besides, it didn't make any difference to me if he marked on every piece of paper in the store.

I always managed to make my trips on Saturdays as that was "coon hunters'" day. I didn't have to stand around on the outside of the circle any more and listen to the coon hunters. I'd get right up in the middle and say my piece with the rest of them.

20   I didn't have to tell any whoppers for some of the things my dogs did were almost unbelievable anyhow. Oh, I guess I did make things a little bigger than they actually were but I never did figure a coon hunter told honest-to-goodness lies. He just kind of stretched things a little.

I could hold those coon hunters spellbound with some of my hunting tales. Grandpa would never say anything while I was telling my stories. He just puttered around the store with a silly little grin on his face. Once in a while when I got too far off the beaten path, he would come around and cram a bar of soap in my pocket. My face would get all red, I'd cut my story short, fly out the door, and head for home.

The coon hunters were always kidding me about my dogs. Some of the remarks I heard made me fighting mad. "I never saw hounds so small, but I guess they are hounds, at least they look like it." "I don't believe Little Ann is half as smart as he says she is. She's so little those old coons think she's a rabbit. I bet she sneaks right up on them before they realize she's a dog." "Some of these nights a big old coon is going to carry her off to his den and raise some little coon puppies."

I always took their kidding with a smile on my face, but it made my blood boil like the water in Mama's teakettle. I had one way of shutting them up. "Let's all go in the store," I'd say, "and see who has the most hides in there."

It was true that my dogs were small, especially Little Ann. She could walk under an ordinary hound; in fact, she was a regular midget. If it had not been for her long ears, no one could have told that she was a hound. Her actions weren't those of a hunting hound. She was constantly playing. She would play with our chickens and young calves, with a piece of paper or a corncob. What my little girl lacked in size, she made up in sweetness. She could make friends with a tomcat.

Old Dan was just the opposite. He strutted around with a belligerent and tough attitude. Although he wasn't a tall dog, he was heavy. His body was long and his chest broad and thick. His legs were short, big, and solid. The muscles in his body were hard and knotty. When he walked, they would twist and jerk under the skin.

He was a friendly dog. There were no strangers to him. He loved everyone. Yet he was a strange dog. He would not hunt with another hound, other than Little Ann, or another hunter, not even my father. The strangest thing about Old Dan was that he would not hunt, even with me, unless Little Ann was with him. I found this out the first night I tried it.

Little Ann had cut the pad of her right foot on a sharp, jagged flint rock. It was a nasty cut. I made a little boot of leather and put it on her wounded foot. To keep her from following me, I locked her in the corncrib.

Two nights later I decided to take Old Dan hunting for a while. He followed me down to the river bottoms and disappeared in the thick timber. I waited and waited for him to strike a trail. Nothing happened. After about two hours, I called to him. He didn't come. I called and called. Disgusted, I gave up and went home.

Coming up through the barn lot, I saw him rolled up in a ball on the ground in front of the corncrib. I immediately understood. I walked over and opened the door. He jumped up in the crib, smelled Little Ann's foot, twisted around in the shucks, and lay down by her side. As he looked at me, I read this message in his friendly gray eyes, "You could've done this a long time ago."

I never did know if Little Ann would hunt by herself or not. I am sure she would have, for she was a smart and understanding dog, but I never tried to find out.

Little Ann was my sisters' pet. They rubbed and scratched and petted her. They would take her down to the creek and give her baths. She loved it all.

If Mama wanted a chicken caught, she would call Little Ann. She would run the chicken down and hold it with her paws until Mama came. Not one feather would be harmed. Mama tried Old Dan once. Before she got the chicken, there wasn't much left but the feathers.

By some strange twist of nature, Little Ann was destined to go through life without being a mother. Perhaps it was because she was stunted in growth, or maybe because she was the runt in a large litter. That may have had something to do with it.

Where the Red Fern Grows 685

21 Critical Thinking and Reading
You might want to point this out to students as one of the main ideas of the novel. As Billy's appearance in town was strange, so too are his dogs' appearances strange to the other hunters. Yet all three have proven their value and abilities. How important is appearance to a person's true character? Why do people often judge others based on appearance? Are such judgments valid?

22 **Literary Focus** You could point out that the conflict of this chapter has been established. What is the conflict that Billy and his dogs face?

During the fur season, November through February, I was given complete freedom from work. Many times when I came home, the sun was high in the sky. After each hunt, I always took care of my dogs. The flint rocks and saw briers were hard on their feet. With a bottle of peroxide and a can of salve I would doctor their wounds.

I never knew what to expect from Old Dan. I never saw a coon hound so determined or one that could get into so many predicaments. More than one time, it would have been the death of him if it hadn't been for smart Little Ann.

22   One night, not long after I had entered the bottoms, my dogs struck the trail of an old boar coon. He was a smart old fellow and had a sackful of tricks. He crossed the river time after time. Finally, swimming to the middle and staying in the swift current, he swam downstream.

Knowing he would have to come out somewhere, my dogs split up. Old Dan took the right side. Little Ann worked the other side. I came out of the bottoms onto a gravel bar and stood and watched them in the moonlight.

Little Ann worked downriver, and then she came up. I saw her when she passed me going up the bank, sniffing and searching for the trail. She came back to me. I patted her head, scratched her ears, and talked to her. She kept staring across the river to where Old Dan was searching for the trail.

She waded in and swam across to help him. I knew that the coon had not come out of the river on her side. If he had, she would have found the trail. I walked up to a riffle, pulled off my shoes, and waded across.

My dogs worked the riverbank, up and down. They circled far out into the bottoms. I could hear the loud snuffing of Old Dan. He was bewildered and mad. I was getting a thrill from it all, as I had never seen them fooled like this.

Old Dan gave up on his side, piled into the river, and swam across to the side Little Ann had worked. I knew that it was useless for him to do that.

I was on the point of giving up, calling them to me, and going elsewhere to hunt, when I heard the bawl of Little Ann. I couldn't believe what I heard. She wasn't bawling on a trail. She was sounding the tree bark. I hurried down the bank.

There was a loud splash. I saw Old Dan swimming back. By this time, Little Ann was really singing a song. In the bright moonlight, I could see Old Dan clearly. His powerful front legs were churning the water.

Then I saw a sight that makes a hunter's heart swell with pride. Still swimming, Old Dan raised his head high out of the water and bawled. He couldn't wait until he reached the bank to tell Little Ann he was coming. From far out in the river he told her.

Reaching the shallows, he plowed out of the river onto a sand bar. Not even taking time to shake the water from his body, again he raised his head and bawled, and tore out down the bank.

In a trot, I followed, whooping to let them know I was coming. Before I reached the tree, Old Dan's deep voice was making the timber shake.

The tree was a large birch, standing right on the bank of the river. The swift current had eaten away at the footing, causing it to lean. The lower branches of the tree dangled in the water.

I saw how the smart old coon had pulled his trick. Coming in toward the bank from midstream, he had caught the dangling limbs and climbed up. Exhausted from the long swim, he stayed there in the birch thinking he had outsmarted my dogs. I

Grammar in Action

A good writer such as Wilson Rawls writes paragraphs that are well organized. One way to smoothly connect the ideas in a paragraph, to make sure that they flow logically from one to the next, is to use **transitions.** Transitions help to connect ideas while pointing out their logical order. The following are some common transitions:

after	behind	for example	one
above	earlier	last	soon
away	in front of	meanwhile	therefore
before	finally	next	until

Notice how Rawls uses transitions in the following paragraph to connect the ideas and show their relationship to one another:

One night, not long *after* I had entered the bottoms, my dogs struck the trail of an old boar coon. He was a smart old fellow and had a sackful of tricks. He crossed the river time *after* time. *Finally,* swimming to the middle and staying in the swift current, he swam downstream.

The transitions in this paragraph help clarify the chronological order of events.

couldn't understand how Little Ann had found him.

It was impossible to fall the tree toward the bottoms. It was too much off balance. I did the next best thing. I cut a long elder switch. Unbuckling one of my suspenders, I tied it to the end and climbed the tree.

The coon was sitting in a fork of a limb. Taking my switch, I whopped him a good one and out he came. He sailed out over the river. With a loud splash, he hit the water and swam for the other side. My dogs jumped off the bank after him. They were no match against his expert swimming. On reaching the other bank, he ran downriver.

Climbing down out of the tree, I picked up my ax and lantern, and trotted down to another riffle and waded across. I could tell by the bawling of my dogs, they were close to the coon. He would have to climb a tree, or be caught on the ground.

All at once their voices stopped. I stood still and waited for them to bawl treed. Nothing happened. Thinking the coon had taken to the river again, I waited to give them time to reach the opposite bank. I waited and waited. I could hear nothing. By then I knew he had not crossed over. I thought perhaps they had caught him on the ground. I hurried on.

I came to a point where a slough of crystal-clear water ran into the river. On the other side was a bluff. I could hear one of my dogs over there. As I watched and waited, I heard a dog jump in the water. It was Little Ann. She swam across and came up to me. Staying with me for just a second, she jumped in the slough and swam back to the other side.

I could hear her sniffing and whining. I couldn't figure out where Old Dan was. By squatting down and holding the lantern high over my head, I could dimly see the op-posite bank. Little Ann was running up and down. I noticed she always stayed in one place of about twenty-five yards, never leaving that small area.

She ran down to the water's edge and stared out into the slough. The horrible thought came that Old Dan had drowned. I knew a big coon was capable of drowning a dog in water by climbing on his head and forcing him under.

As fast as I could run, I circled the slough, climbed up over the bluff, and came down to where Little Ann was. She was hysterical, running up and down the bank and whining.

I tied my lantern on a long pole, held it out over the water, and looked for Old Dan's body. I could see clearly in the clear spring waters, but I couldn't see my dog anywhere. I sat down on the bank, buried my face in my hands, and cried. I was sure he was gone.

Several minutes passed, and all that time Little Ann had never stopped. Running here and there along the bank, she kept sniffing and whining.

I heard when she started digging. I looked around. She was ten feet from the water's edge. I got up and went over to her. She was digging in a small hole about the size of a big apple. It was the air hole for a muskrat den.

I pulled Little Ann away from the hole, knelt down, and put my ear to it. I could hear something, and feel a vibration in the ground. It was an eerie sound and seemed to be coming from far away. I listened. Finally I understood what the noise was.

It was the voice of Old Dan. Little Ann had opened the hole up enough with her digging so his voice could be heard faintly. In some way he had gotten into that old muskrat den.

I knew that down under the bank, in the

Where the Red Fern Grows 687

Students Activity 1. Analyze another paragraph from *Where the Red Fern Grows* to see how Rawls uses transitions to create links between ideas. Identify the transitions and explain how they link the ideas in the sentences.

Student Activity 2. Write a short paragraph describe Billy's relationship with his dogs. Use transitions to link your ideas clearly and smoothly.

water, the entrance to the den could be found. Rolling up my sleeve, I tried to find it with my hand. I had no luck. It was too far down.

There was only one thing to do. Leaving my ax and lantern, I ran for home. Picking up a long-handled shovel, I hurried back.

The sun was high in the sky before I had dug Old Dan out. He was a sight to see, nothing but mud from the tip of his nose to the end of his tail. I held on to his collar and led him down to the river to wash him off. The water there was much warmer than the cold spring water of the slough.

After washing him, I turned him loose. Right back to the hole he ran. Little Ann was already digging. I knew the coon was still there. Working together, we dug him out.

After the coon was killed, I saw what had made him so smart. His right front foot was twisted and shriveled. At one time he must have been caught in a trap and had pulled himself free. He was an old coon. His face was almost white. He was big and heavy and had beautiful fur.

Tired, muddy, wet, and hungry, I started for home.

I've often wondered how Old Dan got into that old muskrat den. Perhaps there was another entrance I had overlooked. I'll never know.

One night, far back in the mountains, in a place called "The Cyclone Timber," Old Dan really pulled a good one.

Many years before my time, a terrible cyclone had ripped its way through the mountains, leaving its scar in the form of fallen timber, twisted and snarled. The path of the cyclone was several miles wide and several miles long. It was a wonderful place to hunt as it abounded with game.

My dogs had struck the trail of a coon about an hour before. They had really been warming him up. I knew it was about time for him to take up a tree, and sure enough, I heard the deep voice of Old Dan telling the world he had a coon up a tree.

I was trotting along, going to them, when his voice stopped. I could hear Little Ann, but not Old Dan. I wondered why, and was a little scared, for I just knew something had happened. Then I heard his voice. It seemed louder than it had been before. I felt much better.

When I came up to the tree I thought Little Ann had treed Old Dan. She was sitting on her haunches staring up and bawling the tree bark. There, a good fifteen feet from the ground, with his hind legs planted firmly in the center of a big limb, and his front feet against the trunk of the tree, stood Old Dan, bawling for all he was worth.

Above him some eight or nine feet was a baby coon. I was glad it was a young one, for if it had been an old one, he would have jumped out. Old Dan would have followed, and he surely would have broken all of his legs.

From where I was standing, I could see it was impossible for Old Dan to have climbed the tree. It was dead and more of an old snag than a tree, with limbs that were crooked and twisted. The bark had rotted away and fallen off, leaving the trunk bare and slick as glass. It was a good ten feet up to the first limb. I couldn't figure out how Old Dan had climbed that tree. There had to be a solution somewhere.

Walking around to the other side, I saw how he had accomplished his feat. There in the bottom was a large hole. The old tree was hollow. Stepping back, I looked up and could see another hole, which had been hidden from me because of Old Dan's body.

23 He had simply crawled into the hole at the bottom, climbed up the hollow of the tree, and worked his way out on the limb. In some way he had turned around and reared up, placing his front feet against the trunk.

There he was. I didn't know what to do. I couldn't cut the tree down and I was afraid

23 **Discussion** What does this incident reveal about Dan's character? Do you think that a dog can climb a tree?

24 **Critical Thinking and Reading**
What steps does Billy take in solving the problem of getting Dan out of the tree?

25 **Literary Focus** The narrator is introducing the conflict of this chapter as the struggle of Billy and Dan to help Ann out of a predicament. What might that predicament be?

to climb it for fear I would scare the coon into jumping out. If he did, Old Dan would jump, too, and break his legs.

I ran plan after plan around in my mind. None would work. I finally came to the conclusion that I had to climb the tree and get ahold of that crazy dog. I blew out my lantern, pulled off my shoes and socks, and started shinnying up the tree. I prayed that the coon wouldn't jump out.

Inching along, being as quiet as I could, I made it up to Old Dan and grabbed his collar. I sat down on the limb, and held him tight. He would bawl now and then, and all but burst my eardrums. I couldn't drop him to the ground, and I couldn't climb down with him. I couldn't sit there on that limb and hold him all night. I would be no better off when daylight came.

Glancing at the hole by my side gave me the solution to my problem. I thought, "If he came out of this hole, he can go back in it."

That was the way I got my dog down from the tree. This had its problems, too. In the first place, Old Dan didn't want to be put in the hole head first. By scolding, pushing, shoving, and squeezing, I finally got him started on his way.

Like a fool, I sat there on the limb, waiting to see him come out at the bottom, and come out he did. Turning around, bawling as he did, right back in the hole he went. There was nothing I could do but sit and wait. I understood why his voice had stopped for a while. He just took time out to climb a tree.

Putting my ear to the hole, I could hear him coming. Grunting and clawing, up he came. I helped him out of the hole, turned him around, and crammed him back in. That time I wasn't too gentle with my work. I was tired of sitting on the limb, and my bare feet were getting cold.

I started down the same time he did. He beat me down. Looking over my shoulder, I saw him turn around and head back for the hole. I wasn't far from the ground so I let go. The flint rocks didn't feel too good to my feet when I landed.

I jumped to the hole just in time to see the tip end of his long tail disappearing. I grabbed it. Holding on with one hand, I worked his legs down with my other, and pulled him out. I stopped his tree-climbing by cramming rocks and chunks into the hole.

How the coon stayed in the tree, I'll never know, but stay he did. With a well-aimed rock, I scared him out. Old Dan satisfied his lust to kill.

I started for home. I'd had all the hunting I wanted for that night.

Chapter 11

I had often wondered what Old Dan would do if Little Ann got into some kind of a predicament. One night I got my answer.

For several days a northern blizzard had been blowing. It was a bad one. The temperature dropped down to ten below. The storm started with a slow cold drizzle and then sleet. When the wind started blowing, everything froze, leaving the ground as slick as glass.

Trapped indoors, I was as nervous as a fish out of water. I told Mama I guessed it was just going to storm all winter.

She laughed and said, "I don't think it will, but it does look like it will last for a while."

She ruffled up my hair and kissed me between the eyes. This did rile me up. I didn't like to be kissed like that. It seemed that I could practically rub my skin off and still feel it, all wet and sticky, and kind of burning.

Sometime on the fifth night, the storm blew itself out and it snowed about three inches. The next morning I went out to my doghouse. Scraping the snow away from the

Grammar in Action

Writers use **vivid, specific words** to create a lively, colorful picture. These words may be verbs, nouns, adjectives or adverbs. Vivid, specific language appeals to the senses and makes descriptions precise and memorable. Therefore, the more vivid and specific words you use in your sentences, the clearer the description will be for the reader. Notice how Wilson Rawls uses vivid, specific words to make the baying of the dogs come alive.

The deep "Ou-ou-ou's" of Old Dan and the sharp "Aw-aw-aw-aw's" of Little Ann bored a hole in the inky-black night. The vibrations rolled and quivered in the icy silence.

Rawls puts you right on the scene with his choice of words. Yo can feel the bitter cold, see the pitch-black night, and hear th howling of the hounds reverberating in the air. Compare thes sentences to the following.

The low barking of old Dan and the high barking of Little Ann made a great deal of noise in the dark night. The noise echoed in the cold silence.

two-way door, I stuck my head in. It was as warm as an oven. I got my face washed all over by Little Ann. Old Dan's tail thumped out a tune on the wall.

I told them to be ready because we were going hunting that night. I knew the old ringtails would be hungry and stirring for they had been denned up during the storm.

That evening as I was leaving the house, Papa said, "Billy, be careful tonight. It's slick down under the snow, and it would be easy to twist an ankle or break a leg."

I told him I would and that I wasn't going far, just down back of our fields in the bottoms.

"Well, anyway," he said, "be careful. There'll be no moon tonight and you're going to see some fog next to the river."

Walking through our fields I saw my father was right about it being slick and dark. Several times I slipped and sat down. I couldn't see anything beyond the glow of my lantern, but I wasn't worried. My light was a good one, and Mama had insisted that I make two little leather pouches to cover the blades of my ax.

Just before I reached the timber, Old Dan shook the snow from the underbrush with his deep voice. I stopped and listened. He bawled again. The deep bass tones rolled around under the tall sycamores, tore their way out of the thick timber, traveled out over the fields, and slammed up against the foothills. There they seemed to break up and die away in the mountains.

Old Dan was working the trail slowly and I knew why. He would never line out until Little Ann was running by his side. I thought she would never get there. When she did, her beautiful voice made the blood pound in my temples. I felt the excitement of the hunt as it ate its way into my body. Taking a deep breath, I reared back and whooped as loud as I could.

The coon ran upriver for a way and then, cutting out of the bottoms, he headed for the mountains. I stood and listened until their voices went out of hearing. Slipping and sliding, I started in the direction I had last heard them. About halfway to the foothills I heard them coming back.

Somewhere in the rugged mountains, the coon had turned and headed toward the river. It was about time for him to play out a few tricks and I was wondering what he would do. I knew it would be hard for him to hide his trail with snow on the ground, and I realized later that the smart old coon knew this, too.

As the voices of my dogs grew louder, I could tell that they were coming straight toward me. Once I started to blow out my lantern, thinking that maybe I could see them when they crossed our field, but I realized I didn't stand a chance of seeing the race in the skunk-black night.

Down out of the mountains they brought him, singing a hound-dog song on his heels. The coon must have scented me, or seen my lantern. He cut to my right and ran between our house and me. I heard screaming and yelling from my sisters. My father started whooping.

I knew my whole family was out on the porch listening to the beautiful voices of my little red hounds. I felt as tall as the tallest sycamore on the riverbank. I yelled as loud as I could. Again I heard the squealing of my sisters and the shouts of my father.

The deep "Ou-ou-ou's" of Old Dan and the sharp "Aw-aw-aw-aw's" of Little Ann bored a hole in the inky-black night. The vibrations rolled and quivered in the icy silence.

The coon was heading for the river. I could tell my dogs were crowding him, and wondered if he'd make it to the water. I was hoping he wouldn't, for I didn't want to wade the cold water unless I had to do it.

I figured the smart old coon had a reason

Where the Red Fern Grows 691

26 Literary Focus The narrator builds suspense by giving a clue to what is going to happen. Why does this make you want to continue reading?

27 Discussion Billy feels proud when he discovers that his family is listening. Why is this important to him?

Student Activity 1. Rewrite the following paragraph using vivid, specific words to make it lively and exciting.

The boy lay still in the barn. Would they find him? The boy looked about to see if there was a better place to be. Perhaps he should move to the upstairs area. Suddenly, noise was heard coming toward the barn. The children came in, saying, "We won! We won! We found you, John."

Student Activity 2. Write a description of some exciting adventure you witnessed or imagined. Make it come alive for the reader by using vivid words and specific details.

28 Discussion Based on what you know about Grandpa's knowledge of raccoon hunting, what do you think might happen?

29 Reading Strategy You could have students summarize the clues that were given in this chapter about this event.

for turning and coming back to the river and wondered what trick he had in mind. I remembered something my grandfather had told me. He said, "Never underestimate the cunning of an old river coon. When the nights are dark and the ground is frozen and slick, they can pull some mean tricks on a hound. Sometimes the tricks can be fatal."

I was halfway through the fog-covered bottoms when the voices of my dogs stopped. I stood still, waited, and listened. A cold silence settled over the bottoms. I could hear the snap and crack of sap-frozen limbs. From far back in the flinty hills, the long, lonesome howl of a timber wolf floated down in the silent night. Across the river I heard a cow moo. I knew the sound was coming from the Lowery place.

Not being able to hear the voices of my dogs gave me an uncomfortable feeling. I whooped and waited for one of them to bawl. As I stood waiting I realized something was different in the bottoms. Something was missing.

I wasn't worried about my dogs. I figured that the coon had pulled some trick and sooner or later they would unravel the trail. But the feeling that something was just not right had me worried.

I whooped several times but still could get no answer. Stumbling, slipping, and sliding, I started on. Reaching the river, I saw it was frozen over. I realized what my strange uneasy feeling was. I had not been able to hear the sound of the water.

As I stood listening I heard a gurgling out in the middle of the stream. The river wasn't frozen all the way across. The still eddy waters next to the banks had frozen, but out in the middle, where the current was swift, the water was running, leaving a trough in the ice pack. The gurgling sound I had heard was the swift current as it sucked its way through the channel.

The last time I had heard my dogs they were downstream from me. I walked on, listening.

I hadn't gone far when I heard Old Dan. What I heard froze the blood in my veins. He wasn't bawling on a trail or giving the tree bark. It was one, long, continuous cry. In his deep voice there seemed to be a pleading cry for help. Scared, worried, and with my heart beating like a churn dasher, I started toward the sound.

I almost passed him but with another cry he let me know where he was. He was out on the ice pack. I couldn't see him for the fog. I called to him and he answered with a low whine. Again I called his name. This time he came to me.

He wasn't the same dog. His tail was between his legs and his head was bowed down. He stopped about seven feet from me. Sitting down on the ice, he raised his head and howled the most mournful cry I had ever heard. Turning around, he trotted back out on the ice and disappeared in the fog.

I knew something had happened to Little Ann. I called her name. She answered with a pleading cry. Although I couldn't see her, I guessed what had happened. The coon had led them to the river. Running out on the ice, he had leaped across the trough. My dogs, hot on the trail, had followed. Old Dan, a more powerful dog than Little Ann, had made his leap. Little Ann had not made it. Her small feet had probably slipped on the slick ice and she had fallen into the icy waters. Old Dan, seeing the fate of his little friend, had quit the chase and come back to help her. The smart old coon had pulled his trick, and a deadly one it was.

I had to do something. She would never be able to get out by herself. It was only a matter of time until her body would be paralyzed by the freezing water.

Laying my ax down, I held my lantern

out in front of me and stepped out on the ice. It started cracking and popping. I jumped back to the bank. Although it was thick enough to hold the light weight of my dogs, it would never hold me.

Little Ann started whining and begging for help. I went all to pieces and started crying. Something had to be done and done quickly or my little dog was lost. I thought of running home for a rope or for my father, but I knew she couldn't last until I got back. I was desperate. It was impossible for me to swim in the freezing water. I wouldn't last for a minute. She cried again, begging for the one thing I couldn't give her, help.

I thought, "If only I could see her maybe I could figure out some way I could help."

Looking at my lantern gave me an idea. I ran up the bank about thirty feet, turned, and looked back. I could see the light, not well, but enough for what I had in mind. I grabbed my lantern and ax and ran for the bottoms.

I was looking for a stand of wild cane. After what seemed like ages, I found it. With the longest one I could find, I hurried back. After it was trimmed and the limber end cut off, I hung the lantern by the handle on the end of it and started easing it out on the ice.

I saw Old Dan first. He was sitting close to the edge of the trough, looking down. Then I saw her. I groaned at her plight. All I could see was her head and her small front paws. Her claws were spread out and digging into the ice. She knew if she ever lost that hold she was gone.

Old Dan raised his head and howled. Hound though he was, he knew it was the end of the trail for his little pal.

I wanted to get my light as close to Little Ann as I could, but my pole was a good eight feet short. Setting the lantern down, I eased the pole from under the handle. I thought, "I'm no better off than I was before. In fact I'm worse off. Now I can see when the end comes."

Little Ann cried again. I saw her claws slip on the ice. Her body settled lower in the water. Old Dan howled and started fidgeting. He knew the end was close.

I didn't exactly know when I started out toward my dog. I had taken only two steps when the ice broke. I twisted my body and fell toward the bank. Just as my hand closed on a root I thought my feet touched bottom, but I wasn't sure. As I pulled myself out I felt the numbing cold creep over my legs.

It looked so hopeless. There didn't seem to be any way I could save her.

At the edge of the water stood a large sycamore. I got behind it, anything to blot out that heartbreaking scene. Little Ann, thinking I had deserted her, started crying. I couldn't stand it.

I opened my mouth to call Old Dan. I wanted to tell him to come on and we'd go home as there was nothing we could do. The words just wouldn't come out. I couldn't utter a sound. I lay my face against the icy cold bark of the sycamore. I thought of the prayer I had said when I had asked God to help me get two hound pups. I knelt down and sobbed out a prayer. I asked for a miracle which would save the life of my little dog. I promised all the things that a young boy could if only He would help me.

Still saying my prayer and making promises, I heard a sharp metallic sound. I jumped up and stepped away from the tree. I was sure the noise I heard was made by a rattling chain on the front end of a boat.

I shouted as loud as I could. "Over here. I need help. My dog is drowning."

I waited for an answer. All I could hear were the cries of Little Ann.

Again I hollered. "Over here. Over on the bank. Can you see my light? I need help. Please hurry."

Where the Red Fern Grows   693

I held my breath waiting for an answering shout. I shivered from the freezing cold of my wet shoes and overalls. A straining silence settled over the river. A feathery rustle swished by in the blackness. A flock of low-flying ducks had been disturbed by my loud shouts. I strained my ears for some sound. Now and then I could hear the lapping slap of the ice-cold water as it swirled its way through the trough.

I glanced to Little Ann. She was still holding on but I saw her paws were almost at the edge. I knew her time was short.

I couldn't figure out what I had heard. The sound was made by metal striking metal, but what was it? What could have caused it?

I looked at my ax. It couldn't have made the sound as it was too close to me. The noise had come from out in the river.

When I looked at my lantern I knew that it had made the strange sound. I had left the handle standing straight up when I had taken the pole away. Now it was down. For some unknown reason the stiff wire handle had twisted in the sockets and dropped. As it had fallen it had struck the metal frame, making the sharp metallic sound I had heard.

As I stared at the yellow glow of my light, the last bit of hope faded away. I closed my eyes, intending to pray again for the help I so desperately needed. Then like a blinding red

694   The Novel

Literary element: Plot. Students might have an easier time understanding the pattern of events in the plot if they can trace the events graphically on a diagram like the following:

conflict   rising action climax   resolution

You could trace the events of the episode in Chapter 11 on the diagram as an example. The conflict is Billy's struggle to save

Little Ann from drowning in the frozen river. The action rises as Billy tries different ways to save her as she slips further into the river. The climax is reached when Billy slowly drags Little Ann out of the river. The resolution of the conflict is when Billy lights the fire and warms himself and Little Ann and we know they will be alright. The remainder of the chapter is the **denouement,** where remaining details such as Billy saying a thankful prayer and his catching a cold, are related to conclude the episode.

For further practice, have students use the diagram to trace the events of one of the hunting episodes described in Chapters 8–10. You might want to coordinate this activity with the **Analyzing Literature** questions on page 697.

flash the message of the lantern bored its way into my brain. There was my miracle. There was the way to save my little dog. In the metallic sound I had heard were my instructions. They were so plain I couldn't help but understand them. The bright yellow flame started flickering and dancing. It seemed to be saying, "Hurry. You know what to do."

Faster than I had ever moved in my life I went to work. With a stick I measured the water in the hole where my feet had broken through the ice. I was right. My foot had touched bottom. Eighteen inches down I felt the soft mud.

With my pole I fished the lantern back to the bank. I took the handle off, straightened it out, and bent a hook in one end. With one of my shoelaces I tied the wire to the end of the cane pole. I left the hook sticking out about six inches beyond the end of it.

I started shouting encouragement to Little Ann. I told her to hang on and not to give up for I was going to save her. She answered with a low cry.

With the hook stuck in one of the ventilating holes in the top of my light, I lifted it back out on the ice and set it down. After a little wiggling and pushing, I worked the hook loose and laid the pole down.

I took off my clothes, picked up my ax, and stepped down into the hole in the icy water. It came to my knees. Step by step, breaking the ice with my ax, I waded out.

The water came up to my hips, and then to my waist. The cold bite of it took my breath away. I felt my body grow numb. I couldn't feel my feet at all but I knew they were moving. When the water reached my armpits I stopped and worked my pole toward Little Ann. Stretching my arms as far out as I could, I saw I was still a foot short. Closing my eyes and gritting my teeth, I moved on. The water reached my chin.

I was close enough. I started hooking at the collar of Little Ann. Time after time I felt the hook almost catch. I saw I was fishing on a wrong angle. She had settled so low in the water I couldn't reach her collar. Raising my arms above my head so the pole would be on a slant I kept hooking and praying. The seconds ticked by. I strained for one more inch. The muscles in my arms grew numb from the weight of the pole.

Little Ann's claws slipped again. I thought she was gone. At the very edge of the ice, she caught again. All I could see now were her small red paws and her nose and eyes.

By Old Dan's actions I could tell he understood and wanted to help. He ran over close to my pole and started digging at the ice. I whopped him with the cane. That was the only time in my life I ever hit my dog. I had to get him out of the way so I could see what I was doing.

Just when I thought my task was impossible, I felt the hook slide under the tough leather. It was none too soon.

As gently as I could I dragged her over the rim of the ice. At first I thought she was dead. She didn't move. Old Dan started whining and licking her face and ears. She moved her head. I started talking to her. She made an effort to stand but couldn't. Her muscles were paralyzed and the blood had long since ceased to flow. **30**

At the movement of Little Ann, Old Dan threw a fit. He started barking and jumping. His long red tail fanned the air.

Still holding onto my pole, I tried to take a step backward. My feet wouldn't move. A cold gripping fear came over me. I thought my legs were frozen. I made another effort to lift my leg. It moved. I realized that my feet were stuck in the soft muddy bottom.

I started backing out, dragging the body of my little dog. I couldn't feel the pole in my

Where the Red Fern Grows 695

30 Literary Focus This point is the climax of the events in this chapter. Billy and Ann are not completely safe, but he has pulled her from the river. The conflict, the struggle to save Ann, has been resolved.

31 **Literary Focus** The resolution of the events occurs quickly once the conflict is resolved.

32 **Discussion** Why does Billy feel this way when his mother kisses him? What does he really mean when he says that he doesn't want to feel silly and babylike, but he does want to be treated like a coon hunter?

Reader's Response Which of Billy's experiences did you find most exciting? Why?

Closure and Extension

ANSWERS TO THINKING ABOUT THE SELECTION
Recalling

1. Billy promises his dogs that if they get the raccoon up into a tree, then he will take care of the rest and get the raccoon.
2. Billy's feelings as the dogs are chasing the first raccoon are wonderful. He cries with happiness at first and then is excited and proud.
3. Old Dan reacts to Billy's taking him hunting without Ann by going back to the farm and refusing to hunt.
4. Billy and the dogs go down to the river after dark. The dogs search for the trail of a raccoon and begin the chase when they discover one. Billy tries to follow as the dogs chase the raccoon, who tries to lose the dogs by pulling various tricks. Finally, the exhausted raccoon climbs a tree to escape pursuit. Billy then uses his axe or climbs the tree himself to knock the raccoon out of the tree to where the dogs are waiting.

Interpreting

5. Billy is happy to be treated like a man because young people desire to be treated as adults. Father's attitudes toward Billy have changed because Billy has taken on a lot of responsibility and has displayed maturity in his actions.
6. Billy insists on cutting down the sycamore by himself because he promised his dogs he would. He felt that it was his responsibility alone to uphold that promise. The

696

---

hands. When my feet touched the icy bank, I couldn't feel that either. All the feeling in my body was gone.

I wrapped Little Ann in my coat and hurried into my clothes. With the pole I fished my light back.

Close by was a large drift. I climbed up on top of it and dug a hole down through the ice and snow until I reached the dry limbs. I poured half of the oil in my lantern down into the hole and dropped in a match. In no time I had a roaring fire.

I laid Little Ann close to the warm heat and went to work. Old Dan washed her head with his warm red tongue while I massaged and rubbed her body.

I could tell by her cries when the blood started circulating. Little by little her strength came back. I stood her on her feet and started walking her. She was weak and wobbly but I knew she would live. I felt much better and breathed a sigh of relief.

After drying myself out the best I could, I took the lantern handle from the pole, bent it back to its original position, and put it back on the lantern. Holding the light out in front of me, I looked at it. The bright metal gleamed in the firelight glow.

I started talking to it. I said, "Thanks, old lantern, more than you'll ever know. I'll always take care of you. Your globe will always be clean and there'll never be any rust or dirt on your frame."

I knew if it had not been for the miracle of the lantern, my little dog would have met her death on that night. Her grave would have been the cold icy waters of the Illinois River.

Out in the river I could hear the cold water gurgling in the icy trough. It seemed to be angry. It hissed and growled as it tore its way through the channel. I shuddered to think of what could have happened.

Before I left for home, I walked back to the sycamore tree. Once again I said a

696   The Novel

prayer, but this time the words were different. I didn't ask for a miracle. In every way a young boy could, I said "thanks." My second prayer wasn't said with just words. All of my heart and soul were in it.

On my way home I decided not to say anything to my mother and father about Little Ann's accident. I knew it would scare Mama and she might stop my hunting.

Reaching our house, I didn't hang the lantern in its usual place. I took it to my room and set it in a corner with the handle standing up.

The next morning I started sneezing and came down with a terrible cold. I told Mama I had gotten my feet wet. She scolded me a little and started doctoring me.

For three days and nights I stayed home. All this time I kept checking the handle of the lantern. My sisters shook the house from the roof to the floor with their playing and romping, but the handle never did fall.

I went to my mother and asked her if God answered prayers every time one was said. She smiled and said, "No, Billy, not every time. He only answers the ones that are said from the heart. You have to be sincere and believe in Him."

She wanted to know why I had asked.

I said, "Oh, I just wondered, and wanted to know."

She came over and straightened my suspenders, saying, "That was a very nice question for my little Daniel Boone to ask."

Bending over, she started kissing me. I finally squirmed away from her, feeling as wet as a dirt dauber's nest. My mother never could kiss me like a fellow should be kissed. Before she was done I was kissed all over. It always made me feel silly and baby-like. I tried to tell her that a coon hunter wasn't supposed to be kissed that way, but Mama never could understand things like that.

I stomped out of the house to see how my dogs were.

---

action makes his family proud of his willpower and honor.
7. Students can give any three of the following examples. Billy cuts down the big tree to keep his promise to the dogs. The dogs refuse to let Billy go anywhere without them. Old Dan refuses to hunt without Little Ann. Ann and Billy get Dan out of the underground muskrat den. Billy gets Dan down from the tree unhurt. Dan and Billy save Ann from the freezing river waters.
8. Old Dan is relentless, strong, and

stubborn. Little Ann is smart and never gets fooled by a raccoon. Their skills complement each other because what one dog lacks, the other dog has. Between them they have all of the attributes of a great hunting dog.

Applying

9. Answers will differ. Suggested Response: It is important for people to keep promises because doing so enables people to trust each other. People know that they can count on you and what you say if you keep your promises.

Challenge In what ways have Billy's conflicts helped him to grow as a character?

ANSWERS TO ANALYZING LITERATURE

1. Students should describe any two of the following episodes. Billy's dogs tree their first raccoon in the big sycamore and Billy spends two days cutting it down. Dan gets caught in the underground den of a muskrat and Billy has to dig him out. Dan climbs up a hollow tree in

THINKING ABOUT THE SELECTION

Recalling

1. What commitment does Billy make to his dogs just before the first hunt?
2. Describe Billy's feelings as his dogs are chasing the first raccoon.
3. How does Old Dan react when Billy takes him hunting without Little Ann?
4. Describe what occurs during a typical hunt.

Interpreting

5. In Chapter 8 Billy realizes that his father, "doesn't even talk to me like I was a boy any more. He talks to me like I was a man." Why does this realization make Billy so happy? Why have Father's reactions to Billy changed?
6. Why does Billy insist on cutting down the big sycamore and doing it by himself? How does this action make his family feel about him?
7. Give three examples of the bond of love and faithfulness between Billy and the dogs.
8. Compare and contrast the hunting skills of Old Dan and Little Ann. How do they complement each other?

Applying

9. Billy decides that he must cut down a tree that he has enjoyed for years to fulfill a promise he made to his dogs. Why is it important for people to keep promises?

ANALYZING LITERATURE

Understanding Plot Development

The sequence of events in a novel is the plot. In *Where the Red Fern Grows,* the events occur in **episodes,** separate incidents that together make up the plot. Each episode has a conflict that reaches a climax and is resolved.

1. Briefly describe two episodes that occur while Billy and the dogs are hunting.
2. What is the climax of each episode?
3. How is each episode resolved?

CRITICAL THINKING AND READING

Solving Problems

Like the characters in novels, you may face problems that are difficult to resolve. Here is a problem-solving strategy that you can apply in many situations. First, define the problem clearly. Then consider possible solutions and compare the possible outcomes to each solution. Finally, decide on the best solution, supporting your choice with reasons.

Billy uses this strategy when Little Ann is about to slip into the icy river. He quickly goes over the problem: she fell through the ice and must be rescued. Then, he considers several possible solutions: he could run back to the house for help or he could swim out to get her. He decides that neither of these solutions is practical. Finally, he realizes that the best solution is to reach Little Ann with the lantern handle attached to a cane pole.

1. Review the process Billy went through in Chapters 2–5 to solve the problem of getting hunting dogs.
2. Using the problem-solving strategy described here, devise a way that Billy can use to prevent his dogs from following him to Grandfather's store.

THINKING AND WRITING

Writing a News Article

Imagine that you are a reporter for the local newspaper in Billy's county. You are in Grandfather's store one day, and you hear about Billy and his dogs. Write a news article about an episode in the plot. A news article answers the questions *Who? What? When? Where? Why?* and *How?* Include the answers to these questions in your report. When you revise, be sure you have included specific details about the episode. Add an eye-catching headline that will make people want to read your article.

Challenge Describe the conflict, climax, and resolution of the episode when Billy travels to and from Talhequah.

ANSWERS TO CRITICAL THINKING AND READING

1. As you review this process with students, you might want to mention that Billy's problem was defined clearly at the beginning of Chapter 2: he wanted two hound dogs. He then attempted several unsuccessful solutions. He asked, then begged, both his parents, and he even tried to bribe his mother by saying that he would buy her a new dress and some hats. The outcomes to these solutions were identical; his parents could not afford to buy hound dogs. Finally, Billy came up with a solution that worked: saving money for the dogs himself.
2. Answers will differ, but students should offer several possible solutions. Have them choose the best one and support their choice with valid reasons. Possible solutions might include Billy's sisters distracting the dogs while he sneaks off, giving the dogs food to distract them, or waiting until the dogs are away from the farm.

THINKING AND WRITING

Publishing Student Writing
You might organize a class magazine to publish students' composition assignments. You could divide the class into groups that would each be responsible for a different aspect of the magazine. One group could handle art, another group could handle layout, and another group could be in charge of producing made-up advertisements. You might want to be in charge of choosing the articles and compositions that appear in the magazine, you could have part or all of the class decide, or you could include every student's work.

---

pursuit of a raccoon and Billy has to climb up and force him back down. Ann falls into the river when it is partially frozen and Billy has to save her life by wading into the water and hooking her collar with a piece of wire on the end of a pole.
2. The climax of the big sycamore episode occurs when the tree gets blown over by the wind after Billy can no longer chop. The climax of the episode when Dan is caught underground occurs when Ann alerts Billy to where Dan is after

Billy thought Dan had drowned in the river. The climax of the hollow tree episode occurs when Billy finally gets Dan out of the tree. The climax of the episode of Little Ann's near-drowning occurs when Billy finally hooks the lantern handle around Ann's collar and pulls her from the freezing water.
3. The resolution of the big sycamore episode occurs when the dogs catch the raccoon that was in the tree and Billy apologizes to the tree for cutting it down. The epi-

sode of Old Dan in the muskrat den is resolved when Billy digs him out with a shovel and the dogs then catch the old raccoon. The episode of Old Dan up in the hollow tree is resolved when Billy knocks the raccoon out of the tree and Dan kills it. The episode of Little Ann in the freezing river is resolved by Billy dragging her off the ice, building a fire to dry and warm both Ann and himself, and catching a bad cold from the ordeal.

Focus

Literary Focus You might first ask students to describe the setting they have already read about. Be sure that they include details relating to the time in which the story is set, as well as the physical details. Then you could ask students how these details have affected Billy and his family and how they have affected the plot.

Look For It might be helpful to give **less advanced** students examples of how a different setting would affect the story. For example, if the story were set in Hawaii, Billy would not want hound dogs because there would be no raccoons to hunt. If the story was set in the time when settlers first arrived in Oklahoma, Billy might have been too busy clearing land and helping to raise food for the family to have the time to hunt.

Writing/Prior Knowledge You might find it more productive to assign specific areas and time periods to **less advanced** students. For example, you could have students write about how their lives would be different if they lived in the Arctic, the desert, or during the time when dinosaurs lived.

Vocabulary The words in this section are straightforward and most students should have no problems with them.

Where the Red Fern Grows, Chapters 12–15

Setting in a Novel

The **setting** of a novel is the place and the time of the events. Setting is often closely related to other elements in the story. *Where the Red Fern Grows* is set in the farm country and river bottoms of the Illinois River in the Ozark Mountains during the early 1900's. This setting is reflected in the character's manner of living, and therefore, in the events in the novel.

Look For

You have already been introduced to the setting in this novel. As you continue reading, look for how the details of the setting affect the characters and the plot. Would this story have been the same if it had occurred anywhere else? Why or why not?

Writing

Think about the region where you live and how it affects your life. Write about how your setting affects your thoughts and your actions, as well as how it affects others around you. Consider how your life would be different if you lived anywhere else.

Vocabulary

Knowing the following words will help you as you read Chapters 12–15 of *Where the Red Fern Grows*.

leering (lir′ iŋ) *v.*: Looking with harmful intent (p. 699)

jubilant (jōo′b'l ənt) *adj.*: Joyful and triumphant (p. 718)

gloated (glōt′'d) *v.*: Gazed or grinned in scornful triumph (p. 720)

Objectives

1 To understand setting
2 To infer the effect of setting on other aspects of the novel
3 To understand synonyms
4 To write about setting

Support Material

Teaching Portfolio
Teacher Backup, p. 1077
Grammar in Action Worksheet, *Finding Adverbs*, p. 1083; *Recognizing Linking Verbs,* p. 1085; *Using Prepositional Phrases,* p. 1087; *Understanding* Lay *and* Lie, p. 1089
Usage and Mechanics Worksheet, p. 1091
Vocabulary Check, p. 1092

Analyzing Literature Worksheet, *Understanding Setting,* p. 1093
Language Worksheet, *Using Synonyms,* p. 1094
Selection Test, p. 1095

Chapter 12

The fame of my dogs spread all over our part of the Ozarks. They were the best in the country. No coon hunter came into my grandfather's store with as many pelts as I did. Grandpa never overlooked an opportunity to brag. He told everyone the story of my dogs, and the part he had played in getting them.

Many was the time some farmer, coming to our home, would say, "Your Grandpa was telling me you got three big coons over in Pea Vine Hollow the other night." I would listen, knowing I only got one, or maybe none, but Grandpa was my pal. If he said I caught ten in one tree, it was just that way.

Because of my grandfather's bragging, and his firm belief in my dogs and me, a terrible thing happened.

One morning, while having breakfast, Mama said to Papa, "I'm almost out of corn meal. Do you think you can go to the mill today?"

Papa said, "I intended to butcher a hog. We're about out of meat." Looking at me, he said, "Shell a sack of corn. Take one of the mules and go to the mill for your mother."

With the help of my sisters, we shelled the corn. Throwing it over our mule's back, I started for the store.

On arriving at the millhouse, I tied my mule to the hitching post, took my corn, and set it by the door. I walked over to the store and told Grandpa I wanted to get some corn ground.

He said, "I'll be with you in just a minute."

As I was waiting, I heard a horse coming. Looking out, I saw who it was and didn't like what I saw. It was the two youngest Pritchard boys. I had run into them on several occasions during pie suppers and dances.

The Pritchards were a large family that lived upriver about five miles. As in most small country communities, there is one family that no one likes. The Pritchards were it. Tales were told that they were bootleggers, thieves, and just all-around "no-accounts." The story had gone round that Old Man Pritchard had killed a man somewhere in Missouri before moving to our part of the country.

Rubin was two years older than I, big and husky for his age. He never had much to say. He had mean-looking eyes that were set far back in his rugged face. They were smoky-hued and unblinking, as if the eyelids were paralyzed. I had heard that once he had cut a boy with a knife in a fight over at the saw-mill.

Rainie was the youngest, about my age. He had the meanest disposition of any boy I had ever known. Because of this he was disliked by young and old. Wherever Rainie went, trouble seemed to follow. He was always wanting to bet, and would bet on anything. He was nervous, and could never seem to stand still.

Once at my grandfather's store, I had given him a piece of candy. Snatching it out of my hand, he ate it and then sneered at me and said it wasn't any good. During a pie supper one night, he wanted to bet a dime that he could whip me.

My mother told me always to be kind of Rainie, that he couldn't help being the way he was. I asked, "Why?" She said it was because his brothers were always picking on him and beating him.

On entering the store, they stopped and glared at me. Rubin walked over to the counter. Rainie came over to me.

Leering at me, he said, "I'd like to make a bet with you."

I told him I didn't want to bet.

He asked if I was scared.

"No. I just don't want to bet," I said.

Where the Red Fern Grows   699

Presentation

Motivation/Prior Knowledge Have students imagine that someone has challenged them to a contest involving something that they are particularly proud of, such as an athletic skill or knowledge of a subject. Would they accept the challenge? In what kind of situations might it be unwise to accept a challenge?

Thematic Idea Billy seems to have little remorse about the raccoons he and his dogs hunt and kill. For a different perspective on hunters and hunting, you could refer to "Last Cover," on page 57. The story involves the relationship between two boys and a wild fox.

Purpose-Setting Question What is the role of the setting in these chapters of the novel?

1 Reading Strategy You might want to have students summarize the events that contributed to this fame and the role that Grandpa has played. What makes these dogs so special?

2 Literary Focus Billy includes setting in his description of the Pritchard family, saying "as in most *small country communities,* there is one family that no one likes." Is this true only for small country communities? Could there be such a family in a city neighborhood?

3 Discussion What is the meaning of the *deposition?* Should you be kind to those who are mean in every case? Why or why not?

4 Discussion What impression does this description of Rainie give you? What would you think of Rainie if you did not know anything about him?

5 Clarification A "turkey gobbler's wattle" is the fleshy, bright red piece of skin that hangs from the chin of the turkey.

4 His neck and ears looked as though they hadn't been washed in months. His ferret-like eyes kept darting here and there. Glancing down to his hands, I saw the back of his right sleeve was stiff and starchy from the constant wiping of his nose.

He saw I was looking him over, and asked if I liked what I saw.

I started to say, "No," but didn't, turned, and walked away a few steps.

Rubin ordered some chewing tobacco.

"Aren't you a little young to be chewing?" Grandpa asked.

"Ain't for me. It's for my dad," Rubin growled.

Grandpa handed two plugs to him. He paid for it, turned around, and handed one plug to Rainie. Holding the other up in front of him, he looked it over. Looking at Grandpa, he gnawed at one corner of it.

Grandpa mumbled something about how kids were brought up these days. He came from behind the counter, saying to me, "Let's go grind that corn."

The Pritchard boys made no move to follow us out of the store.

"Come on," Grandpa said. "I'm going to lock up till I get this corn ground."

"We'll just stay here. I want to look at some of the shirts," said Rubin.

"No, you won't," said Grandpa. "Come on, I'm going to lock up."

Begrudgingly, they walked out.

I helped Grandpa start the mill and we proceeded to grind the corn. The Pritchard boys had followed us and were standing looking on.

Rainie walked over to me. "I hear you have some good hounds," he said.

I told him I had the best in the country. If he didn't believe me, he could just ask my grandfather.

He just leered at me. "I don't think they're half as good as you say they are," he said. "Bet our old blue tick hound can out-hunt both of them."

I laughed, "Ask Grandpa who brings in the most hides."

"I wouldn't believe him. He's crooked," he said.

I let him know right quick that my grandfather wasn't crooked.

"He's a storekeeper, ain't he?" he said.

I glanced over at Grandpa. He had heard the remark made by Rainie. His friendly old face was as red as a turkey gobbler's wattle. **5**

The last of my corn was just going through the grinding stones. Grandpa pushed a lever to one side, shutting off the power. He came over and said to Rainie, "What do you do? Just go around looking for trouble. What do you want, a fight?"

Rubin sidled over. "This ain't none of your business," he said. "Besides, Rainie's not looking for a fight. We just want to make a bet with him."

Grandpa glared at Rubin. "Any bet you would make sure would be a good one all right. What kind of a bet?"

Rubin spat a mouthful of tobacco juice on the clean floor. He said, "Well, we've heard so much about them hounds of his, we just think it's a lot of talk and lies. We'd like to make a little bet; say about two dollars."

I had never seen my old grandfather so mad. The red had left his face. In its place was a sickly, paste-gray color. The kind old eyes behind the glasses burned with a fire I had never seen.

In a loud voice, he asked, "Bet on what?"

Rubin spat again. Grandpa's eyes followed the brown stain in its arch until it landed on the clean floor and splattered.

With a leering grin on his ugly, dirty face, Rubin said, "Well, we got an old coon up in our part of the country that's been there a long time. Ain't no dog yet ever been smart enough to tree him, and I—"

Rainie broke into the conversation. "He ain't just an ordinary coon. He's an old-timer. Folks call him the 'ghost coon.' Believe me, he is a ghost. He just runs hounds long enough to get them all warmed up, then climbs a tree and disappears. Our old blue hound has treed him more times than—"

Rubin told Rainie to shut up and let him do the talking. Looking over at me, he said, "What do you say? Want to bet two dollars your hounds can tree him?"

I looked at my grandfather, but he didn't help me.

I told Rubin I didn't want to bet, but I was pretty sure my dogs could tree the ghost coon.

Rainie butted in again, "What's the matter? You 'yellow'?"

I felt the hot blood rush into my face. My stomach felt like something alive was crawling in it. I doubled up my right fist and was on the point of hitting Rainie in one of his eyes when I felt my grandfather's hand on my shoulder.

I looked up. His eyes flashed as he looked at me. A strange little smile was tugging at the corner of his mouth. The big artery in his neck was pounding out and in. It reminded me of a young bird that had fallen out of a nest and lay dying on the ground.

Still looking at me, he reached back and took his billfold from his pocket, saying, "Let's call that bet." Turning to Rubin, he said, "I'm going to let him call your bet, but now you listen. If you boys take him up there to hunt the ghost coon, and jump on him and beat him up, you're sure going to hear from me. I don't mean maybe. I'll have both of you taken to Tahlequah and put in jail. You had better believe that."

Rubin saw he had pushed my grandfather far enough. Backing up a couple of steps, he said, "We're not going to jump on him. All we want to do is make a bet."

Grandpa handed me two one-dollar bills, saying to Rubin, "You hold your money and he can hold his. If you lose, you had better pay off." Looking back to me, he said, "Son, if you lose, pay off."

I nodded my head.

I asked Rubin when he wanted me to come up for the hunt.

He thought a minute. "You know where that old log slide comes out from the hills onto the road?" he asked.

I nodded.

"We'll meet you there tomorrow night about dark," he said.

It was fine with me, I said, but I told him not to bring his hounds because mine wouldn't hunt with other dogs.

He said he wouldn't.

I agreed to bring my ax and lantern.

As they turned to leave, Rainie smirked. "Sucker!" he said.

I made no reply.

After the Pritchard boys had gone, my grandfather looked at me and said, "Son, I have never asked another man for much, but I sure want you to catch the ghost coon."

I told him if the ghost coon made one track in the river bottoms, my dogs would get him.

Grandpa laughed.

"You'd better be getting home. It's getting late and your mother is waiting for the corn meal," he said.

I could hear him chuckling as he walked toward his store. I thought to myself, "There goes the best grandpa a boy ever had."

Lifting the sack of meal to the back of my old mule, I started for home. All the way, I kept thinking of Old Dan, Little Ann, ghost coons, and the two ugly, dirty Pritchard boys. I decided not to tell my mother and father anything about the hunt for I knew Mama wouldn't approve of anything I had to do with the Pritchards.

6 Discussion Why do people often get upset when others suggest that they are "yellow" or cowards?

7 Discussion Why does Grandpa call Rainie's bet? What is the purpose of his threat?

8 Reading Strategy You could have students summarize some of the reasons why Billy feels this way about his grandfather. Based on what they have read, do students agree with Billy?

The following evening I arrived at the designated spot early. I sat down by a red oak tree to wait. I called Little Ann over to me and had a good talk with her. I told her how much I loved her, scratched her back, and looked at the pads of her feet.

"Sweetheart," I said, "you must do something for me tonight. I want you to tree the ghost coon for it means so much to Grandpa and me."

She seemed to understand and answered by washing my face and hands.

I tried to talk to Old Dan, but I may as well have talked to a stump for all the attention he paid to me. He kept walking around sniffing here and there. He couldn't understand why we were waiting. He was wanting to hunt.

Rubin and Rainie showed up just at dark. Both had sneers on their faces.

"Are you ready?" Rubin asked.

"Yes," I said, and asked him which way was the best to go.

"Let's go downriver a way and work up," he said. "We're sure to strike him coming upriver, and that way we've got the wind in our favor."

"Are these the hounds that we've been hearing so much about?" Ranie asked.

I nodded.

"They look too little to be any good," he said.

I told him dynamite came in little packages.

He asked me if I had my two dollars.

"Yes," I said.

He wanted to see my money. I showed it to him. Rubin, not to be outdone, showed me his.

We crossed an old field and entered the river bottoms. By this time it was quite dark. I lit my lantern and asked which one wanted to carry my ax.

"It's yours," Rainie said. "You carry it."

Not wanting to argue, I carried both the lantern and the ax.

Rainie started telling me how stingy and crooked my grandfather was. I told him I hadn't come to have any trouble or to fight. All I wanted to do was to hunt the ghost coon. If there was going to be any trouble, I would just call my dogs and go home.

Rubin had a nickel's worth of sense, but Rainie had none at all. Rubin told him if he didn't shut up, he was going to bloody his nose. That shut Rainie up.

Old Dan opened up first. It was a beautiful thing to hear. The deep tones of his voice rolled in the silent night.

A bird in a canebrake on our right started chirping. A big swamp rabbit came running down the riverbank as if all hell was close to his heels. A bunch of mallards, feeding in the shallows across the river, took flight with frightened quacks. A feeling that only a hunter knows slowly crept over my body. I whooped to my dogs, urging them on.

Little Ann came in. Her bell-like tones blended with Old Dan's, in perfect rhythm. We stood and listened to the beautiful music, the deep-throated notes of hunting hounds on the hot-scented trail of a river coon.

Rubin said, "If he crosses the river up at the Buck Ford, it's the ghost coon, as that's the way he always runs."

We stood and listened. Sure enough, the voices of my dogs were silent for a few minutes. Old Dan, a more powerful swimmer than Little Ann, was the first to open up after crossing over. She was close behind him.

Rubin said, "That's him, all right. That's the ghost coon."

They crossed the river again.

We waited.

Rainie said, "You may as well get your money out now."

I told him just to wait a while, and I'd show him the ghost coon's hide.

This brought a loud laugh from Rainie, which sounded like someone had dropped an empty bucket on a gravel bar and then had kicked it.

The wily old coon crossed the river several times, but couldn't shake my dogs from his trail. He cut out from the bottoms, walked a rail fence, and jumped from it into a thick canebrake. He piled into an old slough. Where it emptied into the river, he swam to the middle. Doing opposite to what most coons do, which is swim downstream, he swam upstream. He stopped at an old drift in the middle of it.

Little Ann found him. When she jumped him from the drift, Old Dan was far down-river searching for the trail. If he could have gotten there in time, it would have been the

Critical Thinking and Reading
Ask the students to infer the effect of the setting on the hunt for the ghost coon. How would the hunt be different if the Ghost Coon lived in a flat, marshy area? How would the hunt be different if it took place during daylight?

last of the ghost coon, but Little Ann couldn't do much by herself in the water. He fought his way free from her, swam to our side, and ran upstream.

I could hear Old Dan coming through the bottoms on the other side, bawling at every jump. I could feel the driving power in his voice. We heard him when he hit the water to cross over. It sounded like a cow had jumped in.

Little Ann was warming up the ghost coon. I could tell by her voice that she was close to him.

Reaching our side, Old Dan tore out after her. He was a mad hound. His deep voice was telling her he was coming.

We were trotting along, following my dogs, when I heard Little Ann's bawling stop.

"Wait a minute," I said. "I think she has treed him. Let's give her time to circle the tree to make sure he's there."

Old Dan opened up bawling treed. Rubin started on.

"Something's wrong," I said. "I can't hear Little Ann."

Rainie spoke up, "Maybe the ghost coon ate her up."

I glared at him.

Hurrying on, we came to my dogs. Old Dan was bawling at a hole in a large sycamore that had fallen into the river.

At that spot, the bank was a good ten feet above the water level. As the big tree had fallen, the roots had been torn and twisted from the ground. The jagged roots, acting as a drag, had stopped it from falling all the way into the stream. The trunk lay on a steep slant from the top of the bank to the water. Looking down, I could see the broken tangled mass of the top. Debris from floods had caught in the limbs, forming a drift.

Old Dan was trying to dig and gnaw his way into the log. Pulling him from the hole, I held my lantern up and looked down into the dark hollow. I knew that somewhere

down below the surface there had to be another hole in the trunk, as water had filled the hollow to the river level.

Rubin, looking over my shoulder, said, "That coon couldn't be in there. If he was, he'd be drowned."

I agreed.

Rainie spoke up. "You ready to pay off?" he asked. "I told you them hounds couldn't tree the ghost coon."

I told him the show wasn't over.

Little Ann had never bawled treed, and I knew she wouldn't until she knew exactly where the coon was. Working the bank up and down, and not finding the trail, she swam across the river and worked the other side. For a good half-hour she searched that side before she came back across to where Old Dan was. She sniffed around the hollow log.

"We might as well get away from here," Rainie said. "They ain't going to find the ghost coon."

"It sure looks that way," Rubin said.

I told them I wasn't giving up until my dogs did.

"You just want to be stubborn," Rubin said. "I'm ready for my money now."

I asked him to wait a few minutes.

"Ain't no use," he said. "No hound yet ever treed that ghost coon."

Hearing a whine, I turned around. Little Ann had crawled up on the log and was inching her way down the slick trunk toward the water. I held my lantern up so I could see better. Spraddle-legged, claws digging into the bark, she was easing her way down.

"You'd better get her out of there," Rubin said. "If she gets down in that old tree top, she'll drown."

Rubin didn't know my Little Ann.

Once her feet slipped. I saw her hind quarters fall off to one side. She didn't get scared. Slowly she eased her legs back up on the log.

11

Grammar in Action

Rawls makes us see the actions of Billy and his dogs. How? By using specific nouns, active verbs, and effective modifiers. **Adverbs** are modifiers that show *how, when, where, how often,* and *to what extent* characters perform their actions. Consider these examples:

HOW?   *Slowly* and *carefully* she worked her way through the tangled masses.

WHEN?	I arrived at the designated spot *early*.
WHERE?	Let's go *downriver* a way and work up.
HOW OFTEN?	*Once* her feet slipped.
TO WHAT EXTENT?	Rubin swung his pole, missed the coon, and *almost* hit Little Ann.

Remember that adverbs can describe verbs (as in the sentences above), adjectives, or other adverbs, as in these examples:

Billy was *certainly* worried about Little Ann. [describes adjective *worried*]

Billy approached the coon *very* cautiously. [describes the adverb *cautiously*]

I made no reply. I just watched and waited.

Little Ann eased herself into the water. Swimming to the drift, she started sniffing around. In places it was thin and her legs would break through. Climbing, clawing, and swimming, she searched the drift over, looking for the lost trail.

I saw when she stopped searching. With her body half in the water, and her front feet curved over a piece of driftwood, she turned her head and looked toward the shore. I could see her head twisting from side to side. I could tell by her actions that she had gotten the scent. With a low whine, she started back.

I told Rubin, "I think she smells something."

Slowly and carefully she worked her way through the tangled mass. I lost sight of her when she came close to the undermined bank. She wormed her way under the overhang. I could hear her clawing and wallowing around, and then out from under the bank came the biggest coon I had ever seen, the ghost coon.

He came out right over Little Ann. She caught him in the old treetop. I knew she was no match for him in that tangled mass of limbs and logs. He fought his way free and swam for the opposite bank. She was right behind him.

Old Dan didn't wait, look, or listen. He piled off the ten-foot bank and disappeared from sight. I looked for him. I knew he was tangled in the debris under the surface. I started to take off my overalls, but stopped when I saw his red head shoot up out of the water. Bawling and clawing his way free of the limbs and logs, he was on his way.

On reaching midstream, the ghost coon headed downriver with Little Ann still on his tail.

We ran down the riverbank. I could see my dogs clearly in the moonlight. The ghost coon was about fifteen feet ahead of Little Ann. About twenty-five yards behind them came Old Dan, trying so hard to catch up. I whooped to them.

Rubin grabbed a pole, saying, "He may come out on this side."

Knowing the ghost coon was desperate, I wondered what he would do. Reaching a gravel bar below the high bank, we ran out on it to the water's edge. Then the ghost coon did something that I never expected. Coming even with us, he turned from midstream and came straight for us.

I heard Rubin yell, "Here he comes!"

He churned his way through the shallows and ran right between us. Rubin swung his pole, missed the coon, and almost hit Little Ann. The coon headed for the river bottoms with her right on his heels.

The bawling of Little Ann and our screaming and hollering made so much noise, I didn't hear Old Dan coming. He tore out of the river, plowed into me, and knocked me down.

We ran through the bottoms, following my dogs. I thought the ghost coon was going back to the sycamore log but he didn't. He ran upriver.

While hurrying after them, I looked over at Rainie. For once in his life, I think he was excited. He was whooping and screaming, and falling over logs and limbs.

I felt good all over.

Glancing over at me, Rainie said, "They ain't got him yet."

The ghost coon crossed the river time after time. Seeing that he couldn't shake Old Dan and Little Ann from his trail, he cut through the river bottoms and ran out into an old field.

At this maneuver, Rubin said to Rainie, "He's heading for that tree."

"What tree?" I asked.

"You'll see," Rainie said. "When he gets tired, he always heads for that tree. That's

12 **Enrichment** To give students a better idea of the size and strength of raccoons, you might want to show them some photos of the animals. Also, you could remind them that some raccoons can weigh as much as twenty-five pounds. You can find photographs of raccoons on pages 344–345 of *The Animal Kingdom,* by Robert T. Orr (New York: Macmillan, 1965), in many encyclopedias, or other books on animals.

Notice that Rawls uses adverbs sparingly. These modifiers, like all that he uses, convey colorful and essential meanings to the actions they describe.

Student Activity 1. Find five more examples of adverbs in *Where the Red Fern Grows*. Which of the five questions above do these adverbs answer?

Student Activity 2. Write sentences about the novel using the following adverbs. Underline any verbs, adjectives, or other adverbs that they modify.

fearfully	always	suddenly
there (place)	sometimes	carefully

13 Discussion Why does the Pritchard boys' knowledge of the ghost coon impress Billy? Do you think his view of them is changing?

14 Clarification *Bur oak* is another name for the North American white oak.

where he gets his name, the ghost coon. He just disappears."

"If he disappears, my dogs will disappear with him," I said.

Rainie laughed.

13 I had to admit one thing. The Pritchard boys knew the habits of the ghost coon. I knew he couldn't run all night. He had already far surpassed any coon I had ever chased.

"They're just about there," Rubin said.

Just then I heard Old Dan bark treed. I waited for Little Ann's voice. I didn't hear her. I wondered what it could be this time.

"He's there all right," Rubin said. "He's in that tree."

"Well, come on," I said. "I want to see that tree."

"You might as well get your money out," Rainie said.

I told him he had said that once before, back on the riverbank.

Chapter 13

14 Coming up to the tree, I could see it was a huge bur oak. It wasn't tall. It was just the opposite, rather low and squatty. The top was a thick mass of large limbs, and it hadn't shed all of its leaves yet.

It stood by itself in an old field. There were no other trees within fifty yards of it. About fifteen feet to the left were the remains of a barbed-wire fence. An old gate hung by one rusty hinge from a large corner post. I could tell that at one time a house had stood close by.

Rubin saw me looking around. "A long time ago some Indians lived here and farmed these fields," he said.

I walked around the tree looking for the coon, but could see very little in the dark shadows.

"Ain't no use to look," Rubin said. "He won't be there."

Rainie spoke up. "This ain't the first time we've been to this tree," he said.

Rubin told Rainie to shut up. "You talk too much," he said.

In a whining voice, Rainie said, "Rubin, you know the coon ain't in that tree. Make him pay off and let's go home. I'm getting tired."

I told Rubin I was going to climb the tree.

"Go ahead," he said. "It won't do you any good."

The tree was easy to climb. I looked all over it, on each limb, and in every dark place. I looked for a hollow. The ghost coon wasn't there. I climbed back down, scolded Old Dan to stop his loud bawling, and looked for Little Ann.

I saw her far up the old fence row, sniffing and running here and there. I knew the ghost coon had pulled a real trick, but I couldn't figure out what it was. Little Ann had never yet barked treed. I knew if the coon was in the tree she wouldn't still be searching for a trail.

Old Dan started working again.

My dogs covered the field. They circled and circled. They ran up and down the barbed-wire fence on both sides.

I knew the coon hadn't walked the barbed wire. Ghost or no ghost, he couldn't do that. I walked over to the old gate and looked around. I sat down and stared up into the tree. Little Ann came to me.

Old Dan, giving up his search, came back to the tree and bawled a couple of times. I scolded him again.

Rubin came over. Leering at me, he said, "You give up?"

I didn't answer.

Little Ann once again started searching for the lost trail. Old Dan went to help her.

Rainie said, "I told you that you couldn't tree the ghost coon. Why don't you pay off so we can go home?"

I told him I hadn't given up. My dogs were still hunting. When they gave up, I would, too.

Rubin said, "Well, we're not going to stay here all night."

Looking back to the tree, I thought perhaps I had overlooked something. I told Rubin I was going to climb it again.

He laughed, "Go ahead. Won't do any good. You climbed it once. Ain't you satisfied?"

"No, I'm not satisfied," I said. "I just don't believe in ghost coons."

Rubin said, "I don't believe in ghosts either, but facts are facts. To tell you the truth, I've climbed that tree a dozen times and there just ain't no place in it for a coon to hide."

Rainie spoke up. "Our old blue hound has treed the ghost coon in this tree more times than one. Maybe you two don't believe in ghosts, but I do. Why don't you pay off so we can get away from here?"

"I'll climb it one more time," I said. "If I can't find him, I'll pay off."

Climbing up again, I searched and searched. When I got through, I knew the ghost coon wasn't in that tree. When I came down, I saw my dogs had given up. That took the last resistance out of me. I knew if they couldn't find the ghost coon, I couldn't.

Digging the two one-dollar bills out of my pocket, I walked over to Rubin. Little Ann was by my side. I handed my money over, saying, "Well, you won it fair and square."

With a grin on his face, Rubin took my money. He said, "I bet this will break your old grandpa's heart."

I didn't reply.

Reaching down, I caught Little Ann's head in my hands. Looking into her warm friendly eyes, I said, "It's all right, little girl, we haven't given up yet. We'll come back. We may never catch the ghost coon, but we'll run him until he leaves the country.

She licked my hands and whined.

A small breeze began to stir. Glancing up into the tree, I saw some leaves shaking. I said to Rubin, "Looks like the wind is coming up. It may blow up a storm. We'd better be heading for home."

Just as I turned, I saw Little Ann throw up her head and whine. Her body grew stiff and taut. I watched her. She was testing the wind. I knew she had scented something in the breeze. Stiff-legged, head high in the air, she started walking toward the tree. Almost there, she turned back and stopped. I knew she had caught the scent but could only catch it when a breeze came.

Looking at Rubin, I said, "I haven't lost that two dollars yet."

Another breeze drifted out of the river bottoms. Little Ann caught the scent again. Slowly she walked straight to the large gatepost, reared up on it with her front feet, and bawled the most beautiful tree bark I ever heard in my life.

Old Dan, not understanding why Little Ann was bawling, stood and looked. He walked over to the post, reared up on it, and sniffed. Then, raising his head, he shook the dead leaves in the bur oak tree with his deep voice.

I looked at Rainie. Laughing, I said, "There's your ghost coon. Now what do you think of my dogs?"

For once he made no reply.

Going over to the post, I saw it was a large black locust put there many years ago to hang the gate. Looking up at the tree, I saw how the ghost coon had pulled his trick. One large long limb ran out and hung di-

708

15 Discussion What does Billy mean by this statement? Do you agree with him? Why or why not? Can you think of other examples concerning predatory animals and their prey?

16 Literary Focus The description of the area where the ghost coon is treed creates a feeling of mystery. Which details contribute to this feeling? How has this affected the boys?

rectly over the gate. It was a drop of a good twelve feet from the branch to the top of the gatepost, but I knew we weren't after an ordinary coon. This was the ghost coon.

I said to Rubin, "Boost me up and I'll see if the post is hollow."

After breaking off a long jimpson weed to use as a prod, I got up on Rubin's shoulder, and he raised me up. The post was hollow. Not knowing how far down the hole went, I started the switch down. About halfway, I felt something soft. I gave it a hard jab.

I heard him coming. He boiled out right in my face. I let go of everything. Hitting the ground, I rolled over on my back and looked up.

For a split second, the ghost coon stayed on top of the post, and then he jumped. My dogs were on him the instant he hit the ground. The fight was on.

I knew the coon didn't have a chance as he wasn't in the waters of the river. He didn't give up easily even though he was on dry land. He was fighting for his life and a good account he gave. He fought his way to freedom, and made it back to the bur oak tree. He was a good six feet up the side when Old Dan, leaping high in the air, caught him and pulled him back down.

At the foot of the tree, the fight went on. Again the ghost coon fought his way free. This time he made it and disappeared in the dark shadows of the tree. Old Dan was furious. Never before had I seen a coon get away from him.

I told Rubin I would climb up and run him out. As I started climbing, I saw Little Ann go to one side and Old Dan to the other. My dogs would never stay together when they had treed a coon, so that any way he left a tree, he was met by one of them.

About halfway up, far out on a limb, I found the ghost coon. As I started toward him, my dogs stopped bawling. I heard something I had heard many times. The sound was like the cry of a small baby. It was the cry of a ringtail coon when he knows it is the end of the trail. I never liked to hear this cry, but it was all in the game, the hunter and the hunted.

As I sat there on the limb, looking at the old fellow, he cried again. Something came over me. I didn't want to kill him.

I hollered down and told Rubin I didn't want to kill the ghost coon.

He hollered back, "Are you crazy?"

I told him I wasn't crazy. I just didn't want to kill him.

I climbed down.

Rubin was mad. He said, "What's the matter with you?"

"Nothing," I told him. "I just don't have the heart to kill the coon."

I told him there were plenty more; why kill him? He had lived here a long time, and more than one hunter had listened to the voices of his hounds bawling on his trail.

Rainie said, "He's chicken-livered, that's what it is."

I didn't like that but, not wanting to argue, I didn't say anything.

Rubin said, "I'll go up and run him out."

"I won't let my dogs kill him," I said.

Rubin glared at me. "I'm going up and run that coon out," he said. "If you stop your dogs, I'm going to beat you half to death."

"Do it anyway, Rubin," Rainie said.

"I've a good mind to," said Rubin.

Just as Rubin started to climb the tree, Old Dan growled. He was staring into the darkness. Something was coming.

"What's that?" I asked.

"I don't know," Rubin said. "Don't sound like anything I ever heard."

"It's ghosts," Rainie said. "Let's get away from here."

An animal was coming out of the darkness. It was walking slowly in an odd way, as

15

16

Primary Source: Tall Tales

Oral literature—tall tales, legends, songs and jokes—is an important part of Ozark Mountain culture. On page 664, Billy refers to the tall tales told by his grandfather and other coon hunters. If the Pritchard boys had not seen the coon, it is possible that the story of the ghost coon might have grown into a local legend. Here is an Ozark yarn involving a raccoon hunting, taken from *We Always Lie to Strangers,* by Randolph Vance.

I have often heard coon-hunters tell of killing seven or eight coons in one tree, on the same night. These tales may be true, for all I know, since I never did much coon-hunting. But the yarn which follows is a typical backwoods tale. An old hunter near Hiwasse, Arkansas, told me that the best coon-dogs in Benton County treed (a coon) one night at a big hickory, with a large cavity just above the first fork. When the hunters came up, they were astonished to see the trunk of the tree swell to several times its proper size, and then gradually return to normal, while a great cloud of steam poured out of the hole above the fork. This performance was repeated at regular intervals. When the tree

if it were walking sideways. The hair on the back of my neck stood straight out.

As the animal came closer, Rainie said, "Why, it's Old Blue. How did he get loose?"

It was a big blue tick hound. Around his neck was a piece of rope about three feet long. One could see that the rope had been gnawed in two. The frayed end had become entangled in a fair-sized dead limb. Dragging the limb was what made the dog look so odd. I felt much better when I found out what it was.

The blue tick hound was like the Pritchards, mean and ugly. He was a big dog, tall and heavy. His chest was thick and solid. He came up growling. The hair on his back was standing straight up. He walked stiff-legged around Old Dan, showing his teeth.

I told Rainie he had better get hold of his dog, or there was sure to be a fight.

"You better get hold of your dog," he said. "I'm not worried about Old Blue. He can take care of himself."

I said no more.

"Don't make no difference now whether you kill the ghost coon or not," Rubin said. "Old Blue will take care of him."

I knew the killing of the coon was out of my control, but I didn't want to see him die. I said to Rubin, "Just give back my two dollars and I'll go home. I can't keep you from killing him, but I don't have to stay and see it."

"Rubin, don't give him the money," Rainie said. "He ain't killed the ghost coon."

"That's right," Rubin said. "You ain't, and I wouldn't let you now, even if you wanted to."

was cut down the hunters killed thirty-seven coons, and many more escaped in the confusion. "They was packed in that holler like sardines in a can," the old man explained. "We figgered out that them coons all got to breathin' together, just like a lot of soldiers a-marchin' in step. Every time they'd breathe out, the tree would skrink up ag'in, an' we'd see the steam a-comin' out of the holler."

Discuss the yarn with students. You might speculate on what true incident might have been the origin to this yarn. What yarn might grow out of the story of the ghost coon?

17 Reading Strategy You could have students review other events in the story when Billy's dogs came to each other's aid. Based on these events, are students surprised that Ann is helping Dan? How great a sacrifice would the dogs make for each other?

I told them my dogs had treed the ghost coon and that was the bet, to tree the ghost coon.

"No, it wasn't," Rubin said. "You said you would kill him."

"It was no such thing," I said. "I've done all I said I would."

Rubin walked up in front of me. He said, "I ain't going to give you the money. You didn't win it fair. Now what are you going to do about it?"

I looked into his mean eyes. I started to make some reply, but decided against it.

He saw my hesitation, and said, "You better get your dogs and get out of here before you get whipped."

In a loud voice, Rainie said, "Bloody his nose, Rubin."

I was scared. I couldn't whip Rubin. He was too big for me. I started to turn and leave when I thought of what my grandfather had told them.

"You had better remember what my grandpa said," I reminded them. "He'll do just what he said he would."

Rubin didn't hit me. He just grabbed me and with his brute strength threw me down on the ground. He had me on my back with my arms outspread. He had a knee on each arm. I made no effort to fight back. I was scared.

"If you say one word to your grandpa about this," Rubin said, "I'll catch you hunting some night and take my knife to you."

Looking up into his ugly face, I knew he would do just what he said. I told him to let me up and I would go and not say anything to anyone.

"Don't let him up, Rubin," Rainie said. "Beat him, or hold him and let me do it."

Just then I heard growling, and a commotion off to one side. The blue hound had finally gotten a fight out of Old Dan. Turning my head sideways, I could see them standing on their hind legs, tearing and slashing at

each other. The weight of the big hound pushed Old Dan over.

I told Rubin to let me up so we could stop the fight.

He laughed, "While my dog is whipping yours, I think I'll just work you over a little." So saying, he jerked my cap off, and started whipping me in the face with it.

I heard Rainie yell, "Rubin, they're killing Old Blue."

Rubin jumped up off me.

I clambered up and looked over to the fight. What I saw thrilled me. Faithful Little Ann had gone to the assistance of Old Dan.

I knew my dogs were very close to each other. Everything they did was done as a combination, but I never expected this. It is a very rare occasion for a female dog to fight another dog, but fight she did.

I could see that Little Ann's jaws were glued to the throat of the big hound. She would never loosen that deadly hold until the last breath of life was gone.

Old Dan was tearing and slashing at the soft belly. I knew the destruction his long sharp teeth were causing.

Again Rainie yelled, "Rubin, they're killing him. They're killing Old Blue. Do something quick."

Rubin darted over to one side, grabbed my ax from the ground, and said in a loud voice, "I'll kill them hounds."

At the thought of what he was going to do with the ax, I screamed and ran for my dogs. Rubin was about ten feet ahead of me, bent over, running with the ax held out in front of him. I knew I could never get to them in time.

I was screaming, "No, Rubin, no!"

I saw the small stick when it whipped up from the ground. As if it were alive, it caught between Rubin's legs. I saw him fall. I ran on by.

Reaching the dogfight, I saw the big hound was almost gone. He had long since ceased fighting. His body lay stretched full-length on the ground. I grabbed Old Dan's collar and pulled him back. It was different with Little Ann. Pull as I might, she wouldn't let go of the hound's throat. Her jaws were locked.

I turned Old Dan loose and, getting astraddle of Little Ann, I pried her jaws apart with my hands. Old Dan had darted back in. Grabbing his collar again, I pulled them off to one side.

The blue hound lay where he was. I thought perhaps he was already dead, and then I saw him move a little.

Still holding my dogs by their collars, I looked back. I couldn't understand what I saw. Rubin was laying where he had fallen. His back was toward me, and his body was bent in a "U" shape. Rainie was standing on the other side of him, staring down.

I hollered and asked Rainie, "What's the matter?"

He didn't answer. He just stood as though in a trance, staring down at Rubin.

I hollered again. He still didn't answer. I didn't know what to do. I couldn't turn my dogs loose. They would go for the hound again.

Again I hollered at Rainie, asking him to come and help me. He neither moved nor answered. I had to do something.

Looking around, my glance fell on the old barbed-wire fence. I led my dogs to it. Holding onto their collars with one hand, I worked a rusty barbed wire backwards and forwards against a staple until it broke. Running the end of it under their collars, I tied them up. They made two or three lunges toward the hound, but the wire held.

I walked over and stopped at Rainie's side. I again asked, "What's the matter?"

He said not a word.

I could see that Rainie was paralyzed with fright. His mouth and eyes were opened wide, and his face was as white as chalk. I laid my hand on his shoulder. At the touch of my hand, he jumped and screamed. Still screaming, he turned and started running. I watched him until he disappeared in the darkness.

Looking down at Rubin, I saw what had paralyzed Rainie. When Rubin had tripped, he had fallen on the ax. As it entered his stomach, the sharp blade had sunk to the eye of the double-bitted ax.

Turning my back to the horrible sight, I closed my eyes. The muscles in my stomach knotted and jerked. A nauseating sickness spread over my body. I couldn't look at him.

I heard Rubin whisper. Turning around, I knelt down by his side with my back to the ax. I couldn't understand what he was whispering. Kneeling down closer, I heard and understood. In a faint voice, he said, "Take it out of me."

I hesitated.

Again he pleaded. "Please take it out of me."

Turning around, I saw his hands were curled around the protruding blade as if he himself had tried to pull it from his stomach.

How I did it, I'll never know. Putting my hands over his and pressing down, I pulled the ax from the wound. The blood gushed. I felt the warm heat as it spread over my hands. Again the sickness came over me. I stumbled to my feet and stepped back a few paces.

Seeing a movement from Rubin, I thought he was going to get up. With his hands, he pushed himself halfway up. His eyes were wide open, staring straight at me. Stopping in his effort of getting up, still staring at me, his mouth opened as if to say something. Words never came. Instead, a large red bubble slowly worked its way out of his mouth and burst. He fell back to the ground. I knew he was dead.

Scared, not knowing what to do, I called

18 Discussion Why does Rainie run away? Was anyone at fault for what happened to Rubin? Support your answer.

19 Literary Focus You could point out to students how the setting affects the way Papa reacts to the tragedy. He must get Grandpa because "he is the only man in the country that has the authority to move the body." How would a similar situation be handled today?

18 for Rainie. I got no answer. I called his name again and again. I could get no reply. My voice echoed in the darkness of the silent night. A cold chill ran over my body.

I suppose it is natural at a time like that for a boy to think of his mother. I thought of mine. I wanted to get home.

Going over to my dogs, I glanced to where the blue hound was. He was trying to get up. I was glad he wasn't dead.

Picking up my lantern, I thought of my ax. I left it. I didn't care if I never saw it again.

Knowing I couldn't turn my dogs loose, I broke off enough of the wire to lead them. As I passed under the branches of the bur oak tree, I looked up into the dark foliage. I could see the bright eyes of the ghost coon. Everything that had happened on this terrible night was because of his very existence, but it wasn't his fault.

I also knew he was a silent witness to the horrible scene. Behind me lay the still body of a young boy. On my left a blue tick hound lay torn and bleeding. Even after all that had happened, I could feel no hatred for the ghost coon and was not sorry I had let him live.

Arriving home, I awakened my mother and father. Starting at my grandfather's mill, I told everything that had happened. I left nothing out. My mother had started crying long before I had completed my story. Papa said nothing, just sat and listened. When I had finished, he kept staring down at the floor in deep thought. I could hear the sobbing of my mother in the silence. I walked over to her. She put her arms around me and said, "My poor little boy."

Getting to his feet, Papa reached for his coat and hat. Mama asked him where he was going.

19 "Well, I'll have to go up there," he said. "I'm going to get Grandpa, for he is the only man in the country that has authority to move the body."

Looking at me, he said, "You go across the river and get Old Man Lowery, and you may as well go on up and tell the Bufords, too. Tell them to meet us at your grandfather's place."

I hurried to carry the sad message.

The following day was a nasty one. A slow, cold drizzle had set in. Feeling trapped indoors, I prowled from room to room. I couldn't understand why my father hadn't come back from the Pritchards'. I sat by the window and watched the road.

Understanding my feelings, Mama said, "Billy, I wouldn't worry. He'll be back before long. It takes time for things like that."

"I know," I said, "but you would think he would've been back by now."

Time dragged slowly by. Late in the afternoon, I saw Papa coming. Our old mule was jogging along. Water was shooting out from under his feet in small squirts at every step.

Papa had tied the halter rope around the mule's neck. He was sitting humped over, with his hands jammed deep in the pockets of his patched and worn mackinaw. I felt sorry for him. He was soaking wet, tired, sleepy, and hungry.

Telling Mama, "Here he is," I grabbed my jumper and cap, and ran out to the gate and waited.

I was going to ask him what had happened at the Pritchards' but on seeing his tired face and wet clothes, I said, "Papa, you had better go in to the fire. I'll take care of the mule, and do the feeding and milking."

"That would be fine," he said.

After doing the chores, I hurried to the house. I couldn't wait any longer. I had to find out what had happened.

Walking into the front room, I saw my father had changed clothes. He was standing in front of the fireplace, drinking coffee.

712   *The Novel*

Grammar in Action

Although most of Rawls' writing involves describing action and showing specific details, sometimes he must tell his readers *what something is* or *appears to be* or *what someone is feeling*. In these cases, a writer uses verbs that are not active, but merely link a subject with a predicate. Such **linking verbs** are used in *Where The Red Fern Grows* to show the relationship between other words in a sentence.

The following day *was* a nasty one.
I *felt* bad about the death of Rubin.
He *was* soaking wet, tired, sleepy, and hungry.
There *are* people like the Pritchards all through the hills.
Mama wished they *were* more friendly.

Notice how the linking verbs act as equal signs in the sentences; the predicates either rename or describe their subjects. As you can see, the most common linking verb is *be*. In addition, these verbs often serve to link subjects and verbs:

appear	grow	seem	stay
become	look	smell	taste
feel	remain	sound	turn

"Boy, that's bad weather, isn't it?" he said.

I said it was, and asked him about Rubin.

"We went to the old tree and got Rubin's body," Papa said. "We were on our way back to the Pritchards' when we met them. They were just this side of their place. They had started to look for him. Rainie had been so dazed when he got home, they couldn't make out what he was trying to tell them, but they knew it must have been something bad. They wanted to know what had happened. I did my best to explain the accident. It hit Old Man Pritchard pretty hard. I felt sorry for him."

Mama asked how Mrs. Pritchard was taking it.

Papa said he didn't know as he never did get to see any of the womenfolks. He said they were the funniest bunch he had ever seen. He couldn't understand them. There wasn't one tear shed that he could see. All of the men had stayed out at the barn. They never had been invited in for a cup of coffee or anything.

Mama asked when they were to have the funeral.

"They have their own graveyard right there on the place," Papa said. "Old Man Pritchard said they would take care of everything, and didn't want to bother people. He said it was too far for anyone to come, and it was bad weather, too."

Mama said she couldn't help feeling sorry for Mrs. Pritchard, and wished they were more friendly.

I asked Papa about Rainie.

Papa said, "According to what Old Man Pritchard said, Rainie just couldn't seem to get over the shock. They were figuring on taking him into town to see the doctor."

In a stern voice, Papa said, "Billy, I don't want you fooling around with the Pritchards any more. You have plenty of country around here so you don't have to go there to hunt."

I said I wouldn't.

I felt bad about the death of Rubin. I didn't feel like hunting and kept having bad dreams. I couldn't forget the way he had looked at me just before he died. I moped and wandered around in a daze. I wanted to do something but didn't know what it was.

I explained my feelings to my mother. She said, "Billy, I feel the same way and would like to do something to help, but I guess there's nothing we can do. There are people like the Pritchards all through the hills. They live in little worlds of their own and are all alone. They don't like to have outsiders interfere."

I told my mother I had been thinking about how dangerous it was to carry an ax while hunting, and I had decided I'd save a few coon hides and get a good gun. Boy, I just shouldn't have mentioned getting a gun. My mother got "sitting-hen" mad.

"You're not getting a gun," she said. "I won't have that at all. I told you a long time ago you could have one when you are twenty-one years old, and I mean just that. I worry enough with you out there in the hills all hours of the night, running and jumping, but I couldn't stand it if I knew you had a gun with you. No, sir. You can just forget about a gun."

"Yes, Mama," I said, and sulked off to my room.

Lying on my bed, still trying to figure out what I could do to help, I glanced over to the wall. There, tied in a small bundle, was just what I needed.

Some time back my sisters had made some flowers for Decoration Day.[1] They had given me a small bouquet for my room. Taking them down, I could see they had faded a little, and looked rather old, but they were

_____
1. Decoration Day: Memorial Day.

20 Critical Thinking and Reading
You might want to discuss how the setting might have had an effect on the Pritchard family. Ask students to make inferences about the effect of setting on their lives. Are there people like the Pritchards who "live in little worlds of their own and are all alone" and who do not live in the hills?

20

Student Activity 1. Locate five other examples of linking verbs in *Where the Red Fern Grows*. Identify the subject and the predicate that are linked by the linking verb. Do the predicates rename or describe their subjects?

Student Activity 2. Choose five of the verbs from the list and write sentences in which they are used as linking verbs. Make sure that the subject "equals" the predicate.

21 Discussion How does this description of Mrs. Pritchard and Papa's statement that Mr. Pritchard was "hit . . . pretty hard" by the news of Rubin's death differ from the impressions you had previously of the Pritchard family? Does it alter your impression of them?

22 Discussion Why does Billy feel better after paying his respects to Rubin's grave? What is the "funny feeling" that he refers to? Why was Billy unable to hunt before this?

still pretty. I blew the dust off and straightened the crinkled petals. Putting them inside my shirt, I left the house.

I hadn't gone far when I heard something behind me. It was my dogs. I tried to tell them I wasn't going hunting. I just had a little business to attend to, and if they would go back, I'd take them out that night. It was no use. They couldn't understand.

Circling around through the flats, I came to the hollow above the Pritchards' place. Down below me, I could see the graveyard, and the fresh mound of dirt. As quietly as I could, I started easing myself down the mountainside.

Old Dan loosened a rock. The farther it bounced, the louder it got. It slammed up against a post oak tree and sounded like a gunshot. I held my breath and watched the house. No one came out.

I glared at Old Dan. He wagged his tail, and just to show off, he sat down on his rear and started digging at a flea with his hind leg. The way his leg was thumping in the leaves, anyone could have heard it for a mile. I waited until he quit thumping before starting on.

Reaching the bottom, I had about twenty yards of clearing to cross, but the grass and bushes were pretty thick. Laying down on my stomach, with my heart beating like a triphammer, I wiggled my way to Rubin's grave. I laid the flowers on the fresh mound of earth, and then turned around and scooted for the timber.

Just as we reached the mountaintop, my foot slipped and I kicked loose a large rock. Down the side of the mountain it rolled. This time the blue tick hound heard the noise. He came out from under the house bawling. I heard a door slam and Mrs. Pritchard came out. She stood looking this way and that way.

The hound ran up to the graveyard and started sniffing and bawling. Mrs. Pritchard

followed him. Seeing the flowers on Rubin's grave, she picked them up and looked at them. She scolded the hound, and then looked up at the hillside. I knew she couldn't see me because the timber was too thick, but I felt uncomfortable anyway.

Scolding the hound again, she knelt down and arranged the flowers on the grave. Taking one more look at the hillside, she started back. Halfway to the house, I saw her reach down and gather the long cotton skirt in her hand and dab at her eyes.

I felt much better after paying my respects to Rubin. Everything looked brighter, and I didn't have that funny feeling any more.

All the way home my dogs kept running out in front of me. They would stop, turn around, and look at me. I had to smile, for I knew what they wanted. I stopped and petted them a little and told them that as soon as I got home and had my supper, we would go hunting.

Chapter 14

A few days later, on his way back from the mill, one of the Hatfield boys stopped at our place. He told me my grandfather wanted to see me. It was unusual for Grandpa to send for me and it had me worried. I figured that he wanted to talk to me about the death of Rubin Pritchard. I always enjoyed talking to my grandpa but I didn't want to talk about Rubin's death. Every time I thought of him, I lived the horrible tragedy all over again.

After a practically sleepless night, the next morning I started for the store. I was walking along deep in thought when Little Ann zipped by me. She was as happy as a young gray squirrel. She wiggled and twisted and once she barked at me. I looked behind me. There was Old Dan trotting along. He stopped when I turned around. Little Ann came up to me. I scolded them and tried to explain that I wasn't going hunting. I was just going up to the store to see what my grandpa wanted. They couldn't, or didn't, want to understand.

I picked up a small stick and slapped my leg with it. In a deep voice I said, "Now you go home, or I'm going to wear you out."

This hurt their feelings. With their tails between their legs and trotting side by side, they started back. Every little way they would stop and look back at me. It was too much. I couldn't stand it. I began to feel bad all over.

"Well, all right," I said. "Come on, you can go, but, Dan, if there are any dogs around the store, and you get in a fight, I won't take you hunting for a whole year, and I mean that," although I knew I didn't.

They came running, tickled to death. Little Ann took one of her silly spells. She started nipping at the long red tail of Old Dan. Not getting any reaction from him, she jumped over him. She barked at him. He wouldn't even look at her. She ran around in front of him and laid down in the trail, acting like a cat ready to spring. Stiff-legged, he walked up close to her, stopped, and showed his teeth. I laughed out loud. I knew he wouldn't bite her any more than he would bite me. He was just acting tough because he was a boy dog.

After several attempts to get him to play, Little Ann gave up. Together they started sniffing around in the underbrush.

As I walked up in front of the store, Grandpa hollered at me from the barn. I went over to him. Right away he wanted to know all about Rubin's accident. He listened while I told the story over again.

After I had had my say, Grandpa stood looking down at the ground. There was a deep frown on his face, and a hurt look in his eyes. His quietness made me feel uneasy. He finally raised his head and looked at me. What I could see in his friendly old face tore

at my heart. It seemed that there were more wrinkles than I had ever seen before. His uncombed, iron-gray hair looked almost white. I noticed that his wrinkled old hand trembled as he rubbed the wire-stiff stubble on his chin.

In a low voice that quivered as he talked, he said, "Billy, I'm sorry about all this. Truly sorry. I can't help but feel that in a way it was my fault."

"No, Grandpa," I said, "it wasn't your fault. It wasn't anyone's fault. It just happened and no one could help it."

"I know," he said, "but if I hadn't called Rubin's bet, nothing would have happened. I guess when a man gets old he doesn't think straight. I shouldn't have let those boys get under my skin."

"Grandpa," I said, "Rubin and Rainie could get under anybody's skin. You couldn't help that. Why, they get under everyone's skin that gets close to them."

"Yes, I know," he said, "but still I acted like a fool. Billy, I had no idea things were going to turn out like they did, or I wouldn't have called that bet."

Wanting to change the conversation, I said, "Grandpa, we won that bet fair and square, but they took my money anyway."

I saw the fire come back to his eyes. This made me feel better. He was more like the Grandpa I loved.

"That's all right," he said. "We'll just forget the whole thing."

He stepped over and laid his hand on my shoulder. In a solemn voice, he said, "We won't talk about this again. Now, I want you to forget it ever happened because it wasn't your fault. Oh, I know it's hard for a boy to ever completely forget something like that. All through your life you'll think of it now and then, but try not to let it bother you, and don't ever feel guilty about it. It's not good for a young boy to feel that way."

I nodded my head, thinking if people

23 Discussion People often look back on events and wish they had done something differently. Why is this reaction so common? Why do people feel this way?

would just stop questioning me about Rubin's death, maybe I could forget.

Grandpa said, "Well, the accident wasn't the only thing I wanted to talk to you about. I've got something else—something I think will help us both forget a lot of things."

The twinkle in Grandpa's eyes reminded me of what my father had said: "Seems like that old man can cook up more deals than anyone in the country."

I didn't care how many deals Grandpa cooked up. He was still the best grandpa in the whole wide world.

"What have you got?" I asked.

"Come over to the store," he said, "and I'll show you."

On our way over, I heard him mutter, "I hope this doesn't turn out like the ghost-coon hunt."

On entering the store, Grandpa walked to the post office department, and came back with a newspaper in his hand. He spread it out on the counter.

Pointing with his finger, he said in a loud voice, "Look, there!"

I looked. The large black letters read: CHAMPIONSHIP COON HUNT TO BE HELD. My eyes

popped open. Again I read the words.

Grandpa was chuckling.

I said, "Boy, if that isn't something. A championship coon hunt." Wide-eyed, I asked, "Where are they having this hunt, and what does it have to do with us?"

Grandpa was getting excited. Off came his glasses and out came the old red handkerchief. He blew his breath on the lens and polished them. He snorted a time or two, reared back, and almost shouted, "Do with us? Why it has everything to do with us. All my life I've wanted to go to one of these big coon hunts. Why I've even dreamed about it. And now the opportunity has come. Yes, sir, now I can go." He paused. "That is, if it's all right with you."

I was dumbfounded. I said, "All right with me? Why, Grandpa, you know it's all

Literary element: Character.

Up to this point in the novel, students have concentrated primarily on the main character, Billy. However, there are several important minor characters as well. Minor characters are those who take part in the action but are not the focus of attention. Perhaps the most important minor character in the novel is Grandpa.

Grandpa plays a large role in the narrative and is more fully developed than any of the other minor characters. We get to know his strengths and his weaknesses.

You might want to have students discuss Grandpa's character. Ask students for words that describe Grandpa. Make sure they include Grandpa's weaknesses as well as his strengths. Write these words as headings for separate columns on the chalkboard. Then ask students to recall the actions taken and statements made by Grandpa and Billy that are examples of these traits. Write the actions and statements under the appropriate headings on the chalkboard. After students have completed this chart, ask them how Grandpa influences Billy. What worth-

right with me, but what have I got to do with it?"

Grandpa was so excited I thought he was going to burst a blood vessel.

Talking excitedly, he said, "I've got it all fixed, Billy. We can enter Old Dan and Little Ann in this championship hunt."

I was so surprised at what Grandpa had said I couldn't utter a word. At first I was scared and then a wonderful feeling came over me. I felt the excitement of the big hunt as it burned its way into my body. I started breathing like I had been running for a hundred miles. After several attempts, I croaked, "Can just any dog be in this hunt?"

Grandpa almost jumped as he answered,

"No, sir, not just any hound can be entered. They have to be the best, and they have to be registered, too."

He started talking with his hands. Pointing to a chair, he said, "Sit down and I'll tell you all about it."

Grandpa calmed down a little and started talking in a serious voice. "Billy," he said, "it takes some doing to have a set of dogs entered in this hunt. I've been working on this for months. I've written letters on top of letters. I've even had several good friends in town helping me. You see, I've kept a record of all the coons your dogs have caught, and believe me, their catch is up there with the best of them. Now, I have already paid the entry fee and everything is fixed. All we have to do is go."

"Entry fee? How much did it cost?" I asked.

"You let me worry about that," he said. "Now what do you say? Want to give it a whirl? I understand the winner receives a gold cup, and you never can tell, we might come home with it. We have as good a chance as anyone else."

Grandpa had me so worked up by this time, I didn't think anyone else had any good hounds but me.

I reared back and blurted, "It's all right with me, Grandpa. Just tell me what to do."

Grandpa flew out of gear like a Model-T Ford. He slapped the counter with his hand. In a pent-up voice, he said, "That's the boy! That's the way I like to hear a coon hunter talk."

With a questioning look on his face, he asked, "Didn't I see your dogs with you when you came up?"

"Yes, they followed me," I said. "They're outside."

"Well, call them in," he said. "I've got something for them."

I called to them. Little Ann came in the store, walking like she was scared. Old Dan

while qualities does Billy learn from Grandpa? Students should get at qualities such as understanding, kindness, sense of humor, trust.

You might have students write their own charts to keep in their notebooks. Then, as they read further they can add any new information about Grandpa's character.

came to the door and stopped. I tried to coax him in. It was no use. My dogs, never being allowed in the house, were scared to come in.

Grandpa walked over to a hoop of cheese and cut off two chunks about the size of my fist. He walked to the door, talking to Old Dan. "What's the matter, boy?" he said. "You scared to come in? Well, that shows you're a good dog."

He handed him a piece of the cheese. I heard it rattle in his throat as he gulped it down.

Grandpa came back and set Little Ann up on the counter. He chuckled as he broke the cheese up in small pieces and fed her.

"Yes, sir," he said, "I think we have the best darn coon hounds in these Ozark Mountains, and just as sure as shootin', we're going to win that gold cup."

Grandpa didn't have to say that. The way I was feeling, I already had the cup. All I had to do was go and get it.

Finished with his feeding of Little Ann, Grandpa said, "Now, let's see. The hunt starts on the twenty-third. That's about—well, let's see—this is the seventeenth." Counting on his fingers he finally figured it out. "That's six days from now," he said in a jubilant voice.

I nodded my head.

"We can leave here early on the morning of the twenty-second," he said, "and barring accidents, we should make the campground in plenty of time for the grand opening."

I asked how we were going.

"We'll go in my buggy," he said. "I'll load the tent and everything the night before."

I asked him what he wanted me to bring.

"Nothing," he said, "but these two little hounds, and you be here early; and I believe I'd let these dogs rest, 'cause we want them in tiptop shape when we get there."

I saw the thinking wrinkles bunch up on Grandpa's forehead.

"You reckon your daddy would like to go?" he asked. "As late in the fall as it is, I don't think he's too busy, is he?"

"No, our crops are all gathered," I said. "We've been clearing some of the bottom land, but that's almost done now."

"Well, ask him," he said. "Tell him I'd like to have him go."

"I'll ask him," I said, "but you know how Papa is. The farm comes first with him."

"I know," Grandpa said, "but you ask him anyway, and tell him what I said. Now it's getting late and you had better be heading for home."

I was almost to the door when Grandpa said, "Wait a minute."

He walked over behind the candy counter and shook out one of the quarter sacks. He filled it up to the brim, bounced it on the counter a few times, and dropped in a few more gumdrops.

With a twinkle in his eye, and a smile on his face, he handed it to me saying, "Save some for your sisters."

I was so choked up I couldn't say anything. I took it and flew out the door, calling to my dogs.

On my way home I didn't walk on the ground. I was way up in the clouds just skiping along. With a song, I told the sycamore trees and the popeyed gray squirrels how happy I was.

Little Ann sensed my happiness. She pranced along on the trail. With a doggish grin on her face, she begged for a piece of candy, which I so gladly gave.

Even Old Dan felt the pleasant atmosphere. His long red tail fanned the air. Once he raised his head and bawled. I stood still and listened to the droning tones of his deep voice. The sound seemed to be trapped for an instant in the thick timber. It rolled around under the tall white sycamores, beat its way through the wild cane, and found freedom out over the clear blue waters of the

Literary element: Setting

The setting usually provides more than a backdrop for the action. The description of the setting can evoke a mood, it can introduce a particular culture or people, and it can bring the action to life.

Sometimes the words used to describe the setting in the novel also help to create a **mood** or an **atmosphere.** The mood or atmosphere is the feeling created in part by the description.

For example, two sentences in the descriptive passage on pages 718–719, reinforce Billy's feelings of expectancy and happiness: "The silence seemed strained and expectant, like a young boy waiting for a firecracker to explode" (p. 718) and "All around me the happy atmosphere resumed its natural state" (p. 719).

On the other hand, the words used to describe the setting at the end of the hunt for the ghost coon on page 706 create an atmosphere of mystery and foreboding. The tree "stood by itself in an old field," near "the remains of a barbed wire fence," and "an old gate." Indians had lived and farmed there "a long time ago." Billy "could see very little in the dark shadows."

The setting in a novel can also expose readers to a particular

river. The sound, following the river's course, rolled like the beat of a jungle drum.

As the echo died away in the distance, silence settled over the bottoms. The gray squirrels stopped their chattering. The wild birds quit their singing. I stood still. No sound could be heard. It seemed that all the creatures of the wild were holding their breath. I gazed up to the towering heights of the tall trees. No leaf was stirring. The silence seemed strained and expectant, like a young boy waiting for a firecracker to explode.

I looked at Old Dan. He was standing perfectly still, with his right front foot raised and his long ears fanned open. He seemed to be listening, and challenging any living creature to make a noise.

The silence was broken by the "Whee-e-e-e" of a red-tailed hawk. This seemed to be a signal. All around me the happy atmosphere resumed its natural state.

I heard the "Bam, bam, bam" of a woodpecker high in the top of a box elder snag. The cry of a kingfisher and the scream of a bluejay blended perfectly with the drumlike beat. A barking red squirrel, glued to the side of a hackberry tree, kept time to the music with the beat of his tail.

24 Each noise I heard and each sight I saw was very familiar to me but I never grew tired of listening and watching. They were a God-sent gift and I enjoyed them all.

25 As I skipped along, it was hard for me to realize all the wonderful things that had happened to me in such a few short years. I had two of the finest little hounds that ever bawled on the trail of a ringtail coon. I had a wonderful mother and father and three little sisters. I had the best grandpa a boy ever had, and to top it all, I was going on a championship coon hunt. It was no wonder that my heart was bursting with happiness. Wasn't I the luckiest boy in the world?

Everyone was just sitting down to supper when I got home. My sisters quit the table for the candy. I told them to divide it equally. The oldest one asked if I wanted any of it.

"No," I said. "I brought it all for you." Of course, I didn't tell them about the four pieces I had in my pocket.

They thanked me with their clear blue eyes.

I guess it's pretty hard for a young boy to fool his mama. She took one look at me and called me over. She ruffled up my hair, kissed me, and said, "If my little boy's eyes get any bigger they're going to pop right out of his head. Now tell me, what are you so happy about?"

Before I could say anything, Papa chuckled and asked, "What's going on between you and your grandpa? What are you and that old man cooking up now?"

As fast as I could talk I started telling about the big coon hunt. I told how hard Grandpa had been working to have my dogs entered, and how he had already paid my entry fee.

Catching my breath and looking at Papa, I said, "We're going in his buggy and he wants you to go."

I waited in silence for his reply. Papa sat there staring off into space, sipping his coffee and saying nothing. I knew he was thinking.

In the silence I was sure I could hear my heart thumping.

I said, "Papa, please go. We'll have a lot of fun and besides the winner receives a big golden cup."

He scratched his head and said, "Billy, I'd sure like to go, but I don't see how I can with all this work around here."

I was beginning to think that Papa wasn't going to go. Then Mama started talking.

"Work?" she said. "Why, all the work is practically done. I don't know of one thing you couldn't put off for a few days. Why don't

24 **Literary Focus** The description of Billy's surroundings in these paragraphs is vivid and creates a specific mood. Ask students if they can visualize in their minds the area that Billy is walking through. What mood do they feel? What elements of the description do they particularly admire?

25 **Reading Strategy** You might want to have students supply events that support each of these statements. Do they agree with Billy that his hounds are among the finest, that his mother, father, and sisters are wonderful, that he has the best grandfather? Why or why not?

way of life. In *Where the Red Fern Grows,* we come to learn much about the geography, the plant life, and the animals of the Ozark Mountain region of Oklahoma. Through the description of Billy and the other characters we learn something about the people who lived in the Ozarks during the 1920's.

Finally, the realistic descriptions of the settings in this novel brings the action alive for the readers. Through these descriptions we are able to imagine everything the characters see, hear, and smell.

You might want to have students write their own descriptions of settings. You could divide the class into groups and have each group select a place to describe. The setting might be a real place, a place students have read about, or a place they create from their imaginations. Groups should begin by brainstorming for descriptive words and phrases. The words and phrases should be vivid, precise, and appeal to different senses. Then the groups should arrange their details in a logical, easy-to-follow order. When groups are ready to write their settings, have them focus on presenting one main impression.

you go? You haven't been anywhere since I don't know when."

"It's not only the work I'm thinking of," Papa said, "It's you and the girls."

"Why, don't worry about the girls and me," Mama said. "We'll be all right. Besides, it'll be several months yet before I need any help."

When Mama said this, it dawned on me. I had been so busy with my coon hunting I hadn't noticed anything unusual. Mama's tummy was all swelled up. She was going to have a baby. I felt guilty for not having noticed. I went over and put my arms around her and kissed her.

Papa spoke up. "It's sure going to be a big hunt," he said. "I heard something about it up at the store one day."

"Grandpa said there would be hunters there from everywhere," I said, "and some of the best coon hounds in the country."

"Do you think you have a chance to win the cup?" Papa asked.

I started to answer him when the little one piped up. "They can't beat Old Dan and Little Ann," she said. "I just bet they can't."

Everyone laughed at her serious remark. I would have kissed her but she had candy, corn bread, and molasses all over her face.

I told Papa I didn't know how good those dogs were, but there was one thing I did know. If they beat mine, they would have to hunt harder than they ever had before.

After I had had my say about the dogs, a silence settled over the dining room. Everyone was looking at Papa and waiting for his answer.

I saw a pleased smile spread over his face. He stood up. "All right, I'll go," he said, "and, by golly, we'll bring that gold cup back, too."

My sisters started clapping their hands and squealing with delight. A satisfied smile spread over my mother's face.

At that moment I'm sure no boy in the world could have been happier than I. Tears of happiness rolled down my cheeks. Mama wiped them away with her apron.

In the midst of all the excitement, my little sister, saying not a word, climbed down from her chair. No one said anything. We just watched her.

Still clutching a spoon in her small hand, she came around the table and walked up to me. Looking down at the floor, in a bashful voice, she asked. "Can I have the gold cup?"

Putting my finger under her sticky little chin, I tilted her head up. I smiled as I looked into her clear blue eyes. I said, "Honey, if I win it, I'll give it to no one but you."

I had to cross my heart and hope to die several times before she was satisfied.

Back in her chair she gloated over the others. "You just wait and see," she said. "It'll be all mine, nobody's but mine, and I'll put my banty eggs in it."

"Silly, you don't put banty eggs in a gold cup," the oldest one said. "They're just made to look at."

That night I dreamed about gold cups, little red hounds, and coons as big as rain barrels. Once I woke myself up whooping to my dogs.

The next few days were busy ones for me. Knowing that Papa and I would be gone for several days, I did everything I could to make things convenient for Mama. I chopped a large pile of wood and stacked it close to the kitchen door. To make it easy for her to feed our stock, I cut some poles from the hillside and boxed up one of the stalls in the barn. I filled it full of hay so she wouldn't have to climb the ladder to the loft.

Papa laid down the law to my sisters about being good and helping Mama while we were gone.

The day before we were to leave, I was as nervous as a June bug in a henhouse. The

Commentary: Hawks

When Billy explains to his father that Little Ann is gun shy (p. 721), he mentions that "Grandpa shot a chicken hawk." The chicken hawk he refers to was probably one of the seventeen kinds of hawks that live in various parts of North America. They have been called chicken hawks because they occasionally raid poultry farms. As Billy's comment reveals, many people, especially at the time this story is set, believed that all hawks should be shot on sight because they occasionally feed on the livestock of farmers. In fact, these birds of prey are beneficial to the balance of nature.

There are two main groups of hawks that inhabit our continent, *bird hawks* and *buzzard hawks*. Bird hawks have slender bodies and long wings. They feed primarily on other birds and mice. Types of bird hawks include the now rare goshawk, the sharp-shinned hawk, and Cooper's hawk. Buzzard hawks have larger, heavier bodies than bird hawks. They have broad wings and wide, rounded tails. They feed on lizards, snakes, frogs, and rodents. The red-tailed and red-shouldered hawks are among the more common species of buzzard hawks.

The flight of hawks is quite beautiful. They soar in wide

day seemed endless. A few of the miserable hours were spent talking to my dogs. I told them all about the big hunt and how important it was.

"Now if you don't win the golden cup," I said, "I won't be mad because I know you will do your best."

Old Dan wouldn't even look at me, and paid no attention to what I said. He was sulking because I hadn't been taking him hunting. When I talked to Little Ann, it was different. She listened and seemed to understand everything I said.

I dreaded to go to bed that night. I thought sleep would be impossible. I must have been more tired than I thought I was. I fell asleep almost immediately. Old Red, our rooster, woke me at daybreak, crowing his fool head off.

It was a beautiful morning, clear and frosty.

After a good breakfast, we kissed Mama good-bye and started for the store.

I'm sure there were a lot of coon hunters in the Ozarks, but on that morning none could have felt as big and important as I. Walking along by the side of my father, I threw out my chest and tried hard to keep pace with his long strides. He noticed and laughed.

"You'll have to grow a little bit," he said, "before you can take steps that long."

I didn't say anything, I just smiled.

Hearing a noise overhead, I looked up. The gray ones were winging their way southward. I listened to their talking and wondered what they were saying.

Looking to the mountains around us, I saw that the mysterious artist who comes at night had paid us a visit. I wondered how he could paint so many different colors in one night: red, wine, yellow, and rust.

My dogs were trotting along in front of us. I smiled at the way their hind quarters shifted to the right. Little Ann would jump and bounce and try to get Old Dan to play, but the solemn old boy just jogged along, heedless of everything.

"You know," Papa said, "she doesn't even act like a hound. She is bouncing and playing all the time. Why, she acts more like a little pup than a hound."

"Yes, I know," I said. "I've noticed that myself, but you know one thing, Papa, she's the smartest dog I've ever seen. Why, some of the things she does are almost unbelievable."

"Yes, I know," said Papa, "but still it's strange, very strange."

"There's only one thing wrong with her, Papa," I said.

"Yes, what's that?" he asked.

"You won't believe it," I said, "but she's gun-shy."

"Gun-shy? How do you know she's gun-shy?" Papa asked.

"I didn't know for a long time," I said, "until one day when I was hoeing corn down in the field by the old slough. She and Old Dan were digging in a bank after a ground hog. Across the river some fishermen started shooting a gun. It scared Little Ann, and she came running to me, shaking all over."

"Aw," Papa said, "maybe you just thought she was scared."

"No, I didn't, Papa," I said. "It happened again up at the store one day. Grandpa shot a chicken hawk. When the gun went off, it scared her half to death. No, she's gun-shy all right."

"Aw, well," Papa said, "that doesn't mean anything. A lot of dogs are afraid of guns."

"I know," I said, "but you wouldn't think she would be that way. I believe if I had a gun of my own I could break her of being gun-shy."

Papa looked at me. He said, "From what your mother says, you won't be getting a gun for some time yet."

"Yes, I know," I said.

Where the Red Fern Grows 721

26

26 **Discussion** In what ways has Billy grown up since the beginning of the story? Why is it important for young people to be thought of as adults?

circles high above the earth with their wings outstretched. Their flight conveys a feeling of grace and economy of motion. More important than their beauty is the hawk's role in keeping nature in balance. When you see a hawk soaring gracefully above the earth, it is probably watching a meadow or other clearing for field mice or rats. Their predation on these species is important to keep the populations of such creatures in check. For these reasons, it is important to protect the hawk and promote its survival. Fortunately, there are laws in the United States that protect these birds from being hunted.

When we reached the store we saw the team was already hitched to the buggy and was standing in front of the store. Grandpa had loaded the tent and several boxes of groceries.

27 I had never seen him in such high spirits. He slapped Papa on the back, saying, "I'm sure glad you could go with us. It'll do you good to get out once in a while."

Papa laughed and said, "It looked like I had to go or have everyone in the family mad at me."

Looking in the buggy I saw my ax. I didn't think I ever wanted to see it again, but for some reason it didn't look like I thought it would. There was no blood on it and it looked harmless enough laying there all clean and bright.

Grandpa saw me looking at it. He came over.

"I kept it a few days," he said, "just in case the marshal wanted to ask some questions. Everything seems to be all right now, and we may need a good ax on this hunt."

Grandpa sensed how I felt about the ax. He waited in silence for my answer.

The excitement of the hunt was so strong in me, even the sight of the ax brought back only a fleeting remembrance of Rubin's accident.

I said, "Yes, we will need one. Besides, it's a good one and there's no use in throwing it away."

Grandpa laughed, reached over, and screwed my cap around on my head, saying, "That's the boy, that's what I wanted you to say. Now, you better go to the barn and get some hay and make a bed in the buggy box for your dogs."

"Aw, Grandpa," I said, "they can walk. They don't ever get tired; besides, they're used to walking."

"Walk!" Grandpa almost shouted. "They're not going to walk. No, sir, not if I can help it. You want them to be footsore when we get there?"

Papa chuckled and said, "We can't win a gold cup with two sore-footed hounds, can we?"

"Of course not," Grandpa said. "Now, you go and get that hay like I said."

As I turned to go to the barn I couldn't help but smile. It made me feel good to have my papa and grandpa so concerned about my dogs.

I had taken only a few steps when Grandpa said, "Oh, wait a minute."

I stopped and turned around.

Walking up to me and glancing toward the house as he did, he whispered, "In that empty kraut barrel in the harness room, there's a jug of corn liquor. Cover it up in the hay so your grandma won't see it and bring it back with you."

With a twinkle in his eye, he said, "You never can tell when we'll need some medicine."

I knew my father wouldn't drink any of the liquor, but if Grandpa wanted to take along a whole barrel, it was all right with me.

Just when I thought we were ready to leave, Grandma came bustling out.

Grandpa got nervous. He whispered and asked, "Did you hide the jug good?"

I nodded my head.

Grandma handed Grandpa a pair of long-handle underwear and a scarf, saying, "I knew you'd forget something."

Grandpa snorted but knew there was no use arguing with her.

She started picking around in the groceries, asking about salt, pepper, and matches.

"Nannie, we've got everything," he said. "You must think I'm a baby and don't know how to pack a grub box."

"A baby," Grandma snorted. "Why, you're worse than a baby. At least they have

Grammar in Action

Prepositions—such as *inside, around, of, in,* and *beyond*—are words that shows the relationship between nouns or noun phrases and other words in a sentence. Together a preposition and its noun phrase are called a **prepositional phrase.** Wilson Rawls uses prepositional phrases throughout *Where the Red Fern Grows* to add detail and depth to his sentences. Often, more than one prepositional phrase occurs in one sentence.

He waited *in silence for my answer.*
Over a dim and rocky road, in a northeasterly direction, our buggy moved on.
One *of the girls* threw two cold biscuits out *in the back yard to Old Dan.*

Prepositional phrases serve as either adjectives or adverbs in sentences. Because they are modifiers, the sentences are still complete sentences without them. Read the above sentences aloud without the prepositional phrases to appreciate the detail and texture that they add.

a little sense. You don't have any at all. An old codger like you out chasing a coon all over the hills."

At her biting remark, I thought Grandpa was going to blow up. He snorted like Daisy, our milk cow, when she had seen a booger.

I crawled up in the buggy box with my dogs and hung my feet out.

Grandma came over and asked me about warm clothes. I told her I had plenty.

She kissed me good-bye and we were on our way.

Chapter 15

Over a dim rocky road, in a northeasterly direction, our buggy moved on.

I noticed that the road stayed at the edge of the foothills, but always in sight of the river.

About the middle of the afternoon we stopped at a small stream to water the team. Papa asked Grandpa if he intended to go all the way to the campground before stopping.

"No," he said, "I figure to put up for the night when we reach Bluebird Creek. With a good early start in the morning we can make the campgrounds in plenty of time to pitch our tent and set up camp."

Late that evening we reached Bluebird Creek. We didn't set up our tent. With a tarp we made a lean-to and built a large fire out in front of it.

While Grandpa fed and watered the team, Papa and I carried our bedding to the shelter and made down our beds.

Grandpa said, "While we're cooking supper, you see to your dogs. Feed them and fix them a warm bed."

"I figure to cook them some corn-meal mush," I said. "That's what they're used to eating."

"Mush!" Grandpa growled. "They're not going to have mush, not if I can help it."

He walked over to a grocery box, mumbling as he did, "Mush! A hound can't hunt on a bellyful of that stuff."

He came back and handed me two large cans of corned-beef hash, saying, "Here. Reckon they'll eat this."

I wanted to hug my old grandpa's neck. "Sure, Grandpa," I said, "They'll love that."

Opening one of the cans, I dumped it out on a piece of bark in front of Old Dan. He sniffed at it and refused to eat. I laughed, for I knew why. While I was opening the other can, Grandpa came over.

"What's the matter," he asked. "Won't he eat it?"

"Sure, Grandpa," I said, "he'll eat, but not before Little Ann gets her share."

With the second can opened, I fed her on another piece of bark. Both of them started eating at the same time.

With an astonished look on his face, Grandpa exclaimed, "Well, I'll be darned. I never saw anything like that. Why, I never saw a hound that wouldn't eat. Did you train them to do that?"

"No, Grandpa," I said. "They've always been that way. They won't take anything away from each other, and everything they do, they do it as one."

Papa had overheard our conversation. He said, "You think that's strange. You should have seen what I saw one day.

"One of the girls threw two cold biscuits out in the back yard to Old Dan. He stood and looked at them for a bit, then, picking both of them up in his mouth, he trotted around the house. I followed just to see what he was going to do. He walked up in front of the doghouse, laid them down, and growled; not like he was mad. It was a strange kind of a growl. Little Ann came out of the doghouse and each of them ate a biscuit. Now, I saw this with my own eyes. Believe me, those dogs are close to each other—real close."

Where the Red Fern Grows 723

28 **Literary Focus** You could point out to students that the setting of rural Oklahoma during the 1920's is reflected in the mode of transportation and the necessity of camping out during their journey to the coon hunt. How would this journey be different if the story was set in the 1980's?

29 **Discussion** Do you think this is realistic behavior for dogs? What other unusual characteristics have the dogs exhibited?

Student Activity 1. With a partner, list all of the prepositions you can think of. Many of them show location. You may want to use *Where the Red Fern Grows* as a source.

Student Activity 2. Find five examples of sentences in the novel that contain more than one prepositional phrase. What words in the sentences do the phrases describe?

Student Activity 3. Write three original sentences about *Where the Red Fern Grows* using at least two prepositional phrases in each. Underline the prepositional phrases and draw an arrow to the words they describe.

After Papa had stopped talking, silence settled over the camp.

Grandpa stood staring at my dogs. In a slow voice, as if he were picking his words, he said, "You know, I've always felt like there was something strange about those dogs. I don't know just what it is, and I can't exactly put my finger on it, yet I can feel it. Maybe it's just my imagination. I don't rightly know."

Turning to my father, he said, "Did you ever notice the way they watch this boy? They see every move he makes."

Papa said, "Yes, I've noticed a lot of things they have done. In fact, I could tell you of a few that you would never believe, but right now here's something you had better believe. Supper is ready."

While I was helping myself to hot dutch-oven corn bread, fried potatoes, and fresh side meat, Grandpa poured the coffee. Instead of the two cups I expected to see, he set out three and filled them to the brim with the strong black liquid.

I had never been allowed to drink coffee at home and didn't exactly know what to do. I glanced at Papa. He seemed too busy with his eating to pay any attention to me. Taking the bull by the horns, I reached over and ran my finger through the cup's handle. I held my breath as I walked over and sat down by a post oak stump. Nothing was said. Grandpa and Papa paid no attention to what I did. My head swelled up as big as a number-four washtub. I thought, "I'm not only big enough to help Papa with the farm. Now I'm big enough to drink coffee."

With supper over and the dishes washed, Grandpa said, "Well, we had better turn in as I want to get an early start in the morning."

Long after Grandpa and Papa had fallen asleep, I lay thinking of the big hunt. My thoughts were interrupted when the wonders of night life began to stir in the silence around us.

From a ridge on our right a red fox started barking. He was curious and, in his small way, challenging the intruders that had dared to stop in his wild domain. From far back in the flinty hills, the monotonous calls of a hoot owl floated down in the silent night. It was the mating call and was answered from a distant mountain.

I could hear the stamping feet of our horses, and the grinding, crunching noise made by their strong teeth as they ate the hard, yellow kernels of corn in their feed boxes. A night hawk screamed as he winged his way through the starlit night. An eerie screech from a tree close by made shivers run up and down my spine. It was a screech owl.

I didn't like to hear the small owl, for there was a superstition in the mountains concerning them. It was said that if you heard one owl it meant nothing at all, but if you heard more than one, it meant bad luck.

I lay and listened to the eerie twittering sound. It was coming from the left of our camp. The creepy noise stopped, and for several moments there was silence. When next I heard the cry, it was coming from the right. I sat up in alarm. Had I heard two owls?

My movement had awakened Grandpa. In a sleepy voice, he asked, "What's the matter? Can't you sleep? What are you sitting up like that for?"

"Grandpa, I heard two screech owls," I said.

Grunting and mumbling, he sat up. Rubbing the sleep from his eyes, he said, "You heard two screech owls. Why, that's nothing. I've heard two—oh, I see. You're thinking of the bad-luck superstition. There's nothing to that; nothing at all. Now you lie down and go to sleep. Tomorrow is going to be a big day."

724　*The Novel*

I tried hard to fall asleep, but couldn't. I couldn't get the owls out of my mind. Had I really heard two? Were we going to have bad luck? Surely nothing bad could happen. Not on such a wonderful hunt.

I found peace in my mind by telling myself that the owl had changed trees. Yes, that was it. He had simply flown out of one tree to another.

The next morning, while having breakfast, Grandpa started kidding me about the screech owls.

"I wish you could have caught one of those owls last night," he said. "We could have boiled him in our coffee pot. I've heard there is nothing like strong hoot-owl coffee."

"It wasn't a hoot owl, Grandpa," I said. "It was a screech owl. I don't know for sure if I heard one or two. It could have been just one." Pointing to a small red oak, I said, "I think the first time I heard him, he was over there. The next time, it was over in that direction. Maybe he changed trees. I sure hope so."

Grandpa saw I was bothered. "You don't believe that hogwash superstition, do you? Bad luck! Baw, there's nothing to it."

Papa laughed, and said, "These mountains are full of that jinx stuff. If a man believed it all, he'd go crazy."

The encouraging words from Papa and Grandpa helped some, but there was still some doubt. It's hard for a young boy to completely forget things like that.

Breakfast over, and our gear stowed back in the buggy, we left Bluebird Creek.

On that day Grandpa drove a little faster than he had on the previous one. I was glad of this, for I was anxious to reach the campground.

About noon he stopped the team. I heard him ask Papa, "Is this Black Fox Hollow?"

"No," Papa said. "This is Waterfall. Black Fox is the next one over. Why?"

"Well," Grandpa said, "there's supposed to be a white flag in the mouth of Black Fox. That's where we leave the road. The camp is in the river bottoms."

By this time I was so excited, I stood up in the buggy box so I could get a better view.

"Maybe you ought to step them up a little, Grandpa," I said. "It's getting pretty late."

Papa joined in with his loud laughter. "You just take it easy," he said. "We'll get there in plenty of time. Besides, these mares can't fly."

I saw the flag first. "There it is, Grandpa," I shouted.

"Where?" he asked.

"Over there. See, tied on that grapevine."

As we left the main road, I heard Papa say, "Boy, look at all those tracks. Sure has been a lot of traveling on this road."

"That smoke over there must be coming from the camps," Grandpa said.

When we came in sight of the camp, I couldn't believe what I saw. I stared in amazement. I had never seen so many people at one gathering. Tents were spread out over an acre and a half of ground; all colors, shapes, and sizes. There were odd-looking cars, buggies, wagons, and saddle horses.

I heard Grandpa say almost in a whisper, "I knew there would be a lot of people here but I never expected so many."

I saw the astonished look on my father's face.

Off to one side of the camp, under a large black gum tree, we set up our tent. I tied my dogs to the buggy, and fixed a nice bed for them under it. After everything was taken care of, I asked if I could look around the camp.

"Sure," Grandpa said. "Go any place you want to go, only don't get in anyone's way."

I started walking through the large camp. Everyone was friendly. Once I heard a

31 **Discussion** What are superstitions? Why are some people more superstitious than others? Do you think all people are superstitious to some degree?

32 **Reading Strategy** Billy is comparing the appearance of his dogs with others at the campsite. Based on previous incidents involving Billy and his dogs, you could have students question whether the dogs' appearance will affect their performance during the coon hunt.

voice say, "That's the boy who owns the two little red hounds. I've heard they're pretty good."

If my head had gotten any bigger, I know it would have burst.

I walked on, as straight as a canebrake cane.

I looked at the hounds. They were tied in pairs here and there. I had seen many coon hounds but none that could equal these. There were redbones, blue ticks, walkers, and bloodhounds. I marveled at their beauty. All were spotlessly clean with slick and glossy coats. I saw the beautiful leather leashes and brass-studded collars.

32 I thought of my dogs. They were tied with small cotton ropes, and had collars made from old checkline leather.

As I passed from one set of dogs to another, I couldn't help but wonder if I had a chance to win. I knew that in the veins of these hounds flowed the purest of breeded blood. No finer coon hounds could be found anywhere. They came from the Smoky Mountains of Tennessee, the bayou country of Louisiana, the Red River bottoms of Texas, and the flinty hills of the Ozarks.

Walking back through the camp, I could feel the cold fingers of doubt squeezing my heart. One look at my dogs drove all doubt away. In the eyes of Little Ann it seemed I could read this message: "Don't worry. Just wait. We'll show them."

That night, Grandpa said, "Tomorrow they'll have a contest for the best-looking hound. Which one are you going to enter?"

I told him I didn't think I'd enter either one of my dogs. They were so little. I didn't think they had a chance.

Grandpa got all huffed up. He said, "It

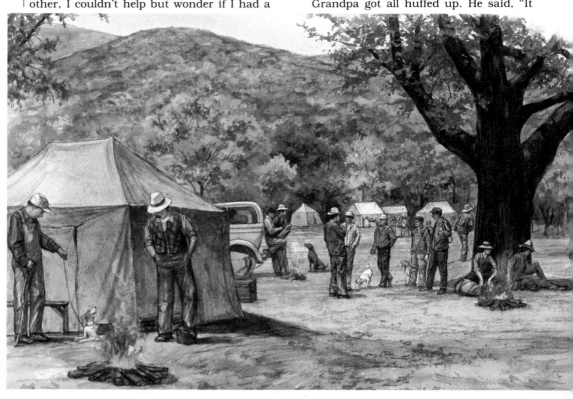

Grammar in Action

Many people have trouble with certain verbs, using incorrect principal parts or confusing two verbs with similar meanings. Two troublesome verbs are *lay* and *lie,* which are often confused because they are similar in appearance, sound, and meaning. Notice how the character Billy confuses these two verbs in the following sentence:

Shaking my finger at her, I said, "If you *lay* down and roll, I'll wear you out," although I knew I wouldn't.

Like Billy, many people confuse these two verbs. The verb *lay* means "to put down, or place." Billy should have used the verb *lie,* which means "to rest in a reclining position." The easiest way to avoid confusing the two verbs is to memorize their meanings and their principal parts. The principal parts of the two verbs are as follows:

Present	Present Participle	Past	Past Participle
lay	(am) laying	laid	(have) laid
lie	(am) laying	lay	(have) lain

Student Activity 1. Decide whether the forms of the verbs *lay* and *lie* are used correctly in the following sentences.

doesn't make any difference how little they are. They're coon hounds, aren't they?"

I asked him if he had seen any of the other hounds.

He said, "Yes, I've seen them all. Sure they're big and good dogs, too, but it makes no difference. I don't care if your dogs are no bigger than a snuff can. They still have a chance. Now, which one are you going to enter?"

I couldn't decide. I said, "I'll think it over tonight and let you know tomorrow."

The next morning when I stepped outside the tent I saw the men everywhere. They were combing and brushing their dogs, and getting them pruned for the beauty contest. Beautiful combs and brushes were used to brush expensive oils into their glossy hair.

Going over to my dogs, I stood and looked at them. I started to untie Old Dan but, taking a closer look at him, I could see he could never win a beauty contest. His face and ears were a mass of old scars, caused

from the many fights with tough old coons and bobcats. I held his head in my hands and felt sorry for him, but loved him that much more.

I looked Little Ann over and couldn't see any scars. I laughed because I knew why. She was too smart to walk right up in the face of a fight. She would wait until Old Dan took hold and then dart in.

I untied her rope and walked her over to our tent.

My father and grandfather were gone. No doubt they were in some tent visiting old friends and making new ones.

Looking around to find something I could use to groom my dog, I saw Grandpa's open suitcase. There, right on top, was the very thing I needed, his beautiful bone-handled hairbrush and his ivory comb. Picking them up, I turned them over and over in my hand.

Little Ann stood looking at me. Impulsively I reached down and raked her from shoulder to hip with the brush. She seemed to like it. I knew I shouldn't do it, but I decided to use them.

Knowing I had no oils, I got some butter from our grocery box. With the homemade butter and Grandpa's hair set, I brushed her until she shone. All the time I was grooming her, she tried to lick the butter from my hands.

The job completed, I stepped back and inspected her. I was surprised at the change. Her short red hair glistened and every one was in perfect place.

Shaking my finger at her, I said, "If you lay down and roll, I'll wear you out," although I knew I wouldn't.

Hearing a lot of movement outside, I looked out. Men were setting their dogs on a long table which had been built in the center of the campground. Leading Little Ann to it, I picked her up and set her on the table, too.

I told her to act like a lady. She wagged

33

33 Discussion Do you think using Grandpa's brush is all right? What does this action reveal about Billy's maturing process?

Where the Red Fern Grows   727

1. The workmen will come and *lie* the new carpet this afternoon.

2. The rotten tomatoes had *lain* in the refrigerator all weekend.

3. She made sure that she carefully *laid* the glass bowl on the table.

4. *Lying* his cards on the table, the gambler started to smile.

5. Johnny has decided to *lay* down and take a rest.

Student Activity 2. Fill in the blanks of the following sentences with the correct principal part of either *lie* or *lay*.

1. The two dogs were _____ side by side in the grass.

2. We always _____ a towel on the sand when we go to the beach.

3. He has _____ asleep for the past twenty minutes.

4. After we came home yesterday, I _____ down for a nap.

5. Fred got into trouble when he _____ his dirty clothes on mom's best table cloth.

her tail as though she understood. I untied the rope and stepped back.

After the dogs were all lined up, the judging started. Four judges walked around and around the table, looking at them from all angles. When one of them would point at a hound, he was taken down and eliminated from the contest. Dog after dog was disqualified. Little Ann was still on the table.

My eyes were wide, my throat dry, and my heart thumping. One judge stopped in front of Little Ann. My heart stopped, too. Reaching over, he patted her on the head.

Turning to me, he asked, "Is this your dog?"

I couldn't speak. I just nodded my head.

He said, "She's a beautiful hound."

He walked on down the line. My heart started beating again.

There were eight dogs left. Little Ann was still holding her own. Then there were four. I was ready to cry. Two more were taken down. Little Ann and a big walker hound owned by a Mr. Kyle were the only ones left. The judges couldn't seem to make up their minds.

Everyone started shouting, "Walk them! Walk them!"

I didn't know what they meant.

Mr. Kyle and I were told to go to one end of the table. Our dogs were placed at the other end. Mr. Kyle snapped his fingers and called to his dog.

The big hound started walking toward his master. What a beautiful sight it was. He walked like a king. His body was stiff and straight, his head high in the air, his large muscles quivered and jerked under his glossy coat, but something went wrong. Just before he reached the end, he broke his stride, turned, and jumped down from the table.

A low murmur ran through the crowd.

It was my turn. Three times I tried to call to Little Ann. Words just wouldn't come out. My throat was too dry. The vocal cords refused to work, but I could snap my fingers. That was all I needed. She started toward me. I held my breath. There was silence all around me.

As graceful as any queen, with her head high in the air, and her long red tail arched in a perfect rainbow, my little dog walked down the table. With her warm gray eyes staring straight at me, on she came. Walking up to me, she laid her head on my shoulder. As I put my arms around her, the crowd exploded.

During the commotion I felt hands slapping me on the back, and heard the word "congratulations" time after time. The head judge came over and made a speech. Handing me a small silver cup, he said, "Congratulations, son. It was justly won."

The tears came rolling. I gathered my dog up in my arms and walked to our tent. Grandpa followed, proudly carrying the cup.

That evening the head judge stepped up on the table. He had a small box in his hand. He shouted, "Over here, men! I have some announcements to make."

We all gathered around.

In a loud voice, he said, "Gentlemen, the contest will start tonight. I'm sure most of you men have been in these hunts before. For those of you who haven't, I will explain the rules. Each night five sets of dogs will be taken out to hunt. A judge will go along with each pair of hounds. Every morning, the judges will turn in that night's catch. The two hounds that tree the most coons will qualify for the championship runoff. The other four sets will be eliminated from the hunt. Of course, if there is a tie, both sets will qualify. On the following nights, only those hounds tying the first night's score, or getting more, will be in the runoff.

"Now, gentlemen, this hunt must be carried out in a sportsmanlike way. If the coon is treed where he can't be caught, such as in a bluff, it will not be counted. You must catch the coon, skin it, and turn the hide over to your judge.

"You are allowed to take an ax, a lantern, and a gun with bird shot, which you can use to get a coon out of a tree.

"Twenty-five sets of hounds have been entered in the hunt. In this box, I have twenty-five cards. Everyone in the contest will now line up for the drawing. The card you draw will tell you what night your hounds are to hunt."

Walking along in the line, I noticed the beautiful red coats, the caps, and the soft leather boots worn by the other hunters. I felt out of place in my faded blue overalls, old sheepskin coat, and scuffed and worn shoes, but to the wonderful men it made no difference. They treated me like a man, and even talked to me like a man.

When it came my time to draw, my hand was shaking so hard I could hardly get it in the box. Pulling the card out, I saw I had drawn the fourth night.

After the hunters had left, we stood around our campfires sipping strong black coffee and listening to the baying of the hounds. Time after time, we heard the tree bark.

Once two hounds came close to the camp, hot on a trail. We listened to their steady bawling. All at once they stopped.

After several minutes of waiting, a hunter said, "You know what? That old coon took to the river and in some way has fooled those dogs."

Another one said, "Yes, sir, he sure has."

A friendly hunter looked at me and asked, "Do you think he could have fooled your dogs?"

Thinking his question over, I said, "You know, sometimes when I am hunting, away

back in the mountains or down on the river, I sing a little song I made up myself. One of the verses goes like this:

> *You can swim the river, Old Mister Ringtail,*
> *And play your tricks out one by one.*
> *It won't do any good, Old Mister Ringtail,*
> *My Little Ann knows every one.*

The hunters roared with laughter. Some slapped me on the back.

Tired and sleepy, but with a smile on my face, I went off to bed.

The next morning two blue tick hounds, from the Smoky Mountains of Tennessee, came out in the lead with three big coons to their credit. The other four sets were eliminated.

The following morning all five sets of dogs were eliminated. None had even tied the blue ticks, although two sets had gotten two coons, and one of these had treed a third one in a bluff.

That day, while eating dinner, my grandfather asked me if my dogs had ever treed three coons in one night.

I said, "Yes, four different times, but that's all."

"Where do you think we should hunt on our night?" Papa asked.

I told him if we could get our judge to go with us in the buggy, we would be better off if we could go far downriver and get out of the range where other dogs had hunted.

He said, "That's a good idea. I'll go to see the judges about it."

While I was washing the dishes, Grandpa said, "I think I'll shave."

I should've left the tent then, but I wasn't done with my dish-washing.

With a pin, Grandpa hung a small mirror on the tent wall. After much snorting, mum-

Where the Red Fern Grows 729

34 Discussion Why do these men treat Billy as an equal? In what way are they different from the people in Tahlequah?

35 Discussion Why is Billy in charge of deciding where the group will hunt?

Enrichment The types of dogs that Billy refers to (blue tick, black and tan) are different breeds of dogs from the hound group. The dogs used for hunting raccoons are called scent hounds because they hunt by scent. A dog's sense of smell is its most highly developed sense, enabling it to detect some odors that are a million times too faint for people to detect. Dogs recognize objects primarily by smell as people recognize them by sight. Scientists believe that dogs were the first animals domesticated by humans and that our first associations with dogs began more than 12,000 years ago.

Reader's Response If you were Billy, what would you be thinking and feeling as you first entered the camp of the Championship Coon Hunt?

Closure and Extension

ANSWERS TO THINKING ABOUT THE SELECTION
Recalling

1. Rubin and Rainie are dirty and mean looking and are disliked by just about everyone. They always seem to be looking for trouble.
2. Grandfather calls Rainie's bet because he is annoyed by the two boys' rude behavior. They insulted him as well as Billy and ridiculed Billy's dogs. He also has faith in Billy's dogs.
3. Billy decides that he is not going to kill the ghost coon after he finally corners it in the tree.
4. The hunt for the ghost coon ends when Billy's dogs get into a fight with the Pritchards' dog. Rubin, who is going to try and kill Billy's dogs, trips and falls on the axe he is carrying.
5. Grandfather's reasons for arranging the trip to the Championship Coon Hunt include the fact that he always dreamed of being in such a hunt and he finally has the opportunity. He thinks that Dan and Ann are two of the best coon hounds in the country. He also wants to put Rubin's death

730

---

bling, and screwing of his face this way and that, the job was completed. Dabbing a little water on his iron-gray hair, he reached for his brush and comb.

From the corner of my eye I watched him. I had tried to clean the beautiful brush but hadn't been able to get all the short red hair from it.

With two fingers, Grandpa pulled some of the hair from the bristles. Holding it in front of him, he looked it over carefully. Then, bending over close to the mirror, peeking over his glasses, he inspected his head. Straightening up, he looked at the brush again. Turning around quickly, he looked straight at me and said, "Say, young—"

Not waiting for anything more, I scooted for the door. Crawling under the buggy, I lay down between my dogs. I knew he wouldn't be mad at me, but it would be best to stay away for a while.

The third night, the blue ticks were tied by two black and tan hounds from the bayou country of Louisiana.

All that day I was restless. I prowled through the camp. Every little while I would go and see how Old Dan and Little Ann were. Once I took two weenies from our groceries. I heated them and gave them to my dogs for a treat. Old Dan swallowed his down in one gulp, and looked at me as if to say, "Is that all?" Little Ann ate hers in a ladylike way. I could have sworn I saw a small grin on her face.

Grandpa was hopping around like a grasshopper, going here and there. Once, passing a tent, I heard his voice. I knew he was bragging about my dogs. I smiled to myself.

Another hunter stopped me and asked, "Is it true that your hounds have treed six coons in one night, three up in one tree, or is that old man just blowing off steam?"

I told him my grandfather had a little steam, but he was the best grandpa a boy ever had.

He patted me on the head, turned, and walked away laughing.

THINKING ABOUT THE SELECTION
Recalling

1. Describe the Pritchard boys.
2. Why does Grandfather call Rainie's bet?
3. What happens when Billy finally corners the ghost coon in the tree?
4. How does the hunt for the ghost coon end?
5. What are Grandfather's reasons for arranging the trip for Billy, Papa and himself to the Championship Coon Hunt?

Interpreting

6. Compare and contrast Billy and the Pritchards.

730 *The Novel*

7. Why do Billy and the Pritchards want to catch the ghost coon so badly?
8. What are Billy's feelings after the death of Rubin? How do you think he will change as a result of Rubin's death?
9. Why is it important to Billy that he is treated as an equal by the men at the Championship Coon Hunt? Do you think he deserves to be treated this way? Why or why not?

Applying

10. Throughout the novel, Billy has experiences that contribute to his maturing. Discuss some of Billy's responsibilities and experiences and compare them to your own.

---

and its effects on Billy behind them.

Interpreting

6. Comparisons between Billy and the Pritchards should include that they dress similarly and live in the same setting, that they share an interest in hunting for raccoons, and that they know the habits and strategies of raccoons. The contrasts include the following: In appearance Billy is clean, the Pritchards dirty. Billy's

manner is polite and he honors his part of the bet, while the Pritchards are rude and belligerent and they refuse to pay Billy after he has won the bet.
7. They want to catch the ghost coon badly because it is especially smart and resourceful. It has escaped from previous hunters enough times to earn the nickname "ghost coon."
8. Billy feels badly, has no desire to hunt, and has bad dreams following the death of Rubin. He cannot forget the incident and

would like to do something but does not know what action to take. Answers will differ. Suggested Response: Billy will be more careful about accepting challenges or bets. He will also be more careful in handling his axe.
9. It is important to Billy that he is treated as an equal because most young people want to be treated like adults. It is also important because it shows Billy that the other hunters respect him for his hunting abilities and

ANALYZING LITERATURE

Appreciating Setting in a Novel

Setting is the physical background and time period in which a novel takes place. In *Where the Red Fern Grows,* the setting has an important influence on the characters and the plot of the story.

1. Describe the features of the river bottoms as Billy sees them.
2. What aspects of the setting make coon hunting challenging?
3. How has the setting helped to shape Billy's character?

CRITICAL THINKING AND READING

Inferring the Effect of Setting

The setting in *Where the Red Fern Grows* affects other aspects of the novel. You can make inferences about its effect on the plot and the characters. For example, Billy would not have walked all the way to Tahlequah if the events took place in today's world of cars and buses.

1. How does the setting of Tahlequah make the characters living there different from Billy?
2. How do the surroundings noted on page 718 affect Billy's mood?
3. How would the events of the story differ if Billy's family lived in Tahlequah?

UNDERSTANDING LANGUAGE

Using Synonyms

Synonyms are words that have similar meanings. However, most synonyms are not exactly alike. In this novel, Wilson Rawls uses a number of synonyms to describe the dogs' cries in different situations. The dogs *whimper* and *cry* when they get confused. They *whine* in anticipation when they catch the scent of a raccoon. Big Dan *howls* in despair when Little Ann falls into the icy river.

Following are four synonyms. Use a dictionary to find their differences in meaning. Complete each sentence with the synonym that best fits the meaning of the sentence. Use each word only once.

    dark   dim   murky   gloomy

1. The cave was so _____ that he couldn't see two inches in front of his face.
2. The fog from the ocean made it difficult to see through the _____ air.
3. The _____ atmosphere of the forest gave me the creeps.
4. Obscured by the clouds, the sun was so _____ that it gave off little warmth.

THINKING AND WRITING

Writing About Setting

Imagine that you have a friend in another country who is going to visit you for the first time. Write your friend a letter describing where you live. As you plan your letter, refer to the description of your region that you wrote before reading these chapters. Keep in mind that this person is completely unfamiliar with your country. As you review your letter, be sure you have included the effect of your surroundings on your thoughts, actions, and appearance.

(Answers begin on p. 730.)

ANSWERS TO CRITICAL THINKING AND READING

1. Suggested Response: The setting of Tahlequah makes the characters different from Billy in several ways. Tahlequah has schools; the children are probably more educated and are accustomed to being around others their own age. The people are used to living among more people. They also have more goods and services available to them. The town probably is more in touch with what is happening in the rest of the country; consequently, the people there have a broader perspective.
2. The surroundings on this page create happy, content feelings in Billy. He is reminded of all of the good things in his life and feels as if he is the luckiest boy in the world.
3. Answers will differ. Suggested Response: Billy might not have hunted as much. He would have been in school much of the time. His father might have had a better-paying job, and Billy would not have had to save money himself to pay for the dogs. Billy would not have known the Pritchard boys. Billy would not have visited his grandfather's store as much.

Challenge How might the events of the story differ if Billy's family lived on the same farm, but during the 1980's instead of the 1920's?

ANSWERS TO UNDERSTANDING LANGUAGE

1. dark	3. gloomy
2. murky	4. dim

THINKING AND WRITING

Publishing Student Writing You could ask for student volunteers to change their letters into descriptive essays for publication in the school or community newspaper. If possible, have students bring in photographs depicting the area described to accompany the essays.

do not look down on him because he is so young. Billy deserves to be treated as an equal because he has proved his and the dogs' hunting skills. He has also shown that he is mature for his age.

Applying

10. Answers will differ, but some of the experiences and responsibilities that could be compared include the following: saving money to buy an important item; traveling somewhere alone; helping parents work.

ANSWERS TO ANALYZING LITERATURE

1. The river bottoms, as Billy sees them, include fields and woods with sycamore, box elder, and oak trees and stands of wild cane and bushes. The river varies in depth and has riffles to cross over and drifts of sand and branches. There are also sloughs of clear spring water near the river. The background of these sights is foothills and mountains.
2. The aspects of the setting that make coon hunting a challenge are the river, the trees (both alive and dead), the heavy underbrush, and the dark of night.
3. The setting has helped shape Billy's character because he has learned from working on the farm that hard work produces results. He has also developed a love of the outdoors and hunting.

Literary Focus It might be helpful to review the incidents in the narrative where Billy experienced different emotions in his relationship with the dogs. For example, he felt joy when he saw the dogs for the first time; he experienced fear when Little Ann was caught in the freezing river; he felt contentment when he was returning home from the store with the news of the Championship Coon Hunt. What other emotions does Billy experience in his relationship with his dogs? Relate incidents from the narrative when these other emotions were displayed. What do all of these differing emotions point out about a loving relationship?

Look For You might have **more advanced** students try to determine other general statements Rawls is making about life. Remind them that these themes are developed not only in these final chapters but throughout the novel.

Writing/Prior Knowledge You could have **more advanced** students compare the relationship they write about with the relationship Billy has with his dogs. If they have chosen Billy's relationship as their subject, you could refer them to "Luke Baldwin's Vow," on page 95, and have them compare Billy's relationship to the relationship Luke has with this dog.

Vocabulary If less advanced students have difficulty with the vocabulary, you could have them pronounce each word aloud.

GUIDE FOR READING

Where the Red Fern Grows, Chapters 16–20

Theme in a Novel

A **theme** is a general idea about life presented through the characters and their actions in a novel. In your reading to this point, you have seen a deepening relationship between Billy and his dogs. With his dogs, Billy has experienced many emotions, including joy, fear, and contentment. Billy's feelings and his relationship with his dogs point out a theme.

Look For

As you read these last chapters, take note of how the bond of love between the dogs and Billy is expressed. What general statement about life is Wilson Rawls making through Billy and his dogs?

Writing

Many people experience a relationship with their animals similar to the one Billy has with his dogs. Write about the feelings involved in a relationship you have had or have with a pet. If you do not have any experiences with animals, write about someone you know who does, or write about Billy's relationship with his dogs.

Vocabulary

Knowing the following words will help you as you read Chapters 16–20 of *Where the Red Fern Grows*.

haggard (hag′ ərd) *adj.:* Having a worn look from sleeplessness (p. 746)

predatory (pred′ə tôr′ē) *adj.:* Living by capturing and feeding on other animals (p. 753)

sinews (sin′ yōōs) *n.:* Tendons (p. 754)

berserk (bər surk′) *adj.:* Into a violent or destructive rage (p. 754)

lithe (līth) *adj.:* Flexible and supple (p. 754)

disembowel (dis′ im bou′ əl) *v.:* Take out the inner organs (p. 755)

scourge (skʉrj) *n.:* The cause of serious trouble (p. 756)

entrails (en′ trālz) *n.:* The inner organs of animals (p. 757)

Objectives

1 To identify and understand theme
2 To evaluate a novel
3 To understand derived words
4 To write a book review

Support Material

Teaching Portfolio

Teacher Backup, p. 1097
Grammar in Action Worksheets, *Identifying Transitive Verbs*, p. 1104; *Identifying Intransitive Verbs*, p. 1106; *Varying Sentence Length*, p. 1108; *Making Comparisons*, p. 1110
Usage and Mechanics Worksheet, p. 1112
Vocabulary Check, p. 1113

Critical Thinking and Reading Worksheet, *Evaluating a Novel*, p. 1114
Language Worksheet, *Using Derived Words*, p. 1115
Selection Test, p. 1116

Chapter 16

In the afternoon our judge came over and introduced himself. He told us he'd be going with us that night.

About sundown we piled in our buggy and drove a few miles downriver. I noticed other hunters doing the same thing. Everyone was trying to get away from the already-hunted territory.

It was dark by the time Grandpa stopped. I untied the ropes from my dogs. Little Ann reared up on me and whined. Old Dan walked off a few yards, stretched his body, and dragged his claws through the soft bottom soil. Opening his mouth, he let out one loud bawl, and then disappeared in the thick timber. Little Ann was right on his heels.

We took off after them.

Grandpa got nervous. He said to me, "Don't you think you ought to whoop to them?"

I told him to wait a little while. There would be plenty of time for whooping.

He snorted and said he thought a hunter always whooped to his dogs.

"I do, Grandpa," I said, "but not before they strike a trail."

We walked on. Every now and then we would stop and listen. I could hear the loud snuffing of Old Dan. Once we caught a glimpse of Little Ann as she darted across an opening that was bathed in moonlight. She was as silent as a ghost and as quick as a flitting shadow.

Papa said, "It sure is a beautiful night for hunting."

The judge said, "You can't beat these Ozark Mountain nights for beauty. I don't care where you go."

Grandpa started to say something. His voice was drowned out by the bell-like cry of Little Ann.

In a whisper, I said, "Come on, Dan. Hurry and help her."

As if in answer to my words, his deep voice hammered its way up through the river bottoms. I felt the blood tingling in my veins. That wonderful feeling that only a hunter knows crept over my body.

Looking over at Grandpa, I said, "Now you can whoop."

Jerking off his hat and throwing back his head, he let out a yell. It wasn't a whoop, or a screech, it was about halfway in between. Everyone laughed.

The coon was running upriver toward our campground. We turned and followed. I could tell by the dogs' voices that they were running side by side, and were hot on the trail. Closing my eyes, I could almost see them running, bodies stretched to their fullest length, legs pounding up and down, white steam rolling from their hot breath in the frosty night. **1**

Grandpa got tangled up in some underbrush, and lost his hat and spectacles. It took us a while to find the glasses. Papa said something about getting them wired on with baling wire. Grandpa snorted. The judge laughed.

The coon crossed the river and ran on upstream. Soon my dogs were out of hearing distance. I told Papa we had better stay on our side of the river and keep going until we could hear them again.

Twenty minutes later we heard them coming back. We stopped.

"I think they have crossed back to our side," I said.

All at once the voices of my dogs were drowned out by a loud roar.

"What in the world was that?" Grandpa said.

"I don't know," the judge said. "Reckon it was wind or thunder?"

About that time we heard it again.

Where the Red Fern Grows 733

Presentation

Motivation/Prior Knowledge
You might consider leading the class in a discussion of the feelings and thoughts people have when a loved person or animal dies. While people experience sadness and grief they often experience positive feelings as well. Pleasant memories of shared experiences and respect for things learned from those who have died help people. The passage of time also helps, as does religious faith.

Thematic Idea Another selection that deals with the theme of the bond of love that develops between people and animals is "A Secret for Two" on page 45.

Purpose-Setting Question In what ways do Billy and his dogs express their love for each other?

1 Literary Focus You could point out that Billy knows his dogs so well that he can predict what they will do and how they look. How does Billy know these things?

2 Discussion Is Grandpa's behavior during the coon hunt in keeping with his character? Why is the misfortune of someone often funny to everyone else?

3 Discussion How is this coon hunt different from the previous hunts? Do you think that being in unfamiliar territory will help or hinder the dogs?

The judge started laughing. "I know now what it is," he said. "Those hounds have run that coon right back by our camp. The noise we heard was the other hunters whooping to them."

Everyone laughed.

A few minutes later I heard my dogs bawling treed. On reaching the tree, Papa ran his hand back under his coat. He pulled out Grandpa's gun.

"That's a funny-looking gun," the judge said. "It's a 410-gauge pistol, isn't it?"

"It's the very thing for this kind of work," Papa said. "You couldn't kill a coon with it if you tried, especially if you're using bird shot. All it will do is sting his hide a little."

At the crack of the gun, the coon gave a loud squall and jumped. My dogs lost no time in killing him.

We skinned the coon, and soon were on our way again.

The next time my dogs treed, they were across the river from us. Finding a riffle, we pulled off our shoes and started across.

Grandpa very gingerly started picking his way. His tender old feet moved from one smooth rock to another. Everything was fine until we reached midstream, where the current was much swifter. He stepped on a loose round rock. It rolled and down he went.

As the cold river water touched his body, he let out a yell that could have been heard for miles. He looked so funny we couldn't keep from laughing.

Papa and the judge helped him to his feet. Laughing every step of the way, we finally reached the other side. Grandpa kept going in his wet clothes until we reached the tree where the dogs were.

After killing the coon, we built a large fire so Grandpa could dry his clothes. He'd get up as close to the fire as he could, and turn this way and that. He looked so funny standing there with his long underwear steaming. I started rolling with laughter.

734 *The Novel*

He looked over at me and snapped, "What's so funny?"

I said, "Nothing."

"Well, why are you laughing?" he said.

At this remark, Papa and the judge laughed until their eyes watered.

Mumbling and grumbling, Grandpa said, "If you fellows were as cold as I am, you wouldn't be laughing."

We knew we shouldn't be laughing, but we couldn't help ourselves.

The judge looked at his watch. "It's after three o'clock," he said. "Do you think they'll tree another one?"

As if to throw the words back in the judge's face, Old Dan opened up. I stood up and whooped. "Whoo-e-e! Get him, Dan! Get him! Put him up a little tree."

There was a mad scramble. Grandpa tried to put his britches on backwards. The judge and Papa ran over to help him with his shoes. Each one tried to put a shoe on the wrong foot. I was laughing so hard I could do nothing.

A hundred yards from the fire, I realized we had forgotten the coonskins. I ran back for them.

My dogs had jumped the coon in swampland. He tore out for the river bottoms. I could tell they were close to him by their fast bawling. All at once their baying stopped. We stood still and listened. Old Dan bawled treed a few more times and then stopped.

Grandpa asked, "What's happened?"

I told him the coon had probably pulled some kind of trick.

Coming up to my dogs, we saw they were working up and down an old rail fence. We stood and watched. Every now and then, Old Dan would rear up on a large hackberry tree that was standing about seven feet from the fence and bawl treed.

As yet Little Ann had not bawled the tree bark. We watched her. She was working everywhere. She climbed up on the rail fence and followed its zigzag course until she disappeared in the darkness.

I told Papa I was sure the coon had walked the rail fence and in some way had fooled my dogs.

Old Dan would keep coming back to the hackberry tree. He would rear up on it and bawl treed. We walked up to him. Looking the tree over, we could see that the coon wasn't in it.

4 Reading Strategy Based on what they know about Little Ann, you might have students predict whether or not she will figure out the coon's trick.

5 Literary Focus Billy will not give up because of the faith and love he has for his dogs. Would this bond be affected if the dogs fail and they lose the coon hunt?

The judge said, "It looks like he has them fooled."

"Maybe you had better call them off," Grandpa said. "We can go someplace else and hunt. We've got to get one more coon, even if I have to tree it myself."

For some reason, no one laughed at his remark.

"It's almost daylight," Papa said.

"Yes, that's what has me worried," I said. "We don't have time to do any more hunting. If we lose this one, we're beat."

Hearing the word beat, Grandpa began to fidget. He asked me, "What do you think happened? How did that coon fool them?"

"I don't know for sure," I said. "He walked that rail fence. The hackberry tree has something to do with his trick, but I don't know what."

"Son," the judge said, "I wouldn't feel too badly if I were you. I've seen some of the very best hounds fooled by a smart old coon."

Regardless of all the discouraging talk, the love and belief I had in my little red hounds never faltered. I could see them now and then, leaping over old logs, tearing through the underbrush, sniffing and searching for the lost trail. My heart swelled with pride. I whooped, urging them on.

In a low voice, the judge said, "I'll say one thing. They don't give up easily."

Birds began to chirp all around us. The sky took on a light gray color. Tiny dim stars were blinking the night away.

"It looks like we're beat," Papa said. "It's getting daylight."

At that moment, the loud clear voice of a redbone hound, bawling treed, rang through the river bottoms. It was the voice of Little Ann.

Sucking in a mouthful of air, I held it. I could feel my heart pounding against my ribs. I closed my eyes tight and gritted my teeth to keep the tears from coming.

"Let's go to them," Grandpa said.

"No, wait a minute," I said.

"Why?" he asked.

'Wait till Old Dan gets there," I said. "It's daylight now, and if we walk up to the tree, the coon will jump out. It's hard to keep a coon in a tree after daylight. Let's wait until Old Dan gets there. Then if he jumps, he won't have a chance to get away."

"The boy's right," the judge said. "It's hard to keep a coon in a tree after daybreak."

Just then we heard Old Dan. His deep voice shattered the morning silence. Searching for the lost trail, he had crossed the fence and worked his way out into an old field. Turning around, we saw him coming. He was a red blur in the gray morning shadows. Coming to the trail fence, and without breaking his stride, he raised his body into the air. About halfway over and while still in the air he bawled.

Hitting the ground with a loud grunt, he ran past us. Everyone whooped to him. Ahead was a deep washout about ten feet wide. On the other side was a canebrake. His long red body, stretched to its fullest length, seemed to float in the air as he sailed over it. We could hear the tall stalks rattling as he plowed his way through them. A bunch of sleepy snow birds rose from the thick cane, flitted over, and settled in a row on the old rail fence.

Nearing the tree, we could see it was a tall sycamore, and there high in the top was the coon.

Grandpa threw a fit. He hopped around whooping and hollering. He threw his old hat down on the ground and jumped up and down on it. Then he ran over and kissed Little Ann right on the head.

After we killed and skinned the coon, the judge said, "Let's walk back to that old fence. I think I know how the old fellow pulled his trick."

Primary Source

Billy's knowledge of coon hunting, knowing the coon's tricks and the habits of his dogs, is not unlike that of real coon hunters. These excerpts are from "Listening in the Dark," by Bill Tarrant in the January, 1989 *Field & Stream* magazine.

. . . "That coon's put the hurt on 'em . . . the dogs have lost him and they don't know where he's at."

I sit up higher and peer into the dark. This young man speaks with authority. He laughs and says, "He's one of those big, smart ones."

"How's that?" I ask.

"Because that coon could have gone to tree all right, but then he leaped to another tree. What we call a tap. He climbed up a tree a little way and jumped off somewhere he thought the dogs couldn't scent him . . . in a brushpile or a honeysuckle thicket. Then he wiggled his way through there and come out the other end."

. . . I start to speak when a deep, resonant, lopped-off bawl pierces the valley. "They treed already?" I ask.

"Yep," says Fitch.

"That voice," I inquire, "what would you call that voice right now?"

Back at the fence, the judge stood and looked around for a few minutes. Smiling, he said, "Yes, that's how he did it."

"How?" Grandpa asked.

Still smiling, the judge said, "That old coon walked this rail fence. Coming even with the hackberry tree, he leaped up on its side, and climbed up. Notice how thick the timber is around here. See that limb way up there in the top, the one that runs over and almost touches the sycamore?"

We saw what he meant.

"The coon walked out on that limb," he said, "leaped over, and caught the sycamore limb. Repeating this over and over, from tree to tree, he worked his way far out into the river bottoms. What I can't figure out is how that hound found him."

Gazing at Little Ann, he shook his head and said, "I've been hunting coons and judging coon hunts for forty years, but I've never seen anything like that.

He looked at me. "Well, son," he said, "you have tied the leading teams. There's only one more night of eliminations. Even if some of them get more than three coons, you will still be in the runoff, and from what I've seen here tonight, you have a good chance of winning the cup."

6 ⎡ I knew that Little Ann had scented the coon in the air, the same as she had the ghost coon. I walked over and knelt down by her side. The things I wanted to say to her I couldn't, for the knot in my throat, but I'm sure she understood. ⎣

As we came into the campground, the hunters came out of their tents and gathered around us. The judge held up the three big coon hides. There was a roar from the crowd.

One man said, "That was the most beautiful sight I've ever seen."

"What was a beautiful sight?" Grandpa asked.

"Last night those little red hounds brought that coon right through camp."

The judge said, "We figured they did when we heard the noise."

Laughing, the man said, "We heard them when they ran up the other side of the river. Way up above here they crossed over. We could tell they were coming back so we doused all the fires and, sure enough, they came right through camp. Those two little hounds weren't fifty yards behind the coon, running side by side. Boy, they were picking them up and laying them down, and bawling every time their feet touched the ground. I'll tell you, it was the prettiest sight I ever saw."

When the judge started telling about the last coon Little Ann had treed I took my dogs over to our tent and fed and watered them. After they had had their fill, I gave them a good rubdown with a piece of gunny sack. Taking them out to the buggy, I tied them up. I stood and watched while they twisted around in the hay making their bed.

That day I tried to get some sleep in our tent, but the soaking Grandpa had taken in the river had given him a cold, causing him to snore. I never heard such a racket in all my life. I'd have sworn he rattled the paper sacks in our grocery boxes. Taking a blanket, I went out to my dogs. Little Ann had wiggled up as close to Old Dan as she could. Prying them apart, I lay down between them and fell asleep.

The last night of the eliminations turned out like the second night. None of the judges turned in more than two hides.

That day, about noon, the owners of the other winning teams and I were called for a conference with the head judge. He said, "Gentlemen, the eliminations are over. Only three sets of hounds are left for the runoff. The winner of tonight's hunt will receive the gold cup. If there is a tie for the championship, naturally there will be another runoff." 7

6 **Discussion** What do you think Billy wanted to say to Little Ann? What is he feeling?

7 **Reading Strategy** You might want to have the students predict the outcome of the runoff.

"That's a short, ringing chop."

"How does that differ from a locate?"

"A locate is when they hit the trail and they got a long, howling bawl. You can tell. When they run a coon and bawl it's just a straight-line bawl. When they strike, it depends on whether it's a hot or cold trail. When it's cold they're going to be real long in voice, just like they were saying, 'It's r-e-e-e-a-l c-o-o-o-o-o-o-o-o-l-d.' It'll be a long bawl.

"But if it's a real hot track, they'll run it just like they're barking treed. If they're right on that coon . . . if they can see him . . . they're going to run it just like they're treein'. The coon can't stand it when they're running like that. The faster they bark, more or less, the hotter the track."

The article also reveals that Billy's love for hunting coons is not unique. The author writes:

I'm proud of Fitch's running commentary when I tell him, "You've really analyzed this coon hunting."

He says, "I don't know what I'd rather do—breathe or hunt coon."

8 Discussion Why do you think everyone wants Billy to win the Gold Cup? What does this reflect about the men involved in the hunt?

9 Literary Focus This is another example of the bond between Billy and his dogs. Do you think the dogs are aware of the importance of the hunt? Do you understand Billy? What feelings do you think they are conveying to Billy?

He shook hands with each of us and wished us good luck.

Tension began to build up in the camp. Here and there hunters were standing in small groups, talking. Others could be seen going in and out of tents with rolls of money in their hands. Grandpa was the busiest one of all. His voice could be heard all over the camp. Men were looking at me, and talking in low tones. I strutted like a turkey gobbler.

That evening, while we were having supper, a hunter dropped by. He had a small box in his hand. Smiling, he said, "Everyone has agreed that we should have a jackpot for the winner. I've been picked to do the collecting."

Grandpa said, "You may as well leave it here now."

Looking at me, the hunter said, "Son, I think almost every man in this camp is hoping you win it, but it's not going to be easy. You're going up against four of the finest hounds there are." Turning to my father, he said, "Did you know the two big walker hounds have won four gold cups?"

Very seriously, Papa said, "You know I have two mules down on my place. One is almost as big as a barn. The other one isn't much bigger than a jack rabbit, but that little mule can outpull the big one every time."

Smiling, the hunter turned to leave. He said, "You could be right."

Papa asked me again where I thought we should start hunting.

I had been thinking about this all day. I said, "You remember where we jumped the last coon in the swamp?"

Papa said, "Yes."

"Well, the way I figure, more than one coon lives in that swamp," I said. "It's a good place for them as there are lots of crawfish and minnows in those potholes. If a hound jumps one there, he has a good chance to tree him."

Papa asked, "Why?"

"It's a long way back to the river, and about the same distance to the mountains," I said. "Either way he runs, a dog can get pretty close to him, and so he would have to take to a tree."

That evening we climbed into Grandpa's buggy and headed for the swamp. It was dark by the time we reached it.

Grandpa handed Papa his gun, saying, "You're getting to be a pretty good shot with this thing."

"I hope I get to shoot it a lot tonight," Papa said.

Under my breath, I said, "I do, too."

After untying the ropes from my dogs, I held onto their collars for a minute. Pulling them up close, I knelt down and whispered, "This is the last night. I know you'll do your best."

They seemed to understand and tugged at their collars. When I turned them loose, they started for the timber. Just as they reached the dark shadows, they stopped, turned around, and stared straight at me for an instant.

The judge saw their strange actions. Laying a hand on my shoulder, he asked, "What did they say, son?"

I said, "Nothing that anyone could understand, but I can feel that they know this hunt is important. They know it just as well as you or I."

It was Little Ann who found the trail. Before the echo of her sharp cry had died away, Old Dan's deep voice floated out of the swamp.

"Well, let's go," Papa said eagerly.

"No, let's wait a minute," I said.

"Wait? Why?" Grandpa asked.

"To see which way he's going to run," I said.

The coon broke out of the swamp and headed for the river. Listening to my dogs, I could tell they were close to him. I said to Papa, "I don't think he'll ever make it to the river. They're right on his heels now."

By the time we had circled the swamp, they were bawling treed.

The judge said, "Boy, that was fast."

10 I felt my father's hand on my shoulder. Looking at me, he smiled and nodded his head. Papa and I knew I had judged the coon perfectly. He didn't have time to reach the river or the mountains.

My dogs had treed the coon in a tall ash which stood about fifty yards from the river. I knew the fifty yards had saved us a good hour, because he could have pulled trick after trick if he had gotten in the water.

We spied the coon in the topmost branches. At the crack of the gun, he ran far out on a limb and jumped. He landed in an old fallen treetop. He scooted through it. Coming out on the other side, he ran for the river. The tangled mass of limbs slowed my dogs and they all but tore the treetop apart getting out of it. The coon was just one step ahead of them as they reached the river. We heard them hit the water.

Running over, we stood and watched the fight. The coon was at home in the river. He crawled up on Old Dan's head, trying to force him under. Before he could do it, Little Ann reached up and pulled him off.

In a scared voice, Papa said, "That water looks deep to me."

"Maybe you had better call them off," said the judge. "That's a big coon and he could drown one of them easily in that deep water."

"Call them off?" I said. "Why, you couldn't whip them off with a stick. There's no use for anyone to get scared. They know exactly what they're doing. I've seen this more times than one."

Grandpa was scared and excited. He was jumping up and down, whooping and hollering.

Papa raised the gun to aim.

I jumped and grabbed his arm. "Don't do that," I yelled. "You're sure to hit one of my dogs."

Round and round in the deep water the fight went on. The coon climbed on Old Dan's head and sank his teeth in one of his long tender ears. Old Dan bawled with pain. Little Ann swam in and caught one of the coon's hind legs in her mouth. She tried hard to pull him off. All three disappeared under the water.

I held my breath.

The water churned and boiled. All three came to the top about the same time. The coon was between the bank we were standing on and my dogs. He swam toward us. They caught him again just as he reached shore. He fought his way free and ran for a large sycamore. Old Dan caught him just as he started up. I knew that was the end of the fight.

After it was all over and the coon had been skinned, Grandpa said, "I hope we don't have to go through that again tonight. For a while I sure thought your dogs were goners."

The judge said, "Well, have you ever seen that? Look over there!"

Old Dan was standing perfectly still, with eyes closed and head hanging down. Little Ann was licking at his cut and bleeding ears.

11 "She always does that," I said. "If you'll watch, when she gets done with him, he'll do the same for her."

We stood and watched until they had finished doctoring each other. Then, trotting side by side, they disappeared in the darkness.

We followed along, stopping now and then to listen.

Chapter 17

Looking up the sky, Papa said, "That doesn't look good up there. I think we are in for a storm."

The sky had turned a dark gray. Fast-

10 **Critical Thinking and Reading** Billy's hunting skills are proving to be important to the success of his dogs. Do you think it is realistic for Billy to have so much skill? Explain.

11 **Literary Focus** This is a good example of the unusually close feelings the dogs have for one another. Can you think of other examples where the dogs acted in an unusual way in displaying their close relationship?

12 **Discussion** How does the coming storm affect the conflict? Does it heighten your interest? What trait of Billy's character is revealed by his insistence on continuing despite the weather?

moving clouds were rolling through the heavens.

Grandpa said, "Looks like we're going to get some wind, too."

Scared and thinking everyone might want to stop hunting because of a few clouds, I said, "If a storm is brewing, it's a good night to hunt. All game stirs just before a storm."

Thirty minutes later, Papa said, "Listen."

We stood still. A low moaning sound could be heard in the tops of the tall sycamores.

Grandpa said, "I was afraid of that. We're going to get some wind."

We heard a rattling in the leaves and underbrush. It was beginning to sleet. The air turned cold and chilly.

From far downriver, we heard the deep baying of a hound on a trail. It was Old Dan. Seconds later, the rhythmic crying of Little Ann could be heard. Swallowing the lump that had jumped up in my throat, I whooped as loud as I could.

The ground was turning white with sleet. The storm had really set in. We hurried along.

I said to Papa, "If this keeps up that old coon won't run long. He'll head for his den."

"If it gets much worse," Grandpa said, "I know some coon hunters that won't be running very long. They'll be frozen too stiff to run."

The judge asked if there was any danger of getting lost.

"I don't know," Papa said. "It's all strange country to me."

My dogs' voices sounded far away. I knew they were much closer than they sounded as they were downwind from us. Finding three large sycamores growing close together, we stopped on the leeward[1] side.

Papa shouted above the wind, "I don't

___

1. **leeward** (lē′ wərd) *adj.*: Sheltered from the wind.

know if we can take much more of this."

"It is bad," Grandpa replied, "and it looks like it's going to get worse."

"You can't see over fifteen feet now," the judge said. "Do you think we can find the buggy?"

"I think we can find the buggy all right," Papa said.

I could no longer hear the voices of my dogs. This had me worried. I didn't want to leave them out in the storm.

"Can anyone hear the hounds?" Grandpa asked.

"I can't," Papa said.

The judge spoke up. "Fellows, I think we'd better go in," he said. "There's no telling where they are. They may have crossed the river."

Scared and knowing I had to do something, I said, "They're closer than you think, probably treed by now. You can't hear them for this wind." I begged, "Let's go a little farther."

There was no reply and no one made a move to leave the shelter of the trees.

Taking a few steps, I said, "I'll take the lead. Just follow me."

"Billy, we couldn't find them," Papa said. "You can't see or hear a thing. We had better start back for camp."

"I think so, too," the judge said.

At this remark, I cried, "I've been out in storms like this before, all by myself. I've never left my dogs in the woods, and I'm not going to now, even if I have to look for them by myself."

No one answered.

"Please go just a little farther," I begged. "I just know we'll hear them."

Still no one spoke or made a move to go on.

Stepping over to my father, I buried my faces in his old mackinaw coat. Sobbing, I pleaded with him not to turn back.

He patted my head. "Billy," he said, "a

___

Grammar in Action

Much of a story's meaning lies in its verbs, and there are several different kinds. Some action verbs, for example, require a noun to receive and complete their action. Think of the verb *find*. A person doesn't just find, he or she must find *something*. Verbs such as *find*, that require a direct object to complete their meaning, are called **transitive verbs.** Look at these transitive verbs from Rawls' novel:

Thirty minutes later, Papa *said*, "Listen." [said what? He said "Listen."]

We *heard* a rattling in the leaves and underbrush. [heard what? We heard a rattling.]
No one *made* a move to go on.
I *buried* my face in his old mackinaw coat

These sentences would make no sense without the nouns that follow the verbs and complete their meaning. These verbs *need* direct objects. Caution students, however, that the same word can be a transitive verb in one sentence and not in another. This quality depends upon *how* they function in sentences.

Student Activity 1. Find five other examples of transitive verbs in *Where the Red Fern Grows*. What are the nouns that receive their actions and complete their meanings?

man could freeze to death in this storm, and besides, your dogs will give up and come in."

13 "That's what has me worried," I cried. "They won't come in. They won't, Papa. Little Ann might, but not Old Dan. He'd die before he'd leave a coon in a tree."

Papa was undecided. Making up his mind, he stepped away from the tree and said to the others, "I'm going on with him. You fellows coming, or going back?"

He turned and followed me. Grandpa and the judge fell in behind him.

By this time the ground was covered with a thin white layer of sleet. We kept slipping and falling. I could hear Grandpa mumbling and grumbling. The wind-driven sleet stung our skin like thousands of pricking needles. Strong gusts of wind growled and moaned through the tops of the tall timber.

Once during a momentary lull of the storm, I thought I heard the baying of a hound. I told my father I thought I had heard Old Dan.

"From which direction?" he asked.

"From that way," I said, pointing to our left.

We started on. A few minutes later Papa stopped. He shouted to my grandfather, "Did you hear anything?"

"No," Grandpa shouted back. "I can't hear anything in this storm."

"I thought I did, but I'm not sure," the judge said.

"Where was it coming from?" Papa asked.

"Over that way," the judge said, pointing to our right.

"That's the way it sounded to me," Papa said.

At that moment, all of us heard the deep voice of Old Dan.

"It sounds as if they're close," Grandpa said.

"Let's split up," said the judge. "Maybe one of us can find them."

"No," Papa said, "it'd be easy to get lost in the storm."

"I think they're more to the right of us," I said.

"I do, too," Papa said.

We trudged on. Old Dan bawled again. The sound of his voice seemed to be all around us.

"The way that wind is whipping the sound through this timber," the judge said, "we'd be lucky if we ever found them."

Papa shouted over the roar of the wind, "We can't take much more of this. We'll freeze to death."

The men were giving up. I felt the knot again as it crawled up in my throat. Salt water froze on my eyelashes. Kneeling down, I put my ear close to the icy ground in hopes I could hear my dogs, but I couldn't hear anything above the roar of the blizzard.

Standing up, I peered this way and that. All I could see was a white wall of whirling sleet. I closed my eyes and said a silent prayer and hoped for a miracle.

We heard a sharp crack and a loud crashing noise. A large limb, torn from a tree by the strong wind, fell to the ground. The sharp crack of the limb gave me the idea. Shouting to my father, I said, "Shoot the gun. If my dogs are close enough to hear it, maybe Little Ann will come to us." 14

Papa didn't hesitate. Pointing the gun high over his head, he pulled the trigger. The sharp crack rang out into the teeth of the storm.

We waited.

Just when I had given up all hope and had sunk to the lowest depth of despair, out of the white wall of driving sleet, my little dog came to me. I knelt down and gathered her in my arms.

Taking one of the lead ropes from my pocket, I tied it to her collar. I said, "Find him, little girl. Please find Old Dan."

Right then I didn't care about coons,

Where the Red Fern Grows　741

13 **Literary Focus** Billy will not return without his dogs because he knows that Dan will never give up. What is revealed by Billy's willingness to risk his own health for his dogs? Why do you think the others decide to stay with him?

14 **Reading Strategy** Have students recall other situations in which Billy has thought of a solution to a problem that appears hopeless. What seems to trigger his ideas? Do you think Billy will find the dogs now?

Student Activity 2. Tell whether the verbs in these sentences are transitive or not. Tell why.
1. The water churned and boiled.
2. My dogs treed the coon in a tall ash.
3. Grandpa jumped up and down.

Student Activity 3. Use the following verbs as transitive verbs in sentences of your own about Billy and his pups. Underline the nouns that receive the action of the verbs. *point, give, love, pat, keep, see.*

15 **Critical Thinking and Reading**
Does the setting described by the author seem realistic? Can you picture the scenery in your mind?

16 **Discussion** Old Dan did not give up the trail despite the weather, and Little Ann, guided by pure instinct, led the men to him. What does this behavior reveal about the animals' characters? Are their actions consistent with what you know already about them?

gold cups, or anything. All I wanted was my dogs.

I don't know how she did it. Straight into the face of the storm she led us. Time after time she would stop and turn her head this way and that. I knew she couldn't scent or see anything. Instinct alone was guiding her. Over a winding and twisting trail, we followed.

Coming out of the bottoms, she led us into a thick canebrake. The tall stalks sheltered us from the storm. The roaring of the wind didn't seem as loud. Like ghostly figures, large trees loomed out of the almost solid mass. Falling and stumbling, we kept pushing on.

Grandpa shouted, "Hold up a minute. I'm just about all in."

We stopped.

"Do you think that hound knows what she's doing?" the judge asked. "Maybe we're just running around in circles."

Looking at me, Papa said, "I hope she does. Some of these canebrakes cover miles. If we get lost in here, we'll be in bad shape."

Grandpa said, "I think we've gone too far. The last time I heard Old Dan, he sounded quite close."

"That was because the wind carried the sound," I said.

The judge spoke up, "Fellows, no dog is worth the lives of three men. Now let's do the smart thing and get out of here while we can. Our clothes are wet. If we keep on wandering around in this jungle, we'll freeze to death. It doesn't look like this blizzard is ever going to let up."

I could hear the roar of the blizzard back in the thick timber of the bottoms. Two large limbs being rubbed together by the strong wind made a grinding creaking sound. The tall slender cane around us rattled and swayed.

I could feel the silence closing in. I knew the judge's cold logic had had its effect on my father and grandfather. The men had given up. There was no hope left for me.

Kneeling down, I put my arms around Little Ann. I felt the warm heat from her moist tongue caressing my ear. Closing my eyes, I said, "Please, Dan, bawl one more time, just one more time."

I waited for my plea to be answered.

With its loud roaring, the north wind seemed to be laughing at us. All around, tall stalks of cane were weaving and dancing to the rattling rhythm of their knife-edged blades.

My father tried to talk above the wind, but his words were lost in the storm. Just before another blast, clear as a foghorn on a stormy sea, Old Dan's voice rang loud and clear. It seemed louder than the roar of the wind or the skeleton-like rustling of the tall swaying cane.

I jumped to my feet. My heart did a complete flip-flop. The knot in my throat felt as big as an apple. I tried to whoop, but it was no use. Little Ann bawled and tugged on the rope.

There was no mistaking the direction. We knew that Little Ann had been right all along. Straight as an arrow, she had led us to him.

Old Dan was treed down in a deep gully. I slid off the bank and ran to him. His back was covered with a layer of frozen sleet. His frost-covered whiskers stood out straight as porcupine quills.

I worked the wedges of ice from between his toes, and scraped the sleet from his body with my hands. Little Ann came over and tried to wash his face. He didn't like it. Jerking loose from me, he ran over to the tree, reared up on it, and started bawling.

Hearing shouting from the bank above me, I looked up. I could dimly see Papa and the judge through the driving sleet. At first I thought they were shouting to me, but on peering closer I could see that they had their

backs to me. Catching hold of some long stalks of cane that were hanging down from the steep bank, I pulled myself up.

Papa shouted in my ear, "Something has happened to your grandfather."

Turning to the judge, he said, "He was behind you. When was the last time you saw him?"

"I don't know for sure," the judge said. "I guess it was back there when we heard the hound bawl."

"Didn't you hear anything?" Papa asked.

"Hear anything?" the judge exclaimed. "How could I hear anything in all that noise? I thought he was behind me all the time, and didn't miss him until we got here."

I couldn't hold back the tears. My grandfather was lost and wandering in that white jungle of cane. Screaming for him, I started back.

Papa caught me. He shouted, "Don't do that."

I tried to tear away from him but his grip on my arm was firm.

"Shoot the gun," the judge said.

Papa shot time after time. It was useless. We got no answer.

Little Ann came up out of the washout. She stood and stared at me. Turning, she disappeared quickly in the thick cane. Minutes later we heard her. It was a long, mournful cry.

The only times I had ever heard my little dog bawl like that were when she was baying at a bright Ozark moon, or when someone played a French harp or a fiddle close to her ear. She didn't stop until we reached her.

Grandpa lay as he had fallen, face down in the icy sleet. His right foot was wedged in the fork of a broken box elder limb. When the ankle had twisted, the searing pain must have made him unconscious.

Papa worked Grandpa's foot free and turned him over. I sat down and placed his head in my lap. While Papa and the judge massaged his arms and legs, I wiped the frozen sleet from his eyes and face.

Burying my face in the iron-gray hair, I cried and begged God not to let my grandfather die.

"I think he's gone," the judge said.

"I don't think so," Papa said. "He took a

Where the Red Fern Grows 743

17 **Discussion** What does this statement reveal about Grandpa? Do you think he is being brave or unwise by ignoring the pain? Explain.

bad fall when that limb tripped him, but he hasn't been lying here long enough to be frozen. I think he's just unconscious."

Papa lifted him to a sitting position and told the judge to start slapping his face. Grandpa moaned and moved his head.

"He's coming around," Papa said.

I asked Papa if we could get him back to the gully where Old Dan was. I had noticed there was very little wind there and we could build a fire.

"That's the very place," he said. "We'll build a good fire and one of us can go for help."

Papa and the judge made a seat by catching each other's wrists. They eased Grandpa between them.

By the time we reached the washout, Grandpa was fully conscious again, and was mumbling and grumbling. He couldn't see why they had to carry him like a baby.

After easing him over the bank and down into the gully, we built a large fire. Papa took his knife and cut the boot from Grandpa's swollen foot. Grandpa grunted and groaned from the pain. I felt sorry for him but there was nothing I could do but look on.

Papa examined the foot. Shaking his head, he said, "Boy, that's a bad one. It's either broken or badly sprained. I'll go for some help."

Grandpa said, "Now wait just a minute. I'm not going to let you go out in that blizzard by yourself. What if something happens to you? No one would know."

"What time is it?" he asked.

The judge looked at his watch. "It's almost five o'clock," he said.

"It's not long till daylight," Grandpa said. "Then if you want to go, you can see where you're going. Now help me get propped up against this bank. I'll be all right. It doesn't hurt any more. It's numb now."

"He's right," the judge said.

"Think you can stand it?" Papa asked.

Grandpa roared like a bear. "Sure I can stand it. It's nothing but a sprained ankle. I'm not going to die. Build that fire up a little more."

While Papa and the judge made Grandpa comfortable, I carried wood for the fire.

17

"There's no use standing around gawking at me," Grandpa said. "I'm all right. Get the coon out of that tree. That's what we came for, isn't it?"

Up until then, the coon-hunting had practically been forgotten.

The tree was about thirty feet from our fire. We walked over and took a good look at it for the first time. My dogs, seeing we were finally going to pay some attention to them, started bawling and running around the tree.

Papa said, "It's not much of a tree, just an old box elder snag. There's not a limb on it."

"I can't see any coon," said the judge. "It must be hollow."

Papa beat on its side with the ax. It gave forth a loud booming sound. He said, "It's hollow all right."

He stepped back a few steps, scraped his feet on the slick ground for a good footing, and said, "Stand back, and hold those hounds. I'm going to cut it down. We need some wood for our fire anyway."

Squatting down between my dogs, I held onto their collars.

Papa notched the old snag so it would fall away from our fire. As the heavy ax chewed its way into the tree, it began to lean and crack. Papa stopped chopping. He said to the judge, "Come on and help me. I think we can push it over now."

After much grunting and pushing, snapping and popping, it fell.

I turned my dogs loose.

On hitting the ground, the snag split

Grammar in Action

Transitive verbs require direct objects to complete their meanings, but other verbs do not. **Intransitive verbs** can stand on their own or they can be followed by adverbs or adverb phrases that modify their meaning. Their meaning is self-contained; they do not need a noun to receive their action. For example, Rawls uses these intransitive verbs in *Where the Red Fern Grows*.

We *waited*.
Papa didn't *hesitate*.

We *stood* still.
After much grunting and pushing, it *fell*.
Grandpa *grunted* and *groaned* from the pain.

It is important to point out, however, that the transitive or intransitive nature of a verb depends on how it is used in a sentence. Many verbs can be either transitive or intransitive:

The wind-driven sleet *stung* our skin. [Transitive]
When the wind hit my eyes, they *stung*. [Intransitive]

Good writers use a variety of verbs in their writing—*linking verbs, transitive verbs, intransitive verbs*—for each gives a different rhythm to their sentences and contributes a different dimension to their story.

and broke up. Goggle-eyed, I stood rooted in my tracks and watched three big coons roll out of the busted old trunk.

One started up the washout, running between us and the fire. Old Dan caught him and the fight was on. The second coon headed down the washout. Little Ann caught him.

Hearing a loud yell from Grandpa, I looked that way. Old Dan and the coon were fighting close to his feet. He was yelling and beating at them with his hat. The judge and Papa ran to help.

The third coon started climbing up the steep bank close to me. Just before reaching the top, his claws slipped in the icy mud. Tumbling end over end, down he came. I grabbed up a stick and threw it at him. Growling and showing his teeth, he started for me. I threw the fight to him then and there. Some ten yards away I looked back. He was climbing the bank. That time he made it and disappeared in the thick cane.

Hearing a squall of pain from Little Ann, I turned. The coon was really working her over. He had climbed up on her back and was tearing and slashing. She couldn't shake him off. Grabbing a club from the ground, I ran to help her.

Before we had killed our coon, Old Dan came tearing in. We stood and watched the fight. When the coon was dead, Papa picked it up and we walked back to the fire.

"How many coons were in that old snag?" Papa asked.

"I saw three," I said. "The one that got away climbed out over there." I pointed in the direction the coon had taken.

I never should have pointed. My dogs turned as one, and started bawling and clawing their way up the steep bank. I shouted and scolded, but to no avail. They disappeared in the rattling cane.

We stood still, listening to their voices.

The sound died away in the roaring storm. Sitting down close to the fire, I buried my face in my arms and cried.

I heard the judge say to my father, "This beats anything I have ever seen. Why, those dogs can read that boy's mind. He just pointed at that bank and away they went. I never saw anything like it. I can't understand some of the things they have done tonight. Hounds usually aren't that smart. If they were collies, or some other breed of dog, it would be different, but they're just redbone hounds, hunting dogs."

Papa said, "Yes, I know what you mean. I've seen them do things that I couldn't understand. I'd never heard of hounds that ever had any affection for anyone, but these dogs are different. Did you know they won't hunt with anyone but him, not even me?"

Hearing my grandfather call my name, I went over and sat down by his side. Putting his arm around me, he said, "Now, I wouldn't worry about those dogs. They'll be all right. It's not long till daylight. Then you can go to them."

I said, "Yes, but what if the coon crosses the river? My dogs will follow him. If they get wet they could freeze to death."

"We'll just have to wait and hope for the best," he said. "Now straighten up and quit that sniffling. Act like a coon hunter. You don't see me bawling, and this old foot is paining me something awful."

I felt better after my talk with Grandpa.

"Come on, let's skin these coons," Papa said.

I got up to help him.

After the skins were peeled from the carcasses, I had an idea. Holding one up close to the fire until it was warm, I took it over and wrapped it around Grandpa's foot. Chuckling, he said, "Boy, that feels good. Heat another skin the same way."

I kept it up for the rest of the night.

Where the Red Fern Grows 745

18 **Reading Strategy** You might have students predict what might happen to Dan and Ann.

19 **Literary Focus** What do these statements show about Billy's dogs and their relationship with him? How do Papa and the judge seem to feel about them?

20 **Discussion** Why does Grandpa's advice make Billy feel better? Why do you think he seems to know what to say to Billy?

Student Activity 1. Find five other examples of intransitive verbs in *Where the Red Fern Grows*.

Student Activity 2. Use the following words as intransitive verbs in sentences about Billy and his pups: *kneel, fight, mumble, care, listen, land*.

Student Activity 3. Use these words as transitive verbs in one sentence and intransitive verbs in another sentence: *point, cross, climb*.

21 **Discussion** What does searching for the lost party in a dangerous storm indicate about the men involved in the coon hunt?

22 **Discussion** Do you agree with the judge that Dan and Ann knew that Billy needed another raccoon to win? What have the dogs done to make him believe this?

Chapter 18

Just before dawn, the storm blew itself out with one last angry roar. It started snowing. A frozen silence settled over the canebrake.

Back in the thick timber of the river bottoms, the sharp snapping of frozen limbs could be heard. The tall stalks of wild cane looked exhausted from the hellish night. They were drooping and bending from the weight of the frozen sleet.

I climbed out of the deep gully and listened for my dogs. I couldn't hear them. Just as I started back down the bank, I heard something. I listened. Again I heard the sound.

Papa was watching me. "Can you hear the dogs?" he asked.

"No, not the dogs," I said, "but I can hear something else."

"What does it sound like?" he asked.

"Like someone whooping," I said.

Papa and the judge hurried up the bank. We heard the sound again. It was coming from a different direction.

"The first time I heard it," I said, "it was over that way."

"It's the men from camp," the judge said. "They're searching for us."

We started whooping. The searchers answered. Their voices came from all directions. The first one to reach us was Mr. Kyle. He looked haggard and tired. He asked if everything was all right.

"Yes, we're all right," Papa said, "but the old man has a bad ankle. It looks like we'll have to carry him out."

21 "Your team broke loose and came back to camp about midnight," Mr. Kyle said. "This really spooked us. We were sure something bad had happened. Twenty-five of us have been searching since then."

Several men climbed down the bank and went over to Grandpa. They looked at his an-

kle. One said, "I don't think it's broken, but it sure is a bad sprain."

"You're in luck," another one said. "We have one of the best doctors in the state of Texas in our camp, Dr. Charley Lathman. He'll have you fixed up in no time."

"Yes," another said, "and if I know Charley, he's probably got a small hospital with him."

Back in the crowd, I heard another man say, "You mean that Lathman fellow, who owns those black and tan hounds, is a doctor?"

"Sure is," another said. "One of the best."

Mr. Kyle asked where my dogs were. I told him that they were treed somewhere.

"What do you mean, treed somewhere?" he asked.

Papa explained what had happened.

With a wide-eyed look on his face, he said, "Do you mean to tell me those hounds stayed with the tree in that blizzard?"

I nodded.

Looking at me, he said, "Son, I hope they have that coon treed, because you need that one to win the cup. Those two walker hounds caught three before the storm came up. When it got bad, all the hunters came in."

22 The judge spoke up. "I'll always believe that those hounds knew that boy needed another coon to win," he said. "If you fellows had seen some of the things those dogs have done, you'd believe it, too."

One hunter walked over to the broken snag. "Three out of one tree," he said. "No wonder, look here! That old snag was half-full of leaves and grass. Why, it was a regular old den tree."

Several of the men walked over. I heard one say, "I've seen this happen before. Remember that big hunt in the Red River bottoms, when the two little beagle hounds treed four coons in an old hollow snag? They won the championship, too."

"I wasn't there but I remember reading about it," one said.

"Say, I don't see Benson," Mr. Kyle said.

The men started looking at each other.

"He was searching farther downriver than the rest of us," one fellow said. "Maybe he didn't hear us shouting."

Some of the men climbed out of the gully. They started whooping. From a distance we heard an answering shout.

"He hears us," someone said. "He's coming."

Everyone looked relieved.

Mr. Benson struck the washout a little way above us. He was breathing hard, as if he'd been running. He started talking as soon as he was within hearing distance.

"It scared me when I first saw them," he said. "I didn't know what they were. They looked like white ghosts. I'd never seen anything like it."

A hunter grabbed Mr. Benson by the shoulder, shaking him. "Get ahold of yourself, man," he said. "What are you talking about?"

Mr. Benson took a deep breath to control himself, and started again in a much calmer voice. "Those two hounds," he said. "I found them. They're frozen solid. They're nothing but white ice from the tips of their noses to the ends of their tails."

Hearing Mr. Benson's words, I screamed and ran to my father. Everything started whirling around and around. I felt light as a feather. My knees buckled. I knew no more.

Regaining consciousness, I opened my eyes and could dimly see the blurry images of the men around me. A hand was shaking me. I could hear my father's voice but I couldn't understand his words. Little by little the blackness faded away. My throat was dry and I was terribly thirsty. I asked for some water.

Mr. Benson came over. He said, "Son,

I'm sorry, truly sorry. I didn't mean it that way. Your dogs are alive. I guess I was excited. I'm very sorry."

I heard a deep voice say, "That's a hell of a thing to do. Come running in here saying the dogs are frozen solid."

Mr. Benson said, "I didn't mean it to sound that way. I said I'm sorry. What more do you want me to do?"

The deep voice growled again. "I still think it was a hell of a thing for a man to do."

Mr. Kyle took over. "Now let's not have any more of this," he said. "We have work to do. We've been standing here acting like a bunch of schoolkids. All this time that old man has been lying there suffering. A couple of you men cut two poles and make a stretcher to carry him."

While the men were getting the poles, Papa heated the coonskins again and rewrapped Grandpa's foot.

With belts and long leather laces from their boots, the hunters made a stretcher. Very gently they put Grandpa on it.

Again Mr. Kyle took command. "Part of us will start for camp with him," he said. "The others will go after the dogs."

"Here, take this gun," Papa said. "I'll go with him."

Looking at me, Mr. Kyle said, "Come on, son. I want to see your hounds."

Mr. Benson led the way. "As soon as we get out of this cane," he said, "we may be able to hear them. They have the coon treed in a big black gum tree. You're going to see a sight. Now I mean a sight. They've walked a ring around that tree clear down through the ice and snow. You can see the bare ground."

"Wonder why they did that?" someone asked.

"I don't know," Mr. Benson replied, "unless they ran in that circle to keep from freezing to death, or to keep the coon in the tree."

23 Discussion Do you think the dogs knew that they would freeze to death if they stopped running?

24 Literary Focus You could have the students reread these paragraphs and discuss both men's statements. Do they agree with Mr. Kyle? Why or why not? What do they think of the other man's statement? How might these statements relate to the theme?

I figured I knew why my dogs were covered with ice. The coon had probably crossed the river, maybe several times. Old Dan and Little Ann would have followed him. They had come out of the river with their coats dripping wet, and the freezing blast of the blizzard had done the rest.

Nearing the tree, we stopped and stared.

"Did you ever see anything like that?" Mr. Benson asked. "When I first saw them, I thought they were white wolves."

My dogs hadn't seen us when we came up. They were trotting round and round. Just as Mr. Benson had said, we could see the path they had worn down through the ice and snow till the bare black earth was visible. Like ghostly white shadows, around and around they trotted.

In a low voice, someone said, "They know that if they stop they'll freeze to death."

"It's unbelievable," said Mr. Kyle. "Come on. We must do something quick."

With a choking sob, I ran for my dogs.

On hearing our approach, they sat down and started bawling treed. I noticed their voices didn't have that solid ring. Their ice-covered tails made a rattling sound as they switched this way and that on the icy ground.

A large fire was built. Standing my dogs close to the warm heat, the gentle hands of the hunters went to work. With handkerchiefs and scarves heated steaming hot, little by little the ice was thawed from their bodies.

23 "If they had ever lain down," someone said, "they would've frozen to death."

"They knew it," another said. "That's why they kept running in that circle."

"What I can't understand is why they stayed with the tree," Mr. Benson said. "I've seen hounds stay with a tree for a while, but not in a northern blizzard."

"Men," said Mr. Kyle, "people have been trying to understand dogs ever since the be-ginning of time. One never knows what they'll do. You can read every day where a dog saved the life of a drowning child, or lay down his life for his master. Some people call this loyalty. I don't. I may be wrong, but I call it love—the deepest kind of love."

After these words were spoken, a thoughtful silence settled over the men. The **24** mood was broken by the deep growling voice I had heard back in the washout.

"It's a shame that people all over the world can't have that kind of love in their hearts," he said. "There would be no wars, slaughter, or murder; no greed or selfishness. It would be the kind of world that God wants us to have—a wonderful world."

After all the ice was thawed from my dogs and their coats were dried out, I could see they were all right. I was happy again and felt good all over.

One of the hunters said, "Do you think those hounds are thawed out enough to fight a coon?"

"Sure, just run him out of that tree," I said.

At the crack of the gun, the coon ran far out on a big limb and stopped. Again the hunter sprinkled him with bird shot. This time he jumped. Hitting the ground, he crouched down.

Old Dan made a lunge. Just as he reached him, the coon sprang straight up and came down on his head. Holding on with his claws, the coon sank his teeth in a long tender ear. Old Dan was furious. He started turning in a circle, bawling with pain.

Little Ann was trying hard to get ahold of the coon but she couldn't. Because of his fast circling, Old Dan's feet flew out from under him and he fell. This gave Little Ann a chance. Darting in, her jaws closed on the back of the coon's neck. I knew the fight was over.

Arriving back at camp, I saw that all the

tents had been taken down but ours. A hunter said, "Everyone was in a hurry to get out before another blizzard sets in."

Papa told me to take my dogs into the tent as Grandpa wanted to see them.

I saw tears in my grandfather's eyes as he talked to them. His ankle was wrapped in bandages. His foot and toes were swollen to twice their normal size. They had turned a greenish-yellow color. Placing my hand on his foot, I could feel the feverish heat.

Dr. Lathman came over. "Are you ready to go now?" he asked.

Snorting and growling, Grandpa said, "I told you I wasn't going anywhere till I see the gold cup handed to this boy."

Turning to face the crowd, Dr. Lathman said, "Men, let's get this over. I want to get this man to town. That's one of the meanest sprains I've ever seen and it should be in a cast, but I don't have any plaster of Paris with me."

The hunter who had come by our tent collecting the jackpot money came up to me. Handing me the box, he said, "Here you are, son. There's over three hundred dollars in this box. It's all yours."

Turning to the crowd, he said, "Fellows, I can always say this. On this hunt I've seen two of the finest little coon hounds I ever hope to see."

There was a roar of approval from the crowd.

Looking down, I saw the box was almost full of money. I was shaking all over. I tried to say "Thanks," but it was only a whisper. Turning, I handed the box to my father. As his rough old hands closed around it, I saw a strange look come over his face. He turned and looked at my dogs.

Some of the men started shouting, "Here it is!"

The crowd parted and the judge walked through. I saw the gleaming metal of the gold cup in his hand. After a short speech, he handed it to me, saying, "Son, this makes me very proud. It's a great honor to present you with this championship cup."

The crowd exploded. The hunters' shouts were deafening.

I don't know from where the two silly old tears came. They just squeezed their way out. I felt them as they rolled down my cheeks. One dropped on the smooth surface of the cup and splattered. I wiped it away with my sleeve.

Turning to my dogs, I knelt down and showed the cup to them. Little Ann licked it. Old Dan sniffed one time, and then turned his head away.

The judge said, "Son, there's a place on the cup to engrave the names of your dogs. I can take it into Oklahoma City and have it done, or you can have it done yourself. The engraving charge has already been paid by the association."

Looking at the cup, it seemed that far down in the gleaming shadows I could see two wide blue eyes glued to a windowpane. I knew that my little sister was watching the road and waiting for our return. Looking back at the judge, I said, "If you don't mind, I'll take it with me. My grandfather can send it in for me."

Laughing, he said, "That's all right." Handing me a slip of paper, he said, "This is the address where you should send it."

Grandpa said, "Now that that's settled, I'm ready to go to town." Turning to Papa, he said, "You'll have to bring the buggy, and I wish you'd look after my stock. I know Grandma will want to go in with us and there'll be no one there to feed them. Tell Bill Lowery to come up and take care of the store. You'll find the keys in the usual place."

"We'll take care of everything," Papa said. "Don't worry about a thing. I don't intend to stop until we get back, because it looks like we're in for some more bad weather."

I went over and kissed Grandpa good-

Where the Red Fern Grows 749

25 Discussion How is Billy feeling right now? Why are all the other hunters so excited that Billy won?

25

bye. He pinched my cheek, and whispered, "We'll teach these city slickers that they can't come up here and beat our dogs."

I smiled.

Grandpa was carried out and made comfortable in the back seat of Dr. Lathman's car. I stood and watched as it wheezed and bounced its way out of sight.

"While I'm harnessing the team," Papa said, "you take the tent down and pack our gear."

On the back seat of the buggy, I made a bed out of our bed-clothes. Down on the floor boards, I fixed a nice place for my dogs.

All through the night, the creaking wheels of our buggy moved on. Several times I woke up. My father had wrapped a tarp around himself. Reaching down, I could feel my dogs. They were warm and comfortable.

Early the next morning, we stopped for breakfast. While Papa tended to the team, I turned my dogs loose and let them stretch.

"We made good time last night," Papa said. "If everything goes right, we'll be home long before dark."

Reaching Grandpa's store in the middle of the afternoon, Papa said, "I'll put the team in the barn and feed the stock while you unload the buggy."

Coming back from the barn, he said, "In the morning, I'll go over and tell Bill Lowery to come up and open the store."

Looking around, he said, "It snowed more here than it did where we were hunting."

Feeling big and important, I said, "I don't like the looks of this weather. We'd better be scooting for home."

Papa laughed. "Sure you're not in a

hurry to get home to show off the gold cup?" he asked.

A smile was my only answer.

Two hundred yards this side of our home, the road made a turn around a low foothill shutting our house off from view.

Papa said, "You're going to see a scramble as soon as we round that bend."

It was more of a stampede than a scramble. The little one came out first, and all but tore the screen door from its hinges. The older girls passed her just beyond the gate. In her hurry, she slipped and fell face down in the snow. She started crying.

The older girls ran up asking for the cup.

Holding it high over my head, I said, "Now wait a minute. I've got another one for you two." I held the small silver cup out to them.

While they were fighting over it, I ran to the little one. Picking her up, I brushed the snow from her long, braided hair and her tear-stained face. I told her there was no use to cry. I had brought the gold cup to her, and no one else was going to get it.

Reaching for the cup, she wrapped her small arms around it. Squeezing it up tight, she ran for the house to show it to Mama.

Mama came out on the porch. She was just as excited as the girls were. She held out her arms. I ran to her. She hugged me and kissed me.

"It's good to have you home again," she said.

"Look what I have, Mama," the little one cried, "and it's all mine."

She held the golden cup out in her two small hands.

As Mama took the beautiful cup, she looked at me. She started to say something but was interrupted by the cries from the other girls.

"We have one, too, Mama," they cried, "and it's just as pretty as that one."

"It's not either," the little one piped in a defiant voice. "It's not even as big as mine."

"Two cups!" Mama exclaimed. "Did you win two!"

"Yes, Mama," I said. "Little Ann won that one all by herself."

The awed expression on my mother's face was wonderful to see. Holding a cup in each hand, she held them out in front of her.

"Two," she said. "A gold one and a silver one. Who would have thought anything so wonderful could have happened to us. I'm so proud; so very proud."

Handing the cups back to the girls, she walked over to Papa. After kissing him, she said, "I just can't believe everything that has happened. I'm so glad you went along; Did you enjoy yourself?"

With a smile on his face, Papa almost shouted, "Enjoy myself? Why, I never had such a time in my life."

His voice trailed off to a low calm, "That is, except for one thing. Grandpa had a bad accident."

"Yes, I know," Mama said. "One of Tom Logan's boys was at the store when they arrived. He came by and told us all about it. The doctor said it wasn't as bad as it looked, and he was pretty sure Grandpa would be home in a few days."

I was happy to hear this news, and could tell by the pleased look on my father's face, he was glad to hear it, too.

On entering the house, Papa said, "Oh, I almost forgot." He handed the box of money to Mama.

"What's this?" she asked.

"Oh, it's just a little gift from Old Dan and Little Ann," Papa said.

Mama opened the box. I saw the color drain from her face. Her hands started trembling. Turning her back to us, she walked over and set it on the mantel. A peaceful silence settled over the room. I could hear the clock ticking away. The fire in the fireplace crackled and popped.

Where the Red Fern Grows 751

27 **Reading Strategy** Have students predict what the family might do with the three hundred dollars. Do you think the money will change the family in any way?

28 **Reading Strategy** Students could question Mama's actions as Billy has. Why did she act that way? How does she feel about the dogs?

29 **Discussion** Do you think Billy is correct about what his parents were discussing?

27 Turning from the mantel, Mama looked straight at us. Her lips were tightly pressed together to keep them from quivering. Walking slowly to Papa, she buried her face in his chest. I heard her say, "Thank God, my prayers have been answered."

There was a celebration in our home that night. To me it was like a second Christmas.

Mama opened a jar of huckleberries and made a large cobbler. Papa went to the smokehouse and came back with a hickory-cured ham. We sat down to a feast of the ham, huge plates of fried potatoes, ham gravy, hot corn bread, fresh butter, and wild bee honey.

During the course of the meal, the entire story of the championship hunt was told, some by Papa but mostly by me.

Just when everything was so perfect and peaceful, an argument sprang up between the two oldest girls. It seemed that each wanted to claim the silver cup. Just when they were on the verge of sawing it in two, so each would have her allotted share, Papa settled the squabble by giving the oldest one a silver dollar. Once again peace and harmony was restored.

That night as I was preparing for bed, a light flashed by my window. Puzzled, I tiptoed over and peeked through the pane. It was Mama. Carrying my lantern and two large plates heaped high with food, she was heading for the doghouse. Setting the light down on the ground in front of it, she called to my dogs. While they were eating, Mama did something I couldn't understand. She knelt down on her knees in prayer.

After they had eaten their food, Mama started petting them. I could hear her voice but couldn't make out her words. Whatever she was saying must have pleased them. Little Ann wiggled and twisted. Even Old Dan wagged his long red tail, which was very unusual.

Papa came out. I saw him put his arm around Mama. Side by side they stood for several minutes looking at my dogs. When they turned to enter the house, I saw Mama dab at her eyes with her apron.

28 Lying in bed, staring into the darkness, I tried hard to figure out the strange actions of my parents. Why had Mama knelt in prayer in front of my dogs? Why had she wept?

I was running all the why's around in my mind when I heard them talking.

"I know," Papa said, "but I think there's a way. I'm going to have a talk with Grandpa. I don't think that old foot of his is ever going to be the same again. He's going to need some help around the store."

I knew they were talking about me, but I couldn't understand what they meant. Then I thought, "Why, that's it. They want me to help Grandpa." That would be all right with me. I could still hunt every night.

29 Feeling smart for figuring out their conversation, I turned over and fell asleep.

Chapter 19

Although the winning of the cups and the money was a big event in my life, it didn't change my hunting any. I was out after the ringtails every night.

I had been hunting the river bottoms hard for about three weeks. On that night, I decided to go back to the Cyclone Timber country. I had barely reached the hunting ground when my dogs struck a trail. Old Dan opened up first.

They struck the trail on a ridge and then dropped down into a deep canyon, up the other side, and broke out into some flats. I could tell that the scent was hot from their steady bawling. Three times they treed the animal.

Every time I came close to the tree, the animal would jump, and the race would be

Grammar in Action

Good writers vary their sentences to make their writing more interesting and readable. Varying the structure and length of sentences as well as sentence openers makes writing come alive. Notice how Wilson Rawls uses varied sentence structure, length, and openers to make the passage fast-paced and exciting.

> The silence was shattered by one long, loud bawl from Old Dan. I'd never heard my dog bawl like that. It was different.

His voice rang out over the mountains, loud and clear. The vibration of the deep tones rolled in the silence of the frosty night, on and on, out over the flats, down in the canyons, and died away in the rimrocks, like the cry of a lost soul. Old Dan had voiced his challenge to the devil cat.

Rawls's sentences swing from one long sentence to a pair of short ones. The length and style of the sentence beginning *The vibrations of the deep tones . . .* reflects the action Rawls is describing. The long series of prepositional phrases evokes the echo of Old Dan's bark. By intermixing simple and complex sentences, and including different types of phrases, Rawls makes the action more lively and interesting.

on. After a while, I knew it wasn't a coon. I decided it was a bobcat.

I didn't like to have my dogs tree the big cats, for their fur wasn't any good, and all I could expect was two cut-up hounds.

They could kill the largest bobcat in the hills, and had on several occasions, but to me it was useless. The only good I could see in killing one was getting rid of a vicious predatory animal.

The fourth time they treed, they were on top of a mountain. After the long chase, I figured the animal was winded and would stay in the tree. In a trot I started to them.

As I neared the tree, Little Ann came to me, reared up, and whined. By her actions, I knew something was wrong. I stopped. In the moonlight, I could see Old Dan sitting on his haunches, staring up at the tree and bawling.

The tree had lots of dead leaves on it. I knew it was a large white oak because it is one of the last trees in the mountains to lose its leaves.

Old Dan kept bawling. Then he did something he had never done before. For seconds his deep voice was still, and silence settled over the mountains. My eyes wandered from the tree to him. His lips were curled back and he snarled as he stared into the dark foliage of the tree. His teeth gleamed white in the moonlight. The hair on his neck and along his back stood on end. A low, deep, rumbling growl rolled from his throat.

30 I was scared and I called to him. I wanted to get away from there. Again I called, but it was no use. He wouldn't leave the tree, for in his veins flowed the breeded blood of a hunting hound. In his fighting heart, there was no fear.

I set the lantern down and tightened my grip on the handle of the ax. Slowly I started walking toward him. I thought, "If I can get close enough to him, I can grab his collar." I kept my eyes on the tree as I edged forward. Little Ann stayed by my side. She, too, was watching the tree.

Then I saw them—two burning, yellow eyes—staring at me from the shadowy foliage of the tree. I stopped, petrified with fear.

The deep baying of Old Dan stopped and again the silence closed in.

I stared back at the unblinking eyes.

I could make out the bulk of a large animal, crouched on a huge branch, close to the trunk of the big tree. Then it moved. I heard the scratch of razor-sharp claws on the bark. It stood up and moved out of the shadows on to the limb. I saw it clearly as it passed between the moon and me. I knew what it was. It was the devil cat of the Ozarks, the mountain lion.

The silence was shattered by one long, loud bawl from Old Dan. I'd never heard my dog bawl like that. It was different. His voice rang out over the mountains, loud and clear. The vibration of the deep tones rolled in the silence of the frosty night, on and on, out over the flats, down in the canyons, and died away in the rimrocks, like the cry of a lost soul. Old Dan had voiced his challenge to the devil cat.

There was a low cough and a deep growl from the lion. I saw him crouch. I knew what was coming. My hands felt hot and sweaty on the smooth ash handle of the ax. With a blood-curdling scream he sprang from the tree with claws outspread and long, yellow fangs bared.

Old Dan didn't wait. Rearing up on his hind legs, he met the lion in the air. The heavy weight bowled him over and over. He wound up in a fallen treetop.

The impact of the two bodies threw the lion off balance. Little Ann darted in. Her aim was true. I heard the snap of her steel-trap jaws as they closed on his throat.

With a squall of pain and rage, the big cat rolled over on his side, dragging Little

Where the Red Fern Grows   753

30 Discussion Why is Billy scared? What happened differently from other times when the dogs treed an animal?

Student Activity 1. Find three other paragraphs from *Where the Red Fern Grows* in which Rawls effectively varies his sentence structure, length, and openers. Explain how Rawls's use of varied sentences in each paragraph is effective.

Student Activity 2. Rewrite the following paragrah, varying sentence length, structure and openers, to make it more lively and interesting.

Mario was fifteen years old. He had come to this country two years ago. He lived with his father, mother and two sisters. They lived in a four-story apartment building. Mario hoped someday to live in a house surrounded by grass and trees. He thought he might be able to have a dog if he lived in such a place.

Ann with him. His right paw reached out and curved over her shoulder. Sinews tightened and razor-sharp claws dug inward. With a cry of pain, she loosened her hold. I saw the blood squirting from the deep wound in her shoulder. She ignored it and bored back into the fight.

Old Dan, stunned for an instant from the impact of the lion's body, fought his way from the treetop. Bawling the cry of the damned, he charged back in.

I went berserk, and charged into the fight.

There in the flinty hills of the Ozarks, I fought for the lives of my dogs. I fought with the only weapon I had, the sharp cutting blade of a double-bitted ax.

Screaming like a madman, with tears running down my face, I hacked and chopped at the big snarling mountain cat.

Once, feeling the bite of the sharp blade, the devil cat turned on me. His yellow slitted eyes burned with hate. The long, lithe body dipped low to the ground. The shoulder muscles knotted and bulged. I tried to jump back but my foot slipped and I dropped to my knees. I knew I was trapped. With a terrifying scream he sprang.

I never saw my dogs when they got be-

tween the lion and me, but they were there. Side by side, they rose up from the ground as one. They sailed straight into those jaws of death, their small, red bodies taking the ripping, slashing claws meant for me.

I screamed and charged back into the fight, swinging my ax, but I was careful not to hit one of my dogs.

The battle raged on and on, down the side of the mountain, over huckleberry bushes, fallen logs, and rocks. It was a rolling, tumbling mass of fighting fury. I was in the middle of it all, falling, screaming, crying and backing away at every opportunity.

I had cut the big cat several times. Blood showed red on the bit of the ax, but as yet I had not gotten in the fatal lick. I knew it had to be soon for my dogs were no match against the razor-sharp claws and the long, yellow fangs.

The screams of the big cat and the deep

Primary Source

Billy calls the mountain lion a "devil cat," and expresses the opinion that the only good that could come from his dogs killing a bobcat would be "getting rid of a vicious predatory animal." As this excerpt from *Vanishing Wildlife* by Roy Pinney attests, predatory animals such as mountain lions are misunderstood, and killing them usually does more harm than good:

> Authenticated reports of mountain lions attacking humans are extremely rare. This fact, however, has made little

impact on most people. The average person still considers the mountain lion a dangerous animal; for this reason, it has been widely and systematically exterminated. In many instances, the results have been disastrous. In Yellowstone National Park and in Kaibab National Forest, for example, where both mountain lions and wolves were wiped out as a result of well-organized campaigns, the deer population increased so alarmingly that it did permanent damage to the top soil and forest, and tens of thousands of the deer died from starvation . . . If for no other reason than this, the mountain lion deserves to be regarded as an invaluable part of our wildlife scene.

bellowing voices of my dogs echoed through the mountains as if the demons of hell had been turned loose. Down the side of the mountain, the terrible fight went on, down to the very bottom of the canyon.

The big cat had Old Dan by the throat. I knew he was seeking to cut the all-important vein, the jugular. At the pitiful bawl of Old Dan, Little Ann, throwing caution to the wind, ran in and sank her teeth in the lion's tough neck.

With her claws digging into the mountain soil, she braced herself, and started

pulling. The muscles in her small legs knotted and quivered. She was trying hard to pull the devil cat's fangs from the throat of Old Dan.

In the rays of a bright Ozark moon, I could see clearly. For an instant I saw the broad back of the big cat. I saw the knotty bulge of steel-bound muscle, the piston-like jerk of the deadly hind claws, trying for the downward stroke that could disembowel a dog.

Raising the ax high over my head, I brought it down with all the strength in my body. My aim was true. Behind the shoulders, in the broad muscular back, the heavy blade sank with a sickening sound. The keen edge cleaved through the tough skin. It seemed to hiss as it sliced its way through bone and gristle.

I left the ax where it was, sunk to the eye in the back of the devil cat.

He loosened his hold on the throat of Old Dan. With a scream of pain, he reared up on his hind legs and started pawing the air. Little Ann dangled from his neck, still holding on. Her eyes were shut tight and her small feet were digging and clawing at the body.

Old Dan, spewing blood from a dozen wounds, leaped high in the air. His long, red body sailed in between the outspread paws of the lion. I heard the snap of his powerful jaws as they closed on the throat.

The big cat screamed again. Blood gurgled and sprayed. In a bright red mist, it rained out over the underbrush and rattled like sleet on the white oak leaves. In a boxer's stance, he stood and clawed the air. His slitted eyes turned green with hate. He seemed to be unaware of the two hounds hanging from his body, and kept staring at me. I stood in a trance and stared back at the ghastly scene.

The breath of life was slowly leaving him.

Where the Red Fern Grows 755

To determine just how important these animals are, a group of scientists made a study of a remote mountainous area in California a few years ago. At that time there was an estimated population of 600 mountain lions in the region. In the course of the study it was found that these 600 lions took a toll of about 21,600 deer, probably fawns and weak or older deer, for the most part. It was calculated that an equal number of deer, mainly prime bucks useful as breeding stock, were killed every year by hunters. Significantly, despite the combined annual toll, the deer in the area were on the increase. The Kaibab herd is notably defective, with a high proportion of deformed, undersized, scrawny deer, the result of overcrowding and total lack of predator weeding out of inferior specimens.

As a result of the extensive misconceptions about mountain lions, they have been hunted to near extiction.

He was dying on his feet but refusing to go down. My ax handle stuck straight out from his back. Blood, gushing from the mortal wound, glistened in the moonlight. A shudder ran through his body. He tried once again to scream. Blood gurgled in his throat.

31 It was the end of the trail for the scourge of the mountains. No more would he scream his challenge from the rimrocks to the valley below. The small, harmless calves and the young colts would be safe from his silent stalk.

He fell toward me. It seemed that with his last effort he was still trying to get at me.

As his heavy body struck the ground, something exploded in my head. I knew no more.

When I came to, I was sitting down. It was silent and still. A bird, disturbed by the fight, started chirping far up on the side of the mountain. A small winter breeze rustled some dead leaves in the deep canyon. A cold, crawling chill crept over my body.

I looked over at the lion. My dogs were still glued to his lifeless body. In his dying convulsions the ax had become dislodged from the wound. It lay there in the moonlight, covered with blood.

My numb brain started working. I thought of another time the ax had been covered with blood. I don't know why I thought of Rubin Pritchard at that time, or why I thought of these words I had often heard: "There is a little good in all evil."

I got to my feet and went over to my dogs. I knew I had to inspect them to see how badly they were hurt. It wasn't too hard to get Little Ann to loosen her hold. I examined her body. She was cut in several places, but nothing fatal. The only bad wound she had was in her shoulder. It was nine inches long and down to the clean, white bone. She started licking it immediately.

It was different with Old Dan. Try as I might, he wouldn't turn loose. Maybe he could remember the night in the cave when he was a pup. How the big cat had screamed and how he had bawled back at him.

I took hold of his hind legs and tried to pull him loose. It was no use. He knew that the hold he had was a deadly one and he wasn't going to let go. I tried to tell him it was all over, that the lion was dead, to turn loose as I wanted to see how badly he was hurt. He couldn't understand and wouldn't even open his eyes. He was determined to hold on until the body turned cold and stiff.

With my ax handle, I pried apart his locked jaws. Holding on to his collar, I led him off to one side. I couldn't turn him loose as I knew if I did, he would go back to the lion.

With one hand I started examining him. I ran my fingers through the short, red hair. I could feel the quivering muscles and the hot, sweaty skin. He was a bloody mess. His long, velvety ears were shredded. His entire body was a mass of deep, raw, red wounds. On both sides of his rib carriage, the sharp claws had laid the flesh open to the bone.

His friendly old face was pitiful to see. A razor-sharp claw had ripped down on an angle across his right eye. It was swollen shut. I wondered if he would ever see from that eye again.

Blood dripped from his wounds and fell on the white-oak leaves. I saw he was bleeding to death. With tears running down my cheeks, I did the only thing a hunter could do. I raked the leaves away and let his blood drip on the black mountain soil. Mixing it into a mud, I worked it into his wounds to stop the flow of blood.

With my ax in one hand and holding onto his collar with the other, we climbed out of the canyon. I knew if I could get him far enough away from the lion he wouldn't go back.

On reaching the top, I saw the yellow glow of my lantern. I turned Old Dan loose and walked over and picked it up.

Not knowing exactly where I was, I looked down out of the mountains to get my bearings. Beyond the foothills and fields I could see the long, white, crooked line of steam, marking the river's course. Following the snakelike pattern with my eyes, in no time I knew exactly where I was, for I knew every bend in the river.

Anxious to get home so I could take care of my dogs, I turned to call to them. Little Ann was close by. She was sitting down, licking at the wound in her shoulder. I saw the shadowy form of Old Dan sniffing around the tree where the lion had been treed.

32 As I stood and watched him in the moonlight, my heart swelled with pride. Wounded though he was, he wanted to make sure there were no more lions around.

I called to him. In a stiff-legged trot he came to me. I caught hold of his collar and gave him another inspection. In the lantern light I could see the mudcaked wounds clearly. The bleeding had almost stopped. I felt much better.

Little Ann came over. I knelt down and put my arms around them. I knew that if it hadn't been for their loyalty and unselfish courage I would have probably been killed by the slashing claws of the devil cat.

"I don't know how I'll ever pay you back for what you've done," I said, "but I'll never forget it."

Getting up, I said, "Come on, let's go home so I can take care of those wounds."

I hadn't gone far when I heard a cry. At first I thought it was a bird, or a night hawk. I stood still and listened. I glanced at Little Ann. She was looking behind me. I turned around and looked for Old Dan. He was nowhere in sight.

The cry came again, low and pitiful. Instantly Little Ann started back the way we had come. I followed as fast as I could run.

I found Old Dan lying on his side, pleading for help. What I saw was almost more than I could stand. There, tangled in the low branches of a huckleberry bush, were the entrails of my dog. With a gasping cry I knelt down by his side.

I knew what had happened. Far back in the soft belly, the slashing, razor-sharp claws of the lion had cut into the hollow. In my inspections I had overlooked the wound. His entrails had worked out and had become entangled in the bush. The forward motion of his body had done the rest.

He whimpered as I laid my hand on his head. A warm, red tongue flicked out at it. With tears in my eyes, I started talking to him. "Hang on, boy," I said. "Everything will be all right. I'll take care of you."

With trembling hands, I unwound the entrails from the bush. With my handkerchief I wiped away the gravel, leaves, and pine needles. With fingers that shook, I worked the entrails back into the wound.

Knowing that I couldn't carry him and the ax and lantern, I stuck the ax deep in the side of a white oak tree. I blew out the lantern and hung the handle over the other blade. I wrapped my dog in my old sheepskin coat and hurried for home.

Arriving home, I awakened my mother and father. Together we doctored my dogs. Old Dan was taken care of first. Very gently Mama worked the entrails out and in a pan of warm soapy water, washed them clean of the pine needles, leaves, and grit.

"If I only knew what I was doing," Mama said, as she worked, "I'd feel better."

With gentle hands, she worked the entrails back through the opening. The wound was sewn up and bandaged with a clean white cloth.

Where the Red Fern Grows 757

32 Discussion What do Dan's actions reflect about his character? Do you think his actions were realistic?

33 **Discussion** Why does Billy's family care about the dogs so much? Have the dogs helped the family?

34 **Reading Strategy** You might have the students summarize the events in the story that support this statement. What love does Dan have other than Billy and hunting?

35 **Discussion** When the dogs save Billy's life, "they looked just like one." In what other ways do the dogs seem to act like two parts of a single thing? What does this reflect about their relationship?

Little Ann wasn't hard to doctor. I held her head while Mama cleaned her wounds with peroxide. Feeling the bite of the strong liquid, she whined and licked at my hands.

"It's all right, little girl," I said. "You'll be well in no time."

I opened the door and watched her as she limped off to the doghouse.

Hearing a whimper, I turned around. There in the doorway to the room stood my sisters. I could tell by the looks on their faces that they had been watching for some time. They looked pitiful standing there in their long white gowns. I felt sorry for them.

"Will Little Ann be all right?" my oldest sister asked.

"Yes," I said, "she'll be all right. She only had one bad wound and we've taken care of that."

"Old Dan's hurt bad, isn't he?" she said. I nodded my head.

"How bad is it?" she asked.

"It's bad," I said. "He was cut wide open." They all started crying.

"Now here," Mama said, going over, "you girls get back in bed. You'll take a death of cold being up like this in your bare feet."

"Mommie," the little one said. "God won't let Old Dan die, will He?"

"I don't think so, honey," Mama said. "Now off to bed."

33 | They turned and walked slowly back to their room.

"The way your dogs are cut up," Papa said, "it must have been a terrible fight."

"It was, Papa," I said. "I never saw anything like it. Little Ann wouldn't have fought the lion if it hadn't been for Old Dan. All she was doing was helping him. He wouldn't quit. He just stayed right in there till the end. I even had to pry his jaws loose from the lion's throat after the lion was dead."

Glancing at Old Dan, Papa said, "It's in his blood, Billy. He's a hunting hound, and the best one I ever saw. He only has two loves—you and hunting. That's all he knows." | 34

"If it hadn't been for them, Papa," I said, "I probably wouldn't be here now."

"What do you mean," Mama said, "you wouldn't be here now?"

I told them how the lion had leaped at me and how my dogs had gotten between him and me.

"They were so close together," I said, "when they came up off the ground they looked just like one." | 35

There was a moaning sigh from Mama. She covered her face with her hands and started crying.

"I don't know," she sobbed, "I just don't know. To think how close you came to being killed. I don't think I can stand any more."

"Now, now," Papa said, as he walked over and put his arms around her. "Don't go all to pieces. It's all over. Let's be thankful and do our best for Old Dan."

"Do you think he'll die, Papa?" I asked.

"I don't know, Billy," Papa said, shaking his head. "He's lost an awful lot of blood and he's a mighty sick dog. All we can do now is wait and see."

Our wait wasn't long. My dog's breathing grew faster and faster, and there was a terrible rattling in his throat. I knelt down and laid his head in my lap.

Old Dan must have known he was dying. Just before he drew one last sigh, and a feeble thump of his tail, his friendly gray eyes closed forever.

At first I couldn't believe my dog was dead. I started talking to him. "Please don't die, Dan," I said. "Don't leave me now."

I looked to Mama for help. Her face was as white as the bark on a sycamore tree and the hurt in her eyes tore at my heart. She opened her mouth to say something but words wouldn't come out.

Grammar in Action

Sometimes the easiest way for a writer to show his readers a detail is to compare it with something else. Rawls makes comparisons often through his novel by using the words *like* and *as*.

Grandpa roared *like a bear.*

I looked to Mama for help. Her face was *as white as the bark on a sycamore tree . . .*

Beyond the foothills and fields I could see the long, white, crooked line of the stream, marking the river's course.

Following the *snakelike* pattern with my eyes, in no time I knew exactly where I was.

Writers—and thoughtful readers—get more meaning out of comparisons than first meets the eye. Grandpa, for example, is like a bear in many ways: he is strong, cunning, and proud. Perhaps Mama is like a sycamore tree because she provides comfort for her family; her arms may be like branches; her roots dig deep. The stream may be snakelike because it will bring death in the following scene. The meaning and power of such rich comparisons lies in the imagination of the reader.

Student Activity 1. Find five other sentences in which Wilson Rawls uses comparisons. For each sentence, explain what is being compared.

Feeling as cold as an arctic wind, I got up and stumbled to a chair. Mama came over and said something. Her words were only a murmur in my ears.

Very gently Papa picked Old Dan up in his arms and carried him out on the porch. When he came back in the house, he said, "Well, we did all we could do, but I guess it wasn't enough."

I had never seen my father and mother look so tired and weary as they did on that night. I knew they wanted to comfort me, but didn't know what to say.

Papa tried. "Billy," he said, "I wouldn't think too much about this if I were you. It's not good to hurt like that. I believe I'd just try to forget it. Besides, you still have Little Ann."

I wasn't even thinking about Little Ann at that moment. I knew she was all right.

"I'm thankful that I still have her," I said, "but how can I forget Old Dan? He gave his life for me, that's what he did—just laid down his life for me. How can I ever forget something like that?"

Mama said, "It's been a terrible night for all of us. Let's go to bed and try to get some rest. Maybe we'll all feel better tomorrow."

"No, Mama," I said. "You and Papa go on to bed. I think I'll stay up for a while. I couldn't sleep anyway."

Mama started to protest, but Papa shook his head. Arm in arm they walked from the room.

Long after my mother and father had retired, I sat by the fire trying to think and couldn't. I felt numb all over. I knew my dog was dead, but I couldn't believe it. I didn't want to. One day they were both alive and happy. Then that night, just like that, one of them was dead.

I didn't know how long I had been sitting there when I heard a noise out on the porch. I got up, walked over to the door, and listened. It came again, a low whimper and a scratchy sound.

I could think of only one thing that could have made the noise. It had to be my dog. He wasn't dead. He had come back to life. With a pounding heart, I opened the door and stepped out on the porch.

What I saw was more than I could stand. The noise I had heard had been made by Little Ann. All her life she had slept by Old Dan's side. And although he was dead, she had left the doghouse, had come back to the porch, and snuggled up close to his side.

She looked up at me and whimpered. I couldn't stand it. I didn't know I was running until I tripped and fell. I got to my feet and ran on and on, down through our fields of shocked corn, until I fell face down on the river's bank. There in the gray shadows of a breaking dawn, I cried until I could cry no more.

The churring of gray squirrels in the bright morning sun told me it was daylight. I got to my feet and walked back to the house.

Coming up through our barn lot, I saw my father feeding our stock. He came over and said, "Breakfast is about ready."

"I don't want any breakfast, Papa," I said. "I'm not hungry and I have a job to do. I'll have to bury my dog."

"I tell you what," he said. "I'm not going to be very busy today, so let's have a good breakfast and then I'll help you."

"No, Papa," I said. "I'll take care of it. You go and eat breakfast. Tell Mama I'm not hungry."

I saw a hurt look in my father's eyes. Shaking his head, he turned and walked away.

From rough pine slabs, I made a box for my dog. It was a crude box but it was the best I could do. With strips of burlap and corn shucks, I padded the inside.

Up on the hillside, at the foot of a beauti-

Where the Red Fern Grows   759

36 **Discussion** Do you think it is good advice to try to forget about the death of someone you love?

37 **Reading Strategy** Billy wants to bury Dan without any help. You could have students summarize other projects that Billy has insisted on doing alone.

Student Activity 2. Read these comparisons from earlier in *Where the Red Fern Grows*. Now that you have nearly finished the novel, discuss the rich possibilities of their meanings.
1. "It scared me when I first saw them," he said. "I didn't know what they were. They looked like white ghosts." (*page 747*)
2. I saw the knotty bulge of stell-bound muscle, the piston-like jerk of the deadly hind claws, trying for the downward stroke that could disembowel a dog. (*page 755*)

ful red oak tree, I dug his grave. There where the wild mountain flowers would grow in the spring, I laid him away.

I had a purpose in burying my dog up there on the hillside. It was a beautiful spot. From there one could see the country for miles, the long white crooked line of the river, the tall thick timber of the bottoms, the sycamore, birch, and box elder. I thought perhaps that on moonlight nights Old Dan would be able to hear the deep voices of the hounds as they rolled out of the river bottoms on the frosty air.

After the last shovel of dirt was patted in place, I sat down and let my mind drift back through the years. I thought of the old K. C. Baking Powder can, and the first time I saw my pups in the box at the depot. I thought of the fifty dollars, the nickels and dimes, and the fishermen and blackberry patches.

38 I looked at his grave and, with tears in my eyes, I voiced these words: "You were worth it, old friend, and a thousand times over."

In my heart I knew that there in the grave lay a man's best friend.

Two days later, when I came in from the bottoms where my father and I were clearing land, my mother said, "Billy, you had better look after your dog. She won't eat."

I started looking for her. I went to the barn, the corncrib, and looked under the porch. I called her name. It was no use.

I rounded up my sisters and asked if they had seen Little Ann. The youngest one said she had seen her go down into the garden. I went there, calling her name. She wouldn't answer my call.

I was about to give up, and then I saw her. She had wiggled her way far back under the thorny limbs of a blackberry bush in the corner of the garden. I talked to her and tried to coax her out. She wouldn't budge. I got down on my knees and crawled back to her. As I did, she raised her head and looked at me.

Her eyes told the story. They weren't the soft gray eyes I had looked into so many times. They were dull and cloudy. There was no fire, no life. I couldn't understand.

39 I carried her back to the house. I offered her food and water. She wouldn't touch it. I noticed how lifeless she was. I thought perhaps she had a wound I had overlooked. I felt and probed with my fingers. I could find nothing.

My father came and looked at her. He shook his head and said, "Billy, it's no use. The life has gone out of her. She has no will to live."

He turned and walked away.

I couldn't believe it. I couldn't.

With eggs and rich cream, I made a liquid. I pried her mouth open and poured it down. She responded to nothing I did. I carried her to the porch, and laid her in the same place I had laid the body of Old Dan. I covered her with gunny sacks.

All through the night I would get up and check on her. Next morning I took warm fresh milk and again I opened her mouth and fed her. It was a miserable day for me. At noon it was the same. My dog had just given up. There was no will to live.

That evening when I came in from the fields, she was gone. I hurried to my mother. Mama told me she had seen her go up the hollow from the house, so weak she could hardly stand. Mama had watched her until she had disappeared in the timber.

I hurried up the hollow, calling her name. I called and called. I went up to the head of it, still calling her name and praying she would come to me. I climbed out onto the flats; looking, searching, and calling. It was no use. My dog was gone.

I had a thought, a ray of hope. I just knew I'd find her at the grave of Old Dan. I hurried there.

I found her lying on her stomach, her hind legs stretched out straight, and her front feet folded back under her chest. She had laid her head on his grave. I saw the trail where she had dragged herself through the leaves. The way she lay there, I thought she was alive. I called her name. She made no movement. With the last ounce of strength in her body, she had dragged herself to the grave of Old Dan.

Kneeling down by her side, I reached out and touched her. There was no response, no whimpering cry or friendly wag of her tail. My little dog was dead.

I laid her head in my lap and with tear-filled eyes gazed up into the heavens. In a choking voice, I asked, "Why did they have to die? Why must I hurt so? What have I done wrong?"

I heard a noise behind me. It was my mother. She sat down and put her arm around me.

"You've done no wrong, Billy," she said. "I know this seems terrible and I know how it hurts, but at one time or another, everyone suffers. Even the Good Lord suffered while He was here on earth."

"I know, Mama," I said, "but I can't understand. It was bad enough when Old Dan died. Now Little Ann is gone. Both of them gone, just like that."

"Billy, you haven't lost your dogs altogether," Mama said. "You'll always have their memory. Besides, you can have some more dogs."

I rebelled at this. "I don't want any more dogs," I said. "I won't ever want another dog. They wouldn't be like Old Dan and Little Ann."

"We all feel that way, Billy," she said. "I do especially. They've fulfilled a prayer that I thought would never be answered."

"I don't believe in prayers any more," I said. "I prayed for my dogs, and now look, both of them are dead."

Mama was silent for a moment; then, in a gentle voice, she said, "Billy, sometimes it's hard to believe that things like this can happen, but there's always an answer. When you're older, you'll understand better."

"No, I won't," I said. "I don't care if I'm a hundred years old, I'll never understand why my dogs had to die."

As if she were talking to someone far away, I heard her say in a low voice, "I don't know what to say. I can't seem to find the right words."

Looking up to her face, I saw that her eyes were flooded with tears.

"Mama, please don't cry," I said. "I didn't mean what I said."

"I know you didn't," she said, as she squeezed me up tight. "It's just your way of fighting back."

I heard the voice of my father calling to us from the house.

"Come now," Mama said. "I have supper ready and your father wants to talk to you. I think when you've heard what he has to say, you'll feel better."

"I can't leave Little Ann like this, Mama," I said. "It'll be cold tonight. I think I'll carry her back to the house."

"No, I don't think you should do that," Mama said. "Your sisters would go all to pieces. Let's make her comfortable here."

Raking some dead leaves into a pile, she picked Little Ann up and laid her in them. Taking off my coat, I spread it over her body. I dreaded to think of what I had to do on the morrow.

My father and sisters were waiting for us on the porch. Mama told them the sad story.

40 **Critical Thinking and Reading** You could have students evaluate this event. Why did Ann crawl to Dan's grave? What does this action reflect about the dogs' relationship with each other? Is this action believable?

41 **Discussion** Why are memories so important to people who have lost loved ones? How do they help people get over the loss?

My sisters broke down and started crying. They ran to Mama and buried their faces in her long cotton dress.

Papa came over and laid his hand on my shoulder. "Billy," he said, "there are times in a boy's life when he has to stand up like a man. This is one of those times. I know what you're going through and how it hurts, but there's always an answer. The Good Lord has a reason for everything He does."

"There couldn't be any reason for my dogs to die, Papa," I said. "There just couldn't. They hadn't done anything wrong."

Papa glanced at Mama. Getting no help from her, he said, "It's getting cold out here. Let's go in the house. I have something to show you."

"Guess what we're having for supper," Mama said, as we turned to enter the house. "Your favorite, Billy, sweet potato pie. You'll like that, won't you?"

I nodded my head, but my heart wasn't in it.

Papa didn't follow us into the kitchen. He turned and entered his bedroom.

When he came into the room, he had a small shoe box in his hand. I recognized the box by the bright blue ribbon tied around it. Mama kept her valuables in it.

A silence settled over the room. Walking to the head of the table, Papa set the box down and started untying the ribbon. His hands were trembling as he fumbled with the knot. With the lid off, he reached in and started lifting out bundles of money.

After stacking them in a neat pile, he raised his head and looked straight at me. "Billy," he said, "you know how your mother has prayed that some day we'd have enough money to move out of these hills and into town so that you children could get an education."

I nodded my head.

"Well," he said, in a low voice, "because of your dogs, her prayers have been answered. This is the money earned by Old Dan and Little Ann. I've managed to make the farm feed us and clothe us and I've saved every cent your furs brought in. We now have enough."

"Isn't it wonderful," Mama said. "It's just like a miracle."

"I think it is a miracle," Papa said. "Remember, Billy said a prayer when he asked for his pups and then there were your prayers. Billy got his pups. Through those dogs your prayers were answered. Yes, I'm sure it is a miracle."

"If he gave them to me, then why did he take them away?" I asked.

"I think there's an answer for that, too," Papa said. "You see, Billy, your mother and I had decided not to separate you from your dogs. We knew how much you loved them. We decided that when we moved to town we'd leave you here with your grandpa for a while. He needs help anyway. But I guess the Good Lord didn't want that to happen. He doesn't like to see families split up. That's why they were taken away."

I knew my father was a firm believer in fate. To him everything that happened was the will of God, and in his Bible he could always find the answers.

Papa could see that his talk had had very little effect on me. With a sorrowful look on his face, he sat down and said, "Now let us give thanks for our food and for all the wonderful things God has done for us. I'll say a special prayer and ask Him to help Billy."

I barely heard what Papa had to say.

During the meal, I could tell that no one was enjoying the food. As soon as it was over, I went to my room and lay down on the bed.

Mama came in. "Why don't you go to

Literary element: Theme.

An important theme in this novel is the idea that accepting setbacks and facing responsibility are important steps in the passage from childhood to adulthood. At the beginning of the novel, Billy reacts in a childish way when his parents refuse his request for new hound pups. Throughout the novel he matures, working to save money for the hounds, learning to solve problems on his own, and accepting responsibility for his actions. In the end, Billy is able to accept the loss of the dogs he loves as much as he loves his family.

Have students discuss how Billy learns and grows throughout the novel. To initiate discussion, write the following list on the chalkboard:

1. Billy's trip to Tahlequah
2. Cutting down the big tree
3. The death of Dan and Ann

For each incident in the list, have a student briefly recount what happened. Then have the class discuss what Billy learned. What did he learn about life that helped him to mature?

The trip to Tahlequah forced Billy to take care of himself and to stand up for things he cared about. He also learned that

bed," she said, "and get a good night's sleep. You'll feel better tomorrow."

"No, I won't, Mama," I said. "I'll have to bury Little Ann tomorrow."

"I know," she said, as she turned my covers down. "I'll help if you want me to."

"No, Mama," I said, "I don't want anyone to help. I'd rather do it all by myself."

"Billy, you're always doing things by yourself," Mama said. "That's not right. Everyone needs help some time in his life."

"I know, Mama," I said, "but, please, not this time. Ever since my dogs were puppies, we've always been together—just us three. We hunted together and played together. We even went swimming together.

"Did you know, Mama, that Little Ann used to come every night and peek in my window just to see if I was all right? I guess that's why I want to be by myself when I bury her."

"Now say your prayers and go to sleep. I'm sure you'll feel better in the morning."

I didn't feel like saying any prayers that night. I was hurting too much. Long after the rest of the family had gone to bed, I lay staring into the darkness, trying to think and not able to.

Some time in the night I got up, tiptoed to my window, and looked out at my doghouse. It looked so lonely and empty sitting there in the moonlight. I could see that the door was slightly ajar. I thought of the many times I had lain in my bed and listened to the squeaking of the door as my dogs went in and out. I didn't know I was crying until I felt the tears roll down my cheeks.

Mama must have heard me get up. She came in and put her arms around me. "Billy," she said, in a quavering voice, "you'll just have to stop this. You're going to make yourself sick and I don't think I can stand any more of it."

"I can't, Mama," I said. "It hurts so much, I just can't. I don't want you to feel bad just because I do."

"I can't help it, Billy," she said. "Come now and get back in bed. I'm afraid you'll catch cold."

After she had tucked me in, she sat on the bed for a while. As if she were talking to the darkness, I heard her say, "If only there were some way I could help—something I could do."

"No one can help, Mama," I said. "No one can bring my dogs back."

"I know," she said, as she got up to leave the room, "but there must be something—there just has to be."

After Mama had left the room, I buried my face in my pillow and cried myself to sleep.

The next morning I made another box. It was smaller than the first one. Each nail I drove in the rough pine boards caused the knot in my throat to get bigger and bigger.

My sisters came to help. They stood it for a while, then with tears streaming, they ran for the house.

I buried Little Ann by the side of Old Dan. I knew that was where she wanted to be. I also buried a part of my life along with my dog. |42

Remembering a sandstone ledge I had seen while prowling the woods, I went there. I picked out a nice stone and carried it back to the graves. Then, with painstaking care, I carved their names deep in its red surface.

As I stood looking at the two graves, I tried hard to understand some of the things my father had told me, but I couldn't—I was still hurting and still had that empty feeling.

I went to Mama and had a talk with her.

"Mama," I asked, "do you think God made a heaven for all good dogs?"

"Yes," she said, "I'm sure He did."

sometimes people wrongly judge others by appearance rather than by character.

By cutting down the big tree, Billy kept his word even to his dogs. He learned that it is important to keep your word and to finish a job, even if the job is very difficult to accomplish.

The death of Dan and Ann was the most difficult experience for Billy. Yet he learned that the loss was not complete. Their death meant that the family was able to move into town, something Billy's parents had always dreamed about. Despite the extreme pain this loss caused Billy, he found that sometimes good things can come as a result of painful ones. He also learned not to let painful memories block out wonderful ones.

"Do you think He made a place for dogs to hunt? You know—just like we have here on our place—with mountains and sycamore trees, rivers and cornfields, and old rail fences? Do you think He did?"

"From what I've read in the Good Book, Billy," she said, "He put far more things up there than we have here. Yes, I'm sure He did."

I was thinking this over when Mama came up to me and started tucking my shirt in. "Do you feel better now?" she asked.

"It still hurts, Mama," I said, as I buried my face in her dress, "but I do feel a little better."

"I'm glad," she said, as she patted my head. "I don't like to see my little boy hurt like this."

Chapter 20

The following spring we left the Ozarks. The day we moved I thought everyone would be sad, but it was just the opposite. Mama seemed to be the happiest one of all. I could hear her laughing and joking with my sisters as they packed things. She had a glow in her eyes I had never seen before and it made me feel good.

I even noticed a change in Papa. He didn't have that whipped look on his face any more. He was in high spirits as we carried the furniture out to our wagon.

After the last item was stored in the wagon, Papa helped Mama to the spring seat and we were ready to go.

"Papa, would you mind waiting a few minutes?" I asked, "I'd like to say good-bye to my dogs."

"Sure," he said, smiling. "We have plenty of time. Go right ahead."

Nearing the graves, I saw something different. It looked like a wild bush had grown up and practically covered the two little mounds. It made me angry to think that an old bush would dare grow so close to the graves. I took out my knife, intending to cut it down.

When I walked up close enough to see what it was, I sucked in a mouthful of air and stopped. I couldn't believe what I was seeing. There between the graves, a beautiful red fern had sprung up from the rich mountain soil. It was fully two feet tall and its long red leaves had reached out in rainbow arches curved over the graves of my dogs.

I had heard the old Indian legend about the red fern. How a little Indian boy and girl were lost in a blizzard and had frozen to death. In the spring, when they were found, a beautiful red fern had grown up between their two bodies. The story went on to say that only an angel could plant the seeds of a red fern, and that they never died; where one grew, that spot was sacred.

Remembering the meaning of the legend, I turned and started hollering for Mama.

"Mama! Mama!" I shouted. "Come here! And hurry! You won't believe it."

In a frightened voice, she shouted back, "What is it, Billy? Are you all right?"

"I'm all right, Mama," I shouted, "but hurry. You just won't believe it." 43

Holding her long skirt in her hand and with a frightened look on her face, Mama came puffing up the hillside. Close behind her came Papa and my sisters.

"What is it, Billy?" Mama asked, in a scared voice. "Are you all right?"

"Look!" I said, pointing at the red fern.

Staring wide-eyed, Mama gasped and covered her mouth with her hand. I heard her say, almost in a whisper, "Oh-h-h-h, it's a red fern—a sacred red fern."

She walked over and very tenderly started fingering the long red leaves. In an awed voice, she said, "All my life I've wanted to see one. Now I have. It's almost unbelievable.

Commentary

Billy refers to "old Indian legend" of the red fern on page 764. Although it may or may not be an actual legend, Billy was probably referring to a legend of the Cherokees.

The legends of the Cherokee people can be divided into four categories. There are sacred legends that explain things such as the creation of the Earth, animal stories that explain unusual behavior or markings on animals, local legends, and historical legends. The legend of the red fern, if it is an actual legend, would probably be categorized as a local legend.

44 Literary Focus Billy's relationship with the dogs has lasted from the time they were very young until their deaths. He has experienced many different emotions associated with them. Why do you think Billy feels better? What does this reflect about the nature of people who lose someone they love?

"Don't touch it, Mama," my oldest sister whispered. "It was planted by an angel."

Mama smiled and asked, "Have you heard the legend?"

"Yes, Mama," my sister said. "Grandma told me the story, and I believe it, too."

With a serious look on his face, Papa said, "These hills are full of legends. Up until now I've never paid much attention to them, but now I don't know. Perhaps there is something to the legend of the red fern. Maybe this is God's way of helping Billy understand why his dogs died."

"I'm sure it is, Papa," I said, "and I do understand. I feel different now, and I don't hurt any more." | 44

"Come," Mama said, "let's go back to the wagon. Billy wants to be alone with his dogs for a while."

Just as they turned to leave, I heard Papa murmur in a low voice, "Wonderful indeed is the work of our Lord."

As I stood looking at the two graves, I noticed things I hadn't seen before. Wild violets, rooster heads, and mountain daisies had completely covered the two little mounds. A summer breeze gushed down from the rugged hills. I felt its warm caress as it fanned my face. It hummed a tune in the underbrush and rustled the leaves on the huge red oak. The red fern wavered and danced to the music of the hills.

Where the Red Fern Grows 765

Taking off my cap, I bowed my head. In a choking voice, I said, "Good-bye, Old Dan and Little Ann. I'll never forget you; and this I know—if God made room in heaven for all good dogs, I know He made a special place for you."

With a heavy heart, I turned and walked away. I knew that as long as I lived I'd never forget the two little graves and the sacred red fern.

Not far from our home, the road wound its way up and over a hill. At the top Papa stopped the team. We all stood up and looked back. It was a beautiful sight, one I'll never forget.

As I stood and looked at the home of my birth, it looked sad and lonely. There was no spiral of lazy blue smoke twisting from the rock chimney, no white leghorn hen chasing a June bug, no horse or cow standing with head down and tail switching.

I saw I had left the door to the barn loft open. A tuft of hay hung out. It wavered gently in the warm summer breeze.

Something scurried across the vacant yard and disappeared under the barn. It was Samie, our house cat. I heard my little sister say in a choking voice, "Mommie, we forgot Samie."

There was no answer.

45 To the left, I could see our fields and the zigzag lines of rail fences. Farther down, I could see the shimmering whiteness of the tall sycamores. My vision blurred as tears came to my eyes.

The sorrowful silence was broken by my mother's voice. She asked, "Billy, can you see it?"

"See what, Mama?" I asked.

"The red fern," she said.

My oldest sister spoke up. "I can see it," she said.

Rubbing my eyes, I looked to the hillside above our home. There it stood in all its wild beauty, a waving red banner in a carpet of green. It seemed to be saying, "Good-bye, and don't worry, for I'll be here always."

Hearing a sniffling, I turned around. My three little sisters had started crying. Mama said something to Papa. I heard the jingle of the trace chains as they tightened in the singletrees.

Our wagon moved on.

I have never been back to the Ozarks. All I have left are my dreams and memories, but if God is willing, some day I'd like to go back—back to those beautiful hills. I'd like to walk again on trails I walked in my boyhood days.

Once again I'd like to face a mountain breeze and smell the wonderful scent of the redbuds, and papaws, and the dogwoods. With my hands I'd like to caress the cool white bark of a sycamore.

I'd like to take a walk far back in the flinty hills and search for a souvenir, an old double-bitted ax stuck deep in the side of a white oak tree. I know the handle has long since rotted away with time. Perhaps the rusty frame of a coal-oil lantern still hangs there on the blade.

I'd like to see the old home place, the barn and the rail fences. I'd like to pause under the beautiful red oaks where my sisters and I played in our childhood. I'd like to walk up the hillside to the graves of my dogs.

I'm sure the red fern has grown and has completely covered the two little mounds. I know it is still there, hiding its secret beneath those long, red leaves, but it wouldn't be hidden from me for part of my life is buried there, too.

Yes, I know it is still there, for in my heart I believe the legend of the sacred red fern.

Closure and Extension

ANSWERS TO THINKING ABOUT THE SELECTION
Recalling

1. Billy decides where the group will hunt, guides the group as they chase the dogs, and convinces them to stay out in the storm.
2. The dogs save Billy by leaping up at the mountain lion, coming between it and Billy.
3. The results of the fight with the mountain lion are the deaths of Dan and Ann. Dan dies from the wounds he received, and Ann dies from loneliness and grief.

4. Billy's reaction to the deaths of his dogs includes anger because their deaths seemed unjust and sadness and loss because of the close relationship and great love he had for the dogs.
5. The legend of the red fern is that an Indian boy and girl froze to death in a blizzard and were not found until the following spring. When they were found a red fern had grown between the bodies. The story concludes that only an angel can plant the seeds for a red fern and the fern will never die.

The spot where the plant grows is considered sacred.

Interpreting

6. Billy and Ann risk their lives to help Dan because they love him to the extent that they will give up their own lives.
7. Answers will differ. Suggested Response: Ann dies because she had been so close to Dan for all of her life that when he died she could not continue life without him and simply gave up.

8. Answers may differ. Suggested Response: The title is a reference to where the narrator's dogs and his wonderful life with those dogs are buried.

Applying

9. Answers will differ. Students will probably suggest that accepting the death of someone you care for is difficult because of the loss in your own life of the support the person gave you. It often seems unfair that the person was taken

THINKING ABOUT THE SELECTION

Recalling

1. In what ways is Billy the leader of his group during the championship hunt?
2. How do the dogs save Billy from the mountain lion?
3. What is the result of the fight with the mountain lion?
4. Describe Billy's reaction to the deaths of his dogs.
5. What is the legend of the Red Fern?

Interpreting

6. Why do Billy and Little Ann risk their lives to help Old Dan as he is fighting the lion?
7. Why does Little Ann die?
8. What is the meaning of the novel's title?

Analyzing

9. Why is it so difficult to accept the loss of someone or something you care for?

ANALYZING LITERATURE

Understanding Theme

A **theme**, or general idea about life, is revealed through the events of a novel. In the various episodes of this novel, Billy has developed a strong and loving relationship with his dogs.

1. What theme is Wilson Rawls presenting through this relationship?
2. What episodes in the story support the theme that hard work is very rewarding?

CRITICAL THINKING AND READING

Evaluating a Novel

Evaluating a novel means judging carefully how good it is. You comment on its strengths and weaknesses, using your knowledge of literary elements. It is important to remember that when you evaluate, your judgment must be supported by evidence in the novel, not by personal likes and dislikes. For example, if you think the characters in a novel are unrealistic, then by supporting your judgment with details, you could conclude that the work was unsuccessful.

Answer the following questions about *Where the Red Fern Grows*. Support your answers with details from the novel.

1. Do the characters seem like real people? Why or why not?
2. Do the conflicts in the plot hold your interest?
3. Is the setting described realistically?

UNDERSTANDING LANGUAGE

Understanding Derived Words

By adding prefixes or suffixes to a word, you can form new words. For example, you can derive several words from the verb *believe*. If you add the suffix *-able,* you create the adjective *believable.* If you then add the prefix *un-,* the word has the opposite meaning: *unbelievable.* Other words from *believe* are *believability* and *believably.*

Create derived words from the following words.

1. appear
2. touch
3. tangle
4. forgive
5. settle
6. play

THINKING AND WRITING

Writing a Book Review

A **book review** is a discussion and evaluation of ideas in a book. Write a book review of *Where the Red Fern Grows*. Begin with an introduction that identifies the author and the title of the book and gives a brief, one- or two-sentence description of the events. In the body of the review, evaluate one of the elements you studied in the four sections of the novel: character, plot, setting, or theme. You might review your answers to the questions in the **Critical Thinking and Reading** activity, Evaluating a Novel. End with a concluding sentence that provides your judgment of the book. As you revise, be sure you have supported your comments with specific examples.

Where the Red Fern Grows 767

(Answers begin on p. 766.)

ANSWERS TO CRITICAL THINKING AND READING

1. Answers will differ and should include evaluations of all the major characters, including the two dogs. For example, Billy is a realistic character because he experiences many of the feelings and emotions of a boy his age. Details from the story include his feelings while in Tahlequah, his feelings about the deaths of his dogs, and his relationships with his mother, father, and grandfather.
2. Answers will differ, and students should support their opinions with details from the story. Students may find that some conflicts held their interest better than others.
3. Suggested Response: In general, the setting was described realistically and helped set the mood and the action of the story.

ANSWERS TO UNDERSTANDING LANGUAGE

Answers will differ. Possible answers:
1. disappear
2. untouchable
3. entangle
4. unforgiving
5. settlement
6. misplay

Writing Across the Curriculum
You might want to have students research and report on various aspects of the flora, fauna, and geography of the Ozark Mountain region. Students could report on raccoons, the trees mentioned in the story, the geography of the Ozark Mountains, or another subject relating to this aspect of the novel. You might inform the Science department of the assignment. Science teachers might provide guidance for students in conducting research and might give them extra credit.

---

away. It is also sad that someone you loved is now gone.

Challenge What do you think are Billy's feelings about the family moving into town?

ANSWERS TO ANALYZING LITERATURE

1. The theme that Rawls is presenting is that people experience many different emotions and feelings in relationships with those they love. In true, loving relationships, negative emotions accompany positive emotions.
2. The episode in which Billy saves his money to buy the dogs, the episodes where Ann does not give up the hunt and finds the raccoon, the episode where Billy cuts down the big tree to honor his promise to the dogs, and the episode where the family is able to move into town all support the theme that hard work pays off.

Challenge Ask students to give examples of relationships or experiences with which they are familiar that convey any of the themes of the novel. These examples can be from books, movies, television programs, or their own lives.

FOCUS ON READING

Distinguishing Facts from Opinions

Most material that you read contains statements of fact and opinion. By determining which statements are facts and which are opinions, you will gain a greater understanding of what the author is saying and whether or not you agree with it. You will be able to evaluate the material.

Facts

A **fact** is a statement that can be checked to see if it is true or false. Look at the following sentences:

> Wilson Rawls wrote *Where the Red Fern Grows*.
> Grandpa wrote a letter to a place in Arkansas to get Billy two hunting dogs.

Both sentences are factual because the facts they contain can be checked. However, the first sentence is true, whereas the second is false because the place Grandpa wrote to was in Kentucky. You could check these facts by referring back to the book. Often you will have to use reference books and articles to prove facts.

Opinions

An **opinion** differs from a fact because it cannot be checked. It is someone's belief, judgment, or feeling. Carefully read the following sentences to find the differences between them:

> *Where the Red Fern Grows* is the best book Wilson Rawls ever wrote.
> "*Where the Red Fern Grows,* written by Wilson Rawls, is the best book in our library.

The word *best* makes the first sentence a statement of opinion or judgment. Someone else may think one of the other books Wilson Rawls authored was his best. The second sentence, on the other hand, contains both facts and opinions. It is a fact that the novel was written by Wilson Rawls; however, the word *best* indicates an opinion.

Signals

Distinguishing between facts and opinions can be difficult because sentences may contain both and some sentences that seem to be facts may prove to be opinions. Looking for signal words can help you accurately identify facts and opinions.

Watch for words such as "I (we) think," and "I (we) feel," for they signal a statement of belief or opinion. Positive judgments are indicated by words such as "best," "fantastic," or "helpful"; whereas negative judgments are suggested by words such as "awful," "offensive," or "harmful." Words like "never" and "always" often signal an exaggerated statement of opinion. And "must," "should," and "have to" clearly indicate a command or suggestion and thus show that the statement is expressing someone's feeling or opinion.

Guidelines

- If the statement can be proven to be true or false, it is a fact.
- If the statement expresses a belief or a judgment of feeling, it is an opinion.
- If the statement contains words such as "think," "great," "horrible," "never," or "must," it is usually an opinion.

Activity

Read each of the following statements. Identify whether each is a fact (F), an opinion (O), or a mixture of both (BOTH).

1. The marshal bought Billy a bottle of soda pop.
2. Old Dan and Little Ann were the best hunting dogs in the Ozarks.
3. Billy had three adorable little sisters.
4. Billy saved fifty dollars, which was a tremendous amount of money for a young boy to accumulate.

Activity

Read this passage and answer the questions that follow.

Where the Red Fern Grows is the story of a young boy's growing-up years in the Ozarks. It is told by Billy Coleman, now a grown man, who is reminiscing about his youth. He recalls the training of Old Dan and Little Ann, the nighttime coon hunts, and the tremendous love that developed between a boy and his dogs. His dogs became the finest hunting team in his part of the Ozarks. This story is always exciting and everyone loves it. You must read the book.

1. Identify two statements of fact.
2. Identify two statements of opinion.
3. Identify one mixed statement.
4. Identify the signal words that indicate an opinion.

YOU THE WRITER

Assignment

1. Imagine that you are going to write a novel. Since you want to get to know one of the characters in the novel better—from the inside out—have this person write a diary entry.

Prewriting. Jot down facts about this character as they come to you: name, age, school, the names of parents, sisters, brothers. Describe this character's attitudes. Ask and answer questions.

Writing. Organize your material in chronological order. Try to include at least one encounter with another person. Include some dialogue.

Revising. Evaluate your composition. Ask yourself this question: Have I created a real person, one with a clear identity? Have I included the specific details that will make my character jump off the page?

Assignment

2. Plan a novel about two characters with contrasting personalities who come into conflict. Write an essay in which you describe the different personalities and the conflict.

Prewriting. Look around you at people you know who have contrasting personalities. Jot down notes comparing and contrasting them.

Writing. In your thesis sentence, tell the reader in a general way what each of the characters is like. Then indicate that one day they came into conflict with each other. Finally, trace the chain of events leading to the crisis that brings them into conflict.

Revising. Check to see that you have told your "story" in a step-by-step way. Also check to see that you have described the personalities of the characters.

Assignment

3. Some novels are told through an exchange of letters. Write *two* letters, one from character A to character B, and one from character B to character A. In the letters, have the characters discuss a problem they have with a third character.

Prewriting. Before you write, establish the personalities of each of the three characters. In fact, try to make the two characters writing the letters opposites.

Writing. Now write your letters. Tell the story of the problem the letter writers have with the third person in chronological order. Let the first letter tell the first part of the story and the second letter tell the rest.

Revising. Check to see that your sentences are smooth. Tie your thoughts together more tightly by combining sentences.

YOU THE CRITIC

Assignment

1. Identify a character in the novel you have read who changes in an important way. Then write an essay in which you show (1) the character's personality before the change, (2) the event or sequence of events that changed him or her, (3) the change itself, and (4) the effect the character's change had on the story.

Prewriting. Make a brief outline. Fill in the outline, telling (1) what the character was like before the change, (2) what caused him or her to change, (3) what he or she was like after the change, and (4) how the character's change affected the story.

Writing. Now write your essay. Start by identifying the character you are going to write about and indicating that he or she underwent a change that affected the story. In your body paragraphs, cover each of the four topics. Include a citation from the novel.

Revising. When you revise, check to see that you have answered the question fully. Have you covered all four of the sections?

Assignment

2. Identify two minor characters in the novel you read. Then write an essay in which you (1) describe their personalities, (2) tell what motivates them to take the actions they do, and (3) show that the actions they take play a role in moving the story along.

Prewriting. Before you write, divide a sheet of paper into two columns. In the left-hand column, list the major characters. In the right-hand column, list the minor characters. Then choose two characters from the right-hand column and jot down notes about them.

Writing. Write your essay. In the opening paragraph, state your thesis, or main idea. Divide the body into three paragraphs, one for each section of the question. Conclude by summing up the points.

Revising. When you revise, make sure you have followed each of the three steps in the assignment.

Assignment

3. Write an essay about a person in the novel whom you like or admire. Explain why you like or admire this person.

Prewriting. Look over the novel again and examine your reactions to each of the characters. Which ones do you like or admire? Which ones don't you like? Choose one character and freewrite.

Writing. Now write your essay. First identify the character you like or admire. Then, in your thesis statement, indicate the qualities and actions that make this character sympathetic. In your body paragraphs, discuss these qualities and actions in detail. Refer to specific things this person says and does in the novel.

Revising. When you revise, tighten the connections between your ideas by using transitional words and phrases.

You the Critic   771

1. Has the student clearly indicated the character and the change the character underwent?
2. Has the student indicated the cause of the change?
3. Has the student made clear how the character's change affected the novel?
4. Is the composition free from grammar, usage, and mechanics errors?

Guidelines for Evaluating Assignment 2

1. Has the student stated the main idea in the first paragraph?
2. Has the student described the personalities of two minor characters and their motivation?
3. Has the student given a paragraph to each character?
4. Is the essay free of grammar, usage, and mechanics errors?

Guidelines for Evaluating Assignment 3

1. Has the student identified the character he or she admires?
2. Has the student clearly indicated the admirable qualities of this character?
3. Has the student given specific examples of the character's words or behavior?
4. Is the essay free from grammar, usage, and mechanics errors?

HANDBOOK OF WRITING ABOUT LITERATURE

SECTION 1: UNDERSTANDING THE WRITING PROCESS

Lesson 1: Prewriting

Writing is a process that involves several stages:

1. *Prewriting:* planning your writing
2. *Drafting:* creating a first version, or draft, of your writing
3. *Revising:* making improvements in your draft
4. *Proofreading:* checking for errors in grammar and usage, spelling, punctuation, capitalization, and manuscript form
5. *Publishing,* or *Sharing:* letting others read what you have written

This lesson will teach you the steps of prewriting.

STEP 1: ANALYZE THE SITUATION

To *analyze* something is to divide it into parts, or elements, and then to study these parts. Before writing, you should always analyze the elements of the writing situation in which you find yourself. To do so, ask yourself the following questions:

1. *Topic* (the subject you will be writing about): What exactly are you going to write about? Can you state your subject in a sentence? Is your subject too broad or too narrow?
2. *Purpose* (what you want your writing to accomplish): Do you want your writing to explain? to describe? to persuade? to tell a story? to entertain? What do you want your audience to learn or to understand?
3. *Audience* (the people who will read or listen to your writing): Who is your audience? What might they already know about your subject?
   - What basic facts will you have to provide for them?

4. *Voice* (the way your writing will sound to your reader): What impression do you want to make? Do you want to sound formal or informal? Should you sound cool and reasoned or full of emotion?
5. *Content* (the subject and all the information you will provide about it): How much do you already know about this subject? What else do you need to find out? What libraries can you consult for newspapers, books, magazines, and other resources? Are there people you can ask for information?
6. *Form* (the shape that your writing will take, including its length and its organization): How do you picture your finished work? How long will it be? Will it be one paragraph or several? Will you use a special form like a verse or a drama? In what order will you present your information?

When you begin your prewriting, try to answer these questions. Doing so will help you to clarify your goals. If you are writing a paper for school, your teacher may give you a topic or may ask that the writing take a specific form. However, many decisions about the writing will still be up to you.

STEP 2: MAKE A PLAN

After thinking about the writing situation, you may find that you need more information. If so, you must decide how to gather this information. On the other hand, you may find that you already have too much information—that your topic is too broad. If this is the case, then you must decide how to narrow your topic. If you have the right amount of information but don't know how to present it clearly, you will have to choose a way to organize your information.

STEP 3: GATHER INFORMATION

There are many ways to gather information, to narrow a topic, and to organize ideas. You must find ways that work well for you. The following are some ways that you can try:

1. *Brainstorming:* Discuss the topic with a group of people. Follow these rules in your discussion: Try to generate as many ideas as possible. Do not pause to evaluate your ideas. This can be done later. Do not allow any member of the group to make negative comments about what another member says.
2. *Freewriting:* Write down everything that comes to your mind about the topic. Don't worry about spelling or about writing complete, grammatical sentences. Simply write nonstop for one to five minutes. Then read your freewriting and look for ideas you can use in your first draft.
3. *Clustering:* Write your topic in the middle of a piece of paper and circle it. Then write all the ideas you can think of that relate to your topic in circles around the main topic. Connect your circles with lines that show how your ideas, or subtopics, branch out from your main topic. You may even think of some ideas that branch off from your subtopics. If you need to narrow your topic, you might select one of your subtopics as a new main topic.
4. *Analyzing:* Divide your topic into parts that you can consider separately. Make notes about each part. Then study how the parts are related both to each other and to the main topic.
5. *Questioning:* Make a list of questions about the topic. Begin your questions with words like *who, what, where, when, why,* and *how.* Then answer the questions by doing research to find the information you need.
6. *Using Outside Sources:* Talk to other people about your topic. Conduct formal interviews. Read relevant books, pamphlets, newspapers, magazines, and reference works. Watch movies or television shows or listen to radio programs that deal with your topic.
7. *Making Charts* or *Lists:* Make a list or chart of relevant information. Possibilities include a time line, an ordered list of events, a pros-and-cons chart, a list of reasons, or a list of parts.

Any of these methods for finding information can be also used to identify a topic in the first place.

STEP 4: ORGANIZE YOUR NOTES

Once you have gathered enough information, you will have to organize it. Careful organization will make your writing easy to read and understand. The following methods of organization are common:

1. *Time Order,* or *Chronological Order:* organization in order of occurence (from earliest to latest, for example)
2. *Spatial Order:* organization by position in space (from left to right, for example)
3. *Degree Order:* organization by size, amount, or intensity (from coldest to warmest, for example)
4. *Priority Order:* organization by importance, value, usefulness, or familiarity (from worst to best, for example)

CASE STUDY: PREWRITING

Pilar's English teacher asked the students in her class to write single paragraphs about their hobbies. Pilar chose to write about reading. Here are her preliminary notes for her paragraph:

- Topic: reading as a hobby
- Purpose: to inform

- Audience: my classmates and teacher

- Voice: informal and probably with some feelings

- Content: not sure. I have so many thoughts and feelings about reading, I don't know what to say.

- Form: single paragraph

Pilar reviewed her notes and decided that she needed to define her purpose more clearly. She decided to try freewriting:

> I really enjoy reading—especially about kids my age and families. Some of my friends share my interests, but others prefer fantasy or adventure or travel reading—other friends don't read much. Too bad—they're missing something special. . . .

Pilar read her freewriting and realized that her purpose could be to persuade non-reading classmates that reading is fun. Pilar decided to gather more ideas and information by using the questioning technique:

> What kinds of books do I enjoy? Where do I read? Why do I read? How do I read? When do I read? Whose books do I enjoy?
> I love stories about kids like me. I usually read on the floor or all cozy in bed. I read for lots of reasons: to find out what other kids' lives are like (seeing how they manage things), for privacy, for company, because a friend has suggested the book, to get out of a grouchy mood, and also because I've liked other things by the writer. I read with or without a snack, with lots of noise or in silence. I usually read before bedtime to relax. I enjoy just about any books about kids.

Pilar looked over her notes and decided that in her paragraph she would first introduce the topic, "Why reading is a pleasurable hobby." Then she would give reasons why she enjoys reading, choosing three reasons and organizing them by degree, from least to most important.

ACTIVITIES AND ASSIGNMENTS

A. Answer the following questions about the case study.

1. Find the section of Pilar's notes in which she analyzed the writing situation. Which parts of her earliest notes needed to be expanded? Which were sufficient?

2. Why did Pilar freewrite? Why did she list questions and answer them?

B. Choose one of the following topics or one of your own: *sports, travel, pets,* or *outer space.* Prepare to write a paragraph about your topic. Follow these steps:

1. Make notes about the topic, purpose, audience, voice, content, and form of your paragraph.

2. Review your notes. Decide on a plan of action. To analyze the writing situation and to gather ideas, use prewriting techniques such as freewriting, clustering, analyzing, questioning, consulting outside sources, and making charts or lists.

3. Organize your notes, then make a rough outline for your paragraph. Your outline should include your main topic and two or three subtopics, or parts of the main topic. Under each subtopic, list specific details that you will include in your writing. Save your prewriting notes in a folder.

Lesson 2: Drafting and Revising

WRITING A DRAFT

Drafting follows prewriting and is the second stage in the writing process. When drafting, you simply write down ideas and information in sentence form. The following are important points to remember about drafting:

1. Write your rough draft slowly or quickly—whichever way works for you. Some writers like to work from detailed, thorough outlines and to write very slowly, correcting and polishing as they go. Other writers prefer to jot down brief outlines, write their rough drafts very quickly, and then go back to make corrections and revisions. Each of these methods is perfectly OK. Only you can decide which approach works best for you.

2. Do not try to make your rough draft a finished product. The main point of a draft is to get your ideas down on paper. Once this is done, you can go back and make improvements. Save concern over spelling, punctuation, and so on for the revision and proofreading stages of the writing process.

3. Refer to your prewriting notes as you draft. Do not ramble on about unrelated subjects—stick to your main topic.

4. Keep your audience and purpose in mind as you write. Try not to speak above or below the heads of your audience. Make sure that the ideas and information that you include are consistent with your purpose.

5. Be flexible. Don't be afraid to set aside earlier ideas if later ones work better. If you have already written part of a draft and a more interesting aspect of your topic comes to mind, use it! Remember, too, that you can always do more prewriting activities to gather more information or to focus your thinking.

6. Write as many rough drafts as you need. After you have written one draft, you might review it and realize that you need to add more information, to change your purpose, or to narrow your focus. If this happens, try some more prewriting activities and then write another draft. When you have a draft you are satisfied with, you are ready to go on to the next stage of the writing process—revising.

REVISING YOUR DRAFT

Revising is the process of reworking what you have written to make it as good as it can be. As you revise, use the Checklist for Revision on the next page. If you answer "no" to any of the questions on the checklist, then you will have to change, or revise, your draft accordingly.

EDITORIAL SYMBOLS

When you revise a rough draft, use the standard editorial symbols in the chart on the next page.

CASE STUDY: DRAFTING AND REVISING

Pilar used her prewriting notes from the last lesson to begin drafting her paragraph. Here is the beginning of her first rough draft:

> I love reading stories about kids like me for many reasons, and I think you should too. I like the privacy and also because a friend has suggested the book. I especially like to find out about other kids. How they handle their lives.

Pilar stopped writing and looked at her draft. She had given the three reasons she enjoyed reading and now had nothing more to say. She realized that her paragraph would never con-

Drafting and Revising   777

<table>
<tr><td colspan="2">**CHECKLIST FOR REVISION**</td></tr>
</table>

CHECKLIST FOR REVISION

Topic and Purpose
- ☐ Is my topic clear?
- ☐ Does the writing have a specific purpose?
- ☐ Does the writing achieve its purpose?

Audience
- ☐ Will everything that I have written be clear to my audience?
- ☐ Will my audience find the writing interesting?
- ☐ Will my audience respond in the way I would like?

Voice, Word Choice
- ☐ Is the impression that my writing conveys the one that I intended it to convey?
- ☐ Is my language appropriately formal or informal?
- ☐ Have I avoided vague, undefined terms?
- ☐ Have I used vivid, specific nouns, verbs, and adjectives?
- ☐ Have I avoided jargon that my audience will not understand?
- ☐ Have I avoided clichés?
- ☐ Have I avoided slang, odd connotations, euphemisms, and gobbledygook (except for novelty or humor)?

Content/Development
- ☐ Have I avoided including unnecessary or unrelated ideas?
- ☐ Have I developed my topic completely?
- ☐ Have I supplied examples or details that support the statements that I have made?
- ☐ Are my sources of information unbiased, up-to-date, and authoritative?
- ☐ Are any quotations that I have used verbatim, or word-for-word?

Form
- ☐ Have I followed a logical method of organization?
- ☐ Have I used transitions, or connecting words, to make the organization clear?
- ☐ Does the writing have a clear introduction, body, and conclusion?

SYMBOL	MEANING	EXAMPLE
	move text	She wants to go also
	delete	Meghan is quite very happy.
∧	insert	of *that* book
⊂	close up; no space	dish washer
⊙	insert period	was free
	insert comma	pencils, books and pens
	add apostrophe	childrens books
	add quotation marks	The Raven
∿	transpose	to quickly run
¶	begin paragraph	book. If
/	make lower case	the President
≡	capitalize	president Adams

778   *Handbook of Writing About Literature*

vince someone that reading was an interesting and fun hobby. Pilar set two goals for her next draft:

1. to keep her purpose more clearly in mind as she wrote, and
2. to give more reasons for her argument, with details to make the reasons persuasive.

Pilar wrote several more drafts of her paragraph. Here is her revised final draft:

Have you considered reading as a hobby?

When you have a free hour alone to relax ~~by~~ yourself you might try reading a good book.

Ask freinds ~~who know you~~ to reccomend

good books they think you'll like, or read

something ~~or other~~ by a Writer you enjoyed in
Find a comfortabel place to read and
school. ~~Get comfy,~~ see what happens.
Here's what happens for me.
Reading gives me both privacy and ~~I like the~~

company at the same time. When I'm involved

in a book I'm away from my every day world. I

can discover places, people, and information I
most of all,
might never otherwise have known. I especially

like finding out about how other kids live their
situations I might find myself in
lifes. I actually learn about ~~real life.~~ And see

ways I might handle my own life. Maybe you'll
for
enjoy reading ~~because of~~ some of the same

reasons I do. Its a pleasure.

ACTIVITIES AND ASSIGNMENTS

A. Answer the following questions about the revised final draft in the case study:

1. Has Pilar corrected all the errors in her draft? Why isn't it necessary for all the errors to be corrected in the revision stage?
2. Why did Pilar delete material in the second and third sentences?
3. Why did Pilar add the sentence "Here's what happens for me"?
4. Why did Pilar delete the phrase "I like the" before the word "company"?
5. Why did Pilar take out the word "kids" in the third from the last sentence?
6. What transitional words did Pilar add to indicate that she was about to give the last reason why she enjoys reading?
7. Why did Pilar replace the words "real life" with other words?
8. What other revisions did Pilar make? Why did she make them?

B. Using your prewriting notes from the last lesson, write the rough draft of a paragraph on your topic. Then revise the draft until you are pleased with it.

Follow these steps for drafting and revising your paragraph:

1. Introduce your topic in a sentence or two.
2. Write the body of your paragraph, referring as necessary to your rough outline and to your prewriting notes. Do not spend time worrying about spelling and mechanics at this stage.
3. Write a conclusion of one or two sentences. In the conclusion, sum up the main idea of your paragraph.
4. Revise your draft, using the Checklist for Revision. Be sure that you can answer "yes" to every question. If not, use editorial symbols to make the necessary corrections.

Lesson 3: Proofreading and Publishing

PROOFREADING YOUR FINAL DRAFT

Once you have finished revising your rough draft, the next step is to make a clean copy and then proofread it. When you *proofread,* you check for errors in grammar and usage, spelling, punctuation, capitalization, and manuscript form. Use the checklist at right when proofreading.

If your answer to any of the questions in the checklist is "no," use editorial symbols to make the necessary corrections on your final draft. Refer to a dictionary, writing textbook, or handbook of style as necessary.

PUBLISHING, OR SHARING YOUR WORK

After proofreading your final, revised draft, you are ready for the final step in the writing process—sharing your work with others. Much of the writing that you do for school will be handed in to your teachers. However, you can share your writing with other people as well. These are some of the many ways in which you can share your work:

1. Share your writing in a small group by reading it aloud or by passing it around for others to read.
2. Read your work aloud to the class.
3. Make copies of your writing for members of your family or for your friends.
4. Display your work on a classroom bulletin board.
5. Save your writing in a folder for later publication. At the end of the year, choose the best pieces from your folder and bind them together. Share the collection with your relatives and friends.
6. Submit your writing to the school literary magazine, or start a literary magazine for your school or for your class.
7. Submit your writing to your school or community newspaper.

CHECKLIST FOR PROOFREADING

Grammar and Usage
- ☐ Are all of my sentences complete? That is, have I avoided sentence fragments?
- ☐ Do all of my sentences express only one complete thought? That is, have I avoided run-on sentences?
- ☐ Do the verbs I have used agree with their subjects?
- ☐ Have all the words in my paper been used correctly? Am I sure about the meanings of all of these words?
- ☐ Is the thing being referred to by each pronoun (*I, me, this, each,* etc.) clear?
- ☐ Have I used adjectives and adverbs correctly?

Punctuation
- ☐ Does every sentence end with a punctuation mark?
- ☐ Have I used commas, semicolons, colons, hyphens, dashes, parentheses, quotation marks, and apostrophes correctly?

Spelling
- ☐ Am I absolutely sure that each word has been spelled correctly?

Capitalization
- ☐ Have I capitalized any words that should not be capitalized?
- ☐ Should I capitalize any words that I have not capitalized?

Manuscript Form
- ☐ Have I indented the first line(s) of my paragraph(s)?
- ☐ Have I written my name and the page number in the top, right-hand corner of each page?
- ☐ Have I double spaced the manuscript?
- ☐ Is my manuscript neat and legible?

---

780   *Handbook of Writing About Literature*

8. Enter your writing in literary contests for student writers.
9. Submit your writing to a magazine that publishes work by young people.

CASE STUDY: PROOFREADING AND PUBLISHING

After revising her final draft, Pilar made a fresh, clean copy. Then she was ready for the proofreading stage. She read the Checklist for Proofreading on the previous page and applied each question to her revised draft. She found several errors. Pilar's paragraph with the proofreading corrections that she made is in the right-hand column.

Pilar made a clean final copy of her paragraph. Then she shared her paragraph with other students in a small-group discussion.

ACTIVITIES AND ASSIGNMENTS

A. Answer the following questions about the case study:
1. What errors in spelling did Pilar correct during proofreading?
2. What capitalization error did Pilar correct?
3. What run-on sentence did she correct? How did she do this?
4. What punctuation errors did Pilar correct?
5. What error in manuscript form did she correct?
6. Are there any changes that you think should still be made in Pilar's paragraph?

Proofread to correct any errors in your draft. Share the final copy of your paragraph with your family, your teacher, and your classmates.

B. Make a clean copy of your revised draft from the last lesson. Then use the Checklist for Proofreading to check your revised draft. Using editorial symbols, make any necessary corrections on your final draft.

Have you considered reading as a hobby? When you have a free hour alone to relax, try reading a good book. Ask friends to recommend good books they think you'll like, or read something by a writer you enjoyed in school. Find a comfortable place to read, see what happens. Here's what happens for me: Reading gives me both privacy and company at the same time. When I'm involved in a book, I'm away from my everyday world. I can discover places, people, and information I might never otherwise have known. Most of all, I especially like finding out about how others live their lifes. I actually learn about situations I might find myself in and see ways I might handle my own life. Maybe you'll enjoy reading for some of the same reasons I do. Its a pleasure.

ANSWERS TO ACTIVITIES AND ASSIGNMENTS, SECTION A.

1. Pilar corrected a series of grammer, usage, spelling, punctuation, capitalization, and manuscript errors.
2. She changed the capital "w" in "writers" to lowercase.
3. She corrected the sentence beginning with "Find a comfortable..." by separating the two clauses with the conjunction "and."
4. She added two commas and an apostrophe. She replaced a period with a colon.
5. She indicated the first line of the paragraph.
6. Answers will differ. If students suggest corrections, be sure that they give valid reasons for each change.

Motivation for Writing You might write the names of the five senses across the top of the chalkboard so that each word has beneath it a column. Ask students for words that appeal to each of the five senses. For example, a word that appeals to the sense of hearing is *buzz*; a word that appeals to the sense of touch is *coarse*; a word that appeals to the sense of smell is *reek*; a word that describes taste is *bitter*; and a word that appeals to the sense of sight is *bright*. Explain to students that these words create images in a reader's mind. Writers use images to make their descriptions vivid and memorable. Tell them that writing about images will help them to understand and appreciate images in literature.

SECTION 2: UNDERSTANDING THE PARTS OF A LITERARY WORK: ANALYSIS AND INTERPRETATION

Lesson 4: Writing About Images

WHAT IS AN IMAGE?

An *image* is a portrayal, in words, of a sight, sound, touch, taste, or smell. This haiku contains images of sight:

> The snake slid away,
> But the eyes that glared at me,
>   Remained in the grass.
>   —Kyoshi (trans. R. H. Blyth)

The following lines contain images of touch:

> Ah grief and sadness!
> The fishing line trembles
>   In the autumn breeze.
>   —Buson (trans. R. H. Blyth)

These lines contain images of sound:

> The silence!
> The voice of the cicada
>   Penetrates the rocks.
>   —Bashō (trans. R. H. Blyth)

WHY DO WRITERS USE IMAGES?

Writers use images for two purposes:
1. To create pictures, in words, of people, places, and things, and
2. To create feelings, or moods

Consider the use of images in the following poem:

THE RUNNER

Walt Whitman

On a flat road runs the well-trained runner,
He is lean and sinewy with muscular legs.
He is thinly clothed, he leans forward as he runs,
With lightly closed fists and arms partially rais'd.

The images in this poem
1. Create a picture of a lean, swift runner, and
2. Create a mood of intense concentration.

CASE STUDY: WRITING ABOUT IMAGES

Prewriting

Roberto's English teacher asked the class to write an analysis of a favorite poem. Roberto chose to write about the use of images in the following poem:

OLD FLORIST

Theodore Roethke

That hump of a man bunching
  chrysanthemums
Or pinching-back asters, or planting azaleas,
Tamping and stamping dirt into pots,—
How he could flick and pick
Rotten leaves or yellowy petals,
Or scoop out a weed close to flourishing roots,
Or make the dust buzz with a light spray,
Or drown a bug in one spit of tobacco juice,
Or fan life into wilted sweet-peas with his hat,
Or stand all night watering roses, his feet blue
  in rubber boots.

Roberto began by looking up the words he didn't know in a dictionary. He made a list of their definitions:

- chrysanthemums: plants with colorful, showy flowers

- asters: plants with daisylike flowers of various colors

- azaleas: shrubs with flowers of various colors

- tamping: packing down tightly

Roberto reread the poem with these definitions in mind. Next Roberto made a chart in his notes of the images in the poem:

- Images of sight: every line includes visual images of the "hump of a man" who actively, busily tends to his colorful flowers

- Images of sound:
  "tamping and stamping dirt"
  "make the dust buzz with a light spray"
  "drown a bug in one spit of tobacco juice"

- Images of touch:
  "tamping and stamping dirt into pots"
  "flick and pick rotten leaves or yellowy petals"
  "fan life into wilted sweet-peas with his hat"

- Images of taste:
  none

- Images of smell:
  none directly, but flowers and earth suggest fragrances

Roberto decided to write about how Roethke uses images to create a vivid picture of the florist carefully tending to his plants. He made the following rough outline for his writing:

- Topic sentence:
  tell what poem I'm writing about.
  state my purpose—to show how Roethke uses images to create a vivid picture of the florist.

- Body:
  describe the images of sight, sound, and touch in the poem.

- Conclusion:
  suggest that the images contribute to the mood of the poem—reader feels the florist's loving, attentive attitude toward his plants.

Drafting and Revising

Using his outline and his prewriting notes, Roberto wrote a draft of his analysis. Then he read what he had written and decided that it could be made much clearer. Some of his sentences were not really related to his topic. Roberto revised his draft, making his writing clearer and more focused.

Proofreading and Publishing

Roberto made a clean copy of his revised draft. He used the Checklist for Proofreading, on page 780, to help him to correct errors in grammar and usage, spelling, punctuation, capitalization, and manuscript form. Then Roberto made a clean final copy of his paper and shared it with a small group of classmates. First he read the Roethke poem aloud to them. Then he read his analysis of the poem. He and his classmates each discussed their thoughts about the poem and learned quite a bit from one another.

ACTIVITIES AND ASSIGNMENTS

A. Write a paragraph such as Roberto might have written, based on prewriting notes in the case study. Follow these steps when writing, revising, proofreading, and publishing your draft:

1. Reread "Old Florist." As you read, ask yourself whether there are any images not mentioned in Roberto's notes that you would like to include in your paragraph. If there are, add them to your own prewriting notes.
2. Write a topic sentence that tells what your paragraph will be about.
3. In the body of your paragraph, describe the images in the poem, and tell to what senses these images appeal.
4. Write a conclusion of one or two sentences that sums up the feeling that the images create in the reader.

Writing About Images 783

5. Revise your rough draft to make sure that your paragraph is clear and well organized. Also make sure that your writing accomplishes its purpose and does not stray from your topic.

6. Make a clean copy of your revised draft, and proofread this copy for errors in grammar and usage, spelling, punctuation, capitalization, and manuscript form.

7. Share your final, proofread draft with friends and with your teacher.

B. Choose one of these poems and write a paragraph about its images: "The Village Blacksmith," on page 431; "The Highwayman," on page 437; "The Pheasant," on page 466; "The Bat," on page 472; "Seal," on page 475; one of the haiku on pages 478 and 479; "Washed in Silver," on page 484; "The Flower-Fed Buffaloes," on page 488; "My Mother Pieced Quilts," on page 494; "In Just—," on page 500; or "Stopping by Woods on a Snowy Evening," on page 504. Follow these steps when planning and writing your paragraph:

1. Read the poem carefully several times. Look up any words that you don't know in a dictionary.

2. In your prewriting notes, make a chart with columns labeled *sight, sound, touch, taste,* and *smell.* Fill it in with the images used in the poem.

3. Make notes telling what picture or pictures are created by the images. Also tell what mood you feel is created by the images.

4. Write a topic sentence that tells the name of the poem and that summarizes the main point you plan to make about its images.

5. Write several body sentences that present the images used in the poem.

6. Write a concluding sentence or two to sum up your paragraph. You might want to conclude by telling how the images in the poem create a certain mood or feeling.

7. Revise your paragraph carefully. Add any important details that you left out. Make sure that you have made all your ideas clear to the reader. Check to see that your writing is well organized and that it doesn't stray from the topic.

8. Proofread your paragraph, using the Checklist for Proofreading on page 780.

9. Share your proofread paragraph with your classmates and with your teacher.

Lesson 5: Writing About Sound

SOUND AND MEANING

When you hear written words read aloud, you may discover that they have another dimension of meaning. Read the following haiku aloud, and listen to the sounds of the words:

As lightning flashes . . .
Zig-zag screeches of the heron
Flying in the dark
—Bashō

The way the poem sounds gives the reader a richer sense of the way its subjects—the lightning and the heron—sound. The words *flashes, zig-zag,* and *screeches* all sound like what they mean. In both prose and poetry, the sounds and the meanings of words often go hand in hand.

TECHNIQUES INVOLVING SOUND

Writers can use many literary devices to add a dimension of sound to their writing. The following devices of sound are commonly used in literature.

Read the entries in the Handbook of Literary Terms, on page 832, for more detailed explanations of the terms listed in the chart. Then read the following case study.

CASE STUDY: WRITING ABOUT SOUND

André's English class was studying the use of devices of sound in poetry. For a writing assignment about sound, André chose the following poem:

BROADWAY, TWILIGHT

Tom Prideaux

Roaring, clanking,
Sirens screaming
In confusion;
Pink and yellow,
Shifting, gleaming
In profusion.

Above the deepening blue
The stars blink calmly through.

SOUND DEVICES	
Onomatopoeia: words that sound like what they mean, like *bleep, crunch,* and *chirp*	*Assonance:* repetition of vowel sounds, as in "young, fuzzy puppy"
Euphony: pleasant sounds, like those used by Langston Hughes in the following lines from "Harlem Night Song": Come, Let us roam the night together Singing	*Meter:* words with a regular rhythm as in "The sun is shining brightly now"
	Parallelism: repetition of grammatical patterns, as in *"through the door* and *up the stairs"*
Cacophony: harsh, jarring sounds, as in "twisted, crushed, junked automobiles"	*Repetition:* the repeated use of a sound, word, phrase, sentence, rhythmical pattern, or grammatical pattern. Forms of repetition include alliteration, consonance, assonance, meter, parallelism, and rhyme.
Alliteration: repetition of initial consonant sounds, as in "winding way"	
Consonance: repetition of internal consonant sounds, as in "The spotted kitten slept quietly on matted fur"	

Motivation for Writing You might remind students that in poetry, the sounds of the words can add to a poem's meaning. This is why it is often important to read a poem aloud to appreciate it fully. To illustrate this point, you might have students read aloud one of the poems from the poetry unit. Ask how the sounds contribute to the meaning and tone of the poem. Tell students that writing about sound in a poem will increase their understanding and appreciation of poetry.

Prewriting

First André read Prideaux's poem aloud several times, listening carefully to its sounds. Then, to gather information for his writing, he made a copy of the poem and marked it as follows:

1. He underlined examples of onomatopoeia.
2. He circled all the rhyming words.
3. He underlined, twice, all the repeated sounds he could find.
4. In the margins he noted examples of alliteration, consonance, assonance, and parallelism.
5. He also marked the stresses, or beats, in each line of the poem to show meter.

Here is André's marked copy of the poem:

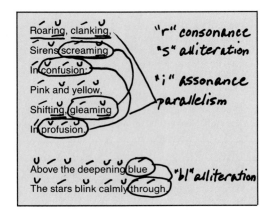

Next André made a detailed list in his notes of the sound devices used in the poem:

- Onomatopoeia: "Roaring," "clanking," and "screaming" all sound like what they describe.

- Cacophony: The first stanza has many harsh-sounding words that describe the "confusion."

- Euphony: The second stanza is melodious compared to the first.

- Meter: pounding beat in the first stanza—almost every word has stressed first syllable. The second stanza flows peacefully, quietly.

- Rhyme: screaming/gleaming; confusion/profusion; pink/blink; blue/through.

- Repetition:
  Alliteration: "Sirens screaming," "blue . . . blink"
  Consonance: "Roaring . . . Sirens screaming"
  Assonance: "Pink . . . Shifting . . . In"
  Parallelism: "Roaring, clanking"/"Shifting, gleaming"; "In confusion"/"In profusion."

André reviewed the poem and his notes. He made an observation about the poem as a whole that he thought he could use in the introduction to his paragraph. He added this observation to his notes:

> title foreshadows contrast between the sounds, colors, and movement of a busy street (Broadway) and the calm beauty of the overhead twilight sky

André wanted to make a rough outline before he began writing. He considered two possible ways to organize his paragraph. He could organize sequentially—line by line in the order of the poem—or he could use a topic organization and discuss each sound device in turn. He decided to use the topic organization.

Drafting and Revising

Using his prewriting notes and his rough outline, André wrote a rough draft. This is the beginning of his rough draft:

> In his poem "Broadway: Twilight, Tom Prideaux uses a whole lot of sound devices, to show what broadway looks and sounds like, specially in contrast to the calm, darkning twilight sky. First of all, the otomatopia really lets the reader hear the street noises "Roaring, clanking,/Sirens screaming," the first two lines,

start things off with a bang. Second of all, Mr. Prideaux uses lot of repetition devices. The short *i* sound is assonance in every single one of the first six lines: "roaring, clanking," "screaming/in confusion;/Pink", "shifting, gleaming/In profusion." For consonance the *r* sound repeats three times in the first six words. The *ing* sound too occurs five times in the first stanza. In line 2 the alliteration of "Sirens screaming" repeats the *s* sound.

André finished his draft, revised it, and copied it over.

Proofreading and Publishing

André carefully proofread his revised draft for errors in grammar and usage, spelling, punctuation, capitalization, and manuscript form. Then he shared his paper with a small group of classmates before giving it to his teacher.

ACTIVITIES AND ASSIGNMENTS

A. Finish André's rough draft, using information from André's prewriting notes. Then revise and proofread the rough draft. Make sure that you correct all of André's errors in spelling and mechanics. Share your final, proofread draft with your classmates.

B. Write a two-paragraph composition on the use of sound in one of the following poems: "The Highwayman," on page 437; "Feelings About Words," on page 486; "The Flower-Fed Buffaloes," on page 488; or "In Just—," on page 500. Follow these steps when writing your paper:

1. Read the poem aloud several times, and listen carefully to its sounds.
2. Make a copy of the poem. If it is an especially long poem, you may decide to write about only one or two stanzas.

3. Mark your copy of the poem as follows:
   a. Underline examples of onomatopoeia once.
   b. Circle rhyming words.
   c. Underline repeated sounds twice.
   d. In the margins, note examples of alliteration, consonance, assonance, parallelism, and repeated words.
4. Read the section on Meter in the Handbook of Literary Terms and Techniques, on page 839. Then choose one stanza of your poem, and mark its feet and stresses, as follows:

There was an old man with a beard,
Who said, "It is just as I feared!—
Two Owls and a Hen, four Larks and a
Wren,
Have all built their nests in my
beard!

5. Organize your notes. Write a rough outline for your paper.
6. Use your prewriting notes and your outline to write a rough draft. In your first paragraph, be sure that you inform your readers about the following:
   a. the title and author of the poem you are writing about
   b. the topic of your paper—the poet's use of sound devices, and
   c. the meter and rhyme scheme of the poem.
      In the second paragraph of your draft, discuss the remaining devices of sound used in the poem.
7. Revise your rough draft. Then make a clean copy of your revised draft, and proofread it for errors in grammar and usage, spelling, punctuation, capitalization, and manuscript form.
8. Share your proofread draft with your classmates before handing it in.

Writing About Sound   787

Lesson 6: Writing About Figures of Speech

WHAT IS A FIGURE OF SPEECH?

A *figure of speech* is language that is not meant to be taken literally. Consider these lines from a novel by Zora Neale Hurston:

> Phoeby's hungry listening helped Janie to tell her story. So she went on thinking back to her young years and explaining them to her friend in soft, easy phrases while all round the house, the night time put on flesh and blackness.

Listening can't literally be "hungry," nor can night "put on flesh and blackness." The reader understands that these ideas are meant to be interpreted figuratively—that the writer is using figures of speech.

The following figures of speech are often used in literature:

FIGURES OF SPEECH

Hyperbole: exaggeration for emphasis:

"I'm so tired I could sleep for a month and a half."

Personification: speaking or writing about a subject that isn't human as though it were:

"The sky wore her fanciest, most colorful dress."

Simile: a comparison between two subjects, using *like* or *as:*

"The lines on his face were like ditches on a well-traveled road."

Metaphor: a comparison of two subjects that does not use *like* or *as:*

"His room is a pigsty."

WHY WRITERS USE FIGURES OF SPEECH

Writers use figures of speech to express their ideas vividly. Consider the difference between the following passages.

Without figures of speech:
"I enjoyed the rhythm of the rain falling on my rainhat."

With figures of speech:
"The rain tapped a tune on my rainhat, and my brain danced with delight."

The figures of speech in the second passage convey a fuller, more vivid sense of the experience.

HOW WRITERS CREATE FIGURES OF SPEECH

Hyperbole is a relatively simple figure of speech. To create a hyperbole, a writer first thinks of a subject and of a quality or characteristic of the subject:

Subject: myself
Quality: tiredness

Next the writer creates a sentence exaggerating the quality:

I'm so tired I could sleep for a month and a half.

Simile and metaphor are more complex. As with hyperbole, the writer thinks of a subject and of a quality or characteristic of the subject. For example, the subject might be a room, and the characteristic might be its messiness. Then the writer thinks of some other subject that has the same characteristic, such as a pigsty. Then the writer can put the two together, using *like* or *as,* to form a simile:

His room is like a pigsty.

If the writer makes the comparison without using *like* or *as,* the result is a metaphor:

His room is a pigsty.

Personification works just like metaphor. The difference is that one of the two subjects is human and the other is not. The nonhuman subject is described as having some human characteristics.

CASE STUDY: WRITING ABOUT FIGURES OF SPEECH

Verlinda's English teacher asked the class to write a paragraph about the figures of speech used in a poem. Verlinda decided to write about the following poem:

CONSTRUCTION

Patricia Hubbell

The house frames hang like spider webs
Dangling in the sun,
While up and down the wooden strands
The spider workers run.
They balance on the two-by-fours,
They creep across the beams,
While down below, the heap of wood,
A spider-stockpile, gleams.
The spider-workers spin the web
And tack it tight with nails.
They ready it against the night
    When all work ends.

Verlinda studied the poem carefully and decided that the figure of speech most important to it was metaphor. The speaker of the poem was comparing the work of the men to the work of spiders. Verlinda made the following notes:

- Poem: "Construction," by Patricia Hubbell

- Figure of speech used: metaphor

- Two subjects being compared: men working at a construction site and spiders working on a web

- Similarities between the two subjects:
    "house frames hang like spider webs"
    Workers move like spiders, running "up and down," sometimes creeping.
    Materials gleam in sun like a spider's materials.
    Both building a structure that must be well fastened before night comes.

Verlinda reviewed her prewriting and organized her information in a rough outline.

Drafting and Revising

Verlinda used her prewriting notes to write a rough draft of her paragraph. Here is that draft, with Verlinda's corrections and revisions:

In her poem "Construction" the poet Patricia Hubbell ~~Hubbell~~ uses metaphor to ~~give forth~~ create a vivid, unusual portrait of an ordinary scene. Just as People stop to admire spiders at work, the reader of this poem stops to admire construction workers building a house. In fact, The central metaphor of the poem compares construction workers to spiders and ~~a house is like a web~~ an unfinished house to a web. By using the metaphor of the spiders Hubbell gives ~~a new~~ her readers look at ~~the~~ the construction worker's job delicate grace and even magic of arts. Hubbell describes the "spider workers as skilfully moving about, running, balancing and creeping across the wooden strands. The house itself looks like a web, having frames that "hang like spider webs" furthermore, The materials in the workers stock pile look like a spiders stock pile. ~~They~~ Finally, like spiders, gleem gleaming in the sun. The workers must make sure that the structure ~~that their~~ they are building is well fastened before night comes.

Proofreading and Publishing

Verlinda made a clean final copy of her paragraph for her teacher, who displayed it on the bulletin board.

ANSWERS TO ACTIVITIES AND ASSIGNMENTS, SECTION A.

1. Suggested response: She moved the sentence to the end of the paragraph because it sums up the main idea of the paragraph.
2. She combined the sentence which begins "Just as..." with the sentence which begins "The reader." Suggested response: She combined these two sentences to make her comparison more vivid and coherent.
3. Verlinda added "Just as."
4. She added "having frames that 'hang like spider webs.'"
5. The errors Verlinda caught were as follows: the quotation marks in line 1, the spelling of *Hubbell* and the comma in line 2, the period instead of a comma in line 9, the spelling of *creeping* in line 12, and the lack of an apostrophe in the word *spider's* in line 15. The errors she missed include the missing comma following the poem's title in line 1, and the word *stockpile* written as two words in line 15.

ACTIVITIES AND ASSIGNMENTS

A. Answer the following questions about the revised draft in the case study.
1. Why do you think Verlinda moved the sentence that begins "By using the metaphor" to the end of her paragraph?
2. What sentences did Verlinda combine? Why do you think she did so?
3. What transitional words, or transitions, did Verlinda add?
4. What specific details and evidence from the poem did Verlinda add?
5. What errors in spelling and punctuation did Verlinda catch during revision? What errors in punctuation and spelling remain in her draft?

B. Write a paragraph on figures of speech in one of the following poems: "Upon Mistress Susanna Southwell, Her Feet," on page 464; "The Pheasant," on page 466; "Fog," on page 468; "Washed in Silver," on page 484; "My Mother Pieced Quilts," on page 494; or "Mother to Son," on page 518. Follow these steps:
1. Read the poem several times. Then copy the poem by hand onto a sheet of paper. Writing out the poem in this way lets you become familiar with the author's exact words.
2. On the copy, underline all the figures of speech that you can find. List them on a separate sheet of paper under the following headings: *Hyperbole, Personification, Simile,* and *Metaphor.*
3. Decide which figure of speech you think is the most important to the meaning of the poem as a whole. Make prewriting notes about this figure of speech, explaining how it works and how it contributes to the poem as a whole.
4. Use your prewriting notes to develop your paragraph. Begin with a topic sentence. In the body of your paragraph, cite evidence from the poem. Conclude with a sentence that briefly summarizes the main idea of your paragraph.
5. Revise your paragraph. Then make a clean final copy and proofread it. Use the Checklist for Proofreading on page 780. Finally, share the proofread copy with your family and friends before giving it to your teacher.

Lesson 7: Writing About Setting

WHAT IS SETTING?

The *setting* of a story, novel, poem, or play is the time and place in which the action occurs. However, when creating a setting, a writer tells more than the date and the location. The writer also reveals details about elements of the environment such as weather, scenery, rooms, local customs, clothing, and dialects.

The second chapter of Wilson Rawls's novel *Where the Red Fern Grows,* on page 629, contains a detailed description of setting. The author includes sensory images and details about the landscape, local customs, and the time of year:

> Our home was in a beautiful valley far back in the rugged Ozarks. The country was new and sparsely settled. The land we lived on was Cherokee land, allotted to my mother because of the Cherokee blood that flowed in her veins. It lay in a strip from the foothills of the mountains to the banks of the Illinois River in northeastern Oklahoma.... Mama had picked the spot for our log house. It nestled at the edge of the foothills in the mouth of a small canyon, and was surrounded by a grove of huge red oaks. Behind our house one could see miles and miles of the mighty Ozarks. In the spring the aromatic scent of wild flowers, redbuds, papaws, and dogwoods, drifting on the wind currents, spread over the valley and around our home.

WHY DO WRITERS CREATE SETTINGS?

Writers create settings to serve various functions, or purposes, as shown in the chart, Uses of Setting.

CASE STUDY: WRITING ABOUT SETTING

Kyra read James Baldwin's "Caleb's Brother," on page 119. She thought that the

---

USES OF SETTING

To create a mood, or atmosphere: For example, a description of a log cabin nestled in a beautiful mountain canyon creates a peaceful, happy mood. On the other hand, details about a wet, dark tunnel might create a scary mood.

To inform readers about different ways of life: Through such details as customs, clothing, and speech patterns, a reader can get a sense of what it would be like to grow up in the backwoods of the Ozarks or to be a small boy living in a big city.

To make the action of a literary work seem more real: The vivid details of a setting can take readers to imaginary or faraway times and places.

To contribute to the conflict, or struggle, in a work: For example, a work set in the Arctic Circle might involve a character's struggle to survive extremely cold weather.

To symbolize, or stand for, some idea that the writer wants to emphasize: For example, if a story opens in the Ozarks in the springtime, its setting might symbolize hopeful beginnings and growth. A winter setting, on the other hand, might symbolize death.

---

setting was important to the story, so she decided to write a composition about the setting in "Caleb's Brother" for her English class.

Prewriting

Kyra reread "Caleb's Brother," paying careful attention to the setting. She narrowed the topic of her composition to the setting in one particular scene in the story, the scene in which Leo, wet and lonely, walks home in the rain and finds no one on his stoop.

Writing About Setting 791

Motivation for Writing To help students get a good idea about what setting is and how setting can affect people and events, you might write the date and your location on the chalkboard. Your location might include the name of the town, the county, or the state in which you reside. Explain to students that this is the setting, the time and the place, in which they live. Ask them how their setting affects them. For example, the climate in their location has an effect on how they dress. Also, people living in this time generally spend more time watching television than people did in the past.

The setting can also influence the plot, characters, and theme in works of literature. Writing about setting will help students understand setting and how it can affect other elements in literature.

To gather information, Kyra made the following chart in her prewriting notes:

SETTING	DETAILS
long avenue	"stretched straight before me, endless"
familiar buildings	"dark, silent shapes, great masses of wet rock"
men on stoops	"stood against the walls or against the stoops, made faceless by the light in the hallway behind them"
rain and splashing	"rain was falling harder"; "cars sloshed by, sending up sheets of water"
music and voices in the distance	"heard music faintly, and many voices"
woman ahead	"walked, very fast, head down"

Kyra looked over her prewriting chart and made notes about the function of the setting in the scene:

- *Function of setting:*
    To provide a backdrop for the story
    To emphasize the mood of emptiness and loneliness
    To symbolize Leo's struggle with loneliness
    To make the story realistic

Kyra decided that the two most important functions of the setting were to create a mood and to symbolize Leo's conflict with loneliness. She wrote a topic sentence and made a rough outline for her paper.

Drafting and Revising

Kyra used her prewriting notes and her outline to write the following draft of her composition:

An important use of setting in James Baldwins "Caleb's Brother is the scene when Leo walks home alone in the dark, cold, rain. This setting does more than provide a backdrop for the action of the story, it emphasizes little Leo's feelings of isolation, and it symbolizes Leo's conflict. Leo's big brother is suppose to take him to the movies every saturday. His brother, however, is usually busy with his friends, though, so that he sends Leo off alone. Because of his youth, Leo must ask at the theater until he finds someone to take him in. This also makes him feel badly. On this rainy day, Leo does'nt ask anyone to take him in, and no body offers. Feeling lousy, Leo heads home. Specific details about the setting that create the mood of loneliness include the men who seem to have no faces. Faces are the physical part of people that we relate to, so Leo has no way of relating to these men. Music and voices remind the reader and perhaps Leo too that others are not lonelie. The weather adds to Leo's pain. The pouring rain and the splashing cars emphasize the wet, cold elements that punch at Leo's spirit. A woman, almost running, her head down, seems to be in the act of fleeing away from Leo she is another person rejecting him. His very own building stoop is empty. Nobody is there for him at home. The whole setting underlines Leo's feelings of painful loneliness and rejection. These are the feelings Leo battles each week when his brother sends him off alone.

Kyra revised her composition to cut out details that didn't relate to setting and to make it more clearly organized. She also added some direct quotations from the story to make her writing more interesting.

Proofreading and Publishing

Kyra made a fresh copy of her revised draft and proofread it carefully. Then she made a clean final copy and shared it with her parents and with her English teacher.

ACTIVITIES AND ASSIGNMENTS

A. Rewrite the draft in the case study, adding some direct quotations from the story "Caleb's Brother." Use the quotations from Kyra's prewriting chart or any others that you think are helpful or interesting. Then revise the draft so that it is well organized and clear. Make a fresh copy of the revised draft, and proofread this copy for errors in grammar and usage, spelling, punctuation, capitalization, and manuscript form. Share your final copy with your classmates and with your teacher.

B. Choose one of the following works for a composition on setting: "All Summer in a Day," on page 107; "The Trout," on page 113; "The Third Level," on page 127; "Rip Van Winkle," on page 133; "The Highwayman," on page 437; "The Cremation of Sam McGee," on page 445; or "Annabel Lee," on page 455. Follow these steps when planning and writing your paper:

1. Read your chosen work once. Ask yourself what the setting is, and whether setting is more important in particular scenes in the work. You may want to select one setting to write about if the work has several different settings. Then read the work again, paying careful attention to the details that help to create the setting.

2. Write a topic sentence for your composition. Make a chart in your prewriting notes like the one in the case study, listing specific examples from the work to support your topic sentence.

3. Decide what the most important function of the setting is. Is the most important function to create a mood? to show a particular lifestyle? to make the story realistic? to create a conflict? to symbolize an important idea? Your topic sentence should reflect what this most important function is. Now make a rough outline for your composition.

4. Write a draft of your paper based on your notes and your outline. Revise the draft using the Checklist for Revision on page 778.

5. Make a clean copy of your draft for proofreading. Proofread your writing, using the Checklist for Proofreading on page 780. Make a final copy of your composition, and share it with your classmates and with your teacher.

Lesson 8: Writing About Plot

WHAT IS PLOT?

Plot is the sequence of events—what happens and how it happens—in a short story, a novel, a play, or a narrative poem. To enjoy and interpret any work that tells a story, you must understand its plot.

WHAT ARE THE PARTS OF A PLOT?

To analyze a plot, you can group the events of a story into parts. Here is an example of a plot that can be divided into parts:

A girl wants a racing bicycle. She works for eight months after school and weekends in a supermarket to earn the money to buy it. When she has just saved enough money to buy the bicycle, the money is stolen from her house. The girl then works another six months in the bicycle shop. She finally is able to buy the bicycle, and she becomes a state champion bicycle racer.

Major sections of a plot include the following:

1. *The inciting incident:* This is an event that creates the *central conflict,* or struggle. In the example, the inciting incident occurs when the girl decides that she wants an expensive racing bicycle but realizes that she has no money to buy it.
2. *The development:* This is the part of the story in which the struggle takes place. In the example the development takes place when the girl is working in the supermarket.
3. *The climax:* This is the high point of interest and suspense in the story. In the example, the climax occurs when the girl's money is stolen.
4. *The resolution:* This is the point at which the central conflict is ended, or resolved. In the example the resolution occurs when the girl finally gets her new bicycle.

Not all plots have this exact structure. For example, in some stories the inciting incident takes place before the beginning of the work. In the example, if the girl were already working in the supermarket at the opening of the story, the inciting incident would have occurred before the story began.

In some stories the climax and the resolution are the same event. If, in the example, the girl had decided she no longer wanted a bicycle when she discovered that her money had been stolen, then the climax and the resolution would have occurred at the same time.

Some stories have a section before the inciting incident. This section, called the *exposition,* introduces the reader to the setting and the characters. Other stories have a section that follows the resolution, called the *denouement.* The denouement gives the writer the chance to answer any questions that might remain in the reader's mind.

WHAT ARE SOME SPECIAL TECHNIQUES OF PLOT?

There are a number of special techniques writers use to make their plots more interesting. The following are some of the most common:

1. *Suspense:* This is the feeling of excitement or tension the reader experiences as the action of the plot unfolds. A writer creates suspense by raising questions in the reader's mind. In the example the writer might add suspense by creating stumbling blocks for the girl that keep the reader wondering, "Will she get the bicycle?"
2. *Foreshadowing:* This is a hint or clue about an event that will occur later in the story. In the example the writer could use foreshadowing

794 *Handbook of Writing About Literature*

by having the girl's brother warn her that she shouldn't leave a large amount of money in the house.

3. *Flashback:* This is a section in a story where the action is interrupted to tell about an earlier event. In the example, when the girl discovers that her money has been stolen, the writer might insert a flashback in which the girl remembers how hard she had worked to earn that money. After the flashback ended, the narrative would return to the present action.

4. *Surprise ending:* This is an ending that catches the reader off guard with an unexpected turn of events. In the example there would be a surprise ending if the girl found out that her money hadn't been stolen after all.

WHAT IS CONFLICT?

Conflict is a struggle between opposing forces. Without some sort of conflict, there would be no basis for a plot. The central conflict of a story occurs when the main character must fight against some force or make an important decision. There may also be minor conflicts taking place in a story at the same time as the central conflict.

Conflicts are either external or internal. An *external conflict* takes place when a person or group struggles against another person or group or against a nonhuman force such as a storm or a car that won't start.

An *internal conflict* takes place within a person's mind. For example, a character in a story might be torn between risking his or her life to save someone else and not taking the chance.

CASE STUDY: WRITING ABOUT PLOT

Maria's English class learned how plot is used in literary works. Then her teacher asked the class to choose a short story and analyze its plot. Maria selected Ernest Hemingway's "A Day's Wait," on page 205.

Prewriting

Maria read the short story twice. She thought about what the central conflict was, and she decided that it was an internal conflict—the boy struggling against his fear of dying. Then Maria used freewriting to list the events in the story. She grouped the events into parts of the plot, as follows:

- Inciting incident: The boy looks sick and feverish, so his father sends him to bed and calls a doctor. The doctor says that the boy has a fever of one hundred and two.

- Development: The boy continues to look worse and starts to act strange. His father can't understand what is bothering him so much.

- Climax: After the boy's father has taken his temperature, the boy asks how long it will be before he dies. Suddenly Papa—and the reader—realize that the boy has expected to die all along.

- Resolution: Papa discovers that the boy, who only knows about French thermometers, thinks that his 102-degree fever will kill him. He explains the difference between American and European thermometers, and the boy realizes that he is not going to die.

Maria also made notes about the conflict and about special plot devices used in the short story:

- Conflict: At first it appears to be external—the boy against his illness. At the climax of the story, however, the reader discovers that the conflict is really internal—the boy struggling to be brave in the face of death.

- Suspense: Throughout the development, the reader wonders what is wrong with the boy and what is going to happen to him.

Maria made a rough outline for her composition. Her outline showed how she would organize the information from her prewriting notes.

Drafting and Revising

Maria wrote the first draft of her composition very quickly. Then she went back and carefully revised what she had written. She made sure everything she said in her paper was closely related to her topic—the plot of "A Day's Wait."

Proofreading and Publishing

Maria made a fresh copy of her paper and proofread it carefully. She shared her final copy with her class by reading it aloud to them.

ACTIVITIES AND ASSIGNMENTS

A. Read the short story "A Day's Wait," on page 205. Then use Maria's prewriting notes from the case study to write a paragraph about the plot of the story. Follow these steps:
1. Write a topic sentence that tells what your paragraph will be about. Do not begin your sentence with the words *This paragraph will be about.* You might start off with the words *The fascinating plot of Ernest Hemingway's "A Day's Wait"* . . .
2. Write the body of your paragraph. Explain the parts of the plot and include quotations from the story to support your main points.
3. Write a concluding sentence for your paragraph. In this concluding sentence, tell how Hemingway's handling of the plot, especially the news revealed in the climax, makes the story enjoyable to read.

4. Revise and proofread your paragraph. Share it with your classmates in a small-group discussion.

B. Choose one of the following works for a paragraph on plot: "Rikki-tikki-tavi," on page 13; "The Ransom of Red Chief," on page 25; "A Boy and a Man," on page 37; "A Secret for Two," on page 45; "Zoo," on page 51; "The Highwayman," on page 437; or "Oranges," on page 459. Follow these steps when planning and writing your paragraph:
1. Read the work once. Ask yourself what the central conflict in the work is, and write this conflict in your notes. Then read the work a second time, paying careful attention to the parts of the plot and to special plot devices.
2. Make a chart in your prewriting notes with spaces for *Exposition, Inciting incident, Development, Climax, Resolution, Denouement, Suspense, Foreshadowing, Flashback,* and *Surprise ending.* Fill in the chart with information from the story or poem. Bear in mind that some stories do not contain all these parts.
3. Write a topic sentence that tells what the main idea of your paragraph will be.
4. Write the body of your paragraph, describing the parts of the plot. Include evidence, such as quotations from the work, to support your ideas.
5. Write a concluding sentence that sums up your paragraph by telling how the plot makes the work interesting to read.
6. Revise your paragraph, making sure all of your ideas are clear. Then proofread your paragraph for errors in grammar and usage, spelling, punctuation, capitalization, and manuscript form. Share your paragraph with your classmates and with your teacher.

Lesson 9: Writing About Character

TYPES OF CHARACTER

A *character* is a person or animal who takes part in the action of a short story, novel, poem, or play. The main character is called the *protagonist*. What happens to the protagonist is usually the focus of the literary work. Other characters in the work may be *major characters*—characters who play important roles—or *minor characters*—characters who play less important roles. In some works the protagonist struggles against another major character who is called the *antagonist*.

CHARACTERIZATION

Characterization is a process of showing what a character is really like. Writers use many techniques to characterize the people and animals in their works. In *direct characterization* the writer simply tells the reader what a character is like. A statement such as ''Danny felt lonely and frightened'' is a direct characterization.

In *indirect characterization* the writer shows what a character is like by describing what the character says or does, how a character looks, or what other characters say about him or her.

ELEMENTS OF CHARACTER

A well-developed character—just like a real person—has many different *traits,* or characteristics. The following are some traits that help a reader understand a character fully:

1. *Appearance:* What does the character look like? What does the character wear? What can you learn about the character from his or her appearance?
2. *Personality:* Does the character tend to be emotional or rational? shy or outgoing? talented or clumsy? happy or sad? caring or cold? a leader or a follower? honest or dishonest?
3. *Background:* Where did the character grow up? What experiences has he or she had? What is the character's social status? occupation? How much schooling has the character had? What are his or her hobbies or skills?
4. *Motivation:* What makes the character do what he or she does? What does the character like or dislike? What are the character's wishes, goals, desires, dreams, and needs?
5. *Relationships:* How is the character related to other characters in the work? How does the character interact with other characters? Does the character have many friends or many enemies?
6. *Conflict:* Is the character involved in some struggle? If so, is this an internal conflict—one that takes place within the character's mind—or an external conflict—a struggle between the character and some outside force? Is the conflict ever resolved? If so, how?
7. *Change:* Does the character change in the course of the work? Does he or she learn or grow? That is, is the character static (unchanging) or dynamic (changing)?

When planning a paper about a character, follow these steps:

1. Determine what character you are dealing with—the main character, another major character, or a minor character.
2. As you read the work, pay close attention to details that show what the character is like. Note what the narrator says about the character, what other characters say about the character, and what the character says and does.
3. Answer the questions from the lesson about appearance, personality, background, motivation, relationships, conflict, and change. Find

evidence in the work to support your answers.

4. Choose one aspect of the character to focus on in your paper. Write a topic sentence about this aspect of the character.

5. Find evidence from your prewriting notes to support your topic sentence.

CASE STUDY: WRITING ABOUT CHARACTER

Marc's English teacher asked the class to choose a main character from a short story and to write a composition about that character. Marc decided to write about the character Colin in Paul Annixter's "Last Cover," on page 57.

Prewriting

Marc read the story once. To gather information for his paper, he did some freewriting. He imagined that he was describing Colin to someone who knew nothing about him, and he wrote down everything he knew and felt about Colin.

Marc then reread the story to gather more evidence about the characterization of Colin. He made the chart displayed in the right-hand column as part of his prewriting notes.

Marc added several more details to his chart so that he would have plenty of evidence to support his topic sentence.

Next, Marc reviewed his notes to decide which aspect of Annixter's characterization of Colin would be the focus of his paper. He wrote the following topic sentence for his composition:

> Although Colin may appear to be weak, he is really very strong inside.

Marc made a rough outline for his composition to organize his information.

Drafting and Revising

Marc used his prewriting notes and his outline to write a draft of his composition. Here is his unrevised first draft:

> The main character of Paul Annixter's short story, "Last Cover," an eleven-year-old boy

TRAIT AND SPECIFIC EXAMPLE	WHAT THE EXAMPLE SAYS ABOUT COLIN
Appearance: "small for his age, delicate and blond, his hair much lighter and softer than mine, his eyes deep and wide and blue"	frail, probably quiet and thoughtful, not a "typical" eleven-year-old boy
Relationships: "the fox became Colin's whole life"; father gives him a hard time, scorns his art: "'white-livered' interpretation of nature through pen and pencil instead of rod and rifle"	devoted to a wild animal—maybe even more than to humans; in conflict with father over art
Interests: "growing love of wild things"; "threatened to break the family tradition with his leaning toward art"	loner; independent thinker; mind of his own

named Colin. He is "small for his age, delicate," with soft, light hair. He's often sick. From his appearance, he looks frail. He's not a "typical" country boy all day outside and can't wait to go hunting with the men. He's really good at drawing. Colin's dad hates the interest in art. He wants Colin to be an outdoorsman. He gives Colin a hard time. Colin doesn't give in though. Although Colin may appear to be weak, he is really very strong inside.

Colin's real love is the wild fox he found as a kit and raised that is named Bandit. Bandit has grown up and returned to the wild. Now the fox and his wife, unafraid of people, have become experts at raiding neighborhood farms. Bandit must be killed. Colin turns out to be really tuff. He hides out with the fox the day the farmers hunt for it. But he seems to understand and except that Bandit must be killed. Hes not a crybaby this time. The fox gets killed that night, and colin really shows strength and matureness. He uses drawing to help himself deal with his grief. When Colin's father sees it, even he is proud of his son. You would be too. Colin's strength is nice.

Marc read his first draft and realized that it needed major revisions. He revised the draft, adding more specific details and making his sentences clearer.

Proofreading and Publishing

Marc made a clean copy of his draft and proofread it carefully. Then he shared his final copy with his teacher, who displayed it on the class bulletin board.

ACTIVITIES AND ASSIGNMENTS

A. Revise and proofread the draft from the case study. Follow these steps:

1. Read "Last Cover," on page 57. Then read Marc's rough draft, noting how it is organized. What is the topic sentence? Is the rest of the composition directly related to the topic sentence? Is there enough evidence to support the topic sentence? If you answered "no" to either of the last two questions, revise Marc's draft accordingly.
2. Use the Checklist for Revision on page 778 to finish revising the draft.

3. Make a clean copy of the revised draft, and proofread this copy for errors in grammar and usage, spelling, punctuation, capitalization, and manuscript form. Share your final copy with a small group of your classmates.

B. Choose one of the following short stories for a paragraph about character: "The Sneaker Crisis," on page 67; "The Luckiest Time of All," on page 75; "Amigo Brothers," on page 79, "Stolen Day," on page 89; "Two Kinds," on page 95; or "Caleb's Brother," on page 119. Follow these steps:

1. Read the story and choose a main character to write about. Freewrite about the character as though you were describing him or her to a friend.
2. Reread the story to find details to support your description of the character. List your information in a chart like the one Marc made in the case study.
3. Choose one aspect of your character that you think is especially interesting. Write a topic sentence to indicate you are going to write about this aspect. Then make a rough outline for your paragraph that shows how you will organize your information when you write.
4. Write a draft of your paragraph according to your outline. Then revise it to make it clear and specific.
5. Proofread your draft using the Checklist for Proofreading on page 780. Make a clean final copy of your paragraph.
6. Share your paragraph with your classmates in a small-group discussion. Then share it with your teacher.

Lesson 10: Writing About Narration and Point of View

WHAT IS NARRATION?

Narration is the act of telling a story, or *narrative*. Narratives include short stories, novels, dramas, nonfictional narrative essays, and narrative poems. The voice that tells the story is called the *narrator*. The type of narrator a work has determines the point of view.

WHAT IS POINT OF VIEW?

Point of view refers to the narrative voice, the voice that tells a story. Imagine a grandmother telling you a story about when she was young. She will use many first-person pronouns (*I, me, us, our,* and so on) because she is a character in her own story. Now imagine that the grandmother is telling a fairy tale to a small child. She will no longer refer to herself or use first-person pronouns. Instead, the grandmother will use many third-person pronouns such as *she, his,* and *them* to talk about the characters because she is telling the story from outside the action.

To determine the point of view of a particular story, you must first ask whether the narrator is a character in the story. If the narrator does take part in the action, then the story is told from the *first-person point of view.* If the narrator is outside the action, then the story is told from the *third-person point of view.*

In addition to deciding whether the writer has used a first-person or third-person point of view, you must decide how much the narrator knows about what each of the characters thinks and feels. A narrator who can tell about the thoughts and feelings of all the characters is *omniscient,* or "all-knowing." A narrator who knows only what goes on in the mind of one major or minor character is *limited.* If the narrator does not discuss the thoughts or feelings of any of the characters but reports only what they do, then the story has an *objective narrator.*

CASE STUDY: WRITING ABOUT NARRATION AND POINT OF VIEW

Linda's English class was given an assignment to write a composition describing the point of view in a short story. Linda decided to write about point of view in Jack Finney's "The Third Level," on page 127.

Prewriting

Linda read the short story quickly and noticed that the narrator referred to himself as "I" throughout the narrative and that he participated in the action of the story. She then knew that the story was told from the first-person point of view.

Next she asked herself whether the narrator was omniscient, limited, or objective. The narrator, Charley, had expressed his own thoughts and feelings, so Linda knew that the voice was not objective. She reread the story and looked for clues that would help her to determine whether the point of view was omniscient or limited. She realized that the narrator did not view the events of the story through several characters' eyes, so she concluded that "The Third Level" was told from the first-person limited point of view.

Linda needed a plan of action for gathering information for her composition. She decided to try the questioning method. She listed the following questions in her prewriting notes:

What do I know about the narrator, and how do I know it?
How would the story be different if it were told by a different narrator? (Consider one or two possibilities.)

What advantages are there to the story's being told from this point of view?
Why do I think the author chose this point of view?

Linda answered the questions, using specific examples and details from the story. Then she looked at the information she had gathered and made a rough outline for her composition.

Drafting and Revising

Linda used her prewriting notes and her outline to write a first draft of her composition. Then she revised her paper, using standard editorial symbols to mark her changes. At right is Linda's revised draft.

Proofreading and Publishing

Linda made a fresh copy of her composition. She proofread it carefully. Then she shared it with a friend in her class who had also enjoyed "The Third Level."

ACTIVITIES AND ASSIGNMENTS

A. Answer the following questions based on the case study:
1. What error in manuscript form did Linda correct at the beginning of her composition?
2. Why did Linda eliminate the sentence *I think this because of what he says*?
3. Why did Linda change *the train station* to *Grand Central Station* and *another century* to *the nineteenth century*?
4. What other changes did Linda make? Why did she make them?

B. Choose one of the following short stories for a one- or two-paragraph composition about point of view: "A Secret for Two," on page 45; "Last Cover," on page 57; "Amigo Brothers," on page 79; "Two Kinds," on page 95; "Caleb's Brother," on page 119; "Hallucination," on page

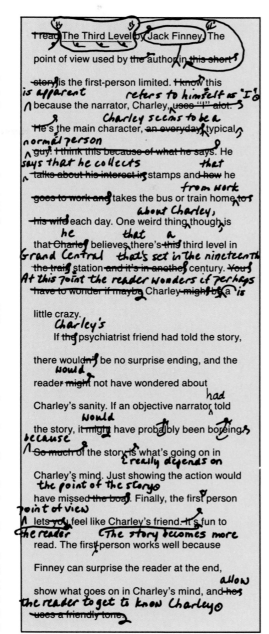

1. She indicates that the first line of the paragraph should be indented.
2. She eliminates the line because it does not provide evidence from the story.
3. Linda made this change to make her facts more specific.
4. She made a number of changes that clarify her ideas. She also corrected a number of spelling, punctuation, and grammatical errors.

Writing About Narration and Point of View 801

179; or "A Day's Wait," on page 205. Follow these steps:

1. Read the story carefully. Determine what point of view is used in the story. Is it first person or third person? omniscient, limited, objective, or subjective?
2. In your prewriting notes, write the answers to the questions that Linda asked herself in the case study. Read the story a second time, noting any important details about the point of view.
3. Make a rough outline that shows how you will organize your information when you write your paper.
4. Write a topic sentence that states the title, author, and point of view of your chosen story.
5. Write the rest of your composition from your outline and your prewriting notes.
6. Revise your paper and then proofread it carefully. Make a clean final copy and share it with your classmates and with your teacher.

Lesson 11: Writing About Theme

WHAT IS THEME?

The *theme* of a literary work is its central message, or insight into life. Theme is more than a statement of what a work is about—it is a statement of what the work means. For example, the story "A Secret for Two," on page 45, is about what happens to a man and his horse, but this subject is not the story's theme. The theme is that a relationship can be so strong that one member of the pair can't go on without the other.

Not every literary work has a theme, or "something to say." A wonderful ghost story or a good mystery, for example, might simply be entertaining.

HOW WRITERS PRESENT THEMES

A theme may be stated directly or it may be implied. For example, in "Utzel and His Daughter, Poverty," one of the characters states the theme directly. Also the framed motto Utzel hangs on the wall indicates the theme.

Often the writer of a literary work does not state his or her theme directly. Instead, the reader must decide what the message of the work is, based on other elements of the work such as the outcome of the plot. Such a theme is implied.

To understand the theme of a work, you often must think a lot about it and read it several times.

STATING THE THEME

Consider the theme of this poem:

SONG FORM
LeRoi Jones
(Imamu Amiri Baraka)

Morning uptown, quiet on the street,
no matter the distinctions that can be
made, quiet, very quiet, on the street.
Sun's not even up, just some kid and me,
skating, both of us, at the early sun, and
amazed there is grace for us, without our
having to smile too tough, or be very pleasant
even to each other. Merely to be merely to be

The poem is about how the speaker and "some kid" find themselves both skating on a quiet street at sunrise. The two are surprised because at this quiet hour they can go about their ways peacefully, just being themselves.

Here is one way of stating the theme: "The quiet of early morning can be magical." Here's another way: "Tensions between people let up when people can just be themselves." Different readers will state the theme, or significance of the poem, in different ways.

CASE STUDY: WRITING ABOUT THEME

Zoraida's English class was given an assignment to write one or two paragraphs about the theme of a short story. Zoraida decided to write about the theme of Piri Thomas's "Amigo Brothers," on page 79.

Prewriting

Zoraida read the story once straight through. Then she wrote down what she thought the theme might be.

• *Possible themes:*
 Thinking positively and working hard will lead to success.
 Boxing is a good way to stay out of trouble.
 It is important to work hard for individual success, but a close friendship is more important than individual success.

Zoraida thought her third statement of the theme best captured the meaning of the story. She reread the story with that theme in mind, and she decided the story in fact supported that

Motivation for Writing You might stress to students that the theme is the central idea in a literary work. All of the other elements—plot, characters, and setting—contribute to the theme of the work. Themes that students might be familiar with include the idea that crime doesn't pay, that good will triumph over evil, or that true love is stronger than any obstacles between two people. You might ask students if they are familiar with any stories, plays, television shows, or movies which convey such themes.

Explain to students that writing about theme helps them to understand and appreciate the central idea of a work of literature. They might also be able to apply the idea presented in the theme to their own experiences.

theme. She did some freewriting about the theme of the story, then, using ideas from her freewriting and referring to the story for details, Zoraida made a chart of events in the story that communicate its theme. This is her chart:

Theme: It is important to work hard for individual success, but a close friendship is more important than individual success.	
Felix and Antonio are the best of friends and both dream of becoming the lightweight champion of the world	same age; train for boxing together; worked hard and think positively; are good fighters
Felix and Antonio find out they will be boxing each other for the Boys Club Championship	both "sense wall rising between them"; agree they must both fight to win; decide to not see each other again until after the fight; train hard to prepare
Felix and Antonio prepare for the fight by trying to put their feelings for each other aside	Felix stays in the South Bronx, decides that he is the Champion and Antonio is the Challenger; Antonio decides Felix must be just an opponent with another face; both hope to knock the other out quickly to avoid hurting him
Felix and Antonio fight as hard and fairly as they can and try to win	both are knocked down once; both hold punches at the bell; they must be separated at the end of the last round
Their friendship proves to be stronger than their desire to win the fight	they walk out of the ring arm-in-arm before the decision of the fight is announced

Drafting and Revising

Zoraida used her prewriting notes to make a rough outline. She began her rough draft with an introduction stating the title of the story, its author, and its theme. As she wrote, she kept her purpose in mind—to show how the story supported her statement of the theme. In the body of her paper she cited examples from the story and gave reasons for her interpretation of the theme. Finally, Zoraida concluded by restating the theme and commenting on it. When she finished her draft, Zoraida revised it carefully, paying attention to whether she had supported her topic sentence.

Proofreading and Publishing

Zoraida proofread her revised draft for errors. Then she made two copies—one for her English teacher and another for her writing folder.

ACTIVITIES AND ASSIGNMENTS

A. If you haven't already done so, read "Amigo Brothers," on page 79. Then, using Zoraida's prewriting notes from the case study, write a one- or two-paragraph composition about the theme of the story. Follow these steps:
1. Add to Zoraida's notes any important details that were omitted.
2. Write a topic sentence that states the theme of "Amigo Brothers."
3. Use Zoraida's prewriting notes and your additions to write your composition. Remember to refer to the story for details to support your topic sentence.
4. Write a concluding sentence that restates the theme; comment on the theme.
5. Revise your composition, using the Checklist for Revision on page 778. Then proofread for errors in spelling and mechanics, using the Checklist for Proofreading on page 780. Share your work with a classmate before giving it to your English teacher.

B. Choose one of the stories from the Theme section of your text, and write a paragraph or two about its themes. In your composition, explain how the story suggests that theme. Your purpose is to convince your reader that the story does, in fact, have the theme you think it has. Follow these steps:

1. Read the short story once. Write down possible themes. Remember to use a full sentence to state each theme. Think about your themes. Ask yourself which version of the theme best describes the significance of the story.

2. Reread the story. Then freewrite about the theme, asking yourself these questions: What do I mean by my statement of theme? What reasons in the story support my statement of the theme?

3. Make a chart of evidence from the story, supporting your statement of its theme.

4. Write a topic sentence that gives the name and author of the work and that states its theme.

5. Write several body sentences supporting your view of the theme by giving evidence from the story.

6. Write a concluding sentence that sums up and comments on the theme.

7. Revise your composition carefully. Add any important details you may have left out. Delete unnecessary or repeated words. Then copy over your revised composition and carefully proofread it.

8. Make a clean final copy. Share this copy with a classmate before giving it to your English teacher.

SECTION 3: UNDERSTANDING THE WORK AS A WHOLE: INTERPRETATION AND SYNTHESIS

Lesson 12: Writing About a Short Story

To write about a work as a whole, you must understand it thoroughly. You must consider each of its parts separately before you can interpret the meaning of the entire work. Here is a list of questions about the parts of a short story. After you have read a short story carefully, ask yourself the following questions:

1. *Author:* Who is the author of the story?
2. *Title:* What is the story's title? Does the title suggest the story's subject or theme?
3. *Setting:* What are the time and place of the story? What mood is created by the setting? Does the setting determine the action or conflict of the story?
4. *Point of view:* Is the story written from the first-person or third-person point of view? Is the narrator limited or omniscient?
5. *Central conflict:* What is the central conflict, or struggle, of the story? Is this conflict internal or external? If the conflict is external, is it a conflict between two people, between a person and nature, between a person and society, or between a person and a supernatural force?
6. *Plot:* What are the major events of the story? What happens in the introduction? What is the inciting incident? What happens during the development? What is the climax of the story? How is the central conflict resolved, or ended? What, if anything, happens after the resolution? That is, does the story have a denouement?

    What special plot devices are used in the story? Does the story make use of foreshad-owing or flashbacks? Is the story suspenseful? If so, what expectations on the part of the reader create this suspense? Does the story have a surprise ending?
7. *Characterization:* Who is the main character, or protagonist? Who are the other major and minor characters? What is revealed in the story about each character's appearance, personality, background, motivations, and relationships? What conflicts do these characters face? Which of these characters change in the course of the story and in what ways? What roles do the minor characters play in advancing the action of the story?
8. *Devices of sound and figures of speech:* Does the story make use of special devices of sound such as onomatopoeia or parallelism? of figures of speech such as metaphor or hyperbole?
9. *Theme:* What is the theme, or message, of the story? How is this theme revealed?

In this lesson you will learn how to write a composition of several paragraphs that explains your interpretation of a short story. Your composition will have three main parts: an introduction, a body, and a conclusion. The introduction will include a thesis statement—a sentence that makes an important general point about the story. The body will give specific examples from the story that support the thesis statement. Your answers to the questions in the preceding list will provide these examples. Finally, the conclusion will restate the thesis statement and sum up the main point of your composition.

CASE STUDY: WRITING ABOUT A SHORT STORY

Dewayne's English teacher asked the class to write a three- or four-paragraph composition about a favorite short story. The composition was supposed to state the theme of the story and explain how other aspects of the story work to reveal the theme. Dewayne decided to write about Gwendolyn Brooks's ''Home,'' on page 175.

Prewriting

To gather information for his composition, Dewayne answered the questions in the list. Here are his prewriting notes:

- Author: Gwendolyn Brooks

- Title: ''Home.'' The title suggests the subject of the story.

- Setting: The time is the late afternoon. The place is the front porch of the characters' home. The mood created by the setting is one of comfort and familiarity. The setting does determine the conflict of the story—the members of the family do not want to leave their home.

- Point of view: third-person omniscient

- Central conflict: The three women struggle to hide their true feelings about moving from their home. The conflicts are internal.

- Plot:
  Introduction—The setting is described and the mood is established.
  Inciting incident—Papa is faced with getting an extension on his homeowner's loan (This event takes place before the opening scene of the story).
  Development—During the course of the conversation between Mama and the girls, their feelings about their home are revealed, and the reader realizes how important it is that Papa get the extension.
  Climax—Papa returns home, and he and Mama go inside to discuss what happened with the loan.
  Resolution—Mama comes back onto the porch and tells the girls that everything is fine.
  Denouement—Helen, relieved, says proudly that she wants to give a party so that her friends can see that her family owns a house.
  Special devices—Suspense is created by the reader's wondering whether the family will have to leave their home.

- Characterization: There are three main characters—Mama, Maud Martha, and Helen. Papa is a minor character. Mama and Helen are alike in their trying to act cheerful about the prospect of moving to a city flat. Maud Martha is less successful at hiding the way she really feels.

- Theme: The theme of the story is that people often try to hide painful feelings by saying things they don't mean.

Drafting and Revising

Dewayne used his prewriting notes and his rough outline to write a draft of his composition. Then he revised it carefully. His revised draft was clear and well organized.

Dewayne used his notes to make a rough outline of his composition:

- Introduction (paragraph 1): Include author, title, setting, and thesis statement. Thesis statement: ''The theme of Gwendolyn Brooks's 'Home' is that people often deal with painful emotions by saying things they don't really mean.''

- Body (paragraph 2): Explain how plot reveals theme. The plot revolves around the conversation on the porch. Thus the characterizations of Mama, Maud Martha, and

Helen, through dialogue, are essential to the story.

- Body (paragraph 3): Explain how point of view reveals theme. The narrator is omniscient and can describe the thoughts of the characters. Thus the narrator can reveal the contrast between the characters' words and their true feelings.

- Conclusion (paragraph 4): Restate thesis statement and sum up the main point(s) of the composition. Say that the story has an important message that applies to real life.

ACTIVITIES AND ASSIGNMENTS

A. Write a draft of a four-paragraph composition from the notes and the rough outline in the case study. Revise the draft, and then proofread it. Make a clean final copy of the composition and share it with a small group of your classmates.

B. Choose one of the following short stories for a three- or four-paragraph composition analysis: "The Ransom of Red Chief," on page 25; "A Boy and a Man," on page 37; "Amigo Brothers," on page 79; "All Summer in a Day," on page 107; "Utzel and His Daughter, Poverty," on page 149; or "The Hummingbird That Lived Through Winter," on page 197. Follow these steps when planning and writing your composition:

1. Read the story carefully. In your prewriting notes, answer the questions listed in this lesson.
2. Write a thesis statement that tells the theme of the story.
3. Decide what important elements of the story—setting, point of view, conflict, plot, characterization, devices of sound, or figures of speech—support your thesis statement. Choose one or two of these elements to discuss in the body of your composition.
4. Make a rough outline showing how you will organize the information in your notes in the paragraphs of your composition.
5. Write a draft of your composition based on your outline. Be sure to include quotations from the story to support your points. Also make sure that your writing does not stray from its purpose, which is to support your thesis statement with evidence from the story.
6. Revise your draft using the Checklist for Revision on page 778. Then make a clean copy of the draft and proofread it. Make a final copy of your composition and share it with your classmates and with your teacher.

Lesson 13: Writing About a Poem

Before writing about a poem, you must understand it thoroughly. Poetry is often very compact—that is, it uses few words to express many ideas. Therefore, you must understand the meaning and significance of each word and phrase before you can write about the poem as a whole. Here is a list of steps you should follow when planning a composition about a poem:

1. Read the poem once, silently, and note any words you do not know. Look up these words in a dictionary and write down their definitions. Reread the poem with the definitions in mind.
2. Read the poem aloud, listening for any special devices of sound such as rhythm, rhyme, onomatopoeia, and alliteration.
3. Read the poem again, silently. This time pay close attention to the images and to the figures of speech in the poem.
4. Paraphrase the poem. That is, restate each sentence of the poem in your own words. As you do so, think not only about what is stated directly in the poem but also about what is suggested or implied.

In your prewriting notes, answer the following questions about the poem:

1. *Author:* Who is the poem's author?
2. *Title:* What is the title of the poem? Does the title suggest the poem's subject or theme?
3. *Genre:* What is the poem's genre, or type? Is it a *lyric poem*—a highly musical work that expresses emotion? Is it a *narrative poem*—one that tells a story? Is it a *dramatic poem*—one that contains characters who speak dialogue? Is it a *concrete poem*—one with a shape that suggests its meaning?
4. *Stanza form:* Is the poem divided into stanzas? If so, how many lines does each stanza have? Is the poem written in some standard stanza form such as couplets, quatrains, sonnet form, haiku form, or limerick form? Does each stanza function as a separate unit of meaning, like a paragraph in a composition?
5. *Devices of sound:* Is the poem in free verse or in some regular meter? If the poem has a regular meter, how many feet are in an average line? What kind of foot is most common in the poem?

   Does the poem have a regular rhyme scheme, or pattern of rhyming words? If so, what is this rhyme scheme?

   Does the poem make use of onomatopoeia? alliteration? consonance? assonance? internal rhyme? euphony? cacophony? parallelism? repetition? Does it have a refrain? What examples can you find of these devices?
6. *Imagery:* Does the poem contain images of sight? of sound? of taste? of touch? of smell? What effects do these images have?
7. *Figures of speech:* Does the poem contain examples of metaphor? of simile? of personification? of hyperbole? Does the poet make use of symbols? allusions? irony? What effect is created by the figures of speech in the poem?
8. *Other literary devices:* What is the poem's general mood? Does this mood change in the course of the poem?

   What is the poem's setting? How is the setting related to the poem's mood? to the action of the poem?

   What seems to be the poem's central message, or theme? What do you think the writer's purpose was?

   Is the poem written in complete sentences?

Does the poem use punctuation, capitalization, or spacing in special ways? Are there any words not in the dictionary that the poet has created for some purpose?

Does the poem invite the reader to contrast two or more things?

9. *Questions about lyric poems:* What can you infer about the poem's speaker? Does the poem give you any hints about the speaker's background, situation, personality, emotional state, or views?

Is the speaker of the poem addressing anyone in particular? If so, whom? What can you infer about the relationship between the speaker and the speaker's audience?

10. *Questions about narrative and dramatic poems:* What can you infer about the main speaker of the poem? Is the poem told from the first-person or the third-person point of view?

How many characters appear in the poem? What can you infer about these characters? about the relationships between or among them?

Does this poem tell a story? If so, does this story involve a conflict? What is the plot of the poem?

If you have questions about any of the terms in the preceding list, refer to the Handbook of Literary Terms and Techniques on page 832.

CASE STUDY: WRITING ABOUT A POEM

Bob's English teacher asked the class to write a three- or four-paragraph composition about a poem. The composition was supposed to do two things:
1. state an important idea about the poem, and
2. give evidence from the poem that shows how the idea was expressed by the poet.

Bob decided to write about Vachel Lindsay's "The Flower-Fed Buffaloes," on page 488.

Prewriting

Bob knew that his first task was to under-stand the poem thoroughly. He began by reading the poem to himself. He then looked up the word *trundle* in a dictionary and found that it meant "to roll along."

Next Bob read the poem aloud and listened carefully for any devices of sound. Then he looked for examples of imagery and figurative language. He asked himself what the poem meant and *paraphrased,* or restated, the poem in his prewriting notes. Finally, he answered the questions from the lesson and added this information to his notes. Here is a section from Bob's notes:

- Author: Vachel Lindsay

- Title: "The Flower-Fed Buffaloes." The title suggests the subject and theme of the poem: Buffaloes were beautiful creatures, fed on flowers.

- Devices of sound: The poem is written in a regular meter. There are many rhyming words at the ends of lines—spring/sing, ago/low, and wheat/sweet.

  There are several examples of alliteration: "wheels *s*pin by/In the *s*pring that *s*till is *s*weet" and "*L*eft us, *l*ong ago . . . *l*ying *l*ow." The alliteration of *l* sounds and the euphony throughout the poem create the effect of a lullaby—perhaps a gentle good-night song to the buffaloes. The phrases *no more* and *lying low* are repeated for effect near the end of the poem.

- Images:
  Sight—buffaloes roaming about the prairie, grazing amidst flowers, grasses, and wheat fields
  Sound—locomotive singing, buffaloes bellowing
  Taste—none (What does a flower taste like?)
  Touch—grass tossing, wheels spinning, buffaloes trundling
  Smell—"perfumed grass," "sweet" spring

- Figures of speech: The poet describes locomotives as singing and prairie flowers as lying low. These personifications suggest that even the scenery "feels" the happy mood of the first part of the poem.

- Mood: The mood shifts from happy and carefree in the first part of the poem to sad in the last part. The setting—the prairie in springtime—helps to convey the joyful atmosphere in the first eight lines.

- Theme: The poet's purpose seems to be to express sadness over the fact that the buffaloes have disappeared from the prairie. He wants to keep the buffaloes from disappearing from people's memories as well.

Bob made the following rough outline from his prewriting notes.

- Introductory paragraph: Tell what poem I'm writing about—author and title. Include a thesis statement: "The poem shows the sadness of the buffaloes' disappearance but allows the buffaloes to live on in people's memories."

- Body paragraph 1: Describe how devices of sound help to create moods of happiness and then sadness.

- Body paragraph 2: Describe how the images in the poem contribute to the contrasting moods in the poem.

- Concluding paragraph: Sum up mood of poem. Restate thesis statement in light of what I've written in the body paragraphs.

Drafting and Revising

Bob wrote a draft of his composition from his prewriting notes and his outline. Then he revised his work, adding more quotations from the poem to support his ideas.

Proofreading and Publishing

Bob made a fresh copy of his composition. He proofread it for errors in spelling and mechanics. Then he made a clean final copy of his paper and read it aloud to the class.

ACTIVITIES AND ASSIGNMENTS

A. Using the notes and the rough outline from the case study, write a draft of Bob's composition. Feel free to add any important ideas that are missing from Bob's prewriting notes. Revise and proofread the composition. Then share it with your classmates and with your teacher.

B. Choose one of the following poems for a three- or four-paragraph composition: "Oranges," on page 459; "The Pheasant," on page 466; "The Pasture," on page 473; "The Courage That My Mother Had," on page 492; "In Just—," on page 500; "Season at the Shore," on page 508; "Mother to Son," on page 518; or "Father William," on page 525. Follow these steps in planning and writing your paper.

1. Follow the steps in this lesson for reading and thinking about the poem. List your questions and answers about the poem in your prewriting notes. Then look over your notes and decide what important point about the poem will be the main idea of your composition.
2. Make a rough outline showing how you will organize your information into three or four paragraphs.
3. Write a thesis statement that tells the main point of your composition. Include this thesis statement in the first paragraph, or introduction, of your rough draft.
4. Finish your draft according to your outline.
5. Revise your draft using the Checklist for Revision on page 778.
6. Make a clean copy of your revised draft, and proofread this copy for errors in grammar and usage, spelling, punctuation, capitalization, and manuscript form. Then make a final copy of your composition and share it with your friends and with your teacher.

Writing About a Poem   811

Motivation for Writing You might explain to students that writing about drama, like writing about poetry, short stories, or other forms of literature, will enable them to better understand and appreciate the components that make up drama. By carefully thinking about and analyzing elements such as staging, dialogue, and acting, students will develop an idea about what is involved in writing and performing a play.

Lesson 14: Writing About Drama

In many respects drama is like other forms of literature. Dramas have plots, conflicts, settings, and characters, as do short stories, novels, and narrative poems. They also express themes and make use of special literary devices such as imagery, sound, and figurative language. Therefore, when writing about dramas, you will use many of the same methods discussed in previous sections of this handbook.

However, drama differs from other types of literature in one very important respect. Dramas are intended to be performed before an audience, not merely to be read. When you read a drama, you should constantly imagine what it would be like to watch actors and actresses perform the drama. The characters should come alive in your mind as you imagine how they would move and speak on stage.

In its printed form, drama reflects the fact that it has been written to be performed. It is made up of dialogue and stage directions. Each line of *dialogue*—the words to be spoken by the actors—follows the name of the character who will speak it. When specific instructions are needed about how the play is to be performed, the writer gives *stage directions*. Stage directions give information about how the actors will move and speak; how the stage should look to the audience; what properties, or movable pieces, should be used by the actors; and what special effects of sound and lighting should be used during the production.

When writing about a drama, you can write about it solely as a work of literature, or you can write about it as a performance. The following are some possible approaches to writing about drama.

The Drama as Literature:

1. Choose a character who intrigues you, and write about how that character changes during the course of the drama.
2. Write an analysis of the plot of the drama. Explain the parts of the plot, including the introduction, the inciting incident, the development, the climax, the resolution, and the denouement.
3. Explain the theme of the drama, and relate this theme to other elements of the work that reveal the theme.

The Drama as Performance:

1. Choose a character who intrigues you, and write about how that character should be portrayed in an actual production.
2. Choose a scene from the drama, and write a description of a stage setting for that scene as it would be viewed from the audience.
3. Write a review of an actual performance of the drama. Comment on the quality of the acting, the set, the costumes, the lighting, and the sound.

CASE STUDY: WRITING ABOUT DRAMA

Kenneth's English class was asked to write a composition about a drama. Kenneth chose a play that he especially liked, *The Dying Detective,* on page 233.

Prewriting

To find a topic for his composition, Kenneth decided to do some freewriting:

Reading this play was fun because I kept trying to figure out how or if Holmes was going to live. As literature, the play has wonderful suspense and a surprise ending. As performance, the setting might make the drama even better by adding to the suspense. Actually seeing Holmes pale and near death, getting sicker instead of healthier, adds to the already strong drama.

Kenneth read over his prewriting and found an interesting idea for his composition. He realized that he could write about how the visual elements of the performance—the stage set and what Holmes looks like—contribute to the effectiveness of the play.

Kenneth's next step was to draft a topic sentence. He wanted his topic sentence to express the main idea of his composition and to guide him in gathering more information for his writing. Here is the first draft of Kenneth's topic sentence:

> When I read *The Dying Detective,* by Michael and Mollie Hardwick based on a story by Sir Arthur Conan Doyle, I especially enjoyed the suspense and Sherlock Holmes's pale face and what the set looked like.

Kenneth read his topic sentence and realized that it would need to be revised for several reasons. First, the sentence was confusing. It wasn't at all clear whether he had actually seen the play or had merely read it. Second, the sentence was too specific—details such as "Holmes's pale face" should be saved for the body of the composition.

Kenneth decided that his main idea would best be stated in two sentences. He therefore wrote two introductory sentences, as follows:

> In *The Dying Detective,* by Michael and Mollie Hardwick from a story by Sir Arthur Conan Doyle, the literary and performance elements work well together. Suspense is created by the plot and reinforced by the setting and by Holmes's physical appearance.

Kenneth needed a plan of action for gathering information. First, he decided to do more freewriting about the plot. He wrote about all the major events in the plot and commented on those moments when the suspense was greatest. Second, he made a chart of information about the setting and about Holmes's physical appearance. In the first column he listed specific details from the drama about the setting and about Holmes's appearance. In the second column he listed the impact each detail had on the reader or on the audience.

The last step in Kenneth's prewriting activities was to make a rough outline for his composition. Here is Kenneth's rough outline:

- Introductory paragraph: Tell what I'm going to write about in general. Include topic sentence.
- Body paragraph 1: Describe how the plot creates suspense.
- Body paragraph 2: Describe how the visual elements—the set and Holmes's appearance—add to the suspense created by the plot.
- Concluding paragraph: Sum up what I've written. Say that the drama is well worth reading or watching.

Drafting and Revising

Kenneth wrote a draft of his composition according to his outline. He included many specific details from the drama to support the points he wanted to make. Then he revised his draft so that it was clear and easy to read.

Proofreading and Publishing

Kenneth made a fresh copy of his revised draft and proofread it carefully. Then he made a final copy of his composition and read it aloud to a small group of his classmates before turning it in to his teacher.

ACTIVITIES AND ASSIGNMENTS

A. Using Kenneth's prewriting from the case study, write a composition about some aspect of *The Dying Detective,* on page 233. Follow these steps:

1. Read the drama carefully. Review Kenneth's introductory sentences and outline. You may decide to use these or you may decide to

choose a new topic and to develop your own notes, topic sentence, and outline. In either case, do some freewriting about the play to gather ideas for your composition.

2. Write a draft of your composition. Make sure that it has a clear introduction, body, and conclusion.

3. Revise your rough draft carefully, using the Checklist for Revision on page 778. Then make a clean copy and proofread it for errors in grammar and usage, spelling, punctuation, capitalization, and manuscript form. Refer to the Checklist for Proofreading on page 780.

4. Make a final copy of your composition, and share this copy with a small group of your

B. Write a three- or four-paragraph composition about *Grandpa and the Statue,* on page 219, or *The Monsters Are Due on Maple Street,* on page 247. Follow these steps when planning and writing your composition:

1. Read carefully the drama you have chosen. Review the possible approaches to writing about drama explained in this lesson. Then freewrite to find a specific topic for your composition.

2. Write a topic sentence that tells what your composition will be about. Do not include details from the drama in this sentence—keep the sentence general.

3. Do some more prewriting activities, such as charting or clustering, to gather ideas and information. Then make a rough outline that tells what information you will include in each paragraph of your composition.

4. Write a draft of your composition. Revise the draft using the Checklist for Revision on page 778. Make a clean copy of your revised draft and proofread it using the Checklist for Proofreading on page 780. Share the final copy of your composition with your class mates and with your teacher.

SECTION 4: JUDGING A LITERARY WORK: EVALUATION

Lesson 15: Evaluating a Literary Work

WHAT IS EVALUATION?

Imagine that your older brother, who knows that you have just finished reading Quentin Reynold's "A Secret for Two," on page 45, asks you what you thought of the story. If you merely reply, "I liked it," he will probably ask you, "Well, *why* did you like it?" Then you might say something like, "I thought the theme of the story was important. Also, the characters really came alive. I could relate to the way Pierre felt about his horse because of the way I feel about our dog." This is an *evaluation* of, or a judgment about, the short story.

An evaluation tells what you think is good— or bad—about a literary work. It is an opinion about the quality of the work, not a fact about it. A statement such as "This story is about a man and a horse" is a fact. The statement "This story's main character is easy to relate to" is an evaluation.

CRITERIA FOR EVALUATION

In the preceding example, "A Secret for Two" was evaluated according to two *criteria,* or standards: the importance of the theme and the characterization of Pierre. The following are some common criteria for evaluating literary works:

1. *Originality or inventiveness:* One quality often found in great literature is originality. Originality means dealing with a topic that has never been written about before or exploring a topic in a new and imaginative way. A work that lacks originality is trite or a cliché and probably will not get a favorable evaluation.

2. *Consistency or completeness of effect:* A literary work is usually aimed at creating a certain effect. For example, in "The Sneaker Crisis," on page 67, Shirley Jackson tries to create the effect of humor. The authors of *The Dying Detective,* on page 233, have tried to create the effect of suspense. Literature is often evaluated according to how well the author has achieved an effect. Consider the following haiku:

1.   A dog walks up and
     Quickly licks a young boy's face
     And then disappears.

2.   Bounding mass of fur
     Pink tongue on astonished cheek
     Grateful little boy

Each of these poems describes the same incident involving a boy and a dog. However, in the first poem, the effect is spoiled by the word *walks,* which is vague and inappropriate. The word *bounding,* in the second poem, is more appropriate and contributes to the effect of the poem as a whole.

3. *Importance:* Some literary works are judged to be better than others because they deal with matters of greater importance. For example, Walt Whitman's poem "Miracles," on page 531, might be considered a greater work than either of the haiku in the previous example because it deals with a more serious topic— the wonder to be found in every aspect of life on earth.

4. *Moral or ethical message:* Sometimes literary works are evaluated according to the moral or ethical messages they convey. How a work will be evaluated depends on whether the

Evaluating a Literary Work 815

Motivation for Writing You might want to lead the class in a discussion of what evaluation means. Tell students that when they are asked such questions as "What do you think of this book?" or "How did you like that flavor of ice cream?" they are being asked to evaluate. Explain that we evaluate countless things in our lives, including clothes, food, television programs, books, even other people. More often than not, in casual conversations we do not think very carefully about what we are asked to evaluate; we usually base our response on our basic reaction to the thing being evaluated. However, in this lesson, students will learn how to evaluate literary works carefully and completely. Learning this will help them evaluate literature, as well as other things, in a logical and factual manner.

person evaluating the work agrees or disagrees with the message in the work. For example, a person who agrees with the statement "People shouldn't expect life to be easy" would probably have good things to say about Langston Hughes's poem "Mother to Son," on page 518.

5. *Clarity:* No matter what ideas an author wants to convey in a literary work, the work will not be evaluated favorably unless the author expresses them clearly. Clarity does not mean easiness—a work may be difficult without being unclear. However, an author cannot be careless when expressing ideas and still write great literature.

CASE STUDY: EVALUATING A LITERARY WORK

Janet's English teacher asked the class for advice in selecting the literature for next year's seventh-grade students. The teacher asked each student to select a work from the text and to write an evaluation of that work, telling why it should be included in next year's reading. Janet chose Shel Silverstein's poem "Sarah Cynthia Sylvia Stout Would Not Take the Garbage Out," on page 451.

Prewriting

To gather ideas for her evaluation, Janet tried freewriting about why she liked the poem. Here is Janet's freewriting:

I love it! This is me! I hate to take the trash out, and my parents nag me all the time. This poet is the first one to make a joke out of something so usually grown-up serious as taking out the garbage. You can almost smell and feel the yucky junky accumulating garbage . . . .

Janet now had a general idea of why she liked the poem. She was ready to choose some criteria for her evaluation. She looked at the list of criteria in this lesson and made the following addition to her prewriting notes:

- Originality: This is the first poem I've ever seen that deals with not taking the garbage out.

- Effect: The humorous effect is definitely achieved! Silverstein does this in three ways. First, the vivid images of the items in Sarah's trash make garbage seem funny and reminds the reader of his or her own messy garbage. Second, the poet uses hyperbole to exaggerate what might happen if one didn't take the garbage out for a really long time. Third, the poem has many instances of alliteration, which make the descriptions seem even funnier.

Next Janet made a chart listing specific examples from the poem to support her evaluation. Here is the first part of that chart.

LITERARY DEVICE AND EXAMPLES	EFFECT
Alliteration: b sounds throughout poem; "*black burned buttered toast*"	makes poem slide, just like oozing, creeping pile of garbage; descriptions seem even sillier
Images: "brown bananas"; "gloppy glumps of cold oatmeal"; "pizza crusts"; "greasy napkins"	reader can really imagine how the garbage looks, smells, and feels

Janet finished her chart and then made a rough outline for her evaluation.

Drafting and Revising

Janet wrote the first draft of her evaluation. First she wrote a topic sentence that introduced the title and author of the poem and the purpose of her writing—to explain why the poem should be used in next year's seventh-grade classes. Then she wrote the specific reasons why she thought the poem was a good one, giving examples from the poem to support her reasons. Finally, she wrote a concluding sentence that summed up the main point of her evaluation. She revised her draft carefully, making sure that all of her points were clear.

Proofreading and Publishing

Janet made a clean copy of her revised draft and proofread it. Then she shared the final copy of her evaluation with her class discussion group and with her teacher.

ACTIVITIES AND ASSIGNMENTS

A. Read "Sarah Cynthia Sylvia Stout Would Not Take the Garbage Out," on page 451. Then write an evaluation of the poem, using the prewriting notes in the case study. If you do not agree with any of Janet's main points, write your own reaction to the poem. Be sure that you can support your ideas with specific examples. Revise and proofread your draft, and share the final copy of your evaluation with a small group of your classmates.

B. Write an evaluation of one of the following works: "Zoo," on page 51; "The Sneaker Crisis," on page 67; "All Summer in a Day," on page 107; "Home," on page 175; *The Monsters Are Due on Maple Street*," on page 247; "A Time of Beginnings," on page 343; "The Night the Bed Fell," on page 363; "Endlessness," on page 387; "Annabel Lee," on page 455; "Fog," on page 468; "Feelings About Words," on page 486; "Stopping by Woods on a Snowy Evening," on page 504; or "I'm Nobody," on page 521. Follow these steps:

1. Read the work carefully. Then freewrite about why you liked or did not like the work. If there are elements that you like and others that you dislike in the work, write about both.
2. Ask yourself what criteria—originality, effect, importance, moral or ethical message, or clarity—could be applied to your chosen work. Then write in your notes whether the work fulfills each criterion.
3. Gather examples from the work to support your judgments. List these in a chart in your prewriting notes.
4. Make a rough outline for your paper. Then write a first draft of your evaluation.
5. Revise your draft, making sure that all of your main points are clear and that you have included specific examples from the work to support your statements.
6. Proofread your evaluation carefully. Then make a clean final copy of your paper, and share this copy with your classmates and with your teacher.

Lesson 16: Writing a Comparative Evaluation

WHAT IS A COMPARATIVE EVALUATION?

Imagine that a classmate of yours shows you two poems. After you have read the poems, your classmate asks you, "Which did you like better?" When you answer that question, supporting your opinion with evidence from the two poems, you are giving a *comparative evaluation.* You are evaluating both poems according to certain criteria, and you are making a judgment about which poem does a better job of meeting each criterion.

When choosing literary works to compare, you should not select two that are completely unlike each other. For example, you would probably not try to compare Shel Silverstein's poem "Sarah Cynthia Sylvia Stout Would Not Take the Garbage Out," on page 451, to James Baldwin's short story "Caleb's Brother," on page 119. One is a humorous poem, while the other is a serious short story. It is better to compare two works that have something in common, such as the same author, the same subject, the same form, or the same theme.

STEPS IN WRITING A COMPARATIVE EVALUATION

Your first step is to select two works to compare and to decide what feature of the works you will be comparing. List these in your notes as follows:

- Works to be compared: Quentin Reynold's short story "A Secret for Two," on page 45, and Paul Annixter's short story "Last Cover," on page 57.

- Feature to be compared: how a relationship between a human being and an animal is shown

The next step is to study each work and to make notes about the feature you are comparing. Decide which writer has done a better job of handling the feature, and list reasons why you think this is true.

When you write your composition, begin by explaining your topic and purpose in your introductory paragraph. Then write one paragraph about each of the works you are comparing. Finally, write a concluding paragraph that summarizes your reasons for believing one work is better than the other.

CASE STUDY: WRITING A COMPARATIVE EVALUATION

Eddie's English teacher asked the class to write a comparative evaluation of two poems by Robert Frost: "The Pasture," on page 473, and "Stopping by Woods on a Snowy Evening," on page 504.

Prewriting

Eddie began by reading both poems carefully. He read them silently and then aloud. Next he did some freewriting to gather ideas about why he liked one poem better than the other. Here is Eddie's freewriting:

I like "The Pasture" better, I think—I like the way it invites me to join in the poem. I can picture the calf and the spring when the speaker says what he's going to do. The "Woods" poem is nice, too, but it's cold and lonely. Nature in that poem is silent and dark, not lively and inviting as in "The Pasture."

Next Eddie needed to gather information. He made the chart on page 819 to compare the literary elements in each poem.

LITERARY ELEMENT	"THE PASTURE"	"STOPPING BY WOODS ON A SNOWY EVENING"
Point of view	first person—speaking directly to reader	first person—addressed to no one in particular
Character	farmer	a person who enjoys nature
Setting	farm; farmer is about to do chores: clean spring, fetch newborn calf—farmer invites reader along	deep in the woods on a dark, snowy winter night; nobody around except speaker and his horse
Images	"watch the water clear"; touch images of mother cow licking calf and calf's tottering	tinkle of harness bells; sound of snowflakes falling; darkness; woods filling with snow
Subject	speaker describes how he enjoys nature and invites the reader to enjoy it with him	speaker tells about his own enjoyment of nature
Theme	nature is worth seeing and it's a thing to be shared	nature is lovely
Figures of speech	none	personification of horse "thinking"
Sound	repetition of last line of each stanza; lines 2 and 3 rhyme in each 2-line stanza; meter regular except for last line of each stanza	last line repeated twice; lines 1, 2, and 4 rhyme in each stanza except in last; line 3 rhymes with lines 1, 2, and 4 of next stanza; meter regular

Eddie needed to decide on two or three literary elements to serve as the criteria for his evaluation. Eddie knew that another student writing about the same two poems could evaluate them completely differently and say that "Stopping by Woods on a Snowy Evening" was the better poem. Therefore, he wanted to be sure that he could back up his judgment with plenty of facts about both poems. He chose the three elements he thought would best support his evaluation: subject, images, and setting.

Eddie made the following rough outline for his composition:

- Introductory paragraph:
  Give titles and authors of works to be compared.
  Tell what opinion about the works will be supported.
  Tell what criteria will be used.
- First body paragraph:
  Discuss "Stopping by Woods on a Snowy Evening";

Writing a Comparative Evaluation 819

Subject
Images
Setting
Give evaluation based on criteria.

- Second body paragraph:
Discuss "The Pasture";
Subject
Images
Setting
Give evaluation based on criteria.

- Concluding paragraph:
Sum up evaluation, say that "The Pasture" has a more friendly tone and is therefore more fun to read and easier to relate to.

Drafting and Revising

Eddie used his prewriting notes and his outline to write the first draft of his composition. Then he revised it several times, making sure that all of his main points were clear and were backed up with evidence from the poems.

Proofreading and Publishing

Eddie proofread his revised draft and made a clean final copy of his evaluation. He read his paper aloud to the class, and he and his classmates discussed their opinions of the two poems he had evaluated.

ACTIVITIES AND ASSIGNMENTS

A. Read "The Pasture," on page 473, and "Stopping by Woods on a Snowy Evening," on page 504. Then, using the prewriting notes and the rough outline in the case study, write a draft of Eddie's evaluation. Revise and proofread your paper carefully, and discuss the evaluation with a small group of your classmates. In your discussion, give reasons why you agree or disagree with Eddie's judgment.

B. Write a comparative evaluation based on one of the following pairs of literary works: "The Bat," on page 472, and "Seal," on page 475; "The Courage That My Mother Had," on page 492, and "Mother to Son," on page 518; or "All Summer in a Day," on page 107, and "The Third Level," on page 127. Follow these steps:
1. Read the works carefully. Then freewrite about why you liked one better than the other.
2. Set up a comparison chart like the one in the case study, and fill in this chart with specific information from the two works.
3. Sum up your opinion about the works in a sentence or two, stating why you like one better than the other. Then choose two or three criteria you think best support your opinion.
4. Make an outline for your composition like the one in the case study. Then write a draft of your evaluation, including many specific examples from the works to support your main points.
5. Revise your draft, making sure that all of your ideas are expressed clearly. Then proofread your composition for errors in spelling and mechanics.
6. Share the final copy of your evaluation with a small group of your classmates who wrote about the same two works that you did. Discuss the reasons why your evaluations were similar or different. Then share your evaluation with your teacher.

SECTION 5: WRITING CREATIVELY
Lesson 17: Writing a Short Story

FINDING A STORY IDEA

Short stories contain many elements, such as setting, conflict, plot, character, point of view, and theme. Brainstorming about any of these elements can lead to an idea for a story. The following are some ways to find an interesting idea for a short story:

1. Think of a time and a place that interest you. The place might be a real one—a place you have visited or would like to visit—or it might be an imaginary one, such as an Earth colony on another planet in the distant future.
2. Think of a conflict that interests you. You might pick an external conflict, such as an argument between two people, or an internal conflict, such as one person's struggle to make an important decision.
3. Think of an interesting person whom you know. Create a character who is like this person in some way.
4. Think of an important idea or belief that you would like others to think about. Make this idea the theme of your short story, and try to think of a situation in which the idea might be tested or shown to be true. This situation will be the basis of the plot of your short story.

DEVELOPING YOUR IDEA

Once you have an idea for one part of your story, you must develop the other parts. To do this, answer the following questions:

1. *Setting:* When does the action of the story occur? Where does the story take place? What images of sight, sound, touch, taste, and smell can I use to describe this place?
2. *Character:* Who is the main character in the story? What is the character's name? How does this character look, act, and talk? What is this character's personality like? What kind of background does this character have? What is this character's relationship to other characters? What does this character love and hate? Will the character change in the course of the story? Will there be one major character with whom this character is in conflict? Will there be other major and minor characters in the story? What will each of these characters be like? What roles will they play in the story? How will they be related to the main character?
3. *Conflict:* What will be the central conflict that the main character is involved in? Will this conflict be within the character's own mind? Will it be a conflict between the character and some outside force, such as nature, another person, or society?
4. *Plot:* What events will occur in the story, and in what order?

   Introduction: What background information will you need to supply about the setting? about the characters?

   Inciting incident: What event will introduce the central conflict of the story?

   Development: What events will occur as a result of the central conflict? How will this conflict develop?

   Climax: What will be the high point of interest or suspense in the story?

   Resolution: What event will resolve, or end, the conflict?

   Denouement: What, if anything, will happen after the conflict is resolved?
5. *Theme:* What will be the central point, or insight, of the story? How will the insightful idea be revealed?

Writing a Short Story   821

Motivation for Writing You might ask students if they have ever wondered how a writer comes up with ideas and develops them into short stories. If students were to ever want to write a short story, how would they go about it? Where would they begin? Explain that in this lesson students will learn how to come up with a good idea, develop it into a story, and write the story.

6. *Point of view:* Will the story be told by one of the characters or by an outside narrator? That is, will it be told from the first-person or the third-person point of view? Will the narrator be limited or omniscient?

DRAFTING YOUR STORY

Use your answers to the preceding questions to write your story. Begin with an introduction that grabs the attention of the reader. Then describe the events of the story in the order in which they happen. Be sure to use lots of specific details to keep the story interesting. Develop suspense by keeping the reader wondering what will happen next. If you like, you may use special literary techniques such as foreshadowing, flashbacks, and a surprise ending.

CASE STUDY: WRITING A SHORT STORY

Todd's English teacher asked the class to write a short story. Todd decided to try brainstorming in order to come up with an idea for his story. Here is a section from his prewriting notes:

- Setting: the beach in summer; my living room; the school playground; this year; a sunny day; far in the future; the planet Venus

- Conflict: don't want to leave the beach but my parents say I have to; bored to death and don't know what to do; competing to make the softball team; aliens are attacking the planet

- Character: myself; my little sister; Rudy, my best friend; Cesar, my next-door neighbor; a kid from Venus; a pro basketball player; a race car driver

Todd looked over his brainstorming notes and decided to set his story in his living room because this setting was familiar to him. He decided to create an internal conflict in which his main character struggles against boredom on a rainy afternoon. There would be two major characters in the story, one based on himself and the other based on his best friend, Rudy. He named these characters Jeremy and Raoul. One minor character in Todd's story would be Jeremy's mother.

Todd made the following notes about the events that would take place in his story:

- Inciting incident: Jeremy and Raoul have nothing to do. It's winter, cold and wet outside, so they want to stay indoors and find something to do in Jeremy's living room.

- Conflict: The conflict is really internal. Both boys want to think of something fun and interesting to do. They are both irritable, though, and blame each other for not coming up with any good ideas.

- Development: The boys discuss various ideas but can't agree on anything. They are growing more and more annoyed with each other.

- Climax: Jeremy and Raoul have a big argument about how the other one never has any good ideas for anything to do. They wrestle on the floor of the living room, almost knocking over one of Jeremy's mother's favorite vases. Jeremy's mother comes into the room and says that if the boys do not settle down, Raoul will have to go home. They decide to read the newspaper to see if anything interesting is going on in the rest of the world.

- Resolution: The boys start talking about how much fun it would be to work on a newspaper. One of them suggests that they start their own newspaper to report about life in their school and in their town. Their problem is solved, and they begin making plans excitedly.

Drafting and Revising

Todd used his prewriting notes to write a draft of his short story. Then he revised his story, adding more dialogue and specific details to make it more interesting and vivid.

Proofreading and Publishing

Todd made a fresh copy of his story and proofread it for errors in spelling and mechanics. He made two final copies and submitted one to his English teacher and the other to his school literary magazine.

ACTIVITIES AND ASSIGNMENTS

A. Use Todd's prewriting notes in the case study to write the short story that he planned. Revise the story, adding more specific details where necessary. Then proofread the story and share your final copy with your classmates and your teacher.

B. Write an original short story. Follow these steps:

1. Use the guidelines for brainstorming in this lesson to find an interesting idea for your story. When you have decided on an idea for one part of your story, develop the other parts by answering the questions listed in this lesson.

2. Use your notes to write a rough draft of your story. Begin with a brief introduction of the setting and the characters. Then tell the events of the plot in the order in which they happen. Make sure that by the end of your story the central conflict has been resolved.

3. Revise your draft, adding details and dialogue where necessary to make your story more interesting and fun to read.

4. Proofread your story for errors in grammar and usage, spelling, punctuation, capitalization, and manuscript form. Then share the final copy of your story with your classmates and with your teacher.

Motivation for Writing You might want to ask students if they have ever wondered how poets come up with ideas and develop them into poems. Ask students what they believe are the most important aspects of poetry. Explain that in this lesson they will learn about three verse forms of poetry, which they will be able to use to write an original poem.

Lesson 18: Writing a Poem

There are many kinds of poems and many ways to go about writing them. In this lesson you will learn about three simple verse forms. Then you will have the chance to write some verses of your own.

THREE VERSE FORMS

1. *Haiku:* The haiku is a form of verse that originated in Japan. The purpose of a haiku is to capture a brief moment and to describe it vividly to the reader. A haiku usually contains images of sight, sound, touch, taste, or smell that help the reader to experience the subject of the poem.

   A haiku consists of three unrhymed lines. The first and third lines have five syllables and the second line has seven syllables. The following is an example of haiku:

   > The falling flower
   > I saw drift back to the branch
   > Was a butterfly.
   > —Moritake

   Notice how the author has used the visual image of a falling flower to describe the movement of a fluttering butterfly. As you read the poem, count the syllables in each line. You will see that this haiku follows the 5–7–5 pattern.

2. *Concrete poems:* A concrete poem is one whose words are arranged on the page to form a visual picture. The shape of a concrete poem often is related to the poem's subject. William Jay Smith's poem "Seal," on page 475, is a concrete poem. Its shape reminds the reader of the slippery, fluid motion of a seal.

3. *Couplets:* A couplet is a pair of rhymed lines. The lines in a couplet usually have the same number of beats, or stresses, and usually have a similar rhythm. Many poems are made up of couplets. For example, Robert P. Tristam Coffin's "The Pheasant," on page 466, is composed of couplets:

   > A pheasant cock sprang into view,
   > A living jewel, up he flew.

Notice the rhyming words at the end of the lines in the couplet. Read the lines aloud and listen for the rhythmical pattern in each line. You will hear the patterns are similar for each of the lines in the couplet.

CASE STUDY: WRITING A POEM

Joel's English teacher asked the class to write a poem in one of the verse forms they had studied in this lesson.

Prewriting

Joel needed to think of a topic for his poem. He brainstormed for five minutes, writing all the ideas he could think of on a piece of paper. Then he selected the idea he liked best: *Games My Dad and I Used to Play.* Joel remembered that his father used to help him to fall asleep by making him laugh. He decided that the topic of his poem would be the game he called "Mr. Pillow-Head." He then wrote details in his prewriting notes about how the game was played.

Next Joel needed to decide what form of verse he would use for his poem. He knew that he could not describe the game in only three lines, so he would not write a haiku. He considered writing a concrete poem, but he did not think that arranging the poem in the shape of a pillow would add much to its meaning. He decided that he would write a poem in couplets.

Drafting and Revising

Joel wrote the following first draft of his poem:

> There were times when I was small
> When I couldn't sleep at all.
> I'd lie awake in bed
> 'Til Dad came in and said,
> "Why can't you get to sleep?
> Have you tried counting sheep?"
> "Yes, Dad," I'd say, and then
> It was that time again.
> He'd take my pillow, turn away,
> Then reappear, and next he'd say
> As I was laughing 'til I was red,
> "Hello! I'm Mr. Pillow-Head."
> When that was done, he'd tuck me in
> And I'd fall asleep, my face in a grin.

Joel read his poem aloud, listening to the rhythmical pattern of the lines. Then he revised his poem, changing some words to make it flow more easily. He also added more vivid adjectives and verbs.

Proofreading and Publishing

Joel made a clean copy of his poem and proofread it for errors in spelling and punctuation. Then he made two final copies—one for his father and one for his teacher.

ACTIVITIES AND ASSIGNMENTS

A. Revise Joel's poem, making any necessary changes to smooth the rhythm. Also add some more vivid adjectives and verbs to describe the action of the poem. Make a clean copy of the poem and proofread it carefully. Then share your final copy with a small group of your classmates, and discuss the changes that they made in Joel's poem.

B. Write a poem of your own. Decide what verse form you would like to use, then follow one of the following sets of directions.

Haiku:

1. Choose a scene or an event you would like to describe in a haiku. Make a list of images related to that scene or event in your prewriting notes.
2. Make a list of vivid adjectives and verbs that describe the subject of your haiku. If you would like to use a figure of speech—a simile, metaphor, personification, or hyperbole—write down ideas for these in your notes also.
3. Write several versions of each line of the haiku. Make sure that the syllable count is 5–7–5.
4. Select the version of each line that is the most descriptive and that goes best with the other lines of the haiku.

Concrete poem:

1. Choose a subject that could easily be represented by a simple shape.
2. Make a list of images that describe the subject of your poem.
3. Write a description of your subject using the images from your list.
4. Arrange the words of your description on a page to form a picture of your subject.

Couplets:

1. Choose a subject that you can describe in a few short lines.
2. Describe your subject in one to three sentences.
3. Choose a few sets of rhyming words that will fit into your description.
4. Rewrite your sentences in verse form, inserting your rhyming words so that they fall at the ends of the lines in your poem.
5. Rewrite your lines as necessary so that both lines in each couplet contain the same number of beats, or stresses.

When you have finished drafting your poem, read it aloud and listen to how it sounds. Revise it as necessary to make it sound the way you would like it to. Proofread your poem and share your final copy with your classmates and with your teacher.

Lesson 19: Writing a Short Dramatic Sketch

A *dramatic sketch* is a short scene that makes a single point. The purpose of the scene may be to convey an important message or merely to make the audience laugh; that is, a dramatic sketch may be serious or comic.

ELEMENTS OF A DRAMATIC SKETCH

A dramatic sketch is written in the same form as a full-length drama. It is made up of dialogue and stage directions. *Dialogue,* or the words spoken by each character in the sketch, follows the names of the characters who speak it. The characters' names are written in capital letters. The following is a line of dialogue from *A Christmas Carol: Scrooge and Marley:*

> SCROOGE. Remember it! I would know it blind-folded! My bridge, my church, my winding river!

Stage directions are notes that tell important details such as what the setting of the sketch should look like, what special effects of lighting or sound should be used, and how the characters should move and speak. They appear in square brackets or parentheses and are italicized or underlined. Note the stage directions in this passage from *The Dying Detective:*

> HOLMES. [*Cheerfully.*] The best way of success-fully acting a part is to *be* it. I give you my word that for three days I have neither tasted food nor drink until you were good enough to pour me out that glass of water. But it's the tobacco I find most irksome.
>
> [*We hear the thud of footsteps running upstairs off-stage.*]
>
> Hello, hello! Do I hear the step of a friend?

[INSPECTOR MORTON *hurries in.*]

PLANNING A DRAMATIC SKETCH

Before you begin writing a dramatic sketch, you need to decide whether your sketch will be serious or comic, what its setting will be, what characters will be involved, and what events will take place.

When you plan your setting, keep in mind the fact that when the sketch is performed, the set will have to be constructed on a stage. It is easier to build a set that looks like a living room than to build one that looks like the view from a mountain peak! In your prewriting notes, list the time and place where your sketch will occur. Then write down important details about the setting that will be essential to the action of the sketch.

Next, make a list of the characters that will participate in the action of your sketch, and describe each of them briefly. Make note of the way you want each character to look, move, and speak.

Finally, make a list of the events that will occur in your sketch. Make sure that the sketch has a definite beginning, middle, and end.

WRITING THE SKETCH

Begin your sketch with a title and a list of characters. Then use stage directions to describe, briefly, the setting of the sketch. After these stage directions, begin the dialogue of the characters.

As you write the dialogue, insert stage directions wherever necessary to tell how the characters should move or speak. You don't need to describe every single action in detail or tell how every line should be spoken. Include stage di-

826   *Handbook of Writing About Literature*

rections only when they are necessary to understand the action of the sketch. However, it is important always to indicate when characters enter and exit the stage.

When writing dialogue, it is a good idea to stop from time to time and read the lines aloud. Make sure that your dialogue sounds natural and believable.

CASE STUDY: WRITING A SHORT DRAMATIC SKETCH

Laura's English teacher asked the class to write a short dramatic sketch based on one of Aesop's fables. Laura decided to use "The Fox and the Crow," on page 547.

Prewriting

Laura read the fable several times and tried to imagine seeing it performed on stage. To gather information about what each character would be like, she made the following prewriting notes:

FOX:

- Appearance: red fur; wears black and yellow plaid pants, black high-top sneakers, black suspenders; smiles a lot, showing gleaming white teeth
- Personality: sly; sneaky; a smooth talker; smart
- Speech: an enthusiastic speaker; strong, smooth voice

CROW:

- Appearance: shiny black feathers; wears a yellow bonnet
- Personality: flirtatious; vain
- Speech: speaks slowly and carefully; uses formal language

Next Laura made a chart to list details about the setting of her sketch:

- Time: a fall day
- Place: a country road
- Lighting: afternoon sun
- Other details: The action occurs at a large oak tree on which the crow is perched.
- Properties: cheese

In her prewriting notes, Laura listed, in order, the events that would take place in her sketch. She organized the events into a beginning, a middle, and an end, as follows:

- Beginning:
  The fox strolls down a country road, wondering how he can get something to eat.
  The fox spots the crow in the tree with cheese in her beak.
  The fox gets an idea.

- Middle:
  The fox flatters the crow and asks her to sing.
  The crow starts to sing and drops the cheese on the ground.
  The fox grabs the cheese and eats it happily.

- End:
  The fox tells the crow, "Do not trust flatterers."

Drafting and Revising

Laura wrote the title of her sketch at the top of her page, and below it she listed the cast of characters with a brief description of each. Then she wrote a description of the setting in brackets and underlined it.

Next, Laura wrote the dialogue of her sketch, adding stage directions wherever she wanted to describe particular movements or ways of speaking by the characters. When she had finished her draft, she read the dialogue aloud and revised it to make it sound more natural.

Proofreading and Publishing

Finally, Laura proofread her dramatic sketch and made a clean final copy of it. This she shared with her teacher, who suggested that Laura plan a performance of the sketch for the class.

ACTIVITIES AND ASSIGNMENTS

A. Using the prewriting notes from the case study, write a short dramatic sketch based on "The Fox and the Crow." Follow the same steps that Laura did in the case study. When you have finished the first draft of the sketch, revise and proofread it carefully. Then make a clean final copy of your sketch, and share this copy with your classmates and with your teacher.

B. Write your own short dramatic sketch based on one of the following works: "The Town Mouse and the Country Mouse," on page 545; "The Boy and the Wolf," on page 553; "Prometheus the Fire-Bringer," on page 563; "Baucis and Philemon," on page 577; or "Narcissus," on page 585. Follow these steps:

1. Select one of the works and read it carefully. Try to imagine what it would be like to see the story acted out on a stage.
2. Make a chart in your prewriting notes to gather information about the characters in your sketch. Fill in the chart with details about how each character should look, act, and speak.
3. List in your notes the important details about the setting of your sketch. Be sure to include a list of the properties, or movable objects, that will appear on stage.
4. List the events that will take place in the sketch. Make sure that your sketch has a beginning, a middle, and an end.
5. Write the title and the list of characters at the top of your page. Then use stage directions to describe the setting of the sketch.
6. Write the dialogue of your sketch. Include stage directions whenever you want to indicate a special effect of lighting or sound or to tell how a character should move or speak.
7. Revise your draft, making sure that all of the dialogue sounds natural. Then proofread your revised draft for errors in grammar and usage, spelling, punctuation, and capitalization.
8. Make a clean final copy of your dramatic sketch, and share this copy with your teacher. If you wish to do so, you could suggest that the sketch be performed for the class.

Lesson 20: Writing a Personal Essay

The purpose of a *personal essay* is to share your thoughts and experiences with others. Writing a personal essay is similar to writing a composition about literature in several ways. First, you use the writing process—prewriting, drafting, revising, proofreading, and publishing. Second, you have a main idea that you support with evidence. Third, your essay has an introduction, a body, and a conclusion.

However, a personal essay differs from the compositions that you have written in other parts of this handbook in one very important way. The evidence that you use to support your main idea does not come from literary works but from your own experiences and ideas. A personal essay allows you to share a part of your life with your readers. The topic of such an essay should be something especially important or meaningful to you.

Once you have decided on a topic for your essay, you must decide what your purpose in writing about that topic will be. You might want to tell a story, to describe something, to explain something, or to persuade people to believe or to do something. Your purpose will determine what techniques you will use when writing your essay.

When you know the topic and the purpose of your essay, you should write a thesis statement that tells both of these. The following are examples of thesis statements for different types of essays:

1. *Narrative essay:* Last Thanksgiving I had a very funny experience at my grandmother's house.
2. *Descriptive essay:* The mountains of Vermont are among the most beautiful in the world.
3. *Expository essay:* Learning how to perform tricks with a yo-yo can be easy if you know the proper technique.

4. *Persuasive essay:* The school cafeteria should not raise the price of milk for students.

To gather information to support your thesis statement, use techniques such as freewriting, clustering, questioning, and making lists or charts. In some cases it is helpful to conduct interviews. If you are writing a narrative essay, you could make a time line of the events you will write about. If you are writing a descriptive essay, you could list all the images of sight, sound, touch, taste, and smell that describe your subject. For an expository essay, try listing all the steps or parts of the thing that you are explaining. To gather evidence for a persuasive essay, make a chart listing the pros and cons of the idea that you are trying to convince your readers to accept.

CASE STUDY: WRITING A PERSONAL ESSAY

Adam was asked by his English teacher to write a personal essay about a place that was especially meaningful to him.

Prewriting

Adam needed to think of a place to write about. To gather ideas for topics, he listed all the familiar places he could think of:

Grandma's living room
my bedroom
the alley behind my house
the school baseball diamond
the local swimming pool
the public library
the amusement park we visited last summer

Adam decided to write about his own room. The purpose of his essay would be to describe his room. To collect ideas about why his room was special to him, he used the questioning

Motivation for Writing You might ask students why almost everyone enjoys telling anecdotes about themselves to friends and others. You could explain that sharing your thoughts and experiences with others is a good way to let others know about you, your likes and dislikes, your joys and frustrations. People enjoy hearing about your thoughts and experiences because they get to know and understand you better and because they may have experienced similar events and feelings. For the same reasons, personal essays can be an enjoyable and rewarding experience. Writing about your own thoughts and experiences allows you to think carefully about them and even to understand them and their influence on you better. In this lesson, students will learn some techniques in writing personal essays.

technique. He listed the following questions in his prewriting notes:

What people do I associate with my room?
What does my room look like?
What events do I associate with my room?
What objects do I associate with my room?

Then Adam answered the questions:

I think of having friends visit—we play Monopoly or write stories or just talk. I love the desk in the corner against my wall. I especially think of the bottom drawer in my chest where I keep all my letters from friends—they're nice to reread when I feel lonely. I like to look out the window at the lawn of the library next door—in different seasons I see different things. Sometimes I just do nothing—stretch out on my bed. When I close my door, nobody can enter without knocking—privacy!

Next Adam wrote several possible topic statements for his essay. Here are the sentences that he considered:

I like my room a lot.
I'm happy in my room.
My room is important to me because there I feel a wonderful sense of privacy.

Adam was pleased with his third topic sentence because it told the main idea of his essay. The evidence he had collected in his prewriting would support this main idea.

Adam's next step was to make a rough outline. He wanted to organize his information into an introduction, a body, and a conclusion for his essay. Here is Adam's rough outline:

• Introduction: State place and briefly tell what it means.

• Body: Provide specific examples to show the reader what the place means.

• Conclusion: Restate main idea and say something interesting about it.

Drafting and Revising

Adam used his notes and his outline to write a draft of his essay. Then he revised the draft. Here is Adam's draft with his revisions marked in standard editorial symbols:

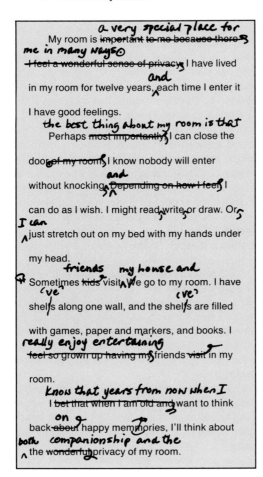

Proofreading and Publishing

Adam made a clean copy of his essay and proofread it for errors in spelling and mechanics. Then he shared his essay with his friends and with his teacher.

ACTIVITIES AND ASSIGNMENTS

A. Answer the following questions about the case study:

1. What changes did Adam make in his topic sentence? How did these changes make it a better topic sentence?
2. What run-on sentence did Adam correct when he revised his essay? what sentence fragment?
3. Where did Adam change a sentence in which the language was too informal?
4. What spelling errors did Adam correct?
5. Where did Adam combine sentences to make his writing smoother?
6. What other changes did Adam make? Why did he make them?

B. Write your own personal essay about a place that is important to you. Your purpose will be to describe the place and to show why it is significant to you. Follow these steps when planning and writing your essay:

1. Think of a place that is special to you. Try brainstorming to gather possible ideas.
2. To gather information about the place you have chosen to write about, try any of the following prewriting techniques: freewriting, clustering, analyzing, questioning, or making charts or lists.
3. Write a topic sentence that tells the main idea of your essay. Make sure that the information you have gathered during prewriting supports this main idea.
4. Make a rough outline for the rest of your essay. Organize your information under three headings: introduction, body, and conclusion.
5. Write a draft of your essay according to your outline.
6. Revise your essay. Make sure that all your ideas are clear and are supported by specific information about your special place.
7. Proofread your essay using the Checklist for Proofreading on page 780. Then make a clean final copy, and share this copy with your classmates and with your teacher.

HANDBOOK OF LITERARY TERMS AND TECHNIQUES

ALLITERATION *Alliteration* is the repetition of initial consonant sounds. Writers use alliteration to create musical effects and to draw attention to certain words or ideas. Shel Silverstein uses alliteration for humorous effect in the title of his poem "*Sarah Cynthia Sylvia Stout*," on page 451. In the following lines from "Who Has Seen the Wind," Christina Rossetti uses alliteration to imitate the sound of the wind:

Who *h*as seen the wind
Neither you nor I:
But *wh*en the trees bow down their heads
The *w*ind is passing by.

In "The Highwayman," on page 437, Alfred Noyes uses alliteration to imitate the sound of horseshoes on a stone pavement:

Over the *c*obbles he *c*lattered and
*c*lashed in the dark innyard.

ALLUSION An *allusion* is a reference to a well-known person, place, event, literary work, or work of art. Understanding what a writer is saying often depends on recognizing allusions. E.E. Cummings's "goat-footed balloonman" in the poem "In Just—," on page 500, is an allusion to Greek myths about the god Pan. Pan was a goat-footed god associated with spring.

ANAPEST See *Meter.*

ANECDOTE An *anecdote* is a brief story about an interesting, amusing, or strange event. Writers tell anecdotes for specific reasons. For example, in "Cat on the Go," on page 351, James Herriot tells several anecdotes about the character named Oscar. Herriot tells these anecdotes to amuse the reader and to reveal Oscar's unusual personality.

ANTAGONIST An *antagonist* is a character or force in conflict with a main character, or protagonist. In "Rikki-tikki-tavi," on page 13, there are two antagonists, the cobras Nag and Nagaina. The protagonist is the mongoose, Rikki.
See *Conflict* and *Protagonist.*

ATMOSPHERE See *Mood.*

AUTOBIOGRAPHY *Autobiography* is a form of nonfiction in which a person tells his or her own life story. This text contains several excerpts from autobiographies, including the selections from Ernesto Galarza's *Barrio Boy,* on page 337, and from Jade Snow Wong's *Fifth Chinese Daughter,* "A Time of Beginnings," on page 343.
Because autobiographies are about real people and events, they are a form of nonfiction. The best autobiographies contain many elements of short stories, including plots, settings, and characters. Most autobiographies, including *Barrio Boy,* are written in the first person. However, a few autobiographies, like *Fifth Chinese Daughter,* are written in the third person.
See *Biography, Nonfiction,* and *Point of View.*

BALLAD A *ballad* is a songlike poem that tells a story, often one dealing with adventure and romance. Most ballads are written in four- to six-line stanzas and have regular rhythms and rhyme schemes. A ballad often features a refrain—a regularly repeated line or group of lines.
The following stanza is from the traditional English ballad "Willie O'Winsbury":

The king has called on his merry men all,
By thirty and by three,
Saying, "Fetch me this Willie O'Winsbury,
For hanging he shall be."

Originally, ballads were not written down. They were composed orally and then sung. As these early *folk ballads* passed from singer to singer, they often changed dramatically. As a result, folk ballads usually exist in many different forms.

Many writers of the modern era have used the ballad form to create *literary ballads*—written imitations of folk ballads. The influence of the ballad tradition can be seen in Alfred Noyes's "The Highwayman," on page 437. While Noyes's poem is not written in typical ballad form, it does tell a story of adventure in rhyming stanzas.

See *Oral Tradition* and *Refrain.*

BIOGRAPHY   *Biography* is a form of nonfiction in which a writer tells the life story of another person. Examples from the text include "Eugenie Clark and the Sleeping Sharks," on page 319, and "Winslow Homer: America's Greatest Painter," on page 395. Because biographies deal with real people and real events, they are classified as nonfiction.

See *Autobiography* and *Nonfiction.*

BLANK VERSE   *Blank verse* is poetry written in unrhymed iambic pentameter lines. The following lines from Robert Frost's "Birches" are written in blank verse:

When I see birches bend to left and right
Across the lines of straighter darker trees,
I like to think some boy's been swinging them.

See *Meter.*

CHARACTER   A *character* is a person or animal who takes part in the action of a literary work. The *main character* is the most important character in a story, poem, or play. A *minor character* is one who takes part in the action but who is not the focus of attention. In Pearl Buck's "The Old Demon," on page 155, the main character is Mrs. Wang. Her grandson and his wife are minor characters.

Characters are sometimes classified as flat or round. A *flat character* is one-sided and often stereotypical. A *round character,* on the other hand, is fully developed and exhibits many traits—often both faults and virtues. In O. Henry's "The Ransom of Red Chief," on page 25, Sam, Bill, and Red Chief are flat characters. In Washington Irving's "Rip Van Winkle," on page 133, the title character is round, or fully developed.

Characters can also be classified as dynamic or static. A *dynamic character* is one who changes in the course of the work. A *static character* is one who does not change. Rip Van Winkle is a dynamic character. Sam, Bill, and Red Chief are static characters.

See *Characterization, Hero/Heroine,* and *Motivation.*

CHARACTERIZATION   *Characterization* is the act of creating and developing a character. Writers use two major methods of characterization—direct and indirect.

When describing a character *directly,* a writer simply states the character's traits, or characteristics. In "A Secret for Two," on page 45, Quentin Reynolds describes Jacques directly, saying, "Jacques was a kind man."

When describing a character *indirectly,* a writer depends on the reader to draw conclusions about the character's traits. Sometimes the writer describes the character's appearance, actions, or speech. At other times the writer tells what other participants in the story say and think about the character. The reader then draws his or her own conclusions.

See *Character* and *Motivation.*

CINQUAIN   See *Stanza.*

CLIMAX　See *Plot.*

CONCRETE POEM　A *concrete poem* is one with a shape that suggests its subject. The poet arranges the letters, punctuation, and lines to create an image, or picture, on the page. William Jay Smith's "Seal," on page 475, is a concrete poem. Its swirling shape suggests the form of a seal's body and the way the seal moves.

CONFLICT　A *conflict* is a struggle between opposing forces. Conflict is one of the most important elements of stories, novels, and plays because it causes the action.

There are two kinds of conflict: external and internal. An *external conflict* is one in which a character struggles against some outside force. For example, in "A Boy and a Man," on page 37, the character Rudi struggles against nature to save the life of a man who has fallen into a crevasse.

An *internal conflict* is one that takes place within the mind of a character. The character struggles to make a decision, take an action, or overcome a feeling. For example, in "A Day's Wait," on page 205, the character Schatz struggles with his feelings of fear and despair because he believes he is dying.
See *Climax, Plot* and *Resolution.*

COUPLET　See *Stanza.*

DACTYL　See *Stanza.*

DENOUEMENT　See *Plot.*

DESCRIPTION　A *description* is a portrait, in words, of a person, place, or object. Descriptive writing uses images that appeal to the five senses—sight, hearing, touch, taste, and smell. See *Image.*

DEVELOPMENT　See *Plot.*

DIALECT　A *dialect* is the form of a language spoken by people in a particular region or group. The English language is divided into many dialects. British English differs from American English. The English spoken in Boston differs from that spoken in Charleston, Chicago, Houston, or San Francisco. This variety adds richness to the language. Dialects differ in pronunciation, grammar, and word choice.

Writers use dialects to make their characters seem realistic. In the following selection from Lucille Clifton's "The Luckiest Time of All," on page 75, the character speaking uses a dialect from the rural southern United States:

> It was just this time, spring of the year, and me and my best friend Ovella Wilson, who is now gone, was goin to join the Silas Greene. Usta be a kinda show went all through the South, called it the Silas Greene show. Somethin like the circus. Me and Ovella wanted to join that thing and see the world. Nothin wrong at home or nothin, we just wanted to travel and see new things and have high times. Didn't say nothin to nobody but one another. Just up and decided to do it.

DIALOGUE　A *dialogue* is a conversation between characters. In poems, novels, and short stories, dialogue is usually set off by quotation marks:

> "And you just been wandering around in the rain all night?"
> I shook my head. "Yes."
> —James Baldwin, "Caleb's Brother"

In a play, dialogue follows the names of the characters, and no quotation marks are used:

> MONAGHAN. I see it all right, but it's all broke!
> SHEEAN. *Broke!* They brought it from France on a boat. They had to take it apart, didn't they?
> —Arthur Miller, *Grandpa and the Statue*

See *Drama.*

DIMETER　See *Meter.*

DRAMA A *drama* is a story written to be performed by actors. Although a drama is meant to be performed, one can also read the *script,* or written version, and imagine the action. The script of a drama is made up of dialogue and stage directions. The *dialogue* is the words spoken by the actors. The *stage directions,* usually printed in italics, tell how the actors should look, move, and speak. They also describe the setting and effects of sound and lighting.

Dramas are often divided into parts called *acts.* The acts are often divided into smaller parts called *scenes. The Dying Detective,* on page 233, is a one-act drama. All of its action takes place in one act that has three scenes.

DRAMATIC IRONY See *Irony.*

DYNAMIC CHARACTER See *Character.*

ESSAY An *essay* is a short, nonfiction work about a particular subject. Most essays have a single major focus and a clear introduction, body, and conclusion.

There are many types of essays. A *narrative essay,* like "Rattlesnake Hunt," on page 369, tells a story about a real-life experience. An *expository essay,* like the excerpt from *These Were the Sioux,* on page 411, relates information or provides explanations. A *persuasive essay,* like "Letter Writing," on page 381, presents and supports an opinion. Most essays contain passages that describe people, places, or objects. However, there are very few purely descriptive essays.
See *Description, Exposition, Narration,* and *Persuasion.*

EXPOSITION *Exposition* is writing or speech that explains, informs, or presents information. This Handbook of Literary Terms is an example of exposition. So are the introductions to the selections in this text.

In the plot of a story or drama, the *exposition,* or introduction, is the part of the work that introduces the characters, setting, and basic situation.
See *Plot.*

EXTENDED METAPHOR In an *extended metaphor,* as in a regular metaphor, a subject is spoken or written of as though it were something else. However, extended metaphor differs from regular metaphor in that several comparisons are made. Carl Sandburg uses extended metaphor in his poem "Fog," on page 468. The poem points out a number of similarities between fog and a cat. Like a cat, the fog is silent and moves stealthily.
See *Metaphor.*

FABLE A *fable* is a brief story, usually with animal characters, that teaches a lesson, or moral. The moral is usually stated at the end of the fable.

The fable is an ancient literary form found in many cultures. The fables written by Aesop, a Greek slave who lived in the sixth century B.C., are still popular with children today. Many familiar expressions, such as "crying wolf," "sour grapes," and "crying over spilt milk," come from Aesop's fables. Other famous writers of fables include La Fontaine, the seventeenth-century French poet, and James Thurber, the twentieth-century American humorist. Thurber called his works fables for our time. Many of Thurber's fables have surprise endings. See the fables by Aesop and Thurber on pages 545, 547, and 549.
See *Irony* and *Moral.*

FANTASY *Fantasy* is highly imaginative writing that contains elements not found in real life. Joan Aiken's "The Third Wish," on page 3, is a fantasy. The story contains such unreal, fantastic elements as a talking animal, magic wishes,

and a swan that changes into a woman and back again. Many science fiction stories, such as Isaac Asimov's "Hallucination," on page 179, contain elements of fantasy.
See *Science Fiction.*

FICTION   *Fiction* is prose writing that tells about imaginary characters and events. Short stories and novels are works of fiction. Some writers base their fiction on actual events and people, to which they add invented characters, dialogue, settings, and plots. Other writers of fiction rely on imagination alone to provide their materials.
See *Narration, Nonfiction,* and *Prose.*

FIGURATIVE LANGUAGE   *Figurative language* is writing or speech that is not meant to be taken literally. The many types of figurative language are known as *figures of speech.* Common figures of speech include hyperbole, metaphor, personification, and simile.

Writers use figurative language to state ideas in vivid and imaginative ways. For example, in "The River," by Javier Héraud, the speaker uses figurative language to express his own wildness:

I am a river,
I flow each moment more
  furiously,
more violently

The speaker does not mean, literally, that he is a river. However, by using figurative language to compare himself to a river, the speaker conveys the idea of his wildness vividly and imaginatively.
See *Metaphor, Personification, Simile,* and *Symbol.*

FIGURE OF SPEECH   See *Figurative Language.*

FLASHBACK   A *flashback* is a section of a literary work that interrupts the sequence of events to relate an event from an earlier time. Arthur Miller uses this technique extensively in his play *Grandpa and the Statue,* on page 219. The play's action shifts from the present, when Monaghan is an adult in an army hospital, to the past, when Monaghan is a child in Brooklyn.

FLAT CHARACTER   See *Character.*

FOLK BALLAD   See *Ballad.*

FOLK TALE   A *folk tale* is a story composed orally and then passed from person to person by word of mouth. Folk tales originated among people who could neither read nor write. These people entertained one another by telling stories aloud, often ones dealing with heroes, adventure, magic, or romance. Eventually, modern scholars like Wilhelm and Jakob Grimm began collecting these stories and writing them down. In this way folk tales have survived into the present day. The Brothers Grimm collected many European folk tales and published these as *Grimm's Fairy Tales.* The Grimm's tales include such famous stories as "Cinderella," "Rapunzel," and "The Bremen Town Musicians." In the United States, scholars have also collected folk tales. These tales deal with such fanciful heroes as Pecos Bill, Paul Bunyan, Mike Fink, and Davy Crockett. "The Little Lizard's Sorrow," on page 615, is a retelling of a Vietnamese folk tale.
See *Fable, Legend, Myth,* and *Oral Tradition.*

FOOT   See *Meter.*

FORESHADOWING   *Foreshadowing* is the use, in a literary work, of clues that suggest events that have yet to occur. Writers use foreshadowing to build their readers' expectations and to create suspense. For example, at the beginning of *The Monsters Are Due on Maple Street,* on page 247, the narrator makes the following statement:

NARRATOR'S VOICE. Maple Street. Six-forty-four P.M. on a late September evening. [*A pause*] Maple Street in the last calm and reflective moment . . . before the monsters came!

The narrator's comment foreshadows, or predicts, what will happen later in the play. It leads the reader or audience to feel suspense and to expect the arrival of monsters. Later the reader or audience is surprised to find out who the monsters really are.

FREE VERSE   *Free verse* is poetry not written in a regular rhythmical pattern, or meter. Walt Whitman's "Miracles," on page 531, is written in free verse. So are the traditional Chippewa Indian song, "A Song of Greatness" on page 520, and Langston Hughes's "Mother to Son" on page 518.

In a free verse poem the poet is free to write lines of any length or with any number of strong stresses, or beats. Free verse is therefore less constraining than *metrical verse,* in which every line must have a certain length and a certain number of stresses.
See *Meter.*

GENRE   A *genre* is a division or type of literature. Literature is commonly divided into three major genres: poetry, prose, and drama. Each major genre is in turn divided into lesser genres, as follows:

1. *Poetry:* lyric poetry, concrete poetry, dramatic poetry, narrative poetry, epic poetry
2. *Prose:* fiction (novels and short stories) and nonfiction (biography, autobiography, letters, essays, and reports)
3. *Drama:* serious drama and tragedy, comic drama, melodrama, and farce

See *Drama, Poetry,* and *Prose.*

HAIKU   *Haiku* is a three-line Japanese verse form. The first and third lines of a haiku have five syllables. The second line has seven syllables. A writer of haiku uses images to create a single,

vivid picture, generally of a scene from nature. See the examples of haiku on pages 478 and 479.

HEPTAMETER   See *Meter.*

HEPTASTICH   See *Stanza.*

HERO/HEROINE   A *hero* or *heroine* is a character whose actions are inspiring or noble. Often heroes and heroines struggle mightily to overcome foes or to escape difficulties. This is true, for example, of Demeter in "Demeter and Persephone," on page 557, and of Prometheus in "Prometheus the Fire-Bringer," on page 563. The most obvious examples of heroes and heroines are the larger-than-life characters in myths and legends. However, characters who are more ordinary than Demeter and Prometheus can also act heroically. For example, in Alfred Noyes's poem on page 437, the landlord's daughter, Bess, sacrifices her own life to save that of the highwayman. This is a heroic deed, and Bess is therefore a heroine.

Note that the term *hero* was originally used only for male characters and the term *heroine* for female characters. However, it is now acceptable to use *hero* to refer to females as well as to males.

HEXAMETER   See *Meter.*

HUBRIS   *Hubris* is the fault of excessive pride. In "Narcissus," on page 585, and in "Phaëthon, Son of Apollo," on page 571, the central characters are guilty of hubris.

IAMB   See *Meter.*

IMAGE   An *image* is a word or phrase that appeals to one or more of the five senses. Writers use images to describe how their subjects look, sound, feel, taste, and smell. In the following lines from the poem "Kansas Land," Gordon

Parks uses images of sight, sound, and smell to re-create the natural wonders of life in Kansas:

> Cloud tufts billowing across the round
>   blue sky.
> Butterflies to chase through grass high
>   as the chin.
> Junebugs, swallowtails, red robin and
>   bobolink,
> Nights filled with soft laughter, fire
>   flies and restless stars,
> The winding sound of crickets rubbing
>   dampness from their wings.
> Silver September rain, orange-red-brown
>   Octobers and white Decembers with
>   hungry
> Smells of hams and pork butts curing in
>   the smokehouse.

IMAGERY   See *Image.*

INCITING INCIDENT   See *Plot.*

IRONY   *Irony* is the general name given to literary techniques that involve surprising, interesting, or amusing contradictions. In *verbal irony,* words are used to suggest the opposite of their usual meaning. In *dramatic irony,* there is a contradiction between what a character thinks and what the reader or audience knows to be true. In *irony of situation,* an event occurs that directly contradicts the expectations of the characters, the reader, or the audience. O. Henry uses irony in his short story "The Ransom of Red Chief," on page 25. In this story, two men kidnap a young boy in a seemingly easy scheme to get ransom money. In an ironic twist, the boy proves to be so wild and mischievous that the two men end up paying his father to take him back.

IRONY OF SITUATION   See *Irony.*

LEGEND   A *legend* is a widely told story about the past, one that may or may not have a foundation in fact. Every culture has its own legends—its familiar, traditional stories. Examples of leg-

ends in the text include "Ojeeg, the Hunter, and the Ice Man," on page 593, and "Popocatepetl and Ixtlaccihuatl," on page 599. The former is a legend from the Micmac Indians of Canada. The latter is a legend from the Aztec Indians of Mexico.
See *Oral Tradition.*

LIMERICK   A *limerick* is a humorous, rhyming, five-line poem with a specific meter and rhyme scheme. Most limericks have three strong stresses in lines 1, 2, and 5 and two strong stresses in lines 3 and 4. Most follow the rhyme scheme *aabba.* See the limericks by Oliver Herford on page 529.

LYRIC POEM   A *lyric poem* is a highly musical verse that expresses the observations and feelings of a single speaker. Examples of lyric poems in the text include "My Mother Pieced Quilts," on page 494, and "I'm Nobody," on page 521.

MAIN CHARACTER   See *Character.*

METAMORPHOSIS   A *metamorphosis* is a change in shape, or form. Many ancient Greek and Roman myths involve characters who undergo dramatic changes. One famous collection of these myths, by the Roman poet Ovid, is called *Metamorphoses.*

   In the myth of "Narcissus," on page 585, a conceited young man who loves to gaze at his own reflection in a pool is transformed into a flower. In this same myth a talkative young woman named Echo is changed into a bodiless voice that can only repeat what is said to her. These metamorphoses are inflicted on Narcissus and Echo as punishments for their misdeeds.
See *Myth.*

METAPHOR   A *metaphor* is a figure of speech in which something is described as though it were something else. A metaphor, like a simile, works by pointing out a similarity between two unlike things. In "A Far Cry From Africa," the West Indian poet Derek Walcott uses the following metaphor:

A wind is ruffling the tawny pelt
Of Africa.

A "tawny pelt" is a brownish-yellow animal hide. By comparing Africa to a tawny pelt, Walcott suggests two similarities. First, the African grasslands are like a tawny pelt because they are brownish-yellow in color. Second, Africa itself is like that proud, strong animal that wears a tawny pelt—the lion.
See *Extended Metaphor* and *Simile.*

METER   The *meter* of a poem is its rhythmical pattern. This pattern is determined by the number and types of stresses, or beats, in each line. To describe the meter of a poem, you must *scan* its lines. *Scanning* involves marking the stressed and unstressed syllables, as follows:

The life | I lead | I want | to be

As you can see, each strong stress is marked with a slanted line (´) and each weak stress with a horseshoe symbol (˘). The weak and strong stresses are then divided by vertical lines (|) into groups called *feet.*

The following types of feet are common in English poetry:

1. *Iamb:* a foot with one weak stress followed by one strong stress, as in the word "begin"

2. *Trochee:* a foot with one strong stress followed by one weak stress, as in the word "people"

3. *Anapest:* a foot with two weak stresses followed by one strong stress, as in the phrase "on the sea"

4. *Dactyl:* a foot with one strong stress followed by two weak stresses, as in the word "happiness"

5. *Spondee:* a foot with two strong stresses, as in the word "downtown"

6. *Pyrrhic:* a foot with two weak stresses, as in the last foot of the word "unev|enly"

7. *Amphibrach:* a foot with a weak syllable, one strong syllable, and another weak syllable, as in "the shimmer|ing sunlight"

8. *Amphimacer:* a foot with a strong syllable, one weak syllable, and another strong syllable, as in "Jack and Jill"
Depending on the type of foot that is most common in them, lines of poetry are described as *iambic, trochaic, anapestic,* or *dactylic.*

Lines are also described in terms of the number of feet that occur in them, as follows:

1. *Monometer:* verse written in one-foot lines

Thus I
Pass by
And die

    —Robert Herrick, "Upon His Departure"

2. *Dimeter:* verse written in two-foot lines

There was | a woman
Who lived | on a hill.
If she's | not gone,
She lives | there still.

    —Anonymous

3. *Trimeter:* verse written in three-foot lines

Where dips | the rock|y highland
Of Sleuth | Wood in | the lake,
There lies | a leaf|y island
Where flapp|ing her|ons wake

The drows|y wat|er rats;

    —W.B. Yeats, "The Stolen Child"

4. *Tetrameter:* verse written in four-foot lines

When wear|y with | the long | day's care,
  And earth|ly change | from pain | to pain,
And lost, | and read|y to | despair,
  Thy kind | voice calls | me back | again

    —Emily Brontë, "To Imagination"

5. *Pentameter:* verse written in five-foot lines

Amidst | these scenes, | O Pil|grim, seek'st|
  thou Rome?
Vain is | thy search|—the pomp | of Rome | is
  fled

    —Francisco de Quevedo, "Rome in Her Ruins"

A six-foot line is called a *hexameter.* A line with seven feet is a *heptameter.*

A complete description of the meter of a line tells both how many feet there are in the line and what kind of foot is most common. Thus the lines from Quevedo's poem would be described as *iambic pentameter,* with one variation, a trochee, in the second line. *Blank verse* is poetry written in unrhymed iambic pentameter. Poetry that does not have a regular meter is called *free verse.*
See *Blank Verse* and *Free Verse.*

MINOR CHARACTER See *Character.*

MONOMETER See *Meter.*

MOOD *Mood,* or *atmosphere,* is the feeling created in the reader by a literary work or passage. Writers use many devices to create mood, including images, dialogue, setting, and plot. Often a writer creates a mood at the beginning of a work and then sustains this mood throughout. Sometimes, however, the mood of the work changes dramatically. For example, the mood of most of "A Boy and a Man," on page 37, is tense and suspenseful. This mood changes after the man is rescued from the crevasse.

MORAL A *moral* is a lesson taught by a literary work. A fable usually ends with a moral that is directly stated. For example, Aesop's fable "The Fox and the Crow," on page 547, ends with the moral "Do not trust flatterers." A poem, novel, short story, or essay often suggests a moral that is not directly stated. The moral must be drawn by the reader, based on other elements in the work.
See *Fable.*

MOTIVATION A *motivation* is a reason that explains or partially explains a character's thoughts, feelings, actions, or speech. Writers try to make their characters' motivations, or motives, as clear as possible. If the motives of a main character are not clear, then the character will not be believable.

Characters are often motivated by needs such as hunger or comfort. They are also motivated by feelings such as fear, love, and pride. In "Last Cover," on page 57, Colin's fierce, protective love for his pet fox motivates him to go into the woods each day and to create a beautiful drawing. In turn, admiration for Colin's drawing motivates Father to support Colin's plan to become an artist.

MYTH A *myth* is a fictional tale that explains the actions of gods or heroes or the origins of elements of nature. Myths are part of the oral tradition. They are composed orally and then passed from generation to generation by word of mouth. Every ancient culture has its own mythology, or collection of myths. The stories on pages 557–585 of your text are retellings, in writing, of myths from ancient Greece and Rome. These Greek and Roman myths, known collectively as *classical mythology,* tell about such gods and

heroes as Zeus, Demeter, Apollo, and Prometheus. The myths of "Narcissus," on page 585, and of "Baucis and Philemon," on page 577, explain the origins of items in nature such as narcissus flowers, echoes, linden trees, and oaks.
See *Oral Tradition.*

NARRATION *Narration* is writing that tells a story. The act of telling a story is also called *narration.* Fictional works such as novels and short stories are examples of narration. So are poems that tell stories, such as "The Cremation of Sam McGee," on page 445. Narration can also be found in many kinds of nonfiction, including autobiographies, biographies, and newspaper reports. A story told in fiction, nonfiction, poetry, or even in drama is called a *narrative.*
See *Narrative Poem* and *Narrator.*

NARRATIVE See *Narration.*

NARRATIVE POEM A *narrative poem* is a story told in verse. Narrative poems often have all the elements of short stories, including characters, setting, conflict, and plot. Examples of narrative poems include "The Highwayman," on page 437, and "Annabel Lee," on page 455.

NARRATOR A *narrator* is a speaker or character who tells a story. A *third-person narrator* is one who stands outside the action and speaks about it. A *first-person narrator* is one who tells a story *and* participates in its action.

In some dramas, like *The Monsters Are Due on Maple Street,* on page 247, there is a separate character called "The Narrator" who introduces, comments on, and concludes the play.
See *Point of View.*

NONFICTION *Nonfiction* is prose writing that presents and explains ideas or that tells about real people, places, objects, or events. Autobiographies, biographies, essays, reports, letters, memos, and newspaper articles are all types of nonfiction.
See *Fiction.*

NOVEL A *novel* is a long work of fiction. Novels contain all of the elements of short stories, including characters, plot, conflict, and setting. However, novels are much longer than short stories. The writer of novels, or novelist, can therefore develop these elements more fully than a writer of short stories can. In addition to its main plot, a novel may contain one or more subplots, or independent, related stories. A novel may also have several themes. This text contains one full-length novel, *Where the Red Fern Grows,* by Wilson Rawls, on page 629.
See *Fiction.*

OCTAVE See *Stanza.*

ONOMATOPOEIA *Onomatopoeia* is the use of words that imitate sounds. *Crash, buzz, screech, hiss, neigh, jingle,* and *cluck* are examples of onomatopoeia. *Chickadee, towhee,* and *whippoorwill* are onomatopoeic names of birds.

In her poem "Onomatopoeia," Eve Merriam uses words to re-create the sounds of water splashing from a faucet:

> The rusty spigot
> sputters,
> utters
> a splutter,
> spatters a smattering of drops,
> gashes wider;
> slash,
> splatters,
> scatters,
> spurts,
> finally stops sputtering
> and plash!
> gushes rushes splashes
> clear water dashes.

ORAL TRADITION The *oral tradition* is the passing of songs, stories, and poems from generation to generation by word of mouth. Folk songs, folk tales, legends, and myths all come from the oral tradition. No one knows who first created these stories and poems. They are *anonymous.*

Here is an anonymous poem from the oral tradition:

Monday's child is fair of face,
Tuesday's child is full of grace,
Wednesday's child is full of woe,
Thursday's child has far to go,
Friday's child is loving and giving,
Saturday's child works hard for its
    living,
And a child that is born on the Sabbath
    day
Is fair and wise and good and gay.

See *Folk Tale, Legend,* and *Myth.*

PARALLELISM   See *Repetition.*

PENTAMETER   See *Meter.*

PERSONIFICATION   *Personification* is a type of figurative language in which a nonhuman subject is given human characteristics. In "Feelings About Words," on page 486, Mary O'Neil personifies words, describing some as "lazy" and some as full of "pride" and "pomp." In the following lines from the poem "Minor Elegy," Henriqueta Lisboa personifies death:

How do you recognize death?
Maybe she looks gray.
Does she give out calling cards, with
    her name correctly embossed?
Will she waylay us in the hall?

PERSUASION   *Persuasion* is writing or speech that attempts to convince the reader to adopt a particular opinion or course of action. Newspaper editorials and letters to the editor are examples of persuasion. So are advertisements and campaign speeches given by political candidates. In "How to Enjoy Poetry," on page 375,

James Dickey attempts to persuade the reader to start reading poetry.

PLOT   *Plot* is the sequence of events in a literary work. In most novels, dramas, short stories, and narrative poems, the plot involves both characters and a central conflict. The plot usually begins with an *exposition* that introduces the setting, the characters, and the basic situation. This is followed by the *inciting incident,* which introduces the central conflict. The conflict then increases during the *development* until it reaches a high point of interest or suspense, the *climax.* The climax is followed by the *falling action* or end, of the central conflict. Any events that occur during the falling action make up the *resolution* or *denouement.*

Some plots do not have all of these parts. Some stories begin with the inciting incident and end with the resolution. In some the inciting incident has occurred before the opening of the story.
See *Conflict.*

POETRY   *Poetry* is one of the three major types of literature, the others being prose and drama. Defining *poetry* more precisely isn't easy, for there is no single, unique characteristic that all poems share. Poems are often divided into lines and stanzas and often employ regular rhythmical patterns, or meters. However, some poems are written out just like prose, and some are written in free verse. Most poems make use of highly concise, musical, and emotionally charged language. Many also make use of imagery, figurative language, and special devices of sound such as rhyme.

Major types of poetry include lyric poetry, narrative poetry, and concrete poetry. E.E. Cummings's "In Just—," on page 500, and Teresa Palomo Acosta's "My Mother Pieced Quilts," on page 494, are both lyric poems. Alfred Noyes's "The Highwayman," on page 437, is a narrative poem. William Jay Smith's "Seal," on page 475, is a concrete poem.

Other forms of poetry include *dramatic poetry,* in which characters speak in their own voices, and *epic poetry,* in which the poet tells a long, involved tale about gods or heroes.
See *Concrete Poem, Genre, Lyric Poetry,* and *Narrative Poetry.*

POINT OF VIEW   *Point of view* is the perspective, or vantage point, from which a story is told. Three commonly used points of view are first person, omniscient third person, and limited third person.

In stories told from the *first-person point of view,* the narrator is a character in the story and refers to himself or herself with the first-person pronoun *I.* The story "Two Kinds," on page 95, is told by a first-person narrator—the story's main character.

The two kinds of third-person point of view, limited and omniscient, are called "third person" because the narrator uses third-person pronouns such as *he* and *she* to refer to the characters. There is no *I* telling the story.

In stories told from the *omniscient third-person point of view,* the narrator knows and tells about what each character feels and thinks. "Rikki-tikki-tavi," on page 13, is written from the omniscient third-person point of view.

In stories told from the *limited third-person point of view,* the narrator relates the inner thoughts and feelings of only one character, and everything is viewed from this character's perspective. "A Boy and a Man," on page 37, is written from the limited third-person point of view.
See *Narrator.*

PROSE   *Prose* is the ordinary form of written language. Most writing that is not poetry, drama, or song is considered prose. Prose is one of the major genres of literature and occurs in two forms: fiction and nonfiction.
See *Fiction, Genre,* and *Nonfiction.*

PROTAGONIST   The *protagonist* is the main character in a literary work. In "Rikki-tikki-tavi," on page 13, the protagonist, or main character, is Rikki, the mongoose.
See *Antagonist* and *Character.*

PYRRHIC   See *Meter.*

QUATRAIN   See *Stanza.*

REFRAIN   A *refrain* is a regularly repeated line or group of lines in a poem or song. In the following lines from a traditional Eskimo poem, the refrain has been italicized:

I wonder what the dear south wind
    has on its mind
    as it blows past?
Does it think about the small people
    who live north of us?
Does it think of them,
    as it blows past?

REPETITION   *Repetition* is the use, more than once, of any element of language—a sound, word, phrase, clause, or sentence. Repetition is used in both prose and poetry. In prose a situation or character may be repeated with some variations. A subplot, for example, may repeat, with variations, the circumstances presented in the main plot. Poets make use of many varieties of repetition. *Rhyme, alliteration,* and *rhythm* are all repetitions of sounds or sound patterns. A *refrain* is a repeated line. Patterns of rhythm and rhyme may be repeated throughout a long poem, as in "The Cremation of Sam McGee," by Robert Service, on page 445.

The following poem makes use of a type of repetition called *parallelism.* In parallelism a grammatical pattern is repeated but the words are changed.

Grandfather sings, I dance.
Grandfather speaks, I listen.
Now I sing, who will dance?
I speak, who will listen?

Grandfather hunts, I learn.
Grandfather fishes, I clean.
Now I hunt, who will learn?
I fish, who will clean?

Grandfather dies, I weep.
Grandfather buried, I am left alone.
When I am dead, who will cry?
When I am buried, who will be alone?
—Shirley Crawford, "Grandfather"

See *Alliteration, Meter, Plot, Rhyme,* and *Rhyme Scheme.*

RESOLUTION See *Plot.*

RHYME *Rhyme* is the repetition of sounds at the end of words. Poets use rhyme to lend a songlike quality to their verses and to emphasize certain words and ideas. Many traditional poems contain *end rhymes,* or rhyming words at the ends of lines. See, for example, the end rhymes in Robert Frost's "The Pasture," on page 473. Another common device is the use of *internal rhymes,* or rhyming words within lines. Notice, for example, the internal rhymes in the following passage from Edgar Allan Poe's "Annabel Lee," on page 455:

For the moon never *beams* without
    bringing me *dreams*
    Of the beautiful Annabel Lee;
And the stars never *rise* but I see
    the bright *eyes*
    Of the beautiful Annabel Lee

See *Rhyme Scheme.*

RHYME SCHEME A *rhyme scheme* is a regular pattern of rhyming words in a poem. To indicate the rhyme scheme of a poem, one uses lowercase letters. Each rhyme is assigned a different letter, as follows:

Under a spreading chestnut *tree*	a
The village smithy *stands;*	b
The smith, a mighty man is *he,*	a
With large and sinewy *hands;*	b
And the muscles of his brawny *arms*	c
Are strong as iron *bands.*	b

—Henry Wadsworth Longfellow, "The
    Village Blacksmith"

The rhyme scheme of these lines is thus *ababcb.*

RHYTHM *Rhythm* is the pattern of beats, or stresses, in spoken or written language.
See *Meter.*

ROUND CHARACTER See *Character.*

SCAN/SCANNING See *Meter.*

SCENE See *Drama.*

SCIENCE FICTION *Science fiction* is writing that tells about imaginary events that involve science or technology. Many science fiction stories are set in the future. "All Summer in a Day," on page 107, is a science fiction story. In this story Ray Bradbury describes events that take place in the future on the planet Venus. *The Monsters Are Due on Maple Street,* on page 247, is a science fiction drama.

SENSORY LANGUAGE *Sensory language* is writing or speech that appeals to one or more of the five senses.
See *Image.*

SESTET See *Stanza.*

SETTING The *setting* of a literary work is the time and place of the action. The time includes not only the historical period—the past, present, or future—but also the year, the season, the time of day, and even the weather. The place may be a specific country, state, region, community, neighborhood, building, institution, or home. Details such as dialects, clothing, customs, and modes of transportation are often used to establish setting.

In most stories the setting serves as a backdrop—a context in which the characters interact. In some stories the setting is crucial to the plot. For example, the weather on the planet Venus is central to the plot of Ray Bradbury's story "All Summer in a Day," on page 107. Setting can also help to create a mood, or feeling. In "The Third Level," on page 127, the writer's description of a summer evening in a small Illinois town creates a mood of peace and innocence:

> It's a wonderful town still, with big old frame houses, huge lawns and tremendous trees whose branches meet overhead and roof the streets. And in 1894, summer evenings were twice as long, and people sat out on their lawns, the men smoking cigars and talking quietly, the women waving palm-leaf fans, with the fireflies all around, in a peaceful world. To be back there with the First World War still twenty years off, and World War II over forty years in the future . . . I wanted two tickets for that.

See *Mood.*

SHORT STORY A *short story* is a brief work of fiction. Like a novel, a short story presents a sequence of events, or plot. The plot usually deals with a central conflict faced by a main character, or protagonist. Like a lyric poem, a short story is concise and creates a single effect, or dominant impression, on its reader. The events in a short story usually communicate a message about life or human nature. This message, or central idea, is the story's *theme.*
See *Conflict, Plot,* and *Theme.*

SIMILE A *simile* is a figure of speech that makes a direct comparison between two unlike subjects using either *like* or *as.* Everday speech often contains similes such as "pale as a ghost,"
"good as gold," "spread like wildfire," and "clever as a fox."

Writers use similes to describe people, places, and things vividly. Poets, especially, create similes to point out new and interesting ways of viewing the world. In the following poem, Maxine Kumin uses a simile that compares the wings of moths beating against a screen to the end of a piece of film hitting the spool of a movie projector:

> Once he puts out the light
> moth wings on the window screen slow
> and drop away *like film lapping the spool*
> *after the home movie runs out.*
> —Maxine Kumin, "The Hermit Has a
> Visitor"

SPEAKER The *speaker* is the imaginary voice assumed by the writer of a poem. In other words, the speaker is the character who tells the poem. This character, or voice, often is not identified by name. The speaker in the following lines, by poet Sylvia Plath, is a mirror:

> I am silver and exact. I have no
> preconceptions.
> Whatever I see I swallow immediately
> Just as it is, unmisted by love or dislike.
> I am not cruel, only truthful—
> —Sylvia Plath, "Mirror"

See *Narrator.*

SPONDEE See *Meter.*

STAGE DIRECTIONS *Stage directions* are notes included in a drama to describe how the work is to be performed or staged. Stage directions are usually printed in italics and enclosed within parentheses or brackets. Some stage directions describe the movements, costumes, emotional states, and ways of speaking of the characters. For example, these stage directions from *The Dying Detective,* on page 233, tell how the characters should move:

[She exits with WATSON's things. HOLMES groans again and flings out an arm restlessly. WATSON comes to the audience's side of the bed and sits on it.]

The following stage directions, from the same play, tell how the actor playing Holmes should sound:

HOLMES [Urgently]. No, no! Keep back!

Stage directions may also describe special effects of lighting or sound, as follows:

[We hear the thud of footsteps running upstairs offstage.]

See *Drama.*

STANZA   A *stanza* is a group of lines in a poem, considered as a unit. Many poems are divided into stanzas that are separated by spaces. Stanzas often function just like paragraphs in prose. Each stanza states and develops a single main idea.

Stanzas are commonly named according to the number of lines found in them, as follows:

1. *Couplet:* a two-line stanza
2. *Tercet:* a three-line stanza
3. *Quatrain:* a four-line stanza
4. *Cinquain:* a five-line stanza
5. *Sestet:* a six-line stanza
6. *Heptastich:* a seven-line stanza
7. *Octave:* an eight-line stanza

Robert P. Tristam Coffin's "The Pheasant," on page 466, is written in couplets:

The fierceness flowed out of his eyes
And left them meek and large and wise.

Gentleness relaxed his head,
He lay in jeweled feathers, dead.

Robert Frost's "Stopping by Woods on a Snowy Evening," on page 504, is written in quatrains:

Whose woods these are I think I know.
His house is in the village, though;

He will not see me stopping here
To watch his woods fill up with snow.

My little horse must think it queer
To stop without a farmhouse near
Between the woods and frozen lake
The darkest evening of the year.

Division into stanzas is common in traditional poetry and is often accompanied by rhyme. Notice, for example, that in each of the stanzas from the Frost poem, the first, second, and fourth lines rhyme. That is, each stanza follows the rhyme scheme *aaba.* However, some rhyming poems are not divided into stanzas, and some poems divided into stanzas do not contain rhyme. See, for example, Nikki Giovanni's "Winter," on page 502, which is divided into unrhymed quatrains.

STATIC CHARACTER   See *Character.*

SUBPLOT   See *Novel.*

SURPRISE ENDING   A *surprise ending* is a conclusion that is unexpected. Sometimes a surprise ending follows a false resolution. The reader thinks that the conflict has already been resolved but then is confronted with a new twist that changes the outcome of the plot. Often a surprise ending is *foreshadowed,* or subtly hinted at, in the course of the work. Writer O. Henry was a master of the surprise ending. See the surprise ending of his story "The Ransom of Red Chief," on page 25.
See *Foreshadowing* and *Plot.*

SUSPENSE   *Suspense* is a feeling of anxious uncertainty about the outcome of events in a literary work. Writers create suspense by raising questions in the minds of their readers. For example, in "A Day's Wait," on page 205, Ernest Hemingway raises questions about why the boy is acting so strangely and whether the boy will recover from his illness. In "A Boy and a Man," on page 37, James Ullman makes the reader wonder whether the character Rudi will succeed in saving the life of the explorer trapped in the crevasse.

SYMBOL   A *symbol* is anything that stands for or represents something else. Symbols are common in everyday life. A dove with an olive branch in its beak is a symbol of peace. A blindfolded woman holding a balanced scale is a symbol of justice. A crown is a symbol of a king's status and authority.

TERCET   See *Stanza.*

TETRAMETER   See *Meter.*

THEME   A *theme* is a central message, concern, or purpose in a literary work. A theme can usually be expressed as a generalization, or general statement, about human beings or about life. The theme of a work is not a summary of its plot. The theme is the central idea that the writer communicates.

A theme may be stated directly by the writer, although this is unusual. In "Utzel and His Daughter, Poverty," on page 149, Isaac Bashevis Singer states his theme directly: "all a man possesses he gains through work, and not by lying in bed and being idle." This statement is a generalization that applies to all human beings. Singer illustrates this theme by telling the story of what happens to Utzel and his daughter.

Most themes are not directly stated but are implied. When the theme is implied, the reader must figure out what the theme is by looking carefully at what the work reveals about people or about life.

TRIMETER   See *Meter.*

TROCHEE   See *Meter.*

VERBAL IRONY   See *Irony.*

HANDBOOK OF CRITICAL THINKING AND READING TERMS

ABSTRACT *adj.* Anything that is not concrete or definite is *abstract*. Examples of abstract words include *truth, beauty, justice, goodness,* and *freedom.* A writer can express an abstract idea clearly by using concrete examples or details. Suppose that a writer wants to describe a beautiful summer day. A good writer will avoid writing a sentence like "It was a beautiful day" because the word *beautiful* is too abstract. Instead, the writer will use description to create concrete images of a beautiful day. For instance, the writer might describe sunlight shining through green leaves or clouds drifting in a clear blue sky. These details make make the abstract idea of beauty quite clear.

ANALOGY *n.* An *analogy* is a comparison of two unlike subjects. In the following passage, an analogy is drawn between atoms and the solar system:

> An atom is like a little solar system. Where the sun would be is the nucleus of the atom made up of neutrons and protons. Circling the nucleus, like planets, are electrons. Most of the area of the atom, like most of the solar system, is empty space.

For an analogy to work, the two subjects being compared must have one or more characteristics in common. An analogy can be expressed using a variety of literary techniques, such as simile, metaphor, and extended metaphor. See the entries for these terms in the Handbook of Literary Terms and Techniques.

ANALYSIS *n.* *Analysis* is the process of studying the parts of a whole. Analyzing something is like taking a machine apart to see how it works. These are the steps you should take when conducting an analysis:

1. Break the whole down into its parts.
2. Study the characteristics of each part.
3. Notice how the parts are related to one another and to the whole.

The study of literature involves analysis. Suppose, for example, that you wish to study a short story. To do so, you must look carefully at each of its parts—setting, characters, plot, and theme. Then you must think about how the parts are related to one another.

ARGUMENT *n.* An *argument* is a set of reasons for accepting some conclusion. Andrew A. Rooney's essay "Letter Writing," on page 381, presents an argument supporting the conclusion that "there ought to be a five-cent stamp for personal letters." Rooney states this conclusion in his first paragraph and then provides reasons to support this conclusion in the rest of his essay.

Whenever you write about a literary work in a paper or in an essay test, you must present an argument. That is, you must present a set of reasons for accepting a conclusion about the work. Suppose, that you are writing about the narrator's mother in the short story "Two Kinds," on page 95. You might decide to argue that the mother's expectations for her daughter are too great. If so, you would state this conclusion. Then you would support it by giving reasons, or evidence, from the story. For instance, the mother first wants her daughter to be the next Shirley Temple, then tries to get her to memorize different facts, and then makes her take piano lessons even though her daughter has no desire to be a "genius." In the end, these expectations cause her daughter to rebel against her and to stop trying to learn to play the piano.

Short essays or summaries of literary works are also called *arguments*. Thus, if you wrote a summary of the plot of "Two Kinds," you would be presenting the argument of the story.
See *Conclusion, Deduction, Evidence, Induction,* and *Inference.*

BANDWAGON/SNOB APPEAL See *Propaganda Techniques.*

CATEGORIZATION *n.* *Categorization* is the process of placing objects or ideas into groups or classes. When you categorize something, you follow these steps:
1. List the object's characteristics.
2. Place the object into a group with other things that have the same characteristics or qualities.
3. Find or create a name for the group. For example, the selection from Ernesto Galarza's book *Barrio Boy,* on page 337, belongs to the category of literature called "nonfiction." Nonfiction is based on real-life experiences.

CAUSE AND EFFECT *n. phrase* When one event precedes and brings about another event, the first is said to be a *cause* and the second an *effect.* For example, in "The Third Wish," on page 3, Leita grows thin and pale because she is unhappy being human. Unhappiness is the cause; thinness and paleness are the effects.

Without cause and effect, works of literature would have no plots. Literary plots rely on a series of causes and effects to advance the story.

CIRCULAR REASONING/BEGGING THE QUESTION See *Logical fallacy.*

COMPARISON *n.* *Comparison* is the process of observing and pointing out similarities. If you were to write a comparison of Felix and Antonio, the main characters in "Amigo Brothers," on page 79, you might say that both are good boxers, confident, and close friends. You might also mention that both conquer their pre-fight jitters and learn the value of giving their best.
See *Contrast.*

CONCLUSION *n.* A *conclusion* is an idea that follows reasonably from another idea or group of ideas. In his essay "Letter Writing," on page 381, Andrew A. Rooney's conclusion that "there ought to be a five-cent stamp for personal letters" follows from the evidence presented: a telephone call cannot take the place of a letter because it cannot be saved or re-read, and the rising cost of stamps discourages letter writing.

CONTRAST *n.* *Contrast* is the process of observing and pointing out differences.
See *Comparison.*

DEDUCTION *n.* *Deduction* is a form of argument in which the conclusion has to be true if the premises are true. Consider, for example, the following argument:

Premise: Peter Jennings is a newscaster.
Premise: Peter Jennings hosts *World News Tonight.*
Premise: *World News Tonight* is a television show.
Conclusion: Peter Jennings is on television.

This argument is a deduction because if you agree that the premises are true, then you must agree that the conclusion is true.
See *Generalization* and *Inference.*

DEFINITION *n.* *Definition* is the process of explaining the meaning of a word or a phrase. The following are some types of definitions:
1. *Ostensive definition:* the actual naming of an object. If a child points to a ball and says "ball," she has given an ostensive definition of the word *ball.*
2. *Lexical definition:* the definition found in the dictionary. There are different kinds of lexical definitions, including definition by synonym, definition by antonym, definition by examples, and genus and differentia definition.
   a. *Definition by synonym* uses a word or

phrase that has the same meaning as the word being defined:

A house is a "dwelling."

b. *Definition by antonym* uses a word or phrase that has the opposite meaning from the word being defined:

Scrooge is *penurious.* That is, he is not generous.

c. *Definition by example* uses a list of related terms, or examples, to which the word being defined applies:

The Empire State Building and the Sears Tower are both *skyscrapers.*

d. In a definition by *genus and differentia,* the object being defined is placed in a large group and is then defined by how it differs from the other objects in the group:

To be defined: *licorice whip*
Genus, or group: candy
Differentia: thin, string-shaped,
        red or black color
Definition: A *licorice whip* is a thin, string-
        shaped piece of red or black
        candy.

Lexical definitions should be used to define key terms when writing about literature.

EITHER/OR FALLACY   See *Logical Fallacy.*

EVALUATION *n.*   *Evaluation* is the process of making judgments about the quality or value of something. When you evaluate a literary work, you analyze and interpret it. You can judge the work once you have taken the time to understand it. If you do not understand the work, then you will not be able to support your evaluation with facts. If you judge a work to be boring but do not support your evaluation by citing passages where the description is too long or where the writer uses too many words to get an idea across, then your evaluation is vague. To convince your reader to agree with you, you will

have to cite specific examples from the work. See *Opinion* and *Judgment.*

EVIDENCE *n.*   *Evidence* is factual information presented to support an argument. When you write an evaluation, you must present evidence from the work to support your claims. For example, in "Home," on page 175, you could argue that all of the family members are concerned about losing their home, but downplay their fears to avoid disappointment. You could support this argument by pointing out that Mama talks of moving to a nicer apartment and that Helen claims that she does not want to bring friends to the house. Their real feelings show when the author reveals their thoughts and when they try to hold back their tears. Also, after they find out that they can remain, Helen decides to have a party. This information is evidence in support of the argument. Without supporting facts, you would not know if the argument was valid or if it was merely an opinion.
See *Fact, Reason,* and *Support.*

FACT *n.*   A *fact* is a statement that is true by definition or that can be proved by observation. Some facts are known by definition: A bicycle has two wheels. Others can be proved through observation: The sun rises in the east and sets in the west.

Writers use facts as evidence to support their conclusions or opinions. Facts are also used to tell the reader about the characters or the setting of the work. Whenever you speak or write, you should present facts to support any opinions that you express.
See *Opinion.*

FALSE ANALOGY   See *Logical Fallacy.*

GENERALIZATION *n.*   A *generalization* is a broad statement, one that applies to more than one thing. You will know that a generalization is false if you can find contrary examples. For example, suppose you feel that your teenage brother is a good driver, and then you hear someone say that all teenagers are bad drivers. You will know that this generalization is false because your brother is a teenager and a good driver. Therefore, *all* teenagers are not bad drivers.

Generalizations are often used in arguments. The following is a *deductive argument* beginning with a generalization:

Premise: (generalization) Rikki-tikki-tavi wants to kill all snakes.
Conclusion: Rikki wants to kill Nag and Nagaina.

Inductive arguments often end with a generalization:

Premise: Maple trees lose their leaves in the fall.
Premise: Oak trees lose their leaves in the fall.
Conclusion: (generalization) Many trees lose their leaves in the fall.

Always avoid overgeneralizations in your writing. To do so, use *qualifiers,* words that limit statements. Such words include *many, some, a couple, almost,* and *nearly.* For example, a qualifier transforms the overgeneralization that all teenagers are bad drivers into a true generalization: Some teenagers are bad drivers.
See *Conclusion* and *Stereotype.*

INDUCTION *n.* *Induction* is a form of argument in which the conclusion is probably, but not necessarily, true. The conclusion of an inductive argument is usually a generalization, as in the following example:

My house is red.
My aunt's house is red.
My best friend's house is red.
My neighbor's house is red.
Conclusion: Many houses are red.

Inductive arguments can be disproved by finding counter examples—ones that contradict the conclusion. For example, if the conclusion of the preceding argument were that *all* houses are red, it would be easy to find an example that would disprove this conclusion.
See *Generalization* and *Inference.*

INFERENCE *n.* An *inference* is any logical or reasonable conclusion. The conclusions of inductive and deductive arguments are inferences. Whenever you read someone's work or have a conversation with someone, you must make inferences. For example, if a writer tells you that a character is smiling and laughing, you can infer that the character is happy. Likewise, if someone tells you in a telephone conversation that she has a fever and is coughing, you can infer that she is sick. The number of conclusions that you can draw is limited only by your thoughtfulness and by the information that you can gather. Whenever you read or listen, think about the language and draw conclusions, or inferences, from it.
See *Conclusion, Deduction,* and *Induction.*

INTERPRETATION *n.* *Interpretation* is the process of determining the meaning or significance of speech, writing, art, music, or actions. The following steps should be taken when interpreting a literary work:
1. Read the work carefully and actively by questioning, predicting, clarifying, summarizing, and pulling it all together.
2. Break the work down into its parts for analysis. Study the characteristics of and relationships between these parts.
3. Draw conclusions about the meaning of the work from your analysis. Support your general conclusion with specific facts.

An interpretation of a work is often a statement of its central message, or theme. The interpretation must be supported by facts drawn from careful reading and analysis of the work. For example, if you were to interpret the story "Hallucination," on page 179, you might say: "The theme of Isaac Asimov's story 'Hallucination' is that fear closes the mind and prevents a person from being receptive to new ideas." You would then use examples from the story as evidence to support your general interpretation. See *Analysis.*

JUDGMENT *n.* A *judgment* is a statement about the quality or value of something. Personal opinions are judgments, not facts. Judgments are not facts because they are subjective. However, sound judgments are ones that are supported by facts.
See *Evaluation* and *Opinion.*

LOADED WORDS See *Propaganda Techniques.*

LOGICAL FALLACY *n. phrase* A *logical fallacy* is a flaw in reasoning. The following logical fallacies are all quite common:
1. *Overgeneralization:* This fallacy occurs when a conclusion goes far beyond what the evidence can support. "All teenagers love rock music" is an example of overgeneralization.
2. *Post hoc, ergo propter hoc:* (Latin, literally, "After this, therefore because of this"). This fallacy occurs when someone falsely concludes that one event caused a second event to occur simply because it occurred before the second event. Suppose, for example, that you get sick while hiking and conclude that the mountain air caused it. If you then find out that your sickness is due to food poisoning, you will realize that your first explanation was an example of the *post hoc* fallacy.
3. *The either/or fallacy:* This fallacy occurs when one reduces the alternatives or possibilities to only two when in fact there are more. Often, one of the alternatives is completely unacceptable, leaving only one choice. The statement "Either you learn to love camping, or you will never appreciate nature" is an example of the either/or fallacy.
4. *Circular reasoning/begging the question:* This fallacy occurs when one fails to provide any logical support for an opinion. This fallacy is known as *begging the question* because the writer or speaker is asking his or her audience to accept an opinion without sufficient proof. The statement "San Francisco is a more beautiful city than New York because it is more scenic" is an example of circular reasoning and begging the question.
5. *False analogy:* This fallacy occurs when superficial similarities are used to support a major conclusion. One cannot assume that just because two things are similar in some ways they will be similar in all ways. Frequently, writers and speakers try to compare their opinion or position to another that is more familiar and accepted. Because the two views have surface similarities, they hope that acceptance of one will encourage acceptance of the other. For example, the statement "Workers are like machines and can therefore be disposed of when they wear out" is an example of false analogy.

MAIN IDEA *n. phrase* The *main idea* is the central point a speaker or writer wants to communicate. Main ideas in essays are usually stated at the beginning, in the thesis statement, or at the end, in the conclusion. In some literary works the main idea is not stated directly but is implied by statements in the work or by the work as a whole.
See *Purpose.*

OBJECTIVE *adj.* Something is *objective* if it has an existence independent of any particular person's attitudes, ideas, or beliefs. An objective statement is a fact that can be verified, or proved, by anyone. For example, the statement "Arthur Miller wrote the play *Grandpa and the Statue*" is objective because anyone can check to see whether the statement is true. However, the statement "Miller's play is lighthearted and frivolous" is subjective. This statement expresses one person's attitude toward the play after seeing or reading it. Other people might

reasonably disagree with this opinion.
See *Subjective*.

OPINION *n.*   An *opinion* is a statement that cannot be proved true or false. Often it can be supported by facts but is not itself a fact. There are different kinds of opinions. *Judgments* are opinions about the value or quality of things. The statement "'When the Frost is on the Punkin' is a wonderful poem" is a judgment. A *prediction* is an opinion about the future. "Cars will eventually run on electricity" is a prediction. A *statement of obligation* is an opinion about what people should or should not do. "If you see someone cheating on a test, you should tell the teacher" is a statement of obligation.

When you express an opinion in writing or in conversation, you should be able to support your opinion with facts. If you cannot, others can dismiss it as being unsound or merely personal. If you can support your opinion with facts, others can use your facts to decide whether to agree or disagree with your opinion.
See *Facts, Judgment,* and *Prediction*.

OVERGENERALIZATION   See *Logical Fallacy*.

PARAPHRASE *n.*   A *paraphrase* is a restatement in different words. Paraphrasing is a helpful technique to use when you want to make sure you understand what someone is saying. It is particularly helpful when you are interpreting a literary work. Putting the writer's meaning into your own words can help you to understand the work.

Paraphrasing is also helpful when you want to quote someone else's thoughts or ideas but don't want to quote his or her exact words. Remember that paraphrases, like word-for-word quotations, must be credited to their sources.

POST HOC, ERGO PROPTER HOC   See *Logical Fallacy*.

PREDICTION *n.*   *Prediction* is the act of making statements about the future. Writers use the technique of foreshadowing to give readers clues or hints about what will happen next. Readers do not always have to rely on clues from writers, however. Frequently readers can predict what will happen because they have read stories with similar plots or because they know how certain types of people, and thus characters, would act in a given situation.

A prediction leads a reader to have certain expectations. If a reader predicts that the hero will walk into the villain's trap, the reader will experience suspense until this event occurs or fails to occur. Writers create expectations to heighten the reader's involvement.
See *Opinion*.

PROBLEM SOLVING *n. phrase   Problem solving* is the process by which a person comes up with an answer to some question or a way out of some difficulty. Problem solving is something that everyone does every day. The process of solving a problem often involves the following steps:
1. Define the problem.
2. Examine the circumstances surrounding the problem.
3. Decide what the result or goal should be once the problem is solved.
4. Take action to reach the desired outcome or goal.

If a problem is particularly difficult, it is helpful to try the following problem-solving strategies:
1. Break the problem down into parts and solve the parts separately.
2. Think of a simpler problem of the same type that you have solved before. Apply part or all of your previous solution to your current difficult problem.
3. Restate the problem in your own words.
4. Ask someone to help you with parts of the problem that are especially difficult.
5. Ask "What if" questions to come up with

possible solutions. Test each solution.

6. Define the key terms or concepts involved in the problem.
7. Try diagramming, freewriting, and other techniques for generating ideas.
8. Use means/ends analysis. That is, at each step in the solution, compare where you are to where you want to be.

See *Analysis.*

PROPAGANDA TECHNIQUE *n. phrase* A *propaganda technique* is used by a writer or speaker to mislead an audience by appealing to its emotions. Several common propaganda techniques follow:

1. *Bandwagon* is the technique of pressuring people to accept some belief or to take some action merely because other people are doing so.
2. *Loaded words* are those that have strong positive or negative connotations. Loaded words with positive connotations are called *purr words.* Such words include *natural, intelligent,* and *strong. Snarl words,* on the other hand, have negative connotations. Such words include *unnatural, dumb,* and *weak.*
3. *Transfer* is the technique of attempting to get people to associate their positive feelings about one thing with another, unrelated thing. An advertiser who uses red, white, and blue banners may be attempting to get people to associate patriotism with buying particular products.
4. *Unreliable testimonial* is a personal endorsement made by someone who is not qualified to make the endorsement. The following advertisement provides an example: "As a professional athlete, I care about what I eat. So I choose Crunchy Flakes because they are nutritious. If you care about your health like me, you'll buy Crunchy Flakes."

PURPOSE *n.* The *purpose* is the goal or aim of a literary work. A work may serve any of a number of different purposes. Sometimes writers or speakers try to persuade their audiences to accept certain points of view. At other times a writer or speaker may attempt to explain a concept, tell a story, describe an event, or merely entertain. A single work may have more than one purpose. For example, "The Mystery and Wonder of Words" on page 401 entertains the reader, conveys knowledge about the origins of words, and instills curiosity about language.
See *Main Idea.*

REALISTIC DETAILS/FANTASTIC DETAILS *n. phrases* A *realistic detail* is one that is drawn from actual or possible experience. A *fantastic detail* is one that is not based on actual experience but is improbable or imaginary. Realistic details lend believability to fiction, poetry, and drama. The reader feels that he or she is reading about real people, places, and events. The use of fantastic details heightens the reader's interest and forces him or her to think imaginatively. Some stories use both realistic and fantastic details. For example, in "Hallucination," on page 179, Isaac Asimov uses realistic details such as grass, insects, and human beings to make his story believable. He also uses fantastic details such as another planet, a time in the future, and thinking insects.

REASON *n.* A *reason* is a statement given in support of some conclusion. As a verb, *to reason* refers to the human ability to think logically and rationally.
See *Argument* and *Conclusion.*

SOURCE *n.* A *source* is anything from which ideas and information are obtained. Libraries are filled with sources. Works of fiction, newspapers, dictionaries, and reference books are all sources. Television shows, computerized information services, and movies are sources, too. Even your own experiences and those of other people are sources. Writers use various sources of information to support their ideas.

As a writer, you must be sure to credit the sources that you use either in the text of your writing or in footnotes or end notes. Failing to attribute statements or facts to their proper sources tricks the reader into believing that what is really someone else's thought or idea is your own. Such plagiarism should be avoided at all costs.

Some sources are better than others. Sources that are current and unbiased are best. *Firsthand,* eyewitness accounts are excellent sources. These are preferable to *secondhand* sources. Secondhand sources usually get their information from firsthand sources and then re-tell it. "Winslow Homer: America's Greatest Painter," on page 395, is H.N. Levitt's second-hand account of Winslow Homer's life and work. Levitt used various sources of information and then wrote this article based on his analysis of the information. "These Were the Sioux," on page 411, is a firsthand account in which Mari Sandoz recounts her own experiences with the Sioux Indians.

STEREOTYPE *n.* A *stereotype* is a generalization applied to a whole group of people. It is a fixed or conventional notion or characterization. Some common stereotypes are the mad scientist and the absent-minded professor. Most stereotypes are misleading and false. For instance, children who have no brothers or sisters are often stereotyped as being spoiled, always getting their way, and manipulating adults into doing what they want them to do. However, these things are not true of all such children, and the stereotype leads to unfair or absurd conclusions. Therefore, you should avoid using stereotypes in your work.

Writers of short stories often resort to stereotyping because they have very little space in which to develop complete, rounded characters. However, even when used in works of fiction, stereotypes can lead to unwarranted over-generalizations about groups of people. See *Generalization.*

SUBJECTIVE *adj.* Something is *subjective* if it has to do with personal experience rather than some objective reality. People's feelings about literary works are subjective because they are internal experiences. When you evaluate a literary work, you state your subjective impressions of it. However, your statements must be supported by objective, factual evidence. See *Objective.*

SUMMARIZE *v.* To *summarize* something is to restate it briefly in different words. For example, a brief summary of *A Christmas Carol: Scrooge and Marley* might read as follows:

> Scrooge is a very stingy businessman whose partner, Marley, was equally stingy, if not stingier than Scrooge. After Marley dies, Scrooge continues his stingy ways. Then, one Christmas Eve, Marley's ghost visits Scrooge and tells him that three visions will appear to him that night: the Ghost of Christmas Past, the Ghost of Christmas Present, and the Ghost of Christmas Yet-to-Come. At first Scrooge is disbelieving, but eventually he becomes receptive to the lessons being taught to him. By morning, Scrooge is a changed person.

SUPPORT *v.* To *support* a statement is to provide evidence for it. See *Evidence.*

TIME ORDER *n. phrase* *Time order* is organization by order of occurrence. Events are told in time order in most novels, plays, short stories, and narrative poems. Many types of nonfiction, including autobiographies, biographies, and histories, also use time order. Time order is sometimes called *chronological order.*

TRANSFER See *Propaganda Technique.*

UNRELIABLE TESTIMONIAL See *Propaganda Technique.*

GLOSSARY

READING THE GLOSSARY ENTRIES

The words in this glossary are from selections appearing in your textbook. Each entry in the glossary contains the following parts:

1. Entry Word. This word appears at the beginning of the entry, in boldface type.

2. Pronunciation. The symbols in parentheses tell how the entry word is pronounced. If a word has more than one possible pronunciation, the most common of these pronunciations is given first.

3. Part of Speech. Appearing after the pronunciation, in italics, is an abbreviation that tells the part of speech of the entry word. The following abbreviations have been used:

n. noun   **p.** pronoun   **v.** verb

adj. adjective   **adv.** adverb   **conj.** conjunction

4. Definition. This part of the entry follows the part-of-speech abbreviation and gives the meaning of the entry word as used in the selection in which it appears.

KEY TO PRONUNCIATION SYMBOLS USED IN THE GLOSSARY

The following symbols are used in the pronunciations that follow the entry words:

Symbol	Key Words	Symbol	Key Words
a	asp, fat, parrot	b	bed, fable, dub
ā	ape, date, play	d	dip, beadle, had
ä	ah, car, father	f	fall, after, off
		g	get, haggle, dog
e	elf, ten, berry	h	he, ahead, hotel
ē	even, meet, money	j	joy, agile, badge
		k	kill, tackle, bake
i	is, hit, mirror	l	let, yellow, ball
ī	ice, bite, high	m	met, camel, trim
		n	not, flannel, ton
ō	open, tone, go	p	put, apple, tap
ô	all, horn, law	r	red, port, dear
o͞o	ooze, tool, crew	s	sell, castle, pass
o͝o	look, pull, moor	t	top, cattle, hat
yo͞o	use, cute, few	v	vat, hovel, have
yo͝o	united, cure, globule	w	will, always, swear
oi	oil, point, toy	y	yet, onion, yard
ou	out, crowd, plow	z	zebra, dazzle, haze
u	up, cut, color	ch	chin, catcher, arch
ur	urn, fur, deter	sh	she, cushion, dash
		t/h	thin, nothing, truth
ə	a in ago	t/h	then, father, lathe
	e in agent	zh	azure, leisure
	i in sanity	ŋ	ring, anger, drink
	o in comply	'	[indicates that a
	u in focus		following l or n is a
ər	perhaps, murder		syllabic consonant, as in
			able (ā' b'l)]

This pronunciation key is from *Webster's New World Dictionary,* Second College Edition. Copyright © 1986 by Simon & Schuster. Used by permission.

A

abet (ə bet')   *v.* To help or encourage

abode (ə bōd')   *n.* Home

accessible (ak ses' ə b'l)   *adj.* Easy to get

acknowledge (ak näl' ij)   *v.* To recognize and admit

adamant (ad' ə mənt)   *adj.* Unyielding; inflexible

addled (ad' 'ld)   *adj.* Muddled and confused

adhesive (əd hē' siv)   *adj.* Sticking

aeon (ē' än)   *n.* A very long period of time

aesthetic (es t/het' ik)   *adj.* From an artistic point of view

akimbo (ə kim' bō)   *adv.* Hands on hips, with elbows pointing outward

algae (al' jē)   *n.* Plants like seaweed that live in water or damp places

allay (ə lā')   *v.* To put to rest; calm

amber (am' bər)   *n.* A brownish-yellow substance; *adj.* of a brownish-yellow color

ambulance (am' byə ləns)   *n.* A specially equipped vehicle for carrying the sick or wounded

amends (ə mendz')   *n.* Things given or done to make up for injury or loss

amiss (ə mis')   *adv.* In a wrong way; improper

Anglophile (aŋ' glə fīl)   *n.* A person who is strongly devoted to England, its people, customs, or influence

anoint (ə noint')   *v.* To rub oil or ointment on

anonymous (ə nän' ə məs)   *adj.* With no name known

apparition (ap' ə rish' ən)   *n.* Ghost

appease (ə pēz')   *v.* To satisfy

appraisal (ə prā' z'l)   *n.* Judgment of something's or someone's quality

apprehensive (ap' rə hen' siv)   *adj.* Anxious; fearful

apprentice (ə pren' tis)   *v.* To receive financial support and instruction in a trade in return for work

apt (apt)   *adj.* Inclined; likely

aptitude (ap' tə to͞od')   *n.* Talent; ability

arched (ärchd)   *adj.* Curved

arid (ar' id)   *adj.* Dry and barren

Arkansas (är' k'n sô')   [< Fr. < Siouan tribal name; ? "downstream people"] State of the south central United States

arrogant (ar' ə gənt)   *adj.* Proud; self-important

arroyo (ə roi' ō)   *n.* A dry gully or ravine

assent (ə sent')   *n.* Agreement

assortment (ə sôrt' mənt)   *n.* A group or collection of different kinds of things

astonish (ə stän' ish)   *v.* To amaze

astrophysics (as' trō fiz' iks)   *n.* The science of the physical properties of the stars, planets, and other heavenly bodies

asunder (ə sun' dər)   *adv.* Into parts or pieces

audible (ô' də b'l)   *adj.* Loud enough to be heard

avarice (av' ər is)   *n.* Greed for riches

awe (ô)   *n.* A mixed feeling of fear and wonder

B

banish (ban′ ish) *v.* To send into exile

bantam (ban′ təm) *n.* A small chicken

bark (bärk) *n.* Any boat, especially a small sailing boat

barometer (bə räm′ ə tər) *n.* An instrument for measuring atmospheric pressure

barrage (bə räzh′) *n.* A heavy attack

barrio (bär′ ē ō) *n.* Part of a town or city where most of the people are Hispanic

bay (bā) *v.* To bark with deep, prolonged tones

beam (bēm) *v.* To shine brightly

belligerent (bə lij′ ər ənt) *adj.* Showing a readiness to fight

bellow (bel′ ō) *v.* To roar with a powerful, reverberating sound

bellows (bel′ ōz) *v.* A device for quickening the fire by blowing air on it

berserk (bər surk′) *adj.* Into a violent or destructive rage

beset (bi set′) *v.* Covered; set thickly with

besiege (bi sēj′) *v.* To surround

bias (bī′ əs) *n.* Preference; leaning; prejudice

bilious (bil′ yəs) *adj.* Bad-tempered; cross

billow (bil′ ō) *v.* To surge or swell

bleachers (blēch′ ərz) *n* Benches stacked in rows for spectators at sporting events

blemish (blem′ ish) *n.* A defect or scar

bog (bäg) *n.* A small marsh or swamp

bonnet (bän′ it) *n.* [Brit.] An automobile hood

brandish (bran′ dish) *v.* To wave in a threatening way

bravado (brə vä′ dō) *n.* Pretended courage

brawn (brôn) *n.* Physical strength

breeches (brich′ iz) *n.* Trousers that reach to or just below the knee

brooch (brōch) *n.* A large ornamental pin worn on a dress

brutality (broo tal′ ə tē) *n.* Violence; harshness

buffet (bə fā′) *n.* A piece of furniture with drawers and cupboards for dishes, table linen, and so on

burly (bur′ lē) *adj.* Heavy and muscular

burrow (bur′ ō) *v.* To dig a hole or tunnel, especially for shelter

bustle (bus′ l) *v.* To hurry

C

calabash (kal′ ə bash′) *n.* A large fruit that is dried and made into a bowl or cup

calico (kal′ ə kō) *n.* A coarse and cheap cloth

calligrapher (kə lig′ rə fər) *n.* Someone skilled in the art of beautiful handwriting

camouflage (kam′ ə fläzh′) *v.* Disguise

candy (kan′ dē) *v.* To coat with sugar

canebrake (kān′ brāk) *n.* A dense growth of cane plants

cant (kant) *v.* To tilt

cantankerous (kan taŋ′ kər əs) *adj.* Bad-tempered

cantonment (kan tän′ mənt) *n.* Temporary quarters assigned to troops

canvas (kan′ vəs) *n.* Closely woven cloth used for tents and sails

carp (kärp) *n.* A fresh-water fish living in a pond or other quiet water

cascade (kas kād′) *n.* A waterfall or anything tumbling like water

casement (kās′ mənt) *n.* A window frame that opens on hinges

castings (kas′ tiŋz) *n.* Waste material

cataract (kat′ ə rakt′) *n.* An eye disease in which the lens becomes clouded over, causing partial or total blindness

catastrophe (kə tas′ trə fē) *n.* A sudden disaster or misfortune

catgut (kat′ gut′) *n.* A tough string or thread used in surgery

chemistry (kem′ is trē) *n.* The chemical makeup and reaction of substances

Cherokee (cher′ ə kē) *n.* [< tribal name *Tsárăgĭ,* prob. < Choctaw *chiluk-ki,* "cave people"] A member of a tribe of Iroquoian Native Americans most of whom were moved from the southeast United States to Oklahoma

chivalrous (shiv′ 'l rəs) *adj.* Courteous

chloroform (klôr′ ə förm′) *n.* A substance used at one time as an anesthetic

chortle (chôr′ t'l) *v.* To make an amused chuckling or snorting sound

clamor (klam′ ər) *v.* To cry out; to demand loudly

clan (klan) *n.* A group of people, often relatives

claret (klar′ it) *adj.* Purplish-red

cleft (kleft) *v.* Split or opened

coarse (kôrs) *adj.* Inferior; crude; common

comely (kum′ lē) *adj.* Attractive; pretty

collaborate (kə lab′ ə rāt′) *v.* Work together

comforter (kum′ fər tər) *n.* A long, woolen scarf

commence (kə mens′) *v.* To begin

commit (kə mit′) *v.* To deliver for safekeeping; entrust; **commit to memory** to learn by heart

commotion (kə mō′ shən) *n.* Noisy reaction; confusion

comparable (käm′ pər ə b'l) *adj.* Similar

compel (kəm pel′) *adj.* To have a powerful effect

competent (käm′ pə tənt) *adj.* Capable

complaint (kəm plānt′) *n.* An illness

compulsion (kəm pul′ shən) *n.* A driving force

concave (kän kāv′) *adj.* Hollow and curved like the inside of an empty ball

conceivable (kən sē′ və b'l) *adj.* Imaginable

concussion (kən kush′ ən) *n.* Violent shaking

confound (kən found′) *v.* To confuse

consolation (kän′ sə lā′ shən) *n.* Something that makes one feel better

conspire (kən spīr′) *v.* To combine; to work together

consternation (kän′ stər nā′ shən) *n.* Sudden confusion and frustration

consultation (kän′ s'l tā′ shən) *n.* Discussion

conventional (kən ven′ shən 'l) *adj.* Ordinary; usual

convey (kən vā′) *v.* To make known

corroborate (kə räb′ ə rāt′) *v.* Confirm; support

councilor (koun′ sə lər) *n.* Adviser

countenance (koun′ tə nəns) *n.* Face

coupe (koo pā′) *n.* A small, two-door automobile

court (kôrt) *v.* To try to win someone's love

covet (kuv′ it) *v.* To envy

covey (kuv′ ē) *n.* A small flock of birds
crafty (kraf′ tē) *adj.* Sly, cunning
cremate (krē′ māt) *v.* To burn to ashes
crevasse (kri vas′) *n.* Deep crack
crotchet (kräᴄh′ it) *n.* A peculiar or stubborn idea
crucial (krōō′ sʰəl) *adj.* Of great importance
cul-de-sac (kul′ də sak′) *n.* A blind alley; a deadend street
culprit (kul′ prit) *n.* Guilty person
cunning (kun′ iŋ) *adj.* Skillful; clever
cupidity (kyōō pid′ ə tē) *n.* Strong desire for wealth
curdle (kur′ d′l) *v.* To thicken; clot
currency (kur′ ən sē) *n.* Money

D

dabbling (dab′ liŋ) *n.* The act of dipping lightly in water
dark (därk) *adj.* Entirely or partly without light
data (dāt′ ə) *n.* Information
dawdle (dôd′ ′l) *v.* Waste time by being slow
debut (dā byōō′) *n.* First appearance before the public
decipher (di sī′ fər) *v.* To make out the meaning of
decreed (di crēd′) *v.* Officially ordered
deference (def′ ər əns) *n.* Respect
defiant (di fī′ ənt) *adj.* Boldly resisting
definitive (di fin′ ə tiv) *adj.* Final; the last word
deft (deft) *adj.* Skillful
defy (di fī′) *v.* To boldly oppose or resist
deign (dān) *v.* To graciously agree to do something beneath one
delude (di lōōd′) *v.* To fool; to mislead
deluge (del′ yōōj) *n.* A great flood or rush of anything
demeanor (di mēn′ ər) *n.* Outward behavior; manner
democracy (di mäk′ rə sē) *n.* Government in which the people hold the ruling power
democrat (dem′ ə krat′) *n.* A person who believes in and upholds government by the people
demon (dē′ mən) *n.* Evil spirit
denumerable (di nōō′ mər ə b′l) *adj.* Countable; said of a set whose elements can be put in a one-to-one correspondence with the natural integers
derelict (der′ ə likt′) *v.* An abandoned ship
derive (di rīv′) *n.* To receive from someone or something
desolate (des′ ə lit) *adj.* Lonely; solitary
despair (di sper′) *n.* Loss of hope
despise (di spīz′) *v.* Look down on with scorn
despondent (di spän′ dənt) *adj.* Lacking hope; depressed
destitute (des′ tə tōōt′) *adj.* Living in complete poverty
deteriorate (di tir′ ē ə rāt′) *v.* To become worse
dignitary (dig′ nə ter′ ē) *n.* Person holding a high position or office
diligent (dil′ ə jənt) *adj.* Careful, steady effort
dim (dim) *adj.* Not bright; somewhat dark; not clearly seen
disdain (dis dān′) *v.* To scorn; regard as unworthy
disembowel (dis′ im bou′ əl) *v.* To take out the inner organs
dispel (dis pel′) *v.* To scatter and drive away
disposition (dis′ pə zishʰ′ ən) *n.* Arrangement
dissever (di sev′ ər) *v.* To separate
dissuade (di swäd′) *v.* To advise someone against an action

distemper (dis tem′ pər) *v.* An infectious virus disease of young dogs
distinct (dis tiŋkt′) *adj.* Separate and different
distinction (dis tiŋk′ sʰən) *n.* Difference of meaning
distracted (dis trakt′ id) *adj.* With the mind drawn away in another direction
distraught (dis′ trôt′) *adj.* Extremely upset
divisor (də vī′ zər) *n.* The number or quantity by which the dividend is divided to produce the quotient
domestic (də mes′ tik) *adj.* Of the home and family
dominion (də min′ yən) *n.* Region over which one rules
dote (dōt) *v.* To be extremely fond
downy (doun′ ē) *adj.* Soft and fluffy, like soft, fine feathers
draggled (drag′ ′ld) *adj.* Wet and dirty
dreaded (dred′ əd) *adj.* Feared

E

ecstatic (ik stat′ ik) *adj.* Delighted
edifice (ed′ ə fis) *n.* Large structure
elevation (el′ ə vā′ sʰən) *n.* A high place
elusive (i lōō′ siv) *adj.* Hard to find
emaciated (i mā′ sʰē āt′ əd) *adj.* Extremely thin, starving
emblem (em′ bləm) *n.* Sign; symbol
emerge (i murj′) *v.* To become visible
emit (i mit′) *v.* To send out or utter
emphatic (im fat′ ik) *adj.* Felt with emphasis; forceful; definite
enamel (i nam′ ′l) *n.* Glassy colored substance used as coating on metal, glass, and pottery
encounter (in koun′ tər) *n.* Meeting
endow (en dou′) *v.* Provide with some talent or quality
entice (in tīs′) *v.* To tempt
entrails (en′ trālz) *n.* The inner organs of animals
epidemic (ep′ ə dem′ ik) *n.* Outbreak of a contagious disease
equivalent (i kwiv′ ə lənt) *n.* A thing similar to another thing
esteem (ə stēm′) *v.* To respect; to hold in high regard
evident (ev′ ə dent) *adj.* Obvious
ewer (yōō′ ər) *n.* A large water pitcher with a wide mouth
exclaim (iks klām′) *v.* To cry out; speak or say suddenly and vehemently
expectant (ik spek′ tənt) *adj.* Showing eager waiting
exquisite (eks′ kwi zit) *adj.* Very beautiful, especially in a delicate way
extract (ik strakt′) *v.* To draw out
extricate (eks′ trə kāt) *v.* To set free; disentangle
exuberance (ig zōō′ bər əns) *n.* High spirits
exultation (eg′ zəl tā′ sʰən) *n.* Rejoicing

F

falter (fôl′ tər) *v.* To show uncertainty; act hesitantly
fanciful (fan′ si fəl) *adj.* Playfully imaginative
fantasia (fan tā′ zʰə) *n.* A musical composition of no fixed form, with a structure determined by the composer's fancy
fantasize (fan′ tə sīz) *v.* To have daydreams; indulge in fantasies

fare (fer) *n.* Food

favoritism (fā′ vər it iz′m) *n.* Showing special kindness

feed (fēd) *n.* The tiny particles that minnows feed on

feint (fānt) *v.* To pretend to make an attack

fennel (fen′ 'l) *n.* A tall herb

fiasco (fē as′ kō) *n.* A complete failure

file (fīl) *v.* To move in line

firing (fīr′ iŋ) *n.* The application of heat to harden or glaze pottery

firmament (fur′ mə mənt) *v.* The sky, viewed poetically as a solid arch or vault

fitting (fit′ iŋ) *adj.* Suitable; proper

flagon (flag′ ən) *n.* A container for liquids with a handle, narrow neck, spout, and sometimes a lid

flat (flat) *n.* An apartment

flatterer (flat′ ər ər) *n.* One who praises a person insincerely in order to gain something for oneself

flaunt (flônt) *v.* To display; to show off

fledgling (flej′ liŋ) *n.* A young bird

flinch (flinch) *v.* To move back, as if away from a blow

flit (flit) *v.* To fly lightly and rapidly

flock (fläk) *n.* Group of sheep

flush (flush) *v.* To drive from hiding

fluster (flus′ tər) *v.* To make nervous

forlorn (fər lôrn′) *adj.* Hopeless; miserable

formidable (fôr′ mə də b'l) *adj.* Impressive

forthwith (fôrth′ with′) *adv.* At once

fortitude (fôr′ tə tōōd′) *n.* Firm courage

fragile (fraj′ 'l) *adj.* Delicate; easily broken

fraudulent (frô′ jə lənt) *adj.* Acting with fraud; deceit

free-lance (frē′ lans′) *adj.* Working independently by selling services to individual buyers

G

gabardine (gab′ ər dēn′) *n.* A cloth of wool, cotton, rayon, or other material, used for suits and dresses

gaiter (gāt′ ər) *n.* Covering for the leg extending from the instep to the ankle or knee

galleon (gal′ ē ən) *n.* A large Spanish ship of the 15th and 16th centuries, used as both a warship and a trader

gambol (gam′ b'l) *n.* Play, frolic

garment (gär′ mənt) *n.* An article of clothing; costume

gaunt (gônt) *adj.* Thin and bony

gaze (gāz) *v.* To look intently and steadily

geology (jē äl′ ə jē) *n.* The science dealing with the physical nature and history of the earth

ghastly (gast′ lē) *adj.* Ghostlike; frightful

girdle (gər′ d'l) *n.* A belt or sash for the waist

glacier (glā′ shər) *n.* Large mass of ice and snow

gleeful (glē′ fəl) *adj.* Merry

glint (glint) *v.* To gleam, flash, or glitter

gloat (glōt) *v.* To gaze or grin in scornful triumph

gloomy (glōōm′ ē) *adj.* Causing gloom; dismal; depressing

glossy (glôs′ ē) *adj.* Smooth and shiny

gnarled (närld) *adj.* Knotty and twisted

gnawing (nô′ iŋ) *adj.* Tormenting; bothering

gourd (gôrd) *n.* The fruit of a certain kind of plant; the dried, hollowed shell of this fruit used as a drinking cup or dipper

gout (gout) *n.* A disease characterized by swelling and pain in the hands and feet

grave (grāv) *adj.* Serious

grieve (grēv′) *v.* To feel sorrow for a loss

grisly (griz′ lē) *adj.* Horrible

grizzled (griz′ 'ld) *adj.* Gray

grotesque (grō tesk′) *n.* A strange or distorted character

grouse (grous) *n.* A group of game birds

gumption (gump′ shən) *n.* Courage and enterprise

H

haggard (hag′ ərd) *adj.* Looking worn from grief or illness

harass (hə ras′) *v.* To trouble or worry

haughty (hôt′ ē) *adj.* Showing pride in oneself and contempt for others

haunch (hônch) *n.* An animal's lower back; hip

hearth (härth) *n.* The stone or brick floor of a fireplace

heartily (härt′ 'l ē) *adv.* Warmly; completely

heed (hēd) *n.* Attention

henceforth (hens fôrth′) *adv.* From this time on

herpetologist (hur′ pə täl′ ə jist) *n.* Someone who studies reptiles and amphibians

hexagonal (hek sag′ ə n'l) *n.* Six-sided

hissing (his′ iŋ) *v.* Making a sound like a prolonged *s*

holocaust (häl′ ə kôst′) *n.* In ancient times an offering burned to the gods

hummock (hum′ ək) *n.* Area of fertile, wooded land, higher than the surrounding swamp

hunch (hunch) *v.* To stand with one's back bent

hurl (hurl) *v.* To throw with force or violence

Husky (hus′ kē) *n.* A strong dog used for pulling a sled over the snow

hymn (him) *n.* A song of praise

I

idiograph (id′ ē ə graf′) *n.* A symbol that stands for a thing or idea without expressing the sounds that make up its name

immeasurable (i mezh′ ər ə b'l) *adj.* So great that it cannot be measured

immense (i mens′) *adj.* Vast

impartiality (im pär′ shē al′ i tē) *n.* Fairness; not taking sides

impetuous (im pech′ oo wəs) *adj.* Moving with great force or violence

implore (im plôr′) *v.* To beg

impressive (im pres′ iv) *adj.* Having a strong effect on the mind or emotions

improvise (im′ prə vīz′) *v.* To make with the tools and materials at hand, usually to fill an unforeseen and immediate need

incense (in′ sens) *n.* Any of various substances that produce a pleasant odor when burned

incessant (in ses′ 'nt) *adj.* Without stopping

incomprehensible (in′ käm pri hen′ seb'l) *adj.* Not able to be understood

incredulous (in krej′ oo ləs) *adj.* Unwilling or unable to believe

incubation (in′ kyə bā′ shən) *n.* The phrase in a disease between the infection and the first appearance of symptoms

indifferent (in dif′ ər ənt) *adj.* Uninterested

industrious (in dus′ trē əs) *adj.* Hard-working

inert (in urt′) *adj.* Without power to move

inertia (in ur′ shə) *n.* The tendency of an object to remain at rest if it is at rest, or to remain moving if it is moving—unless it is disturbed by an outside force

inevitable (in ev′ ə tə b′l) *adj.* Certain to happen

inflammatory (in flam′ ə tôr′ ē) *adj.* Characterized by pain and swelling

ingenious (in jēn′ yəs) *adj.* Clever and inventive

insolent (in′ sə lənt) *adj.* Disrespectful

integer (in′ tə jər) *n.* Any positive or negative whole number

interact (in′ tər akt′) *v.* To affect and be affected by

interplanetary (in′ tər plan′ ə ter′ ē) *adj.* Between planets

interpreter (in tur′ prə tər) *n.* Someone who translates from one language to another

interrogation (in ter′ ə gā′ shən) *n.* Situation where people are formally questioned

intervene (in′ tər vēn′) *v.* To step into a situation

interwoven (in′ tər wō′ vən) *adj.* Mixed together

intricacy (in′ tri kə sē) *n.* The quality of being hard to follow or understand

intrigue (in trēg′) *v.* To fascinate

invariable (in ver′ ē ə b′l) *adj.* Not changing; uniform

ironical (ī rän′ i k′l) *adj.* In a different way from what is expected

irrevocable (i rev′ ə kə b′l) *adj.* Unchangeable

J

jubilant (jōō′ b′l ənt) *adj.* Joyful and triumphant

judicious (jōō dish′ əs) *adj.* Wise

K

keener (kēn′ ər) *adj.* Sharper and quicker

Kentucky (kən tuk′ ē) [<Iroquoian (Wyandot), level land, plain] Eastern central state of the United States

kiln (kiln) *n.* An oven to bake pottery

kilometer (ki läm′ ə tər) *n.* 1,000 meters or about ⅝ of a mile

kindling (kin′ dliŋ) *n.* Bits of dry wood for starting a fire

L

lackadaisical (lak′ ə dā′ zi kəl) *adj.* Showing a lack of interest

lackluster (lak′ lus′ tər) *adj.* Lacking brightness; dull

laconic (lə kän′ ik) *adj.* Using few words

lacy (lā′ sē) *adj.* Having a delicate, open pattern, like lace

lament (lə ment′) *v.* To express deep sorrow for; mourn

lariat (lar′ ē it) *n.* A rope for tethering grazing horses; lasso

latent (lāt′ 'nt) *adj.* Hidden and not fully developed

lattice (lat′ is) *n.* An openwork structure of crossed strips or bars of wood, metal, and the like

leer (lir′) *v.* To look with harmful intent

leeward (lē′ wərd) *adj.* Sheltered from the wind

legacy (leg′ ə sē) *n.* Something handed down by a parent or an ancestor

lethal (lē′ t*h*əl) *adj.* Deadly

liability (lī ə bil′ ə tē) *n.* A disadvantage

lichen (lī′ kən) *n.* Any of a large group of small plants

limerick (lim′ ər ik) *n.* A nonsense poem of five lines

lithe (līt*h*) *adj.* Flexible and supple

loathe (lōt*h*) *v.* To hate

lollop (läl′ əp) *v.* To move in a clumsy or relaxed way, bobbing up and down or from side to side

lorry (lôr′ ē) *n.* [Brit.] A motor truck

lute (lōōt) *n.* An old-fashioned stringed instrument like a guitar

M

machete (mə shet′ ē) *n.* Large, heavy-bladed knife

madly (mad′ lē) *adv.* Insanely; wildly or furiously; foolishly; extremely

majestic (mə jes′ tik) *adj.* Grand; lofty

malleable (mal′ ē ə b′l) *adj.* Able to be hammered, pounded, or pressed into various shapes without breaking

maneuver (mə nōō′ vər) *n.* A planned movement or procedure

mantle (man′ t′l) *n.* A loose, sleeveless cloak or cape

marred (märd) *v.* Disturbed

martial (mär′ shəl) *adj.* Suitable for war

masterful (mas′ tər fəl) *adj.* Able to force one's will on others

mastiff (mas′ tif) *n.* A large, powerful, smooth-coated dog with hanging lip and drooping ears

maxim (mak′ sim) *n.* Wise saying

meager (mē′ gər) *adj.* Of poor quality; small in amount

meek (mēk) *adj.* Patient and mild

melancholy (mel′ ən käl′ ē) *adj.* Sad, gloomy

menace (men′ is) *n.* Danger, threat

menage (mə näz*h*′) *n.* Household

mesa (mā′ sə) *n.* A flat tableland with steep sides

mesmerize (mez′ mər īz′) *v.* To hypnotize

mesmerizing (mez′ mər īz′ iŋ) *adj.* Hypnotizing

metamorphose (met′ ə môr′ fōz) *v.* To change

metamorphosis (met′ ə môr′ fə sis) *n.* A change of form

milling (mil′ iŋ) *v.* Moving in a circular or random motion

mined (mīnd) *adj.* Filled with buried explosives that are set to go off when stepped on

miracle (mir′ ə k′l) *n.* An event or action that apparently contradicts known scientific laws and is hence thought to be due to supernatural causes

misanthrope (mis′ ən thrōp′) A person who hates or mistrusts everyone

Missouri (mi zoor′ ē) [<Algonquian, literally, people of the big canoes] Middle Western state of the central United States

mobilize (mō′ bə līz′) *v.* To put into motion

mock (mäk) *v.* To copy

moil (moil) *v.* To toil and slave

momentum (mō men′ təm) *n.* The increasing force of a moving object

monarch (män′ ərk) *n.* A ruler; king or queen

monitoring (män′ ə tər′ iŋ) *v.* Watching or keeping track of

monogrammed (män′ ə gramd′) *adj.* Having a design made up of two or more letters

monotone (män′ ə tōn) *v.* A single, unchanging tone

moor (moor) *n.* Rolling land with swamps

morbid (môr′ bid) *adj.* Of, having, or caused by disease; unhealthy

morgue (môrg) *n.* A place where the bodies of dead persons are kept to be examined or identified before burial

morose (mə rōs′) *adj.* Gloomy; ill-tempered

mortal (môr′ t'l) *n.* A being who must eventually die

mortality (môr tal′ ə tē) *n.* Having to die someday

mortician (môr tish′ ən) *n.* An undertaker; funeral director

mortuary (môr′ chōō wer′ ē) *n.* A place where dead bodies are kept before burial or cremation, such as a morgue or funeral home

mosaic (mō zā′ ik) *adj.* Made of different pieces combined to form a whole

mourning (môr′ niŋ) *v.* Feeling sorrow for the death of a loved one

murder (mur′ dər) *v.* To kill unlawfully and with malice

murky (mur′ kē) *adj.* Heavy and obscure with smoke or mist

mush (mush) *v.* To travel by foot over snow, usually with a dog sled

muslin (muz′ lin) *n.* A plain, strong kind of cotton cloth

mustache (mus′ tash) *n.* The hair on the upper lip of men

mutilated (myōōt′ 'l āt′ əd) *adj.* Damaged or injured

mutton (mut′ 'n) *n.* Sheep

muzzled (muz′ 'ld) *adj.* Prevented from talking or expressing an opinion

N

narcissism (när′ sə siz′m) *n.* Self-love; excessive interest in one's own appearance, comfort, importance, or abilities

neurophysiology (noor′ ō fiz′ ē äl′ ə jē) *n.* The study of the brain and nervous system

nimble (nim′ b'l) *adj.* Moving quickly and lightly

nonchalant (nän′ shə länt′) *adj.* Casual

O

obliging (ə blīj′ iŋ) *adj.* Ready to do favors

obsequious (əb sē′ kwē əs) *adj.* Much too willing to serve or obey; overly submissive

obsidian (əb sid′ ē ən) *n.* A hard, usually dark-colored or black, volcanic glass

obstinate (äb′ stə nit) *adj.* Stubborn

odious (ō′ dē əs) *adj.* Disgusting; offensive

oil painting (oil′ pānt′ iŋ) *n.* A picture painted in oil colors

ominous (äm′ ə nəs) *adj.* Threatening

ontogeny (än täj′ ə nē) *n.* The life cycle of a simple organism or individual

ooze (ōōz) *v.* To flow or leak slowly

opalescent (ō′ pə les′ 'nt) *adj.* Showing a play of colors like an opal

opaque (ō pāk′) *adj.* Not letting light pass through

organdy (ôr′ gən dē) *n.* Thin, crisp cotton fabric used for items like dresses and curtains

ostler (äs′ lər) *n.* Someone who takes care of horses at an inn or stable

outskirts (out′ skurtz) *n.* Part or district remote from the center or midst

Ozark (ō′ zärk) **Mountains** [< Fr. *aux Arcs,* to the (region of the) Arc (Arkansa) Indians] Highland region in N.W. Arkansas, SW Missouri, and NE Oklahoma

P

pandemic (pan dem′ ik) *adj.* Prevalent over a whole area; universal

paradox (par′ ə däks′) *n.* A statement that seems contradictory, unbelievable, or absurd but that may actually be true in fact

parasite (par′ ə sīt) *n.* An animal that lives on another organism in order to get food, protection, or both

passive (pas′ iv) *adj.* Inactive

pathetic (pə thet′ ik) *adj.* Arousing pity, sorrow, and sympathy

pathological (path′ ə läj′ i k'l) *adj.* Due to or involving disease

pauper (pô′ pər) *n.* An extremely poor person

peeved (pēvd) *adj.* Irritated

perilous (per′ əl əs) *adj.* Dangerous

perpetual (pər pech′ oo wəl) *adj.* Never stopping

persistent (pər sis′ tənt) *adj.* Constantly recurring

perspective (pər spek′ tiv) *n.* The appearance of objects or scenes as determined by their relative distance and positions; a specific point of view

pestilent (pes′ t'l ənt) *adj.* Deadly; annoying

petrol (pet′ rəl) *n.* [Brit.] Gasoline

phantasmagoria (fan taz′ mə gôr′ ē ə) *n.* An early type of magic-lantern show consisting of various optical illusions

phantom (fan′ təm) *n.* Something that seems to appear to the sight but has no physical existence

philanthropy (fi lan′ thrə pē) *n.* A desire to help mankind; benevolence

philharmonic (fil′ här män′ ik) *adj.* Loving or devoted to music

philosophy (fi läs′ ə fē) *n.* Originally, love of, or the search for wisdom or knowledge

phylogeny (fī läj′ ə nē) *n.* The development of a species or group

pilgrimage (pil′ grəm ij) *n.* A long journey to a place of interest

pious (pī′ əs) *adj.* Good; virtuous

plaiting (plāt′ iŋ) *n.* Braiding

plankton (plaŋk′ tən) *n.* Very small animal and plant life that floats or drifts in the water

pliant (plī′ ənt) *adj.* Easily bent; adaptable

poise (poiz) *v.* To balance

pomegranate (päm′ gran′ it) *n.* A round fruit with a red, leathery rind and many seeds

pomp (pämp) *n.* Impressive show or display

ponderous (pän′ dər əs) *adj.* Very heavy, bulky

posting (pōs′ tiŋ) Notice of the racing time of each swimmer

pound (pound) *n.* A unit of money used by the British

precipitation (pri sip′ ə tā′ shən) *n.* Great speed

precipitous (pri sip′ ə təs) *adj.* Very steep

predatory (pred′ ə tôr′ ē) *adj.* Living by capturing and feeding on other animals

predestined (prē des′ tind) *adj.* In this case, marked to die early

preen (prēn) *v.* To dress up; show pride in one's appearance

preening (prēn′ iŋ) *n.* The act of cleaning and trimming feathers with a beak

preferable (pref′ ər ə b'l) *adj.* More desirable

premium (prē′ mē əm) *n.* An additional charge

prescribed   (pri skrib''d)   *adj.* Advised as a medicine by a doctor

presently   (prez' 'nt lē)   *adv.* In a little while

presumptuous   (pri zump' choo wəs)   *n.* Overstepping ordinary bounds of courtesy

prevalent   (prev' ə lənt)   *adj.* Widely accepted

priming   (prī' miŋ)   *n.* The explosive used to set off the charge in a gun

prodigy   (präd' ə jē)   *n.* A child of unusually high talent

proffer   (präf' ər)   *v.* To offer

profound   (prə found')   *adj.* Deeply or intensely felt

prolapse   (pro' laps)   *n.* An internal organ that has fallen out of place

Promethean   (prə mē' thē ən)   *adj.* Life-bringing, creative, or courageously original

prominent   (präm' ə nənt)   *adj.* Widely and favorably known

promissory   (präm' i sôr' ē)   **notes**   *n.* Written promises to pay someone a certain sum of money

prone   (prōn)   *adj.* Lying face downward

prose   (prōz)   *n.* Nonpoetic language

providence   (präv' ə dəns)   *n.* A godsend; a valuable gift

provisional   (prə vizh' ən 'l)   *adj.* Temporary; depending on future events

provision   (prō vizh' ən)   *n.* A stock of food and supplies

psychology   (sī käl' ə jē)   *n.* The science dealing with the mind

pummel   (pum' 'l)   *v.* To hit with repeated blows

pungent   (pun' jənt)   *adj.* Sharp-smelling

Q

quaff   (kwäf)   *v.* To drink in a thirsty way

quail   (kwāl)   *v.* To draw back in fear

quarry   (kwôr' ē)   *v.* To carve out of the ground

quaver   (kwā' vər)   *v.* To shake or tremble

quicksilver   (kwik' sil' vər)   *adj.* Quick; changeable; unpredictable; like the chemical element mercury, which is silver-white and flows easily

quip   (kwip)   *v.* To make a witty remark

quiver   (kwiv' ər)   *n.* A case for arrows

R

radiant   (rā' dē ənt)   *adj.* Shining brightly

rancid   (ran' sid)   *adj.* Spoiled and bad smelling

rapt   (rapt)   *adj.* Giving complete attention; totally carried away by something

rash   (rash)   *adj.* Reckless

realm   (relm)   *n.* A kingdom

reconnoiter   (rē' kə noit' ər)   *v.* To look around

refuge   (ref' yōōj)   *n.* A place of safety or shelter

refute   (ri fyōōt')   *v.* To prove someone wrong

regalia   (ri gāl' yə)   *n.* Splendid clothes and decorations

register   (rej' is tər)   *n.* A record containing a list of names

relate   (ri lāt')   *v.* To tell

relevant   (rel' ə vənt)   *adj.* Relating to the matter at hand; to the point

relish   (rel' ish)   *v.* To especially enjoy

remit   (ri mit')   *v.* To forgive or pardon; put back

remonstrance   (ri män' strəns)   *n.* The act of protesting or pleading

render   (ren' dər)   *v.* To melt down

repellent   (ri pel' ənt)   *n.* Something that pushes away

reproach   (ri prōch')   *v.* To blame; scold

resigned   (ri zīn' 'd)   *adj.* In a yielding and uncomplaining manner

resilient   (ri zil' yənt)   *adj.* Springing back into shape

resin   (rez' 'n)   *n.* A sticky brownish or yellowish substance that comes from evergreen trees

resolute   (rez' ə lōōt')   *adj.* Of firm purpose

resourceful   (ri sôrs' fəl)   *adj.* Able to deal effectively with problems

retrospect   (ret' rə spekt')   *n.* A looking back on the past

reverie   (rev' ər ē)   *n.* Dreamy thinking or imagining

revoke   (ri vōk')   *v.* To cancel, withdraw

rheumatism   (rōō' mə tiz'm)   *n.* Pain and stiffness of the joints and muscles

riffle   (rif' 'l)   *n.* A shallow area in a stream

rigorous   (rig' ər əs)   *adj.* Strict; thorough

rind   (rīnd)   *n.* Tough outer layer or skin

rite   (rīt)   *n.* Religious observance

rodeo   (rō' dē ō')   *n.* A public exhibition or competition of the skills of cowboys

rouge   (rōōzh)   *n.* A reddish cosmetic used to color the cheeks

rout   (rout')   *v.* To completely defeat

ruff   (ruf)   *n.* A band of fur around the necks of animals or birds

runt   (runt)   *n.* The smallest animal of a litter

S

saffron   (saf' rən)   *n.* An orange-yellow color

sage   (sāj)   *n.* A very wise man

saline   (sā' līn)   *n.* A salt solution

sanction   (saŋk' shən)   *n.* Support

sanctuary   (saŋk' choo wer' ē)   *n.* A place of protection

sauciness   (sô' sē nes)   *n.* Liveliness; spirit

saunter   (sôn' tər)   *v.* To walk about idly; stroll

savor   (sā vər)   *v.* To enjoy

scale   (skāl)   *n.* A series of musical tones

scapegoat   (skāp' gōt)   *n.* A person or group blamed for the mistakes or crimes of others

scorn   (skôrn)   *n.* A strong dislike for someone or something thought to be inferior

scour   (skour)   *v.* To clean by rubbing vigorously

scourge   (skurj)   *n.* The cause of serious trouble

scowl   (skoul)   *v.* To frown

scrim   (skrim)   *n.* A light, semi-transparent curtain

scrooge   (skrōōj)   *n.* A hard, miserly misanthrope

scurry   (skur' ē)   *v.* To run hastily; scamper

scuttle   (skut' 'l)   *v.* To run or move quickly; scurry

seismology   (sīz mäl' ə jē)   *n.* A geophysical science dealing with earthquakes and related phenomena

sentimental   (sen' tə men' t'l)   *adj.* Acting from feeling rather than from practical motives

sepulcher   (sep' 'l kər)   *n.* Grave; tomb

seraph   (ser' əf)   *n.* Angel

serenity   (sə ren' ə tē)   *n.* Calmness

severe   (sə vir')   *adj.* Harsh

sexton   (seks' tən)   *n.* A church official in charge of ringing the bells

shadowing   (shad' ō iŋ)   *v.* Shading an area in a picture or painting

sheen (shēn) *n.* Brightness; shininess

shilling (shil' iŋ) *n.* A British coin worth five pennies

shrew (shrōō) *n.* A small, slender, mouselike animal with soft, brown fur and a long, pointed snout

shrewdest (shrōōd' əst) *adj.* Cleverest

shrouded (shroud' əd) *adj.* Hidden from view

shudder (shud' ər) *v.* To shake

sibling (sib' liŋ) *n.* A brother or sister

sieve (siv) *n.* A utensil with many tiny openings; strainer

sinew (sin' yōō) *n.* Tendon

sinewy (sin' yōō wē) *adj.* Tough and strong

skids (skidz) *n.* Planks or logs on which a heavy object can be slid

slacken (slak' 'n) *v.* To become less active

slither (slith' ər) *v.* To slide

slough (slōō) *n.* A swamp, bog, or marsh that is part of an inlet or backwater

sluggish (slug' ish) *adj.* Lacking energy

sluice (slōōs) *n.* An artificial channel or passage for water, having a gate or valve at its head to regulate the flow

smartly (smärt' lē) *adv.* Sharply

snorkel (snôr' k'l) *v.* To swim underwater using a snorkel, or breathing tube, that extends above the surface of the water

snowshoes (snō' shōōz') *n.* Racket-shaped pieces of wood crisscrossed with strips of leather, worn on the feet to prevent sinking in deep snow

snug (snug) *adj.* Cozy; comfortable

solemn (säl' əm) *adj.* Serious; somber

solemnize (säl' əm nīz) *v.* To honor

somber (säm' bər) *adj.* Dark and solemn

somnolent (säm' nə lent) *adj.* Sleepy, drowsy

spectacle (spek' tə k'l) *n.* Something to look at; unusual display

spectacles (spek' tə k'lz) *n.* A pair of eyeglasses

spectator (spek' tā tər) *n.* A person who sees or watches something without taking an active part

specter (spek' tər) *n.* A ghost or ghostlike appearance

spectral (spek' trəl) *adj.* Like a specter; phantom; ghostly

spectroscope (spek' trə skōp') *n.* An optical instrument used for forming spectra for study

spittoon (spi tōōn') *n.* A jarlike container into which people spit

squat (skwät) *adj.* Short and heavy

stable (stā' b'l) *n.* A building in which horses or cattle are sheltered and fed

staccato (stə kät' ō) *adj.* Made up of sharp, separate little elements

stalk (stôk) *v.* To walk slowly and stiffly

stealthy (stel' thē) *adj.* Secretly; slyly

steed (stēd) *n.* A high-spirited riding horse

stern (sturn) *adj.* Strict; unyielding

still (stil) *n.* A photograph made from a single frame of a motion picture and used for advertising it

straggly (strag' lē) *adj.* Spread out

straightforward (strāt' fôr' wərd) *adj.* Direct; frank; honest

strand (strand) *n.* The ocean shore

stride (strīd) *v.* To walk with long steps, especially in a vigorous manner

strive (strīv) *v.* To struggle

stubble (stub' 'l) *n.* Short stumps of corn or grain

studio (stōō' dē ō') A room or rooms where an artist or photographer works

subscribe (səb skrīb') *v.* To support

subservient (səb sur' vē ənt) *adj.* Inferior

subtle (sut' 'l) *adj.* Delicately skillful or clever

succession (sək sesh' ən) *n.* The act of coming after another in order

succulent (suk' yoo lent) *adj.* Juicy

supercilious (sōō' pər sil' ē əs) *adj.* Proud; scornful

supple (sup' 'l) *adj.* Flexible

surge (surj) *v.* To move in a violent swelling motion

surpass (sər pas') *v.* To be superior to

surreptitious (sur' əp tish' əs) *adj.* Secret

susceptible (sə sep' tə b'l) *adj.* Responsive

sustain (sə stān') *v.* To support

swarm (swôrm) *v.* To be filled or crowded

swerve (swurv) *n.* A curving motion

sylvan (sil' vən) *adj.* Of or characteristic of woods and forests

T

tableau (tab' lō) *n.* A dramatic scene or picture

taco (tä' kō) *n.* A Mexican dish consisting of a fried, folded tortilla filled with chopped meat, shredded lettuce, and the like

taint (tānt) *n.* A trace

taut (tôt) *adj.* Tightly stretched

tawny (tô' nē) *adj.* Yellowish-brown

teak (tēk) *n.* Yellowish-brown wood

technology (tek näl' ə jē) *n.* The ideas of science applied to practical problems

tedious (tē' dē əs) *adj.* Long and boring

tempest (tem' pist) *n.* A violent storm

tentative (ten' tə tiv) *adj.* Hesitant; uncertain

tepid (tep' id) *adj.* Not warm or cold; lukewarm

termagant (tur' mə gənt) *adj.* Scolding

testimony (tes' ti mō' nē) *n.* Statement or declaration

tether (teth' ər) *v.* to fasten with a rope or chain

thistle (this' 'l) *n.* A stubborn, weedy plant with sharp leaves and usually purplish flowers

threadbare (thred' ber') *adj.* Worn, shabby

tiered (tird) *adj.* Stacked in rows

titanic (tī tan' ik) *adj.* Having great size, strength, or power

torrent (tôr' ənt) *n.* A flood

totter (tät' ər) *v.* To rock or shake as if about to fall; to be unsteady

tracheotomy (trā' kē ät' ə mē) *n.* An operation in which the trachea, or windpipe, is cut to make an artificial breathing hole

transformation (trans' fər mā' shən) *n.* A change in condition and outward appearance

translucent (trans lōō' s'nt) *adj.* Clear

transmission (trans mish' ən) *n.* The passage of radio waves through space between the transmitting station and the receiving station

trebly (tre' blē) *adv.* Three times as much; triply

tribulation (trib' yə lā' shən) *n.* Great misery or distress

trident (trīd' 'nt) *n.* A spear with three points

trifle (trī' f'l) *n.* Something of little value or importance

triumphant (trī um′ fənt)   *adj.* Rejoicing for victory; exulting in success

trundle (trun′ d'l)   *v.* To move on wheels or as if on wheels

tumultuous (tōō mul′ choo wəs)   *adj.* Noisy and violent

turmoil (tur′ moil′)   *n.* Uproar; confusion

U

unanimous (yoo nan′ ə məs)   *adj.* Based on complete agreement

unbiased (un′ bī′ əst)   *adj.* Without prejudice; fair

undeleterious (un del′ ə tir′ ē əs)   *adj.* Healthy, full of well-being

unique (yōō nēk′)   *adj.* Highly unusual or rare

unison (yōō′ nə sən)   *n.* Complete agreement; harmony

unrequited (un′ ri kwī′ t'd)   *adj.* Unreturned

urchin (ur′ chin)   *n.* A mischievous boy

usurp (yōō surp′)   *v.* To take without right

utilize (yōōt′ 'l īz′)   *v.* To make useful

V

vacancy (vā′ kən sē)   *n.* Emptiness

vanquish (vaŋ′ kwish)   *v.* To overcome

varmint (vär′ mənt)   *n.* An animal regarded as troublesome

veer (vir)   *v.* To change direction

verdict (vur′ dikt)   *n.* A decision or judgment

verge (vurj)   *n.* The edge or brink

verisimilitude (ver′ ə si mil′ ə tōōd′)   *n.* The appearance of being true or real

vertebrate (vur′ tə brāt′)   *n.* An animal with a backbone

vibrant (vī′ brənt)   *adj.* Throbbing with life and activity; lively; energetic

vicar (vik′ ər)   *n.* A parish priest in the Anglican Church

virago (vi rä′ gō)   *n.* A quarrelsome woman

visage (viz′ ij)   *n.* Face

vital (vīt′ 'l)   *adj.* Essential to life; living

vitality (vī tal′ ə tē)   *n.* The power to live or go on living

vitalize (vīt′ 'l īz′)   *n.* To make vital; give life to

vital signs (vīt′ 'l sīnz′)   *n.* Indicators of the efficient functioning of the body; especially pulse, temperature, and respiration

vitamin (vīt′ ə min)   *n.* Any of a number of complex organic substances found in most foods

vixen (vik′ s'n)   *n.* A female fox

void (void)   *n.* Emptiness

W

waft (wâft)   *v.* Carry

wages (wāj′ əz)   *n.* Money paid to an employee for work done

warbler (wôr′ blər)   *n.* Songbird

wassail (wäs′ 'l)   *n.* A spiced drink used in celebrating

watercolor (wôt′ ər kul′ ər)   *n.* A pigment or coloring matter that is mixed with water for use as a paint; a painting done with such paints

wee (wē)   *adj.* Very small, tiny

wheedle (hwē′ d'l)   *v.* To persuade a person by flattery or coaxing

whimper (hwim′ pər)   *v.* To make low, crying sounds; complain

wicker (wik′ ər)   *n.* A thin, flexible twig

wigwam (wig′ wäm)   *n.* A shelter with a rounded top made by certain Native American groups

willful (wil′ fəl)   *adj.* Wanting one's own way; self-willed

wily (wī′ lē)   *adj.* Sly

wince (wins)   *v.* Draw back

winnow (win′ ō)   *v.* To beat as with wings

wistfully (wist′ fəl lē)   *adj.* Showing vague yearnings

wither (with′ ər)   *v.* Dry up

wonderful (wun′ dər fəl)   *adj.* That causes wonder; marvelous; amazing

wonderland (wun′ dər land′)   *n.* An imaginary land full of wonders

wonderment (wun′ dər mənt)   *n.* Astonishment

wonderworker (wun′ dər wurk′ ər)   *n.* One who performs miracles or wonders

wondrous (wun′ drəs)   *adj.* Wonderful; extraordinary

Y

yearn (yurn)   *v.* Want very much

yucca (yuk′ ə)   *adj.* Plants with stiff sword-shaped leaves and white flowers

INDEX OF FINE ART

INDEX OF SKILLS

ANALYZING LITERATURE

CRITICAL THINKING AND READING

READING IN THE CONTENT AREAS

SPEAKING AND LISTENING

STUDY AND RESEARCH

THINKING AND WRITING

UNDERSTANDING LANGUAGE

INDEX OF TITLES BY THEMES

INDEX OF AUTHORS AND TITLES

Page numbers in italics refer to biographical information.

Index of Authors and Titles   877

ACKNOWLEDGMENTS (continued)

Atheneum Publishers, an imprint of Macmillan Publishing Co.
"Construction" from *8 A.M. Shadows* by Patricia Hubbell. Copyright © 1965 by Patricia Hubbell. Andrew A. Rooney, "Letter Writing" from *And More By Andy Rooney* by Andrew A. Rooney. Copyright © 1982 Essay Productions, Inc. Reprinted with permission of Atheneum Publishers, an imprint of Macmillan Publishing Co.

Elizabeth Barnett, Literary Executor of the Estate of Norma Millay Ellis
"The Courage That My Mother Had" by Edna St. Vincent Millay. From *Collected Poems,* Harper & Row. Copyright © 1954 by Norma Millay Ellis. Reprinted by permission.

Gwendolyn Brooks
"Home" from *The World of Gwendolyn Brooks,* Harper & Row. Reprinted by permission of the author.

Clarion Books/Ticknor & Fields, a Houghton Mifflin Company, and The Bodley Head, Ltd.
"The Pointing Finger" from *Sweet and Sour: Tales from China* by Carol Kendall and Yao-wen Li. Copyright © 1980 by Carol Kendall and Yao-wen Li. Reprinted by permission.

Don Congdon Associates, Inc.
"All Summer in a Day" by Ray Bradbury. Copyright © 1954 by Ray Bradbury; renewed 1982 by Ray Bradbury. "The Third Level" by Jack Finney. Copyright © 1950 by *Collier's;* renewed 1977 by Jack Finney. Reprinted by permission of Don Congdon Associates, Inc.

Congdon & Weed, Inc.
"No Gumption" from *Growing Up* by Russell Baker. Copyright © 1982 by Russell Baker. Reprinted by permission of Congdon & Weed, Inc.

Harold Courlander
"All Stories are Anansi's" from *The Hat-Shaking Dance and Other Ashanti Tales from Ghana* by Harold Courlander with Albert Kofi Prempeh. Copyright © 1957 by Harcourt Brace Jovanovich, Inc.; 1985 by Harold Courlander. Reprinted by permission of the author.

Current History, Inc.
"A puppy whose hair was so flowing" by Oliver Herford. From *The Century Magazine,* copyright 1912. Reprinted by permission of Current History, Inc.

Delacorte Press
"The Luckiest Time of All" excerpted from the book *The Lucky Stone* by Lucille Clifton. Copyright © 1979 by Lucille Clifton. Reprinted by permission of Delacorte Press.

Delacorte Press/Seymour Lawrence
"Seal" excerpted from the book *Laughing Time* by William Jay Smith. Copyright © 1953, 1955, 1956, 1957, 1959, 1968, 1974, 1977, 1980 by William Jay Smith. Reprinted by permission of Delacorte Press/Seymour Lawrence.

Devin-Adair Publishers
"The Trout" from *The Man Who Invented Sin and Other Stories* by Sean O'Faolain. The Devin-Adair Company, 1948, renewed in 1976.

Adriaan de Wit for the Estate of Dorothy de Wit
"Ojeeg, the Hunter, and the Ice Man" retold by Dorothy de Wit in *The Talking Stone,* edited by Dorothy de Wit. Copyright © 1979 by Dorothy de Wit. Reprinted by permission.

Dodd, Mead & Company, Inc.
Reprinted by permission of Dodd, Mead & Company, Inc. from *Circle of the Seasons* by Edwin Way Teale. Copyright 1953 by Edwin Way Teale. Copyright renewed 1981 by Nellie D. Teale.

Doubleday, a division of Bantam, Doubleday, Dell Publishing Group, Inc.
"The Ransom of Red Chief" from *The Tales of O. Henry* by O. Henry. "The Third Wish" by Joan Aiken first appeared in *All and More* copyright © 1974 by Joan Aiken from, *Not What You Expected.* Excerpts from *Tell Me How Long the Train's Been Gone* by James Baldwin. Copyright © 1968 by James Baldwin. "Broadway, Twilight" by Tom Prideaux from *Creative Youth* edited by Hughes Mearns. Copyright 1925 by Doubleday. Text of *Where the Red Fern Grows* by Woodrow Wilson Rawls. Copyright © 1961 by Woodrow Wilson Rawls and copyright © 1961 by the Curtis Publishing Company. "The Bat" copyright 1938 by Theodore Roethke from *The Collected Poems of Theodore Roethke.* "Old Florist" by Theodore Roethke, copyright 1946 by Harper & Brothers from *The Collected Poems of Theodore Roethke.* Reprinted by permission of Doubleday.

E. P. Dutton, a division of New American Library
"The Flower-Fed Buffaloes" from *Going-to-the-Stars* by Vachel Lindsay. Copyright 1926 by D. Appleton & Co., renewed 1954 by Elizabeth C. Lindsay. A Hawthorn book. Reprinted by permission of E. P. Dutton, a division of New American Library.

Exposition-Phoenix Press Inc.
"Life" from *One and Many* by Naomi Long Madget. Copyright 1956. Reprinted by permission of Exposition-Phoenix Press Inc.

Farrar, Straus and Giroux, Inc.
Excerpt titled "The Sneaker Crisis" from *Raising Demons* by Shirley Jackson. Copyright 1953, 1954, 1956, 1957 by Shirley Jackson. Copyright renewed © 1985 by Laurence Hyman, Barry Hyman, and Sarah Hyman Elias. "Utzel and His Daughter, Poverty" from *Stories for Children* by Isaac Bashevis Singer. Copyright © 1962, 1967, 1968, 1970, 1972, 1973, 1974, 1975, 1976, 1979, 1980, 1984 by Isaac

Bashevis Singer. Excerpt from "A Far Cry From Africa" from *Collected Poems 1948–1984* by Derek Walcott. Copyright © 1962, 1963, 1964 and 1986 by Derek Walcott. Reprinted by permission of Farrar, Straus and Giroux, Inc.

Harcourt Brace Jovanovich, Inc.
"Eugenie Clark and the Sleeping Sharks" from *Wild Animals, Gentlemen Women,* copyright © 1978 by Margery Facklam. "Morning—'The Bird Perched for Flight'" from "The Heron and the Astronaut" in *Earth Shine,* copyright © 1969 by Anne Morrow Lindbergh. "Fog" from *Chicago Poems* by Carl Sandburg, copyright 1916 by Holt, Rinehart and Winston, Inc.; renewed 1944 by Carl Sandburg. "The Boy and the Wolf" adapted by Louis Untermeyer from *The Magic Circle* by Louis Untermeyer, copyright 1952 by Harcourt Brace Jovanovich, Inc.; renewed 1980 by Bryna Ivens Untermeyer, Lawrence S. Untermeyer, and John F. Moore. Excerpt by Alice Walker copyright © 1974 from her volume "In Search of Our Mothers' Gardens" by Alice Walker. "Women" copyright © 1970 by Alice Walker, from her volume *Revolutionary Petunias & Other Poems.* Reprinted by permission of Harcourt Brace Jovanovich, Inc.

Harper & Row, Publishers, Inc.
"Rikki-tikki-tavi" from *The Jungle Book* by Rudyard Kipling. Haiku, "The Falling Flower" by Moritake from *Poetry Handbook: A Dictionary of Terms,* 4th edition by Babette Deutsch (Thomas Y. Crowell). Copyright © 1957, 1962, 1969, 1974 by Babette Deutsch. "The Highwayman" from *Collected Poems* by Alfred Noyes (J. B. Lippincott). Chapter 2, "A Boy and a Man" from *Banner in the Sky* by James Ramsey Ullman (J. B. Lippincott). Copyright 1954 by James Ramsey Ullman. Reprinted by permission of Harper & Row, Publishers, Inc.

Harper & Row, Publishers, Inc. and Olwyn Hughes
Excerpt from "Mirror" from *The Collected Poems of Sylvia Plath* by Sylvia Plath. Copyright © 1960, 1965, 1971, 1981 by Ted Hughes.

Harvard University Press and the Trustees of Amherst College
"I'm Nobody! Who are you?" by Emily Dickinson. Reprinted by permission of the publishers and the Trustees of Amherst College from *The Poems of Emily Dickinson,* edited by Thomas H. Johnson, Cambridge, Mass.: The Belknap Press of Harvard University Press, Copyright 1951, © 1955, 1979, 1983 by The President and Fellows of Harvard College.

William Heinemann, Ltd.
"The Gentlemen of the Jungle" by Jomo Kenyatta from *African Short Stories* selected and edited by Chinua Achebe and C. L. Innes. Copyright 1985 by Chinua Achebe and C. L. Innes. Reprinted by permission of William Heinemann, Ltd.

Lawrence Hill and Company
"Last Cover" reprinted from *The Best Nature Stories of Paul Annixter* by Jane and Paul Annixter by permission of Lawrence Hill and Company. Copyright 1974.

Edward D. Hoch
"Zoo" by Edward D. Hoch, © 1958 by King-Size Publications, Inc.; © renewed 1986 by Edward D. Hoch. Reprinted by permission of the author.

The Hokuseido Press
Haiku poems ("The silence!" by Bashō; "Ah, grief and sadness!" by Buson; and "The snake slid away" by Kyoshi) from *Haiku,* translated by R. H. Blyth, The Hokuseido Press, 1971. Reprinted by permission of The Hokuseido Press.

Henry Holt and Company, Inc.
Lines from "Birches" copyright © 1969 by Holt, Rinehart and Winston, Inc; copyright © 1962 by Robert Frost; copyright © 1975 by Lesley Frost Ballantine; "The Pasture" copyright 1939, © 1967, 1969 by Holt, Rinehart and Winston, Inc.; and "Stopping by Woods on a Snowy Evening" copyright 1923, © 1969 by Holt, Rinehart and Winston, Inc.; copyright 1951 by Robert Frost. From *The Poetry of Robert Frost* edited by Edward Connery Lathem. Reprinted by permission of Henry Holt and Company, Inc.

Houghton Mifflin Company
"Endlessness" from *Realm of Numbers* by Isaac Asimov. Copyright © 1959 by Isaac Asimov. "A Song of Greatness" from *The Children Sing in the Far West* by Mary Austin. Copyright 1928 by Mary Austin. Copyright © renewed 1956 by Kenneth M. Chapman and Mary C. Wheelwright. "Phaëthon, Son of Apollo" from *Greek Myths* by Olivia Coolidge. Copyright 1949 and copyright © renewed 1977 by Olivia Coolidge. "The Village Blacksmith" from *The Poetical Works of Longfellow,* Cambridge Edition, 1975. Lines from "Patterns" from *The Complete Poetical Works of Amy Lowell.* Copyright © 1955 by Hougton Mifflin Company; copyright © renewed 1983 by Houghton Mifflin Company, Brinton P. Roberts, Esquire, and G. D'Andelot Belin, Esquire. "Icarus and Daedalus" from *Old Greek Folk Stories Told Anew* by Josephine Preston Peabody. The Riverside Press. Reprinted by permission of Houghton Mifflin Company.

Jeremy Ingalls
"Prometheus the Fire-Bringer," one of her fifteen stories in her *A Book of Legends* initially published by Harcourt Brace and Company in 1941. Copyright purchased by author in 1950. Copyright © 1950, 1968 by Jeremy Ingalls. Reprinted by permission of the author.

International Creative Management, Inc.
Grandpa and the Statue by Arthur Miller. Copyright © 1945, 1973 by Arthur Miller. "Feelings About Words" from *Words, Words, Words* by Mary O'Neill. Copyright © 1966 by Mary O'Neill. *The Monsters Are Due on Maple Street* by Rod Serling. Copyright © 1960 by Rod Serling. Reprinted by permission of International Creative Management, Inc.

International Paper Company
"How to Enjoy Poetry" by James Dickey from the Power of

the Printed Word Program. Reprinted by permission of International Paper Company.

Japan Publications, Inc.
"On sweet plum blossoms," "Has spring come indeed?" and "Temple bells die out" by Bashō. Reprinted from *One Hundred Famous Haiku* by Daniel C. Buchanan, with permission from Japan Publications © 1973.

Johns Hopkins University Press
Lines from "Rome in Her Ruins" by Francisco de Quevedo, translated by Felicia D. Hemans. Reprinted from *Ten Centuries of Spanish Poetry: An Anthology in English Verse with Original Texts* edited by Eleanor L. Turnbull. Copyright 1955 by The Johns Hopkins Press. Reprinted by permission.

Alfred A. Knopf, Inc.
"Amigo Brothers" adapted by permission of Alfred A. Knopf, Inc. from *Stories from El Barrio* by Piri Thomas. Copyright © 1978 by Piri Thomas. "Mother to Son" copyright 1926 by Alfred A. Knopf, Inc., and renewed 1954 by Langston Hughes. Reprinted from *Selected Poems of Langston Hughes,* by permission of the publisher. Lines from "Harlem Night Song" copyright 1926 and renewed 1954 by Langston Hughes. Reprinted from *Selected Poems of Langston Hughes,* by permission of the publisher. "Annabel Lee" from *The Complete Poems and Stories of Edgar Allan Poe, with Selections from His Writings,* edited by Arthur Hobson Quinn. Lines from "The Puritan's Ballad" from *Collected Poems of Elinor Wylie* by Elinor Wylie; copyright 1928 by Alfred A. Knopf, Inc. and renewed 1965 by Edwina C. Rubinstein, by permission of Alfred A. Knopf, Inc.

H. N. Levitt
"Winslow Homer: America's Greatest Painter" by H. N. Levitt from *Boy's Life,* September 1986. Copyrighted H. N. Levitt 1986. Reprinted by permission of the author.

Little, Brown and Company
"Baucis and Philemon" from *Mythology* by Edith Hamilton. Copyright 1942 by Edith Hamilton; copyright © renewed 1969 by Dorian Fielding Reid and Doris Fielding Reid. "The Porcupine" from *Verses from 1929 On* by Ogden Nash. Copyright 1944 by Ogden Nash. First appeared in *The Saturday Evening Post.* By Permission of Little, Brown and Company.

Liveright Publishing Company
"In Just—" is reprinted from *Tulips & Chimneys* by E. E. Cummings by permission of Liveright Publishing Corporation. Copyright 1923, 1925 and renewed 1951, 1953 by E. E. Cummings. Copyright © 1973, 1976 by the Trustees for the E. E. Cummings Trust. Copyright © 1973, 1976 by George James Firmage.

Sterling Lord Literistic, Inc.
"Song Form" from *Black Magic Poetry 1961–1967* by Amiri Baraka (LeRoi Jones). Copyright © 1969 by Amiri Baraka (LeRoi Jones). Reprinted by permission of Sterling Lord Literistic, Inc.

Macmillan of Canada, a division of Canada Publishing Corporation
"Narcissus" from *Four Ages of Man: The Classical Myths* © 1962 by Jay MacPherson. Reprinted by permission of Macmillan of Canada, a division of Canada Publishing Corporation.

Macmillan Publishing Company
"The Pheasant" from *Collected Poems* by Robert P. Tristram Coffin. Copyright 1935 by Macmillan Publishing Company, renewed 1963 by Margaret Coffin Halvosa. "The Town Mouse and the Country Mouse" and "The Fox and the Crow" from *The Fables of Aesop: Selected, Told Anew and Their History Traced* by Joseph Jacobs. Copyright © 1964 by Macmillan Publishing Company. "When the Frost is on the Punkin" from *The Complete Works of James Whitcomb Riley,* Vol. 2 (Indianapolis: Bobbs-Merrill, 1913). Reprinted with permission of Macmillan Publishing Company.

Macmillan Publishing Company and The Society of Authors on behalf of the copyright owner, Mrs. Iris Wise
"Washed in Silver" from *Collected Poems* by James Stephens. Copyright 1915 by Macmillan Publishing Company, renewed 1943 by James Stephens. Reprinted with permission of Macmillan Publishing Company.

Macmillan Publishing Company and A. P. Watt Ltd.
Lines from "The Stolen Child" from *Collected Poems of W.B. Yeats* (New York: Macmillan, 1956).

McIntosh and Otis, Inc.
From *These Were the Sioux* by Mari Sandoz. Copyright © 1961 by Mari Sandoz. Reprinted by permission of McIntosh and Otis, Inc.

William Morrow & Company, Inc.
"Winter" from *Cotton Candy on a Rainy Day* by Nikki Giovanni. Copyright © 1978 by Nikki Giovanni. By permission of William Morrow & Company, Inc.

John Murray (Publishers) Ltd.
"The Dying Detective" from *The Game's Afoot* by Michael and Mollie Hardwick. Copyright © Michael & Mollie Hardwick 1969.

New American Library
"Miracles" from *Leaves of Grass* by Walt Whitman.

New Directions Publishing Corporation
Lines from "Garden" by H.D., *Collected Poems 1912–1944.* Copyright © 1982 by the Estate of Hilda Doolittle. Reprinted by permission of New Directions Publishing Corporation.

Harold Ober Associates Inc.
"Stolen Day" by Sherwood Anderson, originally published in *This Week* Magazine. Copyright 1941 by United Newspapers

Magazine Corp. Copyright renewed 1968 by Eleanor Copenhaver Anderson. "The Old Demon" by Pearl S. Buck, originally published in *Cosmopolitan.* Copyright 1939 by Pearl S. Buck. Copyright © renewed 1966 by Pearl S. Buck. Reprinted by permission of Harold Ober Associates Inc.

The Peter Pauper Press
Haiku, "As lightning flashes..." by Bashō from *Cherry-Blossoms: Japanese Haiku,* Series III. Copyright © 1960 by The Peter Pauper Press. Reprinted by permission of The Peter Pauper Press, White Plains, NY.

Prentice-Hall, Inc.
"The Mystery and Wonder of Words" from the book *Wonders in Words* by Maxwell Nurnberg, © 1968. Used by permission of the publisher, Prentice-Hall, Inc., Englewood Cliffs, NJ.

The Putnam Publishing Group
"Rip Van Winkle" from *A Legend of the Kaatskill Mountains* by Washington Irving. G. P. Putnam & Sons, 1871. "Two Kinds" by Amy Tan from *The Joy Luck Club* by Amy Tan. Copyright © 1989 by Amy Tan. "The Cremation of Sam McGee" by Robert Service from *Collected Poems of Robert Service.* Reprinted by permission of the Putnam Publishing Group.

Random House, Inc.
"Father William" from *The Complete Works of Lewis Carroll* by Lewis Carroll. Lines from "Minor Elegy" by Henriqueta Lisboa, translated by Willis Barnstone and Nelson Cerqueira. Reprinted from *A Book of Women Poets from Antiquity to Now* edited by Aliki Barnstone and Willis Barnstone, Schocken Books. Reprinted by permission.

Marian Reiner
Haiku by Buson, Otsuji, and Kyorai from *More Cricket Songs: Japanese Haiku* translated by Harry Behn. Copyright © 1971 by Harry Behn. All rights reserved. Reprinted by permission of Marian Reiner.

Marian Reiner for Eve Merriam
"Onomatopoeia" from *It Doesn't Always Have to Rhyme* by Eve Merriam. Copyright © 1964 by Eve Merriam. All Rights Reserved. Reprinted by permission of Marian Reiner for the author.

Estate of Quentin Reynolds
"A Secret for Two" by Quentin Reynolds. Copyright 1936 Crowell-Collier Publishing Co. Reprinted by permission.

St. Martin's Press, Inc. and Harold Ober Associates Inc.
"Cat on the Go" from *All Things Wise and Wonderful* by James Herriot. Copyright © 1976, 1977 by James Herriot. Reprinted by permission of St. Martin's Press, Inc., New York and Harold Ober Associates Inc.

William Saroyan Foundation
"The Hummingbird That Lived Through Winter" from *Dear Baby* by William Saroyan. Copyright 1935, 1936, 1939, 1941, 1942, 1943, 1944 by William Saroyan. Reprinted by permission of the William Saroyan Foundation.

Charles Scribner's Sons, an imprint of Macmillan Publishing Co.
"A Day's Wait" from *Winner Take Nothing* by Ernest Hemingway. Copyright 1933 Charles Scribner's Sons; copyright renewed © 1961 Mary Hemingway. "Rattlesnake Hunt," excerpt from *Cross Creek* by Marjorie Kinnan Rawlings. Copyright 1942 Marjorie Kinnan Rawlings; copyright renewed © 1970 Norton Baskin. Reprinted by permission of Charles Scribner's Sons, an imprint of Macmillan Publishing Co.

Leslie Marmon Silko
From "Humaweepi, the Warrior Priest" by Leslie Marmon Silko. Reprinted by permission of the author.

Simon & Schuster, Inc.
Pronunciation key from *Webster's New World Dictionary—Second College Edition.* Copyright © 1984 by Simon & Schuster, Inc. Reprinted by permission.

Gary Soto and Poetry
"Oranges" by Gary Soto. First appeared in *Poetry,* copyright © 1983 by The Modern Poetry Association and is reprinted by permission of the author and the Editor of *Poetry.*

Rosemary A. Thurber
"The Fox and the Crow" by James Thurber. Copyright © 1950 James Thurber. Copyright © 1978 Helen Thurber. From *Further Fables for Our Time,* published by Simon & Schuster, Inc. "The Night the Bed Fell" by James Thurber. Copyright © 1933, 1961 James Thurber. From *My Life and Hard Times,* published by Harper & Row. Reprinted by permission.

TriQuarterly
Lines from "The River" by Javier Héraud, translated by Paul Blackburn. From *TriQuarterly,* No. 13–14, Fall/Winter issue, 1969. Copyright © 1969 by *TriQuarterly,* Evanston, IL. Reprinted by permission of the publisher.

University of Notre Dame Press
From *Barrio Boy* by Ernesto Galarza. © 1971 by University of Notre Dame Press. Reprinted by permission.

University of Pittsburgh Press
Lines from "A Forgotten Man's Song about the Winds" (Talitgak traditional) reprinted from *Eskimo Poems from Canada and Greenland* translated by Tom Lowenstein, by permission of the University of Pittsburgh Press. © 1973 by Tom Lowenstein.

Viking Penguin Inc.
"The Legend of the Hummingbird" from *Once in Puerto Rico* by Pura Belpré. Copyright © 1973 by Pura Belpré. Lines

from "The Hermit Has a Visitor" from *Our Ground Time Here Will Be Brief* by Maxine Kumin. Copyright © 1972 by Maxine Kumin. "Season at the Shore" from *Times Three* by Phyllis McGinley. Copyright 1954 by Phillis McGinley, renewed © 1982 by Phyllis Hayden Blake. Originally published in *The New Yorker*. Reprinted by permission of Viking Penguin Inc.

Mai Vo-Dinh
"The Little Lizard's Sorrow" from *The Toad is the Emperor's Uncle, Animal Folktales from Viet-Nam,* told and illustrated by Vo-Dinh. Copyright © 1970 by Mai Vo-Dinh. Reprinted by permission of the author.

Western Publishing Company, Inc.
"The Bride of Pluto" (retitled "Demeter and Persephone") adapted from *Golden Treasury of Myths and Legends* by Anne Terry White. © 1959 Western Publishing Company, Inc. Reprinted by permission.

Jade Snow Wong and Curtis Brown, Ltd.
From "A Time of Beginnings" in *No Chinese Stranger* by Jade Snow Wong. Copyright © 1975 by Jade Snow Wong. Reprinted by permission of the author and Curtis Brown, Ltd.

Juliet Wood (née Piggott)
"Popocatepetl and Ixtlaccihuatl" from *Mexican Folk Tales* by Juliet Piggott. Copyright © 1973 Juliet Piggott. Reprinted by permission of the author.

Writers & Artists Agency
A Christmas Carol: Scrooge and Marley adapted from Charles Dickens by Israel Horovitz. Reprinted by permission.

Note: Every effort has been made to locate the copyright owner of material reprinted in this book. Omissions brought to our attention will be corrected in subsequent editions.

ART CREDITS

Cover and Title Page: *Sally,* Joseph De Camp, oil on canvas, 26 × 23", Worcester Art Museum, Worcester, Massachusetts; **p. 1:** *The Boating Party,* 1893/1894, Mary Cassatt, The National Gallery of Art, Washington, Chester Dale Collection; **p. 5:** *Bouquet with Flying Lovers,* c. 1934–47, Marc Chagall, The Tate Gallery, London; **p. 8:** Glass mosaic wall mural: Landscape—Base and Fountain, c. 1905–15 (detail), Tiffany Studios, The Metropolitan Museum of Art, Gift of Lillian Nassau, 1976, and Gift of Mrs. L. Groves Geer, 1978; **p. 11:** Ufer, Walter (1876–1936), 1984-66, *The Callers,* oil on canvas, executed ca. 1926, 50½ × 50½", National Museum of American Art, Smithsonian Institution, Gift of Mr. and Mrs. Crosby Kemper, Jr.; **p. 12:** *Rudyard Kipling* (detail), 1899, P. Burne-Jones, National Portrait Gallery, London; **p. 55:** *Four Girls,* August Macke, Three Lions; **p. 58:** *Brer Fox,* Bob Kuhn, Sportsman's Edge/King Gallery; **p. 61:** *The Courtship,* Bonnie Marris, The Greenwich Workshop, Inc.; **p. 63:** *September Gathering,* George Harkins, Glen C. Janss Collection; **p. 75:** Johnson, William H., *Mom and Dad* (or) *Portrait of a Lady with Kittens,* 1944, National Museum of American Art, Smithsonian Institution, Gift of the Harmon Foundation; **p. 89:** *A Country Lad,* Winslow Homer, Cooper-Hewitt Museum, Smithsonian Institution; **p. 91:** *Young Fisherman,* 1889, Louis Michel Eilshemius, Hirshhorn Museum and Sculpture Garden, Smithsonian Institution. Gift of Joseph H. Hirshhorn, 1966; **p. 98:** *Atelier,* Byron Birdsall, Artique, Ltd.; **p. 105:** *Early Summer on the Farm,* Karl Rodko, Three Lions; **p. 108:** *Sunrise IV,* 1937, Arthur Dove. Hirshhorn Museum and Sculpture Garden, Smithsonian Institution; **p. 114:** Thomas Worthington Whittredge, *Forest Interior,* 1882, oil on canvas, 69.9 × 69.9 cm, Roger McCormick Fund, 1981.643, © 1987 The Art Institute of Chicago. All rights reserved. **p. 119:** Johnson, William H., *Jim,* 1930, National Museum of American Art, Smithsonian Institution, Gift of the Harmon Foundation; **p. 122:** *Harlem Nocturne,* 1952, Alice Neel, Courtesy Robert Miller Gallery, New York: **p. 132:** *Washington Irving* (detail), Daniel Huntington, National Portrait Gallery, Smithsonian Institution; **p. 133:** *Rip in the Mountains,* Albertus Del Orient Brower, Shelburne Museum, Shelburne, Vermont; **p. 136:** *Rip at the Inn,* Albertus Del Orient Brower, Shelburne Museum, Shelburne, Vermont; **p. 139:** *Rip Van Winkle Asleep,* Albertus Del Orient Brower, Shelburne Museum, Shelburne, Vermont; **p. 142:** *Return of Rip Van Winkle,* 1829, John Quidor, National Gallery of Art, Washington, Laurie Platt Winfrey, Inc.; **p. 147:** Winslow Homer, American, 1836–1910, *The Four Leaf Clover,* 1873, oil on canvas, 14¼" × 20⅜", 70.150, © 1987 The Detroit Institute of Arts, Bequest of Robert H. Tannahill; **p. 154:** *Pearl S. Buck* (detail), Vita P. Solomon, National Portrait Gallery, Smithsonian Institution, Gift of the Pearl S. Buck Foundation; **p. 175:** Evergood, Philip, *Her World,* 1948, The Metropolitan Museum of Art, Arthur Hoppock Hearn Fund, 1950. Copyright © 1986 by The Metropolitan Museum of Art; **p. 214:** *Parade Curtain After Picasso,* 1980, oil on canvas, 48 × 60", © David Hockney, 1980; **p. 220:** Pennies for the Pedestal, *The Herald,* April 3, 1885, courtesy of the New York Historical Society, New York City: **p. 226:** *Wake of the Ferry II,* 1907, John Sloan, The Phillips Collection, Washington, D.C.; **p. 229:** *The Unveiling of the Statue of Liberty,* 1880, Edward Moran, Museum of the City of New York; **p. 232:** *Sir Arthur Conan Doyle* (detail), 1927, H. L. Gates, National Portrait Gallery, London; **p. 308:** *Reclining Woman,* 1952, John Robinson, Private Collection, Courtesy of the artist; **p. 317:** Johnson, Malvin Gray, *Self Portrait,* 1934, National Museum of American Art, Smithsonian Institution, Gift of the Harmon Foundation; **p. 349:** Fairfield Porter, *Iced Coffee,* Courtesy Private Collection, Brookline, Massachusetts; **pp. 364, 365, 366:** Copyright © 1933, 1961, James Thurber, from *My Life and Hard Times,* published by Harper & Row; **p. 376:** van Gogh, Vincent, *The Starry Night* (1889), oil on canvas, 29 × 39¼", Collection, The Museum of Modern Art, New York. Acquired through the Lillie P. Bliss Bequest; **p. 378:** Delaunay, Robert, *Simultaneous Contrasts: Sun and Moon* (1913. Dated on painting 1912), oil on canvas, 53" diameter, Collection, The Museum of Modern Art, New York, Mrs. Simon Guggenheim Fund; **p. 382:** *Girl Writing,* 1941, Milton Avery, The Phillips

Collection, Washington, D.C.; **p. 385:** Lawrence, Jacob, *The Library*, 1960, National Museum of American Art, Smithsonian Institution, Gift of S. D. Johnson & Son, Inc.; **p. 391:** Victor Vasarely, *Reytey*, 1968, Collection, Solomon R. Guggenheim Museum, New York, Photo: Carmelo Guadagno; **p. 396:** Homer, Winslow, *Prisoners from the Front,* The Metropolitan Museum of Art, Gift of Mrs. Frank B. Porter, 1922 (22.207), Copyright © 1980 by the Metropolitan Museum of Art; **p. 398:** Homer, Winslow, *The Gulf Stream,* Copyright © 1980 by the Metropolitan Museum of Art, The Metropolitan Museum of Art, Wolfe Fund, 1906; Catherine Lorillard Wolfe Collection; **p. 402:** Stuart Davis, *Owh! in San Pao,* 1951, oil on canvas, 52¼ × 41¾″, Collection of Whitney Museum of American Art, Purchase, Acq. #52.2; **p. 404:** Stuart Davis, *The Paris Bit,* 1959, oil on canvas, 46 × 60″, Collection of Whitney Museum of American Art, Purchase, with funds from the Friends of the Whitney Museum of American Art, Acq. #59.38; **p. 410:** *Mari Sandoz* (detail) by Louise Austen, University Archives, Love Library, University of Nebraska; **p. 412:** Catlin, George, *Chee-A-Ka-Tchee, Wife of Not-To-Way,* 1835–1836, National Museum of American Art, Smithsonian Institution, Gift of Mrs. Joseph Harrison, Jr.; **p. 415:** *Sioux Encampment,* Jules Tavernier, c. 1874–1884, oil on canvas, 171.5 × 99 cm, The Oakland Museum, Oakland, CA, The Kahn Collection, Laurie Platt Winfrey, Inc.; **p. 428:** *Springtime Fantasy,* Adolphe Faugeron, Three Lions; **p. 433:** *Henry Wadsworth Longfellow* (detail), Thomas B. Read, National Portrait Gallery, Smithsonian Institution; **p. 435:** *The Boy,* Thomas Hart Benton, Three Lions; **p. 455:** MacDonald, J. E. H., *Belgium,* 1915, oil on cardboard, 52.7 × 74.9 cm (20¾″ × 29½″), Art Gallery of Ontario, Toronto, Purchase, 1963, 62/21, Photo, Larry Ostrom, Art Gallery of Ontario; **p. 451:** *Waterfall No. III, Iao Valley,* Georgia O'Keeffe, 1939, Art Resource, **p. 462:** *Carl Sandburg* (detail), 1951, Emerson C. Burkhart, National Portrait Gallery, Smithsonian Institution; **p. 464:** John Newbery, ''Little Goody-Two-Shoes,'' 1766 ed., from *Illustrators of Children's Books, 1744–1945,* by Bertha Mahoney, Boston, Hornbook, 1947, The New York Public Library, Astor, Lenox and Tilden Foundations; **p. 467:** *Ring-Necked Pheasant,* 1977, © 1977 Roger Tory Peterson, Courtesy of the artist and Mill Pond Press, Inc., Venice, FL 33495; **p. 476** (detail) and **p. 479:** *Ravens in Moonlight,* 1882, Gengyo, Omni Photo Communications, © LEA; **p. 481:** *Young Girls at the Piano,* Pierre Auguste Renoir, Joslyn Art Museum, Omaha, Nebraska; **p. 482:** James Stephens (detail), Sir William Rothenstein, The Tate Gallery, London; **p. 486:** *Dominant Curve,* April 1936, Wassily Kandinski, Solomon R. Guggenheim Museum, New York, Photo, David Heald; **p. 489:** *The Buffalo Trail,* 1867–68, Albert Bierstadt, American, 1830–1902, oil on canvas, 32 × 48 in. (81.3 × 122.0 cm), Gift of Mrs. Maxim Karolik for the Karolik Collection of American Paintings, 1815–1865, Courtesy, Museum of Fine Arts, Boston; **p. 490;** *Edna St. Vincent Millay* (detail), 1934, Charles Ellis, National Portrait Gallery, Smithsonian Institution; **p. 493:** *Portrait of Henriette,* Andrew Wyeth, Courtesy of the San Antonio Museum Association, San Antonio, TX; **p. 497:** MacDonald,

J. E. H., Canadian, 1873–1932, *Mist Fantasy,* 1922, oil on canvas, 93.7 × 66.7 cm, Art Gallery of Ontario, Toronto, Gift of Mrs. S. J. Williams in memory of F. Elinor Williams, 1927; **p. 498:** *Edward Estlin Cummings* (detail), 1958, *Self Portrait,* National Portrait Gallery, Smithsonian Institution; **p. 506:** *John Singer Sargent* (detail), James Whitcomb Riley, Indianapolis Museum of Art; **p. 515:** *Snapshot at the Beach,* 1891, 19th Century, Three Lions; **p. 516:** *Langston Hughes* (detail) by Winold Reiss, c. 1925, National Portrait Gallery, Smithsonian Institution, Gift of W. Tjark Reiss in memory of his father, Winold Reiss; **p. 519:** Edmund Archer, *Organdy Collar* (1936), oil on canvas, 19 × 16″, Collection of Whitney Museum of American Art, Purchase, Acq. #38.49; **pp. 525, 526:** *You Are Old Father William,* 1865, Sir John Tenniel, The Granger Collection 931.11; **p. 531:** *Good Fortune,* René Magritte, Museum Boymans-Van Beuningen, Rotterdam; **p. 538:** *Classical Fable,* © 1986 Thomas McKnight, Chalk & Vermilion; **p. 541:** *Chariot of the Moon,* Frederic E. Church, Courtesy of The Cooper-Hewitt Museum, Smithsonian Institution: **p. 543:** *The Blue Horse,* Franz Marc, Three Lions; **p. 549:** Original art by James Thurber, © 1956 by James Thurber; **p. 555:** *Hector and Andromache,* Giorgio De Chirico, Scala/Art Resource; **p. 570:** (detail) and **p. 573:** *The Fall of Phaëthon,* Peter Paul Rubens; **p. 576:** *Philemon and Baucis* (detail), 1658, Rembrandt van Rijn, National Gallery of Art, Washington, Widener Collection; **p. 580:** (detail) and **582:** *Daedalus and Icarus,* Albrecht Durer, **p. 584:** Claude: *Landscape* (detail), *Narcissus,* 1644, The Granger Collection, C. 19; **p. 585:** *Narciso Alla Fonte,* Caravaggio, Scala/Art Resource; **p. 587:** Rousseau, Henri, *The Sleeping Gypsy,* 1897, oil on canvas, 51″ × 6′7″, Collection, The Museum of Modern Art, New York, Gift of Mrs. Simon Guggenheim; **pp. 598** (detail) and **600:** *Erupting Volcano,* 1943, Dr. Atl (Gerardo Murillo), Laurie Platt Winfrey; **p. 603:** *Quetzalcoatl,* from Codex Borbonicus (copy), Mixtec, ca. A.D. 1500, M.N.A.H., Biblioteca, Laurie Platt Winfrey, Inc.; **p. 610:** *Spider,* 1887, Odilon Redon, Lithograph printed in black sheet, 11 × 8⁹/₁₆″ (28 × 21.7 cm), Collection, the Museum of Modern Art, New York, Mrs. Bertram Smith Fund; *On the Trail,* Winslow Homer, National Gallery of Art, Washington, Gift of Ruth K. Henschel in memory of her husband, Charles R. Henschel; **p. 627:** *Hunter in the Adirondacks,* 1892 (detail), Winslow Homer, Courtesy of the Harvard University Art Museums (Fogg Art Museum), Anonymous gift.

PHOTOGRAPH CREDITS

p. 24: UPI/Bettmann News Photos; **p. 36:** AP/Wide World Photos; **p. 38:** Keith Gunnar/Bruce Coleman; **p. 44:** AP/Wide World Photo; **p. 50:** Patricia M. Hoch; **p. 56:** New York Public Library Picture Collection; **p. 66:** AP/Wide World Photo; **p. 74:** Rollie McKenna; **p. 88:** UPI/Bettmann Newsphotos; **p. 94:** Robert Foothorap, G. P. Putnam's Sons; **p. 100:** Courtesy of the author; **p. 110:** Burk Uzzle/Archive Pictures; **p. 106:** Thomas Victor; **p. 112:** Godfrey Graham, Little Brown & Co.; **p. 118:** Thomas Victor; **p. 128:** Culver

Pictures; **p. 130:** Illinois State Historical Society; **p. 148:** Thomas Victor, **p. 166:** Thomas Victor; **p. 168:** Peter Menzel/Wheeler Pictures; **p. 171:** Ralph Loony/Shostal #401, 518; **p. 172:** Gary Meszaros/Bruce Coleman; **p. 174:** Mark Leighton, UPI/Bettmann News Photos; **p. 178:** Thomas Victor; **p. 196:** The Bettmann Archive; **p. 200:** John Moss; **p. 208:** Larry Burrows © Time, Inc., 1959; **p. 218:** Thomas Victor; **p. 246:** International Creative Management; **p. 248:** Frank Wing/Stock Boston; **p. 255:** Jean-Pierre Pieuchot/The Image Bank; **p. 259:** D. Carroll/The Image Bank; **p. 262:** The Granger Collection; **p. 265, 269, 275, 278, 284, 288, 298, 302:** The Guthrie Theatre; **p. 313:** Harvey Lloyd/The Stock Market; **p. 315:** Thomas Victor; **p. 318:** Dave Gannon; **p. 320:** Norman Owen Tomalin/Bruce Coleman; **pp. 324–25:** Ron and Valerie Taylor/Bruce Coleman; **p. 328:** Thomas Victor; **p. 330:** Russell Baker; **p. 333:** Russell Baker; **p. 336:** Mae Galorza: **p. 339:** Rodney Jones; **p. 342:** Courtesy of the author; **pp. 344, 346–47:** Jade Snow-Wong; **p. 350:** John Wyand; **p. 352:** Mike Mazzaschi/Stock Boston; **p. 357:** Louis Panuse/DPI; **p. 362:** UPI/Bettmann News Photo: **p. 368:** AP/Wide World Photo; **p. 369:** M. P. Kahl/Bruce Coleman; **pp. 370–71:** Wendell Metzen/Bruce Coleman; **p. 374:** Thomas Victor; **p. 380:** AP/Wide World Photo; **p. 386:** Thomas Victor; **p. 394:** John Kleinhans; **p. 406:** AP/Wide World Photo: **p. 421:** NASA 68-HC-853; **p. 422:** Bettmann Archives; **p. 436:** New York Public Library Picture Collection; **p. 444:** AP/Wide World Photo; **p. 450:** AP/Wide World Photo; **p. 454:** UPI/Bettmann News Photos; **p. 458:** Diane Trejo; **p. 462:** (top) New York Public Library Picture Collection; (middle) AP/Wide World Photo; **pp. 468–69:** Andrei Lloyd/The Stock Market; **p. 470;** (top) AP/Wide World: (bottom) Dmitri Kessel, *Life* magazine, © Time, Inc.; **p. 472:** S. C.

Bisserot/Bruce Coleman; **p. 474:** Sonja H. Smith; **p. 482:** (middle) John Gannon; (bottom) The Bettmann Archives; **pp. 484–85:** Harald Sund; **p. 495:** Photography, Rod Hansen/Collection of the Yakima Valley Museum and Historical Assoc.; **p. 498:** (bottom) Dmitri Kessel, *Life* magazine © Time, Inc.; **p. 500:** David Herman/Shostal 508–529; **p. 503:** Gordon R. Gainer/Stock Market; **p. 505:** D. S. Henderson/The Image Bank; **p. 506:** (top) AP/Wide World; **p. 509:** Jerry Simions/Shostal Assoc. 502–945; **p. 513:** David Barnes/Stock Market; **p. 516:** (second down) Courtesy of the Huntington Library; (third down) Granger Collection; (bottom) Courtesy of the author; **p. 517:** Raymond R. Patterson; **p. 523:** Declan Haun/Black Star; **p. 524:** New York Public Library Picture Collection; **p. 528:** New York Public Library Picture Collection; **p. 532:** UPI/Bettmann News Photos; **p. 548:** UPI/Bettmann News Photo; **p. 588:** Lois and George Cox/Bruce Coleman; **p. 590:** Bob and Clara Calhoun/Bruce Coleman; **p. 628:** Courtesy Doubleday and Co.

ILLUSTRATION CREDITS

pp. 14, 18–19: Miriam Shottland/Tania Kimche; **pp. 27, 31, 33:** Dan Brown/ARTCO, Gail Thurm; **pp. 46, 51, 52, 67, 72, 80, 84, 151, 156, 161, 181, 184, 186, 192:** The Art Source; **p. 197:** Ed Acuna/ARTCO, Gail Thurm; **pp. 234, 241, 432, 438–439, 441, 448, 545:** The Art Source; **pp. 552, 553:** Miriam Shottland/Tania Kimche; **pp. 557, 559:** The Art Source: **pp. 562, 563, 567:** Tim Hilderbrandt/Jeff Lavaty; **pp. 595, 608, 617–618, 630–631, 639, 648, 655, 661, 669, 677, 684, 689, 694, 703, 709, 716–717, 726–727, 735, 743, 750, 754–755, 765:** The Art Source.